DATAPEDIA
of the United States

American History in Numbers

FOURTH EDITION, 2007

DATAPEDIA
of the United States

American History in Numbers

FOURTH EDITION, 2007

Edited by
George Thomas Kurian
and
Barbara A. Chernow

BERNAN PRESS
Lanham, MD

ISBN: 978–1–59888–083–0

2008   2007   4   3   2   1

Bernan Press
4611-F Assembly Drive
Lanham, MD 20706
Email: info@bernan.com
www.bernan.com

CONTENTS

v

SECTION III Industry and Services

Comparative Time Lines   202

Chapter 10 Labor

Highlights   211

Chapter 11 Construction and Housing

Highlights   243

Chapter 12 Manufacturing

Highlights   263

Chapter 16 Distribution and Services

SECTION IV Health, Social Welfare, and Law Enforcement

Chapter 17 Health

Chapter 18 Food and Nutrition

Chapter 19 Social Welfare

Chapter 20 Criminal Justice

SECTION V Education, Society, and Leisure

Chapter 21 Education and Learning

Chapter 22 Arts, Entertainment, Recreation, and Travel

EDITORIAL AND PRODUCTION STAFF

Researchers
Christi De Larco, Head Researcher
Alexandr Gelfand, Research Assistant

Production
Kathy B. Cleghorn, Production Manager
Chenelle A. Warner, Production Editor
Kristin Fritz, Proofreader

Composition
Robert Eckert
Carol Walma
Nancy Benson

Indexer
Gerald McClanahan

Designer
Paula Goldstein

INTRODUCTION

Datapedia of the United States: American History in Numbers, Fourth Edition, is a comprehensive desk reference that continues and enhances *Historical Statistics of the United States from Colonial Times. Datapedia* brings together into one source a compendium of the most significant historical statistics of the United States from 1790 to 2007, as well as demographic and other select data projections through 2050. *Datapedia* provides a complete and convenient profile of the United States covering all its vital sectors—including the labor market, social welfare, and national defense.

Organization of the Fourth Edition:
Familiar Format and New Features
Those familiar with *Datapedia* will find that this edition retains the features of its previous edition, but has been reorganized into seven sections containing a total of 31 chapters. The data is presented in a reader-friendly format, balanced by highlights and graphics. In addition, two new features have been added. First, each section opens with a series of timelines that enable the reader to pinpoint significant events and to compare developments in each of the chapters included in that section. Second, each chapter ends with an essay about a subject that is particularly relevant to our times, such as the Cost of the War in Iraq, Campaign Finance Reform, and e-Commerce.

Expanded areas of coverage include statistics and analyses on the following topics:

- Health and Health Care
- Food and Nutrition
- Education and Learning
- Law Enforcement, Courts, and Prisons
- Arts, Entertainment, Recreation, and Travel
- Politics and Elections
- Public Finance
- National Defense

Datapedia includes more than 345 data tables that have been expertly selected, compiled, and analyzed. For the period of 1790 to 1970, the data is based entirely on *Historical Statistics.* For the time period following, *Datapedia* is based on the annual *Statistical Abstract of the United States* as well as other government data from the sources indicated at the bottom of each table.

Generally, only national data are shown. Some exceptions are made where regional or state statistics are useful for the correct interpretation of data or where national data in the subject field cannot be summarized effectively. Of course, in the early part of many series, the data are limited to the geographic area of the original 13 colonies—that is, the Atlantic seaboard.

In general, only absolute rather than derived data are included because one-dimensional aggregates at gross levels offer somewhat greater flexibility to the user. Criteria for inclusion vary, but in most cases are based on the quantity and quality of the data available and the extent to which they enhance our understanding of historical trends. Additionally, certain series are presented only for years in which a national census was held.

History of Statistics
Before the first census of 1790, the collection of statistics was not considered as a primary function of the U.S.

government. The accuracy of the limited data that was collected, however, was much higher, given that our nation was significantly smaller—literally and figuratively—comparative to today. Although some of this data—from the early years of our republic—have been lost, much of the data have been gathered from fugitive documents. Further, the quality of the statistical tables spanning over two centuries is remarkably even.

As our country developed, the complexity of statistical operations grew as well as the techniques for data collection and analysis. Data collection and analysis became a routine function of the government as well as independent researchers and scholars. Statistics began to be viewed as not only a means to measure and analyze the current state of our society but also to predict future trends, which is one of the intended uses of *Datapedia*.

Projective statistics and number crunching, in general, have been greatly facilitated by the introduction of computers in the twentieth century. Although data experts still are, and will continue to be, an integral part of data gathering and interpretation, automated computer processes have provided us with raw and refined data of exceptionally high quality. Technological advancements have also resulted in increased access to government statistics via the posting of a myriad of data on many government Web sites.

Most, if not all, of the data organized in this edition is publicly available online. However, the task of gathering them from a number of sources within the government and assembling them into a logical and understandable format is impractical for most data users. Additionally, even though current statistics are readily available, obtaining historical time series data often is time-consuming and difficult. Definitions and other documentation can be inconvenient to find as well. Continuing the tradition of *Historical Statistics, Datapedia* greatly simplifies the task of researching and analyzing data from an historical perspective; and, according to *American Reference Books Annual,* "presents a plethora of interesting and often hard-to-find data in a user-friendly format."

The data in this edition meet the publication standards of the federal statistical agencies from which they were obtained. Every effort has been made to select data that are accurate, meaningful, and useful. All statistical data are subject to error arising from sampling variability, reporting errors, incomplete coverage, imputation, and other causes. The responsibility of the editor and publisher of *Datapedia* is limited to reasonable care in the reproduction and presentation of data obtained from established sources.

George Thomas Kurian
Barbara A. Chernow
Editors

ACKNOWLEDGEMENTS

Datapedia of the United States: American History in Numbers, Fourth Edition, would not have been possible without the foresight of the founding editor George Thomas Kurian. Recognizing that a compilation of historical statistics was too valuable to be lost to the public, Mr. Kurian first collaborated with Bernan Press in 1994 in the publication of the first edition of *Datapedia* and again in 2001 and 2004 for the second and third editions. So, first and foremost, thanks are due to Mr. Kurian for his role in ensuring the continuity of the *Datapedia* series and for his guidance in the production of the fourth edition, for which he was joined by a coeditor, Barbara A. Chernow.

Special thanks are also due to Jo A. Wilson and Katherine DeBrandt of Bernan Press, who ensured a smooth transition from the third to the fourth edition and reviewed material as it was completed for accuracy, quality, and presentation.

I am extremely grateful for each person's respective contributions and commitment to helping Bernan Press fulfill the research needs of our customers.

Kenneth E. Lawrence
Publisher
Bernan Press

ABOUT THE EDITORS

George Thomas Kurian is a noted encyclopedist, researcher, and president of the New York-based Encyclopedia Society. Mr. Kurian has authored nearly 25 encyclopedias and over 30 other reference books. The reference books he has authored include the *Atlas of the Third World, Dictionary of World Politics, Encyclopedia of American Studies, Encyclopedia of the World's Nations, Global Data Locator, Historical Guide to U. S. Government,* and *Sourcebook of Global Statistics.*

Barbara A. Chernow is a career encyclopedist, researcher, and reference book editor who served as associate editor of *The Papers of Alexander Hamilton,* managing editor of the *Macmillan Encyclopedia of Architects,* and coeditor of the *Columbia Encyclopedia,* fifth edition. Dr. Chernow is the author of *Beyond the Internet: Successful Research Strategies, Robert Morris: Land Speculator* and a contributor to journals and books, including the *Encyclopedia of New York City,* on the subject of early American history and finance.

DATAPEDIA
of the United States

American History in Numbers

FOURTH EDITION, 2007

Demographics

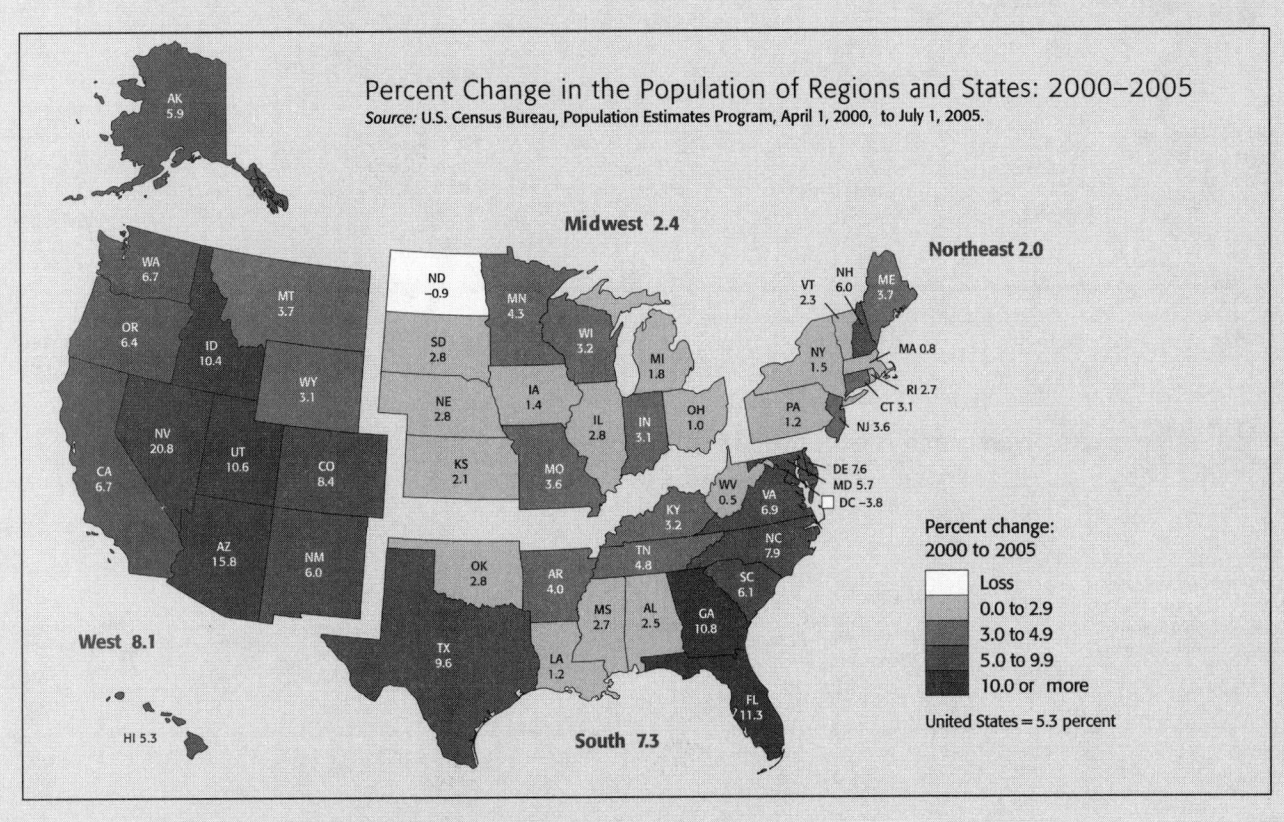

Percent Change in the Population of Regions and States: 2000–2005
Source: U.S. Census Bureau, Population Estimates Program, April 1, 2000, to July 1, 2005.

AK
5.9

Midwest 2.4

Northeast 2.0

WA
6.7

MT
3.7

ND
−0.9

MN
4.3

VT
2.3

NH
6.0

ME
3.7

OR
6.4

ID
10.4

WY
3.1

SD
2.8

WI
3.2

MI
1.8

NY
1.5

MA 0.8

NV
20.8

UT
10.6

CO
8.4

NE
2.8

IA
1.4

OH
1.0

PA
1.2

RI 2.7

CT 3.1

NJ 3.6

CA
6.7

KS
2.1

IL
2.8

IN
3.1

MO
3.6

DE 7.6

MD 5.7

DC −3.8

AZ
15.8

NM
6.0

OK
2.8

AR
4.0

WV
0.5

KY
3.2

VA
6.9

TN
4.8

NC
7.9

West 8.1

TX
9.6

LA
1.2

MS
2.7

AL
2.5

GA
10.8

SC
6.1

FL
11.3

HI 5.3

South 7.3

Percent change:
2000 to 2005

Loss
0.0 to 2.9
3.0 to 4.9
5.0 to 9.9
10.0 or more

United States = 5.3 percent

Population

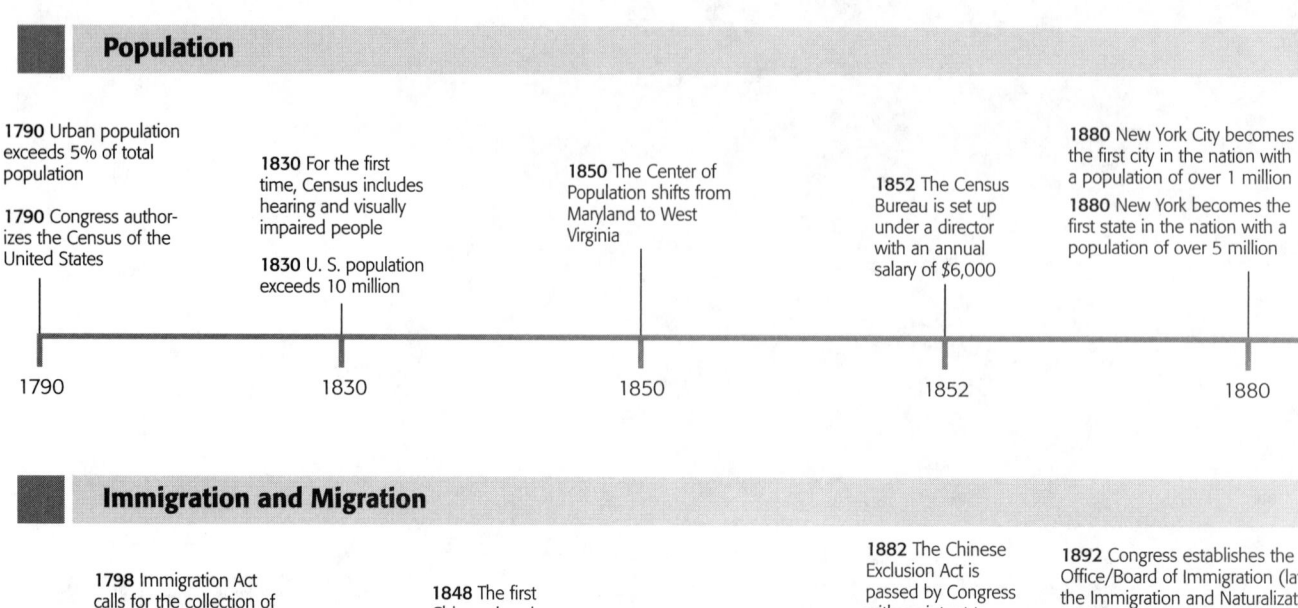

1790 Urban population exceeds 5% of total population

1790 Congress authorizes the Census of the United States

1830 For the first time, Census includes hearing and visually impaired people

1830 U. S. population exceeds 10 million

1850 The Center of Population shifts from Maryland to West Virginia

1852 The Census Bureau is set up under a director with an annual salary of $6,000

1880 New York City becomes the first city in the nation with a population of over 1 million

1880 New York becomes the first state in the nation with a population of over 5 million

| 1790 | 1830 | 1850 | 1852 | 1880 |

Immigration and Migration

1798 Immigration Act calls for the collection of data on the arrival of aliens in the United States

1790 Congress authorizes the collection of naturalization data

1819 Congress passes the first act governing immigration to the United States

1848 The first Chinese immigrant arrives

1861 The first Japanese immigrant arrives

1870 The first Australian immigrant arrives

1882 The Chinese Exclusion Act is passed by Congress with an intent to curb immigration of Chinese workers

1891 William D. Owen is named first superintendent of the Immigration Bureau

1892 Congress establishes the Office/Board of Immigration (later the Immigration and Naturalization Service (INS) and authorizes the collection of immigration statistics

| 1790 | 1798 | 1819 | 1848 | 1861 | 1870 | 1882 | 1891 | 1892 |

Births and Deaths

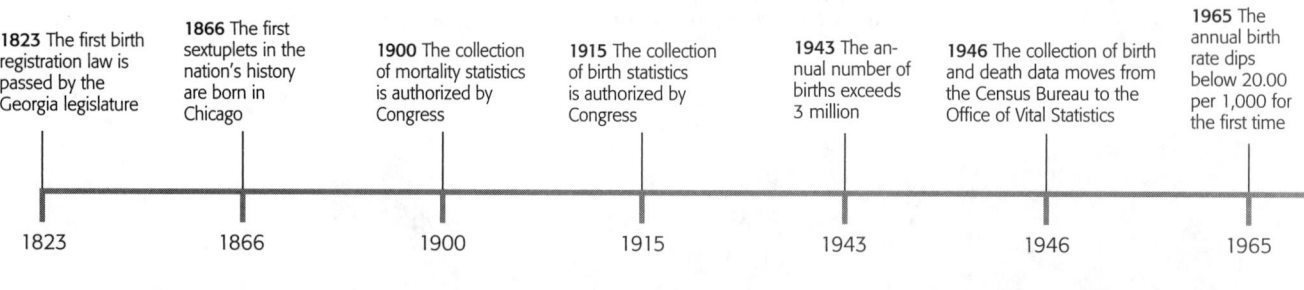

1823 The first birth registration law is passed by the Georgia legislature

1866 The first sextuplets in the nation's history are born in Chicago

1900 The collection of mortality statistics is authorized by Congress

1915 The collection of birth statistics is authorized by Congress

1943 The annual number of births exceeds 3 million

1946 The collection of birth and death data moves from the Census Bureau to the Office of Vital Statistics

1965 The annual birth rate dips below 20.00 per 1,000 for the first time

| 1823 | 1866 | 1900 | 1915 | 1943 | 1946 | 1965 |

Marriage, Divorce, and Alternative Living Arrangements

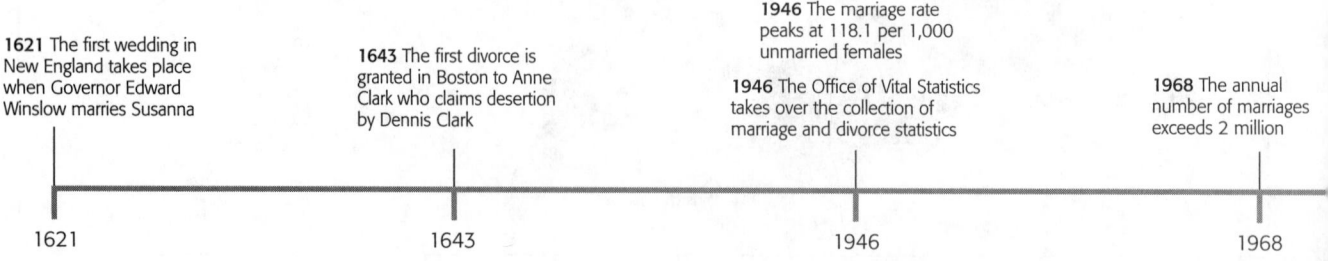

1621 The first wedding in New England takes place when Governor Edward Winslow marries Susanna

1643 The first divorce is granted in Boston to Anne Clark who claims desertion by Dennis Clark

1946 The marriage rate peaks at 118.1 per 1,000 unmarried females

1946 The Office of Vital Statistics takes over the collection of marriage and divorce statistics

1968 The annual number of marriages exceeds 2 million

| 1621 | 1643 | 1946 | 1968 |

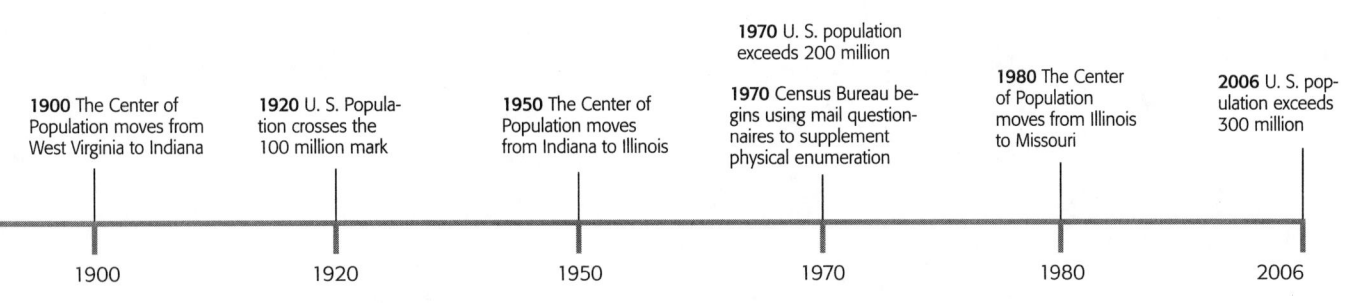

1900 The Center of Population moves from West Virginia to Indiana

1920 U. S. Population crosses the 100 million mark

1950 The Center of Population moves from Indiana to Illinois

1970 U. S. population exceeds 200 million

1970 Census Bureau begins using mail questionnaires to supplement physical enumeration

1980 The Center of Population moves from Illinois to Missouri

2006 U. S. population exceeds 300 million

| 1900 | 1920 | 1950 | 1970 | 1980 | 2006 |

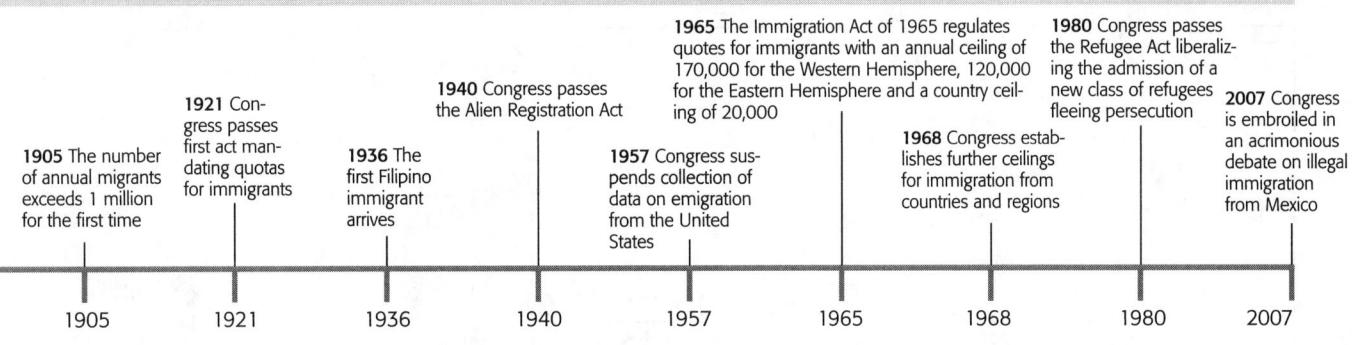

1905 The number of annual migrants exceeds 1 million for the first time

1921 Congress passes first act mandating quotas for immigrants

1936 The first Filipino immigrant arrives

1940 Congress passes the Alien Registration Act

1957 Congress suspends collection of data on emigration from the United States

1965 The Immigration Act of 1965 regulates quotes for immigrants with an annual ceiling of 170,000 for the Western Hemisphere, 120,000 for the Eastern Hemisphere and a country ceiling of 20,000

1968 Congress establishes further ceilings for immigration from countries and regions

1980 Congress passes the Refugee Act liberalizing the admission of a new class of refugees fleeing persecution

2007 Congress is embroiled in an acrimonious debate on illegal immigration from Mexico

| 1905 | 1921 | 1936 | 1940 | 1957 | 1965 | 1968 | 1980 | 2007 |

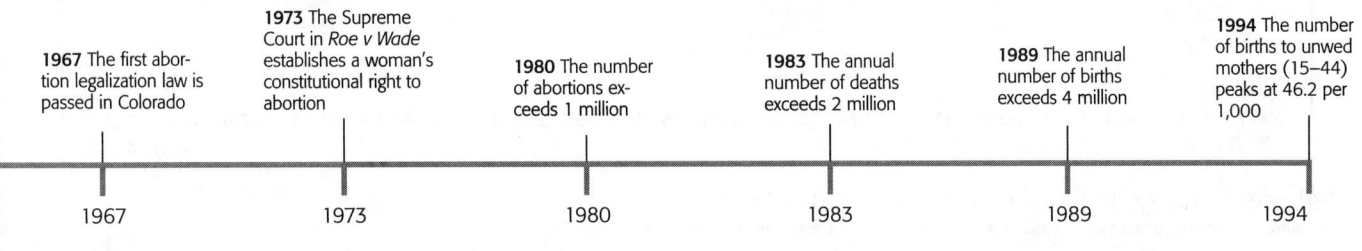

1967 The first abortion legalization law is passed in Colorado

1973 The Supreme Court in *Roe v Wade* establishes a woman's constitutional right to abortion

1980 The number of abortions exceeds 1 million

1983 The annual number of deaths exceeds 2 million

1989 The annual number of births exceeds 4 million

1994 The number of births to unwed mothers (15–44) peaks at 46.2 per 1,000

| 1967 | 1973 | 1980 | 1983 | 1989 | 1994 |

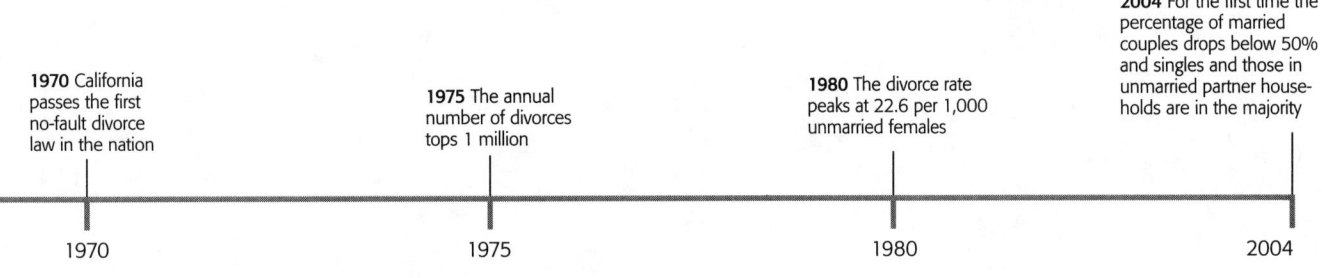

1970 California passes the first no-fault divorce law in the nation

1975 The annual number of divorces tops 1 million

1980 The divorce rate peaks at 22.6 per 1,000 unmarried females

2004 For the first time the percentage of married couples drops below 50% and singles and those in unmarried partner households are in the majority

| 1970 | 1975 | 1980 | 2004 |

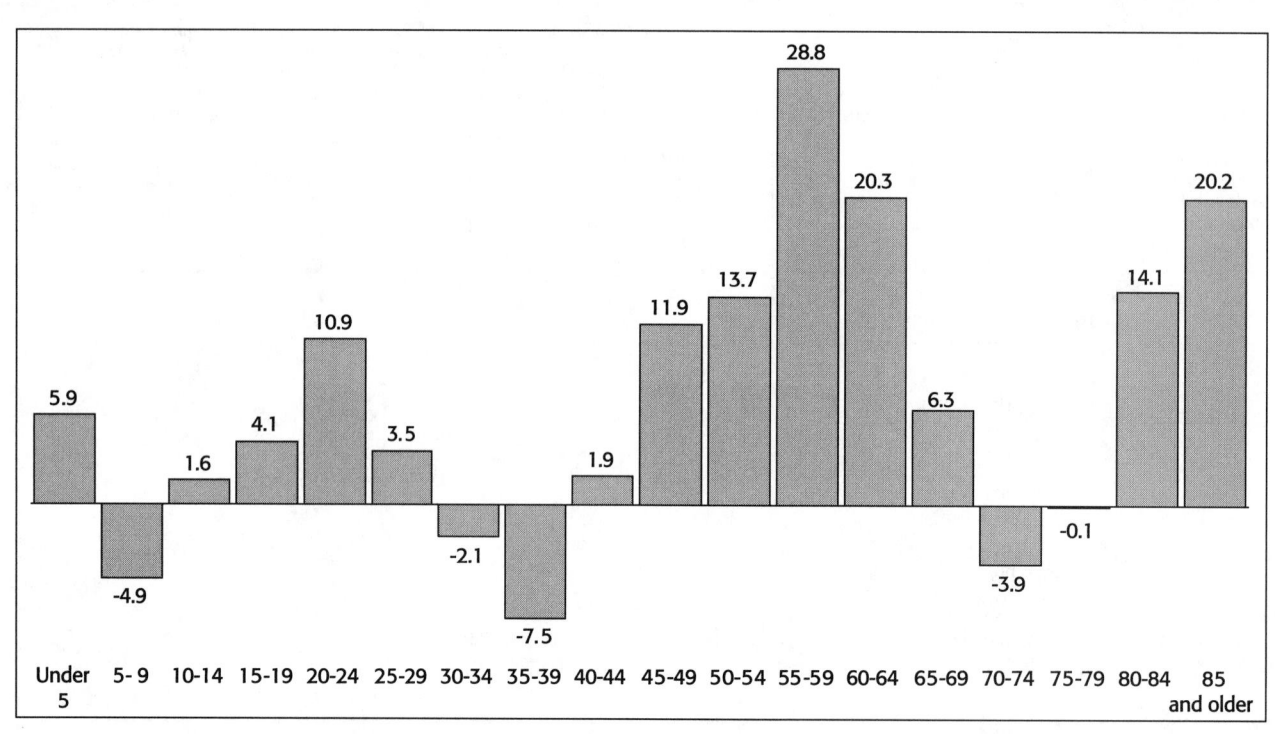

Percent Change in Population by Age, 2000–2005
Source: U.S. Census Bureau. Population Estimates Program, April 1, 2000, and July 1, 2005.

CHAPTER 1

Population

HIGHLIGHTS

1 The Census of the United States was authorized by an Act of Congress, dated March 1, 1790, providing for "the enumeration of the United States." The first census cost $44,377 and utilized the services of 17 marshals and 650 assistants. It counted a population of 3,939,326 in 16 states and the Ohio Territory. Virginia was the most populous state with 746,610 inhabitants, and Rhode Island the least with 68,825 inhabitants. New York City had a population of 33,131, Philadelphia 28,522, and Boston 18,320.

2 Between 1790 and 2000, the Center of Population moved from Maryland to Missouri.

Year	North Latitude	West Latitude	Approximate Location
1790	39 16 30	76 11 12	21 miles east of Baltimore, MD
1850	38 59 00	81 19 00	23 miles SE of Parkersburg, WV
1900	38 09 36	85 48 54	6 miles SE of Columbus, IN
1950	38 50 21	89 09 33	8 miles NNW of Olney, IL
1960	38 35 58	89 15 35	6.5 miles NW of Centralia, IL
1970	38 27 47	89 42 22	5.3 miles SSE of Mescoutah, IL
1980	38 08 13	90 34 26	.25 miles west of De Soto, MO
1990	37 52 20	91 12 55	10 miles SE of Steelville, MO
2000	37 41 49	91 48 34	3 miles E of Edgar Springs, MO

3 Until 1830, people who were hearing, speech, and visually impaired were excluded from the census.

4 The fifth census in 1830 was the first in which the population of the United States exceeded 10 million; the first census in which the count exceeded 100 million was that of 1920; and the first in which the count exceeded 200 million was that of 1970.

5 The 1890 census was the first to utilize enumerating machines.

6 The first states to exceed one million in population were New York, Virginia, and Pennsylvania in 1820. The first state to exceed five million in population was New York in 1880. New York was also the first state to exceed 10 million, in 1920. California became the first state to exceed 20 million, in 1980, and 30 million, in 2000.

7 New York City was the first city to exceed one million in population (exceeding Brooklyn, which was then an independent city) in 1880. In 2000, nine cities exceeded one million in population.

8 Census counts are subject to a margin of error, which has been measured since 1940. Estimated between 1.2 percent and 5.4 percent, the errors generally result from an undercount of certain segments of population.

9 Data on the urban population were first published in 1870. Urban centers were defined as locations with a population of 8,000 or more. In 1880 and 1890, that figure was reduced to 4,000, and in 1900, to 2,500. This definition, with minor modifications, was accepted in later censuses up to and including 1940. In 1950, the Census Bureau adopted the concept of the urbanized area and delineated boundaries for unincorporated places. The urban population was defined as all persons living in urbanized areas and, outside these areas, in all places incorporated or unincorporated, which had 2,500 inhabitants or more. This definition has remained substantially unchanged in subsequent censuses. Minor modifications of this definition are employed in some states. For the 2000 Census, a population density threshold was added.

10 Rural population is subdivided into two categories: rural farm and rural nonfarm. The definition of rural nonfarm is based on the size of the farm and the cash value of the farm produce.

11 The first attempt to define metropolitan population was made in the 1910 census. Metropolitan districts were defined for cities of 200,000 or more. Each metropolitan district included contiguous minor civil divisions that met certain rules of proximity and population density. In 1950, metropolitan districts were replaced by Standard Metropolitan Areas (SMAs), and the name and definitions were revised each decade through the twentieth century. Metropolitan Areas were defined in terms of entire counties, except in New England where the definitions were in terms of cities or towns. In general, an urbanized area is defined as a city (or twin cities) of 50,000 or more and the surrounding closely settled areas. From time to time, new metropolitan areas were created and boundaries of others changed. As a result, data over time may not be comparable. In 2003, a new set of standards was developed to define Core Based Statistical Areas, which include Metropolitan Statistical Areas and Micropolitan Statistical Areas, smaller areas including cities with cohesive groups of counties. The new system is defined in terms of entire counties, even in the New England states.

12 The classification by race in censuses reflects common usage rather than strict biological stock. The data are obtained primarily through self-classification. The standard racial categories are White, Black, Native American, Asian and Pacific Islander, and Hispanic (which may be Black or White). The 1990 census was the first to include an "other race" category that provided for a write-in entry. The census of 1860 was the first in which Native Americans were distinguished from other ethnic groups; however, it excluded those Native Americans living on reservations. The 2000 Census was the first that permitted individuals to specify more than one race, resulting in specific data for persons of multiracial descent.

13 There are no official measures to determine the number of civilian American residents living abroad. The census only counts citizens who are members of the military or employees of the American government working overseas. A 2004 trial census in France, Kuwait, and Mexico taken to determine the viability of measuring the American population abroad was unsuccessful, with only a few thousand questionnaires returned from Americans in all three countries. The cost of this trial census was approximately $1450 per individual compared to approximately $56 spent per domestic household in the 2000 census. According to estimates, between four to eight million Americans live abroad.

14 The population of the United States doubled five times between the first decennial census of 1790 and the seventeenth census in 1950. The first three doublings took 25 years each through 1865. The fourth required 35 years from 1865 to 1900. The fifth doubling took half a century, to 1950. A sixth doubling is projected to occur by about 2010, 60 years since the last doubling.

15 Between 1790 and 1860, the annual increase of population exceeded 3 percent, with the highest being 3.6 percent from 1800 to 1810, and again in the 1840s and the 1850s. In the remaining four decades of the twentieth century and the first decade of the twentieth century, the rate of growth ranged from 2.7 percent to 2.1 percent. The growth rate slumped to 1.5 percent between 1910 and 1920, rose to 1.6 percent in the following decade, and then plummeted to 0.7 percent during the Depression in the 1930s. It rebounded to 1.9 percent in the 1950s (known as the Baby Boom) and was followed by a rate of 1.3 percent in the 1960s as the Boom ended. In the 1970s (the Baby Bust), the growth rate fell to 1.1 percent and remained at 1.0 percent through the 1980s. During the 1990s, the growth rate jumped back to 1.3 percent, but the first few years of the twenty-first century have seen a return to a slower growth of 1.1 percent.

16 The highest decennial jump in population was 36.4 percent reported in the third census in 1810, followed by 35.9 percent in 1850, 35.6 percent in 1860, and 35.1 percent in 1800. The lowest was 7.3 percent reported in 1940, followed by 9.8 percent in 1990, and 11.4 percent in 1980.

17 The United States had more males than females until the end of World War II in 1945. Since then the sex ratio has been in favor of females. However, more male children are born, so that males are in the majority until age 34.

18 Urbanized areas and urban clusters (two definitions of urban areas) accounted for 79 percent of the population and 77.6 percent of the housing units, but only 2.6 percent of the land area in 2000. The West had the most urban population with 88.6 percent of its population living in urban areas, followed by the Northeast (84.4 percent), the Midwest (74.7 percent), and the South (72.8 percent). The most urban states were California and New Jersey, with 94.4 percent, Nevada (91.5 percent), Hawaii (91.5 percent) Massachusetts (91.4 percent), Rhode Island (90.0 percent), Florida (89.3 percent), Utah (88.2 percent), Arizona (88.2 percent), and Illinois (87.8%). The least urban state was Vermont with 38.2 percent, followed by Maine (40.2 percent), and West Virginia (46.1 percent).

19 In 1790, the percentage of the urban population was 5.4 percent. In 2000, it was 79 percent.

20 Two-thirds of America's most populous cities are located in coastal counties. As of July 2005, 152.2 million people lived in coastal counties (53 percent of the U.S. population), a loss of 1 percent compared with 1970. Thirty-three percent lived on the Atlantic coast, 6 percent on the Gulf of Mexico, 10 percent on the Great Lakes, and 14 percent on the Pacific Coast.

21 In the first census in 1790, the density of population was only 4.5 per square mile of land area. It reached 10.6 in 1860, 17.8 in 1890, 26 in 1910, 34.7 in 1930, 42.6 in 1950, 64 in 1980, 70.3 in 1990, 79.6 in 2000, and 83.8 in 2005. The state with the greatest density of population was New Jersey with 1,175.3, followed by Rhode Island with 1,029.9 (District of Columbia was 8,966.1). The state with the least density of population was Alaska with 1.2.

22 Blacks or African Americans alone comprised 12.3 percent of the population in 2000, compared with 15.7 percent in 1850. Nearly 55 percent of Blacks lived in the South, 18.8 percent in the Midwest, 17.6 percent in the Northeast, and 8.9 percent in the West.

23 Arizona has the fastest growing population, overtaking Nevada for the first time in 19 years, with a growth rate of 3.6 compared to 3.5 for Nevada. Other fast growing states include Ohio (2.6), Georgia (2.5), Texas (2.5), and Utah (2.4). Five states lost population in this time period: New York (0.1), Michigan (0.1), District of Columbia (0.1), Rhode Island (0.6), and Louisiana (4.9).

24 From April 1, 2000 to July 1, 2006, New York lost 422,481 of its residents through internal migration, Ohio lost 145,718, and Massachusetts lost 89,812. Louisiana lost 308,248, but that was mainly the result of Hurricane Katrina. The greatest gains through internal migration were registered in Florida (1,863,728), Texas (1,253,486), and California (774,198).

25 The change in the population of Whites from 2000 to 2005 was 4.3 percent compared with 6.2 percent for Blacks, 7.5 percent for American Indian and Alaska Native, 19.8 percent for Asians, and 20.9 percent for Hispanics.

26 From 2004 to 2005, 13.9 percent of the population was mobile (39,887,000, age 1+). This means that people moved from their original house to a different house. Of these, 19.7 percent moved to a different country and 8.5 percent moved to a different state. Lower-income people tend to move more often than higher income people. Fourteen percent of those with no income or a household income of less than $5,000 moved, compared with nine percent of those with an income of more than $75,000.

27 Significant disparities exist in the regional distribution of races. While Whites are distributed fairly equally over the four main regions (Northeast, Midwest, South, and West), 54.8 percent of Blacks are concentrated in the South and only 9.1 percent in the West. Nearly 47.6 percent of Native Americans are found in the West and only 6.4 percent in the Northeast. Asians and Hispanics also are more numerous in the West, with 55.7 percent and 45.2 percent, respectively. One-third of all Hispanics live in California and another one-sixth in Texas. New York has the largest African American population (3.409 million), followed by Texas (2.528 million), Florida (2.634 million), Georgia (2.463 million), and California (2.436 million).

28 The number of senior citizens in the United States is projected to grow from 36.696 million in 2005 to 40.244 million in 2010. Those from 45 to 64 years of age will grow in number from 72.8 million to 81 million, while those from 18 to 44 years of age will increase slightly from 112 million to 113 million during the same period. In 2002, there were 4.593 million senior citizens over the age of 85.

29 In 2000, there were 258 Metropolitan Statistical Areas (MSAs) and 18 Consolidated Metropolitan Statistical Areas (CMSAs), inhabited by 80.3 percent of the population. New Jersey was the only state considered 100 percent metropolitan. Other states with a more than 90 percent metropolitan population included California (96.7 percent), Massachusetts (96.1 percent), Connecticut (95.6 percent), Rhode Island (94.1 percent), Florida (92.8 percent), Maryland (92.7 percent), and New York (92.1 percent). Vermont and Wyoming are the most rural states with 72.2 percent and 70.0 percent of their population respectively in nonmetropolitan areas.

30 In 2002, there were 19,448 incorporated places in the United States, of which 9 have more than a million inhabitants and 16,706 fewer than 10,000. Incorporated places with populations under 25,000 represent a smaller proportion (28.9 percent) of the U.S. population than in 1980 (34.1 percent). Places with populations between 25,000 and 249,999 now account for 42.7 percent, up from 37.2 percent in 1980.

31 Of the large metropolitan areas with populations of 250,000 or more, Las Vegas-Paradise, Nevada grew the most at 24.3 percent from 2000 to 2005. Naples-Marco Island, Florida (22.2 percent), and Provo–Orem, Utah (20.2 percent) were also among the places with a high percentage change.

32 In 2000, five tribes accounted for 36.9 percent of the 4.119 million American Indian and Alaska Natives alone or in combination: Cherokee (17.7 percent), Navajo (7.2 percent), Latin American Indian (4.4 percent), Choctaw (3.9 percent), and Sioux (3.7 percent). 25.7 percent of American Indians and Alaska Natives alone live below the poverty level.

33 The percentage of foreign-born population increased from 6.9 percent in 1950 to 12.4 percent in 2005. Mexicans accounted for almost one-third of the foreign born.

34 Foreign-language speakers have been increasing in number in the United States since 1950: 30.5 million people speak Spanish; 1.8 million speak French; 1.1 million speak German; 2.3 million speak Chinese; 1.1 million speak Vietnamese; and 1.3 million speak Tagalog.

35 Of Americans of European ancestry, those of German descent are the most numerous—an estimated 49 million—followed by Irish (34.7 million), English (27.8 million), Italian (17.2 million), Polish (9.8 million), and French (9.5 million).

36 The average American family size in 2005 was 3.18. Of the total number of 74.3 million family households, 14 million are headed by females. Nonfamily households have become more common since the 1960s. Of the 36.7 million nonfamily households, 19.7 million are headed by females.

37 In 2002, 73.3 percent of White family households have two parents, compared with 38.4 percent of Black family households. Fifty-four percent of Black family households are run by single mothers and 6.9 percent by single fathers.

38 According to the Census Bureau, the U.S. population reached the 300 million mark on October 17, 2006. It took only 39 years to reach that milestone from 200 million. In contrast, it took 52 years for the population to increase from 100 million (1915) to 200 million (1967).

39 New York City has the greatest number of people who speak another language at home other than English at 3,385,082, followed by Los Angeles (2,127,362) and Chicago (859,499).

Table 1-1. Area and Population of the United States, 1790–2000

(Square miles, number, and percent.)

Year	Land area (square miles)	Resident population			
		Number	Increase from preceding census		Per square mile of land area
			Number	Percent[1]	
2000 (Apr. 1)[2]	3 537 439	281 422 509	32 704 207	13.1	79.6
1990 (Apr. 1)[2]	3 536 278	248 718 302	22 176 103	9.8	70.3
1980 (Apr. 1)[2]	3 539 289	226 542 199	23 240 168	11.4	64.0
1970 (Apr. 1)[2]	3 536 855	203 302 031	23 978 856	13.4	57.5
1960 (Apr. 1)*	3 540 911	179 323 175	28 625 814	19.0	50.6
1960 (Apr. 1)[3]	2 968 054	178 464 236	27 766 875	18.4	60.1
1950 (Apr. 1)	2 974 726	150 697 361	19 028 086	14.5	50.7
1940 (Apr. 1)	2 977 128	131 669 275	8 894 229	7.2	44.2
1930 (Apr. 1)	2 977 128	122 775 046	17 064 426	16.1	41.2
1920 (Jan. 1)	2 969 451	105 710 620	13 738 354	14.9	35.6
1910 (Apr. 15)	2 969 565	91 972 266	15 977 691	21.0	31.0
1900 (June 1)	2 969 834	75 994 575	13 046 861	20.7	25.6
1890 (June 1)	2 969 640	62 947 714	12 791 931	25.5	21.2
1880 (June 1)	2 969 640	50 155 783	10 337 334	26.0	16.9
1870 (June 1)	2 969 640	[4]39 818 449	8 375 128	26.6	13.4
1860 (June 1)	2 969 640	31 443 321	8 251 445	35.6	10.6
1850 (June 1)	2 940 042	23 191 876	6 122 423	35.9	7.9
1840 (June 1)	1 749 462	17 069 453	4 203 433	32.7	9.8
1830 (June 1)	1 749 462	12 866 020	3 227 567	33.5	7.4
1820 (Aug. 17)	1 749 462	9 638 453	2 398 572	33.1	5.5
1810 (Aug. 6)	1 681 828	7 239 881	1 931 398	36.4	4.3
1800 (Aug. 4)	864 746	5 308 483	1 379 269	35.1	6.1
1790 (Aug. 2)	864 746	3 929 214	. . .	. . .	4.5

Source: U.S. Census Bureau.
[1]1970, 1980, 1990, and 2000 census counts reflect corrections made since original publication
[2]Based on interval since preceding census which is not always exactly 10 years.
[3]Conterminous United States (excludes Alaska and Hawaii).
[4]Revised to include adjustment of 1,260,078 for under enumeration in the southern states. Unrevised census count is 38,558,371.
* = First year for which figures include Alaska and Hawaii.
. . . = Not available.

Table 1-2. Annual Population Estimates for the United States, 1790–2004

(Number in thousands.)

Year	Total including Armed Forces overseas	Total resident population	Civilian resident population
2004	293 907	293 655	292 414
2003	291 028	290 789	289 538
2002	288 173	287 941	286 695
2001	285 329	285 102	283 887
2000	282 402	282 192	280 968
1999	279 295	279 040	277 841
1998	276 115	275 854	274 633
1997	272 912	272 647	271 394
1996	269 667	269 394	268 108
1995	266 557	266 278	264 927
1994	263 436	263 126	261 714
1993	260 255	259 919	258 446
1992	256 894	256 514	254 929
1991	253 493	252 981	251 370
1990	250 132	249 623	247 983
1989	247 342	246 819	245 131
1988	245 021	244 499	242 817
1987	242 804	242 289	240 550
1986	240 651	240 133	238 412
1985	238 466	237 924	236 219
1984	236 348	235 825	234 110
1983	234 307	233 792	232 097
1982	232 188	231 664	229 995
1981	229 966	229 466	227 818
1980	227 726	227 225	225 621
1979	225 055	224 567	222 969
1978	222 585	222 095	220 467
1977	220 239	219 760	218 106
1976	218 035	217 563	215 894
1975	215 973	215 465	213 789
1974	213 854	213 342	211 636
1973	211 909	211 357	209 600
1972	209 896	209 284	207 511
1971	207 661	206 827	204 866
1970	205 052	203 984	201 895
1969	202 677	201 385	199 145
1968	200 706	199 399	197 113
1967	198 712	197 457	195 264
1966	196 560	195 576	193 420
1965	194 303	193 526	191 605
1964	191 889	191 141	189 141
1963	189 242	188 483	186 493
1962	186 538	185 771	183 677
1961	183 691	182 992	181 143
1960	180 671	179 979	178 140
1959*	177 830	177 135	175 277
1959	177 073	176 289	174 521
1958	174 141	173 320	171 485
1957	171 274	170 371	168 400
1956	168 221	167 306	165 373
1955	165 275	164 308	162 311
1954	162 391	161 164	159 059
1953	159 565	158 242	155 975
1952	156 954	155 687	153 292
1951	154 287	153 310	151 009
1950	151 684	151 235	150 203
1949	149 188	148 665	147 578
1948	146 631	146 093	145 168
1947	144 126	143 446	142 566
1946	141 389	140 054	138 385
1945	139 928	132 481	127 573
1944	138 397	132 885	126 708
1943	136 739	134 245	127 499
1942	134 860	133 920	130 942
1941	133 402	133 121	131 595
1940	132 122	131 954	131 658
1939	130 880	. . .	. . .
1938	129 825	. . .	. . .
1937	128 825	. . .	. . .
1936	128 053	. . .	. . .
1935	127 250	. . .	. . .
1934	126 374	. . .	. . .
1933	125 579	. . .	. . .
1932	124 840	. . .	. . .
1931	124 040	. . .	. . .

* = First year for which figures include Alaska and Hawaii.
. . . = Not available.

Table 1-2. **Annual Population Estimates for the United States, 1790—2004—***Continued*

(Number in thousands.)

Year	Total including Armed Forces overseas	Total resident population	Civilian resident population
1930	123 077	...	...
1929	121 767	...	...
1928	120 509	...	...
1927	119 035	...	...
1926	117 397	...	...
1925	115 829	...	...
1924	114 109	...	...
1923	111 947	...	...
1922	110 049	...	...
1921	108 538	...	...
1920	106 461	...	...
1919	[1]104 514	...	...
1918	[1]103 208	...	...
1917	[1]103 268	...	...
1916	101 961	...	...
1915	100 546	...	...
1914	99 111	...	...
1913	97 225	...	...
1912	95 335	...	...
1911	93 863	...	...
1910	92 407	...	...
1909	90 490	...	...
1908	88 710	...	...
1907	87 008	...	...
1906	85 450	...	...
1905	83 822	...	...
1904	82 166	...	...
1903	80 632	...	...
1902	79 163	...	...
1901	77 584	...	...
1900	76 094	...	...
1899	74 799	...	...
1898	73 493	...	...
1897	72 189	...	...
1896	70 885	...	...
1895	69 580	...	...
1894	68 275	...	...
1893	66 970	...	...
1892	65 666	...	...
1891	64 361	...	...
1890	63 056	...	...
1889	61 775	...	...
1888	60 496	...	...
1887	59 217	...	...
1886	57 938	...	...
1885	56 658	...	...
1884	55 379	...	...
1883	54 100	...	...
1882	52 821	...	...
1881	15 542	...	...
1880	50 262	...	...
1879	49 208	...	...
1878	48 174	...	...
1877	47 141	...	...
1876	46 107	...	...
1875	45 073	...	...
1874	44 040	...	...
1873	43 006	...	...
1872	41 972	...	...
1871	40 938	...	...
1870	39 905	...	...
1869	39 051	...	...
1868	38 213	...	...
1867	37 376	...	...
1866	36 538	...	...
1865	35 701	...	...
1864	34 863	...	...
1863	34 026	...	...
1862	33 188	...	...
1861	32 351	...	...

[1]Total population, including Armed Forces overseas (in thousands): 1917 = 103,414; 1918 = 104,550; 1919 = 105,063; civilian population (in thousands): 1917 = 102,796; 1918 = 101,488; 1919 = 104,158. . . . = Not available.

Table 1-2. Annual Population Estimates for the United States, 1790–2004—*Continued*

(Number in thousands.)

Year	Total including Armed Forces overseas	Total resident population	Civilian resident population
1860	31 513	...	...
1859	30 687	...	...
1858	29 862	...	...
1857	29 037	...	...
1856	28 212	...	...
1855	27 386	...	...
1854	26 561	...	...
1853	25 736	...	...
1852	24 911	...	...
1851	24 086	...	...
1850	23 261	...	...
1849	22 631	...	...
1848	22 018	...	...
1847	21 406	...	...
1846	20 794	...	...
1845	20 182	...	...
1844	19 569	...	...
1843	18 957	...	...
1842	18 345	...	...
1841	17 733	...	...
1840	17 120	...	...
1839	16 684	...	...
1838	16 264	...	...
1837	15 843	...	...
1836	15 423	...	...
1835	15 003	...	...
1834	14 582	...	...
1833	14 162	...	...
1832	13 742	...	...
1831	13 321	...	...
1830	12 901	...	...
1829	12 565	...	...
1828	12 237	...	...
1827	11 909	...	...
1826	11 580	...	...
1825	11 252	...	...
1824	10 942	...	...
1823	10 596	...	...
1822	10 268	...	...
1821	9 939	...	...
1820	9 618	...	...
1819	9 379	...	...
1818	9 139	...	...
1817	8 899	...	...
1816	8 659	...	...
1815	8 419	...	...
1814	8 179	...	...
1813	7 939	...	...
1812	7 700	...	...
1811	7 460	...	...
1810	7 244	...	...
1809	7 031	...	...
1808	6 838	...	...
1807	6 644	...	...
1806	6 451	...	...
1805	6 258	...	...
1804	6 065	...	...
1803	5 872	...	...
1802	5 679	...	...
1801	5 486	...	...
1800	5 297	...	...
1799	5 159	...	...
1798	5 021	...	...
1797	4 883	...	...
1796	4 745	...	...
1795	4 607	...	...
1794	4 469	...	...
1793	4 332	...	...
1792	4 194	...	...
1791	4 056	...	...
1790	3 929	...	...

Source: U.S. Census Bureau.
. . . = Not available.

Table 1-3. Annual Estimates and Projections of the Population, by Sex, 1900—2050

(Number in thousands. As of July 1. 1900—1939 and 2003—2005, resident population; 1940—2002, total population, including Armed Forces overseas.)

Year	Total	Sex	
		Male	Female
Projections			
2050	419 854	206 477	213 377
2040	391 946	192 405	199 540
2030	363 584	178 563	185 022
2020	335 805	165 093	170 711
2015	322 366	158 489	163 877
2010	308 936	151 815	157 121
Estimates			
2005	296 410	146 000	150 441
2004	293 657	144 535	149 121
2003	290 850	143 058	147 792
2002	288 600	141 856	146 744
2001	285 545	140 268	145 277
2000	282 434	138 647	143 787
1999	279 295	137 022	142 273
1998	276 115	135 355	140 760
1997	272 912	133 703	139 209
1996	269 667	132 046	137 621
1995	266 557	130 459	136 098
1994	263 436	128 869	134 566
1993	260 255	127 266	132 990
1992	256 894	125 580	131 314
1991	253 492	123 869	129 624
1990	250 132	122 162	127 970
1989	247 342	120 739	126 603
1988	245 021	119 550	125 472
1987	242 804	118 416	124 388
1986	240 651	117 324	123 327
1985	238 466	116 217	122 249
1984	236 348	115 142	121 206
1983	234 307	114 113	120 195
1982	232 188	113 052	119 135
1981	229 966	111 956	118 010
1980	227 726	110 859	116 867
1979	225 055	109 584	115 472
1978	222 585	108 424	114 161
1977	220 239	107 335	112 905
1976	218 035	106 309	111 727
1975	215 973	105 366	110 607
1974	213 854	104 391	109 463
1973	211 909	103 506	108 402
1972	209 896	102 591	107 305
1971	207 661	101 567	106 094
1970	205 052	100 354	104 698
1969	202 677	99 287	103 390
1968	200 706	98 426	102 280
1967	198 712	97 564	101 148
1966	196 560	96 620	99 941
1965	194 303	95 609	98 694
1964	191 889	94 518	97 371
1963	189 242	93 303	95 939
1962	186 538	92 066	94 472
1961	183 691	90 740	92 952
1960	180 671	89 320	91 352
1959*	177 830	87 995	89 834
1959	177 073	87 621	89 453
1958	174 141	86 236	87 905
1957	171 274	84 892	86 382
1956	168 221	83 434	84 786
1955	165 275	82 030	83 246
1954	162 391	80 647	81 744
1953	159 565	79 295	80 270
1952	156 954	78 061	78 893
1951	154 287	76 792	77 496

* = First year for which figures include Alaska and Hawaii.

Table 1-3. Annual Estimates and Projections of the Population, by Sex, 1900–2050–*Continued*

(Number in thousands. As of July 1. 1900–1939 and 2003–2005, resident population; 1940–2002, total population, including Armed Forces overseas.)

Year	Total	Sex	
		Male	Female
1950	151 684	75 539	76 146
1949	149 188	74 335	74 853
1948	146 631	73 130	73 502
1947	144 126	71 946	72 180
1946	141 389	70 631	70 757
1945	139 928	70 035	69 893
1944	138 397	69 378	69 020
1943	136 739	68 546	68 194
1942	134 860	67 597	67 263
1941	133 402	66 920	66 482
1940	132 122	66 352	65 770
1939	130 880	65 713	65 166
1938	129 825	65 235	64 590
1937	128 825	64 790	64 035
1936	128 053	64 460	63 594
1935	127 250	64 110	63 140
1934	126 374	63 726	62 648
1933	125 579	63 384	62 195
1932	124 840	63 070	61 770
1931	124 040	62 726	61 314
1930	123 077	62 297	60 780
1929	121 767	61 680	60 087
1928	120 509	61 101	59 408
1927	119 035	60 397	58 638
1926	117 397	59 588	57 809
1925	115 829	58 813	57 016
1924	[1]114 109	257 985	56 124
1923	[1]111 947	256 861	55 086
1922	[1]110 049	255 886	54 163
1921	108 538	55 292	53 246
1920	106 461	54 291	52 170
1919	104 514	53 103	51 411
1918	103 208	51 974	51 234
1917	103 268	52 788	50 480
1916	101 961	52 234	49 727
1915	100 546	51 573	48 973
1914	99 111	50 883	48 228
1913	97 225	49 957	47 268
1912	95 335	49 025	46 310
1911	93 863	48 290	45 573
1910	92 407	47 554	44 853
1909	90 490	46 545	43 945
1908	88 710	45 594	43 116
1907	87 008	44 682	42 326
1906	85 450	43 841	41 609
1905	83 822	42 965	40 857
1904	82 166	42 089	40 077
1903	80 632	41 262	39 370
1902	79 163	40 483	38 680
1901	77 584	39 649	37 935
1900	76 094	38 867	37 227

Source: U.S. Census Bureau.
[1]Estimates including Armed Forces overseas, in thousands: 1917 = 103,414; 1918 = 104,550; 1919 = 105,063.
[2]Estimates including Armed Forces overseas, in thousands: 1917 = 52,934; 1918 = 53,316; 1919 = 53,658.

Table 1-4. Annual Estimates and Projections of the Population, by Age, 1900–2050

(Number in thousands. As of July 1. 1900–1939 and 2003–2005, resident population; 1940–2002, total population, including Armed Forces overseas.)

Year	Total	Under 5 years	5–14 years	15–24 years	25–34 years	35–44 years	45–54 years	55–64 years	65 years and over
Projections									
2050	419 854 000	28 080 000	54 495 000	52 869 000	52 804 000	51 796 000	47 383 000	45 721 000	86 705 000
2040	391 946 000	26 299 000	50 503 000	49 721 000	49 755 000	47 008 000	46 981 000	41 629 000	80 049 000
2030	363 584 000	24 272 000	47 329 000	46 639 000	44 935 000	46 676 000	42 902 000	39 378 000	71 453 000
2020	335 805 000	22 932 000	44 478 000	42 229 000	45 065 000	42 816 000	40 921 000	42 732 000	54 632 000
2010	308 936 000	21 426 000	40 473 000	43 012 000	41 646 000	41 121 000	44 827 000	36 186 000	
Estimates									
2005	296 410 000	20 304 000	40 397 000	42 077 000	40 143 000	43 863 000	42 483 000	30 356 000	36 790 000
2004	293 657 000	20 061 000	40 745 000	41 697 000	40 022 000	44 105 000	41 617 000	29 077 000	36 333 000
2003	290 850 000	19 778 000	40 960 000	41 255 000	39 859 000	44 404 000	40 806 000	27 834 000	35 952 000
2002	288 600 205	19 609 147	41 037 286	40 682 017	40 011 623	44 966 018	40 090 235	26 601 968	35 601 911
2001	285 545 032	19 363 555	41 118 564	40 072 966	39 897 632	45 188 663	39 234 294	25 316 092	35 353 266
2000	282 434 382	19 212 382	41 076 678	39 433 066	39 937 925	45 200 232	38 057 687	24 436 064	35 080 348
1999	279 294 713	19 135 544	40 819 824	38 770 905	40 278 512	45 129 860	36 584 022	23 778 205	34 797 841
1998	276 115 288	19 144 923	40 335 509	38 103 329	40 861 616	44 801 737	35 237 881	23 011 134	34 619 159
1997	272 911 760	19 232 671	39 854 729	37 403 286	41 454 232	44 282 377	34 183 418	22 099 486	34 401 561
1996	269 667 391	19 408 272	39 295 639	36 897 544	41 922 421	43 604 756	32 805 569	21 590 141	34 143 049
1995	266 557 091	19 626 505	38 645 220	36 776 907	42 167 847	42 765 129	31 486 001	21 320 178	33 769 304
1994	263 435 673	19 776 862	38 025 965	36 649 961	42 456 594	41 877 423	30 158 761	21 159 304	33 330 803
1993	260 255 352	19 729 275	37 367 359	36 591 319	42 791 562	40 974 857	28 870 496	21 028 673	32 901 811
1992	256 894 189	19 528 041	36 676 867	36 578 817	43 155 535	40 045 547	27 555 069	20 998 319	32 355 994
1991	253 492 503	19 208 046	36 037 085	36 717 342	43 431 090	39 413 148	25 828 059	21 046 109	31 811 624
1990	250 131 894	18 856 447	35 289 633	37 131 327	43 425 039	37 865 692	25 214 557	21 101 920	31 247 279
1989	247 341 697	18 508 058	34 713 629	37 613 503	43 448 348	36 494 304	24 640 816	21 241 283	30 681 756
1988	245 021 414	18 195 420	34 255 539	38 380 551	43 337 953	35 257 516	23 956 847	21 513 981	30 123 607
1987	242 803 533	18 052 205	33 807 104	39 125 882	43 039 473	34 298 910	23 102 870	21 750 923	29 626 166
1986	240 650 755	17 962 501	33 572 632	39 797 597	42 569 828	33 080 761	22 665 712	21 994 127	29 007 597
1985	238 466 283	17 841 621	33 692 290	40 241 164	41 906 305	31 766 587	22 466 729	22 135 408	28 416 179
1984	236 348 292	17 694 905	33 788 200	40 705 554	41 159 818	30 575 414	22 392 473	22 154 421	27 877 507
1983	234 307 207	17 546 883	33 921 777	41 270 714	40 396 793	29 336 099	22 362 154	22 112 114	27 360 673
1982	232 187 835	17 227 829	34 102 523	41 915 663	39 597 137	28 095 288	22 431 804	22 030 110	26 787 481
1981	229 966 237	16 892 719	34 360 528	42 464 817	39 073 237	26 454 383	22 585 741	21 914 015	26 220 797
1980	227 726 463	16 451 184	34 838 688	42 755 321	37 602 918	25 867 299	22 749 367	21 754 230	25 707 456
1979	225 055 487	16 062 882	35 391 774	42 698 483	36 202 624	25 175 999	22 942 025	21 447 956	25 133 744
1978	222 584 545	15 735 004	36 219 589	42 442 086	34 963 103	24 436 821	23 173 601	21 112 290	24 502 051
1977	220 239 425	15 563 659	37 033 667	42 039 541	33 998 226	23 562 471	23 370 355	20 779 661	23 891 845
1976	218 035 164	15 617 115	37 758 862	41 520 290	32 758 856	23 093 851	23 622 096	20 385 993	23 278 101
1975	215 973 199	16 121 483	38 240 018	40 811 662	31 471 262	22 830 830	23 756 641	20 045 008	22 696 295
1974	213 853 928	16 486 729	38 715 753	40 017 005	30 225 400	22 825 489	23 808 746	19 713 323	22 061 483
1973	211 908 788	16 850 846	39 308 434	39 240 266	28 939 077	22 810 067	23 807 018	19 428 146	21 524 934
1972	209 896 021	17 101 353	39 945 515	38 449 007	27 623 937	22 859 507	23 686 132	19 210 749	21 019 821
1971	207 660 677	17 243 968	40 490 468	37 947 543	25 958 294	22 978 047	23 518 574	18 962 323	20 561 460
1970	205 052 174	17 166 191	40 772 280	36 535 203	25 323 532	23 149 652	23 316 402	18 682 185	20 106 729
1969	202 677 000	17 376 000	40 884 000	35 236 000	24 681 000	23 383 000	23 047 000	18 390 000	19 680 000
1968	200 706 000	17 913 000	40 772 000	34 090 000	23 990 000	23 731 000	22 758 000	18 088 000	19 365 000
1967	198 712 000	18 563 000	40 496 000	33 196 000	23 156 000	24 038 000	22 440 000	17 752 000	19 071 000
1966	196 560 000	19 208 000	40 051 000	32 012 000	22 725 000	24 276 000	22 125 000	17 408 000	18 755 000
1965	194 303 000	19 824 000	39 426 000	30 773 000	22 465 000	24 447 000	21 839 000	17 077 000	18 541 000
1964	191 889 000	20 165 000	38 783 000	29 519 000	22 396 000	24 562 000	21 580 000	16 758 000	18 127 000
1963	189 242 000	20 342 000	38 124 000	28 223 000	22 410 000	24 584 000	21 346 000	16 436 000	17 778 000
1962	186 538 000	20 469 000	37 435 000	26 909 000	22 494 000	24 519 000	21 124 000	16 131 000	17 457 000
1961	183 691 000	20 522 000	37 031 000	25 242 000	22 692 000	24 392 000	20 875 000	15 847 000	17 089 000
1960	180 671 000	20 341 000	35 735 000	24 576 000	22 919 000	24 221 000	20 578 000	15 625 000	16 675 000
1959*	177 830 000	20 175 000	34 564 000	23 988 000	23 169 000	24 023 000	20 262 000	15 401 000	16 248 000
1959	177 073 000	20 055 000	34 390 000	23 890 000	23 062 000	23 917 000	20 189 000	15 357 000	16 213 000
1958	174 141 000	19 768 000	33 322 000	23 162 000	23 430 000	23 693 000	19 857 000	15 139 000	15 771 000
1957	171 274 000	19 379 000	32 515 000	22 311 000	23 737 000	23 496 000	19 513 000	14 973 000	15 353 000
1956	168 221 000	18 895 000	31 423 000	21 869 000	24 015 000	23 160 000	19 143 000	14 815 000	14 902 000
1955	165 275 000	18 467 000	30 248 000	21 667 000	24 175 000	22 818 000	18 824 000	14 586 000	14 489 000
1954	162 391 000	17 962 000	29 092 000	21 641 000	24 233 000	22 571 000	18 501 000	14 350 000	14 040 000
1953	159 565 000	17 548 000	27 880 000	21 658 000	24 233 000	22 359 000	18 171 000	14 135 000	13 582 000
1952	156 954 000	17 228 000	26 656 000	21 796 000	24 197 000	22 109 000	17 881 000	13 918 000	13 169 000
1951	154 287 000	17 252 000	25 055 000	22 018 000	24 085 000	21 833 000	17 623 000	13 654 000	12 768 000
1950	151 684 000	16 331 000	24 477 000	22 260 000	23 932 000	21 557 000	17 400 000	13 364 000	12 362 000
1949	149 188 000	15 607 000	23 770 000	22 570 000	23 729 000	21 187 000	17 260 000	13 145 000	11 921 000
1948	146 631 000	14 919 000	23 089 000	22 866 000	23 494 000	20 794 000	17 107 000	12 824 000	11 538 000
1947	144 126 000	14 406 000	22 257 000	23 122 000	23 236 000	20 421 000	16 970 000	12 528 000	11 185 000
1946	141 389 000	13 244 000	21 844 000	23 382 000	22 954 000	20 073 000	16 820 000	12 244 000	10 828 000
1945	139 928 000	12 979 000	21 599 000	23 705 000	22 734 000	19 787 000	16 642 000	11 988 000	10 494 000
1944	138 397 000	12 524 000	21 573 000	23 999 000	22 511 000	19 505 000	16 419 000	11 719 000	10 147 000
1943	136 739 000	12 016 000	21 699 000	24 065 000	22 194 000	19 226 000	16 199 000	11 472 000	9 867 000
1942	134 860 000	11 301 000	21 823 000	24 093 000	21 911 000	18 950 000	15 976 000	11 220 000	9 584 000
1941	133 402 000	10 850 000	22 089 000	24 074 000	21 691 000	18 692 000	15 759 000	10 959 000	9 288 000

* = First year for which figures include Alaska and Hawaii.

Table 1-4. Annual Estimates and Projections of the Population, by Age, 1900–2050—*Continued*

(Number in thousands. As of July 1. 1900–1939 and 2003–2005, resident population; 1940–2002, total population, including Armed Forces overseas.)

Year	Total	Under 5 years	5–14 years	15–24 years	25–34 years	35–44 years	45–54 years	55–64 years	65 years and over
1940	132 122 000	10 579 000	22 363 000	24 033 000	21 446 000	18 422 000	15 555 000	10 694 000	9 031 000
1939	130 880 000	10 148 000	22 701 000	23 819 000	21 176 000	18 178 000	15 336 000	10 487 000	8 764 000
1938	129 825 000	10 176 000	23 146 000	23 655 000	20 953 000	18 001 000	15 077 000	10 310 000	8 508 000
1937	128 825 000	10 009 000	23 564 000	23 487 000	20 723 000	17 866 000	14 785 000	10 132 000	8 258 000
1936	128 053 000	10 044 000	23 942 000	23 309 000	20 505 000	17 783 000	14 495 000	9 949 000	8 027 000
1935	127 250 000	10 170 000	24 213 000	23 130 000	20 275 000	17 712 000	14 208 000	9 739 000	7 804 000
1934	126 374 000	10 331 000	24 402 000	22 963 000	20 022 000	17 640 000	13 933 000	9 502 000	7 582 000
1933	125 579 000	10 612 000	24 531 000	22 820 000	19 750 000	17 569 000	13 684 000	9 249 000	7 363 000
1932	124 840 000	10 903 000	24 614 000	22 716 000	19 484 000	17 504 000	13 481 000	8 992 000	7 147 000
1931	124 040 000	11 179 000	24 629 000	22 617 000	19 242 000	17 412 000	13 296 000	8 735 000	6 928 000
1930	123 077 000	11 372 000	24 631 000	22 487 000	19 039 000	17 270 000	13 096 000	8 477 000	6 705 000
1929	121 767 000	11 734 000	24 470 000	22 151 000	18 941 000	16 921 000	12 761 000	8 315 000	6 474 000
1928	120 509 000	11 978 000	24 320 000	21 811 000	18 953 000	16 540 000	12 430 000	8 178 000	6 299 000
1927	119 035 000	12 111 000	24 152 000	21 430 000	18 948 000	16 172 000	12 092 000	8 003 000	6 127 000
1926	117 397 000	12 189 000	23 906 000	21 037 000	18 867 000	15 847 000	11 786 000	7 805 000	5 960 000
1925	115 829 000	12 316 000	23 614 000	20 691 000	18 720 000	15 576 000	11 521 000	7 605 000	5 786 000
1924	114 109 000	12 269 000	23 358 000	20 314 000	18 557 000	15 337 000	11 278 000	7 387 000	5 609 000
1923	111 947 000	12 119 000	23 089 000	19 798 000	18 231 000	15 066 000	11 068 000	7 165 000	5 411 000
1922	110 049 000	12 031 000	22 788 000	19 402 000	17 924 000	14 823 000	10 899 000	6 951 000	5 231 000
1921	108 538 000	11 879 000	22 515 000	19 140 000	17 747 000	14 665 000	10 721 000	6 791 000	5 080 000
1920	106 461 000	11 631 000	22 158 000	18 821 000	17 416 000	14 382 000	10 505 000	6 619 000	4 929 000
1919	104 514 000	11 536 000	21 849 000	18 465 000	16 912 000	14 008 000	10 402 000	6 456 000	4 886 000
1918	103 208 000	11 606 000	21 732 000	18 071 000	16 445 000	13 879 000	10 293 000	6 356 000	4 826 000
1917	103 268 000	11 527 000	21 369 000	18 836 000	16 913 000	13 647 000	10 068 000	6 194 000	4 714 000
1916	101 961 000	11 442 000	21 008 000	18 872 000	16 776 000	13 388 000	9 846 000	6 026 000	4 603 000
1915	100 546 000	11 347 000	20 660 000	18 844 000	16 580 000	13 130 000	9 613 000	5 866 000	4 501 000
1914	99 111 000	11 244 000	20 816 000	18 796 000	16 370 000	12 875 000	9 398 000	5 711 000	4 401 000
1913	97 225 000	11 082 000	19 904 000	18 649 000	16 070 000	12 562 000	9 135 000	5 542 000	4 281 000
1912	95 335 000	10 915 000	19 503 000	18 477 000	15 772 000	12 252 000	8 875 000	5 372 000	4 169 000
1911	93 863 000	10 796 000	19 214 000	18 355 000	15 530 000	12 003 000	8 657 000	5 234 000	4 074 000
1910	92 407 000	10 671 000	18 950 000	18 212 000	15 274 000	11 759 000	8 454 000	5 101 000	3 986 000
1909	90 490 000	10 509 000	18 670 000	17 871 000	14 923 000	11 471 000	8 204 000	4 964 000	3 878 000
1908	88 710 000	10 364 000	18 440 000	17 526 000	14 585 000	11 202 000	7 974 000	4 840 000	3 779 000
1907	87 008 000	10 220 000	18 240 000	17 184 000	14 257 000	10 945 000	7 755 000	4 724 000	3 684 000
1906	85 450 000	10 092 000	18 067 000	16 864 000	13 952 000	10 705 000	7 554 000	4 621 000	3 595 000
1905	83 822 000	9 944 000	17 888 000	16 526 000	13 631 000	10 461 000	7 350 000	4 517 000	3 505 000
1904	82 166 000	9 791 000	17 697 000	16 178 000	13 315 000	10 211 000	7 150 000	4 410 000	3 414 000
1903	80 632 000	9 645 000	17 524 000	15 858 000	13 019 000	9 974 000	6 964 000	4 313 000	3 335 000
1902	79 163 000	9 502 000	17 360 000	15 555 000	12 737 000	9 745 000	6 788 000	4 220 000	3 256 000
1901	77 584 000	9 336 000	17 158 000	15 242 000	12 442 000	9 504 000	6 606 000	4 122 000	3 174 000
1900	76 094 000	9 181 000	16 966 000	14 951 000	12 161 000	9 273 000	6 437 000	4 026 000	3 099 000

Source: U.S. Census Bureau.

Table 1-5. Resident Population, by Sex, 1790–2005

(Number. 2001–2005 Resident population data was reported by U.S. Census Bureau in thousands; prior years were reported as number.)

Year	Total	Male	Female
2005	296 410 000	146 000 000	150 411 000
2004	293 657 000	144 535 000	149 121 000
2003	290 850 000	143 058 000	147 792 000
2002	287 985 000	141 542 000	146 442 000
2001	285 108 000	140 016 000	145 092 000
2000[1]	281 421 906	138 053 563	143 368 343
1990[1]	248 709 873	121 239 418	127 470 455
1980[1]	226 545 805	110 047 513	116 498 292
1970[1]	203 211 926	98 912 192	10 429 973
1960*	179 323 175	88 331 494	90 991 681
1960	178 464 236	87 864 510	90 599 726
1950	150 697 361	74 833 239	75 864 122
1940	131 669 275	66 061 592	65 607 683
1930	122 775 046	62 137 080	60 637 966
1920	105 710 620	53 900 431	51 810 189
1910	91 972 266	47 332 277	44 639 989
1900	75 994 575	38 816 448	37 178 127
1890	62 947 714	32 237 101	30 710 613
1880	50 155 783	25 518 820	24 636 963
1870	38 558 371	19 493 565	19 064 806
1860	31 443 321	16 085 204	15 358 117
1850	23 191 876	11 837 660	11 354 216
1840	17 069 453	8 688 532	8 380 921
1830	12 866 020	6 532 489	6 333 531
1820	9 638 453	4 896 605	4 741 848
1810	7 239 881	. . .	. . .
1800	5 308 483	. . .	. . .
1790	3 929 214	. . .	. . .

Source: U.S. Census Bureau.
[1]See Table 1-1 for total numbers that reflect corrections since the original publications.
* = First year for which figures include Alaska and Hawaii.
. . . = Not available.

Table 1-6. Median Age of Population, by Race and Sex, 1790–2005

(Age in years.)

Year	All races			White			Black		
	Total	Male	Female	Total	Male	Female	Total	Male	Female
2005	36.2	34.9	37.6	37.6	...	...	30.9	...	...
2004	36.0	34.7	37.4	37.5	...	...	30.8	...	...
2003	35.9	34.5	37.2	37.3	...	...	30.6	...	...
2002	35.7	34.4	37.0	37.1	...	...	30.4	...	...
2001	35.6	34.2	36.8	36.9	...	...	30.2	...	...
2000	35.3	34.0	36.5	36.6	...	...	30.0	...	...
1999	35.2	...	...	...	...	...	...	...	...
1998	34.9	...	...	...	...	...	...	...	...
1997	34.7	...	...	...	...	...	...	...	...
1996	34.4	...	...	...	...	...	...	...	...
1995	34.2	...	...	...	...	...	...	...	...
1994	33.9	...	...	...	...	...	...	...	...
1993	33.6	...	...	...	...	...	...	...	...
1992	33.4	32.3	34.6	34.4	...	...	28.4	...	...
1991	33.1	31.9	34.3	34.1	...	...	28.2	...	...
1990	32.8	31.6	34.0	33.8	...	...	27.9	...	...
1989	32.6	31.6	33.8	33.6	32.5	34.7	27.7	26.3	29.1
1988	32.0	31.2	33.5	33.3	32.1	34.4	27.5	26.1	28.8
1987	31.7	30.9	33.3	33.0	31.9	34.2	27.2	25.8	28.5
1986	31.6	30.6	33.0	32.7	31.5	33.9	26.9	25.5	28.2
1985	31.5	30.3	32.7	32.4	31.2	33.6	26.6	25.2	27.8
1984	31.2	30.0	32.8	32.2	31.0	33.4	26.3	24.9	27.6
1983	30.9	29.6	32.2	31.8	30.5	33.1	25.8	24.4	27.2
1982	30.6	29.4	31.9	31.5	30.2	32.8	25.5	24.1	26.8
1981	30.3	29.1	31.6	31.2	29.9	32.5	25.2	23.9	26.5
1980	30.0	28.8	31.3	30.9	29.6	32.2	24.9	23.6	26.2
1979	29.8	38.9	31.3	30.9	29.7	32.2	24.6	23.5	25.9
1978	29.5	28.6	31.0	30.6	29.4	32.0	24.3	23.2	25.5
1977	29.2	28.2	30.6	30.3	29.0	31.6	24.1	22.9	25.2
1976	28.9	...	...	...	...	...	...	...	...
1975	28.8	27.6	30.3	29.6	28.4	31.0	23.4	22.2	24.6
1974	28.7	27.4	29.8	29.5	28.2	30.8	23.2	21.9	24.3
1973	28.4	...	...	...	...	...	...	...	...
1972	28.2	26.8	29.4	29.2	...	...	23.0	...	...
1971	28.0	...	...	...	...	...	...	...	...
1970	28.1	26.8	29.3	28.9	27.6	30.2	22.4	21.0	23.6
1960*	29.5	28.7	30.3	30.3	29.4	31.1	23.5	22.3	24.5
1960	29.6	28.7	30.4	30.3	29.5	31.2	23.5	22.3	24.5
1950	30.2	29.9	30.5	30.8	30.4	31.1	26.1	25.8	26.4
1940	29.0	29.1	29.0	29.5	29.5	29.5	25.3	25.3	25.3
1930	26.5	26.7	26.2	26.9	27.1	26.6	23.5	23.7	23.3
1920	25.3	25.8	24.7	25.6	26.1	25.1	22.3	22.8	22.0
1910	24.1	24.6	23.5	24.5	24.9	23.9	20.8	21.0	20.7
1900	22.9	23.3	22.4	23.4	23.8	22.9	19.5	19.5	19.5
1890	22.0	22.3	21.6	22.5	22.9	22.1	18.1	17.9	18.3
1880	20.9	21.2	20.7	21.4	21.6	21.1	...	...	...
1870	20.2	20.2	20.1	20.4	20.6	20.3	18.3	17.8	18.8
1860	19.4	19.8	19.1	19.7	20.1	19.3	17.5	17.5	17.5
1850	18.9	19.2	18.6	19.2	19.5	18.8	17.4	17.3	17.4
1840	17.8	17.9	17.8	17.9	18.0	17.8	17.6	17.5	17.6
1830	17.2	17.2	17.3	17.3	17.2	17.3	17.2	17.1	17.3
1820	16.7	16.6	16.8	16.6	16.5	16.6	17.2	17.1	17.4
1810	...	...	...	16.0	15.9	16.1	...	...	...
1800	...	...	...	16.0	15.7	16.3	...	...	...
1790	...	...	...	...	(¹)	...	...	...	...

Source: U.S. Census Bureau.
¹Median falls in the open-ended age group, 16 years and over, which includes 50.3 percent of the White male population.
* = First year for which figures include Alaska and Hawaii.
... = Not available.

Table 1-7. Marital Status of the Population, by Age and Sex, 1890–2005

(Number. Marital status for 1980 and following years reported by U.S. Census Bureau in thousands; prior years reported as number. Excludes members of Armed Forces except those living off post or with their families on post.)

Year	Female Total	Never married	Married	Widowed	Divorced	Status not reported	Male Total	Never married	Married	Widowed	Divorced	Status not reported
18 Years and Over												
2005	112 329 000	24 318 000	63 971 000	11 105 000	12 932 000	-	104 848 000	29 608 000	63 318 000	2 723 000	9 200 000	-
18 to 19 years old	3 805 000	3 622 000	168 000	3 000	13 000	-	3 760 000	3 701 000	55 000	0	3 000	-
20 to 24 years old	10 110 000	7 546 000	2 376 000	17 000	171 000	-	10 282 000	8 868 000	1 304 000	8 000	103 000	
25 to 29 years old	9 674 000	3 995 000	5 084 000	31 000	563 000	-	9 812 000	5 399 000	4 060 000	4 000	348 000	
30 to 34 years old	9 956 000	2 347 000	6 709 000	53 000	847 000	-	9 842 000	3 138 000	6 031 000	21 000	652 000	
35 to 39 years old	10 376 000	1 616 000	7 326 000	87 000	1 347 000	-	11 189 000	2 304 000	6 904 000	45 000	1 006 000	
40 to 44 years old	11 489 000	1 387 000	8 183 000	185 000	1 734 000	-	11 189 000	1 964 000	7 827 000	56 000	1 343 000	
45 to 54 years old	21 399 000	2 073 000	14 841 000	661 000	3 822 000	-	20 526 000	2 665 000	14 865 000	176 000	2 820 000	
55 to 64 years old	15 481 000	946 000	10 331 000	1 474 000	2 730 000	-	14 032 000	899 000	10 932 000	344 000	1 857 000	
65 to 74 years old	9 913 000	406 000	5 655 000	2 772 000	1 079 000	-	8 463 000	408 000	6 646 000	692 000	717 000	
75 years old and over	10 126 000	380 000	3 298 000	5 822 000	626 000	-	6 682 000	262 000	4 694 000	1 377 000	351 000	
2004	110 883 000	23 655 000	63 282 000	11 141 000	12 804 000	-	103 641 000	29 561 000	62 483 000	2 641 000	8 956 000	-
18 to 19 years old	3 552 000	3 391 000	147 000	-	14 000	-	3 923 000	3 868 000	49 000	-	6 000	
20 to 24 years old	10 060 000	7 581 000	2 326 000	11 000	142 000	-	10 241 000	8 850 000	1 308 000	2 000	81 000	
25 to 29 years old	9 460 000	3 855 000	5 004 000	42 000	559 000	-	9 535 000	5 395 000	3 812 000	8 000	320 000	
30 to 34 years old	10 127 000	2 400 000	6 797 000	67 000	863 000	-	10 018 000	3 223 000	6 085 000	20 000	690 000	
35 to 39 years old	10 477 000	1 534 000	7 408 000	135 000	1 400 000	-	10 306 000	2 410 000	6 864 000	30 000	1 002 000	
40 to 44 years old	11 560 000	1 406 000	8 227 000	162 000	1 765 000	-	11 213 000	1 978 000	7 767 000	54 000	1 414 000	
45 to 54 years old	20 974 000	1 949 000	14 691 000	633 000	3 701 000	-	20 070 000	2 437 000	14 715 000	203 000	2 715 000	
55 to 64 years old	14 823 000	796 000	9 973 000	1 458 000	2 596 000	-	13 543 000	797 000	10 756 000	293 000	1 697 000	
65 to 74 years old	9 880 000	365 000	5 589 000	2 768 000	1 158 000	-	8 352 000	370 000	6 630 000	626 000	726 000	
75 years old and over	9 970 000	378 000	3 121 000	5 865 000	606 000	-	6 440 000	233 000	4 497 000	1 405 000	305 000	
2003	110 115 000	23 333 000	62 834 000	11 288 000	12 660 000	-	102 313 000	28 577 000	62 087 000	2 692 000	8 957 000	-
18 to 19 years old	3 689 000	3 486 000	198 000	-	5 000	-	3 858 000	3 794 000	61 000	2 000	2 000	
20 to 24 years old	9 903 000	7 463 000	2 274 000	16 000	150 000	-	9 953 000	8 563 000	1 297 000	-	93 000	
25 to 29 years old	9 330 000	3 760 000	5 028 000	36 000	505 000	-	9 366 000	5 112 000	3 914 000	14 000	327 000	
30 to 34 years old	10 329 000	2 349 000	6 995 000	58 000	928 000	-	10 177 000	3 371 000	6 105 000	21 000	678 000	
35 to 39 years old	10 766 000	1 544 000	7 617 000	134 000	1 471 000	-	10 503 000	2 289 000	7 142 000	21 000	1 051 000	
40 to 44 years old	11 556 000	1 411 000	8 199 000	185 000	1 762 000	-	11 199 000	1 953 000	7 896 000	67 000	1 284 000	
45 to 54 years old	20 617 000	1 797 000	14 521 000	640 000	3 658 000	-	19 578 000	2 117 000	14 439 000	202 000	2 821 000	
55 to 64 years old	14 229 000	801 000	9 463 000	1 487 000	2 478 000	-	13 158 000	757 000	10 430 000	292 000	1 679 000	
65 to 74 years old	9 831 000	337 000	5 505 000	2 888 000	1 101 000	-	8 268 000	383 000	6 415 000	726 000	744 000	
75 years old and over	9 864 000	383 000	3 034 000	5 844 000	602 000	-	6 253 000	239 000	4 390 000	1 347 000	277 000	
2002	108 712 000	23 036 000	62 037 000	11 404 000	12 236 000	-	100 611 000	28 107 000	61 212 000	2 632 000	8 659 000	-
18 to 19 years old	3 880 000	3 640 000	222 000	2 000	16 000	-	4 026 000	3 943 000	76 000	-	7 000	
20 to 24 years old	9 722 000	7 195 000	2 354 000	8 000	164 000	-	9 670 000	8 261 000	1 350 000	3 000	56 000	
25 to 29 years old	9 158 000	3 700 000	4 901 000	33 000	524 000	-	9 141 000	4 904 000	3 875 000	7 000	356 000	
30 to 34 years old	10 270 000	2 362 000	6 888 000	75 000	946 000	-	10 079 000	3 429 000	6 012 000	15 000	623 000	
35 to 39 years old	10 947 000	1 613 000	7 831 000	102 000	1 402 000	-	11 109 000	2 255 000	7 315 000	32 000	1 094 000	
40 to 44 years old	11 506 000	1 320 000	8 295 000	215 000	1 677 000	-	11 109 000	1 852 000	7 909 000	66 000	1 284 000	
45 to 54 years old	20 209 000	1 799 000	14 172 000	672 000	3 566 000	-	19 302 000	2 113 000	14 219 000	215 000	2 755 000	
55 to 64 years old	13 497 000	715 000	8 992 000	1 407 000	2 384 000	-	12 363 000	818 000	9 688 000	318 000	1 538 000	
65 to 74 years old	9 876 000	346 000	5 457 000	3 018 000	1 053 000	-	8 243 000	304 000	6 561 000	706 000	672 000	
75 years old and over	9 647 000	347 000	2 922 000	5 872 000	506 000	-	5 984 000	228 000	4 210 000	1 271 000	275 000	
2001	105 584 000	33 077 000	61 209 000	2 540 000	8 758 000	-	113 451 000	28 056 000	61 889 000	11 526 000	11 980 000	-
2000	104 863 000	22 089 000	60 436 000	11 054 000	11 284 000	-	96 900 000	26 124 000	59 631 000	2 601 000	8 544 000	-
18 to 19 years old	4 009 000	3 727 000	270 000	2 000	10 000	-	4 082 000	4 011 000	70 000	-	1 000	
20 to 24 years old	9 232 000	6 720 000	2 333 000	11 000	168 000	-	9 208 000	7 710 000	1 397 000	-	101 000	
25 to 29 years old	9 326 000	3 627 000	5 106 000	18 000	575 000	-	8 943 000	4 625 000	3 967 000	9 000	342 000	
30 to 34 years old	9 897 000	2 172 000	6 758 000	63 000	904 000	-	9 621 000	2 899 000	5 996 000	15 000	712 000	
35 to 39 years old	11 288 000	1 610 000	8 061 000	131 000	1 486 000	-	11 032 000	2 241 000	7 440 000	42 000	1 308 000	
40 to 44 years old	11 382 000	1 341 000	8 163 000	172 000	1 706 000	-	11 103 000	1 740 000	7 842 000	54 000	1 467 000	
45 to 54 years old	18 742 000	1 606 000	13 191 000	725 000	3 220 000	-	17 889 000	1 697 000	13 660 000	157 000	2 377 000	
55 to 64 years old	12 251 000	606 000	8 333 000	1 441 000	1 871 000	-	11 137 000	612 000	8 809 000	329 000	1 387 000	
65 to 74 years old	9 748 000	363 000	5 424 000	3 055 000	906 000	-	8 051 000	348 000	6 411 000	667 000	625 000	
75 years old and over	8 988 000	317 000	2 799 000	5 435 000	438 000	-	5 838 000	242 000	4 044 000	1 327 000	225 000	
1999	103 867 000	21 865 000	59 918 000	10 944 000	11 141 000	-	95 853 000	25 782 000	58 986 000	2 542 000	8 543 000	-
18 to 19 years old	3 910 000	3 655 000	248 000	-	6 000	-	3 999 000	3 921 000	75 000	-	4 000	
20 to 24 years old	9 121 000	6 585 000	2 350 000	9 000	178 000	-	8 937 000	7 434 000	1 419 000	-	83 000	
25 to 29 years old	9 482 000	3 690 000	5 244 000	27 000	520 000	-	9 157 000	4 776 000	3 966 000	4 000	411 000	
30 to 34 years old	10 069 000	2 223 000	6 801 000	46 000	1 000 000	-	9 767 000	2 997 000	6 062 000	11 000	696 000	
35 to 39 years old	11 340 000	1 727 000	8 084 000	120 000	1 410 000	-	11 189 000	2 357 000	7 528 000	46 000	1 258 000	
40 to 44 years old	11 248 000	1 233 000	8 007 000	180 000	1 827 000	-	10 967 000	1 738 000	7 658 000	61 000	1 511 000	
45 to 54 years old	18 088 000	1 408 000	12 873 000	689 000	3 118 000	-	17 144 000	1 474 000	13 089 000	182 000	2 399 000	
55 to 64 years old	11 942 000	593 000	8 043 000	1 488 000	1 819 000	-	10 967 000	596 000	8 770 000	310 000	1 289 000	
65 to 74 years old	9 816 000	385 000	5 503 000	3 074 000	856 000	-	8 027 000	277 000	6 389 000	705 000	656 000	
75 years old and over	8 851 000	366 000	2 767 000	5 311 000	407 000	-	5 700 000	212 000	4 029 000	1 222 000	237 000	

- = Quantity zero.

Table 1-7. Marital Status of the Population, by Age and Sex, 1890–2005–*Continued*

(Number. Marital status for 1980 and following years reported by U.S. Census Bureau in thousands; prior years reported as number. Excludes members of Armed Forces except those living off post or with their families on post.)

Year	Female						Male					
	Total	Never married	Married	Widowed	Divorced	Status not reported	Total	Never married	Married	Widowed	Divorced	Status not reported
1998	102 403 000	21 043 000	59 255 000	11 027 000	11 078 000	-	95 009 000	25 518 000	58 601 000	2 567 000	8 322 000	-
18 to 19 years old	3 780 000	3 565 000	211 000	-	5 000	-	3 807 000	3 706 000	91 000	-	10 000	-
20 to 24 years old	8 788 000	6 178 000	2 372 000	17 000	222 000	-	8 826 000	7 360 000	1 332 000	-	113 000	-
25 to 29 years old	9 546 000	3 689 000	5 298 000	35 000	525 000	-	9 450 000	4 822 000	4 219 000	10 000	398 000	-
30 to 34 years old	10 282 000	2 219 000	7 044 000	55 000	964 000	-	10 076 000	2 939 000	6 345 000	20 000	773 000	-
35 to 39 years old	11 392 000	1 626 000	8 145 000	138 000	1 484 000	-	11 299 000	2 444 000	7 598 000	44 000	1 213 000	-
40 to 44 years old	11 015 000	1 095 000	8 016 000	166 000	1 738 000	-	10 756 000	1 676 000	7 633 000	50 000	1 397 000	-
45 to 54 years old	17 459 000	1 263 000	12 345 000	697 000	3 154 000	-	16 598 000	1 481 000	12 665 000	150 000	2 303 000	-
55 to 64 years old	11 582 000	538 000	7 847 000	1 526 000	1 671 000	-	10 673 000	572 000	8 559 000	275 000	1 266 000	-
65 to 74 years old	9 882 000	425 000	5 420 000	3 155 000	882 000	-	7 992 000	328 000	6 331 000	707 000	626 000	-
75 years old and over	8 677 000	446 000	2 558 000	5 239 000	433 000	-	5 533 000	190 000	3 829 000	1 311 000	202 000	-
1997	101 414 000	20 503 000	58 748 000	11 056 000	11 107 000	-	94 154 000	25 375 000	57 886 000	2 686 000	8 208 000	-
18 to 19 years old	3 715 000	3 426 000	277 000	4 000	8 000	-	3 783 000	3 687 000	89 000	-	7 000	-
20 to 24 years old	8 737 000	6 145 000	2 362 000	17 000	214 000	-	8 751 000	7 266 000	1 363 000	2 000	121 000	-
25 to 29 years old	9 647 000	3 708 000	5 337 000	25 000	576 000	-	9 613 000	4 947 000	4 249 000	11 000	406 000	-
30 to 34 years old	10 570 000	2 070 000	7 407 000	52 000	1 041 000	-	10 426 000	3 155 000	6 367 000	20 000	884 000	-
35 to 39 years old	11 432 000	1 549 000	8 259 000	100 000	1 523 000	-	11 323 000	2 177 000	7 908 000	25 000	1 212 000	-
40 to 44 years old	10 735 000	1 093 000	7 725 000	178 000	1 738 000	-	10 470 000	1 607 000	7 481 000	33 000	1 349 000	-
45 to 54 years old	16 894 000	1 192 000	12 092 000	650 000	2 960 000	-	16 119 000	1 393 000	12 286 000	156 000	2 285 000	-
55 to 64 years old	11 210 000	523 000	7 517 000	1 485 000	1 685 000	-	10 265 000	595 000	8 205 000	331 000	1 134 000	-
65 to 74 years old	9 930 000	413 000	5 310 000	3 294 000	913 000	-	8 085 000	348 000	6 392 000	758 000	588 000	-
75 years old and over	8 544 000	385 000	2 460 000	5 251 000	449 000	-	5 318 000	199 000	3 547 000	1 351 000	221 000	-
1996	100 425 000	20 023 000	58 822 000	11 070 000	10 511 000	-	92 741 000	24 893 000	57 617 000	2 476 000	7 755 000	-
18 to 19 years old	3 580 000	3 300 000	273 000	1 000	6 000	-	3 610 000	3 525 000	77 000	-	8 000	-
20 to 24 years old	8 861 000	6 070 000	2 529 000	10 000	252 000	-	8 792 000	7 126 000	1 561 000	-	106 000	-
25 to 29 years old	9 709 000	3 650 000	5 426 000	26 000	607 000	-	9 752 000	5 075 000	4 264 000	12 000	402 000	-
30 to 34 years old	10 819 000	2 215 000	7 481 000	58 000	1 066 000	-	10 638 000	3 147 000	6 565 000	32 000	895 000	-
35 to 39 years old	11 388 000	1 487 000	8 262 000	122 000	1 518 000	-	11 091 000	2 303 000	7 611 000	19 000	1 159 000	-
40 to 44 years old	10 417 000	1 009 000	7 566 000	157 000	1 685 000	-	10 182 000	1 443 000	7 320 000	47 000	1 372 000	-
45 to 54 years old	16 260 000	1 025 000	11 869 000	699 000	2 667 000	-	15 324 000	1 247 000	11 889 000	124 000	2 064 000	-
55 to 64 years old	10 992 000	512 000	7 617 000	1 390 000	1 474 000	-	10 092 000	501 000	8 315 000	299 000	976 000	-
65 to 74 years old	10 057 000	384 000	5 514 000	3 301 000	858 000	-	8 213 000	359 000	6 494 000	788 000	571 000	-
75 years old and over	8 341 000	370 000	2 285 000	5 306 000	379 000	-	5 048 000	167 000	3 521 000	1 156 000	203 000	-
1995	99 588 000	19 312 000	58 931 000	11 080 000	10 266 000	-	92 008 000	24 628 000	57 730 000	2 282 000	7 367 000	-
18 to 19 years old	3 494 000	3 202 000	277 000	2 000	13 000	-	3 522 000	3 441 000	80 000	-	-	-
20 to 24 years old	9 119 000	6 087 000	2 769 000	17 000	247 000	-	9 023 000	7 285 000	1 638 000	-	100 000	-
25 to 29 years old	9 712 000	3 429 000	5 576 000	17 000	689 000	-	9 689 000	4 944 000	4 337 000	6 000	401 000	-
30 to 34 years old	11 088 000	2 111 000	7 758 000	69 000	1 150 000	-	10 900 000	3 075 000	6 887 000	11 000	927 000	-
35 to 39 years old	11 200 000	1 408 000	8 103 000	120 000	1 569 000	-	11 041 000	2 241 000	7 561 000	35 000	1 204 000	-
40 to 44 years old	10 163 000	881 000	7 519 000	159 000	1 604 000	-	9 931 000	1 390 000	7 260 000	46 000	1 234 000	-
45 to 54 years old	15 672 000	959 000	11 617 000	655 000	2 441 000	-	15 022 000	1 214 000	11 848 000	153 000	1 807 000	-
55 to 64 years old	10 878 000	467 000	7 543 000	1 405 000	1 463 000	-	9 878 000	494 000	8 097 000	275 000	1 011 000	-
65 to 74 years old	10 117 000	408 000	5 571 000	3 352 000	786 000	-	8 097 000	342 000	6 549 000	693 000	513 000	-
75 years old and over	8 147 000	360 000	2 196 000	5 284 000	305 000	-	4 906 000	201 000	3 474 000	1 062 000	168 000	-
1994	98 765 000	19 458 000	58 113 000	11 073 000	10 120 000	-	91 222 000	24 727 000	57 028 000	2 221 000	7 245 000	-
18 to 19 years old	3 454 000	3 152 000	278 000	3 000	21 000	-	3 462 000	3 375 000	80 000	2 000	5 000	-
20 to 24 years old	9 338 000	6 162 000	2 931 000	11 000	234 000	-	9 221 000	7 469 000	1 658 000	5 000	89 000	-
25 to 29 years old	9 861 000	3 476 000	5 689 000	29 000	667 000	-	9 765 000	4 910 000	4 422 000	9 000	424 000	-
30 to 34 years old	11 212 000	2 228 000	7 703 000	80 000	1 202 000	-	11 108 000	3 298 000	6 940 000	6 000	864 000	-
35 to 39 years old	11 078 000	1 420 000	7 959 000	135 000	1 563 000	-	10 892 000	2 094 000	7 603 000	31 000	1 164 000	-
40 to 44 years old	9 906 000	909 000	7 358 000	146 000	1 492 000	-	9 651 000	1 255 000	7 104 000	31 000	1 262 000	-
45 to 54 years old	15 068 000	892 000	10 977 000	705 000	2 494 000	-	14 454 000	1 185 000	11 362 000	137 000	1 770 000	-
55 to 64 years old	10 805 000	440 000	7 500 000	1 501 000	1 364 000	-	9 933 000	539 000	8 034 000	327 000	1 033 000	-
65 to 74 years old	10 163 000	386 000	5 520 000	3 476 000	781 000	-	7 924 000	390 000	6 353 000	695 000	486 000	-
75 years old and over	7 880 000	393 000	2 199 000	4 986 000	302 000	-	4 812 000	211 000	3 471 000	980 000	150 000	-
1993	97 441 000	18 639 000	57 708 000	11 214 000	9 880 000	-	89 692 000	23 618 000	56 832 000	2 468 000	6 778 000	-
18 to 19 years old	3 244 000	2 918 000	312 000	-	14 000	-	3 263 000	3 162 000	96 000	-	6 000	-
20 to 24 years old	9 016 000	6 019 000	2 796 000	7 000	194 000	-	8 786 000	7 113 000	1 575 000	7 000	91 000	-
25 to 29 years old	9 836 000	3 258 000	5 765 000	25 000	789 000	-	9 767 000	4 727 000	4 595 000	11 000	435 000	-
30 to 34 years old	11 171 000	2 153 000	7 760 000	58 000	1 200 000	-	11 089 000	3 333 000	6 919 000	15 000	822 000	-
35 to 39 years old	10 861 000	1 362 000	8 010 000	121 000	1 367 000	-	10 606 000	2 085 000	7 300 000	33 000	1 189 000	-
40 to 44 years old	9 577 000	867 000	7 065 000	181 000	1 465 000	-	9 298 000	1 008 000	7 091 000	51 000	1 148 000	-
45 to 54 years old	14 655 000	798 000	10 760 000	648 000	2 448 000	-	13 847 000	951 000	11 153 000	142 000	1 602 000	-
55 to 64 years old	11 042 000	469 000	7 629 000	1 594 000	1 349 000	-	10 205 000	670 000	8 251 000	380 000	904 000	-
65 to 74 years old	10 249 000	376 000	5 537 000	3 607 000	728 000	-	8 114 000	389 000	6 502 000	765 000	458 000	-
75 years old and over	7 790 000	419 000	2 074 000	4 972 000	326 000	-	4 717 000	180 000	3 350 000	1 064 000	124 000	-

- = Quantity zero.

Table 1-7. Marital Status of the Population, by Age and Sex, 1890–2005–*Continued*

(Number. Marital status for 1980 and following years reported by U.S. Census Bureau in thousands; prior years reported as number. Excludes members of Armed Forces except those living off post or with their families on post.)

Year	Female						Male					
	Total	Never married	Married	Widowed	Divorced	Status not reported	Total	Never married	Married	Widowed	Divorced	Status not reported
1992	96 599 000	18 576 000	57 133 000	11 325 000	9 565 000	-	88 663 000	23 220 000	56 162 000	2 529 000	6 752 000	-
18 to 19 years old	3 303 000	2 974 000	308 000	-	21 000	-	3 283 000	3 207 000	76 000	-	-	-
20 to 24 years old	9 048 000	5 940 000	2 895 000	11 000	201 000	-	8 800 000	7 067 000	1 612 000	2 000	119 000	-
25 to 29 years old	10 108 000	3 356 000	5 916 000	26 000	811 000	-	10 024 000	4 882 000	4 644 000	13 000	485 000	-
30 to 34 years old	11 260 000	2 122 000	7 856 000	83 000	1 200 000	-	11 101 000	3 262 000	6 991 000	10 000	837 000	-
35 to 39 years old	10 595 000	1 334 000	7 808 000	115 000	1 337 000	-	10 358 000	1 905 000	7 331 000	51 000	1 071 000	-
40 to 44 years old	9 470 000	795 000	7 032 000	187 000	1 456 000	-	9 148 000	839 000	7 117 000	57 000	1 134 000	-
45 to 54 years old	13 910 000	744 000	10 238 000	642 000	2 285 000	-	13 114 000	957 000	10 424 000	128 000	1 606 000	-
55 to 64 years old	11 114 000	445 000	7 739 000	1 659 000	1 271 000	-	10 036 000	559 000	8 249 000	351 000	877 000	-
65 to 74 years old	10 174 000	451 000	5 395 000	3 648 000	681 000	-	8 266 000	383 000	6 536 000	841 000	506 000	-
75 years old and over	7 616 000	413 000	1 947 000	4 953 000	301 000	-	4 533 000	159 000	3 180 000	1 076 000	118 000	-
1991	95 833 000	18 542 000	56 840 000	11 289 000	9 161 000	-	87 762 000	22 925 000	55 850 000	2 385 000	6 602 000	-
18 to 19 years old	3 479 000	3 146 000	317 000	1 000	14 000	-	3 436 000	3 320 000	116 000	-	1 000	-
20 to 24 years old	9 148 000	5 862 000	3 035 000	7 000	243 000	-	8 839 000	7 048 000	1 696 000	2 000	93 000	-
25 to 29 years old	10 436 000	3 369 000	6 260 000	42 000	764 000	-	10 331 000	4 827 000	4 997 000	7 000	500 000	-
30 to 34 years old	11 150 000	2 086 000	7 861 000	82 000	1 121 000	-	10 988 000	2 999 000	7 052 000	13 000	925 000	-
35 to 39 years old	10 313 000	1 203 000	7 648 000	124 000	1 339 000	-	10 066 000	1 769 000	7 202 000	18 000	1 077 000	-
40 to 44 years old	9 320 000	818 000	6 857 000	185 000	1 459 000	-	8 966 000	897 000	6 921 000	55 000	1 092 000	-
45 to 54 years old	13 258 000	740 000	9 738 000	681 000	2 100 000	-	12 428 000	920 000	9 950 000	1 231 000	1 435 000	-
55 to 64 years old	11 184 000	417 000	7 867 000	1 704 000	1 196 000	-	10 161 000	602 000	8 326 000	326 000	908 000	-
65 to 74 years old	10 081 000	488 000	5 370 000	3 562 000	661 000	-	8 156 000	381 000	6 594 000	751 000	430 000	-
75 years old and over	7 464 000	412 000	1 885 000	4 902 000	264 000	-	4 391 000	161 000	2 997 000	1 090 000	142 000	-
1990	91 955 000	27 505 000	55 833 000	2 333 000	6 283 000	-	99 838 000	22 718 000	56 797 000	11 477 000	8 845 000	-
1980	82 054 000	13 977 000	51 767 000	10 479 000	5 831 000	-	74 101 000	17 434 000	50 825 000	1 972 000	3 871 000	-
18 to 19 years old	4 184 000	3 465 000	689 000	3 000	26 000	-	4 042 000	3 808 000	232 000	-	2 000	-
20 to 24 years old	10 246 000	5 148 000	4 705 000	23 000	370 000	-	9 801 000	6 721 000	2 924 000	2 000	154 000	-
25 to 29 years old	9 357 000	1 947 000	6 584 000	33 000	792 000	-	9 076 000	2 940 000	5 650 000	8 000	479 000	-
30 to 34 years old	8 561 000	810 000	6 695 000	102 000	954 000	-	8 270 000	1 298 000	6 310 000	11 000	651 000	-
35 to 44 years old	13 042 000	728 000	10 612 000	292 000	1 411 000	-	12 297 000	904 000	10 358 000	45 000	989 000	-
45 to 54 years old	11 670 000	552 000	9 222 000	821 000	1 074 000	-	10 962 000	699 000	9 347 000	176 000	740 000	-
55 to 64 years old	11 034 000	504 000	7 713 000	2 082 000	735 000	-	9 870 000	565 000	8 414 000	397 000	495 000	-
65 to 74 years old	8 549 000	480 000	4 282 000	3 444 000	342 000	-	6 549 000	357 000	5 346 000	557 000	290 000	-
75 years old and over	5 411 000	344 000	1 264 000	3 677 000	126 000	-	3 234 000	142 000	2 244 000	776 000	71 000	-
1970												
14 years and over	71 485 878	20 426 937	47 001 412	2 130 932	1 926 597	-	77 910 094	17 624 105	47 666 431	9 615 280	3 004 278	-
14 years	2 136 818	2 111 778	20 768	2 451	1 821	-	2 049 056	2 019 680	22 010	5 421	1 945	-
15–19 years	9 718 189	9 315 441	381 500	8 529	12 719	-	9 485 229	8 358 248	1 073 147	23 038	30 796	-
15–17 years	6 071 485	5 986 895	74 740	5 057	4 793	-	5 825 133	5 553 582	250 529	12 382	8 640	-
18 and 19 years	3 646 704	3 328 546	306 760	3 472	7 926	-	3 660 096	2 804 666	822 618	10 656	22 156	-
20–24 years	7 761 209	4 207 592	3 329 772	12 878	110 967	-	8 354 509	3 030 876	5 054 321	56 508	212 804	-
25–29 years	6 569 924	1 288 594	5 066 314	19 196	195 830	-	6 810 076	827 906	5 616 300	71 530	294 340	-
30–34 years	5 607 593	601 868	4 803 203	19 574	182 948	-	5 868 858	435 897	5 055 678	86 494	290 789	-
35–44 years	11 261 731	884 372	9 895 931	75 546	405 882	-	11 860 315	672 255	10 187 753	353 760	646 547	-
45–54 years	11 138 181	711 099	9 813 513	186 144	427 425	-	11 996 408	662 506	9 728 095	942 796	663 011	-
55–64 years	8 858 893	574 425	7 587 085	364 665	332 718	-	9 827 148	669 051	6 677 855	1 988 096	492 146	-
65 years and over	8 433 330	631 768	6 103 326	1 441 949	256 287	-	11 658 495	947 686	4 251 272	6 087 637	371 900	-
1960*												
14 years and over	61 315 358	15 313 822	42 630 422	2 071 910	1 299 204	-	64 961 189	12 320 199	42 905 285	7 880 607	1 855 098	-
14 years	1 402 724	1 394 426	7 756	163	379	-	1 345 136	1 330 089	14 250	391	406	-
15–19 years	6 698 837	6 437 186	254 377	1 784	5 490	-	6 588 597	5 528 745	1 033 804	4 751	21 297	-
15–17 years	4 341 635	4 290 310	48 850	897	1 578	-	4 174 262	3 886 610	277 151	1 874	5 627	-
18 and 19 years	2 357 202	2 146 876	205 527	887	3 912	-	2 417 335	1 642 135	756 653	2 877	15 670	-
20–24 years	5 283 228	2 807 784	2 417 552	4 780	53 112	-	5 519 937	1 567 622	3 833 956	17 252	101 107	-
25–29 years	5 333 282	1 111 768	4 117 072	9 548	94 894	-	5 537 104	582 114	4 772 006	37 047	145 937	-
30–34 years	5 840 287	694 924	5 000 763	17 246	127 354	-	6 111 422	422 915	5 423 228	74 109	191 170	-
35–44 years	11 739 191	948 784	10 410 091	76 436	303 880	-	12 336 341	748 766	10 741 606	374 216	471 753	-
45–54 years	10 139 671	749 390	8 896 768	182 260	311 253	-	10 485 709	738 266	8 379 825	921 258	446 360	-
55–64 years	7 569 153	605 187	6 351 408	380 508	232 050	-	8 138 691	648 264	5 375 362	1 819 043	296 022	-
65 years and over	7 308 985	564 373	5 174 635	1 399 185	170 792	-	8 898 252	753 418	3 331 248	4 632 540	181 046	-
1950												
14 years and over	54 601 105	14 399 840	36 866 055	2 263 850	1 071 360	-	57 102 295	11 418 335	37 576 800	6 734 275	1 372 885	-
14 years	1 090 929	1 080 370	6 660	1 670	1 320	-	1 047 370	1 039 610	6 980	565	215	-
15–19 years	5 323 470	5 146 610	166 955	4 995	4 910	-	5 321 755	4 412 565	887 615	5 260	16 315	-
15–17 years	3 187 510	3 151 360	30 410	3 460	2 280	-	3 116 230	2 893 350	217 325	2 055	3 500	-
18 and 19 years	2 135 960	1 995 250	136 545	1 535	2 630	-	2 205 525	1 519 215	670 290	3 205	12 815	-
20–24 years	5 559 265	3 281 540	2 217 810	9 060	50 855	-	5 878 040	1 898 910	3 856 760	25 280	97 090	-
25–29 years	5 904 975	1 404 860	4 381 375	15 485	103 255	-	6 277 480	833 040	5 227 960	57 490	158 990	-
30–34 years	5 562 315	734 195	4 690 995	20 945	116 180	-	5 896 625	546 245	5 082 260	91 945	176 175	-
35–44 years	10 402 195	996 570	9 046 675	94 865	264 085	-	10 837 650	900 480	9 140 055	409 250	387 865	-
45–54 years	8 484 515	725 355	7 267 615	240 755	250 790	-	8 687 605	680 150	6 737 675	967 595	302 185	-
55–64 years	6 540 100	551 185	5 320 670	495 140	173 105	-	6 633 170	525 405	4 310 160	1 636 660	160 945	-
65 years and over	5 734 250	479 155	3 767 300	1 380 935	106 860	-	6 522 600	581 930	2 327 335	3 540 230	73 105	-

- = Quantity zero.
* = First year for which figures include Alaska and Hawaii.

Table 1-7. Marital Status of the Population, by Age and Sex, 1890–2005–*Continued*

(Number. Marital status for 1980 and following years reported by U.S. Census Bureau in thousands; prior years reported as number. Excludes members of Armed Forces except those living off post or with their families on post.)

Year	Female						Male					
	Total	Never married	Married	Widowed	Divorced	Status not reported	Total	Never married	Married	Widowed	Divorced	Status not reported
1940												
14 years and over	50 553 748	17 593 379	30 192 334	2 143 612	624 423	-	50 549 176	13 935 866	30 090 488	5 700 202	822 620	-
14 years	1 218 116	1 216 784	1 247	60	25	-	1 187 614	1 184 094	3 353	110	57	-
15–19 years	6 180 153	6 073 165	104 935	1 031	1 022	-	6 153 370	5 425 023	713 940	6 423	8 984	-
15–17 years	3 684 780	3 670 287	14 002	311	180	-	3 629 909	3 461 246	165 131	1 729	1 803	-
18 and 19 years	2 495 373	2 402 878	90 933	720	842	-	2 523 461	1 962 777	548 809	4 694	7 181	-
20–24 years	5 692 392	4 109 304	1 557 104	8 394	17 590	-	5 895 443	2 781 001	3 025 923	32 751	55 768	-
25–29 years	5 450 662	1 964 118	3 417 046	20 973	48 525	-	5 645 976	1 288 092	4 185 325	71 878	100 681	-
30–34 years	5 070 312	1 050 199	3 912 820	36 714	70 579	-	5 172 076	761 698	4 155 872	128 256	126 250	-
35–44 years	9 164 794	1 283 994	7 551 974	155 405	173 421	-	9 168 426	950 876	7 430 791	537 584	249 175	-
45–54 years	7 962 019	885 004	6 590 954	328 130	157 931	-	7 550 052	654 312	5 736 614	991 448	167 678	-
55–64 years	5 409 180	577 170	4 245 427	488 620	97 963	-	5 163 025	462 407	3 254 768	1 365 044	80 806	-
65 years and over	4 406 120	433 641	2 810 827	1 104 285	57 367	-	4 613 194	429 363	1 583 902	2 566 708	33 221	-
1930												
14 years and over	45 035 691	16 143 512	26 311 682	2 022 588	488 688	69 221	43 970 842	12 465 795	26 159 771	4 728 565	572 574	44 137
14 years	1 206 486	1 205 662	761	42	21	-	1 175 899	1 171 393	4 241	167	98	-
15–19 years	5 757 825	5 645 359	100 362	1 513	1 348	9 243	5 794 290	5 032 174	731 967	12 337	12 371	5 441
15–17 years	3 493 718	3 482 706	10 553	281	178	-	3 465 118	3 279 560	179 404	3 284	2 870	-
18 and 19 years	2 264 107	2 162 653	89 809	1 232	1 170	9 243	2 329 172	1 752 614	552 563	9 053	9 501	5 441
20–24 years	5 336 815	3 779 443	1 500 493	17 657	221 990	17 322	5 533 563	2 547 057	2 857 665	56 375	62 464	10 002
25–29 years	4 860 180	1 785 413	2 977 004	39 013	50 229	8 521	4 973 428	1 079 923	3 697 645	102 041	89 124	4 695
30–34 years	4 561 786	965 945	3 468 176	59 493	62 669	5 503	4 558 635	603 048	3 715 648	148 571	88 219	3 149
35–44 years	8 816 319	1 261 705	7 189 452	218 881	137 180	9 101	8 382 521	839 130	6 832 581	547 562	157 650	5 598
45–54 years	6 803 569	776 863	5 551 146	357 047	111 471	7 042	6 214 514	564 466	4 673 539	872 676	98 874	4 959
55–64 years	4 367 500	442 505	3 407 751	445 262	66 499	5 483	4 029 398	360 188	2 499 285	1 119 802	45 881	4 242
65 years and over	3 325 211	280 617	2 116 537	883 680	37 371	7 006	3 308 594	268 416	1 147 200	1 869 034	17 893	6 051
1920												
14 years and over	37 861 085	13 969 763	21 823 326	1 754 302	234 519	79 175	36 134 659	10 608 384	21 301 014	3 909 736	272 736	42 789
14 years	1 033 297	1 029 971	3 173	118	35	-	1 012 968	1 007 088	5 554	269	57	-
15–19 years	4 673 792	4 567 770	96 374	1 830	759	7 059	4 756 764	4 137 650	596 542	12 239	6 017	4 316
15–17 years	2 828 546	2 815 533	12 521	384	108	-	2 861 030	2 711 081	145 390	3 091	1 468	-
18 and 19 years	1 845 246	1 752 237	83 853	1 446	651	7 059	1 895 734	1 426 569	451 152	9 148	4 549	4 316
20–24 years	4 527 045	3 200 623	1 280 318	20 511	10 280	15 313	4 749 976	2 164 051	2 483 697	65 414	28 582	8 232
25–29 years	4 538 433	1 789 721	2 662 124	51 470	22 856	12 062	4 548 258	1 048 285	3 336 501	117 389	41 243	4 842
30–34 years	4 130 783	995 869	3 023 357	74 454	28 080	9 023	3 940 410	588 119	3 155 854	152 893	40 188	3 356
35–44 years	7 359 904	1 188 586	5 873 308	220 700	63 592	13 718	6 730 934	767 882	5 426 434	485 493	75 027	6 098
45–54 years	5 653 095	677 420	4 580 056	329 976	56 162	9 481	4 845 590	464 838	3 587 794	739 058	48 562	5 146
55–64 years	3 461 865	337 592	2 697 429	386 587	34 249	6 008	3 069 807	257 029	1 878 478	906 362	23 451	4 487
65 years and over	2 483 071	182 211	1 607 187	668 656	18 506	6 511	2 450 144	173 442	830 160	1 430 621	9 609	6 312
1910												
14 years and over	33 247 336	13 455 690	18 066 188	1 466 839	155 604	103 015	30 904 861	9 826 911	17 667 119	3 167 432	184 621	58 778
14 years	935 974	934 980	898	82	14	-	912 148	908 435	3 482	198	33	-
15–19 years	4 527 282	4 448 067	51 877	1 110	347	25 881	4 536 321	3 985 764	513 239	10 261	3 650	23 407
15–17 years	2 688 370	2 667 874	4 990	252	70	15 184	2 683 806	2 543 264	121 803	2 697	867	15 175
18 and 19 years	1 838 912	1 780 193	46 887	858	277	10 697	1 852 515	1 442 500	391 436	7 564	2 783	8 232
20–24 years	4 580 290	3 432 161	1 100 093	18 815	6 732	22 489	4 476 694	2 163 683	2 225 362	55 354	20 370	11 925
25–29 years	4 244 348	1 816 137	2 353 525	45 092	15 503	14 091	3 935 655	981 556	2 823 935	95 385	29 153	5 626
30–34 years	3 656 768	951 820	2 611 244	65 339	19 068	9 297	3 315 417	535 170	2 619 959	128 942	28 109	3 237
35–44 years	6 153 366	1 026 502	4 873 153	198 701	42 688	12 322	5 504 321	628 516	4 410 310	411 896	49 269	4 330
45–54 years	4 488 929	499 751	3 658 931	286 222	36 502	7 523	3 881 059	331 573	2 904 043	610 386	31 934	3 123
55–64 years	2 674 403	222 950	2 112 699	312 420	21 675	4 659	2 379 698	167 991	1 479 454	714 452	15 200	2 601
65 years and over	1 985 976	123 322	1 303 768	539 058	13 075	7	1 963 548	124 223	687 335	1 140 558	6 903	4 529
1900												
14 years and over	26 286 316	11 053 813	13 920 057	1 173 509	83 828	55 109	24 951 254	8 319 285	13 784 538	2 706 332	114 476	26 923
14 years	793 340	792 267	667	33	7	366	775 224	770 742	3 783	126	30	543
15–19 years	3 750 451	3 706 382	37 781	871	194	5 223	3 805 638	3 374 814	415 682	9 336	2 418	3 388
20–24 years	3 624 580	2 812 113	782 907	14 332	3 322	11 906	3 710 436	1 913 552	1 726 296	52 545	13 124	4 919
25–29 years	3 323 543	1 520 782	1 746 620	38 781	8 218	9 142	3 205 898	882 875	2 209 357	91 847	18 461	3 358
30–34 years	2 901 321	800 664	2 025 729	58 312	10 307	6 309	2 654 718	441 409	2 071 698	121 944	17 384	2 283
35–44 years	4 872 781	826 201	3 840 575	174 535	22 630	8 840	4 339 166	481 668	3 451 375	372 677	29 953	3 493
45–54 years	3 402 458	349 429	2 797 354	230 656	19 498	5 521	2 994 983	234 413	2 212 223	526 456	19 111	2 780
55–64 years	2 062 424	156 823	1 644 373	245 424	12 297	3 507	1 940 111	128 954	1 172 904	626 271	9 566	2 416
65 years and over	1 555 418	89 152	1 044 051	410 565	7 355	4 295	1 525 080	90 858	521 220	905 130	4 129	3 743
1890												
14 years and over	21 397 501	9 331 617	11 176 124	811 110	48 708	29 942	20 239 343	6 906 714	11 101 645	2 144 496	71 584	14 904
14 years	723 158	723 015	23	-	1	119	695 801	694 281	1 411	17	12	80
15–19 years	3 248 711	3 230 935	16 746	137	28	965	3 308 852	2 987 949	313 983	4 845	1 101	974
20–24 years	3 104 893	2 505 460	585 748	7 610	1 468	4 607	3 091 783	1 601 266	1 444 712	36 456	6 931	2 418
25–29 years	2 698 311	1 240 797	1 421 407	26 601	4 340	5 166	2 529 466	641 988	1 805 064	69 965	10 588	1 861
30–34 years	2 425 664	642 827	1 728 930	43 777	5 832	4 298	2 152 966	326 306	1 717 204	96 797	11 161	1 498
35–44 years	3 705 648	568 511	2 997 030	120 796	12 837	6 474	3 346 031	330 139	2 698 266	296 302	18 899	2 425
45–54 years	2 627 024	239 928	2 213 901	157 920	11 393	3 882	2 430 878	171 454	1 796 979	447 370	13 080	1 995
55–64 years	1 630 373	111 144	1 342 414	166 686	7 835	2 294	1 499 997	86 573	905 627	499 420	6 721	1 656
65 years and over	1 233 719	69 100	869 925	287 583	4 974	2 137	1 183 569	66 758	418 399	693 324	3 091	1 997

Source: U.S. Census Bureau.
- = Quantity zero.

Table 1-8. Population of Regions, by Race and Residence, 1790–2000

(Number in thousands.)

Year	Total population	Race			Residence	
		White	Black	Other	Urban	Rural
Northeast						
2000[1]	53 594	41 534	6 100	5 961	45 226	8 368
1990	50 809	42 069	5 613	5 214	40 092	10 717
1980	49 137	42 328	4 849	1 950	38 904	10 232
1970	49 041	44 311	4 344	386	39 450	9 591
1960	44 678	41 522	3 028	127	35 840	8 838
1950	39 478	37 399	2 018	61	31 373	8 105
1940	35 977	34 567	1 370	40	27 568	8 409
1930	34 427	33 237	1 147	43	26 707	7 720
1920	29 662	28 958	679	25	22 404	7 258
1910	25 869	25 361	484	23	18 563	7 305
1900	21 047	20 638	385	24	13 911	7 136
1890	17 407	17 122	270	15	10 266	7 141
1880	14 507	14 274	229	4	7 370	7 137
1870	12 299	12 117	180	2	5 448	6 851
1860	10 594	10 438	156	(2)	3 787	6 807
1850	8 627	8 447	150	-	2 289	6 338
1840	6 761	6 619	142	-	1 253	5 508
1830	5 542	5 417	125	-	785	4 758
1820	4 360	4 246	114	-	480	3 880
1810	3 487	3 384	102	-	380	3 107
1800	2 636	2 553	83	-	245	2 391
1790	1 968	1 901	67	-	160	1 809
Midwest						
2000[1]	64 393	53 834	6 500	4 060	48 105	16 288
1990	59 669	52 018	5 716	2 833	42 774	16 894
1980	58 666	52 195	5 337	1 334	41 466	17 388
1970	56 572	51 641	4 572	359	40 481	16 091
1960	51 619	48 003	3 446	170	35 481	16 138
1950	44 461	42 119	2 228	114	28 491	15 970
1940	40 143	38 640	1 420	83	23 437	16 706
1930	38 594	37 151	1 262	181	22 351	16 243
1920	34 020	33 164	793	62	17 776	16 244
1910	29 889	29 279	543	66	13 487	16 401
1900	26 333	25 776	496	61	10 165	16 168
1890	22 410	21 914	431	65	7 418	14 992
1880	17 364	16 961	386	17	4 198	13 166
1870	12 981	12 699	273	10	2 702	10 279
1860	9 097	8 900	184	13	1 263	7 833
1850	5 404	5 268	136	-	499	4 904
1840	3 352	3 262	89	-	129	3 222
1830	1 610	1 569	42	-	42	1 569
1820	859	841	18	-	10	850
1810	292	286	7	-	3	290
1800	51	50	1	-	-	51
South						
2000[1]	100 237	72 819	18 982	8 436	73 008	27 229
1990	85 446	65 582	15 829	8 452	58 656	26 790
1980	73 572	58 949	14 048	2 364	50 414	24 958
1970	62 795	50 420	11 970	405	40 540	22 255
1960	54 973	43 477	11 312	185	32 160	22 813
1950	47 197	36 850	10 225	122	22 956	24 241
1940	41 666	31 659	9 905	103	15 290	26 375
1930	37 858	27 674	9 362	882	12 904	24 953
1920	33 126	24 132	8 912	81	9 300	23 826
1910	29 389	20 547	8 749	92	6 623	22 767
1900	24 524	16 522	7 923	79	4 421	20 103
1890	20 028	13 193	6 761	74	3 261	16 767
1880	16 517	10 555	5 954	7	2 017	14 500
1870	12 288	7 863	4 421	4	1 497	10 791
1860	11 133	7 034	4 097	2	1 067	10 067
1850	8 983	5 630	3 352	-	744	8 239
1840	6 951	4 309	2 642	-	463	6 488
1830	5 708	3 546	2 162	-	301	5 407
1820	4 419	2 776	1 644	-	204	4 216
1810	3 461	2 191	1 268	-	143	3 318
1800	2 622	1 704	918	-	78	2 544
1790	1 961	1 271	690	-	42	1 919

[1]In 2000, White and Black are "one race only" with "2 or more races" included in "other."
[2]Less than 0.5.
- = Quantity zero.

Table 1-8. Population of Regions, by Race and Residence, 1790–2000—*Continued*

(Number in thousands.)

Year	Total population	Race			Residence	
		White	Black	Other	Urban	Rural
West						
2000[1]	63 198	43 274	3 077	16 847	56 022	7 176
1990	52 786	40 017	2 828	15 087	45 531	7 255
1980	43 172	34 890	2 262	6 020	36 211	6 961
1970	34 804	31 377	1 695	1 732	28 854	5 950
1960	28 053	25 830	1 086	1 137	21 787	6 266
1950	20 190	18 574	571	416	14 027	6 163
1940	14 379	13 350	171	363	8 409	5 969
1930	12 324	10 802	120	974	7 199	5 125
1920	9 214	8 567	79	258	4 773	4 440
1910	7 082	6 544	51	231	3 391	3 691
1900	4 309	3 873	30	188	1 718	2 591
1890	3 134	2 872	27	203	1 161	1 974
1880	1 801	1 612	12	144	544	1 257
1870	991	910	6	74	256	735
1860	619	551	4	64	99	520
1850	179	178	1	-	11	167

Source: U.S. Census Bureau.
[1]In 2000, White and Black are "one race only" with "2 or more races" included in "other."
- = Quantity zero.

Table 1-9. Population of States, by Race, 1790–2005

(Number in thousands, except population per square mile.)

Year	Resident population		Race	
	Total	Per square mile of land area[1]	White	Black
Alabama				
2005	4 558	89.8	3 253	1 203
2004	4 525	89.3	3 233	1 193
2003	4 502	88.7	3 221	1 184
2002	4 480	88.4	3 208	1 177
2001	4 467	88.0	3 204	1 170
2000	4 447	87.6	3 163	1 156
1990	4 041	79.6	2 976	1 021
1980	3 890	76.7	2 873	996
1970	3 444	67.9	2 534	903
1960	3 267	64.4	2 284	980
1950	3 062	59.9	2 080	980
1940	2 833	55.5	1 849	983
1930	2 646	51.8	1 701	945
1920	2 348	45.8	1 447	901
1910	2 138	41.7	1 229	908
1900	1 829	35.7	1 001	827
1890	1 513	29.5	834	678
1880	1 263	24.6	662	600
1870	997	19.4	521	476
1860	964	18.8	526	438
1850	772	15.0	427	345
1840	591	11.5	335	256
1830	310	6.0	190	119
1820	128	2.5	85	42
1810[2]	9	...	...	...
1800[2]	1	...	...	...
Alaska				
2005	664	1.2	468	24
2004	658	1.1	465	24
2003	649	1.1	459	24
2002	641	1.1	454	24
2001	632	1.1	449	23
2000	627	1.1	435	22
1990	550	1.0	415	22
1980	402	0.7	310	14
1970	303	0.5	237	9
1960	226	0.4	179	7
1950	129	0.2	93	-
1940[3]	73	0.1	39	([4])
1930[5]	59	0.1	29	([4])
1920	55	0.1	28	([4])
1910	64	0.1	36	([4])
1900	64	0.1	30	([4])
1890	32	...	4	...
1880	33	...	([4])	...
Arizona				
2005	5 939	52.3	5 188	216
2004	5 740	50.5	5 024	203
2003	5 578	49.1	4 889	193
2002	5 438	48.0	4 772	186
2001	5 296	46.7	4 653	178
2000	5 131	45.2	3 874	159
1990	3 665	32.3	2 963	111
1980	2 718	23.9	2 241	75
1970	1 771	15.6	1 605	53
1960	1 302	11.5	1 170	43
1950	750	6.6	655	26
1940	499	4.4	427	15
1930	436	3.8	379	11
1920	334	2.9	291	8
1910	204	1.8	171	2
1900	123	1.1	93	2
1890	88	0.8	56	1
1880	40	0.4	35	([4])
1870	10	0.1	10	([4])

[1]Beginning 1970 persons per square mile were calculated on the basis of land area data from the 2000 census.
[2]Population of those parts of Mississippi Territory now in present state. Population per square mile, sex, race and age detail for Alabama included with Mississippi.
[3]Census taken October 1, 1939.
[4]Less than 500.
[5]Census taken October 1, 1929.
... = Not available.
- = Quantity zero.

Table 1-9. Population of States, by Race, 1790–2005—*Continued*

(Number in thousands, except population per square mile.)

| Year | Resident population | | Race | |
	Total	Per square mile of land area[1]	White	Black
Arkansas				
2005	2 779	53.4	2 261	437
2004	2 750	52.9	2 238	434
2003	2 726	52.3	2 221	430
2002	2 707	52.0	2 207	428
2001	2 692	51.7	2 197	425
2000	2 673	51.3	2 139	419
1990	2 351	45.1	1 945	374
1980	2 286	43.9	1 890	374
1970	1 923	36.9	1 566	352
1960	1 786	34.3	1 396	389
1950	1 910	36.3	1 482	427
1940	1 949	37.0	1 466	483
1930	1 854	35.2	1 375	478
1920	1 752	33.4	1 280	472
1910	1 574	30.0	1 131	443
1900	1 312	25.0	945	367
1890	1 128	21.5	819	309
1880	803	15.3	592	211
1870	484	9.2	362	122
1860	435	8.3	324	111
1850	210	4.0	162	48
1840	98	1.9	77	20
1830	30	0.6	26	5
1820	14	0.1	13	2
1810	1	...	...	...
California				
2005	36 132	231.7	27 823	2 434
2004	35 842	230.1	27 655	2 430
2003	35 457	227.5	27 404	2 421
2002	34 988	225.2	27 085	2 409
2001	34 527	221.2	26 774	2 398
2000	33 872	217.2	20 170	2 264
1990	29 760	191.1	20 524	2 209
1980	23 668	151.8	18 031	1 819
1970	19 953	128.1	17 761	1 400
1960	15 717	100.8	14 455	884
1950	10 586	67.5	9 915	462
1940	6 907	44.1	6 597	124
1930	5 677	36.2	5 408	81
1920	3 427	22.0	3 265	39
1910	2 378	15.3	2 260	22
1900	1 485	9.5	1 403	11
1890	1 213	7.8	1 112	11
1880	865	5.5	767	6
1870	560	3.6	499	4
1860	380	2.4	323	4
1850	93	0.6	92	1
Colorado				
2005	4 665	45.0	4 211	191
2004	4 602	44.4	4 156	189
2003	4 548	43.9	4 111	186
2002	4 498	43.5	4 071	183
2001	4 427	42.6	4 011	180
2000	4 301	41.5	3 560	165
1990	3 294	31.8	2 905	133
1980	2 890	27.9	2 571	102
1970	2 207	21.3	2 112	66
1960	1 754	16.9	1 701	40
1950	1 325	12.8	1 297	20
1940	1 123	10.8	1 107	12
1930	1 036	10.0	1 019	12
1920	940	9.1	924	11
1910	799	7.7	783	11
1900	540	5.2	529	9
1890	413	4.0	405	6
1880	194	1.9	191	2
1870	40	0.4	39	(4)
1860	34	0.3	34	(4)

[1]Beginning 1970 persons per square mile were calculated on the basis of land area data from the 2000 census.
[4]Less than 500.
... = Not available.

Table 1-9. Population of States, by Race, 1790–2005—*Continued*

(Number in thousands, except population per square mile.)

Year	Resident population		Race	
	Total	Per square mile of land area[1]	White	Black
Connecticut				
2005	3 510	724.5	2 982	354
2004	3 499	723.2	2 980	351
2003	3 486	719.0	2 976	348
2002	3 458	714.3	2 961	344
2001	3 432	707.0	2 948	339
2000	3 406	702.9	2 780	165
1990	3 287	678.5	2 859	274
1980	3 108	641.4	2 799	217
1970	3 032	625.9	2 835	181
1960	2 535	523.2	2 424	107
1950	2 007	409.7	1 952	53
1940	1 709	348.9	1 675	33
1930	1 607	328.0	1 577	29
1920	1 381	286.4	1 359	21
1910	1 115	231.3	1 099	15
1900	908	188.5	892	15
1890	746	154.8	733	12
1880	623	129.2	611	12
1870	537	111.5	528	10
1860	460	95.5	452	9
1850	371	76.9	363	8
1840	310	64.3	302	8
1830	298	61.8	290	8
1820	275	57.1	267	8
1810	262	54.3	255	7
1800	251	52.1	245	6
1790	238	49.4	233	6
Delaware				
2005	844	431.8	631	174
2004	830	425.1	625	169
2003	818	418.5	618	165
2002	806	413.3	612	162
2001	795	407.5	607	158
2000	784	401.1	585	151
1990	666	341.0	535	112
1980	594	304.2	488	96
1970	548	280.6	466	78
1960	446	228.3	384	61
1950	318	160.8	274	44
1940	267	134.7	231	36
1930	238	120.5	206	33
1920	223	113.5	193	30
1910	202	103.0	171	31
1900	185	94.0	154	31
1890	168	85.7	140	28
1880	147	74.6	120	26
1870	125	63.6	102	23
1860	112	57.1	91	22
1850	92	46.6	71	20
1840	78	39.7	59	20
1830	77	39.1	58	19
1820	73	37.0	55	17
1810	73	37.0	55	17
1800	64	32.7	50	14
1790	59	30.1	46	13

[1]Beginning 1970 persons per square mile were calculated on the basis of land area data from the 2000 census.

Table 1-9. Population of States, by Race, 1790–2005—*Continued*

(Number in thousands, except population per square mile.)

| Year | Resident population | | Race | |
	Total	Per square mile of land area[1]	White	Black
District of Columbia				
2005	551	8,966.1	209	314
2004	554	9,015.0	206	321
2003	558	9,175.6	203	328
2002	565	9,298.0	203	335
2001	569	9,313.1	202	341
2000	572	9 316.4	176	343
1990	607	9 884.4	180	400
1980	638	10 396.3	172	449
1970	757	12 323.6	209	538
1960	764	12 440.3	345	412
1950	802	13 150.5	518	281
1940	663	10 870.3	474	187
1930	487	7 981.5	354	132
1920	483	7 292.9	327	110
1910	331	5 517.8	236	94
1900	279	4 645.3	192	87
1890	230	3 972.3	155	76
1880	178	3 062.5	118	60
1870	132	2 270.7	88	43
1860	75	1 294.5	61	14
1850	52	891.2	38	14
1840	34	485.7	24	10
1830	30	442.6	21	9
1820	23	367.1	16	7
1810	15	266.9	10	5
1800	8	156.6	6	2
Florida				
2005	17 790	329.9	14 307	2 799
2004	17 385	322.6	14 017	2 721
2003	16 993	315.6	13 737	2 644
2002	16 678	309.9	13 520	2 577
2001	16 351	304.1	13 291	2 510
2000	15 982	296.4	12 465	2 336
1990	12 938	239.9	10 749	1 760
1980	9 746	180.7	8 185	1 343
1970	6 789	125.9	5 719	1 042
1960	4 952	91.7	4 064	880
1950	2 771	51.1	2 166	603
1940	1 897	35.0	1 382	514
1930	1 468	27.1	1 035	432
1920	968	17.7	638	329
1910	753	13.7	444	309
1900	529	9.6	297	231
1890	391	7.1	225	166
1880	269	4.9	143	127
1870	188	3.4	96	92
1860	140	2.6	78	63
1850	87	1.6	47	40
1840	54	1.0	28	27
1830	35	0.6	18	16

[1]Beginning 1970 persons per square mile were calculated on the basis of land area data from the 2000 census.

Table 1-9. Population of States, by Race, 1790–2005—*Continued*

(Number in thousands, except population per square mile.)

| Year | Resident population | | Race | |
	Total	Per square mile of land area[1]	White	Black
Georgia				
2005	9 073	156.7	6 001	2 700
2004	8 918	152.5	5 929	2 635
2003	8 747	150.0	5 839	2 572
2002	8 582	147.8	5 752	2 512
2001	8 416	144.8	5 664	2 452
2000	8 186	141.4	5 327	2 350
1990	6 478	111.9	4 600	1 747
1980	5 463	94.3	3 947	1 465
1970	4 590	79.2	3 391	1 187
1960	3 943	68.1	2 817	1 123
1950	3 445	58.9	2 381	1 063
1940	3 124	53.4	2 038	1 085
1930	2 909	49.7	1 837	1 071
1920	2 896	49.3	1 689	1 206
1910	2 609	44.4	1 432	1 177
1900	2 216	37.7	1 181	1 035
1890	1 837	31.3	978	859
1880	1 542	26.3	817	725
1870	1 184	20.2	639	545
1860	1 057	18.0	592	466
1850	906	15.4	522	285
1840	691	11.8	408	284
1830	517	8.8	297	220
1820	341	5.8	190	151
1810	252	4.3	145	107
1800	163	1.5	102	60
1790	83	0.6	53	30
Hawaii				
2005	1 275	198.5	342	30
2004	1 262	196.6	336	28
2003	1 248	195.8	328	28
2002	1 234	193.8	322	27
2001	1 222	190.6	316	25
2000	1 212	188.6	294	22
1990	1 108	172.6	370	27
1980	965	150.2	319	17
1970	769	119.9	298	8
1960	633	98.5	202	5
1950	500	78.0	115	3
1940	423	66.0	104	([4])
1930	368	57.5	80	1
1920	256	39.9	55	([4])
1910	192	30.0	44	1
1900	154	24.0	29	([4])
Idaho				
2005	1 429	17.3	1 365	8
2004	1 395	16.8	1 334	8
2003	1 368	16.5	1 308	7
2002	1 344	16.2	1 286	7
2001	1 321	16.0	1 265	6
2000	1 293	15.6	1 177	5
1990	1 007	12.2	950	3
1980	944	11.4	902	3
1970	713	8.6	699	2
1960	667	8.1	657	2
1950	589	7.1	581	1
1940	525	6.3	519	1
1930	445	5.4	439	1
1920	432	5.2	426	1
1910	326	3.9	319	1
1900	162	1.9	154	([4])
1890	89	1.1	82	([4])
1880	33	0.4	29	([4])
1870	15	0.2	11	([4])

[1]Beginning 1970 persons per square mile were calculated on the basis of land area data from the 2000 census.
[4]Less than 500.

Table 1-9. Population of States, by Race, 1790–2005—*Continued*

(Number in thousands, except population per square mile.)

Year	Resident population		Race	
	Total	Per square mile of land area[1]	White	Black
Illinois				
2005	12 763	229.6	10 131	1 928
2004	12 712	228.7	10 102	1 924
2003	12 650	227.6	10 063	1 921
2002	12 587	226.7	10 024	1 917
2001	12 519	224.6	9 982	1 914
2000	12 419	223.4	9 125	1 877
1990	11 431	205.6	8 953	1 694
1980	11 427	205.6	9 233	1 675
1970	11 114	199.9	9 600	1 426
1960	10 081	181.3	9 010	1 037
1950	8 712	155.8	8 046	646
1940	7 897	141.2	7 504	387
1930	7 631	136.4	7 295	329
1920	6 485	115.7	6 299	182
1910	5 639	100.6	5 527	109
1900	4 822	86.1	4 735	85
1890	3 826	68.3	3 768	57
1880	3 078	55.0	3 031	46
1870	2 540	45.4	2 511	29
1860	1 712	30.6	1 704	8
1850	851	15.2	846	5
1840	476	8.5	472	4
1830	157	2.8	155	2
1820	55	1.0	54	1
1810	12	0.1	12	1
Indiana				
2005	6 272	174.9	5 554	555
2004	6 227	173.9	5 522	547
2003	6 196	172.7	5 505	540
2002	6 155	171.7	5 477	533
2001	6 126	170.5	5 460	526
2000	6 080	169.5	5 320	510
1990	5 544	154.6	5 021	432
1980	5 490	153.1	5 004	415
1970	5 194	144.9	4 820	357
1960	4 662	130.0	4 389	269
1950	3 934	108.7	3 759	174
1940	3 428	94.7	3 305	122
1930	3 239	89.4	3 126	112
1920	2 930	81.3	2 849	81
1910	2 701	74.9	2 640	60
1900	2 516	70.1	2 459	58
1890	2 192	61.1	2 147	45
1880	1 978	55.1	1 939	39
1870	1 681	46.8	1 656	25
1860	1 350	37.6	1 339	11
1850	988	27.5	977	11
1840	686	19.1	679	7
1830	343	9.6	338	4
1820	147	4.1	146	1
1810	25	0.6	24	1
1800	6	(6)	5	(4)

[1]Beginning 1970 persons per square mile were calculated on the basis of land area data from the 2000 census.
[4]Less than 500.
[6]Less than 1/10 of a person.

Table 1-9. Population of States, by Race, 1790–2005—*Continued*

(Number in thousands, except population per square mile.)

Year	Resident population		Race	
	Total	Per square mile of land area[1]	White	Black
Iowa				
2005	2 966	53.1	2 816	69
2004	2 953	52.9	2 807	67
2003	2 941	52.7	2 799	66
2002	2 934	52.6	2 796	65
2001	2 931	52.3	2 796	64
2000	2 926	52.4	2 749	62
1990	2 777	49.7	2 683	48
1980	2 914	52.2	2 839	42
1970	2 824	50.6	2 783	33
1960	2 758	49.4	2 729	25
1950	2 621	46.8	2 600	...
1940	2 538	45.3	2 521	17
1930	2 471	44.1	2 453	17
1920	2 404	43.2	2 384	19
1910	2 225	40.0	2 209	15
1900	2 232	40.2	2 219	13
1890	1 912	34.4	1 901	11
1880	1 625	29.2	1 615	10
1870	1 194	21.5	1 188	6
1860	675	12.1	674	1
1850	192	3.5	192	(4)
1840	43	0.2	43	(4)
Kansas				
2005	2 745	33.5	2 453	162
2004	2 734	33.4	2 445	161
2003	2 724	33.3	2 438	160
2002	2 712	33.2	2 431	160
2001	2 701	32.9	2 424	158
2000	2 688	32.9	2 314	154
1990	2 478	30.3	2 232	143
1980	2 364	28.9	2 168	126
1970	2 247	27.5	2 122	107
1960	2 179	26.6	2 079	91
1950	1 905	23.2	1 829	73
1940	1 801	21.9	1 734	65
1930	1 881	22.9	1 812	66
1920	1 769	21.6	1 709	58
1910	1 691	20.7	1 634	54
1900	1 470	18.0	1 416	52
1890	1 428	17.5	1 377	50
1880	996	12.2	952	43
1870	364	4.5	346	17
1860	107	1.3	106	1
Kentucky				
2005	4 173	105.0	3 771	313
2004	4 142	104.4	3 746	310
2003	4 117	103.7	3 727	308
2002	4 089	103.0	3 704	305
2001	4 067	102.3	3 688	303
2000	4 042	101.7	3 641	296
1990	3 685	92.8	3 392	263
1980	3 661	92.1	3 379	259
1970	3 219	81.2	2 982	231
1960	3 038	76.5	2 820	216
1950	2 945	73.9	2 742	202
1940	2 846	70.9	2 631	214
1930	2 615	65.2	2 388	226
1920	2 417	60.2	2 181	236
1910	2 290	57.0	2 028	262
1900	2 147	53.4	1 862	285
1890	1 859	46.3	1 590	268
1880	1 649	41.0	1 377	271
1870	1 321	32.9	1 099	222
1860	1 156	28.8	919	236
1850	982	24.4	761	221
1840	780	19.4	590	190
1830	688	17.1	519	170
1820	564	14.0	435	129
1810	407	10.1	324	82
1800	221	5.5	180	41
1790	74	1.8	61	13

[1]Beginning 1970 persons per square mile were calculated on the basis of land area data from the 2000 census.
[4]Less than 500.
. . . = Not available.

Table 1-9. Population of States, by Race, 1790–2005—*Continued*

(Number in thousands, except population per square mile.)

Year	Resident population		Race	
	Total	Per square mile of land area[1]	White	Black
Louisiana				
2005	4 524	103.8	2 898	1 497
2004	4 507	103.7	2 893	1 487
2003	4 490	103.2	2 889	1 478
2002	4 475	102.9	2 885	1 470
2001	4 465	102.5	2 885	1 462
2000	4 469	102.6	2 856	1 452
1990	4 220	96.9	2 839	1 299
1980	4 206	96.6	2 912	1 238
1970	3 641	83.7	2 541	1 087
1960	3 257	74.8	2 212	1 039
1950	2 684	59.4	1 797	882
1940	2 364	52.3	1 512	849
1930	2 102	46.5	1 323	776
1920	1 799	39.6	1 097	700
1910	1 656	36.5	941	714
1900	1 382	30.4	730	651
1890	1 119	24.6	558	559
1880	940	20.7	455	484
1870	727	16.0	362	364
1860	708	15.6	357	350
1850	518	11.4	255	262
1840	352	7.8	158	194
1830	216	4.8	89	126
1820	153	3.4	74	80
1810	77	2.2	34	42
Maine				
2005	1 322	42.8	1 281	10
2004	1 315	42.7	1 275	9
2003	1 308	42.3	1 270	9
2002	1 297	41.9	1 260	8
2001	1 286	41.7	1 251	8
2000	1 275	41.3	1 236	7
1990	1 228	39.8	1 208	5
1980	1 125	36.4	1 110	3
1970	992	32.2	985	3
1960	969	31.4	963	3
1950	914	29.4	911	1
1940	847	27.3	845	1
1930	797	25.7	795	1
1920	768	25.7	766	1
1910	742	24.8	740	1
1900	694	23.2	682	1
1890	661	22.1	659	1
1880	649	21.7	647	1
1870	627	21.0	625	2
1860	628	21.0	627	1
1850	583	19.5	582	1
1840	502	16.8	500	1
1830	399	13.4	398	1
1820	298	10.0	297	1
1810	229	7.7	228	1
1800	152	5.1	151	1
1790	97	3.2	96	1

[1]Beginning 1970 persons per square mile were calculated on the basis of land area data from the 2000 census.

Table 1-9. Population of States, by Race, 1790–2005—*Continued*

(Number in thousands, except population per square mile.)

Year	Resident population		Race	
	Total	Per square mile of land area[1]	White	Black
Maryland				
2005	5 600	573.0	3 587	1 640
2004	5 561	568.7	3 583	1 617
2003	5 512	563.6	3 574	1 590
2002	5 442	558.4	3 548	1 561
2001	5 380	550.0	3 526	1 534
2000	5 296	541.9	3 391	1 477
1990	4 781	489.1	3 394	1 190
1980	4 217	431.5	3 159	958
1970	3 922	401.5	3 195	699
1960	3 101	317.2	2 574	518
1950	2 343	237.1	1 955	386
1940	1 821	184.2	1 518	302
1930	1 632	165.0	1 354	276
1920	1 450	145.8	1 205	244
1910	1 295	130.3	1 063	232
1900	1 188	119.5	952	235
1890	1 042	104.9	826	216
1880	935	94.0	725	210
1870	781	78.6	605	175
1860	687	69.1	516	171
1850	583	58.6	418	165
1840	470	47.3	318	152
1830	447	45.0	291	156
1820	407	41.0	260	147
1810	381	38.3	235	145
1800	342	34.4	216	125
1790	320	32.0	209	111
Massachusetts				
2005	6 399	816.2	5 549	439
2004	6 407	818.4	5 573	434
2003	6 418	820.6	5 601	429
2002	6 412	819.9	5 615	422
2001	6 395	813.7	5 620	415
2000	6 349	809.8	5 367	343
1990	6 016	767.4	5 405	300
1980	5 737	731.8	5 363	221
1970	5 689	725.7	5 478	176
1960	5 149	656.9	5 023	112
1950	4 691	596.2	4 612	73
1940	4 317	545.9	4 258	55
1930	4 250	537.4	4 193	52
1920	3 852	479.2	3 804	45
1910	3 366	418.8	3 325	38
1900	2 805	349.0	2 770	32
1890	2 239	278.5	2 215	22
1880	1 783	221.9	1 764	19
1870	1 457	181.3	1 443	14
1860	1 231	153.1	1 221	10
1850	995	123.7	985	9
1840	738	91.7	729	9
1830	610	75.9	603	7
1820	523	65.1	516	7
1810	472	58.7	465	7
1800	423	52.6	417	6
1790	379	47.1	373	5

[1]Beginning 1970 persons per square mile were calculated on the basis of land area data from the 2000 census.

Table 1-9. Population of States, by Race, 1790–2005—*Continued*

(Number in thousands, except population per square mile.)

| Year | Resident population | | Race | |
	Total	Per square mile of land area[1]	White	Black
Michigan				
2005	10 121	178.2	8 230	1 451
2004	10 104	178.0	8 226	1 449
2003	10 078	177.5	8 215	1 446
2002	10 039	176.9	8 195	1 443
2001	10 003	175.9	8 176	1 438
2000	9 938	175.0	7 966	1 413
1990	9 295	163.6	7 756	1 292
1980	9 262	163.1	7 872	1 199
1970	8 875	156.4	7 833	991
1960	7 823	137.7	7 086	718
1950	6 372	111.7	5 918	442
1940	5 256	92.2	5 040	208
1930	4 842	84.9	4 664	169
1920	3 668	63.8	3 602	60
1910	2 810	48.9	2 785	17
1900	2 421	42.1	2 399	16
1890	2 094	36.4	2 073	15
1880	1 637	28.5	1 615	15
1870	1 184	20.6	1 167	12
1860	749	13.0	736	7
1850	398	6.9	395	3
1840	212	3.7	212	1
1830	32	0.2	31	(4)
1820	9	(6)	9	(4)
1810	5	0.1	5	(4)
Minnesota				
2005	5 133	64.5	4 601	218
2004	5 097	64.1	4 580	212
2003	5 062	63.6	4 562	204
2002	5 024	63.1	4 541	196
2001	4 985	62.5	4 520	189
2000	4 919	61.8	4 400	172
1990	4 375	55.0	4 130	95
1980	4 076	51.2	3 936	53
1970	3 805	47.8	3 736	35
1960	3 414	42.9	3 372	22
1950	2 982	37.3	2 954	14
1940	2 792	34.9	2 769	10
1930	2 564	32.0	2 543	9
1920	2 387	29.5	2 369	9
1910	2 076	25.7	2 059	7
1900	1 751	21.7	1 737	5
1890	1 310	16.2	1 296	4
1880	781	9.7	777	2
1870	440	5.4	438	1
1860	172	2.1	169	(4)
1850	6	(6)	6	(4)

[1]Beginning 1970 persons per square mile were calculated on the basis of land area data from the 2000 census.
[4]Less than 500.
[6]Less than 1/10 of a person.

Table 1-9. Population of States, by Race, 1790–2005—*Continued*

(Number in thousands, except population per square mile.)

Year	Resident population		Race	
	Total	Per square mile of land area[1]	White	Black
Mississippi				
2005	2 921	62.3	1 788	1 079
2004	2 901	61.9	1 780	1 069
2003	2 881	61.4	1 772	1 059
2002	2 866	61.2	1 767	1 051
2001	2 858	60.9	1 766	1 045
2000	2 845	60.6	1 746	1 034
1990	2 573	54.9	1 633	915
1980	2 521	53.7	1 615	887
1970	2 217	47.3	1 633	816
1960	2 178	46.4	1 258	916
1950	2 179	46.1	1 189	986
1940	2 184	46.1	1 106	1 075
1930	2 010	42.4	998	1 010
1920	1 791	38.6	854	935
1910	1 797	38.8	786	1 009
1900	1 551	33.5	641	908
1890	1 290	27.8	545	743
1880	1 132	24.4	479	650
1870	828	17.9	383	444
1860	791	17.1	354	437
1850	607	13.1	296	311
1840	376	8.1	179	197
1830	137	2.9	70	66
1820	75	1.6	42	33
1810[2]	31	0.4	23	17
1800[2]	8	0.3	5	4
Missouri				
2005	5 800	84.2	4 952	667
2004	5 760	83.5	4 922	661
2003	5 719	82.8	4 893	656
2002	5 681	82.3	4 866	650
2001	5 643	81.7	4 840	643
2000	5 595	81.2	4 748	629
1990	5 117	74.3	4 486	548
1980	4 917	71.4	4 346	514
1970	4 677	67.9	4 177	480
1960	4 320	62.7	3 923	391
1950	3 955	57.1	3 656	297
1940	3 785	54.6	3 539	244
1930	3 629	52.4	3 404	224
1920	3 404	49.5	3 225	178
1910	3 293	47.9	3 135	157
1900	3 107	45.2	2 945	161
1890	2 679	39.0	2 528	150
1880	2 168	31.6	2 023	145
1870	1 721	25.0	1 603	118
1860	1 182	17.2	1 063	119
1850	682	9.9	592	90
1840	384	5.6	324	60
1830	140	2.1	115	26
1820	67	1.0	56	11
1810	20	...	17	4

[1] Beginning 1970 persons per square mile were calculated on the basis of land area data from the 2000 census.
[2] Population of those parts of Mississippi Territory now in present state. Population per square mile, sex, race and age detail for Alabama included with Mississippi.
... = Not available.

Table 1-9. Population of States, by Race, 1790–2005—*Continued*

(Number in thousands, except population per square mile.)

Year	Resident population		Race	
	Total	Per square mile of land area[1]	White	Black
Montana				
2005	936	6.4	852	4
2004	927	6.4	845	3
2003	918	6.3	837	3
2002	910	6.2	831	3
2001	906	6.2	828	3
2000	902	6.2	817	3
1990	799	5.5	741	2
1980	787	5.4	740	2
1970	694	4.8	663	2
1960	675	4.6	651	1
1950	591	4.1	572	1
1940	559	3.8	540	1
1930	538	3.7	520	1
1920	549	3.8	534	2
1910	376	2.6	361	2
1900	243	1.7	226	2
1890	143	1.0	128	1
1880	39	0.3	35	(4)
1870	21	0.1	18	(4)
Nebraska				
2005	1 759	22.9	1 619	76
2004	1 748	22.7	1 610	75
2003	1 738	22.6	1 604	74
2002	1 727	22.5	1 596	72
2001	1 719	22.3	1 591	72
2000	1 711	22.3	1 533	69
1990	1 578	20.5	1 487	57
1980	1 570	20.4	1 490	48
1970	1 483	19.3	1 433	40
1960	1 411	18.4	1 375	29
1950	1 326	17.3	1 301	19
1940	1 316	17.2	1 298	14
1930	1 378	18.0	1 360	14
1920	1 296	16.9	1 279	13
1910	1 192	15.5	1 180	8
1900	1 066	13.9	1 057	6
1890	1 063	13.8	1 047	9
1880	452	5.9	450	2
1870	123	1.6	122	1
1860	29	0.2	29	(4)
Nevada				
2005	2 415	22.0	1 981	187
2004	2 333	21.3	1 925	176
2003	2 242	20.4	1 859	166
2002	2 168	19.8	1 805	158
2001	2 095	19.2	1 753	150
2000	1 998	18.2	1 502	135
1990	1 202	10.9	1 013	79
1980	800	7.3	700	51
1970	489	4.5	448	28
1960	285	2.6	263	13
1950	160	1.5	150	4
1940	110	1.0	104	1
1930	91	0.8	85	1
1920	77	0.7	71	(4)
1910	82	0.7	74	1
1900	42	0.4	35	(4)
1890	47	0.4	39	(4)
1880	62	0.6	54	(4)
1870	42	0.4	39	(4)
1860	7	0.1	7	(4)

[1]Beginning 1970 persons per square mile were calculated on the basis of land area data from the 2000 census.
[4]Less than 500.

Table 1-9. Population of States, by Race, 1790–2005—*Continued*

(Number in thousands, except population per square mile.)

Year	Resident population		Race	
	Total	Per square mile of land area[1]	White	Black
New Hampshire				
2005	1 310	146.1	1 258	13
2004	1 299	144.9	1 250	12
2003	1 288	143.6	1 240	12
2002	1 275	142.2	1 230	11
2001	1 259	140.4	1 216	11
2000	1 236	137.8	1 236	9
1990	1 109	123.7	1 087	7
1980	921	102.7	910	4
1970	738	82.3	733	3
1960	607	67.7	604	2
1950	533	59.1	532	1
1940	492	54.5	491	(4)
1930	465	51.6	464	1
1920	443	49.1	442	1
1910	431	47.7	430	1
1900	412	45.6	411	1
1890	377	41.7	376	1
1880	347	38.4	346	1
1870	318	35.2	318	1
1860	326	36.1	326	(4)
1850	318	35.2	317	1
1840	285	31.5	284	1
1830	269	29.8	269	1
1820	244	27.0	243	1
1810	214	23.7	214	1
1800	184	20.4	184	1
1790	142	15.7	142	1
New Jersey				
2005	8 718	1,175.3	6 680	1 262
2004	8 685	1,172.8	6 680	1 256
2003	8 640	1,164.6	6 672	1 248
2002	8 576	1,158.1	6 649	1 238
2001	8 505	1,143.9	6 622	1 227
2000	8 414	1 134.4	6 105	1 142
1990	7 730	1 044.5	6 130	1 037
1980	7 365	992.9	6 127	925
1970	7 168	966.8	6 350	770
1960	6 067	817.8	5 539	515
1950	4 835	642.8	4 512	319
1940	4 160	553.1	3 931	227
1930	4 041	537.3	3 830	209
1920	3 156	420.0	3 037	117
1910	2 537	337.7	2 446	90
1900	1 884	250.7	1 812	70
1890	1 445	192.3	1 397	48
1880	1 131	150.5	1 092	39
1870	906	120.6	875	31
1860	672	89.4	647	25
1850	490	65.2	466	24
1840	373	49.7	352	22
1830	321	42.7	300	21
1820	278	36.9	258	20
1810	246	32.7	227	19
1800	211	28.1	194	17
1790	184	24.5	170	14

[1]Beginning 1970 persons per square mile were calculated on the basis of land area data from the 2000 census.
[4]Less than 500.

Table 1-9. Population of States, by Race, 1790–2005—*Continued*

(Number in thousands, except population per square mile.)

| Year | Resident population | | Race | |
	Total	Per square mile of land area[1]	White	Black
New Mexico				
2005	1 928	15.9	1 630	47
2004	1 903	15.7	1 610	45
2003	1 879	15.4	1 592	43
2002	1 855	15.3	1 575	42
2001	1 833	15.1	1 559	40
2000	1 819	15.0	1 214	34
1990	1 515	12.5	1 146	30
1980	1 303	10.7	978	24
1970	1 016	8.4	916	20
1960	951	7.8	876	17
1950	681	5.6	630	8
1940	532	4.4	492	5
1930	423	3.5	391	3
1920	360	2.9	335	6
1910	327	2.7	305	2
1900	195	1.6	180	2
1890	160	1.3	143	2
1880	120	1.0	109	1
1870	92	0.7	90	(4)
1860[7]	94	0.4	83	(4)
1850[8]	62	0.3	62	(4)
New York				
2005	19 255	407.8	14 217	3 347
2004	19 281	407.2	14 262	3 361
2003	19 228	406.5	14 247	3 364
2002	19 165	405.8	14 227	3 364
2001	19 091	402.7	14 201	3 360
2000	18 976	401.9	12 894	3 014
1990	17 990	381.0	13 385	2 859
1980	17 558	371.9	13 961	2 402
1970	18 237	386.4	15 834	2 169
1960	16 782	355.4	15 287	1 418
1950	14 830	309.3	13 872	918
1940	13 479	281.2	12 880	571
1930	12 588	262.6	12 153	413
1920	10 385	217.9	10 172	198
1910	9 114	191.2	8 967	134
1900	7 269	152.5	7 157	99
1890	6 003	126.0	5 924	70
1880	5 083	106.7	5 016	65
1870	4 383	92.0	4 330	52
1860	3 881	81.4	3 832	49
1850	3 097	65.0	3 048	49
1840	2 429	51.0	2 379	50
1830[9]	1 919	40.3	1 868	45
1820	1 373	28.8	1 333	39
1810	959	20.1	919	40
1800	589	12.4	556	31
1790	340	7.1	314	26

[1]Beginning 1970 persons per square mile were calculated on the basis of land area data from the 2000 census.
[4]Less than 500.
[7]Includes population of area taken to form part of Arizona Territory in 1863.
[8]Data for Territory of New Mexico which included parts of present states of Arizona and New Mexico, and smaller parts of Colorado and Nevada.
[9]Includes 5,602 persons for whom sex, race and age detail are not available.

Table 1-9. Population of States, by Race, 1790–2005—*Continued*

(Number in thousands, except population per square mile.)

Year	Resident population		Race	
	Total	Per square mile of land area[1]	White	Black
North Carolina				
2005	8 683	178.3	6 434	1 889
2004	8 540	175.3	6 333	1 861
2003	8 422	172.6	6 252	1 836
2002	8 313	170.8	6 178	1 813
2001	8 198	168.1	6 101	1 788
2000	8 049	165.2	5 804	1 738
1990	6 629	136.2	5 008	1 456
1980	5 882	120.7	4 458	1 319
1970	5 082	104.4	3 902	1 126
1960	4 556	93.5	3 399	1 116
1950	4 062	82.7	2 983	1 047
1940	3 572	72.7	2 568	981
1930	3 170	64.5	2 235	919
1920	2 559	52.5	1 784	763
1910	2 206	45.3	1 501	698
1900	1 894	38.9	1 264	624
1890	1 618	33.2	1 055	561
1880	1 400	28.7	867	531
1870	1 071	22.0	678	392
1860	993	20.4	630	362
1850	869	17.8	553	316
1840	753	15.5	485	269
1830	738	15.1	473	265
1820	639	13.1	419	220
1810	556	11.4	376	179
1800	478	9.8	338	140
1790	394	8.1	288	106
North Dakota				
2005	637	9.2	588	5
2004	636	9.2	588	5
2003	633	9.2	586	4
2002	634	9.2	587	4
2001	636	9.2	591	4
2000	642	9.3	593	4
1990	639	9.3	604	4
1980	653	9.5	626	3
1970	618	9.0	599	2
1960	632	9.2	620	1
1950	620	8.8	608	(4)
1940	642	9.2	631	(4)
1930	681	9.7	672	(4)
1920	647	9.2	640	(4)
1910	577	8.2	570	1
1900	319	4.5	312	(4)
1890	191	2.7	182	(4)
1880[10]	37	0.9	133	(4)
1870[10]	2	0.1	13	(4)
1860[10]	5	(6)	3	-

[1]Beginning 1970 persons per square mile were calculated on the basis of land area data from the 2000 census.
[4]Less than 500.
[6]Less than 1/10 of a person.
[10]North and South Dakota comprised Dakota Territory. Population per square mile, sex and age detail for South Dakota included with North Dakota.
- = Quantity zero.

Table 1-9. Population of States, by Race, 1790–2005—*Continued*

(Number in thousands, except population per square mile.)

| Year | Resident population | | Race | |
	Total	Per square mile of land area[1]	White	Black
Ohio				
2005	11 464	280.0	9 759	1 368
2004	11 450	279.8	9 763	1 361
2003	11 432	279.3	9 762	1 353
2002	11 405	278.9	9 757	1 343
2001	11 385	277.8	9 758	1 332
2000	11 353	277.3	9 645	1 301
1990	10 847	264.9	9 522	1 155
1980	10 798	263.7	9 597	1 077
1970	10 652	260.3	9 647	970
1960	9 706	237.0	8 910	786
1950	7 947	193.8	7 428	513
1940	6 908	168.0	6 567	339
1930	6 647	161.6	6 335	309
1920	5 759	141.4	5 572	186
1910	4 767	117.0	4 655	111
1900	4 158	102.1	4 060	97
1890	3 672	90.1	3 585	87
1880	3 198	78.5	3 118	80
1870	2 665	65.4	2 602	63
1860	2 340	57.4	2 303	37
1850	1 980	48.6	1 955	25
1840	1 519	37.3	1 502	17
1830	938	23.3	928	10
1820	581	14.5	577	5
1810	231	5.7	229	2
1800	45	1.1	45	([4])
Oklahoma				
2005	3 548	51.7	2 785	275
2004	3 524	51.3	2 767	272
2003	3 505	51.1	2 755	270
2002	3 487	50.9	2 743	268
2001	3 466	50.4	2 728	266
2000	3 451	50.3	2 628	261
1990	3 146	45.8	2 584	234
1980	3 025	44.1	2 598	205
1970	2 559	37.3	2 280	172
1960	2 328	33.9	2 108	153
1950	2 233	32.4	2 033	146
1940	2 336	33.7	2 104	169
1930	2 396	34.6	2 131	172
1920	2 028	29.2	1 821	149
1910	1 657	23.9	1 445	138
1900	790	11.4	670	56
1890	259	3.7	173	22
Oregon				
2005	3 641	37.9	3 305	66
2004	3 591	37.4	3 264	64
2003	3 563	37.1	3 241	63
2002	3 522	36.7	3 208	62
2001	3 473	36.2	3 168	60
2000	3 421	35.6	2 962	56
1990	2 842	29.6	2 637	46
1980	2 633	27.4	2 491	37
1970	2 091	21.8	2 032	26
1960	1 769	18.4	1 732	18
1950	1 521	15.8	1 497	12
1940	1 090	11.3	1 076	3
1930	954	9.9	939	2
1920	783	8.2	769	2
1910	673	7.0	655	1
1900	414	4.3	395	1
1890	318	3.3	302	1
1880	175	1.8	163	([4])
1870	91	1.0	87	([4])
1860	52	0.5	52	([4])
1850[11]	12	([6])	13	([4])

[1]Beginning 1970 persons per square mile were calculated on the basis of land area data from the 2000 census.
[4]Less than 500.
[6]Less than 1/10 of a person.
[11]Population total of those parts of Oregon Territory taken to form part of Washington Territory in 1853 and 1859 excluded from Oregon included under Washington. Population per square mile, sex, race and age detail for Washington included with Oregon.

Table 1-9. Population of States, by Race, 1790–2005—*Continued*

(Number in thousands, except population per square mile.)

| Year | Resident population | | Race | |
	Total	Per square mile of land area[1]	White	Black
Pennsylvania				
2005	12 430	277.3	10 688	1 318
2004	12 394	276.8	10 681	1 305
2003	12 365	275.9	10 681	1 291
2002	12 324	275.2	10 669	1 279
2001	12 296	274.2	10 666	1 269
2000	12 281	274.0	10 484	1 225
1990	11 882	265.1	10 520	1 090
1980	11 864	264.7	10 652	1 047
1970	11 794	263.3	10 738	1 017
1960	11 319	252.6	10 454	853
1950	10 498	233.1	9 854	638
1940	9 900	219.8	9 427	470
1930	9 631	213.8	9 196	431
1920	8 720	194.5	8 433	285
1910	7 665	171.0	7 468	194
1900	6 302	140.6	6 142	157
1890	5 258	117.3	5 148	108
1880	4 283	95.5	4 197	86
1870	3 522	78.6	3 457	65
1860	2 906	64.8	2 849	57
1850	2 312	51.6	2 258	54
1840	1 724	38.5	1 676	48
1830	1 348	30.1	1 310	38
1820	1 049	23.4	1 017	30
1810	810	18.1	787	23
1800	602	13.4	586	16
1790	434	9.7	424	10
Rhode Island				
2005	1 076	1,029.9	957	66
2004	1 080	1,034.2	962	66
2003	1 076	1,029.9	960	65
2002	1 069	1,023.7	956	63
2001	1 058	1,013.4	949	62
2000	1 048	1 003.2	891	47
1990	1 003	960.3	917	39
1980	947	906.4	897	28
1970	947	908.9	915	25
1960	859	822.5	839	18
1950	792	748.5	777	14
1940	713	674.2	702	11
1930	687	649.8	677	10
1920	604	566.4	594	10
1910	543	508.5	532	10
1900	429	401.6	419	9
1890	346	323.8	338	7
1880	277	259.2	270	6
1870	217	203.7	212	5
1860	175	163.7	171	4
1850	148	138.3	144	4
1840	109	102.0	106	3
1830	97	91.1	94	4
1820	83	77.8	79	4
1810	77	72.1	73	4
1800	69	64.8	65	4
1790	69	64.5	65	4

[1]Beginning 1970 persons per square mile were calculated on the basis of land area data from the 2000 census.

Table 1-9. Population of States, by Race, 1790–2005—*Continued*

(Number in thousands, except population per square mile.)

| Year | Resident population | | Race | |
	Total	Per square mile of land area[1]	White	Black
South Carolina				
2005	4 255	141.3	2 911	1 245
2004	4 198	139.4	2 867	1 235
2003	4 147	137.7	2 831	1 223
2002	4 103	136.4	2 801	1 213
2001	4 060	134.9	2 770	1 204
2000	4 012	133.2	2 696	1 185
1990	3 487	115.8	2 407	1 040
1980	3 122	103.7	2 147	949
1970	2 591	86.0	1 794	789
1960	2 383	79.1	1 551	829
1950	2 117	69.9	1 293	822
1940	1 900	62.1	1 084	814
1930	1 739	56.8	944	794
1920	1 684	55.2	819	865
1910	1 515	49.7	679	836
1900	1 340	44.0	558	782
1890	1 151	37.7	462	689
1880	996	32.6	391	604
1870	706	23.1	290	416
1860	704	23.1	291	412
1850	669	21.9	275	394
1840	594	19.5	259	335
1830	581	19.1	258	323
1820	503	16.5	237	265
1810	415	13.6	214	201
1800	346	11.3	196	149
1790	249	8.2	140	109
South Dakota				
2005	776	10.2	687	6
2004	771	10.2	683	6
2003	765	10.1	679	6
2002	760	10.0	677	5
2001	758	10.0	676	5
2000	755	9.9	669	5
1990	696	9.2	638	5
1980	691	9.1	640	3
1970	666	8.8	630	2
1960	681	9.0	653	2
1950	653	8.5	629	1
1940	643	8.4	619	1
1930	693	9.1	670	(4)
1920	637	8.3	619	1
1910	584	7.6	564	1
1900	402	5.2	381	1
1890	349	4.5	328	(4)
1880[10]	98	...	97	1
1870[10]	12	...	11	(4)
1860[10]	...	...	...	(4)
				...

[1]Beginning 1970 persons per square mile were calculated on the basis of land area data from the 2000 census.
[4]Less than 500.
[10]North and South Dakota comprised Dakota Territory. Population per square mile, sex and age detail for South Dakota included with North Dakota.
... = Not available.

Table 1-9. Population of States, by Race, 1790–2005—*Continued*

(Number in thousands, except population per square mile.)

Year	Resident population		Race	
	Total	Per square mile of land area[1]	White	Black
Tennessee				
2005	5 963	144.7	4 810	1 003
2004	5 893	143.2	4 759	990
2003	5 842	141.7	4 725	978
2002	5 790	140.7	4 692	966
2001	5 747	139.3	4 665	954
2000	5 689	138.0	4 563	933
1990	4 877	118.3	4 048	778
1980	4 591	111.4	3 835	726
1970	3 924	95.3	3 294	621
1960	3 567	86.5	2 978	587
1950	3 292	78.8	2 760	531
1940	2 916	69.5	2 407	509
1930	2 617	62.4	2 139	478
1920	2 338	56.1	1 886	452
1910	2 185	52.4	1 711	473
1900	2 021	48.5	1 540	480
1890	1 768	42.4	1 337	431
1880	1 542	37.0	1 139	403
1870	1 259	30.2	936	322
1860	1 110	26.6	827	283
1850	1 003	24.1	757	246
1840	829	19.9	641	189
1830	682	16.4	536	146
1820	423	10.1	340	83
1810	262	6.3	216	46
1800	106	2.5	92	14
1790	36	0.8	32	4
Texas				
2005	22 860	87.3	19 017	2 673
2004	22 472	85.9	18 715	2 629
2003	22 099	84.5	18 421	2 590
2002	21 722	83.2	18 129	2 549
2001	21 334	81.5	17 828	2 507
2000	20 852	79.6	14 800	2 405
1990	16 987	64.9	12 775	2 022
1980	14 229	54.4	11 198	1 710
1970	11 197	42.8	9 717	1 399
1960	9 580	36.6	8 375	1 187
1950	7 711	29.3	6 727	977
1940	6 415	24.3	5 488	924
1930	5 825	22.1	4 967	855
1920	4 663	17.8	3 918	742
1910	3 897	14.8	3 205	690
1900	3 049	11.6	2 427	621
1890	2 236	8.5	1 746	488
1880	1 592	6.1	1 197	393
1870	819	3.1	565	253
1860	604	2.3	421	183
1850	213	0.8	154	59
Utah				
2005	2 470	30.1	2 316	24
2004	2 421	29.1	2 271	23
2003	2 379	28.6	2 233	22
2002	2 337	28.2	2 195	21
2001	2 288	27.6	2 150	20
2000	2 233	27.2	1 993	18
1990	1 723	21.0	1 616	12
1980	1 461	17.8	1 383	9
1970	1 059	12.9	1 032	7
1960	891	10.8	874	4
1950	689	8.4	677	3
1940	550	6.7	543	1
1930	508	6.2	500	1
1920	449	5.5	442	1
1910	373	4.5	367	1
1900	277	3.4	272	1
1890	211	2.6	206	1
1880	144	1.8	142	(4)
1870	87	1.1	86	(4)
1860	40	0.3	40	(4)
1850	11	(6)	11	(4)

[1]Beginning 1970 persons per square mile were calculated on the basis of land area data from the 2000 census.
[4]Less than 500.
[6]Less than 1/10 of a person.

Table 1-9. Population of States, by Race, 1790–2005—*Continued*

(Number in thousands, except population per square mile.)

Year	Resident population		Race	
	Total	Per square mile of land area[1]	White	Black
Vermont				
2005	623	67.4	604	4
2004	621	67.2	603	4
2003	619	66.9	601	4
2002	616	66.7	598	3
2001	613	66.3	595	3
2000	609	65.8	589	3
1990	563	60.8	555	2
1980	511	55.3	507	1
1970	444	48.1	443	1
1960	390	42.2	389	1
1950	378	40.7	377	(4)
1940	359	38.7	359	(4)
1930	360	38.8	359	1
1920	352	38.6	352	1
1910	356	39.0	354	2
1900	344	37.7	343	1
1890	332	36.4	331	1
1880	332	36.4	331	1
1870	331	36.2	330	1
1860	315	34.5	314	1
1850	314	34.4	313	1
1840	292	32.0	291	1
1830	281	30.8	280	1
1820	236	25.9	235	1
1810	218	23.9	217	1
1800	154	16.9	154	1
1790	85	9.4	85	(4)
Virginia				
2005	7 567	191.1	5 567	1 505
2004	7 481	188.4	5 520	1 487
2003	7 383	186.6	5 462	1 469
2002	7 286	184.2	5 404	1 450
2001	7 192	181.5	5 348	1 431
2000	7 079	178.8	5 120	1 390
1990	6 187	156.3	4 792	1 163
1980	5 347	135.0	4 230	1 009
1970	4 648	117.5	3 762	861
1960	3 967	100.2	3 142	816
1950	3 319	83.2	2 582	734
1940	2 678	67.1	2 016	661
1930	2 422	60.7	1 770	650
1920	2 309	57.4	1 618	690
1910	2 062	51.2	1 390	671
1900	1 854	46.1	1 193	661
1890	1 656	41.1	1 020	635
1880	1 513	37.6	881	632
1870	1 225	30.4	712	513
1860[12]	1 220	24.8	1 047	549
1850[12]	1 119	22.1	895	527
1840[12]	1 025	19.3	748	502
1830[12]	1 044	18.9	701	520
1820[12]	938	16.6	610	465
1810[12]	878	15.2	557	426
1800[12]	808	13.7	518	367
1790[12]	692	11.6	442	306

[1]Beginning 1970 persons per square mile were calculated on the basis of land area data from the 2000 census.
[4]Less than 500.
[12]Sex, race and age detail for West Virginia, 1790–1860, included with Virginia.

Table 1-9. **Population of States, by Race, 1790–2005—***Continued*

(Number in thousands, except population per square mile.)

| Year | Resident population | | Race | |
	Total	Per square mile of land area[1]	White	Black
Washington				
2005	6 288	94.5	5 343	222
2004	6 207	93.2	5 288	217
2003	6 131	92.1	5 237	213
2002	6 066	91.2	5 196	209
2001	5 992	90.0	5 147	204
2000	5 894	88.6	4 821	190
1990	4 867	73.1	4 309	150
1980	4 132	62.1	3 779	106
1970	3 409	51.3	3 251	71
1960	2 853	42.9	2 752	49
1950	2 379	35.6	2 316	31
1940	1 736	25.9	1 698	7
1930	1 563	23.3	1 522	7
1920	1 357	20.3	1 320	7
1910	1 142	17.1	1 109	6
1900	518	7.8	496	3
1890	357	5.3	341	2
1880	75	1.1	67	(4)
1870	24	0.4	22	(4)
1860[13]	12	0.1	11	(4)
1850[11]	1	...	...	...
West Virginia				
2005	1 817	75.5	1 730	58
2004	1 813	75.4	1 726	58
2003	1 810	75.2	1 725	58
2002	1 805	74.8	1 720	58
2001	1 801	74.8	1 718	58
2000	1 808	75.1	1 719	57
1990	1 793	74.5	1 726	56
1980	1 950	81.0	1 875	65
1970	1 744	72.4	1 673	67
1960	1 860	77.2	1 770	89
1950	2 006	83.3	1 890	115
1940	1 902	79.0	1 784	118
1930	1 729	71.8	1 614	115
1920	1 464	60.9	1 377	86
1910	1 221	50.8	1 157	64
1900	959	39.9	915	43
1890	763	31.8	730	33
1880	618	25.7	593	26
1870	442	18.4	424	18
1860[12]	377	...	...	...
1850[12]	302	...	...	...
1840[12]	225	...	...	...
1830[12]	177	...	...	...
1820[12]	137	...	...	...
1810[12]	105	...	...	...
1800[12]	79	...	...	...
1790[12]	56	...	...	...

[1]Beginning 1970 persons per square mile were calculated on the basis of land area data from the 2000 census.
[4]Less than 500.
[11]Population total of those parts of Oregon Territory taken to form part of Washington Territory in 1853 and 1859 excluded from Oregon included under Washington. Population per square mile, sex, race and age detail for Washington included with Oregon.
[12]Sex, race and age detail for West Virginia, 1790–1860, included with Virginia.
[13]Includes population of Idaho and parts of Montana and Wyoming.
. . . = Not available.

Table 1-9. Population of States, by Race, 1790–2005—*Continued*

(Number in thousands, except population per square mile.)

Year	Resident population		Race	
	Total	Per square mile of land area[1]	White	Black
Wisconsin				
2005	5 536	101.9	4 986	331
2004	5 504	101.4	4 963	327
2003	5 472	100.8	4 940	324
2002	5 439	100.2	4 918	320
2001	2 404	99.5	4 895	314
2000	5 364	98.8	4 770	304
1990	4 892	90.1	4 513	245
1980	4 706	86.6	4 443	183
1970	4 418	81.3	4 259	128
1960	3 952	72.8	3 859	75
1950	3 435	62.8	3 393	28
1940	3 138	57.3	3 113	12
1930	2 939	53.7	2 916	11
1920	2 632	47.6	2 617	5
1910	2 334	42.2	2 321	3
1900	2 069	37.4	2 058	3
1890	1 693	30.6	1 681	2
1880	1 315	23.8	1 310	3
1870	1 055	19.1	1 051	2
1860	776	14.0	774	1
1850	305	5.5	305	1
1840	31	0.4	31	([4])
Wyoming				
2005	509	5.2	483	4
2004	506	5.2	480	4
2003	502	5.2	476	4
2002	499	5.1	474	4
2001	494	5.1	470	4
2000	494	5.1	455	4
1990	454	4.7	427	4
1980	470	4.8	446	3
1970	332	3.4	323	3
1960	330	3.4	323	2
1950	291	3.0	284	3
1940	251	2.6	247	1
1930	226	2.3	221	1
1920	194	2.0	190	1
1910	146	1.5	140	2
1900	93	0.9	89	1
1890	63	0.6	59	1
1880	21	0.2	19	([4])
1870	9	0.1	9	([4])

Source: U.S. Census Bureau.
[1]Beginning 1970 persons per square mile were calculated on the basis of land area data from the 2000 census.
[4]Less than 500.

Table 1-10. Mobility Status of the Population by Selected Characteristics, 1947–2005

(Number in thousands. For persons 1 year old and over. Based on comparison of place of residence in immediate prior year and year shown. Excludes members of the Armed Forces except those living off post or with their families on post.)

| Mobility period and characteristic | Total (1,000) | Non-movers | Movers (different house in United States) | | | | | Movers from abroad |
| | | | | Different county | | | | |
			Same county	Same state	Different state, same division¹	Different division, same region	Different region	
2004 to 2005, total	287 136	247 715	22 443	7 776	3 368	930	3 068	1 836
1 to 4 years old	16 243	12 804	2 155	601	247	78	249	108
5 to 9 years old	19 546	16 447	1 868	540	271	58	242	120
10 to 14 years old	20 922	18 335	1 555	455	215	62	193	108
15 to 19 years old	20 661	18 017	1 476	523	225	54	174	190
20 to 24 years old	20 402	14 287	3 553	1 278	431	125	433	296
25 to 29 years old	19 499	14 053	3 118	1 083	431	145	385	285
30 to 44 years old	63 158	53 777	5 243	1 868	809	205	723	531
45 to 64 years old	71 491	66 261	2 709	1 123	593	158	483	164
65 to 74 years old	18 388	17 530	422	168	90	30	123	24
75 to 84 years old	12 981	12 505	263	101	37	13	51	11
85 years old and over	3 845	3 698	79	34	18	2	13	-
Northeast	53 388	48 242	2 831	1 015	516	112	358	315
Midwest	63 983	56 017	4 653	1 576	675	128	679	255
South	103 556	87 869	8 704	3 244	1 397	344	1 320	678
West	66 209	55 588	6 254	1 941	779	347	713	588
Persons 16 years and over	226 105	196 250	16 601	6 102	2 587	729	2 358	1 480
Civilian labor force	147 451	125 752	12 392	4 496	1 790	468	1 587	964
Employed	139 277	119 424	11 358	4 163	1 651	400	1 416	863
Unemployed	8 174	6 328	1 034	333	139	68	171	101
Armed Forces	869	617	76	49	20	13	54	41
Not in labor force	77 786	69 882	4 132	1 557	776	247	717	475
Employed civilians, 16 years and over	139 277	119 424	11 358	4 163	1 651	400	1 416	863
Management, business, and financial	19 878	17 641	1 304	456	199	53	178	47
Professional	28 464	24 796	1 916	850	346	90	341	126
Service	22 609	18 719	2 313	768	280	84	243	201
Sales	16 138	13 738	1 389	512	206	49	187	56
Office and administrative support	19 301	16 734	1 535	545	221	43	170	52
Farming, fishing, and forestry	944	750	100	19	14	-	9	53
Construction and extraction	8 634	6 944	927	357	121	31	82	172
Installation, maintenance, and repair	5 149	4 488	380	170	58	12	37	5
Production	9 598	8 263	794	240	112	19	85	86
Transportation and material moving	8 561	7 351	702	245	95	19	85	64
Persons 15 years and over	230 425	200 129	16 864	6 180	2 635	733	2 384	1 500
Without income	25 279	21 404	1 961	679	385	72	244	534
With income	205 144	178 727	14 903	5 502	2 248	661	2 139	967
Less than $5,000	23 692	20 652	1 555	631	268	102	307	176
$5,000 to $9,999	24 046	20 876	1 837	642	272	61	227	131
$10,000 to $14,999	22 717	19 511	1 962	601	230	67	229	118
$15,000 to $24,999	37 137	31 650	3 201	1 073	439	132	407	235
$25,000 to $34,999	28 431	24 313	2 431	894	331	75	277	111
$35,000 to $49,999	28 468	24 961	1 916	811	328	88	284	79
$50,000 to $74,999	22 529	20 318	1 175	476	230	71	196	65
$75,000 and over	18 124	16 446	826	374	150	65	212	52
Tenure:								
Owner-occupied units	207 326	191 993	8 420	3 457	1 299	414	1 322	423
Renter-occupied units	79 810	55 722	14 023	4 319	2 069	517	1 746	1 414
2003 to 2004	284 367	245 372	22 551	7 842	3 691	992	2 647	1 272
2002 to 2003	282 556	242 463	23 468	7 728	3 752	1 181	2 695	1 269
2001 to 2002	278 160	237 049	23 712	8 066	3 603	193	2 974	1 563
2000 to 2001	275 611	...	...	...	...	...	...	...
1999 to 2000	270 219	...	...	...	...	...	...	...
1998 to 1999	267 933	...	...	...	...	...	...	...
1997 to 1998	265 209	...	...	...	...	...	...	...
1996 to 1997	262 976	...	...	...	...	...	...	...
1995 to 1996	260 406	...	...	...	...	...	...	...
1993 to 1994	255 774	...	...	...	...	...	...	...
1992 to 1993	250 210	...	...	...	...	...	...	...
1991 to 1992	247 380	...	...	...	...	...	...	...
1990 to 1991	244 884	...	...	...	...	...	...	...
1989 to 1990	242 208	...	...	...	...	...	...	...
1985 to 1986	232 998	...	...	...	...	...	...	...
1980 to 1981	221 641	...	...	...	...	...	...	...
1969 to 1970	198 955	160 860	23 225	6 250	7 066	...	...	1 554

Table 1-10. Mobility Status of the Population by Selected Characteristics, 1947–2005—*Continued*

(Number in thousands. For persons 1 year old and over. Based on comparison of place of residence in immediate prior year and year shown. Excludes members of the Armed Forces except those living off post or with their families on post.)

Mobility period and characteristic	Total (1,000)	Non-movers	Movers (different house in United States)					Movers from abroad
			Same county	Different county				
				Same state	Different state, same division[1]	Different division, same region	Different region	
1968 to 1969	196 642	159 310	22 993	6 316	6 625	...	...	1 399
1967 to 1968	194 621	156 735	36 603	6 607	7 035	...	...	1 283
1966 to 1967	192 233	155 710	22 339	6 308	6 553	...	...	1 323
1965 to 1966	190 242	152 656	24 165	6 275	6 263	...	...	883
1964 to 1965	187 974	149 128	25 122	6 597	6 147	...	...	978
1963 to 1964	185 312	148 125	24 089	6 191	6 047	...	...	859
1962 to 1963	182 541	146 109	23 059	5 712	6 640	...	...	1 021
1961 to 1962	179 663	144 445	23 341	5 461	5 562	...	...	854
1960 to 1961	177 354	140 821	24 289	5 493	5 753	...	...	998
1959 to 1960*	174 451	139 766	22 564	5 724	5 523	...	...	874
1958 to 1959	170 658	137 018	22 315	5 419	5 070	...	...	836
1957 to 1958	167 604	133 501	22 023	5 656	5 584	...	...	840
1956 to 1957	164 371	131 648	21 566	5 192	5 076	...	...	889
1955 to 1956	161 497	127 457	22 186	5 859	5 053	...	...	942
1954 to 1955	158 609	126 190	21 086	5 511	4 895	...	...	927
1953 to 1954	155 679	125 654	19 046	4 947	5 034	...	...	998
1952 to 1953	153 038	121 512	20 638	4 626	5 522	...	...	740
1951 to 1952	150 494	120 016	19 874	4 854	5 112	...	...	638
1950 to 1951	148 400	116 936	20 694	5 276	5 188	...	...	306
1949 to 1950	146 864	118 849	19 276	4 360	8 889	...	...	491
1948 to 1949	144 101	116 498	18 792	3 992	4 344	...	...	476
1947 to 1948	141 698	113 026	19 202	4 638	4 370	...	...	462

Source: U.S. Census Bureau. *Statistical Abstract of the United States: 2007* and *Bicentennial Edition: Historical Statistics of the United States, Colonial Times to 1970.*
Note: Northeast comprises New England and Middle Atlantic states.
   New England: Maine, New Hampshire, Vermont, Massachusetts, Rhode Island, and Connecticut.
   Middle Atlantic: New York, New Jersey, and Pennsylvania.

Midwest comprises East North Central and West North Central states.
   East North Central: Ohio, Indiana, Illinois, Michigan, and Wisconsin.
   West North Central: Minnesota, Iowa, Missouri, North Dakota, South Dakota, Nebraska, and Kansas.

South comprises South Atlantic, East South Central and West South Central states.
   South Atlantic: Delaware, Maryland, District of Columbia, Virginia, West Virginia, North Carolina, South Carolina, Georgia, and Florida.
   East South Central: Kentucky, Tennessee, Alabama, and Mississippi.
   West South Central: Arkansas, Louisiana, Oklahoma, and Texas.

West comprises Mountain and Pacific states.
   Mountain: Montana, Idaho, Wyoming, Colorado, New Mexico, Arizona, Utah, and Nevada.
   Pacific: Washington, Oregon, California, Alaska, and Hawaii
[1]U.S. Census Bureau data for 1970 and prior years do not include divisional or regional data. All interstate moves for 1947-1970 are included in this category.
- = Quantity zero or rounds to zero.
Z = Less than 0.5 percent.
* = First year for which figures include Alaska and Hawaii.
. . . = Not available.

Table 1.11. United States Population by Race and Ethnicity, 1970–2005

| | | One Race[1] | | | | | | | Two or More Races | | | | | |
| | | | | | | | | | | Race alone or in Combination[2] | | | | |
	Population[3]	One Race	White	Black	American Indian or Alaska Native	Asian	Native Hawaiian or Other Pacific Islanders	Other Race	Two or More Races	White	Black	American Indian or Alaska Native	Asian	Native Hawaiian or Other Pacific Islanders
Percent Change, 2000 to 2005	**5.3**	5.2	4.3	6.2	7.5	19.8	11.7	...	17.5	4.5	7.1	5.4	19.7	9.1
2005	296 410 000	291 831 000	237 855 000	37 909 000	2 863 000	12 687 000	517 000	...	4 579 000	241 807 000	39 724 000	4 454 000	14 377 000	990 000
2004	293 657 000	289 213 000	236 064 000	37 496 000	2 825 000	12 321 000	506 000	...	4 444 000	239 892 000	39 229 000	4 411 000	13 956 000	975 000
2003	290 850 000	286 539 000	234 241 000	37 082 000	2 788 000	11 933 000	496 000	...	4 311 000	237 947 000	38 733 000	4 368 000	13 514 000	960 000
2002	287 985 000	283 804 000	232 375 000	36 671 000	2 750 000	11 523 000	485 000	...	4 181 000	235 962 000	38 244 000	4 324 000	13 052 000	944 000
2000[4]	281 425 000	277 527 000	228 107 000	35 705 000	2 664 000	10 589 000	463 000	...	3 898 000	231 436 000	37 105 000	4 225 000	12 007 000	907 000
1990	248 709 873	...	199 686 070	29 986 060	1 959 234	7 273 662	(5)	9 804 847	...	...	...	...	...	...
1990 Sample	248 709 873	...	199 827 064	29 930 524	2 015 143	7 226 986	(5)	9 710 156	...	...	...	...	...	...
1980	226 545 805	...	188 371 622	26 495 025	1 420 400	3 500 439	(5)	6 758 319	...	...	...	...	...	...
1980 Sample	226 545 805	...	189 035 012	26 482 349	1 534 336	3 726 440	(5)	5 767 668	...	...	...	...	...	...
1970	203 211 926	...	177 748 975	22 580 289	827 255	1 538 721	(5)	516 686	...	...	...	...	...	...
1970 15% Sample[6]	203 210 158	...	178 119 221	22 539 362	795 110	1 526 401	(5)	230 064	...	...	...	...	...	...
1970 5% Sample	203 193 774	...	178 081 520	22 565 377	...	...	(5)	...	...	...	...	...	...	...
1960[7]	179 323 175	...	158 831 732	18 871 831	551 669	980 337	(5)	87 606	...	...	...	...	...	...
1960[8]	178 464 236	...	158 454 956	18 860 117	508 675	565 443	(5)	75 045	...	...	...	...	...	...
1950	150 697 361	...	134 942 028	15 042 286	343 410	321 033	(5)	48 604	...	...	...	...	...	...
1940[9]	131 669 275	...	118 214 870	12 865 518	333 969	254 918	(5)	(X)	...	...	...	...	...	...
1940 5% Sample[9]	...	...	118 392 040	...	...	...	(5)	(X)	...	...	...	...	...	...
1930	122 775 046	...	110 286 740	11 891 143	332 397	264 766	(5)	(X)	...	...	...	...	...	...
1920	105 710 620	...	94 820 915	10 463 131	244 437	182 137	(5)	(X)	...	...	...	...	...	...
1910	91 972 266	...	81 731 957	9 827 763	265 683	146 863	(5)	(X)	...	...	...	...	...	...
1900	75 994 575	...	66 809 196	8 833 994	237 196	114 189	(5)	(X)	...	...	...	...	...	...
1890[10]	62 947 714	...	55 101 258	7 488 676	248 253	109 527	(5)	(X)	...	...	...	...	...	...
1890[11]	62 622 250	...	54 983 890	747 040	58 806	109 514	(5)	(X)	...	...	...	...	...	...
									Black					
									Total	Free	Slave			
1880	50 155 783	...	43 402 970	6 580 793	66 407	105 613	(5)	...				...	...	...
1870	38 558 371	...	33 589 377	4 880 009	25 731	63 254	(5)	...				...	...	...
1860	31 443 321	...	26 922 537	4 441 830	44 021	34 933	(5)	...	4 441 830	488 070	3 953 760	...	...	...
1850	23 191 876	...	19 553 068	3 638 808	...	...	...	...	3 638 808	434 495	3 204 313	...	...	...
1840	17 063 353	...	14 189 705	2 873 648	...	...	...	...	2 873 648	386 293	2 487 355	...	...	...
1830	12 860 702	...	10 532 060	2 328 642	...	...	...	...	2 328 642	319 599	2 009 043	...	...	...
1820	9 638 453	...	7 866 797	1 771 656	...	...	...	...	1 771 656	233 634	1 538 022	...	...	...
1810	7 239 881	...	5 862 073	1 377 808	...	...	...	...	1 377 808	186 446	1 191 362	...	...	...
1800	5 308 483	...	4 306 446	1 002 037	...	...	...	...	1 002 037	108 435	893 602	...	...	...
1790	3 929 214	...	3 172 006	757 208	...	...	...	...	757 208	59 527	697 681	...	...	...

[1]Prior to the 2000 Census respondents were only given the option to report one race, therefore, data on race from Census 2000 are not directly comparable with those from the 1990 census and previous censuses.
[2]In combination with one or more other races. The sum of the five race groups adds to more than the total population because individuals may report more than one race.
[3]Census data for years 1790-1990 are total population; years 2000-2005 reflect resident population.
[4]The April 1, 2001 population estimates base reflects changes to the Census 2000 population from the Count Question Resolution program and geographic program revisions.
[5]Prior to 2000 Native Hawaiian population and other Pacific Islanders were included with data for Asian population.
[6]Hispanic origin based on Spanish language.
[7]Includes Alaska and Hawaii.
[8]Excludes Alaska and Hawaii.
[9]Hispanic origin based on White population of Spanish mother tongue.
[10]Includes Indian Territory and Indian Reservations.
[11]Excludes Indian Territory and Indian Reservations.
. . . = Not available.
X = Not applicable.

Table 1.11. United States Population by Race and Ethnicity, 1970–2005—*Continued*

Not Hispanic or Latino

	Total Not Hispanic or Latino	One Race[1]						Two or More Races					
									Race alone or in Combination[2]				
		One Race	White	Black	American Indian or Alaska Native	Asian	Native Hawaiian or Other Pacific Islanders	Two or More Races	White	Black	American Indian or Alaska Native	Asian	Native Hawaiian or Other Pacific Islanders
Percent Change, 2000 to 2005	3.1	2.9	1.4	5.9	6.5	19.9	10.3	16.7	1.7	6.6	4.3	19.8	8.0
2005	253 723 000	249 749 000	198 366 000	36 325 000	2 233 000	12 421 000	405 000	3 974 000	201 782 000	37 859 000	3 603 000	13 934 000	812 000
2004	252 319 000	248 459 000	197 843 000	35 950 000	2 207 000	12 061 000	398 000	3 861 000	201 156 000	37 414 000	3 574 000	13 527 000	802 000
2003	250 915 000	247 166 000	197 340 000	35 574 000	2 181 000	11 680 000	391 000	3 750 000	200 551 000	36 970 000	3 546 000	13 099 000	791 000
2002	249 485 000	245 843 000	196 827 000	35 201 000	2 155 000	11 277 000	384 000	3 642 000	199 940 000	36 350 000	3 519 000	12 650 000	779 000
2000[4]	246 118 000	242 712 000	195 577 000	34 314 000	2 097 000	10 357 000	367 000	3 406 000	198 477 000	35 499 000	3 456 000	11 632 000	752 000
1990	...	...	188 128 296	...	...	...	...	...	...	...	...	...	...
1990 Sample	...	...	188 424 773	...	...	...	...	...	...	...	...	...	...
1980	...	...	180 256 366	...	...	...	...	...	...	...	...	...	...
1980 Sample	...	...	180 602 838	...	...	...	...	...	...	...	...	...	...
1970	...	...	...	...	...	...	...	...	...	...	...	...	...
1970 15% Sample[6]	...	...	169 023 068	...	...	...	...	...	...	...	...	...	...
1970 5% Sample	...	...	169 615 394	...	...	...	...	...	...	...	...	...	...
1960[7]	...	...	...	...	...	...	...	...	...	...	...	...	...
1960[8]	...	...	...	...	...	...	...	...	...	...	...	...	...
1950	...	...	...	...	...	...	...	...	...	...	...	...	...
1940[9]	...	...	*116 356 846*	...	...	...	...	...	...	...	...	...	...
1940 5% Sample[9] ..	...	...	116 530 640	...	...	...	...	...	...	...	...	...	...
1930	...	...	...	...	...	...	...	...	...	...	...	...	...
1920	...	...	...	...	...	...	...	...	...	...	...	...	...
1910	...	...	...	...	...	...	...	...	...	...	...	...	...
1900	...	...	...	...	...	...	...	...	...	...	...	...	...
1890	...	...	...	...	...	...	...	...	...	...	...	...	...
1890	...	...	...	...	...	...	...	...	...	...	...	...	...
1880	...	...	...	...	...	...	...	...	...	...	...	...	...
1870	...	...	...	...	...	...	...	...	...	...	...	...	...
1860	...	...	...	...	...	...	...	...	...	...	...	...	...
1850	...	...	...	...	...	...	...	...	...	...	...	...	...
1840	...	...	...	...	...	...	...	...	...	...	...	...	...
1830	...	...	...	...	...	...	...	...	...	...	...	...	...
1820	...	...	...	...	...	...	...	...	...	...	...	...	...
1810	...	...	...	...	...	...	...	...	...	...	...	...	...
1800	...	...	...	...	...	...	...	...	...	...	...	...	...
1790	...	...	...	...	...	...	...	...	...	...	...	...	...

[1]Prior to the 2000 Census respondents were only given the option to report one race, therefore, data on race from Census 2000 are not directly comparable with those from the 1990 census and previous censuses.
[2]In combination with one or more other races. The sum of the five race groups adds to more than the total population because individuals may report more than one race.
[4]The April 1, 2001 population estimates base reflects changes to the Census 2000 population from the Count Question Resolution program and geographic program revisions.
[6]Hispanic origin based on Spanish language.
[7]Includes Alaska and Hawaii.
[8]Excludes Alaska and Hawaii.
[9]Hispanic origin based on White population of Spanish mother tongue.
. . . = Not available.

Table 1.11. United States Population by Race and Ethnicity, 1970–2005—*Continued*

| | | One Race[1] | | | | | | Two or More Races | | | | | |
| | | | | | | | | | Race alone or in Combination[2] | | | | |
	Total Hispanic or Latino	One Race	White	Black	American Indian or Alaska Native	Asian	Native Hawaiian or Other Pacific Islanders	Two or More Races	White	Black	American Indian or Alaska Native	Asian	Native Hawaiian or Other Pacific Islanders
Percent Change, 2000 to 2005	20.9	20.9	21.4	13.9	11.2	14.8	16.9	23.2	21.4	16.2	10.6	18.2	14.5
2005	42 687 000	42 082 000	39 489 000	1 585 000	630 000	267 000	112 000	605 000	40 025 000	1 866 000	851 000	443 000	177 000
2004	41 338 000	40 754 000	38 221 000	1 547 000	619 000	260 000	108 000	583 000	38 736 000	1 815 000	836 000	429 000	173 000
2003	39 935 000	39 373 000	36 901 000	1 508 000	607 000	253 000	105 000	561 000	37 396 000	1 763 000	821 000	415 000	169 000
2002	38 500 000	37 960 000	35 548 000	1 471 000	594 000	246 000	102 000	540 000	36 022 000	1 713 000	805 000	402 000	165 000
2000[4]	35 306 000	34 815 000	32 530 000	1 391 000	566 000	232 000	95 000	491 000	32 959 000	1 606 000	770 000	375 000	155 000
1990	...	22 354 059	...	...	...	...	...	...	...	...	...	...	...
1990 Sample	...	21 900 089	...	...	...	...	...	...	...	...	...	...	...
1980	...	14 608 673	...	...	...	...	...	...	...	...	...	...	...
1980 Sample	...	14 603 683	...	...	...	...	...	...	...	...	...	...	...
1970	...	...	...	...	...	...	...	...	...	...	...	...	...
1970 15% Sample[6]	...	9 589 216	...	...	...	...	...	...	...	...	...	...	...
1970 5% Sample	...	9 072 602	...	...	...	...	...	...	...	...	...	...	...
1960[7]	...	...	...	...	...	...	...	...	...	...	...	...	...
1960[8]	...	...	...	...	...	...	...	...	...	...	...	...	...
1950	...	...	...	...	...	...	...	...	...	...	...	...	...
1940[9]	...	*1 858 024*	...	...	...	...	...	...	...	...	...	...	...
1940 5% Sample[9] ..	...	1 861 400	...	...	...	...	...	...	...	...	...	...	...
1930	...	...	...	...	...	...	...	...	...	...	...	...	...
1920	...	...	...	...	...	...	...	...	...	...	...	...	...
1910	...	...	...	...	...	...	...	...	...	...	...	...	...
1900	...	...	...	...	...	...	...	...	...	...	...	...	...
1890[10]	...	...	...	...	...	...	...	...	...	...	...	...	...
1890[11]	...	...	...	...	...	...	...	...	...	...	...	...	...
1880	...	...	...	...	...	...	...	...	...	...	...	...	...
1870	...	...	...	...	...	...	...	...	...	...	...	...	...
1860	...	...	...	...	...	...	...	...	...	...	...	...	...
1850	...	...	...	...	...	...	...	...	...	...	...	...	...
1840	...	...	...	...	...	...	...	...	...	...	...	...	...
1830	...	...	...	...	...	...	...	...	...	...	...	...	...
1820	...	...	...	...	...	...	...	...	...	...	...	...	...
1810	...	...	...	...	...	...	...	...	...	...	...	...	...
1800	...	...	...	...	...	...	...	...	...	...	...	...	...
1790	...	...	...	...	...	...	...	...	...	...	...	...	...

Source: U.S. Census Bureau. *Statistical Abstract of the United States: 2007* and *Working Paper No. 56: Historical Census Statistics on Population Totals by Race, 1790 to 1990, and by Hispanic Origin, 1970 to 1990, for the United States, Regions, Divisions, and States.*
[1]Prior to the 2000 Census respondents were only given the option to report one race, therefore, data on race from Census 2000 are not directly comparable with those from the 1990 census and previous censuses.
[2]In combination with one or more other races. The sum of the five race groups adds to more than the total population because individuals may report more than one race.
[4]The April 1, 2001 population estimates base reflects changes to the Census 2000 population from the Count Question Resolution program and geographic program revisions.
[6]Hispanic origin based on Spanish language.
[7]Includes Alaska and Hawaii.
[8]Excludes Alaska and Hawaii.
[9]Hispanic origin based on White population of Spanish mother tongue.
[10]Includes Indian Territory and Indian Reservations.
[11]Excludes Indian Territory and Indian Reservations.
. . . = Not available.

Table 1-12. Households, by Number of Persons, 1790–2005

(Number in thousands, percent.)

Year	Number of households	Size of household						
		1 person	2 persons	3 persons	4 persons	5 persons	6 persons	7 or more persons
2005	113 100	29 900	37 200	18 300	16 500	7 200	2 500	1 400
2004	112 000	29 586	37 366	17 968	16 066	7 150	2 476	1 388
2003	111 278	29 431	37 078	17 889	15 967	7 029	2 521	1 364
2002	109 297	28 775	36 240	17 742	15 794	6 948	2 438	1 360
2001[1]	108 209	28 207	35 917	17 444	15 692	6 978	2 555	1 415
2000	104 705	26 724	34 666	17 172	15 309	6 981	2 445	1 428
1999	103 874	26 606	34 262	17 386	15 030	6 962	2 367	1 261
1998	102 528	26 327	32 965	17 331	15 358	7 048	2 232	1 267
1997	101 018	25 402	32 736	17 065	15 396	6 774	2 311	1 334
1996	99 627	24 900	32 526	16 724	15 118	6 631	2 357	1 372
1995	98 990	24 732	31 834	16 827	15 321	6 616	2 279	1 382
1994	97 107	23 611	31 211	16 898	15 073	6 749	2 186	1 379
1993[2]	96 426	23 558	31 041	16 964	14 997	6 404	2 217	1 244
1992	95 669	23 974	30 734	16 398	14 710	6 389	2 126	1 338
1991	94 312	23 590	30 181	16 082	14 556	6 206	2 237	1 459
1990	93 347	22 999	30 114	16 128	14 456	6 213	2 143	1 295
1989	92 830	22 708	29 976	16 276	14 550	6 232	2 003	1 084
1988	91 066	21 889	29 295	16 163	14 143	6 081	2 176	1 320
1987	89 479	21 128	28 602	16 159	13 984	6 162	2 176	1 268
1986	88 458	21 178	27 732	16 088	13 774	6 276	2 138	1 272
1985	86 789	20 602	27 389	15 465	13 631	6 108	2 299	1 296
1984	85 407	19 954	26 890	15 134	13 593	6 070	2 372	1 394
1983	83 918	19 250	26 439	14 793	13 303	6 105	2 460	1 568
1982	83 527	19 354	26 486	14 617	12 868	6 103	2 480	1 619
1981	82 368	18 936	25 787	14 569	12 768	6 117	2 549	1 643
1980	80 776	18 296	25 327	14 130	12 666	6 059	2 519	1 778
1979	77 330	17 201	23 928	13 392	12 274	6 187	2 573	1 774
1978	76 030	16 715	23 334	13 040	11 955	6 356	2 723	1 906
1977	74 142	15 532	22 775	12 794	11 630	6 285	2 864	2 263
1976	72 867	14 983	22 321	12 520	11 407	6 268	3 001	2 367
1975	71 120	13 939	21 753	12 384	11 103	6 399	3 059	2 484
1974	69 859	13 368	21 495	11 913	10 900	6 469	3 063	2 651
1973	68 251	12 635	20 632	11 804	10 739	6 426	3 245	2 769
1972	66 676	12 189	19 482	11 542	10 679	6 431	3 374	2 979
1971	64 778	11 446	18 892	11 071	10 059	6 640	3 435	3 234
1970	63 401	10 851	18 333	10 949	9 991	6 548	3 534	3 195
1969	62 214	10 401	18 034	10 769	9 778	6 387	3 557	3 288
1968	60 813	9 802	17 377	10 577	9 623	6 319	3 627	3 488
1967	59 236	9 200	16 770	10 403	9 559	6 276	3 491	3 550
1966	58 406	9 093	16 679	9 993	9 465	6 257	3 465	3 465
1965	57 436	8 631	16 119	10 263	9 269	6 313	3 327	3 514
1964	56 149	7 821	15 622	10 034	9 565	6 328	3 373	3 405
1963	55 270	7 501	15 279	9 989	9 445	6 240	3 473	3 342
1962	54 764	7 473	15 461	10 077	9 347	6 016	3 368	3 022
1961	53 557	7 112	15 185	9 780	9 390	6 052	3 085	2 953
1960*	52 799	6 917	14 678	9 979	9 293	6 072	3 010	2 851
1959	51 302	6 317	14 538	9 788	9 123	5 793	2 948	2 795
1958	50 402	6 078	14 303	9 715	8 933	5 609	3 002	2 762
1957	49 543	5 451	14 274	9 743	9 096	5 487	2 848	2 644
1956	48 785	5 396	13 827	9 936	9 152	5 287	2 624	2 563
1955	47 788	5 212	13 612	9 725	9 052	5 291	2 568	2 328
1954	46 893	5 032	13 249	9 776	8 820	5 170	2 521	2 325
1953[3]	46 828	6 148	13 530	9 868	8 300	4 658	2 332	1 992
1952[4]	45 464	5 388	13 460	9 908	8 106	4 378	2 142	2 082
1951[4]	44 564	. . .	. . .	. . .	. . .	. . .	. . .	. . .
1950[3]	43 468	4 737	12 529	9 808	7 729	4 357	2 196	2 113
1940[4]	34 949	2 481	8 667	7 829	6 326	4 019	2 377	3 250
1930[4]	29 905	2 357	6 983	6 227	5 235	3 574	2 273	3 255
1900	15 964	814	2 395	2 810	2 698	2 267	1 740	3 257
1890[5]	12 690	457	1 675	2 119	2 132	1 916	1 472	2 919
1790	558	21	44	65	77	78	74	200

[1]Data for March 2001 and later use population controls based on Census 2000 and an expanded sample of households.
[2]Revised based on population from the decennial census for that year.
[3]Covers related persons only; therefore, not strictly comparable with other years.
[4]As of April.
[5]As of June; includes a small number of quasi-households.
* = First year for which figures include Alaska and Hawaii.
. . . = Not available.

Table 1-12. Households, by Number of Persons, 1790–2005—*Continued*

(Number in thousands, percent.)

Year	Percent distribution of number of households						
	1 person	2 persons	3 persons	4 persons	5 persons	6 persons	7 or more persons
2005	26.0	33.0	16.0	15.0	6.0	2.0	1.0
2004	26.0	33.0	16.0	14.0	6.0	2.0	1.0
2003	26.0	33.0	16.0	14.0	6.0	2.0	1.0
2002	26.3	33.2	16.2	14.5	6.4	2.2	1.2
2001[1]	26.1	33.2	16.1	14.5	6.4	2.4	1.3
2000	25.5	33.1	16.4	14.6	6.7	2.3	1.4
1999	25.6	33.0	16.7	14.5	6.7	2.3	1.2
1998	25.7	32.2	16.9	15.0	6.9	2.2	1.2
1997	25.1	32.4	16.9	15.2	6.7	2.3	1.3
1996	25.0	32.6	16.8	15.2	6.7	2.4	1.4
1995	25.0	32.2	17.0	15.5	6.7	2.3	1.4
1994	24.3	32.1	17.4	15.5	7.0	2.3	1.4
1993	24.5	32.3	17.5	15.5	6.6	2.3	1.3
1992	25.1	32.1	17.1	15.4	6.7	2.2	1.4
1991	25.0	32.0	17.1	15.4	6.6	2.4	1.5
1990	24.6	32.3	17.3	15.5	6.7	2.3	1.4
1989	24.5	32.3	17.5	15.7	6.7	2.2	1.2
1988	24.0	32.2	17.7	15.5	6.7	2.4	1.4
1987	23.6	32.0	18.1	15.6	6.9	2.4	1.4
1986	23.9	31.4	18.2	15.6	7.1	2.4	1.4
1985	23.7	31.6	17.8	15.7	7.0	2.6	1.5
1984	23.4	31.5	17.7	15.9	7.1	2.8	1.6
1983	22.9	31.5	17.6	15.9	7.3	2.9	1.9
1982	23.2	31.7	17.5	15.4	7.3	3.0	1.9
1981	23.0	31.3	17.7	15.5	7.4	3.1	2.0
1980	22.7	31.4	17.5	15.7	7.5	3.1	2.2
1979	22.2	30.9	17.3	15.9	8.0	3.3	2.3
1978	22.0	30.7	17.2	15.7	8.4	3.6	2.5
1977	20.9	30.7	17.3	15.7	8.5	3.9	3.1
1976	20.6	30.6	17.2	15.7	8.6	4.1	3.2
1975	19.6	30.6	17.4	15.6	9.0	4.3	3.5
1974	19.1	30.8	17.1	15.6	9.3	4.4	3.8
1973	18.5	30.2	17.3	15.7	9.4	4.8	4.1
1972	18.3	29.2	17.3	16.0	9.6	5.1	4.5
1971	17.7	29.2	17.1	15.5	10.3	5.3	5.0
1970	17.1	28.9	17.3	15.8	10.3	5.6	5.0
1969	16.7	29.0	17.3	15.7	10.3	5.7	5.3
1968	16.1	28.6	17.4	15.8	10.4	6.0	5.7
1967	15.5	28.3	17.6	16.1	10.6	5.9	6.0
1966	15.6	28.6	17.1	16.2	10.7	5.9	5.9
1965	15.0	28.1	17.9	16.1	11.0	5.8	6.1
1964	13.9	27.8	17.9	17.0	11.3	6.0	6.1
1963	13.6	27.6	18.1	17.1	11.3	6.3	6.0
1962	13.6	28.2	18.4	17.1	11.0	6.2	5.5
1961	13.3	28.4	18.3	17.5	11.3	5.8	5.5
1960*	13.1	27.8	18.9	17.6	11.5	5.7	5.4
1959	12.3	28.4	19.1	17.8	11.3	5.7	5.4
1958	12.1	28.4	19.3	17.7	11.1	6.0	5.5
1957	11.0	28.8	19.7	18.4	11.1	5.7	5.3
1956	11.1	28.3	20.4	18.8	10.8	5.4	5.3
1955	10.9	28.5	20.4	18.9	11.1	5.4	4.9
1954	10.7	28.3	20.8	18.8	11.0	5.4	5.0
1953[3]	13.1	28.9	21.1	17.7	9.9	5.0	4.3
1952[4]	11.9	29.6	21.8	17.8	9.6	4.7	4.6
1951[4]	. . .	. . .	. . .	. . .	. . .	. . .	. . .
1950[3]	10.9	28.8	22.6	17.8	10.0	5.1	4.9
1940[4]	7.1	24.8	22.4	18.1	11.5	6.8	9.3
1930[4]	7.9	23.4	20.8	17.5	12.0	7.6	10.9
1900	5.1	15.0	17.6	16.9	14.2	10.9	20.4
1890[5]	3.6	13.2	16.7	16.8	15.1	11.6	23.0
1790	3.7	7.8	11.7	13.8	13.9	13.2	35.8

Source: U.S. Census Bureau.
[1]Data for March 2001 and later use population controls based on Census 2000 and an expanded sample of households.
[3]Covers related persons only; therefore, not strictly comparable with other years.
[4]As of April.
[5]As of June; includes a small number of quasi-households.
* = First year for which figures include Alaska and Hawaii.
. . . = Not available.

Table 1-13. Components of Population Change, 1990–2050
(Number in thousands, percent.)

Year	Population[1]	Net increase		Births		Deaths		Net international migration[2]	
		Total	Percent	Number	Rate per 1,000	Number	Rate per 1,000	Number	Rate per 1,000
Projections									
2050	419 854 000	. . .	. . .	. . .	. . .	. . .	. . .	. . .	. . .
2040	391 946 000	. . .	. . .	. . .	. . .	. . .	. . .	. . .	. . .
2030	363 584 000	. . .	. . .	. . .	. . .	. . .	. . .	. . .	. . .
2020	335 805 000	. . .	. . .	. . .	. . .	. . .	. . .	. . .	. . .
2010	308 936 000	. . .	. . .	. . .	. . .	. . .	. . .	. . .	. . .
Estimates									
2005	296 410 000	2 754 000	0.9	4 129 000		2 425 000		1 050 000	
2004	293 657 000	2 807 000	1.0	4 105 000		2 420 000		1 122 000	
2003	290 809 777	2 835 853	1.0	402 653	14.0	247 680	8.6	128 611	4.5
2002	287 973 924	2 880 111	1.0	402 266	14.1	243 229	8.5	128 974	4.5
2001	285 093 813	2 916 059	1.0	404 731	14.3	241 927	8.6	128 802	4.6
2000 Census	282 177 754	. . .	. . .	. . .	. . .	. . .	. . .	. . .	. . .
1999	272 690 813	2 442 810	0.9	393 847	14.4	234 457	8.6	851 541	3.1
1998	270 248 003	2 464 396	0.9	390 554	14.5	231 979	8.6	853 819	3.2
1997	267 783 607	2 555 035	1.0	389 243	14.5	232 193	8.7	939 450	3.5
1996	265 228 572	2 425 296	0.9	388 196	14.6	231 791	8.7	864 269	3.3
1995	262 803 276	2 476 255	0.9	392 665	14.9	228 436	8.7	784 716	3.0
1994	260 327 021	2 544 413	1.0	397 113	15.3	228 285	8.8	764 208	2.9
1993	257 782 608	2 752 909	1.1	402 712	15.6	222 602	8.6	825 880	3.2
1992	255 029 699	2 876 607	1.1	410 568	16.1	218 011	8.5	773 452	3.0
1991	252 153 092	2 688 696	1.1	413 326	16.4	213 890	8.5	649 430	2.6
1990 Census	248 790 925	. . .	. . .	. . .	. . .	. . .	. . .	. . .	. . .

Source: U.S. Census Bureau.
[1]Population is estimated as of July 1 of the year shown, except that the 1990 and 2000 Census populations are as enumerated on April 1.
[2]Includes net migration of the foreign-born, emigration of natives, net movement from Puerto Rico to the United States, and Armed Forces movement.
 . . . = Not available.

Table 1-14. Population of Major North American Cities, 1750–2005

(Number in thousands.)

Year	1750	1790	1800	1810	1820	1830	1840	1850	1860	1870	1880	1890	1910	1920	1930	1940	1950	1960
Akron	...	...	...	...	...	...	...	3	3	10	17	28	69	208	255	339	410	605
Albany	...	3	5	11	13	24	34	51	62	69	91	95	100	113	127	466	514	715
Albuquerque	...	...	...	...	...	...	...	...	...	...	...	4	11	15	27	69	146	276
Allentown	...	4	4	4	5	6	8	10	8	14	18	25	52	74	93	397	438	545
Anaheim	...	...	...	...	...	...	...	...	...	...	1	1	3	6	11	15	104	704
Atlanta	...	...	...	...	...	...	...	3	10	22	37	66	155	201	270	518	672	1 169
Austin	...	...	...	...	...	...	...	1	2	4	11	15	30	35	53	111	161	232
Baltimore	...	14	26	36	63	81	102	169	212	267	332	434	558	734	805	1 083	1 337	1 804
Birmingham	...	...	...	...	...	...	...	...	...	...	3	26	133	179	260	460	559	747
Boston	16	18	25	33	43	61	93	137	178	251	363	448	671	748	781	2 178	2 370	2 688
Buffalo	...	16	...	...	2	9	18	42	81	118	155	256	424	507	573	958	1 089	1 307
Charleston	...	...	19	25	25	30	29	43	41	49	50	55	59	68	62	121	165	279
Charlotte	...	...	...	...	...	...	...	1	1	4	7	12	34	46	83	152	197	444
Chicago	...	...	...	...	...	...	4	30	109	299	503	1 100	2 185	2 702	3 376	4 826	5 495	6 221
Cincinnati	...	...	...	3	10	25	46	115	161	216	255	297	364	401	451	787	904	1 268
Cleveland	...	...	...	3	10	25	6	17	43	93	160	261	561	797	900	1 267	1 466	1 909
Columbus	...	...	...	...	...	2	6	18	19	31	52	88	182	237	291	389	503	845
Corpus Christi	...	...	...	...	...	...	...	...	...	3	4	4	8	11	28	93	165	267
Dallas	...	...	...	...	...	...	...	...	...	...	10	38	92	159	260	399	615	1 738
Dayton	...	...	...	...	1	3	6	11	20	30	39	61	117	153	201	331	457	727
Denver	...	...	...	...	...	...	...	...	...	5	36	107	213	256	288	408	564	935
Des Moines	...	...	...	...	...	...	...	1	4	12	22	50	86	126	143	196	226	287
Detroit	...	...	...	...	1	2	9	21	46	80	116	206	466	994	1 569	2 377	3 016	3 950
El Paso	...	...	...	...	...	...	...	...	...	...	1	10	39	78	102	131	195	314
Fall River	...	...	...	1	2	4	7	12	14	27	49	74	119	120	115	135	137	100
Ft Lauderdale	...	...	...	...	...	...	...	...	...	...	...	...	...	...	9	18	36	84
Fort Worth	...	...	...	...	...	...	...	...	...	...	7	23	73	106	163	226	361	396
Gary	...	...	...	...	...	...	...	...	...	...	...	...	17	55	100	226	361	395
Grand Rapids	...	...	...	...	...	...	...	3	8	17	32	60	113	138	169	246	288	462
Greensboro	...	...	...	...	...	...	...	...	...	...	2	3	16	20	54	280	337	622
Hartford	...	4	5	4	5	7	9	18	29	37	42	53	99	138	164	296	358	588
Houston	...	...	...	...	...	...	...	2	5	9	17	28	79	138	292	529	807	1 430
Indianapolis	...	...	...	...	...	...	3	8	19	48	75	105	234	314	364	461	552	944
Jacksonville	...	...	...	...	...	...	...	1	2	7	8	17	58	92	130	210	304	530
Jersey City	...	...	...	...	...	...	3	7	29	83	121	163	268	298	317	301	299	611
Kansas City	...	...	...	...	...	...	...	...	4	32	56	133	248	324	400	687	814	1 109
Long Beach	...	...	...	...	...	...	...	...	...	...	...	1	18	56	142	164	251	344
Los Angeles	...	...	...	...	...	...	...	2	4	6	11	50	319	577	1 238	1 504	1 970	2 479
Louisville	...	...	...	1	4	10	21	43	68	101	124	161	224	235	308	451	577	754
Memphis	...	...	...	...	...	...	...	9	23	40	34	64	131	162	253	358	482	727
Miami	...	...	...	...	...	...	...	...	...	...	...	...	5	30	111	268	495	935
Milwaukee	...	...	...	...	...	...	2	20	45	71	116	204	374	457	578	767	871	1 279
Minneapolis	...	...	...	...	...	...	...	...	3	13	47	165	301	381	464	941	1 117	1 598
Nashville	...	...	...	...	...	6	7	10	17	26	43	76	110	118	154	257	322	597
Newark	...	...	...	...	7	11	17	39	72	115	137	182	347	415	442	430	439	1 833
New Orleans	3	5	8	17	27	46	102	116	169	191	216	242	339	387	459	552	685	907
New York	22	33	60	96	131	218	349	696	1 175	1 478	1 912	2 507	4 767	5 620	6 930	6 707	9 556	9 540
Norfolk	...	...	7	...	8	10	11	14	15	19	22	35	67	116	130	259	446	629
Oakland	...	...	...	...	...	...	...	...	2	11	35	49	150	216	284	302	385	368
Oklahoma City	...	...	...	...	...	...	...	...	...	...	...	4	64	91	185	244	325	566
Omaha	...	...	...	...	...	...	...	...	2	16	30	140	124	192	214	325	366	458
Paterson	...	...	...	...	1	...	8	11	20	34	51	78	126	136	139	140	139	144
Philadelphia	12	43	69	95	119	161	206	340	566	674	847	1 047	1 549	1 824	1 951	3 200	3 671	4 343
Phoenix	...	...	...	...	...	...	...	...	...	...	...	3	11	29	48	186	332	664
Pittsburgh	...	...	2	5	7	18	31	68	78	139	235	344	534	588	670	2 083	2 213	2 405
Portland	...	...	...	...	...	...	...	1	3	8	18	46	207	258	302	501	705	822
Providence	3	6	8	10	12	17	23	42	51	69	105	132	224	238	253	677	737	821
Richmond	...	4	6	10	12	16	20	28	38	51	64	81	128	172	183	263	328	457
Rochester	...	2	2	2	2	9	20	36	48	62	89	134	218	296	328	438	488	801
Sacramento	...	...	...	...	...	...	...	7	14	16	21	26	45	66	86	170	277	626
St. Louis	...	...	...	...	4	7	16	78	161	311	351	452	687	773	822	1 432	1 681	2 144
St. Paul	...	...	...	...	...	...	...	1	10	20	41	133	215	235	272	288	311	313
St. Petersburg	...	...	...	...	...	...	...	...	...	...	...	...	4	14	40	61	97	181
Salt Lake City	...	...	...	...	...	...	...	10	8	13	21	45	93	118	140	212	275	576
San Antonio	...	...	...	...	...	...	...	3	8	8	21	38	97	161	232	338	500	736
San Bernardino	...	...	...	...	...	...	...	...	1	3	2	4	13	19	37	161	282	810
San Diego	...	...	...	...	...	...	...	...	1	2	3	16	40	74	148	289	557	1 033
San Francisco	...	...	...	...	...	...	...	35	57	149	234	299	417	507	634	1 462	2 241	2 649
San Jose	...	...	...	...	...	...	...	4	...	9	13	18	29	40	58	175	291	642
Seattle	...	...	...	...	...	...	...	...	...	...	4	43	237	315	366	505	733	1 107
Springfield	...	2	2	3	4	7	11	12	15	27	33	44	89	130	150	365	407	504
Syracuse	...	...	...	...	...	...	7	22	28	43	52	88	137	172	209	295	342	564
Tampa	...	...	...	...	...	...	...	1	...	1	1	6	38	52	101	272	409	809
Toledo	...	...	...	...	...	...	1	4	14	32	50	81	168	243	291	344	396	695
Tucson	...	...	...	...	...	...	...	...	...	...	...	...	13	20	33	73	145	266
Tulsa	...	...	...	...	...	...	...	...	...	...	...	...	18	72	141	193	252	4 758
Virginia Beach	...	...	...	...	...	...	...	...	...	...	...	...	...	...	...	...	5	...
Washington, D.C.	...	...	3	8	13	18	23	40	61	109	178	230	331	438	487	968	1 464	2 097
Wichita	...	...	...	...	...	...	...	...	...	...	5	24	52	72	111	143	222	382
Worcester	...	2	2	3	3	4	7	17	25	41	58	85	146	180	195	253	276	354
Yonkers	...	...	...	...	...	...	...	...	...	...	19	32	80	100	135	143	158	191
Youngstown	...	...	...	...	...	...	...	3	3	8	15	33	79	132	170	474	528	509

Source: U. S. Census Bureau.
[1] Beginning 1940 data reflect Metropolitan Statistical Areas as defined by the U.S. Office of Management & Budget (OMB) according to published standards that are applied to Census Bureau data, formerly *Standard Metropolitan Area, Standard Metropolitan Statistical Area* and *Metropolitan Statistical Area*. The general concept is that of a core area containing a substantial population nucleus, together with adjacent communities having a high degree of economic and social integration with that core.
[2] Population data now contained in Los Angeles Metropolitan Statistical Area data.
[3] Population data now contained in Providence Metropolitan Statistical Area data.
[4] Population data now contained in Miami Metropolitan Statistical Area data.
[5] Population data now contained in Dallas Metropolitan Statistical Area data.
[6] Population data now contained in Chicago Metropolitan Statistical Area data.
[7] Population data now contained in New York Metropolitan Statistical Area data.
[8] Population data now contained in Virginia Beach Metropolitan Statistical Area data.
[9] Population data now contained in San Francisco Metropolitan Statistical Area data.
[10] Population data now contained in Minneapolis Metropolitan Statistical Area data.
[11] Population data now contained in Tampa Metropolitan Statistical Area data.
[12] Reflects population data for Riverside-San Bernardino-Ontario, CA Metropolitan Statistical Area.
. . . = Not available.

Table 1-14. Population of Major North American Cities, 1750–2005—*Continued*

(Number in thousands.)

Year	1970	1980	1990	2000	2001	2002	2003	2004	2005
Akron	679	660	658	696	698	700	701	702	702
Albany	778	836	810	827	829	834	841	845	849
Albuquerque	316	420	599	732	739	753	767	781	798
Allentown	594	635	687	742	749	758	769	780	791
Anaheim	1 421	1 933	[2]	[2]	[2]	[2]	[2]	[2]	[2]
Atlanta	1 596	2 138	3 069	4 282	4 428	4 551	4 675	4 796	4 917
Austin	323	537	846	1 265	1 319	1 346	1 376	1 411	1 453
Baltimore	2 071	2 200	2 382	2 557	2 579	2 597	2 628	2 645	2 656
Birmingham	767	884	957	1 053	1 061	1 066	1 074	1 082	1 090
Boston	2 899	2 806	4 134	4 402	4 428	4 432	4 429	4 419	4 412
Buffalo	1 349	1 243	1 189	1 169	1 164	1 160	1 158	1 154	1 148
Charleston	336	430	507	551	555	563	572	583	595
Charlotte	558	971	1 025	1 340	1 374	1 406	1 439	1 475	1 521
Chicago	6 978	6 060	8 182	9 120	9 203	9 271	9 331	9 393	9 443
Cincinnati	1 385	1 401	1 845	2 014	2 026	2 035	2 046	2 057	2 070
Cleveland	2 064	1 899	2 102	2 148	2 145	2 142	2 140	2 134	2 126
Columbus	1 018	1 244	1 405	1 619	1 639	1 655	1 675	1 691	1 709
Corpus Christi	285	326	368	403	402	404	406	410	414
Dallas	2 378	2 931	3 989	5 196	5 350	5 473	5 585	5 696	5 819
Dayton	853	942	844	848	846	845	845	845	844
Denver	1 239	1 618	1 650	2 193	2 244	2 275	2 300	2 326	2 360
Des Moines	314	368	416	483	490	497	504	512	522
Detroit	4 435	4 488	4 249	4 458	4 473	4 476	4 486	4 490	4 488
El Paso	359	480	592	682	688	694	703	713	722
Fall River	97	93	[3]	[3]	[3]	[3]	[3]	[3]	[3]
Ft Lauderdale	140	158	[4]	[4]	[4]	[4]	[4]	[4]	[4]
Fort Worth	393	385	[5]	[5]	[5]	[5]	[5]	[5]	[5]
Gary	393	385	[6]	[6]	[6]	[6]	[6]	[6]	[6]
Grand Rapids	539	602	646	743	750	757	762	766	771
Greensboro	724	852	540	645	652	656	662	666	675
Hartford	721	716	1 124	1 151	1 158	1 169	1 179	1 183	1 188
Houston	1 999	2 736	3 767	4 741	4 845	4 968	5 074	5 177	5 280
Indianapolis	1 111	1 167	1 294	1 531	1 554	1 576	1 600	1 617	1 641
Jacksonville	622	722	925	1 126	1 148	1 173	1 196	1 224	1 248
Jersey City	608	557	[7]	[7]	[7]	[7]	[7]	[7]	[7]
Kansas City	1 274	1 433	1 637	1 843	1 865	1 888	1 908	1 927	1 948
Long Beach	359	361	[2]	[2]	[2]	[2]	[2]	[2]	[2]
Los Angeles	2 816	2 969	11 274	12 403	12 550	12 692	12 817	12 899	12 924
Louisville	867	957	1 056	1 165	1 172	1 180	1 190	1 199	1 208
Memphis	834	913	1 067	1 208	1 216	1 226	1 238	1 248	1 261
Miami	1 268	1 626	4 056	5 029	5 116	5 206	5 276	5 356	5 422
Milwaukee	1 404	1 397	1 432	1 502	1 505	1 509	1 513	1 513	1 513
Minneapolis	1 965	2 137	2 539	2 981	3 023	3 054	3 083	3 113	3 143
Nashville	699	651	1 048	1 317	1 337	1 352	1 371	1 395	1 423
Newark	2 057	1 879	[7]	[7]	[7]	[7]	[7]	[7]	[7]
New Orleans	1 046	1 256	1 264	1 316	1 312	1 313	1 315	1 318	1 319
New York	9 974	8 275	16 846	18 359	18 500	18 605	18 687	18 755	18 747
Norfolk	733	1 160	[8]	[8]	[8]	[8]	[8]	[8]	[8]
Oakland	362	339	[9]	[9]	[9]	[9]	[9]	[9]	[9]
Oklahoma City	699	861	971	1 098	1 107	1 120	1 132	1 142	1 157
Omaha	543	585	686	769	776	783	792	802	813
Paterson	145	461	[7]	[7]	[7]	[7]	[7]	[7]	[7]
Philadelphia	4 824	4 717	5 436	5 694	5 713	5 740	5 771	5 799	5 823
Phoenix	969	1 509	2 238	3 278	3 383	3 488	3 593	3 713	3 865
Pittsburgh	2 401	2 219	2 468	2 429	2 421	2 414	2 408	2 398	2 386
Portland	1 007	1 298	1 524	1 936	1 976	2 012	2 040	2 062	2 096
Providence	909	926	1 510	1 587	1 597	1 612	1 622	1 627	1 623
Richmond	542	761	949	1 100	1 111	1 126	1 141	1 157	1 176
Rochester	962	971	1 002	1 038	1 039	1 040	1 041	1 041	1 039
Sacramento	804	1 100	1 481	1 809	1 867	1 925	1 975	2 015	2 042
St. Louis	2 411	2 377	2 581	2 702	2 720	2 736	2 753	2 769	2 779
St. Paul	310	270	[10]	[10]	[10]	[10]	[10]	[10]	[10]
St. Petersburg	216	239	[11]	[11]	[11]	[11]	[11]	[11]	[11]
Salt Lake City	705	960	768	972	985	995	1 006	1 019	1 034
San Antonio	888	1 072	1 408	1 719	1 746	1 781	1 815	1 853	1 890
San Bernardino	1 141	1 558	2 589	3 279	3 382	3 503	3 645	3 786	3 910
San Diego	1 358	1 862	2 498	2 825	2 863	2 899	2 921	2 933	2 933
San Francisco	3 107	3 251	3 684	4 137	4 177	4 163	4 155	4 147	4 153
San Jose	1 065	1 295	1 534	1 740	1 745	1 730	1 732	1 738	1 755
Seattle	1 425	1 607	2 559	3 052	3 095	3 122	3 143	3 168	3 203
Springfield	542	515	673	681	680	684	687	687	687
Syracuse	637	643	660	650	650	651	653	653	652
Tampa	1 089	1 614	2 068	2 404	2 443	2 487	2 530	2 587	2 648
Toledo	763	617	654	659	660	659	659	658	657
Tucson	352	531	667	849	861	877	890	907	925
Tulsa	549	657	761	861	868	876	879	881	888
Virginia Beach	172	262	1 451	1 580	1 586	1 604	1 625	1 642	1 647
Washington, D.C.	2 910	3 251	4 122	4 821	4 924	5 010	5 085	5 158	5 215
Wichita	389	442	511	572	575	580	582	584	587
Worcester	372	403	710	753	762	769	775	779	783
Yonkers	204	195	[7]	[7]	[7]	[7]	[7]	[7]	[7]
Youngstown	537	531	614	602	599	596	593	596	593

BOX 1 ■ The Senior Population

One of the most significant demographic changes has been the increase in the number of people who are 65 years of age and older. During the twentieth century, this number of people in this age group in the United States rose from 3 million to 35 million. The oldest-old, those 85 years of age and older, rose from 100,000 to 4.2 million. By 2003, the older population accounted for slightly more than 12% of the total population.

As a result of this shift, governments, families, and businesses need to carefully evaluate the senior population and to collect increasingly refined statistics on its impact on all aspects of life in the United States. Among the issues are:

1. The desire of and necessity for many seniors to work past the age of 65. How does this affect the overall job market and the discretionary spending power of this group? Businesses now have marketing campaigns and products geared to the over-65 group.
2. The drain on social security and Medicare resources as people live longer.
3. Medical research to address new combinations of illnesses, the impact of prescribing so many drugs simultaneously, the long-range impact of critical illnesses, and end-of-life questions.
4. The effect on politics, as candidates and party platforms try to address the concerns of seniors, who are among the most frequent voters in the United States. In states with large retirement populations, such as Florida, senior votes can significantly impact election results.
5. The pressure on children to take care of aging and ill parents.
6. The need for long-term living facilities, including retirement communities, assisted-living facilities, and nursing homes.

In addressing these issues, however, one immediate refinement needs to be made. This group is not evenly divided between men and women. Because women live longer than men, they form the larger part of this demographic, particularly as this older population ages.

Just look at living arrangements. While a majority of senior men, regardless of age, live with a spouse (74.3% of those men 65–74 years, 69.8% of those men 75–84 years, and 56.2% of men 85 years and older), only 53.5% of women who were 65–74 years of age lived with their spouses and, for women 85 years of age or older, the statistic drops to 12.5%. Note that approximately 50.5% of women were widowed or divorced compared with 20.7% of men.

Thus, women are likelier to eventually live with other relatives or in a nursing home or other asissted living facility. In fact, women 65 and older have a two times greater likelihood of living with other relatives than men. Of these women, Hispanic, Asian, and Black women much more commonly live with other relatives than non-Hispanic white women (Hispanic women 36.0%, Asian women 35.8%, Black women 33.5%, non-Hispanic white women 13.6%). Although the percentage of the oldest-old women (85 years and older) living with other relatives declined between 1980 and 2003 (from 43.0% to 28.5%) the actual numbers increased from 483,000 in 1980 to 669,000 in 2003, an increase in real numbers of almost 40%.

According to Census 2000 data, 4.5% of people 65 or older in the United States live in nursing homes. These figures increase with age, with only 1.1% of those 65–74 years of age residing in a nursing home compared to 18.2% of those 85 years of age or older. In 1999 the majority of nursing home residents were women, with the oldest-old women, those 85 or older, making up 41.7% of all older nursing home residents. The male population in nursing homes tends to be younger than the female population, 22.3% of male residents were 65–74 and 39.6% were 75–84 years old.

More refined statistics on alternative living facilities, such as senior-citizen residences and assisted facilities, are not available from the U.S. government.

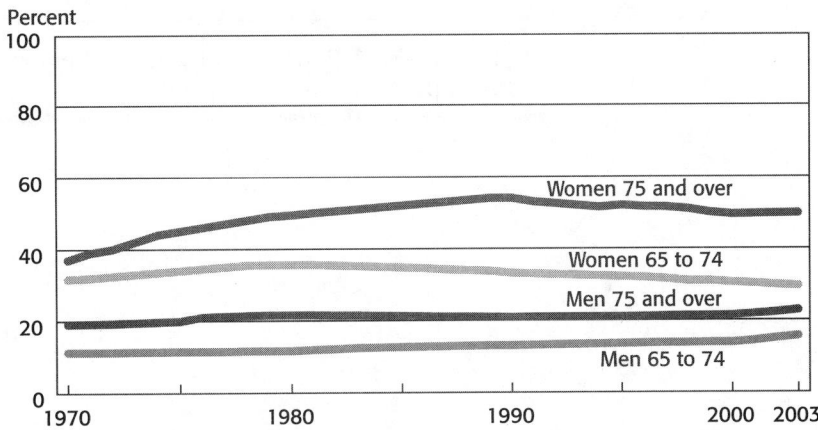

Percent Living Alone Among the Population Aged 65 and Over by Age and Sex: 1970 to 2003

Note: The reference population for these data is the civilian noninstitutionalized population.
Sources: 1970, 1980, and 1990, U.S. Bureau of the Census, 1996; 2000, U.S., Census Bureau, 2000a; 2003, U.S. Census Bureau, 2003a.

Sources:
U.S. Census Bureau. *65+ in the United States: 2005.*
U.S. Census Bureau. *Statistical Abstract of the United States: 2007.*

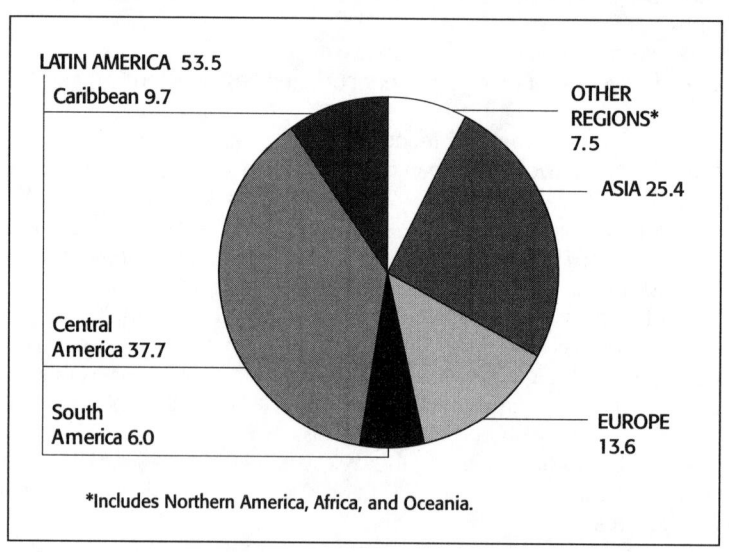

LATIN AMERICA 53.5
Caribbean 9.7
OTHER REGIONS* 7.5
ASIA 25.4
Central America 37.7
South America 6.0
EUROPE 13.6

*Includes Northern America, Africa, and Oceania.

U.S. Foreign-Born Population by World Region of Birth, 2004 (in percent)

Source: U.S. Census Bureau. *Current Population Survey, Annual Social and Economic Supplement, 2004.*

CHAPTER 2

Immigration and Migration

HIGHLIGHTS

1 The continuous record of immigration into the United States began with the Act of 1819. This Act required the captain or master of a vessel arriving at a U.S. port to deliver to the local collector of customs a list or manifest of all passengers taken on board, designating the age, sex, nationality, and occupation of each passenger, as well as the number of passengers who died during the passage. Copies of the manifests were transmitted to the Secretary of State, who reported the information periodically to Congress. Although the reporting of alien arrivals was also required by the Act of 1798 (which expired in 1817), the number of arrivals prior to 1819 is not known. William J. Bromwell, author of *History of Immigration to the United States,* estimates the number of foreign arrivals between the close of the Revolutionary War and 1819 at 250,000. Immigration statistics were compiled by the Department of State from 1820 to 1870, by the Treasury Department's Bureau of Statistics from 1867 to 1895, and since 1892 by the Office or Bureau of Immigration (later the Immigration and Naturalization Service). Annual reports have presented the data on immigration statistics since 1892, with the exception of 1942, when no report was issued because of wartime conditions. Since 1820, reporting on immigration data has undergone many changes. Only arrivals by vessels at Atlantic and Gulf ports were included until 1850, when Pacific ports were added. During the Civil War, Southern ports under Confederate control were excluded. Later, the reporting area was expanded to include outlying possessions: Alaska from 1871 (although irregularly until 1904); Hawaii from 1901; Puerto Rico from 1902; and the Virgin Islands from 1942. The government did not require arrivals at land borders to be counted until 1904, when land border stations were established. By 1908, such arrivals were fully incorporated into the annual totals. In any case, until the first decade of the twentieth century, there were few Canadian or Mexican immigrants in the United States.

2 Since 1933, aliens arriving in the United States have been classified as immigrants or nonimmigrants. Immigrants are nonresident aliens admitted to the United States for permanent residence. Until July 1, 1968, they were further classified into quota and nonquota immigrants. The former were subject to the established quotas of Eastern Hemisphere countries, while nonquota immigrants included natives of the Western Hemisphere and certain groups of special immigrants (classes of immigrants admitted to the United States for political reasons). Since July 1, 1968, this distinction has been abolished in favor of numerical ceilings for regions and countries, but the category of special immigrants has been retained. The collection of data on emigrants has been suspended since 1957. Net immigration data suffer from lack of reliable emigration figures, as well as conflicts in the enumeration of nonimmigrant arrivals.

3 From 1925 to 1929, the annual immigration quota of 164,667 was based on two percent of foreign-born residents of the United States as determined by the 1890 census. The national origin formula provided that the annual quota equal one-sixth of one percent of the number of White inhabitants of the continental United States in 1920, less Western Hemisphere immigrants and their descendants. The annual quota for each nationality was then determined by the same ratio to 150,000 as the number of inhabitants living in the continental United States in 1920 to the total inhabitants (with a minimum of 100). The Act of 1965 replaced the quota system with an annual numerical limitation of 170,000 on the Eastern Hemisphere and 120,000 on the Western Hemisphere, with a ceiling of 20,000 for each country of origin.

4 Before 1882, various state laws excluded certain aliens from admission, such as paupers, felons, and the diseased. The first Chinese Exclusion Law, passed in 1882, also excluded lunatics, idiots, and those likely to become public charges. Nine years later, Congress passed a much broader exclusion law in the Act of 1891. Statistics on excluded aliens were first compiled in 1892. Subsequent acts, principally those of 1917 and 1952, extended the excluded categories to anarchists, criminals, drug traffickers, subversives, and mental and physical defectives.

5 Since the first naturalization statute of 1790, there have been three requirements for immigrants seeking U.S. citizenship: (1) residence in the United States for five years; (2) a good moral character; and (3) an oath to support the Constitution. The residence requirement is only three years for a spouse of a U.S. citizen. Before 1906, individual courts kept naturalization records, but no national data were compiled. Since 1906, all courts have been required to file petitions and certificates of naturalization with the Bureau of Immigration and Naturalization.

6 While most European countries were represented in the immigration totals in the early nineteenth century, the first immigrant from Korea arrived only in 1903, from the Philippines in 1936, from Australia in 1870, and from Japan in 1861.

7 The annual number of immigrants exceeded one million in 12 years: 1905, 1906, 1907, 1910, 1913, 1914, 1989, 1990, 1991, 2001, 2002, and 2005.

8 The Refugee Act of 1980 provides for the admission of refugees and asylum seekers based on United Nations guidelines. Authorized admission ceilings are set annually by the president of the United States in consultation with Congress. After one year of residence, refugees are eligible for immigrant status. Beginning in 1966, Cubans admitted or paroled (admitted without immigration visa) into the United States after 1959 and present in the United States for at least two years could obtain permanent resident status. The Refugee Act of 1980 reduced the residency requirement to one year. In addition, the 125,000 Cuban immigrants admitted to the United States as part of the Muriel boatlift were eligible to become immigrants. Since 1977, refugees from Vietnam, Laos, and Cambodia have been eligible to apply for permanent resident status after living for at least two years (later reduced to one year) in the United States. Other refugee streams have been permitted into the United States under the Refugee Relief Act of 1958 and the Refugees-Escapees-Parolees Act of 1960. A total of 1,013,620 refugees-asylees were admitted in the 1980s and 1,021,266 between 1991 and 2000.

9 The United States has eight metropolitan areas with more than one million foreign-born residents, more than any other country in the world; New York City, Washington DC, Miami, Chicago, Dallas, Houston, Los Angeles, and San Francisco. There are also 29 metropolitan areas with a foreign-born population between 100,000 and 999,000.

Table 2-1. Immigrants, by Region, 1820–2005

(Number.)

Year	All countries[1]	Europe	Asia	America	Caribbean	Central America	South America	Africa
Total, 1820–2005	72 507 559	39 531 157	10 955 326	20 252 870	4 311 400	1 722 416	2 248 435	1 047 481
2005	1 122 373	180 449	382 744	432 748	91 378	52 636	100 811	79 701
2004	957 883	135 663	319 025	408 972	82 116	61 253	69 452	62 623
2003	703 542	102 546	235 339	305 936	67 498	53 283	53 946	45 559
2002	1 059 356	177 059	325 749	477 363	93 914	66 298	73 082	56 002
2001	1 058 902	176 892	336 112	470 794	96 384	72 504	67 880	50 009
1991–2000	9 086 612	1 358 295	2 794 744	4 482 066	977 162	524 538	539 407	354 768
2000	841 002	131 920	254 932	392 461	84 250	60 331	55 143	40 790
1999	646 568	94 373	193 061	312 324	70 386	41 441	41 112	33 740
1998	654 451	92 911	212 799	298 156	72 948	35 368	44 884	37 494
1997	798 378	122 358	258 561	359 619	101 095	43 451	52 600	44 668
1996	915 900	151 898	300 574	407 813	115 991	44 336	61 990	49 605
1995	720 461	132 914	259 984	282 270	96 021	32 020	46 063	39 818
1994	804 416	166 279	282 449	325 173	103 750	40 256	47 505	24 864
1991–1995	5 230 313	764 835	1 574 817	2 711 693	532 492	299 611	283 678	148 463
1991–1994	4 509 852	631 921	1 314 833	2 429 423	436 471	267 591	237 615	108 645
1991–1993	3 705 436	465 642	1 032 384	2 104 250	332 721	227 335	190 110	83 781
1981–1990	7 338 062	761 550	2 738 157	3 615 225	872 051	468 088	461 847	176 893
1971–1980	4 493 314	800 368	1 588 178	1 982 735	741 126	134 640	295 741	80 779
1961–1970	3 321 677	1 123 492	427 642	1 716 374	470 213	101 330	257 940	28 954
1951–1960	2 515 479	1 325 727	153 249	996 944	123 091	44 751	91 628	14 092
1941–1950	1 035 039	621 147	37 028	354 804	49 725	21 665	21 831	7 367
1931–1940	528 431	347 566	16 595	160 037	15 502	5 861	7 803	1 750
1921–1930	4 107 209	2 463 194	112 059	1 516 716	74 899	15 769	42 215	6 286
1911–1920	5 735 811	4 321 887	247 236	1 143 671	123 424	17 159	41 899	8 443
1901–1910	8 795 386	8 056 040	323 543	361 888	107 548	8 192	17 280	7 368
1891–1900	3 687 564	3 555 352	74 862	38 972	33 066	549	1 075	350
1881–1890	5 246 613	4 735 484	69 942	426 967	29 042	404	2 304	857
1871–1880	2 812 191	2 271 925	124 160	404 044	13 957	157	1 128	358
1861–1870	2 314 824	2 065 141	64 759	166 607	9 046	95	1 397	312
1851–1860	2 598 214	2 452 577	41 538	74 720	10 660	449	1 224	210
1841–1850	1 713 251	1 597 442	141	62 469	13 528	368	3 579	55
1831–1840	599 125	495 681	55	33 424	12 301	44	856	54
1821–1830	143 439	98 797	30	11 564	3 834	105	531	16
1820	8 385	7 690	6	387	164	2	11	1

Source: U.S. Department of Homeland Security, Office of Immigration Statistics. *2005 Yearbook of Immigration Statistics.*
Note: From 1820–1867, figures represent alien passengers arrived at seaports; from 1868–1891and 1895–1897, immigrant aliens arrived; from 1892–1894 and 1898–2002, immigrant aliens admitted for permanent residence. From 1892–1903, aliens entering by cabin class were not counted as immigrants. Land arrivals were not completely enumerated until 1908. Data for Czechoslovakia, Soviet Union, and Yugoslavia include independent republics. For this table, fiscal year 1843 covers 9 months ending September 1843; fiscal years 1832 and 1850 cover 15 months ending.

Table 2-2. Immigrants, by Country, 1820–2005

(Number.)

Year	All countries[1]	Total	Europe Northwestern Europe United Kingdom[2]	Ireland[2]	Europe Central Europe Germany[3]	Poland	Commonwealth of Independent States[4]	Italy
2005	1 122 373	176 569	19 800	2 088	9 264	15 352	...	3 066
2004	957 883	133 181	14 915	1 531	7 099	14 326	...	2 346
2003	703 542	100 434	9 527	983	5 064	10 510	...	1 644
2002	1 059 356	173 524	16 297	1 398	8 888	12 711	...	2 578
2001	1 058 902	174 411	18 278	1 505	9 790	11 769	...	3 096
2000	841 002	130 996	13 273	1 296	7 565	10 090	...	2 448
1999	644 787	92 314	7 647	804	5 166	8 773	...	1 512
1998	653 206	90 572	8 976	944	5 440	8 451	...	1 817
1997	797 847	119 764	10 679	998	5 714	12 035	...	1 976
1996	915 560	147 479	13 607	1 731	6 743	15 766	...	2 490
1995	720 177	128 185	12 427	5 315	6 237	13 824	...	2 231
1994	803 993	160 916	16 326	17 256	6 992	28 048	...	2 305
1993	903 916	158 254	18 783	13 590	7 312	27 846	...	2 487
1992	973 445	145 392	19 973	12 226	9 888	25 504	...	2 592
1991	1 826 595	135 234	13 903	4 767	6 509	19 199	...	2 619
1990	1 535 872	112 401	15 928	10 333	7 493	20 537	...	3 287
1989	1 090 924	82 891	14 090	6 961	6 845	15 101	...	2 910
1981–1989	5 801 600	593 200	126 200	22 500	62 600	76 900	58 500	29 600
1971–1980	4 493 300	801 300	123 500	14 100	66 000	43 600	43 200	130 100
1970	373 326	110 653	14 089	1 583	10 632	2 013	836	27 369
1969	358 579	114 052	15 072	1 981	10 380	2 115	574	27 033
1968	454 448	129 022	26 025	2 995	16 590	3 676	974	25 882
1967	361 972	128 775	23 004	2 765	16 595	4 356	876	28 487
1966	323 040	115 898	18 777	3 267	17 654	8 490	768	26 447
1965	296 697	101 468	24 135	5 187	22 432	7 093	632	10 874
1964	292 248	108 215	25 758	6 055	24 494	7 097	763	12 769
1963	306 260	109 066	22 708	5 746	24 727	6 785	591	16 175
1962	283 763	103 989	18 066	5 118	21 477	5 660	753	20 119
1961	271 344	108 532	18 719	5 738	25 815	6 254	996	18 956
1960	265 398	120 178	19 967	6 918	29 452	4 216	856	13 369
1959	260 686	138 191	18 325	6 595	32 039	2 800	775	16 804
1958	253 265	115 198	24 147	9 134	29 498	1 470	641	23 115
1957	326 867	169 625	24 020	8 227	60 353	571	663	19 624
1956	321 625	156 866	19 008	5 607	44 409	263	643	40 430
1955	237 790	110 591	15 761	5 222	29 596	129	523	30 272
1954	208 177	92 121	16 672	4 655	33 098	67	475	13 145
1953	170 434	82 352	16 639	4 304	27 329	136	609	8 432
1952	265 520	193 626	22 177	3 526	104 236	235	548	11 342
1951	205 717	149 545	14 898	3 144	87 755	98	555	8 958
1950	249 187	199 115	12 755	5 842	128 592	696	526	12 454
1949	188 317	129 592	21 149	8 678	55 284	1 673	694	11 695
1948	170 570	103 544	26 403	7 534	19 368	2 447	897	16 075
1947	147 292	83 535	23 788	2 574	13 900	745	761	13 866
1946	108 721	52 852	33 552	1 816	2 598	335	153	2 636
1945	38 119	5 943	3 029	427	172	195	98	213
1944	28 551	4 509	1 321	112	238	292	157	120
1943	23 725	4 920	974	165	248	394	159	49
1942	28 781	11 153	907	83	2 150	343	197	103
1941	51 776	26 541	7 714	272	4 028	451	665	450
1940	70 756	50 454	6 158	839	21 520	702	898	5 302
1939	82 998	63 138	3 058	1 189	33 515	3 072	1 021	6 570
1938	67 895	44 495	2 262	1 085	17 199	2 403	960	7 712
1937	50 244	31 863	1 726	531	10 895	1 212	629	7 192
1936	36 329	23 480	1 310	444	6 346	869	378	6 774
1935	34 956	22 778	1 413	454	5 201	1 504	418	6 566
1934	29 470	17 210	1 305	443	4 392	1 032	607	4 374
1933	23 068	12 383	979	338	1 919	1 332	458	3 477
1932	35 576	20 579	2 057	539	2 670	1 296	636	6 662
1931	97 139	61 909	9 110	7 305	10 401	3 604	1 396	13 399

Note: For years ending Sept. 30 from 1977 to date; prior to that years ending June 30, except 1820–1831 and 1844–1849, years ending Sept. 30; 1833–1842 and 1851–1867, years ending Dec. 31; 1832 covers 15 months ending Dec. 31; 1843, 9 months ending Sept. 30; 1850, 15 months ending Dec. 31; 1868, 6 months ending June 30; 1990–2001, by country of birth; 1906–1989, country of last permanent resident; prior to 1906, countries from which the immigrants came.
[1] For 1820–1867 excludes returning citizens.
[2] Comprises Eire and Northern Ireland.
[3] Includes Austria, 1938 to 1945.
[4] Comprises former Soviet Union.
. . . = Not available.

Table 2-2. Immigrants, by Country, 1820–2005—*Continued*

(Number.)

Year	Asia							America			Africa, total
	Total	Turkey in Asia[6]	China[7]	India	Japan[8]	Korea[9]	Philippines[10]	Total	Canada and New-foundland[11]	Mexico	
2005	400 135	4 614	69 967	84 681	8 768	26 562	60 748	345 575	21 878	161 445	85 102
2004	334 540	3 835	55 494	70 151	7 697	19 766	57 846	342 468	15 569	175 411	66 422
2003	243 918	3 029	40 568	50 228	5 971	12 382	45 250	249 968	11 350	115 585	48 642
2002	340 494	3 375	61 082	70 823	8 248	20 724	51 040	402 949	19 352	218 822	60 101
2001	348 256	3 215	56 267	70 032	9 578	20 532	52 919	405 638	21 752	205 560	53 731
2000	264 413	2 606	45 585	41 903	7 049	15 721	42 343	338 959	16 057	173 493	44 534
1999	198 918	2 215	32 159	30 157	4 202	12 795	30 943	270 719	8 782	147 402	36 578
1998	219 371	2 676	36 854	36 414	5 128	14 222	34 416	252 503	10 130	131 353	40 585
1997	265 674	3 138	41 128	38 048	5 092	14 226	49 102	307 313	11 583	146 833	47 732
1996	307 722	3 657	41 720	44 838	6 007	18 179	55 868	340 428	15 800	163 556	52 875
1995	267 931	2 947	35 463	34 748	4 837	16 047	50 984	231 526	12 932	89 932	42 456
1994	292 589	1 840	53 985	34 921	6 093	16 011	53 535	272 226	16 068	111 398	26 712
1993	358 047	2 204	65 578	40 121	6 908	18 026	63 457	301 380	17 156	126 561	27 783
1992	356 955	2 488	38 907	36 755	11 028	19 359	61 022	384 047	15 205	213 802	27 086
1991	358 533	2 528	33 025	45 064	5 049	26 518	63 596	1 210 981	13 504	946 167	36 179
1990	338 581	2 468	31 815	30 667	5 734	32 301	63 756	957 558	16 812	679 068	35 893
1989	312 149	2 007	32 272	31 175	4 849	34 222	57 034	448 346	12 151	405 172	25 166
1981–1989	2 478 800	18 400	341 800	231 200	37 500	306 500	431 500	2 537 500	102 400	974 200	156 400
1971–1980	1 633 800	18 600	202 500	176 800	47 900	272 000	360 200	1 929 400	114 800	637 200	91 500
1970	90 215	495	6 427	8 795	4 731	8 888	30 507	161 727	26 850	44 821	7 099
1969	72 959	556	5 264	5 205	4 095	5 854	20 263	164 045	29 303	45 748	4 460
1968	56 298	325	4 851	4 165	3 810	3 592	16 086	262 736	41 716	44 716	3 220
1967	57 574	491	7 118	4 129	4 125	3 845	10 336	170 235	34 768	43 034	2 577
1966	40 113	365	2 948	2 293	3 468	2 414	5 894	162 551	37 273	47 217	1 967
1965	20 040	365	1 611	467	3 294	2 139	2 963	171 019	50 035	40 686	1 949
1964	21 279	331	2 684	488	3 774	2 329	2 862	158 644	51 114	34 448	2 015
1963	23 242	307	1 605	965	4 147	2 560	3 483	169 966	50 509	55 986	1 982
1962	20 249	304	1 356	390	4 054	1 463	3 354	155 871	44 272	55 805	1 834
1961	19 495	296	900	292	4 490	1 442	2 628	139 580	47 470	41 476	1 851
1960	21 604	200	1 380	244	5 699	1 410	2 791	119 525	46 668	32 708	1 925
1959	25 259	229	1 702	351	6 248	1 614	2 503	93 061	34 599	22 909	1 992
1958	20 870	197	1 143	323	6 847	1 470	2 034	113 132	45 143	26 791	2 008
1957	20 008	77	2 098	196	6 829	577	1 874	134 160	46 354	49 321	1 600
1956	17 327	48	1 386	185	5 967	579	1 792	144 713	42 363	61 320	1 351
1955	10 935	54	568	194	4 150	263	1 598	110 436	32 435	43 702	1 203
1954	9 970	33	254	144	3 846	175	1 234	95 587	34 873	30 645	1 248
1953	8 231	13	528	104	2 579	75	1 074	77 650	36 283	17 183	989
1952	9 328	12	263	123	3 814	47	1 179	61 049	33 354	9 079	931
1951	7 149	3	335	109	271	21	3 228	47 631	25 880	6 153	845
1950	4 508	13	1 280	121	100	24	729	44 191	21 885	6 744	849
1949	7 595	40	3 415	175	529	39	1 157	49 334	25 156	8 083	995
1948	11 907	16	7 203	263	423	44	1 168	52 746	25 485	8 384	1 027
1947	6 733	22	3 191	432	131	...	910	52 753	24 342	7 558	1 284
1946	2 108	16	252	425	14	...	475	46 066	21 344	7 146	1 516
1945	461	13	71	103	1	...	19	29 646	11 530	6 702	406
1944	231	15	50	41	4	...	4	23 084	10 143	6 598	112
1943	342	36	65	71	20	...	8	18 162	9 761	4 172	141
1942	615	31	179	36	44	...	51	16 377	10 599	2 378	473
1941	1 971	16	1 003	94	289	...	170	22 445	11 473	2 824	564
1940	2 050	7	643	52	102	...	137	17 822	11 078	2 313	202
1939	2 281	15	642	36	102	...	119	17 139	10 813	2 640	218
1938	2 492	11	613	34	93	...	116	20 486	14 404	2 502	174
1937	1 149	13	293	47	132	...	84	16 903	12 011	2 347	155
1936	793	20	273	13	91	...	72	11 786	8 121	1 716	105
1935	682	31	229	32	88	...	(10)	11 174	7 782	1 560	118
1934	597	22	187	28	86	...	...	11 409	7 945	1 801	104
1933	552	27	148	44	75	...	...	9 925	6 187	1 936	71
1932	1 931	43	750	87	526	...	...	12 577	8 003	2 171	186
1931	3 345	139	1 150	123	653	...	...	30 816	22 183	3 333	417

Note: For years ending Sept. 30 from 1977 to date; prior to that years ending June 30, except 1820–1831 and 1844–1849, years ending Sept. 30; 1833–1842 and 1851–1867, years ending Dec. 31; 1832 covers 15 months ending Dec. 31; 1843, 9 months ending Sept. 30; 1850, 15 months ending Dec. 31; 1868, 6 months ending June 30; 1990–2001, by country of birth; 1906–1989, country of last permanent resident; prior to 1906, countries from which the immigrants came.
[6]No record of immigration from Turkey in Asia until 1869.
[7]Beginning 1957, includes Taiwan.
[8]No record of immigration from Japan until 1861.
[9]No record of immigration from Korea prior to 1948.
[10]Philippines included in "All other countries" prior to 1936.
[11]Prior to 1920, Canada and Newfoundland were recorded as British North America.
. . . = Not available.

Table 2-2. Immigrants, by Country, 1820–2005—*Continued*

(Number.)

| | | | Europe | | | | Commonwealth of Independent States[4] | Italy |
| | | | Northwestern Europe | | Central Europe | | | |
Year	All countries[1]	Total	United Kingdom[2]	Ireland[2]	Germany[3]	Poland		
1930	241 700	147 438	31 015	23 445	25 569	9 231	2 772	22 327
1929	279 678	158 598	21 327	19 921	46 751	9 002	2 450	18 008
1928	307 255	158 513	19 958	25 268	45 778	8 755	2 652	17 728
1927	335 175	168 368	23 669	28 545	48 513	9 211	2 933	17 297
1926	304 488	155 562	25 528	24 897	50 421	7 126	3 323	8 253
1925	294 314	148 366	27 172	26 650	46 068	5 341	3 121	6 203
1924	706 896	364 339	59 490	17 111	75 091	28 806	20 918	56 246
1923	522 919	307 920	45 759	15 740	48 277	26 538	21 151	46 674
1922	309 556	216 385	25 153	10 579	17 931	28 635	19 910	40 319
1921	805 228	652 364	51 142	28 435	6 803	95 089	10 193	222 260
1920	430 001	246 295	38 471	9 591	1 001	4 813	1 751	95 145
1919	141 132	24 627	6 797	474	52	(5)	1 403	1 884
1918	110 618	31 063	2 516	331	447	(5)	4 242	5 250
1917	295 403	133 083	10 735	5 406	1 857	(5)	12 716	34 596
1916	298 826	145 699	16 063	8 639	2 877	(5)	7 842	33 665
1915	326 700	197 919	27 237	14 185	7 799	(5)	26 187	49 688
1914	1 218 480	1 058 391	48 729	24 688	35 734	(5)	255 660	283 738
1913	1 197 892	1 055 855	60 319	27 876	34 329	(5)	291 040	265 542
1912	838 172	718 875	57 148	25 879	27 788	(5)	162 395	157 134
1911	878 587	764 757	73 384	29 112	32 061	(5)	158 721	182 882
1910	1 041 570	926 291	68 941	29 855	31 283	(5)	186 792	215 537
1909	751 786	654 875	46 793	25 033	25 540	(5)	120 460	183 218
1908	782 870	691 901	62 824	30 556	32 309	(5)	156 711	128 503
1907	1 285 349	1 199 566	79 037	34 530	37 807	(5)	258 943	285 731
1906	1 100 735	1 018 365	67 198	34 995	37 564	(5)	215 665	273 120
1905	1 026 499	974 273	84 189	52 945	40 574	(5)	184 897	221 479
1904	812 870	767 933	51 448	36 142	46 380	(5)	145 141	193 296
1903	857 046	814 507	33 637	35 310	40 086	(5)	136 093	230 622
1902	648 743	619 068	16 898	29 138	28 304	(5)	107 347	178 375
1901	487 918	469 237	14 985	30 561	21 651	(5)	85 257	135 996
1900	448 572	424 700	12 509	35 730	18 507	(5)	90 787	100 135
1899	311 715	297 349	13 456	31 673	17 476	(5)	60 982	77 419
1898	229 299	217 786	12 894	25 128	17 111	4 726	29 828	58 613
1897	230 832	216 397	12 752	28 421	22 533	4 165	25 816	59 431
1896	343 267	329 067	24 656	40 262	31 885	691	51 445	68 060
1895	258 536	250 342	28 833	46 304	32 173	790	35 907	35 427
1894	285 631	277 052	22 520	30 231	53 989	1 941	39 278	42 977
1893	439 730	429 324	35 189	43 578	78 756	16 374	42 310	72 145
1892	579 663	570 876	42 215	51 383	119 168	40 536	81 511	61 631
1891	560 319	546 085	66 605	55 706	113 554	27 497	47 426	76 055
1890	455 302	445 680	69 730	53 024	92 427	11 073	35 598	52 003
1889	444 427	434 790	87 992	65 557	99 538	4 922	33 916	25 307
1888	546 889	538 131	108 692	73 513	109 717	5 826	33 487	51 558
1887	490 109	482 829	93 378	68 370	106 865	6 128	30 766	47 622
1886	334 203	329 529	62 929	49 619	84 403	3 939	17 800	21 315
1885	395 346	353 083	57 713	51 795	124 443	3 085	17 158	13 642
1884	518 592	453 686	65 950	63 344	179 676	4 536	12 689	16 510
1883	603 322	522 587	76 606	81 486	194 786	2 011	9 909	31 792
1882	788 992	648 186	102 991	76 432	250 630	4 672	16 918	32 159
1881	669 431	528 545	81 376	72 342	210 485	5 614	5 041	15 401
1880	457 257	348 691	73 273	71 603	84 638	2 177	5 014	12 354
1879	177 826	134 259	29 955	20 013	34 602	489	4 453	5 791
1878	138 469	101 612	22 150	15 932	29 313	547	3 048	4 344
1877	141 857	106 195	23 581	14 569	29 298	533	6 599	3 195
1876	169 986	120 920	29 291	19 575	31 937	925	4 775	3 015
1875	227 498	182 961	47 905	37 957	47 769	984	7 997	3 631
1874	313 339	262 783	62 021	53 707	87 291	1 795	4 073	7 666
1873	459 803	397 541	89 500	77 344	149 671	3 338	1 634	8 757
1872	404 806	352 155	84 912	68 732	141 109	1 647	1 018	4 190
1871	321 350	265 145	85 455	57 439	82 554	535	673	2 816

Note: For years ending Sept. 30 from 1977 to date; prior to that years ending June 30, except 1820–1831 and 1844–1849, years ending Sept. 30; 1833–1842 and 1851–1867, years ending Dec. 31; 1832 covers 15 months ending Dec. 31; 1843, 9 months ending Sept. 30; 1850, 15 months ending Dec. 31; 1868, 6 months ending June 30; 1990–2001, by country of birth; 1906–1989, country of last permanent resident; prior to 1906, countries from which the immigrants came.
[1]For 1820–1867 excludes returning citizens.
[2]Comprises Eire and Northern Ireland.
[3]Includes Austria, 1938 to 1945.
[4]Comprises former Soviet Union.
[5]Between 1899 and 1919, included with Austria-Hungary, Germany, and Russia.
. . . = Not available.

Table 2-2. Immigrants, by Country, 1820–2005—*Continued*

(Number.)

Year	Asia							America			Africa, total
	Total	Turkey in Asia[6]	China[7]	India	Japan[8]	Korea[9]	Philippines[10]	Total	Canada and New-foundland[11]	Mexico	
1930	4 535	118	1 589	110	837	...	...	88 104	65 254	12 703	572
1929	3 758	70	1 446	103	771	...	...	116 177	66 451	40 154	509
1928	3 880	80	1 320	102	550	...	...	144 281	75 281	59 016	475
1927	3 669	73	1 471	102	723	...	...	161 872	84 580	67 721	520
1926	3 413	37	1 751	93	654	...	...	144 393	93 368	43 316	529
1925	3 578	51	1 937	65	723	...	...	141 496	102 753	32 964	412
1924	22 065	2 820	6 992	183	8 801	...	...	318 855	200 690	89 336	900
1923	13 705	2 183	4 986	257	5 809	...	...	199 972	117 011	63 768	548
1922	14 263	1 998	4 406	360	6 716	...	...	77 448	46 810	19 551	520
1921	25 034	11 735	4 009	511	7 878	...	...	124 118	72 317	30 758	1 301
1920	17 505	5 033	2 330	300	9 432	...	...	162 666	90 025	52 361	648
1919	12 674	19	1 964	171	10 064	...	...	102 286	57 782	29 818	189
1918	12 701	43	1 795	130	10 213	...	...	65 418	32 452	18 524	299
1917	12 756	393	2 237	109	8 991	...	...	147 779	105 399	17 869	566
1916	13 204	1 670	2 460	112	8 680	...	...	137 424	101 551	18 425	894
1915	15 211	3 543	2 660	161	8 613	...	...	111 206	82 215	12 340	934
1914	34 273	21 716	2 502	221	8 929	...	...	122 695	86 139	14 614	1 539
1913	35 358	23 955	2 105	179	8 281	...	...	103 907	73 802	11 926	1 409
1912	21 449	12 788	1 765	175	6 114	...	...	95 926	55 990	23 238	1 009
1911	17 428	10 229	1 460	524	4 520	...	...	94 364	56 830	19 889	956
1910	23 533	15 212	1 968	1 696	2 720	...	...	89 534	56 555	18 691	1 072
1909	12 904	7 506	1 943	203	3 111	...	...	82 208	51 941	16 251	858
1908	28 365	9 753	1 397	1 040	15 803	...	...	59 997	38 510	6 067	1 411
1907	40 524	8 053	961	898	30 226	...	...	41 762	19 918	1 406	1 486
1906	22 300	6 354	1 544	216	13 835	...	...	24 613	5 063	1 997	712
1905	23 925	6 157	2 166	190	10 331	...	...	25 217	2 168	2 637	757
1904	26 186	5 235	4 309	261	14 264	...	...	16 420	2 837	1 009	686
1903	29 966	7 118	2 209	94	19 964	...	...	11 023	1 058	528	176
1902	22 271	6 223	1 649	93	14 270	...	...	6 698	636	709	37
1901	13 593	5 782	2 459	22	5 269	...	...	4 416	540	347	173
1900	17 946	3 962	1 247	9	12 635	...	...	5 455	396	237	30
1899	8 972	4 436	1 660	17	2 844	...	...	4 316	1 322	161	51
1898	8 637	4 275	2 071	...	2 230	...	...	2 627	352	107	48
1897	9 662	4 732	3 363	...	1 526	...	...	4 537	291	91	37
1896	6 764	4 139	1 441	...	1 110	...	...	7 303	278	150	21
1895	4 495	2 767	539	...	1 150	...	...	3 508	244	116	36
1894	4 690	...	1 170	...	1 931	...	...	3 551	194	109	24
1893	2 392	...	472	...	1 380	...	...	2 593	...	(12)	...
1892	...	...	...	...	...	...	...	...	...	(12)	...
1891	7 678	2 488	2 836	42	1 136	...	...	5 082	234	(12)	103
1890	4 448	1 126	1 716	43	691	...	...	3 833	183	(12)	112
1889	1 725	593	118	59	640	...	...	5 459	28	(12)	187
1888	843	273	26	20	404	...	...	5 402	15	(12)	65
1887	615	208	10	32	229	...	...	5 270	9	(12)	40
1886	317	15	40	17	194	...	...	3 026	17	(12)	122
1885	198	...	22	34	49	...	...	41 203	38 336	323	112
1884	510	...	279	12	20	...	...	63 339	60 626	430	59
1883	8 113	...	8 031	9	27	...	...	71 729	70 274	469	67
1882	39 629	...	39 579	10	5	...	...	100 129	98 366	366	60
1881	11 982	5	11 890	33	11	...	...	127 577	125 450	325	33
1880	5 839	4	5 802	21	4	...	...	101 692	99 744	492	18
1879	9 660	31	9 604	15	4	...	...	33 043	31 286	556	12
1878	9 014	7	8 992	8	2	...	...	27 204	25 592	465	18
1877	10 640	3	10 594	17	7	...	...	24 065	22 137	445	16
1876	22 943	8	22 781	25	4	...	...	24 686	22 505	631	89
1875	16 499	1	16 437	19	3	...	...	26 640	24 097	610	54
1874	13 838	6	13 776	17	21	...	...	35 339	33 020	386	58
1873	20 325	3	20 292	15	9	...	...	40 335	37 891	606	28
1872	7 825	...	7 788	12	17	...	...	42 205	40 204	569	41
1871	7 240	4	7 135	14	78	...	...	48 835	47 164	402	24

Note: For years ending Sept. 30 from 1977 to date; prior to that years ending June 30, except 1820–1831 and 1844–1849, years ending Sept. 30; 1833–1842 and 1851–1867, years ending Dec. 31; 1832 covers 15 months ending Dec. 31; 1843, 9 months ending Sept. 30; 1850, 15 months ending Dec. 31; 1868, 6 months ending June 30; 1990–2001, by country of birth; 1906–1989, country of last permanent resident; prior to 1906, countries from which the immigrants came.
[6]No record of immigration from Turkey in Asia until 1869.
[7]Beginning 1957, includes Taiwan.
[8]No record of immigration from Japan until 1861.
[9]No record of immigration from Korea prior to 1948.
[10]Philippines included in "All other countries" prior to 1936.
[11]Prior to 1920, Canada and Newfoundland were recorded as British North America.
[12]No record of immigration from Mexico for 1886–1893.
... = Not available.

Table 2-2. Immigrants, by Country, 1820–2005—*Continued*

(Number.)

			Europe				Commonwealth of Independent States[4]	Italy
			Northwestern Europe		Central Europe			
Year	All countries[1]	Total	United Kingdom[2]	Ireland[2]	Germany[3]	Poland		
1870	387 203	328 626	103 677	56 996	118 225	223	907	2 891
1869	352 768	315 963	84 438	40 786	131 042	184	343	1 489
1868	138 840	130 090	24 127	32 068	55 831	...	141	891
1867	315 722	283 751	52 641	72 879	133 426	310	205	1 624
1866	318 568	278 916	94 924	36 690	115 892	412	287	1 382
1865	248 120	214 048	82 465	29 772	83 424	528	183	924
1864	193 418	185 233	53 428	63 523	57 276	165	256	600
1863	176 282	163 733	66 882	55 916	33 162	94	77	547
1862	91 985	83 710	24 639	23 351	27 529	63	79	566
1861	91 918	81 200	19 675	23 797	31 661	48	34	811
1860	153 640	141 209	29 737	48 637	54 491	82	65	1 019
1859	121 282	110 949	26 163	35 216	41 784	106	91	932
1858	123 126	111 354	28 956	26 873	45 310	9	246	1 240
1857	251 306	216 224	58 479	54 361	91 781	124	25	1 007
1856	200 436	186 083	44 658	54 349	71 028	20	9	1 365
1855	200 877	187 729	47 572	49 627	71 918	462	13	1 052
1854	427 833	405 542	58 647	101 606	215 009	208	2	1 263
1853	368 645	361 576	37 576	162 649	41 946	33	3	555
1852	371 603	362 484	40 699	159 548	145 918	110	2	351
1851	379 466	369 510	51 487	221 253	72 482	10	1	447
1850	369 980	308 323	51 085	164 004	78 896	5	31	431
1849	297 024	286 501	55 132	159 398	60 235	4	44	209
1848	226 527	218 025	35 159	112 934	58 465	...	1	241
1847	234 968	229 117	23 302	105 536	74 281	8	5	164
1846	154 416	146 315	22 180	51 752	57 561	4	248	151
1845	114 371	109 301	19 210	44 821	34 355	6	1	137
1844	78 615	74 745	14 353	33 490	20 731	36	13	141
1843	52 496	49 013	8 430	19 670	14 441	17	6	117
1842	104 565	99 945	22 005	51 342	20 370	10	28	100
1841	80 289	76 216	16 188	37 772	15 291	15	174	179
1840	84 066	80 126	2 613	39 430	29 704	5	...	37
1839	68 069	64 148	10 271	23 963	21 028	46	7	84
1838	38 914	34 070	5 420	12 645	11 683	41	13	86
1837	79 340	71 039	12 218	28 508	23 740	81	19	36
1836	76 242	70 465	13 106	30 578	20 707	53	2	115
1835	45 374	41 987	8 970	20 927	8 311	54	9	60
1834	65 365	57 510	10 490	24 474	17 686	54	15	105
1833	58 640	29 111	4 916	8 648	6 988	1	159	1 699
1832	60 482	34 193	5 331	12 436	10 194	34	52	3
1831	22 633	13 039	2 475	5 772	2 413	...	1	28
1830	23 322	7 217	1 153	2 721	1 976	2	3	9
1829	22 520	12 523	3 179	7 415	597	...	1	23
1828	27 382	24 729	5 352	12 488	1 851	1	7	34
1827	18 875	16 719	4 186	9 766	432	1	19	35
1826	10 837	9 751	2 319	5 408	511	...	4	57
1825	10 199	8 543	2 095	4 888	450	1	10	75
1824	7 912	4 965	1 264	2 345	230	4	7	45
1823	6 354	4 016	1 100	1 908	183	3	7	33
1822	6 911	4 418	1 221	2 267	148	3	10	35
1821	9 127	5 936	3 210	1 518	383	1	7	63
1820	8 385	7 691	2 410	3 614	968	5	14	30

Note: For years ending Sept. 30 from 1977 to date; prior to that years ending June 30, except 1820–1831 and 1844–1849, years ending Sept. 30; 1833–1842 and 1851–1867, years ending Dec. 31; 1832 covers 15 months ending Dec. 31; 1843, 9 months ending Sept. 30; 1850, 15 months ending Dec. 31; 1868, 6 months ending June 30; 1990–2001, by country of birth; 1906–1989, country of last permanent resident; prior to 1906, countries from which the immigrants came.
[1]For 1820–1867 excludes returning citizens.
[2]Comprises Eire and Northern Ireland.
[3]Includes Austria, 1938 to 1945.
[4]Comprises former Soviet Union.
. . . = Not available.

Table 2-2. Immigrants, by Country, 1820–2005—*Continued*

(Number.)

Year	Asia Total	Turkey in Asia[6]	China[7]	India	Japan[8]	Korea[9]	Philippines[10]	America Total	Canada and New-foundland[11]	Mexico	Africa, total
1870	15 825	...	15 740	24	48	...	...	42 658	40 414	463	31
1869	12 949	2	12 874	3	63	...	...	23 767	21 120	320	72
1868	5 171	...	5 157	...	...	...	...	3 415	2 785	129	3
1867	3 961	...	3 863	2	67	...	...	24 715	23 379	292	25
1866	2 411	...	2 385	17	7	...	...	33 582	32 180	239	33
1865	2 947	...	2 942	5	...	...	...	22 778	21 586	193	49
1864	2 982	...	2 975	6	...	...	...	4 607	3 636	99	37
1863	7 216	...	7 214	1	...	...	...	4 147	3 464	96	3
1862	3 640	...	3 633	5	...	...	...	4 175	3 275	142	12
1861	7 528	...	7 518	6	1	...	...	2 763	2 069	218	47
1860	5 476	...	5 467	5	...	...	...	6 343	4 514	229	126
1859	3 461	...	3 457	2	...	...	...	5 466	4 163	265	11
1858	5 133	...	5 128	5	...	...	...	5 821	4 603	429	17
1857	5 945	...	5 944	1	...	...	...	6 811	5 670	133	25
1856	4 747	...	4 733	13	...	...	...	9 058	6 493	741	6
1855	3 540	...	3 526	6	...	...	...	9 260	7 761	420	14
1854	13 100	...	13 100	...	...	...	...	8 533	6 891	446	...
1853	47	...	42	5	...	...	...	6 030	5 424	162	8
1852	4	...	...	4	...	...	...	7 695	6 352	72	...
1851	2	...	...	2	...	...	...	9 703	7 438	181	3
1850	7	...	3	4	...	...	...	15 768	9 376	597	...
1849	11	...	3	8	...	...	...	8 904	6 890	518	3
1848	8	...	...	6	...	...	...	7 989	6 473	24	10
1847	12	...	4	8	...	...	...	5 231	3 827	62	...
1846	11	...	7	4	...	...	...	5 525	3 855	222	1
1845	6	...	6	...	...	...	...	5 035	3 195	498	4
1844	6	...	3	1	...	...	...	3 740	2 711	197	14
1843	11	...	3	2	...	...	...	2 854	1 502	398	6
1842	7	...	4	2	...	...	...	3 994	2 078	403	3
1841	3	...	2	1	...	...	...	3 429	1 816	352	14
1840	1	...	...	1	...	...	...	3 815	1 938	395	6
1839	...	...	...	...	...	...	...	3 617	1 926	353	10
1838	1	...	...	1	...	...	...	2 990	1 476	211	10
1837	11	...	...	11	...	...	...	3 628	1 279	627	2
1836	4	...	...	4	...	...	...	4 936	2 814	798	6
1835	17	...	8	8	...	...	...	3 312	1 193	1 032	14
1834	6	...	...	6	...	...	...	2 779	1 020	885	1
1833	3	...	...	3	...	...	...	3 282	1 194	779	1
1832	4	...	...	4	...	...	...	2 871	608	827	2
1831	1	...	...	1	...	...	...	2 194	176	692	2
1830	...	...	...	...	...	...	...	2 296	189	983	2
1829	2	...	1	1	...	...	...	3 299	409	2 290	1
1828	3	...	...	3	...	...	...	2 090	267	1089	6
1827	1	...	...	1	...	...	...	580	165	127	4
1826	1	...	...	1	...	...	...	831	223	106	...
1825	1	...	1	...	...	...	...	846	314	68	1
1824	1	...	...	1	...	...	...	559	155	110	...
1823	...	...	...	...	...	...	...	382	167	35	...
1822	1	...	...	1	...	...	...	378	204	5	...
1821	...	...	...	...	...	...	...	303	184	4	2
1820	5	...	1	1	...	...	...	387	209	1	1

Source: U.S. Census Bureau. U.S. Department of Homeland Security, Office of Immigration Statistics. *2005 Yearbook of Immigration Statistics.*
Note: For years ending Sept. 30 from 1977 to date; prior to that years ending June 30, except 1820–1831 and 1844–1849, years ending Sept. 30; 1833–1842 and 1851–1867, years ending Dec. 31; 1832 covers 15 months ending Dec. 31; 1843, 9 months ending Sept. 30; 1850, 15 months ending Dec. 31; 1868, 6 months ending June 30; 1990–2001, by country of birth; 1906–1989, country of last permanent resident; prior to 1906, countries from which the immigrants came.
[6]No record of immigration from Turkey in Asia until 1869.
[7]Beginning 1957, includes Taiwan.
[8]No record of immigration from Japan until 1861.
[9]No record of immigration from Korea prior to 1948.
[10]Philippines included in "All other countries" prior to 1936.
[11]Prior to 1920, Canada and Newfoundland were recorded as British North America.
. . . = Not available.

Table 2-3. Formal Removals and Voluntary Departures of Aliens, 1892–2005

(Number.)

Year	Aliens expelled	
	Formal removals[1]	Voluntary departures[2]
2005	208 521	965 538
2004	204 290	1 036 133
2003	189 856	888 409
2002	150 788	934 463
2001	178 207	1 254 182
2000	186 391	1 675 827
1999	181 194	1 574 803
1998	173 146	1 570 127
1997	114 432	1 440 684
1996	69 680	1 573 428
1995	50 924	1 313 764
1994	45 674	1 029 107
1993	42 542	1 243 410
1992	43 671	1 105 829
1991	33 189	1 061 105
1990	30 039	1 022 533
1989	34 427	830 890
1988	25 829	911 790
1987	24 336	1 091 203
1986	24 592	1 586 320
1985	23 105	1 041 296
1984	18 696	909 833
1983	19 211	931 600
1982	15 216	812 572
1981	17 379	823 875
1980	18 013	719 211
1979	26 825	966 137
1978	29 277	975 515
1977	31 263	867 015
1976,TQ[3]	9 245	190 280
1976	29 226	765 094
1975	24 432	655 814
1974	19 413	718 740
1973	17 346	568 005
1972	16 883	450 927
1971	18 294	370 074
1970	17 469	303 348
1969	11 030	240 958
1968	9 590	179 952
1967	9 728	142 343
1966	9 680	123 683
1965	10 572	95 263
1964	9 167	73 042
1963	7 763	69 392
1962	8 025	54 164
1961	8 181	52 383
1960	7 240	52 796
1959	8 468	56 610
1958	7 875	60 600
1957	5 989	63 379
1956	9 006	80 891
1955	17 695	232 769
1954	30 264	1 074 277
1953	23 482	885 391
1952	23 125	703 778
1951	17 328	673 169
1950	10 199	572 477
1949	23 874	276 297
1948	25 276	197 184
1947	23 434	195 880
1946	17 317	101 945
1945	13 611	69 490
1944	8 821	32 270
1943	5 702	11 947
1942	5 542	6 904
1941	7 336	6 531

[1]Formal removals from the United States pursuant to final orders of exclusion, deportation or removal.
[2]Voluntary departures from the United States that are verified by the Department of Homeland Security. Voluntary departures are a form of relief from formal removal, under which an alien is permitted to depart the United States voluntarily.
[3]Fiscal years through 1976 are from July 1 through June 30. Beginning with October 1976 (fiscal year 1977), fiscal years are from October 1 through September 30. The period from July 1 through September 30, 1976 is a separate fiscal period known as the transition quarter (TQ) and not included in any fiscal year.
. . . = Not available.

Table 2-3. Formal Removals and Voluntary Departures of Aliens, 1892–2005—*Continued*

(Number.)

Year	Aliens expelled	
	Formal removals[1]	Voluntary departures[2]
1940	12 254	8 594
1939	14 700	9 590
1938	17 341	9 278
1937	16 905	8 788
1936	16 195	8 251
1935	13 877	7 978
1934	14 263	8 010
1933	25 392	10 347
1932	26 490	10 775
1931	27 886	11 719
1930	24 864	11 387
1929	31 035	25 888
1928	30 464	19 946
1927	31 417	15 012
1926	31 454	...
1925	34 885	...
1924	36 693	...
1923	24 280	...
1922	18 076	...
1921	18 296	...
1920	14 557	...
1919	11 694	...
1918	8 866	...
1917	17 881	...
1916	21 648	...
1915	26 675	...
1914	37 651	...
1913	23 399	...
1912	18 513	...
1911	25 137	...
1910	26 965	...
1909	12 535	...
1908	12 971	...
1907	14 059	...
1906	13 108	...
1905	12 724	...
1904	8 773	...
1903	9 316	...
1902	5 439	...
1901	3 879	...
1900	4 602	...
1899	4 052	...
1898	3 229	...
1897	1 880	...
1896	3 037	...
1895	2 596	...
1894	1 806	...
1893	1 630	...
1892	2 801	...

Source: U.S. Department of Homeland Security, Office of Immigration Statistics. *2005 Yearbook of Immigration Statistics.*
[1]Formal removals from the United States pursuant to final orders of exclusion, deportation or removal.
[2]Voluntary departures from the United States that are verified by the Department of Homeland Security. Voluntary departures are a form of relief from formal removal, under which an alien is permitted to depart the United States voluntarily.
. . . = Not available.

Table 2-4. Foreign-Stock Population, by Nativity and Parentage, 1890–2000

(Number in millions.)

Year	Foreign born	Foreign parentage	Mixed parentage
2000	28.4	14.8	12.7
1970	9.6	24.0	4.7
1960	9.7	14.1	10.2
1930	14.2	17.5	8.5
1920	13.9	15.8	7.0
1910	13.5	12.9	6.0
1900	10.3	10.7	5.0
1890	9.2	8.1	3.4

Source: U.S. Census Bureau.

Table 2-5. Estimated Undocumented Immigrants, by Selected States and Countries of Origin, 1990–2005.

(Number in thousands.)

	Estimated Population						Percent of Total 2000	Estimated Population 2005	Percent of Total 2005	Percent Change 2000 to 2005
	1990	1992	1994¹		1996	2000				
			Low	High						
U.S. Total	**3500**	**3 379**	**3 500**	**4 000**	**...**	**8 460**	**100.0**	**10 500**	**100.0**	**24.0**
State of Residence										
Arizona	88	57	50	68	115	330	4.0	480	5.0	45.0
California	1476	1 441	1 321	1 784	2 000	2 510	30.0	2 770	26.0	10.0
Colorado	31	22	22	29	45	...	...	...	...	...
Connecticut	...	15	13	46	29	...	...	...	...	...
District of Columbia	...	...	...	...	30	...	...	...	...	...
Florida	239	322	243	385	350	800	9.0	850	8.0	6.0
Georgia	34	28	29	36	32	220	3.0	470	4.0	114.0
Hawaii	...	...	4	25	...	...	...	...	...	...
Illinois	194	176	157	225	290	440	5.0	520	5.0	18.0
Maryland	...	27	29	63	44	...	...	...	...	...
Massachusetts	53	45	42	106	85	...	...	...	...	...
Michigan	...	...	10	53	37	...	...	...	...	...
Nevada	27	...	...	...	24	170	2.0	240	2.0	41.0
New Jersey	95	116	98	168	135	350	4.0	380	4.0	9.0
New Mexico	...	19	14	25	37	...	...	...	...	...
New York	357	449	462	539	540	540	6.0	560	5.0	4.0
North Carolina	26	...	...	...	...	260	3.0	360	3.0	38.0
Ohio	...	...	7	36	...	...	...	...	...	...
Oregon	26	20	21	27	33	...	...	...	...	...
Pennsylvania	...	18	15	51	37	...	...	...	...	...
Texas	438	357	300	427	700	1 090	13.0	1 360	13.0	25.0
Virginia	48	35	37	63	55	...	...	...	...	...
Washington	39	30	32	59	52	...	...	...	...	...
Other States	328	...	...	...	330	1 750	21.0	2 510	24.0	43.0
Country of Origin										
Bahamas, The	...	71	...	...	...	...	...	...	...	...
Brazil	20	...	...	...	...	100	1.0	170	2.0	70.0
Canada	25	97	...	...	120	...	...	...	...	...
China	70	...	...	...	...	190	2.0	230	2.0	21.0
Colombia	51	59	...	...	65	...	...	...	...	...
Dominican Republic	46	40	...	...	75	...	...	...	...	...
Ecuador	37	45	...	...	55	...	...	...	...	...
El Salvador	298	327	...	...	335	430	5.0	470	4.0	9.0
Guatemala	118	129	...	...	165	290	3.0	370	4.0	28.0
Haiti	67	88	...	...	105	...	...	...	...	...
Honduras	42	61	...	...	90	160	2.0	180	2.0	13.0
India	28	28	...	...	33	120	1.0	280	3.0	133.0
Ireland	...	36	...	...	30	...	...	...	...	...
Italy	...	67	...	...	...	...	...	...	...	...
Jamaica	...	42	...	...	50	...	...	...	...	...
Korea	24	...	...	...	30	180	2.0	210	2.0	17.0
Mexico	2040	1 321	...	...	2 700	4 680	55.0	5 970	57.0	28.0
Nicaragua	...	68	...	...	70	...	...	...	...	...
Pakistan	...	30	...	...	41	...	...	...	...	...
Peru	27	...	...	...	30	...	...	...	...	...
Philippines	70	90	...	...	95	200	2.0	210	2.0	5.0
Poland	...	91	...	...	70	...	...	...	...	...
Portugal	...	31	...	...	27	...	...	...	...	...
Trinidad & Tobago	...	39	...	...	50	...	...	...	...	...
Vietnam	...	...	...	...	...	160	2.0	160	2.0	-
Other Countries	537	...	...	...	...	1 950	23.0	2 250	21.0	15.0

Source: U.S. Department of Homeland Security, Office of Immigration Statistics and U.S. Census Bureau.
Note: Unauthorized immigrants refer to foreign-born persons who entered the U.S. without inspection or who violated the terms of a temporary admission and who neither acquired legal permanent resident status nor gained temporary protection against removal by applying for an immigration benefit. Data for 1992 and 1994 supplied by U.S. Census Bureau all other years supplied by Department of Homeland Security or the former Immigration and Naturalization Service. Estimates for 1992–1996 as of October of each year; 1990, 2000 and 2005 as of January.
¹The ranges of estimates supplied by the Bureau of the Census represent indicators of magnitude which the Bureau believes is responsive to the inherent uncertainty in the assumptions underlying these estimates.
... = Not available.
- = Quantity zero or rounds to zero.

BOX 2 ■ Unauthorized Resident Immigrants

The Department of Homeland Security (DHS) defines "unauthorized resident immigrant" as "all foreign-born, non-citizens who are not legal residents." This includes both those people who entered the United States illegally; through an illegal border crossing, immigrant smuggling, or human trafficking, and those who entered the country legally and stayed beyond the allowed time period of their authorized residence.

Because unauthorized immigrants are in this country illegally, there has never been an actual count of their numbers. However, as discussion on the impact of the unauthorized resident immigration population on the social fabric and economy of the U.S. became increasingly polarized in the early 1990s, pressure to gather such statistics increased. Therefore, in 1994, the former Immigration and Naturalization Service began national estimates of the unauthorized immigrant population.

According to the latest estimates by the DHS Office of Immigration Statistics, this population has gone from 3.5 million in 1990 to 10.5 million in 2005—an increase of 300 percent. In the five years from 2000 to 2005 the unauthorized immigrant population increased 24% from 8.5 million. Mexicans account of the majority of unauthorized immigrants currently living in the United

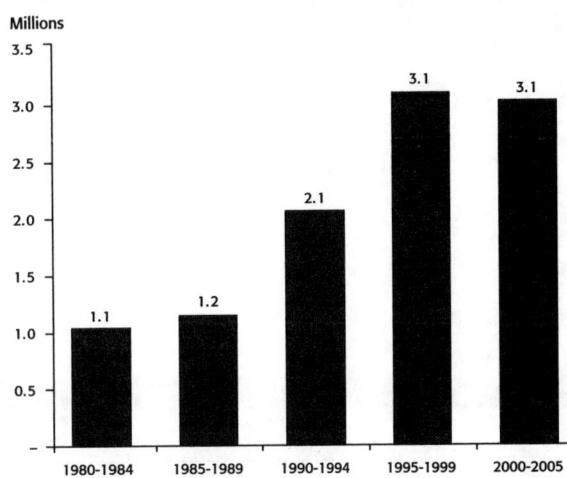

Period of Entry of the Unauthorized Immigrant Population: January 2005
Source: U.S. Department of Homeland Security

States; 57% or nearly 6 million people. El Salvador and Guatemala together account for approximately 8% of the unauthorized immigrant population (470,000 and 370,000, respectively). India and Brazil, while only accounting for 2.7% and 1.6% of the total unauthorized immigrant population, showed the greatest percentage increase from 2000 to 2005 (133% and 70% respectively).

California is home to approximately 2.8 million, or more than one quarter, of all unauthorized immigrants in the United States. Along with California, Texas, Florida, New York, and Illinois continue to have the largest populations of unauthorized immigrants. However, the growth rate of the unauthorized immigrant population in these five states has slowed while several states that have had relatively small unauthorized immigrant populations in the past have shown strong increases from 2000 to 2005: Georgia up 114% with 250,000 additional unauthorized immigrants; Arizona up 45% with 150,000 additional unauthorized immigrants; Nevada up 41% with 70,000 additional unauthorized immigrants.

While the unauthorized immigrant population is estimated to have comprised just 4.9% of the U.S. labor force in 2005 they accounted for 24% of all people in farming occupations, 17% of cleaning occupations, 14% of construction, and 12% of food preparation positions.

Still, these numbers are just estimates calculated by a formula that computes the number of legal foreign-born residents by counting the number of legal admissions, legal temporary migrants, and an estimate of legal immigrants missed in the last census. The number of unauthorized immigrants is then determined by subtracting this number from the Census count for the total foreign-born population. Although the U.S. Census Bueau collects information on a person's place of birth and citizenship, it does not collect information on a non-citizen's visa status. Therefore, even the DHS numbers are at best estimates based on assumptions.

The creation of a viable public policy on immigration is one of the most divisive issues in national politics, and the lack of accurate statistics only clouds legitimate debate. The government needs to determine not only the size of the unauthorized immigrant population, but its cost in terms of use of public services, its contribution to the economy through taxes and consumer spending, whether it is taking jobs from legal residents or filling unwanted positions, the cost of increasing border patrols, the rise in the human trafficking trade across the border, the increase in identity theft to provide documents to illegal immigrants, and a host of other social and economic issues. Then, there is the basic issue of whether people should be allowed to enter illegally under any circumstances.

Sources: U.S. Department of Homeland Security, Office of Immigration Statistics. *Estimates of the Unauthorized Immigrant Population Residing in the United States: January 2005.*

U.S. Department of Homeland Security, Office of Immigration Statistics. *Estimates of the Unauthorized Immigrant Population Residing in the United States: 1990 to 2000.*

Executive Office of the President of the United States, Council of Economic Advisors. *Economic Report of the President,* February 12, 2007.

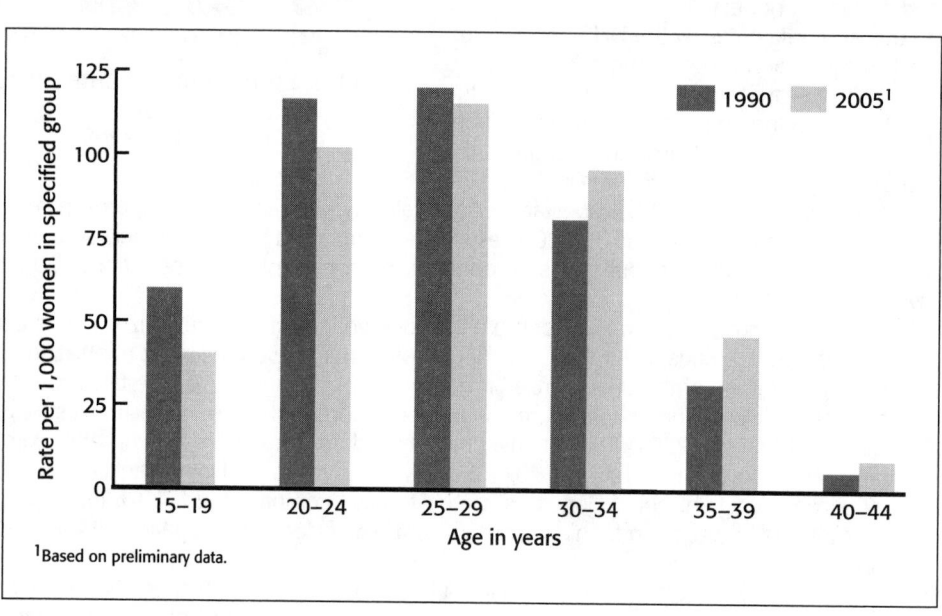

Birth Rates by Age of Mother: United States, 1990 and 2005
Source: U.S. Centers for Disease Control and Prevention, National Center for Health Statistics. National Vital Statistics System.

CHAPTER **3**

Births and Deaths

HIGHLIGHTS

1 Vital statistics on the four key life events—births, deaths, marriages, and divorces—are compiled by the National Center for Health Statistics, successor to the Office of Vital Statistics. From 1900 to 1946, the collection of these data was the responsibility of the Census Bureau.

2 Vital statistics are compiled on the basis of records received from the registration offices of all states, certain cities, and the District of Columbia. Reporting of these events is mandatory in many localities. The annual *Vital Statistics of the United States* summarizes these data, presenting final figures and an annual life table. A life table (also known as a mortality table) is an actuarial table and contains data on life expectancy and death.

3 The annual collection of mortality statistics began in 1900 and the collection of birth statistics in 1915. Since 1933, the entire United States has been included in birth- and death-registration areas. Alaska was added in 1959 and Hawaii in 1960. National statistics on fetal deaths have been compiled since 1922.

4 Birth statistics are based either on complete counts for states participating in the Vital Statistics Cooperative Program or on 50 percent samples. Mortality statistics are compiled in accordance

with the World Health Organization (WHO) regulations based on the *International Statistical Classification of Diseases, Injuries and Causes of Death*. The degree of accuracy of birth data is believed to be more than 99.1 percent. While death data may be nearly as complete as birth data, underreporting may be a problem in isolated areas. The reporting of fetal deaths is likely to be even less complete.

5 Data on illegitimate births are based on estimates. In the 1930s, all states had a queried legitimacy or illegitimacy on birth certificates. This query was removed during the 1940s on grounds of confidentiality. As a result, the data suffer from potential misreporting. The term "illegitimate" was discarded and replaced by "Births to Unmarried Women" in the 1990 census.

6 Overall, the vital statistic rates per 1,000 have dropped precipitously in the United States, and in all developed countries, since 1950. In the United States, the birth rate decreased from 24.1 to 14.0, the death rate from 9.6 to 8.2, and the infant mortality rate from 29.2 to 6.9.

7 The difference in birth rates per 1,000 between White and Black women has narrowed since 1980. The relative rates in 1980 were 15.1 for Whites and 21.3 for Blacks, whereas the corresponding rates in 2004 were 13.5 and 16.0. Fertility rates for Whites have actually increased from 65.6 in 1980 to 66.1 in 2004 while fertility rates for Blacks experienced a significant decline from 84.7 in 1980 to 67.6 in 2004.

8 There were fewer teenage mothers in 2004 than in 1980. Overall teenage births declined from 521,826 in 1980 to 415,262 in 2004. Of these births 17.9 percent were to American Indian, Eskimo, or Aleut teenagers.

9 Utah has the highest birth rate of all states at 21.2, with a correspondingly high fertility rate of 92.3. Other states with high birth rates are Texas (17.0), Arizona (16.3), Idaho (16.2), and Alaska (15.8).

10 The total fertility rate declined from an average of 3,449 (3,326 for Whites and 4,326 for Blacks) in 1960-1964 to 2,046 in 2004 (2,055 for Whites and 2,033 for Blacks). For Whites, this rate represents a rebound from 1976 when the fertility rate bottomed out at 1,738.

11 The percentage of children with low birth weights, defined as below 5 lbs. 8 oz., has increased from 6.8 percent in 1980 to 8.1 percent in 2004. A larger percentage of children born to teenage mothers and unmarried mothers have a lower birth weight (10.3 percent and 35.8 percent respectively).

12 The number of caesareans deliveries rose steadily from 195,000 in 1970 to 1,190,000 in 2004. These deliveries are most common among women 35 years of age and older.

13 The number of abortions in the United States increased from 586,000 in 1972 (around the time of *Roe v. Wade*), to 1,293,000 in 2002, although this figure represents a drop from the peak of 1,609,000 in 1990. Per 1,000 women (15 to 44 years of age), there were 20.8 abortions in 2002, compared with 29.3 in 1980.

14 In 2002 61.9 percent of women used contraception. Of the available methods, the pill was the most popular with 18.9 percent, followed by female sterilization (16.7 percent), and condoms (11.1 percent).

15 Although Americans can expect to live 30.9 years longer than their ancestors did in 1900, the United States trails a number of other developed countries including Japan, Sweden, Switzerland, Norway, Canada, France, Netherlands, Australia, Italy, and Greece in longevity. In 2004, the life expectancy for men was 75.2 years and women 80.4 years, with an average of 77.9 years. Life expectancy for Blacks is five years less than that of Whites: 69.8 for men and 76.5 for women, with an average of 73.3.

16 In the United States, 274 persons die every hour, or about 4.6 persons every minute. The death rate is fairly uniform in all states and regions, around 8.5 per 1,000 population, but is lowest in Alaska at 4.6.

17 In a key area of vital statistics, the United States registered significant gains. Between 1980 and 2003, the infant mortality rate dropped from 12.6 to 6.9 and neonatal deaths from 8.5 to 4.6, both per 1,000 live births. However, the gap between Whites and Blacks continues to persist. Blacks have an infant mortality rate of 14.0 per 1,000 live births compared with 5.7 for Whites.

18 The birthrate of women in their late thirties and forties was at its highest in 2005 since 1965 and 1970 respectively. The birthrate for women 35 to 39 was 46.3 births per 1,000 and for women 45 to 49, it was 0.6 births per 1,000.

19 There were 43,927 children born to American Indian, Eskimo, and Aleut parents in 2004. The states with the greatest numbers were Arizona (6,273), Oklahoma (5,402), New Mexico (3,620), and California (2,976).

Table 3-1. Live Births and Deaths, 1909–2004

(Number in thousands.)

Year	Live births[1]	Deaths[2]
2004	4 112	2 398
2003	4 090	2 448
2002	4 022	2 443
2001	4 026	2 416
2000	4 059	2 403
1999	3 959	2 391
1998	3 942	2 337
1997	3 881	2 314
1996	3 891	2 315
1995	3 900	2 312
1994	3 953	2 279
1993	4 000	2 269
1992	4 065	2 176
1991	4 111	2 170
1990	4 158	2 148
1989	4 041	2 150
1988	3 910	2 168
1987	3 809	2 123
1986	3 757	2 105
1985	3 761	2 086
1984	3 669	2 039
1983	3 639	2 019
1982	3 681	1 975
1981	3 629	1 978
1980	3 612	1 990
1979	3 494	1 914
1978	3 333	1 928
1977	3 327	1 900
1976	3 168	1 909
1975	3 144	1 893
1974	3 160	1 934
1973	3 137	1 973
1972	3 258	1 964
1971	3 556	1 928
1970	3 731	1 921
1969	3 600	1 922
1968	3 502	1 930
1967	3 521	1 851
1966	3 606	1 863
1965	3 760	1 828
1964	4 027	1 798
1963	4 098	1 814
1962	4 167	1 757
1961	4 268	1 702
1960	4 258	1 712
1959	5 245	1 657
1958	4 255	1 648
1957	4 308	1 633
1956	4 218	1 564
1955	4 097	1 529
1954	4 078	1 481
1953	3 965	1 518
1952	3 913	1 497
1951	3 823	1 482
1950	3 632	1 452
1949	3 649	1 444
1948	3 637	1 444
1947	3 817	1 445
1946	3 411	1 396
1945	2 858	1 402
1944	2 939	1 411
1943	3 104	1 460
1942	2 989	1 385
1941	2 703	1 398
1940	2 559	1 417
1939	2 466	1 388
1938	2 496	1 381
1937	2 413	1 450
1936	2 355	1 479
1935	2 377	1 393
1934	2 396	1 397
1933	2 307	1 342
1932	2 440	. . .
1931	2 506	. . .

[1]For 1960–1991 includes births to races not shown separately. For 1992 and later years, unknown race of mother is imputed. 1959–1970, registered live births; 1909–1958, adjusted for under-registration.
[2]Excludes fetal deaths.
. . . = Not available.

Table 3-1. Live Births and Deaths, 1909–2004—*Continued*

(Number in thousands.)

Year	Live births[1]	Deaths[2]
1930	2 618	. . .
1929	2 582	. . .
1928	2 674	. . .
1927	2 802	. . .
1926	2 839	. . .
1925	2 909	. . .
1924	2 979	. . .
1923	2 910	. . .
1922	2 882	. . .
1921	3 055	. . .
1920	2 950	. . .
1919	2 740	. . .
1918	2 948	. . .
1917	2 944	. . .
1916	2 964	. . .
1915	2 965	. . .
1914	2 966	. . .
1913	2 869	. . .
1912	2 840	. . .
1911	2 809	. . .
1910	2 777	. . .
1909	2 718	. . .

Source: U.S. National Center for Health Statistics. *Vital Statistics of the United States,* annual; and *National Vital Statistics Reports (NVSR).*
[1]For 1960–1991 includes births to races not shown separately. For 1992 and later years, unknown race of mother is imputed. 1959–1970, registered live births; 1909–1958, adjusted for under-registration.
[2]Excludes fetal deaths.
. . . = Not available.

Table 3-2. Birth Rate—Total and Fertility Rate for Women 15–44 Years Old, by Race, 1800–2004

(Number in thousands. Birth rates are live births per 1,000 population in specified group. Fertility rates are live births per 1,000 women aged 15–44 years in specified group. Beginning with 1960, population enumerated as of April 1 for census years and estimated as of July 1 for all other years. Beginning with 1970, excludes births to nonresidents of the United States.)

Year	Birth rate, total population			Fertility rate, women 15–44 years[1]		
	Total[2]	White	Black	Total	White	Black
Race of Mother						
2004	14.0	13.5	16.0	66.3	66.1	67.6
2003	14.1	13.6	15.7	66.1	66.1	66.3
2002	13.9	13.5	15.7	64.8	64.8	65.8
2001	14.1	13.7	16.3	65.3	65.0	67.6
2000	14.4	13.9	17.0	65.9	65.3	70.0
1999	14.2	13.7	16.8	64.4	64.0	68.5
1998	14.3	13.8	17.1	64.3	63.6	69.4
1997	14.2	13.7	17.1	63.6	62.8	69.0
1996	14.4	13.9	17.3	64.1	63.3	69.2
1995	14.6	14.1	17.8	64.6	63.6	71.0
1994	15.0	14.3	19.1	65.9	64.2	75.9
1993	15.4	14.6	20.2	67.0	64.9	79.6
1992	15.8	15.0	21.1	68.4	66.1	82.4
1991	16.2	15.3	21.8	69.3	66.7	84.8
1990	16.7	15.8	22.4	70.9	68.3	86.8
1989	16.4	15.4	22.3	69.2	66.4	86.2
1988	16.0	15.0	21.5	67.3	64.5	82.6
1987	15.7	14.9	20.8	65.8	63.3	80.1
1986	15.6	14.8	20.5	65.4	63.1	78.9
1985	15.8	15.0	20.4	66.3	64.1	78.8
1984[3]	15.6	14.8	20.1	65.5	63.2	78.2
1983[3]	15.6	14.8	20.2	65.7	63.4	78.7
1982[3]	15.9	15.1	20.7	67.3	64.8	80.9
1981[3]	15.8	15.0	20.8	67.3	64.8	82.0
1980[3]	15.9	15.1	21.3	68.4	65.6	84.7
Race of Child						
1980[3]	15.9	14.9	22.1	68.4	64.7	88.1
1979[3]	15.6	14.5	22.0	67.2	63.4	88.3
1978[3]	15.0	14.0	21.3	65.5	61.7	86.7
1977[3]	15.1	14.1	21.4	66.8	63.2	88.1
1976[3]	14.6	13.6	20.5	65.0	61.5	85.8
1975[3]	14.6	13.6	20.7	66.0	62.5	87.9
1974[3]	14.8	13.9	20.8	67.8	64.2	89.7
1973[3]	14.8	13.8	21.4	68.8	64.9	93.6
1972[3]	15.6	14.5	22.5	73.1	68.9	99.9
1971[4]	17.2	16.1	24.4	81.6	77.3	109.7
1970[4]	18.4	17.4	25.3	87.9	84.1	115.4
1969[4]	17.9	16.9	24.4	86.1	82.2	112.1
1968[4]	17.6	16.6	24.2	85.2	81.3	112.7
1967[5,6]	17.8	16.8	25.1	87.2	82.8	118.5
1966[4]	18.4	17.4	26.2	90.8	86.2	124.7
1965[4]	19.4	18.3	27.7	96.3	91.3	133.2
1964[4]	21.1	20.0	29.5	104.7	99.8	142.6
1963[4,7]	21.7	20.7	29.7	108.5	103.7	144.9
1962[4,7]	22.4	21.4	30.5	112.2	107.5	148.8
1961[4]	23.3	22.2	34.6	117.2	112.2	153.5
1960*[4]	23.7	22.7	32.1	118.0	113.2	153.6
1959[8]	24.0	22.9	32.9	118.8	113.9	156.0
1958	24.5	23.3	34.3	120.2	114.9	160.5
1957	25.3	24.0	35.3	122.9	117.7	163.0
1956	25.2	24.0	35.4	121.2	116.0	160.9
1955	25.0	23.8	34.7	118.5	113.8	155.3
1954	25.3	24.2	34.9	118.1	113.6	153.2
1953	25.0	24.0	34.1	115.2	111.0	147.3
1952	25.1	24.1	33.6	113.9	110.1	143.3
1951	24.9	23.9	33.8	111.5	107.7	142.1

[1]Computed by relating total births, regardless of age of mother, to women aged 15–44 years.
[2]For 1960–91 includes births to races not shown separately. For 1992 and later years, unknown race of mother is imputed.
[3]Based on 100 percent of births in selected states and on a 50 percent sample of births in all other states.
[4]Based on a 50 percent sample of births.
[5]Based on a 20 to 50 percent sample of births.
[6]For 1800–1970, Black and other.
[7]Figures by race exclude New Jersey; state did not require reporting of race.
[8]Includes Alaska.
* = First year for which figures include Alaska and Hawaii.

Table 3-2. Birth Rate—Total and Fertility Rate for Women 15–44 Years Old, by Race, 1800–2004—*Continued*

(Number in thousands. Birth rates are live births per 1,000 population in specified group. Fertility rates are live births per 1,000 women aged 15–44 years in specified group. Beginning with 1960, population enumerated as of April 1 for census years and estimated as of July 1 for all other years. Beginning with 1970, excludes births to nonresidents of the United States.)

Year	Birth rate, total population			Fertility rate, women 15–44 years[1]		
	Total[2]	White	Black	Total	White	Black
1950	24.1	23.0	33.3	106.2	102.3	137.3
1949	24.5	23.6	33.0	107.1	103.6	135.1
1948	24.9	24.0	32.4	107.3	104.3	131.6
1947	26.6	26.1	31.2	113.3	111.8	125.9
1946	24.1	23.6	38.4	101.9	100.4	113.9
1945	20.4	19.7	26.5	85.9	83.4	106.0
1944	21.2	20.5	27.4	88.8	86.3	108.5
1943	22.7	22.1	28.3	94.3	92.3	111.0
1942	22.2	21.5	27.7	91.5	89.5	107.6
1941	20.3	19.5	27.3	83.4	80.7	105.4
1940	19.4	18.6	26.7	79.9	77.1	102.4
1939	18.8	18.0	26.1	77.6	74.8	100.1
1938	19.2	18.4	26.3	79.1	76.5	100.5
1937	18.7	17.9	26.0	77.1	74.4	99.4
1936	18.4	17.6	25.1	75.8	73.3	95.9
1935	18.7	17.9	25.8	77.2	74.5	98.4
1934	19.0	18.1	26.3	78.5	75.8	100.4
1933	18.4	17.6	25.5	76.3	73.7	97.3
1932	19.5	18.7	26.9	81.7	79.0	103.0
1931	20.2	19.5	26.6	84.6	82.4	102.1
1930	21.3	20.6	27.5	89.2	87.1	105.9
1929	21.2	20.5	27.3	89.3	87.3	106.1
1928	22.2	21.5	28.5	93.8	91.7	111.0
1927	23.5	22.7	31.1	99.8	97.1	121.7
1926	24.2	23.1	33.4	102.6	99.2	130.3
1925	25.1	24.1	34.2	106.6	103.3	134.0
1924	26.1	25.1	34.6	110.9	107.8	135.6
1923	26.0	25.2	33.2	110.5	108.0	130.5
1922	26.2	25.4	33.2	111.2	108.8	130.8
1921	28.1	27.3	35.8	119.8	117.2	140.8
1920	27.7	26.9	35.0	117.9	115.4	137.5
1919	26.1	25.3	32.4	111.2	...	...
1918	28.2	27.6	33.0	119.8	...	...
1917	28.5	27.9	32.9	121.0	...	...
1916	29.1	28.5	...	123.4	121.8	...
1915	29.5	28.9	...	125.0	123.2	...
1914	29.9	29.3	...	126.6	124.6	...
1913	29.5	28.8	...	124.7	122.4	...
1912	29.8	29.0	...	125.8	123.3	...
1911	29.9	29.1	...	126.3	123.6	...
1910	30.1	29.2	...	126.8	123.8	...
1909	30.0	29.2	...	126.8	123.6	...
1900	32.3	30.1	...	...	130.0	...
1890	...	31.5	...	...	137.0	...
1880	39.8	35.2	...	...	155.0	...
1870	...	38.3	...	...	167.0	...
1860	44.3	41.4	...	...	184.0	...
1850	...	43.3	...	...	194.0	...
1840	51.8	48.3	...	...	222.0	...
1830	...	51.4	...	...	240.0	...
1820	55.2	52.8	...	...	260.0	...
1810	...	54.3	...	...	274.0	...
1800	...	55.0	...	...	278.0	...

Source: U.S. National Center for Health Statistics. *National Vital Statistics Reports.*
[1]Computed by relating total births, regardless of age of mother, to women aged 15–44 years.
* = First year for which figures include Alaska and Hawaii.

Table 3-3. Fertility Rate, by Race, 1917–2004

(For 1917–2002 fertility rate reflects the number of births that 1,000 women would have in their lifetime, if at each age, they experienced the birth rates occurring in the specified year. For 2003 and 2004 total fertility rates reflect the sums of birth rates for 5-year age groups multiplied by five.)

Year	Total fertility rate				
	Total[1]	White	Black	American Indian[2]	Asian or Pacific Islander
Race of Mother					
2004	2 046	2 055	2 033	1 735	1 898
2003	2 043	2 061	1 999	1 732	1 873
2002	2 013	2 028	1 991	1 735	1 820
2001	2 034	2 040	2 051	1 747	1 840
2000	2 056	2 051	2 129	1 773	1 892
1999	2 008	2 008	2 083	1 784	1 755
1998	1 999	1 991	2 112	1 851	1 732
1997	1 971	1 955	2 092	1 835	1 758
1996	1 976	1 961	2 089	1 855	1 787
1995	1 978	1 955	2 128	1 879	1 796
1994	2 002	1 958	2 259	1 950	1 834
1993	2 020	1 962	2 351	2 049	1 842
1992	2 046	1 978	2 416	2 136	1 895
1991	2 063	1 988	2 462	2 143	1 928
1990	2 081	2 003	2 480	2 185	2 003
1989	2 014	1 931	2 433	2 249	1 948
1988	1 934	1 857	2 298	2 155	1 984
1987	1 872	1 805	2 198	2 101	1 886
1986	1 838	1 776	2 136	2 083	1 836
1985	1 844	1 787	2 109	2 130	1 885
1984	1 807	1 749	2 071	2 138	1 892
1983	1 799	1 741	2 066	2 182	1 944
1982	1 828	1 767	2 107	2 215	2 016
1981	1 812	1 748	2 118	2 093	1 976
1980	1 840	1 773	2 177	2 165	1 954
Race of Child					
1980	1 808	1 716	2 263	...	...
1978	1 760	1 668	2 218	...	...
1977	1 790	1 703	2 251	...	...
1976	1 738	1 652	2 187	...	...
1975	1 774	1 686	2 243	...	...
1974	1 835	1 749	2 299	...	...
1973	1 879	1 783	2 411	...	...
1972	2 010	1 907	2 601	...	...
1971	2 267	2 161	2 902	...	...
1970	2 480	2 385	3 100	...	...
1969	2 465	2 360	3 043	...	...
1968	2 477	2 368	3 100	...	...
1967	2 573	2 453	3 312	...	...
1966	2 736	2 609	3 545	...	...
1965	2 928	2 780	3 829	...	...
1964	3 208	3 074	4 139	...	...
1963	3 333	3 190	...	...	...
1962	3 474	3 340	...	...	...
1961	3 629	3 502	...	...	...
1960	3 654	3 533	4 542	...	...
1959	3 670	3 544	...	...	...
1958	3 630	3 530	...	...	...
1957	3 680	3 580	...	...	...
1956	3 600	3 500	...	...	...
1955	3 500	3 400	...	...	...
1954	3 460	3 370	...	...	...
1953	3 350	3 270	...	...	...
1952	3 290	3 210	...	...	...
1951	3 200	3 120	...	...	...
1950	3 030	2 950	...	...	...
1949	3 040	2 960	...	...	...
1948	3 030	2 970	...	...	...
1947	3 180	3 170	...	...	...
1946	2 860	2 840	...	...	...
1945	2 420	2 380	...	...	...
1944	2 490	2 450	...	...	...
1943	2 640	2 610	...	...	...
1942	2 550	2 530	...	...	...
1941	2 330	2 280	...	...	...

Note: 1972–1984 Fertility rates are based on 100 percent of births in selected states and on a 50 percent sample of births in all other states. 1970 and 1971 rates are based on a 50 percent sample of births.
[1] For 1970–1991 this category includes births to races not shown separately. For 1992 and later years, unknown race of mother is imputed.
[2] Includes births to Aleuts and Eskimos.
. . . = Not available.

Table 3-3. Fertility Rate, by Race, 1917–2004—*Continued*

(For 1917–2002 fertility rate reflects the number of births that 1,000 women would have in their lifetime, if at each age, they experienced the birth rates occurring in the specified year. For 2003 and 2004 total fertility rates reflect the sums of birth rates for 5-year age groups multiplied by five.)

| Year | Total fertility rate | | | | |
	Total[1]	White	Black	American Indian[2]	Asian or Pacific Islander
1940	2 230	2 180	...	...	...
1939	2 172	2 120	...	...	...
1938	2 222	2 175	...	...	...
1937	2 173	2 121	...	...	...
1936	2 146	2 101	...	...	...
1935	2 189	2 141	...	...	...
1934	2 232	2 181	...	...	...
1933	2 172	2 126	...	...	...
1932	2 319	2 271	...	...	...
1931	2 402	2 369	...	...	...
1930	2 533	2 506	...	...	...
1929	2 532	2 506	...	...	...
1928	2 660	2 632	...	...	...
1927	2 824	2 783	...	...	...
1926	2 901	2 839	...	...	...
1925	3 012	2 949	...	...	...
1924	3 121	3 069	...	...	...
1923	3 101	3 063	...	...	...
1922	3 109	3 072	...	...	...
1921	3 326	3 282	...	...	...
1920	3 263	3 219	...	...	...
1919	3 068	3 025	...	...	...
1918	3 312	3 288	...	...	...
1917	3 333	3 312	...	...	...

Source: U.S. National Center for Health Statistics. *National Vital Statistics Reports.*
Note: 1972–1984 Fertility rates are based on 100 percent of births in selected states and on a 50 percent sample of births in all other states. 1970 and 1971 rates are based on a 50 percent sample of births.
[1]For 1970–1991 this category includes births to races not shown separately. For 1992 and later years, unknown race of mother is imputed.
[2]Includes births to Aleuts and Eskimos.
. . . = Not available.

Table 3-4. Birth Rates of Unmarried Women Ages 15–44 Years, by Age of Mother, 1940–2004

(Rates are live births to unmarried females per 1,000 unmarried females in specified group.)

Year	Births (thousands)	Birth rates						
		15–44 years[1]	15–19 years	20–24 years	25–29 years	30–34 years	35–39 years	40–44 years[2]
2004	1 470	46.1	34.7	72.5	68.6	47.0	23.5	6.0
2003	1 416	44.9	34.8	71.2	65.7	44.0	22.3	5.8
2002	1 366	43.7	35.4	70.5	61.5	40.8	20.8	5.4
2001	1 349	43.8	37.0	71.3	59.5	40.4	20.4	5.3
2000	1 347	44.0	39.0	72.2	58.5	39.3	19.7	5.0
1999	1 308	43.3	39.7	70.8	56.9	38.1	19.0	4.6
1998	1 294	43.3	40.9	70.4	55.4	38.1	18.7	4.6
1997	1 257	42.9	41.4	68.9	53.4	37.9	18.7	4.6
1996	1 260	43.8	42.2	68.9	54.5	40.2	19.9	4.8
1995	1 254	44.3	43.8	68.7	54.3	38.9	19.3	4.7
1994	1 290	46.2	45.8	70.9	57.4	39.6	19.7	4.7
1993	1 240	44.8	44.0	68.5	55.9	38.0	18.9	4.4
1992	1 225	44.9	44.2	67.9	55.6	37.6	18.8	4.1
1991	1 214	45.0	44.6	67.8	56.0	37.9	17.9	3.8
1990	1 165	43.8	42.5	65.1	56.0	37.6	17.3	3.6
1989	1 094	41.6	40.1	61.2	52.8	34.9	16.0	3.4
1988	1 005	38.5	36.4	56.0	48.5	32.0	15.0	3.2
1987	933	36.0	33.8	52.6	44.5	29.6	13.5	2.9
1986	878	34.2	32.3	49.3	42.2	27.2	12.2	2.7
1985	828	32.8	31.4	46.5	39.9	25.2	11.6	2.5
1984	770	31.0	30.0	43.0	37.1	23.3	10.9	2.5
1983	738	30.3	29.5	41.8	35.5	22.4	10.2	2.6
1982	715	30.0	28.7	41.5	35.1	21.9	10.0	2.7
1981	687	29.5	27.9	41.1	34.5	20.8	9.8	2.6
1980[3]	666	29.4	27.6	40.9	34.0	21.1	9.7	2.6
1980[3,4]	448	28.4	27.5	39.7	31.4	18.5	8.4	2.3
1975[4]	399	24.5	23.9	31.2	27.5	17.9	9.1	2.6
1970[4]	361	26.4	22.4	38.4	37.0	27.1	13.6	3.5
1969	361	25.0	20.1	37.4	38.1	27.4	13.6	3.6
1968	339	24.4	19.8	37.3	38.6	28.2	14.9	3.8
1967	318	23.9	18.6	38.3	41.4	29.2	15.4	4.0
1966	302	23.4	17.5	39.1	45.6	33.0	16.4	4.1
1965	291	23.5	16.7	39.9	49.3	37.5	17.4	4.5
1964	276	23.0	15.8	39.9	50.2	37.2	16.3	4.4
1963	259	22.5	15.2	40.3	49.0	33.2	16.1	4.3
1962	245	21.9	14.8	40.9	46.7	29.7	15.6	4.0
1961	240	22.7	15.9	41.7	46.5	28.3	15.4	3.9
1960	224	21.6	15.3	39.7	45.1	27.8	14.1	3.6
1959	221	21.9	15.5	40.2	44.1	28.1	14.1	3.3
1958	209	21.2	15.3	38.2	40.5	27.5	13.3	3.2
1957	202	21.0	15.8	37.3	36.8	26.8	12.1	3.1
1956	194	20.4	15.6	36.4	35.6	24.6	11.1	2.8
1955	183	19.3	15.1	33.5	33.5	22.0	10.5	2.7
1954	177	18.7	14.9	31.4	31.0	20.4	10.3	2.5
1953	161	16.9	13.9	28.0	27.6	17.3	9.0	2.4
1952	150	15.8	13.5	25.4	24.8	15.7	8.2	1.9
1951	147	15.1	13.2	23.2	22.8	14.6	7.6	2.2
1950	142	14.1	12.6	21.3	19.9	13.3	7.2	2.0
1949	133	13.3	12.0	21.0	18.0	11.4	6.8	1.9
1948	130	12.5	11.4	19.8	16.4	10.0	5.8	1.6
1947	132	12.1	11.0	18.9	15.7	9.2	5.6	1.8
1946	125	10.9	9.5	17.3	15.6	7.3	4.4	1.8
1945	117	10.1	9.5	15.3	12.1	7.1	4.1	1.6
1944	105	9.0	8.8	13.1	10.1	7.0	4.0	1.3
1943	98	8.3	8.4	11.4	8.8	6.7	3.8	1.3
1942	97	8.0	8.2	11.0	8.4	6.3	3.8	1.2
1941	96	7.8	8.0	10.5	7.8	6.0	3.7	1.4
1940	90	7.1	7.4	9.5	7.2	5.1	3.4	1.2

Source: U.S. National Center for Health Statistics. *National Vital Statistics Reports, Births: Final Data for 2004.*
Note: Rates for 1980–2002 based on 100 percent of births in selected states and on a 50 percent sample of births in all other states. For 1975–1984 births to unmarried women are estimated for the United States from data for registration areas in which marital status of mother was reported. 1970 Rates based on a 50 percent sample of births.
[1]Rates computed by relating total births to unmarried mothers, regardless of age of mother, to unmarried women aged 15–44 years.
[2]Rates computed by relating births to unmarried mothers aged 40 years and over to unmarried women aged 40–44 years.
[3]In 1980 rates were computed both by previous method of classifying birth rates based on race of child and the new method based on race of mother.
[4]Data for states in which marital status was not reported have been inferred and included with data from the remaining states.

Table 3-5. Expectation of Life at Birth, by Race and Sex, 1900–2015

(Years. Prior to 1929, for death-registration only.)

Year	Total			White			Black[1]		
	Both sexes	Male	Female	Both sexes	Male	Female	Both sexes	Male	Female
Projection									
2015	79.2	76.2	82.2	80.9	78.0	83.8	75.5	71.9	78.9
2010	78.5	75.6	81.4	79.0	76.1	81.8	74.5	70.9	77.8
Estimate									
2004[2]	77.9	75.2	80.4	78.3	75.7	80.8	73.3	69.8	76.5
2003	77.5	74.8	80.1	78.0	75.3	70.5	72.7	69.0	76.1
2002	77.3	74.5	79.9	77.7	75.1	80.3	73.3	69.8	76.5
2001	77.2	74.4	79.8	77.7	75.0	80.2	72.2	68.6	75.5
2000	77.0	74.3	79.7	77.6	74.9	80.1	71.9	68.3	75.2
1999	76.7	73.9	79.4	77.3	74.6	79.9	71.4	67.8	74.7
1998	76.7	73.8	79.5	77.3	74.5	80.0	71.3	67.6	74.8
1997	76.5	73.6	79.4	77.1	74.3	79.9	71.1	67.2	74.7
1996	76.1	73.1	79.1	76.8	73.9	79.7	70.2	66.1	74.2
1995	75.8	72.5	78.9	76.5	73.4	79.6	69.6	65.2	73.9
1990	75.7	72.4	79.0	76.5	73.3	79.6	69.5	64.9	73.9
1989	75.5	72.2	78.8	76.3	73.1	79.5	69.2	64.6	73.7
1988	75.8	72.3	79.1	76.5	73.2	79.8	69.6	65.0	73.9
1987	75.5	72.0	78.9	76.3	72.9	79.6	69.3	64.6	73.8
1986	75.4	71.8	78.8	76.1	72.7	79.4	69.1	64.5	73.6
1985	75.1	71.7	78.5	75.9	72.5	79.2	68.8	64.3	73.3
1984	74.9	71.4	78.3	75.6	72.2	78.9	68.9	64.4	73.2
1983	74.9	71.4	78.3	75.6	72.1	78.9	69.1	64.7	73.4
1982	74.7	71.2	78.2	75.4	71.9	78.8	69.1	64.8	73.4
1981	74.7	71.1	78.2	75.3	71.8	78.7	69.3	65.0	73.4
1980	74.7	71.1	78.2	75.3	71.8	78.7	69.5	65.3	73.6
1979	74.6	71.0	78.1	75.2	71.6	78.7	69.4	65.2	73.5
1978	74.5	70.8	78.1	75.1	71.5	78.7	69.4	65.1	73.6
1977	74.1	70.4	77.8	74.8	71.1	78.4	68.9	64.5	73.2
1976	73.7	70.0	77.4	74.4	70.7	78.1	68.1	63.8	72.5
1975	72.6	68.8	76.6	73.4	69.5	77.3	66.8	62.4	71.3
1974	71.9	68.1	75.8	72.7	68.9	76.6	67.6	62.9	71.3
1973	71.3	67.6	75.3	72.2	68.4	76.1	65.9	61.9	70.1
1972	71.1	67.4	75.1	72.0	68.3	75.9	65.6	61.5	69.9
1971	71.1	67.4	75.0	72.0	68.3	75.8	65.6	61.6	69.7
1970	70.9	67.1	74.8	71.7	68.0	75.6	65.3	61.3	69.4
1969	70.5	66.8	74.3	71.3	67.8	75.1	64.3	60.5	68.4
1968	70.2	66.6	74.0	71.1	67.5	74.9	63.7	60.1	67.5
1967	70.5	67.0	74.2	71.3	67.8	75.1	64.6	61.1	68.2
1966	70.1	66.7	73.8	71.0	67.6	74.7	64.0	60.7	67.4
1965	70.2	66.8	73.7	71.0	67.6	74.7	64.1	61.1	67.4
1964	70.2	66.9	73.7	71.0	67.7	74.6	64.1	61.1	67.2
1963	69.9	66.6	73.4	70.8	67.5	74.4	63.6	60.9	66.5
1962	70.0	66.8	73.4	70.9	67.6	74.4	64.1	61.5	66.8
1961	70.2	67.0	73.6	71.0	67.8	74.5	64.4	61.9	67.0
1960*	69.7	66.6	73.1	70.6	67.4	74.1	63.6	61.1	66.3
1959	69.9	66.8	73.2	70.7	67.5	74.2	63.9	61.3	66.5
1958	69.6	66.6	72.9	70.5	67.4	73.9	63.4	61.0	65.8
1957	69.5	66.4	72.7	70.3	67.7	73.7	63.0	60.7	65.5
1956	69.7	66.7	72.9	70.5	67.5	73.9	63.6	61.3	66.1
1955	69.6	66.7	72.8	70.5	67.4	73.7	63.7	61.4	66.1
1954	69.6	66.7	72.8	70.5	67.5	73.7	63.4	61.1	65.9
1953	68.8	66.0	72.0	69.7	66.8	73.0	62.0	59.7	64.5
1952	68.6	65.8	71.6	69.5	66.6	72.6	61.4	59.1	63.8
1951	68.4	65.6	71.4	69.3	66.5	72.4	61.2	59.2	63.4
1950	68.2	65.6	71.1	69.1	66.5	72.2	60.8	59.1	62.9
1949	68.0	65.2	70.7	68.8	66.2	71.9	60.6	58.9	62.7
1948	67.2	64.6	69.9	68.0	65.5	71.0	60.0	58.1	62.5
1947	66.8	64.4	69.7	67.6	65.2	70.5	59.7	57.9	61.9
1946	66.7	64.4	69.4	67.5	65.1	70.3	59.1	57.5	61.0
1945	65.9	63.6	67.9	66.8	64.4	69.5	57.7	56.1	59.6
1944	65.2	63.6	66.8	66.2	64.5	68.4	56.6	55.8	57.7
1943	63.3	62.4	64.4	64.2	63.2	65.7	55.6	55.4	56.1
1942	66.2	64.7	67.9	67.3	65.9	69.4	56.6	55.4	58.2
1941	64.8	63.1	66.8	66.2	64.4	68.5	53.8	52.5	55.3

[1] Before 1970, Black and others.
[2] Preliminary data.
* = First year for which figures include Alaska and Hawaii.

Table 3-5. Expectation of Life at Birth, by Race and Sex, 1900–2015—*Continued*

(Years. Prior to 1929, for death-registration only.)

Year	Total			White			Black[1]		
	Both sexes	Male	Female	Both sexes	Male	Female	Both sexes	Male	Female
1940	62.9	60.8	65.2	64.2	62.1	66.6	53.1	51.5	54.9
1939	63.7	62.1	65.4	64.9	63.3	66.6	54.5	53.2	56.0
1938	63.5	61.9	65.3	65.0	63.2	66.8	52.9	51.7	54.3
1937	60.0	58.0	62.4	61.4	59.3	63.8	50.3	48.3	52.5
1936	58.5	56.6	60.6	59.8	58.0	61.9	49.0	47.0	51.4
1935	61.7	59.9	63.9	62.9	61.0	65.0	53.1	51.3	55.2
1934	61.1	59.3	63.3	62.4	50.6	64.6	51.8	50.2	53.7
1933	63.3	61.7	65.1	64.3	62.7	66.3	54.7	53.5	56.0
1932	62.1	61.0	63.5	63.2	62.0	64.5	53.7	52.8	54.6
1931	61.1	59.4	63.1	62.6	60.8	64.7	50.4	49.5	51.5
1930	59.7	58.1	61.6	61.4	59.7	63.5	48.1	47.3	49.2
1929	57.1	55.8	58.7	58.6	57.2	60.3	46.7	45.7	47.8
1928	56.8	55.6	58.3	58.4	57.0	60.0	46.3	45.6	47.0
1927	60.4	59.0	62.1	62.0	60.5	63.9	48.2	47.6	48.9
1926	56.7	55.5	58.0	58.2	57.0	59.6	44.6	43.7	45.6
1925	59.0	57.6	60.6	60.7	59.3	62.4	45.7	44.9	46.7
1924	59.7	58.1	61.5	61.4	59.8	63.4	46.6	45.5	47.8
1923	57.2	56.1	58.5	58.3	57.1	59.6	48.3	47.7	48.9
1922	59.6	58.4	61.0	60.4	59.1	61.9	52.4	51.8	53.0
1921	60.8	60.0	61.8	61.8	60.8	62.9	51.5	51.6	51.3
1920	54.1	53.6	54.6	54.9	54.4	55.6	45.3	45.5	45.2
1919	54.7	53.5	56.0	55.8	54.5	57.4	44.5	44.5	44.4
1918	39.1	36.6	42.2	39.8	37.1	43.2	31.1	29.9	32.5
1917	50.9	48.4	54.0	52.0	49.3	55.3	38.8	37.0	40.8
1916	51.7	49.6	54.3	52.5	50.2	55.2	41.3	39.6	43.1
1915	54.5	52.5	56.8	55.1	53.1	57.5	38.9	37.5	40.5
1914	54.2	52.0	56.8	54.9	52.7	57.5	38.9	37.1	40.8
1913	52.5	50.3	55.0	53.0	50.8	55.7	38.4	36.7	40.3
1912	53.5	51.5	55.9	53.9	51.9	56.2	37.9	35.9	40.0
1911	52.6	50.9	54.4	53.0	51.3	54.9	36.4	34.6	38.2
1910	50.0	48.4	51.8	50.3	48.6	52.0	35.6	33.8	37.5
1909	52.1	50.5	53.8	52.5	50.9	54.2	35.7	34.2	37.3
1908	51.1	49.5	52.8	51.5	49.9	53.3	34.9	33.8	36.0
1907	47.6	45.6	49.9	48.1	46.0	50.4	32.5	31.1	34.0
1906	48.7	46.9	50.8	49.3	47.3	51.4	32.9	31.8	33.9
1905	48.7	47.3	50.2	49.1	47.6	50.6	31.3	29.6	33.1
1904	47.6	46.2	49.1	48.0	46.6	49.5	30.8	29.1	32.7
1903	50.5	49.1	52.0	50.9	49.5	52.5	33.1	31.7	34.6
1902	51.5	49.8	53.4	51.9	50.2	53.8	34.6	32.9	36.4
1901	49.1	47.6	50.6	49.4	48.0	51.0	33.7	32.2	35.3
1900	47.3	46.3	48.3	47.6	46.6	48.7	33.0	32.5	33.5

Source: U.S. National Center for Health Statistics. *National Vital Statistics Reports, Births: Final Data for 2004.*
[1]Before 1970, Black and others.
[2]Preliminary data.
* = First year for which figures include Alaska and Hawaii.
. . . = Not available.

Table 3-6. Fetal Death Ratio and Neonatal, Infant, and Maternal Mortality Rates, by Race, 1915–2003

(Prior to 1933, for registration area only.)

Year	Fetal death ratio per 1,000 live births			Neonatal mortality rate[1] per 1,000 live births			Infant mortality rate[2] per 1,000 live births			Maternal mortality rate per 100,000 live births		
	Total	White	Black and other	Total	White	Black and other	Total	White	Black and other	Total	White	Black and other
2003	...	...	...	4.6	3.9	7.4	6.9	5.7	11.1	12.1[3]	8.7[3]	24.9[3]
2002	...	...	...	4.7	3.9	7.5	7.0	5.8	11.4	8.9	6.0	19.7
2001	...	...	...	4.5	3.8	7.4	6.8	5.7	11.3	9.9	7.2	20.2
2000	...	...	...	4.6	3.8	7.6	6.9	5.7	11.4	9.8	7.5	18.0
1999	...	...	...	4.7	3.9	7.9	7.1	5.8	11.9	9.9	6.8	21.4
1998	...	...	...	4.8	4.0	7.9	7.2	6.0	11.9	7.1	5.1	14.9
1997	...	...	...	4.8	4.0	7.7	7.2	6.0	11.8	8.4	5.8	18.3
1996	...	...	...	4.8	4.0	7.9	7.3	6.1	12.2	7.6	5.1	16.9
1995	...	...	...	4.9	4.1	8.1	7.6	6.3	12.6	7.1	4.2	18.5
1994	...	...	...	5.1	4.2	8.6	8.0	6.6	13.5	8.3	6.2	16.2
1993	...	...	...	5.3	4.3	9.0	8.4	6.8	14.1	7.5	4.8	17.6
1992	7.4	6.3	11.7	5.4	4.3	9.2	8.5	6.9	14.4	7.8	5.0	18.2
1991	...	...	...	5.6	4.5	9.5	8.9	7.3	15.1	7.9	5.8	15.6
1990	7.5	6.4	11.9	5.8	4.8	9.9	9.2	7.6	15.5	8.2	5.4	19.1
1989	7.5	6.4	11.4	6.2	5.1	10.3	9.8	8.1	16.3	7.9	5.6	16.5
1988	7.5	6.4	11.4	6.3	5.3	10.3	10.0	8.4	16.1	8.4	5.9	17.4
1987	7.7	6.7	11.5	6.5	5.4	10.7	10.1	8.5	16.5	6.6	5.1	12.0
1986	7.7	6.8	11.2	6.7	5.7	10.8	10.4	8.8	16.7	7.2	4.9	16.0
1985	7.9	7.0	11.3	7.0	6.0	11.0	10.6	9.2	16.8	7.8	5.2	18.1
1984	8.2	7.4	11.5	7.0	6.1	10.9	10.8	9.3	17.1	7.8	5.4	16.9
1983	8.5	7.5	12.4	7.3	6.3	11.4	11.2	9.6	17.8	8.0	5.9	16.3
1982	8.9	7.9	12.7	7.7	6.7	12.0	11.5	9.9	18.3	7.9	5.8	16.4
1981	9.0	8.0	12.8	8.0	7.0	12.5	11.9	10.3	18.8	8.5	6.3	17.3
1980	9.2	8.2	13.4	8.5	7.4	13.2	12.6	10.9	20.2	9.2	6.7	19.8
1979	9.4	8.4	13.8	8.9	7.9	12.9	13.1	11.4	19.8	9.6	6.4	22.7
1978	9.7	8.5	14.7	9.5	8.4	14.0	13.8	12.0	21.1	9.6	6.4	23.0
1977	9.9	8.7	14.6	9.9	8.7	14.7	14.1	12.3	21.7	11.2	7.7	26.0
1976	10.5	9.3	15.2	10.9	9.7	16.3	15.2	13.3	23.5	12.3	9.0	26.5
1975	10.7	9.5	16.0	11.6	10.4	16.8	16.1	14.2	24.2	12.8	9.1	29.0
1974	11.5	10.2	17.0	12.3	11.1	17.2	16.7	14.8	24.9	14.6	10.0	35.1
1973	12.2	10.8	18.6	13.0	11.8	17.9	17.7	15.8	26.2	15.2	10.7	34.6
1972	12.7	11.2	19.5	13.6	12.4	19.2	18.5	16.4	27.7	18.8	14.3	38.5
1971	13.4	11.8	21.2	14.2	13.0	19.6	19.1	17.1	28.5	18.8	13.0	45.3
1970	14.2	12.4	22.6	15.1	13.8	21.4	20.0	17.8	30.9	2.2	1.4	5.6
1969	14.1	12.4	22.5	15.6	14.2	22.5	20.9	18.4	32.9	2.2	1.5	5.6
1968	15.8	13.8	25.6	16.1	14.7	23.0	21.8	19.2	34.5	2.5	1.7	6.4
1967	15.6	13.5	25.8	16.5	15.0	23.8	22.4	19.7	35.9	2.8	2.0	7.0
1966	15.7	13.6	26.1	17.2	15.6	24.8	23.7	20.6	38.8	2.9	2.0	7.2
1965	16.2	13.9	27.2	17.7	16.1	25.4	24.7	21.5	40.3	3.2	2.1	8.4
1964	16.4	14.1	28.2	17.9	16.2	26.5	24.8	21.6	41.1	3.3	2.2	9.0
1963	15.8	13.7	26.7	18.2	16.7	26.1	25.2	22.2	41.5	3.6	2.4	9.7
1962	15.9	13.9	26.7	18.3	16.9	26.1	25.3	22.3	41.4	3.5	2.4	9.6
1961	16.1	14.1	27.0	18.4	16.9	26.2	25.3	22.4	40.7	3.7	2.5	10.1
1960*	16.1	14.1	26.8	18.7	17.2	26.9	26.0	22.9	43.2	3.7	2.6	9.8
1959	16.2	14.2	27.3	19.0	17.5	27.7	26.4	23.2	44.0	3.7	2.6	10.2
1958	16.5	14.5	27.5	19.5	17.8	29.0	27.1	23.8	45.7	3.8	2.6	10.2
1957	16.3	14.5	26.8	19.1	17.5	27.8	26.3	23.3	43.7	4.1	2.8	11.8
1956	16.5	14.6	27.2	18.9	17.5	27.0	26.0	23.2	42.1	4.1	2.9	11.1
1955	17.1	15.2	28.4	19.1	17.7	27.2	26.4	23.6	42.8	4.7	3.3	13.0
1954	17.5	15.5	28.9	19.1	17.8	27.0	26.6	23.9	42.9	5.2	3.7	14.4
1953	17.8	15.9	29.6	19.6	18.3	27.4	27.8	25.0	44.7	6.1	4.4	16.6
1952	18.3	16.1	32.2	19.8	18.5	28.0	28.4	25.5	47.0	6.8	4.9	18.8
1951	18.8	16.7	32.1	20.0	18.9	27.3	28.4	25.8	44.8	7.5	5.5	20.1
1950	19.2	17.1	32.5	20.5	19.4	27.5	29.2	26.8	44.5	8.3	6.1	22.2
1949	19.8	17.5	34.6	21.4	20.3	28.6	31.3	28.9	47.3	9.0	6.8	23.5
1948	20.6	18.3	36.5	22.2	21.2	29.1	32.0	29.9	46.5	11.7	8.9	30.1
1947	21.1	18.7	39.6	22.8	21.7	31.0	32.2	30.1	48.5	13.5	10.9	33.5
1946	22.8	20.4	40.9	24.0	23.1	31.5	33.8	31.8	49.5	15.7	13.1	35.9
1945	23.9	21.4	42.0	24.3	23.3	32.0	38.3	35.6	57.0	20.7	17.2	45.5
1944	27.0	24.5	45.4	24.7	23.6	32.5	39.8	36.9	60.3	22.8	18.9	50.6
1943	26.7	24.2	46.2	24.7	23.7	32.9	40.4	37.5	62.5	24.5	21.1	51.0
1942	28.2	25.5	49.3	25.7	24.5	34.6	40.4	37.3	64.6	25.9	22.2	54.4
1941	29.9	26.5	54.0	27.7	26.1	39.0	45.3	41.2	74.8	31.7	26.6	67.8

[1] Represents deaths of infants under 28 days old, exclusive of fetal deaths.
[2] Represents deaths of infants under 1 year old, exclusive of fetal deaths.
[3] Increase partially reflects the use of separate item on the death certificate on pregnancy status by an increasing number of states.
. . . = Not available.
* = First year for which figures include Alaska and Hawaii.

Table 3-6. Fetal Death Ratio and Neonatal, Infant, and Maternal Mortality Rates, by Race, 1915–2003—*Continued*

(Prior to 1933, for registration area only.)

Year	Fetal death ratio per 1,000 live births			Neonatal mortality rate[1] per 1,000 live births			Infant mortality rate[2] per 1,000 live births			Maternal mortality rate per 100,000 live births		
	Total	White	Black and other	Total	White	Black and other	Total	White	Black and other	Total	White	Black and other
1940	31.3	27.7	56.7	28.8	27.2	39.7	47.0	43.2	73.8	37.6	32.0	77.4
1939	32.0	28.2	59.0	29.3	27.8	39.6	48.0	44.3	74.2	40.4	35.3	76.2
1938	32.1	28.1	61.1	29.6	28.3	39.1	51.0	47.1	79.1	43.5	37.7	84.9
1937	33.4	29.2	63.2	31.3	29.7	42.1	54.4	50.3	83.2	48.9	43.6	85.8
1936	34.4	29.8	66.9	32.6	31.0	43.9	57.1	52.9	87.6	56.8	51.2	97.2
1935	35.8	31.1	68.7	32.4	31.0	42.7	55.7	51.9	83.2	58.2	53.1	94.6
1934	36.2	31.4	70.1	34.1	432.3	445.3	60.1	454.5	494.4	59.3	454.4	489.7
1933	37.0	32.2	71.1	34.0	432.1	445.8	58.1	452.8	491.3	61.9	456.4	496.7
1932	37.8	32.7	74.4	33.5	432.0	443.7	57.6	453.3	486.2	63.3	458.1	497.6
1931	38.2	33.4	74.1	34.6	33.2	45.2	61.6	57.4	93.1	66.1	60.1	111.4
1930	39.2	34.0	79.9	35.7	34.2	47.4	64.6	60.1	99.9	67.3	60.9	117.4
1929	39.5	34.4	79.7	36.9	35.6	47.3	67.6	63.2	102.2	69.5	63.1	119.9
1928	40.2	35.0	81.5	37.2	35.7	48.8	68.7	64.0	106.2	69.2	62.7	121.0
1927	38.8	34.8	74.8	36.1	35.0	46.1	64.6	60.6	100.1	64.7	59.4	113.3
1926	38.1	35.1	73.0	37.9	37.1	48.0	73.3	70.0	111.8	65.6	61.9	107.1
1925	38.1	35.1	73.1	37.8	36.8	49.5	71.7	68.3	110.8	64.7	60.3	116.2
1924	39.3	35.8	76.2	38.6	37.4	51.2	70.8	66.8	112.9	65.6	60.7	117.9
1923	38.9	35.9	71.8	39.5	38.6	49.9	77.1	73.5	117.4	66.5	62.6	109.5
1922	39.4	36.4	73.4	39.7	38.8	49.9	76.2	73.2	110.0	66.4	62.8	106.8
1921	...	...	...	39.7	38.7	50.3	75.6	72.5	108.5	68.2	64.4	107.7
1920	...	...	...	41.5	40.4	55.0	85.8	82.1	131.7	79.9	76.0	128.1
1919	...	...	...	41.5	40.3	55.2	86.6	83.0	130.5	73.7	69.6	124.4
1918	...	...	...	44.2	43.3	60.5	100.9	97.4	161.2	91.6	88.9	139.3
1917	...	...	...	43.4	42.6	58.0	93.8	90.5	150.7	66.2	63.2	117.7
1916	...	...	...	44.1	43.5	68.9	101.0	99.0	184.9	62.2	60.8	117.9
1915	...	...	...	44.4	...	...	99.9	98.6	181.2	60.8	60.1	105.6

Source: U.S. National Center for Health Statistics. *Vital Statistics of the United States,* annual; *National Vital Statistics Report (NSVR)* and the U.S. Census Bureau. *Statistical Abstract of the United States: 2007.*
[1]Represents deaths of infants under 28 days old, exclusive of fetal deaths.
[2]Represents deaths of infants under 1 year old, exclusive of fetal deaths.
. . . = Not available.

Table 3-7. Number of Deaths, Death Rates, and Age-Adjusted Death Rates, by Race and Sex, Selected Years, 1940–2004

(Number, rate per 100,000 population.)

Year	All races[1] Both sexes	Male	Female	White Both sexes	Male	Female	Black Both sexes	Male	Female	American Indian[2] Both sexes	Male	Female	Asian or Pacific Islander[3] Both sexes	Male	Female
Number of Deaths															
2004[4]	2 398 000	1 180 000	1 218 000	2 060 000	1 007 000	1 053 000	285 000	145 000	140 000	13 000	7 000	6 000	40 000	21 000	19 000
2003	2 448 288	1 201 964	1 246 324	2 103 714	1 025 650	1 078 064	291 300	148 022	143 278	13 147	7 106	6 041	40 127	21 186	18 941
2002	2 443 387	1 199 264	1 244 123	2 102 589	1 025 196	1 077 393	290 051	146 835	143 216	12 415	6 750	5 665	38 332	20 483	17 849
2001	2 416 425	1 183 421	1 233 004	2 079 691	1 011 218	1 068 473	287 709	145 908	141 801	11 977	6 466	5 511	37 048	19 829	17 219
2000	2 403 351	1 177 578	1 225 773	2 071 287	1 007 191	1 064 096	285 826	145 184	140 642	11 363	6 185	5 178	34 875	19 018	15 857
1999	2 391 399	1 175 460	1 215 939	2 061 348	1 005 335	1 056 013	285 064	145 703	139 361	11 312	6 092	5 220	33 675	18 330	15 345
1998	2 337 256	1 157 260	1 179 996	2 015 984	990 190	1 025 794	278 440	143 417	135 023	10 845	5 994	4 851	31 987	17 659	14 328
1997	2 314 245	1 154 039	1 160 206	1 996 393	986 884	1 009 509	276 520	144 110	132 410	10 576	5 985	4 591	30 756	17 060	13 696
1996	2 314 690	1 163 569	1 151 121	1 992 966	991 984	1 000 982	282 089	149 472	132 617	10 127	5 563	4 564	29 508	16 550	12 958
1995	2 312 132	1 172 959	1 139 173	1 987 437	997 277	990 160	286 401	154 175	132 226	9 997	5 574	4 423	28 297	15 933	12 364
1994	2 278 994	1 162 747	1 116 247	1 959 875	988 823	971 052	282 379	153 019	129 360	9 637	5 497	4 140	27 103	15 408	11 695
1993	2 268 553	1 161 797	1 106 756	1 951 437	988 329	963 108	282 151	153 502	128 649	9 579	5 434	4 145	25 386	14 532	10 854
1992	2 175 613	1 122 336	1 053 277	1 873 781	956 957	916 824	269 219	146 630	122 589	8 953	5 181	3 772	23 660	13 568	10 092
1991	2 169 518	1 121 665	1 047 853	1 868 904	956 497	912 407	269 525	147 331	122 194	8 621	4 948	3 673	22 173	12 727	9 446
1990	2 148 463	1 113 417	1 035 046	1 853 254	950 812	902 442	265 498	145 359	120 139	8 316	4 877	3 439	21 127	12 211	8 916
1989	2 150 466	1 114 190	1 036 276	1 853 841	950 852	902 989	267 642	146 393	121 249	8 614	5 066	3 548	20 042	11 688	8 354
1988	2 167 999	1 125 540	1 042 459	1 876 906	965 419	911 487	264 019	144 228	119 791	7 917	4 617	3 300	18 963	11 155	7 808
1987	2 123 323	1 107 958	1 015 365	1 843 067	953 382	889 685	254 814	139 551	115 263	7 602	4 432	3 170	17 689	10 496	7 193
1986	2 105 361	1 104 005	1 001 356	1 831 083	952 554	878 529	250 326	137 214	113 112	7 301	4 365	2 936	16 514	9 795	6 719
1985	2 086 440	1 097 758	988 682	1 819 054	950 455	868 599	244 207	133 610	110 597	7 154	4 181	2 973	15 887	9 441	6 446
1984	2 039 369	1 076 514	962 855	1 781 897	934 529	847 368	235 884	129 147	106 737	6 949	4 117	2 832	14 483	8 627	5 856
1983	2 019 201	1 071 923	947 278	1 765 582	931 779	833 803	233 124	127 911	105 213	6 839	4 064	2 775	13 554	8 126	5 428
1982	1 974 797	1 056 440	918 357	1 729 085	919 239	809 846	226 513	125 610	100 903	6 679	3 974	2 705	12 430	7 564	4 866
1981	1 977 981	1 063 752	914 209	1 731 233	925 490	805 743	228 560	127 296	101 264	6 608	4 016	2 592	11 475	6 908	4 567
1980	1 989 841	1 075 078	914 763	1 738 607	933 878	804 729	233 135	130 138	102 997	6 923	4 193	2 730	11 071	6 809	4 262
1970	1 921 031	1 078 478	842 553	1 682 096	942 437	739 659	225 647	127 540	98 107	5 675	3 391	2 284	...	...	...
1960	1 711 982	975 648	736 334	1 505 335	860 857	644 478	196 010	107 701	88 309	4 528	2 658	1 870	...	...	...
1950	1 452 454	827 749	624 705	1 276 085	731 366	544 719	169 606	92 004	77 602	4 440	2 497	1 943	...	...	...
1940	1 417 269	791 003	626 266	1 231 223	690 901	540 322	178 743	95 517	83 226	4 791	2 527	2 264	...	...	...
Death Rate															
2004[4]	820.0	820.0	820.0	860.0	850.0	870.0	740.0	780.0	700.0	410.0	450.0	380.0	300.0	320.0	280.0
2003	841.9	840.3	843.4	890.1	877.6	902.3	763.6	813.7	717.9	422.6	457.6	387.7	303.9	330.0	279.2
2002	847.3	846.6	848.0	895.7	884.0	907.0	768.4	816.7	724.4	403.6	439.6	367.7	299.5	331.4	269.7
2001	848.5	846.4	850.4	895.1	881.9	907.9	773.5	823.9	727.7	392.1	424.2	360.2	303.8	335.0	274.4
2000	854.0	853.0	855.0	900.2	887.8	912.3	781.1	834.1	733.0	380.8	415.6	346.1	296.6	332.9	262.3
1999	857.0	859.2	854.9	901.4	892.1	910.4	788.1	847.4	734.3	399.3	431.8	367.1	296.8	333.2	262.5
1998	847.3	856.4	838.5	889.5	887.3	891.6	782.3	848.2	722.6	397.8	441.9	354.2	293.8	335.4	254.9
1997	848.8	864.6	833.6	889.1	893.3	885.0	789.9	867.1	720.1	402.7	458.2	347.7	294.1	336.8	253.9
1996	859.2	882.8	836.7	896.0	907.1	885.3	819.7	915.3	733.3	399.5	441.5	358.0	294.4	340.2	251.1
1995	868.3	900.8	837.2	901.8	921.0	883.2	846.2	960.2	743.2	409.4	459.4	360.1	294.6	341.4	250.4
1994	866.1	904.2	829.7	897.8	922.6	873.8	849.0	970.2	739.7	408.2	468.8	348.3	294.6	344.0	247.7
1993	872.8	915.0	832.5	902.7	931.8	874.6	864.6	992.2	749.6	419.8	479.6	360.7	288.0	338.1	240.3
1992	848.1	896.1	802.4	875.8	912.2	840.8	841.8	967.6	728.6	406.6	474.1	340.0	282.1	331.1	235.3
1991	857.6	908.8	808.7	883.2	922.7	845.2	861.4	994.8	741.4	405.3	468.9	342.7	278.7	326.9	232.4
1990	863.8	918.4	812.0	888.0	930.9	846.9	871.0	1 008.0	747.9	402.8	476.4	330.4	283.3	334.3	234.3
1989	871.3	926.3	818.9	893.2	936.5	851.8	887.9	1 026.7	763.2	430.5	510.7	351.3	280.9	334.5	229.4
1988	886.7	945.1	831.2	910.5	957.9	865.3	888.3	1 026.1	764.6	411.7	485.0	339.9	282.0	339.0	227.4
1987	876.4	939.3	816.7	900.1	952.7	849.8	868.9	1 006.2	745.7	410.7	483.8	339.0	278.9	338.3	222.0
1986	876.7	944.7	812.3	900.1	958.6	844.3	864.9	1 002.6	741.5	409.5	494.9	325.9	276.2	335.1	219.9
1985	876.9	948.6	809.1	900.4	963.6	840.1	854.8	989.3	734.2	416.4	492.5	342.5	283.4	344.6	224.9
1984	864.8	938.8	794.7	887.8	954.1	824.6	836.1	968.5	717.4	419.6	502.7	338.4	275.9	336.5	218.1
1983	863.7	943.2	788.4	885.4	957.7	816.4	836.6	971.2	715.9	428.5	515.1	343.9	276.1	339.1	216.1
1982	852.4	938.4	771.2	873.1	951.8	798.2	823.4	966.2	695.5	434.5	522.9	348.1	271.3	338.3	207.4
1981	862.0	954.0	775.0	880.4	965.2	799.8	842.4	992.6	707.7	445.6	547.9	345.6	272.3	336.2	211.5
1980	878.3	976.9	785.3	892.5	983.3	806.1	875.4	1 034.1	733.3	487.4	597.1	380.1	296.9	375.3	222.5
1970	945.3	1 090.3	807.8	946.3	1 086.7	812.6	999.3	1 186.6	829.2	...	...	...	...	...	...
1960	954.7	1 104.5	809.2	947.8	1 098.5	800.9	1 038.6	1 181.7	905.0	...	...	...	...	...	...
1950	963.8	1 106.1	823.5	945.7	1 089.5	803.3	...	...	...	...	...	...	...	...	...
1940	1 076.4	1 197.4	954.6	1 041.5	1 162.2	919.4	...	...	...	...	...	...	...	...	...

Note: Rates are based on populations enumerated as of April 1st for census years and estimated as of July 1st for all other years. Beginning 1970, excludes deaths of non-residents of the United States. Data for specified races other than white and black should be interpreted with caution because of inconsistencies between reporting race on death certificates and on censuses and surveys. California, Hawaii, Idaho, Maine, Montana, New York and Wisconsin reported multiple-race data in 2003. The multiple-race data for these states were bridged to the single race categories of the 1977 Office of Management and Budget standards for comparability with other states.

[1]For 1940–1991 includes deaths among races not shown separately; beginning in 1992 records coded as "other races" and records for which race was unknown, not stated, or not classifiable were assigned to the race of the previous record.
[2]Includes Aleuts and Eskimos.
[3]Includes Chinese, Filipino, Hawaiian, Japanese, and Other Asian or Pacific Islander.
[4]Preliminary data.
... = Not available.

Table 3-7. Number of Deaths, Death Rates, and Age-Adjusted Death Rates, by Race and Sex, Selected Years, 1940–2004—*Continued*

(Number, rate per 100,000 population.)

Year	All races[1]			White			Black			American Indian[2]			Asian or Pacific Islander[3]		
	Both sexes	Male	Female	Both sexes	Male	Female	Both sexes	Male	Female	Both sexes	Male	Female	Both sexes	Male	Female
Age-Adjusted Death Rate															
2004[4]	800.0	960.0	680.0	790.0	940.0	670.0	1020.0	1260.0	850.0	650.0	750.0	560.0	450.0	530.0	380.0
2003	832.7	994.3	706.2	817.0	973.9	693.1	1,065.9	1,319.1	885.6	685.0	797.0	592.1	465.7	562.7	392.7
2002	845.3	1,013.7	715.2	829.0	992.9	701.3	1,083.3	1,341.4	901.8	677.4	794.2	581.1	474.4	578.4	395.9
2001	854.5	1 029.1	721.8	836.5	1 006.1	706.7	1 101.2	1 375.0	912.5	686.7	798.9	594.0	492.1	597.4	412.0
2000	869.0	1 053.8	731.4	849.8	1 029.4	715.3	1 121.4	1 403.5	927.6	709.3	841.5	604.5	506.4	624.2	416.8
1999	875.6	1 067.0	734.0	854.6	1 040.0	716.6	1 135.7	1 432.6	933.6	780.9	925.9	668.2	519.7	641.2	427.5
1998	870.6	1 069.4	724.7	849.3	1 042.0	707.3	1 127.8	1 430.5	921.6	770.4	943.9	640.5	522.4	646.9	426.7
1997	878.1	1 088.1	725.6	855.7	1 059.1	707.8	1 139.8	1 458.8	922.1	774.0	974.8	625.3	531.8	660.2	432.6
1996	894.1	1 115.7	733.0	869.0	1 082.9	713.6	1 178.4	1 524.2	940.3	763.6	924.8	641.7	543.2	676.1	439.6
1995	909.8	1 143.9	739.4	882.3	1 107.5	718.7	1 213.9	1 585.7	955.9	771.2	932.0	643.9	554.8	693.4	446.7
1994	913.5	1 155.5	738.6	885.6	1 118.7	717.5	1 216.9	1 592.8	954.6	764.8	953.3	618.8	562.7	702.5	452.1
1993	926.1	1 177.3	745.9	897.0	1 138.9	724.1	1 241.2	1 632.2	969.5	796.4	1 006.3	641.6	565.8	709.9	450.4
1992	905.6	1 158.3	725.5	877.7	1 122.4	704.1	1 206.7	1 587.8	942.5	759.0	970.4	599.4	558.5	697.3	445.8
1991	922.3	1 180.5	738.2	893.2	1 143.1	716.1	1 235.4	1 626.1	963.3	763.9	970.6	608.3	566.2	703.4	453.2
1990	938.7	1 202.8	750.9	909.8	1 165.9	728.8	1 250.3	1 644.5	975.1	716.3	916.2	561.8	582.0	716.4	469.3
1989	950.5	1 215.0	761.8	920.2	1 176.6	738.8	1 275.5	1 670.1	998.1	761.6	999.8	586.3	581.3	729.6	458.4
1988	975.7	1 250.7	781.0	947.6	1 215.9	759.1	1 284.3	1 677.6	1 006.8	718.6	917.4	563.6	584.2	732.0	451.0
1987	970.0	1 246.1	774.2	943.4	1 213.4	753.3	1 263.1	1 650.3	989.7	719.8	899.3	583.7	577.3	732.4	448.1
1986	978.6	1 261.7	778.7	952.8	1 230.5	758.1	1 266.7	1 650.1	994.4	720.8	926.7	549.3	576.4	730.5	445.4
1985	988.1	1 278.1	784.5	963.6	1 249.8	764.3	1 261.2	1 634.5	994.4	731.7	926.1	577.2	586.5	755.4	456.7
1984	982.5	1 271.4	779.8	959.7	1 245.9	760.7	1 236.7	1 600.8	976.9	761.7	946.0	567.9	574.4	724.7	443.1
1983	990.0	1 284.5	783.3	967.3	1 259.4	763.9	1 240.5	1 600.7	980.7	757.3	945.0	605.5	565.1	718.8	428.8
1982	985.0	1 279.9	776.6	963.6	1 255.9	758.7	1 221.3	1 580.4	960.1	757.0	940.1	604.4	550.4	738.2	410.3
1981	1 007.1	1 308.2	792.7	984.0	1 282.2	773.6	1 258.4	1 626.6	986.6	784.6	1 030.2	588.0	544.7	710.3	405.3
1980	1 039.1	1 348.1	817.9	1 012.7	1 317.6	796.1	1 314.8	1 697.8	1 033.3	867.0	1 111.5	662.4	589.9	786.5	425.9
1970	1 222.6	1 542.1	971.4	1 193.3	1 513.7	944.0	1 518.1	1 873.9	1 228.7	...	...	...	...	...	...
1960	1 339.2	1 609.0	1 105.3	1 311.3	1 586.0	1 074.4	1 577.5	1 811.1	1 369.7	...	...	...	...	...	...
1950	1 446.0	1 674.2	1 236.0	1 410.8	1 642.5	1 198.0	...	...	...	...	...	...	...	...	...
1940	1 785.0	1 976.0	1 599.4	1 735.3	1 925.2	1 550.4	...	...	...	...	...	...	...	...	...

Source: National Center for Health Statistics. *Deaths: Final Data for 2003.* U.S. Census Bureau, *Statistical Abstract of the United States: 2007.*
Note: Rates are based on populations enumerated as of April 1st for census years and estimated as of July 1st for all other years. Beginning 1970, excludes deaths of non-residents of the United States. Data for specified races other than white and black should be interpreted with caution because of inconsistencies between reporting race on death certificates and on censuses and surveys. California, Hawaii, Idaho, Maine, Montana, New York and Wisconsin reported multiple-race data in 2003. The multiple-race data for these states were bridged to the single race categories of the 1977 Office of Management and Budget standards for comparability with other states.
[1]For 1940–1991 includes deaths among races not shown separately; beginning in 1992 records coded as "other races" and records for which race was unknown, not stated, or not classifiable were assigned to the race of the previous record.
[2]Includes Aleuts and Eskimos.
[3]Includes Chinese, Filipino, Hawaiian, Japanese, and Other Asian or Pacific Islander.
[4]Preliminary data.
. . . = Not available.

Table 3-8. Legal Abortions and Legal Abortion Ratios, by Selected Patient Characteristics, 1973–2003

(Data are based on reporting by state health departments and by hospitals and other medical facilities.)

Characteristic	1973	1975	1980	1981	1982	1983	1984	1985	1986	1987	1988	1989
Number of legal abortions reported in thousands												
Centers for Disease Control and Prevention	616	855	1,298	1,301	1,304	1,269	1,334	1,329	1,328	1,354	1,371	1,397
Alan Guttmacher Institute[4]	745	1,034	1,554	1,577	1,574	1,575	1,577	1,589	1,574	1,559	1,591	1,567
Abortions per 100 live births[5]												
Total	19.6	27.2	35.9	35.8	35.4	34.9	36.4	35.4	35.4	35.6	35.2	34.6
Age												
Under 15 years	123.7	119.3	139.7	126.4	120.0	148.6	143.9	137.6	116.3	127.5	94.9	88.6
15–19 years	53.9	54.2	71.4	66.8	66.5	72.7	69.7	68.8	65.0	66.8	62.4	56.0
20–24 years	29.4	28.9	39.5	37.9	38.0	40.6	39.9	38.6	38.0	38.6	37.4	36.6
25–29 years	20.7	19.2	23.7	23.2	23.5	24.0	22.6	21.7	22.1	21.8	21.4	21.1
30–34 years	28.0	25.0	23.7	23.7	23.0	22.6	20.0	19.9	19.8	19.6	18.8	18.7
35–39 years	45.1	42.2	41.0	40.3	37.1	36.1	33.4	33.6	31.3	29.7	28.0	27.1
40 years and over	68.4	66.8	80.7	77.6	75.0	70.7	64.0	62.3	59.0	55.5	51.4	49.6
Race												
White[6]	32.6	27.7	33.2	31.2	30.4	30.2	28.8	27.7	26.9	26.7	25.9	25.2
Black or African American[7]	42.0	47.6	54.3	54.4	55.6	49.7	47.5	47.2	48.8	50.0	48.9	49.6
Hispanic origin[8]												
Hispanic or Latino	…	…	…	…	…	…	…	…	…	…	…	…
Not Hispanic or Latino	…	…	…	…	…	…	…	…	…	…	…	…
Marital status												
Married	7.6	9.6	10.5	9.8	9.7	9.0	9.3	8.0	10.2	9.6	8.8	8.1
Unmarried	139.8	161.0	147.6	147.5	142.2	130.8	126.7	117.4	95.8	101.9	102.7	92.1
Previous live births[9]												
0	43.7	38.4	45.7	48.6	48.2	45.5	45.9	45.1	41.5	41.0	37.7	36.8
1	23.5	22.0	20.2	21.9	22.0	21.2	21.9	21.6	21.5	22.2	21.8	21.2
2	36.8	36.8	29.5	32.6	32.4	30.4	32.0	29.9	30.5	31.5	30.4	28.9
3	46.9	47.7	29.8	33.5	32.2	28.9	31.3	18.2	29.7	30.9	29.1	26.5
4 or more[10]	44.7	43.5	24.3	26.6	25.4	21.9	24.4	21.5	22.4	24.7	21.9	22.3
Percent distribution[11]												
Total	100.0	100.0	100.0	100.0	100.0	100.0	100.0	100.0	100.0	100.0	100.0	100.0
Period of gestation												
Under 9 weeks	36.1	44.6	51.7	51.2	50.6	49.7	50.5	50.3	51.0	50.4	48.7	49.8
9–10 weeks	29.4	28.4	26.2	26.8	26.7	26.8	26.4	26.6	25.8	26.0	26.4	25.8
11–12 weeks	17.9	14.9	12.2	12.1	12.4	12.8	12.6	12.5	12.2	12.4	12.7	12.6
13–15 weeks	6.9	5.0	5.1	5.2	5.3	5.8	5.8	5.9	6.1	6.2	6.6	6.6
16–20 weeks	8.0	6.1	3.9	3.7	3.9	3.9	3.9	3.9	4.1	4.2	4.5	4.2
21 weeks and over	1.7	1.0	0.9	1.0	1.1	1.0	0.8	0.8	0.8	0.8	1.1	1.0
Previous induced abortions												
0	…	81.9	67.6	65.3	63.7	62.4	60.5	60.1	59.3	58.5	57.8	58.1
1	…	14.9	23.5	24.3	24.9	25.0	25.7	25.7	26.3	26.5	26.9	26.5
2	…	2.5	6.6	7.5	8.2	9.0	9.4	9.8	9.6	10.3	10.4	9.9
3 or more	…	0.7	2.3	2.9	3.2	3.7	4.3	4.4	4.8	4.7	4.9	5.5

Note: The number of areas reporting adequate data (less than or equal to 15% missing) for each characteristic varies from year to year.

[1]In 1998 and 1999, Alaska, California, New Hampshire, and Oklahoma did not report abortion data to CDC. For comparison, in 1997, the 48 corresponding reporting areas reported about 900,000 legal abortions.

[2]In 2000, 2001, and 2002, Alaska, California, and New Hampshire did not report abortion data to CDC.

[3]In 2003, California, New Hampshire, and West Virginia did not report abortion data to CDC.

[4]No surveys were conducted in 1983, 1986, 1989, 1990, 1993, 1994, 1997, 1998, 2001, or 2002. Data for these years were estimated by interpolation.

[5]For calculation of ratios by each characteristic, abortions with characteristic unknown were distributed in proportion to abortions with characteristic known.

[6]For 1989 and later years, white race includes women of Hispanic ethnicity.

[7]Before 1989, black race includes races other than white.

[8]Reporting area increased from 20–22 states, the District of Columbia (DC), and New York City (NYC) in 1991–1995 to 27 states, DC and NYC, with 12 additional states reporting to CDC, but with more than 15% unknowns, and thus excluded from analysis, for 2002 and 2003. California, Florida, Illinois, and Arizona, states with large Hispanic populations do not report Hispanic ethnicity.

[9]For 1973–1975, data indicate number of living children.

[10]For 1975, data refer to four previous live births, not four or more. For five or more previous live births, the ratio is 47.3.

[11]For calculation of percent distribution by each characteristic, abortions with characteristic unknown were excluded.

… = Not available.

Table 3-8. Legal Abortions and Legal Abortion Ratios, by Selected Patient Characteristics, 1973–2003—*Continued*

(Data are based on reporting by state health departments and by hospitals and other medical facilities.)

1990	1991	1992	1993	1994	1995	1996	1997	1998[1]	1999[1]	2000[2]	2001[2]	2002[2]	2003[3]
1,429	1,389	1,359	1,330	1,267	1,211	1,226	1,186	884	862	857	853	854	848
1,609	1,557	1,529	1,495	1,423	1,359	1,360	1,335	1,319	1,315	1,313	1,303	1,293	...
34.4	33.9	33.4	33.3	32.1	31.1	31.5	30.6	26.4	25.6	24.5	24.6	24.6	24.1
81.8	76.7	79.0	74.2	70.3	66.4	72.6	72.9	75.0	70.9	70.8	74.4	75.3	83.0
51.1	46.2	44.5	44.0	41.4	39.9	41.8	40.7	39.1	37.5	36.1	36.6	36.8	37.4
37.8	37.8	37.9	38.3	36.4	34.8	35.7	34.5	32.9	31.6	30.0	30.4	30.3	30.0
21.8	22.1	22.2	22.6	22.1	22.0	22.8	22.4	21.6	20.8	19.8	20.0	20.0	19.5
19.0	18.7	18.2	17.9	17.1	16.4	16.5	16.1	15.7	15.2	14.5	14.7	14.8	14.4
27.3	26.2	25.3	24.7	23.3	22.3	22.1	20.9	20.0	19.3	18.1	18.0	18.0	17.3
50.6	46.9	45.9	42.8	40.9	38.5	37.8	35.2	33.8	32.9	30.1	30.4	31.0	29.3
25.8	24.6	23.6	23.0	21.6	20.3	20.3	19.4	18.9	17.7	16.7	16.5	16.4	16.5
53.7	50.2	53.8	55.0	53.7	53.1	55.9	54.3	51.2	52.9	50.3	49.1	49.5	49.1
...	30.0	31.4	29.5	28.5	27.1	28.2	26.8	27.3	26.1	22.5	23.0	23.3	22.8
...	33.2	32.3	30.9	29.0	27.9	28.6	27.2	27.1	25.2	23.3	23.2	23.7	23.4
8.7	8.9	8.5	8.4	7.8	7.6	7.9	7.4	7.1	7.0	6.5	6.5	6.5	6.3
86.3	81.5	78.6	78.0	66.5	64.5	65.9	65.9	62.7	60.4	57.0	57.2	57.0	53.8
36.0	34.8	32.6	32.5	30.8	28.6	28.9	26.4	25.5	24.3	22.6	26.4	23.3	22.7
22.7	23.2	22.8	22.8	22.3	22.0	22.4	22.3	21.4	20.6	19.4	18.0	19.4	19.0
31.5	31.9	31.8	31.8	30.9	30.6	31.3	31.0	30.0	29.0	27.4	25.5	27.9	27.1
30.1	31.0	30.9	31.2	30.9	30.7	31.7	31.1	30.5	29.8	28.5	26.4	29.1	28.3
26.6	22.6	24.8	23.5	23.5	23.7	25.0	24.5	24.3	24.2	23.7	21.9	23.6	23.4
100.0	100.0	100.0	100.0	100.0	100.0	100.0	100.0	100.0	100.0	100.0	100.0	100.0	100.0
51.6	52.3	52.1	52.3	53.7	54.0	54.6	55.4	55.7	57.6	58.1	59.1	60.5	60.5
25.3	25.1	24.2	24.4	23.5	23.1	22.6	22.0	21.5	20.2	19.8	19.0	18.4	18.0
11.7	11.5	12.1	11.6	10.9	10.9	11.0	10.7	10.9	10.2	10.2	10.0	9.6	9.7
6.4	6.1	6.0	6.3	6.3	6.3	6.0	6.2	6.4	6.2	6.2	6.2	6.0	6.2
4.0	3.9	4.2	4.1	4.3	4.3	4.3	4.3	4.1	4.3	4.3	4.3	4.1	4.2
1.0	1.1	1.4	1.3	1.3	1.4	1.5	1.4	1.4	1.5	1.4	1.4	1.4	1.4
57.1	56.1	55.1	55.0	54.7	55.1	54.7	53.4	53.8	53.7	54.7	55.5	55.3	55.3
26.9	27.2	27.4	27.3	27.2	26.9	26.9	27.5	27.0	27.1	26.4	25.8	25.8	25.7
10.1	10.6	11.0	11.0	11.1	10.9	11.2	11.5	11.4	11.5	11.3	11.0	11.3	11.2
5.9	6.1	6.5	6.7	7.0	7.1	7.2	7.6	7.8	7.7	7.6	7.7	7.6	7.8

Source: U.S. National Center for Health Statistics. *Health, United States 2006.*
Note: The number of areas reporting adequate data (less than or equal to 15% missing) for each characteristic varies from year to year.
[1]In 1998 and 1999, Alaska, California, New Hampshire, and Oklahoma did not report abortion data to CDC. For comparison, in 1997, the 48 corresponding reporting areas reported about 900,000 legal abortions.
[2]In 2000, 2001, and 2002, Alaska, California, and New Hampshire did not report abortion data to CDC.
[3]In 2003, California, New Hampshire, and West Virginia did not report abortion data to CDC.
. . . = Not available.

Table 3-9. Contraceptive Use by Women, 15 to 44 Years of Age, 1982–2002

(Percent, except total number in thousands. Based on samples of the female population of the United States.)

Contraceptive status and method	1982							1988						
		Race/ethnicity			Marital status				Race/ethnicity			Marital status		
		Non-Hispanic							Non-Hispanic					
	All women[1]	White	Black	Hispanic	Never married	Currently married	Formerly married	All women[1]	White	Black	Hispanic	Never married	Currently married	Formerly married
All women (1,000)	**54 099**	**45 367**	**6 985**	...	**19 164**	**28 231**	**6 704**	**57 900**	**47 077**	**7 679**	...	**21 058**	**29 147**	**7 695**
PERCENT DISTRIBUTION														
Using contraception (contraceptors)[2]	...	...	...	...	...	...	...	...	...	...	...	...	...	...
Female sterilization	...	...	...	...	...	...	...	...	...	...	...	...	...	...
Male sterilization	...	...	...	...	...	...	...	...	...	...	...	...	...	...
Pill	15.6	15.1	19.8	...	18.7	13.4	15.8	18.5	18.4	21.6	...	24.7	15.1	14.5
3-month injectable (Depo-Provera™)	X	X	X	X	X	X	X	X	X	X	X	X	X	X
Intrauterine device (IUD)	4.0	3.9	4.7	...	1.9	4.8	6.4	1.2	1.1	1.7	...	0.6	1.5	2.1
Diaphragm	4.5	5.0	1.8	...	4.7	4.5	3.7	3.5	3.8	1.1	...	2.1	4.6	3.0
Condom	6.7	7.2	3.2	...	4.1	9.8	0.8	8.8	9.2	5.8	...	8.2	10.6	3.4
Periodic abstinence-calendar rhythm	2.2	2.2	1.6	...	0.9	3.2	1.4	1.4	1.4	1.2	...	0.6	2.1	1.1
Periodic abstinence-natural family planning	(3)	(3)	(3)	...	(3)	(3)	(3)	(3)	(3)	(3)	...	(3)	(3)	(3)
Withdrawal	(4)	(4)	(4)	...	(4)	(4)	(4)	(4)	(4)	(4)	...	(4)	(4)	(4)
Other methods[5]	2.5	2.4	3.1	...	2.6	2.3	2.7	2.6	2.5	2.6	...	2.1	3.2	1.7
Not using contraception	...	...	...	...	...	...	...	...	...	...	...	...	...	...
Surgically sterile-female (noncontraceptive)	7.8	7.8	7.3	...	0.8	11.0	14.5	4.7	4.7	5.7	...	0.9	6.2	9.7
Nonsurgically sterile-female or male[6]	...	...	...	...	...	...	...	...	...	...	...	...	...	...
Pregnant or postpartum	5.0	4.8	5.6	...	2.5	7.2	2.6	4.8	4.8	5.0	...	2.4	7.1	2.5
Seeking pregnancy	4.2	4.0	5.4	...	1.2	6.7	2.1	3.8	3.7	3.9	...	1.3	6.0	2.0
Other nonuse	26.9	26.2	29.6	...	59.7	5.0	25.6	25.0	23.8	26.9	...	52.5	4.8	26.6
Never had intercourse or no intercourse in 3 months before interview	19.5	19.9	16.1	...	49.6	0.2	15.1	19.0	18.1	16.7	...	43.5	0.3	19.5
Had intercourse in 3 months before interview	7.4	6.4	13.5	...	10.1	4.8	10.4	6.5	5.7	10.2	...	9.0	4.5	7.1
All other nonusers	...	...	...	...	...	...	...	...	...	...	...	...	...	...

[1]Includes other races, not shown separately.
[2]Percents may not add to the total who were using contraception because more than one method could have been used in the month of interview.
[3]For years 1982 and 1988 periodic abstinence calendar rhythm and natural family planning data are combined.
[4]For years 1982 and 1988 "Withdrawal" is included in "Other methods" total.
[5]Includes implants, injectables, morning-after-pill, suppository, Today(TM) sponge and less frequently used methods.
[6]Persons sterile from illness, accident, or congenital conditions.
- = Quantity zero.
X = Not applicable.
. . . = Not available.

Table 3-9. Contraceptive Use by Women, 15 to 44 Years of Age, 1982–2002—*Continued*

(Percent, except total number in thousands. Based on samples of the female population of the United States.)

Year-group columns. Each year block contains: All women[1]; Race/ethnicity — Non-Hispanic White, Non-Hispanic Black, Hispanic; Marital status — Never married (2002: Never married, not co-habiting), Currently married, Formerly married.

1990 All women[1]	1990 White	1990 Black	1990 Hispanic	1990 Never married	1990 Currently married	1990 Formerly married	1995 All women[1]	1995 White	1995 Black	1995 Hispanic	1995 Never married	1995 Currently married	1995 Formerly married	2002 All women[1]	2002 White	2002 Black	2002 Hispanic	2002 Never married, not co-habiting	2002 Currently married	2002 Formerly married
58 381	**42 968**	**7 510**	**5 500**	**20 788**	**30 561**	**7 033**	**60 201**	**42 522**	**8 210**	**6 702**	**22 679**	**29 673**	**7 849**	**61 561**	**40 420**	**8 587**	**9 107**	**21 568**	**28 327**	**6 096**
...	...	...	...	...	...	...	64.2	...	...	...	62.8	63.6	71.5	61.9	64.5	57.4	59.0	44.0	72.9	64.4
...	...	...	...	...	...	...	17.8	...	...	...	...	...	...	16.7	15.5	22.3	19.9	4.4	21.7	35.3
							7.0	...	...	...	...	...	...	5.7	7.5	1.4	2.6	0.4	11.2	2.2
16.9	17.3	16.7	16.4	21.7	14.5	12.8	17.3	18.8	14.8	13.6	20.4	15.6	14.6	18.9	22.2	12.9	13.0	21.8	17.2	12.3
N/A	N/A	N/A	N/A	X	X	X	1.9	X	X	X	X	X	X	3.3	2.7	5.6	4.3	4.2	2.2	1.7
0.8	0.8	0.8	1.0	0.4	1.0	1.4	0.5	0.5	0.5	0.9	0.3	0.7	0.4	1.3	0.9	0.8	3.2	0.2	1.9	1.9
1.7	1.8	1.0	0.8	0.3	2.9	0.5	1.2	1.5	0.5	0.4	0.5	1.8	0.9	0.2	0.2	0.1	-	0.2	0.2	-
10.5	10.3	11.4	8.9	13.0	9.9	5.6	13.1	13.0	12.5	12.1	13.9	13.3	10.1	11.1	10.7	11.4	10.9	10.3	12.0	8.0
1.6	1.6	0.7	1.9	0.8	2.4	0.4	1.3	1.6	0.7	1.3	0.6	2.3	0.7	0.7	0.8	0.3	0.6	0.2	1.3	0.3
0.2	0.2	-	-	-	0.4	-	0.2	0.3	-	0.1	-	0.4	-	0.2	0.2	0.1	0.3	0.0	0.4	-
0.6	0.6	0.4	0.4	0.7	0.5	0.1	2.0	2.1	0.9	2.0	1.5	2.3	1.8	2.5	2.5	1.5	2.2	1.6	3.0	1.3
2.3	2.2	2.8	2.3	1.6	2.1	5.0	1.1	3.4	6.2	4.7	...	...	...	0.6	0.7	0.5	0.3	0.2	0.7	0.9
...	...	...	...	...	...	...	35.8	...	...	...	37.2	36.4	28.5	38.1	35.5	42.6	41.0	56.0	27.1	35.6
5.2	5.4	6.5	3.2	1.1	6.6	10.9	3.0	3.2	3.7	2.3	...	...	...	1.5	1.7	1.5	0.9	0.4	2.1	3.0
...	...	...	...	...	...	...	1.7	...	...	...	1.1	2.0	2.2	1.6	1.7	1.5	1.7	1.0	2.0	2.5
5.4	5.2	5.5	7.7	3.4	7.3	3.1	4.6	4.3	4.5	6.3	3.1	6.4	1.9	5.3	4.6	5.9	6.9	2.3	7.5	2.2
4.0	3.7	4.7	5.1	1.1	6.6	1.5	4.0	3.7	4.6	4.0	1.5	6.4	2.1	4.2	3.9	4.2	5.2	0.8	6.9	2.0
24.2	23.6	22.1	28.3	50.0	6.6	24.4	22.5	21.1	23.1	26.3	46.8	4.7	18.4	25.5	23.7	29.7	26.4	51.4	8.6	26.0
16.4[7]	15.9[7]	14.5[7]	21.5[7]	38.9[7]	0.6[7]	18.9[7]	17.1	16.1	16.1	20.7	40.4	0.5	12.7	18.1	17.0	19.4	18.7	42.9	2.3	17.7
7.8	7.7	7.6	6.8	11.3	6.0	5.5	5.2	5.0	7.0	5.6	6.4	4.2	5.7	7.4	6.7	10.2	7.7	8.5	6.3	8.2
...	...	...	...	...	...	...	0.2	...	...	...	...	...	...	-	-	0.1	-	-	-	0.1

Source: U.S. Census Bureau. U.S. National Center for Health Statistics.
[1] Includes other races, not shown separately.
[7] 1990 Data includes those women who had never had intercourse and those who had not had intercourse in the last month.
- = Quantity zero.
X = Not applicable.
... = Not available.

BOX 3 ■ Family Planning

Contraceptive choices and preferences vary by age, level of education, race, and ethnicity. One goal of the National Survey of Family Growth, conducted by the National Center for Health Statistics, is to gain data on trends and choices in contraceptive use in the United States. The 1973 National Survey of Family Growth was the first publicly conducted fertility study in the United States. The 1973 and 1976 surveys only included women who were currently or previously married because it was believed that the topics of contraception, sterilization, infertility, pregnancy outcomes and births were too sensitive to discuss with a woman who had never been married. Therefore, data from these surveys is not strictly comparable to data collected in later years. Since 1982 the survey has included all women 15 through 44 years of age, regardless of marital status. The 6th Cycle of the survey conducted in 2002 included interviews with males aged 15 to 44 for the first time.

Overall, in 2002 the oral contraceptive pill was the most popular form of birth control. Thirty-one percent of all women aged 15–44 used the pill as their only, or most effective, form of birth control (11.6 million women), followed by female sterilization 27%. The pill was the leading method for women under 30 but by the age of 35, female sterilization is the most common form of contraception. Use of the pill increases as a woman's level of education increases; only 13% of women with less than a high school diploma were currently using the pill versus 43% women with a college degree.

Female sterilization was more common with older women (50% of women 40–44 years of age compared to 4% of those 20–24 years old), with those women who are less educated (55% of women who have less than a high school diploma compared to 13% of college graduates), and who are Hispanic/Latina (19.9%) or African-American (22.6%). Non-Hispanic white women had a use rate of only 15.4%. Conversely, non-Hispanic white women are the most likely to use male sterilization for contraception with an 8% use rate compared to 3% of Hispanic women and 1% of African-American women.

Condom use has increased from 6.7% in 1982 to 11.1% in 2002 and is most common with younger women; 27% of teens use the condom as their primary or most effective form of contraception versus only 11% of women aged 40–44. However, popularity of the diaphragm and IUD, 8% and 7% respectively in 1982, have decreased to only 0.3% and 2% in 2002.

Teen contraceptive use increased between 1988 and 2002. In 2002, of 15–19 year old females who had had sex within the last three months, 83% had used birth control at their last intercourse (up from 61% in 1988 and 58% in 1990), 34% used the pill, 54% used the condom (up from 38% in 1995), and 20% used both pill and condom (up from 8% in 1995).

Age at first intercourse is directly related to contraceptive use for females. Females who were younger than 15 at the time of their first intercourse had a use rate of about 55% versus a 70% use rate for those 19 or older.

Additionally, the greater the education level of a teen girl's mother, the more likely she will use contraception at first intercourse. Teens whose mothers did not finish high school only had a use rate of 48% in comparison to 72% for those girls whose mothers were college educated.

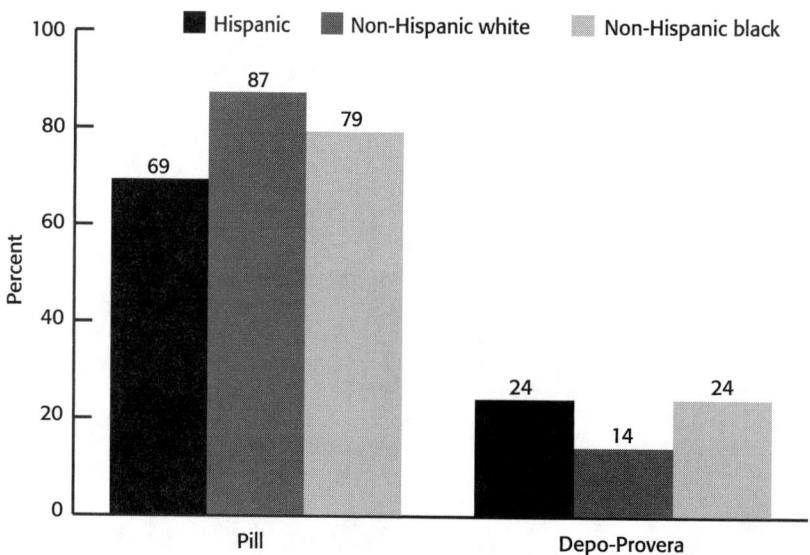

Percentage of Sexually Experienced Women 15–44 Years of Age Who Have Ever Used the Specified Contraceptive Method, by Race and Hispanic Origin: United States, 2002

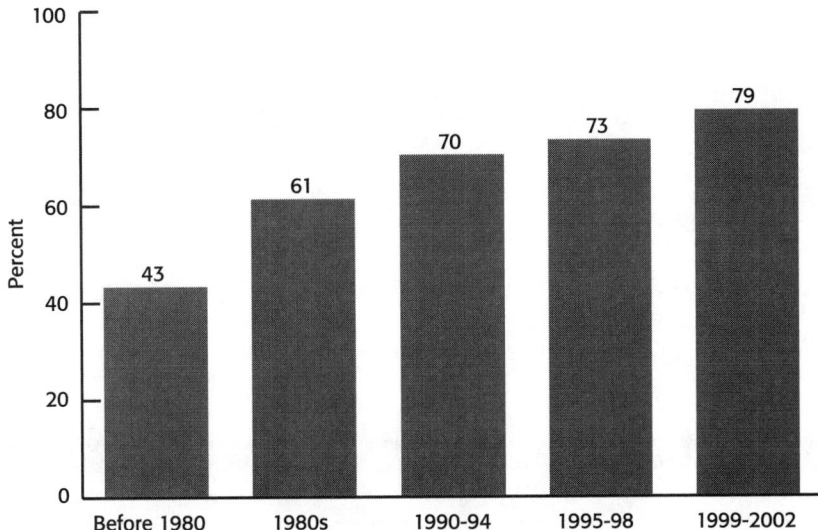

Percentage of Women Who Used a Method of Contraception at Their First Premarital Intercourse, by Year of First Intercourse: United States

While teen contraception use is up, overall, the percent of sexually active women who are at risk of unintended pregnancy has increased from 5.4% in 1995 to 7.4% in 2002. These numbers do not include women who are trying to become pregnant, are currently pregnant, are non-surgically sterile, or are not sexually active.

Family planning medical service use increased between 1995 and 2002 for all ages. Income levels and race did not show significant differences in receipt of such services. However, age was inversely related to medical visits where family planning services were received. Sixty-three percent of women 20–24 years of age received at least one family planning service in the 12 months prior to the interview, while for women 40–44 years of age the figure drops to 20%.

Sources:

U.S. Department of Health and Human Services, Office of Disease Prevention and Health Promotion. *Healthy People 2010, Midcourse Review,* December 2006.

U.S. Centers for Disease Control and Prevention, National Center for Health Statistics. *National Vital Statistics Report, Births: Final Data for 2004,* Vol. 55, No. 1, September 29, 2006.

U.S. Centers for Disease Control and Prevention, National Center for Health Statistics. *Advance Data from Vital and Health Statistics: Use of Contraception and Use of Family Planning Services in the United States: 1982–2002,* No. 350, December 10, 2004.

U.S. Centers for Disease Control and Prevention, National Center for Health Statistics. *Vital and Health Statistics, Teenagers in the United States: Sexual Activity, Contraceptive Use, and Childbearing, 2002,* Series 23, No. 24, December 2004.

U.S. Centers for Disease Control and Prevention, National Center for Health Statistics. *Advance Data from Vital and Health Statistics: Contraceptive Use in the United States: 1982–90,* No. 260, February 14, 1995.

U.S. Census Bureau. *Statistical Abstract of the United States: 1980.*

U.S. Centers for Disease Control and Prevention, National Center for Health Statistics. *Advance Data from Vital and Health Statistics: Contraceptive Efficacy Among Married Women 15–44 Years of Age in the United States, 1970–73,* Number 26, April 6, 1978.

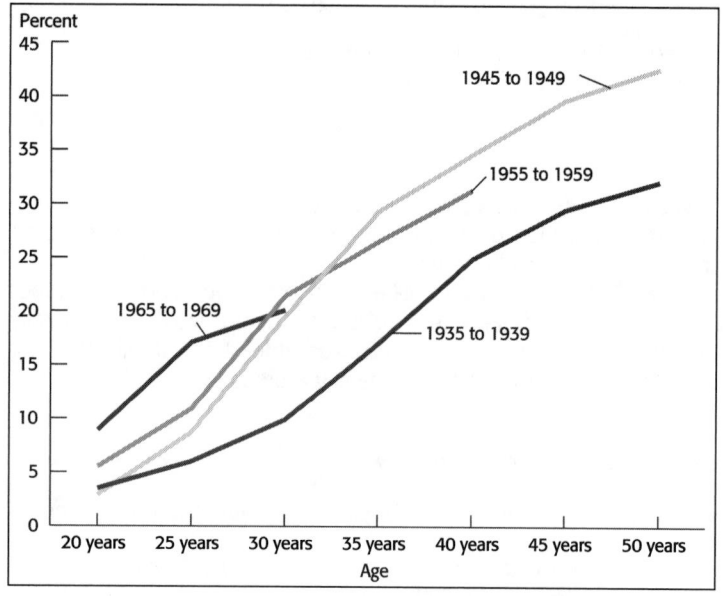

Percent of Men Ever Divorced, Among Those Ever Married by Selected Ages, for Selected Birth Cohorts: 2001
Source: U.S. Census Bureau.

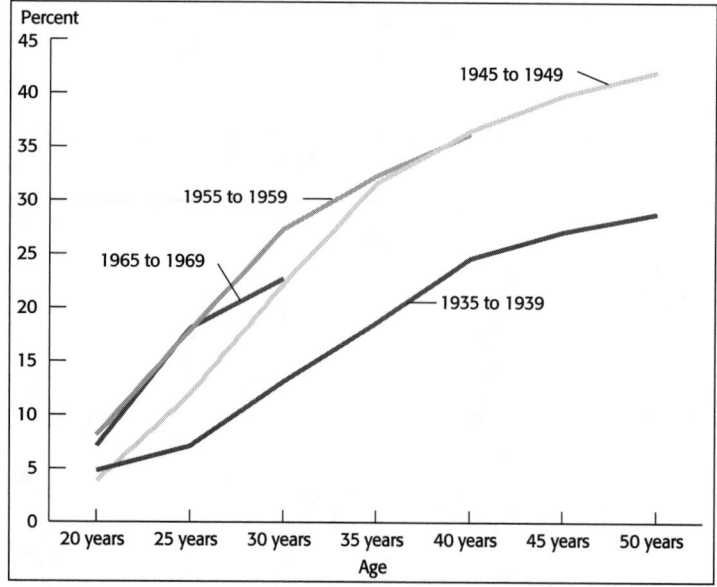

Percent of Women Ever Divorced, Among Those Ever Married by Selected Ages, for Selected Birth Cohorts: 2001
Source: U.S. Census Bureau.

CHAPTER **4**

Marriage, Divorce, and Alternative Living Arrangements

HIGHLIGHTS

1 Statistics on marriages and divorces are compiled by the National Center for Health Statistics, successor to the Office of Vital Statistics. From 1900 to 1946, the collection of these data was the responsibility of the Census Bureau.

2 The divorce rate in 1950 was 2.6 per 1,000 population. The rate climbed to 5.3 in 1981, before leveling off. In 2004, the divorce rate had dropped slightly to 3.7 per 1,000 people.

3 The median age at marriage rose for females from 20.6 in 1970 to 25.5 in 2005 and for males from 22.5 to 27.0 in the same period.

4 The states with the five highest median ages of marriage for men are located on the Atlantic coast. They are New York and Rhode Island (29.9 years each), Massachusetts (29.2 years), and Connecticut and New Jersey (29.1 years each).

5 The median duration of marriage for divorced couples was 7.2 years in 1990. More divorced men and widowers remarry than divorced women and widows. Per 1,000 persons aged 15 and older, 76.2 divorcees and 5.2 widows remarry compared with 105.9 for divorced men and 23.8 widowers.

6 Nevada has the highest rates of both marriage and divorce at 62.5 and 6.4 per 1,000, respectively.

7 The percentage of traditionally married households has been steadily declining and, for the first time, married households are in the minority. Slightly more than 50 percent of American households now have an alternative living arrangement.

Table 4-1. Marriages and Divorces, 1920–2004

(Number in thousands.)

Year	Marriage[1]	Divorces[2]
2004	2 279	. . .
2003	2 245	. . .
2001	2 327	. . .
2000	2 329	. . .
1999	2 358	. . .
1998	2 244	1 135
1997	2 384	1 163
1996	2 344	1 150
1995	2 336	1 169
1994	2 362	1 191
1993	2 334	1 187
1992	2 362	1 215
1991	2 371	1 187
1990	2 443	1 182
1989	2 403	1 157
1988	2 396	1 167
1987	2 403	1 166
1986	2 407	1 178
1985	2 413	1 190
1984	2 477	1 169
1983	2 446	1 158
1982	2 456	1 170
1981	2 422	1 213
1980	2 390	1 189
1979	2 331	1 181
1978	2 282	1 130
1977	2 178	1 091
1976	2 155	1 083
1975	2 153	1 036
1974	2 230	977
1973	2 284	915
1972	2 282	845
1971	2 190	773
1970	2 163	708
1969	2 145	639
1968	2 069	584
1967	1 927	523
1966	1 857	499
1965	1 800	479
1964	1 725	450
1963	1 654	428
1962	1 577	413
1961	1 548	414
1960*	1 523	393
1959	1 494	395
1958	1 451	368
1957	1 518	381
1956	1 585	382
1955	1 531	377
1954	1 490	379
1953	1 546	390
1952	1 539	392
1951	1 595	381
1950	1 667	385
1949	1 580	397
1948	1 811	408
1947	1 992	483
1946	2 291	610
1945	1 613	485
1944	1 452	400
1943	1 577	359
1942	1 772	321
1941	1 696	293

[1]Includes estimates for some states through 1965 and also for 1976 and 1977 and marriage licenses for some states for all years except 1973 and 1975. Beginning 1978, includes nonlicensed marriages in California.
[2]Includes reported annulments and some estimate state figures for all years.
. . . = Not available.
* = First year for which figures include Alaska and Hawaii.

Table 4-1. Marriages and Divorces, 1920–2004—*Continued*

(Number in thousands.)

Year	Marriage[1]	Divorces[2]
1940	1 596	264
1939	1 404	251
1938	1 331	244
1937	1 451	249
1936	1 369	236
1935	1 327	218
1934	1 302	204
1933	1 098	165
1932	982	164
1931	1 061	188
1930	1 127	196
1929	1 233	206
1928	1 182	200
1927	1 201	196
1926	1 203	185
1925	1 188	175
1924	1 185	171
1923	1 230	165
1922	1 134	149
1921	1 164	160
1920	1 274	171

Source: U.S. Census Bureau. U.S. National Center for Health Statistics.
[1]Includes estimates for some states through 1965 and also for 1976 and 1977 and marriage licenses for some states for all years except 1973 and 1975. Beginning 1978, includes nonlicensed marriages in California.
[2]Includes reported annulments and some estimate state figures for all years.
. . . = Not available.
* = First year for which figures include Alaska and Hawaii.

Table 4-2. Marriage Rate, 1920—2005

Year	Marriages per 1,000 population[1]	Marriages per 1,000 unmarried females[2]
2005[3]	7.5	...
2004	7.8	...
2003	7.7	...
2002	7.8	...
2001	8.4	...
2000	8.5	...
1999	8.6	...
1998	8.3	...
1997	8.9	...
1996	8.8	49.7
1995	8.9	50.8
1994	9.1	51.5
1993	9.0	52.3
1992	9.3	53.3
1991	9.4	54.2
1990	9.8	54.5
1989	9.7	54.2
1988	9.8	54.6
1987	9.9	55.7
1986	10.0	56.2
1985	10.1	57.0
1984	10.5	59.5
1983	10.5	59.9
1982	10.6	61.4
1981	10.6	61.7
1980	10.6	61.4
1979	10.4	63.6
1978	10.3	64.1
1977	9.9	63.6
1976	9.9	65.2
1975	10.0	66.9
1974	10.5	72.0
1973	10.9	76.0
1972	10.9	77.5
1971	10.6	76.3
1970	10.6	76.7
1969	10.6	80.0
1968	10.4	79.1
1967	9.7	76.4
1966	9.5	75.6
1965	9.3	75.0
1964	9.0	74.6
1963	8.8	73.4
1962	8.5	71.2
1961	8.5	72.2
1960*	8.5	73.5
1959	8.5	73.6
1958	8.4	72.0
1957	8.9	78.0
1956	9.5	82.4
1955	9.3	80.9
1954	9.2	79.8
1953	9.8	83.7
1952	9.9	83.2
1951	10.4	86.6
1950	11.1	90.2
1949	10.6	86.7
1948	12.4	98.5
1947	13.9	106.2
1946	16.4	118.1
1945	12.2	83.6
1944	10.9	76.5
1943	11.7	83.0
1942	13.2	93.0
1941	12.7	88.5

[1]Includes estimates for some states through 1965 and also for 1976 and 1977 and marriage licenses for some states for all years except 1973 and 1975. Beginning 1978, includes nonlicensed marriages in California.
[2]15 years and over.
[3]Provisional data.
. . . = Not available.
* = First year for which figures include Alaska and Hawaii.

Table 4-2. Marriage Rate, 1920–2005—*Continued*

Year	Marriages per 1,000 population[1]	Marriages per 1,000 unmarried females[2]
1940	12.1	82.8
1939	10.7	73.0
1938	10.3	69.9
1937	11.3	78.0
1936	10.7	74.0
1935	10.4	72.5
1934	10.3	71.8
1933	8.7	61.3
1932	7.9	56.0
1931	8.6	61.9
1930	9.2	67.6
1929	10.1	75.5
1928	9.8	74.1
1927	10.1	77.0
1926	10.2	78.7
1925	10.3	79.2
1924	10.4	80.3
1923	11.0	85.2
1922	10.3	79.7
1921	10.7	83.0
1920	12.0	92.0

Source: U.S. Census Bureau. U.S. National Center for Health Statistics. *National Vital Statistics Report, Births, Marriages, Divorces, and Deaths: Provisional Data for 2005.*
[1]Includes estimates for some states through 1965 and also for 1976 and 1977 and marriage licenses for some states for all years except 1973 and 1975. Beginning 1978, includes nonlicensed marriages in California.
[2]15 years and over.
[3]Provisional data.
. . . = Not available.
* = First year for which figures include Alaska and Hawaii.

Table 4-3. Divorce Rate, 1920–2005

Year	Divorce rate[1] Per 1,000 population[2]	Divorce rate[1] Per 1,000 married females[3]	Divorce rate[1] Median duration of marriage (years)
2005[4]	3.6	...	...
2004	3.8	...	...
2003	3.7	...	...
2002	3.9	...	...
2001	4.0	...	...
2000	4.2	...	...
1999	4.1	...	...
1998	4.2	...	...
1997	4.3	...	...
1996	4.3	...	...
1995	4.4	19.5	...
1994	4.6	19.8	...
1993	4.6	20.5	...
1992	4.8	20.5	...
1991	4.7	21.2	...
		20.9	
1990	4.7	20.9	7.2
1989	4.7	20.4	7.2
1988	4.8	20.7	7.1
1987	4.8	20.8	7.0
1986	4.9	21.2	6.9
1985	5.0	21.7	6.8
1984	5.0	21.5	6.9
1983	5.0	21.3	7.0
1982	5.1	21.7	7.0
1981	5.3	22.6	7.0
1980	5.2	22.6	6.8
1979	5.3	22.8	6.8
1978	5.1	21.9	6.6
1977	5.0	21.1	6.6
1976	5.0	21.1	6.5
1975	4.9	20.3	6.5
1974	4.6	19.3	6.5
1973	4.4	18.2	6.6
1972	4.1	17.0	6.7
1971	3.7	15.7	...
1970	3.5	14.9	6.7
1969	3.2	13.4	6.9
1968	2.9	12.4	7.0
1967	2.6	11.2	7.1
1966	2.5	10.9	7.1
1965	2.5	10.6	7.2
1964	2.4	10.0	7.4
1963	2.3	9.6	7.5
1962	2.2	9.4	7.3
1961	2.3	9.6	7.1
1960*	2.2	9.2	7.2
1959	2.2	9.3	7.0
1958	2.1	8.9	6.4
1957	2.2	9.2	6.7
1956	2.3	9.4	6.5
1955	2.3	9.3	6.4
1954	2.4	9.5	6.4
1953	2.5	9.9	6.1
1952	2.5	10.1	6.1
1951	2.5	9.9	6.0
1950	2.6	10.3	5.8
1949	2.7	10.6	...
1948	2.8	11.2	...
1947	3.4	13.6	...
1946	4.3	17.9	...
1945	3.5	14.4	...
1944	2.9	12.0	...
1943	2.6	11.0	...
1942	2.4	10.1	...
1941	2.2	9.4	...
1940	2.0	8.8	...
1939	1.9	8.5	...
1938	1.9	8.4	...
1937	1.9	8.7	...
1936	1.8	8.3	...
1935	1.7	7.8	...
1934	1.6	7.5	...
1933	1.3	6.1	...
1932	1.3	6.1	...
1931	1.5	7.1	...
1930	1.6	7.5	...
1929	1.7	8.0	...
1928	1.7	7.8	...
1927	1.6	7.8	...
1926	1.6	7.5	...
1925	1.5	7.2	...
1924	1.5	7.2	...
1923	1.5	7.1	...
1922	1.4	6.6	...
1921	1.5	7.2	...
1920	1.6	8.0	...

Source: U.S. Census Bureau. U.S. National Center for Health Statistics. *National Vital Statistics Report, Births, Marriages, Divorces, and Deaths: Provisional Data for 2005.*
[1]Includes reported annulments and some estimated figures for all years.
[2]Divorce rates exclude data for California, Georgia, Hawaii, Indiana, Louisiana, and Minnesota in 2005; California, Georgia, Hawaii, Indiana, and Louisiana, in 2004; California, Hawaii, Indiana, Louisiana, and Oklahoma in 2003; California, Indiana, and Oklahoma in 2002; and California, Colorado, Indiana, and Louisiana for 1998-2001. Populations for these rates also exclude these states.
[3]15 years and over. Population enumerated as of April for 1940, 1950, and 1960 and estimated as of July 1 for all other years; includes Armed Forces abroad for 1941-1946.
[4]Provisional data.
... = Not available.
* = First year for which figures include Alaska and Hawaii.

Table 4-4. Marital History for People 15 Years and Over, by Age and Sex, 2001

(Numbers in thousands, percent. Population represented is the civilian noninstitutionalized adult (15 years and older) population living in the United States.)

Characteristic	Total, 15 years and over		15 years to 19 years	20 to 24 years	25 to 29 years	30 to 34 years	35 to 39 years	40 to 49 years	50 to 59 years	60 to 69 years	70 years and over
	Estimate	90-percent confidence interval									
MEN											
Total (in thousands)	105,850	104,698–107,002	10,186	9,465	9,177	10,069	10,704	21,202	15,694	9,558	9,795
Percent	100.0	-	100.0	100.0	100.0	100.0	100.0	100.0	100.0	100.0	100.0
Never married	30.9	30.2–31.6	99.1	83.9	50.8	29.5	21.5	14.2	6.3	4.3	3.3
Ever married	69.1	68.4–69.8	0.9	16.1	49.2	70.5	78.5	85.8	93.7	95.7	96.7
Married once	53.4	52.6–54.2	0.9	16.0	46.3	60.8	66.2	65.1	62.6	67.5	75.5
Still married[1]	43.7	42.9–44.5	0.6	14.3	39.6	52.3	53.0	53.1	49.5	58.0	58.1
Married twice	12.5	12.0–13.0	-	0.1	2.8	8.7	10.9	17.1	23.2	21.3	16.5
Still married[1]	9.9	9.4–10.4	-	0.1	2.6	7.4	9.1	13.8	17.6	17.0	12.2
Married 3 or more times	3.2	2.9–3.5	-	-	0.1	1.1	1.4	3.6	8.0	6.8	4.7
Still married[1]	2.4	2.2–2.6	-	-	0.1	0.8	1.2	2.9	5.7	5.1	3.5
Ever divorced	21.0	20.4–21.6	0.1	1.0	7.5	15.4	22.9	29.5	40.8	30.9	18.6
Currently divorced	8.8	8.4–9.2	-	0.8	4.7	7.0	12.5	12.5	16.9	9.7	5.5
Ever widowed	3.6	3.3–3.9	-	-	0.1	0.3	0.5	1.3	2.9	7.6	23.1
Currently widowed	2.4	2.2–2.6	-	-	0.1	-	0.2	0.8	1.8	4.5	16.8
WOMEN											
Total (in thousands)	113,777	112,625–114,929	9,764	9,518	9,239	10,211	11,110	22,036	16,626	10,956	14,318
Percent	100.0	-	100.0	100.0	100.0	100.0	100.0	100.0	100.0	100.0	100.0
Never married	24.6	24.0–25.2	96.3	72.4	37.3	21.7	15.6	10.5	6.4	4.1	3.3
Ever married	75.4	74.8–76.0	3.7	27.6	62.7	78.3	84.4	89.5	93.6	95.9	96.7
Married once	58.7	58.0–59.4	3.6	26.5	57.3	67.3	66.8	65.1	65.2	72.9	77.8
Still married[1]	40.7	40.0–41.4	3.1	22.6	47.1	56.2	53.0	48.8	46.4	47.5	29.8
Married twice	13.6	13.1–14.1	0.1	1.1	5.1	10.0	15.7	19.8	22.1	17.4	15.5
Still married[1]	9.1	8.7–9.5	0.1	0.8	4.1	7.9	12.0	14.5	15.3	10.6	6.1
Married 3 or more times	3.1	2.8–3.4	-	-	0.3	1.0	1.8	4.6	6.3	5.6	3.5
Still married[1]	1.9	1.7–2.1	-	-	0.2	0.8	1.5	3.3	4.1	3.1	1.1
Ever divorced	23.1	22.5–23.7	0.2	2.6	11.9	18.6	28.1	35.4	38.9	28.4	17.7
Currently divorced	10.8	10.3–11.3	-	1.6	7.4	9.3	13.7	16.8	17.9	12.6	6.5
Ever widowed	11.6	11.1–12.1	-	0.3	0.5	0.6	1.1	3.5	9.5	23.3	56.3
Currently widowed	10.2	9.8–10.6	-	0.3	0.4	0.4	0.6	2.4	7.1	19.7	52.6

Source: U.S. Census Bureau. Current Population Reports p70-97. *Number, Timing, and Duration of Marriages and Divorces: 2001.*
Note: Figures projected onto U.S. population based on survey of households from the U.S. Census Bureau Survey of Income and Program Participation.
[1]Includes those currently separated.
- = Quantity zero or rounds to zero.

Table 4-5. Percent Reaching Stated Anniversary by Marriage Cohort and Sex for First and Second Marriages, 2001

(Numbers in thousands, percent. Limited to spouses surviving to interview date. Population represented is the civilian noninstitutionalized adult (15 years and older) population living in the United States.)

Sex and year of marriage	Number of marriages (In thousands)	Anniversary[1]							
		5th	10th	15th	20th	25th	30th	35th	40th
FIRST MARRIAGES									
Men									
1955 to 1959	4,100	96.1	89.5	82.2	76.2	72.3	68.7	66.1	63.5
1960 to 1964	5,033	94.0	81.6	71.1	66.1	62.3	60.3	57.7	(X)
1965 to 1969	6,357	93.0	78.3	67.8	62.1	58.0	54.8	(X)	(X)
1970 to 1974	7,436	90.4	72.5	61.3	55.8	52.9	(X)	(X)	(X)
1975 to 1979	7,109	89.3	72.2	63.4	58.4	(X)	(X)	(X)	(X)
1980 to 1984	7,606	89.8	74.5	66.2	(X)	(X)	(X)	(X)	(X)
1985 to 1989	8,048	87.6	74.7	(X)	(X)	(X)	(X)	(X)	(X)
1990 to 1994	7,718	90.1	(X)	(X)	(X)	(X)	(X)	(X)	(X)
Women									
1955 to 1959	5,162	94.0	86.8	78.6	73.1	67.0	64.1	58.9	54.4
1960 to 1964	5,714	93.8	84.0	72.9	66.9	60.9	57.0	53.1	(X)
1965 to 1969	7,138	91.3	77.9	65.7	59.2	55.5	51.9	(X)	(X)
1970 to 1974	8,176	87.8	70.2	60.3	54.1	49.1	(X)	(X)	(X)
1975 to 1979	7,852	84.7	67.7	58.5	52.6	(X)	(X)	(X)	(X)
1980 to 1984	8,448	87.3	71.5	64.2	(X)	(X)	(X)	(X)	(X)
1985 to 1989	8,299	86.6	74.7	(X)	(X)	(X)	(X)	(X)	(X)
1990 to 1994	7,967	86.9	(X)	(X)	(X)	(X)	(X)	(X)	(X)
SECOND MARRIAGES									
Men									
1975 to 1979	1,985	90.8	81.0	57.6	49.0	(X)	(X)	(X)	(X)
1980 to 1984	2,544	90.9	71.8	54.9	(X)	(X)	(X)	(X)	(X)
1985 to 1989	2,881	90.0	72.2	(X)	(X)	(X)	(X)	(X)	(X)
1990 to 1994	2,834	88.8	(X)	(X)	(X)	(X)	(X)	(X)	(X)
Women									
1975 to 1979	2,187	86.3	75.9	55.9	47.2	(X)	(X)	(X)	(X)
1980 to 1984	2,703	89.2	71.0	54.6	(X)	(X)	(X)	(X)	(X)
1985 to 1989	3,008	86.9	67.8	(X)	(X)	(X)	(X)	(X)	(X)
1990 to 1994	3,126	86.8	(X)	(X)	(X)	(X)	(X)	(X)	(X)

Source: U.S. Census Bureau, Current Population Reports P70-97. Number, Timing, and Duration of Marriages and Divorces: 2001.
Note: Figures projected onto U.S. population based on survey of households from the U.S. Census Bureau Survey of Income and Program Participation.
[1]Persons reaching stated anniversary for specified marital order.
X = Not applicable.

Table 4-6. Same-Sex Unmarried Partner Households for the United States and Regions by Metropolitan Residence Status and Selected Characteristics, 2000

	United States	Northeast	Midwest	South	West	In a metropolitan area Total	In central city	Not in central city	Not in metropolitan area
Total households[1]	105 480 101	20 285 622	24 734 532	38 015 214	22 444 733	84 304 885	32 753 918	51 550 967	21 175 216
Total coupled households[2]	59 969 000	11 205 641	14 222 533	21 549 582	12 991 244	47 214 481	15 189 744	32 024 737	12 754 519
Percent of all households	56.9	55.2	57.5	56.7	57.9	78.7	25.3	53.4	21.3
Same-sex unmarried partners									
Total									
Number	594 391	119 246	105 750	209 742	159 653	506 745	247 524	259 221	87 646
Percent of coupled households	1.0	1.1	0.7	1.0	1.21.1	1.6	0.8	0.7	
Sex of partners									
Male partners	301 026	59 328	52 142	107 636	81 920	259 807	135 546	124 261	41 219
Female partners	293 365	59 918	53 608	102 106	77 733	246 938	111 978	134 960	46 427
Percent of households with partners of different races									
Sex of partners									
Male partners	11.5	10.7	8.2	8.7	17.7	...	...	...	...
Female partners	10.0	8.5	7.4	8.0	15.7...	...	...	...	...
Percent of households with only one partner of Hispanic origin									
Sex of partners									
Male partners	6.9	5.9	3.8	5.8	11.1	...	...	...	...
Female partners	5.4	4.3	3.0	4.3	9.2	...	...	...	...
Percent of households with partners of different races or origins									
Sex of partners									
Male partners	15.3	14.2	10.3	12.4	23.2	...	...	...	...
Female partners	12.6	10.8	8.9	10.3	19.7	...	...	...	...

Source: U.S. Census Bureau. *Census 2000 Special Reports, Married-Couple and Unmarried-Partner Households: 2000* and *Technical Note on Same-Sex Unmarried Partner Data From the 1990 and 2000 Censuses.*
Note: For analyses involving unmarried same-sex partners, direct comparison of the 1990 and 2000 Census estimates is not substantively valid. Because the 1990 edit and allocation procedure did not allow same-sex "spouse" combinations to occur, those responses were allocated via statistical model which distributed allocated responses from answers given by respondents in a closely proximate geographic area. This procedure, while ensuring that no same-sex spouse response could be subsequently allocated, produced a set of allocated responses which could have included an "unmarried partner" response as well as any other response that was consistent with the age/sex/marital status profile of the respondent. This would include being allocated as a sibling or relative, for example, or, if the age differences were far enough apart (15 or more years), even a child or parent of the householder. For Census 2000, in order to comply with the 1996 Defense of Marriage Act (H.R. 3396) which instructs all federal agencies only to recognize opposite-sex marriages for the purposes of enacting any agency programs, all same-sex "spouse" responses were invalidated. These responses on Census 2000 were allocated to same-sex "unmarried partner" category rather than randomized allocation of these responses after people had clearly marked a close relationship preference on the census form.
[1]Total includes other types of households including family and nonfamily households which do not contain either spouses or unmarried partners.
[2]Coupled households represent the total of married-couple and unmarried partner households of opposite sex and of same sex.
. . . = Not available.

BOX 4 ■ Unmarried Partner Households

The U.S. Census Bureau began tracking data on unmarried-partner households of both opposite-sex and same-sex couples with the 1990 Census. Before this, only opposite-sex couples were counted. Because there is no documentation attached to unmarried couple partnerships or their dissolution, it is more difficult to verify the accuracy of data provided by couples for the decennial Census and the annual American Community Survey.

The 2000 Census enumerated, 5.5 million couples living together in unmarried-partner households. This number does not include all unmarried partners, only those couples where one person was the householder, the owner or renter of the dwelling in which they resided at the time of the census, are included. The American Community Survey reports that by 2005 the number of unmarried-partner households had grown to approximately 6.0 million.

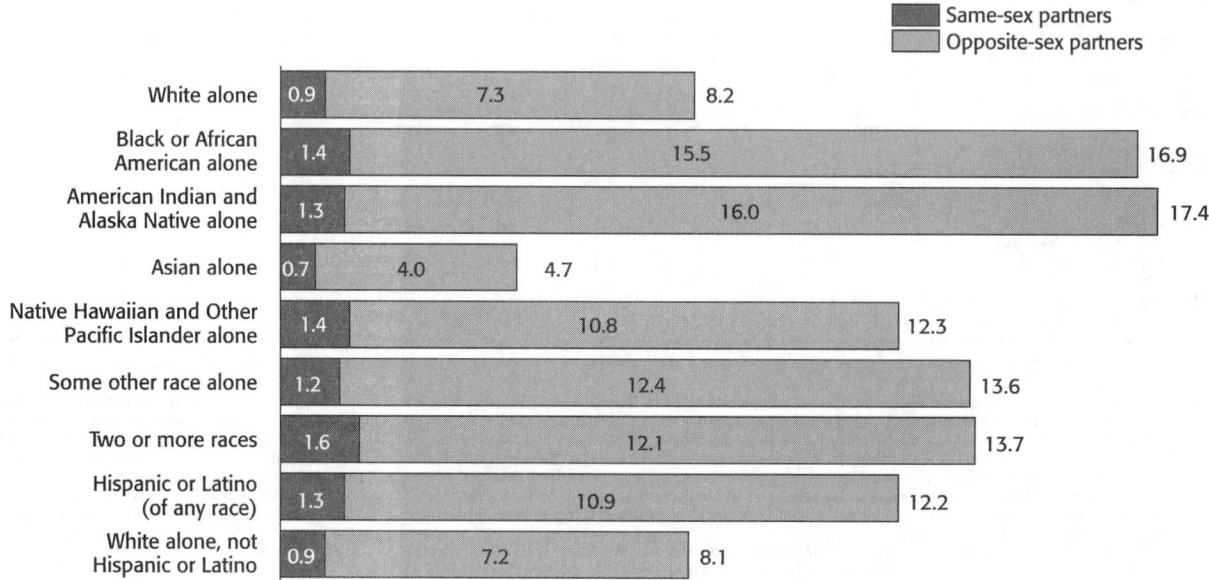

Unmarried-Partner Households by Sex of Partners and Race and Hispanic Origin of Householder: 2000
(Percent of all coupled households. For information on confidentiality protection, nonsampling error and definitions, see www.census.gov/prod/cen2000/docs/sf1.pdf)

Note: Percent same-sex partners and percent opposite-sex partners may not add to total percent unmarried-partner households because of rounding.
Source: U.S. Census Bureau, Census 2000 Summary File 2.

Sources:
U.S. Census Bureau. 2005 American Community Survey.
U.S. Census Bureau. *Married Couple and Unmarried Partner Households: 2000.*
U.S. Census Bureau. Technical Note on Same-Sex Unmarried Partner Data from the 1990 and 2000 Censuses.

Environment

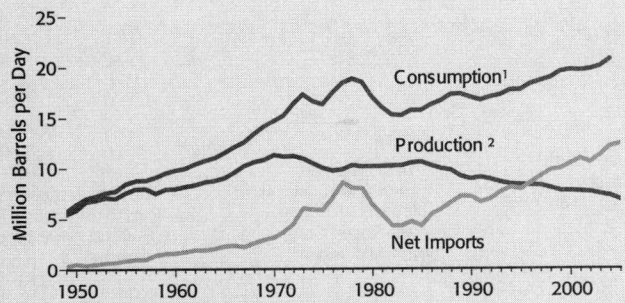

¹ Petroleum products supplied used as an approximation for consumption.
² Crude oil and natural gas plant liquids production.

Petroleum Overview, 1949–2005

When U.S. petroleum production peaked at 11.3 million barrels per day in 1970, net imports stood at 3.2 million barrels per day. By 1996, net imports exceeded production. In 2005, production was 6.8 million barrels per day, and net imports were 12.4 million barrels per day.
Source: U.S. Department of Energy, Energy Information Administration. *Annual Energy Review 2005.*

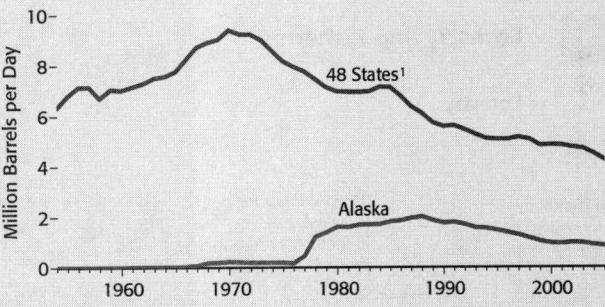

¹ United States excluding Alaska and Hawaii.

48 States and Alaskan Crude Oil Production, 1954–2005

Crude oil production peaked in the 48 States at 9.4 million barrels per day in 1970. As production fell in the 48 States, Alaska's production came on line and helped supply U.S. needs. Alaskan production peaked at 2.0 million barrels per day in 1988; in 2005, production stood at 43 percent of the peak level.
Source: U.S. Department of Energy, Energy Information Administration. *Annual Energy Review 2005.*

Land, Water, and Climate

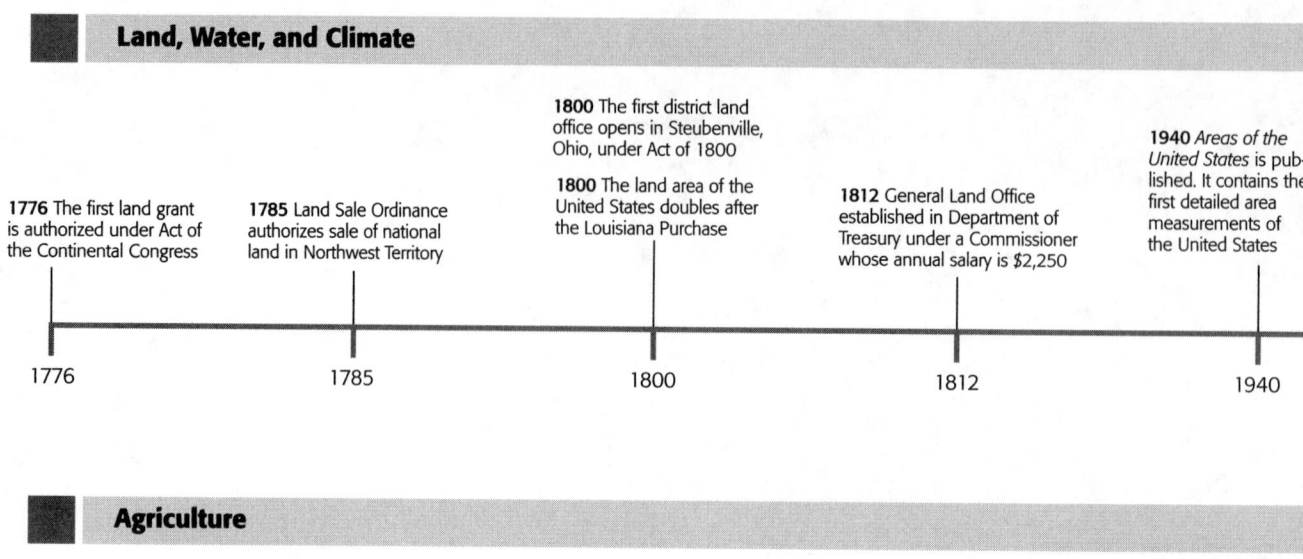

1776 The first land grant is authorized under Act of the Continental Congress

1785 Land Sale Ordinance authorizes sale of national land in Northwest Territory

1800 The first district land office opens in Steubenville, Ohio, under Act of 1800

1800 The land area of the United States doubles after the Louisiana Purchase

1812 General Land Office established in Department of Treasury under a Commissioner whose annual salary is $2,250

1940 *Areas of the United States* is published. It contains the first detailed area measurements of the United States

1776   1785   1800   1812   1940

Agriculture

1735 First Agricultural Experiment is set up near Savannah, Georgia

1785 The first agricultural society, the Philadelphia Society for the Promotion of Agriculture, is founded

1810 The first Agricultural Fair opens at the Berkshire Cattle Show in Pittsfield, Massachusetts

1840 The first Census of Agriculture is held

1855 The first agricultural college opens in Lansing, Michigan

1862 The Agriculture Bureau is established by Act of Congress under Commissioner Isaac Newton who is paid an annual salary of $3000

1863 The Bureau of Agriculture begins publication of agricultural statistics

1867 The National Grange for the Promotion of Husbandry, the first national agricultural organization, is founded in Washington D. C.

1867 Data on livestock are added to the Census of Agriculture

1735   1785   1810   1840   1855   1862   1863   1867

Forestry and Fisheries

Forestry

1626 Plymouth Colony issues first forestry legislation

1799 The first federal forestry legislation authorizes $200,000 for replanting trees

1871 The first recorded forest fire occurs at Peshtigo, north of Green Bay, Wisconsin

1875 American Forestry Association is founded in Chicago with Robert Douglas as first president

1881 The first university-level forestry course is offered at University of Michigan

1626   1799   1871   1875   1881

Fishing

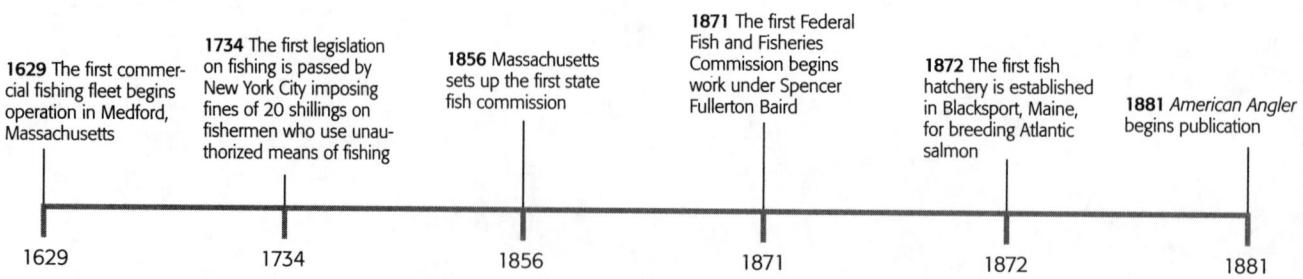

1629 The first commercial fishing fleet begins operation in Medford, Massachusetts

1734 The first legislation on fishing is passed by New York City imposing fines of 20 shillings on fishermen who use unauthorized means of fishing

1856 Massachusetts sets up the first state fish commission

1871 The first Federal Fish and Fisheries Commission begins work under Spencer Fullerton Baird

1872 The first fish hatchery is established in Blacksport, Maine, for breeding Atlantic salmon

1881 *American Angler* begins publication

1629   1734   1856   1871   1872   1881

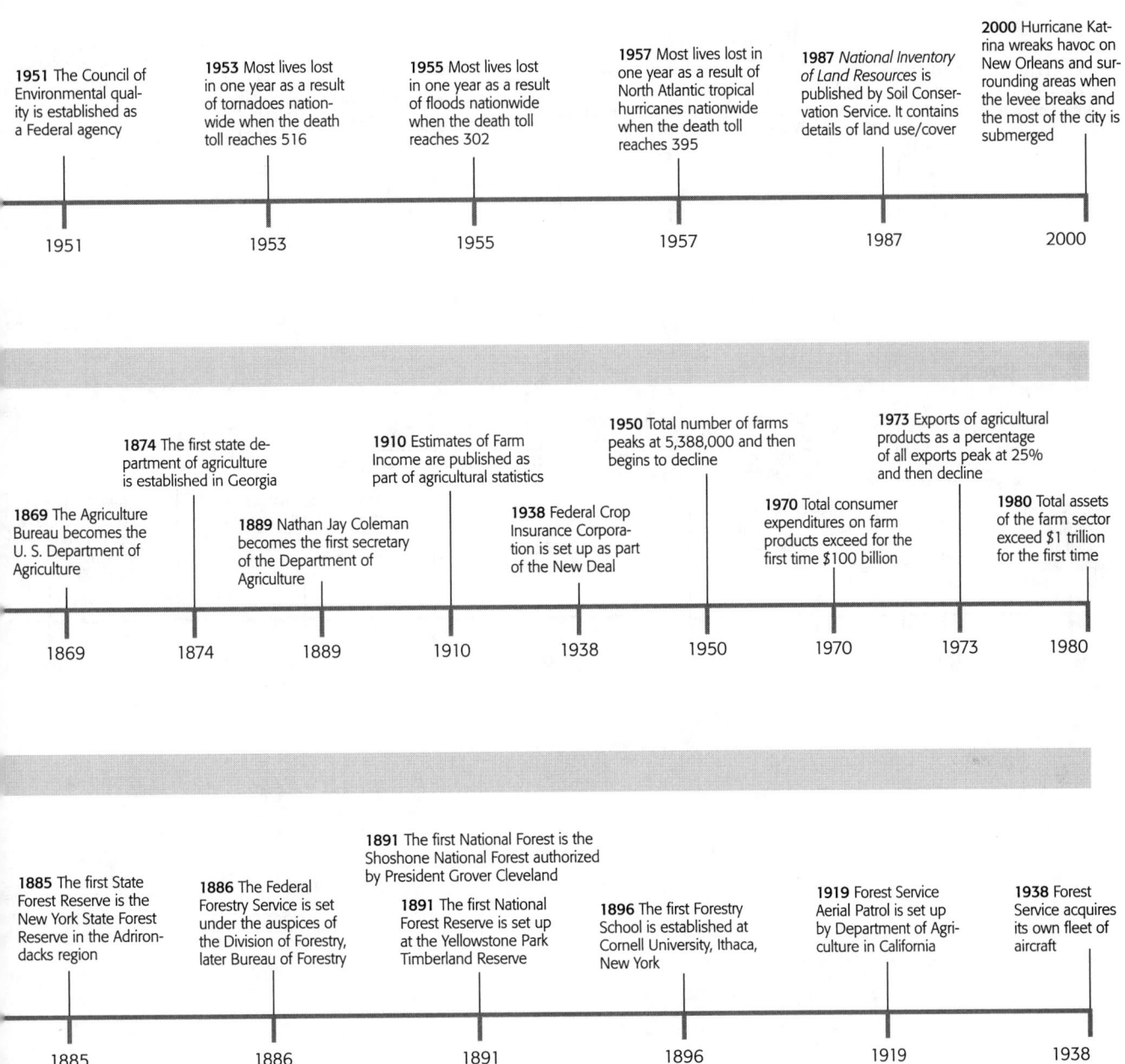

1951 The Council of Environmental quality is established as a Federal agency

1953 Most lives lost in one year as a result of tornadoes nationwide when the death toll reaches 516

1955 Most lives lost in one year as a result of floods nationwide when the death toll reaches 302

1957 Most lives lost in one year as a result of North Atlantic tropical hurricanes nationwide when the death toll reaches 395

1987 *National Inventory of Land Resources* is published by Soil Conservation Service. It contains details of land use/cover

2000 Hurricane Katrina wreaks havoc on New Orleans and surrounding areas when the levee breaks and the most of the city is submerged

1951 1953 1955 1957 1987 2000

1869 The Agriculture Bureau becomes the U. S. Department of Agriculture

1874 The first state department of agriculture is established in Georgia

1889 Nathan Jay Coleman becomes the first secretary of the Department of Agriculture

1910 Estimates of Farm Income are published as part of agricultural statistics

1938 Federal Crop Insurance Corporation is set up as part of the New Deal

1950 Total number of farms peaks at 5,388,000 and then begins to decline

1970 Total consumer expenditures on farm products exceed for the first time $100 billion

1973 Exports of agricultural products as a percentage of all exports peak at 25% and then decline

1980 Total assets of the farm sector exceed $1 trillion for the first time

1869 1874 1889 1910 1938 1950 1970 1973 1980

1885 The first State Forest Reserve is the New York State Forest Reserve in the Adrirondacks region

1886 The Federal Forestry Service is set under the auspices of the Division of Forestry, later Bureau of Forestry

1891 The first National Forest is the Shoshone National Forest authorized by President Grover Cleveland

1891 The first National Forest Reserve is set up at the Yellowstone Park Timberland Reserve

1896 The first Forestry School is established at Cornell University, Ithaca, New York

1919 Forest Service Aerial Patrol is set up by Department of Agriculture in California

1938 Forest Service acquires its own fleet of aircraft

1885 1886 1891 1896 1919 1938

Minerals and Natural Resources

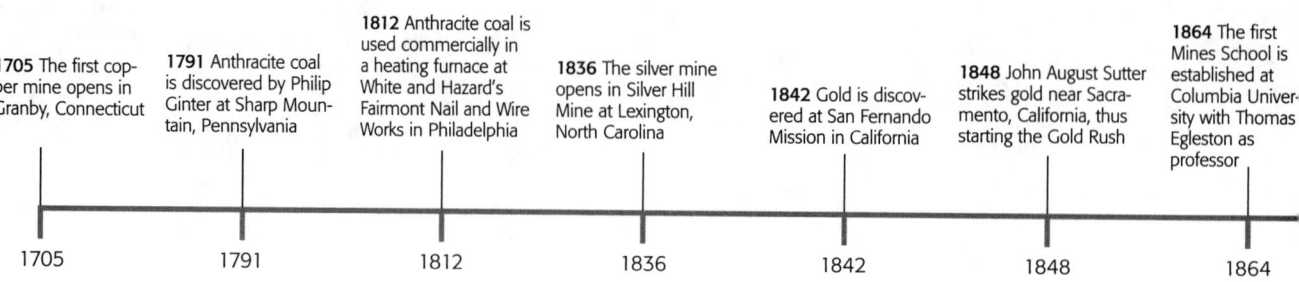

1705 The first copper mine opens in Granby, Connecticut

1791 Anthracite coal is discovered by Philip Ginter at Sharp Mountain, Pennsylvania

1812 Anthracite coal is used commercially in a heating furnace at White and Hazard's Fairmont Nail and Wire Works in Philadelphia

1836 The silver mine opens in Silver Hill Mine at Lexington, North Carolina

1842 Gold is discovered at San Fernando Mission in California

1848 John August Sutter strikes gold near Sacramento, California, thus starting the Gold Rush

1864 The first Mines School is established at Columbia University with Thomas Egleston as professor

1705   1791   1812   1836   1842   1848   1864

Energy

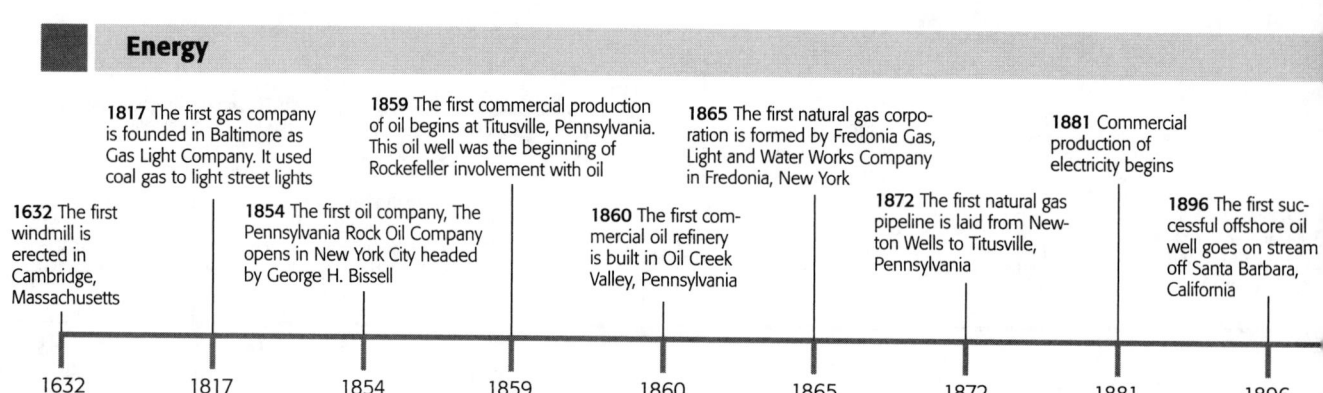

1817 The first gas company is founded in Baltimore as Gas Light Company. It used coal gas to light street lights

1859 The first commercial production of oil begins at Titusville, Pennsylvania. This oil well was the beginning of Rockefeller involvement with oil

1865 The first natural gas corporation is formed by Fredonia Gas, Light and Water Works Company in Fredonia, New York

1881 Commercial production of electricity begins

1632 The first windmill is erected in Cambridge, Massachusetts

1854 The first oil company, The Pennsylvania Rock Oil Company opens in New York City headed by George H. Bissell

1860 The first commercial oil refinery is built in Oil Creek Valley, Pennsylvania

1872 The first natural gas pipeline is laid from Newton Wells to Titusville, Pennsylvania

1896 The first successful offshore oil well goes on stream off Santa Barbara, California

1632   1817   1854   1859   1860   1865   1872   1881   1896

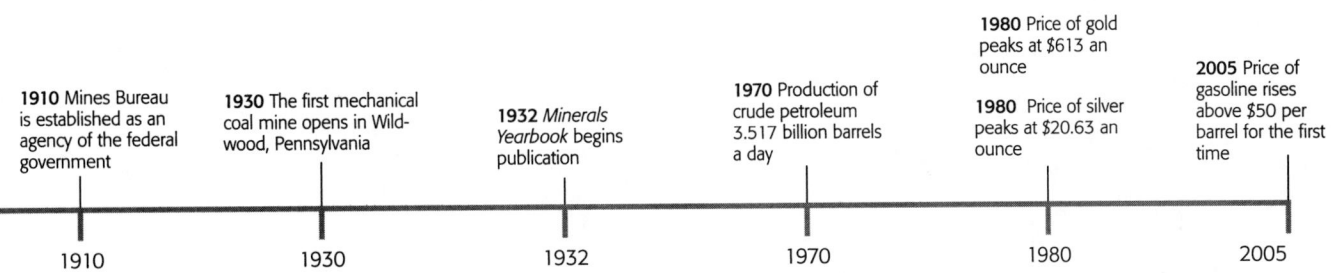

1910 Mines Bureau is established as an agency of the federal government

1930 The first mechanical coal mine opens in Wildwood, Pennsylvania

1932 *Minerals Yearbook* begins publication

1970 Production of crude petroleum 3.517 billion barrels a day

1980 Price of gold peaks at $613 an ounce

1980 Price of silver peaks at $20.63 an ounce

2005 Price of gasoline rises above $50 per barrel for the first time

1910   1930   1932   1970   1980   2005

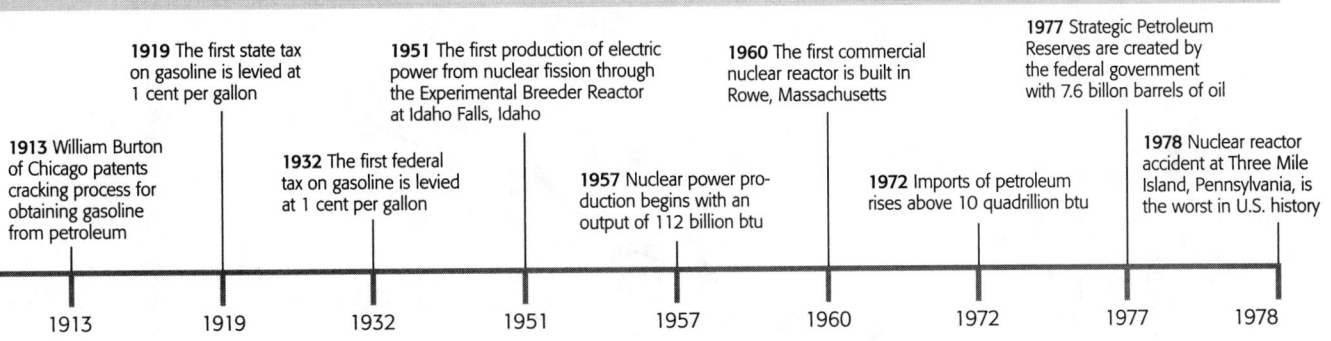

1913 William Burton of Chicago patents cracking process for obtaining gasoline from petroleum

1919 The first state tax on gasoline is levied at 1 cent per gallon

1932 The first federal tax on gasoline is levied at 1 cent per gallon

1951 The first production of electric power from nuclear fission through the Experimental Breeder Reactor at Idaho Falls, Idaho

1957 Nuclear power production begins with an output of 112 billion btu

1960 The first commercial nuclear reactor is built in Rowe, Massachusetts

1972 Imports of petroleum rises above 10 quadrillion btu

1977 Strategic Petroleum Reserves are created by the federal government with 7.6 billon barrels of oil

1978 Nuclear reactor accident at Three Mile Island, Pennsylvania, is the worst in U.S. history

1913   1919   1932   1951   1957   1960   1972   1977   1978

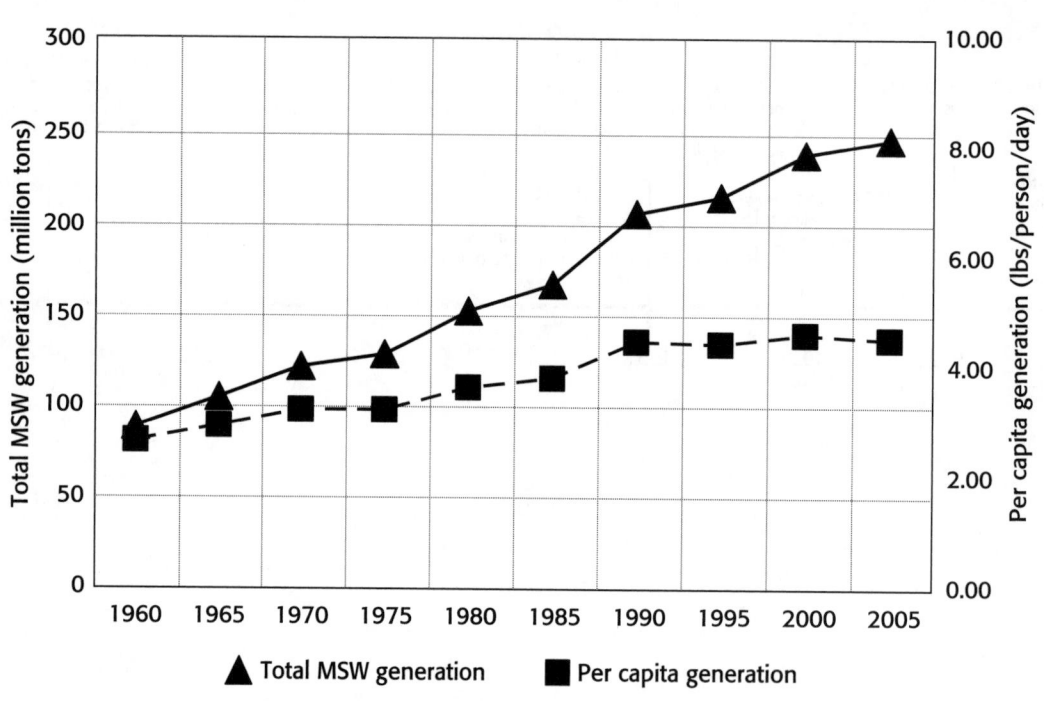

Municipal Solid Waste (MSW) Generation Rates, 1960–2005

Source: U.S. Environmental Protection Agency. *Municipal Solid Waste Generation, Recycling, and Disposal in the United States: Facts and Figures for 2005.*

CHAPTER **5**

Land, Water, and Climate

HIGHLIGHTS

1 When the United States became a republic, its boundaries were unclear. Its territorial claims were based on several treaties that were subject to interpretation. The boundaries themselves were poorly marked and expanded or receded depending on the status of the Indian Wars. From 1781 to 1867, the federal government acquired millions of acres of public domain. From 1781 to 1902, 7 of the original 13 states relinquished their claims to the so-called "Western lands" to the federal government. In 1788, the state of Maryland ceded the present area of the District of Columbia. Between 1810 and 1867, title to the remaining area west of the Mississippi River (except the state of Texas) and to Florida passed to the federal government. The annual report to the General Land Office in 1850 contained the first reference to the areas of the states and territories, although the methods used to obtain the measurements was not indicated. In 1881, the Bureau of the Census initiated the first effort to obtain an accurate and detailed area measurement of the United States. This was revised in 1940 in *Areas of the United States* and presented land and water areas, as well as state, municipal, and county boundaries. Differences in land area figures over time reflect improvements in cartography that made possible a more accurate determination of the outer limits as well as inclusion or exclusion of certain bodies of water. For the 2000 census, area measurements were calculated by computer based on the information contained in a single database, the TIGER (Topologically Integrated Geographic Encoding and Referencing) File. As result, the number of inland water areas increased when coverage was extended to inland bodies of water of at least 40 acres and streams with a width of at least one-eighth of a statute mile. An inventory of the nation's land resources by type of use/cover was conducted by the Soil Conservation Service from 1982 to 1987, and its results were published in 1987 in the *National Inventory of Land Resources*.

2 The state with the largest land area and largest water area is Alaska. Alaska's water area of 91,316 square miles is larger than the land area of all but 11 states.

3 The highest point in the United States is Mount McKinley in Alaska at 20,320 feet (6,198 meters). The lowest point is Death Valley in California at –282 feet (–86 meters).

4 The five Great Lakes—Michigan, Superior, Huron, Erie, and Ontario (including only those portions under the jurisdiction of the United States)—account for 60,178 square miles of water areas. The largest inland lakes outside the Great Lakes are Great Salt Lake (1,836 square miles) and Green Bay (1,396 square miles).

111

5 The Missouri, America's longest river, is 2,565 miles long. There are nine other rivers longer than 1,000 miles: Mississippi (2,340 miles), Yukon (1,980 miles), St. Lawrence (1,900 miles), Arkansas (1,460 miles), Atchafalaya (1,420 miles), Ohio (1,310 miles), Red (1,290 miles), Columbia (1,240 miles), and Snake (1,040 miles).

6 Of the 2,271,343,000 acres of land in the United States, 653,299,000 acres or 28.8 percent is federal land. The percentage of federal land is highest in Nevada (84.5 percent), Alaska (69.1 percent), Utah (57.4 percent), Oregon (53.1 percent), and Idaho (50.2 percent). It is lowest in Connecticut and Rhode Island (0.4 percent each), Iowa and New York (0.8 percent each), and Maine (1.1 percent).

7 In 2000, total water withdrawal (all water withdrawn from natural reservoirs, lakes, rivers, and so on for human consumption and industrial use) per day in the United States was 408 billion gallons or 1,430 gallons per capita. The largest water use was for electric utilities (196 billion gallons per day), followed by irrigation (137 billion gallons per day), public supply (43 billion gallons per day), and industrial use (23 billion gallons per day). Of total water withdrawals, 20.7 percent is ground water and 79.2 percent surface water.

8 The principal agency for environmental monitoring in the United States is the Council on Environmental Quality (CEQ), and the principal agency for pollution abatement and control activities is the Environmental Protection Agency (EPA). CEQ reports data on environmental conditions in its annual *Environmental Quality*. The National Ambient Air Quality Standards (NAAQS) are set by the EPA for particulate matter, sulfur dioxide, petrochemical oxidants (now called ozone), carbon monoxide, and nitrogen oxide. Environmental quality has steadily improved in the United States since the 1970s. In 2002 sulfur dioxide decreased to 15,353,000 tons from 31,218,000 in 1970; volatile organic compounds to 16,544,000 tons from 34,659,000 tons; carbon monoxide to 112,049,000 tons from 204,043,000 tons; lead to 2,627,000 tons (in 1996) from 220,869,000 tons; particular matter (PM-10) to 8,882,000 tons from 13,042,000 tons; and nitrogen dioxide to 21,102,000 tons from 26,883,000 tons in 2002.

9 In 2003, 236.2 million tons of waste were generated nationwide, or 4.4 pounds per capita per day. Of these, 72.3 million tons were recycled and recovered. Paper and paperboard accounted for 35.2 of recycled and recovered materials. The Northeast leads in curbside recycling programs, serving 83 percent of the population. The percentage of population served through recycling programs is lowest in the South at 35 percent.

10 In 2004, there were 1,302 hazardous waste sites in the United States, of which New Jersey had the most at 114 sites, followed by Pennsylvania (96), and California (95). North Dakota is the only state that does not have any hazardous waste sites.

11 In 2006, the United States had 599 species of endangered (those in immediate danger of becoming extinct) plants, 68 species of endangered mammals, 77 species of endangered birds, and 14 species of endangered reptiles. On the threatened species list (those likely to become endangered in the foreseeable future), there were 13 species of mammals, 15 species of birds, 23 species of reptiles, and 146 species of plants.

12 The number of tornadoes and storms has increased in the past 27 years. In 2004, there were 1,819 tornadoes (compared with 656 in 1987 and 701 in 1988). The number of North Atlantic tropical storms and hurricanes varied widely over the years. Between 1994 and 2004, there were 151 tropical storms and hurricanes in the Atlantic coastal states.

13 The lowest temperature on record in the United States was −80°F in Prospect Creek, Alaska. The city with the most precipitation is Mobile, Alabama, with 66.29 inches, but Juneau has the most rainy days—223—in a year. Sault Ste Marie (Michigan) holds the record for the highest average annual snowfall: 117.4 inches.

14 Between 2003 and 2004, land not owned by the federal government in Nevada increased from 5.675 thousand acres to 10.902 thousand acres, a jump of more than 90 percent.

15 The number of people in the Gulf Coast before hurricane Katrina was 11.092 million. In the months following the hurricane, the population decreased to 10.708 million.

Table 5-1. Land Area of the United States, 1790–2000

(Square miles.)

Year	Area		
	Gross area	Land	Water
United States			
2000	3 794 083	3 537 438	256 645
1990	3 787 425	3 536 342	251 083
1980	3 618 770	3 539 289	79 481
1970 (April 1)	3 615 122	3 536 855	78 267
1960 (April 1)	3 615 123	3 540 911	74 212
1950 (April 1)	3 615 211	3 552 206	63 005
Coterminous United States[1]			
1960 (April 1)	3 002 261	2 968 054	54 207
1950 (April 1)	3 022 387	2 974 726	47 661
1940 (April 1)	3 022 387	2 977 128	45 259
1930 (April 1)	3 022 387	2 977 128	45 259
1920 (Jan. 1)	3 022 387	2 969 451	52 936
1910 (April 15)	3 022 387	2 969 565	52 822
1900 (June 1)	3 022 387	2 969 834	52 553
1890 (June 1)	3 022 387	2 969 640	52 747
1880 (June 1)	3 022 387	2 969 640	52 747
1870 (June 1)	3 022 387	2 969 640	52 747
1860 (June 1)	3 022 387	2 969 640	52 747
1850 (June 1)	2 992 747	2 940 042	52 705
1840 (June 1)	1 788 006	1 749 462	38 544
1830 (June 1)	1 788 006	1 749 462	38 544
1820 (Aug. 7)	1 788 006	1 749 462	38 544
1810 (Aug. 6)	1 716 003	1 681 828	34 175
1800 (Aug. 4)	888 811	864 746	24 065
1790 (Aug. 2)	888 811	864 746	24 065

Source: U.S. Census Bureau.
[1]Excludes Alaska and Hawaii.

Table 5-2. Estimated Water Use, 1900–2000

(Billions of gallons, daily average.)

Year	Total water use	Total irrigation[1]	Total public water utilities	Self–supplied use		
				Total rural domestic[2]	Total industrial and miscellaneous[3]	Total steam electric utilities
2000	408	137.0	43.3	5.4	22.3	195.5
1995	402	134.0	43.0	8.9	26.0	190.0
1990	408	137.0	41.0	7.9	30.0	195.0
1985	399	137.0	38.0	7.8	31.0	187.0
1980	440	150.0	34.0	5.6	45.0	210.0
1975	420	140.0	29.0	4.9	45.0	200.0
1974	373	125.0	29.0	4.5	63.0	145.0
1973	361	124.0	29.0	4.5	61.0	142.0
1972	350	122.0	28.0	4.4	59.0	135.0
1971	338	120.0	27.0	4.4	57.0	128.0
1970	327	119.2	27.0	4.3	56.0	120.8
1969	403	156.8	26.6	6.8	83.4	129.6
1968	395	154.6	26.2	6.7	80.9	126.9
1967	388	152.5	25.8	6.7	78.3	124.3
1966	380	150.3	25.4	6.6	75.8	121.6
1965	270	110.8	23.7	4.1	46.4	84.5
1964	362	145.5	24.4	6.4	70.8	114.9
1963	352	142.9	23.8	6.3	68.4	110.8
1962	344	141.2	23.3	6.2	66.6	107.2
1961	335	138.5	22.7	6.1	64.2	103.1
1960[4]	323	135.0	22.0	6.0	61.2	98.7
1958	299	127.5	19.7	5.8	56.4	89.9
1955	264	116.3	16.3	5.4	49.2	76.6
1950	203	100.0	14.1	4.6	38.1	45.9
1946	166	86.4	12.0	3.5	33.0	30.8
1945	170	83.1	12.0	3.2	41.0	31.2
1944	178	80.6	12.0	3.2	48.0	34.6
1940	136	71.0	10.1	3.1	29.0	23.2
1930	110	60.2	8.0	2.9	21.0	18.4
1920	92	55.9	6.0	2.4	18.0	9.2
1910	66	39.0	4.7	2.2	14.0	6.5
1900	40	20.2	3.0	2.0	10.0	5.0

Source: U.S. Census Bureau. U.S. Bureau of Domestic Business Development. U.S. Geological Survey.
[1]Total take including delivery losses but not including reservoir evaporation.
[2]Rural farm and nonfarm household and garden use, and for farm stock and dairies.
[3]For 1900–1960, includes manufacturing industries, mineral industries, rural commercial industries, air conditioning, resorts, hotels, motels, military, and other state and federal agencies and other miscellaneous uses; thereafter, includes manufacturing, mining, and mineral processing, ordance and construction.
[4]Denotes first year for which figures include Alaska and Hawaii.

Table 5-3. Tornadoes, Floods, Tropical Cyclones, and Lightning, 1886–2004

(Number, millions of dollars.)

Year	Tornadoes Number	Lives lost Total	Most in a single tornado	With $500,000 and over in property loss	Floods Lives lost	Property loss ($1,000,000)	Total hurricanes reaching U.S. coast	Lives lost in United States	Property loss ($1,000,000)	Lightning Lives lost
2004	1 819	35	...	...	82	1 696.2	...	34	18 901.8	32
2003	1 376	54	...	...	85	2 540.9	...	14	1 879.5	44
2002	941	55	...	...	49	655.0	1	51	1 104.4	51
2001	1 216	40	...	...	48	1 220.3	0	24	5 187.8	44
2000	1 071	41	...	...	38	1 255.1	0	0	8.1	51
1999	1 343	94	...	...	68	1 420.7	3	19	4 190.1	46
1998	1 424	130	...	...	136	2 324.8	3	9	3 546.6	44
1997	1 148	67	...	...	118	6 910.6	1	1	667.6	42
1996	1 170	26	...	...	131	2 120.7	2	37	1 436.1	52
1995	1 235	30	...	...	80	1 250.5	2	17	5 932.3	85
1994	1 082	69	...	...	91	...	0	9	973.0	69
1993	1 173	33	...	...	103	...	1	2	57.0	43
1992	1 297	39	...	...	62	...	1	27	26 500.0	41
1991	1 132	39	...	...	61	...	1	19	1 500.0	73
1990	1 133	53	...	91	142	...	0	0	57.0	74
1989	856	50	21	60	81	...	4	56	...	...
1988	702	32	5	48	29	...	12	...	...	...
1987	656	59	30	38	82	...	7	...	...	...
1986	764	15	3	75	80	...	6	...	...	...
1985	684	94	18	69	304	...	11	9	...	...
1984	907	122	16	125	126	...	2	4	...	...
1983	931	34	3	95	200	...	2	22	...	...
1982	1 046	64	10	92	155	...	1	...	...	...
1981	783	24	5	55	90	...	2	...	...	...
1980	866	28	5	92	97	...	2	2	...	...
1979	852	84	42	73	100	...	5	11	...	...
1978	788	53	16	59	120	...	2	35	...	...
1977	852	43	22	46	212	...	1	...	...	...
1976	835	44	5	46	187	...	2	9	...	...
1975	920	60	9	42	114	...	1	21	...	...
1974	947	361	34	107	121	...	1	1	...	...
1973	1 102	87	7	76	105	...	1	5	...	...
1972	741	27	6	29	540	...	3	121	...	...
1971	888	156	58	35	74	...	5	8	...	...
1970	649	73	26	30	135	...	4	11	...	...
1969	604	66	32	19	297	...	3	256	...	...
1968	661	131	34	32	31	...	3	9	...	...
1967	912	116	33	41	34	...	2	18	...	...
1966	570	99	58	17	31	...	2	54	...	...
1965	899	298	44	41	119	...	2	75	...	...
1964	713	73	22	22	100	...	6	49	...	...
1963	461	31	5	16	39	...	1	11	...	...
1962	658	28	17	10	19	...	1	4	...	...
1961	682	51	16	22	52	...	3	46	...	...
1960	618	47	16	12	32	...	5	65	...	...
1959	589	58	21	5	25	...	7	24	...	...
1958	565	66	19	9	47	...	1	2	...	...
1957	864	191	44	29	82	...	5	395	...	...
1956	532	83	25	25	42	...	2	21	...	...
1955	593	125	80	14	302	...	5	218	...	...
1954	549	35	6	9	55	...	4	193	...	...
1953	437	516	116	25	40	...	6	2	...	...
1952	236	230	57	19	54	...	2	3	...	...
1951	272	34	6	13	51	...	1	...	...	...
1950	199	70	18	9	93	...	4	19	...	...
1949	249	212	58	13	48	...	3	4	...	...
1948	183	140	33	13	82	...	4	3	...	...
1947	165	313	169	8	55	...	7	53	...	...
1946	106	78	15	7	28	...	4	...	...	...
1945	121	210	69	11	91	...	5	7	...	...
1944	169	275	100	9	33	...	4	64	...	...
1943	152	58	5	8	107	...	4	16	...	...
1942	167	384	65	10	68	...	3	8	...	...
1941	118	53	25	1	47	...	4	10	...	...

. . . = Not available.

Table 5-3. Tornadoes, Floods, Tropical Cyclones, and Lightning, 1886–2004—*Continued*

(Number, millions of dollars.)

Year	Tornadoes				Floods		North Atlantic tropical cyclones (including hurricanes)			Lightning
	Number	Lives lost Total	Most in a single tornado	With $500,000 and over in property loss	Lives lost	Property loss ($1,000,000)	Total hurricanes reaching U.S. coast	Lives lost in United States	Property loss ($1,000,000)	Lives lost
1940	124	65	18	2	60	...	3	51	...	...
1939	152	87	27	3	83	...	3	3	...	...
1938	213	183	32	6	180	...	4	600	...	...
1937	147	29	5	...	142	...	4	...	...	...
1936	151	552	216	6	142	...	7	9	...	...
1935	180	70	11	...	236	...	2	414	...	...
1934	147	47	6	3	88	...	5	17	...	...
1933	258	362	34	9	33	...	7	63	...	...
1932	151	394	37	2	11	...	5	...	...	...
1931	94	36	6	1	...	...	2	...	...	...
1930	192	179	41	6	14	...	1	...	...	...
1929	197	274	40	4	89	...	2	3	...	...
1928	203	92	14	7	15	...	3	1 836	...	...
1927	163	540	92	10	423	...	1	...	...	...
1926	111	144	23	...	16	...	4	269	...	...
1925	119	794	689	3	36	...	2	6	...	...
1924	130	376	85	12	...	...	3	2	...	...
1923	102	109	23	1	...	...	4	...	...	...
1922	108	135	16	5	...	...	1	...	...	...
1921	105	202	61	3	...	...	2	5	...	...
1920	87	498	87	10	...	...	3	2	...	...
1919	64	206	59	2	...	...	2	287	...	...
1918	81	135	36	5	...	...	2	34	...	...
1917	121	509	101	9	...	...	1	5	...	...
1916	90	150	30	1	...	...	8	107	...	...
1915	...	...	...	...	...	...	4	600	...	...
1914	...	...	...	...	...	...	1	...	...	...
1913	...	...	...	...	...	...	3	...	...	...
1912	...	...	...	...	...	...	4	12	...	...
1911	...	...	...	...	...	...	2	17	...	...
1910	...	...	...	...	...	...	2	13	...	...
1909	...	...	...	...	...	...	7	404	...	...
1908	...	...	...	...	...	...	2	...	...	...
1907	...	...	...	...	...	...	3	...	...	...
1906	...	...	...	...	...	...	6	285	...	...
1905	...	...	...	...	...	...	2	...	...	...
1904	...	...	...	...	...	...	3	...	...	...
1903	...	...	...	...	...	...	2	9	...	...
1902	...	...	...	...	...	...	3	...	...	...
1901	...	...	...	...	...	...	6	10	...	...
1900	...	...	...	...	...	...	3	...	...	...
1899	...	...	...	...	...	...	4	...	...	...
1898	...	...	...	...	...	...	6	...	...	...
1897	...	...	...	...	...	...	4	...	...	...
1896	...	...	...	...	...	...	4	...	...	...
1895	...	...	...	...	...	...	4	...	...	...
1894	...	...	...	...	...	...	3	...	...	...
1893	...	...	...	...	...	...	7	...	...	...
1892	...	...	...	...	...	...	3	...	...	...
1891	...	...	...	...	...	...	4	...	...	...
1889	...	...	...	...	...	...	4	...	...	...
1888	...	...	...	...	...	...	6	...	...	...
1887	...	...	...	...	...	...	4	...	...	...
1886	...	...	...	...	...	...	7	...	...	...

Source: U.S. Census Bureau. U.S. National Oceanic and Atmospheric Administration.
. . . = Not available.

Table 5-4. Major U.S. Weather Disasters by Type, Cost, and Number of Deaths: 1980 to 2005

(Covers only weather related disasters costing $1 billion or more. Estimated costs represent actual dollar costs and are not adjusted for inflation.)

Event	Description	Time period	Estimated cost ($1,000,000,000)	Deaths (number)
Hurricane Wilma	Category 3 hurricane makes landfall in southwest Florida, causing considerable damage from major flooding and strong winds in south-east Florida.	October 2005	> 10.0	35
Hurricane Rita	Category 3 hurricane makes landfall on the Texas-Louisiana border coastal region, causing surge/wind damage along the coast and flood damage in FL, MS, LA, AR, and TX.	September 2005	> 8.0	119
Hurricane Katrina	Category 3 hurricane makes landfall as a category 1 near Miami, FL, and on the LA, MS coast, causing massive damage in addition to flood and wind damage in Al, FL, TN, KY, OH, and GA.	August 2005	> 100.0	1 300+
Hurricane Dennis	Category 3 hurricane makes landfall in western Florida causing wind and surge damage, also causing wind and flood damage to GA, MS, and TN.	July 2005	> 2.0	12+
Midwest Drought	Midwest drought causing crop losses in AR, IL, IN, MO, OH, and WI.	Spring–summer 2005	> 1.0	0
Hurricane Jeanne	Category 3 hurricane makes landfall in east-central Florida, causing considerable damage in Florida and some flood damage in GA, SC, NC, VA, MD, DE, NJ, PA, and NY.	September 2004	> 6.9	28
Hurricane Ivan	Category 3 hurricane makes landfall on Gulf coast of Alabama causing significant damage in AL and FL and wind/flood damage in GA, SC, NC, LA, MS, WV, MD, TN, KY, OH, DE, NJ, PA, and NY.	September 2004	> 14.0	57
Hurricane Frances	Category 2 hurricane makes landfall in east-central Florida causing significant damage in FL and considerable flood damage in GA, SC, NC, and NY.	September 2004	> 9.0	48
Hurricane Charley	Category 4 hurricane makes landfall in southwest FL resulting in major damage in FL and some damage in SC.	August 2004	15.0	34
Southern California wildfires	Dry weather, high winds, and resulting wildfires in southern CA burned 743,000 acres and destroyed 3700 homes.	October–November 2003	2.5	22
Hurricane Isabel	Category 2 hurricane makes landfall in eastern NC, causing damage along coasts of NC, VA, and MD with wind damage and flooding in NC, VA, MD, DE, WV, NJ, NY, and PA.	September 2003	5.0	55
Midwest severe storms and tornadoes	Numerous tornadoes over the Midwest, MS River valley, and OH/TN River valleys with record 400 tornadoes in one week.	May 2003	> 3.4	51
Storms and hail	Severe storms and large hail over southern plains, lower MS River valley, and TX.	April 2003	> 1.6	3
Widespread drought	Moderate to extreme drought over large portions of 30 states.	Spring to fall 2002	> 10.0	0
Western fire season	Major fires over 11 western states from Rockies to west coast.	Spring to fall 2002	> 2.0	21
Tropical Storm Allison	Tropical storm produced rainfall and severe flooding in coastal portions of TX and LA and damage in MS, FL, VA, and PA.	June 2001	5.0	43
Midwest and Ohio Valley hail and tornadoes	Storms, tornadoes, and hail in TX, OK, KS, NE, IA, MO, IL, IN, WI, MI, OH, KY, and PA.	April 2001	> 1.9	3
Southern drought/heat wave	Severe drought and heat over south-central and south-eastern states cause significant losses in agriculture and related industries.	Spring–summer 2000	> 4.0	140
Western fire season	Severe fire season in western states.	Spring–summer	> 2.0	0
Hurricane Floyd	Category 2 hurricane in NC, causing severe flooding in NC and some flooding in SC, VA, MD, PA, NY, NJ, DE, RI, CT, MA, and VT.	September 1999	6.0	77
Drought/heat wave	Drought/heat wave over eastern U.S.	Summer 1999	1.0	502
Oklahoma-Kansas tornadoes	Category F4-F5 tornadoes hit OK, KS, TX, and TN.	May 1999	1.6	55
Arkansas-Tennessee tornados	Two outbreaks of tornadoes in 6-day period.	January 1999	1.3	17
Texas flooding	Severe flooding in southeast Texas from 2 heavy rain events with 10–20 inch totals.	October–November 1998	1.0	31
Hurricane Georges	Category 2 hurricane in Puerto Rico, Florida Keys, and Gulf coasts of LA, MS, AL, and FL.	September 1998	5.9	16
Hurricane Bonnie	Category 3 hurricane in eastern NC and VA.	August 1998	1.0	3

Table 5-4. Major U.S. Weather Disasters by Type, Cost, and Number of Deaths: 1980 to 2005—Continued

(Covers only weather related disasters costing $1 billion or more. Estimated costs represent actual dollar costs and are not adjusted for inflation.)

Event	Description	Time period	Estimated cost ($1,000,000,000)	Deaths (number)
Southern drought/heat wave	Severe drought and heat wave from TX/OK to the Carolinas.	Summer 1998	6.0–9.0	200
Minnesota severe storms/hail	Very damaging severe thunderstorms with large hail over wide areas of Minnesota.	May 1998	1.5	1
Southeast severe weather	Tornadoes and flooding related to strong El Nino in the southeast.	Winter/Spring 1998	1.0	132
Northeast ice storm	Intense ice storm hits ME, NH, VT, and NY.	January 1998	1.4	16
Northern plains flooding	Severe flooding in Dakotas and Minnesota due to heavy spring snowmelt.	April–May 1997	3.7	11
MS and OH valleys flooding and tornadoes	Tornadoes and severe flooding hit the states of AR, MO, MS, TN, IL, IN, KY, OH, and WV.	March 1997	1.0	67
West Coast flooding	Flooding from rains and snowmelt in CA, WA, OR, ID, NV, and MT.	December 1996–January 1997	3.0	36
Hurricane Fran	Category 3 hurricane in NC and VA.	September 1996	5.0	37
Southern Plains severe drought	Drought in agricultural areas of TX and OK.	Fall 1995–summer 1996	5.0	0
Pacific Northwest Severe Flooding	Flooding from heavy rain and snowmelt in OR, WA, ID, and MT.	February 1996	1.0	9
Blizzard of '96 followed by flooding	Heavy snowstorm followed by severe flooding in Appalachians, Mid-Atlantic, and Northeast.	January 1996	3.0	187
Hurricane Opal	Category 3 hurricane in FL, AL, parts of GA, TN, and Carolinas.	October 1995	> 3.0	27
Hurricane Marilyn	Category 2 hurricane in Virgin Islands.	September 1995	2.1	13
TX/OK/LA/MS severe weather and flooding	Flooding, hail, and tornadoes across TX, OK, parts of LA, MS, Dallas and New Orleans hardest hit.	May 1995	5.0–6.0	32
California flooding	Flooding from frequent winter storms across much of CA.	January–March 1995	> 3.0	27
Western fire season	Severe fire season in western states due to dry weather.	Summer–Fall 1994	1.0	. . .
Texas flooding	Flooding from torrential rain and thunderstorms across southeast TX.	October 1994	1.0	19
Tropical storm Alberto	Flooding due to 10 to 25 inch rain across GA, AL, part of FL.	July 1994	1.0	32
Southeast ice storm	Intense ice storm in pts of TX, OK, AR, LA, MS, AL, TN, GA, SC, NC, and VA.	February 1994	3.0	9
California wildfires	Out-of-control wildfires over southern CA.	Fall 1993	1.0	4
Midwest flooding	Extreme flooding across central U.S.	Summer 1993	21.0	48
Drought/heat wave	Extreme drought/heat wave across southeastern U.S.	Summer 1993	1.0	16
Storm/Blizzard	"Storm of the Century" hits entire eastern seaboard.	March 1993	5.0–6	270.0
Nor'easter of 1992	Slow-moving storm batters northeast U.S. coast, New England.	December 1992	1.0–2.0	19
Hurricane Iniki	Category 4 hurricane hit Hawaiian island of Kauai.	September 1992	1.8	7
Hurricane Andrew	Category 4 hurricane hit FL and LA.	August 1992	27.0	61
Oakland Firestorm	Oakland, CA firestorm due to low humidity and high winds.	October 1991	2.5	25
Hurricane Bob	Category 2 hurricane—mainly coastal NC, Long Island, and New England.	August 1991	1.5	18
TX/OK/LA/AR flooding	Torrential rains cause flooding along Trinity, Red, and Arkansas rivers.	May 1990	1.0	13
Hurricane Hugo	Category 4 hurricane devastates South and North Carolina with ~20 foot storm surge and severe wind damage after hitting Puerto Rico and the U.S. Virgin Islands.	September 1989	> 9.0	86
Northern Plains Drought	Severe summer drought over much of the northern plains with significant losses to agriculture.	Summer 1989	= 1.0	-
Drought/heat wave	Drought in central and eastern U.S. with very severe losses to agriculture and related industries.	Summer 1988	40.0	5 000–10 000

. . . = Not available or not reported.
- = Quantity zero.

Table 5-4. Major U.S. Weather Disasters by Type, Cost, and Number of Deaths: 1980 to 2005—*Continued*

(Covers only weather related disasters costing $1 billion or more. Estimated costs represent actual dollar costs and are not adjusted for inflation.)

Event	Description	Time period	Estimated cost ($1,000,000,000)	Deaths (number)
Southeast drought/heat wave	Severe summer drought in parts of southeastern U.S. with severe losses to agriculture.	Summer 1986	1.0–1.5	100
Hurricane Juan	Category 1 hurricane hitting Louisiana and Southeast U.S. causing severe flooding.	October–November 1985	1.5	63
Hurricane Elena	Category 3 hurricane causing damage from Florida to Louisiana.	August–September 1985	1.3	4
Florida Freeze	Severe freeze in central/northern Florida, causing losses to citrus industry.	January 1985	1.2	-
1983 Florida Freeze	Severe freeze in central/northern Florida, causing losses to citrus industry.	December 1983	2.0	-
Hurricane Alicia	Category 3 hurricane affecting Texas.	August 1983	3.0	21
Western Storms and Flooding	Storms and flooding related to El Niño, especially in the states of WA, OR, CA, AZ, NV, ID, UT, and MT.	1982–early 1983	1.1	≥ 45
Gulf States Storms and Flooding	Storms and flooding related to El Niño, especially in the states of TX, AR, LA, MS, AL, GA, and FL.	1982–early 1983	1.1	≥ 50
1980 Drought/heat wave	Affecting central and eastern U.S. with damages to agriculture and related industries.	June–September 1980	20.0	~ 10 000

Source: U.S. Census Bureau. *Statistical Abstract of the United States: 2007* and U.S. National Oceanic and Atmospheric Administration, National Climatic Data Center. *Billion Dollar U.S. Weather Disasters, 1980–2005.*
. . . = Not available or not reported.
- = Quantity zero.

Table 5-5. Municipal Solid Waste Generation, Recovery, and Disposal, 1990–2003

(Millions of tons, pounds per person, percent. Covers post-consumer residential and commercial solid wastes which comprise the major portion of typical municipal collections. Excludes mining, agricultural and industrial processing, demolition and construction wastes, sewage sludge, and junked autos and obsolete equipment wastes. Based on material-flows estimating procedure and wet weight as generated.)

Year	1990	1991	1992	1993	1994	1995	1996	1997	1998	1999	2000	2001	2002	2003
Waste Generated	205.2	204.6	208.9	211.8	214.2	211.4	209.2	217.0	223.4	231.0	234.0	231.2	235.5	236.2
Per person per day (lb)	4.5	4.4	4.5	4.5	4.5	4.4	4.3	4.4	4.5	4.6	4.5	4.4	4.5	4.4
Materials Recovered	33.2	37.0	40.6	43.8	50.8	54.9	57.4	60.8	61.1	64.8	68.9	69.3	70.5	72.3
Per person per day (lb)	0.7	0.8	0.9	0.9	1.1	1.1	1.2	1.2	1.2	1.3	1.3	1.3	1.3	1.4
Combustion for Energy Recovery	31.9	30.1	30.5	30.9	31.2	35.5	36.1	36.7	34.4	34.0	33.7	33.6	33.4	33.1
Per person per day (lb)	0.7	0.7	0.7	0.7	0.7	0.7	0.7	0.8	0.7	0.7	0.7	0.7	0.6	0.6
Combustion without Energy Recovery	2.2	2.2	2.2	1.6	1.3	1.0	...	...	...	...	...	...	...	...
Per person per day (lb)	0.05	0.05	0.05	0.03	0.03	0.02	...	...	...	...	...	...	...	...
Landfill, Other Disposal	140.1	135.3	135.7	135.5	130.9	120.9	115.7	119.5	127.1	132.1	131.4	128.3	131.7	130.8
Per person per day (lb)	3.1	2.9	2.9	2.9	2.8	2.5	2.4	2.4	2.6	2.7	2.6	2.5	2.5	2.5
Percent Distribution of Generation														
Paper and paperboard	35.4	34.7	35.5	36.6	37.7	38.6	38.1	38.6	37.7	38.2	37.5	35.7	35.8	35.2
Glass	6.4	6.2	6.3	6.4	6.2	6.1	5.9	5.5	5.7	5.6	5.4	5.4	5.4	5.3
Metals	8.1	8.1	7.7	7.5	7.6	7.5	7.7	7.7	7.5	7.7	7.8	7.9	7.8	8.0
Plastics	8.3	8.7	8.8	9.0	9.0	8.9	9.4	9.9	10.0	10.4	10.5	10.9	11.2	11.3
Rubber and leather	2.8	2.9	2.8	2.7	2.9	2.9	3.0	3.0	3.1	2.7	2.8	2.9	2.8	2.9
Textiles	2.8	3.0	3.2	3.2	3.4	3.5	3.7	3.8	3.9	3.9	4.0	4.2	4.4	4.5
Wood	6.0	6.2	5.9	5.8	5.3	4.9	5.2	5.3	5.4	5.4	5.5	5.7	5.7	5.8
Food wastes	10.1	10.2	10.1	10.0	10.0	10.3	10.4	10.1	11.2	10.9	11.3	11.7	11.6	11.7
Yard wastes	17.1	17.1	16.8	15.7	14.7	14.0	13.3	12.8	12.4	12.0	11.8	12.1	12.0	12.1
Other wastes	3.0	3.1	2.9	3.0	3.2	3.3	3.3	3.3	3.2	3.2	3.2	3.4	3.3	3.2

Source: U.S. Census Bureau. *Statistical Abstract of the United States: 2007.* Franklin Associates, a Division of ERG. *Municipal Solid Waste Generation, Recycling, and Disposal in the United States: Facts and Figures for 2003.*
. . . = Not available.

Table 5-6. National Air Pollutant Emissions, 1970–2002

(Thousands of tons, except as indicated. PM-10 is particulate matter of less than ten microns; PM-2.5 = particulate matter of less than 2.5 microns. Methodologies to estimate data for 1970 to 1980 period and 1985 to present emissions differ.)

Year	Emissions							
	PM-10	PM-10, fugitive dust[1]	PM-2.5	Sulfur dioxide	Nitrogen dioxides	Volatile organic compounds	Carbon monoxide	Lead[2] (tons)
2002	8 882	13 272	6 803	15 353	21 102	16 544	112 049	...
2001	9 118	13 769	6 632	15 932	21 547	17 118	106 295	...
2000	9 440	14 307	7 288	16 347	22 598	17 512	114 467	...
1999	9 391	14 112	7 333	17 545	22 845	18 776	114 541	...
1998	8 343	14 550	6 261	18 944	24 348	18 782	115 380	...
1997	8 393	14 516	6 256	18 840	24 705	19 530	117 910	...
1996	9 014	13 844	6 725	18 385	24 787	20 871	128 858	2 627
1995	8 807	17 012	6 929	18 619	24 956	22 041	126 777	3 929
1994	8 888	19 722	7 541	21 346	25 349	22 569	133 559	4 047
1993	8 411	18 953	7 150	21 772	25 357	22 730	135 901	3 916
1992	8 927	18 170	7 198	22 082	25 260	23 066	140 896	3 810
1991	9 270	18 075	7 320	22 375	25 179	23 577	147 128	4 169
1990	9 689	18 063	7 559	23 076	25 529	24 108	154 186	4 975
1985	11 590	29 734	...	23 307	25 757	27 404	176 844	22 890
1980	7 013	...	...	25 925	27 079	31 106	185 407	74 153
1975	7 671	...	...	28 043	26 337	30 765	188 398	159 659
1970	13 042	...	...	31 218	26 883	34 659	204 043	220 869

Source: U.S. Census Bureau. *Statistical Abstract of the United States: 2007.* U.S. Environmental Protection Agency.
[1]Sources such as agricultural tilling, construction, mining and quarrying, paved roads, unpaved roads, and wind erosion.
[2]Beginning 1996, lead and lead compounds are inventoried through the hazardous air pollutants (HAPs) portion of the National Emission Inventory (NEI) every three years; data for 1997 forward are currently not available.
... = Not available.

BOX 5 ■ Hurricane Katrina

The U.S. Government has declared Hurricane Katrina the costliest and the third deadliest tropical storm to make landfall in the United States, with at least $81 billion in property damages. One year after the storm, the Department of Homeland Security estimated that Federal aid for this disaster had reached $110.6 billion. As of January 31, 2007, the National Flood Insurance Program had paid $15.7 billion dollars on closed claims. Through June 1, 2007, the Federal Emergency Management Agency's (FEMA) Public Assistance program paid $6.7 billion for recovery programs in Louisiana and Mississippi alone, with projected future payments of an additional $2.3 billion.

Katrina made landfall on the Gulf Coast on August 29, 2005 as a Category 3 storm that reached outward from the center of the eye approximately 75 nautical miles, with winds up to 125 miles per hour. Estimates of storm surges are 24 to 28 feet on the Mississippi coast, 15 feet on Coastal Alabama, and 19 feet in New Orleans, where the pressure led to the rupture of many levees. Approximately 80% of New Orleans was flooded in approximately 20 feet of floodwaters within a day of the storm making landfall. The amount of rainfall also varied greatly from 2 inches in areas north of the eye of the storm to14 inches in the hardest hit areas. Precipitation totals of up to 8 inches reached as far inland as portions of the Tennessee valley. Forty-three tornadoes were formed in the wake of Katrina: one in the Florida Keys; 20 in Georgia; 11 in Alabama; and 11 in Mississippi.

The economic and environmental impact of the storm was not limited to the destruction of homes and workplaces but also included significant beach erosion in tourist areas on the Gulf coast, the interruption of a vast majority of the oil refining industry in the Gulf, and several million gallons of oil from damaged refining facilities that were spilled throughout southeastern Louisiana. With adjustments for inflation, it is estimated that Hurricane Katrina had damages approximately double those of Hurricane Andrew in 1992.

Hurricane Katrina National Flood Insurance Program

(Actual figures as of January 31, 2007.)

States affected by Hurricane Katrina	Losses (claims) received	Total closed	Percentage closed	Total $ paid on closed claims
Total	209 374	206 381	98.6	15 661 494 451
Alabama	5 741	5 628	98.0	275 445 207
Florida	8 428	8 397	99.6	115 728 003
Mississippi	19 055	18 653	97.9	2 418 484 220
Louisiana	176 150	173 703	98.6	12 851 837 022

Source: U.S. Department of Homeland Security, Federal Emergency Management Agency. Hurricane Katrina Information.

The Department of Homeland Security has stated that more than 1.5 million people were directly affected by Katrina and more than 800,000 were forced to leave their homes. The Department of Labor reported almost 137,000 people applied for initial unemployment claims in Louisiana and Mississippi between September and December 2005. It is difficult to determine the number of casualties directly related to Hurricane Katrina, but the number is estimated to be at least 1,500.

Controversy has surrounded the Federal Government's response to Hurricane Katrina, particularly in New Orleans. This was the first major disaster after 9/11, and the first test of the Department of Homeland Security's ability to plan for and provide relief in a national emergency. Media images of the destruction and suffering only further fueled the criticisms, which included inadequate planning for evacuation and shelter of the city's least able population, the length of time required for relief supplies to arrive, charges of inaccurate government reports of the situation and efforts to limit media access, the failure to control violence and looting, and a lack of coordination among the various levels of government.

Sources:

Report: Katrina response "a failure of leadership." February 14, 2006. http://www.cnn.com/2006/politics/02/13/katrina.congress/index.html. last accessed August 3, 2007.

Department of Homeland Security, Federal Emergency Management Agency. Hurricane Katrina Information, http://www.fema.gov/hazard/hurricane/2005katrina/index.shtm, last accessed on July 23, 2007.

U.S. Department of Homeland Security, Federal Emergency Management Agency. Hurricane Katrina Flood Recovery (Louisiana) webpage, http://www.fema.gov/hazard/flood/recoverydata/katrina/katrina_la_mmds.shtm, last accessed on July 23, 2007.

U.S. Department of Homeland Security, Federal Emergency Management Agency. FEMA Public Assistance for Louisiana Recovery, June 1, 2007. webpage, http://www.fema.gov/pdf/hazard/hurricane/2005katrina/la_media_report_060107.pdf, last accessed on July 23, 2007.

U.S. Department of Homeland Security, Federal Emergency Management Agency. FEMA Public Assistance For Mississippi Recovery, June 1, 2007. http://www.fema.gov/pdf/hazard/hurricane/2005katrina/ms_media_report_060107.pdf, last accessed on July 23, 2007.

U.S. Department of Homeland Security. Hurricane Katrina: What Government is Doing webpage, http://www.dhs.gov/xprepresp/programs/gc_1157649340100.shtm, last accessed on July 23, 2007.

U.S. Department of Commerce, National Oceanic and Atmospheric Administration. Hurricane Katrina—Most Destructive Hurricane Ever to Strike the U.S. webpage, http://www.katrina.noaa.gov/, last accessed on July 23, 2007.

U.S. Department of Commerce, National Oceanic and Atmospheric Administration, National Hurricane Center. *Tropical Cyclone Report: Hurricane Katrina, 23–30 August, 2005,* December 20, 2005. http://www.nhc.noaa.gov/pdf/TCR-AL122005_Katrina.pdf, as accessed July 23, 2007.

U.S. Department of Commerce, National Oceanic and Atmospheric Administration, National Hurricane Center. The Deadliest, Costliest, and Most Intense United States Tropical Cyclones from 1851 to 2006 (and Other Frequently Requested Hurricane Facts). http://www.nhc.noaa.gov/pdf/NWS-TPC-5.pdf

U.S. Department of Labor. *Monthly Labor Review,* August 2006. Conducting the Mass Layoff Statistics Program: Response and Findings.

$ Billion (2004)[1]

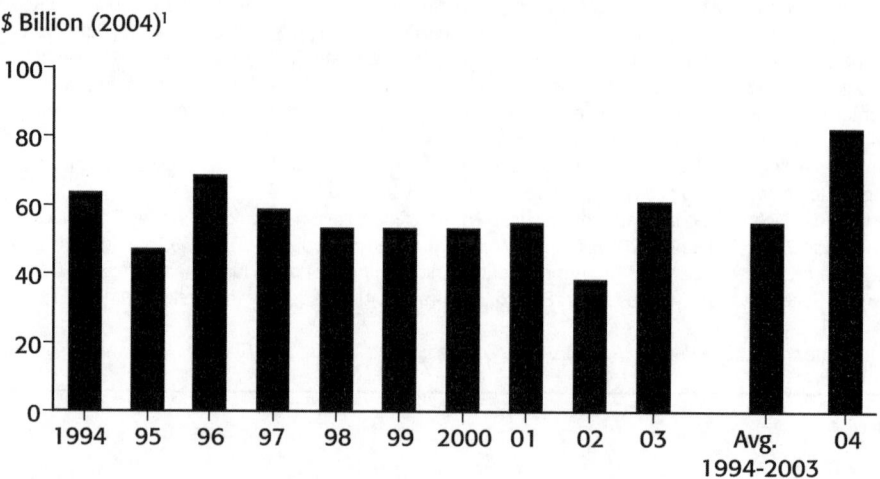

[1]Deflated with the GDP chain-type price index.

Real Net Farm Income, 1994–2004

In 2004, net farm income was 50 percent higher than the average for the previous 10 years.
Source: U.S. Department of Agriculture. Economic Research Service. U.S. and State Farm Income Data.

CHAPTER **6**

Agriculture

HIGHLIGHTS

1 Annual agricultural statistics have been published by the Department of Agriculture since May 1, 1863. The Statistical Reporting Service and the Economic Research Service now compile them. Since 1840, Census of Agriculture has been taken every 10 years. Beginning in 1925, a mid-decade Census of Agriculture has also been taken, based on mailed questionnaires. The first census was limited in scope to domestic animals, production of principal crops, and the value of wool and dairy products. Number of farms, acreage, and value of farmland were first included in 1850, farm tenure in 1880, and classification of farmland by use in 1925.

2 The definition of a farm has varied from census to census. Before 1954, the cutoff was three acres with annual output valued at $150 or more, but farms smaller than three acres were included if the value of output reached the same level. Between 1925 and 1945, farms included places of three or more acres on which there were agricultural operations and places of less than three acres with an annual output of three acres or more. Between 1910 and 1920, the definition was even more liberal, including farms smaller than three acres with less than $250 in output, if they required the continuous services of one person. In 1860

and 1900, there were no acreage or value limits. In 1870, 1880, and 1890, farms smaller than three acres were included only if the value of output exceeded $500. In the census of 1850, no acreage qualification was given, but there was a floor of $100 for value of products. In 1959, the acreage limit was raised to 10 and the value limit to $250 for smaller farms. For the 1974, 1978, 1982, and 1986 Censuses of Agriculture, a farm was defined as any place on which $1,000 or more of agricultural products were produced and/or sold.

3 Estimates of farm population are equally problematic. Since 1960, farm population has been defined as all persons living in rural territory on places of 10 or more acres producing at least $50 worth of agricultural produce. The principal characteristics of farm population are its higher age profile, higher outflow, and higher birth rates. The classification of farm operator was first made in the Census of 1900. It designates a person who operates a farm as an owner, salaried employee, tenant, renter, or sharecropper. Because of the decreasing importance of the cropper system in the South, croppers have not been classified since 1959. Since 1880, farms have been classified by tenure, and since 1900, by race of the owner.

4 Estimates of farm income were started in 1924 on a crop-year basis. Only scattered data on farm income are available for the period before 1910. Willford I. King provides some data for census years from 1850 in *The Wealth and Income of the People of the United States*. The National Industrial Conference Board's *National Income in the United States, 1799 to 1938* provides decennial projections going back to 1800, and the Department of Agriculture's *Gross Farm Income and Indices of Farm Production and Prices in the United States, 1869–1937* extends back to 1869.

5 For many crops, estimates of acreage, production, and prices began in 1866 when the Department of Agriculture began making regular reports. These data are found in *Agricultural Statistics, Crop Production* and *Crop Values*. Data on livestock have been published since 1867, based on the decennial and quintennial Censuses of Agriculture.

6 Early development of the dairy industry is indicated by the export statistics of 1890, which showed the New England states, New York, and Pennsylvania producing considerable amounts of butter and cheese in excess of their consumption requirements. By the middle of the nineteenth century, milk cows were distributed as far west as southern Wisconsin, eastern Iowa, western Missouri and Arkansas, and the eastern third of Texas. By 1860, they had spread to the Pacific coast states. Before 1850, milk, butter, and cheese were produced mainly on farms. Factory cheese production began shortly after 1850; the first condensery was established in 1856 and the first commercial creamery in 1861. Unsweetened condensed milk was first produced in 1885.

7 The share of the farm sector in the economy has steadily declined as the United States moved into postindustrial age. In 1998, agriculture contributed only 2 percent of the $7.9 trillion economy. Although the United States is in many ways the granary of the world, it employs fewer people in that sector today than it did in 1990. The number of farms has declined from 2.440 million in 1980 to 2.101 million in 2005. The land in farms has declined from 1,039 million acres to 933 million acres from 1980 to 2005, and harvested cropland has followed the same trend from 318.9 million acres in 1997 to 302.7 million acres in 2002. However, farm output grew at a slower pace than other sectors of the economy, reaching $258 billion in 2004 from $137.8 billion in 1980.

8 Texas had the most land in farms (129.8 million acres) in 2005, followed by Montana (60.1 million acres), Kansas (47.2 million acres), Nebraska (45.7 million acres), and New Mexico (44.5 million acres). Wyoming led in the average size of farms with 3,739 acres. California leads in the final agricultural sector output with $34.294 billion, followed by Texas with $20.096 billion, and Iowa with $17.177 billion. Texas and Nebraska lead in cattle, California and Wisconsin in dairy products, and Iowa and Illinois in corn and soybeans.

9 Agriculture is one of the strongest export sectors and has always shown a positive trade balance. In 2005, agriculture had a trade balance of $3.7 billion with exports valued at $63.0 billion (7 percent of all exports) and imports of $59.3 billion. The United States accounted for 41.1 percent of the world production of corn and 37.9 percent of soybeans in 2005. In exports, it accounted for 24.8 percent of the wheat, 68.2 percent of corn, 36.9 percent of soybeans, and 41.4 percent of cotton.

10 By cash receipts from farm marketings, the five principal U.S. crops are corn, soybean, vegetables, wheat, and cotton, and which together account for 60 percent of value (corn is considered a cereal, while only sweet corn is considered a vegetable). The most popular vegetable is the potato with a production of $2,903 million in 2005, followed by the tomato ($2,259 million). The most popular fruit is the grape with a production of $3,013 million in 2005, followed by the orange ($1,498 million).

11 The Balance Sheet of the Farming Sector was first attempted in 1944. In 2004, it showed assets of $1.501 trillion, of which real estate accounted for $1.227 billion.

12 Irrigated lands are found primarily in the West and South. California led all states in this respect with 8.713 million acres under irrigation in 1997, or 15.8 percent of all cropland, followed by MO (12.6 percent), and Texas (9.8 percent). Irrigation accounted for withdrawals of 134 billion gallons of water per day.

13 Farms that produce less than $10,000 annually account for 59.3 percent of the number of farms, but only 17.6 percent of the acreage and 1.4 percent of the value of sales. Farms that produce more than $10,000 in sales account for 40.7 percent of the number of farms, 82.4 percent of the acreage, and 98.6 percent of sales.

14 California is the nation's principal farm producer with a total production of 25.9 billion in 2002, followed by Texas and Iowa with a production of $14.7 billion and $12.8 billion respectively.

15 Production of red meat and poultry was 86.8 billion pounds in 2005, of which beef accounted for 24.8 billion pounds and poultry for 40.9 billion pounds.

16 The number of farms producing all the cattle of the United States in 2006 was 97.1 million for a total value of $97.9 billion. Hog and pig farms numbered 61.3 million for a total value of $5.7 billion.

17 Milk produced in 2005 was 177 billion pounds valued at $26.9 billion. Butter production was 1.347 billion pounds, cheese 9.127 billion pounds, plain and fruit flavored yogurt 2.990 billion pounds, and regular ice cream 953 million gallons.

18 New exotic styles of food have created a demand for spices and herbs, almost all of them imported. In 2002, 260,000 tons of spices were imported, including pepper, sesame seed, capsicum, cinnamon, cassia, ginger root, and cumin.

19 American cheese is produced in greater quantities than any of the other cheeses, including all Italian varieties, combined at 3,813 million pounds and 3,805 million pounds respectively.

20 While the number of cows has decreased by more than 50 percent since the 1950s, overall milk production has increased, and the output per cow has more than tripled as a result of factory farms.

21 Canada is the number one export destination for American agricultural products, with that country importing 16.8 percent of 2005 exports, followed by Mexico at 14.9 percent. Since 1990, agricultural exports to Japan have significantly decreased from 20.6 percent to only 12.5 in 2005.

Table 6-1. Farms and Land in Farms, by Size of Farms, 1880–2005

(Farms in thousands, land in farms in thousands of acres.)

Year	Number of farms				Land in farms			
	Total	Under 10 acres	50–99 acres	1,000 acres and over	Total	Under 10 acres	50–99 acres	1,000 acres and over
2005	2 101	...	...	...	933 000	...	...	...
2004	2 113	...	...	...	936 000	...	...	...
2003	2 127	...	...	...	939 000	...	...	...
2002	2 129	179	343	177	938 300	800	24 500	627 600
2001	2 149	...	...	...	942 000	...	...	...
2000	2 167	...	...	...	945 000	...	...	...
1999	2 187	...	...	...	948 000	...	...	...
1998	2 192	...	...	...	952 000	...	...	...
1997	2 216	205	354	177	954 800	900	25 500	616 300
1996	2 191	...	...	...	959 000	...	...	...
1995	2 196	...	...	...	963 000	...	...	...
1994	2 198	...	...	...	966 000	...	...	...
1993	2 202	...	...	...	969 000	...	...	...
1992	1 925	166	283	173	...	...	...	...
1987	2 088	183	311	169	964 500	7 000	22 500	602 000
1982	2 241	188	344	163	...	...	...	...
1978	2 258	151	356	161	986 800	7 000	24 800	599 900
1974	2 314	128	385	155	1 014 800	6 000	25 900	600 400
1969	2 730	162	460	151	1 063 346	568	33 620	578 412
1964	3 158	183	542	145	1 110 185	778	39 590	584 847
1959	3 711	244	658	136	1 123 508	1 053	47 950	554 631
1954[1]	4 782	484	864	130	1 158 192	2 260	62 725	531 482
1950	5 388	489	1 048	121	1 162 643	2 443	75 647	494 856
1945[1]	5 859	595	1 157	113	1 141 615	2 805	83 206	460 006
1940	6 102	509	1 291	101	1 065 114	2 679	93 336	365 772
1935[1]	6 812	571	1 444	89	1 054 515	3 057	104 016	309 701
1930	6 295	362	1 375	81	990 112	1 922	98 700	276 667
1925[1]	6 372	379	1 421	63	924 319	2 097	101 906	224 472
1920	6 454	[2]292	1 475	67	958 677	...	105 631	220 636
1910[1]	6 362	335	1 438	50	[3]881 431	...	103 121	167 082
1900	5 740	268	1 366	47	841 202	1 482	98 600	200 324
1890	4 565	150	1 122	32	...	...	...	...
1880	4 009	139	1 033	29	...	...	...	...

Source: U.S. Census Bureau. U.S. Department of Agriculture.
[1]Excludes Alaska and Hawaii.
[2]Excludes Alaska.
[3]Total includes Alaska and Hawaii.
. . . = Not available.

Table 6-2. Farmers' Marketing, Purchasing, and Service Cooperatives, Memberships, and Business, 1913–2002

(Number, dollars.)

Year	Cooperatives Listed[1]				Estimated memberships[2] (1,000)				Estimated business[3] ($1,000,000)			
	Total	Marketing and related	Farm supply	Service	Total	Marketing and related	Farm supply	Service	Total	Marketing and related	Farm supply	Service
2002	3 140	1 559	1 201	380	2 794	1 049	1 637	107	96 750	69 656	23 679	3 416
2001	3 229	1 606	1 234	389	3 034	1 160	1 746	128	103 269	75 042	24 756	3 471
2000	3 346	1 672	1 277	397	3 085	1 243	1 718	124	99 659	72 065	24 085	3 510
1999	3 466	1 749	1 313	404	3 173	1 283	1 731	159	99 064	71 982	23 177	3 905
1998	3 651	1 863	1 347	441	3 353	1 398	1 774	181	104 667	76 642	24 551	3 473
1997	3 791	1 941	1 386	464	3 424	1 498	1 743	183	106 671	77 843	25 181	3 647
1996	3 884	2 012	1 403	469	3 664	1 682	1 795	187	106 182	79 429	23 653	3 100
1995	4 006	2 074	1 458	474	3 767	1 712	1 846	210	93 818	69 321	21 213	3 284
1994	4 174	2 173	1 496	505	3 986	1 805	1 936	245	89 310	65 545	20 779	2 986
1993	4 244	2 214	1 547	483	4 023	1 830	1 977	216	82 872	60 930	19 218	2 724
1992	4 315	2 218	1 618	479	4 072	1 839	2 021	213	79 284	58 196	18 513	2 575
1991	4 494	2 384	1 689	421	4 059	1 842	2 025	192	76 636	56 203	17 916	2 517
1990	4 663	2 519	1 717	427	4 119	1 882	2 006	232	77 266	57 831	17 088	2 347
1989	4 799	2 550	1 803	446	4 133	1 856	2 035	243	72 129	53 247	16 907	1 974
1988	4 937	2 988	1 836	113	4 196	1 912	2 142	141	66 430	49 067	15 424	1 939
1987	5 109	3 054	1 941	114	4 440	2 026	2 282	132	60 318	44 156	14 271	1 891
1986	5 369	3 260	1 971	138	4 600	2 140	2 310	150	58 396	41 540	15 095	1 760
1985	5 625	3 441	2 036	148	4 783	2 216	2 398	169	65 601	47 321	16 641	1 640
1984	5 782	3 514	2 136	132	4 842	2 317	2 397	128	73 047	54 556	16 969	1 522
1983	5 989	3 647	2 208	134	4 955	2 308	2 553	95	66 755	49 344	15 943	1 468
1982	6 125	3 714	2 299	112	5 136	2 444	2 666	25	69 150	51 394	16 362	1 394
1981	6 211	3 743	2 356	112	5 335	2 452	2 856	27	71 534	53 285	17 059	1 190
1980	6 293	3 808	2 369	116	5 379	2 542	2 805	32	66 254	48 911	16 134	1 209
1979	6 445	3 825	2 507	113	5 627	2 531	3 060	36	56 268	41 693	13 522	1 054
1978	6 600	3 930	2 550	120	5 695	2 595	3 063	37	47 305	35 306	11 052	948
1977	6 736	4 008	2 593	135	5 758	2 655	3 066	37	43 584	32 134	10 558	893
1976	7 535	4 658	2 731	146	5 906	2 812	3 056	39	40 050	29 783	9 412	855
1975	7 645	4 770	2 729	146	6 123	3 127	2 971	25	37 340	28 184	8 412	745
1974	7 755	4 822	2 778	155	6 106	3 111	2 973	22	35 366	26 944	7 764	658
1973	7 854	4 897	2 801	156	6 128	3 118	2 988	22	25 991	19 573	5 915	503
1972	7 797	4 864	2 781	152	6 147	3 134	2 991	22	21 665	16 463	4 740	462
1971	7 995	5 097	2 731	167	6 158	3 105	3 028	25	20 556	15 802	4 340	414
1970	7 790	4 834	2 775	181	6 355	3 103	3 222	30	19 080	14 816	3 873	391
1969	7 747	4 773	2 793	181	6 364	3 141	3 190	33	17 387	13 421	3 615	351
1968	7 940	4 929	2 835	176	6 445	3 225	3 187	34	17 050	13 189	3 545	316
1967	8 125	5 076	2 871	179	6 502	3 298	3 169	34	16 557	12 900	3 339	318
1966	8 329	5 194	2 949	186	6 826	3 636	3 155	36	15 608	12 198	3 085	325
1965	8 583	5 305	3 085	193	7 082	3 791	3 251	40	14 742	11 516	2 910	316
1964	8 847	5 421	3 226	200	7 080	3 613	3 425	42	14 354	11 209	2 832	313
1963	8 907	5 502	3 211	194	7 219	3 582	3 596	41	13 842	10 834	2 704	303
1962	9 039	5 626	3 206	207	7 059	3 420	3 635	44	13 024	10 160	2 561	302
1961	9 163	5 727	3 222	214	7 203	3 473	3 680	50	12 409	9 631	2 472	306
1960*	9 345	5 828	3 297	220	7 274	3 622	3 601	51	12 036	9 330	2 408	298
1959	9 658	6 042	3 387	229	7 559	3 861	3 644	54	11 747	9 103	2 371	273
1958	9 735	6 119	3 383	233	7 487	3 880	3 543	64	10 753	8 318	2 188	247
1957	9 891	6 284	3 373	234	7 673	4 122	3 489	62	10 380	7 999	2 146	235
1956	9 894	6 284	3 375	235	7 732	4 223	3 444	65	9 756	7 495	2 046	215
1955	9 903	6 330	3 346	227	7 604	4 214	3 323	68	9 642	7 425	2 022	196
1954	10 072	6 457	3 374	241	7 608	4 273	3 253	82	9 475	7 339	1 978	158
1953	10 128	6 501	3 378	249	7 475	4 247	3 139	89	9 521	7 366	2 014	142
1952	10 179	6 594	3 324	261	7 364	4 229	3 033	102	9 410	7 377	1 919	115
1951	10 064	6 519	3 283	262	7 091	4 118	2 879	94	8 147	6 362	1 685	100
1950	10 035	6 922	3 113		6 584	4 075	2 509		8 726	7 083	1 643	
1949	10 075	6 993	3 082		6 384	3 973	2 411		9 320	7 700	1 620	
1948	10 135	7 159	2 976		5 890	3 630	2 260		8 635	7 195	1 440	
1947	10 125	7 268	2 857		5 436	3 378	2 058		7 116	6 005	1 111	
1946	10 150	7 378	2 772		5 010	3 150	1 860		6 070	5 147	923	
1945	10 150	7 400	2 750		4 505	2 895	1 610		5 645	4 835	810	
1944	10 300	7 522	2 778		4 250	2 730	1 520		5 160	4 430	730	
1943	10 450	7 708	2 742		3 850	2 580	1 270		3 780	3 180	600	
1942	10 550	7 824	2 726		3 600	2 430	1 170		2 840	2 360	480	
1941	10 600	7 943	2 657		3 400	2 420	980		2 280	1 911	369	

[1]Many cooperatives serve multiple functions; these associations are classified according to the predominant function as indicated by their business volume.
[2]Membership figures contain duplication because farmers are members of more than one cooperative, with an average of about three memberships per active farmer.
[3]Data for years to 1951 are not entirely comparable due to revisions in statistical procedure. Figures through 1950 reflect gross volume, 1951–2002 reflect net volume. Gross business volume includes intercooperative business such as sales of farm products by a regional cooperative for a local member cooperative or sales by a regional to its member local. Net business volume excludes intercooperative business.
* = First year figures include Alaska and Hawaii.

Table 6-2. Farmers' Marketing, Purchasing, and Service Cooperatives, Memberships, and Business, 1913–2002—*Continued*

(Number, dollars.)

Year	Cooperatives Listed[1]				Estimated memberships[2] (1,000)				Estimated business[3] ($1,000,000)			
	Total	Marketing and related	Farm supply	Service	Total	Marketing and related	Farm supply	Service	Total	Marketing and related	Farm supply	Service
1940	10 700	8 051	2 649	(4)	3 200	2 300	900	(4)	2 087	1 729	358	(4)
1939	10 700	8 100	2 600	(4)	3 300	2 410	890	(4)	2 100	1 765	335	(4)
1938	10 900	8 300	2 600	(4)	3 400	2 500	900	(4)	2 400	2 050	350	(4)
1937	10 752	8 142	2 610	(4)	3 270	2 414	856	(4)	2 196	1 883	313	(4)
1936	10 500	8 388	2 112	3 660	2 710	950	1 840	1 586	254			
1935	10 700	8 794	1 906	(4)	3 280	2 490	790	(4)	1 530	1 343	187	(4)
1934	10 900	9 052	1 848	(4)	3 156	2 464	692	(4)	1 365	1 213	152	(4)
1933	11 000	9 352	1 648	(4)	3 000	2 457	543	(4)	1 340	1 200	141	(4)
1932	11 900	10 255	1 645	(4)	3 200	2 667	533	(4)	1 925	1 744	181	(4)
1931	11 950	10 362	1 588	3 000	2 608	392	2 400	2 185	215			
1930	12 000	10 546	1 454	(4)	3 100	2 630	470	(4)	2 500	2 310	190	(4)
1928	11 400	10 195	1 205	(4)	3 000	2 602	398	(4)	2 300	2 172	128	(4)
1926	10 803	9 586	1 217	2 700	2 453	247	2 400	2 265	135			
1924	10 160	9 013	1 140	(4)	...	...	...	...	...	...	...	(4)
1921	7 374	6 476	898	...	...	...	...	1 256	1 198	58		
1915	5 424	5 149	275	651	592	59	636	624	12			
1913	3 099	2 988	111	...	...	...	310	304	6			

Source: U.S. Department of Agriculture. *Cooperative Information Report 1, Section 26, Farm Marketing, Supply and Service Cooperative Historical Statistics.*
Note: Totals may not equal sum of components due to independent rounding.
[1]Many cooperatives serve multiple functions; these associations are classified according to the predominant function as indicated by their business volume.
[2]Membership figures contain duplication because farmers are members of more than one cooperative, with an average of about three memberships per active farmer.
[3]Data for years to 1951 are not entirely comparable due to revisions in statistical procedure. Figures through 1950 reflect gross volume, 1951–2002 reflect net volume. Gross business volume includes intercooperative business such as sales of farm products by a regional cooperative for a local member cooperative or sales by a regional to its member local. Net business volume excludes intercooperative business.
[4]Figures on service cooperatives as a separate category is only available from 1951–2002.
. . . = Not available.

Table 6-3. Balance Sheet of the Farming Sector Business, 1940–2006

(Billions of dollars.)

	Assets							Claims		
		Physical								
				Non-real estate						
Year	Total	Real estate	Livestock and poultry[1]	Machinery and motor vehicles[2]	Crops stored on and off farm[3]	Household equipment and furnishings	Investment and cooperatives	Total[4]	Total liability	Proprietors' equities
2006[5]	1 919.4	1 634.7	80.7	103.5	22.7	70.9	...	1 919.4	226.2	1 693.2
2005	1 805.3	1 520.9	81.1	105.0	24.3	67.5	...	1 805.3	215.6	1 589.6
2004	1 584.8	1 307.6	79.4	102.2	24.4	65.5	...	1 584.8	204.7	1 380.1
2003	1 378.8	1 111.8	78.5	95.9	24.4	62.4	...	1 378.8	196.1	1 182.7
2002	1 304.0	1 045.7	75.6	93.6	23.1	60.4	...	1 304.0	194.1	1 110.0
2001	1 255.9	996.2	78.5	92.8	25.2	58.9	...	1 255.9	185.7	1 070.2
2000	1 203.2	946.4	76.8	90.1	27.9	57.1	...	1 203.2	177.6	1 025.6
1999	1 138.8	887.0	73.2	89.8	28.3	56.5	...	1 138.8	167.7	971.1
1998	1 083.4	840.4	63.4	89.8	29.9	54.7	...	1 083.4	164.6	918.7
1997	1 051.3	808.2	67.1	88.7	32.7	49.7	...	1 051.3	156.9	894.4
1996	1 002.9	769.5	60.3	88.0	31.7	49.0	...	1 002.9	148.6	854.3
1995	965.7	740.5	57.8	87.6	27.4	49.1	...	965.7	143.0	822.8
1994	934.7	704.1	67.9	86.8	23.3	47.6	...	934.7	138.9	795.8
1993	909.2	677.6	72.8	85.4	23.3	46.3	...	909.2	134.3	774.9
1992	867.8	640.8	71.0	84.8	24.2	43.0	...	867.8	131.6	736.2
1991	844.2	624.8	68.1	85.9	22.2	40.5	...	844.2	131.9	712.3
1990	840.6	619.1	70.9	86.3	23.2	38.3	...	840.6	131.1	709.5
1989	813.7	600.1	66.2	84.1	23.9	36.8	...	813.7	131.0	682.7
1988	788.5	582.3	62.2	81.0	23.7	35.9	...	788.5	133.1	655.4
1987	756.5	563.7	58.0	78.7	17.8	35.2	...	756.5	138.5	618.0
1986	722.0	542.4	47.8	79.0	16.3	34.5	...	722.0	151.3	570.7
1985	775.9	586.2	46.3	86.1	22.9	33.3	...	775.9	172.2	603.8
1984	897.8	661.8	49.5	125.8	26.1	32.6	...	897.8	188.8	709.0
1983	959.3	753.4	49.5	101.7	23.7	30.9	...	959.3	186.2	773.1
1982	962.5	750.0	53.0	103.9	25.9	29.7	...	962.5	184.0	778.5
1981	997.9	785.6	53.5	101.1	29.5	28.2	...	997.9	177.7	820.2
1980	1 000.4	782.8	60.6	97.5	32.8	26.7	...	1 000.4	162.4	838.0
1979	914.7	706.1	61.4	91.9	29.9	25.4	...	914.7	147.5	767.2
1978	777.7	601.7	50.1	78.8	23.8	23.2	...	777.7	123.9	653.9
1977	651.5	509.3	31.9	69.3	20.4	20.5	...	651.5	108.4	543.1
1976	590.7	456.5	29.0	63.3	20.6	21.3	...	590.7	94.1	496.6
1975	510.8	383.6	29.4	57.4	20.5	19.9	...	510.8	83.5	427.3
1974	449.2	335.6	24.6	48.5	22.5	18.1	...	449.2	74.7	374.5
1973	418.5	298.3	42.4	39.7	21.4	16.8	...	418.5	66.8	351.7
1972	339.9	243.0	33.7	34.6	12.9	15.7	...	339.9	58.1	281.8
1971	301.8	217.6	27.3	32.4	10.0	14.5	...	301.8	52.8	248.9
1970	278.8	202.4	23.7	30.4	8.7	13.6	...	278.8	48.5	230.3
1969	267.8	295.3	22.8	28.6	8.3	12.8	...	267.8	46.4	221.4
1968	257.2	189.4	20.2	27.7	7.4	12.4	...	257.2	43.9	213.2
1967	246.1	180.9	18.8	26.3	8.0	12.0	...	246.1	42.2	203.9
1966	234.0	171.2	19.0	24.1	8.1	11.6	...	234.0	39.2	194.8
1965	220.8	161.5	17.6	22.4	7.9	11.4	...	220.8	35.8	185.0
1964	204.2	150.5	14.5	21.2	7.0	11.0	...	204.2	32.2	172.1
1963	196.7	142.4	15.9	20.4	7.4	10.7	...	196.7	29.6	167.1
1962	188.9	134.6	17.3	19.9	6.5	10.5	...	188.9	26.7	162.2
1961	181.6	129.1	16.4	19.3	6.5	10.4	...	181.6	24.1	157.5
1960	174.4	123.3	15.6	19.1	6.4	10.0	...	174.4	22.4	151.9
1959	202.1	124.4	17.7	21.8	9.3	9.8	3.9	202.1	23.6	178.5
1958	185.8	115.9	13.9	20.2	7.6	9.9	3.7	185.8	20.4	165.4
1957	177.9	110.4	11.0	20.2	8.3	10.0	3.5	177.9	19.3	158.6
1956	169.6	102.9	10.6	19.3	8.4	10.5	3.2	169.6	18.8	150.8
1955	165.1	98.2	11.2	18.6	9.6	10.0	3.1	165.1	17.6	147.5
1954	161.2	95.0	11.7	18.4	9.2	9.9	2.9	161.2	16.9	144.3
1953	164.3	96.5	14.8	17.4	9.0	9.9	2.7	164.3	16.1	148.2
1952	167.0	95.1	19.5	16.7	8.8	10.3	2.5	167.0	14.7	152.3
1951	151.5	86.6	17.1	14.1	7.9	9.7	2.3	151.5	13.1	138.4
1950	132.5	75.3	12.9	12.2	7.6	8.6	2.1	132.5	12.4	120.1
1949	134.9	76.6	14.4	10.1	8.6	9.1	1.9	134.9	11.4	123.5
1948	127.9	73.7	13.3	7.4	9.0	8.5	1.7	127.9	9.3	118.6
1947	116.4	68.5	11.9	5.3	7.1	7.7	1.5	116.4	8.5	107.9
1946	103.5	61.0	9.7	5.4	6.3	6.1	1.4	103.5	8.0	95.5
1945	94.2	53.9	9.0	6.5	6.7	5.6	1.2	94.2	8.3	85.9
1944	84.6	48.2	9.7	5.4	6.1	5.3	1.1	84.6	8.9	75.7
1943	73.7	41.6	9.6	4.9	5.1	5.0	1.0	73.7	10.0	63.7
1942	62.9	37.5	7.1	4.0	3.8	4.9	0.9	62.9	10.5	52.4
1941	55.0	34.4	5.3	3.3	3.0	4.2	0.9	55.0	10.4	44.6
1940	52.9	33.6	5.1	3.1	2.7	4.2	0.8	52.9	10.0	42.9

Source: U.S. Department of Agriculture, Economic Research Service.
Note: Numbers may not add due to rounding.
[1]Beginning in 1960 excludes horses, mules, and broilers.
[2]Includes only farm share value for trucks and autos.
[3]Includes all non-Commodity Credit Corporation (CCC) crops held on farms plus the value above loan rate for crops held under CCC.
[4]Excludes debt for non-farm purposes.
[5]Preliminary data.
... = Not available.

Table 6-4. Farm Income and Expenses, 1910–2006

(Millions of dollars.)

Year	Net income of farm operators from farming	Realized gross farm income	Realized gross income from farming — Cash receipts from marketing: Total	Crops[1]	Livestock and livestock products	Government payments[2]	Value of farm products consumed in farm households	Gross rental value of farm dwellings
2006P	60 604	298 430	242 700			16 318	...	...
2005	73 834	299 795	238 941	113 962	124 980	24 349	...	...
2004	85 400	296 157	237 878	114 250	123 627	12 965	...	...
2003	60 447	260 855	215 503	109 865	105 638	16 523	...	...
2002	40 227	...	195 001	101 041	93 960	12 415	...	...
2001	55 613	246 500	200 075	93 366	106 709	22 431	...	...
2000	51 320	241 700	192 028	92 394	99 635	23 222	...	...
1999	57 100	234 500	212 900	92 400	98 300	21 500	...	...
1998	56 800	232 100	219 700	101 700	94 000	12 400	...	...
1997	60 400	238 669	230 600	112 400	96 500	7 500	...	...
1996	57 700	235 741	228 400	115 500	92 100	7 300	...	...
1995	52 500	210 743	203 500	95 700	87 800	7 300	...	...
1994	50 700	216 076	208 200	100 300	89 800	7 900	...	...
1993	44 533	204 738	200 300	87 447	90 445	13 400	...	...
1992	47 918	200 534	188 600	85 684	85 636	9 200	...	...
1991	38 600	191 950	184 359	82 077	85 786	8 200	...	...
1990	44 700	198 000	186 000	80 297	89 220	9 300	700	5 600
1989	39 700	191 900	179 900	76 800	84 100	10 900	700	5 500
1988	40 600	174 500	171 900	71 600	79 400	14 500	700	5 400
1987	39 700	168 400	165 100	65 800	76 000	16 700	700	4 900
1986	31 000	156 100	152 800	63 700	71 600	11 800	900	4 600
1985	28 800	161 200	157 900	74 300	69 800	7 700	900	4 700
1984	26 100	168 000	156 100	69 900	72 900	8 400	1 000	4 900
1983	14 200	153 900	151 100	67 200	69 600	9 300	1 000	12 600
1982	23 800	164 100	151 300	72 300	70 300	3 500	1 100	13 100
1981	26 900	166 300	146 000	72 500	69 200	1 900	1 200	12 600
1980	16 100	149 300	143 300	71 700	68 000	1 300	1 200	11 000
1979	27 400	150 700	135 100	62 300	69 200	1 400	1 300	9 300
1978	25 200	128 400	117 300	53 200	59 200	3 000	1 200	8 100
1977	19 900	108 800	99 300	48 600	47 600	1 800	1 200	7 300
1976	18 682	101 812	94 780	48 668	46 112	734	1 334	5 973
1975	25 500	100 600	90 700	45 800	43 100	800	1 100	5 400
1974	26 130	98 340	92 449	51 090	41 359	531	1 295	4 687
1973	33 349	98 911	87 068	41 132	45 936	2 607	1 104	3 913
1972	18 171	70 119	61 190	25 520	35 670	3 961	831	3 474
1971	14 194	60 603	52 859	22 276	30 583	3 145	732	3 226
1970	16 825	57 925	50 522	20 907	29 615	3 717	773	2 913
1969	16 856	55 550	48 143	19 541	28 602	3 794	750	2 863
1968	14 825	50 897	44 117	18 620	25 497	3 462	732	2 586
1967	14 882	48 998	42 693	18 434	24 259	3 079	745	2 481
1966	16 253	49 740	43 294	18 373	24 921	3 277	817	2 352
1965	14 987	44 926	39 350	17 392	21 958	2 463	813	2 300
1964	12 266	42 567	37 233	17 377	19 856	2 181	930	2 223
1963	13 206	42 271	37 398	17 435	19 963	1 696	1 016	2 161
1962	13 215	41 258	36 356	16 294	20 062	1 747	1 076	2 079
1961	12 987	39 771	35 089	15 660	19 429	1 493	1 176	2 012
1960	12 079	38 088	34 154	15 208	18 946	702	1 250	1 981
1959	11 454	37 468	33 511	14 648	18 863	682	1 318	1 957
1958	13 500	37 911	33 456	14 229	19 227	1 089	1 505	1 861
1957	11 325	34 001	29 714	12 338	17 376	1 016	1 484	1 787
1956	11 444	34 274	30 401	14 038	16 363	554	1 585	1 734
1955	11 464	33 138	29 490	13 523	15 967	229	1 678	1 741
1954	12 503	33 589	29 832	13 556	16 276	257	1 789	1 711
1953	13 088	34 986	31 001	14 078	16 923	213	2 007	1 765
1952	15 051	36 759	32 528	14 290	18 238	275	2 220	1 736
1951	15 987	37 055	32 858	13 239	19 619	286	2 304	1 607
1950	13 673	32 271	28 461	12 356	16 105	283	2 063	1 464
1949	12 780	31 628	27 805	12 396	15 409	185	2 230	1 408
1948	17 664	34 722	30 227	13 098	17 129	257	2 733	1 505
1947	15 354	34 146	29 620	13 093	16 527	314	2 765	1 447
1946	15 068	29 539	24 802	11 016	13 786	772	2 662	1 303
1945	12 312	25 813	21 663	9 655	12 008	742	2 356	1 052
1944	11 705	24 448	20 536	9 185	11 351	776	2 181	955
1943	11 736	23 397	19 620	8 127	11 493	645	2 253	879
1942	9 853	18 794	15 565	6 526	9 039	650	1 758	821
1941	6 490	13 851	11 111	4 619	6 492	544	1 429	767

[1]Includes commodities placed under Commodity Credit Corporation (CCC) loans and profits made on loans redeemed.
[2]Government payments reflect payments made directly to all recipients in the farm sector, including landlords.
P = Preliminary.
. . . = Not available.

Table 6-4. Farm Income and Expenses, 1910–2006—*Continued*

(Millions of dollars.)

		Expenses of agricultural production									
		Operating expenses (excluded hired labor)									
Year	Total	Feed purchased	Livestock purchased	Seed purchased[3]	Fertilizer and lime	Repairs	Miscellaneous[4]	Taxes on farm property	Wages paid for hired farm labor[5]	Interest on farm mortgage debt	Net rent to nonfarm landlords
2006[P]	237 826	30 700	18 800	11 300	13 800	...	56 500	8 100	21 800	16 400	10 100
2005	225 961	28 230	19 199	10 426	12 895	...	53 252	8 007	21 962	15 128	10 516
2004	210 758	29 733	18 114	9 625	11 428	...	47 501	7 007	20 506	13 064	9 915
2003	200 409	27 515	16 771	9 425	10 022	...	47 777	6 806	18 780	12 673	10 112
2002	193 358	24 965	14 413	8 925	9 619	...	46 353	6 807	19 113	13 144	9 756
2001	197 133	24 769	15 227	8 222	10 322	...	48 050	6 907	18 775	13 599	11 127
2000	193 111	24 486	15 852	7 519	10 020	...	45 216	6 907	17 943	14 671	11 202
1999	188 274	24 527	13 840	7 212	9 922	...	43 929	6 807	19 808	13 585	11 308
1998	186 502	25 031	12 576	7 212	10 624	...	42 712	7 013	19 120	13 365	11 443
1997	187 637	26 334	13 820	6 711	10 927	...	41 649	6 939	18 410	13 133	11 870
1996	180 970	25 237	11 294	6 212	10 929	...	40 171	6 816	17 331	12 961	12 971
1995	173 819	23 832	12 506	5 462	10 029	...	40 213	6 711	16 294	12 576	10 914
1994	167 191	22 635	13 305	5 373	9 177	...	37 774	6 475	15 310	11 556	11 765
1993	160 500	21 400	14 600	5 200	8 400	9 200	28 200	6 300	15 000	10 800	10 900
1992	152 500	20 100	13 600	4 900	8 300	8 500	24 900	6 200	14 000	11 200	10 800
1991	153 300	19 300	14 100	5 100	8 700	8 600	22 500	5 900	13 900	12 200	9 900
1990	144 300	20 700	14 700	3 600	7 100	7 300	18 800	5 600	12 500	14 500	8 200
1989	140 200	21 000	13 100	3 600	7 200	7 300	19 200	5 100	11 100	14 700	7 900
1988	133 900	20 400	12 800	3 400	6 900	6 800	17 200	4 800	10 400	14 700	7 400
1987	128 700	17 500	11 800	3 300	6 500	6 800	17 500	4 900	10 000	15 000	7 300
1986	125 100	17 500	9 800	3 200	6 800	6 400	15 500	4 600	9 500	16 500	6 100
1985	132 400	16 900	9 200	3 100	7 500	6 400	16 500	4 500	10 000	18 600	7 700
1984	141 900	19 400	9 500	3 400	8 400	6 400	16 900	4 300	9 400	21 100	8 100
1983	139 600	20 600	8 800	2 700	7 100	6 500	17 100	4 500	8 900	21 400	5 200
1982	140 300	18 600	9 700	3 200	8 000	6 400	15 500	4 000	9 400	21 800	5 500
1981	139 400	20 900	9 000	3 400	9 400	7 000	12 400	4 200	8 900	19 900	6 200
1980	133 100	21 000	10 700	3 200	9 500	7 100	11 800	3 900	9 300	16 300	6 100
1979	123 300	19 300	13 000	2 900	7 400	7 300	11 500	3 900	9 000	13 100	6 200
1978	103 200	16 000	10 200	2 600	6 600	6 600	9 500	3 600	8 300	10 200	4 000
1977	89 000	14 000	7 100	2 500	6 500	5 800	6 700	3 700	8 000	8 500	3 400
1976	83 130	14 370	5 871	2 537	6 141	9 096	12 586	3 607	7 037	3 852	4 220
1975	75 100	12 900	5 000	2 100	6 700	4 500	5 600	3 200	6 600	6 400	4 000
1974	72 210	14 513	5 131	2 082	5 808	6 659	10 178	3 096	6 036	3 044	5 100
1973	65 562	13 224	8 065	1 617	3 354	5 229	8 836	2 888	5 232	2 495	5 679
1972	52 809	8 397	6 668	1 115	2 690	4 708	8 312	2 815	4 594	2 132	3 491
1971	47 806	8 049	5 123	1 072	2 633	4 707	7 650	2 704	4 367	1 905	2 246
1970	41 091	7 189	4 345	829	2 222	5 031	5 132	2 957	3 643	1 717	1 302
1969	38 759	6 602	4 219	737	2 084	4 896	4 732	2 732	3 299	1 599	1 297
1968	36 209	5 894	3 676	672	2 130	4 831	4 451	2 515	3 047	1 477	1 307
1967	34 775	6 472	3 391	678	2 124	4 495	4 068	2 275	2 878	1 343	1 305
1966	33 406	6 324	3 498	626	1 952	4 227	3 854	2 108	2 889	1 205	1 442
1965	30 933	5 749	2 913	637	1 754	4 073	3 628	1 943	2 849	1 077	1 328
1964	29 481	5 715	2 420	566	1 701	3 940	3 515	1 833	2 913	952	1 223
1963	29 688	6 128	2 917	553	1 570	3 942	3 315	1 763	2 990	846	1 193
1962	28 639	5 575	3 106	521	1 474	3 944	3 135	1 684	2 961	759	1 132
1961	27 125	5 121	2 730	521	1 373	3 858	2 936	1 597	2 977	686	1 109
1960	26 352	4 923	2 502	510	1 315	3 966	2 829	1 502	2 923	628	1 010
1959	26 106	4 744	2 693	491	1 291	4 069	2 724	1 401	2 882	572	1 011
1958	25 236	4 541	2 702	508	1 206	3 921	2 517	1 306	2 842	521	1 161
1957	23 294	4 035	1 934	510	1 166	3 917	2 332	1 242	2 734	482	1 029
1956	22 374	3 894	1 610	519	1 166	3 785	2 307	1 178	2 641	442	1 109
1955	21 889	3 880	1 539	566	1 185	3 600	2 204	1 141	2 615	402	1 057
1954	21 577	3 906	1 563	525	1 209	3 506	2 077	1 084	2 596	371	1 159
1953	21 275	3 770	1 320	551	1 178	3 541	2 106	1 060	2 736	345	1 214
1952	22 630	4 331	1 918	594	1 184	3 506	2 142	1 033	2 857	318	1 421
1951	22 252	4 144	2 437	551	1 064	3 282	2 064	983	2 921	291	1 368
1950	19 410	3 283	2 004	518	975	2 975	1 763	919	2 811	264	1 233
1949	17 982	3 024	1 529	543	895	2 896	1 702	872	2 806	243	1 107
1948	18 790	3 996	1 589	581	826	2 818	1 580	806	2 990	232	1 370
1947	17 032	3 746	1 379	514	755	2 468	1 421	733	2 783	225	1 455
1946	14 500	3 022	1 170	428	683	2 054	1 185	617	2 532	219	1 401
1945	13 062	2 738	1 011	435	657	1 689	1 081	557	2 299	221	1 064
1944	12 333	2 427	812	440	576	1 608	1 071	499	2 202	230	1 043
1943	11 608	2 135	908	406	505	1 465	1 026	477	2 027	246	1 044
1942	10 040	1 625	877	301	417	1 289	937	466	1 631	272	890
1941	7 781	1 089	635	203	334	1 132	875	463	1 249	284	647

[3]Includes bulbs, plants, and trees.
[4]Includes interest on non real estate debt, marketing, charges, net insurance premiums (crop, fire, wind, and hail) and miscellaneous supplies and services purchased.
[5]Includes values of perquisites.
... = Not available.

Table 6-4. Farm Income and Expenses, 1910–2006—*Continued*

(Millions of dollars.)

Year	Net income of farm operators from farming	Realized gross farm income	Realized gross income from farming			Government payments[2]	Value of farm products consumed in farm households	Gross rental value of farm dwellings
			Cash receipts from marketing					
			Total	Crops[1]	Livestock and livestock products			
1940	4 482	11 059	8 382	3 469	4 913	723	1 210	744
1939	4 414	10 585	7 872	3 336	4 536	763	1 209	741
1938	4 361	10 149	7 723	3 200	4 523	446	1 235	745
1937	6 005	11 367	8 864	3 924	4 940	336	1 434	733
1936	4 308	10 756	8 391	3 649	4 742	278	1 394	693
1935	5 278	9 696	7 120	2 977	4 143	573	1 320	683
1934	2 923	8 568	6 357	3 021	3 336	446	1 125	640
1933	2 555	7 107	5 332	2 486	2 846	131	1 030	614
1932	2 032	6 405	4 748	1 996	2 752	...	993	664
1931	3 344	8 421	6 381	2 540	3 841	...	1 265	775
1930	4 259	11 472	9 055	3 868	5 187	...	1 552	865
1929	6 152	13 938	11 312	5 130	6 182	...	1 713	913
1928	5 981	13 598	10 991	4 956	6 035	...	1 724	883
1927	5 699	13 336	10 733	5 125	5 608	...	1 725	878
1926	5 937	13 302	10 558	4 875	5 683	...	1 875	869
1925	6 734	13 716	11 021	5 545	5 476	...	1 827	868
1924	4 855	12 785	10 225	5 413	4 812	...	1 706	854
1923	5 068	12 167	9 545	4 865	4 680	...	1 772	850
1922	4 343	11 059	8 575	4 300	4 275	...	1 717	767
1921	3 370	10 573	8 058	4 106	3 952	...	1 746	769
1920	7 795	15 944	12 600	6 644	5 956	...	2 509	835
1919	9 078	17 918	14 538	7 603	6 935	...	2 556	824
1918	8 887	16 547	13 467	6 974	6 493	...	2 341	739
1917	8 304	13 410	10 736	5 642	5 094	...	2 003	671
1916	4 570	9 744	7 746	4 035	3 711	...	1 384	614
1915	4 307	8 147	6 392	3 263	3 129	...	1 192	563
1914	4 181	7 793	6 036	2 899	3 137	...	1 228	529
1913	3 728	7 978	6 238	3 077	3 161	...	1 222	518
1912	4 456	7 710	6 008	3 095	2 913	...	1 204	498
1911	3 371	7 213	5 584	2 905	2 679	...	1 165	464
1910	4 176	7 495	5 780	2 929	2 851	...	1 270	445

[1]Includes commodities placed under Commodity Credit Corporation (CCC) loans and profits made on loans redeemed.
[2]Government payments reflect payments made directly to all recipients in the farm sector, including landlords.
. . . = Not available.

Table 6-4. Farm Income and Expenses, 1910–2006—*Continued*

(Millions of dollars.)

		Expenses of agricultural production									
		Operating expenses (excluded hired labor)						Taxes on farm property	Wages paid for hired farm labor[5]	Interest on farm mortgage debt	Net rent to nonfarm landlords
Year	Total	Feed purchased	Livestock purchased	Seed purchased[3]	Fertilizer and lime	Repairs	Miscellaneous[4]				
1940	6 858	998	517	197	306	1 038	784	451	1 029	293	448
1939	6 266	732	465	169	273	959	759	456	988	305	379
1938	5 920	557	368	206	258	907	726	448	979	320	318
1937	6 178	805	332	194	279	879	732	452	988	341	380
1936	5 642	755	283	147	261	749	664	440	868	364	383
1935	5 116	528	312	108	188	717	647	434	775	396	347
1934	4 715	542	183	104	176	608	663	424	679	430	256
1933	4 358	422	199	65	120	554	669	438	617	472	158
1932	4 483	348	193	79	118	521	730	510	669	526	55
1931	5 537	448	253	117	202	635	834	589	914	553	136
1930	6 944	791	362	124	297	785	914	648	1 177	570	321
1929	7 664	919	504	122	300	886	998	651	1 300	582	486
1928	7 757	977	588	134	318	827	1 001	636	1 290	590	496
1927	7 462	892	465	140	267	787	986	620	1 302	593	520
1926	7 372	891	396	142	298	774	1 033	599	1 330	598	425
1925	7 347	988	382	136	299	711	1 021	589	1 267	612	470
1924	7 447	1 116	313	120	264	654	1 030	583	1 248	647	520
1923	7 054	819	304	111	263	637	1 027	590	1 251	679	430
1922	6 614	676	319	109	234	557	1 027	583	1 127	680	368
1921	6 638	710	202	123	249	550	1 052	586	1 170	653	304
1920	8 837	1 254	422	178	390	695	1 263	556	1 790	574	504
1919	8 331	1 097	567	138	358	615	1 143	454	1 515	476	928
1918	7 507	1 106	522	132	311	536	1 024	361	1 337	417	859
1917	6 092	614	414	122	232	464	863	339	1 127	379	825
1916	4 836	517	260	76	193	395	715	304	904	341	534
1915	4 167	411	207	62	165	343	639	284	815	314	403
1914	4 029	414	215	62	195	297	648	261	804	296	355
1913	3 974	406	250	62	175	289	634	257	804	276	340
1912	3 833	419	217	74	161	278	606	225	789	252	343
1911	3 582	350	188	65	168	251	588	215	758	225	331
1910	3 531	426	199	56	152	251	558	195	755	203	320

Source: U.S. Department of Agriculture, Economic Research Service.
[3]Includes bulbs, plants, and trees.
[4]Includes interest on non real estate debt, marketing, charges, net insurance premiums (crop, fire, wind, and hail) and miscellaneous supplies and services purchased.
[5]Includes values of perquisites.

Table 6-5. Consumer Expenditures, Farm Value, and Marketing Bill for All Farm Food Products Purchased by Domestic Civilian Consumers, 1913–2004

(Billions of dollars.)

Year	Consumer expenditures[1]	Farm value	Marketing bill[2]
2004	789	156	633
2003	744	140	604
2002	709	133	577
2001	688	130	558
2000	661	123	538
1999	625	122	503
1998	585	120	465
1997	567	122	445
1996	547	122	425
1995	530	114	416
1994	512	110	403
1993	489	110	380
1992	475	105	369
1991	465	102	364
1990	450	106	344
1989	419	104	316
1988	399	97	302
1987	376	90	285
1986	360	89	271
1985	345	86	259
1984	332	90	242
1983	315	85	230
1982	299	81	218
1981	288	82	206
1980	264	82	183
1979	245	79	166
1978	217	70	147
1977	191	58	133
1976	183	58	125
1975	167	56	111
1974	156	56	98
1973	139	52	87
1972	122	40	82
1971	115	36	79
1970	111	36	75
1969	95	32	63
1968	90	29	61
1967	85	27	58
1966	83	28	55
1965	78	26	52
1964	48	23	51
1963	72	23	49
1962	69	22	47
1961	67	22	45
1960	66	22	44
1959	63	21	42
1958	61	22	40
1957	58	21	38
1956	56	19	36
1955	53	19	34
1954	51	19	32
1953	51	20	32
1952	51	20	30
1951	49	20	29
1950	44	18	26
1949	43	17	26
1948	45	20	25
1947[3]	42	19	23
1947[4]	36	19	18
1946	31	16	16
1945	24	13	12
1944	22	12	11
1943	22	11	11
1942	20	9	10
1941	16	7	9

[1] For 1913–1947, consumer expenditures for farm food eaten away from home are based on retail food store prices.
[2] The difference between expenditures for domestic farm-originated food products and the farm value or payment farmers received for the equivalent farm products.
[3] Comparable with later years. Beginning 1947, a new series based on 1958 benchmark estimate.
[4] Comparable with earlier years.

Table 6-5. Consumer Expenditures, Farm Value, and Marketing Bill for All Farm Food Products Purchased by Domestic Civilian Consumers, 1913–2004—*Continued*

(Billions of dollars.)

Year	Consumer expenditures[1]	Farm value	Marketing bill[2]
1940	14	6	8
1939	15	5	10
1939[5]	13	5	8
1938	13	5	8
1937	14	6	8
1936	14	6	8
1935	14	5	9
1935[5]	13	5	8
1934	12	4	8
1933	11	4	7
1932	11	3	7
1931	13	5	8
1930	16	6	10
1929	18	8	10
1929	17	7	10
1928	16	7	9
1927	16	10	10
1926	16	7	9
1925	16	7	9
1924	14	6	9
1923	14	6	8
1922	13	5	8
1921	13	5	8
1920	16	7	9
1919	15	8	8
1918	13	7	6
1917	12	6	6
1916	10	4	5
1915	8	4	4
1914	8	4	4
1913	7	4	4

Source: U.S. Census Bureau. U.S. Department of Agriculture, Economic Research Service.
Note: May not add due to rounding.
[1]For 1913–1947, consumer expenditures for farm food eaten away from home are based on retail food store prices.
[2]The difference between expenditures for domestic farm-originated food products and the farm value or payment farmers received for the equivalent farm products.
[5]Revised figures according to the commodity flow method; comparable to 1947–1970.

Table 6-6. Acreages of Harvested Crops by Use, and Indexes of Cropland Used for Crops and Crop Production per Acre, 1910–2005[1]

(Acres in millions.)

Year	Acreages of harvested crops by use (million acres)		
	Total[2]	Index (1977 = 100)	Products for domestic use
2005	321	89	. . .
2004	321	89	. . .
2003	324	90	. . .
2002	316	90	. . .
2001	321	90	. . .
2000	325	91	. . .
1999	327	91	. . .
1998	326	91	. . .
1997	332	92	. . .
1996	326	92	. . .
1995	314	88	. . .
1994	321	90	. . .
1993	308	87	. . .
1992	317	89	. . .
1991	318	89	. . .
1990	322	90	239
1989	318	90	215
1988	298	87	179
1987	302	88	196
1986	325	94	229
1985	342	98	263
1984	348	99	252
1983	306	88	182
1982	362	101	249
1981	366	102	237
1980	352	101	215
1979	348	100	232
1978	338	97	224
1977	345	100	232
1976	337	98	240
1975	336	97	236
1974	328	96	229
1973	321	93	225
1972	294	88	203
1971	305	90	243
1970	293	88	225
1969	294	88	233
1968	303	89	249
1967	308	90	239
1966	295	88	226
1965	298	89	222
1964	301	89	227
1963	300	89	223
1962	295	88	229
1961	303	90	[3]1 232
1960	324	94	255
1959	324	95	257
1958	324	94	273
1957	324	95	268
1956	324	98	255
1955	340	100	283
1954	346	100	298
1953	348	100	304
1952	349	100	298
1951	344	102	267
1950	345	100	276
1949	360	102	293
1948	356	100	280
1947	355	99	287
1946	352	98	278
1945	354	98	280
1944	362	100	301
1943	357	100	299
1942	348	98	296
1941	344	97	292

[1]Excludes Alaska and Hawaii.
[2]Area in principal crops harvested as reported by Crop Reporting Board plus acreages in fruits, vegetables for sale, tree nuts, and other minor crops.
[3]1961 and earlier, does not include feed for horses or mules.
. . . = Not available.

Table 6-6. Acreages of Harvested Crops by Use, and Indexes of Cropland Used for Crops and Crop Production per Acre, 1910–2005[1]—*Continued*

(Acres in millions.)

Year	Acreages of harvested crops by use (million acres)		
	Total[2]	Index (1977 = 100)	Products for domestic use
1940	341	97	290
1939	331	96	263
1938	349	98	279
1937	347	100	266
1936	323	99	251
1935	345	100	269
1934	304	99	227
1933	340	100	253
1932	371	102	276
1931	365	101	267
1930	369	101	265
1929	365	100	254
1928	361	99	242
1927	358	99	236
1926	359	98	229
1925	360	98	238
1924	355	97	221
1923	354	97	223
1922	355	97	219
1921	359	97	206
1920	360	97	210
1919	364	99	217
1918	362	98	208
1917	349	94	213
1916	340	92	195
1915	340	92	198
1914	334	90	185
1913	333	90	198
1912	329	89	196
1911	330	89	200
1910	325	87	200

Source: U.S. Census Bureau. U.S. Department of Agriculture, Economic Research Service.
[1]Excludes Alaska and Hawaii.
[2]Area in principal crops harvested as reported by Crop Reporting Board plus acreages in fruits, vegetables for sale, tree nuts, and other minor crops.

Table 6-7. Farm Sector Output and Value Added, 1930–2004

(Billions of dollars. Minus sign (–) indicates decrease.)

ITEM	1930	1940	1950	1960	1970
CURRENT DOLLARS					
Farm output	**10.3**	**9.9**	**31.2**	**35.7**	**51.8**
Cash receipts from farm marketings	9.1	8.2	29.2	33.8	51.3
Crops	3.9	3.3	13.1	14.8	21.8
Livestock	5.2	4.9	16.1	19.0	29.5
Farm products consumed on farms	1.6	1.2	2.1	1.1	0.8
Other farm income	0.0	0.0	0.0	0.2	0.5
Change in farm finished goods inventories	–0.3	0.5	–0.1	0.6	–0.8
Crops	–0.3	0.4	–0.7	0.5	–1.5
Livestock	0.0	0.1	0.6	0.1	0.7
Less: Intermediate goods and services consumed	3.4	4.0	12.5	17.5	28.1
Other than rent	2.9	3.6	11.2	16.1	25.8
Intermediate goods and services purchased, other than rent	2.9	3.6	11.2	16.1	25.8
Less: Change in farm materials and supplies inventories	...	...	...	...	...
Rent paid to nonoperator landlords	0.5	0.5	1.3	1.4	2.3
Equals: Gross farm value added	7.0	5.9	18.7	18.2	23.7
Less: Consumption of fixed capital	0.6	0.6	2.1	3.3	5.3
Equals: Net farm value added	6.4	5.3	16.7	14.9	18.4
Compensation of employees	1.2	1.0	2.8	3.1	4.2
Wage and salary accruals	1.2	1.0	2.8	3.0	3.9
Supplements to wages and salaries	0.0	0.0	0.0	0.1	0.3
Taxes on production and imports	0.4	0.3	0.7	1.1	1.8
Less: Subsidies to operators	0.0	0.6	0.2	0.6	3.3
Net operating surplus	4.7	4.6	13.4	11.3	15.7
Net interest	0.8	0.4	0.4	0.8	2.3
Current transfer payments	0.0	0.0	0.0	0.0	0.0
Proprietors' income and corporate profits with inventory valuation and capital consumption adjustments	4.0	4.1	13.0	10.5	13.3
Proprietors' income	4.0	4.1	12.9	10.5	12.7
Corporate profits	0.0	0.0	0.2	0.0	0.6
Addendum:					
Change in farm inventories[1]	–0.3	0.5	–0.1	0.6	–0.8
CHAINED (2000) DOLLARS					
Farm output, total	...	...	...	...	...
Cash receipts from farm marketings	...	...	...	...	...
Crops	...	...	...	...	...
Livestock	...	...	...	...	...
Farm products consumed on farms	...	...	...	...	...
Other farm income	...	...	...	...	...
Change in farm finished goods inventories	...	...	...	...	...
Crops	...	...	...	...	...
Livestock	...	...	...	...	...
Less: Intermediate goods and services consumed	...	...	...	...	...
Other than rent	...	...	...	...	...
Intermediate goods and services purchased, other than rent	...	...	...	...	...
Less: Change in farm materials and supplies inventories	...	...	...	...	...
Rent paid to nonoperator landlords	...	...	...	...	...
Equals: Gross farm value added	...	...	...	...	...
Less: Consumption of fixed capital	...	...	...	...	...
Equals: Net farm value added	...	...	...	...	...
Change in farm inventories[1]	...	...	...	...	...

Source: U.S. Census Bureau. *Statistical Abstract of the United States: 2007*. U.S. Bureau of Economic Analysis.
[1]Beginning 1991, includes change in farm materials and supplies inventories.
... = Not available.

Table 6-7. Farm Sector Output and Value Added, 1930–2004—*Continued*

(Billions of dollars. Minus sign (–) indicates decrease.)

1980	1985	1990	1995	2000	2001	2002	2003	2004
137.8	**147.7**	**180.1**	**192.0**	**203.6**	**210.8**	**202.1**	**225.8**	**258.0**
140.3	136.3	172.1	194.3	196.6	200.1	194.6	213.3	242.9
72.3	66.5	82.9	107.1	97.0	93.5	100.8	107.8	119.6
68.0	69.8	89.2	87.2	99.5	106.6	93.9	105.6	123.4
1.2	0.9	0.7	0.5	0.6	0.5	0.5	0.5	0.5
2.4	4.6	4.9	6.3	8.4	9.5	10.6	11.6	11.1
–6.1	5.8	2.4	–9.2	–2.0	0.6	–3.7	0.4	3.4
–7.5	7.6	1.9	–9.4	–1.3	1.0	–3.1	1.3	2.6
1.3	–1.8	0.4	0.2	–0.6	–0.4	–0.6	–0.8	0.9
86.4	84.3	103.5	123.5	132.1	137.7	131.2	137.8	145.8
78.9	74.5	92.2	111.1	120.5	120.5	125.6	127.7	135.7
78.9	74.5	92.2	109.2	121.1	125.0	121.7	127.5	135.5
...	...	...	–1.9	0.6	–0.6	1.2	–0.2	–0.2
7.6	9.8	11.3	12.4	11.6	12.0	10.8	10.1	10.1
51.4	63.4	76.6	68.5	71.5	73.1	70.8	88.0	112.2
16.8	18.6	18.6	19.6	21.3	27.4	27.0	27.9	30.1
34.6	44.8	58.0	48.9	50.2	45.7	43.9	60.1	82.2
9.2	9.9	13.4	15.4	19.7	20.9	20.8	20.0	22.5
8.2	8.9	11.7	13.1	17.0	17.9	17.9	17.0	19.7
1.0	1.0	1.8	2.3	2.7	3.0	2.9	2.9	2.8
2.8	3.1	3.8	4.2	4.7	4.8	5.0	5.2	5.4
1.0	6.3	7.6	6.1	19.6	18.3	9.6	13.7	10.7
23.5	38.1	48.5	35.4	45.4	38.3	27.7	48.5	64.9
12.1	14.6	9.9	8.7	10.2	9.6	9.6	8.79.0	
0.0	0.0	0.0	0.0	0.0	0.0	0.0	0.0	0.0
11.4	23.5	38.5	26.7	35.2	28.7	18.1	39.8	55.9
11.3	20.8	31.9	22.7	22.7	19.7	10.6	27.7	35.8
0.1	2.7	6.7	4.0	12.5	9.0	7.5	12.1	20.0
–6.1	5.8	2.4	–11.1	–1.3	0.0	–2.5	0.2	3.2
...	...	**164.5**	**179.6**	**203.6**	**200.7**	**201.4**	**206.3**	**206.1**
...	...	159.0	183.5	196.6	190.1	194.1	194.3	192.8
...	...	77.2	92.3	97.0	91.9	93.4	94.6	94.3
...	...	81.9	90.9	99.5	98.1	100.7	99.5	98.3
...	...	0.7	0.5	0.6	0.5	0.5	0.5	0.4
...	...	4.8	5.8	8.4	9.4	10.1	10.4	9.4
...	...	2.1	–8.8	–2.0	0.6	–3.6	0.4	2.5
...	...	1.6	–7.4	–1.3	1.0	–2.8	1.0	1.8
...	...	0.4	0.3	–0.6	–0.4	–0.6	–0.7	0.7
...	...	117.5	134.4	132.1	135.3	131.3	130.1	130.0
...	...	105.9	121.3	120.5	123.5	120.3	120.4	120.7
...	...	105.9	119.3	121.1	122.9	121.5	120.2	120.5
...	...	...	–2.0	0.6	–0.6	1.2	–0.2	–0.2
...	...	11.7	13.1	11.6	11.8	11.0	9.6	9.3
...	...	49.3	49.6	71.5	65.6	70.1	76.0	75.9
...	...	23.0	21.3	21.3	27.0	26.2	26.7	27.6
...	...	29.4	30.4	50.2	39.0	44.2	49.5	48.8
...	...	2.1	–10.6	–1.3	0.0	–2.5	0.2	2.3

Table 6-8. Value Added to Economy by Agricultural Sector, 1985–2006

(Billions of dollars.)

Item	1985	1986	1987	1988	1989	1990	1991
Value of agricultural sector production	**153.4**	**144.3**	**151.7**	**163.4**	**180.7**	**188.5**	**183.8**
Value of crop production	73.7	63.3	64.5	69.3	81.5	83.2	81.2
Food grains	8.9	5.7	5.8	7.5	8.2	7.5	7.3
Feed crops	22.3	17.0	14.6	14.3	17.0	18.7	19.3
Cotton	3.7	3.4	4.2	4.5	5.0	5.5	5.2
Oil crops	12.4	10.6	11.3	13.5	11.9	12.3	12.7
Tobacco	2.7	1.9	1.8	2.1	2.4	2.7	2.9
Fruits and tree nuts	6.9	7.3	8.1	9.0	9.1	9.4	10.0
Vegetables	8.6	8.9	9.9	9.8	11.6	11.3	11.4
All other crops	8.4	9.1	10.1	10.9	11.6	12.9	13.4
Home consumption	0.2	0.2	0.2	0.2	0.1	0.1	0.2
Value of inventory adjustment[1]	−0.5	−0.7	−1.5	−2.5	4.5	2.8	−1.2
Value of livestock production	69.0	70.7	75.7	78.6	83.5	90.0	87.2
Meat animals	38.7	39.1	44.5	46.7	46.4	51.1	50.1
Dairy products	18.1	17.7	17.7	17.6	19.4	20.2	18.0
Poultry and eggs	11.3	12.7	11.5	12.9	15.4	15.3	15.2
Miscellaneous livestock	2.0	2.0	2.3	2.4	2.5	2.5	2.5
Home consumption	0.7	0.7	0.6	0.6	0.5	0.5	0.5
Value of inventory adjustment[1]	−1.8	−1.5	−0.8	−1.6	−0.7	0.4	1.0
Services and forestry	10.7	10.3	11.4	15.5	15.8	15.3	15.4
Machine hire and custom work	1.5	1.2	1.5	1.5	1.7	1.8	1.8
Forest products sold	1.4	1.5	1.7	1.8	2.0	1.8	1.8
Other farm income	3.2	3.0	3.2	4.5	4.9	4.5	4.7
Gross imputed rental value of farm dwellings	4.7	4.6	5.0	7.7	7.2	7.2	7.2
Purchased inputs	73.5	71.4	76.1	83.4	88.0	92.2	94.3
Farm origin	29.3	30.4	32.6	37.3	38.1	39.5	38.6
Feed purchased	16.9	17.5	17.5	20.2	20.7	20.4	19.3
Livestock and poultry purchased	9.2	9.8	11.8	13.0	12.9	14.6	14.1
Seed purchased	3.1	3.2	3.3	4.1	4.4	4.5	5.1
Manufactured inputs	20.2	18.2	18.1	19.0	20.6	22.0	23.2
Fertilizers and lime	7.5	6.8	6.5	7.7	8.2	8.2	8.7
Pesticides	4.3	4.3	4.5	4.1	5.0	5.4	6.3
Petroleum fuel and oils	6.4	5.3	5.0	4.8	4.8	5.8	5.6
Electricity	1.9	1.8	2.2	2.4	2.6	2.6	2.6
Other purchased inputs	24.1	22.7	25.4	27.1	29.3	30.7	32.5
Repair and maintenance of capital items	6.4	6.4	6.8	7.7	8.4	8.6	8.6
Machine hire and custom work	2.4	2.1	2.1	2.5	2.9	3.0	3.1
Marketing, storage, and transportation expenses	4.1	3.7	4.1	3.5	4.2	4.2	4.7
Contract labor	1.5	1.0	1.3	1.1	1.3	1.6	1.6
Miscellaneous expenses	9.7	9.5	11.2	12.3	12.4	13.4	14.5
Plus: Net government transactions[2]	2.9	7.0	11.5	9.0	5.1	3.1	2.1
Direct Government payments	7.7	11.8	16.7	14.5	10.9	9.3	8.2
Motor vehicle registration and licensing fees	0.3	0.2	0.3	0.3	0.3	0.4	0.3
Property taxes	4.5	4.6	5.0	5.2	5.5	5.8	5.8
Equals: Gross value added	**82.8**	**79.9**	**87.1**	**89.0**	**97.8**	**99.3**	**91.6**
Less: Capital consumption	19.4	17.7	17.2	17.6	18.1	18.1	18.2
Equals: Net value added	**63.3**	**62.2**	**69.9**	**71.4**	**79.7**	**81.2**	**73.5**
Less: Employee compensation	8.5	8.4	8.7	9.8	10.6	12.4	12.2
Less: Net rent received by nonoperator landlords	7.7	6.1	8.3	7.7	8.5	9.0	8.7
Less: Real estate and nonreal estate interest	18.6	16.5	15.0	14.4	14.1	13.5	12.3
Equals: Net farm income	**28.5**	**31.1**	**38.0**	**39.6**	**46.5**	**46.3**	**40.2**

[1]A positive value of inventory change represents current-year production not sold by December 31. A negative value is an offset to production from prior years included in current-year sales.
[2]Direct government payments minus motor vehicle registration and licensing fees and property taxes.

Table 6-8. Value Added to Economy by Agricultural Sector, 1985–2006—*Continued*

(Billions of dollars.)

Item	1992	1993	1994	1995	1996	1997	1998
Value of agricultural sector production	**191.9**	**191.6**	**208.2**	**203.6**	**228.5**	**230.5**	**220.2**
Value of crop production	89.6	82.7	100.5	95.9	115.7	112.5	102.1
Food grains	8.5	8.2	9.5	10.4	10.8	10.4	8.8
Feed crops	20.1	20.2	20.3	24.5	27.2	27.1	22.6
Cotton	5.2	5.2	6.7	6.9	7.0	6.3	6.1
Oil crops	13.3	13.2	14.7	15.5	16.3	19.8	17.4
Tobacco	3.0	2.9	2.7	2.5	2.8	2.9	2.8
Fruits and tree nuts	10.1	10.3	10.3	11.0	11.8	13.0	12.0
Vegetables	11.8	13.7	14.0	15.0	14.4	14.7	15.0
All other crops	14.3	13.9	14.9	15.3	16.1	17.2	17.6
Home consumption	0.2	0.2	0.2	0.2	0.2	0.2	0.2
Value of inventory adjustment[1]	3.2	−5.3	7.2	−5.3	9.0	1.0	−0.3
Value of livestock production	87.1	92.0	89.7	87.8	92.1	96.3	94.2
Meat animals	47.7	51.0	46.7	44.9	44.2	49.7	43.4
Dairy products	19.7	19.3	20.0	19.9	22.8	20.9	24.1
Poultry and eggs	15.5	17.4	18.5	19.1	22.5	22.3	23.0
Miscellaneous livestock	2.7	3.0	3.2	3.4	3.6	3.6	3.8
Home consumption	0.4	0.4	0.3	0.3	0.3	0.2	0.2
Value of inventory adjustment[1]	1.0	1.1	1.1	0.2	−1.1	−0.4	−0.3
Services and forestry	15.2	17.0	18.0	19.9	20.7	21.7	23.9
Machine hire and custom work	1.8	1.9	2.1	1.9	2.2	2.4	2.2
Forest products sold	2.1	2.4	2.6	2.8	2.6	2.8	3.0
Other farm income	4.1	4.6	4.3	5.8	6.2	6.9	8.7
Gross imputed rental value of farm dwellings	7.2	8.1	9.0	9.4	9.8	9.6	10.0
Purchased inputs	92.6	100.0	103.9	108.8	112.2	120.0	117.7
Farm origin	38.6	41.3	41.3	41.8	42.7	46.9	44.8
Feed purchased	20.1	21.4	22.6	23.8	25.2	26.3	25.0
Livestock and poultry purchased	13.6	14.7	13.3	12.5	11.3	13.8	12.6
Seed purchased	4.9	5.2	5.4	5.5	6.2	6.7	7.2
Manufactured inputs	22.7	23.1	24.4	26.1	28.6	29.2	28.1
Fertilizers and lime	8.3	8.4	9.2	10.0	10.9	10.9	10.6
Pesticides	6.5	6.7	7.2	7.7	8.5	9.0	9.0
Petroleum fuel and oils	5.3	5.4	5.3	5.4	6.0	6.2	5.6
Electricity	2.6	2.7	2.7	3.0	3.2	3.0	2.9
Other purchased inputs	31.3	35.5	38.2	40.9	40.8	43.9	44.8
Repair and maintenance of capital items	8.2	9.3	9.2	9.6	10.4	10.6	10.5
Machine hire and custom work	3.1	3.6	3.9	3.9	3.7	4.0	4.6
Marketing, storage, and transportation expenses	4.5	5.6	6.8	7.2	6.9	7.1	6.9
Contract labor	1.7	1.8	1.8	2.0	2.1	2.5	2.4
Miscellaneous expenses	13.7	15.2	16.6	18.2	17.7	19.7	20.4
Plus: Net government transactions[2]	2.7	7.0	1.2	0.4	0.4	0.4	5.3
Direct Government payments	9.2	13.4	7.9	7.3	7.3	7.5	12.4
Motor vehicle registration and licensing fees	0.4	0.4	0.4	0.4	0.4	0.5	0.5
Property taxes	6.1	6.0	6.3	6.4	6.6	6.7	6.6
Equals: Gross value added	**102.0**	**98.7**	**105.5**	**95.2**	**116.7**	**110.9**	**107.8**
Less: Capital consumption	18.3	18.2	18.4	18.9	19.1	19.3	19.6
Equals: Net value added	**83.7**	**80.5**	**87.1**	**76.3**	**97.6**	**91.7**	**88.2**
Less: Employee compensation	12.2	13.1	13.4	14.3	15.1	15.9	16.8
Less: Net rent received by nonoperator landlords	9.2	9.7	9.3	9.6	10.5	11.2	10.9
Less: Real estate and nonreal estate interest	11.6	10.9	11.8	12.6	13.1	13.2	13.5
Equals: Net farm income	**50.7**	**46.7**	**52.6**	**39.8**	**59.0**	**51.3**	**47.1**

[1]A positive value of inventory change represents current-year production not sold by December 31. A negative value is an offset to production from prior years included in current-year sales.
[2]Direct government payments minus motor vehicle registration and licensing fees and property taxes.

Table 6-8. Value Added to Economy by Agricultural Sector, 1970–2006—*Continued*

(Billions of dollars.)

Item	1999	2000	2001	2002	2003	2004	2005	2006P
Value of agricultural sector production	**213.5**	**219.1**	**228.0**	**218.7**	**242.6**	**279.0**	**275.4**	**282.1**
Value of crop production	92.8	94.9	95.0	98.3	109.4	124.0	112.7	119.6
Food grains	6.9	6.5	6.4	6.8	8.0	9.1	8.4	8.7
Feed crops	19.5	20.5	21.5	24.0	24.7	28.2	25.3	29.1
Cotton	4.6	2.9	3.6	3.4	6.5	5.4	5.8	5.5
Oil crops	13.4	13.5	13.3	15.0	18.7	19.8	18.3	18.8
Tobacco	2.3	2.3	1.9	1.7	1.6	1.5	1.1	1.2
Fruits and tree nuts	12.0	12.5	12.0	12.6	13.4	15.5	16.8	17.7
Vegetables	15.0	15.6	15.5	17.2	17.4	17.3	16.9	18.6
All other crops	18.4	18.7	19.2	20.2	20.7	21.0	21.3	21.8
Home consumption	0.2	0.2	0.2	0.2	0.1	0.1	0.1	0.1
Value of inventory adjustment[1]	0.5	2.2	1.5	−2.9	−1.7	6.1	−1.3	−2.0
Value of livestock production	95.2	99.1	106.4	93.5	104.9	124.6	126.9	122.7
Meat animals	45.7	53.0	53.3	48.1	56.2	62.2	64.8	65.3
Dairy products	23.2	20.6	24.7	20.6	21.2	27.4	26.7	23.4
Poultry and eggs	23.0	21.8	24.6	21.2	23.9	29.5	28.9	27.7
Miscellaneous livestock	3.9	4.2	4.1	4.1	4.3	4.4	4.5	4.7
Home consumption	0.1	0.1	0.1	0.1	0.1	0.2	0.3	0.3
Value of inventory adjustment[1]	−0.7	−0.6	−0.4	−0.6	−0.8	0.9	1.7	1.2
Services and forestry	25.4	25.0	26.5	26.9	28.3	30.5	35.8	39.8
Machine hire and custom work	2.0	2.2	2.1	2.2	3.0	3.5	2.8	3.0
Forest products sold	2.7	2.8	2.6	2.5	2.2	2.4	2.5	2.5
Other farm income	10.1	8.7	10.1	10.2	10.5	11.3	12.4	12.5
Gross imputed rental value of farm dwellings	10.6	11.3	11.7	12.0	12.6	13.3	18.2	21.8
Purchased inputs	118.7	121.8	125.7	123.1	130.0	136.5	146.7	154.8
Farm origin	45.5	47.9	48.2	48.3	53.7	57.1	57.9	60.9
Feed purchased	24.5	24.5	24.8	25.0	27.5	30.0	28.2	30.9
Livestock and poultry purchased	13.8	15.9	15.2	14.4	16.8	17.6	19.2	18.7
Seed purchased	7.2	7.5	8.2	8.9	9.4	9.5	10.4	11.3
Manufactured inputs	27.1	28.7	29.4	28.5	28.6	31.4	35.5	37.8
Fertilizers and lime	9.9	10.0	10.3	9.6	10.0	11.4	12.9	13.7
Pesticides	8.6	8.5	8.6	8.3	8.4	8.5	8.9	9.3
Petroleum fuel and oils	5.6	7.2	6.9	6.6	6.8	8.2	10.3	11.0
Electricity	3.0	3.0	3.6	3.9	3.3	3.2	3.4	3.8
Other purchased inputs	46.1	45.2	48.1	46.4	47.7	48.0	53.3	56.1
Repair and maintenance of capital items	10.7	10.9	11.2	10.4	10.3	13.1	11.9	12.9
Machine hire and custom work	4.4	4.1	4.0	4.0	3.5	3.7	3.5	3.6
Marketing, storage, and transportation expenses	7.3	7.5	7.8	7.5	7.4	7.1	8.8	9.0
Contract labor	2.5	2.7	3.1	2.7	3.2	2.6	3.0	3.2
Miscellaneous expenses	21.3	19.9	21.9	21.7	23.3	21.5	26.1	27.4
Plus: Net government transactions[2]	14.3	15.5	13.3	4.0	9.9	5.8	15.8	7.6
Direct Government payments	21.5	22.9	20.7	11.2	17.2	13.3	24.3	16.3
Motor vehicle registration and licensing fees	0.4	0.5	0.5	0.4	0.5	0.5	0.6	0.6
Property taxes	6.8	6.9	6.9	6.8	6.8	7.0	8.0	8.1
Equals: Gross value added	**109.0**	**112.8**	**115.6**	**99.6**	**122.5**	**148.3**	**144.6**	**135.0**
Less: Capital consumption	19.8	20.1	20.6	21.0	21.3	22.3	24.1	25.3
Equals: Net value added	**89.3**	**92.7**	**95.0**	**78.6**	**101.2**	**125.9**	**120.4**	**109.7**
Less: Employee compensation	17.4	17.9	18.8	19.1	18.8	20.6	21.0	21.8
Less: Net rent received by nonoperator landlords	10.4	11.2	11.1	9.8	10.3	9.7	10.5	10.1
Less: Real estate and nonreal estate interest	13.8	14.7	13.6	13.1	12.7	13.1	15.1	17.2
Equals: Net farm income	**47.7**	**48.9**	**51.5**	**36.6**	**59.5**	**82.5**	**73.8**	**60.6**

Source: U.S. Census Bureau, *Statistical Abstract of the United States: 2007.* U.S. Department of Agriculture, Economic Research Service.
Note: Data are consistent with the net farm income accounts and include income and expenses related to the farm operator dwellings. Value of agricultural sector production is the gross value of the commodities and services produced within a year. Net value-added is the sector's contribution to the National economy and is the sum of the income from production earned by all factors-of-production, regardless of ownership. Net farm income is the farm operators' share of income from the sector's production activities. The concept presented is consistent with that employed by the Organization for Economic Co-operation and Development.
[1]A positive value of inventory change represents current-year production not sold by December 31. A negative value is an offset to production from prior years included in current-year sales.
[2]Direct government payments minus motor vehicle registration and licensing fees and property taxes.
P = Preliminary.

Table 6-9. Value of Agricultural Exports and Imports, 1970–2005

(Billions of dollars, percent.)

Year	Trade balance	Exports, domestic products		Imports for consumption	
		Total	Percent of all exports	Total	Percent of all imports
2005	3.7	63.0	7	59.3	4
2004	7.4	61.4	8	54.0	4
2003	12.0	59.4	8	47.4	4
2002	11.2	53.1	8	41.9	4
2001	14.3	53.7	8	39.4	3
2000	12.3	51.2	7	39.0	3
1999	10.7	48.4	8	37.7	4
1998	14.9	51.8	8	36.9	4
1997	21.0	57.2	9	36.1	4
1996	26.8	60.3	10	33.5	4
1995	26.0	56.3	10	30.3	4
1994	19.2	46.2	10	27.0	4
1993	17.7	42.9	10	25.1	4
1992	18.3	43.1	10	24.8	5
1991	16.5	39.3	10	22.9	5
1990	16.6	39.5	11	22.9	5
1989	18.3	40.1	12	21.9	5
1988	16.1	37.1	12	21.0	5
1987	8.3	28.7	12	20.4	5
1986	4.8	26.2	13	21.5	6
1985	9.1	29.0	13	20.0	6
1984	18.5	37.8	17	19.3	6
1983	19.6	36.1	18	16.5	7
1982	21.3	36.6	17	15.3	6
1981	26.4	43.3	18	16.9	6
1980	23.9	41.2	18	17.4	7
1979	18.0	34.7	19	16.7	8
1978	14.6	29.4	21	14.8	9
1977	10.2	23.6	20	13.4	9
1976	12.0	23.0	20	11.0	9
1975	12.6	21.9	21	9.3	10
1974	11.7	21.9	23	10.2	10
1973	9.3	17.7	25	8.4	12
1972	2.9	9.4	19	6.5	12
1971	1.9	7.7	18	5.8	13
1970	1.5	7.3	17	5.8	15

Source: U.S. Census Bureau. *Statistical Abstract of the United States: 2007.* U.S. Department of Agriculture, Economic Research Service.

BOX 6 ■ Use of Pesticides

In 2004, overall pesticide use for agricultural crops in the United States was 494.5 million pounds of active ingredients and 2.1 pounds in active ingredients used per acre. This is slightly lower than in 1990, despite the fact that total agricultural use increased from the 1990 level of 497.7 million pounds of active ingredients to the 1997 level of 587.6 million pounds. In addition, the cost to farmers has increased, so that although farmers used 3.2 million fewer pounds of active ingredients in 2004 than they did in 1990, they incurred increased costs of $3.1 billion.

In total amount, corn and soybeans are the two crops with the greatest amount of pesticide applied (in 2004 corn crops were responsible for 174.6 million pounds of pesticide use; soybeans used 87.8 million pounds). However, these two also cover the greatest acreage of all crops grown. In 2004 there were 74 million acres of soybeans and 73.6 acres of corn planted in the United States. Cotton and potatoes are additional crops with high pesticide use, 56.7 and 62.1 million pounds respectively. While cotton and potato crops cover a relatively small area in comparison to soy and corn (cotton 13.7 million acres, potatoes 1.1 million acres) their yield is far greater; cotton yields 855 bushels per acre and potatoes yield 391 while corn and soy yield 160 and 42.2 respectively.

While agricultural pesticide use has decreased from its peak in the late 1990s, the number of certified organic farms in the United States has also increased. Organic farms use alternative pest control methods, such as crop rotation and biological pest management and are prohibited from using virtually all synthetic chemicals in crop production. In 1992, there were just 935,450 acres of certified organic farmland in the United States. That number more than doubled by 2002 to 1.9 million and then doubled again in just three more years to 4.1 million acres in 2005. The number of organic farms also doubled from 3,587 in 1992 to 7,323 in 2002 but only increased 16% between 2002 and 2005. While the adoption rate of organic farming is high, the overall level is low; only approximately 0.5% of farmland in the United States is certified organic.

Certified Organic Farmland Acreage and Livestock, 2000-2003

(In thousands, except as noted.)

Item	2000	2001	2002	2003	Crop	Certified organic acreage (1,000)	
						2000	2003
						0000	0000
Certified growers (number)	6,592	6,949	7,323	8,035	Corn	78	106
					Wheat	181	234
					Oats	30	46
Certified organic acreage, total	1,776	2,094	1,926	2,197	Barley	42	30
Pastureland and rangeland	557	790	626	745	Rice	27	20
Cropland	1,219	1,305	1,300	1,452	Millet	15	27
					Buckwheat	11	8
					Rye	7	12
					Soybeans	136	122
Certified animals:							
Beef cows	13.8	15.2	23.4	27.3	Dry beans	14	10
Milk cows	38.2	48.7	67.2	74.4	Dry peas and lentils	10	16
Other cows	...	1.0	10.1	11.5			
Hogs and pigs	1.7	3.1	2.8	6.6	Hay and silage	231	328
					Flax	25	15
					Sunflowers	19	7
Sheep and lambs	2.3	4.2	4.9	4.6	Lettuce	11	12
Layer hens	1,114	1,612	1,052	1,591	Tree nuts	4	10
Broilers	1,925	3,286	3,032	6,301	Citrus	7	12
Turkeys	9	99	306	217	Apples	9	14
Unclassified/other poultry	111	17	1,880	671	Grapes	13	21
					Herbs, culinary and medicinal	4	25
					Cotton	15	10
					Trees for maple syrup	12	2

Source: U.S. Census Bureau. Statistical Abstract of the United States: 2007. U.S. Department of Agriculture, Economic Research Service.
... = Not available.

Sources:

U.S. Department of Agriculture, Economic Research Service. Organic Production Data Sets. http://www.ers.usda.gov/
data/organic/

U.S. Census Bureau. *Statistical Abstract of the United States: 2007.*

U.S. Census Bureau. *Statistical Abstract of the United States: 2003.*

U.S. Census Bureau. *Statistical Abstract of the United States: 2001.*

U.S. Census Bureau. *Statistical Abstract of the United States: 2000.*

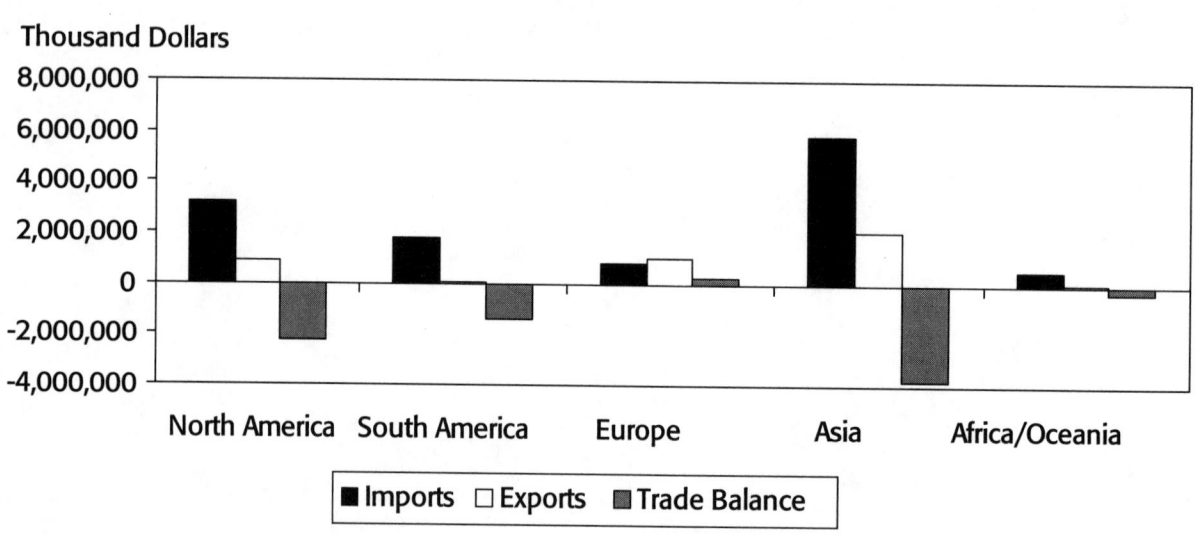

U.S. Trade in Edible Fishery Products, 2005

Source: U.S. National Oceanic and Atmospheric Administration, Office of Science and Technology. *Fisheries of the United States—2005.*

CHAPTER **7**

Forestry and Fisheries

HIGHLIGHTS

1 The National Forest Service is the largest land-owner in the United States and oversees the National Forest System, which covers more than 192 million acres. A forest is defined as land that is at least 10 percent stocked by forest trees of any size. The states with the largest National Forest System in 2004 are Arkansas (21.97 million acres), California (20.77 million acres), Idaho (20.72 million acres), Montana (16.92 million acres), and Oregon (15.67 million acres).

2 Data on lumber were first collected by the Census Office (later the Census Bureau) in 1810. Subsequent statistics were published by this agency for 1819, decennially for 1839 to 1899, and annually from 1904 to 1954, except in 1905, 1906, 1913, 1915 to 1918, 1920, and 1948. Current data are reported in *An Analysis of the Timber Situation in the United States, 1989–2040; Forest Statistics of the United States, U. S. Timber Production, Trade, Consumption and Price Statistics, 1960–1988;* and the annual *Land Areas of the National Forest System.*

3 The total forest area of the United States in 1992 was 754 million acres, of which 360 million acres were in private hands, 116 million acres were federally owned or managed, and 29 million acres were owned by states, counties, and municipalities. Of the total acreage, 168 million acres were in the Northeast, 212 million acres in the South, 142 million acres in the Rockies, and 217 million acres in the West. The net volume of growing stock was 786 billion cubic feet, of which softwood accounted for 450 billion cubic feet.

4 The GDP of timber-related industry was $106.2 billion in 2002, of which paper and allied products accounted for $73.0 billion and wood products for $33.1 billion. The wood manufacturing products industries employed 556,000 persons, and paper, paperboard, and other paper products industries employed 530,000 persons in 2001. In 2002, domestic production of industrial roundwood was 14.9 billion cubic feet; lumber, 7.1 billion cubic feet; plywood and veneer, 1.1 billion cubic feet; and pulp products, 5.7 billion cubic feet.

5 The first comprehensive statistical study of fisheries and fishery industries was produced for the year 1880 by the U.S. National Museum with the cooperation of the Commission of Fisheries and the Superintendent of the Tenth Census. The next general survey was conducted by the Bureau of the Census in 1908, followed by one in 1931 and another in 1950. Since then, annual data have been available for all coastal areas. Annual surveys are also made of the Mississippi River and its tributaries. Extended data are available for landing at the important fishing ports for certain species and for canned and industrial fishery products. Current fishery data are published in the *Current Fishery Statistics* and *Fisheries of the United States* by the National Marine Fisheries Service. Statistics on commercial landed catches of fish are shown as round, salable weight of recoverable meat. Data do not include catches made for personal use by hobby fishermen, or landings by foreign fishing vessels.

6 The fishing species most often caught are whiting, cod, flounder, haddock, herring, lobster, mackerel, and ocean perch in the New England states; menhaden, oysters, and crabs in the Middle Atlantic and Chesapeake Bay states; shrimp, menhaden, and mullet in the South Atlantic and Gulf states; lake trout and white fish in the Great Lakes states; tuna, salmon, sardine, halibut, and mackerel in the Pacific coast states; tuna in Hawaii; and salmon, halibut, and herring in Alaska.

7 The total domestic fish catch in 2004 was 9.6 billion pounds valued at $3.65 billion. Of these, fish for industrial use accounted for 1.875 billion pounds. Menhaden and Pollock account for more than half the fish catch, but salmon has the highest dollar value ($272.730 million). Among shellfish, crabs ($314.428 million) and shrimp ($308.275 million) have the highest dollar value. In 2004, 1.106 billion pounds of fish were canned. Tuna is the most abundant supply in 2004 with 434 million pounds followed by salmon (199 million pounds).

8 Aquaculture has become a major sector of the fishing industry, producing 638.4 million pounds of catfish and 59.7 million pounds foodsize trout in 2005 for a value of $449.9 million and $62.6 million respectively.

9 In 2004, 9.854 billion pounds of fish were imported for human consumption in contrast with just 876 million for industrial use.

10 In 2004, the United States imported 114 million cubic feet of logs and exported 345 million cubic feet.

Table 7-1. National Forest System Areas and Purchases, 1905–2004

(Acres, thousands of dollars, forest area and forest purchases data as of June 30.)

Year	Gross area of national forests and other lands[1]		Gross area approved for national forest purchase	
	Within unit boundaries[2] (thousands of acres)	Under Forest Service administration[3] (thousands of acres)	Total area (acres)	Total price (thousands of dollars)
2004	232 433	192 830	...	...
2003	232 277	192 483	...	...
2002	232 380	192 434	...	...
2001	...	...	...	...
2000	232 189	192 335	...	...
1999	232 730	191 910	...	...
1998	231 624	191 910	...	...
1997	231 808	191 785	...	...
1996	231 687	191 617	...	...
1995	...	...	...	...
1994	...	...	...	...
1993	...	...	...	...
1992	231 502	191 453	...	...
1991	231 502	191 453	...	...
1990	231 443	191 324	51 000	24 000
1989	231 000	191 000	99 000	34 000
1988	230 000	191 000	42 000	235 000
1987	230 000	191 000	87 000	38 000
1986	230 000	191 000	23 000	7 000
1985	230 000	191 000	16 000	6 900
1984	230 000	191 000	8 000	4 200
1983	230 000	191 000	7 000	2 400
1982	230 000	191 000	2 000	1 500
1981	230 000	191 000	111 000	50 400
1980	226 000	187 000	42 000	27 900
1979	226 000	187 000	58 000	30 200
1978	226 000	188 000	51 000	22 500
1977	226 000	188 000	45 000	16 600
1976	226 000	188 000	43 000	12 300
1975	226 000	188 000	12 000	3 300
1974	226 000	187 000	25 000	6 000
1973	226 000	187 000	117 000	17 500
1972	225 000	187 000	79 000	14 752
1971	225 000	187 000	32 000	4 467
1970	226 064	186 900	92 437	11 539
1969	226 045	186 632	126 341	12 353
1968	226 502	186 921	112 767	9 413
1967	227 721	186 799	104 507	7 037
1966	226 519	186 497	171 947	13 307
1965	226 434	186 577	28 507	1 364
1964	225 743	186 476	40 873	1 600
1963	225 584	186 316	24 698	1 795
1962	225 613	186 324	22 556	964
1961	226 110	186 385	10 355	236
1960	226 623	185 772	7 845	114
1959	227 359	185 805	8 716	224
1958	231 080	188 042	10 463	722
1957	231 293	188 013	17 519	416
1956	232 118	188 117	21 376	372
1955	235 728	188 120	18 665	192
1954	235 694	188 138	17 761	109
1953	229 112	181 568	7 969	99
1952	229 165	181 293	10 181	106
1951	229 258	181 255	25 317	265
1950	229 341	181 205	61 078	532
1949	229 175	180 895	60 719	464
1948	228 936	180 528	103 490	739
1947	228 810	180 264	380 471	2 190
1946	228 760	179 726	...	...
1945	228 703	179 381	5	1
1944	228 643	179 101	9	1
1943	228 633	178 508	8 759	38
1942	228 725	178 340	243 522	1 103
1941	228 309	177 653	195 818	805

[1]On January 2, 1954, some 6,910,000 acres of land utilization project lands were transferred to the Forest Service for administration.
[2]Comprises all publicly and privately owned land within authorized boundaries of national forests, purchase units, national grasslands, land utilization projects, research and experimental areas, and other areas.
[3]Federally owned land within the "gross area within unit boundaries."
... = Not available.

Table 7-1. National Forest System Areas and Purchases, 1905–2004—*Continued*

(Acres, thousands of dollars, forest area and forest purchases data as of June 30.)

Year	Gross area of national forests and other lands[1]		Gross area approved for national forest purchase	
	Within unit boundaries[2] (thousands of acres)	Under Forest Service administration[3] (thousands of acres)	Total area (acres)	Total price (thousands of dollars)
1940	228 174	176 779	553 077	2 203
1939	228 784	176 494	534 138	2 275
1938	227 280	175 238	800 113	2 713
1937	226 621	174 405	425 637	2 124
1936	197 435	165 979	289 104	11 535
1935	188 292	163 310	366 184	14 991
1934	188 037	162 591	420 681	10 018
1933	186 837	162 009	667 314	1 221
1932	186 215	161 361	83 086	206
1931	185 252	160 788	547 945	1 944
1930	183 976	160 091	538 048	1 468
1929	184 565	159 751	464 177	1 787
1928	184 404	159 481	261 107	1 996
1927	183 938	158 800	135 088	726
1926	184 124	158 759	191 725	737
1925	184 126	158 395	247 067	1 187
1924	182 817	157 503	130 290	425
1923	182 100	157 237	79 923	348
1922	181 800	156 837	242 169	826
1921	181 820	156 666	112 397	499
1920	180 300	156 032	101 428	451
1919	174 261	153 933	103 355	657
1918	175 951	155 375	185 199	848
1917	176 340	155 220	175 463	853
1916	176 089	155 400	54 898	316
1915	184 506	162 773	282 900	1 618
1914	185 321	163 849	391 114	1 940
1913	186 617	165 517	425 717	2 005
1912	187 406	165 027	287 698	1 627
1911	190 608	168 165	...	...
1910	192 931	168 029	...	...
1909	194 505	172 230	...	...
1908	167 977	147 820	...	...
1907	150 832	132 732	...	...
1906	106 994	94 159	...	...
1905	85 693	75 352	...	...

Source: U.S. Census Bureau. U.S. Forest Service.

[1]On January 2, 1954, some 6,910,000 acres of land utilization project lands were transferred to the Forest Service for administration.

[2]Comprises all publicly and privately owned land within authorized boundaries of national forests, purchase units, national grasslands, land utilization projects, research and experimental areas, and other areas.

[3]Federally owned land within the "gross area within unit boundaries."

... = Not available.

Table 7-2. Domestic Production, Net Imports, and Apparent Consumption of Industrial Products in Roundwood Equivalent, 1900–2005

(Millions of cubic feet, excludes fuelwood.)

Year	Total			Domestic production of lumber	Domestic production of plywood and veneer	Domestic production of pulp products	Logs	
	Domestic production	Net imports	Apparent consumption				Imports	Exports
2005	14 142	3 967	18 110	7 633	1 089	4 591	114	345
2004	15 139	4 201	19 339	7 510	1 086	5 692	73	366
2003	14 571	3 561	18 132	7 131	1 054	5 557	80	356
2002	14 902	2 736	17 637	7 060	1 074	5 708	81	309
2001	14 634	2 846	17 481	6 820	1 067	5 691	70	307
2000	15 436	2 533	17 969	7 199	1 187	5 881	68	331
1999	15 632	2 406	18 038	7 379	1 208	5 813	47	326
1998	15 620	2 206	17 827	7 093	1 201	6 114	30	316
1997	15 703	1 718	17 421	7 103	1 213	6 097	20	384
1996	15 413	1 621	17 034	6 886	1 281	5 908	18	422
1995	15 537	1 625	17 161	6 815	1 303	6 079	13	451
1994	15 306	1 493	16 800	7 052	1 320	5 576	18	429
1993	15 011	1 322	16 334	6 887	1 293	5 423	15	460
1992	14 994	. . .	15 628	6 864	1 265	5 463	7	351
1991	14 780	. . .	15 153	6 677	1 226	5 434	2	331
1990	15 557	784	16 361	7 317	1 423	5 313	4	674
1989	15 413	. . .	. . .	. . .	. . .	. . .	. . .	. . .
1988	14 985	1 245	16 230	6 920	1 630	4 885	15	825
1987	14 670	1 925	16 595	6 990	1 650	4 670	15	705
1986	13 845	2 075	15 920	6 545	1 505	4 545	15	620
1985	12 515	2 270	14 785	5 665	1 420	4 165	20	655
1984	12 725	2 105	14 830	5 770	1 400	4 355	30	600
1983	12 065	1 600	13 665	5 370	1 365	4 165	30	565
1982	10 910	1 020	11 930	4 635	1 135	3 980	20	550
1981	10 710	1 665	11 775	4 395	1 180	4 125	20	435
1980	12 120	900	13 020	5 300	1 175	4 390	25	560
1979	12 510	1 520	14 030	5 680	1 370	4 110	25	665
1978	12 235	1 910	14 145	5 825	1 460	3 745	20	585
1977	11 965	1 515	13 480	5 730	1 425	3 645	30	525
1976	11 815	970	12 785	5 475	1 355	3 805	15	555
1975	10 575	530	11 105	4 890	1 165	3 485	15	455
1974	11 540	950	12 490	5 095	1 150	4 220	15	455
1973	11 925	1 395	13 325	5 670	1 320	3 755	5	575
1972	11 440	1 515	12 960	5 535	1 300	3 520	10	535
1971	11 310	1 565	12 875	5 715	1 225	3 560	15	360
1970	11 115	1 065	12 180	5 355	1 065	3 835	25	430
1969	11 000	1 375	12 370	5 535	1 050	3 585	15	375
1968	11 025	1 275	12 305	5 630	1 120	3 385	15	405
1967	10 410	1 205	11 615	5 360	1 030	3 190	15	310
1966	10 645	1 430	12 075	5 645	1 030	3 190	15	220
1965	10 540	1 385	11 930	5 670	1 030	3 095	10	190
1964	10 170	1 315	11 485	5 635	960	2 865	10	170
1963	9 560	1 360	10 920	5 355	870	2 670	15	150
1962	9 035	1 415	10 450	5 120	800	2 565	20	85
1961	8 745	1 250	9 995	4 945	765	2 475	20	75
1960	8 920	1 220	10 145	5 080	705	2 575	20	45
1959	9 390	1 345	10 735	5 745	720	2 355	20	35
1958	8 530	1 185	9 715	5 160	615	2 165	15	30
1957	8 615	1 155	9 770	5 100	560	2 350	25	25
1956	9 620	1 330	10 950	5 920	590	2 475	30	30
1955	9 225	1 270	10 495	5 785	575	2 200	35	25
1954	8 755	1 190	9 945	5 635	480	1 960	35	25
1953	8 790	1 230	10 020	5 710	475	1 910	40	20
1952	8 775	1 160	9 935	5 820	435	1 810	30	10
1951	8 740	1 205	9 950	5 780	390	1 825	35	15
1950	8 525	1 380	9 910	5 905	345	1 500	45	10
1949	7 355	935	8 290	5 000	320	1 275	30	10
1948	8 375	1 090	9 465	5 750	290	1 470	45	10
1947	8 090	815	8 905	5 500	275	1 370	30	10
1946	7 705	810	8 515	5 295	255	1 260	25	(Z)
1945	6 605	685	7 290	4 365	250	1 140	25	5
1944	7 455	555	8 010	5 115	270	1 160	25	5
1943	7 560	565	8 125	5 325	280	1 030	20	5
1942	8 085	705	8 790	5 645	305	1 130	30	5
1941	8 055	650	8 705	5 680	265	1 075	55	5

Z = Less than 2.5 million cubic feet.
. . . = Not available.

Table 7-2. Domestic Production, Net Imports, and Apparent Consumption of Industrial Products in Roundwood Equivalent, 1900–2005—*Continued*

(Millions of cubic feet, excludes fuelwood.)

Year	Total			Domestic production of lumber	Domestic production of plywood and veneer	Domestic production of pulp products	Logs	
	Domestic production	Net imports	Apparent consumption				Imports	Exports
1940	6 990	420	7 410	4 845	235	930	35	10
1939	6 370	535	6 905	4 470	210	725	...	...
1938	5 570	470	6 040	3 860	195	595	...	...
1937	6 360	610	6 980	4 505	195	640	...	...
1936	5 990	560	6 540	4 295	165	555	...	...
1935	5 090	420	5 515	3 565	145	485	...	...
1934	4 340	355	4 695	2 925	130	430	...	...
1933	4 040	345	4 385	2 665	125	415	...	...
1932	3 400	305	3 705	2 100	120	350	...	...
1931	4 600	335	4 945	3 105	125	400	...	...
1930	6 305	400	6 705	4 560	155	395	...	...
1929	8 045	330	8 375	6 020	200	445	...	...
1928	7 670	290	7 960	5 710	175	400	...	...
1927	7 780	340	8 115	5 790	175	380	...	...
1926	8 215	375	8 595	6 180	145	400	...	...
1925	8 350	360	8 710	6 375	135	345	...	...
1924	8 250	285	8 530	6 140	115	340	...	...
1923	8 535	345	8 880	6 375	115	340	...	...
1922	7 605	290	7 895	5 480	90	340	...	...
1921	6 560	165	6 730	4 505	75	260	...	...
1920	7 770	205	7 975	5 440	80	360	...	...
1919	7 725	125	7 850	5 370	105	330	...	...
1918	7 310	180	7 490	4 955	95	335	...	...
1917	7 940	170	8 110	5 570	90	245	...	...
1916	8 530	165	8 695	6 185	90	325	...	...
1915	8 020	135	8 150	5 750	85	300	...	...
1914	8 565	15	8 550	6 290	85	265	...	...
1913	9 170	165	9 005	6 835	80	260	...	...
1912	9 330	145	9 185	6 990	80	250	...	...
1911	9 020	150	8 870	6 680	80	240	...	...
1910	9 295	80	9 215	6 910	90	220	...	...
1909	9 275	50	9 225	6 910	80	230	...	...
1908	8 725	80	8 645	6 520	70	205	...	...
1907	9 555	115	9 440	7 145	65	235	...	...
1906	9 225	95	9 130	7 145	60	225	...	...
1905	8 625	90	8 535	6 755	35	195	...	...
1904	8 490	150	8 340	6 675	20	190	...	...
1903	8 215	140	8 075	6 445	15	175	...	...
1902	7 880	60	7 820	6 180	10	160	...	...
1901	7 580	110	7 470	5 930	5	150	...	...
1900	7 285	140	7 140	5 680	5	135	...	...

Source: U.S. Census Bureau. U.S. Forest Service.
. . . = Not available.

Table 7-3. Per Capita Consumption of Timber Products, by Major Product, 1900–2005

Year	All products	Industrial roundwood					Fuelwood
		Total	Lumber	Plywood and veneer	Pulp products	Miscellaneous products	
2005	...	48.0	26.0	4.0	16.0	1.0	8.8
2004	...	52.0	26.0	4.0	19.0	1.0	5.2
2003	...	50.0	25.0	4.0	19.0	1.0	5.2
2002	...	61.0	34.0	4.0	21.0	2.0	9.0
2001	...	61.0	33.0	4.0	22.0	2.0	9.0
2000	...	63.0	34.0	5.0	23.0	2.0	9.1
1999	...	65.0	35.0	5.0	23.0	2.0	9.1
1998	...	65.0	34.0	5.0	24.0	2.0	9.1
1997	...	64.0	34.0	5.0	24.0	2.0	9.3
1996	73.8	63.5	34.1	4.9	22.6	1.9	10.3
1995	75.9	64.7	33.8	5.0	24.0	2.0	11.2
1994	76.3	64.3	34.3	5.1	22.7	2.2	12.0
1993	75.0	63.0	33.3	5.0	22.3	2.4	11.9
1992	74.5	62.6	32.8	5.0	22.3	2.4	11.9
1991	72.4	60.4	31.0	5.0	22.2	2.2	12.0
1990	77.4	65.3	34.6	5.6	22.8	2.2	12.1
1989	79.8	67.5	36.9	5.9	22.5	2.2	12.3
1988	81.0	68.5	36.8	7.1	22.6	2.1	12.5
1987	82.9	70.2	38.2	7.5	22.5	2.0	12.7
1986	81.0	68.1	36.7	7.3	22.2	2.0	12.9
1985	78.7	64.2	34.7	6.9	20.7	1.9	14.5
1984	78.9	63.6	34.3	6.9	20.5	1.9	15.3
1983	74.5	60.7	32.2	7.0	19.6	1.9	13.8
1982	67.2	52.8	26.8	5.7	18.5	1.9	14.4
1981	68.1	54.3	27.2	5.8	19.5	1.8	13.8
1980	70.7	57.0	29.6	5.8	19.8	1.8	13.6
1979	74.6	64.8	35.4	7.3	20.3	1.8	9.8
1978	72.4	65.5	36.9	7.8	19.1	1.8	6.9
1977	67.8	63.2	35.8	7.6	18.1	1.7	4.5
1976	62.5	59.8	32.3	7.2	18.6	1.7	2.8
1975	55.8	53.2	28.5	6.2	16.7	1.8	2.6
1974	63.0	60.5	31.2	6.3	21.2	1.8	2.5
1973	68.0	65.6	36.2	7.7	19.8	1.9	2.4
1972	67.9	65.6	36.2	8.1	19.4	1.9	2.3
1971	66.5	64.1	34.7	7.4	20.0	2.0	2.4
1970	64.4	61.7	31.9	6.4	21.4	2.1	2.6
1969	66.4	63.4	33.5	6.3	21.4	2.2	3.1
1968	66.8	63.3	34.4	6.8	19.8	2.4	3.5
1967	65.1	61.2	33.5	5.9	19.2	2.6	3.9
1966	68.1	63.8	34.9	6.1	19.9	2.9	4.3
1965	67.9	63.1	35.6	5.8	18.9	2.9	4.7
1964	65.0	59.9	32.9	5.5	18.7	2.8	5.1
1963	63.3	57.7	32.0	5.0	17.9	2.7	5.6
1962	62.0	56.0	30.9	4.7	17.8	2.5	6.0
1961	61.0	54.4	29.9	4.5	17.3	2.7	6.6
1960	63.3	56.1	30.8	4.2	18.2	2.8	7.2
1959	68.2	60.4	35.2	4.4	17.6	3.0	7.8
1958	64.0	55.5	31.9	3.8	16.5	3.2	8.5
1957	65.9	56.8	31.6	3.5	18.2	3.4	9.1
1956	74.6	64.8	37.5	3.7	19.9	3.6	9.8
1955	73.8	63.3	37.5	3.7	18.1	3.8	10.5
1954	72.3	61.0	36.8	3.1	16.8	4.0	11.3
1953	74.5	62.6	37.7	3.1	17.3	4.2	12.0
1952	75.8	63.0	38.7	2.8	16.9	4.4	12.7
1951	78.6	64.2	38.9	2.6	17.8	4.7	14.4
1950	80.0	65.1	41.8	2.3	15.6	5.1	14.9
1949	74.6	55.7	34.5	2.1	14.1	5.0	18.9
1948	81.9	63.7	40.5	2.0	15.3	5.8	18.2
1947	79.8	61.2	38.1	1.8	14.7	6.5	18.6
1946	78.4	59.4	38.1	1.8	13.3	6.3	18.9
1945	73.2	51.9	31.9	1.7	12.3	6.0	21.3
1944	78.6	57.6	37.7	1.9	11.5	6.5	21.1
1943	79.9	59.5	39.6	1.9	11.3	6.7	20.4
1942	86.3	65.1	43.1	2.2	12.3	7.4	21.2
1941	91.9	65.0	43.4	1.9	11.9	7.7	26.9

Table 7-3. Per Capita Consumption of Timber Products, by Major Product, 1900–2005—*Continued*

Year	All products	Industrial roundwood					Fuelwood
		Total	Lumber	Plywood and veneer	Pulp products	Miscellaneous products	
1940	85.3	55.8	36.4	1.7	10.4	7.3	29.4
1939	84.8	52.8	33.7	1.6	10.1	7.4	32.0
1938	79.8	46.5	29.2	1.5	8.7	7.1	33.3
1937	85.8	54.2	34.1	1.5	10.7	7.9	31.6
1936	84.3	51.1	32.7	1.2	9.4	7.6	33.3
1935	78.8	43.4	27.0	1.1	8.3	7.0	35.5
1934	75.3	37.1	21.8	1.0	7.6	6.8	38.2
1933	74.8	34.9	20.1	1.0	7.2	6.6	39.8
1932	69.6	29.7	15.9	0.9	6.3	6.7	39.9
1931	75.3	39.9	23.9	1.0	7.2	7.8	35.4
1930	85.3	54.5	35.6	1.2	7.9	9.7	30.8
1929	94.8	68.8	47.3	1.6	8.5	11.3	26.0
1928	92.8	66.1	45.1	1.5	8.0	11.5	26.8
1927	95.1	68.2	46.9	1.4	7.8	12.1	26.9
1926	99.3	73.2	51.4	1.2	7.9	12.7	26.1
1925	103.1	75.2	54.0	1.2	7.1	12.9	27.8
1924	104.4	74.7	52.4	1.0	6.8	14.5	29.6
1923	109.5	79.4	56.3	1.0	6.8	15.2	30.2
1922	105.9	71.7	49.2	0.8	6.3	15.4	34.2
1921	101.4	62.0	40.8	0.7	4.7	15.9	39.4
1920	113.1	74.9	50.5	0.8	5.9	17.7	38.2
1919	113.5	74.7	50.6	1.0	4.9	18.2	38.8
1918	112.7	71.7	47.6	0.9	4.8	18.4	41.1
1917	117.5	78.4	53.9	0.9	5.0	18.7	39.1
1916	124.1	85.3	60.6	0.9	4.9	18.9	38.8
1915	120.6	81.1	56.9	0.8	4.6	18.8	39.6
1914	126.4	86.3	61.7	0.9	4.4	19.4	40.1
1913	131.5	92.6	67.0	0.8	4.3	20.5	38.9
1912	135.8	96.4	70.3	0.8	4.1	21.1	39.5
1911	137.4	94.5	68.0	0.9	4.0	22.5	43.0
1910	142.0	99.7	72.5	1.0	3.8	22.5	42.3
1909	144.2	101.9	74.7	0.9	3.7	22.7	42.3
1908	142.3	97.5	71.7	0.8	3.2	21.8	44.8
1907	152.5	108.5	79.7	0.7	3.9	24.3	44.0
1906	152.6	106.9	81.7	0.7	3.5	21.1	45.7
1905	150.2	101.8	78.8	0.4	3.1	19.6	48.3
1904	152.6	101.5	78.7	0.2	3.0	19.5	51.1
1903	154.2	100.2	77.6	0.2	2.9	19.5	54.0
1902	155.6	98.7	76.6	0.1	2.7	19.3	56.8
1901	156.2	96.3	74.5	0.1	2.4	19.2	59.9
1900	156.9	93.8	72.3	0.1	2.2	19.2	63.1

Source: U.S. Census Bureau. U.S. Forest Service.

Table 7-4. Paper and Board Domestic Production, Apparent Consumption, and Waste Paper Consumption, 1809–2002

(Thousands of short tons.)

Year	Paper and board[1]		
	Domestic production	Apparent consumption[2]	Waste paper consumption
2002	89 636	97 227	...
2001	88 913	97 303	...
2000	94 491	103 147	...
1999	97 020	104 873	...
1998	94 510	100 978	...
1997	95 029	99 175	...
1996	90 381	94 287	...
1995	89 509	96 126	...
1994	89 080	95 195	...
1993	84 857	91 013	...
1992	82 868	87 577	...
1991	79 427	84 078	23 500
1990	78 679	85 711	21 700
1989	76 786	84 100	20 200
1988	76 587	84 532	19 700
1987	74 361	82 105	18 700
1986	70 905	77 855	17 900
1985	66 983	74 137	16 400
1984	68 449	75 055	16 700
1983	64 947	69 519	15 600
1982	59 290	63 117	14 600
1981	62 109	66 258	15 000
1980	61 042	64 814	14 900
1979	67 000	72 700	15 400
1978	64 300	70 400	14 800
1977	62 100	66 500	14 100
1976	60 500	64 300	13 600
1975	52 800	56 000	11 700
1974	61 100	65 500	14 000
1973	61 800	67 400	14 100
1972	59 500	64 500	12 925
1971	55 100	59 700	12 100
1970	53 516	58 057	10 594
1969	54 187	59 003	10 939
1968	51 245	55 664	10 222
1967	46 926	51 945	9 888
1966	47 113	52 680	10 564
1965	44 080	49 102	10 231
1964	41 703	46 384	9 843
1963	39 230	43 715	9 613
1962	37 541	42 216	9 075
1961	35 749	40 312	9 018
1959	34 015	38 725	9 414
1958	30 823	35 119	8 671
1957	30 666	35 268	8 493
1956	31 441	36 496	8 836
1955	30 178	34 719	9 041
1954	26 876	31 379	7 857
1953	26 605	31 360	8 531
1952	24 418	29 017	7 881
1951	26 047	30 561	9 071
1950	24 375	29 011	7 956
1949	20 315	24 694	6 600
1948	21 897	26 082	7 585
1947	21 102	24 749	8 009
1946	19 278	22 510	7 278
1945	17 371	19 665	6 800
1944	17 183	19 445	6 859
1943	17 036	19 437	6 368
1942	17 084	19 780	5 495
1941	17 762	20 421	6 075

[1]Excludes defibrated and exploded woodpulp used for hard pressed board.
[2]Beginning 1929, includes changes in newsprint stocks.
. . . = Not available.

Table 7-4. Paper and Board Domestic Production, Apparent Consumption, and Waste Paper Consumption, 1809–2002—*Continued*

(Thousands of short tons.)

Year	Paper and board[1]		
	Domestic production	Apparent consumption[2]	Waste paper consumption
1940	14 484	16 757	4 668
1939	13 510	15 949	4 366
1938	11 381	13 542	. . .
1937	12 837	16 028	. . .
1936	11 976	14 651	. . .
1935	10 479	12 758	3 587
1934	9 187	11 289	. . .
1933	9 190	10 916	. . .
1932	7 998	9 727	. . .
1931	9 382	11 347	. . .
1930	10 169	12 319	. . .
1929	11 140	13 411	3 842
1928	10 403	12 451	. . .
1927	10 002	11 925	. . .
1926	9 794	11 584	. . .
1924	7 930	9 281	. . .
1923	7 871	9 194	. . .
1922	6 875	7 865	. . .
1921	5 333	6 027	. . .
1920	7 185	7 640	. . .
1919	5 966	6 253	1 854
1918	5 938	6 275	. . .
1917	5 804	6 054	. . .
1914	5 153	5 395	1 510
1909	4 121	4 103	984
1904	3 107	3 029	589
1899	2 168	2 168	. . .
1889	935	. . .	. . .
1879	452	. . .	. . .
1869	[3]386	. . .	. . .
1859	127	. . .	. . .
1849	[3]78	. . .	. . .
1839	[3]38	. . .	. . .
1819	[3]12	. . .	. . .
1809	[3]3	. . .	. . .

Source: U.S. Census Bureau. U.S. Department of Agriculture, National Agricultural Statistics Service.
[1]Excludes defibrated and exploded woodpulp used for hard pressed board.
[2]Beginning 1929, includes changes in newsprint stocks.
[3]Estimated from values reported by the Bureau of the Census.
. . . = Not available.

Table 7-5. Yield and Value of Domestic Fisheries, Imports and Exports, 1905–2004

Year	Yield (millions of lbs.)[1] domestic			Value (millions of dollars)		
	Total	For human food	For industrial use[2]	Domestic total	Total imports[3]	Total exports[3]
2004	9 643	7 768	1 875	3 652	...	...
2003	9 507	7 521	1 986	3 347	...	...
2002	9 397	7 205	2 192	3 092	...	...
2001	9 489	7 311	2 178	3 218	...	...
2000	9 069	6 912	2 157	3 549	...	...
1999	9 339	6 832	2 507	3 464	...	...
1998	9 194	7 174	2 020	3 128	...	...
1997	9 846	7 248	2 597	3 447	...	...
1996	9 565	7 474	2 091	3 487	...	...
1995	9 788	7 667	2 121	3 770	...	...
1994	10 461	7 936	2 525	3 807	...	...
1993[4]	10 467	8 214	2 253	3 471	...	...
1992	9 637	7 618	2 019	3 678	...	...
1991	9 484	7 031	2 453	3 308	...	...
1990	9 404	7 041	2 363	3 522	9 048	5 639
1989	8 463	6 204	2 259	3 238	9 604	4 707
1988	7 192	4 588	2 604	3 520	8 872	2 275
1987	6 896	3 946	2 950	3 115	8 818	1 660
1986	6 031	3 393	2 638	2 763	7 626	1 356
1985	6 258	3 294	2 964	2 326	6 679	1 084
1984	6 438	3 320	3 118	2 350	5 883	949
1983	6 439	3 238	3 201	2 355	5 129	1 021
1982	6 367	3 285	3 082	2 390	4 523	1 059
1981	5 977	3 547	2 430	2 388	4 206	1 157
1980	6 482	3 654	2 828	2 237	3 648	1 006
1979	6 267	3 318	2 949	2 234	3 809	1 084
1978	6 028	3 177	2 851	1 854	3 086	906
1977	5 271	2 592	2 319	1 554	2 634	520
1976	5 388	2 775	2 613	1 349	2 328	385
1975	4 877	2 465	2 412	977	1 637	305
1974	4 967	2 496	2 471	932	1 711	262
1973	4 858	2 398	2 460	937	1 583	299
1972	4 806	2 435	2 371	748	1 494	158
1971	5 018	2 441	2 577	651	1 074	139
1970	4 917	2 537	2 380	613	1 037	118
1969	4 337	2 321	2 016	526	844	104
1968	4 160	2 347	1 814	497	823	68
1967	4 055	2 368	1 687	440	708	82
1966	4 366	2 573	1 794	472	720	85
1965	4 777	2 587	2 190	446	601	70
1964	4 541	2 497	2 044	390	564	64
1963	4 847	2 556	2 291	377	501	57
1962	5 354	2 540	2 814	396	490	36
1961	5 187	2 490	2 697	362	401	35
1960	4 942	2 498	2 444	354	363	44
1959	5 122	2 369	2 753	346	370	44
1958	4 747	2 651	2 096	373	331	31
1957	4 789	2 475	2 314	354	299	36
1956	5 268	2 690	2 578	372	283	40
1955	4 809	2 579	2 230	339	259	40
1954	4 762	2 705	2 057	359	252	32
1953	4 487	2 519	1 968	356	246	28
1952	4 432	2 778	1 654	364	240	22
1951	4 433	3 048	1 385	365	212	36
1950	4 901	3 307	1 594	347	198	28
1949	4 804	3 305	1 499	343	152	35
1948	4 513	3 146	1 367	371	157	24
1947	4 349	3 020	1 329	312	110	53
1946	4 467	3 049	1 418	313	130	40
1945	4 598	3 167	1 431	270	101	38
1944	4 533	2 865	1 668	213	78	36
1943	4 162	2 737	1 425	204	67	48
1942	3 875	2 683	1 192	170	40	32
1941	4 900	3 062	1 838	129	41	22

[1]Live weight.
[2]Meal, oil, fish solubles, homogenized condensed fish, shell products, bait, and animal food.
[3]Fish as fish products. Includes Puerto Rico; beginning 1955, imports also include landings of tuna by foreign vessels in American Samoa and imports of tuna into U.S. outlying areas.
[4]Represents record year.
... = Not available.

Table 7-5. Yield and Value of Domestic Fisheries, Imports and Exports, 1905–2004—*Continued*

Year	Yield (millions of lbs.)[1] domestic			Value (millions of dollars)		
	Total	For human food	For industrial use[2]	Domestic total	Total imports[3]	Total exports[3]
1940	4 060	2 675	1 385	96	42	18
1939	4 445	2 713	1 732	98	46	14
1938	4 254	2 639	1 615	94	39	14
1937	4 353	2 703	1 650	101	51	15
1936	4 826	2 854	1 972	95	42	13
1935	4 135	2 583	1 552	83	36	14
1934	4 104	2 434	1 670	77	31	14
1933	2 997	2 087	911	61	305	8
1932	2 612	1 864	748	56	30	8
1931	2 630	2 129	501	77	43	12
1930	3 224	2 478	746	109	51	17
1929	3 491	2 601	890	126	67	24
1928	3 061	2 370	691	114	59	21
1927	2 806	2 172	634	112	56	19
1926	2 871	2 198	673	107	50	20
1925	2 891	2 029	862	105	49	21
1924	2 461	1 874	587	...	46	21
1923	2 726	1 807	919	...	...	...
1922	2 619	1 677	942	...	...	...
1921	2 255	1 451	804	...	...	...
1917	2 676	...	...	71	...	...
1908	2 053	...	...	63	...	...
1907	1 930	...	...	61	...	...
1906	2 046	...	...	59	...	...
1905	2 002	...	...	57	...	...

Source: U.S. Census Bureau. U.S. National Oceanic and Atmospheric Administration, National Marine Fisheries Service.
[1] Live weight.
[2] Meal, oil, fish solubles, homogenized condensed fish, shell products, bait, and animal food.
[3] Fish as fish products. Includes Puerto Rico; beginning 1955, imports also include landings of tuna by foreign vessels in American Samoa and imports of tuna into U.S. outlying areas.
... = Not available.

Table 7-6. Selected Extinct Species of the United States, 2007

Class & Specie	Former habitat	Delisted or declared extinct
Mammals		
Eastern elk (Cervus canadensis canadensis)	United States east of the Great Plains	1880
Birds		
Carolina parakeet (Conuropsis carolinensis carolinensis)	Southeastern United States	~1920
Guam broadbill (Myiagra freycineti)	Guam	2004
Heath hen (Tympanuchus cupido cupido)	Eastern United States	1932
Mariana mallard (Anas oustaleti)	Guam, Tinian, and Saipan of the Marianas Archipelago	2004
Passenger pigeon (Ectopistes migratorius)	Central and eastern North America	1914
Dusky seaside sparrow (Ammodramus maritimus nigrescens)	Florida	1990
Santa Barbara song sparrow (Melospiza melodia graminea)	California	1983
Fishes		
Blackfin cisco (Coregonus nigripinnis)	Lakes Huron, Michigan, Ontario, and Superior	1960s
Deepwater cisco (Coregonus johannae)	Lakes Huron and Michigan	1960s
Amistad Gambusia (Gambusia amistadensis)	Found only in Goodenough Spring, a tributary of the Rio Grande in Val Verde County, Texas	1987
Longjaw cisco (Coregonus alpenae)	Lakes Erie, Huron, and Michigan	1985
Shortnose cisco (Coregonus reighardi)	Lakes Huron, Michigan, and Ontario	1985
Blue pike (Stizostedion vitreum glacum)	Lakes Erie and Ontario	1983
Tecopa Pupfish (Cyprinodon nevadensis calidae)	California	1982
Harelip sucker (Lagochila lacera)	Found in a few clear streams of the upper Mississippi Valley; Scioto River in Ohio; Tennessee River in Georgia; White River in Arkansas; Lake Erie drainage; and Blanchard and Auglaize Rivers in northwestern Ohio	1900
Clams		
Leafshell (Epioblasma flexuosa)	Alabama, Illinois, Indiana, Kentucky, Ohio, and Tennessee	1988
Round combshell (Epioblasma personata)	Illinois, Indiana, Kentucky, and Ohio	1988
Sampson' speralymussel (Epioblasma sampsonii)	Illinois, Indiana, and Kentucky	1984
Scioto pigtoe (Pleurobema bournianum)	Ohio	...
Tennessee riffleshell (Epioblasma propinqua)	Alabama, Illinois, Indiana, Kentucky, Ohio, and Tennessee	1988
Plants		
Bigleaf scurfpea (Orbexilum macrophyllum)	Indiana and Kentucky	...
Thismia americana (Thismia americana)	Illinois	1995

Source: U.S. Fish and Wildlife Service, Division of Endangered Species and the Threatened and Endangered Species System (TESS).
Note: This is a selected list of those species that have been declared extinct in the U.S. and its territories. The U.S. Fish and Wildlife Service has stated that since 1620 more than 500 species have become extinct in the U.S. alone.

Table 7-7. Threatened and Endangered Wildlife and Plant Species by Number, 2006

(As of April. Endangered species: One in danger of becoming extinct throughout all or a significant part of its natural range. Threatened species: One likely to become endangered in the foreseeable future.)

Item	Mammals	Birds	Reptiles	Amphibians	Fishes	Snails	Clams	Crustaceans	Insects	Arachnids	Plants
Total listings	**357**	**273**	**118**	**32**	**149**	**37**	**72**	**22**	**49**	**12**	**748**
Endangered species, total ..	324	252	79	21	87	25	64	19	40	12	600
United States	68	77	14	13	76	24	62	19	36	12	599
Foreign	256	175	65	8	11	1	2	0	4	0	1
Threatened species, total	33	21	39	11	62	12	8	3	9	0	148
United States	13	15	23	10	61	12	8	3	9	0	146
Foreign	20	6	16	1	1	0	0	0	0	0	2

Source: U.S. Census Bureau. *Statistical Abstract of the United States: 2007. U.S. Fish and Wildlife Service.*

BOX 7 ■ Endangered Species

When the Endangered Species Act was passed in 1973, only 77 species were listed, but by March 2007, the list contained 1,009 plants and animals categorized as endangered and 301 listed as threatened. As of November 2006, ten species had recovered and had been removed from the endangered or threatened species list. Sixteen species increased their numbers enough to be reclassified as threatened, and 350 species were stabilized or improved. It is estimated that the Endangered Species Act has prevented 900 species from becoming extinct since 1973. However, in that same time period, seven species have become extinct with an additional 28 suspected to be extinct.

In 2007 the bald eagle had rebounded from a total population of only 417 breeding pairs in 1963 to 9,789 pairs, prompting its removal from the endangered and threatened species list. The grizzly bear in Yellowstone and the gray wolf in Minnesota and the northern Great Lakes region were also removed from the list in 2007.

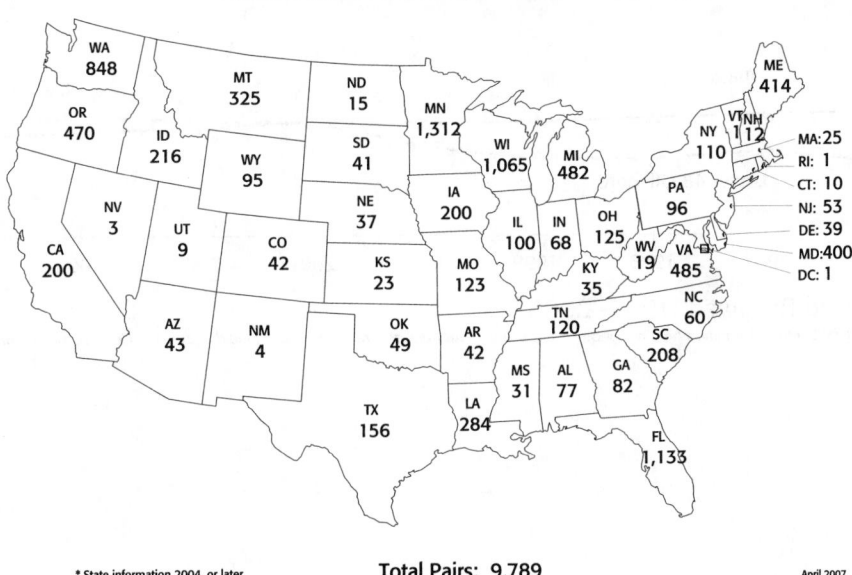

U.S. Fish & Wildlife Service
Estimated Number of Bald Eagle Breeding Pairs (by State)*

* State information 2004, or later   **Total Pairs: 9,789**   April 2007

Sources:
U.S. Interior Department, U.S. Fish and Wildlife Service. *Endangered Species Bulletin,* November 2006.
U.S. Interior Department, U.S. Fish and Wildlife Service. *Endangered Species Bulletin,* July/December 2003.
U.S. Interior Department, U.S. Fish and Wildlife Service. News Releases.
U.S. Interior Department, U.S. Fish and Wildlife Service, Ecological Services. Bald Eagle Population Size. http://www.fws.gov/midwest/eagle/population/index.html

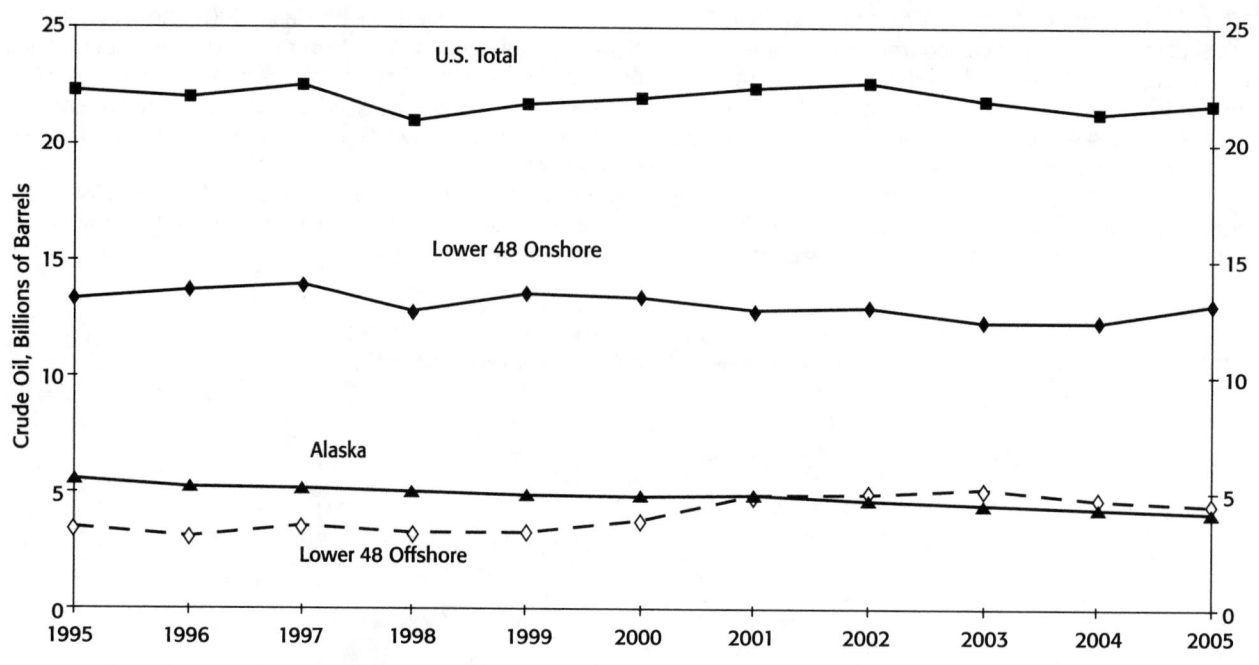

U.S. Crude Oil Proved Reserved, 1995–2005

Source: U.S. Department of Energy, Energy Information Administration. *U.S. Crude Oil, Natural Gas, and Natural Gas Liquids Reserves, 1995–2004 annual reports,* DOE/EIA-0216.

CHAPTER **8**

Minerals and Natural Resources

HIGHLIGHTS

1 The principal source for minerals data is the *Minerals Yearbook* published annually since 1932–1933 by the U.S. Bureau of Mines. For earlier years, the same data are provided by the *Minerals Resources of the United States,* which was published from 1882 until 1932 by the U.S. Geological Survey. Since 1977, mineral fuel data have been collected and published by the Energy Information Administration.

2 Censuses of mineral industries have been conducted by the Bureau of the Census at various intervals since 1840. Since 1967, the census has been conducted every fifth year for years ending in two and seven.

3 Because of poor husbandry of natural resources and unbridled consumption habits, the United States is losing its commanding position in the production of major minerals. In 2005, the United States was 100 percent dependant on foreign supplies for columbium, strontium, manganese, vanadium, and bauxite, 93 percent for tin, 91 percent for the platinum group and tantalum, 82 percent for barite, 78 percent for cobalt, 70 percent for tungsten, 69 percent for chromium, 64 percent for zinc, 57 for silver, 52 percent for nickel, 47 percent for aluminum, 40 percent for copper, and 29 percent for gypsum.

4 In 2002, there were 24,000 mining establishments employing 488,000 workers. Arizona leads all states in non-fuel mineral production with $4.73 billion, followed by California ($3.53 billion), Nevada ($3.64 billion), and Utah ($2.87 billion).

5 The federal government maintains the world's largest stockpile of strategic minerals. In 2001, they included 54,000 tons of tin, 6.8 million troy oz. of silver, 16 million pounds of cobalt, 2.1 million tons of manganese, 69 million pounds of tungsten, 125 million tons of zinc, 21,000 tons of titanium, 108,000 troy oz of platinum, 902,000 short tons of chromium, and 1.0 million carats of diamonds.

6 The United States is the world's largest exporter of coal, producing 1.1 billion tons of coal, or 21.2 percent of world production. The United States is the second largest producer of coal; the first is China. The most significant coal mining states are Wyoming, Kentucky, and West Virginia. The number of mines has declined to 707 in 2000 from 5,598 in 1980, and the number of miners from 225,000 to 72,000 during the same period.

7 Proved U.S. reserves of oil may last for 10 years at current rates of production. The United States fares better in natural gas with reserves of 193 trillion cubic feet in 2004. U.S. production of natural gas accounts for 20 percent in 2003 of the world total, making it the world's second largest gas producer, after Russia. U.S. production of crude oil in 2004 was 1.98 billion barrels, of which Alaska alone accounted for 332 million barrels. U.S. dependence on foreign oil, which was significantly reduced in the 1970s, is once again rising. Imports of foreign oil increased to 3.7 billion barrels compared with 1.9 billion barrels in 1980. The number of oil wells drilled, which peaked in 1990 at close to 602,000, dropped to fewer than 534,000 in 2000. There were 163 operating refineries in 1998, down from 319 in 1980. The refineries total output was 6.3 billion barrels, of which motor gasoline was a little less than half (2.9 billion). Natural gas production was 20.7 trillion cubic feet in 2001 of which Louisiana (5.2) and Texas (6.5) together accounted for 59 percent.

8 The 2005 prices of major minerals are far above those prevailing in 1990. Copper increased from $1.23 to $1.73; platinum from $467 per troy oz. to $900; gold from $385 per oz. to $446; silver from $4.82 per oz. to $7.34; and tin from $3.86 per pound to $5.34.

9 The average weekly wages for an employee in the mining sector in 2005 was $884. The highest average was for coal miners at $1,071, but they also worked the longest average week at 48.5 hours.

10 The United States imported the most gold in 1940 at 3760 tons and exported the most in 1965 at 1140 tons. Between 1992 and 2001, the primary gold production in the United States was more than 300 tons.

Table 8-1. Mineral Production by Type of Mineral, 1985–2004

(Production as measured by mine shipments, mine sales, or marketable production.)

Mineral	1985	1990	1995	2000	2001	2002	2003	2004
FUEL MINERALS								
Coal, total (millions of short tons)	883.6	1,029.1	1,033.0	1,073.6	1,127.7	1,094.3	1,071.8	1,111.5
Bituminous (millions of short tons)	613.9	693.2	613.8	574.3	611.3	572.1	541.5	546.6
Subbituminous (millions of short tons)	192.7	244.3	328.0	409.2	434.4	438.4	442.6	479.6
Lignite (millions of short tons)	72.4	88.1	86.5	85.6	80.0	82.5	86.4	83.5
Anthracite (millions of short tons)	4.7	3.5	4.7	4.6	1.9	1.4	1.3	1.7
Natural gas (marketed production) (trillions of cubic feet)	17.27	18.59	19.51	20.20	20.57	19.88	19.91	19.64
Petroleum (crude) (millions of barrels)[1]	3,275	2,685	2,394	2,131	2,118	2,097	2,073	1,988
Uranium (recoverable content) (millions of pounds)	4.6	8.9	6.0	4.0	2.6	2.3	2.0	2.3
NONFUEL MINERALS								
Asbestos (sales) (1,000 metric tons)	6	(D)	9	5	5	3	0	0
Barite, primary, sold/used by producers (1,000 metric tons)	375	430	543	392	400	420	468	532
Boron minerals, sold or used by producers (1,000 metric tons)	...	1,090	1,190	1,070	...	1,050.0	1,150	1,210
Bromine, sold or used by producers (1,000 metric tons)	231	177	218	228	212	222	216	222
Cement:								
Portland (millions of metric tons)	82	67	73	84	...	85	88	92
Masonry (millions of metric tons)	4	3	4	4	...	4	5	5
Clays (1,000 metric tons)	42,200	42,900	43,000	40,800	39,600	39,300	40,000	41,200
Diatomite (1,000 metric tons)	720	631	722	677	644	624	599	620
Feldspar[2] (1,000 metric tons)	900	630	880	790	800	790	800	770
Fluorspar, finished shipments (1,000 metric tons)	0	64	51	0	...	0	0	0
Garnet (industrial) (1,000 metric tons)		47	46	60	53	39	29	28
Gypsum, crude (millions of metric tons)	19	15	17	20	16	16	17	17
Helium[3] (millions of cubic meters)	118	85	101	98	87	87	87	86
Lime, sold or used by producers (millions of metric tons)	21	16	19	20	19	18	19	20
Mica, scrap/flake, sold/used by producers (1,000 metric tons)	94	109	108	101	98	81	79	99
Peat, sales by producers (1,000 metric tons)	775	721	660	847	870	728	632	741
Perlite, processed, sold or used (1,000 metric tons)	726	576	700	672	588	521	493	508
Phosphate rock (marketable) (millions of metric tons)	42	46	44	39	32	36	35	36
Potash (K_2O equivalent) sales (1,000 metric tons)	1,300	1,710	1,480	1,300	1,200	1,200	1,100	1,300
Pumice & pumicite, producer sales (1,000 metric tons)	617	443	529	1,050	920	956	870	1,490
Salt, common, sold/used by producers (millions of metric tons)	41	37	41	46	42	40	44	47
Sand & gravel, sold/used by producer (millions of metric tons)	1,108	855	935	1,148	1,158	1,157	1,188	1,270
Construction (millions of metric tons)	1,080	829	907	1,120	1,130	1,130	1,160	1,240
Industrial (millions of metric tons)	28	26	28	28	28	27	28	30
Sodium carbonate (natural) (soda ash) (1,000 metric tons)	10,100	9,100	10,100	10,200	10,300	10,500	10,600	11,000
Sodium sulfate (natural) (1,000 metric tons)	(D)	349	327	...	512	500	466	467
Stone[4] (millions of metric tons)	2,600	1,110	2,420	2,810	2,810	2,770	2,870	3,050
Crushed and broken (millions of metric tons)	1,560	1,110	1,260	1,560	1,590	1,510	1,530	1,590
Dimension[5] (1,000 metric tons)	1,040	1,120	1,160	1,250	1,220	1,260	1,340	1,460
Sulfur: Total shipments (1,000 metric tons)	11,500	12,100	10,700	9,450	9,260	9,600	10,100	
Sulfur: Frasch mines (shipments) (1,000 metric tons)	(D)	3,680	3,150	900	0	0	0	0
Talc, and pyrophyllite, crude (1,000 metric tons)	954	1,270	1,060	851	863	828	840	833
Vermiculite concentrate (1,000 metric tons)	(D)	209	171	150	...	...	...	...
METALS								
Antimony ore and concentrate (metric tons)	480	(D)	262	(D)	300	0	0	0
Aluminum (1,000 metric tons)	3,800	4,048	3,375	3,668	2,637	2,707	2,703	2,516
Bauxite (dried) (1,000 metric tons)	...	(D)	(D)	...	...	...	...	...
Beryllium (ore and concentrate) (metric tons)	...	182	202	180	...	80.0	85	90
Copper (recoverable content) (1,000 metric tons)	1,660	1,590	1,850	1,450	1,340	1,140	1,120	1,160
Gold (recoverable content) (metric tons)	340	294	317	353	335	298	277	258
Iron ore (gross weight)[6] (millions of metric tons)	56	57	61	61	46	52	46	56
Lead (recoverable content) (1,000 metric tons)	520	484	386	449	466	440	449	430
Magnesium metal (1,000 metric tons)	(D)	139	142	(D)	66	(D)	(D)	(D)
Manganiferous ore (gross weight)[7] (1,000 metric tons)	(D)	(D)	(D)	0	...	...	...	...
Mercury[8] (metric tons)	(D)	...	(D)	...	...	...	...	...
Molybdenum (concentrate) (1,000 metric tons)	44	62	61	41	38	32	34	42
Nickel (1,000 metric tons)	0	0	2	0	0	0	0	0
Palladium metal (kilograms)	10,200	5,930	5,260	10,300	12,100	14,800	14,000	13,700
Platinum metal (kilograms)	3,200	1,810	1,590	4,390	3,610	4,390	4,170	4,040
Silicon (silicon content) (1,000 metric tons)	425	418	396	367	282	261	253	275
Silver (recoverable content) metric tons	1,860	2,120	1,560	1,860	1,740	1,350	1,240	1,250
Titanium concentrate: Ilmenite (gross weight) (1,000 metric tons)	(D)	(D)	(D)	300	...	300	300	300
Tungsten ore and concentrate[9] (metric tons)	(D)	(D)	0	0	...	0	0	0
Zinc (recoverable content) (1,000 metric tons)	775	515	603	805	842	701	738	715

Source: U.S. Census Bureau. Statistical Abstract of the United States: 2007.
Note: Nonfuels through 1994 from U.S. Bureau of Mines, thereafter U.S. Geological Survey; fuels from U.S. Department of Energy, U.S. Energy Information Administration.
[1]42 gallons per barrel.
[2]Beginning 1992, includes aplite.
[3]Refined.
[4]Excludes abrasive stone, bituminous limestone and sandstone, and ground soapstone, all included elsewhere in table; 1993 excludes dimension stone. Includes calcareous marl and slate.
[5]Includes Puerto Rico, 1990–1996.
[6]Represents shipments; includes byproduct ores.
[7]5 to 35 percent manganiferous ore.
[8]Production from mercury ore only. 1986–1989; mercury recovered as a by products of gold ores only, 1990–1997.
[9]Content of ore and concentrate.
D = Withheld to avoid disclosing individual company data.
... = Not available.

Table 8-2. Net U.S. Imports of Selected Minerals and Metals as Percent of Apparent Consumption, 1985–2005

(Percent. Based on net imports, which equal the difference between imports and exports plus or minus government stockpile and industry stock changes.)

Minerals in rank order of net imports	1985	1990	1995	2000	2001	2002	2003	2004	2005P
Selenium	(D)	33	10	(D)	(D)	(D)	(D)	(D)	(D)
Cadmium	57	46	(²)	6	5	(²)	(²)	21	(²)
Mercury	...	(D)	...	(²)	(²)	...	(²)	(²)	(²)
Bauxite[1]	96	98	99	100	100	100	100	100	100
Columbium	100	100	100	100	100	100	100	100	100
Fluorspar	...	91	92	100	100	100	100	100	100
Manganese	100	100	100	100	100	100	100	100	100
Mica (sheet)	100	100	100	100	100	100	100	100	100
Strontium	100	100	100	100	100	100	100	100	100
Vanadium	(D)	(D)	84	100	100	100	100	100	100
Tin	72	71	84	88	86	88	89	88	93
Platinum	92	78	...	78	92	91	91	92	91
Tantalum	89	86	80	80	81	82	79	88	91
Barite	74	71	65	84	86	78	77	79	82
Potash	76	68	75	80	80	80	80	70	80
Cobalt	94	84	79	78	76	72	79	77	78
Palladium	...	84	...	84	88	82	82	83	78
Tungsten	68	81	90	66	64	69	63	73	70
Chromium	75	80	75	77	60	61	67	70	69
Zinc	70	64	71	72	73	75	72	73	64
Titanium	...	...	70	79	78	74	68	58	63
Silver	...	...	...	43	49	60	65	53	57
Nickel	71	64	60	55	52	52	50	55	52
Aluminum	16	(²)	23	33	38	39	38	44	47
Copper	28	15	27	37	22	37	40	43	40
Gypsum	38	46	29	27	26	23	23	27	29
Sulfur	3	15	21	18	13	19	20	20	23
Iron and steel	22	13	21	18	16	15	10	14	15
Iron ore	21	21	14	10	26	10	12	6	2

Source: U.S. Census Bureau. Statistical Abstract of the United States: 2007.
Note: Through 1994, figures from U.S. Bureau of Mines; thereafter the U.S. Geological Survey, Mineral Commodity Summaries and Minerals Yearbook, and Historical Statistics for Mineral and Material Commodities in the United States. Import and export data from the U.S. Census Bureau.
[1]Includes alumina.
[2]Net exports.
P = Preliminary
D = Withheld to avoid disclosure.
. . . = Not available.

Table 8-3. Selected Mineral Products—Average Prices, 1970–2005

Year	Nonfuels								Fuels		
	Copper,[1] electrolytic (cents per lb.)	Platinum[2] (dol./troy oz.)	Gold (dol.fine oz.)	Silver (dol./fine oz.)	Lead[3] (cents per lb.)	Tin[4] (cents per lb.)	Zinc[5] (cents per lb.)	Sulfur, crude[6] (dol./ metric ton)	Bituminous coal[7,8] (dol. short ton)	Crude petroleum[7] (col. bbl.)	Natural gas[7] (dol./ 1,000 cu. ft.)
2005	173	900	446	7.34	61	534	67	35.00	...	50.26	7.51
2004	134	849	411	6.69	55	555	52	32.50	30.47	36.77	5.49
2003	84	694	365	4.91	44	340	41	28.71	26.73	27.56	4.88
2002	76	543	311	4.62	44	292	39	11.84	26.57	22.51	2.95
2001	77	533	272	4.39	44	315	44	10.01	25.36	21.84	4.00
2000	88	549	280	5.00	44	370	56	24.73	24.15	26.72	3.68
1999	76	379	280	5.25	44	366	53	37.81	23.92	15.56	2.19
1998	79	375	295	5.54	45	373	51	29.14	24.87	10.87	1.96
1997	107	397	332	4.89	47	381	65	36.06	24.64	17.23	2.32
1996	109	398	389	5.19	49	412	51	34.11	25.17	18.46	2.17
1995	138	425	386	5.15	42	416	56	44.46	25.56	14.62	1.55
1994	111	411	385	5.29	37	369	49	30.08	25.68	13.19	1.85
1993	92	370	361	4.30	32	350	46	31.86	26.15	14.25	2.04
1992	107	356	345	3.94	35	402	58	48.14	26.78	15.99	1.74
1991	109	371	363	4.04	34	363	53	71.45	27.49	16.54	1.64
1990	123	467	385	4.82	46	386	75	80.14	27.43	20.03	1.71
1989	131	507	383	5.50	39	520	82	86.62	27.40	15.86	1.69
1988	121	523	438	6.54	37	441	60	85.95	27.66	12.58	1.69
1987	83	553	448	7.01	36	419	42	89.78	28.19	15.40	1.67
1986	66	461	368	5.47	22	383	38	105.22	28.84	12.51	1.94
1985	67	291	318	6.14	19	596	40	106.46	30.78	24.09	2.51
1984	67	357	361	8.14	26	624	49	94.31	30.63	25.88	2.66
1983	77	424	424	11.44	22	655	41	87.24	31.11	26.19	2.59
1982	73	327	376	7.95	26	654	39	108.27	32.15	28.52	2.46
1981	84	446	460	10.52	37	733	45	111.48	31.51	31.77	1.98
1980	101	677	613	20.63	43	846	37	89.06	29.17	21.59	1.59
1979	92	445	308	11.09	53	754	37	55.75	27.31	12.64	1.18
1978	66	261	194	5.40	34	630	31	45.17	22.64	9.00	0.91
1977	67	157	148	4.62	31	535	34	43.68	20.59	8.57	0.79
1976	70	162	125	4.35	23	380	37	45.00	20.11	8.19	0.58
1975	64	164	161	4.42	22	340	39	44.20	19.79	7.67	0.44
1974	77	181	160	4.71	23	396	36	...	16.01	6.87	0.30
1973	59	150	98	2.56	16	228	21	...	8.71	3.89	0.22
1972	51	121	59	1.68	15	178	18	...	7.78	3.39	0.19
1971	52	121	41	1.55	14	167	16	...	7.13	3.39	0.18
1970	58	133	36	1.77	16	174	15	22.41	6.30	3.18	0.17

Source: U.S. Census Bureau. Statistical Abstract of the United States: 2007.
Note: Nonfuels figures, through 1994, from U.S. Bureau of Mines, thereafter, U.S. Geological Survey; fuels figures from U.S. Department of Energy, Energy Information Administration.
[1]Domestic market prices for wirebar, 1970, 1975–77; U.S. producer prices for cathode thereafter.
[2]Average annual dealer prices.
[3]1970, New York prices; beginning 1975, nationwide delivered basis.
[4]Straits tin through 1975; thereafter, composite price.
[5]Prime western. Beginning 1975, delivered price.
[6]F.o.b. (Free on Board) works.
[7]Average value at the point of production or domestic first purchase price.
[8]Through 1978, includes subbituminous coal.

Table 8-4. Crude Petroleum—Production, Value, and Proved Reserves, 1859–2006

(Thousands of 42-gallon barrels, except as indicated.)

Year	Production	Average value at well per bbl. dollars	Estimated proved reserves, Dec. 31
2006	1 875 000	. . .	. . .
2005	1 890 000	. . .	. . .
2004	1 988 000	36.77	21 400 000
2003	2 073 000	27.56	21 900 000
2002	2 097 000	22.51	22 700 000
2001	2 118 000	21.84	22 400 000
2000	2 131 000	26.72	22 000 000
1999	2 147 000	15.56	21 800 000
1998	2 282 000	10.87	21 000 000
1997	2 355 000	17.23	22 500 000
1996	2 366 000	18.46	22 000 000
1995	2 394 000	14.62	22 400 000
1994	2 431 000	13.19	22 500 000
1993	2 499 000	14.25	23 000 000
1992	2 625 000	15.99	23 700 000
1991	2 707 000	16.54	24 700 000
1990	2 685 000	20.03	26 300 000
1989	2 779 000	15.86	26 500 000
1988	2 979 000	12.58	26 800 000
1987	3 047 000	15.40	27 300 000
1986	3 168 000	12.51	26 900 000
1985	3 275 000	24.09	28 400 000
1984	3 250 000	25.88	28 400 000
1983	3 171 000	26.19	27 700 000
1982	3 157 000	28.52	27 900 000
1981	3 129 000	31.77	29 400 000
1980	3 146 000	21.59	29 800 000
1979	3 121 000	12.64	29 800 000
1978	3 178 000	9.00	31 400 000
1977	3 009 000	8.57	31 800 000
1976	2 976 000	8.19	30 900 000
1975	3 057 000	7.67	32 700 000
1974	3 203 000	6.87	34 200 000
1973	3 361 000	3.89	35 300 000
1972	3 455 000	3.39	36 300 000
1971	3 454 000	3.39	38 100 000
1970	3 517 000	3.18	39 000 000
1969	3 371 751	3.09	29 632 000
1968	3 329 042	2.94	30 707 000
1967	3 216 715	2.92	31 377 000
1966	3 027 763	2.88	31 452 000
1965	2 848 514	2.86	31 352 000
1964	2 786 822	2.88	30 991 000
1963	2 752 723	2.89	30 970 000
1962	2 676 189	2.90	31 389 000
1961	2 621 758	2.89	31 759 000
1960	2 574 933	2.88	31 613 000
1959	2 574 590	2.90	31 719 000
1958	2 448 937	3.01	30 536 000
1957	2 616 901	3.09	30 300 000
1956	2 617 283	2.79	30 434 649
1955	2 484 428	2.77	30 012 170
1954	2 314 988	2.77	29 560 746
1953	2 357 082	2.68	28 944 828
1952	2 289 836	2.53	27 960 554
1951	2 247 711	2.53	27 468 031
1950	1 973 574	2.51	25 268 398
1949	1 841 940	2.54	24 649 489
1948	2 020 185	2.60	23 280 444
1947	1 856 987	1.93	21 487 685
1946	1 733 939	1.41	20 873 560
1945	1 713 655	1.22	20 826 813
1944	1 677 904	1.21	20 453 231
1943	1 505 613	1.20	20 064 152
1942	1 386 645	1.19	20 082 793
1941	1 402 228	1.14	19 559 296
1940	1 353 214	1.02	19 024 515
1939	1 264 962	1.02	18 483 012
1938	1 214 355	1.13	17 348 146
1937	1 279 160	1.18	15 507 268
1936	1 099 687	1.09	13 063 400
1935	996 596	0.97	12 400 000
1934	908 065	1.00	12 177 000
1933	905 656	0.67	12 000 000
1932	785 159	0.87	12 300 000
1931	851 081	0.65	13 000 000

Table 8-4. Crude Petroleum—Production, Value, and Proved Reserves, 1859–2006—*Continued*

(Thousands of 42-gallon barrels, except as indicated.)

Year	Production	Average value at well per bbl. dollars	Estimated proved reserves, Dec. 31
1930	898 011	1.19	13 600 000
1929	1 007 323	1.27	13 200 000
1928	901 474	1.17	11 000 000
1927	901 129	1.30	10 500 000
1926	770 874	1.88	8 800 000
1925	763 743	1.68	8 500 000
1924	713 940	1.43	7 500 000
1923	732 407	1.34	7 600 000
1922	557 531	1.61	7 600 000
1921	472 183	1.73	7 800 000
1920	442 929	3.07	7 200 000
1919	378 367	2.01	6 700 000
1918	355 928	1.98	6 200 000
1917	335 316	1.56	5 900 000
1916	300 767	1.10	5 900 000
1915	281 104	0.64	5 500 000
1914	265 763	0.81	5 400 000
1913	248 446	0.95	5 500 000
1912	222 935	0.74	5 400 000
1911	220 449	0.61	5 000 000
1910	209 557	0.61	4 500 000
1909	183 171	0.70	4 200 000
1908	178 527	0.72	4 000 000
1907	332 190	1.44	7 800 000
1906	252 988	1.46	7 600 000
1905	269 434	1.24	7 600 000
1904	234 162	1.72	7 200 000
1903	200 922	1.88	6 800 000
1902	177 534	1.60	6 400 000
1901	69 389	0.96	3 000 000
1900	63 621	1.19	2 900 000
1899	57 071	1.13	2 500 000
1898	55 364	0.80	...
1897	60 476	0.68	...
1896	60 960	0.96	...
1895	52 892	1.09	...
1894	49 344	0.72	...
1893	48 431	0.60	...
1892	50 515	0.51	...
1891	54 293	0.56	...
1890	45 824	0.77	...
1889	35 164	0.77	...
1888	27 612	0.65	...
1887	28 283	0.67	...
1886	28 065	0.71	...
1885	21 859	0.88	...
1884	24 218	0.85	...
1883	23 450	1.10	...
1882	30 350	0.78	...
1881	27 661	0.92	...
1880	26 286	0.94	...
1879	19 914	0.86	...
1878	15 397	1.17	...
1877	13 350	2.38	...
1876	9 133	2.52	...
1875	12 163	1.35	...
1874	10 927	1.17	...
1873	9 894	1.83	...
1872	6 293	3.64	...
1871	5 205	4.34	...
1870	5 261	3.86	...
1869	4 215	5.64	...
1868	3 646	3.62	...
1867	3 347	2.41	...
1866	3 598	3.74	...
1865	2 498	6.59	...
1864	2 116	8.06	...
1863	2 611	3.15	...
1862	3 057	1.05	...
1861	2 114	0.49	...
1860	500	9.59	...
1859	2	16.00	...

Source: U.S. Census Bureau. *Statistical Abstract of the United States: 2007.* U.S. Department of Energy, Energy Information Administration.
. . . = Not available.

Table 8-5. Uranium Reserves and Resources, 2003

(Million Pounds U3O8)

Resource Category and State	Forward-Cost Category (dollars per pound)[1]		
	$30 or Less	$50 or Less	$100 or Less
Reserves[2]	**265**	**890**	**1,414**
New Mexico	84	341	566
Wyoming	106	363	582
Texas	6	23	38
Arizona, Colorado, Utah	45	123	170
Others[3]	24	40	58
Potential Resources[4]			
Estimated Additional Resources	2,180	3,310	4,850
Speculative Resources	1,310	2,230	3,480

Source: U.S. Department of Energy, Energy Information Administration. Annual Energy Review 2005 Report No.DOE/EIA-0384 2005 Report No. DOE/EIA-0384 2005.
[1]Forward costs are all operating and capital costs (in current dollars) yet to be incurred in the production of uranium from estimated resources. Excluded are previous expenditures (such as exploration and land acquisitions), taxes, profit, and the cost of money. Generally, forward costs are lower than market prices. Resource values in forward cost categories are cumulative; that is, the quantity at each level of forward cost includes all reserves/resources at the lower cost in that category.
[2]The Energy Information Administration (EIA) category of uranium reserves is equivalent to the internationally reported category of "Reasonably Assured Resources" (RAR).
[3]California, Idaho, Nebraska, Nevada, North Dakota, Oregon, South Dakota, and Washington.
[4]Shown are the mean values for the distribution of estimates for each forward-cost category, rounded to the nearest million pounds U3O8.

Table 8-6. Technically Recoverable Crude Oil, Natural Gas, and Natural Gas Liquids Resource Estimates, 2004

Region	Crude Oil[1]			Natural Gas (Dry)			Natural Gas Liquids[1]		
	Federal Lands[2]	Non-Federal Lands	Total	Federal Lands[2]	Non-Federal Lands	Total	Federal Lands[2]	Non-Federal Lands	Total
	Billion Barrels			Trillion Cubic Feet			Billion Barrels		
Undiscovered Conventionally Reservoired Fields[3]	**82.54**	**22.51**	**105.05**	**420.14**	**261.78**	**681.92**	**1.8**	**6.25**	**8.05**
Alaska Onshore and State Offshore[4]	3.75	4.68	8.43	33.97	95.37	129.34	0.54	0.61	1.15
Alaska Federal Offshore[5]	24.9	X	24.9	122.6	X	122.6	0	X	0
48 States Onshore and State Offshore[4]	3.79	17.83	21.62	23.97	166.41	190.38	1.26	5.64	6.9
48 States Federal Offshore[5]	50.1	X	50.1	239.6	X	239.6	0	X	0
Discovered Conventionally Reservoired Fields[3] (Ultimate Recovery Appreciation)[6]	**22.03**	**45.67**	**67.7**	**186.7**	**203.3**	**390**	**4.94**	**8.46**	**13.4**
U.S. Onshore and State Offshore[4]	14.33	45.67	60	118.7	203.3	322	4.94	8.46	13.4
U.S. Federal Offshore[5]	7.7	X	7.7	68	X	68	0	X	0
Undiscovered Unconventionally Reservoired Fields[7] (Continuous-Type Deposits (all onshore)	**0.32**	**1.75**	**2.07**	**143.16**	**215.55**	**358.71**	**1.45**	**0.67**	**2.12**
U.S. Total	**104.89**	**69.93**	**174.82**	**750**	**68.63**	**1,430.63**	**8.19**	**15.38**	**23.57**
U.S. Onshore and State Offshore[4]	22.19	69.93	92.12	319.8	680.63	1,000.43	8.19	15.38	23.57
Federal Offshore[5]	82.7	X	82.7	430.2	X	430.2	0	X	0

Source: U.S. Department of Energy, Energy Information Administration. *Annual Energy Review 2005* Report No. DOE/EIA-0384 2005. U.S. Department of the Interior, U.S. Geological Survey, and the Minerals Management Service.
Note: "Technically recoverable" resources are those that are producible using current technology without reference to the economic viability thereof. A value of zero indicates either that none exists in this area or that no estimate of this resource has been made for this area. "48 States" is the United States excluding Alaska and Hawaii.
[1]To the extent that lease condensate is measured or estimated it is included in "Natural Gas Liquids"; otherwise, lease condensate is included in "Crude Oil".
[2]Lands owned or under the jurisdiction of the Federal government, excluding Indian and Native lands even when federally managed in trust.
[3]Conventionally reservoired deposits are discrete subsurface accumulations of crude oil or natural gas usually defined, controlled, or limited by hydrocarbon/water contacts.
[4]Onshore (Federal and State) plus State offshore waters (near-shore, shallow-water areas under State jurisdiction).
[5]Federal offshore jurisdictions (Outer Continental Shelf and deeper water areas seaward of State offshore).
[6]Proved reserves are not included in these estimates. Ultimate recovery appreciation (reserve growth) is the volume by which the estimate of total recovery from a known crude oil or natural gas reservoir or aggregation of such reservoirs is expected to increase during the time between discovery and permanent abandonment. The estimates of ultimate recovery appreciation for onshore and state offshore lands were imputed by assuming that the total estimates reported by the U.S. Geological Survey could be apportioned according to the ratio of 1996 production from onshore federal lands to total U.S. production.
[7]Unconventionally reservoired deposits (continuous-type accumulations) are geographically extensive subsurface accumulations of crude oil or natural gas that generally lack well-defined hydrocarbon/water contacts. Examples include coal bed methane, "tight gas," and auto-sourced oil and gas-shale reservoirs.
X = Not applicable.

Table 8-7. Coal Demonstrated Reserve Base, 2005

(Billion Short Tons.)

Region and State	Anthracite	Bituminous Coal		Subbituminous Coal		Lignite	Total		
		Underground	Surface	Underground	Surface	Surface[1]	Underground	Surface	Total
Appalachian	7.3	70.9	23	0	0	1.1	74.9	27.4	102.3
Alabama	0	1	2.1	0	0	1.1	1	3.2	4.2
Kentucky, Eastern	0	1.3	9.4	0	0	0	1.3	9.4	10.7
Ohio	0	17.6	5.8	0	0	0	17.6	5.8	23.3
Pennsylvania	7.2	19.5	0.9	0	0	0	23.3	4.3	27.6
Virginia	0.1	1	0.6	0	0	0	1.2	0.6	1.7
West Virginia	0	29.4	3.9	0	0	0	29.4	3.9	33.2
Other[2]	0	1.1	0.3	0	0	0	1.1	0.3	1.4
Interior	0.1	117.4	27.3	0	0	12.9	117.5	40.2	157.7
Illinois	0	88	16.6	0	0	0	88	16.6	104.5
Indiana	0	8.8	0.8	0	0	0	8.8	0.8	9.5
Iowa	0	1.7	0.5	0	0	0	1.7	0.5	2.2
Kentucky, Western	0	15.9	3.6	0	0	0	15.9	3.6	19.6
Missouri	0	1.5	4.5	0	0	0	1.5	4.5	6
Oklahoma	0	1.2	0.3	0	0	0	1.2	0.3	1.6
Texas	0	0	0	0	0	12.4	0	12.4	12.4
Other[3]	0.1	0.3	1.1	0	0	0.5	0.4	1.5	1.9
Western	Z	21.8	2.3	121.3	59.6	29.4	143.1	91.3	234.5
Alaska	0	0.6	0.1	4.8	0.6	Z	5.4	0.7	6.1
Colorado	Z	7.8	0.6	3.7	0	4.2	11.5	4.8	16.3
Montana	0	1.4	0	69.6	32.6	15.8	71	48.3	119.3
New Mexico	Z	2.7	0.9	3.5	5.1	0	6.2	6	12.2
North Dakota	0	0	0	0	0	9.1	0	9.1	9.1
Utah	0	5.2	0.3	Z	0	0	5.2	0.3	5.4
Washington	0	0.3	0	1	Z	Z	1.3	0	1.3
Wyoming	0	3.8	0.5	38.7	21.3	0	42.5	21.8	64.3
Other[4]	0	0	0	Z	Z	0.4	0	0.4	0.4
U.S. Total	7.5	210.1	52.6	121.3	59.6	43.4	335.5	159	494.4
States East of the Mississippi River	7.3	183.7	43.9	0	0	1.1	187.6	48.4	236
States West of the Mississippi River	0.1	26.4	8.7	121.3	59.6	42.3	147.8	110.6	258.4

Source: U.S. Department of Energy, Energy Information Administration. *Annual Energy Review 2005* Report No. DOE/EIA-0384 2005.
Note: Data represent remaining measured and indicated coal resources, analyzed and on file, meeting minimum seam and depth criteria, and in the ground as of January 1, 2005. These coal resources are not totally recoverable. Net recoverability with current mining technologies ranges from 0 percent (in far northern Alaska) to more than 90 percent. Fifty-four percent of the demonstrated reserve base of coal in the United States is estimated to be recoverable. Totals may not equal sum of the components due to independent rounding.
[1]Lignite resources are not mined underground in the United States.
[2]Georgia, Maryland, North Carolina, and Tennessee.
[3]Arkansas, Kansas, Louisiana, and Michigan.
[4]Arizona, Idaho, Oregon, and South Dakota.
Z = Less than 0.05 billion short tons.

BOX 8 ■ Arctic Exploration

The world's continued increasing consumption of petroleum and natural gas, coupled with rising oil prices, fuels the exploration for new and untapped energy reserves. At the same time, because the effects of global warming are more concentrated at the poles, scientists have recorded minimum sea ice coverage in the Arctic Ocean. The melting of the polar ice cap has opened new opportunities for the exploitation of what is believed to be 25% of the world's remaining oil and gas reserves, which were previously inaccessible.

Legislation to open up drilling in the Arctic Ocean, the Arctic National Wildlife Refuge, and the waters just outside it, have been repeatedly proposed in the U.S. Congress since the turn of the century. Some see the increased opportunity for extraction as a clear positive with increased access to resources, higher revenues, and jobs. Others, however, feel that the ecosystem of the Arctic zone is already too strained by the warming air and water temperatures, melting of the permafrost and reduction in area and thickness of the polar ice. They believe that the increased traffic, industry, pollution, and potential for oil spills would do irreversible damage.

Russia, Canada, and Norway have petitioned to increase their sovereign waters in the Arctic Ocean, thereby increasing the area in which they could explore and exploit potential reserves. The United States and Denmark, as well as the other nations with coastal land in the Arctic Ocean, may follow suit.

Sources:
U.S. Arctic Research Commission. Report on Goals and Objectives for Arctic Research 2007, for the U.S. Arctic Research Plan. http://www.arctic .gov/publications.htm
Smithsonian Institution. Media Library. http://forces.si.edu/arctic/index.html
U.S. Department of Commerce, National Oceanic and Atmospheric Administration. *State of the Arctic,* October 2006.
Borgerson, Scott. "Breaking the Ice Up North. (Editorial Desk)." *The New York Times* (October 19,2005): A21(L).
"As Polar Ice Turns to Water, Dreams of Treasure Abound. (Foreign Desk)." *The New York Times* (October 10, 2005): A1(L).

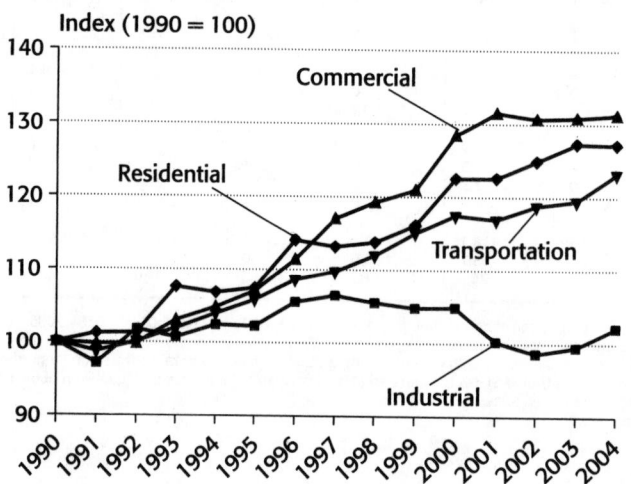

Index (1990 = 100)

U.S. Carbon Dioxide Emissions by Sector,
1990–2004

Note: Sectoral emissions include both direct emissions and emissions attributable to purchased electricity.
Source: U.S. Department of Energy, Energy Information Administraion. *Emissions of Greenhouse Gases in the United States 2004.*

CHAPTER 9

Energy

HIGHLIGHTS

1 Data on the production of electric energy have been available since the beginning of the first commercial production in 1882, but because of the changing bases of measurement and variations in coverage, the information is difficult to evaluate for the years before 1920. The Bureau of the Census conducted censuses of the light and power industries at five-year intervals from 1902 to 1937. The *Electrical World* (McGraw-Hill) and the National Electric Light Association also published considerable data on this early period. Early data on capacity have to be converted from horsepower (hp) to kilowatts (kW) to be comparable. Data on generation also were often reported without allowance for kWh used in generation, and end uses were reported by appliances (such as lamps) rather than as kWh. These variations in measurements, classification, and coverage often resulted in differences as high as 25 percent. Generators in mobile equipment, such as ships, railroads, and barges, are also unaccounted for in the totals.

2 The principal sources of data on energy are the Energy Information Administration, the Edison Electric Institute, and the American Gas Association. Among the EIA annuals are *Annual Energy Review, Electric Power Annual, Natural Gas Annual, Petroleum*

Supply Annual, State Energy Data Report, State Energy Price and Expenditure Report, Financial Statistics of Selected Electric Utilities, Performance Profiles of Major Energy Producers, Annual Energy Outlook, and *International Energy Annual.* The Edison Electric Institute produces the *Statistical Yearbook of Electric Utility Industry* and the *Year-End Summary of the Electric Power Situation in the United States* while the American Gas Association published *Gas Facts.*

3 Energy data were presented formerly in widely varying units, but increasingly are being converted to a common thermal unit, the BTU (British Thermal Unit). A BTU is the amount of energy required to raise the temperature of 1 pound of water 1 degree Fahrenheit at or near 39.2 degrees F. The conversion factors are as follows:

	Production	Consumption
Petroleum (barrel)	5.800 million BTU	5.586 million BTU
Coal (short ton)	21.278 million BTU	20.852 million BTU
Natural Gas (cubic feet)	1,028 BTU	1,028 BTU
Nuclear Power (kWh)	10,676 BTU	10,676 BTU
Geothermal Power (kWh)	20,914 BTU	20,914 BTU
Fossil Fuel (kWh)	10,272 BTU	10,272 BTU

4 Of the total consumption of 100.41 quadrillion BTU in 2004, 40.4 percent is derived from petroleum, 23.0 percent from natural gas, 22.4 from coal, 8.2 percent from nuclear power, and 6.2 percent from renewable sources such as hydroelectric, geothermal, and bio fuels. The United States is more or less self-sufficient in the major energy sources except petroleum, of which the total import consists of 26 quadrillion BTU.

5 The share of coal in both production and consumption has shown remarkable growth. Its production has increased from 14.61 quadrillion BTU in 1970 to 22.71 BTU in 2004. Other alternative forms of energy, once thought of as the wave of the future, have not yet made made an impact on the energy picture.

6 By end-use consumption, residential and commercial use account for 38.9 percent of total energy, industrial use for 33.3 percent, and transportation for 27.8 percent in 2004.

7 Energy prices rose steeply from 1970 to 1985, but have stabilized since then. The average fuel price per million BTU was $1.65 in 1970, $8.40 in 1985, and $9.85 in 2000.

8 In 2001, the average household consumed 92 million BTU at a cost of $1,493 per year. Of total consumption, natural gas accounted for 4.84 quadrillion BTU, electricity for 3.89 quadrillion BTU, and fuel oil for 0.71 quadrillion BTU.

9 The United States has had a negative trade balance in both natural gas and crude oil since 1970. Crude oil imports reached 3.670 billion barrels in 2005 compared with 483 million barrels in 1970. Of the total imports OPEC countries supply 1.738 billion barrels and non-OPEC countries supply 1.932 billion barrels.

10 There are 104 nuclear power plants located in the United States in 31 states. Illinois has the most with 11. Total generation of electric power in 2005 was 780.5 billion kWh or 19.3 percent of total. The United States accounts for slightly less than one-fourth of the 436 nuclear plants worldwide.

11 In 2004, the gas utility had a total of 63,296,000 (of which 58,501,000 were residential), sales of 8.766 quadrillion BTU, and revenues of $79.928 billion.

12 The Strategic Petroleum Reserve grew 7.6 million barrels in 1977 to 688.6 in March of 2007, equivalent to 56 days of oil imports.

13 Solar collectors have yet to realize their potential as inexpensive energy producers. The number of solar collector manufacturers dropped from a high of 225 in 1984 to 26 in 2003, and total shipments declined from 17,191,000 square feet to 11,444,000 square feet.

14 Developed water power in the United States generated 275.573 million kWh in 2000. The Pacific region produced one-half of the total.

15 Ethanol is produced at 128 distillation plants throughout 21 states. Iowa has the largest number with 28, followed by Nebraska (19) Minnesota (16), and South Dakota (14).

16 Texas generated the greatest amount of electricity in 2004. Of the 390.3 billion kWh generated, 38.1 percent came from coal. Wyoming generated only 44.8 billion kWh, but the majority of it (96.7 percent) was derived from coal.

Table 9-1. Energy Overview, 1949–2005

(Billion Btu.)

Year	Production				Trade	
					Imports	
	Fossil Fuels[1]	Nuclear Electric Power	Renewable Energy[2]	Total	Petroleum[3]	Total[4]
2005[P]	54 970 853	8 133 222	6 061 049	69 165 125	28 872 049	34 261 201
2004	55 946 438 [R]	8 221 985 [R]	6 219 752 [R]	70 388 176 [R]	28 208 978 [R]	33 543 175 [R]
2003	56 032 742 [R]	7 958 858	6 144 795 [R]	70 136 396 [R]	26 219 947	31 060 501 [R]
2002	56 783 439	8 143 089	5 932 567 [R]	70 859 096 [R]	24 675 552	29 407 132
2001	58 523 257	8 032 697	5 354 223 [R]	71 910 177 [R]	25 399 534	30 156 633
2000	57 253 678	7 862 349	6 173 193 [R]	71 289 220 [R]	24 531 818	28 972 779
1999	57 505 489	7 610 256	6 599 070	71 714 815	23 133 234	27 252 257
1998	59 204 238	7 067 809	6 569 374 [R]	72 841 420 [R]	22 908 126	26 580 676
1997	58 758 209	6 596 992	7 106 641 [R]	72 461 841 [R]	21 740 472	25 215 350
1996	58 280 604	7 086 674	7 107 038 [R]	72 474 316 [R]	20 285 407	23 701 776
1995	57 439 781	7 075 436	6 619 531 [R]	71 134 748 [R]	18 881 979	22 260 469
1994	57 952 344	6 693 877	6 073 425 [R]	70 719 646 [R]	19 244 037	22 389 924
1993	55 735 528	6 410 499	6 188 871 [R]	68 334 898 [R]	18 510 466	21 272 544
1992	57 589 696	6 479 206	5 930 167 [R]	69 999 070 [R]	16 967 714	19 372 208
1991	57 829 229	6 422 132	6 182 472 [R]	70 433 833 [R]	16 347 774	18 334 826
1990	58 528 539	6 104 350	6 158 162 [R]	70 791 052 [R]	17 117 225	18 817 264
1989	57 468 063	5 602 161	6 336 730 [R]	69 406 954 [R]	17 161 562	18 766 288
1988	57 874 979	5 586 968	5 513 649 [R]	68 975 596 [R]	15 747 008	17 295 931
1987	57 166 750	4 753 933	5 684 932 [R]	67 605 615	14 161 961	15 398 216
1986	56 575 231	4 380 109	6 175 542 [R]	67 130 881 [R]	13 200 846	14 151 407
1985	57 538 724	4 075 563	6 143 728 [R]	67 758 015 [R]	10 609 216	11 780 570
1984	58 849 156	3 552 531	6 487 646 [R]	68 889 333 [R]	11 432 840	12 470 740
1983	54 415 961	3 202 549	6 532 898 [R]	64 151 408 [R]	10 646 788	11 751 804
1982	57 457 816	3 131 148	6 018 352 [R]	66 607 317 [R]	10 777 312	11 861 077
1981	58 529 325	3 007 589	5 471 574	67 008 488	12 639 417	13 719 022
1980	59 007 873	2 739 169	5 485 420	67 232 462 [R]	14 658 259	15 796 247
1979	58 005 609	2 775 827	5 166 379	65 947 815	17 933 196	19 459 809
1978	55 074 118	3 024 126	5 038 938	63 137 182	17 823 568	19 106 170
1977	55 100 782	2 701 762	4 249 002	62 051 547	18 755 525	19 948 129
1976	54 722 896	2 111 121	4 767 792	61 601 809	15 672 116	16 760 058
1975	54 733 273	1 899 798	4 723 494	61 356 565	12 947 546	14 032 389
1974	56 330 758	1 272 083	4 769 395	62 372 236	13 126 685	14 304 274
1973	58 241 491	910 177	4 433 121	63 584 788	13 465 595	14 613 142
1972	58 937 904	583 752	4 398 409	63 920 065	10 298 545	11 387 141
1971	58 041 560	412 939	4 268 335	62 722 834	8 540 125	9 534 770
1970	59 186 071	239 347	4 075 857	63 501 275	7 469 646	8 341 615
1969	56 285 569	153 722	4 101 751	60 541 041	6 902 990	7 676 216
1968	54 306 187	141 534	3 777 541	58 225 261	6 212 622	6 905 114
1967	52 597 132	88 456	3 693 799	56 379 387	5 555 095	6 159 155
1966	50 035 367	64 158	3 434 674	53 534 199	5 628 825	6 145 832
1965	47 234 902	43 164	3 398 036	50 676 101	5 401 965	5 891 935
1964	45 788 951	39 819	3 227 637	49 056 406	4 958 720	5 447 296
1963	44 037 181	38 147	3 098 396	47 173 724	4 650 155	5 086 654
1962	41 731 885	26 394	3 118 714	44 876 994	4 561 672	4 994 279
1961	40 307 136	19 678	2 953 406	43 280 220	4 192 289	4 436 901
1960	39 869 117	6 026	2 928 619	42 803 762	3 998 694	4 187 626
1959	39 045 216	2 187	2 901 339	41 948 742	3 910 109	4 076 278
1958	37 216 322	1 915	2 915 090	40 133 327	3 719 106	3 884 371
1957	40 133 484	112	2 849 194	42 982 790	3 461 019	3 528 983
1956	39 771 452	0	2 850 582	42 622 033	3 166 178	3 206 741
1955	37 363 680	0	2 783 987	40 147 667	2 751 505	2 789 908
1954	33 764 330	0	2 754 099	36 518 430	2 323 614	2 347 876
1953	35 349 336	0	2 831 460	38 180 796	2 284 823	2 313 042
1952	34 976 732	0	2 940 181	37 916 913	2 114 304	2 145 984
1951	35 792 151	0	2 958 464	38 750 615	1 872 279	1 892 425
1950	32 562 667	0	2 977 718	35 540 384	1 886 296	1 912 887
1949	28 748 176	0	2 973 984	31 722 160	1 427 346	1 448 158

[1]Coal, natural gas (dry), crude oil, and natural gas plant liquids.
[2]Electricity net generation from conventional hydroelectric power, geothermal, solar, and wind; consumption of wood, waste, and alcohol fuels; geothermal heat pump and direct energy; and solar thermal direct use energy.
[3]Crude oil and petroleum products. Includes imports into the Strategic Petroleum Reserve.
[4]Also includes natural gas, coal, coal coke, and electricity.
P = Preliminary data.
R = Revised.

Table 9-1. Energy Overview, 1949–2005—*Continued*

(Billion Btu.)

Year	Trade — Exports — Coal	Total[5]	Adjustments[6]	Consumption — Fossil Fuels[7,8]	Nuclear Electric Power	Renewable Energy[1,8]	Total[8,9]
2005[P]	1 273 227	4 640 125	1 108 095	85 955 433	8 133 222	6 061 049	99 894 296
2004	1 253 129	4 433 311	916 421 [R]	86 233 440 [R]	8 221 985 [R]	6 219 752 [R]	100 414 461 [R]
2003	1 117 147	4 053 613 [R]	1 130 039 [R]	84 385 899 [R]	7 958 858	6 144 795 [R]	98 273 323 [R]
2002	1 032 088	3 668 430 [R]	1 369 074	83 994 305	8 143 089	5 932 567 [R]	97 966 872 [R]
2001	1 265 220	3 770 444	−1 798 502	83 182 463	8 032 697	5 354 223 [R]	96 497 865 [R]
2000	1 527 552	4 005 875	2 720 247	84 964 950	7 862 349	6 173 193 [R]	98 976 371 [R]
1999	1 525 108	3 714 999	1 584 575	82 649 963	7 610 256	6 599 070	96 836 647
1998	2 091 677	4 299 200	77 537	81 591 948	7 067 809	6 569 374 [R]	95 200 433 [R]
1997	2 193 135	4 513 987	1 636 843	81 086 024	6 596 992	7 106 641 [R]	94 800 047 [R]
1996	2 368 031	4 633 260	2 682 959	79 978 498	7 086 674	7 107 038 [R]	94 225 791 [R]
1995	2 318 168	4 510 870	2 315 494	77 487 518	7 075 436	6 619 531 [R]	91 199 841 [R]
1994	1 878 801	4 061 144	243 287	76 480 082	6 693 877	6 073 425 [R]	89 291 713 [R]
1993	1 962 467	4 258 368	2 303 121	75 054 900 [9]	6 410 499	6 188 871 [9]	87 652 195 [9,R]
1992	2 681 926	4 936 938	1 580 521	73 518 753	6 479 206	5 930 167 [R]	86 014 860 [R]
1991	2 853 670	5 140 959	1 039 527	71 995 657	6 422 132	6 182 472 [R]	84 667 227 [R]
1990	2 772 273	4 752 479	−125 893	72 459 544	6 104 350	6 158 162 [R]	84 729 945 [R]
1989	2 637 312	4 660 891	1 486 958	73 022 968	5 602 161	6 336 730 [R]	84 999 308 [R]
1988	2 499 010	4 366 448	964 242	71 660 305	5 586 968	5 513 649 [R]	82 869 321 [R]
1987	2 092 954	3 811 934	31 549	68 626 480	4 753 933	5 684 932 [R]	79 223 446 [R]
1986	2 248 436	4 021 467	−435 009	66 147 680	4 380 109	6 175 542 [R]	76 825 812 [R]
1985	2 438 129	4 196 166	1 237 546	66 221 020	4 075 563	6 143 728 [R]	76 579 965 [R]
1984	2 151 306	3 786 148	−780 964	66 617 460	3 552 531	6 487 646 [R]	76 792 960 [R]
1983	2 044 701	3 692 918	935 234	63 289 533	3 202 549	6 532 898 [R]	73 145 527 [R]
1982	2 786 901	4 607 598	−574 645	64 036 625	3 131 148	6 018 352 [R]	73 286 151 [R]
1981	2 944 069	4 307 244	−77 311	67 750 386	3 007 589	5 471 574	76 342 955
1980	2 420 518	3 694 770	−1 053 700	69 984 251	2 739 169	5 485 420	78 280 238 [R]
1979	1 753 277	2 855 108	−1 649 302	72 891 627	2 775 827	5 166 379	80 903 214
1978	1 078 028	1 920 443	−336 538	71 855 989	3 024 126	5 038 938	79 986 371
1977	1 441 875	2 051 891	−1 948 231	70 989 367	2 701 762	4 249 002	77 999 554
1976	1 596 619	2 171 688	−177 806	69 104 082	2 111 121	4 767 792	76 012 373
1975	1 761 300	2 323 252	−1 066 511	65 354 796	1 899 798	4 723 494	71 999 191
1974	1 619 649	2 203 366	−482 264	67 906 091	1 272 083	4 769 395	73 990 880
1973	1 425 200	2 033 086	−456 481	70 316 351	910 177	4 433 121	75 708 364
1972	1 530 788	2 118 310	−484 628	67 695 880	583 752	4 398 409	72 704 267
1971	1 546 119	2 150 898	−817 741	64 595 645	412 939	4 268 335	69 288 965
1970	1 935 500	2 632 135	−1 366 594	63 522 269	239 347	4 075 857	67 844 161
1969	1 534 224	2 125 659	−470 720	61 361 751	153 722	4 101 751	65 620 879
1968	1 380 367	1 998 489	−712 494	58 502 470	141 534	3 777 541	62 419 392
1967	1 352 369	2 115 402	−1 515 034	55 126 873	88 456	3 693 799	58 908 107
1966	1 350 634	1 829 067	−834 419	53 513 987	64 158	3 434 674	57 016 544
1965	1 376 486	1 828 933	−721 883	50 576 504	43 164	3 398 036	54 017 221
1964	1 335 161	1 814 661	−871 864	48 543 050	39 819	3 227 637	51 817 177
1963	1 356 399	1 835 183	−779 035	46 509 283	38 147	3 098 396	49 646 160
1962	1 082 910	1 472 536	−571 031	44 680 770	26 394	3 118 714	47 827 707
1961	980 641	1 376 584	−601 520	42 758 243	19 678	2 953 406	45 739 017
1960	1 023 170	1 477 475	−427 042	42 136 751	6 026	2 928 619	45 086 870
1959	1 051 257	1 533 808	−1 025 490	40 550 068	2 187	2 901 339	43 465 722
1958	1 415 843	2 049 839	−322 832	38 716 702	1 915	2 915 090	41 645 028
1957	2 174 059	3 439 441	−1 285 146	38 925 592	112	2 849 194	41 787 186
1956	1 984 106	2 945 377	−1 129 145	38 888 151	0	2 850 582	41 754 252
1955	1 464 521	2 285 508	−444 096	37 410 105	0	2 783 987	40 207 971
1954	910 509	1 696 301	−530 622	33 877 300	0	2 754 099	36 639 382
1953	980 726	1 866 013	−963 357	34 826 156	0	2 831 460	37 664 468
1952	1 402 980	2 365 131	−949 941	33 799 903	0	2 940 181	36 747 825
1951	1 682 779	2 621 545	−1 047 465	34 008 105	0	2 958 464	36 974 030
1950	786 496	1 465 322	−1 372 181	31 631 956	0	2 977 718	34 615 768
1949	877 294	1 591 760	402 944	29 002 099	0	2 973 984	31 981 503

Source: U.S. Department of Energy, Energy Information Administration. *Annual Energy Review 2005 Report No. DOE/EIA-0384 2005.*
Note: Totals may not equal sum of components due to independent rounding.
[1]Coal, natural gas (dry), crude oil, and natural gas plant liquids.
[5]Also includes natural gas, petroleum, coal coke, and electricity.
[6]A balancing item. Includes stock changes, losses, gains, miscellaneous blending components, and unaccounted-for supply.
[7]Coal, coal coke net imports, natural gas, and petroleum.
[9]Beginning in 1993, ethanol blended into motor gasoline is included in consumption values for both "Fossil Fuels" and "Renewable Energy," but is counted only once in total consumption.
[10]Also includes electricity net imports.
P = Preliminary data.
R = Revised.

Table 9-2. Gas Utility Industry—Customers, Sales, and Revenues, by Type of Service, 1932–2004

Year	Customers[1] (thousands)				Sales[2] (mil. therms[3])				Revenues[2] (mil. of dol)			
	Total[4]	Residential	Commercial	Industrial	Total	Residential	Commercial	Industrial	Total	Residential	Commercial	Industrial
2004	63 297	58 501	4 641	152	87 660	45 660	20 750	17 630	79 929	47 275	18 689	11 230
2003	62 610	57 802	4 661	145	89 270	47 220	21 250	16 720	72 606	43 664	17 349	11 525
2002	62 034	57 293	4 590	149	88 640	45 890	20 550	17 480	57 112	35 062	13 512	6 841
2001	61 385	56 680	4 546	156	86 670	45 250	20 530	14 610	69 150	42 454	16 848	7 513
2000	61 262	56 494	4 610	157	92 320	47 410	20 770	16 980	59 243	35 828	13 339	7 432
1999	60 778	56 017	4 599	159	89 750	46 220	20 670	15 530	47 202	30 095	10 731	4 715
1998	61 528	56 517	4 825	183	87 810	45 340	20 630	13 700	47 084	30 130	11 020	4 189
1997	61 013	55 934	4 881	196	97 220	50 560	23 410	15 930	54 876	34 187	13 203	5 556
1996	60 044	55 222	4 643	177	102 420	53 330	25 180	17 480	53 630	32 942	13 250	5 812
1995	58 728	53 955	4 530	181	92 210	48 030	22 810	19 190	46 436	28 742	11 573	5 571
1994	57 936	53 219	4 475	180	92 480	48 450	22 550	19 920	49 852	30 552	12 276	6 428
1993	57 028	52 358	4 428	181	101 510	50 540	23 970	25 330	50 137	29 787	12 076	7 642
1992	53 132	51 525	4 397	165	99 070	46 940	22 090	27 720	46 178	26 702	10 865	7 913
1991	55 174	50 634	4 322	168	96 010	45 460	21 980	26 310	44 647	25 729	10 669	7 576
1990	54 261	49 802	4 246	166	98 420	44 680	21 920	30 100	45 153	25 000	10 604	8 996
1989	53 356	48 980	4 161	168	105 510	47 980	23 220	32 430	47 493	26 172	11 074	9 666
1988	52 422	48 133	4 069	168	107 050	46 950	23 060	35 440	46 162	24 828	10 681	10 113
1987	51 576	47 362	3 980	180	105 430	43 850	21 560	38 480	45 492	23 622	10 271	11 069
1986	50 704	46 583	3 892	178	111 250	43 810	22 390	43 380	51 201	24 759	11 274	14 495
1985	49 971	45 929	3 816	179	126 160	45 130	23 380	56 350	63 293	26 864	12 722	23 086
1984	49 325	45 367	3 730	180	131 620	46 280	23 960	59 910	67 496	27 485	13 205	26 094
1983	48 799	44 894	3 676	182	128 580	44 500	22 980	59 700	65 837	26 173	12 659	26 315
1982	48 415	44 552	3 631	186	141 830	47 700	24 710	27 950	63 200	23 700	11 666	27 200
1981	47 947	44 149	3 564	187	153 750	46 100	23 760	82 390	56 110	19 180	9 286	27 124
1980	47 223	43 489	3 498	187	154 130	48 260	24 530	78 570	48 303	17 432	8 183	22 215
1979	46 478	42 821	3 423	189	154 400	50 830	24 860	76 410	38 947	14 833	6 624	17 045
1978	45 789	42 183	3 370	189	147 480	51 070	25 000	69 320	32 150	12 939	5 696	13 139
1977	45 274	41 682	3 371	173	143 410	49 460	24 090	67 960	28 303	11 541	4 980	11 455
1976	44 941	41 338	3 372	180	148 140	50 140	24 230	71 920	23 701	9 941	4 075	9 435
1975	44 555	40 950	3 367	184	148 630	49 910	23 870	68 370	19 101	8 445	3 303	6 745
1974	44 267	40 627	3 392	194	160 000	48 650	22 930	81 530	15 242	6 899	2 539	5 391
1973	43 711	40 116	3 331	209	164 800	49 940	22 810	83 710	12 987	6 247	2 172	4 197
1972	42 955	39 428	3 264	209	170 820	51 420	22 760	87 760	12 465	6 094	2 064	3 943
1971	42 242	38 789	3 199	205	166 860	50 400	21 560	86 460	11 357	5 635	1 829	3 569
1970	41 482	38 097	3 131	199	160 435	49 237	20 066	84 392	10 283	5 207	1 620	3 181
1960*	33 054	30 418	2 458	141	92 877	31 881	9 198	47 094	5 617	3 177	723	1 563
1950	24 001	22 146	1 739	100	42 090	13 839	4 104	22 887	1 948	1 177	266	480
1940	17 600	16 381	1 138	73	17 235	5 823	1 598	9 544	872	573	112	182
1932	15 532	14 452	999	73	10 441	4 672	1 193	1 534	723	537	93	91

Source: U.S. Census Bureau. American Gas Association. *Gas Facts,* annual.

[1]Annual average.

[2]Excludes sales for resale.

[3]A therm is equivalent to 100,000 British thermal units. A Btu is the quantity of heat required to raise the temperature of one pound of water one degree F. at or near its point of maximum density.

[4]Includes customers not otherwise categorized.

* = Includes Hawaii.

Table 9-3. Electricity Net Generation: Total (All Sectors), 1949-2005

(Thousand Kilowatthours.)

Year	Fossil Fuels					Nuclear Electric Power	Hydroelectric Pumped Storage[5]
	Total	Coal[1]	Petroleum[2]	Natural Gas[3]	Other Gases[4]		
2005[P]	2 903 275 650	2 014 172 634	121 910 223	751 549 111	15 643 682	780 464 675	−6 568 160
2004	2 825 010 758	1 978 620 218	120 645 844 [R]	708 978 606 [R]	16 766 090	788 528 387 [R]	−8 488 210
2003	2 758 649 951	1 973 736 750	119 405 640	649 907 541	15 600 020	763 732 695	−8 535 065
2002	2 730 166 178	1 933 130 353	94 567 394	691 005 746	11 462 685	780 064 087	−8 742 928
2001	2 677 004 758	1 903 955 943	124 880 222	639 129 120	9 039 473	768 826 308	−8 823 445
2000	2 692 478 478	1 966 264 596	111 220 965	601 038 159	13 954 758	753 892 940	−5 538 860
1999	2 569 669 781	1 881 087 224	118 060 838	556 396 127	14 125 592	728 254 124	−6 096 899
1998	2 547 065 197	1 873 515 690	128 800 173	531 257 104	13 492 230	673 702 104	−4 467 280
1997	2 430 319 913	1 845 015 736	92 554 873	479 398 670	13 350 634	628 644 171	−4 039 905
1996	2 346 018 207	1 795 195 593	81 411 225	455 055 576	14 355 813	674 728 546	−3 088 078
1995	2 293 908 429	1 709 426 468	74 554 065	496 057 945	13 869 951	673 402 123	−2 725 131
1994	2 270 132 580	1 690 693 864	105 900 983	460 218 682	13 319 051	640 439 832	−3 377 825
1993	2 230 741 008	1 690 070 232	112 788 180	414 926 798	12 955 798	610 291 214	−4 035 572
1992	2 138 704 811	1 621 206 039	100 154 163	404 074 372	13 270 237	618 776 263	−4 176 582
1991	2 103 262 931	1 590 622 748	119 751 573	381 553 017	11 335 593	612 565 087	−4 541 435
1990	2 103 780 605	1 594 011 479	126 621 142	372 765 154	10 382 830	576 861 678	−3 507 741
1989[11]	2 108 788 380	1 583 779 139	164 517 957	352 628 866	7 862 418	529 354 717	[10]
1988	1 942 353 039	1 540 652 774	148 899 561	252 800 704	...	526 973 047	[10]
1987	1 854 894 663	1 463 781 289	118 492 571	272 620 803	...	455 270 382	[10]
1986	1 770 924 752	1 385 831 452	136 584 867	248 508 433	...	414 038 063	[10]
1985	1 794 276 363	1 402 128 125	100 202 273	291 945 965	...	383 690 727	[10]
1984	1 758 882 261	1 341 680 752	119 807 913	297 393 596	...	327 633 549	[10]
1983	1 678 021 330	1 259 424 279	144 498 593	274 098 458	...	293 677 119	[10]
1982	1 644 061 443	1 192 004 204	146 797 490	305 259 749	...	282 773 248	[10]
1981	1 755 401 180	1 203 203 232	206 420 775	345 777 173	...	272 673 503	[10]
1980	1 753 796 457	1 161 562 368	245 994 189	346 239 900	...	251 115 575	[10]
1979	1 708 047 407	1 075 037 091	303 525 209	329 485 107	...	255 154 623	[10]
1978	1 646 193 360	975 742 083	365 060 441	305 390 836	...	276 403 070	[10]
1977	1 648 902 277	985 218 596	358 178 822	305 504 859	...	250 883 283	[10]
1976	1 559 003 041	944 390 993	319 988 137	294 623 911	...	191 103 531	[10]
1975	1 441 659 530	852 786 222	289 094 900	299 778 408	...	172 505 075	[10]
1974	1 449 428 547	828 432 921	300 930 538	320 065 088	...	113 975 740	[10]
1973	1 502 852 588	847 651 470	314 342 926	340 858 192	...	83 479 463	[10]
1972	1 421 175 022	771 131 265	274 295 961	375 747 796	...	54 091 135	[10]
1971	1 307 358 661	713 102 454	220 225 423	374 030 784	...	38 104 545	[10]
1970	1 261 467 944	704 394 479	184 183 402	372 890 063	...	21 804 448	[10]
1969	1 177 127 337	706 001 240	137 847 152	333 278 945	...	13 927 839	[10]
1968	1 093 613 136	684 904 580	104 275 833	304 432 723	...	12 528 419	[10]
1967	984 559 872	630 483 363	89 270 724	264 805 785	...	7 655 214	[10]
1966	943 552 534	613 474 800	78 926 172	251 151 562	...	5 519 909	[10]
1965	857 286 609	570 925 951	64 801 224	221 559 434	...	3 656 699	[10]
1964	803 222 210	526 230 019	56 953 712	220 038 479	...	3 342 743	[10]
1963	747 530 402	493 926 719	52 001 610	201 602 073	...	3 211 836	[10]
1962	683 430 067	450 249 238	48 879 536	184 301 293	...	2 269 685	[10]
1961	639 676 043	421 870 669	48 519 376	169 285 998	...	1 692 149	[10]
1960	609 024 037	403 067 357	47 986 893	157 969 787	...	518 182	[10]
1959	571 883 320	378 424 210	46 839 719	146 619 391	...	188 101	[10]
1958	504 496 623	344 365 781	40 371 540	119 759 302	...	164 691	[10]
1957	501 098 089	346 386 207	40 499 357	114 212 525	...	9 670	[10]
1956	478 487 464	338 503 484	35 946 772	104 037 208	...	0	[10]
1955	433 786 447	301 362 698	37 138 308	95 285 441	...	0	[10]
1954	364 354 412	239 145 966	31 520 175	93 688 271	...	0	[10]
1953	337 041 749	218 846 325	38 404 449	79 790 975	...	0	[10]
1952	293 639 515	195 436 666	29 749 761	68 453 088	...	0	[10]
1951	270 531 451	185 203 657	28 712 116	56 615 678	...	0	[10]
1950	232 813 441	154 519 994	33 734 288	44 559 159	...	0	[10]
1949	200 965 261	135 451 320	28 547 232	36 966 709	...	0	[10]

Source: U.S. Department of Energy, Energy Information Administration. *Annual Energy Review 2005 Report No. DOE/EIA-0384 2005.*
Note: Totals may not equal sum of components due to independent rounding.
[1]Anthracite, bituminous coal, subbituminous coal, lignite, waste coal, and coal synfuel.
[2]Distillate fuel oil, residual fuel oil, petroleum coke, jet fuel, kerosene, other petroleum, and waste oil.
[3]Natural gas, plus a small amount of supplemental gaseous fuels that cannot be identified separately.
[4]Blast furnace gas, propane gas, and other manufactured and waste gases derived from fossil fuels.
[5]Pumped storage facility production minus energy used for pumping.
[6]Wood, black liquor, and other wood waste.
[7]Municipal solid waste, landfill gas, sludge waste, tires, agricultural byproducts, and other biomass.
[8]Solar thermal and photovoltaic energy.
[9]Batteries, chemicals, hydrogen, pitch, purchased steam, sulfur, and miscellaneous technologies.
[10]Included in "Conventional Hydroelectric Power."
[11]Through 1988, all data except hydroelectric are for electric utilities only; hydroelectric data through 1988 include industrial plants as well as electric utilities. Beginning in 1989, data are for electric utilities, independent power producers, commercial plants, and industrial plants.
. . . = Not available.
R = Revised.
P=Preliminary.

Table 9-3. Electricity Net Generation: Total (All Sectors), 1949-2005—*Continued*

(Thousand Kilowatthours.)

| | Renewable Energy | | | | | | | |
| Conventional Hydroelectric Power | Biomass | | Geothermal | Solar[8] | Wind | Total | Other[9] | Total |
	Wood[6]	Waste[7]						
265 077 680	37 828 379	23 996 556	15 124 491	541 392	14 597 163	357 165 661	3 650 896	4 037 988 722
268 417 308 [R]	37 576 418 [R]	23 302 172 [R]	14 810 975 [R]	575 155	14 143 741 [R]	358 825 769	6 678 560 [R]	3 970 555 264
275 806 328	37 529 098	23 735 672	14 424 231	534 001	11 187 467	363 216 797	6 120 827	3 883 185 205
264 328 832	38 665 040	22 856 632	14 491 310	554 831	10 354 279	351 250 924	5 713 991	3 858 452 252
216 961 044	35 199 905	21 764 564	13 740 501	542 755	6 737 332	294 946 101	4 689 931	3 736 643 653
275 572 597	37 594 866	23 131 314	14 093 158	493 375	5 593 261	356 478 571	4 793 914	3 802 105 043
319 536 029	37 040 734	22 572 175	14 827 013	495 082	4 487 998	398 959 031	4 023 773	3 694 809 810
323 335 661	36 338 384	22 447 935	14 773 918	502 473	3 025 696	400 424 067	3 571 410	3 620 295 498
356 453 295	36 948 441	21 709 073	14 726 102	511 168	3 288 035	433 636 114	3 611 990	3 492 172 283
347 162 063	36 800 310	20 911 336	14 328 684	521 205	3 234 069	422 957 667	3 571 279	3 444 187 621
310 832 748	36 521 082	20 404 971	13 378 258	496 821	3 164 253	384 798 133	4 103 808	3 353 487 362
260 125 733	37 937 364	19 128 595	15 535 453	486 622	3 447 109	336 660 876	3 666 925	3 247 522 388
280 494 008	37 623 407	18 333 031	16 788 565	462 452	3 005 827	356 707 290	3 487 156	3 197 191 096
253 088 003	36 528 662	17 816 035	16 137 962	399 640	2 887 523	326 857 825	3 719 887	3 083 882 204
288 994 189	33 725 358	15 664 746	15 966 444	471 765	2 950 951	357 773 453	4 738 849	3 073 798 885
292 865 846	32 521 889	13 260 379	15 434 271	367 087	2 788 600	357 238 072	3 615 663	3 037 988 277
271 976 936	27 236 668	9 162 887	14 593 443	250 601	2 112 043	325 332 578	3 829 849	2 967 305 524
226 100 803	935 986	738 258	10 300 079	9 094	871	238 085 091	...	2 707 411 177
252 856 093	783 088	693 941	10 775 461	10 497	3 541	265 122 621	...	2 575 287 666
294 005 219	491 509	685 234	10 307 954	14 032	4 189	305 508 137	...	2 490 470 952
284 310 538	743 294	639 578	9 325 230	10 630	5 762	295 035 032	...	2 473 002 122
324 311 365	461 411	424 540	7 740 504	5 248	6 490	332 949 558	...	2 419 465 368
335 290 855	215 867	162 745	6 075 101	...	2 668	341 747 236	...	2 313 445 685
312 374 013	195 940	124 979	4 842 865	...	...	317 537 797	...	2 244 372 488
263 844 664	245 201	122 628	5 686 163	...	...	269 898 656	...	2 297 973 339
279 182 090	275 366	157 797	5 073 079	...	...	284 688 332	...	2 289 600 364
283 075 976	299 859	198 192	3 888 968	...	...	287 462 995	...	2 250 665 025
283 465 224	197 193	140 434	2 977 630	...	...	286 780 481	...	2 209 376 911
223 598 687	307 634	173 271	3 582 335	...	...	227 661 927	...	2 127 447 487
286 924 238	84 386	182 078	3 616 407	...	...	290 807 109	...	2 040 913 681
303 152 673	17 551	173 568	3 246 172	...	...	306 589 964	...	1 920 754 569
304 211 805	68 523	182 154	2 452 636	...	...	306 915 118	...	1 870 319 405
275 430 574	130 403	197 890	1 965 713	...	...	277 724 580	...	1 864 056 631
275 928 828	130 859	199 774	1 452 795	...	...	277 712 256	...	1 752 978 413
269 531 459	111 330	199 869	547 752	...	...	270 390 410	...	1 615 853 616
250 957 442	136 000	220 450	525 183	...	...	251 839 075	...	1 535 111 467
253 468 237	319 933	...	614 710	...	...	254 402 880	...	1 445 458 056
225 873 158	375 062	...	435 826	...	...	226 684 046	...	1 332 825 601
224 948 605	315 688	...	316 309	...	...	225 580 602	...	1 217 795 688
197 937 538	333 926	...	187 988	...	...	198 459 452	...	1 147 531 895
196 984 345	268 804	...	189 214	...	...	197 442 363	...	1 058 385 671
180 301 506	148 076	...	203 791	...	...	180 653 373	...	987 218 326
168 990 140	127 940	...	167 953	...	...	169 286 033	...	920 028 271
172 015 646	127 796	...	100 462	...	...	172 243 904	...	857 943 656
155 536 444	125 734	...	94 021	...	...	155 756 199	...	797 124 391
149 440 035	140 166	...	33 368	...	...	149 613 569	...	759 155 788
141 154 533	152 877	...	...	...	...	141 307 410	...	713 378 831
143 614 545	175 003	...	...	...	...	143 789 548	...	648 450 862
133 357 930	176 678	...	...	...	...	133 534 608	...	634 642 367
125 236 621	151 678	...	...	...	...	125 388 299	...	603 875 763
116 235 946	276 469	...	...	...	...	116 512 415	...	550 298 862
111 639 772	263 434	...	...	...	...	111 903 206	...	476 257 618
109 617 396	389 418	...	...	...	...	110 006 814	...	447 048 563
109 708 251	481 647	...	...	...	...	110 189 898	...	403 829 413
104 376 120	390 784	...	...	...	...	104 766 904	...	375 298 355
100 884 575	389 585	...	...	...	...	101 274 160	...	334 087 601
94 772 992	386 036	...	...	...	...	95 159 028	...	296 124 289

Table 9-4. Electric Power Sector Energy Consumption, 1949–2005

(Billion Btu.)

| Year | Fossil Fuels | | | | Nuclear Electric Power |
	Coal	Natural Gas[1]	Petroleum	Total	
2005[P]	20 752 225	5 964 841	1 230 286	27 947 352	8 133 222
2004	20 305 035 [R]	5 610 653 [R]	1 212 324 [R]	27 128 012 [R]	8 221 985 [R]
2003	20 184 743	5 263 596	1 204 985	26 653 323	7 958 858
2002	19 782 781	5 785 335	961 313	26 529 429	8 143 089
2001	19 613 673	5 481 200	1 276 552	26 371 425	8 032 697
2000	20 220 171	5 315 657	1 144 320	26 680 148	7 862 349
1999	19 279 487	4 925 561	1 211 350	25 416 398	7 610 256
1998	19 215 682	4 698 402	1 306 235	25 220 319	7 067 809
1997	18 904 538	4 146 099	926 801	23 977 438	6 596 992
1996	18 429 027	3 883 039	817 356	23 129 423	7 086 674
1995	17 466 285	4 325 493	754 597	22 546 374	7 075 436
1994	17 260 875	4 000 109	1 058 783	22 319 767	6 693 877
1993	17 195 927	3 559 807	1 123 789	21 879 524	6 410 499
1992	16 465 595	3 534 068	990 707	20 990 370	6 479 206
1991	16 249 709	3 398 823	1 198 261	20 846 792	6 422 132
1990	16 260 952	3 332 223	1 289 433	20 882 609	6 104 350
1989[5]	16 137 221	3 192 128	1 703 091	21 032 440	5 602 161
1988	15 849 966	2 709 410	1 563 425	20 122 802	5 586 968
1987	15 173 411	2 935 061	1 256 859	19 365 331	4 753 933
1986	14 443 716	2 690 851	1 451 843	18 586 409	4 380 109
1985	14 542 209	3 159 758	1 090 459	18 792 426	4 075 563
1984	14 019 485	3 220 239	1 286 116	18 525 840	3 552 531
1983	13 212 591	2 998 090	1 543 683	17 754 363	3 202 549
1982	12 582 150	3 341 637	1 567 654	17 491 440	3 131 148
1981	12 583 461	3 767 559	2 201 663	18 552 683	3 007 589
1980	12 122 684	3 810 451	2 633 561	18 566 696	2 739 169
1979	11 259 923	3 612 691	3 283 366	18 155 980	2 775 827
1978	10 238 271	3 296 767	3 986 863	17 521 902	3 024 126
1977	10 262 025	3 283 745	3 900 624	17 446 394	2 701 762
1976	9 720 234	3 151 728	3 477 133	16 349 095	2 111 121
1975	8 785 839	3 239 769	3 165 675	15 191 283	1 899 798
1974	8 534 031	3 519 184	3 365 031	15 418 245	1 272 083
1973	8 658 401	3 748 016	3 514 815	15 921 233	910 177
1972	7 810 652	4 084 289	3 097 087	14 992 028	583 752
1971	7 299 131	4 099 275	2 494 999	13 893 405	412 939
1970	7 227 462	4 053 747	2 117 337	13 398 545	239 347
1969	7 219 295	3 595 759	1 571 294	12 386 348	153 722
1968	6 993 639	3 245 494	1 181 450	11 420 583	141 534
1967	6 444 982	2 834 236	1 010 541	10 289 758	88 456
1966	6 301 644	2 696 077	883 230	9 880 951	64 158
1965	5 821 061	2 395 376	722 002	8 938 439	43 164
1964	5 379 553	2 397 228	633 882	8 410 663	39 819
1963	5 050 213	2 210 952	584 707	7 845 871	38 147
1962	4 622 376	2 034 783	559 585	7 216 744	26 394
1961	4 354 953	1 888 996	557 278	6 801 227	19 678
1960	4 227 551	1 785 129	552 715	6 565 395	6 026
1959	4 029 357	1 685 507	551 978	6 266 842	2 187
1958	3 721 340	1 420 903	485 713	5 627 956	1 915
1957	3 855 246	1 382 906	498 383	5 736 534	112
1956	3 789 674	1 282 687	454 719	5 527 079	0
1955	3 458 271	1 193 644	470 747	5 122 663	0
1954	2 840 759	1 206 291	417 409	4 464 458	0
1953	2 777 361	1 070 472	514 298	4 362 131	0
1952	2 557 397	941 971	420 366	3 919 734	0
1951	2 506 808	790 635	399 898	3 697 341	0
1950[P]	2 199 111	650 931	471 666	3 321 708	0
1949	1 995 055	569 375	414 632	2 979 062	0

Source: U.S. Department of Energy, Energy Information Administration. *Annual Energy Review 2005 Report No. DOE/EIA-0384 2005.*
Note: Data are for fuels consumed to produce electricity and useful thermal output. The electric power sector comprises electricity-only and combined-heat-and-power (CHP) plants within the NAICS (North American Industry Classification System) 22 category whose primary business is to sell electricity, or electricity and heat to the public. Totals may not equal the sum of components due to independent rounding.
[1]Natural gas, plus a small amount of supplemental gaseous fuels that cannot be identified separately.
[2]Conventional hydroelectric power.
[3]Wood and waste.
[4]Net imports equal imports minus exports.
[5]Through 1988, data are for electric utilities only. Beginning in 1989, data are for electric utilities and independent power producers.
. . . = Not available.
R = Revised.
P = Preliminary

Table 9-4. Electric Power Sector Energy Consumption, 1949–2005—*Continued*

(Billion Btu.)

Primary Consumption

Renewable Energy						Electricity Net Imports[4]	Total Primary
Hydroelectric Power[2]	Biomass[3]	Geothermal	Solar	Wind	Total		
2 682 052	531 062	317 871	5 544	149 490	3 686 020	84 360	39 850 955
2 656 470 [R]	509 655	311 282 [R]	5 764	141 749 [R]	3 624 920 [R]	38 597	39 013 515 [R]
2 780 551	521 531	303 154	5 469	114 571	3 725 276	21 896	38 359 353
2 649 979	515 655	304 564	5 644	105 334	3 581 176	71 595 [R]	38 325 289 [R]
2 208 671	450 440	288 784	5 608	69 617	3 023 121	75 156	37 502 399
2 767 916	452 754	296 196	5 033	57 057	3 578 955	115 199	38 236 652
3 217 744	453 224	311 619	5 063	45 894	4 033 545	98 924	37 159 122
3 241 286	444 496	310 503	5 124	30 853	4 032 262	88 224	36 408 614
3 581 168	445 973	308 659	5 221	33 581	4 374 601	116 203	35 065 234
3 527 582	438 273	300 329	5 389	33 440	4 305 014	137 144	34 658 255
3 149 392	421 664	279 793	5 123	32 630	3 888 602	133 856	33 644 268
2 620 314	433 889	324 908	5 020	35 560	3 419 692	152 937	32 586 273
2 860 991	414 619	351 116	4 767	30 987	3 662 481	94 910	32 047 414
2 585 662	402 457	337 509	4 133	29 863	3 359 624	86 733	30 915 933
2 984 899	354 351	335 247	4 923	30 796	3 710 217	66 965	31 046 107
3 014 012	316 507	325 601	3 818	29 007	3 688 946	7 888	30 683 793
2 808 182	231 530	307 863	2 614	22 033	3 372 222	37 450	30 044 273
2 301 629	17 285	217 290	94	9	2 536 308	108 399	28 354 477
2 601 572	15 389	229 119	109	37	2 846 226	158 101	27 123 591
3 038 157	12 292	219 178	147	44	3 269 818	122 481	26 358 817
2 937 168	14 447	198 282	111	60	3 150 069	139 655	26 157 712
3 352 809	9 249	164 896	55	68	3 527 076	135 323	25 740 770
3 494 005	3 983	129 339	...	28	3 627 355	120 547	24 704 814
3 232 512	3 355	104 746	...	...	3 340 613	100 026	24 063 227
2 724 925	3 845	123 043	...	...	2 851 813	113 406	24 525 491
2 867 306	4 500	109 776	...	...	2 981 582	71 399	24 358 846
2 896 591	5 156	83 788	...	...	2 985 535	69 381	23 986 723
2 905 420	3 498	64 350	...	...	2 973 268	67 318	23 586 613
2 300 652	5 018	77 418	...	...	2 383 087	59 422	22 590 665
2 942 893	2 764	78 154	...	...	3 023 811	29 378	21 513 405
3 122 285	1 989	70 153	...	...	3 194 427	21 103	20 306 611
3 143 378	2 613	53 158	...	...	3 199 149	43 311	19 932 789
2 826 675	3 411	42 605	...	...	2 872 691	48 715	19 752 816
2 829 445	3 431	31 479	...	...	2 864 355	26 227	18 466 362
2 790 405	3 261	11 862	...	...	2 805 527	12 046	17 123 917
2 599 507	3 740	11 347	...	...	2 614 595	6 688	16 259 175
2 613 763	3 342	13 281	...	...	2 630 386	3 656	15 174 112
2 313 457	3 900	9 416	...	...	2 326 774	- 2 152	13 886 738
2 310 877	3 293	6 886	...	...	2 321 056	- 1 020	12 698 249
2 028 381	3 478	4 170	...	...	2 036 029	3 725	11 984 863
2 026 320	2 810	4 197	...	...	2 033 327	- 482	11 014 449
1 852 542	1 549	4 520	...	...	1 858 612	6 671	10 315 765
1 737 441	1 341	3 726	...	...	1 742 507	334	9 626 860
1 780 151	1 349	2 331	...	...	1 783 831	1 829	9 028 798
1 620 627	1 339	2 181	...	...	1 624 147	7 689	8 452 741
1 569 167	1 508	774	...	...	1 571 449	15 474	8 158 344
1 511 462	1 677	...	...	...	1 513 139	12 127	7 794 295
1 554 805	1 940	...	...	...	1 556 745	11 320	7 197 936
1 480 092	2 008	...	...	...	1 482 100	12 288	7 231 035
1 397 960	1 738	...	...	...	1 399 698	15 519	6 942 296
1 321 695	3 234	...	...	...	1 324 929	13 879	6 461 471
1 304 094	3 209	...	...	...	1 307 303	7 983	5 779 745
1 356 353	5 019	...	...	...	1 361 372	6 852	5 730 355
1 404 274	6 435	...	...	...	1 410 709	7 740	5 338 183
1 360 698	5 331	...	...	...	1 366 029	7 461	5 070 831
1 346 015	5 486	...	...	...	1 351 481	6 094	4 679 283
1 349 185	5 803	...	...	...	1 354 988	5 420	4 339 470

Table 9-5. Consumption for Electricity Generation by Energy Source: Total (All Sectors), 1949–2005

(Billion Btu.)

	Fossil Fuels					Nuclear Electric Power
	Coal[1]	Petroleum[2]	Natural Gas[3]	Other Gases[4]	Total	
2005P	21 009 823	1 317 402	6 692 285	188 617	29 208 127	8 133 222
2004	20 507 591 [R]	1 281 493 [R]	6 329 238 [R]	186 964 [R]	28 305 286 [R]	8 221 985 [R]
2003	20 366 879	1 265 964	5 735 770	156 305	27 524 918	7 958 858
2002	19 996 890	1 014 206	6 249 585	131 231	27 391 912	8 143 089
2001	19 733 840	1 337 107	5 981 907	97 308	27 150 162	8 032 697
2000	20 442 828	1 211 721	5 818 336	125 971	27 598 856	7 862 349
1999	19 467 086	1 284 682	5 441 478	126 387	26 319 633	7 610 256
1998	19 416 802	1 377 768	5 204 838	124 988	26 124 396	7 067 809
1997	19 128 305	984 546	4 657 954	119 412	24 890 217	6 596 992
1996	18 650 317	888 037	4 399 633	158 560	24 096 547	7 086 674
1995	17 687 345	813 192	4 840 068	132 520	23 473 125	7 075 436
1994	17 485 104	1 135 437	4 476 159	136 381	23 233 081	6 693 877
1993	17 424 494	1 202 639	4 026 611	136 230	22 789 974	6 410 499
1992	16 685 503	1 076 405	3 999 460	141 279	21 902 647	6 479 206
1991	16 460 000	1 276 457	3 861 183	125 485	21 723 125	6 422 132
1990	16 477 441	1 366 877	3 751 530	111 750	21 707 598	6 104 350
1989	16 359 471 [10]	1 757 320 [10]	3 581 360 [10]	90 360	21 788 511 [10]	5 602 161 [10]
1988	15 849 966	1 563 425	2 709 410	...	20 122 801	5 586 968
1987	15 173 411	1 256 859	2 935 061	...	19 365 331	4 753 933
1986	14 443 716	1 451 842	2 690 851	...	18 586 409	4 380 109
1985	14 542 209	1 090 459	3 159 758	...	18 792 426	4 075 563
1984	14 019 485	1 286 116	3 220 239	...	18 525 840	3 552 531
1983	13 212 591	1 543 683	2 998 090	...	17 754 364	3 202 549
1982	12 582 150	1 567 654	3 341 637	...	17 491 441	3 131 148
1981	12 583 461	2 201 663	3 767 559	...	18 552 683	3 007 589
1980	12 122 684	2 633 561	3 810 451	...	18 566 696	2 739 169
1979	11 259 923	3 283 366	3 612 691	...	18 155 980	2 775 827
1978	10 238 271	3 986 863	3 296 767	...	17 521 901	3 024 126
1977	10 262 025	3 900 625	3 283 745	...	17 446 395	2 701 762
1976	9 720 234	3 477 132	3 151 728	...	16 349 094	2 111 121
1975	8 785 839	3 165 675	3 239 769	...	15 191 283	1 899 798
1974	8 534 031	3 365 031	3 519 184	...	15 418 246	1 272 083
1973	8 658 401	3 514 816	3 748 016	...	15 921 233	910 177
1972	7 810 652	3 097 088	4 084 289	...	14 992 029	583 752
1971	7 299 131	2 494 999	4 099 275	...	13 893 405	412 939
1970	7 227 462	2 117 337	4 053 747	...	13 398 546	239 347
1969	7 219 295	1 571 294	3 595 759	...	12 386 348	153 722
1968	6 993 639	1 181 450	3 245 494	...	11 420 583	141 534
1967	6 444 982	1 010 541	2 834 236	...	10 289 759	88 456
1966	6 301 644	883 230	2 696 077	...	9 880 951	64 158
1965	5 821 061	722 002	2 395 376	...	8 938 439	43 164
1964	5 379 553	633 882	2 397 228	...	8 410 663	39 819
1963	5 050 213	584 707	2 210 952	...	7 845 872	38 147
1962	4 622 376	559 585	2 034 783	...	7 216 744	26 394
1961	4 354 953	557 277	1 888 996	...	6 801 226	19 678
1960	4 227 551	552 715	1 785 129	...	6 565 395	6 026
1959	4 029 357	551 977	1 685 507	...	6 266 841	2 187
1958	3 721 340	485 713	1 420 903	...	5 627 956	1 915
1957	3 855 246	498 382	1 382 906	...	5 736 534	112
1956	3 789 674	454 719	1 282 687	...	5 527 080	0
1955	3 458 271	470 747	1 193 644	...	5 122 662	0
1954	2 840 759	417 409	1 206 291	...	4 464 459	0
1953	2 777 361	514 298	1 070 472	...	4 362 131	0
1952	2 557 397	420 366	941 971	...	3 919 734	0
1951	2 506 808	399 898	790 635	...	3 697 341	0
1950	2 199 111	471 666	650 931	...	3 321 708	0
1949	1 995 055	414 632	569 375	...	2 979 062	0

Source: U.S. Department of Energy, Energy Information Administration. Annual Energy Review 2005 Report No. DOE/EIA-0384 2005.
Note: Data are for energy consumed to produce electricity. Data also include energy consumed to produce useful thermal output at a small number of electric utility combined-heat-and-power (CHP) plants. This table no longer shows energy consumption by hydroelectric pumped storage plants. The change was made because most of the electricity used to pump water into elevated storage reservoirs is generated by plants other than pumped-storage plants; thus, the associated energy is already accounted for in other data columns in this table (such as "Conventional hydroelectric power," "Coal," "Natural Gas," and so on). Totals may not equal the sum of components due to independent rounding.
[1]Anthracite, bituminous coal, subbituminous coal, lignite, waste coal, and coal synfuel.
[2]Distillate fuel oil, residual fuel oil, petroleum coke, jet fuel, kerosene, other petroleum, and waste oil.
[3]Natural gas, plus a small amount of supplemental gaseous fuels that cannot be identified separately.
[4]Blast furnace gas, propane gas, and other manufactured and waste gases derived from fossil fuels.
[5]Wood, black liquor, and other wood waste.
[6]Municipal solid waste, landfill gas, sludge waste, tires, agricultural byproducts, and other biomass.
[7]Solar thermal and photovoltaic energy.
[8]Batteries, chemicals, hydrogen, pitch, purchased steam, sulfur, and miscellaneous technologies.
[9]Net imports equal imports minus exports. See Note 3, "Electricity Imports and Exports," at end of section.
[10]Through 1988, data are for electric utilities only. Beginning in 1989, data are for electric utilities, independent power producers, commercial plants, and industrial plants.
[11]Through 1988, data are for electric utilities and industrial plants. Beginning in 1989, data are for electric utilities, independent power producers, commercial plants, and industrial plants.
P = Preliminary.
R = Revised.
. . . = Not available.

Table 9-5. Consumption for Electricity Generation by Energy Source: Total (All Sectors), 1949–2005—Continued

(Billion Btu.)

Renewable Energy								Electricity Net Imports[9]	
Conventional Hydroelectric Power	Biomass		Geothermal	Solar[7]	Wind	Total			
	Wood[5]	Waste[6]							
2 714 661	624 746	414 817	317 871	5 544	149 490	4 227 129	32 891	84 360	41 685 730
2 690 078 [R]	533 515 [R]	390 937 [R]	311 282 [R]	5 764	141 749 [R]	4 073 325 [R]	51 299 [R]	38 597	40 690 493 [R]
2 824 533	519 294	383 121	303 154	5 469	114 571	4 150 141	58 718	21 896	39 714 531
2 689 017	605 055	399 088	304 564	5 644	105 334	4 108 702	49 046	71 595 [R]	39 764 345 [R]
2 241 858	486 015	346 561	288 784	5 608	69 617	3 438 444	41 266	75 156	38 737 725
2 811 116	495 833	330 082	296 196	5 033	57 057	3 995 317	46 205	115 199	39 617 926
3 267 575	490 188	331 619	311 619	5 063	45 894	4 452 141	40 787	98 924	38 521 740
3 297 054	474 573	332 198	310 503	5 124	30 853	4 450 305	36 460	88 224	37 767 193
3 640 458	484 321	338 969	308 659	5 221	33 581	4 811 208	36 418	116 203	36 451 038
3 589 656	512 722	323 779	300 329	5 389	33 440	4 765 315	37 122	137 144	36 122 802
3 205 307	479 899	315 691	279 793	5 123	32 630	4 318 443	41 964	133 856	35 042 824
2 683 457	498 447	300 731	324 908	5 020	35 560	3 848 124	39 683	152 937	33 967 702
2 891 613	485 164	288 164	351 116	4 767	30 987	4 051 811	33 713	94 910	33 380 908
2 617 436	480 547	282 739	337 509	4 133	29 863	3 752 227	40 334	86 733	32 261 148
3 015 943	424 640	246 531	335 247	4 923	30 796	4 058 081	58 566	66 965	32 328 870
3 046 391	442 307	211 208	325 601	3 818	29 007	4 058 332	36 035	7 888	31 914 204
2 837 263 [11]	344 584 [10]	150 779 [10]	307 863 [10]	2 614 [10]	22 033 [10]	3 665 137 [10]	39 075	37 450	31 132 333
2 334 265	9 663	7 622	217 290	94	9	2 568 943	...	108 399	28 387 111
2 634 508	8 159	7 230	229 119	109	37	2 879 162	...	158 101	27 156 527
3 071 179	5 134	7 158	219 178	147	44	3 302 839	...	122 481	26 391 838
2 970 192	7 765	6 682	198 282	111	60	3 183 093	...	139 655	26 190 737
3 385 811	4 817	4 432	164 896	55	68	3 560 078	...	135 323	25 773 772
3 527 260	2 271	1 712	129 339	...	28	3 660 610	...	120 547	24 738 070
3 265 558	2 048	1 307	104 746	...	...	3 373 659	...	100 026	24 096 274
2 757 968	2 563	1 282	123 043	...	...	2 884 856	...	113 406	24 558 534
2 900 144	2 861	1 639	109 776	...	...	3 014 420	...	71 399	24 391 683
2 930 686	3 104	2 052	83 788	...	...	3 019 629	...	69 381	24 020 817
2 936 983	2 043	1 455	64 350	...	...	3 004 831	...	67 318	23 618 175
2 333 252	3 210	1 808	77 418	...	...	2 415 688	...	59 422	22 623 267
2 976 265	875	1 889	78 154	...	...	3 057 183	...	29 378	21 546 776
3 154 607	183	1 806	70 153	...	...	3 226 749	...	21 103	20 338 933
3 176 580	711	1 902	53 158	...	...	3 232 351	...	43 311	19 965 991
2 861 448	1 355	2 056	42 605	...	...	2 907 464	...	48 715	19 787 589
2 863 865	1 358	2 073	31 479	...	...	2 898 775	...	26 227	18 500 783
2 824 151	1 167	2 094	11 862	...	...	2 839 273	...	12 046	17 157 663
2 633 547	1 427	2 313	11 347	...	...	2 648 635	...	6 688	16 293 216
2 647 983	3 342	...	13 281	...	...	2 664 606	...	3 656	15 208 332
2 348 629	3 900	...	9 416	...	...	2 361 946	...	− 2 152	13 921 910
2 346 664	3 293	...	6 886	...	...	2 356 843	...	− 1 020	12 734 037
2 061 519	3 478	...	4 170	...	...	2 069 167	...	3 725	12 018 001
2 059 077	2 810	...	4 197	...	...	2 066 085	...	− 482	11 047 205
1 886 314	1 549	...	4 520	...	...	1 892 384	...	6 671	10 349 537
1 771 355	1 341	...	3 726	...	...	1 776 421	...	334	9 660 774
1 816 141	1 349	...	2 331	...	...	1 819 821	...	1 829	9 064 788
1 656 463	1 339	...	2 181	...	...	1 659 983	...	7 689	8 488 577
1 607 975	1 508	...	774	...	...	1 610 257	...	15 474	8 197 152
1 548 465	1 677	...	...	...	...	1 550 142	...	12 127	7 831 298
1 591 967	1 940	...	...	...	...	1 593 907	...	11 320	7 235 099
1 515 613	2 008	...	...	...	...	1 517 621	...	12 288	7 266 555
1 434 711	1 738	...	...	...	...	1 436 449	...	15 519	6 979 048
1 359 844	3 234	...	...	...	...	1 363 078	...	13 879	6 499 619
1 359 772	3 209	...	...	...	...	1 362 981	...	7 983	5 835 424
1 412 859	5 019	...	...	...	...	1 417 878	...	6 852	5 786 861
1 465 812	6 435	...	...	...	...	1 472 247	...	7 740	5 399 721
1 423 795	5 331	...	...	...	...	1 429 126	...	7 461	5 133 928
1 415 411	5 466	...	...	...	...	1 420 877	...	6 094	4 748 679
1 424 722	5 803	...	...	...	...	1 430 525	...	5 420	4 415 007

Table 9-6. Estimated Renewable Energy Consumption: Residential, Commercial, and Industrial Sectors, 1949–2005

(Billion Btu.)

Year	Residential Sector Biomass Wood[3]	Geothermal[4]	Solar[5]	Total	Hydroelectric Power[6]	Commercial Sector[1] Biomass Wood[3]	Waste[7]	Total	Geothermal[4]	Total
2005[P]	420,000	15,900	58,923	494,823	819	70,175	45,673	115,848	13,600	130,267
2004	410,000 [R]	14,000 [R]	58,736 [R]	482,736 [R]	1,052	70,327 [R]	55,462 [R]	125,789 [R]	12,000 [R]	138,841 [R]
2003	400,000 [R]	13,000 [R]	58,151	471,151 [R]	740	71,435 [R]	47,480	118,915 [R]	11,000 [R]	130,655 [R]
2002	380,000 [R]	10,204	58,747	448,951 [R]	130	68,658 [R]	41,964	110,622 [R]	8,753	119,505 [R]
2001	370,000	9,450	59,846	439,296	687	66,788 [R]	39,222	106,010 [R]	8,270	114,967 [R]
2000	430,000 [R]	8,600	61,355	499,955 [R]	1,018	71,469 [R]	47,256	118,725 [R]	7,600	127,343 [R]
1999	400,000 [R]	8,500	63,730	472,230 [R]	1,173	66,621 [R]	53,916	120,537 [R]	6,700	128,410 [R]
1998	380,000 [R]	7,700	64,663	452,363 [R]	1,228	64,014 [R]	54,162	118,176 [R]	7,100	126,504 [R]
1997	440,000 [R]	7,500	65,016	512,516 [R]	1,228	73,386 [R]	57,607	130,993 [R]	5,700	137,921 [R]
1996	540,000 [R]	7,000	65,444	612,444 [R]	1,300	75,668 [R]	53,028	128,696 [R]	5,300	135,296 [R]
1995	520,000 [R]	6,600	64,734	591,334 [R]	1,220	72,379 [R]	40,198	112,577 [R]	4,500	118,297 [R]
1994	520,000 [R]	6,200	63,528	589,728 [R]	957	71,715 [R]	34,522	106,237 [R]	4,200	111,394 [R]
1993	550,000 [R]	6,800	61,691	618,491 [R]	1,028	75,597 [R]	33,392	108,989 [R]	3,400	113,417 [R]
1992	640,000 [R]	6,400	59,753	706,153 [R]	1,266	72,027 [R]	32,452	104,479 [R]	3,200	108,945 [R]
1991	610,000 [R]	5,900	57,765	673,665 [R]	1,369	68,440 [R]	26,485	94,925 [R]	3,000	99,294 [R]
1990	580,000 [R]	5,500	55,900	641,400 [R]	1,432	65,738 [R]	27,765	93,503 [R]	2,800	97,735 [R]
1989	920,000 [R]	5,000	52,677	977,677 [R]	685	76,485 [R]	21,995	98,480 [R]	2,500	101,665 [R]
1988	910,000 [R]	...	...	910,000 [R]	...	32,000	...	32,000	...	32,000
1987	850,000 [R]	...	...	850,000 [R]	...	29,000	...	29,000	...	29,000
1986	920,000 [R]	...	...	920,000 [R]	...	27,000	...	27,000	...	27,000
1985	1,010,000 [R]	...	...	1,010,000 [R]	...	24,000	...	24,000	...	24,000
1984	980,000 [R]	...	...	980,000 [R]	...	22,000	...	22,000	...	22,000
1983	970,000 [R]	...	...	970,000 [R]	...	22,000	...	22,000	...	22,000
1982	970,000 [R]	...	...	970,000 [R]	...	22,000	...	22,000	...	22,000
1981	870,000 [R]	...	...	870,000 [R]	...	21,000	...	21,000	...	21,000
1980	850,000 [R]	...	...	850,000 [R]	...	21,000	...	21,000	...	21,000
1979	728,076	...	...	728,076	...	13,812	...	13,812	...	13,812
1978	621,849	...	...	621,849	...	11,834	...	11,834	...	11,834
1977	541,783	...	...	541,783	...	10,286	...	10,286	...	10,286
1976	481,634	...	...	481,634	...	9,099	...	9,099	...	9,099
1975	425,408	...	...	425,408	...	8,067	...	8,067	...	8,067
1974	370,952	...	...	370,952	...	7,018	...	7,018	...	7,018
1973	354,096	...	...	354,096	...	6,708	...	6,708	...	6,708
1972	379,776	...	...	379,776	...	7,190	...	7,190	...	7,190
1971	381,874	...	...	381,874	...	7,190	...	7,190	...	7,190
1970	400,777	...	...	400,777	...	7,534	...	7,534	...	7,534
1969	415,053	...	...	415,053	...	7,860	...	7,860	...	7,860
1968	425,511	...	...	425,511	...	8,136	...	8,136	...	8,136
1967	433,973	...	...	433,973	...	8,325	...	8,325	...	8,325
1966	454,974	...	...	454,974	...	8,617	...	8,617	...	8,617
1965	468,150	...	...	468,150	...	8,858	...	8,858	...	8,858
1964	499,058	...	...	499,058	...	9,460	...	9,460	...	9,460
1963	536,967	...	...	536,967	...	10,165	...	10,165	...	10,165
1962	560,084	...	...	560,084	...	10,630	...	10,630	...	10,630
1961	586,864	...	...	586,864	...	11,146	...	11,146	...	11,146
1960	626,630	...	...	626,630	...	11,868	...	11,868	...	11,868
1959	646,926	...	...	646,926	...	12,298	...	12,298	...	12,298
1958	688,447	...	...	688,447	...	13,089	...	13,089	...	13,089
1957	701,812	...	...	701,812	...	13,330	...	13,330	...	13,330
1956	738,706	...	...	738,706	...	14,018	...	14,018	...	14,018
1955	775,066	...	...	775,066	...	14,706	...	14,706	...	14,706
1954	799,748	...	...	799,748	...	15,170	...	15,170	...	15,170
1953	831,947	...	...	831,947	...	15,738	...	15,738	...	15,738
1952	899,164	...	...	899,164	...	17,114	...	17,114	...	17,114
1951	958,212	...	...	958,212	...	18,198	...	18,198	...	18,198
1950	1,005,529	...	...	1,005,529	...	19,075	...	19,075	...	19,075
1949	1,055,186	...	...	1,055,186	...	19,986	...	19,986	...	19,986

Source: U.S. Department of Energy, Energy Information Administration. *Annual Energy Review 2005 Report No. DOE/EIA-0384 2005.*
Note: Totals may not equal sum of components due to independent rounding.
[1] Commercial sector, including commercial combined-heat-and-power (CHP) and commercial electricity-only plants.
[2] Industrial sector, including industrial combined-heat-and-power (CHP) and industrial electricity-only plants.
[3] Wood, black liquor, and other wood waste.
[4] Geothermal heat pump and direct use energy. Source: Oregon Institute of Technology, Geoheat Center.
[5] Solar thermal direct use energy and photovoltaic electricity generation. Includes a small amount of commercial sector use.
[6] Conventional hydroelectric power.
[7] Municipal solid waste, landfill gas, sludge waste, tires, agricultural byproducts, and other biomass. Beginning 1989, Energy Information Administration and Office of Coal, Nuclear, Electric, and Alternative Fuels estimates based on information presented in Government Advisory Associates' *Resource Recovery Yearbook* and information provided by the U.S. Environmental Protection Agency.
[8] Ethanol blended into motor gasoline.
P = Preliminary.
R = Revised.
. . . = Not available.

Table 9-6. Estimated Renewable Energy Consumption: Residential, Commercial, and Industrial Sectors, 1949–2005—*Continued*

(Billion Btu.)

Industrial Sector²						Transportation Sector
	Biomass					Biomass
Hydroelectric Power⁶	Wood³	Waste⁷	Total	Geothermal⁴	Total	Alcohol Fuels⁸
31,789	1,238,325	135,756	1,374,081	4,300	1,410,170	339,769
32,556 [R]	1,475,732 [R]	161,853 [R]	1,637,585 [R]	3,800 [R]	1,673,941 [R]	299,314 [R]
43,242	1,363,313	169,634	1,532,947	3,400 [R]	1,579,589 [R]	238,125 [R]
38,908	1,396,435	168,120	1,564,555	4,787	1,608,250	174,685 [R]
32,500	1,442,633	150,272	1,592,905	4,760	1,630,165	146,674
42,183	1,635,925	145,112	1,781,037	4,400	1,827,620	139,320
48,658	1,619,520	171,042	1,790,562	4,100	1,843,320	121,565
54,539	1,603,440	180,344	1,783,784	3,000	1,841,323	116,921
58,062	1,730,613	184,015	1,914,628	3,100	1,975,790	105,813
60,773	1,683,499 [R]	223,549	1,907,048 [R]	2,900	1,970,721	83,563
54,695	1,652,078	195,025	1,847,103	3,000	1,904,798	116,500
62,186	1,579,770	199,247	1,779,017	2,800	1,844,003	108,608
29,593	1,484,345 [R]	181,158	1,665,503 [R]	2,400	1,697,496 [R]	96,986
30,508	1,461,223	178,514	1,639,737	2,200	1,672,445	83,000
29,675	1,409,847	184,674	1,594,521	2,100	1,626,296	73,000
30,947	1,441,912	192,323	1,634,235	1,900	1,667,082	63,000
28,396	1,583,563	200,406	1,783,969	1,800	1,814,165	71,000
32,635	1,625,000	307,706	1,932,706	...	1,965,341	70,000
32,936	1,576,000	281,770	1,857,770	...	1,890,706	69,000
33,021	1,610,000	255,703	1,865,703	...	1,898,724	60,000
33,024	1,645,000	229,635	1,874,635	...	1,907,659	52,000
33,002	1,679,000	203,568	1,882,568	...	1,915,570	43,000
33,255	1,690,000	155,288	1,845,288	...	1,878,543	35,000
33,046	1,516,000	117,693	1,633,693	...	1,666,739	19,000
33,043	1,602,000	86,718	1,688,718	...	1,721,761	7,000
32,838	1,600,000	...	1,600,000	...	1,632,838	...
34,094	1,404,862	...	1,404,862	...	1,438,956	...
31,563	1,400,424	...	1,400,424	...	1,431,987	...
32,601	1,281,245	...	1,281,245	...	1,313,846	...
33,372	1,219,876	...	1,219,876	...	1,253,248	...
32,321	1,063,270	...	1,063,270	...	1,095,591	...
33,202	1,159,074	...	1,159,074	...	1,192,276	...
34,773	1,164,853	...	1,164,853	...	1,199,626	...
34,420	1,112,668	...	1,112,668	...	1,147,088	...
33,746	1,039,998	...	1,039,998	...	1,073,744	...
34,040	1,018,911	...	1,018,911	...	1,052,951	...
34,220	1,014,232	...	1,014,232	...	1,048,452	...
35,172	981,948	...	981,948	...	1,017,120	...
35,787	894,658	...	894,658	...	930,445	...
33,138	901,916	...	901,916	...	935,054	...
32,757	854,943	...	854,943	...	887,700	...
33,772	826,735	...	826,735	...	860,507	...
33,914	774,843	...	774,843	...	808,757	...
35,990	728,179	...	728,179	...	764,169	...
35,836	695,413	...	695,413	...	731,249	...
38,808	679,864	...	679,864	...	718,672	...
37,003	691,973	...	691,973	...	728,976	...
37,162	619,647	...	619,647	...	656,809	...
35,521	616,431	...	616,431	...	651,952	...
36,751	661,409	...	661,409	...	698,160	...
38,149	631,137	...	631,137	...	669,286	...
55,678	576,200	...	576,200	...	631,878	...
56,506	565,897	...	565,897	...	622,403	...
61,538	551,656	...	551,656	...	613,194	...
63,097	552,928	...	552,928	...	616,025	...
69,396	532,237	...	532,237	...	601,633	...
75,537	468,287	...	468,287	...	543,824	...

Table 9-7. Energy Supply and Disposition by Type of Fuel, 1645–2005

(In quadrillion British thermal units (Btu).)

	Production													
		Fossil fuels						Renewable energy[3]						
Year	Production, total[1]	Total	Crude oil[2]	Natural gas liquids	Natural gas	Coal	Nuclear electric power	Renewable energy[1], total	Hydro-electric power	Geothermal	Biofuels (wood & waste)[4]	Solar energy	Wind energy	Hydro-electric pumped storage[5]
2005[14]	69.17	54.97	10.84	2.32	18.76	23.05	8.13	6.06	2.71	0.35	2.78	0.06	0.15	...
2004	70.39	55.95	11.50	2.47	19.26	22.71	8.22	6.22	2.69	0.34	2.98	0.06	0.14	...
2003	70.14	56.03	12.03	2.35	19.69	21.97	7.96	6.14	2.82	0.33	2.81	0.06	0.11	−0.09
2002	70.86	56.78	12.16	2.56	19.44	22.62	8.14	5.93	2.69	0.33	2.75	0.06	0.11	−0.09
2001	71.91	58.52	12.28	2.55	20.20	23.49	8.03	5.35	2.24	0.31	2.67	0.07	0.07	−0.09
2000	71.29	57.25	12.36	2.61	19.66	22.62	7.86	6.17	2.81	0.32	2.92	0.07	0.06	−0.06
1999	71.71	57.51	12.45	2.53	19.34	23.19	7.61	6.60	3.27	0.33	2.89	0.07	0.05	−0.06
1998	72.84	59.20	13.24	2.42	19.61	23.94	7.07	6.57	3.30	0.33	2.84	0.07	0.03	(−Z)
1997	72.46	58.76	13.66	2.50	19.39	23.21	6.60	7.11	3.64	0.32	3.04	0.07	0.03	(−Z)
1996	72.47	58.28	13.72	2.53	19.34	22.68	7.09	7.11	3.59	0.32	3.10	0.07	0.03	(−Z)
1995	71.13	57.44	13.89	2.44	19.08	22.03	7.08	6.62	3.21	0.29	3.02	0.07	0.03	(−Z)
1994	70.72	57.95	14.10	2.39	19.35	22.11	6.69	6.07	2.68	0.34	2.95	0.07	0.04	(−Z)
1993	68.33	55.74	14.49	2.41	18.58	20.25	6.41	6.19	2.89	0.36	2.84	0.07	0.03	(−Z)
1992	70.00	57.59	15.22	2.36	18.38	21.63	6.48	5.93	2.62	0.35	2.87	0.06	0.03	(−Z)
1991	70.43	57.83	15.70	2.31	18.23	21.59	6.42	6.18	3.02	0.35	2.73	0.06	0.03	(−Z)
1990	70.79	58.53	15.57	2.17	18.33	22.46	6.10	6.16	3.05	0.34	2.69	0.06	0.03	(−Z)
1989[13]	69.41	57.47	16.12	2.16	17.85	21.35	5.60	6.34	2.84	0.32	3.10	0.06	0.02	...
1988	68.98	57.87	17.28	2.26	17.60	20.74	5.59	5.51	2.33	0.22	2.96	0.00	0.00	...
1987	67.61	57.17	17.67	2.22	17.14	20.14	4.75	5.68	2.63	0.23	2.82	0.00	0.00	...
1986	67.13	56.58	18.38	2.15	16.54	19.51	4.38	6.18	3.07	0.22	2.88	0.00	0.00	...
1985	67.76	57.54	18.99	2.24	16.98	19.33	4.08	6.14	2.97	0.20	2.98	0.00	0.00	...
1984	68.89	58.85	18.85	2.27	18.01	19.72	3.55	6.49	3.39	0.16	2.94	0.00	0.00	...
1983	64.15	54.42	18.39	2.18	16.59	17.25	3.20	6.53	3.53	0.13	2.88	...	0.00	...
1982	66.61	57.46	18.31	2.19	18.32	18.64	3.13	6.02	3.27	0.10	2.65	...	...	...
1981	67.01	58.53	18.15	2.31	19.70	18.38	3.01	5.47	2.76	0.12	2.59	...	...	...
1980	67.23	59.01	18.25	2.25	19.91	18.60	2.74	5.49	2.90	0.11	2.48	...	...	...
1979	65.95	58.01	18.10	2.29	20.08	17.54	2.78	5.17	2.93	0.08	2.15	...	...	...
1978	63.14	55.07	18.43	2.25	19.49	14.91	3.02	5.04	2.94	0.06	2.04	...	...	...
1977	62.05	55.10	17.45	2.33	19.57	15.75	2.70	4.25	2.33	0.08	1.84	...	...	...
1976	61.60	54.72	17.26	2.33	19.48	15.65	2.11	4.77	2.98	0.08	1.71	...	...	...
1975	61.36	54.73	17.73	2.37	19.64	14.99	1.90	4.72	3.15	0.07	1.50	...	...	...
1974	62.37	56.33	18.57	2.47	21.21	14.07	1.27	4.77	3.18	0.05	1.54	...	...	...
1973	63.58	58.24	19.49	2.57	22.19	13.99	0.91	4.43	2.86	0.04	1.53	...	...	...
1972	63.92	58.94	20.04	2.60	22.21	14.09	0.58	4.40	2.86	0.03	1.50	...	...	...
1971	62.72	58.04	20.03	2.54	22.28	13.19	0.41	4.27	2.82	0.01	1.43	...	...	...
1970	63.50	59.19	20.40	2.51	21.67	14.61	0.24	4.08	2.63	0.01	1.43	...	...	...
1969	60.54	56.29	19.56	2.42	20.45	13.86	0.15	4.10	2.65	0.01	1.44	...	...	...
1968	58.23	54.31	19.31	2.32	19.07	13.61	0.14	3.78	2.35	0.01	1.42	...	...	...
1967	56.38	52.60	18.65	2.18	17.94	13.83	0.09	3.69	2.35	0.01	1.34	...	...	...
1966	53.53	50.04	17.56	2.00	17.01	13.47	0.06	3.43	2.06	0.00	1.37	...	...	...
1965	50.68	47.23	16.52	1.88	15.78	13.06	0.04	3.40	2.06	0.00	1.33	...	...	...
1964	49.06	45.79	16.16	1.80	15.30	12.52	0.04	3.23	1.89	0.00	1.34	...	...	...
1963	47.17	44.04	15.97	1.71	14.51	11.85	0.04	3.10	1.77	0.00	1.32	...	...	...
1962	44.88	41.73	15.52	1.59	13.72	10.90	0.03	3.12	1.82	0.00	1.30	...	...	...
1961	43.28	40.31	15.21	1.55	13.10	10.45	0.02	2.95	1.66	0.00	1.29	...	...	...
1960	42.80	39.87	14.93	1.46	12.66	10.82	0.01	2.93	1.61	0.00	1.32	...	...	...
1959	41.95	39.05	14.93	1.38	11.95	10.78	0.00	2.90	1.55	..	1.35	...	...	...
1958	40.13	37.22	14.20	1.29	10.94	10.78	0.00	2.92	1.59	...	1.32	...	...	...
1957	42.98	40.13	15.18	1.29	10.61	13.06	0.00	2.85	1.52	...	1.33	...	...	...
1956	42.62	39.77	15.18	1.28	10.00	13.31	0.00	2.85	1.43	...	1.42	...	...	...
1955	40.15	37.36	14.41	1.24	9.34	12.37	0.00	2.78	1.36	...	1.42	...	...	...
1954	36.52	33.76	13.43	1.11	8.68	10.54	0.00	2.75	1.36	...	1.39	...	...	...
1953	38.18	35.35	13.67	1.06	8.34	12.28	0.00	2.83	1.41	...	1.42	...	...	...
1952	37.92	34.98	13.28	1.00	7.96	12.73	0.00	2.94	1.47	...	1.47	...	...	...
1951	38.75	35.79	13.04	0.92	7.42	14.42	0.00	2.96	1.42	...	1.53	...	...	...
1950	35.54	32.56	11.45	0.82	6.23	14.06	0.00	2.98	1.42	...	1.56	...	...	...
1949	31.72	28.75	10.68	0.71	5.38	11.97	0.00	2.97	1.42	...	1.55	...	...	...
1948	...	...	...	...	...	...	...	...	...	...	...	...	...	...
1947	...	...	...	...	...	...	...	...	...	...	...	...	...	...
1946	...	...	...	...	...	...	...	...	...	...	...	...	...	...
1945[13]	...	...	...	...	...	...	...	...	...	...	...	...	...	...
1940	...	...	...	...	...	...	...	...	...	...	...	...	...	...
1935	...	...	...	...	...	...	...	...	...	...	...	...	...	...
1930	...	...	...	...	...	...	...	...	...	...	...	...	...	...
1925	...	...	...	...	...	...	...	...	...	...	...	...	...	...
1920	...	...	...	...	...	...	...	...	...	...	...	...	...	...

[1]Includes types of fuel not shown separately.
[2]Includes lease condensate.
[3]Electricity net generation from conventional hydroelectric power, geothermal, solar, and wind; consumption of wood, waste, and alcohol fuels; geothermal heat pump and direct use energy; and solar thermal direct use energy.
[4]Prior to 1945, wood only. Thereafter, wood, waste, and alcohol (ethanol blended into motor gasoline).
[5]Pumped storage facility production minus energy used for pumping.
[13]There are discontinuities in this time series between data prior to 1949 and subsequent years and between 1989 and 1990.
[14]Preliminary.
. . . = Not available.
Z Less than 5 trillion.

Table 9-7. Energy Supply and Disposition by Type of Fuel, 1645–2005—*Continued*

(In quadrillion British thermal units (Btu).)

Year	Production, total[1]	Fossil fuels					Nuclear electric power	Renewable energy[3]						
		Total	Crude oil[2]	Natural gas liquids	Natural gas	Coal		Renewable energy[1], total	Hydro-electric power	Geothermal	Biofuels (wood & waste)[4]	Solar energy	Wind energy	Hydro-electric pumped storage[5]
1915	...	...	...	...	...	...	...	...	...	...	...	...	...	...
1910	...	...	...	...	...	...	...	...	...	...	...	...	...	...
1905	...	...	...	...	...	...	...	...	...	...	...	...	...	...
1900	...	...	...	...	...	...	...	...	...	...	...	...	...	...
1895	...	...	...	...	...	...	...	...	...	...	...	...	...	...
1890	...	...	...	...	...	...	...	...	...	...	...	...	...	...
1885	...	...	...	...	...	...	...	...	...	...	...	...	...	...
1880	...	...	...	...	...	...	...	...	...	...	...	...	...	...
1875	...	...	...	...	...	...	...	...	...	...	...	...	...	...
1870	...	...	...	...	...	...	...	...	...	...	...	...	...	...
1865	...	...	...	...	...	...	...	...	...	...	...	...	...	...
1860	...	...	...	...	...	...	...	...	...	...	...	...	...	...
1855	...	...	...	...	...	...	...	...	...	...	...	...	...	...
1850	...	...	...	...	...	...	...	...	...	...	...	...	...	...
1845	...	...	...	...	...	...	...	...	...	...	...	...	...	...
1835	...	...	...	...	...	...	...	...	...	...	...	...	...	...
1825	...	...	...	...	...	...	...	...	...	...	...	...	...	...
1815	...	...	...	...	...	...	...	...	...	...	...	...	...	...
1805	...	...	...	...	...	...	...	...	...	...	...	...	...	...
1795	...	...	...	...	...	...	...	...	...	...	...	...	...	...
1785	...	...	...	...	...	...	...	...	...	...	...	...	...	...
1775	...	...	...	...	...	...	...	...	...	...	...	...	...	...
1765	...	...	...	...	...	...	...	...	...	...	...	...	...	...
1755	...	...	...	...	...	...	...	...	...	...	...	...	...	...
1745	...	...	...	...	...	...	...	...	...	...	...	...	...	...
1735	...	...	...	...	...	...	...	...	...	...	...	...	...	...
1725	...	...	...	...	...	...	...	...	...	...	...	...	...	...
1715	...	...	...	...	...	...	...	...	...	...	...	...	...	...
1705	...	...	...	...	...	...	...	...	...	...	...	...	...	...
1695	...	...	...	...	...	...	...	...	...	...	...	...	...	...
1685	...	...	...	...	...	...	...	...	...	...	...	...	...	...
1675	...	...	...	...	...	...	...	...	...	...	...	...	...	...
1665	...	...	...	...	...	...	...	...	...	...	...	...	...	...
1655	...	...	...	...	...	...	...	...	...	...	...	...	...	...
1645	...	...	...	...	...	...	...	...	...	...	...	...	...	...

[1]Includes types of fuel not shown separately.
[2]Includes lease condensate.
[3]Electricity net generation from conventional hydroelectric power, geothermal, solar, and wind; consumption of wood, waste, and alcohol fuels; geothermal heat pump and direct use energy; and solar thermal direct use energy.
[4]Prior to 1945, wood only. Thereafter, wood, waste, and alcohol (ethanol blended into motor gasoline).
[5]Pumped storage facility production minus energy used for pumping.
... = Not available.

Table 9-7. Energy Supply and Disposition by Type of Fuel, 1645–2005—*Continued*

(In quadrillion British thermal units (Btu).)

Year	Net imports, total[6]	Net trade								Adjustments
		Exports				Imports				
		Total	Coal	Natural gas	Petroleum (Crude oil)	Total	Coal	Natural gas	Petroleum (Crude oil)[7]	
2005[14]	29.62	4.64	1.27	0.79	0.09	34.26	0.76	4.39	21.94	1.11
2004	29.11	4.43	1.25	0.86	0.06	33.54	0.68	4.37	22.08	0.92
2003	27.01	4.05	1.12	0.69	0.03	31.06	0.63	4.04	21.06	1.13
2002	25.74	3.67	1.03	0.52	0.02	29.41	0.42	4.10	19.92	1.37
2001	26.39	3.77	1.27	0.38	0.04	30.16	0.49	4.07	20.35	−1.80
2000	24.97	4.01	1.53	0.25	0.11	28.97	0.31	3.87	19.78	2.72
1999	23.54	3.71	1.53	0.16	0.25	27.25	0.23	3.66	18.94	1.58
1998	22.28	4.30	2.09	0.16	0.23	26.58	0.22	3.22	18.92	0.08
1997	20.70	4.51	2.19	0.16	0.23	25.22	0.19	3.06	17.88	1.64
1996	19.07	4.63	2.37	0.16	0.23	23.70	0.20	3.00	16.34	2.68
1995	17.75	4.51	2.32	0.16	0.20	22.26	0.24	2.90	15.67	2.32
1994	18.33	4.06	1.88	0.16	0.21	22.39	0.22	2.68	15.34	0.24
1993	17.01	4.26	1.96	0.14	0.21	21.27	0.20	2.40	14.75	2.30
1992	14.44	4.94	2.68	0.22	0.19	19.37	0.10	2.16	13.25	1.58
1991	13.19	5.14	2.85	0.13	0.25	18.33	0.08	1.80	12.55	1.04
1990	14.06	4.75	2.77	0.09	0.23	18.82	0.07	1.55	12.77	−0.13
1989[13]	14.11	4.66	2.64	0.11	0.30	18.77	0.07	1.39	12.60	1.49
1988	12.93	4.37	2.50	0.07	0.33	17.30	0.05	1.30	11.03	0.96
1987	11.59	3.81	2.09	0.05	0.32	15.40	0.04	0.99	10.07	0.03
1986	10.13	4.02	2.25	0.06	0.33	14.15	0.06	0.75	9.00	−0.44
1985	7.58	4.20	2.44	0.06	0.43	11.78	0.05	0.95	6.81	1.24
1984	8.68	3.79	2.15	0.06	0.38	12.47	0.03	0.85	7.30	−0.78
1983	8.06	3.69	2.04	0.06	0.35	11.75	0.03	0.94	7.08	0.94
1982	7.25	4.61	2.79	0.05	0.50	11.86	0.02	0.95	7.42	−0.57
1981	9.41	4.31	2.94	0.06	0.48	13.72	0.03	0.92	9.34	−0.08
1980	12.10	3.69	2.42	0.05	0.61	15.80	0.03	1.01	11.19	−1.05
1979	16.60	2.86	1.75	0.06	0.50	19.46	0.05	1.30	13.83	−1.65
1978	17.19	1.92	1.08	0.05	0.33	19.11	0.07	0.99	13.46	−0.34
1977	17.90	2.05	1.44	0.06	0.11	19.95	0.04	1.04	14.03	−1.95
1976	14.59	2.17	1.60	0.07	0.02	16.76	0.03	0.99	11.24	−0.18
1975	11.71	2.32	1.76	0.07	0.01	14.03	0.02	0.98	8.72	−1.07
1974	12.10	2.20	1.62	0.08	0.01	14.30	0.05	0.99	7.40	−0.48
1973	12.58	2.03	1.43	0.08	0.00	14.61	0.00	1.06	6.89	−0.46
1972	9.27	2.12	1.53	0.08	0.00	11.39	0.00	1.05	4.71	−0.48
1971	7.38	2.15	1.55	0.08	0.00	9.53	0.00	0.96	3.57	−0.82
1970	5.71	2.63	1.94	0.07	0.03	8.34	0.00	0.85	2.81	−1.37
1969	5.55	2.13	1.53	0.05	0.01	7.68	0.00	0.75	2.99	−0.47
1968	4.91	2.00	1.38	0.10	0.01	6.91	0.01	0.67	2.76	−0.71
1967	4.04	2.12	1.35	0.08	0.15	6.16	0.01	0.58	2.40	−1.52
1966	4.32	1.83	1.35	0.03	0.01	6.15	0.00	0.50	2.62	−0.83
1965	4.06	1.83	1.38	0.03	0.01	5.89	0.00	0.47	2.65	−0.72
1964	3.63	1.81	1.34	0.02	0.01	5.45	0.01	0.46	2.58	−0.87
1963	3.25	1.84	1.36	0.02	0.01	5.09	0.01	0.42	2.43	−0.78
1962	3.52	1.47	1.08	0.02	0.01	4.99	0.01	0.42	2.42	−0.57
1961	3.06	1.38	0.98	0.01	0.02	4.44	0.00	0.23	2.25	−0.60
1960	2.71	1.48	1.02	0.01	0.02	4.19	0.01	0.16	2.20	−0.43
1959	2.54	1.53	1.05	0.02	0.01	4.08	0.01	0.14	2.08	−1.03
1958	1.83	2.05	1.42	0.04	0.03	3.88	0.01	0.14	2.06	−0.32
1957	0.09	3.44	2.17	0.04	0.29	3.53	0.01	0.04	2.21	−1.29
1956	0.26	2.95	1.98	0.04	0.17	3.21	0.01	0.01	2.02	−1.13
1955	0.50	2.29	1.46	0.03	0.07	2.79	0.01	0.01	1.69	−0.44
1954	0.65	1.70	0.91	0.03	0.08	2.35	0.01	0.01	1.42	−0.53
1953	0.45	1.87	0.98	0.03	0.12	2.31	0.01	0.01	1.40	−0.96
1952	−0.22	2.37	1.40	0.03	0.15	2.15	0.01	0.01	1.24	−0.95
1951	−0.73	2.62	1.68	0.03	0.17	1.89	0.01	0.00	1.06	−1.05
1950	0.45	1.47	0.79	0.03	0.20	1.91	0.01	0.00	1.06	−1.37
1949	−0.14	1.59	0.88	0.02	0.19	1.45	0.01	0.00	0.91	0.40
1948	...	...	...	...	...	...	...	...	...	...
1947	...	...	...	...	...	...	...	...	...	...
1946	...	...	...	...	...	...	...	...	...	...
1945[13]	...	...	...	...	...	...	...	...	...	...
1940	...	...	...	...	...	...	...	...	...	...
1935	...	...	...	...	...	...	...	...	...	...
1930	...	...	...	...	...	...	...	...	...	...
1925	...	...	...	...	...	...	...	...	...	...
1920	...	...	...	...	...	...	...	...	...	...
1915	...	...	...	...	...	...	...	...	...	...
1910	...	...	...	...	...	...	...	...	...	...
1905	...	...	...	...	...	...	...	...	...	...
1900	...	...	...	...	...	...	...	...	...	...
1895	...	...	...	...	...	...	...	...	...	...
1890	...	...	...	...	...	...	...	...	...	...

[6]Imports minus exports.
[7]Includes imports into the Strategic Petroleum Reserve, which began in 1977.
[13]There are discontinuities in this time series between data prior to 1949 and subsequent years and between 1989 and 1990.
[14]Preliminary.
... = Not available.

Table 9-7. **Energy Supply and Disposition by Type of Fuel, 1645–2005—*Continued***

(In quadrillion British thermal units (Btu).)

Year	Net imports, total[6]	Net trade								Adjustments
		Exports				Imports				
		Total	Coal	Natural gas	Petroleum (Crude oil)	Total	Coal	Natural gas	Petroleum (Crude oil)[7]	
1885	...	...	...	...	...	...	...	...	...	...
1880	...	...	...	...	...	...	...	...	...	...
1875	...	...	...	...	...	...	...	...	...	...
1870	...	...	...	...	...	...	...	...	...	...
1865	...	...	...	...	...	...	...	...	...	...
1860	...	...	...	...	...	...	...	...	...	...
1855	...	...	...	...	...	...	...	...	...	...
1850	...	...	...	...	...	...	...	...	...	...
1845	...	...	...	...	...	...	...	...	...	...
1835	...	...	...	...	...	...	...	...	...	...
1825	...	...	...	...	...	...	...	...	...	...
1815	...	...	...	...	...	...	...	...	...	...
1805	...	...	...	...	...	...	...	...	...	...
1795	...	...	...	...	...	...	...	...	...	...
1785	...	...	...	...	...	...	...	...	...	...
1775	...	...	...	...	...	...	...	...	...	...
1765	...	...	...	...	...	...	...	...	...	...
1755	...	...	...	...	...	...	...	...	...	...
1745	...	...	...	...	...	...	...	...	...	...
1735	...	...	...	...	...	...	...	...	...	...
1725	...	...	...	...	...	...	...	...	...	...
1715	...	...	...	...	...	...	...	...	...	...
1705	...	...	...	...	...	...	...	...	...	...
1695	...	...	...	...	...	...	...	...	...	...
1685	...	...	...	...	...	...	...	...	...	...
1675	...	...	...	...	...	...	...	...	...	...
1665	...	...	...	...	...	...	...	...	...	...
1655	...	...	...	...	...	...	...	...	...	...
1645	...	...	...	...	...	...	...	...	...	...

[6]Imports minus exports.
[7]Includes imports into the Strategic Petroleum Reserve, which began in 1977.
. . . = Not available.

Table 9-7. Energy Supply and Disposition by Type of Fuel, 1645–2005—*Continued*

(In quadrillion British thermal units (Btu).)

		Consumption												
		Fossil fuels						Renewable energy[3]						
Year	Con-sumption, total[7]	Total	Petro-leum[8,9]	Coal Coke net imports	Natural gas[10]	Coal	Nuclear electric power	Renewable energy[3], total	Hydro-electric power[11]	Geo-thermal[12]	Biofuels (wood & waste)[4]	Solar energy	Wind energy	Hydro-electric pumped storage[5]
2005[14]	99.89	85.96	40.44	0.04	22.64	22.83	8.13	6.06	2.71	0.35	2.78	0.06	0.15	...
2004	100.41	86.23	40.59	0.14	23.04	22.47	8.22	6.22	2.69	0.34	2.98	0.06	0.14	...
2003	98.27	84.39	39.05	0.05	22.97	22.32	7.96	6.14	2.82	0.33	2.81	0.06	0.11	−0.09
2002	97.97	83.99	38.40	0.06	23.63	21.90	8.14	5.93	2.69	0.33	2.75	0.06	0.11	−0.09
2001	96.50	83.18	38.33	0.03	22.91	21.91	8.03	5.35	2.24	0.31	2.67	0.07	0.07	−0.09
2000	98.98	84.96	38.40	0.07	23.92	22.58	7.86	6.17	2.81	0.32	2.92	0.07	0.06	−0.06
1999	96.84	82.65	37.96	0.06	23.01	21.62	7.61	6.60	3.27	0.33	2.89	0.07	0.05	−0.06
1998	95.20	81.59	36.93	0.07	22.94	21.66	7.07	6.57	3.30	0.33	2.84	0.07	0.03	(−Z)
1997	94.80	81.09	36.27	0.05	23.33	21.45	6.60	7.11	3.64	0.32	3.04	0.07	0.03	(−Z)
1996	94.23	79.98	35.76	0.02	23.20	21.00	7.09	7.11	3.59	0.32	3.10	0.07	0.03	(−Z)
1995	91.20	77.49	34.55	0.06	22.78	20.09	7.08	6.62	3.21	0.29	3.02	0.07	0.03	(−Z)
1994	89.29	76.48	34.67	0.06	21.84	19.91	6.69	6.07	2.68	0.34	2.95	0.07	0.04	(−Z)
1993	87.65	75.05	33.84	0.03	21.35	19.84	6.41	6.19	2.89	0.36	2.84	0.07	0.03	(−Z)
1992	86.01	73.52	33.53	0.03	20.84	19.12	6.48	5.93	2.62	0.35	2.87	0.06	0.03	(−Z)
1991	84.67	72.00	32.85	0.01	20.15	18.99	6.42	6.18	3.02	0.35	2.73	0.06	0.03	(−Z)
1990	84.73	72.46	33.55	0.00	19.73	19.17	6.10	6.16	3.05	0.34	2.69	0.06	0.03	(−Z)
1989[13]	85.00	73.02	34.21	0.03	19.71	19.07	5.60	6.34	2.84	0.32	3.10	0.06	0.02	(13)
1988	82.87	71.66	34.22	0.04	18.55	18.85	5.59	5.51	2.33	0.22	2.96	0.00	0.00	(13)
1987	79.22	68.63	32.87	0.01	17.74	18.01	4.75	5.68	2.63	0.23	2.82	0.00	0.00	(13)
1986	76.83	66.15	32.20	−0.02	16.71	17.26	4.38	6.18	3.07	0.22	2.88	0.00	0.00	(13)
1985	76.58	66.22	30.92	−0.01	17.83	17.48	4.08	6.14	2.97	0.20	2.98	0.00	0.00	(13)
1984	76.79	66.62	31.05	−0.01	18.51	17.07	3.55	6.49	3.39	0.16	2.94	0.00	0.00	(13)
1983	73.15	63.29	30.05	−0.02	17.36	15.89	3.20	6.53	3.53	0.13	2.88	...	0.00	(13)
1982	73.29	64.04	30.23	−0.02	18.51	15.32	3.13	6.02	3.27	0.10	2.65	...	...	(13)
1981	76.34	67.75	31.93	−0.02	19.93	15.91	3.01	5.47	2.76	0.12	2.59	...	...	(13)
1980	78.28	69.98	34.20	−0.04	20.39	15.42	2.74	5.49	2.90	0.11	2.48	...	...	(13)
1979	80.90	72.89	37.12	0.06	20.67	15.04	2.78	5.17	2.93	0.08	2.15	...	...	(13)
1978	79.99	71.86	37.97	0.12	20.00	13.77	3.02	5.04	2.94	0.06	2.04	...	...	(13)
1977	78.00	70.99	37.12	0.01	19.93	13.92	2.70	4.25	2.33	0.08	1.84	...	...	(13)
1976	76.01	69.10	35.17	−0.00	20.35	13.58	2.11	4.77	2.98	0.08	1.71	...	...	(13)
1975	72.00	65.35	32.73	0.01	19.95	12.66	1.90	4.72	3.15	0.07	1.50	...	...	(13)
1974	73.99	67.91	33.45	0.06	21.73	12.66	1.27	4.77	3.18	0.05	1.54	...	...	(13)
1973	75.71	70.32	34.84	−0.01	22.51	12.97	0.91	4.43	2.86	0.04	1.53	...	...	(13)
1972	72.70	67.70	32.95	−0.03	22.70	12.08	0.58	4.40	2.86	0.03	1.50	...	...	(13)
1971	69.29	64.60	30.56	−0.03	22.47	11.60	0.41	4.27	2.82	0.01	1.43	...	...	(13)
1970	67.84	63.52	29.52	−0.06	21.79	12.26	0.24	4.08	2.63	0.01	1.43	...	...	(13)
1969	65.62	61.36	28.34	−0.04	20.68	12.38	0.15	4.10	2.65	0.01	1.44	...	...	(13)
1968	62.42	58.50	26.98	−0.02	19.21	12.33	0.14	3.78	2.35	0.01	1.42	...	...	(13)
1967	58.91	55.13	25.28	−0.02	17.94	11.91	0.09	3.69	2.35	0.01	1.34	...	...	(13)
1966	57.02	53.51	24.40	−0.02	17.00	12.14	0.06	3.43	2.06	0.00	1.37	...	...	(13)
1965	54.02	50.58	23.25	−0.02	15.77	11.58	0.04	3.40	2.06	0.00	1.33	...	...	(13)
1964	51.82	48.54	22.30	−0.01	15.29	10.96	0.04	3.23	1.89	0.00	1.34	...	...	(13)
1963	49.65	46.51	21.70	−0.01	14.40	10.41	0.04	3.10	1.77	0.00	1.32	...	...	(13)
1962	47.83	44.68	21.05	−0.01	13.73	9.91	0.03	3.12	1.82	0.00	1.30	...	...	(13)
1961	45.74	42.76	20.22	−0.01	12.93	9.62	0.02	2.95	1.66	0.00	1.29	...	...	(13)
1960	45.09	42.14	19.92	−0.01	12.39	9.84	0.01	2.93	1.61	0.00	1.32	...	...	(13)
1959	43.47	40.55	19.32	−0.01	11.72	9.52	0.00	2.90	1.55	...	1.35	...	...	(13)
1958	41.65	38.72	18.53	−0.01	10.66	9.53	0.00	2.92	1.59	...	1.32	...	...	(13)
1957	41.79	38.93	17.93	−0.02	10.19	10.82	0.00	2.85	1.52	...	1.33	...	...	(13)
1956	41.75	38.89	17.94	−0.01	9.61	11.35	0.00	2.85	1.43	...	1.42	...	...	(13)
1955	40.21	37.41	17.25	−0.01	9.00	11.17	0.00	2.78	1.36	...	1.42	...	...	(13)
1954	36.64	33.88	15.84	−0.01	8.33	9.71	0.00	2.75	1.36	...	1.39	...	...	(13)
1953	37.66	34.83	15.56	−0.01	7.91	11.37	0.00	2.83	1.41	...	1.42	...	...	(13)
1952	36.75	33.80	14.96	−0.01	7.55	11.31	0.00	2.94	1.47	...	1.47	...	...	(13)
1951	36.97	34.01	14.43	−0.02	7.05	12.55	0.00	2.96	1.42	...	1.53	...	...	(13)
1950	34.62	31.63	13.32	0.00	5.97	12.35	0.00	2.98	1.42	...	1.56	...	...	(13)
1949	31.98	29.00	11.88	−0.01	5.15	11.98	0.00	2.97	1.42	...	1.55	...	...	(13)
1948	...	...	...	...	...	...	...	...	...	...	...	...	0.03	...
1947	...	...	...	...	...	...	...	...	...	...	...	...	0.03	...
1946	...	...	...	...	...	...	...	...	...	...	...	...	0.03	...
1945[13]	32.67	29.95	10.11	...	3.87	15.97	...	2.70	1.44	...	1.26	...	0.02	...

[3]Electricity net generation from conventional hydroelectric power, geothermal, solar, and wind; consumption of wood, waste, and alcohol fuels; geothermal heat pump and direct use energy; and solar thermal direct use energy.
[4]Prior to 1945, wood only. Thereafter, wood, waste, and alcohol (ethanol blended into motor gasoline).
[5]Pumped storage facility production minus energy used for pumping.
[7]Includes imports into the Strategic Petroleum Reserve, which began in 1977.
[8]Beginning in 1993, ethanol blended into motor gasoline is included in petroleum.
[9]Petroleum products supplied, including natural gas plant liquids and crude oil burned as fuel.
[10]Includes supplemental gaseous fuels.
[11]Through 1988, includes all electricity net imports. From 1989, includes only electricity net imports derived from hydroelectric power.
[12]From 1989, includes electricity imports from Mexico that are derived from geothermal energy.
[13]There are discontinuities in this time series between data prior to 1949 and subsequent years and between 1989 and 1990.
[14]Preliminary.
... = Not available.
Z Less than 5 trillion.

Table 9-7. Energy Supply and Disposition by Type of Fuel, 1645–2005—*Continued*

(In quadrillion British thermal units (Btu).)

| | | Consumption | | | | | | | | | | | |
| | | Fossil fuels | | | | | Nuclear electric power | Renewable energy[3] | | | | | | Hydro-electric pumped storage[5] |
Year	Con-sumption, total[7]	Total	Petro-leum[8,9]	Coal Coke net imports	Natural gas[10]	Coal	Nuclear electric power	Renewable energy[3], total	Hydro-electric power[11]	Geo-thermal[12]	Biofuels (wood & waste)[4]	Solar energy	Wind energy	Hydro-electric pumped storage[5]
1940	25.21	22.96	7.76	...	2.67	12.54	...	2.24	0.88	...	1.36	...	0.00	...
1935	20.44	18.23	5.68	...	1.92	10.63	...	2.20	0.81	...	1.40	...	0.00	...
1930	23.68	21.47	5.90	...	1.93	13.64	...	2.21	0.75	...	1.46	...	0.00	...
1925	22.38	20.18	4.28	...	1.19	14.71	...	2.20	0.67	...	1.53	...	0.00	...
1920	21.34	18.99	2.68	...	0.81	15.50	...	2.35	0.74	...	1.61	...	0.00	...
1915	17.73	15.39	1.42	...	0.67	13.29	...	2.35	0.66	...	1.69	...	0.00	...
1910	16.57	14.26	1.01	...	0.54	12.71	...	2.30	0.54	...	1.77	...	...	...
1905	13.21	10.98	0.61	...	0.37	10.00	...	2.23	0.39	...	1.84	...	...	...
1900	9.59	7.32	0.23	...	0.25	6.84	...	2.27	0.25	...	2.02	...	...	...
1895	7.66	5.27	0.17	...	0.15	4.95	...	2.40	0.09	...	2.31	...	...	...
1890	7.01	4.48	0.16	...	0.26	4.06	...	2.54	0.02	...	2.52	...	...	...
1885	5.65	2.96	0.04	...	0.08	2.84	...	2.68	0.00	...	2.68	...	...	...
1880	5.00	2.15	0.10	...	0.00	2.05	...	2.85	0.00	...	2.85	...	...	...
1875	4.32	1.45	0.01	...	0.00	1.44	...	2.87	0.00	...	2.87	...	...	...
1870	3.95	1.06	0.01	...	0.00	1.05	...	2.89	0.00	...	2.89	...	...	...
1865	3.41	0.64	0.01	...	0.00	0.63	...	2.77	0.00	...	2.77	...	...	...
1860	3.16	0.52	(Z)	...	0.00	0.52	...	2.64	0.00	...	2.64	...	...	...
1855	2.81	0.42	0.00	...	0.00	0.42	...	2.39	0.00	...	2.39	...	...	...
1850	2.36	0.22	0.00	...	0.00	0.22	...	2.14	0.00	...	2.14	...	...	...
1845	1.76	0.00	0.00	...	0.00	...	...	1.76	0.00	...	1.76	...	...	...
1835	1.31	0.00	0.00	...	0.00	...	...	1.31	0.00	...	1.31	...	...	...
1825	0.96	0.00	0.00	...	0.00	...	...	0.96	0.00	...	0.96	...	...	...
1815	0.71	0.00	0.00	...	0.00	...	...	0.71	0.00	...	0.71	...	...	...
1805	0.54	0.00	0.00	...	0.00	...	...	0.54	0.00	...	0.54	...	...	...
1795	0.40	0.00	0.00	...	0.00	...	...	0.40	0.00	...	0.40	...	...	...
1785	0.31	0.00	0.00	...	0.00	...	...	0.31	0.00	...	0.31	...	...	...
1775	0.25	0.00	0.00	...	0.00	...	...	0.25	0.00	...	0.25	...	...	...
1765	0.20	0.00	0.00	...	0.00	...	...	0.20	0.00	...	0.20	...	...	...
1755	0.16	0.00	0.00	...	0.00	...	...	0.16	0.00	...	0.16	...	...	...
1745	0.11	0.00	0.00	...	0.00	...	...	0.11	0.00	...	0.11	...	...	...
1735	0.08	0.00	0.00	...	0.00	...	...	0.08	0.00	...	0.08	...	...	...
1725	0.06	0.00	0.00	...	0.00	...	...	0.06	0.00	...	0.06	...	...	...
1715	0.04	0.00	0.00	...	0.00	...	...	0.04	0.00	...	0.04	...	...	...
1705	0.02	0.00	0.00	...	0.00	...	...	0.02	0.00	...	0.02	...	...	...
1695	0.01	0.00	0.00	...	0.00	...	...	0.01	0.00	...	0.01	...	...	...
1685	0.01	0.00	0.00	...	0.00	...	...	0.01	0.00	...	0.01	...	...	...
1675	0.01	0.00	0.00	...	0.00	...	...	0.01	0.00	...	0.01	...	...	...
1665	0.01	0.00	0.00	...	0.00	...	...	0.01	0.00	...	0.01	...	...	...
1655	(Z)	0.00	0.00	...	0.00	...	...	(Z)	0.00	...	(Z)	...	...	...
1645	(Z)	0.00	0.00	...	0.00	...	...	(Z)	0.00	...	(Z)	...	...	...

Source: U.S. Census Bureau. *Statistical Abstract of the United States: 2007* U.S. Department of Energy, Energy Information Administration.
[3]Electricity net generation from conventional hydroelectric power, geothermal, solar, and wind; consumption of wood, waste, and alcohol fuels; geothermal heat pump and direct use energy; and solar thermal direct use energy.
[4]Prior to 1945, wood only. Thereafter, wood, waste, and alcohol (ethanol blended into motor gasoline).
[5]Pumped storage facility production minus energy used for pumping.
[7]Includes imports into the Strategic Petroleum Reserve, which began in 1977.
[8]Beginning in 1993, ethanol blended into motor gasoline is included in petroleum.
[9]Petroleum products supplied, including natural gas plant liquids and crude oil burned as fuel.
[10]Includes supplemental gaseous fuels.
[11]Through 1988, includes all electricity net imports. From 1989, includes only electricity net imports derived from hydroelectric power.
[12]From 1989, includes electricity imports from Mexico that are derived from geothermal energy.
... = Not available.
Z Less than 5 trillion.

Table 9-8. Nuclear Power Plants—Number, Capacity, and Generation, 1957–2005

Year	Operable generating units[1,2]	Net summer capability[2,3] (mil. kilowatts)	Net generation		Capacity factor[4]
			Total (bil. kilowatt-hours)	Percent of total electric utility generation	
2005	104	99.6	780.5	19.3	89.4
2004	104	99.6	788.5	19.9	90.1
2003	104	99.2	763.7	19.7	87.9
2002	104	98.7	780.1	20.2	90.3
2001	104	98.2	768.8	20.6	89.4
2000	104	97.9	753.9	19.8	88.1
1999	104	97.4	728.3	19.7	85.3
1998	104	97.1	673.7	18.6	78.2
1997	107	99.7	628.6	18.0	71.1
1996	109	100.8	674.7	19.6	76.2
1995	109	99.5	673.4	20.1	77.4
1994	109	99.1	640.4	19.7	73.8
1993	110	99.0	610.3	19.1	70.5
1992	109	100.0	618.8	20.1	70.9
1991	111	99.6	612.6	19.9	70.2
1990	112	99.6	576.9	19.0	66.0
1989	111	98.2	529.4	17.8	62.2
1988	109	94.7	527.0	19.5	63.5
1987	107	93.6	455.3	17.7	57.4
1986	101	85.2	414.0	16.6	56.9
1985	96	79.4	383.7	15.5	58.0
1984	87	69.7	327.6	13.5	56.3
1983	81	63.0	293.7	12.7	54.4
1982	78	60.0	282.8	12.6	56.6
1981	75	56.0	272.7	11.9	58.2
1980	71	51.8	251.1	11.0	56.3
1979	69	49.7	255.2	11.3	58.4
1978	70	50.8	276.4	12.5	64.5
1977	67	46.3	250.9	11.8	63.3
1976	63	43.8	191.1	9.4	54.7
1975	57	37.3	172.5	9.0	55.9
1974	55	31.9	114.0	6.1	47.8
1973	42	22.7	83.5	4.5	53.5
1972	27	14.5	54.1	3.1	. . .
1971	22	9.0	38.1	2.4	. . .
1970	20	7.0	21.8	1.4	. . .
1969	17	4.4	13.9	1.0	. . .
1968	13	2.7	12.5	0.9	. . .
1967	15	2.7	7.7	0.6	. . .
1966	14	1.7	5.5	0.5	. . .
1965	13	0.8	3.7	0.3	. . .
1964	13	0.8	3.3	0.3	. . .
1963	11	0.8	3.2	0.3	. . .
1962	9	0.7	2.3	0.3	. . .
1961	3	0.4	1.7	0.2	. . .
1960	3	0.4	0.5	0.1	. . .
1959	2	0.1	0.2	(Z)	. . .
1958	1	0.1	0.2	(Z)	. . .
1957	1	0.1	(Z)	(Z)	. . .

Source: U.S. Census Bureau. *Statistical Abstract of the United States: 2007.* U.S. Department of Energy, Energy Information Administration.
[1]Total of nuclear generating units holding full-power licenses, or equivalent permission to operate, at the end of the year. Although Browns Ferry 1 was shut down in 1985, the unit has remained fully licensed and thus has continued to be counted as operable during the shutdown.
[2]As of year-end.
[3]Net summer capacity is the steady hourly output that generating equipment is expected to supply to system load, exclusive of auxiliary power, as demonstrated by test at the time of summer peak demand.
[4]Weighted average of monthly capacity factors. Monthly factors are derived by dividing actual monthly generation by the maximum possible generation for the month (number of hours in the month multiplied by the net summer capacity at the end of the month).
Z = less than 50 million or 0.05 percent.
. . . = Not available.

Table 9-9. Energy Consumption, by End-Use Sector, 1949–2005

(Quadrillion Btu, percent. Btu=British thermal unit. For residential and commercial, industrial, and transportation, represents consumption of fossil fuels only.)

Year	Total consumption[1]	Residential and commercial[1]	Industrial[2]	Transportation	Percent of total		
					Residential and commercial[1]	Industrial[2]	Transportation
2005[3]	99.89	39.84	31.98	28.06	39.9	32.0	28.1
2004	100.41	39.02	33.44	27.95	38.9	33.3	27.8
2003	98.27	38.64	32.61	27.02	39.3	33.2	27.5
2002	97.97	38.40	32.72	26.85	39.2	33.4	27.4
2001	96.50	37.51	32.71	26.27	38.9	33.9	27.2
2000	98.98	37.72	34.70	26.55	38.1	35.1	26.8
1999	96.84	36.07	34.81	25.95	37.2	35.9	26.8
1998	95.20	35.05	34.89	25.26	36.8	36.6	26.5
1997	94.80	34.79	35.26	24.75	36.7	37.2	26.1
1996	94.23	34.80	34.98	24.44	36.9	37.1	25.9
1995	91.20	33.34	34.01	23.85	36.6	37.3	26.1
1994	89.29	32.35	33.58	23.37	36.2	37.6	26.2
1993	87.65	32.19	32.70	22.77	36.7	37.3	26.0
1992	86.01	30.94	32.65	22.42	36.0	38.0	26.1
1991	84.67	31.06	31.48	22.12	36.7	37.2	26.1
1990	84.73	30.41	31.90	22.42	35.9	37.7	26.5
1989	85.00	31.12	31.39	22.48	36.6	36.9	26.4
1988	82.87	29.82	30.73	22.32	36.0	37.1	26.9
1987	79.22	28.32	29.43	21.47	35.7	37.2	27.1
1986	76.83	27.70	28.33	20.79	36.1	36.9	27.1
1985	76.58	27.60	28.89	20.09	36.0	37.7	26.2
1984	76.79	27.48	29.65	19.65	35.8	38.6	25.6
1983	73.15	26.46	27.51	19.18	36.2	37.6	26.2
1982	73.29	26.49	27.70	19.09	36.1	37.8	26.0
1981	76.34	25.99	30.84	19.51	34.0	40.4	25.6
1980	78.28	26.43	32.15	19.70	33.8	41.1	25.2
1979	80.90	26.47	33.96	20.47	32.7	42.0	25.3
1978	79.99	26.64	32.73	20.61	33.3	40.9	25.8
1977	78.00	25.87	32.31	19.82	33.2	41.4	25.4
1976	76.01	25.48	31.43	19.10	33.5	41.3	25.1
1975	72.00	24.31	29.45	18.24	33.8	40.9	25.3
1974	73.99	24.05	31.82	18.12	32.5	43.0	24.5
1973	75.71	24.44	32.65	18.61	32.3	43.1	24.6
1972	72.70	24.04	30.95	17.72	33.1	42.6	24.4
1971	69.29	22.96	29.60	16.73	33.1	42.7	24.1
1970	67.84	22.11	29.64	16.10	32.6	43.7	23.7
1969	65.62	21.00	29.11	15.51	32.0	44.4	23.6
1968	62.42	19.67	27.89	14.87	31.5	44.7	23.8
1967	58.91	18.54	26.62	13.75	31.5	45.2	23.3
1966	57.02	17.52	26.40	13.10	30.7	46.3	23.0
1965	54.02	16.51	25.07	12.43	30.6	46.4	23.0
1964	51.82	15.73	24.09	12.00	30.4	46.5	23.2
1963	49.65	15.26	22.73	11.65	30.7	45.8	23.5
1962	47.83	14.84	21.77	11.22	31.0	45.5	23.5
1961	45.74	14.03	20.94	10.77	30.7	45.8	23.5
1960	45.09	13.67	20.82	10.60	30.3	46.2	23.5
1959	43.47	12.80	20.32	10.35	29.4	46.7	23.8
1958	41.65	12.33	19.31	10.00	29.6	46.4	24.0
1957	41.79	11.69	20.20	9.90	28.0	48.4	23.7
1956	41.75	11.70	20.20	9.86	28.0	48.4	23.6
1955	40.21	11.18	19.47	9.55	27.8	48.4	23.8
1954	36.64	10.59	17.15	8.90	28.9	46.8	24.3
1953	37.66	10.34	18.20	9.12	27.5	48.3	24.2
1952	36.75	10.44	17.30	9.00	28.4	47.1	24.5
1951	36.97	10.26	17.67	9.04	27.8	47.8	24.5
1950[3]	34.62	9.89	16.23	8.49	28.6	46.9	24.5
1949	31.98	9.27	14.72	7.99	29.0	46.0	25.0

Source: U.S. Census Bureau. *Statistical Abstract of the United States: 2007.* U.S. Department of Energy, Energy Information Administration.
[1]Commercial sector fuel use, including that at commercial combined-heat-and-power (CHP) and commercial electricity-only plants.
[2]Industrial sector fuel use, including that at industrial combined-heat-and-power (CHP) and industrial electricity-only plants.
[3]Preliminary.

Table 9-10. Consumer Price Estimates for Energy by Source, 1970–2002

(Nominal Dollars per Million Btu.)

			Primary Energy[1]						
			Petroleum						
	Coal	Natural Gas	Distillate Fuel Oil	Jet Fuel	LPG[2]	Motor Gasoline[3]	Residual Fuel Oil	Other[4]	Total
2002	1.3	5.27	8.63	5.33	8.15	10.67	3.98	6.56	8.82
2001	1.29	6.87	9.17	5.72	9.61 [R]	11.35	3.99	6.37 [R]	9.32 [R]
2000	1.24	5.62	9.86	6.6	10.2 [R]	12.01	4.32	6.97	9.91
1999	1.27	4.16	7.19	4.01	6.65	9.31	2.51	5.3	7.33
1998	1.29	4.13	6.57	3.35	6.01 [R]	8.45	2.15	5.04	6.64
1997	1.32	4.53	7.66	4.53	7.43 [R]	9.81	2.93	5.88	7.86
1996	1.33	4.25	7.87	4.82	8.03 [R]	9.85	2.8	6.19	8.02 [R]
1995	1.37	3.73	6.98	4	6.56 [R]	9.22	2.46	5.74	7.29
1994	1.39	4.08	6.99	3.95	6.66 [R]	8.96	2.32	5.47	7.06
1993	1.42	4.1	7.08	4.29	6.23 [R]	8.83	2.26	5.5	7.01
1992	1.45	3.83	7.09	4.52	6.21 [R]	8.96	2.28	5.52	7.07
1991	1.48	3.74	7.29	4.83	6.81 [R]	8.93	2.62	5.74	7.2
1990	1.49	3.82	7.68	5.68	6.77 [R]	9.12	3.17	5.82	7.47
1989	1.48	3.82	6.43	4.39	5.54 [R]	8.02	2.72	5.5	6.43
1988	1.5	3.78	5.83	3.8	5.88 [R]	7.33	2.35	5.26	5.91
1987	1.53	3.77	5.97	4.03	6.07 [R]	7.23	2.86	5.63	6.04
1986	1.62	4.07	5.68	3.92	6.44 [R]	6.79	2.37	5.8	5.73
1985	1.69	4.61	7.22	5.91	6.55 [R]	9.01	4.3	7.55	7.63
1984	1.71	4.75	7.37	6.25	6.93	8.89	4.75	7.67	7.68
1983	1.7	4.72	7.32	6.53	7.17	9.12	4.5	7.6	7.77
1982	1.73	4.23	7.78	7.23	6.66	10.39	4.65	7.87	8.4
1981	1.64	3.43	8.03	7.57	6.18	10.94	4.91	8.67	8.68
1980	1.46	2.86	6.7	6.36	5.64	9.84	3.88	7.04	7.4
1979	1.36	2.31	4.69	3.9	4.5	7.11	2.83	4.7	5.23
1978	1.27	1.95	3.26	2.87	3.6	5.24	2.08	3.45	3.84
1977	1.11	1.76	3.11	2.59	3.65	5.13	2.14	3.27	3.73
1976	1.04	1.46	2.77	2.25	3.21	4.84	1.9	3.08	3.47
1975	1.03	1.18	2.6	2.05	2.97	4.65	1.93	2.94	3.35
1974	0.88	0.89	2.44	1.58	2.81	4.32	1.82	2.6	3.06
1973	0.48	0.73	1.46	0.92	2.02	3.1	0.75	1.58	1.97
1972	0.45	0.68	1.22	0.79	1.52	2.88	0.62	1.49	1.78
1971	0.42	0.63	1.22	0.77	1.49	2.9	0.58	1.45	1.79
1970	0.38	0.59	1.16	0.73	1.46	2.85	0.42	1.38	1.72

Source: U.S. Department of Energy, Energy Information Administration. *Annual Energy Review 2005 Report No. DOE/EIA-0384 2005.*
Note: Prices include taxes where data are available. There are no direct fuel costs for hydroelectric, geothermal, wind, or solar energy.
[1]Consumption-weighted average prices for all sectors, including the electric power sector.
[2]Liquefied petroleum gases.
[3]Beginning in 1993, includes ethanol blended into motor gasoline.
[4]Consumption-weighted average price for asphalt and road oil, aviation gasoline, kerosene, lubricants, petrochemical feedstocks, petroleum coke, special naphthas, waxes, and products.
[5]Wood and waste.
[6]Includes coal coke imports and exports, which are not separately displayed. In 2002, coal coke imports averaged 3.04 dollars per million Btu, and coal coke exports averaged 3.25 dollars per million Btu.
[7]Includes net imports of electricity, which are not separately displayed. Also, in 1981-1992, includes ethanol blended into motor gasoline that is not included in the motor gasoline data for those years.
[8]Electricity-only and combined-heat-and-power (CHP) plants within the NAICS (North American Industry Classification System) 22 category whose primary business is to sell electricity and heat, to the public. Through 1988, data are for electric utilities only; beginning in 1989, data are for electric utilities and independent power producers.
[9]Consumption-weighted average electric power sector price for coal, natural gas, petroleum, nuclear fuel, wood, waste, and net imports of electricity.
[10]Retail electricity prices paid by ultimate customers, reported by electric utilities and, beginning in 1996, other energy service providers.
[11]Consumption-weighted average price for primary energy and retail electricity in the four end-use sectors (residential, commercial, industrial, and transportation); excludes energy in the electric power sector.
R = Revised.

Table 9-10. Consumer Price Estimates for Energy by Source, 1970–2002—*Continued*

(Nominal Dollars per Million Btu.)

Nuclear Fuel	Biomass[5]	Total[6,7]	Electric Power Sector[8,9]	Retail Electricity[10]	Total Energy[6,7,11]
0.44	1.59	5.23	1.51	21.21	10.07
0.44	1.61 [R]	5.79	1.78	21.49 [R]	10.73 [R]
0.46	1.58 [R]	5.71	1.64	20.03 [R]	10.33
0.48	1.34 [R]	4.36	1.31	19.52 [R]	8.53 [R]
0.5	1.27 [R]	4.07	1.3	19.8 [R]	8.2 [R]
0.51	1.15 [R]	4.66	1.36	20.13 [R]	8.8
0.51	1.25 [R]	4.63	1.34	20.16 [R]	8.75
0.54	1.4 [R]	4.23	1.28	20.29 [R]	8.28
0.56	1.39 [R]	4.27	1.35	20.33 [R]	8.3
0.56	1.28 [R]	4.25	1.39	20.38	8.25
0.59	1.32 [R]	4.24 [R]	1.37	20.06	8.13
0.63	1.39 [R]	4.28	1.39	19.84 [R]	8.2
0.67	1.32 [R]	4.45	1.47	19.32 [R]	8.25
0.7	1.42 [R]	4.07 [R]	1.5	18.98	7.55
0.73	2.09 [R]	3.89 [R]	1.47	18.68	7.26
0.71	2.07	3.99	1.55	18.74	7.34
0.7	2.12 [R]	3.97 [R]	1.58	19.05	7.3
0.71	2.47 [R]	4.92 [R]	1.88	19.05	8.37
0.67	2.53 [R]	5.03	2	18.5	8.28
0.58	2.44 [R]	5.11	2	18.62	8.39
0.54	2.6 [R]	5.32	2.03	18.16	8.46
0.48	2.52 [R]	5.24	2.02	16.14	8.03
0.43	2.26	4.57	1.76	13.95	6.89
0.34	1.88	3.47	1.49	11.78	5.21
0.3	1.61	2.71	1.26	10.92	4.23
0.27	1.58	2.58	1.17	10.11	3.98
0.25	1.53	2.34	1.03	9.13	3.57
0.24	1.5	2.19	0.96	8.61	3.33
0.2	1.5	1.94	0.87	7.42	2.87
0.19	1.39	1.29	0.47	5.86	2.02
0.18	1.33	1.18	0.42	5.54	1.84
0.18	1.31	1.15	0.38	5.3	1.76
0.18	1.29	1.08	0.32	4.98	1.65

Table 9-11. Crude Oil and Refined Products—Summary, 1949–2005

(Thousands of barrels.)

Year	Input to refineries	Domestic Production[1] 48 states[2]	Alaska	Total	Imports Total[3]	Strategic reserve	Exports
2005[P]	5,549,521	1,553,570	315,420	1,868,990	3,670,403	0	15,089
2004	5,663,861 [R]	1,650,837 [R]	332,465	1,983,302 [R]	3,692,063 [R]	0	9,783
2003	5,585,875	1,717,871	355,582	2,073,453	3,527,696	0	4,538
2002	5,455,530	1,737,789	359,335	2,097,124	3,336,175	5,767	3,296
2001	5,521,637	1,766,099	351,412	2,117,511	3,404,894	3,912	7,386
2000	5,514,395	1,775,509	355,198	2,130,707	3,319,816	3,006	18,352
1999	5,403,450	1,763,534	383,198	2,146,732	3,186,663	3,040	43,031
1998	5,434,383	1,853,068	428,851	2,281,919	3,177,584	0	40,102
1997	5,351,466	1,881,882	472,949	2,354,831	3,002,299	0	39,308
1996	5,195,265	1,856,018	509,999	2,366,017	2,747,839	0	40,211
1995	5,100,317	1,852,614	541,654	2,394,268	2,638,810	0	34,509
1994	5,061,111	1,862,528	568,948	2,431,476	2,578,072	4,485	36,020
1993	4,968,641	1,921,539	577,494	2,499,033	2,477,230	5,367	35,834
1992	4,908,603	1,997,310	627,322	2,624,632	2,226,341	3,594	32,473
1991	4,855,016	2,050,690	656,349	2,707,039	2,110,532	0	42,385
1990	4,894,379	2,037,377	647,310	2,684,687	2,151,387	9,772	39,653
1989	4,891,381	2,094,793	683,980	2,778,773	2,132,761	20,348	51,683
1988	4,848,175	2,240,980	738,143	2,979,123	1,869,005	18,758	56,713
1987	4,691,783	2,331,423	715,955	3,047,378	1,705,922	26,517	54,964
1986	4,641,296	2,486,942	681,310	3,168,252	1,524,978	17,563	56,205
1985	4,380,741	2,608,320	666,233	3,274,553	1,168,297	43,124	74,513
1984	4,408,183	2,619,295	630,401	3,249,696	1,253,949	72,038	66,233
1983	4,265,068	2,545,472	625,527	3,170,999	1,215,225	85,285	59,948
1982	4,297,355	2,537,805	618,910	3,156,715	1,273,214	60,193	86,279
1981	4,551,725	2,541,287	587,337	3,128,624	1,604,703	93,298	83,166
1980	4,934,169	2,554,719	591,646	3,146,365	1,926,162	16,067	104,935
1979	5,346,388	2,609,975	511,335	3,121,310	2,379,541	24,434	85,707
1978	5,379,753	2,729,596	448,620	3,178,216	2,319,826	58,798	57,728
1977	5,329,883	2,840,064	169,201	3,009,265	2,414,327	7,540	18,255
1976	4,910,240	2,912,782	63,398	2,976,180	1,935,012	X	2,941
1975	4,541,426	2,986,945	69,834	3,056,779	1,498,181	X	2,146
1974	4,428,726	3,131,982	70,603	3,202,585	1,269,155	X	1,074
1973	4,537,254	3,288,580	72,323	3,360,903	1,183,996	X	697
1972	4,280,863	3,382,475	72,893	3,455,368	811,135	X	187
1971	4,087,809	3,374,420	79,494	3,453,914	613,417	X	503
1970	3,967,503	3,433,834	83,616	3,517,450	483,293	X	4,991
1969	3,879,605	3,297,798	73,953	3,371,751	514,114	X	1,436
1968	3,774,360	3,262,838	66,204	3,329,042	472,323	X	1,802
1967	3,582,594	3,186,616	29,126	3,215,742	411,649	X	26,541
1966	3,447,193	3,013,405	14,358	3,027,763	447,120	X	1,477
1965	3,300,842	2,837,386	11,128	2,848,514	452,040	X	1,097
1964	3,223,329	2,775,763	11,059	2,786,822	438,643	X	1,363
1963	3,170,652	2,741,983	10,740	2,752,723	412,660	X	1,698
1962	3,069,631	2,665,930	10,259	2,676,189	411,039	X	1,790
1961	2,987,158	2,615,431	6,327	2,621,758	381,548	X	3,227
1960	2,952,534	2,574,374	559	2,574,933	371,575	X	3,087
1959	2,917,661	2,574,403	187	2,574,590	352,344	X	2,526
1958	2,789,404	2,448,987	0	2,448,987	348,007	X	4,346
1957	2,890,436	2,616,901	0	2,616,901	373,255	X	50,243
1956	2,905,106	2,617,283	0	2,617,283	341,833	X	28,624
1955	2,730,218	2,484,428	0	2,484,428	285,421	X	11,571
1954	2,539,564	2,314,988	0	2,314,988	239,479	X	13,599
1953	2,554,865	2,357,082	0	2,357,082	236,455	X	19,931
1952	2,441,259	2,289,836	0	2,289,836	209,591	X	26,696
1951	2,370,404	2,247,711	0	2,247,711	179,073	X	28,604
1950	2,094,867	1,973,574	0	1,973,574	177,714	X	34,823
1949	1,944,221	1,841,940	0	1,841,940	153,686	X	33,069

Source: U.S. Department of Energy, Energy Information Administration. *Annual Energy Review 2005 Report No. DOE/EIA-0384 2005.* 1949–1975 U.S. Bureau of Mines.
Note: Crude oil includes lease condensate. Includes imports from U.S. possessions and territories. Stocks are as of year end. Totals may not equal sum of components due to independent rounding.
[1]Crude oil production on leases, and natural gas plant liquids (liquefied petroleum gases, pentanes plus, and a small amount of finished petroleum products) production at natural gas processing plants. Excludes what was previously classified as "Field Production" of finished motor gasoline, motor gasoline blending components, and other hydrocarbons and oxygenates; these are now included in "Adjustments."
[2]United States excluding Alaska and Hawaii.
[3]Includes imports for the Strategic Petroleum Reserve (SPR), which began in 1977.
[4]Crude oil stocks in the SPR include non-U.S. stocks held under foreign or commercial storage agreements.
R = Revised
X = Not applicable.

Table 9-11. Crude Oil and Refined Products - Summary, 1949–2005—*Continued*

(Thousands of barrels.)

Refined oil products			Crude oil stocks	
Imports	Exports	Total all imports	Total	Strategic reserve[4]
1,266,956	413,570	4,937,359	1,007,781	684,544
1,119,041 [R]	373,853	4,811,104 [R]	961,341 [R]	675,600
948,805	370,170	4,476,501	907,263	638,388
872,363	355,781	4,208,538	876,705	599,091
928,144	347,033	4,333,038	862,221	550,241
874,270	362,358	4,194,086	826,185	540,678
774,411	299,986	3,961,074	851,723	567,241
730,862	304,655	3,908,446	894,948	571,405
706,671	326,950	3,708,970	868,119	563,429
721,289	318,686	3,469,128	849,669	565,816
585,943	311,968	3,224,753	894,968	591,640
705,549	307,876	3,283,621	928,915	591,670
669,224	330,140	3,146,454	922,465	587,080
660,556	315,109	2,886,897	892,864	574,724
673,231	322,956	2,783,763	893,102	568,508
775,008	273,018	2,926,395	908,387	585,692
809,338	261,777	2,942,099	921,148	579,857
840,135	241,753	2,709,140	889,874	559,515
731,437	223,766	2,437,359	889,643	540,648
746,604	230,168	2,271,582	842,789	511,565
681,211	210,555	1,849,508	814,208	493,316
735,987	197,843	1,989,936	795,881	450,505
628,519	209,906	1,843,744	722,939	379,089
593,144	211,235	1,866,358	643,557	293,827
583,717	133,858	2,188,420	593,805	230,341
602,541	94,321	2,528,703	465,966	107,800
706,946	86,149	3,086,487	430,265	91,191
732,819	74,329	3,052,645	376,281	66,860
800,319	70,333	3,214,646	347,683	7,455
741,399	78,658	2,676,411	285,471	X
712,154	74,282	2,210,335	271,354	X
961,792	79,417	2,230,947	265,020	X
1,099,497	83,716	2,283,493	242,478	X
924,179	81,202	1,735,314	246,395	X
819,463	81,342	1,432,880	259,648	X
764,769	89,467	1,248,062	276,367	X
641,437	83,449	1,155,551	265,227	X
567,046	82,742	1,039,369	272,193	X
514,342	85,519	925,991	248,970	X
492,042	70,923	939,162	238,391	X
448,732	67,191	900,772	220,289	X
388,093	72,516	826,736	230,057	X
362,053	74,216	774,713	237,361	X
348,754	59,600	759,793	252,011	X
318,118	60,336	699,666	244,664	X
292,536	70,819	664,111	239,800	X
297,239	74,541	649,583	257,129	X
272,582	96,292	620,589	262,730	X
201,334	156,944	574,589	281,813	X
183,758	128,762	525,591	266,014	X
170,143	122,617	455,564	265,610	X
144,476	116,134	383,955	258,385	X
141,044	126,660	377,499	274,445	X
138,916	131,492	348,507	271,928	X
129,121	125,448	308,194	255,783	X
132,547	76,483	310,261	248,463	X
81,873	86,307	235,559	253,356	X

Table 9-12. Electric Utility Sales and Average Prices, by End-Use Sector, 1949–2005

| Year | Retail Sales[1] (Thousand kilowatt-hours) | | | | | Current dollars | | |
	Residential	Commercial[3]	Industrial[4]	Transportation[5]	Total Retail Sales	Total	Residential	Commercial[6]
2005[P] ..	1,361,120,301	1,266,700,167	1,016,730,890	8,258,736	3,652,810,094	8.09	9.42	8.68
2004	1,293,586,726 [R]	1,229,044,633	1,018,521,753 [R]	7,064,416 [R]	3,548,217,528 [R]	7.62 [R]	8.97 [R]	8.16 [R]
2003	1,273,597,170 [R]	1,197,198,591 [R]	1,011,617,409 [R]	6,809,728	3,489,222,898 [R]	7.42	8.7	8 [R]
2002	1,265,402,563 [R]	1,205,078,298 [R]	990,139,177 [R]	5,459,847 [R]	3,466,079,885 [R]	7.22 [R]	8.46	7.9 [R]
2001	1,201,147,845 [R]	1,191,204,169 [R]	984,511,441 [R]	5,228,132	3,382,091,587 [R]	7.31 [R]	8.63 [R]	7.95 [R]
2000	1,192,446,491	1,159,346,640	1,064,239,394	5,381,743	3,421,414,268	6.81	8.24	7.43
1999	1,144,923,068	1,103,821,210	1,058,216,608	5,126,194	3,312,087,080	6.64	8.16	7.26
1998	1,130,109,120	1,077,956,920	1,051,203,114	4,961,598	3,264,230,752	6.74	8.26	7.41
1997	1,075,880,095	1,026,626,104	1,038,196,892	4,907,333	3,145,610,424	6.85	8.43	7.59
1996	1,082,511,750	980,061,114	1,033,631,378	4,922,779	3,101,127,021	6.86	8.36	7.64
1995	1,042,501,471	953,117,247	1,012,693,350	4,974,521	3,013,286,589	6.89	8.4	7.69
1994	1,008,481,682	913,105,691	1,007,981,245	4,994,246	2,934,562,864	6.91	8.38	7.73
1993	994,780,818	884,746,341	977,164,250	4,770,931	2,861,462,340	6.93	8.32	7.74
1992	935,938,788	850,006,923	972,713,990	4,705,745	2,763,365,446	6.82	8.21	7.66
1991	955,417,350	855,243,856	946,583,391	4,758,443	2,762,003,040	6.75	8.04	7.53
1990	924,018,699	838,263,106	945,521,695	4,751,165	2,712,554,665	6.57	7.83	7.34
1989	905,524,634	810,855,917	925,658,669	4,770,112	2,646,809,332	6.45	7.65	7.2
1988	892,866,141	784,029,282	896,498,117	4,668,955	2,578,062,495	6.35	7.48	7.04
1987	850,410,251	744,066,688	858,232,919	4,562,361	2,457,272,219	6.37	7.45	7.08
1986	819,088,315	714,721,226	830,530,503	4,413,008	2,368,753,052	6.44	7.42	7.2
1985	793,933,848	689,121,387	836,771,997	4,146,620	2,323,973,852	6.44	7.39	7.27
1984	780,091,660	663,679,536	837,836,126	4,189,072	2,285,796,394	6.25	7.15	7.13
1983	750,948,242	620,292,106	775,999,288	3,714,960	2,150,954,596	6.3	7.2	7
1982	729,519,768	608,747,987	744,949,124	3,224,475	2,086,441,354	6.1	6.9	6.9
1981	722,265,024	595,908,402	825,743,449	3,185,984	2,147,102,859	5.5	6.2	6.3
1980	717,495,000	558,642,792	815,067,000	3,244,208	2,094,449,000	4.7	5.4	5.5
1979	682,819,000	543,411,819	841,903,000	2,965,181	2,071,099,000	4	4.6	4.7
1978	674,466,000	531,439,150 [E]	809,078,000	2,938,850 [E]	2,017,922,000	3.7	4.3	4.4
1977	645,238,971	514,028,685 [E]	786,037,126	3,056,430 [E]	1,948,361,212	3.4	4.1	4.1
1976	606,452,082	491,776,960 [E]	754,068,873	2,948,179 [E]	1,855,246,094	3.1	3.7	3.7
1975	588,140,393	468,296,100 [E]	687,679,652	2,974,482 [E]	1,747,090,627	2.9	3.5	3.5
1974	578,183,693	440,015,803 [E]	684,875,074	2,849,156 [E]	1,705,923,726	2.5	3.1	3
1973	579,231,374	444,505,477 [E]	686,085,180	3,086,750 [E]	1,712,908,781	2	2.5	2.4
1972	538,609,184	412,534,052 [E]	640,977,918	3,039,537 [E]	1,595,160,691	1.9	2.4	2.3
1971	499,531,999	377,493,933 [E]	589,447,990	3,066,355 [E]	1,469,540,277	1.8	2.3	2.2
1970	466,290,588	352,040,593 [E]	570,854,195	3,114,524 [E]	1,392,299,900	1.7	2.2	2.1
1969	426,736,084	324,657,857 [E]	559,385,270	3,054,035 [E]	1,313,833,246	1.6	2.2	2.1
1968	381,569,847	297,174,471 [E]	521,132,904	2,993,795 [E]	1,202,871,017	1.6	2.3	2.1
1967	340,113,936	271,154,289 [E]	485,015,199	2,933,842 [E]	1,099,217,266	1.7	2.3	2.1
1966	316,888,360	251,826,893 [E]	463,603,406	2,825,941 [E]	1,035,144,600	1.7	2.3	2.1
1965	291,012,652	231,126,287 [E]	428,727,266	2,923,108 [E]	953,789,313	1.7	2.4	2.2
1964	271,842,079	216,233,909 [E]	405,049,062	2,933,964 [E]	896,059,014	1.7	2.5	2.2
1963	250,752,651	201,513,284 [E]	377,429,639	2,917,534 [E]	832,613,108	1.8	2.5	2.3
1962	232,801,889	181,964,471 [E]	359,853,731	2,979,638 [E]	777,599,729	1.8	2.6	2.4
1961	214,444,853	167,655,999 [E]	336,825,958	3,023,373 [E]	721,950,183	1.8	2.6	2.4
1960	201,463,381	159,143,787 [E]	324,401,907	3,065,687 [E]	688,074,762	1.8	2.6	2.4
1959	184,544,088	142,983,473 [E]	315,134,503	4,225,813 [E]	646,887,877	...	...	...
1958	169,492,241	127,566,180 [E]	286,549,905	4,254,726 [E]	587,863,052	...	...	...
1957	156,723,271	120,363,169 [E]	293,989,661	4,744,074 [E]	575,820,175	...	...	...
1956	143,476,453	111,423,632 [E]	285,947,447	5,432,959 [E]	546,280,491	...	...	...
1955	128,400,614	102,547,316 [E]	259,974,388	5,825,735 [E]	496,748,053	...	...	...
1954	116,228,286	93,594,893 [E]	208,464,736	5,875,877 [E]	424,163,792	...	...	...
1953	104,146,290	87,024,490 [E]	198,618,114	6,428,002 [E]	396,216,896	...	...	...
1952	93,544,873	80,095,756 [E]	176,127,494	6,395,837 [E]	356,163,960	...	...	...
1951	83,092,821	73,962,588 [E]	166,168,060	7,061,114 [E]	330,284,583	...	...	...
1950	72,200,340	65,971,215 [E]	146,478,732	6,793,039 [E]	291,443,326	...	...	...
1949	66,791,968	58,647,204 [E]	122,590,923	6,481,239 [E]	254,511,334	...	...	...

Source: U.S. Department of Energy, Energy Information Administration. *Annual Energy Review 2005 Report No. DOE/EIA-0384 2005.*
Note: Totals may not equal sum of components due to independent rounding. For "Average retail price" data beginning in 2003, the category "Other" has been replaced by "Transportation," and the categories "Commercial" and "Industrial" have been redefined.
[1]Data represent revenue from electricity retail sales divided by electricity retail sales. Prices include state and local taxes, energy or demand charges, customer service charges, environmental surcharges, franchise fees, fuel adjustments, and other miscellaneous charges applied to end-use customers during normal billing operations. Prices do not include deferred charges, credits, or other adjustments, such as fuel or revenue from purchased power, from previous reporting periods. Through 1979, data are for Classes A and B privately owned electric utilities only. For 1980–1982, data are for selected Class A utilities whose electric operating revenues were $100 million or more during the previous year. For 1983, data are for a selected sample of electric utilities. Beginning in 1984, data are for a census of electric utilities. Beginning in 1996, data also include energy service providers selling to retail customers.
[2]In chained (2000) dollars, calculated by using gross domestic product implicit price deflators.
[3]Commercial sector, including public street and highway lighting, interdepartmental sales, and other sales to public authorities.
[4]Industrial sector. Through 2002, excludes agriculture and irrigation; beginning in 2003, includes agriculture and irrigation.
[5]Transportation sector, including sales to railroads and railways.
[6]Commercial sector. For 1960-2002, prices exclude public street and highway lighting, interdepartmental sales, and other sales to public authorities.
[7]Public street and highway lighting, interdepartmental sales, other sales to public authorities, agriculture and irrigation, and transportation including railroads and railways.
R = Revised.
P = Preliminary
E = Estimate
. . . = Not available.
X = Not applicable.

Table 9-12. Electric Utility Sales and Average Prices, by End-Use Sector, 1949–2005—*Continued*

Average Retail Prices of Electricity (cents per kilowatt-hour)

Industrial[4]	Transportation[5]	Other[7]	Constant (2000) dollars[2]					
			Total	Residential	Commercial[6]	Industrial[4]	Transportation[5]	Other[7]
5.57	7.44	X	7.21	8.4	7.74	4.97	6.63	X
5.27 [R]	7.13 [R]	X	6.98 [R]	8.22 [R]	7.48 [R]	4.83 [R]	6.54 [R]	X
5.12 [R]	7.55 [R]	X	6.98 [R]	8.18 [R]	7.53	4.82 [R]	7.1 [R]	X
4.91 [R]	...	6.75 [R]	6.93	8.12 [R]	7.58 [R]	4.71 [R]	...	6.48 [R]
4.98 [R]	...	7.44 [R]	7.14 [R]	8.43 [R]	7.76 [R]	4.86 [R]	...	7.27 [R]
4.64	...	6.56	6.81	8.24	7.43	4.64	...	6.56
4.43	...	6.35	6.78	8.34	7.42	4.53	...	6.49
4.48	...	6.63	6.99	8.56	7.68	4.64	...	6.87
4.53	...	6.91	7.18	8.84	7.95	4.75	...	7.24
4.6	...	6.91	7.31	8.91	8.14	4.9	...	7.36
4.66	...	6.88	7.48	9.12	8.35	5.06	...	7.47
4.77	...	6.84	7.66	9.28	8.56	5.28	...	7.58
4.85	...	6.88	7.84	9.41	8.76	5.49	...	7.78
4.83	...	6.74	7.89	9.5	8.87	5.59	...	7.8
4.83	...	6.51	7.99	9.52	8.92	5.72	...	7.71
4.74	...	6.4	8.05	9.6	9	5.81	...	7.84
4.72	...	6.25	8.21	9.74	9.17	6.01	...	7.96
4.7	...	6.2	8.39	9.88	9.3	6.21	...	8.19
4.77	...	6.21	8.7	10.18	9.67	6.52	...	8.48
4.93	...	6.11	9.04	10.41	10.11	6.92	...	8.58
4.97	...	6.09	9.24	10.6	10.43	7.13	...	8.74
4.83	...	5.9	9.24	10.57	10.54	7.14	...	8.72
5	...	6.4	9.7	11	10.7	7.7	...	9.8
5	...	5.9	9.7	11	11	8	...	9.4
4.3	...	5.3	9.3	10.5	10.7	7.3	...	9
3.7	...	4.8	8.7	10	10.2	6.9	...	8.9
3.1	...	4	8.1	9.3	9.5	6.3	...	8.1
2.8	...	3.6	8.1	9.4	9.6	6.1	...	7.9
2.5	...	3.5	8	9.6	9.6	5.9	...	8.2
2.2	...	3.3	7.7	9.2	9.2	5.5	...	8.2
2.1	...	3.1	7.6	9.2	9.2	5.5	...	8.2
1.7	...	2.8	7.2	8.9	8.6	4.9	...	8.1
1.3	...	2.1	6.3	7.9	7.5	4.1	...	6.6
1.2	...	2	6.3	8	7.6	4	...	6.6
1.1	...	1.9	6.2	8	7.6	3.8	...	6.6
1	...	1.8	6.2	8	7.6	3.6	...	6.5
1	...	1.7	6.1	8.4	8	3.8	...	6.5
1	...	1.8	6.4	9.2	8.4	4	...	7.2
1	...	1.8	7.1	9.6	8.8	4.2	...	7.5
1	...	1.8	7.3	9.9	9.1	4.3	...	7.8
1	...	1.8	7.5	10.7	9.8	4.4	...	8
1	...	1.8	7.7	11.3	9.9	4.5	...	8.1
1	...	1.8	8.3	11.5	10.6	4.6	...	8.3
1.1	...	1.9	8.4	12.1	11.1	5.1	...	8.8
1.1	...	1.8	8.5	12.2	11.3	5.2	...	8.5
1.1	...	1.9	8.6	12.4	11.4	5.2	...	9
...	...	...	...	...	...	...	...	...
...	...	...	...	...	...	...	...	...
...	...	...	...	...	...	...	...	...
...	...	...	...	...	...	...	...	...
...	...	...	...	...	...	...	...	...
...	...	...	...	...	...	...	...	...
...	...	...	...	...	...	...	...	...
...	...	...	...	...	...	...	...	...
...	...	...	...	...	...	...	...	...
...	...	...	...	...	...	...	...	...
...	...	...	...	...	...	...	...	...
...	...	...	...	...	...	...	...	...
...	...	...	...	...	...	...	...	...

Table 9-13. Emissions of Greenhouse Gases, 1980–2004

Year	Greenhouse Gases				Greenhouse Gases, Based on Global Warming Potential[1]				
	Carbon Dioxide[2,3]	Methane	Nitrous Oxide	HFCs PFCs SF6	Carbon Dioxide[2]	Methane	Nitrous Oxide	HFCs PFCs SF6	Total
	Million Metric Tons of Gas				Million Metric Tons Carbon Dioxide Equivalent[2]				
2004[P]	5,973.00	27.8	1.2	X	5,973.00	639.5	353.7	155.9	7,122.10
2003	5,871.80 [R]	27.6 [R]	1.1	X	5,871.80 [R]	633.9 [R]	335.2 [R]	142.4 [R]	6,983.20 [R]
2002	5,808.50 [R]	27.2 [R]	1.1	X	5,808.50 [R]	626.2 [R]	335.1 [R]	143.1 [R]	6,912.90 [R]
2001	5,785.50 [R]	27.2 [R]	1.1	X	5,785.50 [R]	625.8 [R]	338.8 [R]	133.9 [R]	6,884.10 [R]
2000	5,845.50 [R]	27.8 [R]	1.2 [R]	X	5,845.50 [R]	639.8 [R]	343.5 [R]	142.1 [R]	6,970.80 [R]
1999	5,677.90 [R]	27.9 [R]	1.2 [R]	X	5,677.90 [R]	642.2 [R]	347.1 [R]	137.4 [R]	6,804.70 [R]
1998	5,598.10 [R]	28.4 [R]	1.2 [R]	X	5,598.10 [R]	654.2 [R]	348.8 [R]	137.7 [R]	6,738.80 [R]
1997	5,563.00 [R]	29.4 [R]	1.2 [R]	X	5,563.00 [R]	675.2 [R]	349.1 [R]	122 [R]	6,709.30 [R]
1996	5,499.70 [R]	29.4 [R]	1.2	X	5,499.70 [R]	675.8 [R]	358 [R]	114.3 [R]	6,647.70 [R]
1995	5,312.10 [R]	30.4 [R]	1.2	X	5,312.10 [R]	699.9 [R]	357.6 [R]	94.3 [R]	6,463.90 [R]
1994	5,259.00 [R]	30.4 [R]	1.3 [R]	X	5,259.00 [R]	698.9 [R]	374.5 [R]	87.5 [R]	6,419.90 [R]
1993	5,183.00 [R]	30.4 [R]	1.2	X	5,183.00 [R]	700.2 [R]	349.5 [R]	86.1 [R]	6,318.80 [R]
1992	5,067.80 [R]	31.5 [R]	1.2 [R]	X	5,067.80 [R]	723.6 [R]	349.7 [R]	82.2 [R]	6,223.20 [R]
1991	4,953.00 [R]	31.3 [R]	1.2 [R]	X	4,953.00 [R]	720.7 [R]	342.6 [R]	79.9 [R]	6,096.10 [R]
1990	5,002.30 [R]	31.4 [R]	1.1	X	5,002.30 [R]	721.4 [R]	337 [R]	88.1 [R]	6,148.80 [R]
1989	5,105.80	30.2	1.1	X	5,105.80	693.8	332.8	94.5	6,226.90
1988	5,012.60	30.1	1.1	X	5,012.60	692	316.9	91.3	6,112.80
1987	4,800.20	29.9	1.1	X	4,800.20	688.3	323.4	77.8	5,889.80
1986	4,642.50	29.4	1.1	X	4,642.50	676.5	323.8	75	5,717.80
1985	4,638.30	30	1.1	X	4,638.30	689.7	330.7	70.5	5,729.30
1984	4,655.80	29.8	1	X	4,655.80	684.5	294	75.5	5,709.90
1983	4,408.00	29.1	0.9	X	4,408.00	669.9	270.2	67.1	5,415.30
1982	4,448.80	29.4	1	X	4,448.80	676.8	282.6	55.4	5,463.70
1981	4,704.30	29.2	1	X	4,704.30	671.1	292	74	5,741.30
1980	4,824.70	28.6	1	X	4,824.70	658	287	70.4	5,840.00

Source: U.S. Department of Energy, Energy Information Administration. *Annual Energy Review 2005 Report No. DOE/EIA-0384 2005.*
Note: HFCs = hydrofluorocarbons; PFCs = perfluorocarbons; and SF6 = sulfur hexafluoride. Emissions are from anthropogenic sources. "Anthropogenic" means produced as the result of human activities, including emissions from agricultural activity and domestic livestock. Emissions from natural sources, such as wetlands and wild animals, are not included. Because of the continuing goal to improve estimation methods for greenhouse gases, data are frequently revised on an annual basis in keeping with the latest findings of the international scientific community. Totals may not equal the sum of components due to independent rounding.
[1] Emissions of greenhouse gases are weighted based upon their relative global warming potential (GWP), with carbon dioxide equal to a weight of one. The use of updated estimates of GWP resulted in a number of revisions to previously published data. It is also important to note that revisions in estimated emissions result from revisions in energy consumption as well.
[2] Metric tons of carbon dioxide can be converted to metric tons of carbon equivalent by multiplying by 12/44.
[3] Carbon dioxide data in this table differ from those for the United States in Table 11.19 due to: the exclusion of emissions from international bunker fuels consumption; the inclusion of emissions from geothermal power generation, cement production and other industrial processes, and municipal solid waste combustion; and the inclusion of data for the U.S. territories.
P = Preliminary
X = Not applicable because these gases cannot be summed in native units.
R = Revised.

BOX 9 ■ Development of Alternative Fuel Sources

The development of alternative, nonpetroleum based fuels is considered crucial to decrease the United States' reliance on foreign oil sources. In light of the Iraqi military conflict, rising oil prices and the shutdown of British Petroleum's Prudhoe Bay pipeline, politicians both red and blue voiced the necessity of continuing and expanding research on alternative sources of energy.

George W. Bush, in a State of the Union Address in 2006, announced the Advanced Energy Initiative (AEI), which included plans to decrease U.S. oil imports from the Middle East by 75% by the year 2025. This plan also included funding research on three types of alternative fuels: clean coal technologies, solar energy, and wind energy.

A Democratic Senate passed a bill that would require increased fuel efficiency from auto makers, financial support for ethanol production, and price controls for gasoline.

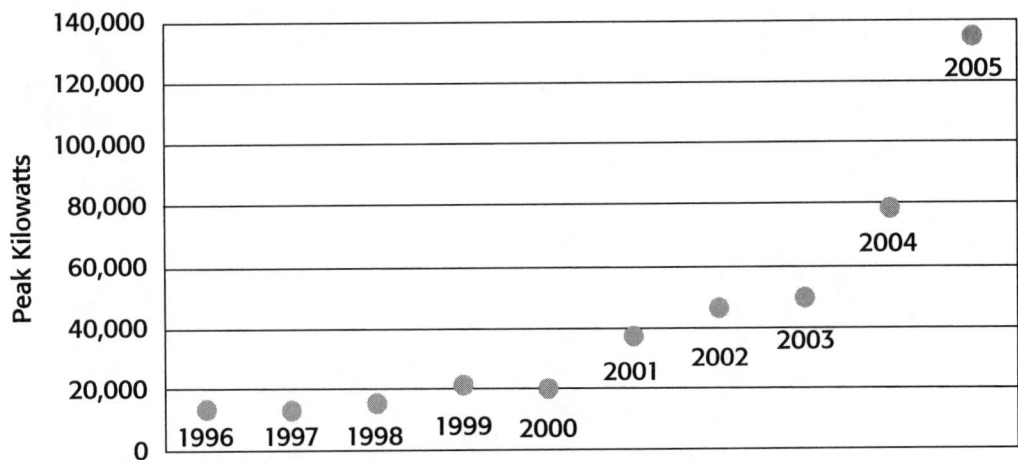

Photovoltalc Domestic Shipments, 1996–2005

Source: Energy Information Administration, Form EIA-63B, "Annual Photovoltalc Macule/Cell Manufacturers Survey."

Sources:
U.S. White House. News & Policies. http://www.whitehouse.gov/news/releases/2006/01/20060131–6.html
United States Senate Committee on Energy and Natural Resources. Press Releases. http://energy.senate.gov/
    public/index.cfm?FuseAction=PressReleases.Detail&PressRelease_id=235326&Month=6&Year=2007&Party=0
U.S. Department of Energy, Energy Information Administration. Solar Thermal and Photovoltaic Collector Manufacturing
    Activities 2005. http://www.eia.doe.gov/cneaf/solar.renewables/page/solarreport/solar.html

Industry and Services

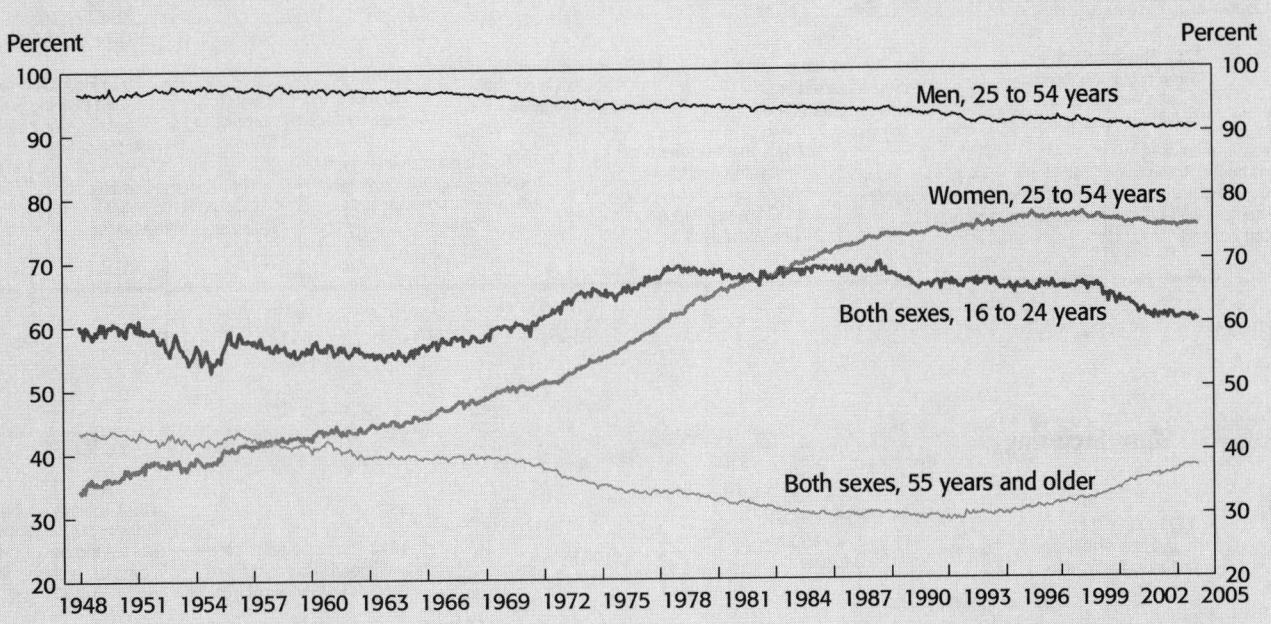

Labor Force Participation Rates for Major Age–Sex Groups, Seasonally Adjusted, 1948–2007

Note: Shaded areas represent recessions. Beginning in 1994, data reflect the introduction of a major redesign of the Current Population Survey. Additional adjustments to population controls were incorporated into the data in January of various years. These changes can affect comparability with data for previous periods.

Labor

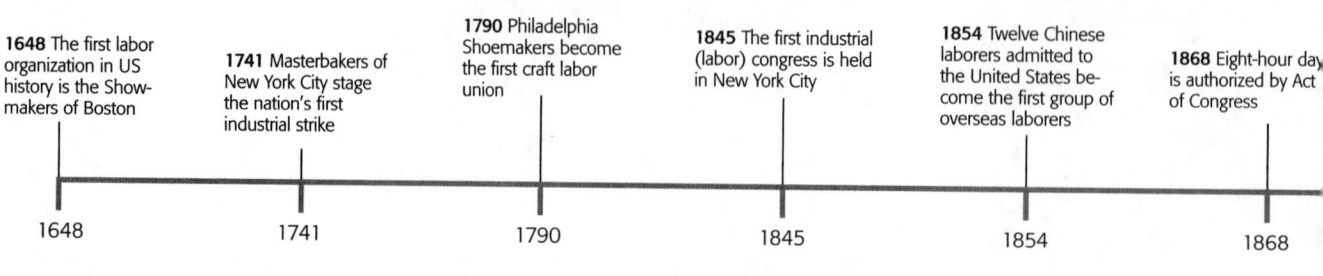

1648 The first labor organization in US history is the Show-makers of Boston

1741 Masterbakers of New York City stage the nation's first industrial strike

1790 Philadelphia Shoemakers become the first craft labor union

1845 The first industrial (labor) congress is held in New York City

1854 Twelve Chinese laborers admitted to the United States become the first group of overseas laborers

1868 Eight-hour day is authorized by Act of Congress

1648   1741   1790   1845   1854   1868

Labor—*continued*

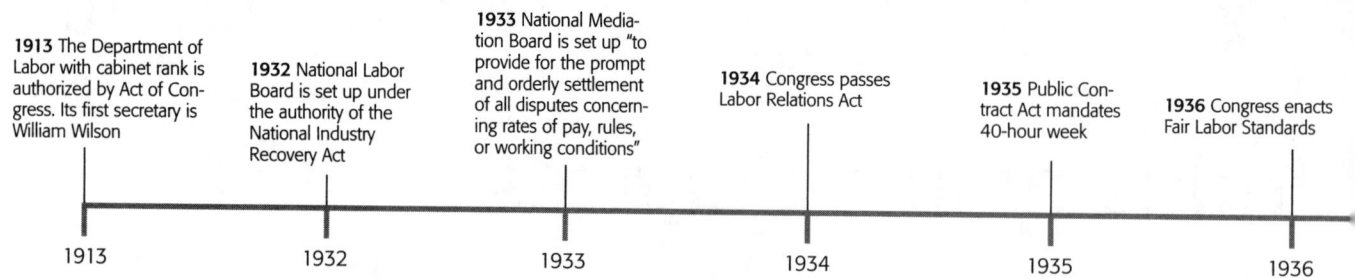

1913 The Department of Labor with cabinet rank is authorized by Act of Congress. Its first secretary is William Wilson

1932 National Labor Board is set up under the authority of the National Industry Recovery Act

1933 National Mediation Board is set up "to provide for the prompt and orderly settlement of all disputes concerning rates of pay, rules, or working conditions"

1934 Congress passes Labor Relations Act

1935 Public Contract Act mandates 40-hour week

1936 Congress enacts Fair Labor Standards

1913   1932   1933   1934   1935   1936

Construction and Housing

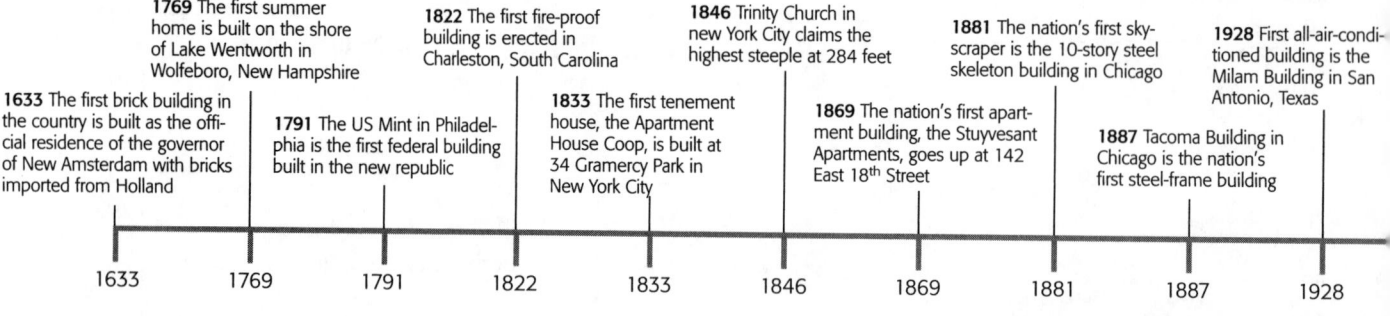

1769 The first summer home is built on the shore of Lake Wentworth in Wolfeboro, New Hampshire

1822 The first fire-proof building is erected in Charleston, South Carolina

1846 Trinity Church in new York City claims the highest steeple at 284 feet

1881 The nation's first sky-scraper is the 10-story steel skeleton building in Chicago

1928 First all-air-conditioned building is the Milam Building in San Antonio, Texas

1633 The first brick building in the country is built as the official residence of the governor of New Amsterdam with bricks imported from Holland

1791 The US Mint in Philadelphia is the first federal building built in the new republic

1833 The first tenement house, the Apartment House Coop, is built at 34 Gramercy Park in New York City

1869 The nation's first apartment building, the Stuyvesant Apartments, goes up at 142 East 18th Street

1887 Tacoma Building in Chicago is the nation's first steel-frame building

1633   1769   1791   1822   1833   1846   1869   1881   1887   1928

Manufacturing

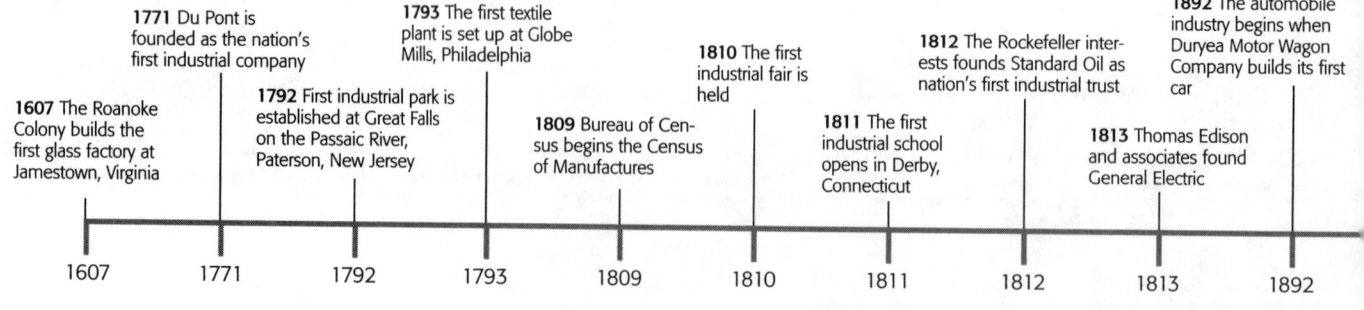

1771 Du Pont is founded as the nation's first industrial company

1793 The first textile plant is set up at Globe Mills, Philadelphia

1810 The first industrial fair is held

1812 The Rockefeller interests founds Standard Oil as nation's first industrial trust

1892 The automobile industry begins when Duryea Motor Wagon Company builds its first car

1607 The Roanoke Colony builds the first glass factory at Jamestown, Virginia

1792 First industrial park is established at Great Falls on the Passaic River, Paterson, New Jersey

1809 Bureau of Census begins the Census of Manufactures

1811 The first industrial school opens in Derby, Connecticut

1813 Thomas Edison and associates found General Electric

1607   1771   1792   1793   1809   1810   1811   1812   1813   1892

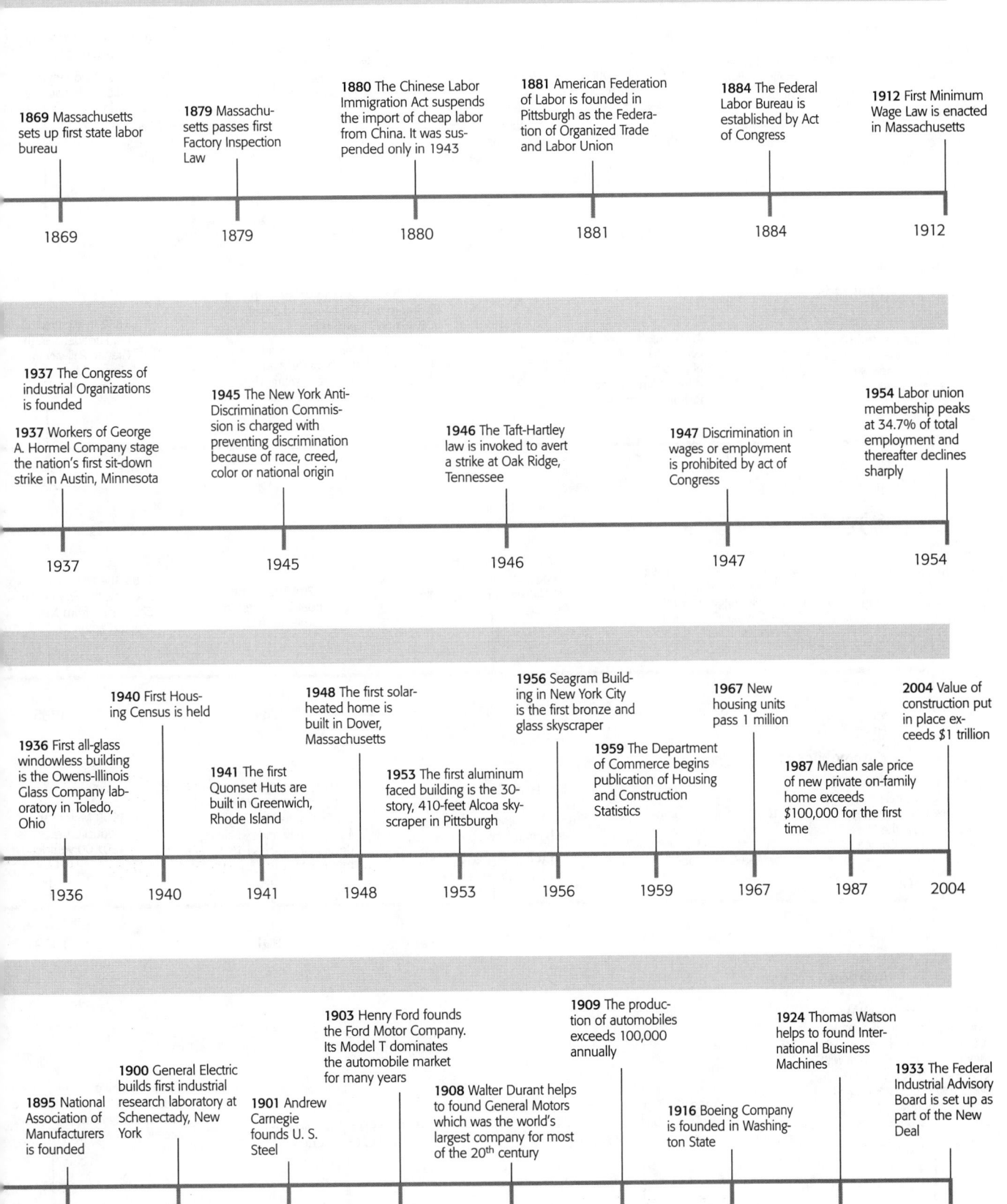

1869 Massachusetts sets up first state labor bureau

1879 Massachusetts passes first Factory Inspection Law

1880 The Chinese Labor Immigration Act suspends the import of cheap labor from China. It was suspended only in 1943

1881 American Federation of Labor is founded in Pittsburgh as the Federation of Organized Trade and Labor Union

1884 The Federal Labor Bureau is established by Act of Congress

1912 First Minimum Wage Law is enacted in Massachusetts

1869 1879 1880 1881 1884 1912

1937 The Congress of industrial Organizations is founded

1937 Workers of George A. Hormel Company stage the nation's first sit-down strike in Austin, Minnesota

1945 The New York Anti-Discrimination Commission is charged with preventing discrimination because of race, creed, color or national origin

1946 The Taft-Hartley law is invoked to avert a strike at Oak Ridge, Tennessee

1947 Discrimination in wages or employment is prohibited by act of Congress

1954 Labor union membership peaks at 34.7% of total employment and thereafter declines sharply

1937 1945 1946 1947 1954

1940 First Housing Census is held

1948 The first solar-heated home is built in Dover, Massachusetts

1956 Seagram Building in New York City is the first bronze and glass skyscraper

1967 New housing units pass 1 million

2004 Value of construction put in place exceeds $1 trillion

1936 First all-glass windowless building is the Owens-Illinois Glass Company laboratory in Toledo, Ohio

1941 The first Quonset Huts are built in Greenwich, Rhode Island

1953 The first aluminum faced building is the 30-story, 410-feet Alcoa skyscraper in Pittsburgh

1959 The Department of Commerce begins publication of Housing and Construction Statistics

1987 Median sale price of new private on-family home exceeds $100,000 for the first time

1936 1940 1941 1948 1953 1956 1959 1967 1987 2004

1903 Henry Ford founds the Ford Motor Company. Its Model T dominates the automobile market for many years

1909 The production of automobiles exceeds 100,000 annually

1924 Thomas Watson helps to found International Business Machines

1900 General Electric builds first industrial research laboratory at Schenectady, New York

1901 Andrew Carnegie founds U. S. Steel

1908 Walter Durant helps to found General Motors which was the world's largest company for most of the 20th century

1916 Boeing Company is founded in Washington State

1933 The Federal Industrial Advisory Board is set up as part of the New Deal

1895 National Association of Manufacturers is founded

1895 1900 1901 1903 1908 1909 1916 1924 1933

Transportation

Roads

1663 The first hard-surfaced road is built by the Dutch from Pahaquarry Mines in New Jersey to Kingston, New York

1785 The first toll road is built from Alexandria, Virginia to Snicker's Gap, Virginia

1806 Great National Pike, also known as the Cumberland Road, is built from Cumberland, Maryland to Vadalia, Illinois

1842 The 2000-mile Oregon Trail from Westport Landing in Missouri to Vancouver in Washington becomes operational

1861 The first divided highway is Savery Avenue in Carver, Massachusetts

1916 The first Federal-State highway program is launched

1916 Office of Road Inquiry is renamed Office of Public Roads and Engineering

1890 The Office of Road Inquiry is set up as the first federal agency for roads

1663 | 1785 | 1806 | 1842 | 1861 | 1890 | 1916

Railroads

1826 The first freight railroad is the Granite Railway Company of Massachusetts

1827 The first railroad for commercial transportation of passengers and freight is the Baltimore and Ohio Railroad Company

1830 The first railroad station is the Baltimore and Ohio Railroad depot in Baltimore, Maryland

1830 The first interstate railroad is the 59-mile Petersburg Railroad chartered between Petersburg, Virginia, and Blakely, North Carolina

1832 In the first railroad accident on the Granite Railway in Quincy, Massachusetts, one person is killed

1826 | 1827 | 1830 | 1832

Shipping

1607 The first ship in the American Colonies is *Virginia of Sahadahock* built in Maine

1679 Commercial vessel *Le Griffon,* a two-masted square rigger, is launched at Cayuga Creek near Niagara River

1763 The first steamboat is built by William Henry in Lancaster, Pennsylvania

1784 The motor boat is invented by James Rumsey

1785 The first trading ship to China, the *Empress of China,* sails from New York to Canton

1607 | 1679 | 1763 | 1784 | 1785

Automobiles

1891 The first automobile is made by Charles Edgar Duryea in Springfield, Massachusetts, for the Duryea Motor Wagon Company

1898 The first automobile truck is made by the Pittsburgh Motor Vehicle Corporation

1899 Jacob German is arrested and jailed for driving at a "reckless speed" of 12 miles per hour in New York City

1899 Illinois issues the first driving license

1901 Connecticut passes first state motor car legislation in Connecticut regulating speeding and penalizing drivers who exceed 15 miles per hour

1909 Motor car production exceeds 100,000 vehicles

1891 | 1898 | 1899 | 1901 | 1909

Aviation

1903 Wilbur and Orville Wright inaugurate the age of aviation with their first airplane flight at Kitty Hawk, North Carolina with Orville Wright at the controls. It has a maximum speed of 31 miles per hour and travels 852 feet in 59 seconds

1909 The first commercial airplane is built by Glenn Curtiss and sold for $5,000

1910 The first pilot's license is issued to Glenn Curtiss

1926 The first piece of aviation legislation is the Air Commerce Act which regulates "the use of aircraft in commerce"

1903 | 1909 | 1910 | 1926

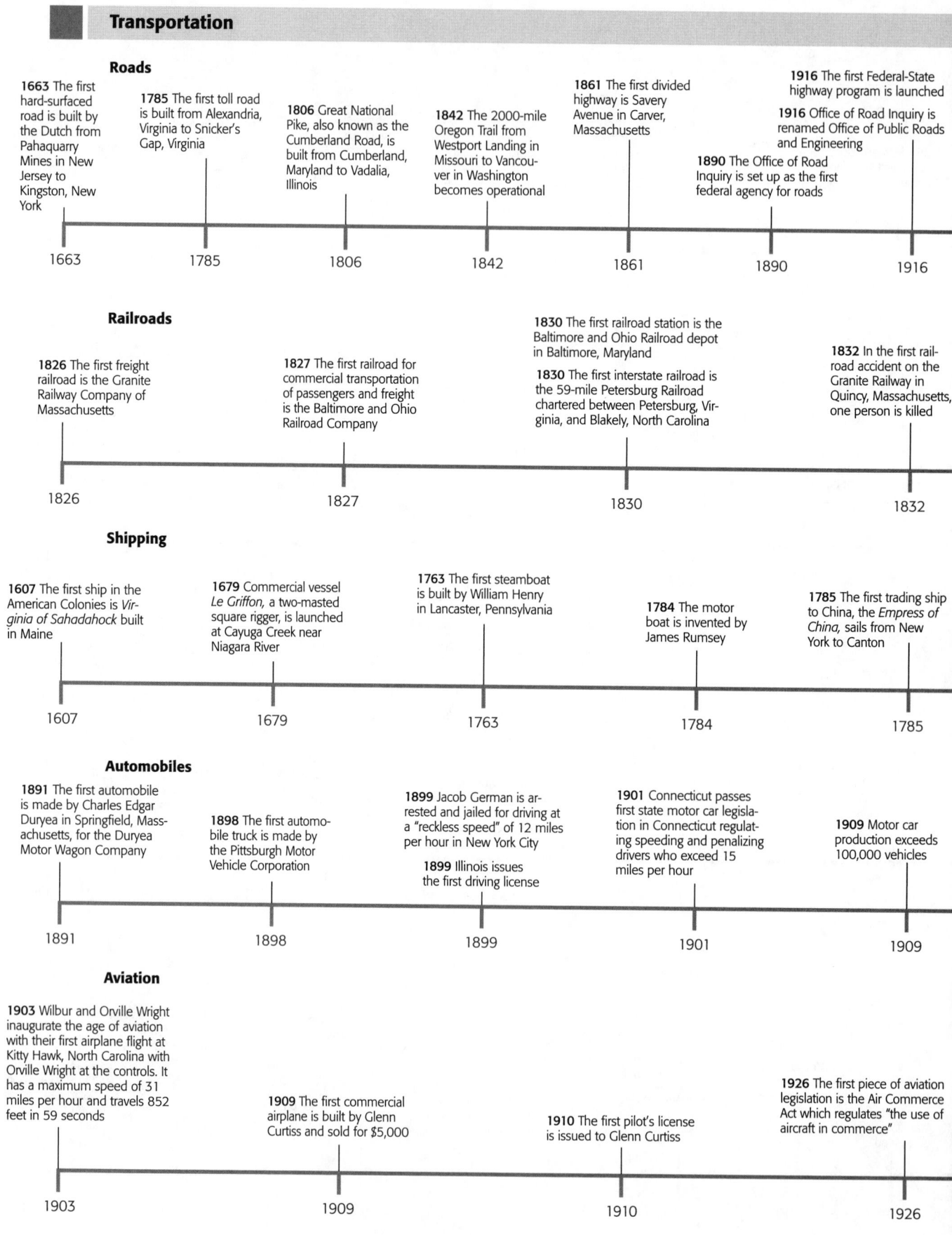

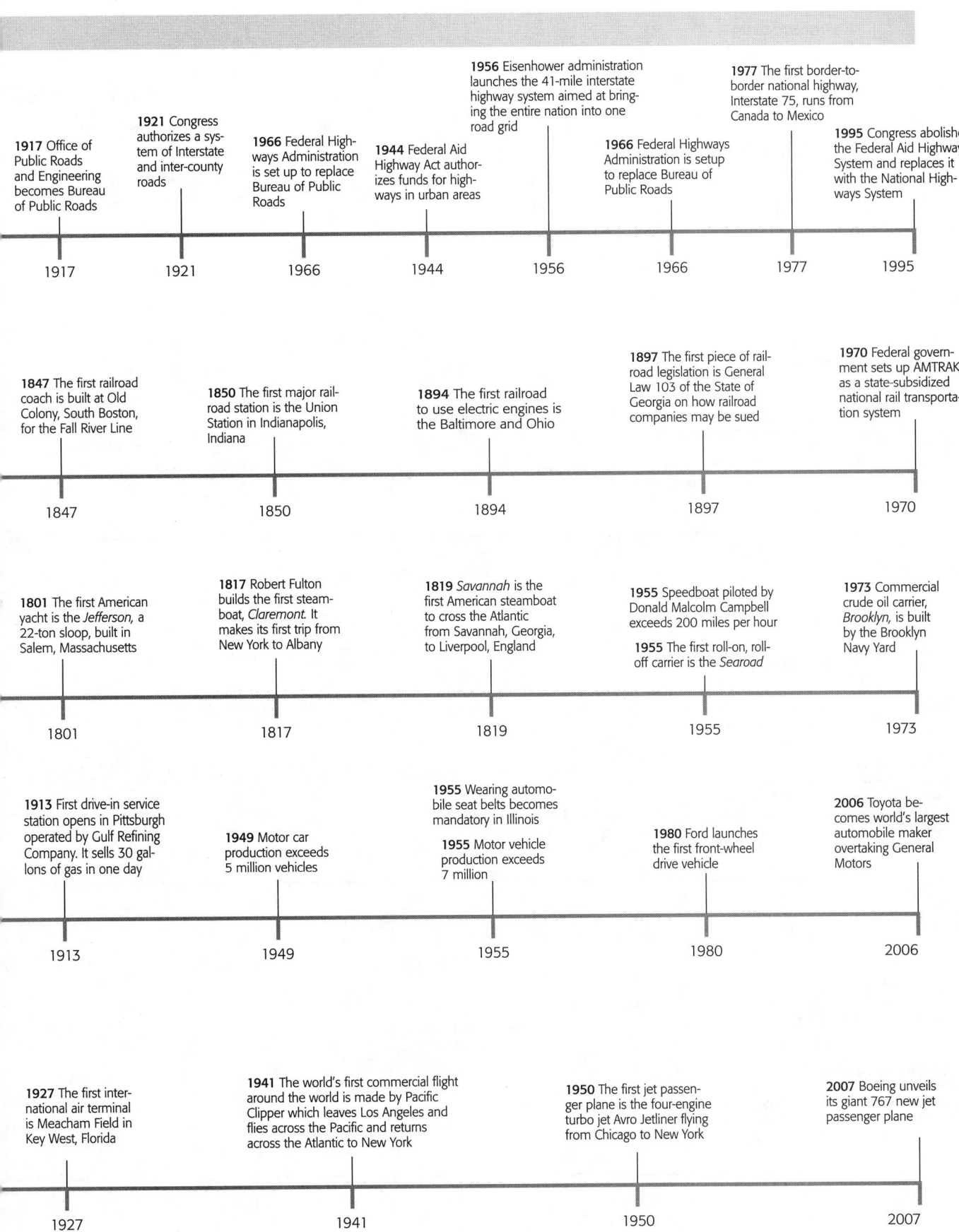

1917 Office of Public Roads and Engineering becomes Bureau of Public Roads

1921 Congress authorizes a system of Interstate and inter-county roads

1966 Federal Highways Administration is set up to replace Bureau of Public Roads

1944 Federal Aid Highway Act authorizes funds for highways in urban areas

1956 Eisenhower administration launches the 41-mile interstate highway system aimed at bringing the entire nation into one road grid

1966 Federal Highways Administration is setup to replace Bureau of Public Roads

1977 The first border-to-border national highway, Interstate 75, runs from Canada to Mexico

1995 Congress abolishes the Federal Aid Highway System and replaces it with the National Highways System

1917   1921   1966   1944   1956   1966   1977   1995

1847 The first railroad coach is built at Old Colony, South Boston, for the Fall River Line

1850 The first major railroad station is the Union Station in Indianapolis, Indiana

1894 The first railroad to use electric engines is the Baltimore and Ohio

1897 The first piece of railroad legislation is General Law 103 of the State of Georgia on how railroad companies may be sued

1970 Federal government sets up AMTRAK as a state-subsidized national rail transportation system

1847   1850   1894   1897   1970

1801 The first American yacht is the *Jefferson,* a 22-ton sloop, built in Salem, Massachusetts

1817 Robert Fulton builds the first steamboat, *Claremont.* It makes its first trip from New York to Albany

1819 *Savannah* is the first American steamboat to cross the Atlantic from Savannah, Georgia, to Liverpool, England

1955 Speedboat piloted by Donald Malcolm Campbell exceeds 200 miles per hour

1955 The first roll-on, roll-off carrier is the *Searoad*

1973 Commercial crude oil carrier, *Brooklyn,* is built by the Brooklyn Navy Yard

1801   1817   1819   1955   1973

1913 First drive-in service station opens in Pittsburgh operated by Gulf Refining Company. It sells 30 gallons of gas in one day

1949 Motor car production exceeds 5 million vehicles

1955 Wearing automobile seat belts becomes mandatory in Illinois

1955 Motor vehicle production exceeds 7 million

1980 Ford launches the first front-wheel drive vehicle

2006 Toyota becomes world's largest automobile maker overtaking General Motors

1913   1949   1955   1980   2006

1927 The first international air terminal is Meacham Field in Key West, Florida

1941 The world's first commercial flight around the world is made by Pacific Clipper which leaves Los Angeles and flies across the Pacific and returns across the Atlantic to New York

1950 The first jet passenger plane is the four-engine turbo jet Avro Jetliner flying from Chicago to New York

2007 Boeing unveils its giant 767 new jet passenger plane

1927   1941   1950   2007

Communications

Telecommunications

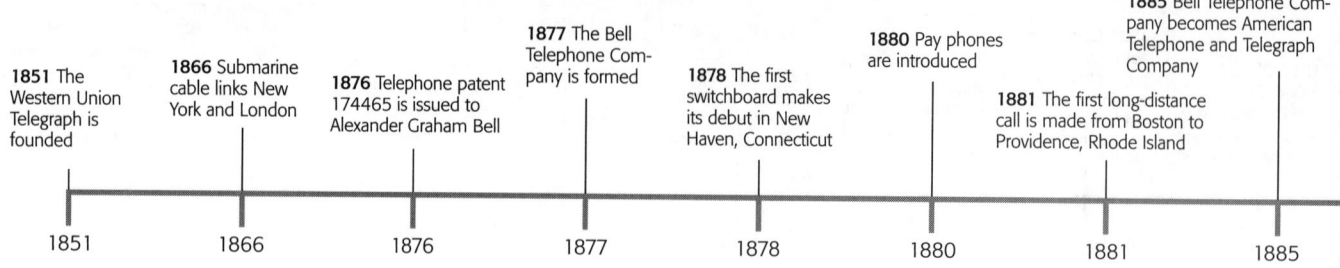

1851 The Western Union Telegraph is founded

1866 Submarine cable links New York and London

1876 Telephone patent 174465 is issued to Alexander Graham Bell

1877 The Bell Telephone Company is formed

1878 The first switchboard makes its debut in New Haven, Connecticut

1880 Pay phones are introduced

1881 The first long-distance call is made from Boston to Providence, Rhode Island

1885 Bell Telephone Company becomes American Telephone and Telegraph Company

1851   1866   1876   1877   1878   1880   1881   1885

Post Office

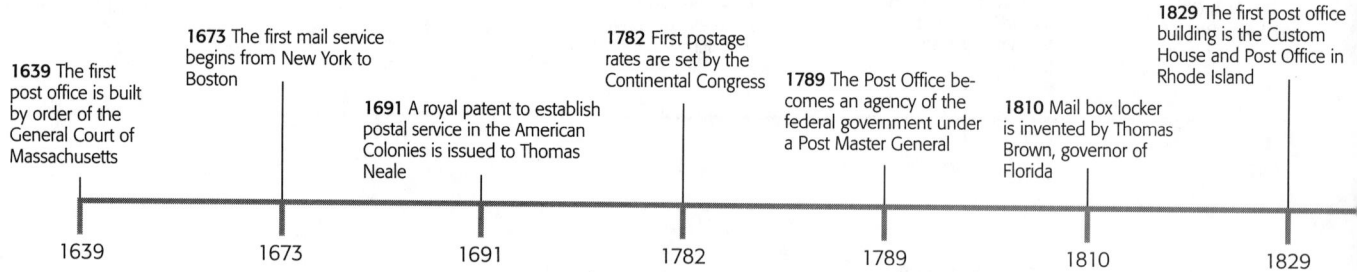

1639 The first post office is built by order of the General Court of Massachusetts

1673 The first mail service begins from New York to Boston

1691 A royal patent to establish postal service in the American Colonies is issued to Thomas Neale

1782 First postage rates are set by the Continental Congress

1789 The Post Office becomes an agency of the federal government under a Post Master General

1810 Mail box locker is invented by Thomas Brown, governor of Florida

1829 The first post office building is the Custom House and Post Office in Rhode Island

1639   1673   1691   1782   1789   1810   1829

Post Office—*Continued*

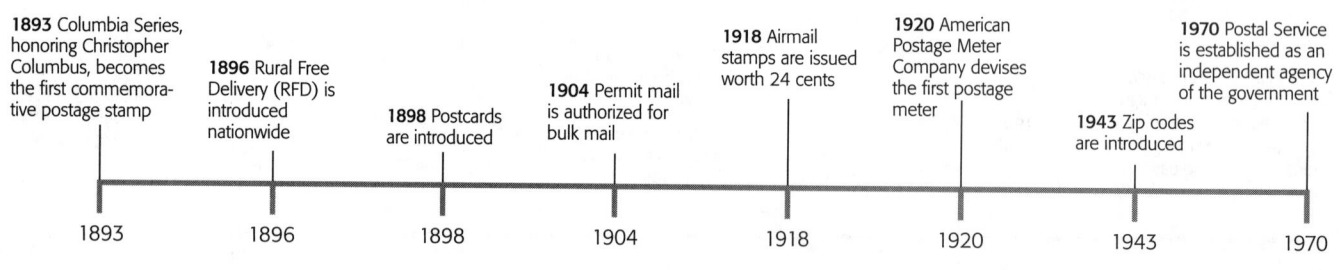

1893 Columbia Series, honoring Christopher Columbus, becomes the first commemorative postage stamp

1896 Rural Free Delivery (RFD) is introduced nationwide

1898 Postcards are introduced

1904 Permit mail is authorized for bulk mail

1918 Airmail stamps are issued worth 24 cents

1920 American Postage Meter Company devises the first postage meter

1943 Zip codes are introduced

1970 Postal Service is established as an independent agency of the government

1893   1896   1898   1904   1918   1920   1943   1970

Television

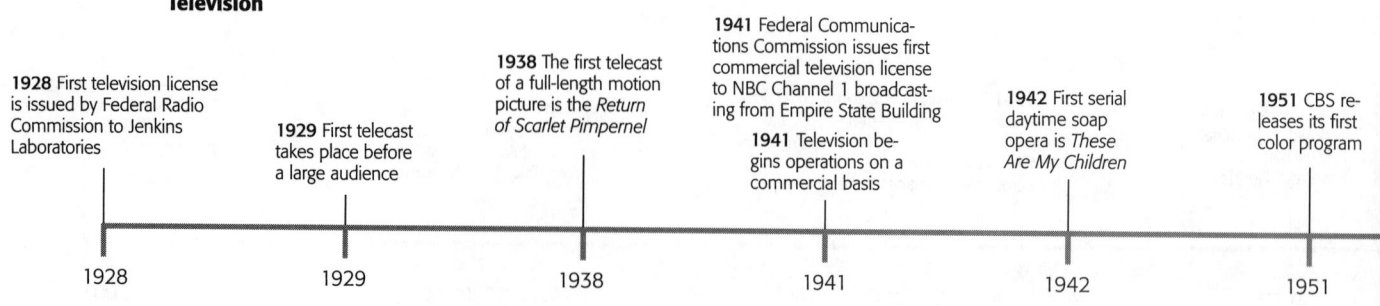

1928 First television license is issued by Federal Radio Commission to Jenkins Laboratories

1929 First telecast takes place before a large audience

1938 The first telecast of a full-length motion picture is the *Return of Scarlet Pimpernel*

1941 Federal Communications Commission issues first commercial television license to NBC Channel 1 broadcasting from Empire State Building

1941 Television begins operations on a commercial basis

1942 First serial daytime soap opera is *These Are My Children*

1951 CBS releases its first color program

1928   1929   1938   1941   1942   1951

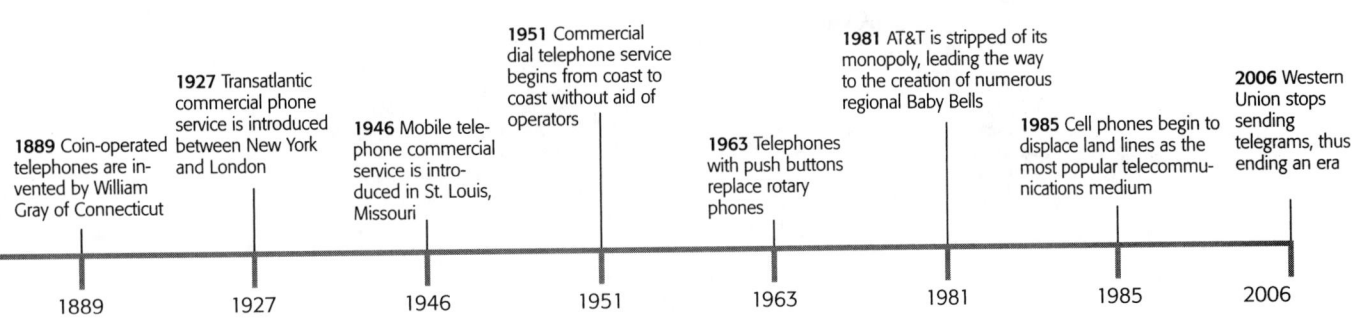

1889 Coin-operated telephones are invented by William Gray of Connecticut

1927 Transatlantic commercial phone service is introduced between New York and London

1946 Mobile telephone commercial service is introduced in St. Louis, Missouri

1951 Commercial dial telephone service begins from coast to coast without aid of operators

1963 Telephones with push buttons replace rotary phones

1981 AT&T is stripped of its monopoly, leading the way to the creation of numerous regional Baby Bells

1985 Cell phones begin to displace land lines as the most popular telecommunications medium

2006 Western Union stops sending telegrams, thus ending an era

1889 1927 1946 1951 1963 1981 1985 2006

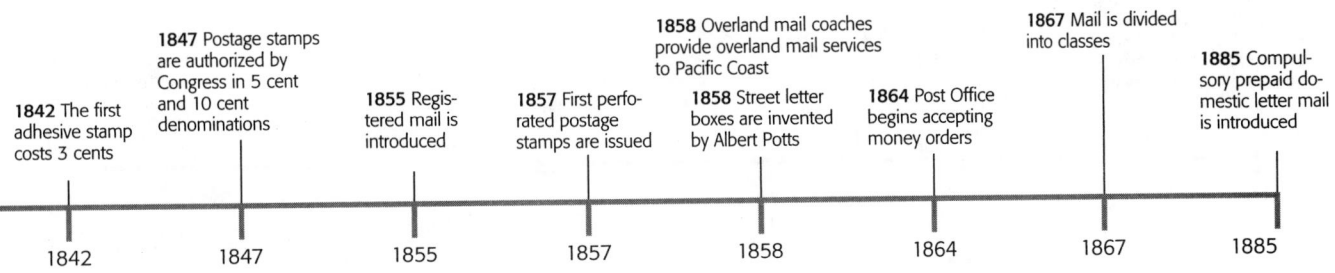

1842 The first adhesive stamp costs 3 cents

1847 Postage stamps are authorized by Congress in 5 cent and 10 cent denominations

1855 Registered mail is introduced

1857 First perforated postage stamps are issued

1858 Overland mail coaches provide overland mail services to Pacific Coast

1858 Street letter boxes are invented by Albert Potts

1864 Post Office begins accepting money orders

1867 Mail is divided into classes

1885 Compulsory prepaid domestic letter mail is introduced

1842 1847 1855 1857 1858 1864 1867 1885

Radio

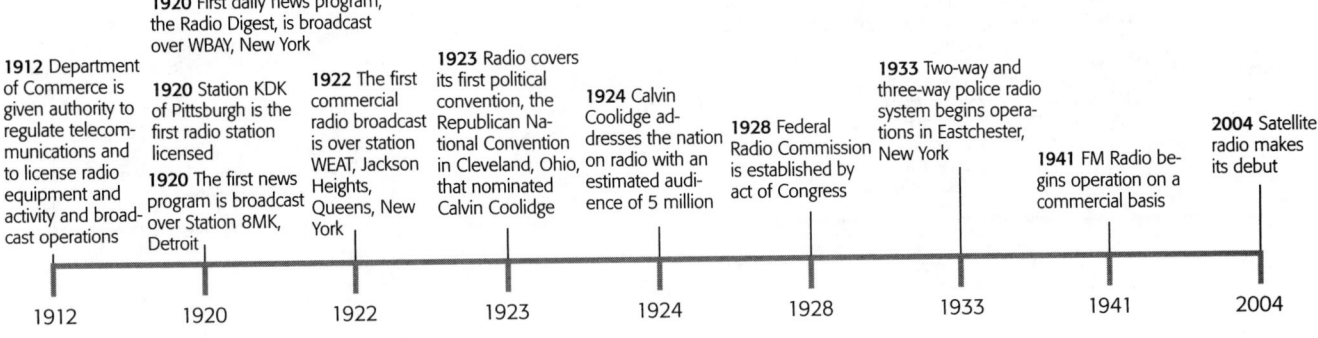

1912 Department of Commerce is given authority to regulate telecommunications and to license radio equipment and activity and broadcast operations

1920 Station KDK of Pittsburgh is the first radio station licensed

1920 The first news program is broadcast over Station 8MK, Detroit

1920 First daily news program, the Radio Digest, is broadcast over WBAY, New York

1922 The first commercial radio broadcast is over station WEAT, Jackson Heights, Queens, New York

1923 Radio covers its first political convention, the Republican National Convention in Cleveland, Ohio, that nominated Calvin Coolidge

1924 Calvin Coolidge addresses the nation on radio with an estimated audience of 5 million

1928 Federal Radio Commission is established by act of Congress

1933 Two-way and three-way police radio system begins operations in Eastchester, New York

1941 FM Radio begins operation on a commercial basis

2004 Satellite radio makes its debut

1912 1920 1922 1923 1924 1928 1933 1941 2004

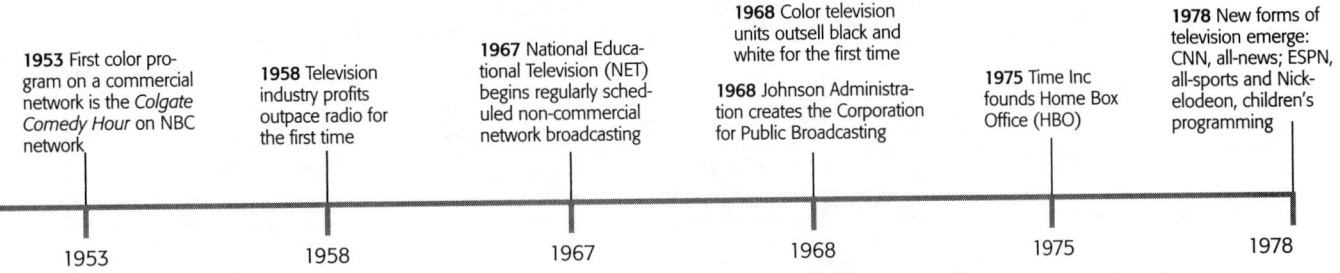

1953 First color program on a commercial network is the *Colgate Comedy Hour* on NBC network

1958 Television industry profits outpace radio for the first time

1967 National Educational Television (NET) begins regularly scheduled non-commercial network broadcasting

1968 Color television units outsell black and white for the first time

1968 Johnson Administration creates the Corporation for Public Broadcasting

1975 Time Inc founds Home Box Office (HBO)

1978 New forms of television emerge: CNN, all-news; ESPN, all-sports and Nickelodeon, children's programming

1953 1958 1967 1968 1975 1978

Communications—*Continued*

Book Publishing

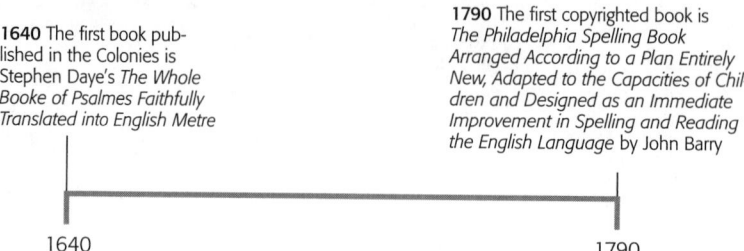

1640 The first book published in the Colonies is Stephen Daye's *The Whole Booke of Psalmes Faithfully Translated into English Metre*

1790 The first copyrighted book is *The Philadelphia Spelling Book Arranged According to a Plan Entirely New, Adapted to the Capacities of Children and Designed as an Immediate Improvement in Spelling and Reading the English Language* by John Barry

1640   1790

Magazines

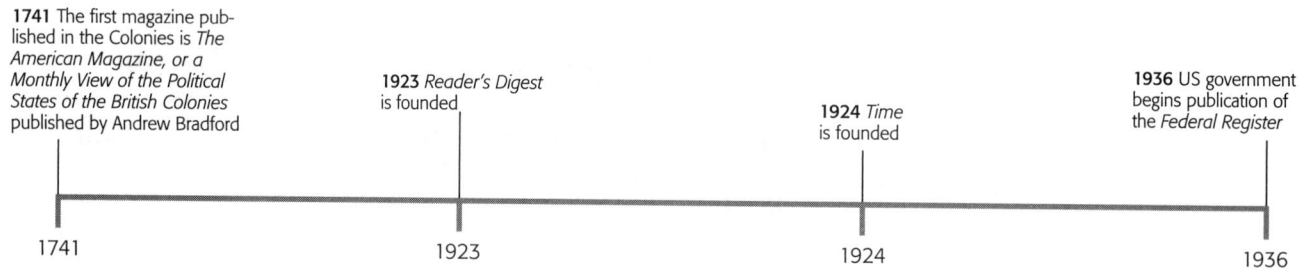

1741 The first magazine published in the Colonies is *The American Magazine, or a Monthly View of the Political States of the British Colonies* published by Andrew Bradford

1923 *Reader's Digest* is founded

1924 *Time* is founded

1936 US government begins publication of the *Federal Register*

1741   1923   1924   1936

Productivity and Technological Development

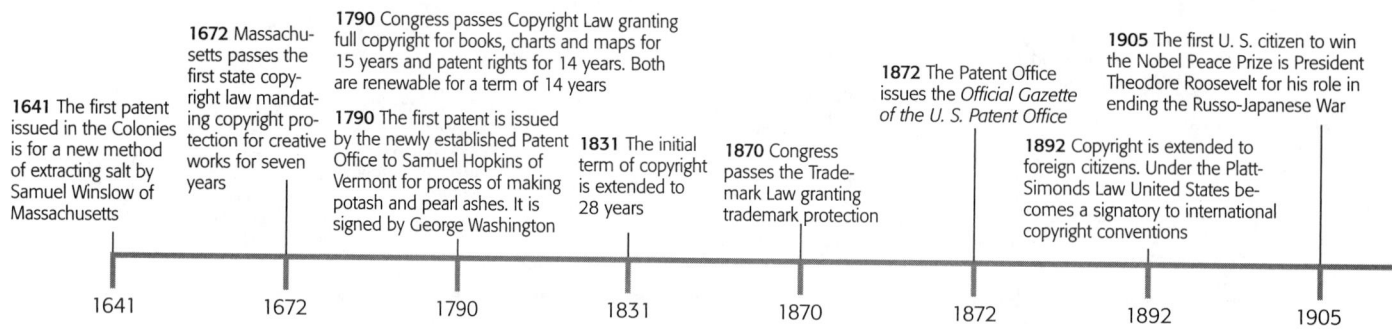

1641 The first patent issued in the Colonies is for a new method of extracting salt by Samuel Winslow of Massachusetts

1672 Massachusetts passes the first state copyright law mandating copyright protection for creative works for seven years

1790 Congress passes Copyright Law granting full copyright for books, charts and maps for 15 years and patent rights for 14 years. Both are renewable for a term of 14 years

1790 The first patent is issued by the newly established Patent Office to Samuel Hopkins of Vermont for process of making potash and pearl ashes. It is signed by George Washington

1831 The initial term of copyright is extended to 28 years

1870 Congress passes the Trademark Law granting trademark protection

1872 The Patent Office issues the *Official Gazette of the U. S. Patent Office*

1892 Copyright is extended to foreign citizens. Under the Platt-Simonds Law United States becomes a signatory to international copyright conventions

1905 The first U. S. citizen to win the Nobel Peace Prize is President Theodore Roosevelt for his role in ending the Russo-Japanese War

1641   1672   1790   1831   1870   1872   1892   1905

Distribution and Services

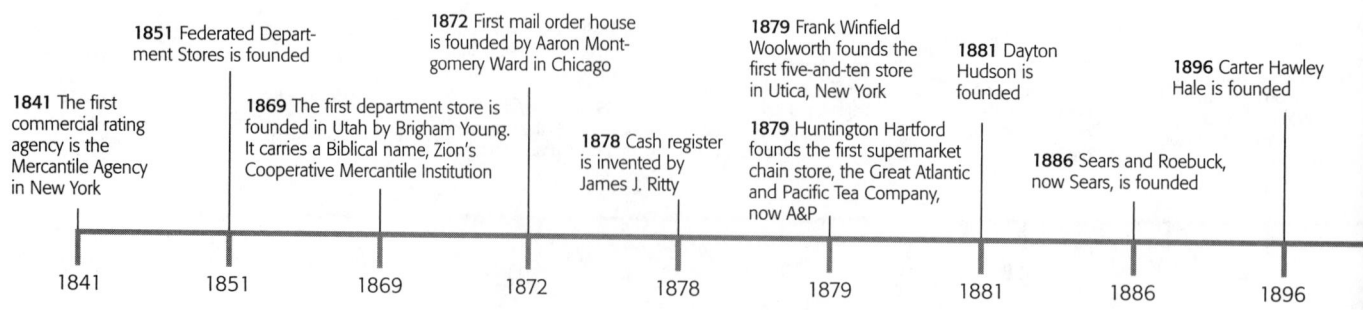

1841 The first commercial rating agency is the Mercantile Agency in New York

1851 Federated Department Stores is founded

1869 The first department store is founded in Utah by Brigham Young. It carries a Biblical name, Zion's Cooperative Mercantile Institution

1872 First mail order house is founded by Aaron Montgomery Ward in Chicago

1878 Cash register is invented by James J. Ritty

1879 Frank Winfield Woolworth founds the first five-and-ten store in Utica, New York

1879 Huntington Hartford founds the first supermarket chain store, the Great Atlantic and Pacific Tea Company, now A&P

1881 Dayton Hudson is founded

1886 Sears and Roebuck, now Sears, is founded

1896 Carter Hawley Hale is founded

1841   1851   1869   1872   1878   1879   1881   1886   1896

Newspapers

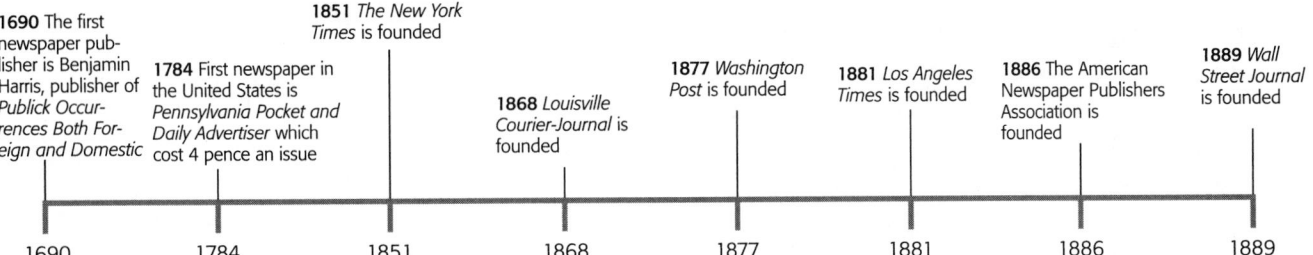

1690 The first newspaper publisher is Benjamin Harris, publisher of *Publick Occurrences Both Foreign and Domestic*

1784 First newspaper in the United States is *Pennsylvania Pocket and Daily Advertiser* which cost 4 pence an issue

1851 *The New York Times* is founded

1868 *Louisville Courier-Journal* is founded

1877 *Washington Post* is founded

1881 *Los Angeles Times* is founded

1886 The American Newspaper Publishers Association is founded

1889 *Wall Street Journal* is founded

1690   1784   1851   1868   1877   1881   1886   1889

Advertising

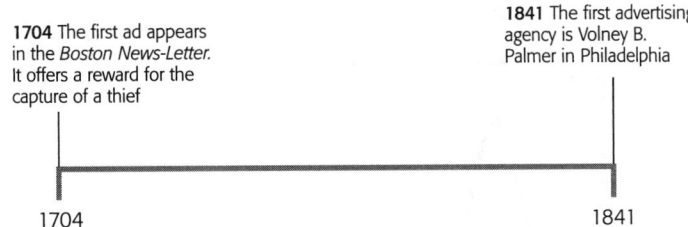

1704 The first ad appears in the *Boston News-Letter*. It offers a reward for the capture of a thief

1841 The first advertising agency is Volney B. Palmer in Philadelphia

1704   1841

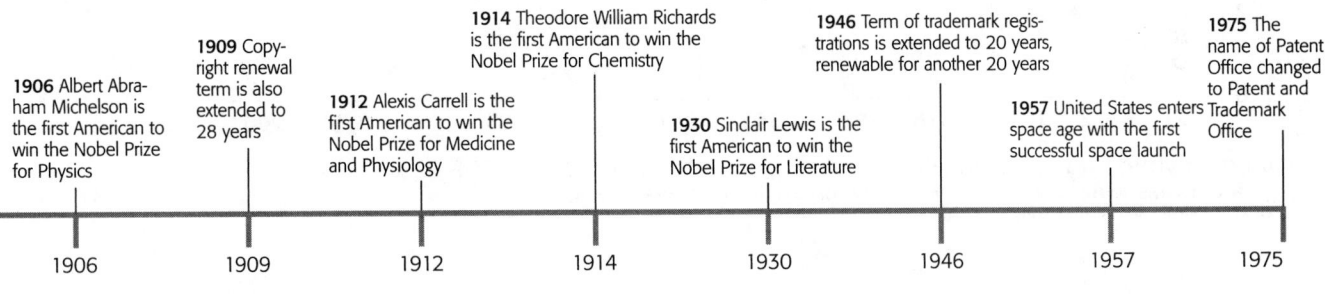

1906 Albert Abraham Michelson is the first American to win the Nobel Prize for Physics

1909 Copyright renewal term is also extended to 28 years

1912 Alexis Carrell is the first American to win the Nobel Prize for Medicine and Physiology

1914 Theodore William Richards is the first American to win the Nobel Prize for Chemistry

1930 Sinclair Lewis is the first American to win the Nobel Prize for Literature

1946 Term of trademark registrations is extended to 20 years, renewable for another 20 years

1957 United States enters space age with the first successful space launch

1975 The name of Patent Office changed to Patent and Trademark Office

1906   1909   1912   1914   1930   1946   1957   1975

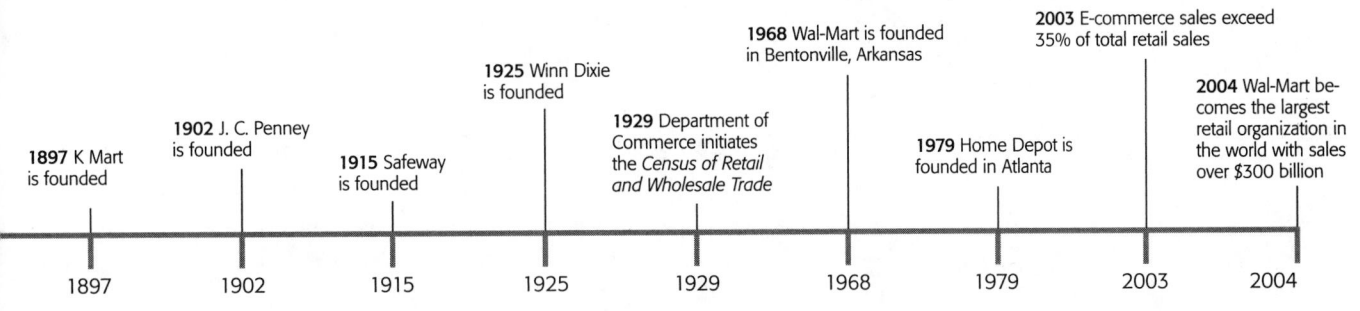

1897 K Mart is founded

1902 J. C. Penney is founded

1915 Safeway is founded

1925 Winn Dixie is founded

1929 Department of Commerce initiates the *Census of Retail and Wholesale Trade*

1968 Wal-Mart is founded in Bentonville, Arkansas

1979 Home Depot is founded in Atlanta

2003 E-commerce sales exceed 35% of total retail sales

2004 Wal-Mart becomes the largest retail organization in the world with sales over $300 billion

1897   1902   1915   1925   1929   1968   1979   2003   2004

Percent

Percent

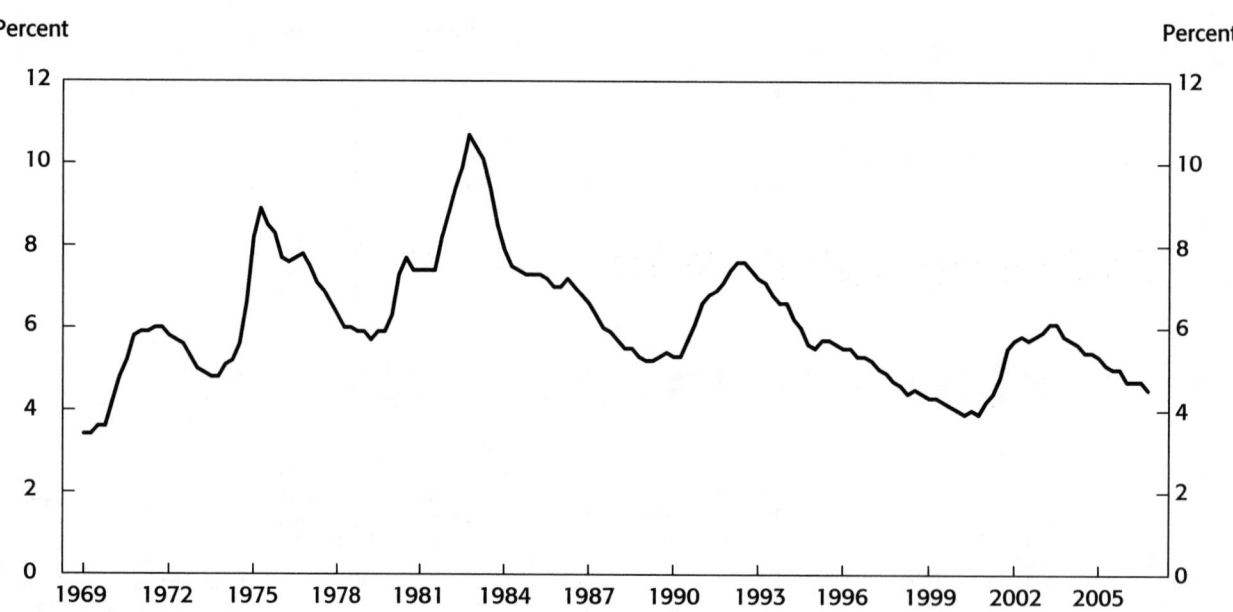

Unemployment Rate, Seasonally Adjusted Quarterly Data, 1969–2006
Note: Shaded regions represent recessions as designated by the National Bureau of Economic Research.
Source: Bureau of Labor Statistics, Current Population Survey.

CHAPTER **10**

Labor

HIGHLIGHTS

1 The techniques for measuring labor force (or work force) data were developed during the late 1930s by the Work Projects Administration (WPA). For every week containing the 12th day of the month, the Bureau of the Census collects data for the Bureau of Labor Statistics. This dataset is part of the former Current Population Survey and is based on a scientifically designed sample of households. The survey includes all employed and unemployed persons as well as self-employed persons, unpaid family workers and domestic servants, and others who do not ordinarily appear on the payrolls of any establishment. Labor force data are also collected in the decennial censuses.

2 The concepts of employment, unemployment, and labor have changed over the years. By current definitions, employed persons are those who work as paid employees or in their own businesses or professions, or on their farm or who work 15 hours or more as unpaid workers in a family enterprise. It also includes those who are temporarily absent from work or business because of illness, vacation, bad weather, labor/

management dispute or personal reasons. Volunteer workers are excluded. Unemployed persons are those who do not work during the survey week, but who make efforts to secure a job and are available for work. The civilian labor force (persons 14 years and over until 1966 and over 16 years thereafter) is the sum of the employed and the unemployed. Data on the size of the armed forces is obtained from the Department of Defense and added to the civilian labor force to obtain the Total Labor Force. For years prior to 1940 (when detailed labor force data became available for the whole nation), the data are based on Stanley Legerbott's *Manpower in Economic Growth: The American Record Since 1800*. Legerbott obtained his data by interpolating between detailed worker rates in the census years and applying the resultant series to unpublished census estimates of population. The gainful worker concept differs from other concepts in that its primary purpose is a count of occupations and occupational status rather than employment. It excludes students as well as women doing housework, but includes retired people who report their former line of work.

211

3 The most sensitive labor force data relate to unemployment. Because they are based on reports of unemployment insurance claims, rates may be generally lower than actual unemployment. They exclude those long-term unemployed who have become discouraged and opted out of the employment market. In earlier years, unemployment estimates were calculated as a residual, that is, the total number of employed persons was deducted from the total civilian labor force. The unemployment rate presents the data on unemployed persons as a percentage of the civilian labor force. The lowest unemployment rate (that is, the closest the United States ever came to the concept of full employment) was achieved in 1944 during wartime (1.2 percent), the highest rates were in 1894 (18.3 percent) and in 1939 (17.2 percent).

4 Economically Active Population is a concept developed by David L. Caplan and M. Claire Casey. It refers to both employed and unemployed workers in the civilian labor force 10 years old and over before 1940, and 14 years and over since 1940. It is similar to the gainful workers concept, which is also based on occupation and marketable skills rather than on employment. The occupational classification system is generally comparable with the system used in the *Dictionary of Occupational Titles*.

5 The most common range of wages for agricultural laborers in the United States in the nineteenth century was from $8 to $12 per month, the same range that prevails in many Third World countries today. Data on wages after the Civil War and before 1900 comes from a number of published reports, such as Joseph D. Weeks's *Report on the Statistics of Wages in the Manufacturing Industries* (1886) and the *Aldrich Reports on Wholesale Prices, on Wages and on Transportation* (1893). Since 1939, private industry employment and payrolls are based principally upon records of the Social Security Programs.

6 The average weekly hours worked and paid for differ from the average hours worked per week, both during times of substantial unemployment as well as times of relative full employment because of the overtime element. The widespread adoption of paid vacations of increasing length and the increasing number of paid holidays raised average weekly hours paid for, while keeping the average weekly hours worked low.

7 The Bureau of Labor Statistics monitors and publishes biennial data on labor unions, their membership dues, collective agreements, and voting rights. Union membership figures are available since 1951 and include the AFL–CIO, the principal labor federation, and independent labor unions. The decline in union membership has consequences not merely in U.S. industry but also in U.S. politics.

8 Data on work stoppages, including strikes and lockouts, were first published in 1881 and at five-year intervals thereafter with the exception of the period from 1906 to 1913. This seven-year lapse occurred while the charge of collecting labor statistics was moved from the Bureau of Labor (which collected these data from 1881 to 1905) to the Department of Labor, which was officially founded in 1913. During the transition period there was no government agency for the collection of labor statistics. Until 1927, these data were quite fragmentary and based on press reports and other secondary sources.

9 Compilation of work injury statistics began in 1910 for the iron and steel industry and by 1925 covered 24 industries. Since 1920, reports have been standardized with the injury-frequency rate defined as the average number of disabling injuries per million people-hours worked.

10 As of February 2007, the civilian labor force consisted of 152,784,000 persons or 50.7 percent of the population. The highest participation rate (91.7 percent) is found among males 25 to 34 years of age, while the lowest (11.5 percent) is found among women 65 years and older. White male participation rate (74.1 percent in 2005) has been historically higher than that of Black male participation rate (67.3 percent in 2005). The civilian labor force participation is expected to decrease to 64.7 percent in 2015, but the decrease will not come from women but from men.

11 Marital status makes a difference in the participation rates of men and women. The participation rate for single women (66.0 percent) is higher than that for married women (60.7 percent). The figures are reversed for men, with single men having a lower rate (70.1 percent) than that for married men (77.2 percent).

12 While the average work week was 39.1 hours in 2005, 10.222 million people work more than 60 hours every week and 14.569 million people work between 49 and 59 hours. More than 7.5 million people hold multiple jobs, and 32.268 million people hold part-time jobs.

13 In 2004, 20.673 million people usually worked at home. This number was almost equally distributed between men (10.780 million) and women (9.893 million). Minorities have not been prominent in this work-at-home population, the overwhelming majority of which is White. The Black work-at-home population numbered 1.247 million and Hispanics numbered 1.255 million.

14 The percentage of workers who have not completed high school declined from 36.1 percent in 1970 to 10.0 percent in 2005, while the percentage of college graduates rose from 14.1 percent to 32.4 percent.

15 Unemployment decreased in 2005 to 5.1 percent but this rate masks serious disparities between certain age groups. Among Blacks 16 to 19 years old, the unemployment rate is 33.3 percent, and among all males in that same age group is 18.6 percent. Unemployment is also higher among certain sectors, such as agriculture (8.3 percent), and leisure and hospitality (7.8 percent). Certain states, such as Mississippi (7.9 percent), Louisiana (7.1 percent), South Carolina, and Alaska (6.8 percent each), have higher than the national average unemployment, while Hawaii (2.8), North Dakota (3.4), and Vermont and Virginia (3.4 percent each), all have lower than average unemployment.

16 Approximately 55.5 percent of workers used computers in their jobs in 2003. Computer use is most widespread in the financial activities industry (82.4 percent), information industry (77.5 percent), and professional and business services industry (68.4 percent).

17 The average hourly earnings, including overtime, doubled in private industry since 1980. In 2005, it was highest in utilities ($26.70) and professional and technical services ($24.14) and lowest in leisure and hospitality ($9.14). In 2004, total annual compensation was highest in securities, commodity contracts, and investments ($193,915). It was lowest in accommodation and food services ($23,266). Highest average annual pay is received in Connecticut ($51,007), New York ($49,941), and New Jersey ($48,064), and the lowest in Montana ($27,830) and South Dakota ($28,281).

18 In constant 1996 dollars, the minimum wage actually decreased from $4.39 in 1955 to $4.04 in 2006, although in current dollars it increased from $0.75 to $5.15.

19 The jobs with the fastest potential growth rate until 2014 are home health aides (56.0 percent), network systems and data communications analysts (54.6 percent), medical assistants (52.1 percent), and physician assistants (49.6 percent).

20 In 2004, there were 49,100 job-related deaths and 10.5 million work-related disabling injuries leading to a loss of 485 million days of production time in future years.

21 Workplace stoppages, such as strikes and lockouts, once a permanent fixture of the industrial landscape, have become scarce. In 2005 there were only 22 work stoppages involving 100,000 workers and the loss of 1.7 million workdays compared with 424 work stoppages in 1974 involving 1,796,000 workers and the loss of 31.8 million workdays. American workers are more satisfied with their work conditions and pay than they have ever been in the previous century.

22 Labor union membership has declined overall from 17.7 million in 1983 to 15.7 million in 2005. Most of the decline is in the private sector where union membership is down from 11.9 million in 1983 to 8.3 million in 2005. This decline is partially offset by a slight increase in union membership in the public sector from 5.7 million to 7.4 million in the same period.

23 People working in the education, training, and library sectors have the highest unionization rate among all occupations at 37 percent.

24 Wyoming has the smallest number of union members (18 thousand), followed by South Dakota (20.5 thousand) and North Dakota (21 thousand). California has the largest number of union members at 2.4 million.

25 There is a significant discrepancy between the salaries of CEOs and their employees. An average CEO of a large company makes approximately 211 times more than the average worker in salary. Compared to other countries, an executive in the United States receives an average of $2.2 million in compensation as contrasted with $1.4 million in Switzerland and $1.2 million in France and the United Kingdom.

26 In 2005, 23,848,000 million people had disabilities. Of those, 19.2 percent are employed at least part time, while 77.6 percent are not in the labor force.

Table 10-1. Labor Force Status of the Population, 1870–2006

(Thousands of people, 16 years and over, except as noted.)

Year	Noninstitutional population[1]	Total labor force[2]	Total civilian labor force	Employed— agriculture	Employed— nonagriculture	Unemployed	Total not in labor force
2006[3]	228 815	...	151 428	2 206	142 221	7 001	77 387
2005[3]	226 082	...	149 320	2 197	139 532	7 591	76 762
2004[3]	223 357	...	147 401	2 232	137 020	8 149	75 956
2003[3]	221 168	...	146 510	2 275	135 461	8 774	74 658
2002	217 570	...	144 863	2 311	134 174	8 378	72 707
2001	215 092	...	143 734	2 299	134 635	6 801	71 359
2000[3]	212 577	...	142 583	2 464	134 427	5 692	69 994
1999[3]	207 753	...	139 368	3 281	130 207	5 880	68 385
1998[3]	205 220	...	137 673	3 378	128 085	6 210	67 547
1997[3]	203 133	...	136 297	3 399	126 159	6 739	66 837
1996	200 591	...	133 943	3 443	123 264	7 236	66 647
1995	198 584	...	132 304	3 440	121 460	7 404	66 280
1994[3]	196 814	...	131 056	3 409	119 651	7 996	65 758
1993	194 838	...	129 200	3 115	117 144	8 940	65 638
1992	192 805	...	128 105	3 247	115 245	9 613	64 700
1991	190 925	...	126 346	3 269	114 449	8 628	64 578
1990[3]	189 164	...	125 840	3 223	115 570	7 047	63 324
1989	186 393	...	123 869	3 199	114 142	6 528	62 523
1988	184 613	123 893	121 669	3 169	111 800	6 701	62 944
1987	182 753	122 122	119 865	3 208	109 232	7 425	62 888
1986[3]	180 587	120 079	117 834	3 163	106 434	8 237	62 752
1985	178 206	117 695	115 461	3 179	103 971	8 312	62 744
1984	176 383	115 763	113 544	3 321	101 685	8 539	62 839
1983	174 215	113 750	111 550	3 383	97 450	10 717	62 665
1982	172 271	112 384	110 204	3 401	96 125	10 678	62 067
1981	170 130	110 812	108 670	3 368	97 030	8 273	61 460
1980	167 745	109 042	106 940	3 364	95 938	7 637	60 806
1979	164 863	107 050	104 962	3 347	95 477	6 137	59 900
1978[3]	161 910	104 368	102 251	3 387	92 661	6 202	59 659
1977	159 033	101 142	99 009	3 283	88 734	6 991	60 025
1976	156 150	98 302	96 158	3 331	85 421	7 406	59 991
1975	153 153	95 955	93 775	3 408	82 438	7 929	59 377
1974	150 120	94 179	91 949	3 515	83 279	5 156	58 171
1973[3]	147 096	91 756	89 429	3 470	81 594	4 365	57 667
1972[3]	144 126	89 484	87 034	3 484	78 669	4 882	57 091
1971	140 216	87 198	84 382	3 394	75 972	5 016	55 834
1970	137 085	85 959	82 771	3 463	75 215	4 093	54 315
1969	134 335	84 240	80 734	3 606	74 296	2 832	53 602
1968	132 028	82 272	78 737	3 817	72 103	2 817	53 291
1967	129 874	80 793	77 347	3 844	70 527	2 975	52 527
1966	128 058	78 893	75 770	3 979	68 915	2 875	52 288
1965	126 513	77 178	74 455	4 361	66 726	3 366	52 058
1964	124 485	75 830	73 091	4 523	64 782	3 786	51 394
1963	122 416	74 571	71 833	4 687	63 076	4 070	50 583
1962[3]	120 153	73 442	70 614	4 944	61 759	3 911	49 539
1961	118 771	73 031	70 459	5 200	60 546	4 714	48 312
1960[4]	117 245	72 142	69 628	5 458	60 318	3 852	47 617
1959	115 329	70 921	68 369	5 565	59 065	3 740	46 960
1958	113 727	70 275	67 639	5 586	57 450	4 602	46 088
1957	112 265	69 729	66 929	5 947	58 123	2 859	45 336
1956	110 954	69 409	66 552	6 283	57 514	2 750	44 402
1955	109 683	68 072	65 023	6 450	55 722	2 852	44 660
1954	108 321	66 993	63 643	6 205	53 904	3 532	44 678
1953[3]	107 056	66 560	63 015	6 260	54 919	1 834	44 041
1952	105 231	65 730	62 138	6 500	53 749	1 883	43 093
1951	104 621	65 117	62 017	6 726	53 235	2 055	42 604
1950	104 995	63 858	62 208	7 160	51 758	3 288	42 787
1949	103 994	62 903	61 286	7 658	49 993	3 637	42 708
1948	103 068	62 080	60 621	7 629	50 714	2 276	42 447
1947	103 418	60 941	59 350	7 890	49 148	2 311	42 477
Decennial Census							
1970 (April)	139 130	82 049	80 051	2 750	73 804	3 497	57 082
1960 (April)[4,5]	124 517	69 877	68 144	4 257	60 383	3 505	54 639
1950 (April)[5]	110 267	59 643	58 646	[6]6 876	[6]48 912	2 858	[6]50 624
1940 (April)[5]	[6]100147	53 011	52 705	8 449	36 621	7 635	47 136
1930 (April)[7]	98 723	48 830	...	10 472	38 358	...	49 893
1920 (Jan)[7]	82 739	41 614	...	10 666	30 948	...	41 125
1910 (April)[7]	71 580	38 167	...	12 388	25 779	...	33 413
1900 (June)[7]	57 950	29 073	...	10 382	18 691	...	28 877
1890 (June)[7]	47 414	23 318	...	9 148	14 170	...	24 095
1880 (June)[7]	36 762	17 392	...	7 714	9 678	...	19 370
1870 (June)[7]	28 229	12 506	...	5 949	6 557	...	15 723

Source: U.S. Census Bureau. U.S. Department of Labor, Bureau of Labor Statistics.
[1]1879–1930, total population includes institutional.
[2]1940–1970, includes armed forces.
[3]Data not strictly comparable with earlier years because of changes in classifications and methods.
[4]Denotes first year for which figures include Alaska and Hawaii.
[5]Data for persons 14 years and over.
[6]Estimated from data based on different sample.
[7]Data for persons 10 years old and over reporting a gainful occupation.
... = Not available.

Table 10-2. Unemployment, 1890–2006

(Percent.)

Year	Percent of civilian labor force
2006[1]	4.6
2005[1]	5.1
2004[1]	5.5
2003[1]	6.0
2002	5.8
2001	4.7
2000[1]	4.0
1999[1]	4.2
1998[1]	4.5
1997[1]	4.9
1996	5.4
1995	5.6
1994[1]	6.1
1993	6.9
1992	7.5
1991	6.8
1990[1]	5.6
1989	5.3
1988	5.5
1987	6.2
1986[1]	7.0
1985	7.2
1984	7.5
1983	9.6
1982	9.7
1981	7.6
1980	7.1
1979	5.8
1978[1]	6.1
1977	7.1
1976	7.7
1975	8.5
1974	5.6
1973[1]	4.9
1972[1]	5.6
1971	5.9
1970	4.9
1969	3.5
1968	3.6
1967	3.8
1966	3.8
1965	4.5
1964	5.2
1963	5.7
1962[1]	5.5
1961	6.7
1960[1,2]	5.5
1959	5.5
1958	6.8
1957	4.3
1956	4.1
1955	4.4
1954	5.5
1953[1]	2.9
1952	3.0
1951	3.3
1950	5.3
1949	5.9
1948	3.8
1947	3.9
1946	3.9
1945	1.9
1944	1.2
1943	1.9
1942	4.7
1941	9.9

[1]Data not strictly comparable with earlier years because of changes in classifications and methods.
[2]First year for which figures include Alaska and Hawaii.

Table 10-2. Unemployment, 1890–2006—*Continued*

(Percent.)

Year	Percent of civilian labor force
1940	14.6
1939	17.2
1938	19.0
1937	14.3
1936	16.9
1935	20.1
1934	21.7
1933	24.9
1932	23.6
1931	15.9
1930	8.7
1929	3.2
1928	4.2
1927	3.3
1926	1.8
1925	3.2
1924	5.0
1923	2.4
1922	6.7
1921	11.7
1920	5.2
1919	1.4
1918	1.4
1917	4.6
1916	5.1
1915	8.5
1914	7.9
1913	4.3
1912	4.6
1911	6.7
1910	5.9
1909	5.1
1908	8.0
1907	2.8
1906	1.7
1905	4.3
1904	5.4
1903	3.9
1902	3.7
1901	4.0
1900	5.0
1899	6.5
1898	12.4
1897	14.5
1896	14.4
1985	13.7
1894	18.4
1893	11.7
1892	3.0
1891	5.4
1890	4.0

Source: U.S. Department of Labor, Bureau of Labor Statistics.

Table 10-3. Unemployment Rates, by Sex and Race in the Civilian Labor Force, 1947–2006

(Percent.)

Year	Total[1]	Male	Female	White[2]	Black[2]
2006	4.6	4.6	4.6	4.0	8.9
2005	5.1	5.1	5.1	4.4	10.0
2004	5.5	5.6	5.4	4.8	10.4
2003	6.0	6.3	5.7	5.2	10.8
2002	5.8	5.9	5.6	5.1	10.2
2001	4.7	4.8	4.7	4.2	8.6
2000	4.0	3.9	4.1	3.5	7.6
1999	4.2	4.1	4.3	3.7	8.0
1998	4.5	4.4	4.6	3.9	8.9
1997	4.9	4.9	5.0	4.2	10.0
1996	5.4	5.4	5.4	4.7	10.5
1995	5.6	5.6	5.6	4.9	10.4
1994	6.1	6.2	6.0	5.3	11.5
1993	6.9	7.2	6.6	6.1	13.0
1992	7.5	7.9	7.0	6.6	14.2
1991	6.8	7.2	6.4	6.1	12.5
1990	5.6	5.7	5.5	4.8	11.4
1989	5.3	5.2	5.4	4.5	11.4
1988	5.5	5.5	5.6	4.7	11.7
1987	6.2	6.2	6.2	5.3	13.0
1986	7.0	6.9	7.1	6.0	14.5
1985	7.2	7.0	7.4	6.2	15.1
1984	7.5	7.4	7.6	6.5	15.9
1983	9.6	9.9	9.2	8.4	19.5
1982	9.7	9.9	9.4	8.6	18.9
1981	7.6	7.4	7.9	6.7	15.6
1980	7.1	6.9	7.4	6.3	14.3
1979	5.8	5.1	6.8	5.1	12.3
1978	6.1	5.3	7.2	5.2	12.8
1977	7.1	6.3	8.2	6.2	14.0
1976	7.7	7.1	8.6	7.0	14.0
1975	8.5	7.9	9.3	7.8	14.8
1974	5.6	4.9	6.7	5.0	10.5
1973	4.9	4.2	6.0	4.3	9.4
1972	5.6	5.0	6.6	5.1	10.4
1971	5.9	5.3	6.9	5.4	9.9
1970	4.9	4.4	5.9	4.5	8.2
1969	3.5	2.8	4.7	3.1	6.4
1968	3.6	2.9	4.8	3.2	6.7
1967	3.8	3.1	5.2	3.4	7.4
1966	3.8	3.2	4.8	3.4	7.3
1965	4.5	4.0	5.5	4.1	8.1
1964	5.2	4.6	6.2	4.6	9.6
1963	5.7	5.2	6.5	5.0	10.8
1962	5.5	5.2	6.2	4.9	10.9
1961	6.7	6.4	7.2	6.0	12.4
1960	5.5	5.4	5.9	5.0	10.2
1959	5.5	5.2	5.9	4.8	10.7
1958	6.8	6.8	6.8	6.1	12.6
1957	4.3	4.1	4.7	3.8	7.9
1956	4.1	3.8	4.8	3.6	8.3
1955	4.4	4.2	4.9	3.9	8.7
1954	5.5	5.3	6.0	5.0	9.9
1953	2.9	2.8	3.3	2.7	4.5
1952	3.0	2.8	3.6	2.8	5.4
1951	3.3	2.8	4.4	3.1	5.3
1950	5.3	5.1	5.7	4.9	9.0
1949	5.9	5.9	6.0	5.6	8.9
1948	3.8	3.6	4.1	3.5	5.9
1947	3.9	4.0	3.7	. . .	. . .

Source: U.S. Census Bureau. *Statistical Abstract of the United States 2007.* U.S. Department of Labor, Bureau of Labor Statistics.
[1]Includes other races, not shown separately.
[2]Beginning 2003, for this race group only. The 2003 Current Population Survey (CPS) allowed respondents to choose more than one race. Beginning 2003, data represent persons who selected this race group only and exclude persons reporting more than one race. The CPS in prior years only allowed respondents to report one race group.
. . . = Not available.

Table 10-4. Unemployment Rates, by Industry (NAICS Basis), 2000–2006

(Percent.)

Year	2000	2001	2002	2003[1]	2004[1]	2005[1]	2006
Total[2]	4.0	4.7	5.8	6.0	5.5	5.1	4.6
Nonagricultural Private Wage and							
Salary Workers	4.1	5.0	6.2	6.3	5.7	5.2	4.7
Mining	4.4	4.2	6.3	6.7	3.9	3.1	3.2
Construction	6.2	7.1	9.2	9.3	8.4	7.4	6.7
Manufacturing	3.5	5.2	6.7	6.6	5.7	4.9	4.2
Durable goods	3.2	5.2	6.9	6.9	5.5	4.6	3.9
Nondurable goods	4.0	5.2	6.2	6.9	5.9	5.3	4.8
Wholesale and retail trade	4.3	4.9	6.1	6.0	5.8	5.4	4.9
Transportation and utilities	3.4	4.3	4.9	5.3	4.4	4.1	4.0
Information	3.2	4.9	6.9	6.8	5.7	5.0	3.7
Financial activities	2.4	2.9	3.5	3.5	3.6	2.9	2.7
Business and professional services	4.8	6.1	7.9	8.2	6.8	6.2	5.6
Education and health services	2.5	2.8	3.4	3.6	3.4	3.4	3.0
Leisure and hospitality	6.6	7.5	8.4	8.7	8.3	7.8	7.3
Other services[3]	3.9	4.0	5.1	5.7	5.3	4.8	4.7
Agriculture and Related Private							
Wage and Salary Workers	9.0	11.2	10.1	10.2	9.9	8.3	7.2
Government Workers	2.1	2.2	2.5	2.8	2.7	2.6	2.3
Self-Employed and Unpaid							
Family Members	2.1	2.1	2.6	2.7	2.8	2.7	2.7

Source: U.S. Census Bureau. *Statistical Abstract of the United States 2007.* U.S. Department of Labor, Bureau of Labor Statistics.
[1]Data not strictly comparable with earlier years because of changes in classifications and methods.
[2]Includes the self-employed, unpaid family workers, and persons with no previous work experience, not shown separately.
[3]Includes private household workers.

Table 10-5. Unemployment Rates, by Industry (SIC Basis), 1948–1999

(Percent.)

Year	Total unemployed[1]	Experienced wage and salary workers								Government
		Agriculture	Wage and salary workers in private nonagricultural industries							
			Mining	Construction	Manufacturing	Transportation and public utilities	Wholesale trade	Finance, insurance, and real estate	Service industries	
1999	4.0	8.9	5.7	7.0	3.6	3.0	5.2	2.3	4.0	2.2
1998	4.5	8.3	3.2	7.5	3.9	3.4	5.5	2.5	4.5	2.3
1997	4.9	9.1	3.8	9.0	4.2	3.5	6.2	3.0	4.6	2.6
1996	5.4	10.2	5.1	10.1	4.8	4.1	6.4	2.7	5.4	2.9
1995	5.6	11.1	5.2	11.5	4.9	4.5	6.5	3.3	5.4	2.9
1994	6.1	11.3	5.4	11.8	5.6	4.8	7.4	3.6	5.9	3.4
1993	6.8	11.7	7.4	14.4	7.2	5.1	7.8	4.1	6.1	3.3
1992	7.5	12.5	8.0	16.8	7.8	5.5	8.4	4.6	6.5	3.6
1991	6.8	11.8	7.8	15.5	7.3	5.3	7.6	4.0	5.7	3.3
1990	5.6	9.8	4.8	11.1	5.8	3.9	6.4	3.0	5.0	3.7
1989	5.3	9.6	5.8	10.0	5.1	3.9	6.0	3.1	4.8	2.7
1988	5.5	10.6	7.9	10.6	5.3	3.9	6.2	3.0	4.9	2.8
1987	6.2	10.5	10.0	11.6	6.0	4.5	6.9	3.1	5.4	3.5
1986	7.0	12.5	13.5	13.1	7.1	5.1	7.6	3.5	6.1	3.6
1985	7.2	13.2	9.5	13.1	7.7	5.1	7.6	3.5	6.2	3.9
1984	7.5	13.5	10.0	14.3	7.5	5.5	8.0	3.7	6.6	4.5
1983	9.6	16.0	17.0	18.4	11.2	7.4	10.0	4.5	7.9	5.3
1982	9.7	14.7	13.4	20.0	12.3	6.8	10.0	4.7	7.6	4.9
1981	7.6	12.1	6.0	15.6	8.3	5.2	8.1	3.5	6.6	4.7
1980	7.1	11.0	6.4	14.1	8.5	4.9	7.4	3.4	5.9	4.1
1979	5.8	9.3	4.9	10.3	5.6	3.7	6.5	3.0	5.5	3.7
1978	6.0	8.9	4.2	10.6	5.5	3.7	6.9	3.1	5.7	3.9
1977	7.0	11.2	3.8	12.7	6.7	4.7	8.0	3.8	6.6	4.2
1976	7.7	11.8	4.6	15.5	7.9	5.0	8.6	4.3	7.2	4.4
1975	8.5	10.4	4.1	18.0	10.9	5.6	8.7	4.9	7.1	4.1
1974	5.6	7.5	3.0	10.7	5.8	3.3	6.5	3.1	5.2	3.0
1973	4.9	7.0	2.9	8.9	4.4	3.0	5.7	2.7	4.8	2.7
1972	5.6	7.7	3.2	10.3	5.6	3.5	6.4	3.4	5.3	3.0
1971	5.9	7.9	4.0	10.4	6.8	3.8	6.4	3.3	5.6	2.9
1970	4.9	7.5	3.1	9.7	5.6	3.2	5.3	2.8	4.7	2.2
1969	3.5	6.1	2.9	6.0	3.3	2.2	4.1	2.1	3.5	1.9
1968	3.6	6.3	3.1	6.9	3.3	2.0	4.0	2.2	3.7	1.8
1967	3.8	6.9	3.4	7.4	3.7	2.4	4.2	2.5	3.9	1.8
1966	3.8	6.6	3.7	8.0	3.2	2.1	4.4	2.1	3.9	1.8
1965	4.5	7.6	5.4	10.1	4.0	2.9	5.0	2.3	4.6	1.9
1964	5.2	9.7	6.7	11.2	5.0	3.5	5.7	2.6	5.3	2.1
1963	5.7	9.2	7.2	13.3	5.7	4.2	6.2	2.7	5.7	2.2
1962	5.5	7.5	7.8	13.5	5.8	4.1	6.3	3.0	5.5	2.1
1961	6.7	9.6	11.1	15.7	7.8	5.3	7.3	3.3	6.2	2.5
1960	5.5	8.3	9.7	13.5	6.2	4.6	5.9	2.4	5.1	2.4
1959	5.5	9.1	9.7	13.4	6.1	4.4	5.8	2.5	5.3	2.2
1958	6.8	10.3	11.0	15.3	9.3	6.1	6.8	2.9	5.7	2.5
1957	4.3	6.9	5.9	10.9	5.1	3.3	4.5	1.8	4.2	1.9
1956	4.1	7.4	6.8	10.0	4.7	3.0	4.5	1.8	4.6	1.7
1955	4.4	7.2	9.1	10.9	4.7	4.0	4.7	2.4	5.2	2.0
1954	5.5	9.0	14.4	12.9	7.1	5.6	5.7	2.3	5.5	2.2
1953	2.9	5.6	4.6	7.2	3.1	2.2	3.4	1.8	3.4	1.5
1952	3.0	4.8	3.8	6.7	3.5	2.3	3.5	1.8	3.6	1.6
1951	3.3	4.4	4.0	7.2	3.9	2.3	3.9	1.5	4.2	1.8
1950	5.3	9.0	6.7	12.2	6.2	4.6	6.0	2.2	6.4	3.0
1949	5.9	7.1	8.9	14.0	8.0	5.9	6.2	2.1	6.8	3.1
1948	3.8	5.5	3.1	8.7	4.2	3.5	4.7	1.8	4.8	2.2

[1]Also includes the self employed, unpaid family workers, and those with no previous work experience, not shown separately.

Table 10-6. Labor Force and Employment, by Super Sector, 1800–2006

(Thousands of people.)

Year	Civilian labor force[1]	Agriculture	Total nonfarm	Total private	Goods-producing	Service-providing	Private service-providing	Natural resources and mining	Construction	Manufac-turing	Trade, trans-portation, and utilities	Wholesale trade
2006	151 428	2 206	136 174	114 184	22 570	113 605	91 615	684	7 689	14 197	26 231	5 898
2005	149 320	2 197	133 703	111 899	22 190	111 513	89 709	628	7 336	14 226	25 959	5 764
2004	147 401	2 232	131 435	109 814	21 882	109 553	87 932	591	6 976	14 315	25 533	5 663
2003	146 510	2 275	129 999	108 416	21 816	108 182	86 599	572	6 735	14 510	25 287	5 608
2002	144 863	2 311	130 341	108 828	22 557	107 784	86 271	583	6 716	15 259	25 497	5 652
2001	143 734	2 299	131 826	110 707	23 873	107 952	86 834	606	6 826	16 441	25 983	5 773
2000	142 583	2 464	131 785	110 996	24 649	107 136	86 346	599	6 787	17 263	26 225	5 933
1999	139 368	3 281	128 993	108 686	24 465	104 528	84 221	598	6 545	17 322	25 771	5 893
1998	137 673	3 378	125 930	106 021	24 354	101 576	81 667	645	6 149	17 560	25 186	5 795
1997	136 297	3 399	122 776	103 113	23 886	98 890	79 227	654	5 813	17 419	24 700	5 664
1996	133 943	3 443	119 708	100 169	23 410	96 299	76 759	637	5 536	17 237	24 239	5 522
1995	132 304	3 440	117 298	97 866	23 156	94 142	74 710	641	5 274	17 241	23 834	5 433
1994	131 056	3 409	114 291	95 016	22 774	91 517	72 242	659	5 095	17 021	23 128	5 247
1993	129 200	3 115	110 844	91 855	22 219	88 625	69 636	666	4 779	16 774	22 378	5 093
1992	128 105	3 247	108 726	89 940	22 095	86 631	67 845	689	4 608	16 799	22 125	5 110
1991	126 346	3 269	108 374	89 829	22 588	85 787	67 241	739	4 780	17 068	22 281	5 185
1990	125 840	3 223	109 487	91 072	23 723	85 764	67 349	765	5 263	17 695	22 666	5 268
1989	123 869	3 199	108 014	90 087	24 045	83 969	66 042	750	5 309	17 985	22 510	5 284
1988	121 669	3 169	105 345	87 806	23 909	81 436	63 897	770	5 233	17 906	21 974	5 153
1987	119 865	3 208	102 088	84 932	23 470	78 618	61 462	771	5 090	17 609	21 302	5 003
1986	117 834	3 163	99 474	82 636	23 318	76 156	59 318	829	4 937	17 552	20 795	4 935
1985	115 461	3 179	97 511	80 978	23 585	73 926	57 393	974	4 793	17 819	20 379	4 915
1984	113 544	3 321	94 530	78 371	23 435	71 095	54 936	1 014	4 501	17 920	19 653	4 788
1983	111 550	3 383	90 280	74 269	22 110	68 171	52 160	997	4 065	17 048	18 668	4 559
1982	110 204	3 401	89 677	73 695	22 550	67 127	51 145	1 163	4 024	17 363	18 457	4 575
1981	108 670	3 368	91 289	75 109	24 118	67 172	50 991	1 180	4 304	18 634	18 604	4 634
1980	106 940	3 364	90 528	74 154	24 263	66 265	49 891	1 077	4 454	18 733	18 413	4 557
1979	104 962	3 347	89 932	73 864	24 997	64 935	48 868	1 008	4 562	19 426	18 303	4 485
1978	102 251	3 387	86 826	71 014	24 156	62 670	46 858	902	4 322	18 932	17 658	4 280
1977	99 009	3 283	82 593	67 334	22 972	59 620	44 362	865	3 940	18 167	16 765	4 055
1976	96 158	3 331	79 502	64 501	22 025	57 477	42 476	832	3 662	17 531	16 128	3 920
1975	93 775	3 408	77 069	62 250	21 318	55 751	40 932	802	3 608	16 909	15 606	3 810
1974	91 949	3 515	78 389	64 086	23 364	55 025	40 721	755	4 095	18 514	15 693	3 823
1973	89 429	3 470	76 912	63 050	23 450	53 462	39 600	693	4 167	18 589	15 349	3 688
1972	87 034	3 484	73 798	60 333	22 299	51 499	38 034	672	3 957	17 669	14 788	3 547
1971	84 382	3 394	71 335	58 323	21 602	49 734	36 721	658	3 770	17 174	14 318	3 424
1970	82 771	3 463	71 006	58 318	22 179	48 827	36 139	677	3 654	17 848	14 144	3 418
1960	. . .	5 458	54 296	45 832	19 182	35 114	26 650	771	2 973	15 438	11 147	2 690
1950	. . .	7 160	45 287	39 167	17 343	27 945	21 824	924	2 405	14 013	9 694	2 255
1940	56 520	. . .	32 407	28 156	12 378	20 029	15 778	927	1 352	10 099	7 043	1 571
1930	48 830	. . .	. . .	. . .	. . .	. . .	. . .	. . .	1 988	9 884	. . .	. . .
1920	41 610	. . .	. . .	. . .	. . .	. . .	. . .	. . .	1 233	11 190	. . .	. . .
1910	37 480	. . .	. . .	. . .	. . .	. . .	. . .	. . .	1 949	8 332	. . .	. . .
1900	29 070	. . .	. . .	. . .	. . .	. . .	. . .	. . .	1 665	5 895	. . .	. . .
1890	23 320	. . .	. . .	. . .	. . .	. . .	. . .	. . .	1 510	4 390	. . .	. . .
1880	17 390	. . .	. . .	. . .	. . .	. . .	. . .	. . .	900	3 290	. . .	. . .
1870	12 930	. . .	. . .	. . .	. . .	. . .	. . .	. . .	780	2 470	. . .	. . .
1860	11 110	. . .	. . .	. . .	. . .	. . .	. . .	. . .	520	1 530	. . .	. . .
1850	8 250	. . .	. . .	. . .	. . .	. . .	. . .	. . .	410	1 200	. . .	. . .
1840	5 660	. . .	. . .	. . .	. . .	. . .	. . .	. . .	290	500	. . .	. . .
1830	4 200	. . .	. . .	. . .	. . .	. . .	. . .	. . .	. . .	. . .	. . .	. . .
1820	3 135	. . .	. . .	. . .	. . .	. . .	. . .	. . .	. . .	. . .	. . .	. . .
1810	2 330	. . .	. . .	. . .	. . .	. . .	. . .	. . .	. . .	75	. . .	. . .
1800	1 900	. . .	. . .	. . .	. . .	. . .	. . .	. . .	. . .	. . .	. . .	. . .

[1]Data affected by changes in population controls in January 2000, January 2003, January 2004, January 2005, and January 2006, therefore, data for the aforementioned years is not strictly comparable to earlier years.
. . . = Not available.

Table 10-6. Labor Force and Employment, by Super Sector, 1800–2006—*Continued*

(Thousands of people.)

Year	Retail trade	Transportation and warehousing	Utilities	Information	Financial activities	Professional and business services	Education and health services	Leisure and hospitality	Other services	Government
2006	15 319	4 466	549	3 055	8 363	17 552	17 838	13 143	5 432	21 990
2005	15 280	4 361	554	3 061	8 153	16 954	17 372	12 816	5 395	21 804
2004	15 058	4 249	564	3 118	8 031	16 395	16 953	12 493	5 409	21 621
2003	14 917	4 185	577	3 188	7 977	15 987	16 588	12 173	5 401	21 583
2002	15 025	4 224	596	3 395	7 847	15 976	16 199	11 986	5 372	21 513
2001	15 239	4 372	599	3 629	7 807	16 476	15 645	12 036	5 258	21 118
2000	15 280	4 410	601	3 631	7 687	16 666	15 109	11 862	5 168	20 790
1999	14 970	4 300	609	3 419	7 648	15 957	14 798	11 543	5 087	20 307
1998	14 609	4 168	613	3 218	7 462	15 147	14 446	11 232	4 976	19 909
1997	14 389	4 027	621	3 084	7 178	14 335	14 087	11 018	4 825	19 664
1996	14 143	3 935	640	2 940	6 969	13 462	13 683	10 777	4 690	19 539
1995	13 897	3 838	666	2 843	6 827	12 844	13 289	10 501	4 572	19 432
1994	13 491	3 701	689	2 738	6 867	12 174	12 807	10 100	4 428	19 275
1993	13 021	3 554	711	2 668	6 709	11 495	12 303	9 732	4 350	18 989
1992	12 828	3 462	726	2 641	6 540	10 970	11 891	9 437	4 240	18 787
1991	12 896	3 463	736	2 677	6 558	10 714	11 506	9 256	4 249	18 545
1990	13 182	3 476	740	2 688	6 614	10 848	10 984	9 288	4 261	18 415
1989	13 108	3 386	732	2 622	6 562	10 555	10 616	9 062	4 116	17 927
1988	12 808	3 290	723	2 585	6 500	10 090	10 063	8 778	3 907	17 540
1987	12 419	3 156	725	2 507	6 385	9 608	9 515	8 446	3 699	17 156
1986	12 078	3 059	723	2 445	6 128	9 211	9 061	8 156	3 523	16 838
1985	11 733	3 012	720	2 437	5 815	8 871	8 657	7 869	3 366	16 533
1984	11 223	2 934	708	2 398	5 553	8 464	8 193	7 489	3 186	16 159
1983	10 635	2 775	699	2 253	5 334	8 039	7 766	7 078	3 021	16 011
1982	10 372	2 817	694	2 317	5 209	7 848	7 515	6 874	2 924	15 982
1981	10 364	2 932	674	2 382	5 163	7 782	7 357	6 840	2 865	16 180
1980	10 244	2 961	651	2 361	5 025	7 544	7 072	6 721	2 755	16 375
1979	10 180	3 005	632	2 375	4 843	7 312	6 767	6 631	2 637	16 068
1978	9 879	2 890	609	2 287	4 599	6 972	6 427	6 411	2 505	15 812
1977	9 359	2 765	585	2 185	4 348	6 587	6 052	6 065	2 359	15 258
1976	8 966	2 667	576	2 111	4 155	6 287	5 756	5 794	2 244	15 001
1975	8 600	2 620	574	2 061	4 047	6 034	5 497	5 544	2 144	14 820
1974	8 536	2 752	582	2 160	4 023	5 974	5 322	5 471	2 078	14 303
1973	8 371	2 718	571	2 135	3 920	5 774	5 092	5 341	1 990	13 862
1972	8 038	2 646	557	2 056	3 784	5 523	4 863	5 121	1 900	13 465
1971	7 657	...	541	2 009	3 651	5 328	4 675	4 914	1 827	13 012
1970	7 463	...	536	2 041	3 532	5 267	4 577	4 789	1 789	12 687
1960	5 589	...	...	1 728	2 532	3 694	2 937	3 460	1 152	8 464
1950	4 580	...	...	1 625	1 825	2 928	2 144	2 769	839	6 120
1940	3 324	...	...	1 196	1 424	2 073	1 470	1 995	578	4 251
1930	...	...	...	...	...	...	...	...	...	...
1920	...	...	...	...	...	...	...	...	...	...
1910	...	...	...	...	...	...	...	...	...	...
1900	...	...	...	...	...	...	...	...	...	...
1890	...	...	...	...	...	...	...	...	...	...
1880	...	...	...	...	...	...	...	...	...	...
1870	...	...	...	...	...	...	...	...	...	...
1860	...	...	...	...	...	...	...	...	...	...
1850	...	...	...	...	...	...	...	...	...	...
1840	...	...	...	...	...	...	...	...	...	...
1830	...	...	...	...	...	...	...	...	...	...
1820	...	...	...	...	...	...	...	...	...	...
1810	...	...	...	...	...	...	...	...	...	...
1800	...	...	...	...	...	...	...	...	...	...

Source: U.S. Department of Labor, Bureau of Labor Statistics. U.S. Census Bureau.
. . . = Not available.

Table 10-7. Average Annual Earnings of Employees, 1929–2004

(Dollars.)

Year	Earnings of full-time employees
2004	43 327
2003	41 468
2002	40 263
2001	39 538
2000	38 762
1999	36 555
1998	35 034
1997	33 429
1996	32 040
1995	30 911
1994	29 922
1993	29 351
1992	28 667
1991	27 192
1990	25 889
1989	24 766
1988	24 032
1987	22 913
1986	21 935
1985	21 079
1984	20 168
1983	19 330
1982	18 488
1981	17 218
1980	15 757
1979	14 376
1978	13 287
1977	12 379
1976	11 620
1975	10 836
1974	9 994
1973	9 298
1972	8 610
1971	. . .
1970	7 564
1969	7 095
1968	6 657
1967	6 230
1966	5 967
1965	5 710
1964	5 503
1963	5 243
1962	5 065
1961	4 884
1960	4 743
1959	4 594
1958	4 375
1957	4 230
1956	4 055
1955	3 851
1954	3 667
1953	3 581
1952	3 402
1951	3 217
1950	2 992
1949	2 844
1948	2 786
1947	. . .
1946	2 359
1945	2 190
1944	2 109
1943	1 951
1942	1 709
1941	1 443
1940	1 299
1939	1 264
1938	1 230
1937	1 258
1936	1 184
1935	1 137
1934	1 091
1933	1 048
1932	1 120
1931	1 275
1930	1 368
1929	1 405

Source: U.S. Census Bureau. U.S. Bureau of Economic Analysis.
. . . = Not available.

Table 10-8. Earnings and Hours of Production Workers in Manufacturing, 1939–2006

(Dollars, number.)

Industry	Average hourly earnings	Average weekly hours	Average weekly earnings
2006	16.80	41.1	690.83
2005	16.56	40.7	673.37
2004	16.15	40.8	658.59
2003	15.74	40.4	635.99
2002	15.29	40.5	618.75
2001	14.76	40.3	595.19
2000	14.32	41.3	590.65
1999	13.85	41.4	573.17
1998	13.45	41.4	557.12
1997	13.14	41.7	548.22
1996	12.75	41.3	526.55
1995	12.34	41.3	509.26
1994	12.04	41.7	502.12
1993	11.70	41.1	480.80
1992	11.40	40.7	464.43
1991	11.13	40.4	449.73
1990	10.78	40.5	436.16
1989	10.35	40.9	423.32
1988	10.05	41.0	412.05
1987	9.77	40.9	399.59
1986	9.59	40.7	390.31
1985	9.40	40.5	380.70
1984	9.05	40.7	368.34
1983	8.70	40.1	348.87
1982	8.36	38.9	325.20
1981	7.86	39.8	312.83
1980	7.15	39.7	283.86
1979	6.57	40.2	264.11
1978	6.05	40.4	244.42
1977	5.55	40.3	223.67
1976	5.09	40.1	204.11
1975	4.71	39.5	186.05
1974	4.31	40.0	172.40
1973	3.97	40.7	161.58
1972	3.70	40.6	150.22
1971	3.45	39.9	137.66
1970	3.23	39.8	128.55
1969	3.07	40.6	124.64
1968	2.89	40.7	117.62
1967	2.71	40.6	110.03
1966	2.60	41.4	107.64
1965	2.49	41.2	102.59
1964	2.41	40.8	98.33
1963	2.34	40.6	95.00
1962	2.27	40.5	91.94
1961	2.20	39.9	87.78
1960	2.15	39.8	85.57
1959[1]	2.08	40.3	83.82
1958	1.99	39.2	78.01
1957	1.93	39.9	77.01
1956	1.84	40.5	74.52
1955	1.74	40.8	70.99
1954	1.66	39.7	65.90
1953	1.63	40.6	66.18
1952	1.53	40.8	62.42
1951	1.45	40.7	59.02
1950	1.32	40.6	53.59
1949	1.25	39.2	49.00
1948	1.20	40.1	48.12
1947	1.10	40.5	44.55
1946	0.95	40.4	38.38
1945	0.90	43.6	39.24
1944	0.91	45.4	41.31
1943	0.86	45.1	38.79
1942	0.74	43.2	31.97
1941	0.61	40.7	24.83
1940	0.53	38.2	20.25
1939	0.49	37.7	18.47

Source: U.S. Department of Labor, Bureau of Labor Statistics.
[1]First year for which figures include Alaska and Hawaii.

Table 10-9. Labor Union Membership as a Percent of Total Employment, 1930–2006

(Number, percent.)

Year	Total union membership	Percent of employed
2006	15 359	12.0
2005	15 685	12.5
2004	15 472	12.5
2003	15 776	12.9
2002	15 979	13.3
2001	16 289	13.5
2000	16 258	13.5
1999	16 477	13.9
1998	16 211	13.9
1997	16 110	14.1
1996	16 269	14.5
1995	16 360	14.9
1994	16 740	15.5
1993	16 598	15.8
1992	16 390	15.8
1991	16 568	16.1
1990	16 740	16.1
1989	16 961	16.4
1988	17 002	16.8
1987	16 913	17.0
1986	16 975	17.5
1985	16 996	18.0
1984	17 340	17.9
1983	17 717	20.1
1980	22 811	25.2
1978	23 306	19.7
1976	21 171	20.3
1974	23 408	21.7
1972	20 893	21.8
1970	20 752	27.4
1969	20 382	27.1
1968	20 258	27.9
1967	19 712	27.9
1966	19 181	28.1
1965	18 519	28.4
1964	17 976	28.9
1963	17 586	29.2
1962	17 630	29.8
1961	17 328	30.2
1960 1	18 117	31.4
1959	18 169	32.1
1958	18 081	33.2
1957	18 431	32.8
1956	18 477	33.4
1955	17 749	33.2
1954	17 955	34.7
1953	17 860	33.7
1952	16 750	32.5
1951	16 750	33.3
1950	15 000	31.5
1949	15 000	32.6
1948	15 000	31.9
1947	15 414	33.7
1946	14 974	34.5
1945	14 796	35.5
1944	14 621	33.8
1943	13 642	31.1
1942	10 762	25.9
1941	10 489	27.9
1940	8 944	26.9
1939	8 980	28.6
1938	8 265	27.5
1937	7 218	22.6
1936	4 164	13.7
1935	3 728	13.2
1934	3 249	11.9
1933	2 857	11.3
1932	3 226	12.9
1931	3 526	12.4
1930	3 632	11.6

Source: U.S. Census Bureau. The Bureau of National Affairs, Inc. *Union Membership and Earnings Data Book: Compilations from the Current Population Survey (2006) Edition),* copyright by Bureau of National Affairs PLUS; authored by Barry Hirsch of Trinity University and David MacPherson of Florida State University.
[1]First year for which figures include Alaska and Hawaii.
. . . = Not available.

Table 10-10. Work Stoppages, Workers Involved, and Days Idle, 1927–2006

(Number, percent.)

Year	Stoppage beginning in the year		Days idle	
	Number[1]	Number of workers involved (thousands)[2]	Number[3]	Percent of estimated total working time[4]
Work Stoppages Involving 1,000 Workers or More				
2006	20	70	2 688	0.01
2005	22	100	1 736	0.01
2004	17	171	3 344	0.01
2003	14	129	4 091	0.01
2002	19	46	660	(5)
2001	29	99	1 151	(5)
2000	39	394	20 419	0.06
1999	17	73	1 996	0.01
1998	34	387	5 116	0.02
1997	29	339	4 497	0.01
1996	37	273	4 889	0.02
1995	31	192	5 771	0.02
1994	45	322	5 020	0.02
1993	35	182	3 981	0.01
1992	35	364	3 989	0.01
1991	40	392	4 584	0.02
1990	44	185	5 926	0.02
1989	51	452	16 996	0.07
1988	40	118	64 381	0.02
1987	46	174	64 481	0.02
1986	69	533	11 861	0.05
1985	54	324	7 079	0.03
1984	62	376	8 499	0.04
1983	81	909	17 461	0.08
1982	96	656	9 061	0.04
1981	145	729	16 908	0.07
1980	187	795	20 844	0.09
1979	235	1 021	20 409	0.09
1978	219	1 006	23 774	0.11
1977	298	1 212	21 258	0.10
1976	231	1 519	23 962	0.12
1975	235	965	17 563	0.09
1974	424	1 796	31 809	0.16
1973	317	1 400	16 260	0.08
1972	250	975	16 764	0.09
1971	298	2 516	35 538	0.19
All Work Stoppages				
1970	5 716	3 305	66 414	0.37
1969	5 700	2 481	42 869	0.24
1968	5 045	2 649	49 018	0.28
1967	4 595	2 870	42 100	0.25
1966	4 405	1 960	25 400	0.15
1965	3 963	1 550	23 300	0.15
1964	3 655	1 640	22 900	0.15
1963	3 362	941	16 100	0.11
1962	3 614	1 230	18 600	0.13
1961	3 367	1 450	16 300	0.11
1960	3 333	1 320	19 100	0.14
1959[7]	3 708	1 880	69 000	0.50
1958	3 694	2 060	23 900	0.18
1957	3 673	1 390	16 500	0.12
1956	3 825	1 900	33 100	0.24
1955	4 320	2 650	28 200	0.22
1954	3 468	1 530	22 600	0.18
1953	5 091	2 400	28 300	0.22
1952	5 117	3 540	59 100	0.48
1951	4 737	2 220	22 900	0.18

[1]Beginning in year indicated.
[2]Workers counted more than once if involved in more than one stoppage during the year.
[3]Resulting from all stoppages in effect in a year, including those that began in an earlier year.
[4]Agricultural and government employees are included in the total working time; private household and forestry and fishery employees are excluded.
[5]Less than .005 percent.
[6]Revised since originally published.
[7]First year for which figures include Alaska and Hawaii.

Table 10-10. Work Stoppages, Workers Involved, and Days Idle, 1927–2006—*Continued*

(Number, percent.)

Year	Stoppage beginning in the year		Days idle	
	Number[1]	Number of workers involved (thousands)[2]	Number[3]	Percent of estimated total working time[4]
1950	4 843	2 410	38 800	0.33
1949	3 606	3 030	50 500	0.44
1948	3 419	1 960	34 100	0.28
1947	3 693	2 170	34 600	0.30
1946	4 985	4 600	116 000	1.04
1945	4 750	3 470	38 000	0.31
1944	4 956	2 120	8 720	0.07
1943	3 752	1 980	13 500	0.10
1942	2 968	840	4 180	0.04
1941	4 288	2 360	23 000	0.23
1940	2 508	577	6 700	0.08
1939	2 613	1 170	17 800	0.21
1938[8]	2 772	688	9 150	0.15
1937	4 740	1 860	28 400	0.43
1936	2 172	789	13 900	0.21
1935	2 014	1 120	15 500	0.29
1934	1 856	1 470	19 600	0.38
1933	1 695	1 170	16 900	0.36
1932	841	324	6 890	0.11
1931	810	342	6 890	0.11
1930	637	183	3 320	0.05
1929	921	289	5 350	0.07
1928	604	314	12 600	0.17
1927	707	330	26 200	0.37

Source: U.S. Census Bureau. U.S. Department of Labor, Bureau of Labor Statistics.
[1]Beginning in year indicated.
[2]Workers counted more than once if involved in more than one stoppage during the year.
[3]Resulting from all stoppages in effect in a year, including those that began in an earlier year.
[4]Agricultural and government employees are included in the total working time; private household and forestry and fishery employees are excluded.
[8]Before 1939, percent of estimated total working time in private nonfarm economy. In 1939 that percent was 0.28.

Table 10-11. Occupational Injury and Illness Incidence Rates in Manufacturing and Mining, 1972–2004

(Incidence rates per 100 full time employees. Beginning 1992, excludes incidents that resulted in fatality.)

Year	Manufacturing	Mining[1]
2004	6.6	3.8
2003	6.8	3.3
2002	7.2	4.0
2001	8.1	4.0
2000	9.0	4.7
1999	9.2	4.4
1998	9.7	4.9
1997	10.3	5.9
1996	10.6	5.4
1995	11.6	6.2
1994	12.2	6.3
1993	12.1	6.8
1992	12.5	7.3
1991	12.7	7.4
1990	13.2	8.3
1989	13.1	8.5
1988	13.1	8.6
1987	11.9	8.5
1986	10.6	7.4
1985	10.4	8.4
1984	10.6	9.7
1983	12.2	8.4
1982	10.2	10.5
1981	11.5	11.6
1980	12.2	11.2
1979	13.3	11.4
1978	13.2	11.5
1977	13.1	10.9
1976	13.3	11.0
1975	13.0	11.0
1974	14.6	11.0
1973	15.3	12.5
1972	15.6	. . .

Source: U.S. Census Bureau. U.S. Department of Labor, Bureau of Labor Statistics.
Note: Except as noted, data refer to any Occupational Safety and Health Administration (OSHA) recordable occupational injury or illness, whether or not it resulted in days away from work, job transfer, or restriction. Incidence rates were calculated as: number of injuries and illnesses divided by total hours worked by all employees during the year, multiplied by 200,000 as base for 100 full-time equivalent workers (working 40 hours per week, 50 weeks per year).
[1]Data for operators in coal, metal, and nonmetal mining are provided to the Bureau of Labor Statistics by the Mine Safety and Health Administration (MSHA). Independent mining contractors are excluded. Data provided by MSHA do not reflect 2002 OSHA recordkeeping requirements; therefore mining estimates are not comparable with those of other industries.
. . . = Not available.

Table 10-12. Federal Minimum Wage Rates, 1938–2006

(Dollars.)

Year	Current dollars
2006	5.15
2005	5.15
2004	5.15
2003	5.15
2002	5.15
2001	5.15
2000	5.15
1999	5.15
1998	5.15
1997	5.15
1996	4.75
1995	4.25
1994	4.25
1993	4.25
1992	4.25
1991	4.25
1990	3.80
1989	3.35
1988	3.35
1987	3.35
1986	3.35
1985	3.35
1984	3.35
1983	3.35
1982	3.35
1981	3.35
1980	3.10
1979	2.90
1978	2.65
1977	2.30
1976	2.30
1975	2.10
1974	2.00
1973	1.60
1972	1.60
1971	1.60
1970	1.60
1969	1.60
1968	1.60
1967	1.40
1966	1.25
1965	1.25
1964	1.25
1963	1.25
1962	1.15
1961	1.15
1960	1.00
1959	1.00
1958	1.00
1957	1.00
1956	1.00
1955	0.75
1954	0.75
1953	0.75
1952	0.75
1951	0.75
1950	0.75
1949	0.40
1948	0.40
1947	0.40
1946	0.40
1945	0.40
1944	0.30
1943	0.30
1942	0.30
1941	0.30
1940	0.30
1939	0.30
1938	0.25

Source: U.S. Census Bureau. *Statistical Abstract of the United States: 2007.* U.S. Employment Standards Administration.

Table 10-13. Self-Employed Workers by Industry and Occupation, 2000–2005

(Thousands.)

Item	2000	2001	2002	2003[1]	2004[1]	2005[1]
Total self-employed	**10 214**	**10 109**	**9 926**	**10 295**	**10 431**	**10 464**
Industry:						
Agriculture and related industries	1 010	988	1 003	951	964	955
Mining	12	21	13	9	13	11
Construction	1 728	1 675	1 598	1 717	1 848	1 830
Manufacturing	334	354	312	325	316	327
Wholesale and retail trade	1 221	1 195	1 163	1 247	1 153	1 251
Transportation and utilities	348	375	369	357	410	442
Information	139	132	145	152	146	126
Financial activities[2]	735	697	675	736	792	785
Professional and business services[3]	1 927	2 001	1 863	1 908	1 993	1 957
Education and health services[4]	1 107	1 090	1 119	1 138	1 105	1 071
Leisure and hospitality[5]	660	631	627	686	660	674
Other services[6]	993	951	1 041	1 071	1 031	1 036
Occupation:						
Management, professional, and related occupations	4 169	4 085	4 064	4 176	4 179	4 085
Service occupations	1 775	1 775	1 786	1 690	1 757	1 774
Sales and office occupations	1 982	1 927	1 883	1 945	1 909	1 986
Natural resources, construction, and maintenance occupations	1 591	1 602	1 503	1 795	1 847	1 864
Production, transportation, and material moving occupations	698	720	690	689	739	756

Source: U.S. Census Bureau. *Statistical Abstract of the United States: 2007.* U.S. Department of Labor, Bureau of Labor Statistics.
Note: For civilian noninstitutional population 16 years old and over. Annual averages of monthly figures. Data represent the unincorporated self-employed; the incorporated self-employed are considered wage and salary workers. Based on the occupational and industrial classification derived from those used in the 2000 Census and are not comparable to those used in the 1990 Census.
[1] Data not strictly comparable with data for earlier years due to changes in classifications and methods.
[2] Includes finance, insurance, real estate, and rental and leasing.
[3] Includes professional and technical services, management, administration, and waste services.
[4] Includes educational services, health care, and social assistance.
[5] Includes arts, entertainment, recreation, accommodation, and food services.
[6] Includes private household workers.

Table 10-14. Marital Status of Women in the Civilian Labor Force, 1960–2005

(Number, percent.)

Year	Female labor force				Female participation rate[1]			
	Total	Single	Married[2]	Other[3]	Total	Single	Married[2]	Other[3]
2005[4]	69 288	19 183	35 941	14 163	59.3	66.0	60.7	49.4
2004[4]	68 421	18 616	35 845	13 961	59.2	65.9	60.5	49.6
2003[4]	68 272	18 397	36 046	13 828	59.5	66.2	61.0	49.6
2002	67 363	18 203	35 477	13 683	59.6	67.4	61.0	49.2
2001	66 848	18 021	35 236	13 592	59.8	68.1	61.2	49.0
2000[4]	66 303	17 849	35 146	13 308	59.9	68.9	61.1	49.0
1999[4]	64 855	17 575	34 372	12 909	60.0	68.7	61.2	49.1
1998[4]	63 714	17 087	33 857	12 771	59.8	68.5	61.2	48.8
1997[4]	63 036	16 492	33 802	12 742	59.8	67.9	61.6	48.6
1996	61 857	15 842	33 618	12 397	59.3	67.1	61.2	48.1
1995	60 944	15 467	33 359	12 118	58.9	66.8	61.0	47.4
1994[4]	60 239	15 333	32 888	12 018	58.8	66.7	60.7	47.5
1993	58 795	15 031	31 980	11 784	57.9	66.2	59.4	47.2
1992	58 141	14 872	31 700	11 570	57.8	66.2	59.3	47.1
1991	57 178	14 681	31 112	11 385	57.4	66.2	58.5	46.8
1990[4]	56 829	14 612	30 901	11 315	57.5	66.7	58.4	47.2
1989	56 030	14 377	30 548	11 104	57.4	68.0	57.8	47.0
1988	54 742	14 194	29 921	10 627	56.6	67.7	56.7	46.2
1987	53 658	13 885	28 381	10 393	56.0	67.4	55.9	45.7
1986	52 413	13 512	28 623	10 277	55.3	67.2	54.9	45.6
1985	51 050	13 163	27 894	9 993	54.5	66.6	53.8	45.1
1984	49 709	12 867	27 199	9 644	53.6	65.6	52.8	44.7
1983	48 503	12 659	26 468	9 376	52.9	65.0	51.8	44.4
1982	47 755	12 460	25 971	9 324	52.6	65.1	51.1	44.8
1980	45 487	11 865	24 980	8 643	51.5	64.4	49.9	43.6
1975	37 475	9 125	21 484	6 866	46.3	59.8	44.3	40.1
1970	31 543	7 265	18 475	5 804	43.3	56.8	40.5	40.3
1965	26 200	5 976	14 829	5 396	39.3	54.5	34.9	40.7
1960	23 240	5 410	12 893	4 937	37.7	58.6	31.2	41.6

Source: U.S. Census Bureau. *Statistical Abstract of the United States 2007.* U.S. Department of Labor, Bureau of Labor Statistics.
[1]Labor force as a percent of the civilian labor force.
[2]Husband present.
[3]Widowed, divorced, or separated.
[4]Data not strictly comparable with earlier years because of changes in classifications and methods.

Table 10-15. Employment Status of the Civilian Noninstitutional Population, by Sex and Race, 1948–2006

(Thousands of people, percent.)

Year	Civilian noninstitutional population	Civilian labor force						Not in labor force
		Total	Participation rate	Employed		Unemployed		
				Total	Employment population ratio[1]	Number	Unemployment rate	
Both Sexes								
2006[2]	228 815	151 428	66.2	144 427	63.1	7 001	4.6	77 387
2005[2]	226 082	149 320	66.0	141 730	62.7	7 591	5.1	76 762
2004[2]	223 357	147 401	66.0	139 252	62.3	8 149	5.5	75 956
2003[2]	221 168	146 510	66.2	137 736	62.3	8 774	6.0	74 658
2002	217 570	144 863	66.6	136 485	62.7	8 378	5.8	72 707
2001	215 092	143 734	66.8	136 933	63.7	6 801	4.7	71 359
2000[2]	212 577	142 583	67.1	136 891	64.4	5 692	4.0	69 994
1999[2]	207 753	139 368	67.1	133 488	64.3	5 880	4.2	68 385
1998[2]	205 220	137 673	67.1	131 463	64.1	6 210	4.5	67 547
1997[2]	203 133	136 297	67.1	129 558	63.8	6 739	4.9	66 837
1996	200 591	133 943	66.8	126 708	63.2	7 236	5.4	66 647
1995	198 584	132 304	66.6	124 900	62.9	7 404	5.6	66 280
1994[2]	196 814	131 056	66.6	123 060	62.5	7 996	6.1	65 758
1993	194 838	129 200	66.3	120 259	61.7	8 940	6.9	65 638
1992	192 805	128 105	66.4	118 492	61.5	9 613	7.5	64 700
1991	190 925	126 346	66.2	117 718	61.7	8 628	6.8	64 578
1990[2]	189 164	125 840	66.5	118 793	62.8	7 047	5.6	63 324
1989	186 393	123 869	66.5	117 342	63.0	6 528	5.3	62 523
1988	184 613	121 669	65.9	114 968	62.3	6 701	5.5	62 944
1987	182 753	119 865	65.6	112 440	61.5	7 425	6.2	62 888
1986	180 587	117 834	65.3	109 597	60.7	8 237	7.0	62 752
1985	178 206	115 461	64.8	107 150	60.1	8 312	7.2	62 744
1984	176 383	113 544	64.4	105 005	59.5	8 539	7.5	62 839
1983	174 215	111 550	64.0	100 834	57.9	10 717	9.6	62 665
1982	172 271	110 204	64.0	99 526	57.8	10 678	9.7	62 067
1981	170 130	108 670	63.9	100 397	59.0	8 273	7.6	61 460
1980	167 745	106 940	63.8	99 303	59.2	7 637	7.1	60 806
1979	164 863	104 962	63.7	98 824	59.9	6 137	5.8	59 900
1978	161 910	102 251	63.2	96 048	59.3	6 202	6.1	59 659
1977	159 033	99 009	62.3	92 017	57.9	6 991	7.1	60 025
1976	156 150	96 158	61.6	88 752	56.8	7 406	7.7	59 991
1975	153 153	93 775	61.2	85 846	56.1	7 929	8.5	59 377
1974	150 120	91 949	61.3	86 794	57.8	5 156	5.6	58 171
1973	147 096	89 429	60.8	85 064	57.8	4 365	4.9	57 667
1972	144 126	87 034	60.4	82 153	57.0	4 882	5.6	57 091
1971	140 216	84 382	60.2	79 367	56.6	5 016	5.9	55 834
1970	137 085	82 771	60.4	78 678	57.4	4 093	4.9	54 315
1969	134 335	80 734	60.1	77 902	58.0	2 832	3.5	53 602
1968	132 028	78 737	59.6	75 920	57.5	2 817	3.6	53 291
1967	129 874	77 347	59.6	74 372	57.3	2 975	3.8	52 527
1966	128 058	75 770	59.2	72 895	56.9	2 875	3.8	52 288
1965	126 513	74 455	58.9	71 088	56.2	3 366	4.5	52 058
1964	124 485	73 091	58.7	69 305	55.7	3 786	5.2	51 394
1963	122 416	71 833	58.7	67 762	55.4	4 070	5.7	50 583
1962	120 153	70 614	58.8	66 702	55.5	3 911	5.5	49 539
1961	118 771	70 459	59.3	65 746	55.4	4 714	6.7	48 312
1960	117 245	69 628	59.4	65 778	56.1	3 852	5.5	47 617
1959	115 329	68 369	59.3	64 630	56.0	3 740	5.5	46 960
1958	113 727	67 639	59.5	63 036	55.4	4 602	6.8	46 088
1957	112 265	66 929	59.6	64 071	57.1	2 859	4.3	45 336
1956	110 954	66 552	60.0	63 799	57.5	2 750	4.1	44 402
1955	109 683	65 023	59.3	62 170	56.7	2 852	4.4	44 660
1954	108 321	63 643	58.8	60 109	55.5	3 532	5.5	44 678
1953	107 056	63 015	58.9	61 179	57.1	1 834	2.9	44 041
1952	105 231	62 138	59.0	60 250	57.3	1 883	3.0	43 093
1951	104 621	62 017	59.2	59 961	57.3	2 055	3.3	42 604
1950	104 995	62 208	59.2	58 918	56.1	3 288	5.3	42 787
1949	103 994	61 286	58.9	57 651	55.4	3 637	5.9	42 708
1948	103 068	60 621	58.8	58 343	56.6	2 276	3.8	42 447

[1]Civilians employed as a percent of the civilian noninstitutional population.
[2]Data not strictly comparable with earlier years because of changes in classifications and methods.

Table 10-15. Employment Status of the Civilian Noninstitutional Population, by Sex and Race, 1948–2006—*Continued*

(Thousands of people, percent.)

Year	Civilian noninstitutional population	Civilian labor force						Not in labor force
		Total	Participation rate	Employed		Unemployed		
				Total	Employment population ratio[1]	Number	Unemployment rate	
Male								
2006[2]	110 605	81 255	73.5	77 502	70.1	3 753	4.6	29 350
2005[2]	109 151	80 033	73.3	75 973	69.6	4 059	5.1	29 119
2004[2]	107 710	78 980	73.3	74 524	69.2	4 456	5.6	28 730
2003[2]	106 435	78 238	73.5	73 332	68.9	4 906	6.3	28 197
2002	104 585	77 500	74.1	72 903	69.7	4 597	5.9	27 085
2001	103 282	76 886	74.4	73 196	70.9	3 690	4.8	26 396
2000[2]	101 964	76 280	74.8	73 305	71.9	2 975	3.9	25 684
1999[2]	99 722	74 512	74.7	71 446	71.6	3 066	4.1	25 210
1998[2]	98 758	73 959	74.9	70 693	71.6	3 266	4.4	24 799
1997[2]	97 715	73 261	75.0	69 685	71.3	3 577	4.9	24 454
1996	96 206	72 087	74.9	68 207	70.9	3 880	5.4	24 119
1995	95 178	71 360	75.0	67 377	70.8	3 983	5.6	23 818
1994[2]	94 355	70 817	75.1	66 450	70.4	4 367	6.2	23 538
1993	93 332	70 404	75.4	65 349	70.0	5 055	7.2	22 927
1992	92 270	69 964	75.8	64 440	69.8	5 523	7.9	22 306
1991	91 278	69 168	75.8	64 223	70.4	4 946	7.2	22 110
1990[2]	90 377	69 011	76.4	65 104	72.0	3 906	5.7	21 367
1989	88 762	67 840	76.4	64 315	72.5	3 525	5.2	20 923
1988	87 857	66 927	76.2	63 273	72.0	3 655	5.5	20 930
1987	86 899	66 207	76.2	62 107	71.5	4 101	6.2	20 692
1986	85 798	65 422	76.3	60 892	71.0	4 530	6.9	20 376
1985	84 469	64 411	76.3	59 891	70.9	4 521	7.0	20 058
1984	83 605	63 835	76.4	59 091	70.7	4 744	7.4	19 771
1983	82 531	63 047	76.4	56 787	68.8	6 260	9.9	19 484
1982	81 523	62 450	76.6	56 271	69.0	6 179	9.9	19 073
1981	80 511	61 974	77.0	57 397	71.3	4 577	7.4	18 537
1980	79 398	61 453	77.4	57 186	72.0	4 267	6.9	17 945
1979	78 020	60 726	77.8	57 607	73.8	3 120	5.1	17 293
1978	76 576	59 620	77.9	56 479	73.8	3 142	5.3	16 956
1977	75 193	58 396	77.7	54 728	72.8	3 667	6.3	16 797
1976	73 759	57 174	77.5	53 138	72.0	4 036	7.1	16 585
1975	72 291	56 299	77.9	51 857	71.7	4 442	7.9	15 993
1974	70 808	55 739	78.7	53 024	74.9	2 714	4.9	15 069
1973	69 292	54 624	78.8	52 349	75.5	2 275	4.2	14 667
1972	67 835	53 555	78.9	50 896	75.0	2 659	5.0	14 280
1971	65 942	52 180	79.1	49 390	74.9	2 789	5.3	13 762
1970	64 304	51 228	79.7	48 990	76.2	2 238	4.4	13 076
1969	62 898	50 221	79.8	48 818	77.6	1 403	2.8	12 677
1968	61 847	49 533	80.1	48 114	77.8	1 419	2.9	12 315
1967	60 905	48 987	80.4	47 479	78.0	1 508	3.1	11 919
1966	60 262	48 471	80.4	46 919	77.9	1 551	3.2	11 792
1965	59 782	48 255	80.7	46 340	77.5	1 914	4.0	11 527
1964	58 847	47 679	81.0	45 474	77.3	2 205	4.6	11 169
1963	57 921	47 129	81.4	44 657	77.1	2 472	5.2	10 792
1962	56 831	46 600	82.0	44 177	77.7	2 423	5.2	10 231
1961	56 286	46 653	82.9	43 656	77.6	2 997	6.4	9 633
1960	55 662	46 388	83.3	43 904	78.9	2 486	5.4	9 274
1959	54 793	45 886	83.7	43 466	79.3	2 420	5.2	8 907
1958	54 033	45 521	84.2	42 423	78.5	3 098	6.8	8 514
1957	53 315	45 197	84.8	43 357	81.3	1 841	4.1	8 118
1956	52 723	45 091	85.5	43 379	82.3	1 711	3.8	7 633
1955	52 109	44 475	85.4	42 621	81.8	1 854	4.2	7 634
1954	51 395	43 965	85.5	41 619	81.0	2 344	5.3	7 431
1953	50 750	43 633	86.0	42 430	83.6	1 202	2.8	7 117
1952	49 700	42 869	86.3	41 682	83.9	1 185	2.8	6 832
1951	49 727	43 001	86.3	41 780	84.0	1 221	2.8	6 725
1950	50 725	43 819	86.4	41 578	82.0	2 239	5.1	6 906
1949	50 321	43 498	86.4	40 925	81.3	2 572	5.9	6 825
1948	49 996	43 286	86.6	41 725	83.5	1 559	3.6	6 710

[1]Civilians employed as a percent of the civilian noninstitutional population.
[2]Data not strictly comparable with earlier years because of changes in classifications and methods.

Table 10-15. Employment Status of the Civilian Noninstitutional Population, by Sex and Race, 1948–2006—*Continued*

(Thousands of people, percent.)

Year	Civilian noninstitutional population	Civilian labor force						Not in labor force
		Total	Participation rate	Employed		Unemployed		
				Total	Employment population ratio[1]	Number	Unemployment rate	
Female								
2006[2]	118 210	70 173	59.4	66 925	56.6	3 247	4.6	48 037
2005[2]	116 931	69 288	59.3	65 757	56.2	3 531	5.1	47 643
2004[2]	115 647	68 421	59.2	64 728	56.0	3 694	5.4	47 225
2003[2]	114 733	68 272	59.5	64 404	56.1	3 868	5.7	46 461
2002	112 985	67 363	59.6	63 582	56.3	3 781	5.6	45 621
2001	111 811	66 848	59.8	63 737	57.0	3 111	4.7	44 962
2000[2]	110 613	66 303	59.9	63 586	57.5	2 717	4.1	44 310
1999[2]	108 031	64 855	60.0	62 042	57.4	2 814	4.3	43 175
1998[2]	106 462	63 714	59.8	60 771	57.1	2 944	4.6	42 748
1997[2]	105 418	63 036	59.8	59 873	56.8	3 162	5.0	42 382
1996	104 385	61 857	59.3	58 501	56.0	3 356	5.4	42 528
1995	103 406	60 944	58.9	57 523	55.6	3 421	5.6	42 462
1994[2]	102 460	60 239	58.8	56 610	55.3	3 629	6.0	42 221
1993	101 506	58 795	57.9	54 910	54.1	3 885	6.6	42 711
1992	100 535	58 141	57.8	54 052	53.8	4 090	7.0	42 394
1991	99 646	57 178	57.4	53 496	53.7	3 683	6.4	42 468
1990[2]	98 787	56 829	57.5	53 689	54.3	3 140	5.5	41 957
1989	97 630	56 030	57.4	53 027	54.3	3 003	5.4	41 601
1988	96 756	54 742	56.6	51 696	53.4	3 046	5.6	42 014
1987	95 853	53 658	56.0	50 334	52.5	3 324	6.2	42 195
1986	94 789	52 413	55.3	48 706	51.4	3 707	7.1	42 376
1985	93 736	51 050	54.5	47 259	50.4	3 791	7.4	42 686
1984	92 778	49 709	53.6	45 915	49.5	3 794	7.6	43 068
1983	91 684	48 503	52.9	44 047	48.0	4 457	9.2	43 181
1982	90 748	47 755	52.6	43 256	47.7	4 499	9.4	42 993
1981	89 618	46 696	52.1	43 000	48.0	3 696	7.9	42 922
1980	88 348	45 487	51.5	42 117	47.7	3 370	7.4	42 861
1979	86 843	44 235	50.9	41 217	47.5	3 018	6.8	42 608
1978	85 334	42 631	50.0	39 569	46.4	3 061	7.2	42 703
1977	83 840	40 613	48.4	37 289	44.5	3 324	8.2	43 227
1976	82 390	38 983	47.3	35 615	43.2	3 369	8.6	43 406
1975	80 860	37 475	46.3	33 989	42.0	3 486	9.3	43 386
1974	79 312	36 211	45.7	33 769	42.6	2 441	6.7	43 101
1973	77 804	34 804	44.7	32 715	42.0	2 089	6.0	43 000
1972	76 290	33 479	43.9	31 257	41.0	2 222	6.6	42 811
1971	74 274	32 202	43.4	29 976	40.4	2 227	6.9	42 072
1970	72 782	31 543	43.3	29 688	40.8	1 855	5.9	41 239
1969	71 436	30 513	42.7	29 084	40.7	1 429	4.7	40 924
1968	70 179	29 204	41.6	27 807	39.6	1 397	4.8	40 976
1967	68 968	28 360	41.1	26 893	39.0	1 468	5.2	40 608
1966	67 795	27 299	40.3	25 976	38.3	1 324	4.8	40 496
1965	66 731	26 200	39.3	24 748	37.1	1 452	5.5	40 531
1964	65 637	25 412	38.7	23 831	36.3	1 581	6.2	40 225
1963	64 494	24 704	38.3	23 105	35.8	1 598	6.5	39 791
1962	63 321	24 014	37.9	22 525	35.6	1 488	6.2	39 308
1961	62 484	23 806	38.1	22 090	35.4	1 717	7.2	38 679
1960	61 582	23 240	37.7	21 874	35.5	1 366	5.9	38 343
1959	60 534	22 483	37.1	21 164	35.0	1 320	5.9	38 053
1958	59 690	22 118	37.1	20 613	34.5	1 504	6.8	37 574
1957	58 951	21 732	36.9	20 714	35.1	1 018	4.7	37 218
1956	58 228	21 461	36.9	20 419	35.1	1 039	4.8	36 769
1955	57 574	20 548	35.7	19 551	34.0	998	4.9	37 026
1954	56 925	19 678	34.6	18 490	32.5	1 188	6.0	37 247
1953	56 305	19 382	34.4	18 749	33.3	632	3.3	36 924
1952	55 529	19 269	34.7	18 568	33.4	698	3.6	36 261
1951	54 895	19 016	34.6	18 181	33.1	834	4.4	35 879
1950	54 270	18 389	33.9	17 340	32.0	1 049	5.7	35 881
1949	53 670	17 788	33.1	16 723	31.2	1 065	6.0	35 883
1948	53 071	17 335	32.7	16 617	31.3	717	4.1	35 737

[1]Civilians employed as a percent of the civilian noninstitutional population.
[2]Data not strictly comparable with earlier years because of changes in classifications and methods.

Table 10-15. Employment Status of the Civilian Noninstitutional Population, by Sex and Race, 1948–2006—*Continued*

(Thousands of people, percent.)

		Civilian labor force						
				Employed		Unemployed		
Year	Civilian noninstitutional population	Total	Participation rate	Total	Employment population ratio[1]	Number	Unemployment rate	Not in labor force
White[2]								
2006[3]	186 264	123 834	66.5	118 833	63.8	5 002	4.0	62 429
2005[3]	184 446	122 299	66.3	116 949	63.4	5 350	4.4	62 148
2004[3]	182 643	121 086	66.3	115 239	63.1	5 847	4.8	61 558
2003[3]	181 292	120 546	66.5	114 235	63.0	6 311	5.2	60 746
2002	179 783	120 150	66.8	114 013	63.4	6 137	5.1	59 633
2001	178 111	119 399	67.0	114 430	64.2	4 969	4.2	58 713
2000[3]	176 220	118 545	67.3	114 424	64.9	4 121	3.5	57 675
1999[3]	173 085	116 509	67.3	112 235	64.8	4 273	3.7	56 577
1998[3]	171 478	115 415	67.3	110 931	64.7	4 484	3.9	56 064
1997[3]	169 993	114 693	67.5	109 856	64.6	4 836	4.2	55 301
1996	168 317	113 108	67.2	107 808	64.1	5 300	4.7	55 209
1995	166 914	111 950	67.1	106 490	63.8	5 459	4.9	54 965
1994[3]	165 555	111 082	67.1	105 190	63.5	5 892	5.3	54 473
1993	164 289	109 700	66.8	103 045	62.7	6 655	6.1	54 589
1992	162 972	108 837	66.8	101 669	62.4	7 169	6.6	54 135
1991	161 759	107 743	66.6	101 182	62.6	6 560	6.1	54 016
1990[3]	160 625	107 447	66.9	102 261	63.7	5 186	4.8	53 178
1989	159 338	106 355	66.7	101 584	63.8	4 770	4.5	52 983
1988	158 194	104 756	66.2	99 812	63.1	4 944	4.7	53 439
1987	156 958	103 290	65.8	97 789	62.3	5 501	5.3	53 669
1986	155 432	101 801	65.5	95 660	61.5	6 140	6.0	53 631
1985	153 679	99 926	65.0	93 736	61.0	6 191	6.2	53 753
1984	152 347	98 492	64.6	92 120	60.5	6 372	6.5	53 855
1983	150 805	97 021	64.3	88 893	58.9	8 128	8.4	53 784
1982	149 441	96 143	64.3	87 903	58.8	8 241	8.6	53 298
1981	147 908	95 052	64.3	88 709	60.0	6 343	6.7	52 856
1980	146 122	93 600	64.1	87 715	60.0	5 884	6.3	52 523
1979	143 894	91 923	63.9	87 259	60.6	4 664	5.1	51 970
1978	141 612	89 634	63.3	84 936	60.0	4 698	5.2	51 979
1977	139 380	87 141	62.5	81 700	58.6	5 441	6.2	52 238
1976	137 106	84 767	61.8	78 853	57.5	5 914	7.0	52 338
1975	134 790	82 831	61.5	76 411	56.7	6 421	7.8	...
1974	132 417	81 281	61.4	77 184	58.3	4 097	5.0	...
1973	130 097	79 151	60.8	75 708	58.2	3 442	4.3	...
1972	127 906	77 275	60.4	73 370	57.4	3 906	5.1	...
1971	124 758	74 963	60.1	70 878	56.8	4 085	5.4	...
1970	122 174	73 556	60.2	70 217	57.5	3 339	4.5	...
1969	119 913	71 778	59.9	69 518	58.0	2 260	3.1	...
1968	117 948	69 976	59.3	67 750	57.4	2 226	3.2	...
1967	116 100	68 699	59.2	66 361	57.2	2 338	3.4	...
1966	114 566	67 276	58.7	65 021	56.8	2 255	3.4	...
1965	113 284	66 137	58.4	63 446	56.0	2 691	4.1	...
1964	111 534	64 921	58.2	61 922	55.5	2 999	4.6	...
1963	109 705	63 830	58.2	60 622	55.3	3 208	5.0	...
1962	107 715	62 750	58.3	59 698	55.4	3 052	4.9	...
1961	106 604	62 656	58.8	58 913	55.3	3 743	6.0	...
1960	105 282	61 915	58.8	58 850	55.9	3 065	5.0	...
1959	103 803	60 952	58.7	58 006	55.9	2 946	4.8	...
1958	102 392	60 293	58.9	56 613	55.3	3 680	6.1	...
1957	101 119	59 754	59.1	57 465	56.8	2 289	3.8	...
1956	99 976	59 428	59.4	57 269	57.3	2 159	3.6	...
1955	98 880	58 085	58.7	55 833	56.5	2 252	3.9	...
1954	97 705	56 816	58.2	53 957	55.2	2 859	5.0	...

[1]Civilians employed as a percent of the civilian noninstitutional population.
[2]The 2003 Current Population Survey (CPS) allowed respondents to choose more than one race. Beginning 2003, data represent persons who selected this race group only and exclude persons reporting more than one race. The CPS in prior years only allowed respondents to report one race group.
[3]Data not strictly comparable with earlier years because of changes in classifications and methods.
. . . = Not available.

Table 10-15. Employment Status of the Civilian Noninstitutional Population, by Sex and Race, 1948–2006—*Continued*

(Thousands of people, percent.)

Year	Civilian noninstitutional population	Civilian labor force						Not in labor force
		Total	Participation rate	Employed		Unemployed		
				Total	Employment population ratio[1]	Number	Unemployment rate	
Black[2]								
2006[3]	27 007	17 314	64.1	15 765	58.4	1 549	8.9	9 693
2005[3]	26 517	17 013	64.2	15 313	57.7	1 700	10.0	9 504
2004[3]	26 065	16 638	63.8	14 909	57.2	1 729	10.4	9 428
2003	25 686	16 526	64.3	14 739	57.4	1 787	10.8	9 161
2002	25 578	16 565	64.8	14 872	58.1	1 693	10.2	9 013
2001	25 138	16 421	65.3	15 006	59.7	1 416	8.6	8 717
2000[3]	24 902	16 397	65.8	15 156	60.9	1 241	7.6	8 505
1999[3]	24 855	16 365	65.8	15 056	60.6	1 309	8.0	8 490
1998[3]	24 373	15 982	65.6	14 556	59.7	1 426	8.9	8 391
1997[3]	24 003	15 529	64.7	13 969	58.2	1 560	10.0	8 474
1996	23 604	15 134	64.1	13 542	57.4	1 592	10.5	8 470
1995	23 246	14 817	63.7	13 279	57.1	1 538	10.4	8 429
1994[3]	22 879	14 502	63.4	12 835	56.1	1 666	11.5	8 377
1993	22 521	14 225	63.2	12 382	55.0	1 844	13.0	8 296
1992	22 147	14 162	63.9	12 151	54.9	2 011	14.2	7 985
1991	21 799	13 797	63.3	12 074	55.4	1 723	12.5	8 002
1990[3]	21 477	13 740	64.0	12 175	56.7	1 565	11.4	7 737
1989	21 021	13 497	64.2	11 953	56.9	1 544	11.4	7 524
1988	20 692	13 205	63.8	11 658	56.3	1 547	11.7	7 487
1987	20 352	12 993	63.8	11 309	55.6	1 684	13.0	7 359
1986	19 989	12 654	63.3	10 814	54.1	1 840	14.5	7 335
1985	19 664	12 364	62.9	10 501	53.4	1 864	15.1	7 299
1984	19 348	12 033	62.2	10 119	52.3	1 914	15.9	7 315
1983	18 925	11 647	61.5	9 375	49.5	2 272	19.5	7 278
1982	18 584	11 331	61.0	9 189	49.4	2 142	18.9	7 254
1981	18 219	11 086	60.8	9 355	51.3	1 731	15.6	7 134
1980	17 824	10 865	61.0	9 313	52.3	1 553	14.3	6 959
1979	17 397	10 678	61.4	9 359	53.8	1 319	12.3	6 718
1978	16 970	10 432	61.5	9 102	53.6	1 330	12.8	6 539
1977	16 605	9 932	59.8	8 540	51.4	1 393	14.0	6 672
1976	16 196	9 561	59.0	8 227	50.8	1 334	14.0	6 635
1975	15 751	9 263	58.8	7 894	50.1	1 369	14.8	6 487
1974	15 329	9 167	59.8	8 203	53.5	965	10.5	6 169
1973	14 917	8 976	60.2	8 128	54.5	846	9.4	5 941
1972	14 526	8 707	59.9	7 802	53.7	906	10.4	5 819
Asian[2,4]								
2006[3]	10 155	6 727	66.2	6 522	64.2	205	3.0	3 427
2005[3]	9 842	6 503	66.1	6 244	63.4	259	4.0	3 339
2004[3]	9 519	6 271	65.9	5 994	63.0	277	4.4	3 248
2003[3]	9 220	6 122	66.4	5 756	62.4	366	6.0	3 098
2002[3]	9 833	6 604	67.2	6 215	63.2	389	5.9	3 229
2001[3]	9 626	6 469	67.2	6 180	64.2	288	4.5	3 158
2000	9 330	6 270	67.2	6 043	64.8	227	3.6	3 060

Source: U.S. Census Bureau. U.S. Department of Labor, Bureau of Labor Statistics.
[1]Civilians employed as a percent of the civilian noninstitutional population.
[2]The 2003 Current Population Survey (CPS) allowed respondents to choose more than one race. Beginning in 2003, data represent persons who selected this race group only and exclude persons reporting more than one race. The CPS in prior years only allowed respondents to report one race group.
[3]Data not strictly comparable with earlier years because of changes in classifications and methods.

Table 10-16. Productivity—Output per Hour, 1947–2005

(1992 = 100.)

Year	Output per hour			
	Business	Nonfarm business	Nonfinancial corporations	Manufacturing
2005	136.6	136.0	. . .	171.2
2004	133.1	132.4	. . .	163.0
2003	128.6	128.0	. . .	154.4
2002	123.6	123.1	128.9	146.2
2001	118.8	118.3	122.7	137.1
2000	115.9	115.5	120.6	134.4
1999	112.7	112.4	116.4	128.3
1998	109.4	109.3	112.8	123.8
1997	106.5	106.4	109.8	118.0
1996	104.5	104.7	107.1	113.9
1995	101.5	102.0	103.4	110.0
1994	101.3	101.5	102.5	106.1
1993	100.4	100.4	100.5	102.7
1992	100.0	100.0	100.0	100.0
1991	95.9	96.1	97.9	95.4
1990	94.4	94.5	95.5	92.9
1989	92.4	92.8	95.2	90.3
1988	91.5	92.1	96.5	90.0
1987	90.1	90.6	94.3	88.3
1986	89.7	90.2	92.5	. . .
1985	87.1	87.5	90.5	. . .
1984	85.2	86.1	88.4	. . .
1983	83.0	84.5	86.1	. . .
1982	80.2	80.8	83.2	. . .
1981	80.8	81.7	82.3	. . .
1980	79.2	80.6	81.0	. . .
1979	79.3	80.7	81.6	. . .
1978	79.3	81.0	82.5	. . .
1977	78.5	80.0	81.4	. . .
1976	77.1	78.7	79.3	. . .
1975	74.8	76.2	76.9	. . .
1974	72.3	74.2	74.0	. . .
1973	73.4	75.3	75.5	. . .
1972	71.2	73.1	74.8	. . .
1971	69.0	70.7	73.3	. . .
1970	66.3	68.0	70.4	. . .
1969	65.0	67.0	70.0	. . .
1968	64.7	66.9	70.0	. . .
1967	62.5	64.7	67.6	. . .
1966	61.2	63.6	66.7	. . .
1965	58.8	61.4	65.6	. . .
1964	56.6	59.6	64.0	. . .
1963	55.0	57.8	63.0	. . .
1962	52.9	55.9	60.9	. . .
1961	50.6	53.5	58.4	. . .
1960	48.9	51.9	56.6	. . .
1959	48.0	51.3	55.7	. . .
1958	46.3	49.4	53.2	. . .
1957	45.0	48.4	. . .	. . .
1956	43.6	47.2	. . .	. . .
1955	43.6	47.5	. . .	. . .
1954	41.9	45.6	. . .	. . .
1953	41.0	44.8	. . .	. . .
1952	39.6	43.8	. . .	. . .
1951	38.5	43.0	. . .	. . .
1950	37.3	41.9	. . .	. . .
1949	34.5	39.3	. . .	. . .
1948	33.7	38.0	. . .	. . .
1947	32.2	37.0	. . .	. . .

Source: U.S. Census Bureau. U.S. Department of Labor, Bureau of Labor Statistics.
. . . = Not available.

Table 10-17. Unemployed Job Seekers Job Search Activities, 2005

(Thousands of people, percent.)

Characteristic	Population		Jobseekers job search methods							Average number of methods used
	Total unemployed	Total seekers[1]	Employer directly	Sent out a resume or filled out application	Placed or answered ads	Friends or relatives	Public employment agency	Private employment agency	Other activities	
Total	7 591	6 657	60.6	55.4	14.8	17.7	18.3	6.7	11.1	1.85
Male	4 059	3 467	61.4	53.2	14.7	19.4	18.4	6.8	11.6	1.86
Female	3 531	3 190	59.8	57.7	15.0	15.8	18.3	6.6	10.6	1.84
White[2]	5 350	4 595	61.1	55.6	15.2	17.7	17.2	6.6	11.6	1.85
Male	2 931	2 440	62.1	53.4	15.0	19.5	17.5	6.9	12.3	1.87
Female	2 419	2 154	59.9	58.2	15.5	15.6	16.8	6.2	10.8	1.83
Black[2]	1 700	1 563	60.3	55.6	14.3	17.1	22.0	6.5	9.2	1.85
Male	844	766	60.6	53.6	14.3	19.1	21.1	6.1	9.3	1.84
Female	856	798	59.9	57.5	14.4	15.1	22.9	6.9	9.1	1.86
Asian[2]	259	245	59.1	47.1	13.2	23.6	16.7	9.5	16.2	1.86
Male	141	134	60.3	45.6	12.6	22.2	15.9	8.3	16.0	1.81
Female	118	110	57.7	49.0	13.9	25.3	17.6	10.9	16.5	1.92
Hispanic[3]	1 191	1 142	61.1	48.6	10.4	22.3	18.0	6.1	8.7	1.80
Male	647	619	63.7	45.4	10.5	25.3	19.0	5.9	8.5	1.82
Female	544	524	58.2	52.2	10.4	18.9	17.0	6.2	9.0	1.76

Source: U.S. Census Bureau, *Statistical Abstract of the United States 2007.* U.S. Department of Labor, Bureau of Labor Statistics.
[1]Excludes persons on temporary layoff.
[2]Data for this race group only. The 2003 Current Population Survey (CPS) allowed respondents to choose more than one race. Beginning 2003, data represent persons who selected this race group only and exclude persons reporting more than one race. The CPS in prior years only allowed respondents to report one race group.
[3]Persons of Hispanic or Latino origin may be of any race.

Table 10-18. Workers with Access to Retirement and Health Care Benefits by Selected Characteristics, 2005

(Percent.)

Characteristic	Retirement benefits			Healthcare benefits			
	All plans[1]	Defined benefit	Defined contribution	Medical care	Dental care	Vision care	Outpatient prescription drug coverage
Total	60	22	53	70	46	29	64
WORKER CHARACTERISTICS							
White-collar occupations	70	25	64	77	54	33	69
Blue-collar occupations	60	26	50	77	47	30	71
Full-time[2]	69	25	62	85	56	35	78
Part-time[2]	27	10	23	22	14	9	20
Union[3]	88	73	49	92	73	57	87
Nonunion[3]	56	16	54	68	43	26	61
Average wage less than $15 per hour	46	12	41	58	34	21	53
Average wage $15 per hour or more	78	35	69	87	62	40	80
ESTABLISHMENT CHARACTERISTICS							
Goods producing[4]	71	33	61	85	56	36	80
Service producing[4]	56	19	51	66	43	27	59
1 to 99 workers	44	10	40	59	31	19	52
100 or more workers	78	37	69	84	65	41	79
GEOGRAPHIC AREAS							
New England division	57	22	51	67	49	25	60
Middle Atlantic division	60	29	50	72	46	34	63
East North Central division	64	25	55	70	46	27	68
West North Central division	64	23	56	66	42	21	64
South Atlantic division	59	17	55	71	46	27	62
East South Central division	59	14	57	72	45	31	67
West South Central division	56	17	52	68	39	23	60
Mountain division	63	19	58	68	43	30	64
Pacific division	55	24	47	73	55	40	66

Source: U.S. Census Bureau, *Statistical Abstract of the United States 2007.* U.S. Department of Labor, Bureau of Labor Statistics.
[1]Employees may have access to both defined benefit and defined contribution plans. Total excludes duplication.
[2]Employees are classified as working either a full-time or part-time schedule based on the definition used by each establishment.
[3]Union workers are those whose wages are determined through collective bargaining.
[4]Based on the Standard Industrial Classification (SIC) Manual, 1987.

Table 10-19. Characteristics of Multiple Jobholders, 2006

(People in thousands, percent.)

Characteristics	Both sexes		Male		Female	
	Number	Rate[1]	Number	Rate[1]	Number	Rate[1]
Total[2]	7 576	5.2	3 822	4.9	3 753	5.6
Race and Hispanic ethnicity:						
White	6 321	5.3	3 199	4.9	3 122	5.8
Black or African American	818	5.2	404	5.5	415	4.9
Asian	249	3.8	127	3.6	122	4.1
Hispanic or Latino ethnicity[3]	598	3.0	337	2.8	261	3.4
Marital status:						
Married, spouse present	4 136	5.1	2 420	5.3	1 716	4.9
Widowed, divorced, or separated	1 308	5.6	440	4.4	868	6.3
Single, never married	2 131	5.3	962	4.4	1 169	6.5
Full- or part-time status:						
Primary job full-time, secondary job part-time	3 981	...	2 233	...	1 748	...
Both jobs part-time	1 676	...	508	...	1 168	...
Both jobs full-time	310	...	208	...	102	...
Hours vary on primary job	1 564	...	849	...	715	...

Source: U.S. Department of Labor, *Bureau of Labor Statistics.*
[1]Multiple jobholders as a percent of all employed persons in specified group.
[2]Includes a small number of persons who work part-time on their primary job and full-time on their secondary job(s), not shown separately. Includes other races not shown separately.
[3]Persons of Hispanic or Latino ethnicity may be of any race.
... = Not available

BOX 10 ■ Mine Safety

Mining has always been one of the most dangerous occupations. The U.S. coal mining industry reached its nadir in 1907 when, over the course of one year, 3,242 people died in mining accidents. The industry, which includes coal mining along with metal and nonmetal mining, made slow but steady safety gains until the early 1980s, when the enforcement of the Federal Mine Safety and Health Act of 1977 caused a rapid decline in the number of mining accidents and fatalities. These declines resulted in the record lows of 26 fatalities in metal and nonmetal mining in 2003, and 22 fatalities in coal mining in 2005.

However, in 2006, the coal mining industry suffered its greatest losses in more than a decade with a total of 47 mining accident fatalities. Among these was the largest single mining disaster in four decades. It occurred at the Sago mine in West Virginia in early January 2006 and resulted in the loss of 12 miners. This accident was followed less than three weeks later by the Aracoma Alma Mine No.1 fire that claimed the lives of two miners. In May of the same year five miners were killed in Kentucky Darby Mine No. 1.

The magnitude of these accidents and the loss of life, unprecedented in recent history, led to bipartisan and almost unanimous support for the most far-reaching mine safety legislation in almost three decades, the Mine Improvement and New Emergency Response (MINER) Act of 2006. This measure was passed unanimously in the Senate and was approved by a 381 to 37 vote in the House of Representatives in June 2006. In addition, the MINER Act had support from both the United Mine Workers of America and the National Mining Association, which represents mining corporations.

The Mine Safety and Health Administration's (MSHA) subsequent investigations into the three accidents determined not only substantial violations of safety codes and regulations by each of the three mines, but it also uncovered deficiencies in the agency's enforcement thereof.

The MSHA's internal investigation into the Sago Mine accident uncovered a substantial history of violations at the mine and an increase in investigations per agency protocol. However, the increase in violations cited by inspection personnel coincided with a lack of managerial oversight and a failure to follow inspection procedure. As a result, the violations were not corrected.

More than a year after the January 19, 2006 accident, the operator of the Aracoma Alma Mine No. 1 was fined a record $1.5 million for safety violations that the MSHA declared constituted "reckless disregard for safety" and were contributory factors in the fire and the consequent deaths of two miners. The MSHA's internal review also determined that these violations were significant and obvious and ought to have been cited by investigators prior to the fatal accident.

Number of Coal Fatalities, 1900–2006

Total 1900–2006: 104,621

Year	Miners	Fatalities	Year	Miners	Fatalities	Year	Miners	Fatalities	Year	Miners	Fatalities
1900	448 581	1 489	1930	644 006	2 063	1960	189 679	325	1990	168 625	66
1901	485 544	1 574	1931	589 705	1 463	1961	167 568	294	1991	158 677	61
1902	518 197	1 724	1932	527 623	1 207	1962	161 286	289	1992	153 128	55
1903	566 260	1 926	1933	523 182	1 064	1963	157 126	284	1993	141 183	47
1904	593 693	1 995	1934	566 426	1 226	1964	150 761	242	1994	143 645	45
1905	626 045	2 232	1935	565 202	1 242	1965	148 734	259	1995	132 111	47
1906	640 780	2 138	1936	584 582	1 342	1966	145 244	233	1996	126 451	39
1907	680 492	3 242	1937	589 856	1 413	1967	139 312	222	1997	126 429	30
1908	690 438	2 445	1938	541 528	1 105	1968	134 467	311	1998	122 083	29
1909	666 552	2 642	1939	539 375	1 078	1969	133 302	203	1999	114 489	35
1910	725 030	2 821	1940	533 267	1 388	1970	144 480	260	2000	108 098	38
1911	728 348	2 656	1941	546 692	1 266	1971	142 108	181	2001	114 458	42
1912	722 662	2 419	1942	530 861	1 471	1972	162 207	156	2002	110 966	27
1913	747 644	2 785	1943	486 516	1 451	1973	151 892	132	2003	104 824	30
1914	763 185	2 454	1944	453 937	1 298	1974	182 274	133	2004	108 734	28
1915	734 008	2 269	1945	437 921	1 068	1975	224 412	155	2005	112 449	22
1916	720 971	2 226	1946	463 079	968	1976	221 255	141	2006	119 248	47
1917	757 317	2 696	1947	490 356	1 158	1977	237 506	139			
1918	762 426	2 580	1948	507 333	999	1978	255 588	106			
1919	776 569	2 323	1949	485 306	585	1979	260 429	144			
1920	784 621	2 272	1950	483 239	643	1980	253 007	133			
1921	823 253	1 995	1951	441 905	785	1981	249 738	153			
1922	844 807	1 984	1952	401 329	548	1982	241 454	122			
1923	862 536	2 462	1953	351 126	461	1983	200 199	70			
1924	779 613	2 402	1954	283 705	396	1984	208 160	125			
1925	748 805	2 518	1955	260 089	420	1985	197 049	68			
1926	759 033	2 234	1956	260 285	448	1986	185 167	89			
1927	759 177	2 231	1957	254 725	478	1987	172 780	63			
1928	682 831	2 176	1958	224 890	358	1988	166 278	53			
1929	654 494	2 187	1959	203 597	293	1989	164 929	68			

Source: U.S. Department of Labor, Mine Safety and Health Administration.

The Darby Mine internal review revealed a history of repeat violations which ought to have resulted in an increase in investigations by MSHA personnel but did not. In addition, a lack of managerial oversight and a failure to follow inspection procedure allowed the violations to go unnoticed and uncorrected.

As a result of the MSHA's internal investigations, the Office of Accountability was established to monitor the agency and determine if established enforcement procedures are being followed.

In 2007, several Democratic members of Congress, the United Mine Workers of America and the AFL-CIO proposed legislation that would advance the dates by which the safety parameters of the MINER Act must be in place, in addition to outlining further safety requirements, increased enforcement power for the MSHA, and increased fines for mine owners and operators.

Sources:

Associated Press. "Federal Inquiry Faults Mine Inspectors; Accountablity Office Will Be Created. (National Desk)." *The New York Times* (June 29, 2007): A26 (L).

"The Disastrous Lessons of Sago. (Sago Mine Disaster, West Virginia)(Editorial)(Brief Article)." *The New York Times* (July 21, 2006): A18 (L).

Heyman, Daniel and Anahad O'Connor. "U.S. Report Cites Lightning and Old Cable in Mine Blast. (National Desk)." *The New York Times* (May 10, 2007): A22 (L).

U.S. Department of Labor, Mine Safety and Health Administration. Coal Fatalities for 1900 Through 2006. http://www.msha.gov/stats/centurystats/coalstats.asp

U.S. Department of Labor, Mine Safety and Health Administration. Injury Trends in Mining. http://www.msha.gov/MSHAINFO/FactSheets/MSHAFCT2.htm

U.S. Department of Labor, Mine Safety and Health Administration. Metal/Nonmetal Fatalities for 1900 Through 2006. http://www.msha.gov/stats/centurystats/mnmstats.asp

U.S. Department of Labor, Mine Safety and Health Administration. Mine Improvement and New Emergency Response Act of 2006. http://www.msha.gov/MinerAct/MineActAmmendmentSummary.asp

U.S. Department of Labor, Mine Safety and Health Administration. Questions and Answers on the Sago Mine Accident. http://www.msha.gov/sagomine/sagoqa01182006.asp

U.S. Department of Labor, Mine Safety and Health Administration. U.S. Labor Department's MSHA Completes Internal Reviews into Fatal Accidents at Sago, Aracoma and Darby Mines. http://www.msha.gov/MEDIA/PRESS/2007/NR070628.pdf

U.S. Department of Labor, Mine Safety and Health Administration. U.S. Labor Department's MSHA Levies $1.5 Million Fine Against Aracoma Mine Operator. http://www.msha.gov/media/press/2007/nr070329.asp

Urbina, Ian. "Stiff Overhaul of Mine Safety Rules Passes Congress.(National Desk)." *The New York Times* (June 8, 2006):A18(L).

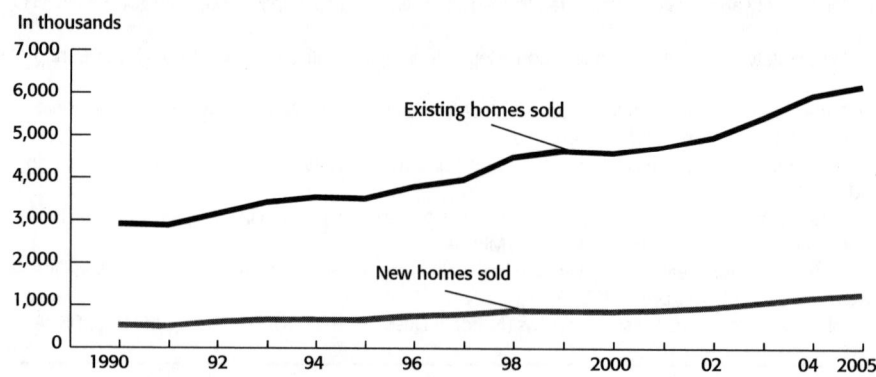

New and Existing Homes Sold: 1990 to 2005
Source: Chart prepared by U.S. Census Bureau.

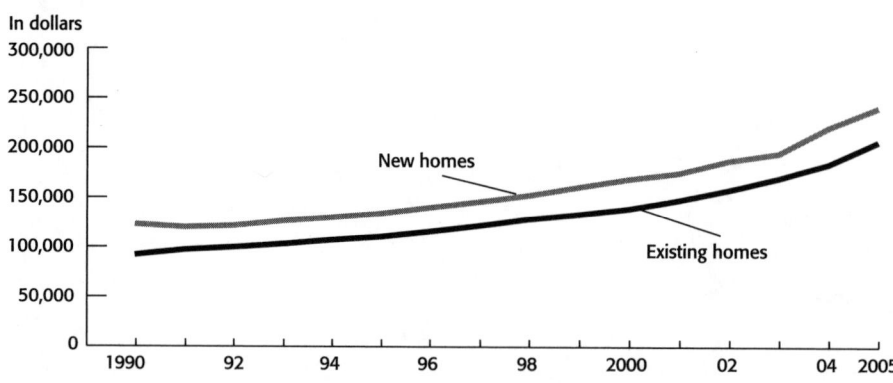

Median Sales Price of Homes: 1990 to 2005
Source: Chart prepared by U.S. Census Bureau.

CHAPTER 11

Construction and Housing

HIGHLIGHTS

1 Housing and construction statistics were collected and published by the Department of Labor until 1959 when the Department of Commerce assumed that responsibility. The Bureau of the Census issues a variety of publications providing data in these fields, including *Current Construction Reports, Housing Starts and Housing Completions, New One Family Houses Sold and for Sale, Price Indexes of New One-Family Houses Sold, Housing Units Authorized by Building Permits, Expenditures for Residential Upkeep and Improvements, Value of New Construction Put in Place,* and *Current Housing Reports.* Other sources include the F. W. Dodge division of McGraw-Hill, the National Association of Home Builders, and the National Association of Realtors. Censuses of the construction industry were first conducted by the Bureau of the Census for 1929, 1935, and 1939; beginning in 1967, a census has been taken every five years, in years ending in 2 and 7.

2 From 1850 to 1930, the Bureau of the Census collected some housing data as part of its censuses of population and agriculture. Beginning in 1940, separate censuses of housing have been taken at 10-year intervals. Beginning in 1970, information on structural characteristics of housing have been included in the censuses.

3 In 2003, 732,175 businesses were involved in construction. They employed 6,381,000 people. In 2005, the value of new construction was $1.144 trillion, with private buildings and structures accounting for $898.970 billion of that amount (of which $642.276 billion was for residential buildings). Private construction included $433.510 billion worth of single-family homes, up from $153.515 billion in 1995. Education construction saw a significant increase, more than doubling in value from $5.699 billion in 1995 to $12.787 billion in 2005.

4 Sales of new single-family homes rose to 1,283,000 in 2005 compared to 545,000 in 1980. Of these, 458,000 were luxury homes valued at $300,000 or more. Median prices of new private one-family homes increased to $240,900 nationwide. The highest prices are in the Northeast ($343,800) and lowest in the South ($197,300).

5 In 2004, the total number of housing units in the United States was 122.672 million, of which 73.754 million were owner-occupied and 36.148 million were rented.

6 Home ownership is part of the American dream, but as of 2005, only 68.9 percent of the population achieved that dream. Home ownership is highest in West Virginia (81.3 percent), Mississippi (78.8 percent), and Alabama (76.6 percent). It is lowest in New York and Colorado because of the high cost of first-time ownership.

7 In 2005, America spent $215.030 billion on home improvement, maintenance, and repairs compared with $115.432 billion in 1990. Average monthly mortgage payments jumped from $329 in 1976 to $804 in 2002, but dropped from 24 percent of personal income to 18.5 percent during the same period of time.

8 Of the 1.636 million new one-family homes completed and sold in 2005, 42 percent have a floor space of 2,400 ft. or more, 39 percent have more than four bedrooms, 66 percent are heated with gas, 89 percent have central air conditioning, 55 percent have a fireplace, and 91 percent have a garage.

9 In 2004, the median gross rent for an apartment nationwide was $694, and 18.9 percent of the apartments had a rent of $1,000 or more.

10 Blacks and Hispanics have a lower home ownership rate than Whites. White home ownership is 72.7 percent, while only 48.1 percent of Blacks and 49.4 percent of Hispanics own homes in 2005. The majority of Blacks and Hispanics live in apartments.

11 In 2003, there were 4,650,000 commercial buildings in the United States, of which 386,000 were educational, 297,000 food service establishments, 129,000 health care, 142,000 lodging, 824,000 office buildings, 277,000 public assembly buildings, 597,000 warehouse and storage buildings, and 370,000 religious buildings.

12 In 2004, Atlanta, GA, had the highest vacancy rate for office buildings (25.8 percent), while the lowest rates were in Des Moines, IA, and Orlando, FL (12.9 percent).

13 Although the quality of American housing has steadily improved during the twentieth century, 7,020,000 homes have signs of mice or rats, 981,000 have holes in floors, 50,000 have no electrical wiring, and 9.049 million have water leakages from inside their home (2005).

14 In 2005, the value of construction put in place by state and local government was $226,954 billion. Of that number, 97 percent went into nonresidential construction.

15 The greatest number of owner-occupied homes is in the South, where more than 28 million people live in their own homes. Of these 99,000 have monthly housing costs of less than $100, while 3.749 million have expenses of $1500 or more.

Table 11-1. Total Housing Inventory, 1965–2005

(Number in thousands.)

Year	All housing units	Vacant Total	Year-round vacant Total	For rent	For sale only	Rented or sold	Held off market Total	Occasional use	Usual residence elsewhere	Other	Seasonal²	Total occupied Total	Owner	Renter
2005	123 925	15 694	11 916	3 721	1 451	1 060	5 684	1 884	1 128	2 672	3 778	108 231	74 553	33 678
2004	122 187	15 599	11 884	3 802	1 307	991	5 784	1 967	1 068	2 749	3 715	106 588	73 575	33 013
2003	120 834	15 274	11 631	3 676	1 308	976	5 671	1 989	994	2 688	3 643	105 560	72 054	33 506
2002¹	119 297	14 332	10 771	3 347	1 220	842	5 362	1 819	995	2 548	3 561	104 965	71 278	33 687
2001	121 480	14 470	10 916	3 203	1 301	882	5 530	1 887	1 064	2 579	3 554	107 010	72 593	34 417
2000	119 628	13 908	10 439	3 024	1 148	856	5 411	1 892	1 037	2 482	3 469	105 720	71 250	34 470
1999	119 044	14 116	10 848	3 119	1 184	956	5 589	1 948	965	2 676	3 268	104 928	70 097	34 831
1998	117 282	13 748	10 516	3 046	1 205	927	5 338	1 792	910	2 636	3 232	103 534	68 638	34 896
1997	115 621	13 419	10 114	2 978	1 133	867	5 136	1 818	885	2 433	3 305	102 202	67 143	35 059
1996	114 139	13 155	9 945	3 008	1 082	834	5 022	1 709	852	2 461	3 209	100 984	66 041	34 943
1995	112 655	12 669	9 570	2 946	1 022	810	4 793	1 667	801	2 325	3 099	99 985	64 739	35 246
1994	110 952	12 257	9 229	2 858	953	772	4 646	1 612	815	2 219	3 028	98 695	63 136	35 558
1993	109 611	11 894	8 937	2 809	894	625	4 609	1 508	994	2 108	2 957	97 717	62 533	35 184
1992	108 316	11 926	8 932	2 769	970	628	4 564	1 443	1 011	2 111	2 994	96 391	61 823	34 568
1991	107 276	12 023	9 137	2 780	1 070	602	4 686	1 494	1 084	2 107	2 886	95 253	61 010	34 242
1990	106 283	12 059	9 128	2 662	1 064	660	4 742	1 485	1 068	2 189	2 931	94 224	60 248	33 976
1989	105 729	12 240	9 349	2 732	1 082	705	4 830	1 565	1 014	2 251	2 891	93 489	59 755	33 734
1988	103 653	11 633	8 533	2 802	968	678	4 085	1 213	887	1 985	3 100	92 020	58 700	33 320
1987	101 811	11 294	8 265	2 752	978	688	3 848	1 066	787	1 996	3 029	90 517	57 915	32 602
1986	99 318	10 173	7 821	2 588	937	683	3 614	991	741	1 883	2 352	89 145	56 844	32 302
1985	97 333	9 446	7 400	2 221	1 006	664	3 510	977	659	1 875	2 046	87 887	56 152	31 736
1984	95 256	8 910	7 080	1 934	947	664	3 535	992	622	1 921	1 830	86 346	55 671	30 675
1983	93 044	8 479	6 693	1 810	862	633	3 389	926	642	1 821	1 787	84 565	54 671	29 894
1982	91 876	8 145	6 369	1 670	843	554	3 302	959	588	1 754	1 776	83 731	54 237	29 495
1981	90 862	8 070	6 136	1 524	759	595	3 259	909	615	1 735	1 934	82 793	54 084	28 709
1980	87 739	8 101	5 996	1 575	734	623	3 064	814	568	1 683	2 106	79 638	52 223	27 415
1979	85 735	7 589	5 893	1 579	607	705	3 003	794	591	1 618	1 696	78 146	50 972	27 174
1978	83 496	6 948	5 260	1 433	524	650	2 653	689	467	1 498	1 688	76 548	49 739	26 810
1977	81 645	6 861	5 224	1 472	574	651	2 528	707	438	1 383	1 637	74 784	48 461	26 324
1976	80 189	6 774	5 190	1 546	598	564	2 482	705	467	1 310	1 584	73 415	47 518	25 897
1975	78 821	6 896	5 202	1 647	591	536	2 429	649	470	1 309	1 694	71 925	46 463	25 462
1974	77 462	6 904	5 155	1 661	557	543	2 393	617	452	1 325	1 750	70 558	45 615	24 943
1973	75 407	6 558	4 851	1 521	467	524	2 340	588	433	1 320	1 706	68 849	44 424	24 425
1972	73 313	6 368	4 665	1 421	432	516	2 297	642	419	1 237	1 703	66 945	43 096	23 849
1971	71 320	6 238	4 559	1 353	422	478	2 307	652	416	1 239	1 680	65 081	41 816	23 266
1970	69 778	6 137	4 391	1 299	427	427	2 238	615	429	1 195	1 746	63 640	40 834	22 806
1969	68 479	6 218	4 437	1 296	408	402	2 332	619	454	1 258	1 782	62 261	40 049	22 211
1968	67 171	6 218	4 446	1 392	439	389	2 227	551	438	1 238	1 772	60 952	38 918	22 034
1967	66 014	6 538	4 762	1 566	499	348	2 349	571	460	1 318	1 776	59 476	37 842	21 634
1966	65 212	6 726	4 909	1 778	522	349	2 261	546	434	1 280	1 817	58 486	37 109	21 377
1965	64 213	6 712	4 853	1 884	548	330	2 092	504	379	1 209	1 860	57 501	36 230	21 271

Source: U.S. Census Bureau, Current Population Survey, Housing Vacancy Survey. *Statistical Abstract of the United States: 2007.*
¹Revised. Based on 2000 census controls.
²Beginning 1986, includes vacant seasonal mobile homes. For years shown, seasonal vacant housing units were underreported prior to 1986.

Table 11-2. Value of Construction Put in Place, 1964–2005

(Millions of dollars.)

Year	Total construction	Private construction						
		Total	Residential			Office[1]	Commercial[1]	Farm nonresidential
			Total[1]	New housing units	Improvements			
2005	1 143 655	898 970	642 276	481 738	160 538	36 823	69 143	7 232
2004	1 034 729	804 235	564 827	417 501	147 326	32 879	64 110	6 400
2003	926 870	702 887	475 941	345 691	130 250	30 579	57 505	5 103
2002	876 802	659 651	421 912	298 841	123 071	35 296	59 008	5 611
2001	868 310	662 247	388 324	279 391	108 933	49 745	63 606	5 135
2000	835 279	649 750	374 457	265 047	109 410	52 407	64 055	5 988
1999	769 461	599 729	350 562	251 271	99 290	45 052	59 376	5 059
1998	706 303	552 001	314 607	223 983	90 624	40 394	55 681	4 284
1997	653 429	502 734	289 014	198 062	90 951	32 813	53 088	3 815
1996	615 900	476 638	281 115	191 114	90 002	26 530	49 381	3 658
1995	557 818	427 885	247 351	171 404	75 947	22 996	44 096	3 014
1994	539 193	418 999	258 561	176 390	82 172	20 443	39 615	3 226
1993	491 033	375 073	225 067	150 911	74 156	19 999	34 396	3 392
1992	463 661	347 814	199 393	...	...	...	...	...
1991	432 592	322 483	166 251	...	...	...	...	...
1990	476 778	369 300	191 103	...	...	...	...	...
1989	477 502	379 328	204 255	...	...	...	...	...
1988	462 012	367 277	204 496	...	...	...	...	...
1987	446 643	355 994	199 652	...	...	...	...	...
1986	433 454	348 872	190 677	...	...	...	...	...
1985	403 416	325 601	160 520	...	...	...	...	...
1984	370 190	299 952	155 015	...	...	...	...	...
1983	311 887	248 437	125 833	...	...	...	...	...
1982	279 332	216 268	84 676	...	...	...	...	...
1981	289 070	224 378	99 241	...	...	...	...	...
1980	273 936	210 290	100 381	...	...	...	...	...
1979	272 873	216 228	116 444	...	...	...	...	...
1978	239 867	189 721	109 838	...	...	...	...	...
1977	200 501	157 418	92 004	...	...	...	...	...
1976	172 132	128 153	68 273	...	...	...	...	...
1975	152 635	109 342	51 581	...	...	...	...	...
1974	155 170	117 038	55 967	...	...	...	...	...
1973	153 781	121 433	65 085	...	...	...	...	...
1972	139 126	109 096	60 693	...	...	...	...	...
1971	122 414	92 715	48 514	...	...	...	...	...
1970	105 890	77 982	35 863	...	...	...	...	...
1969	104 944	77 151	37 214	...	...	...	...	...
1968	96 824	69 386	34 172	...	...	...	...	...
1967	87 221	61 844	28 737	...	...	...	...	...
1966	85 753	61 907	28 611	...	...	...	...	...
1965	81 886	59 966	30 235	...	...	...	...	...
1964	75 097	54 893	30 526	...	...	...	...	...

Note: Represents value of construction put in place during year; differs from building permit and construction contract data in timing and coverage. Includes installed cost of normal building service equipment and selected types of industrial production equipment (largely site fabricated). Excludes cost of shipbuilding, land, and most types of machinery and equipment.
[1]Includes other types of construction, not shown separately.
. . . = Not available.

Table 11-2. Value of Construction Put in Place, 1964–2005—*Continued*

(Millions of dollars.)

Year	Total public construction	State and local consturction								Total federal construction
		Total[1]	Residential	Office	Commercial[1]	Educational[1]	Highway and streets[1]	Water supply, sewage and waste disposal[1]	Conservation and development[1]	
2005	244 686	226 954	6 749	7 365	2 734	64 666	64 750	25 874	2 456	17 732
2004	230 494	212 152	6 319	8 232	2 704	60 149	58 996	24 561	2 010	18 342
2003	223 983	206 071	5 434	8 208	2 958	56 761	57 977	23 933	1 371	17 913
2002	217 150	200 572	5 320	8 156	3 149	54 571	58 286	22 754	1 316	16 578
2001	206 063	190 981	5 005	7 196	3 189	51 289	59 125	20 056	1 396	15 081
2000	185 529	171 362	4 200	6 256	2 543	45 616	53 081	17 221	1 304	14 166
1999	169 732	155 706	4 603	4 521	2 519	41 117	49 174	17 491	1 346	14 025
1998	154 302	139 984	4 340	4 605	1 993	35 015	44 782	16 621	1 444	14 318
1997	150 695	136 608	4 336	4 619	2 227	33 758	43 017	17 008	1 503	14 087
1996	139 263	123 938	4 220	4 404	1 724	28 603	39 500	15 419	1 191	15 325
1995	129 933	114 181	4 043	3 914	1 329	25 743	37 616	13 132	1 265	15 751
1994	120 193	105 753	3 359	3 559	1 075	20 541	37 281	13 365	1 194	14 440
1993	115 960	101 535	3 686	3 192	1 119	19 227	34 353	13 964	1 052	14 424
1992	115 847	101 471	...	...	...	...	...	...	...	14 376
1991	110 109	97 264	...	...	...	...	...	...	...	12 845
1990	107 478	95 379	...	...	...	...	...	...	...	12 099
1989	98 174	86 018	...	...	...	...	...	...	...	12 155
1988	94 735	82 471	...	...	...	...	...	...	...	12 264
1987	90 648	76 596	...	...	...	...	...	...	...	14 052
1986	84 582	72 170	...	...	...	...	...	...	...	12 412
1985	77 815	65 811	...	...	...	...	...	...	...	12 004
1984	70 238	58 998	...	...	...	...	...	...	...	11 240
1983	63 450	52 893	...	...	...	...	...	...	...	10 557
1982	63 064	53 056	...	...	...	...	...	...	...	10 008
1981	64 691	54 278	...	...	...	...	...	...	...	10 413
1980	63 646	54 004	...	...	...	...	...	...	...	9 642
1979	56 646	48 081	...	...	...	...	...	...	...	8 564
1978	50 146	42 000	...	...	...	...	...	...	...	8 146
1977	43 083	35 994	...	...	...	...	...	...	...	7 088
1976	43 980	37 196	...	...	...	...	...	...	...	6 783
1975	43 293	37 205	...	...	...	...	...	...	...	6 088
1974	38 132	33 042	...	...	...	...	...	...	...	5 091
1973	32 348	27 648	...	...	...	...	...	...	...	4 700
1972	30 030	25 786	...	...	...	...	...	...	...	4 244
1971	29 699	25 889	...	...	...	...	...	...	...	3 810
1970	27 908	24 798	...	...	...	...	...	...	...	3 110
1969	27 793	24 643	...	...	...	...	...	...	...	3 150
1968	27 437	24 238	...	...	...	...	...	...	...	3 199
1967	25 377	22 061	...	...	...	...	...	...	...	3 316
1966	23 846	20 043	...	...	...	...	...	...	...	3 803
1965	21 920	18 048	...	...	...	...	...	...	...	3 872
1964	20 203	16 485	...	...	...	...	...	...	...	3 718

Source: U.S. Census Bureau.
Note: Represents value of construction put in place during year; differs from building permit and construction contract data in timing and coverage. Includes installed cost of normal building service equipment and selected types of industrial production equipment (largely site fabricated). Excludes cost of shipbuilding, land, and most types of machinery and equipment.
[1]Includes other types of construction, not shown separately.
. . . = Not available.

Table 11-3. Value of Construction Contracts Awarded (Dodge), by Class of Construction, 1901–2004

(Millions of dollars, includes new structures and alterations to existing structures.)

Year	Total	Nonresidential buildings Total	Commercial	Industrial	Educational and science	Hospital	Public buildings	Religious	Social and recreational	Miscellaneous	Residential buildings	Non-building construction
2004	587 000	161 400	65 600	7 400	43 600	17 200	7 200	4 400	11 700	4 300	331 800	93 800
2003	530 700	155 600	58 900	6 700	47 800	15 600	7 000	4 500	10 800	4 300	283 100	92 000
2002	504 100	155 200	59 700	5 500	45 400	16 100	7 300	5 100	11 500	4 700	248 700	100 200
2001	496 600	169 200	70 300	8 100	47 000	14 400	7 800	4 800	12 000	4 800	219 700	107 700
2000	472 900	173 300	80 900	8 900	40 900	12 400	7 500	4 600	13 800	4 400	208 300	91 300
1999	447 200	168 700	77 200	11 300	37 100	13 600	8 200	4 500	11 600	5 100	195 000	83 500
1998	405 600	154 500	74 000	12 100	30 100	12 900	6 600	4 300	10 800	3 600	179 800	71 300
1997	362 400	138 900	59 800	14 000	28 400	11 900	7 000	3 800	10 000	4 000	153 600	69 800
1996	332 000	120 500	51 900	13 100	23 000	11 100	6 300	2 900	8 100	4 100	146 500	65 100
1995	306 500	114 200	46 600	13 800	22 900	10 800	6 300	2 800	7 100	3 800	127 900	64 400
1994	296 700	101 500	40 800	11 200	21 000	10 500	6 100	2 500	6 500	3 000	133 600	61 600
1993	271 500	88 800	34 200	9 000	19 300	10 500	3 900	2 400	6 800	2 600	123 900	58 900
1992	252 200	87 000	32 800	8 900	17 600	10 900	5 800	2 500	5 500	3 100	110 600	54 600
1991	230 800	86 200	32 700	8 300	19 000	9 600	6 200	2 400	5 100	3 000	94 400	50 200
1990	246 000	95 400	44 800	8 400	16 600	9 200	5 700	2 200	5 300	3 100	100 900	49 700
1989	271 300	106 300	53 600	12 700	15 900	8 800	5 200	2 000	5 000	2 900	116 200	49 000
1988	262 200	97 900	51 600	9 500	14 100	8 200	4 400	2 200	4 700	3 200	116 200	48 100
1987	259 000	98 800	53 700	8 600	13 200	9 000	4 700	2 100	4 300	3 200	114 100	46 100
1986	249 300	91 600	52 400	7 300	11 700	7 900	3 200	2 100	4 200	2 800	115 600	42 100
1985	235 600	92 100	54 600	8 100	10 000	7 800	3 100	2 000	4 000	2 500	102 100	41 400
1984	214 300	82 100	48 200	7 900	8 500	7 400	2 700	1 700	3 300	2 400	95 300	36 900
1983	194 100	67 900	38 300	5 400	7 100	8 500	2 100	1 500	2 900	2 100	88 400	37 800
1982	157 100	64 600	32 300	9 600	6 800	8 000	1 900	1 200	2 800	2 000	55 000	37 500
1981	157 300	65 500	35 200	9 300	6 600	6 400	1 400	1 200	3 400	2 000	56 300	35 400
1980	151 800	56 900	27 700	9 200	7 400	5 400	1 600	1 200	2 700	1 700	60 400	34 500
1979	168 400	50 200	24 400	7 600	6 300	4 800	1 600	1 300	4 100	...	74 600	43 700
1978	159 900	45 000	20 600	9 200	5 700	3 800	1 500	1 200	3 000	...	74 900	39 900
1977	139 700	35 100	13 600	5 400	5 200	4 500	2 300	1 000	3 300	...	62 000	42 600
1976	110 100	30 000	10 200	4 500	4 900	4 500	2 100	900	3 000	...	44 200	35 900
1975	92 700	31 600	9 200	6 800	5 900	3 700	2 100	800	3 100	...	31 300	29 800
1974	93 700	33 200	11 800	5 600	6 300	3 800	2 100	800	2 800	...	33 600	27 000
1973	99 300	31 400	12 800	4 800	5 100	3 300	2 000	700	2 700	...	45 700	22 100
1972	88 885	...	11 369	3 005	4 760	3 516	1 490	640	1 237	1 003	42 882	18 983
1971	80 188	...	9 610	2 619	5 649	3 188	1 493	603	1 296	1 131	34 714	19 883
1970	68 294	24 455	9 056	3 664	5 253	2 811	1 007	575	1 137	952	24 837	19 001
1969	68 294	25 949	9 786	3 915	5 543	2 817	1 154	674	1 116	944	25 633	16 710
1968	61 732	22 513	7 645	3 768	5 347	2 114	1 112	778	954	795	24 838	14 382
1967	54 514	20 139	6 080	3 701	5 216	1 873	959	793	834	683	21 155	13 220
1966	50 150	19 393	5 835	3 623	4 939	1 721	939	825	855	656	17 827	12 930
1965	49 272	17 219	5 457	3 064	4 164	1 515	842	783	800	596	21 248	10 805
1964	47 330	15 522	4 572	2 970	3 554	1 625	789	814	599	598	20 565	11 244
1963	45 546	14 377	4 445	2 274	3 314	1 485	964	755	648	493	20 502	10 667
1962	41 303	13 010	4 216	2 086	3 060	1 079	677	811	704	377	18 039	10 255
1961	37 135	12 115	3 797	1 814	3 015	985	671	805	623	403	16 123	8 897
1960	36 318	12 240	3 725	2 114	3 005	832	679	789	631	464	15 105	8 973
1959	36 269	11 387	3 496	1 880	2 666	865	605	799	601	474	17 150	7 732
1958	35 090	10 948	3 197	1 400	2 907	879	655	746	500	664	14 696	9 446
1957	32 173	11 293	3 267	2 168	2 936	870	470	699	429	455	13 039	7 841
1956	31 612	11 208	3 140	2 381	2 883	678	428	681	422	595	12 862	7 542
1955	24 632	8 497	2 359	1 878	2 134	475	301	551	270	530	11 072	5 063
1954	20 596	7 110	1 816	1 274	2 063	519	249	486	252	452	9 344	4 142
1953	18 804	6 956	1 489	2 051	1 720	434	203	385	222	452	7 840	4 008
1952	18 070	6 695	979	2 558	1 472	444	233	318	153	538	7 963	3 412
1951	17 151	6 823	915	2 883	1 335	581	158	299	136	515	7 605	2 723
1950	16 592	5 182	1 209	1 142	1 180	655	124	336	261	274	8 832	2 578
1949	11 826	3 644	885	559	824	555	119	276	222	204	5 706	2 476
1948	11 121	3 666	975	840	725	405	84	245	232	161	5 299	2 155
1947	9 175	2 716	785	941	392	192	73	118	122	92	4 569	1 890
1946	7 490	2 716	773	1 317	221	131	25	68	93	88	3 142	1 631
1945	3 299	1 850	346	1 027	100	113	16	35	60	153	563	885
1944	1 994	899	81	473	69	59	12	12	33	161	348	746
1943	3 274	1 424	121	766	62	111	25	7	58	274	868	982
1942	8 255	3 897	302	2 228	148	185	102	24	101	808	1 818	2 541
1941	6 007	2 316	471	1 182	141	89	89	53	78	214	1 954	1 738

. . . = Not available.

Table 11-3. Value of Construction Contracts Awarded (Dodge), by Class of Construction, 1901–2004—*Continued*

(Millions of dollars, includes new structures and alterations to existing structures.)

Year	Total	Nonresidential buildings									Residential buildings	Non-building construction
		Total	Commercial	Industrial	Educational and science	Hospital	Public buildings	Religious	Social and recreational	Miscellaneous		
1940	4 004	1 295	318	442	147	94	80	46	63	104	1 597	1 112
1939	3 551	966	247	175	201	83	110	38	82	29	1 334	1 251
1938	3 197	1 072	216	121	334	116	114	36	108	28	986	1 139
1937	2 913	1 156	297	314	223	82	105	37	84	15	905	852
1936	2 675	960	249	198	219	74	102	28	75	14	802	914
1935	1 845	681	165	109	168	47	98	24	55	16	479	685
1934	1 543	551	151	116	112	37	56	18	46	15	249	743
1933	1 256	417	99	128	39	37	51	18	27	19	249	589
1932	1 351	488	123	44	81	48	118	27	34	13	280	583
1931	3 093	1 141	311	116	223	121	181	53	99	36	811	1 141
1930	4 523	1 822	616	257	366	163	140	93	117	71	1 101	1 599
1929	5 751	2 425	929	546	370	152	121	106	147	55	1 916	1 410
1928	6 628	2 438	885	509	390	165	76	128	219	67	2 788	1 402
1927	6 303	2 439	933	376	369	163	80	157	261	102	2 573	1 291
1926	6 381	2 418	921	471	373	133	67	149	252	52	2 671	1 292
1925	6 006	2 202	872	327	419	111	55	153	253	12	2 748	1 057
1924	4 479	1 583	591	233	...	...	...	...	...	...	2 052	844
1923	3 992	1 456	518	313	...	...	...	...	...	...	1 736	801
1922	3 344	1 395	496	278	...	...	...	...	...	...	1 340	609
1921	2 355	998	332	153	...	...	...	...	...	...	879	479
1920[1]	2 564	1 394	444	555	...	...	...	...	...	...	570	600
1919[1]	2 590	1 213	406	498	...	...	...	...	...	...	849	517
1918	1 767	...	...	...	...	...	...	...	...	...	305	...
1917	1 691	...	...	...	...	...	...	...	...	...	355	...
1916	1 413	...	...	...	...	...	...	...	...	...	483	...
1915	978	...	...	...	...	...	...	...	...	...	418	...
1914	775	...	...	...	...	...	...	...	...	...	...	...
1913	917	...	...	...	...	...	...	...	...	...	...	...
1912	923	...	...	...	...	...	...	...	...	...	...	...
1911	828	...	...	...	...	...	...	...	...	...	...	...
1910	859	...	...	...	...	...	...	...	...	...	...	...
1909	166	...	...	...	...	...	...	...	...	...	...	...
1908	112	...	...	...	...	...	...	...	...	...	...	...
1907	129	...	...	...	...	...	...	...	...	...	...	...
1906	125	...	...	...	...	...	...	...	...	...	...	...
1905	107	...	...	...	...	...	...	...	...	...	...	...
1904	97	...	...	...	...	...	...	...	...	...	...	...
1903	104	...	...	...	...	...	...	...	...	...	...	...
1902	119	...	...	...	...	...	...	...	...	...	...	...
1901	120	...	...	...	...	...	...	...	...	...	...	...

Source: U.S. Census Bureau. McGraw-Hill Construction Dodge, a Division of the McGraw-Hill Companies (copyright).
[1]Twenty-five states only. Totals for 27 states are 1919: 2,699; 1920: 2,635.
. . . = Not available.

Table 11-4. Price and Cost Indexes for Construction, 1985–2003

(1996 = 100, Excludes Alaska and Hawaii.)

Name of index	1985	1990	1995	1998	1999	2000	2001	2002	2003
U.S. Census Bureau composite									
Fixed-weighted[1]	71.8	85.5	97.7	106.0	110.3	115.3	120.2	122.7	130.3
Implicit price deflator[2]	71.1	85.0	97.8	106.1	110.4	115.4	119.6	122.6	139,7
U.S. Census Bureau houses under construction[3]									
Fixed-weighted	69.8	84.6	98.1	105.6	110.4	115.4	121.2	124.5	...
Price deflator	68.3	83.4	98.1	105.6	110.4	115.5	121.3	124.7	...
Federal Highway Administration, composite[4]	83.6	88.9	99.8	105.2	111.9	119.3	118.7	121.2	...
Bureau of Reclamation composite[5]	75	85	98	105	107	111	112	114	...
Turner Construction Co.: Building construction[6]	74	87	97	109	113	118	121	123	...
Engineering News-Record[7]									
Buildings	75.8	84.4	97.1	105.8	107.9	110.5	111.6	113.1	...
Construction	74.6	84.2	97.3	105.3	107.8	110.7	112.7	116.3	...
Handy-Whitman public utility[8]									
Buildings	76	85	97	104	107	110	114	116	...
Electric[9]	74	86	98	104	105	109	113	116	...
Gas	75	86	99	104	107	111	114	116	...
Water[10]	76	85	98	104	107	112	116	120	...
C.A. Turner Telephone Plant[11]	77	87	96	102	101	103	106	108	...

Source: U.S. Census Bureau, *Statistical Abstract of the United States: 2004–2005.*
[1]Weighted average of the various indexes used to deflate the Construction Put in Place series. In calculating the index, the weights (i.e., the composition of current dollar estimates in 1996 by category) are held constant.
[2]Derived ratio of total current to constant dollar Construction Put in Place (multiplied by 100).
[3]Excludes value of site.
[4]Based on average contract unit bid prices for composite mile (involving specific average amounts of excavation, paving, reinforcing steel, structural steel, and structural concrete).
[5]Derived from the four quarterly indexes which are weighted averages of costs of labor, materials, and equipment for the construction of dams and reclamation projects.
[6]Based on firm's cost experience with respect to labor rates, materials prices, competitive conditions, efficiency of plant and management, and productivity.
[7]Building construction index computed on the basis of a hypothetical unit of construction requiring 6 bbl. of portland cement, 1,088 M bd. ft. of 2"x4" lumber, 2,500 lb. of structural steel, and 68.38 hours of skilled labor. General construction index based on same materials components combined with 200 hours of common labor.
[8]Based on data covering public utility construction costs in six geographic regions. Covers skilled and common labor.
[9]As derived by U.S. Census Bureau. Covers steam generation plants only.
[10]As derived by U.S. Census Bureau. Reflects costs for structures and improvements at water pumping and treatment plants.
[11]Computed by the Census Bureau by averaging the weighted component indexes published for six geographic regions.
... = Not available.

Table 11-5. Median Sales Price of New Privately Owned One-Family Houses Sold by Region, 1970–2005

(Dollars.)

Year	United States total	Northeast	Midwest	South	West
2005	240 900	343 800	216 900	197 300	332 600
2004	221 000	315 800	205 000	181 100	283 100
2003	195 000	264 500	184 300	168 100	260 900
2002	187 600	264 300	178 000	163 400	238 500
2001	175 200	246 400	172 600	155 400	213 600
2000	169 000	227 400	169 700	148 000	196 400
1999	161 000	210 500	164 000	145 900	173 700
1998	152 500	200 000	157 500	135 800	163 500
1997	146 000	190 000	149 900	129 600	160 000
1996	140 000	186 000	138 000	126 200	153 900
1995	133 900	180 000	134 000	124 500	141 400
1994	130 000	169 000	132 900	116 900	140 400
1993	126 500	162 600	125 000	115 000	135 000
1992	121 500	169 000	115 600	105 500	130 400
1991	120 000	155 900	110 000	100 000	141 100
1990	122 900	159 000	107 900	99 000	147 500
1989	120 000	159 600	108 800	96 400	139 000
1988	112 500	149 000	101 600	92 000	126 500
1987	104 500	140 000	95 000	88 000	111 000
1986	92 000	125 000	88 300	80 200	95 700
1985	84 300	103 300	80 300	75 000	92 600
1984	79 900	88 600	85 400	72 000	87 300
1983	75 300	82 200	79 500	70 900	80 100
1982	69 300	78 200	68 900	66 100	75 000
1981	68 900	76 000	65 900	64 400	77 800
1980	64 600	69 500	63 400	59 600	72 300
1979	62 900	65 500	63 900	57 300	69 600
1978	55 700	58 100	59 200	50 300	61 300
1977	48 800	51 600	51 500	44 100	53 500
1976	44 200	47 300	44 800	40 500	47 200
1975	39 300	44 000	39 600	37 300	40 600
1974	35 900	40 100	36 100	34 500	35 800
1973	32 500	37 100	32 900	30 900	32 400
1972	27 600	31 400	29 300	25 800	27 500
1971	25 200	30 600	27 200	22 500	25 500
1970	23 400	30 300	24 400	20 300	24 000

Source: U.S. Census Bureau. *Statistical Abstract of the United States: 2007.* U.S. Department of Housing and Urban Development.
Note: Composition of regions:
   NORTHEAST: Maine, New Hampshire, Vermont, Massachusetts, Rhode Island, Connecticut, New York, New Jersey, and Pennsylvania.
   MIDWEST: Ohio, Indiana, Illinois, Michigan, Wisconsin, Minnesota, Iowa, Missouri, North Dakota, South Dakota, Nebraska, and Kansas.
   SOUTH: Delaware, Maryland, District of Columbia, Virginia, West Virginia, North Carolina, South Carolina, Georgia, Florida, Kentucky, Tennessee, Alabama, Mississippi, Arkansas, Louisiana, Oklahoma, and Texas.
   WEST: Montana, Idaho, Wyoming, Colorado, New Mexico, Arizona, Utah, Nevada, Washington, Oregon, California, Alaska, and Hawaii.

Table 11-6. Homeownership Rates, by Age of Householder and Household Status, 1985–2005

(Percent.)

Age of householder and household type	1985	1990	1995	2000	2001	2002	2003	2004	2005
United States	63.9	63.9	64.7	67.4	67.8	67.9	68.3	69.0	68.9
AGE									
Less than 25 years old	17.2	15.7	15.9	21.7	22.5	23.0	22.8	25.2	25.7
25 to 29 years old	37.7	35.2	34.4	38.1	38.9	39.0	39.8	40.2	40.9
30 to 34 years old	54.0	51.8	53.1	54.6	54.8	55.0	56.5	57.4	56.8
35 to 39 years old	65.4	63.0	62.1	65.0	65.5	65.2	65.1	66.2	66.6
40 to 44 years old	71.4	69.8	68.6	70.6	70.8	71.7	71.3	71.9	71.7
45 to 49 years old	74.3	73.9	73.7	74.7	75.4	74.9	75.4	76.3	75.0
50 to 54 years old	77.5	76.8	77.0	78.5	78.2	77.8	77.9	78.2	78.3
55 to 59 years old	79.2	78.8	78.8	80.4	81.0	80.8	80.9	81.2	80.6
60 to 64 years old	79.9	79.8	80.3	80.3	81.8	81.5	81.9	82.4	81.9
65 to 69 years old	79.5	80.0	81.0	83.0	82.4	82.8	82.5	83.2	82.8
70 to 74 years old	76.8	78.4	80.9	82.6	82.5	82.5	82.0	84.4	82.9
75 years old and over	69.8	72.3	74.6	77.7	78.1	78.4	78.7	78.8	78.4
Less than 35 years old	39.9	38.5	38.6	40.8	41.2	41.3	42.2	43.1	43.0
35 to 44 years old	68.1	66.3	65.2	67.9	68.2	68.6	68.3	69.2	69.3
45 to 54 years old	75.9	75.2	75.2	76.5	76.7	76.3	76.6	77.2	76.6
55 to 64 years old	79.5	79.3	79.5	80.3	81.3	81.1	81.4	81.9	81.2
65 years old and over	74.8	76.3	78.1	80.4	80.3	80.5	80.5	81.1	80.6
TYPE OF HOUSEHOLD									
Family Households									
Married-couple families	78.2	78.1	79.6	82.4	82.9	83.1	83.3	84.0	84.2
Male householder, no spouse present	57.8	55.2	55.3	57.5	57.9	58.0	57.9	59.6	59.1
Female householder, no spouse present	45.8	44.0	45.1	49.1	49.9	49.2	49.6	50.9	51.0
Nonfamily Households									
One-person	45.8	49.0	50.5	53.6	54.4	54.8	55.2	55.8	55.6
Male householder	38.8	42.4	43.8	47.4	48.2	48.7	50.0	50.5	50.3
Female householder	51.3	53.6	55.4	58.1	59.0	59.4	59.1	59.9	59.6
Other									
Male householder	30.1	31.7	34.2	38.0	38.6	38.8	40.0	41.7	41.7
Female householder	30.6	32.5	33.0	40.6	41.0	41.6	43.1	43.5	44.8

Source: U.S. Census Bureau.

Table 11-7. Shipments of Newly Manufactured Mobile Homes, 1959–2005

(Thousands of Units)

Year	Mobile home shipments
2005 (r)	146.8
2004 (r)	130.7
2003	130.8
2002	168.5
2001	193.1
2000	250.4
1999	348.1
1998	373.1
1997	353.7
1996	363.3
1995	339.9
1994	303.9
1993	254.3
1992	210.5
1991	170.9
1990	188.3
1989	198.1
1988	218.3
1987	232.8
1986	244.3
1985	283.5
1984	295.4
1983	295.8
1982	239.5
1981	240.9
1980	221.6
1979	277.4
1978	275.7
1977	265.6
1976	246.1
1975	212.7
1974	338.3
1973	579.9
1972	575.9
1971	491.7
1970	401.2
1969	412.7
1968	318.0
1967	240.4
1966	217.3
1965	216.5
1964	191.3
1963	150.8
1962	118.0
1961	90.2
1960	103.7
1959	120.5

Source: U.S. Census Bureau. *Manufactured Housing Survey.* 1978–2001 data are compiled from manufacturers' reports to the Institution for Building Technology and Safety (IBTS). Data prior to 1978 were obtained from the Manufactured Housing Institute.
Note: A manufactured, or mobile, home is defined as a movable dwelling, 8 feet or more wide and 40 feet or more long, designed to be towed on its own chassis, with transportation gear integral to the unit when it leaves the factory, and without need of a permanent foundation. These manufactured homes include multiwides and expandable manufactured homes. Excluded are travel trailers, motor homes, and modular housing.
r = Revised data.

Table 11-8. Renter-Occupied Housing Units—Gross Rent by State, 2004

(Thousands, percent.)

State	Total[1] (1,000)	Units with gross rent of—					Median gross rent (dollars)	Gross rent as a percent of household income in the past 12 months				
		$299 or less	$300 to $499	$500 to $749	$750 to $999	$1,000 or more		Less than 15 percent	15 to 24.9 percent	25 to 34.9 percent	35 percent or more	Not computed
United States	**36 148**	**7.6**	**15.4**	**30.7**	**21.3**	**18.9**	**694**	**12.9**	**24.2**	**19.1**	**35.9**	**7.4**
Alabama	493	11.8	29.1	32.0	11.9	3.2	519	13.9	24.0	13.6	33.9	15.4
Alaska	79	3.0	6.0	26.5	30.9	21.2	808	12.6	27.8	19.0	28.2	15.0
Arizona	668	4.3	13.1	40.1	20.8	15.4	691	11.3	22.3	19.3	38.9	8.9
Arkansas	379	11.5	29.9	34.9	9.2	3.3	517	15.5	22.6	17.9	31.6	10.9
California	4 960	3.8	6.7	20.9	25.2	40.1	914	10.1	23.2	20.3	41.2	5.0
Colorado	582	4.6	10.8	35.7	22.3	21.0	724	10.3	22.9	21.0	38.1	5.1
Connecticut	402	7.7	8.5	22.9	31.0	25.3	811	13.5	26.2	19.2	35.2	6.1
Delaware	84	7.2	9.0	30.9	28.0	16.5	743	12.1	27.6	19.4	31.1	7.6
District of Columbia	140	10.4	8.1	25.1	21.1	31.8	799	12.9	24.5	22.3	34.3	6.8
Florida	2 011	4.8	9.2	31.4	28.9	21.0	766	8.9	22.7	21.1	40.8	6.6
Georgia	1 038	8.5	15.8	32.6	25.8	10.8	677	14.5	21.9	18.9	35.9	9.4
Hawaii	176	5.2	8.6	19.8	19.6	34.4	871	10.3	23.2	19.5	33.6	14.2
Idaho	142	8.2	26.7	36.8	13.0	7.4	566	14.6	22.0	20.0	35.1	8.0
Illinois	1 433	7.3	15.2	32.2	23.6	16.9	698	13.7	25.7	17.7	35.6	6.8
Indiana	679	8.9	22.1	41.3	15.3	6.1	589	14.6	28.1	19.4	30.0	8.1
Iowa	308	12.2	27.1	33.2	12.4	4.8	533	14.4	26.5	17.7	30.5	6.6
Kansas	328	11.2	24.3	33.0	15.5	7.4	567	13.4	27.6	19.6	30.0	8.2
Kentucky	492	14.9	28.8	31.4	10.0	3.3	503	15.5	22.7	16.1	33.1	14.8
Louisiana	579	10.8	26.0	34.7	11.6	5.1	540	14.2	20.7	15.0	35.4	15.8
Maine	145	12.2	22.2	33.1	16.3	8.7	582	11.5	28.4	20.0	31.6	10.2
Maryland	634	7.2	8.2	22.2	28.1	29.9	837	14.0	26.4	22.1	31.4	5.3
Massachusetts	863	11.0	9.9	18.2	21.2	35.3	852	12.5	25.7	22.1	33.3	5.5
Michigan	994	7.8	18.1	38.1	20.0	10.9	628	13.4	24.8	19.0	35.4	6.0
Minnesota	507	10.7	13.6	33.2	21.4	14.9	673	13.3	25.3	21.1	33.7	5.3
Mississippi	326	12.7	25.7	31.4	13.0	3.3	529	11.3	21.4	16.5	35.2	13.7
Missouri	674	10.2	24.4	36.9	15.1	5.1	567	13.9	25.9	18.7	31.7	7.5
Montana	116	13.9	26.8	31.8	11.0	5.7	520	15.7	24.4	16.8	32.2	9.3
Nebraska	217	11.2	27.1	35.1	11.0	6.1	547	16.7	25.7	18.7	28.9	9.1
Nevada	338	2.0	7.7	32.9	31.8	22.0	787	11.7	27.4	19.6	35.3	4.8
New Hampshire	135	7.2	8.5	24.1	28.7	27.3	810	11.2	28.9	22.0	33.3	6.7
New Jersey	1 000	6.4	6.3	19.0	31.4	32.9	877	13.3	25.1	19.6	36.6	5.4
New Mexico	219	11.3	26.7	32.8	13.7	7.0	546	15.5	24.2	19.9	31.0	10.2
New York	3 146	7.7	10.8	24.8	24.3	28.8	796	15.0	21.7	18.8	38.9	5.4
North Carolina	1 035	8.2	20.5	37.8	16.6	7.3	610	13.5	23.8	17.7	33.5	11.8
North Dakota	84	15.7	36.0	28.8	5.6	2.7	466	19.4	28.8	14.1	25.6	11.4
Ohio	1 365	9.5	22.0	40.0	16.2	6.8	587	13.8	26.7	17.3	33.9	7.0
Oklahoma	432	7.8	32.9	32.8	11.2	5.5	525	14.6	24.1	16.5	32.6	11.5
Oregon	529	5.6	15.2	37.9	22.7	14.4	681	11.0	24.4	19.8	38.5	4.8
Pennsylvania	1 311	10.1	21.5	32.9	18.5	10.6	611	14.3	24.1	19.6	33.9	6.5
Rhode Island	157	12.1	9.5	28.1	28.3	18.4	740	14.5	22.1	22.7	35.8	6.0
South Carolina	488	9.0	18.8	35.0	16.5	8.2	610	15.9	22.3	15.0	32.6	12.9
South Dakota	93	15.6	28.7	29.0	8.7	4.2	493	15.1	24.8	18.6	26.5	12.3
Tennessee	695	10.2	23.9	37.8	14.3	5.8	564	14.4	24.7	18.0	33.3	9.1
Texas	2 716	6.2	17.8	37.0	20.2	12.2	648	13.5	24.7	18.6	34.3	7.8
Utah	236	5.5	15.8	40.7	22.4	11.1	662	13.9	27.1	18.7	35.1	5.4
Vermont	67	8.7	14.2	34.2	22.8	13.5	674	13.2	27.1	20.7	31.6	6.8
Virginia	878	7.4	13.4	25.2	22.3	25.2	757	13.0	27.2	19.2	32.6	7.4
Washington	868	6.2	11.4	33.4	25.3	19.0	727	9.8	24.5	20.6	39.0	5.9
West Virginia	192	14.8	32.4	28.3	6.5	1.7	461	14.9	19.5	16.0	31.2	16.6
Wisconsin	654	8.1	19.2	43.4	16.9	7.9	609	15.1	27.1	18.4	33.3	5.7
Wyoming	61	10.2	27.9	28.9	10.0	9.4	534	18.4	26.4	17.3	23.8	7.9

Source: U.S. Census Bureau. *Statistical Abstract of the United States: 2007.*
Note: The American Community Survey universe is limited to the household population and excludes the population living in institutions, college dormitories, and other group quarters. Based on a sample and subject to sampling variability.
[1]Includes units with no cash rent.

Table 11-9. Net Stock of Residential Fixed Assets, 1990–2004

(Billions of dollars. End of year estimates.)

Item	1990	1995	1996	1997	1998	1999	2000	2001	2002	2003	2004
Total residential fixed assets	**6 260.2**	**8 028.0**	**8 467.1**	**8 927.5**	**9 507.0**	**10 206.7**	**10 907.4**	**11 711.5**	**12 456.7**	**13 371.0**	**14 773.0**
By type of owner and legal form of organization:											
Private	6 111.0	7 839.8	8 270.6	8 730.6	9 300.1	9 986.7	10 675.7	11 464.8	12 193.1	13 088.1	14 473.3
Corporate	65.7	76.6	80.0	84.6	90.0	94.5	99.5	105.0	110.1	115.9	126.0
Noncorporate	6 045.3	7 763.3	8 190.7	8 646.0	9 210.1	9 892.2	10 576.1	11 359.8	12 083.0	12 972.2	14 347.3
Sole proprietorships and partnerships	731.9	854.7	893.5	949.5	1 011.7	1 068.4	1 126.7	1 188.2	1 244.2	1 308.2	1 419.9
Nonprofit institutions	108.2	117.0	119.7	124.0	129.3	134.4	139.7	145.9	151.3	157.5	168.9
Households	5 205.3	6 791.6	7 177.4	7 572.6	8 069.1	8 689.4	9 309.8	10 025.7	10 687.4	11 506.5	12 758.6
Government	149.2	188.2	196.5	196.8	206.9	219.9	231.7	246.7	263.6	282.9	299.7
Federal	51.8	61.6	63.7	65.9	68.7	72.2	75.4	79.2	82.9	87.9	93.9
State and local	97.3	126.6	132.7	130.9	138.2	147.7	156.4	167.5	180.7	195.0	205.8
By industry:											
Private	6 111.0	7 839.8	8 270.6	8 730.6	9 300.1	9 986.7	10 675.7	11 464.8	12 193.1	13 088.1	14 473.3
Farm	48.7	51.3	52.2	57.9	62.0	67.0	72.2	77.2	80.6	85.5	92.8
Nonfarm	6 062.4	7 788.6	8 218.4	8 672.7	9 238.1	9 919.8	10 603.4	11 387.6	12 112.5	13 002.5	14 380.5
By tenure group:[1]											
Owner occupied	4 515.6	5 987.9	6 344.3	6 712.4	7 174.7	7 752.3	8 328.7	8 996.0	9 614.3	10 377.7	11 538.7
Farm	48.7	51.3	52.2	57.9	62.0	67.0	72.2	77.2	80.6	85.5	92.8
Nonfarm	4 467.0	5 936.7	6 292.1	6 654.5	7 112.7	7 685.3	8 256.4	8 918.8	9 533.7	10 292.2	11 445.9
Tenant-occupied	1 718.8	2 011.3	2 093.3	2 184.6	2 300.6	2 420.6	2 543.0	2 677.2	2 802.0	2 950.4	3 187.7

Source: U.S. Census Bureau. *Statistical Abstract of the United States: 2007.* U.S. Bureau of Economic Analysis.
[1]Excludes stocks of other nonfarm residential assets, which consists primarily of dormitories, and of fraternity and sorority houses.

Table 11-10. Housing Units—Characteristics by Tenure and Region, 2005

(Thousands of units, except as indicated.)

Characteristic	Total housing units	Seasonal	Year-round units							Vacant
			Occupied							
			Total	Owner	Renter	Northeast	Midwest	South	West	
Total units, 2005	**124 377**	**3 845**	**108 871**	**74 931**	**33 940**	**20 337**	**24 955**	**39 722**	**23 858**	**11 660**
Percent distribution	100.0	3.1	87.5	68.8	31.2	18.7	22.9	36.5	21.9	9.4
Units in structure:										
Single family detached	77 703	2 287	69 996	61 699	8 297	11 044	17 707	26 254	14 992	5 420
Single family attached	7 046	197	6 158	3 976	2 182	1 825	1 042	2 035	1 256	691
2 to 4 units	10 071	188	8 379	1 550	6 829	2 604	1 863	2 073	1 840	1 504
5 to 9 units	6 073	125	5 109	502	4 607	917	1 004	1 824	1 364	840
10 to 19 units	5 696	94	4 739	563	4 175	817	902	1 830	1 190	863
20 to 49 units	4 402	125	3 639	436	3 203	1 041	601	964	1 033	638
50 or more units	4 757	186	3 912	689	3 222	1 589	682	809	831	659
Manufactured/mobile home[1] ..	8 630	644	6 940	5 516	1 424	500	1 155	3 932	1 352	1 047
Single-wide	5 584	457	4 257	3 093	1 164	371	843	2 443	600	869
Double-wide	2 897	174	2 558	2 302	255	126	312	1 435	685	165
Triple-wide or larger	118	7	107	103	4	-	-	44	64	4
Year structure built:										
Median year	1973	1972	1973	1974	1970	1956	1968	1978	1976	1971
2005	944	20	512	425	86	40	64	249	159	412
2000 to 2004	9 194	299	8 174	6 622	1 552	716	1 666	3 811	1 980	720
1995 to 1999	8 830	257	7 934	6 312	1 622	663	1 596	3 848	1 827	639
1990 to 1994	7 158	212	6 432	5 195	1 236	649	1 386	2 776	1 620	514
1985 to 1989	8 859	221	7 921	5 369	2 552	1 147	1 373	3 386	2 016	716
1980 to 1984	7 517	275	6 570	4 326	2 245	651	1 011	3 356	1 552	671
1975 to 1979	14 350	409	12 552	7 966	4 586	1 552	2 871	4 916	3 213	1 389
1970 to 1974	10 741	422	9 306	5 894	3 412	1 355	1 983	3 779	2 190	1 012
1960 to 1969	15 192	486	13 499	9 217	4 282	2 467	3 019	4 876	3 136	1 207
1950 to 1959	13 003	366	11 555	8 469	3 086	2 527	3 025	3 490	2 513	1 082
1940 to 1949	7 904	279	6 821	4 458	2 363	1 654	1 497	2 156	1 513	805
1930 to 1939	6 009	183	5 075	3 130	1 945	1 515	1 367	1 280	913	751
1920 to 1929	5 313	127	4 556	2 699	1 857	1 760	1 418	754	624	630
1919 and earlier	9 364	288	7 964	4 848	3 117	3 640	2 678	1 045	602	1 112
Stories in structure:[2]										
1 story	39 963	1 553	34 814	26 278	8 537	1 139	4 031	19 192	10 453	3 596
2 stories	41 189	984	36 283	24 026	12 257	6 187	10 111	11 154	8 832	3 922
3 stories	26 287	393	23 714	16 375	7 340	8 482	8 342	4 353	2 537	2 180
4 to 6 stories	5 819	137	5 128	2 248	2 880	2 932	999	719	478	554
7 or more stories	2 488	135	1 992	488	1 504	1 097	317	372	206	362
Foundation:[3]										
Full basement	26 882	350	24 984	22 612	2 372	8 586	10 745	3 793	1 860	1 547
Partial building	9 431	153	8 735	7 840	894	2 378	3 626	1 590	1 140	544
Crawlspace	22 292	1 151	19 038	15 646	3 392	732	2 575	10 037	5 694	2 103
Concrete slab	25 514	660	23 012	19 317	3 695	1 129	1 720	12 675	7 488	1 843
Other	629	169	384	259	125	44	82	192	66	75
Equipment:										
Lacking complete facilities	5 345	462	1 695	257	1 438	298	345	536	515	3 188
With complete facilities	119 032	3 384	107 177	74 674	32 502	20 038	24 610	39 186	23 343	8 472
Kitchen sink	123 262	3 644	108 656	74 889	33 767	20 296	24 923	39 663	23 775	10 962
Refrigerator	121 035	3 466	108 673	74 856	33 818	20 311	24 909	39 640	23 814	8 895
Cooking stove or range	121 208	3 475	108 140	74 718	33 422	20 179	24 812	39 506	23 642	9 593
Burners only, no stove or range ..	189	32	131	60	71	31	19	37	43	26
Microwave oven only	481	23	397	106	291	104	68	98	126	61
Dishwasher	75 239	1 677	68 508	54 060	14 448	11 132	14 491	26 271	16 614	5 055
Washing machine	95 272	1 979	89 287	71 997	17 290	15 039	20 969	34 138	19 141	4 006
Clothes dryer	92 179	1 949	86 169	70 348	15 821	13 976	20 765	32 893	18 534	4 062
Disposal in kitchen sink	58 906	1 217	53 299	38 595	14 704	5 107	12 423	18 584	17 185	4 390
Trash compactor	4 513	125	4 077	3 343	734	601	659	1 638	1 179	311

[1]Includes trailers. Includes width not reported, not shown separately.
[2]Excludes mobile homes; includes basements and finished attics.
[3]Limited to single-family units.
[4]With and without inserts.
- = Quantity zero or rounds to zero.

Table 11-10. Housing Units—Characteristics by Tenure and Region, 2005—*Continued*

(Thousands of units, except as indicated.)

Characteristic	Total housing units	Seasonal	Year-round units							Vacant
			Occupied							
			Total	Owner	Renter	Northeast	Midwest	South	West	
Main heating equipment:										
Warm-air furnace	76 665	1 727	68 275	50 459	17 817	8 546	20 331	23 735	15 664	6 662
Steam or hot water system	14 074	176	12 880	7 719	5 161	9 496	1 996	588	800	1 018
Electric heat pump	14 551	605	12 484	9 074	3 411	344	664	9 993	1 483	1 462
Built-in electric units	5 607	310	4 699	2 116	2 583	1 065	1 116	918	1 600	598
Floor, wall, or pipeless furnace	5 916	149	5 102	2 172	2 930	443	399	1 300	2 961	664
Room heaters with flue	1 615	111	1 294	752	542	165	172	646	310	211
Room heaters without flue	1 627	76	1 327	881	447	18	42	1 222	45	224
Portable electric heaters	1 127	73	907	441	467	29	20	642	216	146
Stoves	1 171	183	896	742	155	150	143	304	299	93
Fireplaces[4]	251	47	190	166	24	24	22	69	74	15
Other	505	65	298	167	131	18	31	159	90	142
Cooking stoves	148		120	50	70	34	-	50	36	28
None	1 120	324	399	194	205	4	20	96	279	397
Air conditioning: Central	80 511	1 662	72 629	55 849	16 780	6 535	17 401	36 249	12 443	6 220
One or more room units	27 124	579	24 863	14 326	10 537	10 132	5 707	5 697	3 326	1 681
One room unit	14 351	357	12 827	6 166	6 661	4 307	3 558	2 333	2 629	1 167
Two room units	8 166	142	7 641	4 791	2 850	3 473	1 627	2 038	502	382
Three room units or more	4 607	80	4 395	3 369	1 026	2 352	522	1 326	195	132
Source of water:										
Public system or private company	108 210	2 638	95 313	62 991	32 322	17 168	20 874	34 871	22 401	10 260
Well serving 1 to 5 units	15 372	1 014	13 132	11 607	1 525	3 079	4 008	4 648	1 396	1 227
Other	795	194	427	334	93	90	73	203	61	174
Means of sewage disposal:										
Public sewer	98 013	1 976	86 850	55 496	31 355	16 107	20 053	29 617	21 093	9 187
Septic tank, cesspool, chemical toilet	25 976	1 685	21 967	19 403	2 564	4 229	4 888	10 067	2 783	2 323
Other	388	184	54	32	22	-	13	38	2	151

Source: U.S. Census Bureau. *Statistical Abstract of the United States: 2007.*
Note: As of fall. Based on the American Housing Survey. Composition of Regions:
NORTHEAST: Maine, New Hampshire, Vermont, Massachusetts, Rhode Island, Connecticut, New York, New Jersey, and Pennsylvania.
MIDWEST: Ohio, Indiana, Illinois, Michigan, Wisconsin, Minnesota, Iowa, Missouri, North Dakota, South Dakota, Nebraska, and Kansas.
SOUTH: Delaware, Maryland, District of Columbia, Virginia, West Virginia, North Carolina, South Carolina, Georgia, Florida, Kentucky, Tennessee, Alabama, Mississippi, Arkansas, Louisiana, Oklahoma, and Texas.
WEST: Montana, Idaho, Wyoming, Colorado, New Mexico, Arizona, Utah, Nevada, Washington, Oregon, California, Alaska, and Hawaii.
[4]With and without inserts.
- = Quantity zero or rounds to zero.

Table 11-11. Occupied Housing Units and Tenure of Home, 1890–2005

(Number in thousands, percent.)

Year[1]	Total occupied housing units (thousands)	Tenure of homes		Number of renter-occupied units (thousands)
		Owner occupied		
		Number (thousands)	Percent	
2005	108 871	74 931	68.8	33 940
2003[2]	105 842	72 238	68.3	33 604
2001	106 261	72 265	68.0	33 996
1999	102 803	68 796	66.9	34 007
1997	99 487	65 487	65.8	34 000
1995	97 693	63 544	65.0	34 150
1993	94 724	61 252	64.7	33 472
1990	91 947	59 025	64.2	32 923
1987	90 888	58 164	64.0	32 724
1985	88 425	56 145	63.5	32 280
1983	84 638	54 742	64.7	29 914
1981	83 175	54 342	65.3	28 833
1980	80 390	51 795	64.4	28 595
1979	78 572	51 411	65.4	27 160
1978	77 167	50 283	59.4	26 884
1977	75 280	48 765	59.2	26 515
1976	74 005	47 904	64.7	26 101
1975	72 523	46 867	64.6	25 656
1974	62 562	42 157	67.4	20 405
1973	69 337	41 653	64.4	24 684
1970	63 450	39 885	62.9	23 565
1960*	53 024	32 796	61.9	20 227
1956[3]	49 874	30 121	60.4	19 753
1950	42 826	23 560	55.0	19 266
1945[3]	37 600	20 009	53.2	17 591
1940	34 855	15 196	43.6	19 659
1930	29 905	14 002	47.8	15 320
1920	24 353	10 867	45.6	12 944
1910	20 256	9 084	45.9	10 698
1900	15 964	7 205	46.7	8 224
1890	12 690	6 066	47.8	6 624

Source: U.S. Census Bureau.
[1]Figures for 1956 are for December 31; figures for 1945 are for November 1; figures for decennial years 1890 to 1970 are for census dates.
[2]Based on 2000 census controls.
[3]These figures are not comparable with other years; based on sample surveys.
* = First year for which figures include Alaska and Hawaii.

Table 11-12. Housing Units Vacancy Rates, by Region, 1950–2006

(Percent; annual average, except where noted.)

Year	Homeowner vacancy rate					Rental vacancy rate				
	United States	Northeast	Midwest	South	West	United States	Northeast	Midwest	South	West
2006	2.4	1.7	2.6	2.7	2.1	9.7	7.1	12.4	11.6	6.8
2005	1.9	1.5	2.2	2.1	1.4	9.8	6.5	12.6	11.8	7.3
2004	1.7	1.1	2.0	2.0	1.4	10.2	7.3	12.2	12.6	7.5
2003	1.8	1.2	1.7	2.1	1.6	9.8	6.6	10.8	12.5	7.7
2002	1.7	1.2	1.8	1.9	1.6	9.0	5.8	10.1	11.8	6.9
2001	1.8	1.2	1.7	2.1	1.6	8.4	5.3	9.7	11.1	6.2
2000	1.6	1.2	1.3	1.9	1.5	8.0	5.6	8.8	10.5	5.8
1999	1.7	1.4	1.2	2.0	1.7	8.1	6.3	8.6	10.3	6.2
1998	1.7	1.5	1.4	2.0	1.7	7.9	6.7	7.9	9.6	6.7
1997	1.6	1.6	1.2	1.9	1.8	7.7	6.7	8.0	9.1	6.6
1996	1.6	1.6	1.3	1.8	1.7	7.8	7.4	7.9	8.6	7.2
1995	1.5	1.5	1.3	1.7	1.7	7.6	7.2	7.2	8.3	7.5
1994	1.5	1.5	1.1	1.7	1.6	7.4	7.1	6.8	8.0	7.1
1993	1.4	1.3	1.1	1.7	1.4	7.3	7.0	6.6	7.9	7.4
1992	1.5	1.3	1.2	1.7	1.9	7.4	6.9	6.7	8.2	7.1
1991	1.7	1.5	1.3	2.2	1.7	7.4	6.9	6.7	8.9	6.5
1990	1.7	1.6	1.3	2.1	1.8	7.2	6.1	6.4	8.8	6.6
1989	1.8	1.5	1.4	2.2	1.6	7.4	4.7	6.8	9.7	7.1
1988	1.6	1.6	1.2	1.9	1.6	7.7	4.8	6.9	10.1	7.7
1987	1.7	1.2	1.4	2.0	1.8	7.7	4.1	6.8	10.9	7.3
1986	1.6	1.0	1.5	2.1	1.6	7.3	3.9	6.9	10.1	7.1
1985	1.7	1.0	1.6	2.1	2.1	6.5	3.5	5.9	9.1	6.2
1984	1.7	0.8	1.6	2.0	2.0	5.9	3.7	5.9	7.9	5.2
1983	1.5	1.0	1.5	1.8	1.8	5.7	4.0	6.1	6.9	5.2
1982	1.5	1.0	1.6	1.6	1.9	5.3	3.7	6.3	5.8	5.4
1981	1.4	1.1	1.4	1.3	1.7	5.0	3.7	5.9	5.4	5.1
1980	1.4	1.1	1.6	1.3	1.6	5.4	4.2	6.0	6.0	5.2
1979	1.1	0.9	1.1	1.1	1.3	5.0	4.0	5.8	5.8	4.9
1978	1.0	0.8	1.0	1.3	1.0	5.0	4.8	4.8	5.5	4.8
1977	1.2	0.9	0.9	1.7	0.9	5.2	5.1	5.1	5.7	5.0
1976	1.2	1.0	1.0	1.6	1.2	5.6	4.7	5.6	6.4	5.4
1975	1.2	1.0	1.0	1.5	1.5	6.0	4.1	5.7	7.7	6.2
1974	1.2	0.8	1.0	1.5	1.5	6.2	4.2	6.1	8.0	6.2
1973	1.0	0.7	0.9	1.2	1.2	5.8	3.9	5.9	7.1	6.3
1972	1.0	0.8	1.0	1.2	1.1	5.6	3.3	6.1	7.0	6.0
1971	1.0	1.0	1.2	2.0	1.9	5.4	3.0	5.7	7.3	5.7
1970	1.0	0.8	1.0	1.2	1.1	5.3	2.7	5.8	7.2	5.6
1969	1.0	0.8	0.9	1.2	1.2	5.5	3.0	5.7	7.2	6.1
1968	1.1	0.8	1.0	1.4	1.3	5.9	3.7	5.4	7.5	7.1
1967	1.3	0.7	1.0	1.7	2.0	6.8	4.8	5.7	8.0	8.9
1966	1.4	0.9	1.0	1.8	2.1	7.7	5.3	6.5	8.5	10.9
1965	1.5	1.0	1.2	2.0	1.9	8.3	5.6	7.2	9.0	11.9
1964	1.5	1.1	1.3	1.9	1.8	8.3	5.2	7.9	9.1	11.0
1963	1.5	1.0	1.4	1.9	1.9	8.3	5.1	8.7	9.2	10.2
1962	1.4	1.1	1.2	1.7	1.6	8.1	4.7	9.0	9.9	9.5
1961	1.4	1.1	1.2	1.7	1.3	8.7	4.9	9.3	10.4	10.7
1960*	1.3	1.0	1.2	1.6	1.4	8.1	4.9	8.3	9.5	11.0
1959	1.2	1.0	1.1	1.2	1.4	7.0	3.9	7.1	9.4	8.5
1958	1.2	1.0	1.4	1.0	1.2	6.5	3.8	7.3	7.9	7.5
1957	1.0	0.7	0.9	0.9	1.3	5.6	3.4	5.4	6.7	7.4
1956	1.0	0.9	0.8	1.0	1.4	6.1	3.1	5.6	8.1	8.7
1950[1]	0.9	...	...	...	...	...	...	...	...	...

Source: U.S. Census Bureau. Housing Vacancy Survey.
[1] As of April.
* = First year for which figures include Alaska and Hawaii.
. . . = Not available.

Table 11-13. Residential Nonfarm Mortgage Debt Outstanding, by Type of Property, 1925–2005

(Billions of dollars as of December 31.)

Year	Home mortgages[1]	Multi-family residential mortgages
2005	9 149.0	674.5
2004	8 016.2	612.2
2003	7 024.1	557.3
2002	6 244.2	486.7
2001	5 571.3	447.8
2000	5 075.2	405.6
1999	4 674.2	375.8
1998	4 258.5	334.5
1997	3 909.6	300.1
1996	3 674.7	288.0
1995	3 451.2	275.5
1994	3 283.2	269.6
1993	3 106.2	269.1
1992	2 947.3	272.0
1991	2 781.7	284.9
1990	2 614.7	288.3
1989	2 378.9	288.1
1988	2 154.1	275.3
1987	1 920.5	259.2
1986	1 722.0	239.4
1985	1 518.6	205.9
1984	1 321.1	186.1
1983	1 186.1	161.2
1982	1 070.2	146.1
1981	1 030.2	142.4
1980	957.9	142.5
1979	855.7	135.0
1978	738.2	125.2
1977	627.7	114.3
1976	535.0	105.9
1975	473.9	100.7
1974	435.1	100.0
1973	399.8	93.2
1972	357.3	82.9
1971	318.4	70.1
1970	292.1	60.1
1969	278.3	53.2
1968	262.2	48.3
1967	245.1	44.8
1966	231.9	41.3
1965	218.6	38.2
1964	201.4	34.6
1963	184.1	30.0
1962	167.5	26.7
1961	153.3	23.6
1960	140.8	20.8
1959	129.6	18.7
1958	116.8	16.6
1957	107.0	14.6
1956	98.3	14.1
1955	87.5	13.5
1954	75.0	12.7
1953	65.7	12.1
1952	58.2	11.5
1951	51.4	10.6
1950	45.0	9.3
1949	37.4	7.8
1948	33.1	6.7
1947	28.1	5.8
1946	23.0	5.3
1945	18.6	4.9
1944	17.9	5.6
1943	17.8	5.8
1942	18.2	5.8
1941	18.4	5.9
1940	17.4	5.7
1939	16.3	5.6
1938	15.8	4.4
1937	15.5	4.5
1936	15.4	4.6
1935	15.4	4.8
1934	15.6	5.1
1933	15.4	5.7
1932	16.7	6.0
1931	18.1	6.2
1930	18.9	6.5
1929	18.9	6.0
1928	17.9	5.4
1927	16.4	5.0
1926	14.8	4.6
1925	13.0	4.2

Source: Federal Reserve Board. U.S. Census Bureau. *Statistical Abstract of the United States: 2007.* Board of Governors of the Federal Reserve System.
[1]Mortgages on 1 to 4 family properties.

Table 11-14. Profile of Homebuyers by Characteristic, 2004

(Percent, except as indicated.)

Characteristic	Total	Northeast	Midwest	South	West	1st time buyers	Repeat buyers
Age	100	100	100	100	100	100	100
Under 25 years old	5	3	7	5	5	12	1
25 to 34 years old	34	35	37	33	30	54	20
35 to 44 years old	26	29	25	25	24	21	28
45 to 54 years old	18	18	16	18	19	9	24
55 to 64 years old	12	10	9	12	14	3	17
65 to 74 years old	5	3	4	5	6	1	7
75 years old and over	2	2	1	2	2	-	3
Median age (years)	39	39	37	39	41	32	45
Household income	100	100	100	100	100	100	100
Under $25,000	4	3	4	4	5	7	3
$25,000 to 34,999	9	6	10	10	10	14	6
$35,000 to 44,999	11	8	12	10	13	16	6
$45,000 to 54,999	12	10	12	12	12	15	10
$55,000 to 64,999	13	15	15	13	12	15	11
$65,000 to 74,999	10	10	9	10	10	9	10
$75,000 to 84,999	9	9	8	9	9	8	10
$85,000 to 94,999	7	8	7	8	7	5	9
$95,000 to 104,999	7	7	8	7	6	4	9
$105,000 to 114,999	4	4	4	4	4	2	5
$115,000 to 124,999	3	3	2	3	3	2	4
$125,000 to 134,999	2	3	3	2	2	1	3
$135,000 to 149,999	2	3	1	2	2	1	3
$150,000 to 174,999	3	3	2	3	3	1	4
$175,000 to 199,999	1	2	1	2	1	1	2
$200,000 or more	4	6	3	4	4	1	6
Median income ($1,000)	67.1	72.4	63.4	67.3	65	54.5	79.1
Race	100	100	100	100	100	100	100
White	84	87	82	81	77	77	88
Black/African American	6	5	8	9	3	10	4
Asian/Pacific Islander	3	2	3	3	9	4	3
Hispanic/Latino	5	4	4	6	11	7	4
Other	2	1	2	2	3	3	2

Source: U.S. Census Bureau. *Statistical Abstract of the United States: 2007.* NATIONAL ASSOCIATION OF REALTORS®. *Profile of Home Buyers and Sellers, 2004*©.
Note: For the 12 month period ending July 2004, except income for 2003. Based on survey consumers who bought a home between August 2003 and July 2004. Includes condos. Data by region represent region where home was purchased.
- = Represents or rounds to zero.

BOX 11 ■ Home Improvements

In the mid-1990s through the early twenty-first century, the U.S. real estate market experienced tremendous growth, especially in the sale of residential properties. This surge in real estate prices affected not only home sales but also investments in home maintenance, repairs, and improvements. Between 1996 and 2006, expenditures for improvements and repairs of residential housing units increased with one exception. That exception was rental properties with two to four rental units, which experienced a decrease of approximately 32%. Owner-occupied properties with two or more units showed the largest increase in 2006, with expenditures approximately 260% higher than 1996 levels. However, 2006 expenses for these units are only 6% of that spent on owner-occupied single unit properties ($10.5 million compared with $167.2 million).

In both 1996 and 2006 spending on repairs and improvements was greatest in the South and least in the Northeast. In those ten years, spending in the South increased by 245% (from $26.8 million to $65.5 million), but spending in the Northeast grew by 333% (from $14.8 million to $49.4 million). In the meantime, total expenditures in the West almost tripled from $21.4 million to $62.8 million.

In the United States, overall expenses for maintenance and repairs of owner-occupied single unit properties increased 50.7% and alterations to residential structures increased 447% between 1996 and 2006. During this period, spending for structural additions and other property improvements decreased 13.7% and 9.8% respectively.

Spending on improvements for owner-occupied single unit properties in 2006 was the greatest for those homes with a value of $250,000 or more, $85.6 million, however, the greatest spending in 1996 was for those homes with a value of $50,000-$99,999, $15.5 million.

Spending is consistently greater for those homes that were purchased most recently and for those whose owners earn $75,000 or more or are in the age range of 35 to 44 years of age.

Sources:
U.S. Census Bureau. Residential Repairs and Improvement Statistics. http://www.census.gov/const/www/c50index.html

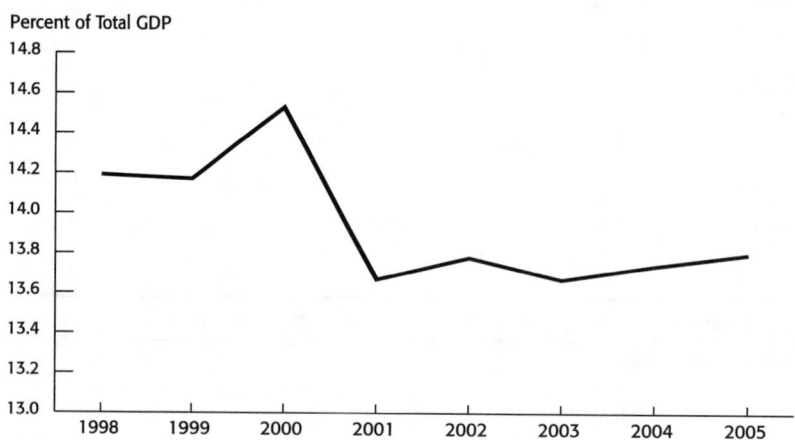

Percent of Total GDP

Manufacturing as a Percent of Total Gross Domestic Product (GDP): 1998 to 2005
Source: U.S. Census Bureau.

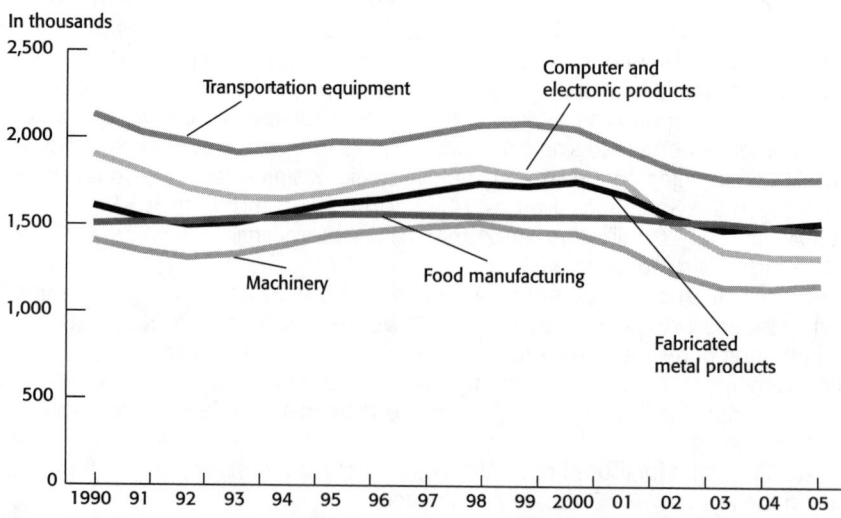

In thousands

Employment in Top Five Manufacturing Industries: 1990 to 2005
Source: U.S. Census Bureau.

CHAPTER 12

Manufacturing

HIGHLIGHTS

1 Manufacturing is defined as the mechanical or chemical transformation of inorganic and organic substances into new products or the assembly of component parts of products. Manufacturing activities were classified from 1947 through 1997 according to the *Standard Industrial Classification (SIC) Manual,* published by the Office of Management and Budget. First issued in 1939, it was revised in 1945, 1957, 1972, and 1987. Beginning in 1997, the SIC codes were replaced with a new system called the North American Industry Classification System (NAICS).

2 The basic source of data on manufactures has been the Census of Manufactures conducted by the Bureau of the Census, beginning in 1809. A census was taken at 10-year intervals thereafter until 1899 (with the exception of 1829), at five-year intervals from 1904 to 1919, and biennially from 1921 to 1939. It was suspended during World War II but resumed in 1947. Legislation enacted in 1948 provided for a Census of Manufactures every five years with annual sample surveys for interim years. The Annual Survey of Manufactures (ASM) is based on a sample of 55,000 establishments out of an approximate total of 200,000. The scope of the census has varied from one census to another. From 1849 to 1899, the minimum size limit of factories was output valued at $500 or more. It was raised to $5,000 or more for 1929 to 1937. Beginning in 1947, the criterion was employment of one or more

persons at any time during the census year. However, these changes have not appreciably affected the historical comparability of the census figures except for the data on the number of establishments. There have also been numerous changes in the definition of manufacturing industries. When the changes result in the omission of an entire industry, the adjustments are generally carried back through the previous censuses. Furthermore, the treatment of nonproduction workers has not been consistent over the years. Personnel in manufacturing industries engaged in distribution and construction have been reported separately since 1939, but not before. Officers of corporations are included as employees, but not proprietors and partners of unincorporated firms, for whom no data have been collected since 1963. Another difference concerns value added in manufacturing. The standard formula for calculating value added by manufacture since 1958 differs from the one used for 1954 and previous years. Before 1958, value added by an establishment was calculated by subtracting the cost of materials, supplies, containers, fuels, electrical energy, and contract work from the value of shipments. This was known as unadjusted value added. Beginning in 1958, the formula was changed to adjusted value added which includes two elements: (1) value added by merchandising (the difference between the sales value and the cost of merchandise sold without further manufacture, processing, and assembly); and (2) an adjustment in the net change in finished goods and work-in-process inventories between the beginning and the end of the year. This concept should not be confused with the National Income Originating in Manufacturing, which is obtained by subtracting from the value of shipments not only the cost of materials, but also other costs such as depreciation charges, state and local taxes, allowances for bad debts, and purchases of services from nonmanufacturing enterprises (engineering and management consultants, advertising, telephone, insurance, royalties, patent fees, and so on). It is therefore a net concept of value added in manufacturing and generally exceeds the latter by about a third.

3 The value added in manufacturing in 2001 was $1.854 trillion, or $165,014 per worker, $82.96 per production worker hour, and $3.13 per dollar of wages.

4 The GDP in manufacturing in 2005 was $1.497 trillion, of which durable goods accounted for $868 billion and nondurable goods for $628 billion. The largest manufacturing sectors in terms of payroll were transportation equipment ($85.128 billion), computer and electronic product ($66.318 billion), and fabricated metal product ($58.581 billion).

5 In 2004, manufacturing employed 13.381 million workers whose total wages amounted to $569.203 billion or $42,537 per worker.

6 The most industrialized state is California with value of shipments in 2004 totaling $388.332 billion, followed by Texas ($385.534 billion), Ohio ($258.799 billion), Michigan ($220.455 billion), Illinois ($210.043 billion), Pennsylvania ($190.341 billion), and Indiana ($183.564 billion).

7 Based on 1997 = 100, the national industrial production index was 110.5 in 2002, and the manufacturing index was 111.4. The fastest growing sectors since 1997 are computers, which jumped to 220.4, and motor vehicles and parts (117.3). Several sectors lost ground, including apparel and leather (72.2) and textile and product mills (82.5).

8 Net manufacturing sales in 2005 were $5.466 trillion, net profit was $524 billion, and net profit after taxes was $406 billion.

9 Alcoholic beverage sales have increased from $72.6 billion in 1990 to $112.3 billion in 2002. From 1990 to 2004, the consumer price index for alcoholic beverages increased from 129.3 to 192.1

10 Official antismoking campaigns and lawsuits against tobacco companies seem to have had an effect on cigarette production and consumption. In 2005, cigarette production was significantly lower at 489 billion than in 1980 (714 billion). However, consumption per person declined from 4,000 in 1980 to 1,700 annually in 2005.

11 Iron and steel were once the bellwether of manufacturing, but they no longer have that role. Nevertheless, the United States is a major producer of steel mill products, producing 131.8 million tons in 2004, up from 109.6 million tons in 1995.

12 The computer industry, slightly more than 20 years old, has become one of the most dynamic sectors. There are manufacturers that produced 24.492 million computers valued at $39.540 billion in 2004. Of these, 15.790 million were personal computers.

13 Home electronic equipment sales have increased from $43 billion in 1990 to $125.910 billion in 2005. Of these, home office products, such as telephones, answering devices, word processors, and fax machines, accounted for $45.032 billion.

14 While the consumption of cigarettes has experienced a decline, the consumption of cigars has almost doubled from 1.9 billion in 1990 to 3.7 in 2005.

15 Alaska has the lowest number of manufacturing establishments (501), which employ 10,000 people and have a payroll of $398 million.

16 In 2004, 35.2 million pairs of shoes were produced in the United States, while an additional 2.124 billion pairs were imported.

Table 12-1. Gross Domestic Product in Manufacturing in Current and Real (2000) Dollars by Industry, 2000-2005

(Billions of dollars.)

Industry	2000	2001	2002	2003	2004	2005
CURRENT DOLLARS						
Gross domestic product, total	9 817.0	10 128.0	10 469.6	10 971.3	11 734.3	12 487.1
Manufacturing	1 426.2	1 341.3	1 352.6	1 369.2	1 420.1	1 496.5
Percent of total	14.53	13.24	12.92	12.48	12.10	11.98
Durable goods	865.3	778.9	774.8	785.5	824.1	868.4
Wood products	31.4	31.3	30.4	33.0	39.2	...
Nonmetallic mineral products	45.7	44.9	45.9	46.2	49.7	...
Primary metals	48.2	41.1	41.9	38.7	50.9	...
Fabricated metal products	121.7	112.0	107.4	109.1	115.4	...
Machinery	109.3	103.2	96.5	95.1	100.2	...
Computer and electronic products	185.6	136.9	124.2	125.6	132.6	...
Electrical equipment, appliances, and components	50.6	49.2	48.8	48.6	48.2	...
Motor vehicles, bodies and trailers, and parts	118.1	103.7	118.9	129.9	120.1	...
Other transportation equipment	64.4	69.2	69.6	65.0	66.9	...
Furniture and related products	32.7	30.2	31.1	30.7	31.4	...
Miscellaneous manufacturing	57.5	57.2	60.0	63.7	69.4	...
Nondurable goods	561.0	562.5	577.9	583.7	596.1	628.1
Food and beverage and tobacco products	154.8	167.1	172.9	170.6	167.9	...
Textile mills and textile product mills	26.5	22.7	21.9	22.7	23.3	...
Apparel and leather and allied products	25.1	22.8	20.9	18.4	18.9	...
Paper products	55.6	48.9	50.3	46.4	48.9	...
Printing and related support activities	49.0	46.9	45.7	44.5	45.9	...
Petroleum and coal products	26.2	33.4	26.2	33.5	34.8	...
Chemical products	157.1	157.2	174.4	181.8	186.0	...
Plastics and rubber products	66.7	63.4	65.5	65.6	70.3	...
CHAINED (2000) DOLLARS						
Gross domestic product, total	9 817.0	9 890.6	10 048.8	10 320.6	10 755.7	11 134.8
Manufacturing	1 426.2	1 346.9	1 384.4	1 410.4	1 478.1	1 536.6
Percent of total	14.53	13.62	13.78	13.67	13.74	13.80
Durable goods	865.3	813.6	827.7	863.2	917.8	970.1
Wood products	31.4	30.9	30.3	31.4	32.4	...
Nonmetallic mineral products	45.7	45.2	45.5	46.6	49.0	...
Primary metals	48.2	43.2	44.1	42.6	46.5	...
Fabricated metal products	121.7	109.4	104.4	107.5	110.7	...
Machinery	109.3	100.4	93.3	92.3	100.7	...
Computer and electronic products	185.6	181.9	185.8	215.0	260.3	...
Electrical equipment, appliances, and components	50.6	48.5	48.8	49.9	49.3	...
Motor vehicles, bodies and trailers, and parts	118.1	104.6	127.5	143.2	139.2	...
Other transportation equipment	64.4	65.2	64.2	57.9	58.0	...
Furniture and related products	32.7	29.1	29.2	28.9	31.0	...
Miscellaneous manufacturing	57.5	55.3	56.4	59.6	66.3	...
Nondurable goods	561.0	533.1	555.7	548.8	563.8	572.8
Food and beverage and tobacco products	154.8	156.0	153.7	153.3	155.8	...
Textile mills and textile product mills	26.5	21.5	21.4	23.1	23.2	...
Apparel and leather and allied products	25.1	22.7	21.1	18.7	19.7	...
Paper products	55.6	48.8	50.8	48.9	53.5	...
Printing and related support activities	49.0	45.3	43.5	42.5	44.4	...
Petroleum and coal products	26.2	23.9	32.5	26.1	24.7	...
Chemical products	157.1	153.1	170.5	172.9	173.6	...
Plastics and rubber products	66.7	61.4	62.9	64.0	70.8	...

Source: U.S. Census Bureau. *Statistical Abstract of the United States: 2007.* Bureau of Economic Analysis.
Note: Data are based on the 1997 North American Industry Classification System (NAICS) codes 31-33. Data include nonfactor charges (capital consumption allowances, indirect business taxes, etc.) as well as factor charges against gross product; corporate profits and capital consumption allowances have been shifted from a company to an establishment basis.
. . . = Not available.

Table 12-2. Manufactures Summary, 1849–2005

(Number, hours, dollars.)

Year[1]	Establishments[2] Total	Establishments[2] With 20 or more employees	Production workers engaged in manufacturing[3,4] (1,000)	Man-hours, production workers (mil.)	Total payroll (mil. dol.)	Value added by manufacture[5,6] (mil. dol.)	Capital expenditures, new (mil. dol.)	End-of-year inventories (mil. dol.)
Factories, Excluding Hand and Neighborhood Industries								
2005	...	...	9 230	19 070	579 891	2 204 095	128 325	466 172
2004	...	...	9 365	19 284	569 704	2 041 434	113 793	428 322
2003	...	...	9 797	19 854	567 602	1 923 415	112 176	409 190
2002	350 828	108 728	10 320	20 432	575 165	1 889 291	123 067	412 328
2001	...	...	11 212	22 384	591 559	1 850 709	142 985	...
2000	...	...	11 944	23 954	617 211	1 973 622	154 479	470 085
1999	...	...	11 977	24 210	601 473	1 954 498	150 325	452 800
1998	...	...	12 190	24 583	586 958	1 891 266	152 708	447 651
1997	362 829	119 748	12 065	24 183	569 809	1 825 688	151 511	433 449
1996	...	...	12 168	25 011	560 518	1 749 662	139 300	427 000
1995	...	...	12 253	25 072	545 363	1 711 442	128 400	421 000
1994	...	...	11 947	24 560	522 566	1 605 980	112 000	397 000
1993	...	...	11 726	23 845	504 363	1 483 054	103 000	383 000
1992	370 912	118 967	11 641	23 563	494 109	1 424 700	103 200	374 000
1991	...	...	11 652	23 383	477 175	1 341 386	103 000	380 000
1990	...	...	12 233	24 463	480 224	1 346 970	105 000	393 000
1989	...	...	12 536	24 934	470 479	1 325 434	98 700	381 000
1988	...	...	12 439	24 815	453 309	1 269 313	81 600	362 000
1987	358 952	120 822	12 280	24 303	428 480	1 165 741	78 600	333 000
1986	...	...	11 765	23 178	402 467	1 035 437	76 400	311 000
1985	...	...	12 174	23 732	396 611	1 000 142	83 100	322 000
1984	...	...	12 573	24 637	384 922	983 228	75 300	330 000
1983	...	...	12 203	23 612	354 232	882 015	61 900	308 000
1982	348 385	117 959	12 401	23 538	341 406	824 118	75 000	307 000
1981	...	...	13 543	26 233	341 320	837 507	78 600	279 000
1980	...	...	13 900	26 746	316 495	773 831	70 100	262 000
1979	...	...	14 538	28 324	298 529	747 481	61 500	239 000
1978	...	...	14 229	27 677	271 541	657 412	55 200	209 000
1977	350 757	113 843	13 691	26 687	242 032	585 166	47 500	188 000
1976	...	...	13 100	25 400	233 000	511 000	40 700	170 000
1975	...	...	12 600	24 100	210 000	442 000	37 300	158 000
1973	...	...	14 200	28 100	193 000	404 000	27 000	125 000
1972	321 000	114 000	13 500	26 700	174 000	354 000	24 100	108 000
1971	...	...	12 900	25 300	156 000	314 000	20 900	102 000
1970	...	...	13 258	26 669	141 886	300 228	22 164	101 285
1969	...	...	14 358	28 600	142 645	304 441	22 291	98 206
1968	...	...	14 041	28 157	132 568	285 059	20 613	90 505
1967	305 680	107 138	13 955	27 838	123 481	261 984	21 503	84 406
1966	...	...	13 827	28 103	117 157	250 880	20 236	77 721
1965	...	...	13 076	26 568	106 643	226 940	16 615	68 009
1964	...	...	12 403	25 246	98 685	206 194	13 294	63 211
1963	306 617	99 352	12 232	24 509	93 283	192 083	11 370	59 913
1962	...	...	12 127	24 270	89 819	179 071	10 436	58 067
1961	...	...	11 779	23 289	83 677	164 281	9 780	54 744
1960	...	...	12 210	24 174	83 673	163 999	10 098	53 560
1959	...	...	12 273	24 444	81 204	161 536	9 140	52 552
1958	299 017	95 278	11 681	22 679	73 875	141 541	9 544	49 947
1957	...	...	12 839	25 208	76 315	147 838	12 144	...
1956	...	...	13 131	26 089	74 015	144 909	11 233	...
1955	...	...	12 954	25 898	69 097	135 023	8 233	...
1954	286 814	90 470	12 372	24 334	62 963	117 032	8 201	40 341
1953	285 000	...	13 501	27 066	66 493	121 659	8 048	...
1952	267 000	...	12 706	25 618	59 598	109 162	7 883	...
1951	262 000	...	12 509	25 264	54 742	102 086	7 782	...

[1]Statistics presented for years ending in 2 and 7 are census data. Interim years are derived in a representative sample of manufacturing establishments canvassed in the Annual Survey of Manufactures (ASM). Also, in census year 1997, collection and publication of census and subsequent ASM data changed from the Standard Industrial Classification (SIC) basis to the North American Industry Classification System (NAICS) basis.

[2]Includes establishments with payroll at any time during year. Beginning in census year 1997, auxiliary establishments associated with manufacturing companies are classified separately. For 1996 and earlier years, establishment counts for auxiliaries are included.

[3]Figures for 2005 represent average number of production workers for the March 12, June 12, September 12, and December 12 pay periods, plus other employees for the payroll period that includes the 12th of March. Figures for earlier years represent the average number of production workers for the payroll periods that include the 12th of March, May, August, and November, plus other employees for the March 12th pay period.

[4]The Bureau of Labor Statistics annual averages for employment in manufacturing indicates 1943 as the year of maximum employment, with 15,147,000 production workers.

[5]Beginning in 1982, all respondents were requested to report their inventories at cost or market prior to adjustment to LIFO cost. This is a change from prior years in which respondents were permitted to value their inventories using any generally accepted accounting method. Consequently, 1982 data for value added are not comparable to prior years.

[6]For 1849–1933, cost of contract work was not subtracted from value of products in calculating value added by manufacture. For 1935–1953, value added by manufacture represents unadjusted value added; beginning 1954, it represents adjusted value, which includes the change during the year in finished goods and work-in-process inventories.

... = Not available.

Table 12-2. Manufactures Summary, 1849–2005—*Continued*

(Number, hours, dollars.)

Year[1]	Establishments[2]		Production workers engaged in manufacturing[3,4] (1,000)	Man-hours, production workers (mil.)	Total payroll (mil. dol.)	Value added by manufacture[5,6] (mil. dol.)	Capital expenditures, new (mil. dol.)	End-of-year inventories (mil. dol.)
	Total	With 20 or more employees						
1950	260 000	...	11 779	23 717	46 643	89 750	5 041	...
1949	...	...	11 016	21 770	41 482	75 367	5 067	...
1947	240 807	...	11 918	24 317	39 696	74 291	5 998	26 129
1939[7]	173 802	...	7 808	...	[8]12 706	24 487	...	9 632
1937	166 794	...	8 569	...	12 830	25 174	...	9 863
1935	167 916	...	7 204	...	9 565	18 553	...	...
1933	139 325	...	5 788	...	[9]6 238	14 008	...	...
1931	171 450	...	6 163	...	...	18 601	...	...
1929	206 663	...	8 370	...	14 284	30 591	...	...
1927	187 629	...	7 848	...	13 123	26 325	...	...
1925	183 877	...	7 871	...	12 958	25 668	...	...
1923	192 096	...	8 194	...	12 997	24 570	...	...
1921	192 059	...	6 476	...	9 870	17 253	...	...
1919	270 231	...	8 465	...	12 427	23 842	...	...
1914	268 436	...	6 602	...	5 016	9 386	...	...
1909	264 810	...	6 262	...	4 106	8 160	...	...
1904	213 444	...	5 182	...	2 991	6 019	...	...
1899	204 754	...	4 502	...	2 259	4 647	...	...
Factories and Hand and Neighborhood Industries								
1899	509 490	...	5 098	...	2 596	5 475	...	...
1889	353 864	...	4 129	...	2 209	4 102	...	...
1879	253 852	...	2 733	...	...	1 973	...	...
1869	252 148	...	2 054	...	...	1 395	...	...
1859	140 433	...	1 311	...	...	854	...	...
1849	123 025	...	957	...	...	464	...	...

Source: U.S. Census Bureau.

[1]Statistics presented for years ending in 2 and 7 are census data. Interim years are derived in a representative sample of manufacturing establishments canvassed in the Annual Survey of Manufactures (ASM). Also, in census year 1997, collection and publication of census and subsequent ASM data changed from the Standard Industrial Classification (SIC) basis to the North American Industry Classification System (NAICS) basis.

[2]Includes establishments with payroll at any time during year. Beginning in census year 1997, auxiliary establishments associated with manufacturing companies are classified separately. For 1996 and earlier years, establishment counts for auxiliaries are included.

[3]Figures for 2005 represent average number of production workers for the March 12, June 12, September 12, and December 12 pay periods, plus other employees for the payroll period that includes the 12th of March. Figures for earlier years represent the average number of production workers for the payroll periods that include the 12th of March, May, August, and November, plus other employees for the March 12th pay period.

[4]The Bureau of Labor Statistics annual averages for employment in manufacturing indicates 1943 as the year of maximum employment, with 15,147,000 production workers.

[5]Beginning in 1982, all respondents were requested to report their inventories at cost or market prior to adjustment to LIFO cost. This is a change from prior years in which respondents were permitted to value their inventories using any generally accepted accounting method. Consequently, 1982 data for value added are not comparable to prior years.

[6]For 1849–1933, cost of contract work was not subtracted from value of products in calculating value added by manufacture. For 1935–1953, value added by manufacture represents unadjusted value added; beginning 1954, it represents adjusted value, which includes the change during the year in finished goods and work-in-process inventories.

[7]Except as noted, figures have been revised by retabulation of returns to exclude data for establishments classified as manufacturing in 1939 but not as nonmanufacturing beginning 1947. Value added by manufacture in 1939, prior to revision and on a basis comparable with prior years, was $24.7 billion.

[8]Figures revised on basis of estimates rather than by retabulation of 1939 reports. Estimates made as follows: For nonproduction employees, by multiplying the retabulated figure for number of production workers by the ratio of all employees to production workers computed from unrevised 1939 data; for salaries and wages, by multiplying the retabulated wage figure by the ratio for salaries and wages also derived from the unrevised 1939 data.

[9]Excludes data for salaried officers of corporations and their salaries; therefore, not strictly comparable with figures for other years.

... = Not available.

Table 12-3. U.S. Multinational Companies, Value Added by Industry of Affiliate and Country, 2003

(Millions of dollars. Minus sign (–) represents loss.)

Country	All industries	Mining	Utilities	Manufacturing Total	Food	Chemicals	Primary and fabricated metals	Machinery
All countries	**704,653**	**70,899**	**11,659**	**346,669**	**22,200**	**74,343**	**13,985**	**17,883**
Canada	83,514	12,266	922	43,983	2,615	4,931	2,155	1,569
Europe	398,533	22,033	4,085	206,620	12,584	49,834	8,592	11,456
Austria	3,715	1	12	1,609	283	166	29	127
Belgium	16,136	13	0	9,853	642	3,380	181	456
Czech Republic	1,875	Z	(D)	1,548	26	83	40	53
Denmark	3,415	681	0	1,232	(D)	140	64	373
Finland	2,169	0	0	568	7	128	4	63
France	41,764	74	0	23,201	1,179	6,078	1,194	1,647
Germany	66,861	1,275	23	36,094	1,709	5,262	2,059	2,592
Greece	1,075	Z	0	488	87	198	49	0
Hungary	2,074	Z	60	1,397	117	21	(D)	23
Ireland	28,287	6	Z	22,409	173	13,808	84	31
Italy	25,252	–16	16	18,412	685	3,304	613	1,387
Luxembourg	890	Z	0	690	0	193	51	Z
Netherlands	25,027	932	17	12,465	1,354	3,499	537	652
Norway	9,639	6,346	Z	2,043	(D)	96	13	226
Poland	3,528	Z	30	2,772	360	193	64	22
Portugal	3,619	Z	Z	2,534	150	186	14	45
Russia	1,782	121	0	952	148	112	0	(D)
Spain	13,323	30	33	8,575	631	2,590	714	478
Sweden	9,210	0	0	5,055	(D)	1,125	131	285
Switzerland	13,035	43	0	3,117	189	1,022	71	243
Turkey	2,714	2	38	2,222	100	237	20	Z
United Kingdom	117,516	9,084	3,725	47,730	4,092	7,903	1,901	2,662
Other	5,627	3,442	(D)	1,655	(D)	110	(D)	(D)
Latin America and Other Western Hemisphere	71,597	8,316	3,625	35,115	4,388	7,911	1,215	2,067
South America	32,520	5,594	3,332	15,629	2,300	4,291	707	1,386
Argentina	5,925	1,714	279	2,926	666	548	25	74
Brazil	14,781	161	2,095	9,659	1,071	2,736	605	1,185
Chile	2,553	497	445	589	57	259	18	10
Colombia	2,549	778	1	660	117	271	6	0
Ecuador	558	247	18	131	12	12	–2	0
Peru	1,631	1,059	52	162	21	56	13	0
Venezuela	3,976	979	397	1,353	272	389	42	111
Other	548	161	44	149	83	21	Z	6
Central America	25,914	563	527	17,365	2,032	3,389	471	628
Costa Rica	788	Z	0	486	62	36	15	1
Honduras	477	0	Z	223	43	6	0	0
Mexico	22,897	561	208	15,965	1,865	3,263	460	628
Panama	464	1	77	54	5	22	0	0
Other	1,288	1	242	638	58	62	–4	0
Other Western Hemisphere	13,162	2,159	–234	2,121	56	231	36	52
Barbados	1,881	Z	0	134	8	3	0	10
Bermuda	5,632	18	Z	42	Z	Z	0	42
Dominican Republic	658	0	(D)	344	25	31	3	0
United Kingdom Islands, Caribbean	1,923	416	–227	1,316	10	0	–9	1
Other	3,069	1,725	(D)	285	14	196	42	Z
Africa	16,881	11,727	(D)	2,040	245	434	125	140
Egypt	1,624	1,337	0	120	(D)	52	11	60
Nigeria	5,004	4,811	51	46	0	4	0	0
South Africa	2,763	–14	0	1,028	52	282	51	78
Other	7,490	5,593	(D)	845	(D)	96	63	2
Middle East	6,831	3,422	(D)	1,707	72	151	15	79
Israel	2,531	Z	0	1,544	64	65	3	47
Saudi Arabia	226	96	1	45	0	27	12	6
United Arab Emirates	955	423	0	90	0	60	0	16
Other	3,119	2,904	(D)	27	8	Z	1	9
Asia and Pacific	127,298	13,135	2,839	57,205	2,296	11,083	1,883	2,572
Australia	23,865	3,361	754	8,928	1,182	1,583	1,251	408
China	8,730	415	126	6,335	260	1,328	246	428
Hong Kong	8,371	Z	(D)	1,236	(D)	192	36	114
India	2,474	40	–7	1,203	37	397	(D)	186
Indonesia	6,130	5,179	163	650	(D)	213	8	6
Japan	38,930	4	0	18,606	168	3,825	(D)	520
Korea, South	5,476	Z	0	3,085	146	413	33	394
Malaysia	5,474	(D)	–1	3,078	9	227	2	22
New Zealand	2,432	84	264	968	(D)	93	15	14
Philippines	2,892	353	687	1,264	143	221	Z	32
Singapore	12,020	56	1	7,807	30	1,690	28	258
Taiwan	4,251	Z	0	1,663	52	547	38	123
Thailand	4,633	1,432	11	2,197	79	270	47	67
Other	1,620	(D)	(D)	182	52	82	Z	Z
International	...	...	...	...	...	...	...	...
Addenda:								
European Union (15)[1]	358,258	12,080	3,825	190,915	11,317	47,960	7,624	10,798
Organization of Petroleum Exporting Countries (OPEC)[2]	19,078	14,038	631	2,309	332	692	62	140

Source: U.S. Census Bureau. *Statistical Abstract of the United States: 2007.* U.S. Bureau of Economic Analysis.
Note: Consists of non-bank U.S. parent companies and their non-bank foreign affiliates. U.S. parent comprises the domestic operations of a multinational and is a U.S. person that owns or controls, directly or indirectly, 10 percent or more of the voting securities of an incorporated foreign business enterprise, or an equivalent interest in an unincorporated foreign business enterprise. A U.S. person can be an incorporated business enterprise. A foreign affiliate is a foreign business enterprise owned or controlled by a U.S. parent company. A majority-owned foreign affiliate (MOFA) is a foreign business enterprise in which a U.S. parent company owns or controls more than 50% of the voting securities.

Table 12-3. U.S. Multinational Companies, Value Added by Industry of Affiliate and Country, 2003—*Continued*

(Millions of dollars. Minus sign (–) represents loss.)

Computers and electronic products	Electrical equipment, appliances, and components	Transportation equipment	Wholesale trade	Information	Finance (except depository institutions) and insurance	Professional, scientific, and technical services	Other industries
35,347	8,379	49,292	110,414	29,417	32,402	36,572	66,621
2,518	678	10,870	6,179	1,573	2,534	1,466	14,591
14,678	5,161	27,432	71,281	19,815	14,927	22,615	37,156
405	45	152	1,362	389	–14	182	175
69	220	946	2,545	146	144	1,698	1,737
79	31	430	126	46	–3	37	(D)
85	Z	9	942	87	29	357	87
175	8	44	1,198	40	–7	164	205
1,489	857	2,806	7,136	985	998	2,004	7,364
2,791	1,685	8,828	17,241	1,605	2,123	3,059	5,441
9	0	0	500	1	46	38	1
7	(D)	384	347	58	10	132	71
3,995	160	111	2,445	2,023	414	567	424
1,463	592	1,053	3,363	806	57	925	1,689
0	2	0	257	2	137	61	–256
492	89	1,490	6,253	1,533	785	1,075	1,967
81	–100	7	394	120	–5	137	604
64	50	544	240	51	111	99	226
119	13	278	752	40	–9	87	215
6	4	77	286	49	95	26	254
402	323	1,961	1,935	307	259	602	1,584
157	56	2,766	1,321	1,823	–145	370	787
386	215	77	7,044	562	183	982	1,104
Z	6	171	359	1	10	28	53
2,403	566	5,233	14,876	9,160	9,665	9,935	13,342
1	(D)	67	361	–19	47	49	(D)
3,272	799	6,868	9,794	3,539	4,636	1,726	4,846
528	229	1,433	3,619	(D)	115	1,068	(D)
10	–26	197	604	445	–270	105	123
517	233	987	1,519	809	164	340	34
Z	8	18	486	189	122	62	163
1	6	56	475	139	53	54	390
0	0	(D)	66	(D)	–25	3	(D)
0	Z	–2	189	103	22	17	28
1	8	131	159	362	64	477	184
0	0	(D)	121	58	–16	9	23
1,541	566	5,440	1,474	654	1,431	466	3,435
(D)	28	0	(D)	13	–8	47	(D)
0	3	(D)	93	Z	5	0	155
1,388	536	5,400	1,012	597	1,418	409	2,726
0	0	(D)	85	Z	12	6	229
(D)	0	0	(D)	44	3	4	(D)
1,203	5	–4	4,702	(D)	3,091	193	(D)
95	5	–4	1,361	180	115	54	37
Z	0	0	2,372	18	2,409	96	676
0	0	0	46	(D)	Z	1	2
1,108	0	0	498	47	145	29	–301
1	0	0	425	4	421	13	(D)
(D)	78	(D)	1,264	65	59	239	(D)
0	0	–4	(D)	3	3	2	(D)
0	0	0	67	0	Z	8	21
(D)	76	(D)	552	91	47	223	836
(D)	2	(D)	(D)	–28	10	5	(D)
(D)	–2	(D)	597	286	167	382	(D)
(D)	–2	(D)	240	326	32	276	114
1	0	Z	50	–79	13	78	22
0	0	Z	283	34	58	23	44
0	0	0	24	6	63	5	(D)
13,610	1,665	3,864	21,299	4,139	10,079	10,144	8,459
106	88	1,583	4,139	1,013	757	2,304	2,608
2,145	487	325	993	192	(D)	214	(D)
158	185	12	3,448	269	1,375	416	(D)
126	28	146	643	135	–81	513	27
–3	10	19	91	Z	–9	1	54
2,262	468	457	6,762	1,647	4,667	5,198	2,046
711	107	472	714	182	719	483	294
2,444	27	19	374	20	134	191	(D)
–4	2	4	707	80	34	148	147
505	21	(D)	202	26	88	42	229
4,224	198	489	1,929	509	762	306	651
529	31	(D)	747	65	1,332	111	332
406	14	117	330	1	231	212	218
1	0	22	219	Z	(D)	4	629
...	...	...	...	...	...	...	...
14,054	4,616	25,676	62,125	18,948	14,480	21,124	34,762
–2	18	150	651	323	138	587	400

[1]The European Union (15) comprises Austria, Belgium, Denmark, Finland, France, Germany, Greece, Ireland, Italy, Luxembourg, the Netherlands, Portugal, Spain, Sweden, and the United Kingdom.
[2]OPEC is the Organization of Petroleum Exporting Countries. Its members are Algeria, Indonesia, Iran, Iraq, Kuwait, Libya, Nigeria, Qatar, Saudi Arabia, the United Arab Emirates, and Venezuela.
D = Data withheld to avoid disclosure.
Z = Less than $500,000.

Table 12-4. Value of Manufactures' Shipments, Inventories, and Orders, 1947–2005

(Billions of dollars, ratio.)

Year	Total shipments	Inventories		Total new orders	Total unfilled orders
		Total[1]	Ratio of inventories to sales[2]		
2005	4 545	440	1.19	4 550	572
2004	4 259	423	1.23	4 208	491
2003	3 972	396	1.23	3 901	470
2002	3 892	444	1.37	3 801	481
2001	3 970	452	1.42	3 875	513
2000	4 209	470	1.37	4 161	545
1999	4 032	453	1.38	3 957	501
1998	3 900	439	1.38	3 808	492
1997	3 835	433	1.39	3 780	508
1996	3 597	421	1.44	3 567	485
1995	3 480	415	1.47	3 427	443
1994	3 238	391	1.48	3 200	431
1993	3 020	371	1.51	2 960	422
1992	2 904	370	1.57	2 635	448
1991	2 878	391	1.65	2 866	515
1990	2 912	405	1.65	2 934	527
1989	2 840	391	1.63	2 875	505
1988	2 695	369	1.57	2 739	471
1987	2 476	338	1.59	2 513	427
1986	2 336	323	1.68	2 342	390
1985	2 334	335	1.73	2 348	384
1984	2 288	340	1.73	2 315	370
1983	2 071	312	1.78	2 105	343
1982	1 960	312	1.95	1 946	309
1981	2 018	283	1.69	2 016	323
1980	1 853	265	1.72	1 876	324
1979	1 727	242	1.68	1 771	301
1978	1 523	212	1.67	1 580	257
1977	1 358	188	1.66	1 381	200
1976	1 186	175	1.77	1 194	177
1975	1 039	160	1.84	1 022	169
1974	1 017	158	1.86	1 048	186
1973	875	124	1.71	912	156
1972	756	108	1.72	770	119
1971	671	103	1.83	671	105
1970	634	102	1.92	624	105
1969	642	98	1.83	648	114
1968	603	91	1.80	608	108
1967	558	85	1.82	565	103
1966	538	78	1.74	557	96
1965	492	68	1.66	506	78
1964	448	63	1.69	459	64
1963	421	60	1.71	426	53
1962	400	58	1.75	401	47
1961	371	55	1.77	373	46
1960*	371	54	1.74	363	44
1959	363	53	1.74	369	52
1958	327	50	1.83	323	47
1957	345	52	1.81	330	53
1956	333	51	1.83	341	68
1955	318	45	1.71	329	60
1954	280	42	1.80	268	48
1953	298	44	1.79	282	60
1952	271	42	1.84	278	76
1951	260	39	1.80	287	67
1950	223	32	1.70	241	41
1949	193	27	1.65	187	24
1948	217	29	1.59	212	31
1947	186	26	0.69	183	34

Source: U.S. Census Bureau, Statistical Abstract of the United States: 2007.
Note: Before 1992, dollars are on the SIC basis; from 1992 forward, dollars are on the NAICS basis.
[1]Beginning in 1982, inventories are stated at current cost and are not comparable to the book value estimates for prior years.
[2]Ratio based on December seasonally-adjusted inventory data, and the monthly average of unadjusted annual shipments.
* = First year for which figures include Alaska and Hawaii.

Table 12-5. Manufacturing Corporations—Sales, Profits, and Stockholders' Equity, 1981–2005

(Billions of dollars.)

Year	Sales (net)	Inventories Net profits Before federal income taxes[1]	After federal income taxes	Stockholders' equity[2]
2005	5 401	522	400	2 410
2004	4 934	448	348	2 206
2003	4 397	306	237	1 952
2002	4 216	196	135	1 804
2002	4 221	197	136	1 805
2001	4 295	83	36	1 843
2000	4 548	381	275	1 823
1999	4 149	355	258	1 569
1998	3 949	315	234	1 483
1997	3 920	331	245	1 463
1996	3 758	307	225	1 348
1995	3 528	275	198	1 241
1994	3 256	244	175	1 110
1993	3 015	118	83	1 040
1992[3]	2 890	31	22	1 035
1991	2 761	99	66	1 064
1990	2 811	158	110	1 044
1989	2 745	188	135	999
1988[4]	2 596	215	154	958
1987	2 378	173	116	901
1986	2 221	129	83	875
1985	2 331	137	88	866
1984	2 335	166	108	864
1983	2 114	133	86	813
1982	2 039	108	71	770
1981	2 145	159	101	743

Source: U.S. Council of Economic Advisors. *Economic Report of the President, 2007.*
Note: Beginning with 2001 data is based on North American Industry Classification System (NAICS). Earlier data are based on the Standard Industrial Classification (SIC). Data are not necessarily comparable from one period to another due to changes in accounting principles, industry classifications, sampling procedures, etc.
[1]In old series, ending with 1973 figures, "income taxes" refers to federal income taxes only, as state and local income taxes had already been deducted. In the new series, beginning with 1974 figures, no income taxes have been deducted.
[2]Annual data are average equity for the year (using four end-of-quarter figures).
[3]Data for 1992 reflect the early adoption of Financial Accounting Standards Board Statement 106 (Employer's Accounting for Post-Retirement Benefits Other Than Pensions) by a large number of companies during the fourth quarter of 1992. Data for 1993 also reflect the adoption of State 106. Corporations must show cumulative effect of a change in accounting principle in the first quarter of the year in which the change is adopted.
[4]Beginning 1988, profits before and after income taxes reflect inclusion of minority stockholders' interest in net income before and after income taxes.

Table 12-6. U.S. Aircraft Shipments, 1981–2005

(Number, millions of dollars.)

Year	TOTAL Units	Value	Civil Total Units	Value	Large transports Units	Value	General aviation[1] Units	Value	Helicopters Units	Value	Military Units	Value
2005	4 518	81 498	4 068	31 498	290	22 116	2 853	8 632	925	750	450	50 000
2004	3 804	74 526	3 384	27 917	283	20 484	2 296	6 918	805	515	420	46 609
2003	3 221	68 006	2 878	27 604	281	21 033	2 080	6 205	517	366	343	40 402
2002	3 251	73 112	2 893	34 965	379	27 547	2 196	7 261	318	157	358	38 147
2001	3 902	77 608	3 557	42 393	526	34 155	2 616	7 991	415	247	345	35 215
2000	4 113	72 669	3 780	38 637	485	30 327	2 802	8 040	493	270	333	34 032
1999	3 799	80 974	3 440	45 174	620	38 171	2 475	6 803	345	200	359	35 800
1998	3 533	75 724	3 115	41 449	559	35 663	2 193	5 534	363	252	418	34 275
1997	2 757	65 129	2 269	31 753	374	26 929	1 549	4 593	346	231	488	33 376
1996	2 220	55 583	1 662	22 156	269	18 915	1 115	3 048	278	193	558	33 427
1995	2 436	49 381	1 625	18 299	256	15 263	1 077	2 842	292	194	811	31 082
1994	2 309	52 718	1 545	20 666	309	18 124	928	2 357	308	185	764	32 052
1993	2 585	59 103	1 630	26 390	408	24 133	964	2 144	258	113	955	32 713
1992	2 585	64 740	1 832	30 732	567	28 750	941	1 840	324	142	753	34 008
1991	3 092	67 510	2 181	29 035	589	26 856	1 021	1 968	571	211	911	38 475
1990	3 321	64 567	2 268	24 476	521	22 215	1 144	2 007	603	254	1 053	40 091
1989	3 709	31 962	2 448	17 129	398	15 074	1 535	1 804	515	251	1 261	14 833
1988	3 323	30 904	2 018	15 860	423	13 603	1 212	1 923	383	334	1 305	15 044
1987	3 010	29 010	1 800	12 148	357	10 507	1 085	1 364	358	277	1 210	16 862
1986	3 262	29 587	2 155	11 859	330	10 309	1 495	1 262	330	288	1 107	17 728
1985	3 610	27 269	2 691	10 385	278	8 448	2 029	1 431	384	506	919	16 884
1984	3 928	21 787	2 992	7 700	185	5 689	2 431	1 681	376	330	936	14 087
1983	4 409	21 769	3 356	9 773	262	8 000	2 691	1 470	403	303	1 053	11 996
1982	6 244	18 446	5 085	8 611	232	6 246	4 266	2 000	587	365	1 159	9 835
1981	11 978	20 093	10 916	13 223	387	9 706	9 457	2 920	1 072	597	1 062	6 870

Source: U.S. Census Bureau. *Statistical Abstract of the United States: 2007.* U.S. Department of Commerce, International Trade Administration.
[1]Excludes off-the-shelf military aircraft.

Table 12-7. Average Hourly Earnings of Production Workers in Manufacturing Industries, by State 2001–2005

(Dollars. Data are based on the North American Industry Classification System (NAICS) 2002. Based on the Current Employment Statistics Program.)

State	2001	2002	2003	2004	2005
United States	**14.76**	**15.29**	**15.74**	**16.15**	**16.56**
Alabama	12.76	13.10	13.56	14.33	14.93
Alaska	11.70	13.24	12.18	12.01	14.22
Arizona	13.80	14.16	14.38	14.20	14.55
Arkansas	12.90	13.30	13.55	13.49	13.71
California	14.69	14.89	15.04	15.36	15.70
Colorado	14.72	15.44	16.89	16.46	15.91
Connecticut	16.42	17.24	17.74	18.35	18.96
Delaware	16.56	16.60	16.91	17.66	17.72
District of Columbia[1]	. . .	. . .	15.76	16.73	16.80
Florida	12.68	13.30	14.09	13.84	13.89
Georgia	12.50	13.38	14.08	14.54	14.56
Hawaii	13.18	13.07	12.90	13.50	14.35
Idaho	13.85	13.80	13.72	14.15	14.96
Illinois	14.66	14.99	15.20	15.61	15.84
Indiana	16.42	17.15	17.84	17.92	18.14
Iowa	14.67	15.32	15.70	16.17	16.25
Kansas	15.48	15.98	15.83	16.57	17.14
Kentucky	15.44	15.73	16.01	16.50	16.64
Louisiana	16.18	17.03	16.86	16.40	17.30
Maine	14.71	15.55	16.28	16.97	17.28
Maryland	14.56	15.21	15.74	16.47	16.98
Massachusetts	15.75	16.25	16.53	16.89	17.67
Michigan	19.45	20.51	21.20	21.51	21.50
Minnesota	14.76	15.06	15.43	16.04	16.63
Mississippi	11.93	12.32	12.89	13.12	13.53
Missouri	16.11	16.80	18.22	17.92	17.43
Montana	14.03	14.43	14.02	14.87	15.61
Nebraska	13.64	14.05	14.86	15.19	15.44
Nevada	13.79	14.62	14.63	14.60	14.98
New Hampshire	13.98	14.21	14.85	15.48	15.87
New Jersey	14.74	15.19	15.45	15.89	16.33
New Mexico	13.27	13.41	13.19	13.13	13.66
New York	16.24	16.75	16.78	17.29	17.77
North Carolina	12.81	13.18	13.66	14.25	14.38
North Dakota	12.77	13.17	14.04	14.35	15.29
Ohio	16.79	17.49	17.99	18.47	19.07
Oklahoma	13.66	14.11	14.13	14.24	14.65
Oregon	14.74	15.06	15.20	15.34	15.49
Pennsylvania	14.37	14.75	14.99	15.16	15.26
Rhode Island	12.68	12.75	12.88	13.03	13.12
South Carolina	13.79	14.00	14.19	14.73	15.23
South Dakota	12.11	12.60	13.13	13.37	13.47
Tennessee	12.88	13.15	13.56	13.84	14.03
Texas	14.04	13.93	13.94	13.98	14.03
Utah	13.76	14.12	14.90	15.38	14.71
Vermont	14.18	14.33	14.54	14.60	15.06
Virginia	14.50	15.20	15.90	16.11	16.40
Washington	17.96	18.15	18.02	18.28	18.83
West Virginia	14.80	15.40	16.05	16.57	17.14
Wisconsin	15.44	15.86	16.12	16.19	16.29
Wyoming	17.26	17.72	16.75	16.58	17.07

Source: U.S. Census Bureau. *Statistical Abstract of the United States: 2007.* U.S. Department of Labor, Bureau of Labor Statistics.
[1]Represents the Washington-Arlington-Alexandria Metropolitan Division.
. . . = Not available.

BOX 12 ■ Outsourcing

International outsourcing, or offshoring, became a topic of debate in the late 1990s, when Americans began to fear that the U.S. labor market would be decimated by the loss of jobs to other countries. Several members of Congress presented legislation that would limit offshoring, primarily by preventing any government contacts from being fulfilled by employees in other countries. Some state legislatures adopted similar legislation.

To date, the effects of outsourcing and offshoring on the world and U.S. economies are not entirely clear. In 2003, the combined gross product of U.S. parent companies and the U.S. affiliates of foreign companies accounted for more than one-fifth of the U.S. gross domestic product. In the same year U.S. parent companies, their foreign affiliates, and U.S. affiliates of foreign companies employed 25 million people in the United States.

As a growing number of companies have branches around the globe, moving work from one location to another is more and more difficult to track. Because globalization and offshoring are relatively new considerations, the government does not yet have a comprehensive method of collecting and analyzing data pertinent to questions on the subject of multinational companies and offshoring. The Bureau of Economic Analysis is, however, currently developing a system that will collect new information from companies, the analysis of which will address topical concerns more fully and rapidly.

The Department of Labor uses Mass Layoff Statistics to try and determine how many people who have been laid off long term have lost their jobs to overseas workers. Beginning in January 2004 company questionnaires from the Bureau of Labor Statistics included questions regarding the movement of work in any layoff and whether the work was moved overseas or within the United States. These figures indicate that in 2004, out of 993,511 workers who suffered long-term layoffs, only 16,197 workers lost jobs that were moved overseas; this is less than two percent.

One of the difficulties in collecting data about offshoring is that companies often do not realize it is occurring. A U.S. parent company could feasibly hire a contractor for set work without knowing that the contractor had, in turn, hired an offshore contractor. Thus, although the first company did not directly move operations overseas, the result of the contract is the same—work that would have previously been completed in the United States was accomplished in another country, resulting in a loss of U.S. jobs.

In addition, it is frequently difficult to determine if layoffs are the result of offshoring, or the result of a business cycle decline, industry specific difficulties, or corporate restructuring which has become increasingly more commonplace.

One point, often omitted from consideration, is whether the United States benefits from offshoring. Many U.S. affiliates of foreign multinational companies do hire U.S. workers. In 2004 U.S. affiliates employed 5.1 million U.S. workers or 4.5% of the private industry work force, down from a high point of 5.0% in 2000.

Sources:

U.S. Bureau of Economic Analysis. *Survey of Current Business.* "A Note on Patterns of Production and Employment by U.S. Multinational Companies". http://www.bea.gov/international/mncglobal.htm

U.S. Bureau of Economic Analysis. *Survey of Current Business.* "U.S. Affiliates of Foreign Companies: Operations in 2004". http://www.bea.gov/international/ai1.htm#fdius

U.S. Department of Labor. *Monthly Labor Review,* August 2005. "Mass Layoff Data Indicate Outsourcing and Offshoring Work"

Kozlow, Ralph, Associate Director for International Economics, U.S. Bureau of Economic Analysis. "Globalization, Offshoring, and Multinational Companies: What Are the Questions, and How Well Are We Doing in Answering Them?" http://www.bea.gov/international/mncglobal.htm

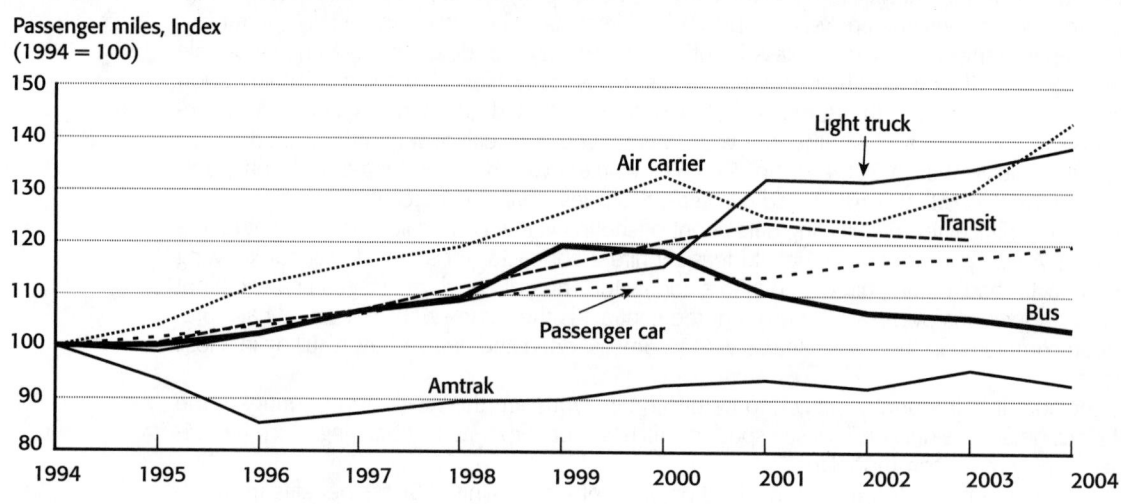

Passenger miles, Index
(1994 = 100)

Index of U.S. Passenger Miles: 1994–2004

CHAPTER **13**

Transportation

HIGHLIGHTS

1 The first transportation agency in the United States, the Office of Road Inquiry, was created in 1894 "to make inquiries in regard to the systems of road management throughout the United States, to make investigations in regard to the best methods of roadmaking, to prepare publications on this subject suitable for publication." It was succeeded by the Office of Public Roads and Rural Engineering in 1916 and by the Bureau of Public Roads in 1918 (called Public Roads Administration between 1939 and 1949). The Bureau was transferred to the Department of Transportation in 1966 and its functions assigned to the Federal Highways Administration. The first survey of highway mileage, revenues, and expenditures was made in 1904, followed by others in 1909 and 1914.

2 In 1912, Congress authorized $500,000 for an experimental program of rural post road construction. However, it was not until the Federal Aid Road Act of 1916 that the Federal-State Highway Program was established on an ongoing basis. In 1921, Congress authorized designation of a system of principal interstate and intercounty roads, limited to 7 percent of the rural mileage then existing. The Federal Aid Highway Act of 1944 specifically authorized the use of funds for highways in urban areas. In addition, the Act provided for the designation of a Federal-Aid secondary system and a national system of interstate highways.

Under President Dwight Eisenhower, the Federal-Aid Highway Act of 1956 established the goal of a 41,000-mile interstate system, which forms the basis of the U.S. road transportation system today. In 1995, Congress abolished the Federal-Aid Highway System and replaced it with the National Highway System (NHS). Roads are classified as (1) arterial highways, (2) collector facilities that link arterials and lower systems, and (3) local roads.

3 The principal sources of highway and motor transport data are the Highway Statistics of the Federal Highway Administration, the Transport Statistics of the United States published by the Interstate Commerce Commission, various surveys and censuses conducted by the U.S. Bureau of the Census, the *Factbook* of the U.S. National Highway Traffic Safety Administration, *Motor Vehicle Facts and Figures* published by the Motor Vehicle Manufacturers Association, *Accident Facts* published by the National Safety Council, and *Transportation in America* published by the Eno Foundation for Transportation.

4 The first federal highway was the Great National Pike, also known as the Cumberland Road, which was built in sections from 1806 to 1840 between Cumberland, Maryland, and Vandalia, Illinois. The total construction cost was $6.821 million.

5 The first hard-surfaced road in what is now the United States was built by the Dutch in 1663. It ran for 100 miles from Pahaquarry Mines in New Jersey to Kingston, New York. The first toll road was the Little River Turnpike built in 1785 from Alexandria, Virginia, to Snicker's Gap, a pass through the Blue Ridge Mountains leading to the Shenandoah Valley.

6 Of the total passenger traffic of 2.498 trillion passenger miles in 2001, private automobiles handled 1.938 trillion passenger miles, air public carriers 488 billion passenger miles, buses 42 billion passenger miles, and railroads 15 billion passenger miles. Of the total freight traffic of 3.733 trillion ton miles, railroads carried 1.558 trillion ton miles, trucks 1.051 trillion ton miles, and inland waterways 494 billion ton miles.

7 Transportation accidents and deaths are closely monitored by the National Highway Traffic Safety Administration. In 2004, there were 6,181,000 motor vehicle accidents and 42,600 deaths, 3,296 railroad accidents and 530 deaths, 30 air carrier accidents and 14 deaths, 1,617 general aviation accidents and 558 deaths. There were 4,904 recreational boating accidents and 676 deaths and 6,222 rail rapid transit accidents and 59 deaths.

8 The total highway mileage in the United States in 2004 was 3,981,512 miles, of which interstates accounted for 46,572 miles, other arterial roads 388,523 miles, collector roads 790,038 miles, local roads 2,746,133 miles, urban roads 884,000 miles, and rural roads 3,079,000 miles. The longest road system is in Texas (303,176 miles), followed by California (169,791 miles).

9 Highways are generally paid for by issuing bonds which are then redeemed by imposing tolls and imposts on highway users. In 2003, imposts on highway users, along with other sources of income, totaled $139.246 billion, while total outstanding highway debt was $119.571 billion.

10 In 2004, motor vehicle registrations totaled 237,243,000 of which automobiles (including taxicabs) accounted for 136,431,000 and motorcycles 5,738,000. California has the largest number of motor vehicles (31.400 million).

11 In 2004, 77.7 percent of the 130.831 million workers commuted to work alone by automobile, 10.1 percent carpooled, and only 4.6 percent used public transportation, while 3.8 percent worked at home. The average travel time to work was 24.7 minutes.

12 Roadway congestion measured in annual person delay was 43,802,000 nationwide in 2003, costing $742 million in delays and fuel costs, or $422 per person. The worst road congestion is in Los Angeles–Long Beach–Santa Ana (623,796,000 hours), followed by New York–Newark, New York–New Jersey-Connecticut (404,480,000 hours), Chicago–Indiana (252,822,000 hours), San Francisco (152,352,000 hours), Dallas–Fort Worth–Arlington (151,840,000 hours), and Washington DC–Virginia–Maryland (145,484).

13 In 2004, there were 10.9 million motor vehicle accidents, involving 10.8 million cars, 8.1 million trucks, and 150,000 motorcycles. Fatalities numbered 46,200, of which 19,100 were car occupants, 4,600 were pedestrians, 4,000 were motorcyclists, and 700 bicyclists. Traffic death rates have decreased significantly since 1972 from 26.2 to 14.5 per 100,000 population, from 44.5 to 17.9 per 100,000 registered vehicles, from 4.3 to 1.4 per 100 million vehicle miles, and from 46.1 to 21.4 per 100,000 licensed drivers. By state, Mississippi has the highest fatality rate at 2.3 per 100 million vehicle miles. In 2004 there were a total of 42,636 alcohol related fatalities.

14 The cost of operating an automobile has increased from 14.4 cents per mile in 1975 to 50.2 cents per mile in 2002. Of the variable costs, gas and oil cost 5.9 cents per mile.

15 Environmental regulations and technology have combined to reduce substantially the average fuel consumption of a car and increase the average number of miles per gallon. The domestic motor fuel consumption in 2004 was 173.7 billion gallons, up from 92.3 billion gallons in 1970. The annual fuel consumption in 2004 was 76 billion gallons for cars, 1 billion gallons for buses, 33.9 billion gallons per truck, and 62.6 billion gallons for vans, pickups, and SUVs. The average miles per gallon for cars increased from 13.5 miles in 1970 to 22.4 in 2004.

16 In 2004, U.S. cars traveled a total of 1.7 trillion miles, buses 6.6 trillion miles, trucks 227 billion miles and vans, pickups and SUVs 1.014 trillion miles. The average annual car mileage is 12,500.

17 In 2004, there were 6,429 mass transit systems (including 1,500 motor bus systems) carrying 9.575 billion people. Buses carried 5.731 billion, heavy rail 2.748 billion, light rail 350 million, and commuter rail 414 million.

18 In 2004, the trucking industry had a fleet of 212,000 trucks and 895,000 truck-tractors with revenues of $185.944 billion.

19 Railroad companies reporting to the Interstate Commerce Commission (ICC) are divided into four groups: (1) regular line-haul; (2) switching and terminal; (3) private or circular (because they are reported on brief circulars); and (4) unofficial. Data on the last three groups are excluded from official statistics. Beginning in 1911, the ICC also divided regular line-haul railroads into Class I, II, and III. Initially, Class I had revenues of more than $1 million, Class II had revenues between $100,000 and $1 million, and Class III had revenues under $100,000. In 1978, the categories were redefined with thresholds for Classes I, II, and III raised to $50 million, $10 to $50 million, and below $10 million respectively. In 1982, the ICC adopted a procedure to adjust the threshold for inflation on the basis of 1978 dollars.

20 The principal sources of information on railways before 1890 is Poor's *Manual of Railroads.* Current data are contained in *Railway Age* and *Yearbook of Railroad Facts* published by the Association of American Railroads.

21 The first interstate railroad was the Petersburg Railroad, chartered by a special act of the General Assembly of Virginia in 1830 and by a special act of the North Carolina legislature in 1831. It ran for 59 miles along the north bank of the Roanoke River from Petersburg, Virginia, to Blakeley, North Carolina. The first railroad for the commercial transportation of passengers and freight was the Baltimore and Ohio Railroad Company, incorporated in 1827.

22 U.S. railroads have downsized in the last decade, resulting in only seven Class I railroads with 158,000 employees (compared with 23 Class I railroads with 302,000 employees in 1985). The total rail line mileage in 2004 was 123,000 railroad line owned and 211,000 railroad track owned. Railroads had operating revenues of $40.617 billion (of which freight generated $39.131 billion) and operating expenditures of $35.107 billion, leaving a net income of $2.867 billion. AMTRAK carried 25.215 billion passengers and had a revenue of 1.433 billion.

23 The principal sources of information on water transportation are *Waterborne Commerce of the United States* issued by the Corps of Engineers of the Department of the Army; *Merchant Fleets of the World* issued by the U.S. Maritime Administration; *The Bulletin* issued by the American Bureau of Shipping; and *World Fleet Statistics* issued by Lloyd's Register of Shipping. Historical statistics on merchant shipping are found in a variety of sources, including *Merchant Marine Statistics, 1924–1965,* Congressional Documents, such as Decadence of American Shipping and Compulsory Pilotage, 1789–1882, publications of the Maritime Commission, especially *Ocean-Going Merchant Fleets of Principal Mar-*

itime Nations, and the censuses of water transportation conducted by the Bureau of the Census and its predecessors. The first census for 1880 was limited to steam vessels (excluding fishing vessels) and those of 1916 and 1926 provided data for all vessels over 5 tons. Changes in maritime law on admeasurement (a determination or comparison of measurements) of gross tonnage have also affected the data. Gross tonnage is a measurement of space, not weight, in which 100 cubic feet (95 cubic feet before 1865) equals one ton. Also, an act in 1874 excluded canal boats and unrigged tonnage from the totals. Other measurements used over the years included duty tonnage (tonnage on which duties were collected), district tonnage (reported by district collectors of customs), registered tonnage, and net tonnage.

24 The United States has six major waterways systems: the Atlantic intracoastal waterway, the Great Lakes, the Gulf intercoastal waterway, the Mississippi River system, the Columbia River, and the Snake River. The Mississippi River with 714.8 million tons accounts for more than two-thirds of the total freight carried in these systems.

25 In 2000, the global merchant fleet consisted of 28,259 vessels with weights over 1,000 gross tons, of which 463 are registered in the United States. Of the 463 ships, 154 are tankers, and 11 are cruise ships.

26 The output of U.S. shipyards has been falling since 1970, bringing shipbuilding, one of the oldest industrial activities in the United States, to the verge of extinction. In 1999, private shipyards employed 99,900 workers compared with 178,000 in 1980 and had only five ships under construction, compared with 69 in 1980.

27 Only scattered data on air transportation are available for the years before 1926. Regular collection of national statistics began with the establishment in that year of an Aeronautical Branch in the Department of Commerce. The Civil Aeronautics Act of 1938 created the Civil Aeronautics Authority, reorganized in 1940 into two separate entities: The Civil Aeronautics Board and the Civil Aeronautics Administration. In 1958, the latter's functions were transferred to the Federal Aviation Agency, which, in turn, was made a part of the Department of Transportation and renamed the Federal Aviation Administration (FAA). The FAA's annual *Statistical Handbook of Civil Aviation* is the principal source of data in this field. Air Transportation data are also presented annually in *Air Transport Facts and Figures,* published by the Air Transport Association of America. A major development in 1978 was the Airline Deregulation Act which encouraged competition among airlines and also blurred the distinction between domestic and international operators.

28 The scheduled airline industry covers certificated route air carriers, commercial operators with large aircraft and commuter airlines. In 2005, these airlines had 738.4 billion passengers against the available seat miles of 1,003.2 billion miles. There were 11.475 million aircraft departures. Total operating revenue was $147.504 billion and operating expenditures were $147.413 billion, leaving a net profit of –$27.402 billion. In 2005 the airline industry employed 552,900 people.

29 In 2004, Atlanta's Hartsfield International Airport topped O'Hare Airport in Chicago as the airport where the most passengers enplaned. In order, the cities with top airports in passengers enplaned after Atlanta and Chicago are Dallas/Fort Worth, Los Angeles, Denver, Las Vegas, Phoenix, Minneapolis, Detroit, Houston, Newark, Orlando, Seattle, San Francisco, New York John F. Kennedy International, Philadelphia, Miami, and Charlotte.

30 There are only two major players in the aircraft industry: Boeing and McDonnell Douglas. In 2002, Boeing was the larger with 158 orders for civil jet transport aircraft; McDonnell Douglas had 16.

31 In 2005 there were 39 aircraft accidents and 22 fatalities.

32 In 2004 there were 19,820 airports in the United States, of which 14,532 were private airports. There were 219,426 active aircraft in the general aviation fleet, of which 9,298 aircraft were turbojet. Of the 618,633 pilots, commercial pilots numbered 122,592. Women make up only 6 percent of all pilots.

33 In 2005, civil U.S. aircraft shipments totaled 4,068 units worth $31.498 billion. Of these, large transports numbered 290, general aviation aircraft 2,853, and helicopters 925.

34 The percentage of on-time arrivals and departures in U.S. airports has been steadily improving. The national average was 77.5 percent for the former and 80.2 percent for the latter in the fourth quarter of 2005. Cincinnati led in on-time arrivals with 84.3 percent and Salt Lake City led with on-time departures with 86.3 percent.

35 There were 6,894 complaints against U.S. airlines in 2005. The most common complaints were flight problems (1,942), baggage (1,586), customer service (800), ticketing/boarding (679), and refunds (529).

36 In 2004, there were 142,000 miles of pipeline valued at $29.552 billion and delivering 6.612 billion barrels of crude oil.

37 The total miles of petroleum pipelines decreased by 31,000 miles between 1980 and 2004, but the net income in the industry rose by 1.411 billion dollars in the same period.

38 There were 7,140,600 delays, cancellations, and diversions in the airline industry in 2005, up substantially from 5,327,400 in 1995.

39 Overall, the United States spent $104.667 billion on highways in 2004. California spent the most at $7.967 billion, followed by Texas ($7.134 billion) and New York ($6.094 billion). Vermont spent the least at only $297 million.

Table 13-1. Transportation-Related Components of U.S. Gross Domestic Product, 1995–2004

(Billions of dollars, percent.)

Item	1995	2000	2001	2002	2003	2004
CURRENT DOLLARS						
Total transportation-related final demand[1]	...	**1 089.5**	**1 103.9**	**1 106.4**	**1 156.9**	**1 227.7**
Total gross domestic product (GDP)	7 397.7	9 817.0	10 128.0	10 649.6	10 971.2	11 734.3
Transportation as a percent of GDP	...	11.1	10.9	10.4	10.5	10.5
Personal consumption of transportation	594.6	853.5	872.3	882.2	928.5	979.1
Motor vehicles and parts	266.7	386.5	407.9	429.3	439.1	441.8
Gasoline and oil	120.2	175.7	171.6	164.5	192.6	230.4
Transportation services	207.7	291.3	292.8	288.4	296.8	306.9
Gross private domestic investment	...	167.4	148.6	132.8	133.9	158.4
Transportation structures	...	6.6	6.9	6.5	6.0	6.5
Transportation equipment	116.1	160.8	141.7	126.3	127.9	151.9
Net exports of transportation-related goods and service[2]	− 43.6	− 109.0	− 108.2	− 112.1	− 125.6	− 135.3
Exports (+)	132.4	179.0	174.3	175.5	174.4	195.1
Civilian aircraft, engines, and parts	26.1	48.1	52.6	50.4	46.7	50.0
Automotive vehicles, engines, and parts	61.3	80.4	75.4	78.9	80.7	89.3
Passenger fares	18.9	20.7	17.9	17.0	15.7	18.9
Other transportation	26.1	29.8	28.4	29.2	31.3	36.9
Imports (−)	176.0	288.0	282.5	287.6	300.0	330.4
Civilian aircraft, engines, and parts	10.7	26.4	31.4	25.5	24.1	24.3
Automotive vehicles, engines, and parts	123.6	195.9	189.8	203.7	210.2	228.2
Passenger fares	14.7	24.3	22.6	20.0	21.0	23.7
Other transportation	27.0	41.4	38.7	38.4	44.7	54.2
Government transportation-related purchases	133.8	177.6	191.2	203.5	220.1	225.5
Federal purchases[3]	16.1	19.2	21.1	26.4	30.6	29.7
State and local purchases[3]	109.3	149.4	160.3	166.6	173.3	179.2
Defense-related purchases[4]	8.4	9.0	9.8	10.5	16.2	16.6
CHAINED (2000) DOLLARS						
Total transportation-related final demand[1]	...	**1 089.5**	**1 098.7**	**1 100.7**	**1 117.1**	**1 139.8**
Total gross domestic product (GDP)	8 031.7	9 817.0	9 890.7	10 048.8	10 320.6	10 755.7
Transportation as a percent of GDP	...	11.1	11.1	11.0	10.8	10.6
Personal consumption of transportation	658.6	853.5	872.1	891.1	913.0	926.3
Motor vehicles and parts	272.3	386.5	405.8	429.0	449.7	457.0
Gasoline and oil	154.5	175.7	178.3	181.9	183.2	185.9
Transportation services	231.8	291.3	288.0	280.2	280.1	283.4
Gross private domestic investment	...	167.4	149.4	132.1	128.6	144.4
Transportation structures	...	6.6	6.6	6.1	5.5	5.7
Transportation equipment	120.6	160.8	142.8	126.0	123.1	138.7
Net exports of transportation-related goods and service[2]	− 46.9	− 109.0	− 108.5	− 114.5	− 126.6	− 132.9
Exports (+)	142.1	179.0	171.6	170.7	164.2	178.6
Civilian aircraft, engines, and parts	30.3	48.1	49.9	46.5	41.5	42.6
Automotive vehicles, engines, and parts	63.4	80.4	75.2	78.3	79.4	87.2
Passenger fares	19.6	20.7	17.8	16.5	13.5	14.8
Other transportation	28.8	29.8	28.7	29.4	29.8	34.0
Imports (−)	189.0	288.0	280.1	285.2	290.8	311.5
Civilian aircraft, engines, and parts	12.4	26.4	30.2	24.2	22.8	22.2
Automotive vehicles, engines, and parts	126.6	195.9	189.9	203.3	208.6	222.7
Passenger fares	17.3	24.3	20.7	17.4	17.9	20.6
Other transportation	32.7	41.4	39.3	40.3	41.5	46.0
Government transportation-related purchases	156.5	177.6	185.7	192.0	202.1	202.0
Federal purchases[3]	18.0	19.2	20.6	25.0	28.2	26.2
State and local purchases[3]	128.8	149.4	155.8	157.3	159.9	161.9
Defense-related purchases[4]	9.7	9.0	9.3	9.7	14.0	13.9

Source: U.S. Census Bureau. *Statistical Abstract of the United States: 2007.* U.S. Department of Transportation, Bureau of Transportation Statistics.
[1]Sum of total personal consumption of transportation, total gross private domestic investment, net exports of transportation-related goods and services, and total government transportation-related purchases.
[2]Sum of exports and imports.
[3]Federal purchases and state and local purchases are the sum of consumption expenditures and gross investment.
[4]Defense-related purchases are the sum of transportation of material and travel.
... = Not available.

Table 13-2. Employment and Earnings in Transportation and Warehousing by Industry, 1995–2005

(Thousands of employees, dollars.)

Industry	2002 NAICS code[1]	1995	2000	2001	2002	2003	2004	2005
Number of Employees								
Transportation and warehousing	**48,49**	**3 838**	**4 410**	**4 372**	**4 224**	**4 185**	**4 249**	**4 347**
Air transportation	481	511	614	615	564	528	515	501
Rail transportation	482	233	232	227	218	218	226	228
Water transportation	483	51	56	54	53	55	56	61
Truck transportation	484	1 249	1 406	1 387	1 339	1 326	1 352	1 393
Transit and ground	485	328	372	375	381	382	385	389
Pipeline transportation	486	54	46	45	42	40	38	38
Scenic and sightseeing	487	22	28	29	26	27	27	30
Support activities	488	430	537	539	525	520	535	551
Couriers and messengers	492	517	605	587	561	562	557	572
Warehousing and storage	493	444	514	514	517	528	558	585
Average Weekly Earnings[2]								
Transportation and warehousing	**48,49**	**513**	**562**	**563**	**580**	**598**	**615**	**619**
Air transportation	481	...	...	...	...	...	...	...
Rail transportation	482	...	...	...	...	...	...	...
Water transportation	483	...	...	...	...	...	...	...
Truck transportation	484	554	635	604	626	652	686	690
Transit and ground	485	356	400	400	422	426	415	412
Pipeline transportation	486	751	826	860	937	1 078	1 100	1 114
Scenic and sightseeing	487	303	360	372	361	369	352	384
Support activities	488	491	549	578	616	658	657	647
Couriers and messengers		343	384	390	398	404	415	408
Warehousing and storage	493	463	558	565	572	567	558	557

Source: U.S. Census Bureau. *Statistical Abstract of the United States: 2007.* U.S. Department of Labor, Bureau of Labor Statistics.
Annual average of monthly figures. Earnings data for air, rail, and water transportation are not available. Based on Current Employment Statistics program. For historical Standard Industrial Classification data, see Bureau of Labor Statistics web site (http://www.bls.gov/ces/cesoldsic.htm).
[1]North American Industry Classification System 2002.
[2]For nonsupervisory workers.
. . . = Not available.

Table 13-3. Transportation Accidents, Deaths, and Injuries, by Mode of Transportation, 1970–2004

(Number.)

| Year and casualty | Land surface | | | Air | | | | Water | | Pipeline[9] | | | |
	Highway[1] (1,000)	Railroad[2]	Rail rapid transit[3]	U.S. air carrier[4]	Commuter air carriers[5]	On demand air carriers[6]	General aviation	Recreational boating[7]	Waterborne (vessel-related)[8]	Gas	Hazardous liquid	Other transit[10]	Hazardous materials[11]
Accidents:													
2004	6 181	3 296	6 222	30	4	66	1 617	4 904	4 962	286	138	14 717	14 740
2003	6 328	2 997	5 554	54	2	74	1 739	5 438	5 163	244	128	14 243	15 162
2002	6 316	2 738	7 078	41	7	60	1 715	5 705	6 008	184	146	23 253	15 117
2001	6 323	3 023	12 406	46	7	72	1 727	6 419	4 958	211	130	45 743	17 794
2000	6 394	2 983	12 782	56	12	80	1 837	7 740	5 403	234	146	47 116	17 557
1999	6 279	2 768	12 196	51	13	74	1 905	7 931	5 526	172	167	46 507	17 616
1998	6 335	2 575	13 516	50	8	77	1 905	8 061	5 767	236	153	46 578	15 497
1997	6 624	2 397	15 151	49	16	82	1 844	8 047	5 504	175	171	46 410	14 070
1996	6 770	2 443	13 748	37	11	90	1 908	8 026	5 260	187	194	45 644	14 077
1995	6 699	2 459	14 327	36	12	75	2 056	8 019	5 349	161	188	48 144	14 853
1990	6 471	2 879	12 178	24	15	107	2 242	6 411	3 613	198	180	77 985	8 879
1985	6 081	3 275	1 014	21	18	157	2 739	6 237	3 439	334	183	. . .	6 019
1980	6 216	8 205	6 789	19	38	171	3 590	5 513	4 624	1 524	246	. . .	15 719
1975	. . .	8 041	. . .	37	48	152	3 995	6 308	3 310	1 338	254	. . .	10 951
1970	. . .	8 095	. . .	55	190	. . .	4 712	3 803	2 582	1 077	351	. . .	. . .
Deaths:													
2004	42.6	530	59	14	0	64	558	676	36	18	5	189	13
2003	42.9	533	49	22	2	42	632	703	53	12	0	185	15
2002	43.0	594	73	0	0	35	581	750	62	11	1	207	9
2001	42.2	550	59	531	13	60	562	681	53	7	0	208	12
2000	41.9	512	80	92	5	71	596	701	53	37	1	215	16
1999	41.7	530	84	12	12	38	619	734	58	18	4	215	9
1998	41.5	577	54	1	0	45	625	815	69	19	2	232	13
1997	42.0	602	77	8	46	39	631	821	48	10	0	198	12
1996	42.1	551	74	380	14	63	636	709	55	48	5	190	120
1995	41.8	567	79	168	9	52	735	829	53	18	3	195	7
1990	44.6	599	117	39	6	51	770	865	85	6	3	222	8
1985	43.8	454	17	526	37	76	956	1 116	131	28	5	. . .	8
1980	51.1	584	83	1	37	105	1 239	1 360	206	15	4	. . .	19
1975	44.5	575	. . .	124	28	69	1 252	1 466	243	8	7	. . .	27
1970	52.6	785	. . .	146	100	. . .	1 310	1 418	178	26	4	. . .	. . .
Injuries:													
2004	2 788	7 790	4 738	19	1	18	266	3 363	198	42	13	14 244	289
2003	2 889	8 149	4 158	30	1	15	322	3 888	227	66	5	14 077	119
2002	2 926	10 104	4 806	24		16	297	4 062	192	49		14 454	136
2001	3 033	9 828	10 641	19	4	24	321	4 274	210	51	10	43 304	168
2000	3 189	10 424	10 848	29	7	12	309	4 355	150	77	4	45 849	251
1999	3 236	10 304	9 665	67	2	15	322	4 315	152	88	20	45 660	264
1998	3 192	10 156	11 059	30	2	10	327	4 612	130	75	6	44 931	195
1997	3 348	10 227	12 285	43	1	23	350	4 555	120	72	5	43 847	221
1996	3 483	10 948	11 093	77	2	22	366	4 442	254	114	13	44 195	1 175
1995	3 465	12 546	11 238	25	17	14	396	4 141	154	53	11	45 958	400
1990	3 231	22 736	10 036	29	11	36	409	3 822	175	69	7	44 520	423
1985	3 363	31 617	1 039	30	14	44	501	2 757	172	108	18	. . .	253
1980	2 848	58 696	6 801	19	14	43	681	2 650	180	177	15	. . .	626
1975	. . .	50 138	. . .	81	6	32	769	2 136	97	214	17	. . .	648
1970	. . .	17 934	. . .	107	. . .	. . .	715	780	105	233	21	. . .	. . .

Source: U.S. Census Bureau. *Statistical Abstract of the United States: 2007.* U.S. Department of Transportation, Bureau of Transportation Statistics.
[1]Data on deaths are from U.S. National Highway Traffic Safety Administration and are based on 30-day definition. Includes only police reported crashes.
[2]Accidents which result in damages to railroad property. Grade crossing accidents are also included when classified as a train accident. Deaths exclude fatalities in railroad-highway grade crossing accidents.
[3]Reporting criteria and source of data changed between 1989 and 1990; these data from 1990 to present are not comparable to earlier years.
[4]Includes scheduled and nonscheduled (charter) air carriers. Represents serious injuries.
[5]All scheduled service. Represents serious injuries.
[6]All nonscheduled service. Represents serious injuries.
[7]Accidents resulting in death; injury or requiring medical treatment beyond first aid; damages exceeding $500; or a person's disappearance.
[8]Covers accidents involving commercial vessels which must be reported to U.S. Coast Guard if there is property damage exceeding $25,000; material damage affecting the seaworthiness or efficiency of a vessel; stranding or grounding; loss of life; or injury causing a person's incapacity for more than 3 days.
[9]Beginning 1985, pipeline accidents/incidents are credited to year of occurrence; prior data are credited to the year filed.
[10]Other Transit includes bus, light rail, commuter rail, demand response, van pool, and automated guideway. Excludes cable car, inclined plane, jitney, and ferry boat.
[11]Incidents, deaths, and injuries involving hazardous materials cover all types of transport. Excludes pipelines and bulk, nonpackaged water incidents.
. . . = Not available.

Table 13-4. Mileage of Rural Roads and Municipal Streets, 1921–2004

(Mileage.)

Year	Total mileage	
	Year[1]	Rural roads
2004	3,997	3,003
2003	3,991	3,036
2002	3,982	3,080
2001	3 963	3 079
2000	3 951	3 092
1999	3 932	3 079
1998[2]	3 920	3 072
1997	3 959	3 116
1996	3 934	3 100
1995	3 912	3 093
1994	3 906	3 093
1993	3 905	3 102
1992	3 902	3 117
1991	3 889	3 139
1990	3 880	3 123
1989	3 877	3 123
1988	3 871	3 132
1987	3 874	3 164
1986	3 880	3 178
1985	3 862	3 171
1984	3 892	3 218
1983	3 880	3 217
1982	3 866	3 226
1981	3 853	3 221
1980	3 955	3 331
1979	3 918	3 224
1978	3 885	3 190
1977	3 867	3 180
1976	3 857	3 209
1975	3 838	3 199
1974	3 816	3 178
1973	3 807	3 176
1972	3 787	3 173
1971	3 759	3 166
1970	3 730	3 169
1969	3 710	3 162
1968	3 684	3 152
1967	3 705	3 184
1966	3 698	3 188
1965	3 690	3 009
1964	3 644	3 003
1963	3 620	3 002
1962	3 600	3 005
1961	3 573	2 995
1960	3 546	2 989
1959*	3 511	2 974
1958	3 479	2 959
1957	3 453	2 952
1956	3 430	2 945
1955	3 418	2 954
1954	3 395	2 941
1953	3 366	2 925
1952	3 343	2 925
1951	3 326	2 925
1950	3 313	2 922
1949	3 322	2 934
1948	3 323	2 929
1947	3 326	2 933
1946	3 316	2 934
1945	3 319	2 939
1944	3 311	2 932
1943	3 311	2 930
1942	3 309	2 925
1941	3 309	2 926

[1] 1980 includes public and nonpublic road mileage; beginning 1985, includes only public road mileage as defined 23 USC 402.
[2] Beginning in 1998, approximately 43,000 miles of Bureau of Land Management roads are excluded.
* = First year for which figures include Alaska and Hawaii.

Table 13-4. Mileage of Rural Roads and Municipal Streets, 1921–2004—*Continued*

(Mileage.)

Year	Total mileage	
	Year[1]	Rural roads
1940	3 287	2 920
1939	3 274	2 913
1938	3 257	2 898
1937	3 245	2 894
1936	3 267	2 920
1935	3 310	3 032
1934	3 309	3 034
1933	3 286	3 029
1932	3 296	3 040
1931	3 291	3 036
1930	3 259	3 009
1929	3 272	3 024
1928	3 262	3 016
1927	3 257	3 013
1926	3 242	3 000
1925	3 246	3 006
1924	3 243	3 004
1923	3 233	2 996
1922	3 196	2 960
1921	3 160	2 925

Source: U.S. Department of Transportation, Bureau of Labor Statistics. U.S. Census Bureau. U.S. Federal Highway Administration.
[1]1980 includes public and nonpublic road mileage; beginning 1985, includes only public road mileage as defined 23 USC 402.

Table 13-5. Public Highway Debt—State and Local Governments, 1970–2004

(Dollars in millions.)

Year	Debt issued			Debt redeemed			Debt outstanding[1]		
	Total	State	Local[2]	Total	State	Local[2]	Total	State	Local[2]
2004	. . .	13 344	. . .	. . .	8 292	. . .	. . .	85 565	. . .
2003	22 127	16 618	5 509	15 171	11 550	3 621	119 571	77 592	41 979
2002	19 089	13 250	5 839	13 537	9 988	3 549	111 226	70 826	40 400
2001	15 697	11 012	4 685	7 230	4 660	2 570	103 342	66 256	37 086
2000	14 513	9 067	5 446	8 623	3 897	4 726	96 383	61 434	34 949
1999	12 822	9 554	3 268	5 808	3 609	2 199	89 778	55 646	34 132
1998	16 412	9 789	6 623	11 735	6 466	5 269	82 599	49 182	33 417
1997	12 347	8 174	4 173	7 043	4 228	2 815	77 501	45 666	31 835
1996	9 728	6 653	3 075	6 380	4 161	2 219	72 197	41 720	30 477
1995	11 305	4 718	6 587	5 634	2 939	2 695	68 733	39 228	29 505
1994	10 833	5 739	5 094	6 178	3 698	2 480	63 062	37 449	25 613
1993	14 178	10 035	4 143	11 554	8 813	2 741	58 373	35 408	22 965
1992	12 988	9 460	3 528	7 809	5 532	2 277	53 539	34 186	19 353
1991	9 516	6 252	3 264	6 142	4 356	1 786	48 316	30 258	18 058
1990	5 708	3 147	2 561	3 120	1 648	1 472	46 586	28 362	18 224
1985	8 194	5 397	2 797	5 294	3 835	1 459	32 690	21 277	11 413
1980	2 381	1 160	1 221	1 987	1 114	873	27 616	20 210	7 406
1970	1 892	1 306	586	1 270	800	470	19 124	14 020	5 133

Source: U.S. Census Bureau. *Statistical Abstract of the United States: 2007.* U.S. Federal Highway Administration.
Note: Long-term obligations. Data are for varying calendar and fiscal years. Excludes duplicated and interunit obligations.
[1]End-of-year.
[2]Local data estimated.
. . . = Not available.

Table 13-6. Motor Vehicle Sales from U.S. Factories, Motor Vehicle Registrations, and Motor Fuel Usage Consumption, 1900–2004

(Number in thousands, millions of gallons.)

Year	Motor-vehicle factory sales[1] (thousands)		Motor-vehicle registration (thousands)		Motor-fuel consumption (millions of gallons)	
	Number of passenger cars	Number of motor trucks and buses[2]	Total	Automobiles	Total	Passenger vehicles
2004	7 467	. . .	237 243	136 431	173 700	76 000
2003	7 143	. . .	231 390	135 670	170 000	75 500
2002	6 964	. . .	229 620	135 921	168 700	75 500
2001	4 884	6 224	230 428	137 633	163 500	73 600
2000	5 504	7 022	221 475	133 621	162 554	73 065
1999	5 428	6 699	216 309	132 432	161 411	73 200
1998	5 677	6 435	211 617	131 839	155 379	71 695
1997	6 070	6 153	207 754	129 749	150 386	69 892
1996	6 140	5 776	206 365	129 728	147 365	69 221
1995	6 310	5 713	201 530	128 387	143 834	68 072
1994	6 549	5 640	198 045	127 883	140 839	68 100
1993	5 962	4 895	194 063	127 327	137 262	67 200
1992	5 685	4 062	190 362	126 581	132 888	65 600
1991	5 407	3 388	188 136	128 300	128 563	64 500
1990	6 050	3 725	188 798	133 700	130 755	69 800
1989	6 807	4 062	187 356	134 559	131 900	74 100
1988	7 105	4 121	184 393	133 836	130 100	73 500
1987	7 085	3 821	178 910	131 482	127 500	73 500
1986	7 516	3 393	175 700	130 004	125 200	73 400
1985	8 002	3 464	171 689	127 885	121 300	71 700
1984	7 621	3 075	166 249	128 158	118 700	70 800
1983	6 739	2 414	163 749	126 444	116 100	70 500
1982	5 049	1 906	159 643	123 702	113 400	69 300
1981	6 255	1 701	158 286	123 098	114 500	69 300
1980	6 400	1 667	155 796	121 601	115 000	70 200
1979	8 419	3 037	151 869	118 429	122 100	77 300
1978	9 165	3 706	148 415	116 573	125 100	81 700
1977	9 201	3 441	142 093	112 288	119 600	80 400
1976	8 500	2 979	138 543	110 189	115 700	79 700
1975	6 713	2 272	132 949	106 706	109 000	74 300
1974	7 331	2 727	129 934	104 856	106 300	75 100
1973	9 658	2 980	125 654	101 985	110 500	78 700
1972	8 824	2 447	118 797	97 082	105 100	73 500
1971	8 585	2 053	112 986	92 718	97 600	69 500
1970	6 547	1 692	108 418	89 244	92 300	67 819
1969	8 224	1 923	105 096	86 858	92 240	63 395
1968	8 822	1 896	100 898	83 605	87 154	59 456
1967	7 437	1 539	96 906	80 399	81 911	56 020
1966	8 598	1 731	93 950	78 125	78 979	54 208
1965	9 306	1 752	90 358	75 258	75 312	49 723
1964	7 752	1 540	86 313	71 995	72 097	48 431
1963	7 638	1 463	82 697	69 038	68 760	46 084
1962	6 933	1 240	79 150	66 085	66 101	44 608
1961	5 543	1 134	75 961	63 421	64 534	42 863
1960	6 675	1 194	73 858	61 671	63 210	41 171
1959*	5 591	1 137	71 354	59 454	61 715	40 879
1958	4 258	877	68 296	56 890	58 589	38 904
1957	6 113	1 107	67 125	55 918	56 954	37 594
1956	5 816	1 104	65 148	54 211	55 149	36 128
1955	7 920	1 249	62 689	52 145	52 565	34 319
1954	5 559	1 042	58 505	48 468	49 118	31 670
1953	6 117	1 206	56 217	46	47 381	30 384
1952	4 321	1 218	53 262	43 823	45 037	28 735
1951	5 338	1 427	51 913	42 688	42 473	26 910
1950	6 666	1 337	49 162	40 339	39 860	25 037
1949	5 119	1 134	44 690	36 458	36 440	23 645
1948	3 909	1 376	41 086	33 355	34 329	22 149
1947	3 558	1 239	37 841	30 849	31 680	20 864
1946	2 149	941	34 373	28 217	28 876	19 502
1945	70	656	31 035	25 797	22 046	14 023
1944	0.6	738	30 479	25 566	19 292	11 805
1943	0.1	700	30 888	36 009	18 642	11 424
1942	223	819	33 004	27 973	22 438	[3]14 974
1941	3 780	1 061	34 894	29 624	26 429	18 502

[1]1960–2005 data from Ward's *Motor Vehicle Facts and Figures 2006*, p. 3.
[2]A substantial portion of the number of trucks and buses consists of chassis only. Includes trucks under 10,000 pounds gross vehicle weight rating (GVWR), such as compact and conventional pickups, sport utility vehicles, minivans, and vans, and trucks and buses over 10,000 pounds GVWR.
[3]Beginning 1942, includes travel by military vehicles.
* = First year for which figures include Alaska and Hawaii.

Table 13-6. Motor Vehicle Sales from U.S. Factories, Motor Vehicle Registrations, and Motor Fuel Usage Consumption, 1900–2004—*Continued*

(Number in thousands, millions of gallons.)

Year	Motor-vehicle factory sales[1] (thousands)		Motor-vehicle registration (thousands)		Motor-fuel consumption (millions of gallons)	
	Number of passenger cars	Number of motor trucks and buses[2]	Total	Automobiles	Total	Passenger vehicles
1940	3 717	755	32 453	27 466	24 038	16 759
1939	2 888	700	31 010	26 226	22 571	15 826
1938	2 020	489	29 814	25 250	21 311	15 069
1937	3 929	891	30 059	25 467	21 115	15 018
1936	3 679	782	28 507	24 183	19 561	14 026
1935	3 274	697	26 546	22 258	17 637	...
1934	2 161	576	25 262	21 545	16 557	...
1933	1 560	329	24 159	20 657	15 367	...
1932	1 104	228	24 391	20 901	15 427	...
1931	1 948	432	26 094	22 396	16 621	...
1930	2 787	575	26 750	23 035	15 777	...
1929	4 455	882	26 705	23 121	15 051	...
1928	3 775	583	24 689	21 362	13 090	...
1927	2 936	465	23 303	20 193	11 936	...
1926	3 692	609	22 200	19 268	10 552	...
1925	3 735	531	20 068	17 481	9 143	...
1924	3 186	417	17 613	15 436	7 809	...
1923	3 625	409	15 102	13 253	6 313	...
1922	2 274	270	12 274	10 704	5 014	...
1921	1 468	148	10 494	9 212	4 064	...
1920	1 906	322	9 239	8 132	3 448	...
1919	1 652	225	7 577	6 679	2 747	...
1918	943	227	6 160	5 555	...	...
1917	1 746	128	5 118	4 727	...	...
1916	1 526	92	3 618	3 368	...	...
1915	896	74	2 491	2 332	...	...
1914	548	25	1 763	1 664	...	...
1913	462	24	1 258	1 190	...	...
1912	356	22	944	902	...	...
1911	199	11	640	619	...	...
1910	181	6	468	548	...	...
1909	124	3	312	306	...	...
1908	64	1.5	198	194	...	...
1907	43	1.0	143	140	...	...
1906	33	0.8	108	106	...	...
1905	24	0.7	79	77	...	...
1904	22	0.7	55	54	...	...
1903	11	...	33	33	...	...
1902	9	...	23	23	...	...
1901	7	...	15	15	...	...
1900	4	...	8	8	...	...

Source: U.S. Department of Transportation, Bureau of Transportation Statistics. U.S. Census Bureau.
[1] 1960–2005 data from Ward's *Motor Vehicle Facts and Figures 2006*, p. 3.
[2] A substantial portion of the number of trucks and buses consists of chassis only. Includes trucks under 10,000 pounds gross vehicle weight rating (GVWR), such as compact and conventional pickups, sport utility vehicles, minivans, and vans, and trucks and buses over 10,000 pounds GVWR.
... = Not available.

Table 13-7. Miles of Travel by Motor Vehicles, 1921–2005

(Million vehicle-miles.)

Year	Total travel, all motor vehicles	Passenger cars[1]	Trucks and combinations	Average miles per vehicle	
				Passenger cars	Trucks alone
2005	2 989 807	1 689 965	1 282 426	. . .	. . .
2004	2 964 788	1 699 890	1 247 975	12 500	27 700
2003	2 890 450	1 672 079	1 202 011	12 300	28 100
2002	2 855 508	1 658 474	1 180 637	12 200	27 100
2001	2 797 287	1 628 332	1 152 239	11 800	26 600
2000	2 746 925	1 600 287	1 128 579	11 900	25 700
1999	2 691 056	1 569 100	1 103 710	11 900	26 000
1998	2 631 522	1 549 577	1 064 655	11 800	25 400
1997	2 561 695	1 502 556	1 042 216	11 600	27 000
1996	2 485 848	1 469 854	999 511	11 300	26 100
1995	2 422 696	1 438 294	968 185	11 200	26 500
1994	2 357 588	1 406 089	934 850	10 800	25 800
1993	2 296 378	1 374 709	905 638	10 500	26 300
1992	2 247 151	1 371 569	860 247	10 600	25 400
1991	2 172 050	1 358 185	798 937	10 300	24 200
1990	2 144 362	1 408 266	720 813	10 300	23 600
1989	2 096 000	1 412 000	679 000	10 200	22 900
1988	2 025 000	1 380 000	639 000	10 000	22 500
1987	1 921 000	1 325 000	591 000	9 700	23 300
1986	1 834 000	1 780 000	551 000	9 500	22 100
1985	1 774 826	1 246 798	514 465	9 400	20 600
1984	1 720 000	1 236 000	480 000	9 200	22 600
1983	1 653 000	1 204 000	444 000	9 100	21 100
1982	1 592 000	1 172 000	417 000	9 100	19 900
1981	1 556 000	1 144 000	408 000	8 900	19 000
1980	1 635 786	1 111 596	399 426	8 800	18 700
1979	1 529 000	1 122 000	401 000	9 100	18 500
1978	1 548 000	1 154 000	385 000	9 500	18 000
1977	1 477 000	1 116 000	346 000	9 500	16 700
1976	1 412 000	1 084 000	312 000	9 400	15 400
1975	1 408 994	1 033 950	282 030	9 300	15 200
1974	1 286 000	1 013 000	262 000	9 200	15 000
1973	1 309 000	1 051 000	256 000	9 900	15 400
1972	1 268 000	1 026 000	229 000	10 200	14 800
1971	1 186 300	970 000	204 000	10 100	14 100
1970	1 171 939	916 700	185 501	10 000	13 600
1969	1 070 575	885 000	172 000	9 900	13 500
1968	1 015 649	850 000	161 000	9 900	12 400
1967	961 553	811 000	149 000	9 800	12 800
1966	930 497	777 000	143 000	9 700	12 500
1965	887 812	722 696	160 434	9 600	10 900
1964	846 500	696 000	146 000	9 700	10 400
1963	805 423	662 000	139 000	9 600	10 400
1962	766 852	627 000	135 000	9 500	10 600
1961	737 535	604 000	129 000	9 500	10 500
1960	718 762	587 012	127 405	9 500	10 700
1959*	700 478	572 000	12 500	9 600	10 700
1958	664 653	540 000	120 000	9 500	10 800
1957	647 004	523 000	118 000	9 300	10 800
1956	631 161	515 000	112 000	9 500	10 500
1955	605 646	493 000	109 000	9 400	10 600
1954	561 963	453 000	105 000	9 300	10 700
1953	544 433	435 000	105 000	9 400	11 000
1952	513 581	410 000	99 000	9 400	10 800
1951	491 093	392 000	95 000	9 200	10 500
1950	458 246	365 000	89 000	9 100	10 300
1949	424 461	342 000	78 000	9 400	9 700
1948	397 957	319 000	74 000	9 600	9 900
1947	370 894	301 000	66 000	9 800	9 600
1946	340 880	281 000	56 000	10 000	9 300
1945	250 173	200 000	46 000	7 800	9 100
1944	212 713	167 000	42 000	6 500	8 900
1943	208 192	162 000	43 000	6 200	9 000
1942	268 224	218 000	47 000	7 800	9 500
1941	333 612	276 000	55 000	9 300	10 600

[1]U.S. Department of Transportation, Federal Highway Administration (FHWA), provides data separately for passenger car and motorcycle in its annual *Highway Statistics* series. However, the 1995 summary report provides updated data for passenger car and motorcycle combined. Passenger car figures in this table were computed by U.S. Department of Transportation, Bureau of Transportation Statistics, by subtracting the most current motorcycle figures from the aggregate passenger car and motorcycle figures.
* = First year for which figures include Alaska and Hawaii.

Table 13-7. Miles of Travel by Motor Vehicles, 1921–2005—*Continued*

(Million vehicle-miles.)

Year	Total travel, all motor vehicles	Passenger cars[1]	Trucks and combinations	Average miles per vehicle	
				Passenger cars	Trucks alone
1940	302 188	250 000	50 000	9 100	10 200
1939	285 402	236 000	47 000	9 000	10 100
1938	271 177	224 000	45 000	8 900	10 000
1937	270 110	224 000	44 000	8 800	9 800
1936	252 128	209 000	41 000	8 600	9 600
1935	228 568	...	...	...	...
1934	215 563	...	...	...	...
1933	200 642	...	...	...	...
1932	200 517	...	...	...	...
1931	216 151	...	...	...	...
1930	206 320	...	...	...	...
1929	197 720	...	...	...	...
1928	172 856	...	...	...	...
1927	158 453	...	...	...	...
1926	140 735	...	...	...	...
1925	122 346	...	...	...	...
1924	104 838	...	...	...	...
1923	84 995	...	...	...	...
1922	67 697	...	...	...	...
1921	55 027	...	...	...	...

Source: U.S. Department of Transportation, Bureau of Transportation Statistics. U.S. Census Bureau. U.S. Federal Highway Administration.
Note: In July 1997, the Federal Highway Administration (FHWA) published revised vehicle-miles data for the highway modes for many years. The major change reflected the reassignment of some vehicles from the passenger car category to the other 2-axle 4-tire vehicle category. This category was calculated prior to rounding. Passenger cars exclude vans, pickups, and SUVs, which are included along with trucks and combinations.
[1]U.S. Department of Transportation, Federal Highway Administration (FHWA), provides data separately for passenger car and motorcycle in its annual *Highway Statistics* series. However, the 1995 summary report provides updated data for passenger car and motorcycle combined. Passenger car figures in this table were computed by U.S. Department of Transportation, Bureau of Transportation Statistics, by subtracting the most current motorcycle figures from the aggregate passenger car and motorcycle figures.
. . . = Not available.

Table 13-8. Motor Vehicle Deaths and Death Rates, 1913–2004

(Rate per 100,000 population.)

Year	Number[1]	Rate[2,3]
2004	46 200	14.5
2003	44 100	14.8
2002	45 400	14.9
2001	43 800	14.8
2000	43 400	14.9
1999	42 400	15.3
1998	43 500	15.4
1997	43 500	15.7
1996	43 600	15.9
1995	43 400	15.9
1994	42 500	15.6
1993	41 900	15.6
1992	43 500	15.4
1991	46 800	16.5
1990	46 800	17.9
1989	47 100	18.4
1988	49 100	19.2
1987	48 300	19.1
1986	47 900	19.1
1985	45 900	18.4
1984	46 200	18.7
1983	44 600	18.2
1982	46 000	19.0
1981	51 400	21.5
1980	53 200	22.5
1979	53 500	22.8
1978	52 400	22.7
1977	49 500	22.1
1976	47 000	21.2
1975	45 900	20.7
1974	46 400	21.4
1973	55 500	25.8
1972	56 300	26.2
1971	54 000	26.5
1970	54 633	25.3
1969	55 791	27.6
1968	55 200	28.8
1967	52 924	27.8
1966	53 041	28.3
1965	49 163	26.5
1964	47 700	26.1
1963	43 564	24.3
1962	40 804	23.1
1961	38 091	22.0
1960	38 137	22.4
1959	37 910	22.7
1958	36 981	22.5
1957	38 702	24.1
1956	39 628	25.1
1955	38 426	24.6
1954	35 586	23.0
1953	37 955	24.9
1952	37 794	25.0
1951	36 996	24.6
1950	34 763	23.3
1949	31 701	21.5
1948	32 259	22.3
1947	32 697	23.0
1946	33 411	24.0
1945	28 076	21.4
1944	24 282	18.3
1943	23 823	17.7
1938–1942 avg.	33 549	25.5
1933–1937 avg.	36 313	29.3
1928–1932 avg.	30 900	26.4
1923–1927 avg.	21 700	19.6
1918–1922 avg.	12 500	12.3
1913–1917 avg.	6 700	7.0

Source: U.S. Census Bureau. U.S. National Highway Traffic Safety Administration.
[1]Deaths that occur within 1 year of accident. National Safety Council. *Injury Facts* ©.
[2]Within 30 days of accident. Based on 30-day definition of traffic deaths.
[3]Based on populations standardized for age (base 1940) to remove influence of changes in age distribution.

Table 13-9. Motor Vehicle Accidents—Number and Deaths, by Type of Accident, 1913–2004

(Number, rate.)

| Year | Total motor vehicle accidents[2] (thousands) | Traffic deaths[1] | | Collision accidents | | | Traffic death rates[4] | |
		Total[3]	Non-collision accidents	With other motor vehicles	With pedestrians	With fixed objects	Per 10,000 motor vehicles	Per 100 million vehicle miles
2004	10 900	46 200	5 200	20 600	5 900	13 300	1.4	1.8
2003	11 800	44 100	5 100	19 800	5 700	12 400	1.5	1.9
2002	18 300	45 400	5 300	19 200	6 100	13 600	1.5	1.9
2001	12 500	43 800	4 900	18 800	6 100	12 800	1.5	1.9
2000	13 400	43 400	4 800	19 100	5 900	12 300	1.5	1.9
1999	11 400	42 400	4 700	18 600	6 100	11 800	1.6	2.0
1998	12 700	43 500	4 600	19 700	5 900	12 200	1.6	2.0
1997	13 800	43 500	4 400	19 900	5 900	12 000	2.1	1.6
1996	11 200	43 600	4 600	19 600	6 100	12 100	1.7	2.1
1995	10 700	43 400	4 400	19 000	6 400	12 100	2.1	1.7
1994	11 200	42 500	4 400	18 900	6 300	11 500	2.1	1.7
1993	11 900	41 900	4 200	18 300	6 400	11 500	2.1	1.7
1992	10 000	41 000	4 100	17 600	6 300	11 700	2.1	1.7
1991	11 300	43 500	4 700	18 200	6 600	12 600	2.2	1.9
1990	11 500	46 800	4 900	19 900	7 300	13 100	2.4	2.1
1989	12 800	47 100	5 000	20 000	7 600	12 600	2.3	2.2
1988	20 600	49 100	5 300	20 900	7 700	13 400	2.5	2.3
1987	20 800	48 300	5 200	20 700	7 500	13 200	2.5	2.4
1986	17 700	47 900	13 100	20 800	8 900	3 300	2.5	2.5
1985	19 300	45 900	12 600	19 900	8 500	3 200	2.6	2.5
1984	18 800	46 200	12 600	20 300	8 600	3 000	2.8	2.6
1983	18 300	44 600	12 200	19 200	8 200	3 100	2.7	2.6
1982	18 100	46 000	12 600	19 800	8 400	3 200	2.9	2.8
1981	18 000	51 400	14 200	22 200	9 400	3 600	3.4	3.2
1980	17 900	53 200	14 700	23 000	9 700	3 700	3.5	3.3
1979	18 100	53 500	15 200	22 200	9 700	3 500	3.5	3.3
1978	18 300	52 400	14 500	22 400	9 600	3 600	3.5	3.3
1977	17 600	49 500	13 700	20 200	9 100	3 400	3.4	3.3
1976	16 800	47 000	13 000	20 100	8 600	3 200	3.4	3.3
1975	16 500	45 900	12 700	19 500	8 400	3 100	3.4	3.4
1974	15 600	46 400	12 800	19 700	8 500	3 100	3.6	3.5
1973	16 600	55 500	15 600	23 600	10 200	3 800	4.4	4.1
1972	17 000	56 300	15 800	23 900	10 300	3 900	4.4	4.3
1971	16 400	54 000	13 700	23 300	10 600	7 100	4.8	4.7
1970	16 000	54 633	[5]15 400	23 200	9 900	[5]3 800	4.9	4.9
1969	15 500	55 791	15 700	23 700	10 100	3 900	5.2	5.2
1968	14 600	54 862	17 400	22 400	9 900	2 700	5.3	5.4
1967	13 700	52 924	16 700	22 000	9 400	2 350	5.4	5.5
1966	13 600	53 041	16 300	22 200	9 400	2 500	5.5	5.7
1965	13 200	49 163	14 900	20 800	8 900	2 200	5.4	5.5
1964	12 300	47 700	14 600	19 600	9 000	2 100	5.5	5.6
1963	11 500	43 564	13 800	17 600	8 200	1 900	5.2	5.4
1962	11 000	40 804	12 900	16 400	7 900	1 750	5.1	5.3
1961	10 400	38 091	12 200	14 700	7 650	1 700	5.0	5.2
1960	10 400	38 137	11 900	14 800	7 850	1 700	5.1	5.3
1959*	10 200	37 910	11 800	14 900	7 850	1 600	5.3	5.4
1958	10 000	36 981	11 600	14 200	7 650	1 650	5.4	5.6
1957	10 200	38 702	11 800	15 400	7 850	1 700	5.7	6.0
1956	10 300	39 628	13 000	15 200	7 900	1 600	6.1	6.3
1955	9 900	38 426	12 100	14 500	8 200	1 600	6.1	6.3
1954	9 550	35 586	11 500	12 800	8 000	1 500	6.1	6.3
1953	9 900	37 955	12 200	13 400	8 750	1 500	6.7	7.0
1952	9 500	37 794	11 900	13 500	8 900	1 450	7.1	7.4
1951	9 400	36 996	11 200	13 100	9 150	1 400	7.1	7.5
1950	8 300	34 763	10 600	11 650	9 000	1 300	7.1	7.6
1949	7 600	31 701	9 100	10 500	8 800	1 100	7.1	7.5
1948	8 200	32 259	8 950	10 200	9 950	1 000	7.9	8.1
1947	8 400	32 697	8 800	9 900	10 450	1 000	8.6	8.8
1946	6 150	33 411	8 900	9 400	11 600	950	9.7	9.8
1945	5 500	28 076	6 600	7 150	11 000	800	9.1	11.2
1944	4 800	24 282	5 600	5 700	9 900	700	8.0	11.4
1943	4 400	23 823	5 690	5 300	9 900	700	7.7	11.4
1942	5 200	28 309	6 740	7 300	10 650	850	8.6	10.6
1941	7 000	39 969	9 450	12 500	13 550	1 350	11.5	12.0

[1]Totals may not equal sums of various types because totals for most types are estimated, and these have been rounded.
[2]Covers only accidents occurring on the road. Data are estimated. Year-to-year comparisons should be made with caution.
[3]Deaths that occur within 1 year of accident. Includes collision categories not shown separately.
[4]Within 30 days of accident. Based on 30-day definition of traffic deaths.
[5]Data based on improved reporting procedure; therefore, not entirely comparable with previous years.
* = First year for which figures include Alaska and Hawaii.

Table 13-9. Motor Vehicle Accidents—Number and Deaths, by Type of Accident, 1913–2004—*Continued*

(Number, rate.)

Year	Total motor vehicle accidents[2] (thousands)	Traffic deaths[1]					Traffic death rates[4]	
		Total[3]	Non-collision accidents	Collision accidents			Per 10,000 motor vehicles	Per 100 million vehicle miles
				With other motor vehicles	With pedestrians	With fixed objects		
1940	6 100	34 501	7 800	10 100	12 700	1 100	10.6	11.4
1939	5 700	32 386	7 900	8 700	12 400	1 000	10.4	11.4
1938	5 800	32 582	7 350	8 900	12 850	940	10.9	12.0
1937	7 000	39 643	9 690	10 320	15 500	1 160	13.2	14.7
1936	...	38 089	9 410	9 500	15 250	1 060	13.4	15.1
1935	...	36 369	9 720	8 750	14 350	1 010	13.7	15.9
1934	...	36 101	9 820	8 110	14 480	1 040	14.3	16.8
1933	...	31 363	8 680	6 470	12 840	900	13.0	15.6
1932	...	29 500	7 000	6 070	11 490	800	12.2	16.1
1931	...	33 700	7 850	6 820	13 370	870	13.0	17.0
1930	...	32 900	8 730	5 880	12 900	720	12.4	17.4
1929	...	31 200	8 430	5 400	12 250	620	11.8	17.3
1928	...	28 000	7 360	4 310	11 420	540	11.4	17.4
1927	...	25 800	7 280	3 430	10 820	500	11.2	17.7
1926	...	23 400	...	...	...	...	10.6	18.0
1925	...	21 900	...	...	...	...	11.0	17.9
1924	...	19 400	...	...	...	...	11.0	...
1923	...	18 400	...	...	...	...	12.2	...
1922	...	15 300	...	...	...	...	...	...
1921	...	13 900	...	...	...	...	...	...
1920	...	12 500	...	...	...	...	...	...
1919	...	11 200	...	...	...	...	...	...
1918	...	10 700	...	...	...	...	...	...
1917	...	10 200	...	...	...	...	...	...
1916	...	8 200	...	...	...	...	...	...
1915	...	6 600	...	...	...	...	...	...
1914	...	4 700	...	...	...	...	...	...
1913	...	4 200	...	...	...	...	...	...

Source: U.S. Census Bureau. U.S. National Highway Traffic Safety Administration. National Safety Council, *Injury Facts.*
[1]Totals may not equal sums of various types because totals for most types are estimated, and these have been rounded.
[2]Covers only accidents occurring on the road. Data are estimated. Year-to-year comparisons should be made with caution.
[3]Deaths that occur within 1 year of accident. Includes collision categories not shown separately.
[4]Within 30 days of accident. Based on 30-day definition of traffic deaths.
. . . = Not available.

Table 13-10. Domestic Motor Fuel Consumption, by Type of Vehicle, 1970–2003

(Billions of gallons, miles per gallon. Minus sign (−) indicates a decrease.)

Year	Annual fuel consumption (billion gallons)					Average mileage per gallon				
	All vehicles[1]	Annual percent change[2]	Cars[1]	Buses[3]	Vans, pickups, SUVs	Trucks[4]	All vehicles[1]	Cars[1]	Buses[3]	Vans, pickups, SUVs	Trucks[4]
2003	169.6	0.5	74.6	1.0	56.3	37.6	17.0	22.3	6.9	17.7	5.7
2002	168.7	3.2	75.5	1.0	55.2	36.8	16.9	22.0	6.8	17.5	5.8
2001	163.5	0.6	73.6	1.0	53.5	35.2	17.1	22.1	6.9	17.6	5.9
2000	162.5	0.7	73.1	1.1	52.9	35.2	16.9	21.9	6.8	17.4	5.8
1999	161.4	3.9	73.2	1.1	52.8	33.9	16.7	21.4	6.7	17.0	6.0
1998	155.4	3.3	71.7	1.1	50.5	32.0	16.9	21.6	6.7	17.2	6.1
1997	150.4	2.0	69.9	1.0	49.4	29.9	17.0	21.5	6.7	17.2	6.4
1996	147.4	2.5	69.2	1.0	47.4	29.6	16.9	21.2	6.6	17.2	6.2
1995	143.8	2.1	68.1	1.0	45.6	29.0	16.8	21.1	6.6	17.3	6.1
1994	140.8	2.5	68.1	1.0	44.1	27.7	16.7	20.8	6.6	17.3	6.1
1993	137.3	3.3	67.2	0.9	42.9	26.2	16.7	20.6	6.6	17.4	6.1
1992	132.9	3.3	65.6	0.9	40.9	25.5	16.9	21.0	6.6	17.3	6.0
1991	128.6	−1.7	64.5	0.9	38.2	25.0	16.9	21.2	6.7	17.0	6.0
1990	130.8	−0.8	69.8	0.9	35.6	24.5	16.4	20.3	6.4	16.1	6.0
1989	131.9	1.4	74.1	0.9	33.3	23.5	15.9	18.0	6.0	16.1	6.1
1988	130.1	2.0	73.5	0.9	32.7	22.9	15.6	18.8	5.8	15.4	6.0
1987	127.5	1.8	73.5	0.9	30.6	22.5	15.1	18.0	5.8	14.9	5.9
1986	125.2	3.2	73.4	0.9	29.1	21.9	14.7	17.4	5.3	14.6	5.8
1985	121.3	2.2	71.7	0.8	27.4	21.4	14.6	17.5	5.4	14.3	5.8
1984	118.7	2.2	70.8	0.8	25.6	21.4	14.5	17.4	5.7	14.0	5.7
1983	116.1	2.4	70.5	0.9	23.9	20.8	14.2	17.1	5.9	13.7	5.6
1982	113.4	−1.0	69.3	1.0	22.7	20.4	14.1	16.9	5.9	13.5	5.5
1981	114.5	−0.4	69.3	1.1	23.7	20.4	13.6	16.5	5.9	12.5	5.3
1980	115.0	−5.9	70.2	1.0	23.8	20.0	13.3	16.0	6.0	12.2	5.4
1970	92.3	4.8	67.8	0.8	12.3	11.3	12.0	13.5	5.5	10.0	5.5

Source: U.S. Census Bureau. *Statistical Abstract of the United States: 2007.* U.S. Department of Transportation, Federal Highway Administration.
Comprises all fuel types used for propulsion of vehicles under state motor fuels laws. Excludes federal purchases for military use.
[1]Motorcycles included with cars through 1994; thereafter in total, not shown separately.
[2]Change from immediate prior year.
[3]Includes school buses.
[4]Includes combinations.

Table 13-11. Average Cost of Owning and Operating an Automobile, 1975–2005

(Dollars, percent.)

Year	Average total cost per mile (current cents)					Average total cost per 15,000 miles (current dollars)		
	Total cost	Gas[1]	Gas as a percent of total cost	Maintenance[2]	Tires	Total cost	Variable cost	Fixed cost[3]
2005	52.2	9.5	18.2	4.9	0.7	7,834	2,265	5,569
2004	56.2	6.5	11.6	5.4	0.7	8,431	1,890	6,541
2003	51.7	7.2	13.9	4.1	1.8	7,754	1,965	5,789
2002	50.2	5.9	11.8	4.1	1.8	7 534	1 770	5 764
2001	51.0	7.9	15.5	3.9	1.8	7 654	2 040	5 614
2000	49.1	6.9	14.1	3.6	1.7	7 363	1 829	5 534
1999	47.0	5.6	11.9	3.3	1.7	7 050	1 590	5 460
1998	46.1	6.2	13.4	3.1	1.4	6 908	1 605	5 303
1997	44.8	6.6	14.7	2.8	1.4	6 723	1 620	5 103
1996	42.6	5.6	13.1	2.8	1.2	6 389	1 440	4 949
1995	41.2	5.8	14.1	2.6	1.2	6 185	1 440	4 745
1994	39.4	5.6	14.2	2.5	1.0	5 916	1 365	4 551
1993	38.7	5.9	15.2	2.4	0.9	5 804	1 380	4 424
1992	38.8	5.9	15.2	2.2	0.9	5 824	1 350	4 474
1991	37.3	6.6	17.7	2.2	0.9	5 601	1 455	4 146
1990	33.0	5.4	16.4	2.1	0.9	4 954	1 260	3 694
1985	23.2	5.6	24.0	1.2	0.7	3 484	1 113	2 371
1980	21.2	5.9	27.9	1.1	0.6	3 176	1 143	2 033
1975	14.4	4.8	33.4	1.0	0.7	2 154	968	1 186

Source: U.S. Department of Transportation, Bureau of Transportation Statistics. *National Transportation Statistics 2005.* American Automobile Association. *Your Driving Costs.*
Note: All figures reflect the average cost of operating a vehicle 15,000 miles per year in stop and go conditions. Methodological changes in 1985 and 2004 make it difficult to compare costs before and after those years.
Prior to 1985, the cost figures are for a mid-sized, current model, American car equipped with a variety of standard and optional accessories. After 1985, the cost figures represent a composite of three current model American cars. The 2004 fuel costs are based on average late-2003 U.S. prices from AAA's Fuel Gauge Report: www.fuelgaugereport.com. Insurance figures are based on a full-coverage policy for a married 47-year-old male with a good driving record living in a small city and commuting three to ten miles daily to work. The policy includes $100,000/$300,000 level coverage with a $500 deductible for collision coverage and a $100 deductible for comprehensive coverage. Depreciation costs are based on the difference between new-vehicle purchase price and its estimated trade-in-value at the end of five years. American Automobile Association analysis covers vehicles equipped with standard and optional accessories including automatic transmission, air conditioning, power steering, power disc brakes, AM/FM stereo, driver- and passenger-side air bags, anti-lock brakes, cruise control, tilt steering wheel, tinted glass, emissions equipment, and rear-window defogger.
[1]Prior to 2004, data include oil cost.
[2]Beginning in 2004, data include oil cost.
[3]Fixed costs (ownership costs) include insurance, license, registration, taxes, depreciation, and finance charges.

Table 13-12. Motor Vehicle Sales and Inventories, 1967–2006

Year	Retail sales of new passenger cars						Retail inventories of new domestic passenger cars (thousands of units, end of period)		
	Thousands of units, not seasonally adjusted			Millions of units, seasonally adjusted annual rate			Not seasonally adjusted	Seasonally adjusted	Inventory to sales ratio
	Total	Domestic	Imports	Total	Domestic	Imports			
2006	7 781	5 436	2 345	7.8	5.4	2.3	1 036	1 177	2.5
2005	7 667	5 480	2 187	7.7	5.5	2.2	932	1 069	2.3
2004	7 505	5 350	2 155	7.5	5.4	2.2	1 033	1 163	2.4
2003	7 615	5 527	2 087	7.6	5.5	2.1	1 131	1 238	2.7
2002	8 102	5 871	2 231	8.1	5.9	2.2	1 148	1 242	2.5
2001	8 422	6 323	2 099	8.4	6.3	2.1	956	984	2.3
2000	8 852	6 833	2 019	8.9	6.8	2.0	1 377	1 398	2.8
1999	8 697	6 982	1 715	8.7	7.0	1.7	1 368	1 410	2.3
1998	8 142	6 764	1 378	8.1	6.8	1.4	1 324	1 367	2.2
1997	8 273	6 906	1 366	8.3	6.9	1.4	1 330	1 342	2.2
1996	8 527	7 254	1 273	8.5	7.3	1.3	1 363	1 376	2.4
1995	8 636	7 129	1 507	8.6	7.1	1.5	1 619	1 631	2.6
1994	8 990	7 255	1 735	9.0	7.3	1.7	1 437	1 449	2.3
1993	8 518	6 734	1 784	8.5	6.7	1.8	1 365	1 377	2.4
1992	8 214	6 277	1 938	8.2	6.3	1.9	1 276	1 288	2.3
1991	8 175	6 137	2 038	8.2	6.1	2.0	1 283	1 296	2.6
1990	9 300	6 897	2 403	9.3	6.9	2.4	1 408	1 418	2.6
1989	9 777	7 078	2 699	9.8	7.1	2.7	1 669	1 687	3.1
1988	10 546	7 539	3 006	10.5	7.5	3.0	1 601	1 601	2.3
1987	10 171	7 081	3 090	10.2	7.1	3.1	1 680	1 716	2.8
1986	11 406	8 215	3 191	11.4	8.2	3.2	1 500	1 515	2.0
1985	10 978	8 205	2 774	11.0	8.2	2.8	1 630	1 619	2.5
1984	10 390	7 952	2 439	10.4	8.0	2.4	1 415	1 411	2.1
1983	9 179	6 793	2 386	9.2	6.8	2.4	1 352	1 350	2.0
1982	7 979	5 758	2 221	8.0	5.8	2.2	1 126	1 127	2.2
1981	8 534	6 209	2 326	8.5	6.2	2.3	1 471	1 495	3.6
1980	8 982	6 581	2 400	9.0	6.6	2.4	1 449	1 440	2.7
1979	10 559	8 230	2 329	10.6	8.2	2.3	1 691	1 667	2.6
1978	11 164	9 164	2 000	11.2	9.2	2.0	1 729	1 731	2.2
1977	11 046	8 971	2 075	11.0	9.0	2.1	1 731	1 743	2.3
1976	9 994	8 492	1 502	10.0	8.5	1.5	1 465	1 494	1.9
1975	8 538	6 951	1 587	8.5	7.0	1.6	1 419	1 468	2.2
1974	8 774	7 362	1 412	8.8	7.4	1.4	1 672	1 730	3.4
1973	11 350	9 589	1 762	11.4	9.6	1.8	1 600	1 654	2.5
1972	10 873	9 253	1 621	10.9	9.3	1.6	1 311	1 379	1.7
1971	10 228	8 662	1 566	10.2	8.7	1.6	1 447	1 512	2.1
1970	8 403	7 119	1 283	8.4	7.1	1.3	1 220	1 294	3
1969	9 582	8 464	1 117	9.6	8.5	1.1	1 467	1 542	2.4
1968	9 655	8 625	1 030	9.7	8.6	1.0	1 449	1 525	2.1
1967	8 347	7 568	779	8.3	7.6	0.8	1 773	1 251	1.9

Table 13-12. Motor Vehicle Sales and Inventories, 1967–2006—*Continued*

Year	Retail sales of new trucks and buses								Unit sales of cars and light trucks (millions of units, seasonally adjusted annual rate)		
	Thousands of units, not seasonally adjusted				Millions of units, seasonally adjusted annual rate						
		0–10,000 pounds		10,001 pounds and over		0–10,000 pounds		10,001 pounds and over			
	Total	Domestic	Imports		Total	Domestic	Imports		Total	Domestic	Imports
2006	9 268.2	7 376.8	1 346.6	544.4	9.3	7.4	1.3	0.5	16.5	12.8	3.7
2005	9 777.3	8 065.4	1 215.5	496.5	9.8	8.1	1.2	0.5	16.9	13.5	3.4
2004	9 792.7	8 114.6	1 246.2	431.6	9.8	8.1	1.2	0.4	16.9	13.5	3.4
2003	9 356.9	7 801.4	1 227.2	328.4	9.4	7.8	1.2	0.3	16.6	13.3	3.3
2002	9 035.3	7 646.9	1 066.3	322.4	9.0	7.6	1.1	0.3	16.8	13.5	3.3
2001	9 046.3	7 718.4	977.8	350.1	9.0	7.7	1.0	0.3	17.1	14.0	3.1
2000	8 953.4	7 650.8	840.8	461.9	9.0	7.6	0.8	0.5	17.3	14.5	2.9
1999	8 784.2	7 420.0	762.9	521.3	8.7	7.4	0.8	0.5	16.9	14.4	2.5
1998	7 815.8	6 745.3	646.2	424.3	7.8	6.7	0.6	0.4	15.5	13.5	2.0
1997	7 217.8	6 270.4	571.2	376.2	7.2	6.3	0.6	0.4	15.1	13.2	1.9
1996	6 921.8	6 131.8	430.9	359.1	6.9	6.1	0.4	0.4	15.1	13.4	1.7
1995	6 469.8	5 690.9	390.5	388.4	6.5	5.7	0.4	0.4	14.7	12.8	1.9
1994	6 407.3	5 658.2	396.3	352.8	6.4	5.7	0.4	0.4	15.0	12.9	2.1
1993	5 667.8	5 000.5	364.5	302.8	5.7	5.0	0.4	0.3	13.9	11.7	2.1
1992	4 892.2	4 247.0	395.9	249.3	4.9	4.2	0.4	0.2	12.9	10.5	2.3
1991	4 355.4	3 605.6	528.8	221.0	4.4	3.6	0.5	0.2	12.3	9.7	2.6
1990	4 837.0	3 956.8	602.7	277.5	4.8	4.0	0.6	0.3	13.9	10.9	3.0
1989	5 055.9	4 113.6	630.3	312.0	5.1	4.1	0.6	0.3	14.5	11.2	3.3
1988	5 231.9	4 199.7	697.9	334.3	5.2	4.2	0.7	0.3	15.4	11.7	3.7
1987	4 991.5	3 792.0	912.2	287.3	5.0	3.8	0.9	0.3	14.9	10.9	4.0
1986	4 912.1	3 671.4	967.2	273.5	4.9	3.7	1.0	0.3	16.1	11.9	4.2
1985	4 741.7	3 618.4	828.3	295.0	4.8	3.6	0.8	0.3	15.4	11.8	3.6
1984	4 093.1	3 207.2	607.7	278.2	4.1	3.2	0.6	0.3	14.2	11.2	3.0
1983	3 117.3	2 465.2	463.3	188.8	3.1	2.5	0.5	0.2	12.1	9.3	2.8
1982	2 562.8	1 967.5	410.4	184.9	2.6	2.0	0.4	0.2	10.4	7.7	2.6
1981	2 255.6	1 581.7	447.6	226.3	2.3	1.6	0.4	0.2	10.6	7.8	2.8
1980	2 487.4	1 731.1	484.6	271.7	2.5	1.7	0.5	0.3	11.2	8.3	2.9
1979	3 589.7	2 730.2	469.4	390.1	3.6	2.7	0.5	0.4	13.8	11.0	2.8
1978	4 256.8	3 481.1	335.9	439.8	4.2	3.5	0.3	0.4	15.0	12.6	2.3
1977	3 813.0	3 112.8	323.1	377.1	3.8	3.1	0.3	0.4	14.5	12.1	2.4
1976	3 300.5	2 738.3	237.5	324.7	3.3	2.7	0.2	0.3	13.0	11.2	1.7
1975	2 350.9	2 052.6	...	298.3	2.4	2.1	...	0.3	10.6	9.0	1.6
1974	2 604.0	2 180.1	...	423.9	2.6	2.2	...	0.4	11.0	9.5	1.4
1973	3 005.1	2 509.4	...	495.7	3.0	2.5	...	0.5	13.9	12.1	1.8
1972	2 559.9	2 122.5	...	437.4	2.6	2.1	...	0.4	13.0	11.4	1.6
1971	2 031.9	1 693.0	...	338.9	2.0	1.7	...	0.3	11.9	10.4	1.6
1970	1 745.8	1 408.5	...	337.3	1.7	1.4	...	0.3	9.8	8.5	1.3
1969	1 935.6	1 551.1	...	384.5	1.9	1.6	...	0.4	11.1	10.0	1.1
1968	1 807.5	1 464.2	...	343.3	1.8	1.5	...	0.3	11.1	10.1	1.0
1967	1 523.5	1 193.8	...	329.7	1.5	1.2	...	0.3	9.5	8.8	0.8

Source: U.S. Bureau of Commerce, Bureau of Economic Analysis.
... = Not available.

Table 13-13. Motor Vehicle Travel, by Type of Vehicle, 1970–2004

	Vehicle miles of travel (billions)						Average annual miles per vehicle (1,000)					
		Passenger vehicles						Passenger vehicles				
Year	Total[1]	Cars[1]	Motorcycles	Buses[2]	Vans, pickups, SUVs	Trucks[3]	Total[1]	Cars[1]	Motorcycles	Buses[2]	Vans, pickups, SUVs	Trucks[3]
2004	2 963	1 705	10	6.6	1 014	227	12.2	12.5	1.7	8.3	11.0	27.7
2003	2 890	1 672	10	6.8	984	218	12.2	12.3	1.8	8.7	11.3	28.1
2002	2 856	1 658	10	6.8	966	215	12.2	12.2	1.9	9.0	11.4	27.1
2001	2 797	1 628	10	7.1	943	209	11.9	11.8	2.0	9.4	11.2	26.6
2000	2 747	1 600	11	7.6	923	206	12.2	11.9	2.4	10.2	11.7	25.7
1999	2 691	1 569	11	7.7	901	203	12.2	11.9	2.5	10.5	12.0	26.0
1998	2 632	1 550	10	7.0	868	196	12.2	11.8	2.7	9.8	12.2	25.4
1997	2 562	1 503	10	6.8	851	191	12.1	11.6	2.6	9.8	12.1	27.0
1996	2 486	1 470	10	6.6	817	183	11.8	11.3	2.6	9.4	11.8	26.1
1995	2 423	1 438	10	6.4	790	178	11.8	11.2	2.5	9.4	12.0	26.5
1994	2 358	1 416	...	6.4	765	170	11.7	10.8	...	9.6	12.2	25.8
1993	2 296	1 385	...	6.1	746	160	11.6	10.5	...	9.4	12.4	26.3
1992	2 247	1 381	...	5.8	707	153	11.6	10.6	...	9.0	12.4	25.4
1991	2 172	1 367	...	5.8	649	150	11.3	10.3	...	9.1	12.2	24.2
1990	2 144	1 418	...	5.7	575	146	11.1	10.3	...	9.1	11.9	23.6
1989	2 096	1 412	...	5.7	536	143	10.9	10.2	...	9.1	11.7	22.9
1988	2 026	1 380	...	5.5	502	138	10.7	10.0	...	8.9	11.5	22.5
1987	1 921	1 325	...	5.3	457	134	10.5	9.7	...	8.9	11.1	23.3
1986	1 835	1 280	...	4.7	424	127	10.1	9.5	...	7.9	10.8	22.1
1985	1 775	1 256	...	4.5	391	124	10.0	9.4	...	7.5	10.5	20.6
1984	1 720	1 236	...	4.6	358	122	10.0	9.2	...	8.0	11.2	22.6
1983	1 653	1 204	...	5.2	328	116	9.8	9.1	...	8.9	10.5	21.1
1982	1 595	1 172	...	5.8	306	111	9.6	9.1	...	10.4	10.3	19.9
1981	1 555	1 144	...	6.2	296	109	9.5	8.9	...	11.5	10.2	19.0
1980	1 527	1 122	...	6.1	291	108	9.5	8.8	...	11.5	10.4	18.7
1975	1 328	1 040	...	6.1	201	81	9.6	9.3	...	13.1	9.8	15.2
1970	1 110	920	...	4.5	123	62	10.0	10.0	...	12.0	8.7	13.6

Source: U.S. Census Bureau. *Statistical Abstract of the United States: 2007.* U.S. Department of Transportation, Federal Highway Administration.
Note: Travel estimates based on automatic vehicle classification data.
[1]Motorcycles included with cars through 1994.
[2]Includes school buses.
[3]Includes combinations.
. . . = Not available.

Table 13-14. Class I Intercity Motor Carriers of Passengers, 1990–2002

(Number, dollars.)

Year	Number of intercity carriers[1]	Operating revenue (millions of dollars)			Operating expenses (millions of dollars)	Operating income (millions of dollars)	Revenue passengers (millions)			Average fare, intercity regular route (dollars)
		Number	Intercity regular route	Other			Total	Intercity regular route passengers	Other passengers	
2002	12	1 070	907	163	1 046	25	32	30	2	30.11
2001	12	1 076	917	158	1 039	36	32	30	2	30.27
2000	12	1 088	920	168	1 035	53	33	31	2	29.46
1999	14	1 014	864	150	1 014	0.2	43	33	10	26.16
1998	15	999	860	139	947	52	47	37	10	23.14
1997	17	1 000	834	165	948	52	52	41	12	20.57
1996	17	912	771	141	878	33	37	34	4	22.85
1995	20	917	767	150	899	18	43	38	5	20.10
1994	20	870	718	152	919	−48	41	36	4	19.77
1993	21	928	747	182	880	48	40	35	5	21.32
1990	21	943	739	204	1 026	−83	44	37	7	20.22

Source: U.S. Census Bureau. *Statistical Abstract of the United States: 2004–2005.* U.S. Department of Transportation, Bureau of Transportation Statistics.
[1]Excludes carriers preponderantly in local or suburban service and carriers engaged in transportation of both property and passengers.

Table 13-15. Public Transit Equipment, Passengers, and Passenger Revenue, 1922–2004

(Number, dollars.)

Year	Heavy rail[1]	Commuter rail[2]	Light rail[3]	Trolley buses[4]	Motor buses[5]	Total revenue and nonrevenue passengers (millions)	Passenger revenue (millions of dollars)	Employees (thousands)	Employee payroll (millions of dollars)
2004	10 858	6 228	1 622	597	81 033	9 575	9 775	359	12 487
2003	10 754	5 959	1 482	672	77 328	9 434	9 149	351	11 634
2002	10 718	5 724	1 445	600	76 190	9 623	8 649	374	11 197
2001	10 718	5 498	1 366	600	76 076	9 653	8 891	371	10 627
2000	10 311	5 498	1 577	652	75 013	9 363	8 746	360	10 400
1999	10 362	5 550	1 180	657	74 228	9 168	8 282	338	...
1998	10 296	5 536	1 076	646	72 142	8 750	7 970	328	...
1997	10 228	5 426	1 078	655	72 770	8 374	7 546	321	...
1996	10 243	5 240	1 114	675	71 678	7 948	7 416	315	...
1995	10 166	5 164	1 048	695	67 107	7 763	6 801	311	8 213
1994	10 282	5 126	1 051	643	68 123	7 949	6 756	294	...
1993	10 282	4 982	1 001	653	64 850	...	6 351	299	7 932
1992	10 391	5 164	1 055	665	63 080	...	6 152	279	7 671
1991	10 478	5 126	1 092	551	60 377	...	6 037	276	7 395
1990	10 419	5 007	913	832	58 714	8 799	5 891	273	7 226
1989	10 506	4 472	755	725	58 919	8 931	5 420	272	6 898
1988	10 539	4 649	831	710	62 572	8 666	5 225	276	6 675
1987	10 168	4 686	766	671	63 017	8 735	5 114	277	6 324
1986	10 386	4 440	697	680	66 218	8 777	5 113	278	6 119
1985	9 326	4 035	717	676	64 285	8 636	4 575	270	5 843
1984	9 083	4 075	733	664	67 294	8 829	4 448	263	5 488
1983	9 943	4 423	1 013	686	62 093	7 889	3 172	195	3 921
1982	9 867	4 497	1 016	763	62 114	7 741	3 077	194	3 731
1981	9 801	4 465	1 075	751	60 393	7 964	2 701	193	3 494
1980	9 641	4 500	1 013	823	59 411	8 567	2 557	187	3 281
1979	9 522	...	...	725	54 490	8 130	2 436	178	3 025
1978	9 567	...	...	593	52 866	7 616	2 271	165	2 741
1977	9 639	...	...	645	51 968	7 286	2 280	163	2 547
1976	9 714	...	...	685	52 382	7 081	2 161	163	2 404
1975	9 608	...	1 061	703	50 811	6 972	1 861	160	2 236
1974	9 403	...	...	718	48 700	6 935	1 940	153	1 967
1973	9 387	...	...	794	48 286	6 660	1 798	141	1 624
1972	9 423	...	...	1 030	49 075	6 567	1 729	138	1 455
1971	9 325	...	...	1 037	49 150	6 847	1 741	139	1 393
1970	10 548	...	1 262	1 050	49 700	7 332	1 639	138	1 274
1969	10 665	...	...	1 082	49 600	7 803	1 555	141	1 184
1968	10 745	...	...	1 185	50 000	8 019	1 470	144	1 110
1967	10 645	...	...	1 244	50 180	8 172	1 457	146	1 055
1966	10 680	...	...	1 326	50 130	8 083	1 385	144	995
1965	10 664	...	1 549	1 453	49 600	8 253	1 340	145	964
1964	10 614	...	...	1 865	49 200	8 328	1 326	145	917
1963	10 634	...	...	2 155	49 400	8 400	1 316	147	892
1962	11 084	...	...	3 161	48 800	8 695	1 330	149	878
1961	11 419	...	...	3 593	49 000	8 883	1 321	152	856
1960	11 866	...	2 856	3 826	49 600	9 395	1 335	156	857
1959*	11 983	...	...	4 297	49 500	9 557	1 308	159	832
1958	12 201	...	...	4 848	50 100	9 732	1 282	165	831
1957	12 759	...	...	5 412	50 800	10 389	1 320	177	840
1956	13 225	...	...	5 748	51 400	10 941	1 351	186	852
1955	14 532	...	...	6 157	52 400	11 529	1 359	198	864
1954	15 600	...	...	6 598	54 000	12 392	1 410	211	895
1953	17 234	...	...	6 941	54 700	13 902	1 449	220	913
1952	19 176	...	...	7 180	55 980	15 119	1 438	227	903
1951	20 604	...	...	7 071	57 660	16 125	1 412	232	872

[1]An electric railway with capacity for heavy volume of traffic. Characterized by high speed and rapid acceleration passenger rail cars operating singly in multi-car trains on fixed rails. Also known as "rapid rail", "subway", "elevated (railway)", or "metropolitan railway (metro)".
[2]An electric or diesel propelled railway for urban passenger train service consisting of local short distance travel operating between a central city and adjacent suburbs. Service must be operated on a regular basis by or under contract with a transit operator for the purpose of transporting passengers within urbanized areas, or between urbanized areas and out-lying areas, usually with only one or two stations in the central business district. Intercity rail is excluded except for that portion of such service that is operated by or under contract with a public transit agency for predominantly commuter services. "Predominantly commuter service" means that for any given trip segment (i.e., distance between any two stations), more than 50 percent of the average daily ridership travels on the train at least three times a week. Also known as "regional rail" or "suburban rail".
[3]Lightweight passenger rail cars operating singly (or in short, usually two-car, trains) on fixed rails in right-of-way that is not separated from other traffic for much of the way. Driven electrically with power drawn from an overhead electric line via trolley or a pantograph. Also known as "streetcar", "tramway", or "trolley car".
[4]Electric rubber-tired passenger vehicles, manually steered and operated singly on city streets. Propelled by a motor drawing current through overhead wires via trolleys, from a central power source not on board the vehicle. Also known as "trolley coach" or "trackless trolley".
[5]Rubber-tired passenger vehicles operating on fixed routes and schedules over roadways. Vehicles are powered by diesel, gasoline, battery, or alternative fuel engines contained within the vehicle.
. . . = Not available.
* = First year for which figures include Alaska and Hawaii.

Table 13-15. Public Transit Equipment, Passengers, and Passenger Revenue, 1922–2004—*Continued*

(Number, dollars.)

Year	Heavy rail[1]	Commuter rail[2]	Light rail[3]	Trolley buses[4]	Motor buses[5]	Total revenue and nonrevenue passengers (millions)	Passenger revenue (millions of dollars)	Employees (thousands)	Employee payroll (millions of dollars)
1950	22 986	...	...	6 504	56 820	17 246	1 387	240	835
1949	24 728	...	...	6 366	57 035	19 008	1 420	253	841
1948	26 280	...	...	5 687	58 540	21 368	1 417	261	829
1947	30 158	...	...	4 707	56 917	22 540	1 324	266	790
1946	33 479	...	...	3 916	52 450	23 372	1 332	261	713
1945	36 377	...	...	3 711	49 670	23 254	1 314	242	632
1944	37 199	...	...	3 561	48 400	23 017	1 297	242	599
1943	37 505	...	...	3 501	47 100	22 000	1 236	239	554
1942	37 508	...	...	3 385	46 000	18 000	979	219	462
1941	37 670	...	...	3 029	39 300	14 085	759	205	386
1940	37 662	...	...	2 802	35 000	13 098	702	203	360
1939	40 372	...	...	2 184	32 600	12 837	682	202	352
1938	42 605	...	...	2 032	28 500	12 645	663	202	344
1937	45 312	...	...	1 655	27 500	13 246	690	209	348
1936	48 103	...	...	1 136	23 900	13 146	686	206	328
1935	50 466	...	...	578	23 800	12 226	642	204	311
1934	54 118	...	...	441	18 700	12 038	...	204	303
1933	58 124	...	...	310	17 200	11 327	...	201	287
1932	...	...	...	...	...	12 025	...	...	...
1931	...	...	...	...	...	13 924	...	...	...
1930	...	...	...	...	...	15 567	...	...	...
1929	...	...	...	...	...	16 985	...	...	...
1928	...	...	...	...	...	16 989	...	...	...
1927	...	...	...	...	...	17 201	...	...	...
1926	...	...	...	...	...	17 234	...	...	...
1925	...	...	...	...	...	16 651	...	...	...
1924	...	...	...	...	...	16 301	...	...	...
1923	...	...	...	...	...	16 311	...	...	...
1922	...	...	...	...	...	15 735	...	...	...

Source: U.S. Department of Transportation, Bureau of Transportation Statistics. U.S. Census Bureau. American Public Transportation Association. *Public Transportation Fact Book* and *Transit Fact Book.*

[1]An electric railway with capacity for heavy volume of traffic. Characterized by high speed and rapid acceleration passenger rail cars operating singly in multi-car trains on fixed rails. Also known as "rapid rail", "subway", "elevated (railway)", or "metropolitan railway (metro)".
[2]An electric or diesel propelled railway for urban passenger train service consisting of local short distance travel operating between a central city and adjacent suburbs. Service must be operated on a regular basis by or under contract with a transit operator for the purpose of transporting passengers within urbanized areas, or between urbanized areas and outlying areas, usually with only one or two stations in the central business district. Intercity rail is excluded except for that portion of such service that is operated by or under contract with a public transit agency for predominantly commuter services. "Predominantly commuter service" means that for any given trip segment (i.e., distance between any two stations), more than 50 percent of the average daily ridership travels on the train at least three times a week. Also known as "regional rail" or "suburban rail".
[3]Lightweight passenger rail cars operating singly (or in short, usually two-car, trains) on fixed rails in right-of-way that is not separated from other traffic for much of the way. Driven electrically with power drawn from an overhead electric line via trolley or a pantograph. Also known as "streetcar", "tramway", or "trolley car".
[4]Electric rubber-tired passenger vehicles, manually steered and operated singly on city streets. Propelled by a motor drawing current through overhead wires via trolleys, from a central power source not on board the vehicle. Also known as "trolley coach" or "trackless trolley".
[5]Rubber-tired passenger vehicles operating on fixed routes and schedules over roadways. Vehicles are powered by diesel, gasoline, battery, or alternative fuel engines contained within the vehicle.
... = Not available.

Table 13-16. U.S. Scheduled Airline Industry, 1926–2005

(Number, gallons, and miles per hour.)

Year	Number of operators	Aircraft in service[1]	Persons employed	Revenue miles flown (thousands)	Revenue passengers carried, unduplicated[2] (thousands)	Revenue passenger-miles flown (millions)	Ton-miles flown: Express and freight (thousands)	Ton-miles flown: Mail (thousands)	Fuel consumed[3] (millions of gallons)	Average available seats	Average speed (mph)
2005	...	...	552 900	...	738 400	778 900	26 812 000	1 195 000	...	...	...
2004	...	...	569 500	...	702 900	733 600	26 682 000	1 296 000	...	...	...
2003	...	...	569 800	...	646 300	656 900	25 363 000	1 372 000	...	...	...
2002	...	...	601 400	...	612 900	641 100	23 243 000	1 348 000	...	...	...
2001	...	...	672 000	...	622 100	651 700	20 119 000	1 885 000	...	...	...
2000	...	...	680 000	...	666 200	692 800	21 443 000	2 445 000	...	...	...
1999	...	...	646 400	...	636 000	652 000	19 317 000	2 296 000	...	...	...
1998	...	...	621 100	...	612 900	618 100	18 131 000	...	...	...	...
1997	...	...	586 500	...	594 700	603 400	17 959 000	...	...	...	...
1996	...	...	564 400	...	581 200	578 800	15 301 000	...	...	...	...
1995	...	...	547 000	...	547 800	540 700	14 578 000	2 343 000	...	...	...
1994	...	...	539 800	...	528 800	519 400	13 792 000	...	...	...	...
1993	...	...	537 100	...	488 500	489 700	11 944 000	...	...	...	...
1992	...	...	540 400	...	475 100	478 600	11 130 000	...	...	...	...
1991	...	...	533 600	...	452 300	448 000	10 225 000	...	...	...	...
1990	60	4 665	545 000	4 491 000	466 000	457 900	10 600 000	2 004 000	16 252	151.9	408
1989	62	4 477	507 000	4 193 000	454 000	432 700	10 275 000	1 911 000	15 624	152.1	406
1988	66	4 439	481 000	4 141 000	455 000	423 300	9 632 000	1 837 000	15 094	153.1	409
1987	68	4 231	457 000	3 988 000	448 000	404 500	8 260 000	1 758 000	14 461	152.9	413
1986	74	3 799	422 000	3 725 000	419 000	366 500	7 344 000	1 081 000	13 682	153.4	409
1985	86	2 860	355 000	3 320 000	382 000	336 400	6 020 000	1 659 000	12 603	152.5	409
1984	87	2 692	345 000	3 133 000	345 000	305 100	6 566 000	1 618 000	11 470	153.7	414
1983	84	2 618	329 000	2 809 000	319 000	281 800	6 092 000	1 480 000	10 526	154.1	415
1982	98	2 468	330 000	2 699 000	294 000	259 600	5 482 000	1 404 000	10 268	153.0	408
1981	98	2 523	350 000	2 703 000	286 000	248 800	5 686 000	1 374 000	10 810	147.2	403
1980	72	2 505	371 000	2 816 000	297 000	255 200	5 742 000	1 342 000	11 311	143.1	405
1979	52	2 466	341 000	2 791 000	317 000	262 000	5 964 000	1 225 000	11 369	139.9	406
1978	34	2 345	329 000	2 520 000	275 000	226 800	5 818 000	1 181 000	10 534	140.0	409
1977	32	2 234	314 000	2 419 000	240 000	193 200	4 109 000	1 039 000	10 296	136.9	408
1976	32	2 271	303 000	2 320 000	223 000	179 000	3 855 000	1 001 000	9 832	134.1	406
1975	33	2 260	290 000	2 241 000	205 000	162 800	4 796 000	1 109 000	9 507	130.4	403
1974	31	2 244	305 000	2 258 000	208 000	162 900	3 760 000	1 016 000	9 546	127.7	402
1973	33	2 361	312 000	2 448 000	202 000	161 900	3 692 000	1 048 000	10 671	123.8	404
1972	37	2 361	305 000	2 376 000	191 000	152 406	3 354 000	1 049 000	9 985	118.1	404
1971	38	2 389	285 000	2 378 000	173 000	132 687	3 023 000	1 154 000	9 841	115.3	405
1970	33	2 437	242 206	2 013 484	153 408	104 156	1 966 009	705 711	...	110.4	350
1969	33	2 423	255 386	2 000 269	158 405	102 717	1 916 472	801 416	27	109.8	394
1968	38	2 317	244 742	1 715 857	145 774	87 508	1 578 992	564 084	113	100.8	373
1967	39	2 194	223 381	1 462 240	128 479	75 487	1 314 409	405 352	223	94.4	354
1966	40	2 027	196 298	1 178 458	105 789	60 591	1 108 691	291 277	332	91.2	320
1965	40	1 896	169 952	1 088 112	92 073	51 887	943 128	225 992	448	89.2	314
1964	40	1 863	153 243	957 575	79 139	44 141	743 963	189 782	507	86.1	297
1963	40	1 832	143 112	888 793	69 366	38 457	603 725	174 439	554	83.4	287
1962	40	1 831	138 673	827 694	60 738	33 623	554 599	166 801	696	79.4	274
1961	41	1 867	136 987	795 165	56 900	31 062	454 142	150 452	743	72.9	253
1960	42	1 594	133 717	820 756	56 352	30 567	386 933	135 923	922	65.5	235
1959	39	1 596	132 042	841 925	54 955	29 308	344 728	120 308	1 142	58.7	223
1958	39	1 546	119 746	784 200	48 297	25 375	294 018	107 018	1 188	55.8	220
1957	40	1 494	119 333	791 265	48 761	25 379	268 791	100 218	1 165	53.7	215
1956	40	1 347	103 489	694 050	41 738	22 399	247 255	94 523	1 005	52.4	213
1955	42	1 212	95 548	627 336	38 025	19 852	229 966	88 751	912	51.2	208
1954	43	1 175	84 765	556 880	32 343	16 802	189 765	82 768	776	50.1	206
1953	44	1 139	84 651	525 374	28 721	14 794	179 063	74 106	692	46.1	198
1952	46	1 078	79 687	465 477	25 010	12 559	162 047	70 443	588	42.7	191
1951	49	981	72 898	411 878	22 652	10 590	144 790	64 734	...	39.6	185
1950	52	960	61 903	369 826	17 345	8 007	152 223	47 740	418	37.5	180
1949	51	913	59 886	355 501	15 081	6 752	123 603	41 889	375	35.0	179
1948	39	878	60 416	338 217	13 168	5 976	102 360	38 198	332	32.4	172
1947	27	810	58 998	325 054	12 890	6 105	64 637	33 086	294	30.0	168
1946	23	674	69 182	309 889	12 213	5 945	38 590	32 969	236	25.3	160
1945	19	421	50 313	208 969	6 576	3 360	22 175	65 103	135	19.7	155
1944	18	288	31 198	138 732	4 046	2 177	16 974	51 146	90	19.1	156
1943	18	204	29 654	105 355	3 020	1 632	15 618	36 067	65	18.3	...
1942	19	186	26 910	111 341	3 137	1 418	11 896	21 167	69	17.9	...
1941	19	370	19 223	134 406	33 464	1 385	5 257	13 108	82	17.5	...

[1]Figures for 1961–1971 for domestic airlines are for total aircraft in service, domestic and international.
[2]Duplication has been eliminated where the same passengers were carried on more than one route of an air carrier, but still exists where the same passengers were carried by more than one air carrier.
[3]Shows gasoline prior to 1970; jet fuel beginning in 1970.
... = Not available.

Table 13-16. U.S. Scheduled Airline Industry, 1926–2005—*Continued*

(Number, gallons, and miles per hour.)

Year	Number of operators	Aircraft in service[1]	Persons employed	Revenue miles flown (thousands)	Revenue passengers carried, unduplicated[2] (thousands)	Revenue passenger-miles flown (millions)	Ton-miles flown Express and freight (thousands)	Mail (thousands)	Fuel consumed[3] (millions of gallons)	Average available seats	Average speed (mph)
1940	19	369	15 984	110 101	32 523	1 052	3 476	10 118	66	16.5	...
1939	418	4 276	410 639	82 925	31 561	683	2 713	8 611	47	14.7	...
1938	516	5 260	59 008	68 610	31 077	480	2 182	7 449	38	13.9	...
1937	22	291	7 586	66 791	3 887	412	2 162	6 698	34	12.5	...
1936	24	280	7 079	64 307	...	6 439	1 866	5 741	31	10.7	...
1935	26	363	5 945	55 918	...	6 316	1 098	4 133	27	10.3	...
1934	24	423	4 201	41 526	...	6 190	7 597	82 237	19	8.9	...
1933	25	418	4 369	49 256	...	6 175	7 423	92 568	22	7.6	...
1932	32	456	4 020	45 894	...	6 127	7 290	92 701	20	6.6	...
1931	39	490	4 314	43 109	...	6 107	7 221	93 140	16	...	...
1930	43	497	2 778	32 645	...	685	7 101	...	12	...	...
1929	38	442	1 958	22 729	...	...	770	...	6	...	...
1928	34	268	101 496	10 528	...	...	759	...	2	...	...
1927	18	...	...	5 856	...	...	713	...	1	...	...
1926	13	...	...	4 318	...	...	71	...	1	...	...

Source: U.S. Census Bureau. Air Transport Association of America. *Air Transport Annual Report.*
[1]Figures for 1961–1971 for domestic airlines are for total aircraft in service, domestic and international.
[2]Duplication has been eliminated where the same passengers were carried on more than one route of an air carrier, but still exists where the same passengers were carried by more than one air carrier.
[3]Shows gasoline prior to 1970; jet fuel beginning in 1970.
. . . = Not available.

Table 13-17. Air Transportation Accidents, 1927–2005

(Number.)

Year	Domestic scheduled air carriers[1]		
	Total accidents	Number of fatal accidents	Total passenger fatalities[2]
2005[P]	39	3	22
2004	30	2	14
2003	54	2	22
2002	41	0	0
2001	46	6	531
2000	56	3	92
1999	51	2	12
1998	50	1	1
1997	49	4	8
1996	37	5	380
1995	36	3	168
1994	23	4	239
1993	23	1	1
1992	18	4	33
1991	26	4	62
1990	24	6	39
1989	28	11	278
1988	30	3	285
1987	34	5	232
1986	24	3	8
1985	21	7	526
1984	16	1	4
1983	23	4	15
1982	15	3	233
1981	25	4	4
1980	15	-	38
1979	18	5	352
1978	19	4	16
1977	18	2	75
1976	21	2	36
1975	29	2	122
1974	43	7	460
1973	32	6	217
1972	43	7	186
1971	39	6	194
1970	31	1	-
1969	37	7	132
1968	44	11	258
1967	43	8	226
1966	50	4	59
1965	55	6	205
1964	45	6	106
1963	39	4	48
1962	35	5	158
1961	56	5	124
1960	62	[3]10	326
1959	61	9	209
1958	42	4	114
1957	44	4	32
1956	55	4	143
1955	44	5	8 156
1954	54	9	4 16
1953	37	5	86
1952	44	6	46
1951	45	11	142
1950	39	4	96
1949	35	8	96
1948	56	5	83
1947	44	8	199
1946	33	9	75
1945	40	8	76
1944	30	5	48
1943	23	2	22
1942	23	5	55
1941	27	4	35

[1]From 1927 to 1994, includes scheduled revenue operators only. Beginning 1995, including all flights by U.S. air carriers operating under 14 CF4 121. Figures between 1980 and 1990 represent both domestic and international flights. Beginning 1997, includes aircraft with 10 or more seats, previously operating under 14 CFR 135.
[2]Other than persons aboard aircraft who were killed, fatalities resulting from the September 11, 2001 terrorist acts are excluded.
[3]Includes two midair collisions nonfatal to air carrier occupants.
- = Quantity zero.
P = Preliminary.

Table 13-17. Air Transportation Accidents, 1927–2005—*Continued*

(Number.)

Year	Domestic scheduled air carriers[1]		
	Total accidents	Number of fatal accidents	Total passenger fatalities[2]
1940	30	3	35
1939	28	2	9
1938	23	5	25
1937	42	5	40
1936	65	8	44
1935	58	8	15
1934	71	8	17
1933	100	9	8
1932	108	16	19
1931	118	13	25
1930	88	9	24
1929	124	21	14
1928	85	11	14
1927	25	4	1

Source: U.S. Census Bureau. *Statistical Abstract of the United States: 2003.* U.S. National Transportation Safety Board.
[1]From 1927 to 1994, includes scheduled revenue operators only. Beginning 1995, including all flights by U.S. air carriers operating under 14 CF4 121. Figures between 1980 and 1990 represent both domestic and international flights. Beginning 1997, includes aircraft with 10 or more seats, previously operating under 14 CFR 135.
[2]Other than persons aboard aircraft who were killed, fatalities resulting from the September 11, 2001 terrorist acts are excluded.

Table 13-18. Airports, Aircraft, and Pilots 1927–2004

(Number.)

Year	Airports and landing fields[1]		Total civil aircraft[2]	Certified airplane pilots[3]			
	Total	Lighted		Total	Airline transport	Commercial	Private
2004	19 820	...	...	618 633	142 160	122 592	235 994
2003	19 581	...	...	625 011	143 504	123 990	143 504
2002	19 572	...	...	631 762	144 708	125 920	245 230
2001	19 306	...	...	612 274	144 702	120 502	243 823
2000	19 281	...	...	625 581	141 596	121 858	251 561
1999	19 098	...	...	635 472	137 642	124 261	258 749
1998	18 770	...	...	618 298	134 612	122 053	247 226
1997	18 345	4 832	200 000	616 000	131 000	125 000	248 000
1996	18 292	4 847	198 600	622 000	127 000	129 000	254 000
1995	18 224	4 838	195 500	639 184	123 877	133 980	261 399
1994	18 343	4 830	281 000	654 000	117 000	139 000	284 000
1993	18 317	4 842	279 000	665 000	117 000	143 000	284 000
1992	17 846	4 831	277 000	683 000	116 000	146 000	288 000
1991	17 581	4 811	275 500	692 000	112 000	148 000	293 000
1990	17 490	4 822	275 900	702 659	107 732	149 666	299 111
1989	17 446	4 443	274 800	700 000	102 000	145 000	293 000
1988	17 327	4 890	272 700	694 000	97 000	143 000	300 000
1987	17 015	4 922	275 100	700 000	91 000	144 000	301 000
1986	16 582	4 954	275 700	709 000	87 000	148 000	306 000
1985	16 319	4 941	274 900	709 540	82 740	151 632	311 086
1984	16 075	4 889	271 500	722 000	79 000	155 000	322 000
1983	16 029	4 878	264 900	718 000	75 000	159 000	319 000
1982	15 831	4 844	259 000	733 000	73 000	165 000	322 000
1981	15 476	4 795	261 600	764 000	70 000	169 000	329 000
1980	15 161	4 738	259 400	827 071	69 569	183 442	357 479
1979	14 746	4 631	251 500	815 000	64 000	182 000	343 000
1978	14 574	4 567	236 800	799 000	56 000	186 000	338 000
1977	14 117	4 483	215 300	784 000	50 000	189 000	327 000
1976	13 770	4 362	205 900	744 000	45 000	188 000	309 000
1975	13 251	4 171	196 300	728 000	43 000	189 000	306 000
1974	13 062	3 999	188 000	734 000	41 000	192 000	306 000
1973	12 700	3 880	179 800	715 000	38 000	182 000	299 000
1972	12 405	3 827	170 800	751 000	38 000	196 000	321 000
1971	12 070	3 759	166 800	741 000	36 000	192 000	313 000
1970	11 261	3 554	154 450	732 729	34 430	186 821	303 779
1969	11 050	3 430	190 749	720 028	31 442	176 585	299 491
1968	10 470	3 312	179 285	691 695	28 607	164 458	281 728
1967	10 126	3 149	166 598	617 931	25 817	150 135	253 312
1966	9 673	2 988	155 132	548 757	23 917	131 539	222 427
1965	9 566	2 878	142 078	479 770	22 440	116 665	196 393
1964	9 490	2 773	137 189	431 041	21 572	108 428	175 574
1963	8 814	2 672	129 975	378 700	20 269	96 341	152 209
1962	8 084	2 481	124 273	830 220	23 220	275 495	531 505
1961	7 715	2 299	117 904	804 707	22 042	268 707	513 958
1960	6 881	2 133	111 580	783 232	20 985	262 437	499 810
1959	6 426	1 943	105 309	758 368	19 364	255 377	483 627
1958	6 018	1 809	98 893	731 078	18 303	245 541	467 234
1957	6 412	1 713	93 189	702 519	16 900	237 149	448 470
1956	7 028	1 399	87 531	669 079	15 295	221 096	432 688
1955	6 839	1 247	85 320	643 201	13 700	211 142	418 359
1954	6 977	1 108	92 067	613 695	13 341	201 441	398 913
1953	6 760	1 050	91 102	585 974	12 757	195 363	377 854
1952	6 042	1 858	89 313	581 218	11 357	193 575	376 286
1951	6 237	...	88 545	580 574	10 813	197 900	371 861
1950	6 403	1 670	92 809	...	...	...	...
1949	6 484	1 480	92 622	525 174	9 025	187 769	328 380
1948	6 414	1 521	95 997	491 306	7 762	176 846	306 699
1947	5 759	1 447	94 821	433 241	7 059	181 912	244 270
1946	4 490	1 019	81 002	400 061	7 654	203 251	189 156
1945	4 026	1 007	37 789	296 895	5 815	162 873	128 207
1944	3 427	964	27 919	183 383	3 046	68 449	111 888
1943	2 769	859	27 180	173 206	2 315	63 940	106 951
1942	2 809	700	27 170	166 626	2 177	55 760	108 689
1941	2 484	662	26 013	129 947	1 587	34 578	93 782
1940	2 331	776	17 928	69 829	1 431	18 791	49 607
1939	2 280	735	13 772	33 706	1 197	11 677	20 832
1938	2 374	719	11 159	22 983	1 159	7 839	13 985
1937	2 299	720	10 836	17 681	1 064	6 411	10 206
1936	2 342	705	9 229	15 952	842	7 288	7 822
1935	2 368	698	9 072	14 805	736	7 362	6 707
1934	2 297	664	8 322	13 949	676	7 484	5 789
1933	2 188	626	9 284	13 960	554	7 635	5 771
1932	2 117	701	10 324	18 594	330	7 967	10 297
1931	2 093	680	10 780	17 739	...	8 513	9 226
1930	1 782	640	9 818	15 280	...	7 847	7 433
1929	1 550	...	9 922	10 430	...	6 165	4 265
1928	1 364	...	5 104	4 887	...	...	...
1927	1 036	...	2 740	1 572	...	...	...

Source: U.S. Census Bureau. U.S. Department of Transportation, Bureau of Transportation Statistics. U.S. Federal Aviation Administration.
[1]Existing airports, heliports, seaplane bases, etc. recorded with the Federal Aviation Administration (FAA). Beginning 1954, includes military airports with joint civil and military use. Prior to 1954, all military fields are included. Includes U.S. outlying areas. Airport type definitions: Public - publicly owned and under control of a public agency; Private - owned by a private individual or corporation (may or may not be open for public use.)
[2]1946–1952 includes gliders. Beginning 1950 and until 1994, includes active and inactive aircraft; after 1994, active aircraft only.
[3]Beginning 1963, data are for active certified airplane pilots only. Also beginning 1963, total includes student, helicopter, glider, and other pilots, not shown separately.
... = Not available.

Table 13-19. Top Airports in 2005—Passengers Enplaned, 1992-2005

(Number in thousands, rank.)

Airport	1992 Total passengers	1992 Rank	1994 Total passengers	1994 Rank	2002 Total passengers	2002 Rank	2004 Total passengers	2004 Rank	2005 Total passengers	2005 Rank
All airports	**454 060**	**X**	**501 197**	**X**	**558 705**	**X**	**654 634**	**X**	**681 949**	**X**
Total, top 40	**343 114**	**X**	**382 759**	**X**	**428 111**	**X**	**502 586**	**X**	**525 418**	**X**
Atlanta, Georgia (William B Hartsfield-Atlanta International)	19 705	3	25 630	2	34 927	1	40 413	1	41 633	1
Chicago, Illinois (Chicago O'Hare International)	28 948	1	29 700	1	27 029	2	33 801	2	33 762	2
Dallas/Fort Worth, Texas (Dallas/Ft Worth International)	24 671	2	25 117	3	22 759	3	27 563	3	27 713	3
Los Angeles, California (Los Angeles International)	18 395	4	19 721	4	19 397	4	22 892	4	22 966	4
Las Vegas, Nevada (McCarran International)	9 347	12	10 435	14	15 581	7	19 413	6	20 705	5
Denver, Colorado (Denver International)	13 595	6	14 640	5	16 077	5	19 856	5	20 206	6
Phoenix, Arizona (Phoenix Sky Harbor International)	10 787	7	12 427	7	15 952	6	19 123	7	20 078	7
Houston, Texas (George Bush Intercontinental)	8 358	21	9 626	17	13 343	10	16 707	10	18 185	8
Minneapolis/St. Paul, Minnesota (Minneapolis-St Paul International)	10 055	11	10 456	13	14 639	8	17 282	8	17 824	9
Detroit, Michigan (Detroit Metro Wayne County)	10 425	10	11 822	8	13 939	9	16 871	9	17 364	10
Orlando, Florida (Orlando International)	8 765	16	8 863	21	12 133	12	13 752	12	14 914	11
Newark, New Jersey (Newark International)	10 479	8	11 782	9	11 138	15	14 139	11	14 819	12
New York, New York (John F Kennedy International)	8 468	20	8 894	20	7 293	28	13 243	15	14 474	13
Philadelphia, Pennsylvania (Philadelphia International)	6 968	23	7 537	24	2 788	19	12 713	16	14 157	14
Seattle, Washington (Seattle-Tacoma International)	8 572	19	9 936	15	12 222	11	13 744	13	13 964	15
San Francisco, California (San Francisco International)	14 208	5	14 309	6	11 253	14	13 504	14	13 830	16
Charlotte, North Carolina (Charlotte-Douglas International)	8 239	22	9 370	18	10 147	16	11 394	18	13 193	17
Miami, Florida (Miami International)	9 076	15	10 810	11	7 444	26	11 521	17	12 145	18
Boston, Massachusetts (Gen. Edward Lawrence Logan International)	9 320	13	10 609	12	9 174	20	11 094	19	11 555	19
New York, New York (La Guardia)	9 252	14	9 780	16	9 889	17	10 998	20	11 539	20
Cincinnati, Ohio (Greater Cincinnati)	4 916	27	5 441	28	9 882	18	10 617	21	11 164	21
Washington, District of Columbia (Washington Dulles International)	4 479	28	4 218	35	4 978	37	9 392	23	11 022	22
Salt Lake City, Utah (Salt Lake City International)	6 096	25	7 825	23	7 718	23	8 868	26	10 551	23
Fort Lauderdale, Florida (Fort Lauderdale-Hollywood International)	3 499	38	4 500	32	7 676	25	9 273	24	9 707	24
Baltimore, Maryland (Baltimore-Washington International)	3 648	35	5 481	27	8 949	21	9 794	22	9 547	25
Tampa, Florida (Tampa International)	4 398	30	5 416	29	7 317	27	8 067	28	8 811	26
San Diego, California (San Diego International/Lindbergh Field)	5 657	26	6 160	26	7 114	30	8 089	27	8 568	27
Chicago, Illinois (Chicago Midway)	1 983	56	4 049	36	7 770	22	9 236	25	8 381	28
Washington, District of Columbia (Ronald Reagan Washington National)	6 837	24	6 975	25	5 715	33	7 233	30	8 351	29
Honolulu, Hawaii (Honolulu International)	8 742	17	8 494	22	7 169	29	7 830	29	8 107	30
Oakland, California (Metropolitan Oakland International)	3 104	42	3 992	38	5 977	31	6 825	31	6 936	31
Portland, Oregon (Portland International)	3 588	36	4 864	30	5 795	32	6 267	32	6 667	32
St. Louis, Missouri (Lambert-St Louis International)	10 436	9	11 453	10	11 748	13	5 884	34	6 327	33
Memphis, Tennessee (Memphis International)	3 339	39	3 454	43	4 702	38	5 287	35	5 628	34
Cleveland, Ohio (Cleveland-Hopkins International)	3 785	34	4 665	31	5 003	36	5 245	36	5 374	35
San Jose, California (San Jose International)	3 137	41	4 016	37	5 028	35	5 190	37	5 234	36
San Juan, Puerto Rico (Luis Munoz Marin International)	. . .	. . .	4 377	33	4 472	39	5 074	38	5 166	37
Sacramento, California (Sacramento International)	2 489	49	2 791	50	4 107	40	4 768	40	5 049	38
Kansas City, Missouri (Kansas City International)	3 515	37	4 236	34	5 105	34	5 003	39	5 010	39
Santa Ana, California (John Wayne)	. . .	. . .	3 188	45	3 890	42	4 621	42	4 791	40

Source: U.S. Census Bureau. U.S. Department of Transportation, Bureau of Transportation Statistics.
Note: For calendar year. Airports ranked by total passengers enplaned by large certificated U.S. air carriers on scheduled and nonscheduled operations, at all airports served within the 50 states, the District of Columbia, and other U.S. areas designated by the Federal Aviation Administration. Data for commuter, and foreign-flag air carriers are not included.
X = Not applicable.
. . . = Not available.

Table 13-20. Railroad Mileage and Equipment, 1896–2004

(Number.)

Year	Total mileage of track[1]	Equipment[2]			
		Total locomotives in service[3]	Passenger-train cars in service, railroad only	Freight-train-cars in service[4]	
				Number	Average capacity[5]
December 31					
2004	211 000	22 015	...	474	94.3
2003	200 000	20 774	...	467	93.7
2002	200 000	20 506	...	478	93.1
2001	204 000	19 745	...	500	92.7
2000	205 000	20 028	...	560	92.3
1999	207 000	20 256	...	579	92.2
1998	224 000	20 261	...	576	92.4
1997	225 000	19 684	...	568	92.2
1996	228 000	19 269	...	571	91.6
1995	228 000	18 812	...	583	88.6
1994	232 000	18 505	...	591	88.1
1993	236 000	18 161	...	587	88.0
1992	238 000	18 004	...	605	88.0
1991	242 000	18 344	...	633	87.9
1990	244 000	18 835	...	659	87.5
1989	248 000	19 015	...	682	87.8
1988	251 000	19 364	2 332	725	86.4
1987	261 000	19 647	2 350	749	85.0
1986	262 000	20 790	2 307	799	84.1
1985	269 000	22 548	2 502	867	83.2
1984	264 000	24 117	2 580	948	83.4
1983	270 000	25 448	2 610	1 007	82.4
1982	275 000	26 795	3 736	1 039	81.6
1981	278 000	27 421	3 945	1 111	80.5
1980	292 000	28 094	4 347	1 168	78.5
1979	300 000	28 097	2 400	1 217	77.7
1978	310 000	27 400	2 400	1 227	76.9
1977	311 000	27 667	5 700	1 287	75.5
1976	313 000	27 612	5 600	1 332	73.8
1975	324 000	27 846	6 471	1 359	72.9
1974	327 000	28 084	7 080	1 375	71.6
1973	329 000	27 790	7 363	1 395	70.5
1972	331 000	27 358	7 763	1 411	69.6
1971	335 000	27 189	8 869	1 422	68.4
1970	336 000	27 077	11 378	1 424	67.1
1969	364 915	29 090	12 630	1 464 194	65.8
1968	366 238	29 448	14 816	1 484 571	64.3
1967	368 030	29 874	17 822	1 510 963	63.4
1966	370 104	30 124	18 974	1 523 741	61.4
1965	370 636	30 061	20 022	1 515 169	59.8
1964	372 300	30 296	21 510	1 517 564	58.2
1963	374 522	30 506	22 616	1 542 456	56.8
1962	376 290	30 701	23 430	1 581 213	56.3
1961	379 415	30 889	24 433	1 635 342	55.7
1960	381 745	31 178	25 746	1 690 396	55.4
1959	383 912	31 539	27 419	1 708 116	55.0
1958	385 264	31 616	28 999	1 755 775	54.8
1957	386 978	32 391	29 564	1 777 557	54.5
1956	389 668	32 593	30 817	1 738 631	54.0
1955	390 965	33 533	32 118	1 723 747	53.7
1954	392 580	35 033	33 035	1 761 386	53.7
1953	393 736	37 251	34 106	1 801 874	53.5
1952	394 631	39 697	34 942	1 783 352	53.2
1951	395 831	42 473	36 326	1 777 878	52.9
1950	396 380	42 951	37 359	1 745 778	52.6
1949	397 232	43 272	38 006	1 778 811	52.4
1948	397 203	44 474	39 406	1 785 067	51.9
1947	397 355	44 344	39 057	1 759 758	51.5
1946	398 037	45 511	38 697	1 768 400	51.3
1945	398 054	46 253	38 633	1 787 073	51.1
1944	398 437	46 305	38 217	1 797 012	50.8
1943	398 730	45 406	38 331	1 784 472	50.7
1942	399 627	44 671	38 446	1 773 735	50.5
1941	403 625	44 375	38 334	1 732 673	50.3

[1]Includes multiple main tracks, yard tracks, and sidings owned by both line-haul and switching and terminal. (Includes estimate for class II and III railroads.)
[2]Includes switching and terminal companies.
[3]For 1890–1927, number of locomotives; for 1928, number of units, except for steam locomotives. (A unit is the least number of wheel bases together with superstructure cabable of independent propulsion, but not necessarily equipped with an independent control.)
[4]Excludes caboose cars. Class I railroads only.
[5]For 1916–1956, represents steam locomotives and freight cars of class I railroads, excluding switching and terminal companies; for 1957–1967, includes all class I locomotives, excluding switching and terminal companies.
... = Not available.

Table 13-20. Railroad Mileage and Equipment, 1896–2004—*Continued*

(Number.)

		Equipment[2]			
				Freight-train-cars in service[4]	
Year	Total mileage of track[1]	Total locomotives in service[3]	Passenger-train cars in service, railroad only	Number	Average capacity[5]
1940	405 975	44 333	38 308	1 684 171	50.0
1939	408 350	45 172	38 977	1 680 519	49.7
1938	411 324	46 544	39 931	1 731 096	49.4
1937	414 572	47 555	40 949	1 776 428	49.2
1936	416 381	48 009	41 390	1 790 043	48.8
1935	419 228	49 541	42 426	1 867 381	48.3
1934	422 401	51 423	44 884	1 973 247	48.0
1933	425 664	54 228	47 677	2 072 632	47.5
1932	428 402	56 732	50 598	2 184 690	47.0
1931	429 823	58 652	52 096	2 245 904	47.0
1930	429 883	60 189	53 584	2 322 267	46.9
1929	429 054	61 257	53 838	2 323 683	46.3
1928	427 750	63 311	54 800	2 346 751	45.8
1927	424 737	65 348	55 729	2 378 800	45.5
1926	421 341	66 847	56 855	2 403 967	45.1
1925	417 954	68 098	56 814	2 414 083	44.8
1924	415 028	69 486	57 451	2 411 627	44.3
1923	412 993	69 414	57 159	2 379 131	43.8
1922	409 359	68 518	56 827	2 352 483	43.1
1921	407 531	69 122	56 950	2 378 510	42.5
1920	403 580	68 942	56 102	2 388 424	42.4
1919	403 891	68 977	56 290	2 426 889	41.9
1918	402 343	67 936	56 611	2 397 943	41.6
1917	400 353	66 070	55 939	2 379 472	41.5
1916	397 014	65 595	55 193	2 329 475	40.9
June 30					
1916	394 944	65 314	54 774	2 343 378	40.5
1915	391 142	66 502	55 810	2 341 567	39.7
1914	387 208	67 012	54 492	2 349 734	39.1
1913	379 508	65 597	52 717	2 298 478	38.3
1912	371 238	63 463	51 583	2 229 163	37.4
1911	362 824	62 463	49 906	2 208 997	36.9
1910	351 767	60 019	47 179	2 148 478	35.9
1909	342 351	58 219	45 664	2 086 835	35.3
1908	333 646	57 698	45 292	2 100 784	34.9
1907	327 975	55 388	43 973	1 991 557	33.8
1906	317 083	51 672	42 262	1 837 914	32.2
1905	306 797	48 357	40 713	1 731 409	30.8
1904	297 073	46 743	39 752	1 692 194	30.1
1903	283 822	43 871	38 140	1 653 782	29.4
1902	274 196	41 225	36 987	1 546 101	. . .
1901	265 352	39 584	35 969	1 464 328	. . .
1900	258 784	37 663	34 713	1 365 531	. . .
1899	250 143	36 703	33 850	1 295 510	. . .
1898	245 334	36 234	33 595	1 248 826	. . .
1897	242 013	35 986	33 626	1 221 730	. . .
1896	239 140	35 950	33 003	1 221 887	. . .

Source: U.S. Census Bureau. Association of American Railroads. *Railroad Racts, Statistics of Railroads of Class 1* and *Analysis of Class 1 Railroads.*
[1]Includes multiple main tracks, yard tracks, and sidings owned by both line-haul and switching and terminal. (Includes estimate for class II and III railroads.)
[2]Includes switching and terminal companies.
[3]For 1890–1927, number of locomotives; for 1928, number of units, except for steam locomotives. (A unit is the least number of wheel bases together with superstructure cabable of independent propulsion, but not necessarily equipped with an independent control.)
[4]Excludes caboose cars. Class I railroads only.
[5]For 1916–1956, represents steam locomotives and freight cars of class I railroads, excluding switching and terminal companies; for 1957–1967, includes all class I locomotives, excluding switching and terminal companies.
. . . = Not available.

Table 13-21. Railroad Freight Traffic, 1912–2005

(Thousands of revenue-tons.)

Year	Total revenue freight originated (Class I railroads in carloads)
December 31	
2005	1 899 000
2004	1 844 000
2003	1 799 000
2004	1 767 000
2001	1 742 000
2000	1 738 000
1999	1 717 000
1998	1 649 000
1997	1 585 000
1996	1 611 000
1995	1 550 000
1994	1 470 000
1993	1 397 000
1992	1 399 000
1991	1 383 000
1990	1 425 000
1989	1 403 000
1988	1 429 000
1987	1 372 000
1986	1 306 000
1985	1 312 100
1984	1 429 400
1983	1 292 600
1982	1 268 600
1981	1 453 000
1980	1 492 400
1979	1 502 100
1978	1 390 400
1977	1 394 700
1976	1 370 000
1975	1 395 100
1974	1 530 000
1973	1 532 000
1972	1 448 000
1971	1 391 000
1970	1 484 110
1969	1 472 620
1968	1 430 441
1967	1 406 668
1966	1 447 852
1965	1 386 090
1964	1 353 117
1963	1 283 382
1962	1 231 415
1961	1 191 154
1960	1 237 575
1959	1 228 277
1958	1 185 951
1957	1 374 884
1956	1 440 937
1955	1 389 346
1954	1 217 005
1953	1 376 046
1952	1 343 294
1951	1 467 023
1950	1 343 308
1949	1 213 911
1948	1 488 612
1947	1 514 985
1946	1 342 230
1945	1 404 080
1944	1 471 366
1943	1 462 314
1942	1 403 612
1941	1 209 559
1940	994 728
1939	886 794
1938	757 470
1937	998 398
1936	942 538
1935	775 588
1934	750 951
1933	684 592
1932	630 989
1931	871 412

Table 13-21. Railroad Freight Traffic, 1912–2005—
Continued

(Thousands of revenue-tons.)

Year	Total revenue freight originated (Class I railroads in carloads)
1930	1 123 530
1929	1 303 048
1928	1 248 989
1927	1 243 171
1926	1 296 651
1925	1 206 655
1924	1 146 747
1923	1 234 692
1922	980 516
1921	898 191
1920	1 202 219
1919	1 045 148
1918	1 209 957
1917	1 210 247
1916	1 150 456
June 30	
1916	878 761
1915	982 892
1914	1 026 817
1913	889 999
1912	866 398

Source: U.S. Census Bureau. Association of American Railroads. *Freight Commodity Statistics.*

Table 13-22. Number and Size of the U.S. Flag Merchant Fleet and Its Share of the World Fleet, 1985–2004

(Oceangoing ships of 1,000 gross tons and over.)

	1985	1990	1995	2000	2001	2002	2003	2004
World fleet	25 555	23 596	25 608	28 318	28 296	28 761	28 650	29 035
U.S. fleet	737	636	509	454	443	426	418	412
U.S. share of the world fleet (percent)	2.9	2.7	2.0	1.6	1.6	1.5	1.5	1.4
Freighters, Total	417	367	295	286	283	276	209	205
DWT (thousands)	7 353	7 265	6 517	6 680	6 635	6 404	5 092	5 043
General cargo[1]	209	166	142	136	132	126	123	121
DWT (thousands)	2 980	2 605	2 472	2 362	2 162	1 838	1 810	1 784
Containership	104	92	81	90	91	90	86	84
DWT (thousands)	2 651	2 856	2 600	3 058	3 200	3 292	3 282	3 259
Partial containerships	63	59	3	...	...	...	...	...
DWT (thousands)	904	836	57	...	...	...	...	...
RO/RO	41	50	69	60	60	60	65	65
DWT (thousands)	818	968	1 388	1 260	1 273	1 273	1 431	1 431
Tankers, Total	258	233	181	142	130	120	109	104
DWT (thousands)	15 534	15 641	11 028	8 447	7 532	6 552	5 792	5 640
Petroleum/chemical[2] ships	244	219	167	142	130	120	109	104
DWT (thousands)	14 574	14 681	10 123	8 447	7 532	6 552	5 792	5 640
Liquefied petroleum/natural gas ships	14	14	14	...	...	...	...	...
DWT (thousands)	960	960	905	...	...	...	...	...
Combination/passenger and cargo, Total	37	10	13	11	13	12	15	18
DWT (thousands)	299	91	115	99	105	100	91	108
Bulk carriers, Total	25	26	20	15	17	18	20	20
DWT (thousands)	1 152	1 270	925	604	706	797	837	837

Source: U.S. Department of Transportation, Bureau of Transportation Statistics and Maritime Administration.
Note: Excludes nonmerchant type &/or U.S. Navy-owned vessels currently in the National Defense Reserve Fleet. Excludes ships operating exclusively on the Great Lakes and inland waterways and special types, such as: channel ships, icebreakers, cable ships, and merchant ships owned by military forces. All data are as of December 31 of year shown, except 2004 data as of July 1.
[1]Includes barge carriers.
[2]Includes integrated tug/barges.
DWT = Deadweight tons.
. . . = Data do not exist.
RO/RO = Roll on/roll off vessels.

Table 13-23. Waterborne Commerce, by Type of Commodity, 1995–2004

(Millions of short tons.)

Commodity	1995	2000[1]	2001	2003	2004 Total	2004 Domestic	2004 Foreign imports	2004 Foreign exports
TOTAL [1]	2 240.4	2 424.6	2 386.8	2,394.3	2,551.9	1,047.1	1,089.1	415.8
Coal	324.5	297.0	303.3	281.2	306.1	222.9	29.4	53.7
Petroleum and Petroleum Products	907.1	1 044.0	1 048.6	1,080.5	1,127.1	365.4	697.8	63.8
Crude petroleum	504.6	571.4	573.6	604.5	616.2	84.4	531.6	0.1
Petroleum products[1]	402.5	472.4	475.0	476.1	510.9	281.0	166.3	63.7
Gasoline	114.4	125.2	127.7	126.4	149.1	87.3	50.7	11.1
Distillate fuel oil	76.7	91.7	91.1	101.7	139.1	69.0	53.9	16.2
Residual fuel oil	111.9	131.6	133.7	116.7	92.9	77.7	14.0	1.3
Chemicals and Related Products	153.7	172.4	169.7	171.3	180.3	75.8	43.8	60.7
Fertilizers	35.7	35.1	39.0	35.2	34.3	13.4	7.5	13.4
Other chemicals and related products	118.0	137.3	130.6	136.1	146.0	62.4	36.3	47.3
Crude Material, Inedible[1]	381.7	380.3	354.0	358.0	390.3	229.4	108.6	52.3
Forest products, wood and chips	47.2	33.1	27.1	23.6	27.8	9.7	9.7	8.4
Pulp and waste paper	14.9	13.6	13.8	16.1	17.5	0.1	2.0	15.4
Soil, sand, gravel, rock, and stone	152.5	165.0	162.6	170.8	179.8	134.3	41.5	3.9
Limestone	54.0	67.4	68.9	64.7	73.2	54.9	15.5	2.8
Phosphate rock	10.7	3.4	1.7	5.7	6.4	3.6	2.8	0.0
Sand and gravel	77.0	79.0	77.5	85.3	83.6	72.2	10.5	0.9
Iron ore and scrap	104.9	97.9	76.8	80.9	94.8	63.1	16.2	15.4
Marine shells	0.5	0.3	0.3	0.1	-	-	-	-
Nonferrous ores and scrap	27.9	29.2	25.7	26.2	25.4	7.1	15.4	2.9
Sulphur, clay and salt	23.4	11.3	10.3	8.4	8.3	1.0	2.6	4.8
Slag	1.9	4.0	4.4	3.6	6.2	3.0	3.1	0.0
Other nonmetal minerals	8.4	25.9	33.1	28.3	30.5	11.0	18.1	1.4
Primary Manufactured Goods	106.3	153.0	137.1	134.7	159.6	43.0	98.4	18.2
Papers products	13.1	12.1	11.9	11.8	13.1	0.3	6.4	6.5
Lime, cement and glass	33.9	55.9	52.1	49.1	55.3	18.6	35.1	1.6
Primary iron and steel products	44.1	57.1	46.6	41.7	54.0	15.9	36.6	1.5
Primary nonferrous metal products	12.3	25.5	23.8	28.6	32.6	8.1	16.2	8.3
Primary wood products	2.9	2.5	2.7	3.3	4.6	0.1	4.2	0.3
Food and Farm Products	303.2	283.3	281.9	265.7	271.3	86.9	35.2	149.2
Fish	3.6	2.4	2.4	2.6	2.9	0.1	1.7	1.1
Grain[1]	167.9	145.2	140.7	130.1	141.8	53.1	1.3	87.4
Corn	105.0	88.2	87.9	78.2	86.4	37.6	0.1	48.7
Wheat	48.5	43.4	40.3	37.3	44.8	12.4	0.1	32.3
Oilseeds	46.1	57.6	61.5	56.9	48.4	19.4	0.5	28.5
Soybeans	42.0	47.3	49.4	49.7	42.7	17.2	0.1	25.4
Vegetables products	9.0	8.9	8.8	8.3	9.1	0.9	4.1	4.1
Processed grain and animal feed	33.0	23.1	22.4	20.3	19.3	6.7	0.8	11.8
Other agricultural products	43.5	46.1	46.1	47.5	49.7	6.7	26.8	16.2
All Manufacturing Equipment, Machinery and Products	57.0	83.6	80.3	90.0	102.7	20.6	67.2	15.0
Waste and Scrap, not elsewhere classified	5.4	4.3	3.5	3.1	3.0	3.0	-	-
Unknown or Not Elsewhere Classified	1.6	6.8	8.2	9.7	11.6	0.1	8.6	2.9

Source: U.S. Census Bureau. U.S. Army Corps of Engineers.
Note: Domestic trade includes all commercial movements between United States ports and on inland rivers, Great Lakes, canals, and connecting channels of the United States, Puerto Rico, and Virgin Islands.
[1]Includes commodities not shown separately.
- = Quantity zero or rounds to zero.

Table 13-24. Top 25 World Merchant Fleets by Flag and Type, 2005

Flag of Registry	Total		Tanker[1]		Dry Bulk[2]	
	No.	DWT	No.	DWT	No.	DWT
Top 25 registries	13 211	776 689 255	3 813	331 968 823	5 398	323 271 924
Total all registries	15 819	868 733 213	4 457	368 119 651	6 327	357 806 857
Top 25 as a percent of total	83.5	89.4	85.6	90.2	85.3	90.3
Panama	3 415	203 437 127	672	61 267 978	1 718	112 676 858
Liberia	1 410	88 832 748	565	50 608 159	331	19 936 853
Greece	555	51 899 956	235	30 139 575	269	19 437 133
Hong Kong	721	48 739 763	87	11 426 647	496	32 532 381
Bahamas	729	46 911 796	235	26 413 600	319	16 175 530
Marshall Islands	644	46 028 621	333	31 861 780	153	9 264 175
Singapore	699	44 619 141	289	26 223 289	180	12 336 140
Malta	745	35 353 729	185	13 370 377	438	19 482 921
Cyprus	696	30 453 506	93	6 241 801	373	18 742 535
China	803	27 496 237	127	6 333 829	372	14 551 392
Norwegian Int'l[6]	370	18 883 291	215	10 578 951	104	7 222 535
Isle of Man	177	12 977 297	112	8 828 365	42	3 466 291
United States	295	12 604 530	95	5 500 216	62	2 391 658
India	201	12 440 711	118	8 704 380	76	3 575 699
Germany	277	12 147 563	18	659 091	5	502 546
Italy	248	10 210 585	125	5 109 928	40	3 126 922
South Korea	177	10 181 158	10	571 390	122	8 313 809
Japan	123	10 029 061	48	5 310 415	48	3 961 802
Iran	118	9 022 357	35	6 170 089	40	1 789 317
United Kingdom	208	8 740 406	53	2 105 500	21	1 587 552
Danish Int'l[6]	134	8 585 386	41	2 680 880	4	321 829
St. Vincent & the Grenadines	216	7 341 117	12	620 961	119	5 106 973
Belgium	43	6 756 063	22	4 308 245	16	2 285 998
Bermuda	85	6 584 222	23	2 121 524	26	3 626 865
Malaysia	122	6 412 884	65	4 811 853	24	856 210

[1]Includes: Petroleum Tankers, Chemical Carriers, LNG Carriers, LNG/LPG Carriers, LPG Carriers.
[2]Includes: Bulk Vessels, Bulk Containerships, Cement Carriers, Wood Chip Carriers, Ore/Bulk/Oil Carriers, Bulk/Oil Carriers, Lakers.
[6]International Shipping Registry which is an open registry under which a ship flies the flag of a specified nation but is exempt from certain taxation and other regulations.

Table 13-24. Top 25 World Merchant Fleets by Flag and Type, 2005—*Continued*

Flag of Registry	Containership[3]			Roll-on/Roll-off[4]		General Cargo[5]	
	No.	DWT	TEU's	No.	DWT	No.	DWT
Top 25 registries	2 382	94 000 907	6 870 944	579	10 232 680	1 039	17 214 921
Total all registries	2 837	106 234 517	7 748 373	703	12 427 776	1 495	24 144 412
Top 25 as a percent of total	84.0	88.5	88.7	82.4	82.3	69.5	71.3
Panama	541	22 132 290	1 601 251	244	3 852 650	240	3 507 351
Liberia	415	16 727 439	1 253 420	37	565 767	62	994 530
Greece	44	2 215 783	159 450	1	10 270	6	97 195
Hong Kong	81	3 636 167	272 804	5	83 780	52	1 060 788
Bahamas	68	2 692 249	190 795	30	609 661	77	1 020 756
Marshall Islands	121	3 921 760	300 481	5	77 182	32	903 724
Singapore	177	5 016 385	351 898	30	586 127	23	457 200
Malta	48	1 311 048	85 324	8	94 947	66	1 094 436
Cyprus	139	3 910 717	285 967	6	96 956	85	1 461 497
China	87	3 224 260	229 053	7	95 225	210	3 291 531
Norwegian Int'l[6]	1	33 855	2 835	48	1 025 810	2	22 140
Isle of Man	15	549 409	38 315	0	0	8	133 232
United States	74	3 110 662	225 627	56	1 415 521	8	186 473
India	4	99 612	6 233	0	0	3	61 020
Germany	248	10 896 410	825 787	3	36 200	3	53 316
Italy	25	926 928	67 811	52	977 020	6	69 787
South Korea	35	1 125 888	78 868	3	67 559	7	102 512
Japan	11	518 994	35 180	15	227 094	1	10 756
Iran	11	408 942	30 748	0	0	32	654 009
United Kingdom	104	4 609 620	350 641	20	289 489	10	148 245
Danish Int'l[6]	78	5 440 293	378 108	4	41 299	7	101 085
St. Vincent & the Grenadines	4	50 173	3 374	2	40 929	79	1 522 081
Belgium	5	161 820	11 186				
Bermuda	19	620 046	41 961	2	28 015	15	187 772
Malaysia	27	660 157	43 827	1	11 179	5	73 485

Source: U.S. Department of Transportation, Maritime Administration. *World Merchant Fleet 2005.* Clarkson Research Studies, Vessel Registers.
Note: Vessel capacities are expressed in deadweight (DWT) which is the total weight (metric tons) of cargo, fuel, fresh water, stores and crew which a ship can carry when immersed to its load line. For containerships, capacities are also expressed in twenty-foot equivalent units (TEU). A TEU is a nominal unit of measure equivalent to a 20'x8'x8' shipping container.
[3]Includes: Fully Cellular Containerships, Refrigerated Container Carriers.
[4]Includes: Roll on-Roll off Vessels, Roll on-Roll off/Containerships, Car Carriers.
[5]Includes: General Cargo Carriers, Partial Containerships, Refrigerated Ships, Barge Carriers, Barge Carriers, Livestock Carriers.
[6]International Shipping Registry which is an open registry under which a ship flies the flag of a specified nation but is exempt from certain taxation and other regulations.

Table 13-25. Freight Carried on Major U.S. Waterways, 1980–2004

(Millions of tons.)

Waterway	1980	1985	1990	1995	2000	2001	2002	2003	2004
Atlantic intracoastal waterway ..	4.0	3.1	4.2	3.5	3.1	2.5	1.9	1.9	2.3
Great Lakes	183.5	148.1	167.1	177.7	187.5	171.4	167.2	156.5	178.4
Gulf intracoastal waterway	94.5	102.5	115.5	117.9	113.8	112.2	107.7	117.8	123.3
Mississippi River system[1]	584.2	527.8	659.6	710.1	715.5	714.8	712.8	676.8	699.8
Mississippi River mainstem	441.5	384.0	475.6	520.2	515.6	504.2	501.7	478.0	496.9
Ohio River system[2]	179.3	203.9	260.0	267.6	274.4	281.8	280.9	261.3	271.5
Columbia River	49.2	42.4	51.4	57.1	55.2	50.3	45.0	47.2	53.5
Snake River	5.1	3.5	4.8	6.8	6.7	5.6	4.3	5.3	5.7

Source: U.S. Census Bureau. *Statistical Abstract of the United States: 2007.* U.S. Army Corps of Engineers.
[1]Main channels and all tributaries of the Mississippi, Illinois, Missouri, and Ohio Rivers.
[2]Main channels and all navigable tributaries and embayments of the Ohio, Tennessee, and Cumberland Rivers.

Table 13-26. Hazardous Shipments—Value, Tons, and Ton-Miles, 2002

Mode of transportation	Value (million dollars)		Tons (1,000)		Ton-miles (millions)		Average miles per shipment
	Total	Percent	Total	Percent	Total	Percent	
All modes	**660 181**	**100.0**	**2 191 519**	**100.0**	**326 727**	**100.0**	**136**
Single modes	**644 489**	**97.6**	**2 158 533**	**98.5**	**311 897**	**95.5**	**105**
Truck[1]	419 630	63.6	1 159 514	52.9	110 163	33.7	86
For-hire truck	189 803	28.8	449 503	20.5	65 112	19.9	285
Private truck	226 660	34.3	702 186	32.0	44 087	13.5	38
Rail	31 339	4.7	109 369	5.0	72 087	22.1	695
Water	46 856	7.1	228 197	10.4	70 649	21.6	(S)
Air (includes truck and air)	1 643	0.2	64	-	85	-	2 080
Pipeline[2]	145 021	22.0	661 390	30.2	(S)	(S)	(S)
Multiple modes	**9 631**	**1.5**	**18 745**	**0.9**	**12 488**	**3.8**	**849**
Parcel, U.S. Postal Service or courier	4 268	0.6	245	-	119	-	837
Other multiple modes	5 363	0.8	18 500	0.8	12 369	3.8	1 371
Other and unknown modes	**6 061**	**0.9**	**14 241**	**0.6**	**2 342**	**0.7**	**57**
Class of material	**660 181**	**100.0**	**2 191 519**	**100.0**	**326 727**	**100.0**	**136**
Class 1, explosives	7 901	1.2	5 000	0.2	1 568	0.5	651
Class 2, gasses	73 932	11.2	213 358	9.7	37 262	11.4	95
Class 3, flammable liquids	490 238	74.3	1 788 986	81.6	218 574	66.9	106
Class 4, flammable solids	6 566	1.0	11 300	0.5	4 391	1.3	158
Class 5, oxidizers and organic peroxides	5 471	0.8	12 670	0.6	4 221	1.3	407
Class 6, toxic (poison)	8 275	1.3	8 459	0.4	4 254	1.3	626
Class 7, radioactive materials	5 850	0.9	57	-	44	-	(S)
Class 8, corrosive materials	38 324	5.8	90 671	4.1	36 260	11.1	301
Class 9, miscellaneous dangerous goods	23 625	3.6	61 018	2.8	20 153	6.2	368

Source: U.S. Census Bureau. *Statistical Abstract of the United States: 2007.* U.S. Department of Transportation, Bureau of Transportation Statistics.
[1]Truck as a single mode includes shipments that went by private truck only, for-hire truck only, or a combination of private truck and for-hire truck.
[2]Commodity Flow Survey data exclude shipments of crude oil.
- = Quantity zero or rounds to zero.
S = Data do not meet publication standards due to high sampling variability or other reasons.

Table 13-27. Prohibited Items Intercepted at U.S. Airport Screening Checkpoints, 2002–2005

(Passengers boarding aircraft in thousands. For the calendar year. Transportation Security Administration (TSA) assumed responsibility for airport security on February 17, 2002, and by November 19, 2002, TSA assumed control over all passenger screenings from private contractors. TSA data are incomplete for 2002.)

Year	2002	2003	2004	2005
Passengers boarding aircraft total (1,000)[1]	612 876	646 275	702 921	738 568
Domestic	560 107	592 412	640 698	670 360
International	52 769	53 863	62 222	68 208
Total prohibited items	4 185 916	6 167 497	7 103 560	15 886 014
Knife[2]	1 147 843	1 969 003	2 055 306	1 822 846
Other cutting items[3]	2 063 729	3 029 318	3 409 724	3 276 936
Club[4]	13 134	25 578	28 998	20 531
Box cutter	37 504	21 396	22 428	21 319
Firearm[5]	983	638	254	(NA)
Incendiary[6]	83 086	485 792	697 242	371 711
Lighters[7]	(X)	(X)	(X)	9 420 653
Other[8]	839 637	635 772	889 608	952 018

Source: U.S. Census Bureau. *Statistical Abstract of the United States: 2007.* U.S. Department of Homeland Security, Transportation Security Administration. Air Transport Association of America. Air Transport Annual Report.
[1]Data comes from the Air Transport Association.
[2]Knife includes any length and type except round-bladed, butter, and plastic cutlery.
[3]Other cutting instruments refers to, e.g., scissors, screwdrivers, swords, sabers, and ice picks.
[4]Club refers to baseball bats, night sticks, billy clubs, bludgeons, etc.
[5]Firearm refers to items like pistols, revolvers, rifles, automatic weapons, shotguns, and parts of guns and firearms.
[6]Incendiaries refer to categories of ammunition and gunpowder, flammables/irritants, and explosives.
[7]As of April 14, 2005, passengers are prohibited from carrying all lighters on their person or in carry-on luggage onboard an airplane.
[8]Other refers to tools, self-defense items, and sporting goods (excluding baseball bats).
. . . = Not available.
X = Not applicable.

BOX 13 ■ Transportation for Disabled People

Americans with disabilities represent 18% of the U.S. population (51.2 million people) and are more likely than the nondisabled to encounter transportation difficulties. Although all riders describe similar reasons for transportation difficulties, they occur with greater frequency for those with disabilities: 12% of people with disabilities said they have difficulty accessing transportation versus only 3% of people without disabilities. "No or limited public transportation" was the difficulty most frequently cited by both groups (33% of those with disabilities compared with 47% without disabilities). Other transportation difficulties listed by those with disabilities were "don't have a car," 26%; "disability makes transportation hard to use," 17%; or "no one to depend on," 12%.

More than half of the 3.5 million people in the United States who are homebound have disabilities. This group tends to be older, with an average age of 66 and with more severe disabilities. Of those who are homebound and disabled, 29% cite difficulty accessing transportation as one of the reasons they never leave home.

The largest difference in transportation between those with disabilities and those without was in private motor vehicle driving (65% of those with disabilities versus 88% of those without). Additionally, those drivers with disabilities are more likely to place limitations on their driving than their counterparts without disabilities.

Percent of Disabled and Nondisabled that Limit or Restrict Driving

	Disability status			
	Disabled		Nondisabled	
Types of limitations or restrictions	Percent	Standard Error	Percent	Standard Error
Drive less often than used to	64.53	2.42	32.20	1.26
Avoid driving at night	51.50	2.21	25.78	1.08
Drive less in bad weather	66.34	2.09	49.75	1.39
Avoid high-speed roads and highways	38.42	1.97	21.77	1.05
Avoid busy roads and intersections	51.67	2.13	39.98	1.20
Drive slower than speed limits	22.02	1.66	14.92	0.99
Avoid left hand turns	11.37	1.49	8.41	0.71
Avoid driving during rush hours	57.98	1.90	41.99	1.44
Avoid driving unfamiliar roads or places	38.01	2.08	27.48	1.05
Avoid driving distances > 100 miles	47.24	2.13	21.91	1.06

Source: U.S. Department of Transportation, Bureau of Transportation Statistics. *2002 National Transportation Availability and Use Survey.*
Note: This table contains the weighted percent or weighted mean and the standard error.

Sources:

U.S. Census Bureau. *U.S. Census Bureau News, Facts for Features,* (CB07-FF.10) May 29, 2007. http://www.census.gov/Press-Release/www/2007/cb07ff-10.pdf

U.S. Department of Transportation, Bureau of Transportation Statistics. *Freedom to Travel.* http://www.bts.gov/publications/freedom_to_travel/

U.S. Department of Transportation, Bureau of Transportation Statistics. *Issue Brief: Transportation Difficulties Keep Over Half a Million Disabled at Home,* April 2003. http://www.bts.gov/publications/issue_briefs/number_03/pdf/entire.pdf

U.S. Department of Transportation, Bureau of Transportation Statistics. Travel Patterns of Older Americans with Disabilities. http://www.bts.gov/programs/bts_working_papers/2004/paper_01/

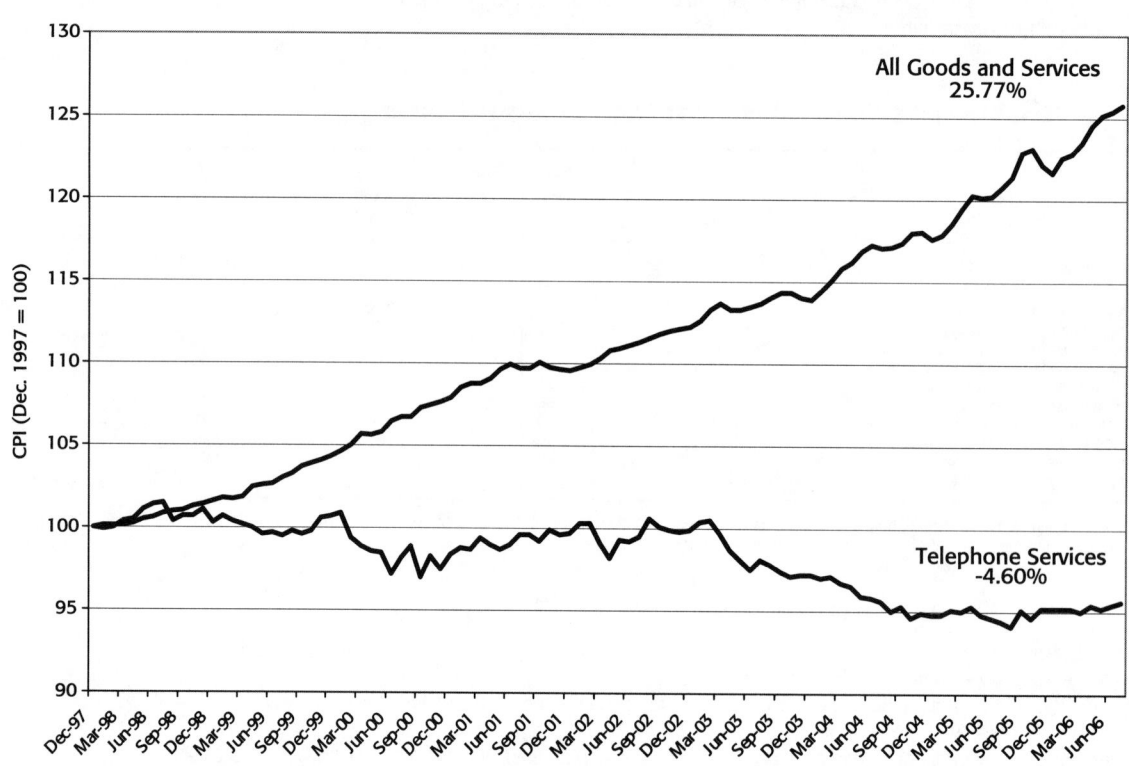

Consumer Price Indices

CHAPTER **14**

Communications

HIGHLIGHTS

1 Communication systems are regulated primarily by the Federal Communications Commission and also by the Interstate Commerce Commission. The bulk of the regional telephone services are provided by the so-called Baby Bells, but the telecommunications industry has been transformed beyond recognition by new communications technology. There is no longer any distinction between local and regional providers and carriers and national ones, and all communications companies are engaged not only in telephones, but in video, Internet, satellites, data transmission, cellulars, interactives, and a host of other new services. AT&T continues to be the largest communications company, closely followed by MCI (owned by Worldcom) and Sprint. Until the 1980s, AT&T was a virtual monopoly, controlling virtually all local and interstate facilities and services. Through Western Union, it controlled production facilities as well. The number of companies within AT&T (known as American Bell Telephone Company until 1900) varied from time to time. At its peak in 1915/1916, it included 39 companies, but subsequent consolidations reduced it to 25. At the time of its breakup, it included 21 totally owned and controlled regional companies (AT&T owned 100 percent of the outstanding shares, although these companies operated under their own names), one subsidiary of one of these regional companies, two companies in which it had substantial minority interests (Cincinnati Bell and Southern New England Telephone Company), Bell Telephone Laboratories, and Western Electric Company.

2 An interesting footnote in the history of U.S. communications is the story of the rise and fall of Western Union Telegraph. Founded in 1851 as the New York and Mississippi Valley Printing and Telegraph Company, it emerged within a few decades as the sole telegraph company in the United States. Western Union developed close contractual ties with the railways, constructing telegraph pole lines along railroad rights-of-way and using railroad stations and personnel for pickup and delivery of telegraph messages. Western Union's most serious rival was the Postal Telegraph which was acquired in the 1880s by Mackay's Commercial Cable Company (later IT&T). Postal Telegraph merged with the Western Union in 1943, but shortly thereafter telegraph was rendered obsolete by other modern forms of communication. On January 27, 2006, Western Union stopped sending telegrams completely. Most of the telegrams sent during the last few days were by people wanting to be the last ones to send a Western Union telegram.

3 Another nineteenth century technological breakthrough that became obsolete was the submarine cable. The first successful cable linking North America with Europe was laid in 1866. The first telegraph rate on cable (presumably from New York to London) was $100 for 100 words. Subsequently, it was reduced, first to $50 and later to $25. By 1868, the rate had fallen to $15.75 and by 1885 to $4.00. By 1916, the New York to London rate was $.17 cents per word. Radio was not a significant factor in overseas communication until the Radio Corporation of America entered the field as successor to the Marconi Company, which was the first company to utilize and market the invention of wireless.

4 Among all forms of communications, federal control has been most effective in radio and television. In 1912, the Department of Commerce was given authority to license radio equipment, operators and broadcast stations, which began operation in 1921. On February 23, 1927, Congress established the Federal Radio Commission; its powers were transferred to the Federal Communications Commission (FCC) in 1934.

5 Statistics on radio and television are provided in the annual reports of the FCC as well as its *Statistics of the Communications Industry.* Unlike the telephone and telegraph, radio and television are not common carriers (public utilities that are subject to strict government supervision) and therefore are not subject to rate or earnings regulation. Statistics on radio and television broadcasting stations are presented in terms of licensed and authorized stations, the former generally referring to operating stations. FM radio was authorized as a regular service in 1941; in the same year the first commercial station was licensed. Noncommercial FM is a separate service with a specific spectrum allocation. Television was first authorized on a regular commercial basis on July 1, 1941, and two stations in New York were the first to begin operations. Time series broadcast advertising was first developed by L. D. H. Weld of McCann-Erickson Advertising Agency and continued after his death in 1946 by Hans Zeisel and others.

6 The first mail service was started in the colonies in 1673 between New York and Boston, a distance of 260 miles. The trip took two weeks on horseback; much of that time was spent waiting for ferries. Mail was not inexpensive. At a time when a decent day's wage was 50 cents, a letter from New York to Philadelphia cost $3.50, and from New York to Williamsburg, Virginia, $11.50. The first postage rates were fixed by the Continental Congress in 1782. In the early days the recipient rather than the sender paid the postage. In 1847, postage stamps were introduced, and in 1885, compulsory prepayment for all domestic letter mail was established. Postcards were introduced in 1898. It was not until 1863 that mail was divided into classes. Local rates were often improvised because no one knew for sure how much it cost to transport mail. The first letter rate on the Pony Express (which operated between Missouri and California during 1860 and 1861) was $5 for a half ounce; it was later reduced to $2 and then $1. Rates continued to fall well into the twentieth century, reaching their lowest in 1928 and 1946 when a first-class postage stamp cost only 5 cents. Postage rates have been rising since then, while telephone rates have done the opposite. In 1915, it cost $20.70 to call New York from San Francisco, but only 5 cents to mail a letter; in 1999, it cost only 7 cents for the same long distance call (for one minute), but 33 cents to mail a letter.

7 Since 1970, contrary to popular perceptions and prejudices against "snail mail," the U.S. Postal Service has become one of the most efficient and productive businesses in the nation. Although the number of post offices is down from 30,326 in 1980 to 27,385 in 2005, the number of pieces of mail handled grew from 106.311 billion to 211.743 billion, the number of employees from 667,000 to 803,000, and operating revenues from $19.253 billion to $69.907 billion during the same period.

8 A book has never been properly defined, but according to the United Nations Educational, Scientific, and Cultural Organization (UNESCO) it is any printed and bound publication longer than 49 pages that is not a periodical. Book publishing statistics, compiled from a number of sources, are not strictly comparable over time and may vary depending on what is included as well as what is excluded. The legal requirement of copyright and deposit of copies with the Library of Congress ensures that the publication of the vast majority of books is documented. The International Standard Book Number (ISBN) system also has the same effect, although compliance is voluntary.

9 In 2001, book publishers employed 89,700 paid employees, with an annual payroll of $4,803 million. The book title output, the most important industry indicator, has increased from 46,738 in 1990 to 96,080 in 2000. The subjects with most titles are sociology and economics (12,039), fiction (11,808), science (7,140), history (6,948), religion (5,086), and medicine (4,817). Average hardcover prices have gone up from $24.64 in 1980 to $60.80 in 2000 and trade paperback prices from $8.60 to $29.48.

10 The number of daily newspapers declined from 1,745 in 1980 to 1,452 in 2005. Fewer people read newspapers in 2005 than in 1970. Total paid circulation of dailies has fallen from 62.1 million to 55.3 million during this period. In per capita terms, the circulation has fallen from 0.30 to 0.18. Per capita circulation is highest in Virginia (0.41) and lowest in Maryland (.09).

11 Total advertising expenditures in all media were $237.4 billion in 2002. The share of each medium is determined by the nature of the special audience that is being addressed. The highest is television at 24.3 percent, followed by direct mail (19.3 percent), newspapers (18.7 percent), radio (8.0 percent), the "Yellow Pages" (5.8 percent), magazines (4.6 percent), and business papers (1.8 percent).

12 The total value of recording media shipments (including CDs, cassettes, and albums) was $12.270 billion in 2005, down from $14.324 billion in 2000.

13 Deregulation of the telecommunications industry has encouraged competition. In 2004, there were 4,636 service providers (including 2,681 local service providers), and the gross sectoral revenue had grown to $291.123 billion. That same year, there were 268 million access lines handling 425 billion local calls and 81 billion toll calls. International calls numbered 7.350 billion. The telecommunications industry had operating revenues in 2004 of $356.113 billion and operating expenses of $314.103 billion.

14 The United States is fast approaching total saturation in the utilization of all media. In 2004, access to telephones was 94.2 percent, radio 99.0 percent, and television 98.2 percent. Cable is behind with 67.5 percent (2005), computers 61.8 percent (2003), and internet access 54.6 percent (2003).

15 There were 3.079 billion books sold in 2005. Juvenile paperbacks sold the largest number with 606.4 million books.

16 The number of average basic cable television subscribers dropped from 66.732 million people in 2001 to 65.337 million in 2005, but total revenue during the same time period increased from $42.557 billion to $66.414 billion.

17 Forty-three percent of people who had a broadband connection at home tended to use the Internet as their news source, while only 26 percent of people with a dial-up connection did so. Local television still remains the news medium of choice for 59 percent of all adults and 60 percent of all Internet users.

Table 14-1. Radio and Television Stations, Sets Produced, and Households with Sets, 1921–2005

(Number, as of June 30, except as noted.)

Year	Operation broadcast stations[1]			Cable television		Households with	
	Standard broadcast (AM)[2]	Frequency modulation (FM), commercial[2]	Television (TV), commercial[3]	Systems	Total subscribers (households, in thousands)	Radio sets (thousands)[2]	Television sets (thousands)[3]
2005	4 758	6 215	1 370	. . .	. . .	. . .	112 000
2004	4 770	6 217	1 366	8 869	. . .	108 300	110 000
2003	4 802	6 207	1 349	9 038	. . .	106 700	108 000
2002	4 804	6 161	1 333	9 339	. . .	105 100	107 000
2001	4 727	6 051	1 309	9 924	73 000	101 900	104 000
2000	4 685	5 892	1 288	10 243	69 300	100 500	103 000
1999	4 783	5 766	1 243	10 700	68 500	. . .	101 000
1998	4 793	5 662	1 221	10 845	67 000	. . .	100 000
1997	4 762	5 542	1 195	10 950	65 900	98 000	99 000
1996	4 857	5 419	1 174	11 119	64 600	98 000	98 000
1995	4 909	5 296	1 161	11 218	63 000	98 000	97 000
1994	4 913	5 109	1 145	11 214	60 500	98 000	94 000
1993	4 994	4 971	1 138	11 217	58 800	97 300	93 000
1992	4 961	4 785	1 118	11 075	57 200	96 600	92 000
1991	4 985	4 570	1 098	10 704	55 800	95 500	93 000
1990	4 987	4 392	1 092	9 575	54 900	94 400	94 000
1989	4 975	4 269	1 061	9 050	47 800	92 800	90 000
1988	4 932	4 155	1 028	8 500	43 800	91 100	89 000
1987	4 902	4 041	968	7 900	41 000	89 900	87 000
1986	4 863	3 944	919	7 600	37 500	88 100	86 000
1985	4 718	3 875	883	6 844	31 300	87 100	87 000
1984	4 754	3 716	841	6 200	30 000	86 700	84 000
1983	4 733	3 527	813	5 600	25 000	. . .	83 300
1982	4 668	3 380	777	4 825	21 000	. . .	81 500
1981	4 634	3 349	756	4 375	18 300	. . .	79 900
1980	4 589	3 282	734	4 225	15 500	78 600	78 000
1979	4 511	3 036	723	4 150	14 100	. . .	74 500
1978	4 459	2 922	714	3 875	13 000	. . .	72 900
1977	4 474	3 007	697	3 832	11 900	. . .	71 200
1976	. . .	701	3 681	10 800	. . .	69 600	
1975	4 463	2 767	706	3 506	9 800	71 400	69 000
1974	4 305	2 413	694	3 158	8 700	. . .	. . .
1973	4 295	2 278	692	2 991	7 300	. . .	. . .
1972	4 273	2 229	690	2 841	6 000	. . .	. . .
1971	4 250	2 122	688	2 639	5 300	. . .	. . .
1970	4 323	2 196	677	2 490	4 500	62 000	59 000
1970[4,5]	. . .	. . .	. . .	. . .	. . .	246 108	60 594
1969	4 254	2 018	680	2 260	3 600	60 600	58 250
1968	4 203	1 850	655	2 000	2 800	58 500	56 670
1967	4 135	1 708	626	1 770	2 100	57 500	55 130
1966	4 075	1 515	613	1 570	1 575	57 000	53 850
1965	4 025	1 343	589	1 325	1 275	55 200	52 700
1964	3 976	1 181	582	1 200	1 085	54 000	51 600
1963	3 860	1 120	581	1 000	950	52 300	50 300
1962	3 745	1 012	571	800	850	51 305	48 855
1961	3 602	889	553	700	725	50 695	47 200
1960*	3 483	741	579	640	650	50 193	45 750
1960[4]	. . .	. . .	. . .	. . .	. . .	48 504	46 312
1959	3 377	622	566	560	550	*49 450	*43 950
1958	3 253	548	556	525	450	48 500	41 924
1957	3 079	530	519	500	350	47 600	38 900
1956	2 896	530	496	450	300	46 800	34 900
1955	2 732	540	458	400	150	45 900	30 700
1954	2 583	553	402	300	65	45 100	26 000
1953	2 458	580	198	150	30	44 800	20 400
1952	2 355	629	108	70	14	42 800	15 300
1951	2 281	649	107	. . .	. . .	41 900	10 320

[1]Includes Alaska, Hawaii, Puerto Rico, Guam and Virgin Islands for all years. Prior to 1948, the FCC did not keep records on the number of stations on the air. Therefore, data for 1933–1948 are for authorized stations and may include a number that were actually not on the air.

[2]1970–1995 as of December 31, except as noted. Source: M Street Corp. as reported by Radio Advertising Bureau New York, NY, through 1992, Radio Facts, annual (copyright); beginning 1993, Radio Marketing Guide and Fact Book for Advertisers, annual (copyright). Number of stations on the air compiled from Federal Communications Commission reports. 1985 data as of February 1986. Beginning 1996, Federal Communications Commission, unpublished data as of September 30.

[3]1970–1975, as of September of prior year; all other years as of January of year shown. Excludes Alaska and Hawaii. Data from Television Bureau of Advertising, Inc., Trends in Television, annual (copyright). Beginning 1997, Federal Communications Commission, unpublished data.

[4]Census figures, as of April 1.

[5]In 1970 census of housing, only battery-operated radios were enumerated.

. . . = Not available.

* = First year for which figures include Alaska and Hawaii.

Table 14-1. Radio and Television Stations, Sets Produced, and Households with Sets, 1921–2005—*Continued*

(Number, as of June 30, except as noted.)

Year	Operation broadcast stations[1]			Cable television		Households with	
	Standard broadcast (AM)[2]	Frequency modulation (FM), commercial[2]	Television (TV), commercial[3]	Systems	Total subscribers (households, in thousands)	Radio sets (thousands)[2]	Television sets (thousands)[3]
1950	2 144	691	104	...	...	40 700	3 875
1950[4]	...	...	...	...	...	40 411	5 030
1949	2 066	737	69	...	...	39 300	940
1948	2 034	1 020	108	...	...	37 623	172
1947	1 795	918	66	...	...	35 900	14
1946	1 215	511	30	...	...	33 998	8
1945	955	53	9	...	...	33 100	...
1944	924	52	9	...	...	32 500	...
1943	912	48	8	...	...	30 800	...
1942[6]	925	42	10	...	...	30 600	...
1941	897	49	2	...	...	29 300	...
1940	847	...	...	...	...	28 500	...
1940[4]	...	...	...	...	...	28 048	...
1939	778	...	...	...	...	27 500	...
1938	743	...	...	...	...	26 667	...
1937	704	...	...	...	...	24 500	...
1936	656	...	...	...	...	22 869	...
1935	623	...	...	...	...	21 456	...
1934	593	...	...	...	...	20 400	...
1933	598	...	...	...	...	19 250	...
1932	604	...	...	...	...	18 450	...
1931	612	...	...	...	...	16 700	...
1930	618	...	...	...	...	13 750	...
1930[4]	...	...	...	...	...	12 049	...
1929	606	...	...	...	...	10 250	...
1928	677	...	...	...	...	8 000	...
1927	681	...	...	...	...	...	...
1926	528	...	...	...	...	...	...
1925	571	...	...	...	...	...	...
1924	530	...	...	...	...	...	...
1923	556	...	...	...	...	...	...
1922	30	...	...	...	...	...	...
1921[7]	1	...	...	...	...	...	...

Source: U.S. Census Bureau.

[1]Includes Alaska, Hawaii, Puerto Rico, Guam and Virgin Islands for all years. Prior to 1948, the FCC did not keep records on the number of stations on the air. Therefore, data for 1933–1948 are for authorized stations and may include a number that were actually not on the air.

[2]1970–1995 as of December 31, except as noted. Source: M Street Corp. as reported by Radio Advertising Bureau New York, NY, through 1992, Radio Facts, annual (copyright); beginning 1993, Radio Marketing Guide and Fact Book for Advertisers, annual (copyright). Number of stations on the air compiled from Federal Communications Commission reports. 1985 data as of February 1986. Beginning 1996, Federal Communications Commission, unpublished data as of September 30.

[3]1970–1975, as of September of prior year; all other years as of January of year shown. Excludes Alaska and Hawaii. Data from Television Bureau of Advertising, Inc., Trends in Television, annual (copyright). Beginning 1997, Federal Communications Commission, unpublished data.

[4]Census figures, as of April 1.

[6]Authorization of new radio stations and production of radio receivers for commercial use halted from April 1942 until October 1945.

[7]First station to receive regular license as of September 15; other stations in operation experimentally.

... = Not available.

Table 14-2. Cable and Pay TV—Summary, 1975–2005

(Thousands. Cable TV for calendar year. Pay TV as of December 31 of year shown.)

	Cable TV				Pay TV						Pay units penetration of homes passed	Pay units penetration of homes with
	Average basic subscribers (1,000)	Average monthly basic rate (dollars)	Revenue[1] (million dollars)		Units[2] (1,000)			Monthly rate (dollars)				
Year			Total	Basic	Total pay[3]	Pay cable	Non-cable delivered premium	All pay weighted average[3]	Pay cable	Non-cable delivered premium		
2005[4]	65 337	39.63	66 414	31 075	125 662	81 128	44 534	10.08	10.16	9.93	102	192
2004	65 727	38.14	60 008	30 080	122 248	80 753	41 495	10.03	10.11	9.88	101	186
2003	66 050	36.59	54 352	29 000	119 927	78 939	40 988	9.37	9.45	9.23	102	182
2002	66 472	34.71	48 733	27 690	118 575	77 292	41 283	9.19	9.29	9.00	103	178
2001	66 732	32.87	42 577	26 324	115 325	75 433	39 892	8.95	9.10	8.66	102	173
2000	66 250	30.37	37 070	24 142	102 590	65 918	36 672	8.69	8.81	8.48	92	155
1999	65 500	28.92	34 095	22 732	88 455	59 005	29 450	8.73	8.85	8.50	81	135
1998	64 650	27.81	31 191	21 574	80 605	55 280	25 325	8.58	8.74	8.22	75	125
1997	63 600	26.48	28 931	20 213	72 785	51 933	20 852	8.31	8.43	8.00	69	114
1996	62 300	24.41	26 195	18 249	63 705	49 728	13 977	7.98	8.12	7.50	61	102
1995	60 550	23.07	24 137	16 763	55 723	46 798	8 925	8.29	8.54	6.99	54	92
1994	58 373	21.62	21 531	15 144	47 478	42 528	4 950	8.19	8.33	6.99	47	81
1993	[5]56 200	19.39	22 809	13 528	42 010	37 113	...	9.27	9.11	...	48	75
1992	54 300	19.08	21 079	12 433	40 893	36 879	...	10.29	10.17	...	48	78
1991	52 570	18.10	19 426	11 418	39 983	36 569	...	10.35	10.27	...	45	75
1990	50 520	16.78	17 582	10 174	39 902	39 751	...	10.35	10.30	...	46	77
1989	47 500	15.21	15 378	8 670	39 055	38 916	...	10.25	10.20	...	47	79
1988	44 160	13.86	13 409	7 345	37 085	36 777	...	10.24	10.17	...	48	81
1987	41 160	12.18	11 563	6 016	33 528	33 232	...	10.25	10.23	...	46	79
1986	38 170	10.67	9 955	4 887	31 033	30 668	...	10.35	10.31	...	45	78
1985	35 440	9.73	8 831	4 138	29 885	29 418	...	10.29	10.25	...	46	82
1984	32 800	8.98	7 738	3 534	28 815	27 754	...	10.03	9.96	...	48	84
1983	29 430	8.61	6 485	3 041	24 515	22 818	...	9.82	9.70	...	47	84
1982	25 250	8.30	5 032	2 515	19 395	17 007	...	9.49	9.30	...	42	76
1981	21 100	7.99	3 675	2 023	14 310	12 239	...	9.16	8.92	...	37	67
1980	17 500	7.69	2 609	1 615	8 581	7 336	...	8.91	8.62	...	26	47
1979	15 000	7.40	1 942	1 332	5 157	4 480	...	8.54	8.24	...	20	36
1978	13 400	7.13	1 513	1 147	2 473	2 182	...	8.16	8.01	...	12	23
1977	12 200	6.86	1 207	1 004	1 138	1 047	...	8.03	7.92	...	7	13
1976	11 000	6.45	932	851	611	568	...	7.96	7.87	...	11	22
1975	9 800	6.50	804	764	194	194	...	...	7.85	...	11	24

Source: U.S. Census Bureau. *Statistical Abstract of the United States: 2007.* Kagan Research, LLC. *Broadband Cable Financial Databook 2004©*; *Cable Program* Investor, December 16, 2004, March 30, 2006, and various other publications.
Note: A pay unit is a subscription service; the average cable household subscribes to 1.5 (2004).
[1]Includes installation revenue, subscriber revenue, and nonsubscriber revenue; excludes telephony and high-speed access.
[2]Individual program services sold to subscribers.
[3]Includes multipoint distribution service (MDS), satellite TV (STV), multipoint multichannel distribution service (MMDS), satellite master antenna TV (SMATV), C-band satellite, and DBS satellite. Includes average pay unit price based on data for major premium pay movie services.
[4]2005 data is estimated.
[5]Weighted average representing 8 months of unregulated basic rate and 4 months of FCC rolled-back rate.
. . . = Not available.

Table 14-3. Recording Media—Manufacturers' Shipments and Value, 1985–2005

(Number in millions, millions of dollars. Minus sign (–) indicates returns greater than shipments.)

Medium	1985	1990	1995	1996	1997	1998	1999	2000	2001	2002	2003	2004	2005
UNIT SHIPMENTS[1]													
Total[2,3]	**653.0**	**865.7**	**1 112.7**	**1 137.2**	**1 063.4**	**1 123.9**	**1 160.6**	**1 079.2**	**968.5**	**859.7**	**798.4**	**958.0**	**1 301.8**
Compact Discs	22.6	286.5	722.9	778.9	753.1	847.0	938.9	942.5	881.9	803.3	746.0	767.0	705.4
Compact disc singles	...	1.1	21.5	43.2	66.7	56.0	55.9	34.2	17.3	4.5	8.3	3.1	2.8
Cassettes	339.1	442.2	272.6	225.3	172.6	158.5	123.6	76.0	45.0	31.1	17.2	5.2	2.5
Cassette singles	...	87.4	70.7	59.9	42.2	26.4	14.2	1.3	-1.5	-0.5	...	...	...
Albums—Long Playing and Extended Play ..	167.0	11.7	2.2	2.9	2.7	3.4	2.9	2.2	2.3	1.7	1.5	1.4	1.0
Vinyl singles	120.7	27.6	10.2	10.1	7.5	5.4	5.3	4.8	5.5	4.4	3.8	3.5	2.3
Music video	...	9.2	12.6	16.9	18.6	27.2	19.8	18.2	17.7	14.7	19.9	32.8	33.8
Digital Video Disc video	...	...	...	...	...	0.5	2.5	3.3	7.9	10.7	17.5	29.0	27.8
Digital Video Disc audio	...	...	...	...	...	...	...	...	0.3	0.4	0.4	0.3	0.5
Super Audio Compact Disc	...	...	...	...	...	...	...	...	...	...	1.3	0.8	0.5
Download single	...	...	...	...	...	...	...	...	...	...	...	139.4	366.9
Download album	...	...	...	...	...	...	...	...	...	...	...	4.6	13.6
Kiosk													0.7
Mobile[4]	...	...	...	...	...	...	...	...	...	...	...	...	170.0
Subscription	...	...	...	...	...	...	...	...	...	...	...	...	1.3
VALUE													
Total	**4 378.8**	**7 541.1**	**12 320.3**	**12 533.8**	**12 236.8**	**13 711.2**	**14 584.7**	**14 323.7**	**13 740.9**	**12 614.2**	**11 854.4**	**12 338.1**	**12 269.5**
Compact Discs	389.5	3 451.6	9 377.4	9 934.7	9 915.1	11 416.0	12 816.3	13 214.5	12 909.4	12 044.1	11 232.9	11 446.5	10 520.2
Compact disc singles	...	6.0	110.9	184.1	272.7	213.2	222.4	142.7	79.4	19.6	36.0	15.0	10.9
Cassettes	2 411.5	3 472.4	2 303.6	1 905.3	1 522.7	1 419.9	1 061.6	626.0	363.4	209.8	108.1	23.7	13.1
Cassette singles	...	257.9	236.3	189.3	133.5	94.4	48.0	4.6	-5.3	-1.6	...	...	...
Albums—Long Playing and Extended Play ..	1 280.5	86.5	25.1	36.8	33.3	34.0	31.8	27.7	27.4	20.5	21.7	19.3	14.2
Vinyl singles	281.0	94.4	46.7	47.5	35.6	25.7	27.9	26.3	31.4	24.9	21.5	19.9	13.2
Music video	...	172.3	220.3	236.1	323.9	508.0	376.7	281.9	329.2	288.4	399.9	607.2	602.2
Digital Video Disc video	...	...	...	...	...	12.2	66.3	80.3	190.7	236.3	369.6	561.0	539.8
Digital Video Disc audio	...	...	...	...	...	...	...	...	6.0	8.5	8.0	6.5	11.2
Super Audio Compact Disc	...	...	...	...	...	...	...	...	...	...	26.3	16.6	10.0
Download single	...	...	...	...	...	...	...	...	...	...	...	138.0	363.3
Download album	...	...	...	...	...	...	...	...	...	...	...	45.5	135.7
Kiosk													1.0
Mobile[4]	...	...	...	...	...	...	...	...	...	...	...	...	421.6
Subscription	...	...	...	...	...	...	...	...	...	...	...	...	149.2

Source: U.S. Census Bureau. *Statistical Abstract of the United States: 2007.* Recording Industry of America. *2005 Year-end Statistics©* and earlier issues.
Note: Based on reports of Recording Industry of America member companies who distributed approximately 84 percent of the prerecorded music in 2005. These data are supplemented by other sources.
[1]Net units, after returns.
[2]Total number of units excludes subscriptions.
[3]Includes other formats not listed separately.
[4]Includes Master Ringtunes, Ringbacks, Full Length Downloads and other mobile.
. . . = Not available.

Table 14-4. Postal Service—Post Offices, Revenues, Expenditures, and Pieces of Mail Handled, 1789–2005

(Number; thousands of dollars; for years ending June 30; includes Alaska, Hawaii, Puerto Rico.)

Year	Post offices[1]	Revenues[2,3] (thousands of dollars)	Expenditures[2,4] (thousands of dollars)	Pieces of mail handled (thousands)
2005	27 385	69 907 000	68 283 000	211 743 000
2004	27 505	68 996 000	65 851 000	206 106 000
2003	27 556	68 529 000	63 902 000	202 185 000
2002	27 791	66 463 000	65 234 000	202 822 000
2001	27 876	65 834 000	65 640 000	207 463 000
2000	27 876	64 540 000	62 992 000	207 882 000
1999	27 893	62 755 000	60 642 000	201 644 000
1998	38 159	60 116 000	57 786 000	196 905 000
1997	38 019	58 331 000	54 873 000	190 888 000
1996	38 212	56 544 000	53 113 000	183 440 000
1995	28 392	54 509 000	50 730 000	180 734 000
1994	28 657	49 576 000	48 455 000	177 100 000
1993	28 728	47 986 000	46 322 000	171 200 000
1992	28 837	47 105 000	45 653 000	166 400 000
1991	28 912	44 202 000	43 291 000	165 900 000
1990	28 959	40 074 000	40 490 000	166 301 000
1989	29 083	38 920 000	38 370 000	161 600 000
1988	29 203	35 939 000	36 119 000	161 000 000
1987	29 319	32 297 000	32 520 000	153 900 000
1986	29 344	31 021 000	30 716 000	147 400 000
1985	29 557	28 956 000	29 207 000	140 100 000
1984	29 750	26 474 000	26 357 000	131 500 000
1983	29 990	24 699 000	24 083 000	119 400 000
1982	30 155	23 628 000	22 826 000	114 000 000
1981	30 242	20 781 000	21 369 000	110 100 000
1980	30 326	19 253 000	19 413 000	106 311 000
1979	30 449	17 999 000	17 529 000	99 800 000
1978	30 518	15 841 000	16 220 000	98 900 000
1977	30 521	14 622 000	15 310 000	92 200 000
1976	30 521	12 747 000	13 923 000	89 800 000
1975	30 754	11 590 000	12 578 000	89 300 000
1974	31 000	10 857 000	11 295 000	90 100 000
1973	31 385	9 913 000	9 926 000	89 700 000
1972	31 686	9 347 000	9 522 000	87 200 000
1971	31 947	8 751 000	8 955 000	87 000 000
1970	32 002	7 701 695	7 867 269	84 881 833
1969	32 064	7 025 898	7 168 489	82 004 501
1968	32 260	6 423 515	6 543 920	79 516 731
1967	32 626	5 101 982	6 249 027	78 366 572
1966	33 121	4 784 186	5 726 523	75 607 302
1965	33 624	4 483 390	5 275 840	71 873 166
1964	34 040	4 276 123	4 927 825	69 676 477
1963	34 498	3 879 128	4 698 528	67 852 738
1962	34 797	3 557 041	4 331 617	66 493 190
1961	34 955	3 423 059	4 249 414	64 932 859
1960	35 238	3 276 588	3 873 953	63 674 604
1959	35 750	3 035 232	3 640 368	61 247 220
1958	36 308	2 550 221	3 440 810	60 129 911
1957	37 012	2 496 614	3 044 438	59 077 633
1956	37 515	2 419 354	2 883 305	56 441 216
1955	38 316	2 349 477	2 712 150	55 233 564
1954	39 405	2 268 517	2 667 664	52 213 170
1953	40 609	2 091 714	2 742 126	50 948 156
1952	40 919	1 947 316	2 666 860	49 905 875
1951	41 193	1 776 816	2 341 399	46 908 410
1950	41 464	1 677 487	2 222 949	45 063 737
1949	41 607	1 571 851	2 149 322	43 555 108
1948	41 695	1 410 971	1 687 805	40 280 374
1947	41 760	1 299 141	1 504 799	37 427 706
1946	41 751	1 224 572	1 353 654	36 318 158
1945	41 792	1 314 240	1 145 002	37 912 067
1944	42 161	1 112 877	1 068 987	34 930 685
1943	42 654	966 227	952 529	32 818 262
1942	43 358	859 817	873 950	30 117 633
1941	43 739	812 828	836 859	29 235 791

[1] Excludes branches and stations.
[2] Accounting basis changed from cash to accrual basis in 1954; from accrual basis to accrued cost basis in 1963.
[3] Net revenues after refunds of postage. Includes operating reimbursements, stamped envelope purchases, indemnity claims, and miscellaneous revenue and expenditure offsets. Shown in year which gave rise to the earnings.
[4] Shown in year in which obligation was incurred.

Table 14-4. Postal Service—Post Offices, Revenues, Expenditures, and Pieces of Mail Handled, 1789–2005—*Continued*

(Number; thousands of dollars; for years ending June 30; includes Alaska, Hawaii, Puerto Rico.)

Year	Post offices[1]	Revenues[2,3] (thousands of dollars)	Expenditures[2,4] (thousands of dollars)	Pieces of mail handled (thousands)
1940	44 024	766 949	807 629	27 749 467
1939	44 327	745 955	784 550	26 444 846
1938	44 586	728 634	772 308	26 041 979
1937	44 877	726 201	772 743	25 801 279
1936	45 230	665 343	753 616	23 571 315
1935	45 686	630 795	696 503	22 331 752
1934	46 506	586 733	630 733	20 625 827
1933	47 641	587 631	699 887	19 868 456
1932	48 159	588 172	793 684	24 306 744
1931	48 733	656 463	802 485	26 544 352
1930	49 063	705 484	803 667	27 887 823
1929	49 482	696 948	782 344	27 951 548
1928	49 944	693 634	725 700	26 837 005
1927	50 266	683 122	714 577	26 686 556
1926	50 601	659 820	679 704	25 483 529
1925	50 957	599 591	639 282	. . .
1924	51 266	572 949	587 377	. . .
1923	51 613	532 828	556 851	23 054 832
1922	51 950	484 854	545 644	. . .
1921	52 168	463 491	620 994	. . .
1920	52 641	437 150	454 323	. . .
1919	53 084	[5]436 239	362 498	. . .
1918	54 347	[5]388 976	324 834	. . .
1917	55 414	329 726	319 839	. . .
1916	55 935	312 058	306 204	. . .
1915	56 380	287 248	298 546	. . .
1914	56 810	287 935	283 544	. . .
1913	58 020	266 620	262 068	18 567 445
1912	58 729	246 744	248 525	17 588 659
1911	59 237	237 880	237 649	16 900 552
1910	59 580	224 129	229 977	14 850 102
1909	60 144	203 562	221 004	14 004 577
1908	60 704	191 479	208 352	13 364 069
1907	62 658	183 585	190 238	12 255 666
1906	65 600	167 933	178 450	11 361 091
1905	68 131	152 827	167 399	10 187 506
1904	71 131	143 582	152 362	9 502 460
1903	74 169	134 224	138 784	8 887 467
1902	75 924	121 848	124 786	8 085 447
1901	76 945	111 631	115 555	7 424 390
1900	76 688	102 354	107 740	7 129 990
1899	75 000	95 021	101 632	6 576 310
1898	73 570	89 013	98 054	6 214 447
1897	71 022	82 665	94 077	5 781 002
1896	70 360	82 499	90 933	5 693 719
1895	70 064	76 983	87 180	5 134 281
1894	69 805	75 080	84 994	4 919 090
1893	68 403	75 897	81 582	5 021 841
1892	67 119	70 930	76 981	4 776 575
1891	64 329	65 932	73 060	4 369 900
1890	62 401	60 882	66 260	4 005 408
1889	58 999	56 176	62 317	3 860 200
1888	57 376	52 695	56 458	3 576 100
1887	55 157	48 838	53 006	3 495 100
1886	53 614	43 948	51 005	3 747 000
1885	51 252	42 561	50 046	. . .
1884	48 434	43 326	47 225	. . .
1883	46 820	45 509	43 283	. . .
1882	46 231	41 876	40 482	. . .
1881	44 512	36 785	39 593	. . .

[1]Excludes branches and stations.
[2]Accounting basis changed from cash to accrual basis in 1954; from accrual basis to accrued cost basis in 1963.
[3]Net revenues after refunds of postage. Includes operating reimbursements, stamped envelope purchases, indemnity claims, and miscellaneous revenue and expenditure offsets. Shown in year which gave rise to the earnings.
[4]Shown in year in which obligation was incurred.
[5]For 1918 and 1919, includes $44,500,000 and $71,392,000, respectively, war-tax revenue accruing from increased postage.
. . . = Not available.

Table 14-4. Postal Service—Post Offices, Revenues, Expenditures, and Pieces of Mail Handled, 1789–2005—*Continued*

(Number; thousands of dollars; for years ending June 30; includes Alaska, Hawaii, Puerto Rico.)

Year	Post offices[1]	Revenues[2,3] (thousands of dollars)	Expenditures[2,4] (thousands of dollars)	Pieces of mail handled (thousands)
1880	42 989	33 315	36 543	. . .
1879	40 588	30 042	33 450	. . .
1878	38 253	29 278	34 165	. . .
1877	37 345	27 532	33 486	. . .
1876	36 383	28 644	33 263	. . .
1875	35 547	26 791	33 611	. . .
1874	34 294	26 471	32 126	. . .
1873	33 244	22 997	29 085	. . .
1872	31 863	21 915	26 658	. . .
1871	30 345	20 037	24 390	. . .
1870	28 492	18 880	23 999	. . .
1869	27 106	17 314	23 698	. . .
1868	26 481	16 292	22 731	. . .
1867	25 163	15 237	19 235	. . .
1866	29 389	14 387	15 352	. . .
1865	28 882	14 556	13 695	. . .
1864	28 878	12 438	12 645	. . .
1863	29 047	11 164	11 314	. . .
1862	28 875	8 300	11 125	. . .
1861	28 586	8 349	13 607	. . .
1860	28 498	8 518	14 875	. . .
1859	28 539	7 968	15 754	. . .
1858	27 977	7 487	12 722	. . .
1857	26 586	7 354	11 508	. . .
1856	25 565	6 921	10 405	. . .
1855	24 410	6 642	9 968	. . .
1854	23 548	6 256	8 577	. . .
1853	22 320	5 241	7 983	. . .
1852	20 910	5 185	7 108	. . .
1851	19 796	6 411	6 278	. . .
1850	18 417	5 500	5 213	. . .
1849	16 749	4 705	4 479	. . .
1848	16 159	4 555	4 327	. . .
1847	15 146	3 880	3 980	. . .
1846	14 601	3 487	4 076	. . .
1845	14 183	4 290	4 321	. . .
1844	14 103	4 237	4 299	. . .
1843	13 814	4 296	4 375	. . .
1842	13 733	4 547	4 628	. . .
1841	13 778	4 408	4 500	. . .
1840	13 468	4 544	4 718	. . .
1839	12 780	4 485	4 637	. . .
1838	12 519	4 239	4 431	. . .
1837	11 767	4 102	3 288	. . .
1836	11 091	3 408	2 842	. . .
1835	10 770	2 994	2 757	. . .
1834	10 693	2 824	2 911	. . .
1833	10 127	2 617	2 930	. . .
1832	9 205	2 259	2 266	. . .
1831	8 686	1 998	1 936	. . .
1830	8 450	1 851	1 933	. . .
1829	8 004	1 707	1 782	. . .
1828	7 530	1 660	1 690	. . .
1827	7 300	1 525	1 470	. . .
1826	6 150	1 448	1 367	. . .
1825	5 677	1 307	1 229	. . .
1824	5 182	1 198	1 188	. . .
1823	4 043	1 130	1 157	. . .
1822	4 709	1 117	1 168	. . .
1821	4 650	1 059	1 165	. . .

[1]Excludes branches and stations.
[2]Accounting basis changed from cash to accrual basis in 1954; from accrual basis to accrued cost basis in 1963.
[3]Net revenues after refunds of postage. Includes operating reimbursements, stamped envelope purchases, indemnity claims, and miscellaneous revenue and expenditure offsets. Shown in year which gave rise to the earnings.
[4]Shown in year in which obligation was incurred.
. . . = Not available.

Table 14-4. Postal Service—Post Offices, Revenues, Expenditures, and Pieces of Mail Handled, 1789–2005—*Continued*

(Number; thousands of dollars; for years ending June 30; includes Alaska, Hawaii, Puerto Rico.)

Year	Post offices[1]	Revenues[2,3] (thousands of dollars)	Expenditures[2,4] (thousands of dollars)	Pieces of mail handled (thousands)
1820	4 500	1 112	1 161	. . .
1819	4 000	1 205	1 118	. . .
1818	3 618	1 230	1 036	. . .
1817	3 459	1 003	917	. . .
1816	3 260	962	804	. . .
1815	3 000	1 043	748	. . .
1814	2 670	730	727	. . .
1813	2 708	703	631	. . .
1812	2 610	649	540	. . .
1811	2 403	587	499	. . .
1810	2 300	552	496	. . .
1809	2 012	507	498	. . .
1808	1 944	461	463	. . .
1807	1 848	479	454	. . .
1806	1 710	446	417	. . .
1805	1 558	421	377	. . .
1804	1 405	389	338	. . .
1803	1 258	352	322	. . .
1802	1 114	327	282	. . .
1801	1 025	320	255	. . .
1800	903	281	214	. . .
1799	677	265	188	. . .
1798	639	233	179	. . .
1797	554	214	150	. . .
1796	468	195	132	. . .
1795	453	161	118	. . .
1794	450	129	90	. . .
1793	209	105	72	. . .
1792	195	67	55	. . .
1791	89	46	37	. . .
1790	75	38	32	. . .
1789	75	[6]8	[6]8	. . .

Source: U.S. Census Bureau. U.S. Postal Service
[1]Excludes branches and stations.
[2]Accounting basis changed from cash to accrual basis in 1954; from accrual basis to accrued cost basis in 1963.
[3]Net revenues after refunds of postage. Includes operating reimbursements, stamped envelope purchases, indemnity claims, and miscellaneous revenue and expenditure offsets. Shown in year which gave rise to the earnings.
[4]Shown in year in which obligation was incurred.
[6]For three months only.
. . . = Not available.

Table 14.5. Software Publishers (NAICS 5112)—Estimated Revenue and Inventories for Employer Firms: 2001 Through 2003

[Estimates are based on data from the 2003 Service Annual Survey and administrative data. Estimates for 2002 and prior years have been revised to reflect historical corrections to individual responses. Dollar volume estimates are published in millions of dollars; consequently results may not be additive. Except where indicated, estimates have been adjusted using results of the 1997 Economic Census]

Item	2003	2002	2001	Percent change 2003/2002	Percent change 2002/2001
Revenue					
Total	89,889	88,846	90,591	1.2	−1.9
Sources of Revenue					
System software publishing, total	31,497	31,459	31,842	0.1	−1.2
Operating systems software	10,390	10,010	9,217	3.8	8.6
Network software	8,493	7,963	7,543	6.6	5.6
Database management software	8,077	8,602	9,929	−6.1	−13.4
Development tools and programming languages software	3,233	3,535	3,717	−8.5	−4.9
Other systems software	1,305	1,348	1,437	−3.2	−6.1
Application software publishing, total	38,492	37,473	37,297	2.7	0.5
General business productivity and home use applications	19,113	17,940	16,980	6.5	5.7
Cross-industry application software	10,561	10,643	11,580	−0.8	−8.1
Vertical market application software	7,699	7,717	7,414	−0.2	4.1
Utilities software	845	850	943	−0.6	−9.9
Other application software	274	323	380	−15.1	−15.0
Custom application design and development services	S	S	S	S	S
Customization and integration of packaged software	3,357	4,029	4,045	−16.7	−0.4
Information technology consulting services	4,743	5,004	5,847	−5.2	−14.4
Application service provisioning	S	S	S	S	S
Business process management services	322	S	S	S	S
Re-sale of computer hardware and software	S	S	S	S	S
Information technology related training services	885	1,173	1,245	−24.5	−5.8
Other services revenue	8,768	7,459	7,667	17.5	−2.7
Breakdown of Revenue					
System software publishing, total	31,497	31,459	31,842	0.1	−1.2
Personal computer software	7,357	6,767	5,759	8.7	17.5
Enterprise software	16,456	16,504	17,931	−0.3	−8.0
Mainframe computer software	7,300	7,798	8,153	−6.4	−4.4
Other system software	S	S	NA	S	NA
Application software publishing, total	38,492	37,473	37,297	2.7	0.5
Personal computer software	14,270	13,116	12,218	8.8	7.4
Enterprise software	21,403	22,457	23,362	−4.7	−3.9
Mainframe computer software	S	S	1,717	S	S
Other application software	S	S	NA	S	NA
Inventories at End of Year					
Total	1,811	2,072	1,671	−12.6	24.0
Finished goods and work-in-process	1,417	1,691	1,310	−16.2	29.1
Materials, supplies, fuel, etc	394	381	361	3.4	5.5

NA Not available. S Estimate does not meet publication standards because of high sampling variability or poor response quality. Unpublished estimates derived from this table by subtraction are subject to these same limitations and should not be attributed to the U.S. Census Bureau.

Note: Estimates cover taxable and tax-exempt firms and are not adjusted for price changes. The introduction and appendixes give information on confidentiality protection, sampling error, nonsampling error, sample design, and definitions. Links to this information on the Internet may be found at www.census.gov/svsd/www/cv.html. Appendix A, Table A-3.1.7 provides estimated measures of sampling variability (coefficients of variation).

Table 14-6. Newspaper, Periodical, Database, and Directory Publishers—Estimated Revenue, Printing Expenses, and Inventories, 1999–2004

(Millions of dollars.)

Item	Newspaper publishers (NAICS 51111)					
	1999	2000	2001	2002	2003	2004
Revenue	**48 414**	**51 507**	**46 039**	**46 402**	**47 443**	**48 599**
Source of revenue:			41 139	41 105	41 756	42 670
Print	...	...	9 094	9 213	9 383	9 149
Subscription and sales	...	...	32 045	31 892	32 372	33 521
Advertising	...	...	401	583	718	902
Internet	...	...	(S)	(S)	(S)	(S)
Subscription and sales	...	...	296	455	554	716
Advertising	...	...	150	161	149	103
Other media	...	...	52	60	(S)	(S)
Subscription and sales	...	...	99	101	94	67
Advertising	...	...				
Contract printing	...	...	1 728	1 708	1 628	1 622
Distribution of flyers, inserts, etc.	...	...	908	996	1 163	1 251
Graphic design services	...	...	(S)	(S)	(S)	(S)
Market research	...	...	2	2	(S)	4
Archival sales services	...	...	24	22	25	26
Sales or licensing of rights of content	...	...	67	44	73	77
Rental or sales of mailing lists	...	...	13	(S)	7	7
Non-newspaper publishing	...	...	252	298	361	200
Publishing services for others	...	...	11	12	19	21
Other revenue	...	...	1 335	1 450	1 536	1 705
Breakdown of revenue by type of publication:						
General interest publications	...	...	40 553	40 272	40 926	41 461
Special interest publications	...	...	1 136	1 141	1 049	1 166
Other publications	...	...	...	(S)	647	(S)
Expenses: Purchased printing	**3 427**	**3 352**	**2 639**	**2 412**	...	...
Inventories at end of year	**737**	**786**	**730**	**700**	**762**	**754**
Finished goods and work-in-process	43	51	62	78	106	90
Materials, supplies, fuel, etc.	694	736	668	621	656	664

. . . = Not available.
S = Data do not meet publication standards.

Table 14-6. Newspaper, Periodical, Database and Directory Publishers—Estimated Revenue, Printing Expenses, and Inventories, 1999–2004—*Continued*

(Millions of dollars.)

Item	Periodical publishers (NAICS 51112)					
	1999	2000	2001	2002	2003	2004
Revenue	**37 901**	**39 834**	**40 189**	**39 757**	**39 560**	**41 760**
Source of revenue:						
Print	...	...	31 763	31 119	29 931	31 020
Subscription and sales	...	...	13 381	13 276	12 126	12 231
Advertising	...	...	18 382	17 844	17 805	18 788
Internet	...	...	1 312	1 329	1 446	1 528
Subscription and sales	...	...	888	915	1 071	994
Advertising	...	...	(S)	(S)	374	(S)
Other media	...	...	2 209	2 405	2 647	2 932
Subscription and sales	...	...	2 119	2 329	2 573	2 863
Advertising	...	...	(S)	76	73	(S)
Contract printing	...	...	944	706	643	700
Distribution of flyers, inserts, etc.	...	...	108	121	(S)	(S)
Graphic design services	...	...	(S)	(S)	(S)	(S)
Market research	...	...	...	...	...	...
Archival sales services	...	...	...	...	...	...
Sales or licensing of rights of content	...	...	247	281	300	(S)
Rental or sales of mailing lists	...	...	164	172	168	170
Non-newspaper publishing	...	...	...	...	...	...
Publishing services for others	...	...	347	(S)	321	(S)
Other revenue	...	...	3 035	3 215	3 906	4 485
Breakdown of revenue by type of publication:						
General interest publications	...	...	17 004	16 693	16 396	16 812
Special interest publications	...	...	18 280	16 695	16 051	17 169
Other publications	...	...	...	(S)	1 576	(S)
Expenses: Purchased printing	4 287	4 981	4 426	4 246	...	...
Inventories at end of year	**1258**	**1340**	**1 672**	**1 711**	**1 578**	**1 708**
Finished goods and work-in-process	877	879	1 251	1 282	1 183	1 243
Materials, supplies, fuel, etc.	381	462	421	429	(S)	466

. . . = Not available.
S = Data do not meet publication standards.

Table 14-6. Newspaper, Periodical, Database and Directory Publishers—Estimated Revenue, Printing Expenses, and Inventories, 1999–2004—*Continued*

(Millions of dollars.)

Item	Database and directory publishers (NAICS 51114)					
	1999	2000	2001	2002	2003	2004
Revenue	**15 433**	**16 657**	**18 933**	**18 992**	**19 181**	**20 249**
Source of revenue:						
Print	...	...	13 594	13 471	13 504	14 101
Subscription and sales	...	...	795	713	745	719
Advertising	...	...	12 799	12 758	12 759	13 382
Internet	...	...	496	596	760	786
Subscription and sales	...	...	(S)	(S)	(S)	(S)
Advertising	...	...	276	315	479	548
Other media	...	...	1 795	1 809	1 456	1 659
Subscription and sales	...	...	1 734	1 767	1 414	1 617
Advertising	...	...	(S)	42	42	42
Contract printing	...	...	230	(S)	(S)	(S)
Distribution of flyers, inserts, etc.	...	...	...	...	...	...
Graphic design services	...	...	...	...	...	...
Market research	...	...	...	...	...	...
Archival sales services	...	...	112	(S)	(S)	(S)
Sales or licensing of rights of content	...	...	1 205	1 333	1 344	1 340
Rental or sales of mailing lists	...	...	...	...	...	...
Non-newspaper publishing	...	...	35	33	65	71
Publishing services for others	...	...	...	...	...	...
Other revenue	...	...	1 465	1 440	1 717	1 962
Breakdown of revenue by type of publication:						
General interest publications	...	...	...	...	...	...
Special interest publications	...	...	...	...	...	...
Other publications	...	...	...	...	...	...
Expenses: Purchased printing	1 198	1 112	1229	(S)	...	...
Inventories at end of year	**408**	**398**	**428**	**(S)**	**(S)**	**(S)**
Finished goods and work-in-process	383	370	406	(S)	(S)	(S)
Materials, supplies, fuel, etc.	...	...	22	(S)	(S)	(S)

Source: U.S. Census Bureau.
Note: For taxable and tax-exempt employer firms. Estimates have been adjusted to the results of the 2002 Economic Census. Based on the North American Industry Classification System (NAICS) 1997.
. . . = Not available.
S = Data do not meet publication standards.

Table 14-7. Book Publishers—Estimated Revenue, Printing Expenses, and Inventories, 2000–2004

(Millions of dollars, percent. Minus sign (–) indicates decrease.)

Item	2000	2001	2002	2003	2004	Percent change 2003–2004
Revenue, total	**25 236**	**25 831**	**26 926**	**26 058**	**26 786**	**2.8**
Books, print, total	...	20 996	22 208	21 600	22 271	3.1
Books, internet, total	...	1 484	1 390	1 439	1 497	4.0
Books, other media, total	...	810	982	808	800	−0.9
Sale or licensing of rights to content	...	295	272	228	266	16.7
Contract printing services	...	184	233	(S)	222	(S)
Fulfillment services	...	140	143	148	169	13.7
Rental or sale of mailing lists	...	(S)	7	(S)	(S)	(S)
Publishing services for others	...	37	51	57	(S)	(S)
Other services revenue	...	1 876	1 640	1 545	1 499	−3.0
Breakdown of revenue:						
Books, print	...	20 996	22 208	21 600	22 271	3.1
Textbooks	...	7 196	7 706	7 276	7 349	1.0
Children's books	...	2 682	2 817	(S)	(S)	(S)
General reference books	...	1 617	1 698	1 810	(S)	(S)
Professional, technical, and scholarly books	...	3 051	3 414	3 118	(S)	(S)
Adult trade	...	5 428	5 502	5 602	5 778	3.1
Other books	...	1 021	1 071	(S)	(S)	(S)
Books, Internet	...	1 484	1 390	1 439	1 497	4.0
Textbooks	...	109	120	(S)	112	(S)
Children's books	...	(S)	(S)	(S)	(S)	(S)
General reference books	...	(S)	34	(S)	39	(S)
Professional, technical, and scholarly books	...	1 258	1 164	1 219	1 269	4.1
Adult trade	...	60	64	(S)	(S)	(S)
Other books	...	(S)	(S)	(S)	(S)	(S)
Books, other media	...	810	982	808	800	−0.9
Textbooks	...	149	147	(S)	(S)	(S)
Children's books	...	51	104	(S)	(S)	(S)
General reference books	...	27	36	44	47	7.1
Professional, technical, and scholarly books	...	284	435	349	321	−8.1
Adult trade	...	220	170	(S)	87	(S)
Other books	...	79	91	(S)	(S)	(S)
Expenses: Purchased printing	4 229	4 212	...	...	...	...
Inventories at end of year	4 229	4 050	4 281	4 177	3 981	−4.7
Finished goods and work-in-process	3 463	3 896	4 112	4 034	3 835	−4.9
Materials, supplies, fuel, etc.	263	154	169	144	146	1.4

Source: U.S. Census Bureau.
Note: For taxable and tax-exempt employer firms. For North American Industry Classification System 51113. Estimates have been adjusted to the results of the 2002 Economic Census. Based on the North American Industry Classification System, 1997.
S = Data do not meet publication standards.

Table 14-8. Books Sold—Quantity and Value of U.S. Domestic Consumer Expenditures, 2004–2009

(Number in millions, millions of dollars.)

Type of Publication	Net Publisher Shipments[1] (millions)						Domestic Consumer Expenditures (million dollars)					
	2004	2005	2006 projection	2007 projection	2008 projection	200 projection	2004	2005	2006 projection	2007 projection	2008 projection	2009 projection
Total	**2 966.2**	**3 078.9**	**3 150.1**	**3 171.2**	**3 183.0**	**3 228.2**	**49 146.6**	**51 919.8**	**53 723.8**	**55 546.9**	**57 194.3**	**58 875.2**
Trade	1 613.1	1 689.8	1 747.3	1 748.1	1 747.5	1 776.1	23 394.4	24 571.1	25 362.6	25 992.3	26 553.2	27 086.2
Adult	785.8	810.4	828.3	841.8	848.3	861.0	14 952.1	15 532.4	15 937.2	16 370.1	16 670.0	16 985.4
Hardback	396.9	406.4	413.8	419.2	421.0	424.7	9 036.3	9 387.6	9 631.4	9 904.1	10 095.2	10 330.8
Paperback	388.9	404.0	414.5	422.6	427.2	436.3	5 915.8	6 144.8	6 305.8	6 466.0	6 574.8	6 654.6
Juvenile	827.3	879.4	919.0	906.2	899.3	915.1	5 369.3	5 883.0	6 185.9	6 298.4	6 500.5	6 643.7
Hardback	253.4	273.0	274.7	277.4	302.8	279.5	2 489.0	2 727.1	2 755.3	2 831.4	3 122.1	2 927.4
Paperback	574.0	606.4	644.4	628.9	596.5	635.7	2 880.3	3 155.9	3 430.6	3 467.0	3 378.4	3 716.3
Mass market paperbacks—rack sized	576.7	573.7	571.1	568.7	562.3	558.7	3 073.0	3 155.7	3 239.5	3 323.8	3 382.7	3 457.1
Religious	241.1	255.5	266.9	278.0	288.9	300.0	4 104.0	4 436.7	4 725.7	5 013.5	5 322.2	5 628.5
Hardback	85.3	91.0	97.1	101.2	105.2	109.2	2 436.6	2 634.1	2 847.8	3 018.2	3 207.2	3 391.7
Paperback	155.8	164.5	169.8	176.9	183.7	190.8	1 667.4	1 802.6	1 877.9	1 995.3	2 115.0	2 236.8
Professional	274.0	278.9	282.7	286.7	290.9	295.9	10 275.3	10 680.4	11 046.6	11 415.8	11 798.1	12 192.4
Hardback	97.8	99.2	100.0	101.0	96.9	96.2	6 428.0	6 695.8	6 923.4	7 175.8	7 428.8	7 553.5
Paperback	176.1	179.8	182.7	185.8	194.0	199.7	2 791.9	2 908.5	3 017.5	3 112.2	3 218.9	3 465.5
University press	24.7	24.5	24.6	24.7	24.6	24.7	547.1	582.3	639.9	655.8	667.4	682.0
Hardback	9.3	9.1	9.2	9.3	9.3	9.3	267.4	279.5	305.8	310.9	315.7	320.5
Paperback	15.4	15.5	15.3	15.4	15.4	15.4	279.7	302.8	334.1	344.9	351.7	361.5
Elementary/high school text ..	159.5	179.8	181.6	189.6	194.2	199.0	4 622.0	5 320.0	5 507.6	5 892.9	6 187.6	6 493.7
Hardback	56.1	63.2	64.9	67.7	69.4	71.1	2 307.3	2 654.6	2 793.4	2 989.0	3 138.5	3 295.4
Paperback	103.4	116.6	116.8	121.9	124.9	127.9	2 314.7	2 665.4	2 714.2	2 903.9	3 049.1	3 198.3
College text	77.1	76.5	75.9	75.4	74.4	73.8	6 203.8	6 329.3	6 441.4	6 576.6	6 665.8	6 792.4
Hardback	34.2	33.8	33.5	33.3	32.8	32.6	4 156.6	4 221.5	4 289.8	4 379.9	4 439.3	4 523.7
Paperback	42.9	42.7	42.4	42.2	41.6	41.3	2 047.2	2 107.8	2 151.6	2 196.7	2 226.5	2 268.7

Source: U.S. Census Bureau. *Statistical Abstract of the United States: 2007.* Book Industry Study Group, Inc. *Book Industry Trends, 2006©.*
Note: Includes all titles released by publishers in the United States and imports which appear under the imprints of American publishers. Due to changes in methodology and scope, these data are not comparable to those previously published.
[1]Represents net publishers' shipments after returns. Multivolume sets, such as encyclopedias, are counted as one unit.

Table 14-9. Periodicals—Average Retail Prices, 2001–2006

(Dollars. Reflects prices for an annual subscription.)

Subject	2001	2002	2003	2004	2005	2006
Agriculture	585	631	686	777	834	890
Anthropology	246	300	342	372	397	416
Art and architecture	107	134	144	160	172	185
Astronomy	918	1 256	1 353	1 500	1 577	1 724
Biology	1 094	1 089	1 206	1 316	1 427	1 548
Botany	814	880	939	1 036	1 134	1 238
Business and economics	491	527	582	643	699	746
Chemistry	2 140	2 432	2 596	2 845	3 012	1 756
Education	261	300	328	366	405	442
Engineering	1 217	1 305	1 412	1 523	1 648	1 756
Food science	818	897	969	1 085	1 188	1 292
General science	755	810	886	954	1 013	1 098
General works	76	181	197	217	232	241
Geography	685	746	819	882	937	984
Geology	884	1 012	1 081	1 171	1 260	1 323
Health sciences	781	808	881	964	1 046	1 132
History	115	132	152	171	189	201
Language and literature	108	120	135	153	166	176
Law	158	159	174	192	200	225
Library and information science	267	286	316	350	390	437
Math and computer science	968	981	1 047	1 134	1 205	1 278
Military and naval science	345	346	400	432	489	538
Music	77	96	105	110	127	130
Philosophy and religion	140	156	174	195	211	226
Physics	2 012	2 178	2 333	2 538	2 695	2 850
Political science	212	288	321	367	399	437
Psychology	340	358	388	437	471	516
Recreation	120	146	156	169	195	206
Sociology	311	332	365	412	452	491
Technology	1 057	1 151	1 241	1 360	1 464	1 560
Zoology	820	973	1 033	1 091	1 161	1 259

Source: U.S. Census Bureau. Library Journal. *Library Journal,* April 15, 2006 (Copyright 2006, a publication of Reed Business Information, a division of Reed Elsevier.)

Table 14-10. Telephone Systems—Summary, 1990–2003

(Covers principal carriers filing annual reports with Federal Communications Commission.)

Item	1990	1995	1996	1997	1998	1999	2000	2001[1]	2002[1]	2003[1]
LOCAL EXCHANGE CARRIERS[2]										
Carriers (number)[3]	51	53	51	51	52	52	52	30	29	28
Access lines (millions)	130	166	178	194	205	228	245	253	262	268
Business access lines (millions)	36	46	49	53	57	57	58	54	54	49
Residential access lines (millions)	89	101	104	108	110	115	115	112	103	99
Other access lines (public, mobile, special) (millions)	6	19	25	33	38	55	72	87	105	120
Number of local calls (originating) (billions)	402	484	504	522	544	554	537	515	459	425
Number of toll calls (originating) (billions)	63	94	95	101	97	102	106	98	90	81
Gross book cost of plant (billions of dollars)	240	284	296	309	325	342	362	360	367	368
Depreciation and amortization reserves (billions of dollars)	89	127	138	149	163	176	190	194	210	222
Net plant (billions of dollars)	151	157	158	160	161	166	172	166	157	146
Total assets (billions of dollars)	180	197	198	198	200	204	214	208	195	182
Total stockholders equity (billions of dollars)	74	72	74	72	70	67	72	66	58	47
Operating revenues (billions of dollars)	84	96	101	103	108	113	117	109	103	108
Local revenues (billions of dollars)	37	46	50	52	55	58	60	55	51	51
Interstate access revenues (billions of dollars)	19	22	23	24	25	27	29	28	28	36
Intrastate access revenues (billions of dollars)	6	7	8	8	8	8	8	7	6	(4)
Toll revenues (billions of dollars)	14	11	10	9	8	7	6	5	4	4
Miscellaneous and uncollectible revenues (billions of dollars)	8	9	10	10	11	12	14	14	13	17
Operating expenses (billions of dollars)[5]	62	72	74	75	78	79	81	77	79	83
Net operating income (billions of dollars)[6]	14	14	16	16	18	20	20	19	23	9
Net income (billions of dollars)	11	11	13	12	12	13	15	11	8	4
Employees (thousands)	569	447	437	435	436	436	434	386	333	303
Compensation of employees (billions of dollars)	23	21	23	22	23	24	24	23	23	23
Average monthly residential local telephone rate (dollars)[7]	19.24	20.01	19.95	19.88	19.76	19.93	20.78	22.62	23.38	24.31
Average monthly single-line business telephone rate (dollars)[7]	41.21	41.80	41.81	41.67	41.29	41.21	41.80	42.43	43.59	43.75
LONG DISTANCE CARRIERS										
Number of carriers with presubscribed lines (number)	325	583	621	...	...	...	...	...	...	...
Number of presubscribed lines (millions)	132	153	159	...	...	...	...	...	...	...
Total toll service revenues (billions of dollars)[8]	67	90	...	101	105	108	110	99	84	77
Interstate switched access minutes (billions of dollars)	307	432	468	497	519	553	567	538	486	444
INTERNATIONAL TELEPHONE SERVICE[9]										
Number of U.S. billed calls (millions)	984	2 830	3 520	4 259	4 477	5 305	5 742	6 265	5 926	7 350
Number of U.S. billed minutes (millions)	8 030	15 889	19 325	22 753	24 250	28 515	30 135	33 287	35 063	42 664
End-User U.S. billed revenues (millions of dollars)	8 059	14 335	14 598	15 662	14 726	14 980	14 909	11 380	9 773	8 944
U.S. carrier end-user revenue net of settlements with foreign carriers (millions of dollars)	5 188	9 397	8 939	10 232	10 242	10 379	10 982	8 034	6 931	5 964
Revenue from private-line service (millions of dollars)	201	514	661	851	921	1 216	1 480	1 467	988	620
Revenue from resale service (millions of dollars)	167	1 756	3 637	4 112	4 798	4 528	7 600	5 341	4 871	5 420

Source: U.S. Census Bureau. *Statistical Abstract of the United States: 2007*. U.S. Federal Communications Commission.
[1]Beginning 2001, detailed financial data only filed by regional Bell-operating companies. Access lines and calls reported by about 50 reporting companies.
[2]Gross operating revenues, gross plant, and total assets of reporting carriers estimated at more than 90 percent of total industry. New accounting rules became effective in 1988; prior years may not be directly comparable on a one-to-one basis. Includes Virgin Islands, and prior to 1991, Puerto Rico.
[3]Beginning 1985, the number of carriers dropped due to a change in the reporting threshold for carriers from $1 million to $100 million in annual operating revenue.
[4]Beginning 2003, included in interstate revenues.
[5]Excludes taxes.
[6]After tax deductions.
[7]Based on surveys conducted by FCC.
[8]Series revised to include all toll revenues: toll, wireless, incumbent local exchange carriers (ILECs) and competitive local exchange carriers (CLECs).
[9]Beginning 1991, data are for all U.S. points, and include calls to and from Alaska, Hawaii, Puerto Rico, Guam, the U.S. Virgin Islands, and offshore U.S. points. Beginning 1991, carriers first started reporting traffic to and from Canada and Mexico. Data for Canada and Mexico in prior years are staff estimates.
... = Not available.

Table 14-11. Cellular and Other Wireless Telecommunications Carriers—Estimated Revenue and Expenses, 2001–2004

(Millions of dollars, percent. Minus sign (−) indicates decrease.)

Item	2001	2002	2003	2004	Percent change 2003–2004
Operating revenue	**82 521**	**96 530**	**109 933**	**125 693**	**14.3**
Mobile total	71 531	83 879	94 818	106 989	12.8
Mobile telephony services	70 903	83 319	94 260	106 232	12.7
Local access and use	52 349	62 489	72 830	80 624	10.7
Mobile value-added services	2 382	2 904	3 396	4 281	26.1
Mobile long distance	5 127	6 073	5 402	6 972	29.1
Mobile all distance	8 669	10 158	10 799	12 078	11.8
Dedicated network services	(S)	(S)	(S)	(S)	(S)
Other mobile telephony revenue	2 377	1 696	(S)	2 271	(S)
Messaging services	441	351	386	217	−43.6
Mobile dispatch services	187	209	(S)	(S)	(S)
Carrier services	2 868	2 738	2 415	2 340	−3.1
Network access	1 149	1 197	1 334	1 029	−22.9
Other carrier services	1 718	1 541	1 081	1 311	21.3
Other telecommunications services	2 515	3 181	3 890	4 300	10.5
Other services revenue	5 607	6 733	8 810	12 064	36.9
Operating expenses	**75 587**	**86 636**	**92 018**	**99 729**	**8.4**
Annual payroll	11 164	10 440	11 967	13 513	12.9
Employer contributions to employee benefit plans	2 155	2 348	2 930	3 886	32.6
Contract labor	...	1 729	1 822	(S)	(S)
Total materials and supplies	...	...	1 447	1 391	−3.9
Computer and other business equipment and supplies	...	...	680	525	−22.7
Other materials, parts, and supplies	...	...	768	866	12.7
Total purchased services	...	...	14 801	16 951	14.5
Custom coded software and system design and support services	...	...	442	335	−24.3
Data processing and other computer services	...	...	426	481	13.1
Communication services	...	1 335	1 729	2 165	25.2
Advertising and promotional services	4 301	4 727	5 187	6 103	17.7
Electricity	...	246	277	325	17.4
Fuels (except motor fuels)	...	...	4	4	−5.0
Professional services[1]	...	...	1 197	1 415	18.2
Lease and rental payments	3 137	3 572	4 216	4 887	15.9
All other	...	...	1 326	1 238	−6.7
Access charges	6 902	6 564	6 795	6 746	−0.7
Depreciation	16 739	16 240	19 313	20 606	6.7
Universal service contributions and other similar charges	651	616	840	1 174	39.6
Taxes and license fees	...	681	769	1 101	43.2
Other	27 739	31 872	31 333	32 582	4.0

Source: U.S. Census Bureau. *Statistical Abstract of the United States: 2007.*
Note: For taxable and tax-exempt employer firms. Covers NAICS 513322. Estimates have been adjusted to the results of the 2002 Economic Census. Based on the North American Industry Classification System (NAICS), 1997.
[1] Includes management consulting, administration, and other professional services.
. . . = Not available.
S = Data do not meet publication standards.

Table 14-12. Households With Computers and Internet Access by Selected Characteristic, 2001 and 2003

(Percent. As of October.)

Charaacteristic	2001							
	Households with computers				Households with Internet access			
	Total	Rural[1]	Urban[1]	Central City[1]	Total	Rural[1]	Urban[1]	Central City[1]
All households	**56.5**	**55.6**	**56.7**	**51.5**	**50.5**	**48.7**	**51.1**	**45.7**
Age of householder:								
Under 25 years old	51.1	41.3	53.0	50.9	44.7	33.5	46.7	45.3
25 to 34 years old	62.5	61.5	62.8	57.5	57.3	55.4	58.8	53.9
35 to 44 years old	69.9	71.2	69.4	62.1	62.6	62.3	63.4	54.3
45 to 54 years old	66.9	68.0	66.4	59.9	60.9	61.1	61.3	53.4
55 years old or over	39.1	38.0	39.5	35.5	33.9	32.1	35.0	29.9
Sex:								
Male	...	...	...	...	...	...	...	...
Female	...	...	...	...	...	...	...	...
Education of householder:								
Elementary	16.0	13.4	17.1	16.9	11.2	10.4	11.6	11.5
Some high school	28.2	27.6	28.4	25.5	22.7	22.4	22.6	19.8
High school graduate or GED[2]	46.5	50.0	45.0	39.0	39.8	42.1	39.3	32.5
Some college	64.5	68.5	63.2	58.4	57.7	60.2	57.3	52.0
Bachelor's degree or more	79.8	81.1	79.5	76.7	75.2	75.1	75.0	72.0
Household income:								
Under $5,000	25.9	17.9	28.2	24.5	20.5	12.5	23.0	20.2
$5,000 to $9,999	19.2	16.4	20.1	20.6	14.4	11.0	15.5	14.5
$10,000 to $14,999	25.7	24.3	26.3	24.3	19.4	18.1	20.7	19.3
$15,000 to $19,999	31.8	29.4	32.6	33.9	23.6	21.0	25.3	24.6
$20,000 to $24,999	40.1	40.0	40.1	36.4	31.8	31.7	32.4	28.7
$25,000 to $34,999	49.7	49.4	49.9	49.9	42.2	40.5	43.7	41.3
$35,000 to $49,999	64.3	64.7	64.2	64.4	56.4	55.0	57.5	56.2
$50,000 to $74,999	77.7	78.1	77.6	75.8	71.4	70.6	71.7	70.5
$75,000 to $99,999[3]	89.0	89.0	88.9	86.4	85.4	84.8	85.5	83.8
$100,000 to $149,999	...	...	...	...	...	...	...	...
$150,000 or more	...	...	...	...	...	...	...	...

[1]The "urban" category includes those areas classified as having a population density of at least 1,000 persons per square mile and a total population of at least 50,000, as well as cities, villages, boroughs (except in Alaska and New York), towns (except in the six New England states, New York, and Wisconsin), and other designated census areas having 2,500 or more persons. A "central city" is the largest city within a "metropolitan" area as defined by the Census Bureau. Additional cities within the metropolitan area can also be classified as central cities if they meet certain employment, population, and employment/residence ratio requirements. All areas not classified by the Census Bureau as urban are defined as rural and generally include communities less than 2,500 persons.
[2]GED = General Education Development (GED) certificate.
[3]Data for 2001 based on household income level of "$75,000 and over".

Table 14-12. Households With Computers and Internet Access by Selected Characteristic, 2001 and 2003—*Continued*

(Percent. As of October.)

	2003							
	Households with computers				Households with Internet access			
Charaacteristic	Total	Rural[1]	Urban[1]	Central City[1]	Total	Rural[1]	Urban[1]	Central City[1]
All households	**61.8**	**61.9**	**61.7**	**56.9**	**54.6**	**54.1**	**54.8**	**49.3**
Age of householder:								
Under 25 years old	56.5	52.5	57.2	56.6	46.9	43.3	47.5	46.0
25 to 34 years old	68.6	71.6	67.8	64.3	60.2	62.1	59.7	56.1
35 to 44 years old	73.2	75.3	72.6	65.8	65.2	66.2	64.9	57.0
45 to 54 years old	71.9	71.5	72.1	65.3	65.1	63.9	65.6	58.4
55 years old or over	46.6	46.7	46.6	41.5	40.8	40.3	40.9	35.4
Sex:								
Male	65.6	64.2	66.2	61.3	58.6	56.3	59.5	54.2
Female	57.4	58.6	57.1	52.5	50.1	51.1	49.8	44.4
Education of householder:								
Elementary	20.6	18.1	21.6	20.7	14.0	12.7	14.5	13.2
Some high school	32.7	34.7	32.0	28.0	24.3	26.3	23.6	20.1
High school graduate or GED[2]	51.1	56.5	48.7	43.0	43.0	47.5	41.1	34.6
Some college	70.6	73.3	69.7	65.4	62.4	64.8	61.6	56.7
Bachelor's degree or more	83.3	84.4	83.0	80.1	78.3	79.3	78.1	74.3
Household income:								
Under $5,000	35.6	29.8	37.0	33.6	26.8	20.0	28.4	24.3
$5,000 to $9,999	26.9	24.4	27.5	27.0	20.0	17.7	20.6	20.4
$10,000 to $14,999	31.7	31.7	31.7	32.2	23.7	23.6	23.7	23.2
$15,000 to $19,999	38.2	36.7	38.8	37.8	29.4	26.9	30.3	28.8
$20,000 to $24,999	46.1	47.7	45.5	45.6	36.7	36.6	36.7	37.8
$25,000 to $34,999	55.4	55.7	55.4	54.7	45.6	46.3	45.4	44.5
$35,000 to $49,999	71.1	72.6	70.6	70.0	62.8	62.3	63.0	62.0
$50,000 to $74,999	81.9	82.4	81.7	81.7	76.0	75.8	76.1	75.1
$75,000 to $99,999[3]	88.1	87.9	88.2	85.6	84.1	84.1	84.1	81.7
$100,000 to $149,999	92.9	92.2	93.2	89.8	90.4	89.7	90.6	86.0
$150,000 or more	94.7	95.0	94.7	92.3	92.4	91.6	92.5	91.8

Source: U.S. Census Bureau. *Statistical Abstract of the United States: 2007.* U.S. Department of Commerce, National Telecommunications and Information Administration.
Note: Based on the Current Population Survey and subject to sampling error.
[1]The "urban" category includes those areas classified as having a population density of at least 1,000 persons per square mile and a total population of at least 50,000, as well as cities, villages, boroughs (except in Alaska and New York), towns (except in the six New England states, New York, and Wisconsin), and other designated census areas having 2,500 or more persons. A "central city" is the largest city within a "metropolitan" area as defined by the Census Bureau. Additional cities within the metropolitan area can also be classified as central cities if they meet certain employment, population, and employment/residence ratio requirements. All areas not classified by the Census Bureau as urban are defined as rural and generally include communities less than 2,500 persons.
[2]GED = General Education Development (GED) certificate.
[3]Data for 2001 based on household income level of "$75,000 and over".

Table 14-13. Internet Access and Usage and Online Service Usage, 1997-2005; and by Characteristic, 2005

(Number in thousands, percent.)

Characteristic	Total adults	Any online/ Internet usage in the past 30 days	Have Internet access			Used the Internet in the last 30 days		
			Home, work or other	Home	Work	Home, work or other	Home	Work
Total adults, 1997	193 462	31 686	46 305	25 500	22 931	29 127	16 640	13 806
Total adults, 2000	199 438	90 458	112 949	77 621	50 476	86 289	65 471	40 449
Total adults, 2003	209 657	131 839	165 898	128 549	73 315	128 417	107 604	62 159
Total adults, 2004	213 454	134 440	168 582	132 395	73 570	130 964	111 052	61 469
Total adults, 2005[1] **......**	**215 800**	**140 507**	**172 050**	**137 866**	**77 044**	**138 037**	**118 047**	**65 252**
PERCENT DISTRIBUTION								
Total	100.0	100.0	100.0	100.0	100.0	100.0	100.0	100.0
Age:								
18 to 34 years old	31.2	36.6	33.6	32.0	33.3	36.8	34.4	33.9
35 to 54 years old	39.4	44.1	42.4	44.6	52.3	44.2	45.5	52.3
55 years old and over	29.4	19.3	24.0	23.4	14.4	19.0	20.1	13.7
Sex:								
Male	48.2	48.4	48.4	49.2	50.3	48.3	48.9	50.2
Female	51.8	51.6	51.6	50.8	49.7	51.7	51.1	49.8
Census region:[2]								
Northeast	19.1	19.8	20.1	20.8	20.5	19.8	20.4	20.3
Midwest	22.5	23.0	23.8	22.6	22.2	23.1	22.6	22.1
South	36.2	33.6	33.3	33.0	34.0	33.4	33.0	33.7
West	22.2	23.5	22.8	23.6	23.3	23.6	24.0	23.8
Household size:								
1 to 2 persons	46.9	42.2	43.5	41.1	42.4	42.1	41.7	42.7
3 to 4 persons	37.4	42.1	40.6	43.0	43.4	42.3	43.1	43.7
5 or more persons	15.7	15.7	15.8	15.9	14.2	15.6	15.3	13.6
Any child in household	41.7	46.0	44.5	45.6	47.5	46.1	46.1	47.4
Marital status:								
Single	24.8	26.3	25.1	22.6	23.0	26.3	23.9	22.7
Married	56.5	60.5	59.4	64.5	64.6	60.5	64.0	64.8
Other	18.7	13.2	15.5	12.9	12.4	13.2	12.1	12.5
Educational attainment:								
Graduated college plus	25.2	35.4	30.3	34.5	46.2	35.7	38.0	49.6
Attended college	27.2	33.7	30.7	32.0	32.0	33.9	33.8	31.8
Did not attend college	47.6	31.0	39.0	33.5	21.8	30.4	28.2	18.6
Employed full-time	52.9	63.3	59.0	61.2	87.5	63.6	63.2	88.8
Employed part-time	11.3	12.9	12.2	12.5	12.1	12.9	12.9	10.8
Occupation of employed:								
Professional	13.3	19.2	16.3	18.5	30.2	19.5	20.6	31.1
Management/business/ financial	9.4	13.2	11.4	12.8	20.9	13.4	13.9	22.8
Sales/office	16.0	20.8	18.7	18.8	29.0	21.0	19.9	30.0
Natural resources/construction/ maintenance	6.8	6.1	6.6	6.5	5.6	6.1	5.8	4.8
Other	18.7	16.8	18.3	17.1	13.8	16.6	15.8	10.9
Type of firm of employed:								
Business	35.8	41.5	38.7	39.6	52.1	41.7	40.9	53.1
Government	10.2	13.6	12.1	13.2	21.5	13.8	14.1	21.7
Other	18.2	21.1	20.3	20.9	26.0	21.1	21.1	24.8
Household income:								
Less than $50,000	48.0	33.1	38.8	30.9	21.4	32.7	29.1	19.4
$50,000 to $74,999	19.8	23.2	22.4	23.6	23.2	23.2	23.2	22.5
$75,000 to $149,999	25.0	33.5	29.8	34.7	41.8	33.8	36.3	43.7
$150,000 or more	7.2	10.2	8.9	10.8	13.6	10.3	11.5	14.4

Source: U.S. Census Bureau. *Statistical Abstract of the United States: 2007.* Mediamark Research, Inc. *CyberStats,* spring 1997 and 2000, and fall 2003, 2004, and 2005 (copyright).
Note: For persons 18 years old and over. As of spring for 1997 and 2000; as of fall beginning 2003. Based on sample and subject to sampling error.
[1]Includes other labor force status, not shown separately.
[2]Composition of regions:
   NORTHEAST: Maine, New Hampshire, Vermont, Massachusetts, Rhode Island, Connecticut, New York, New Jersey, and Pennsylvania.
   MIDWEST: Ohio, Indiana, Illinois, Michigan, Wisconsin, Minnesota, Iowa, Missouri, North Dakota, South Dakota, Nebraska, and Kansas.
   SOUTH: Delaware, Maryland, District of Columbia, Virginia, West Virginia, North Carolina, South Carolina, Georgia, Florida, Kentucky, Tennessee, Alabama, Mississippi, Arkansas, Louisiana, Oklahoma, and Texas.
   WEST: Montana, Idaho, Wyoming, Colorado, New Mexico, Arizona, Utah, Nevada, Washington, Oregon, California, Alaska, and Hawaii.

| **BOX 14 ■ Google** |

Google, Inc., the firm that began in 1998 as a search engine, appears to be in the process of becoming a diversified communications empire and is at the center of some heated controversies. In June 2007, according to Nielsen/NetRatings, Google Search held 52.7% of the Internet search share in the United States. While their majority lead has been gradually diminishing, the number two ranked search engine, Yahoo!, still only held 20.2% of the U.S. market in the same time period.

In addition to specialized search engines focusing on everything from the U.S. government and patents to Shakespeare and maps, Google also has an extensive advertising business, has acquired online video sharing Web site YouTube, provides the online applications Gmail, Docs, Spreadsheets, Google Talk, and Page Creator, and has partnered with Sprint/Nextel to provide search services complete with advertising on its 2.5 GHz broadband wireless network.

Google's acquisition of one of the largest online advertisers, DoubleClick, Inc., in April 2007, has raised concerns that in combining forces, the new conglomeration may hold more private information on individuals than any other organization. DoubleClick's programs track individual users' traffic online, while Google maintains search and browsing histories, as well as E-mail accounts. With Docs and Spreadsheets, Google has full access to files that individuals upload or create. These remain, unencrypted, on Google's server. The concerns are not just that Google may misuse this private information, but that the site might be vulnerable to hackers and might become a target for government search warrants and subpoenas. For example, in 2006, the Department of Justice subpoenaed millions of search queries. Google successfully countered that the subpoena was excessive and an invasion of user privacy.

In the summer of 2007, the Federal Trade Commission was still investigating the merger, but it has not yet ruled on it. In addition, subcommittees in both the House of Representatives and the Senate have called for Google executives to testify in hearings regarding the acquisition.

Google has also helped shape the parameters of the future Federal Communications Commission (FCC) auction of the 700 MHz Band spectrum in January 2008. The 700 MHz band is currently used for analog television, but it will be freed up once the FCC-mandated switch to digital television occurs in early 2009.

Google has been one of the main players appealing to the FCC to require more open systems in an effort to create a third form of broadband in addition to DSL and cable. Google's CEO sent a letter to the Chairman of the FCC stating that the company would bid a minimum of $4.6 billion in the upcoming auction if the FCC agreed to set regulations requiring all 700 MHz licensees to:

- Accept all wireless devices, allowing phone and PDA portability when changing providers.
- Allow customers to access and use software applications without restrictions.
- Provide resellers with wholesale bandwidth.
- Allow other networks to interconnect on a licensee's wireless network.

The FCC did adopt the first two suggestions but not the last two. By the summer of 2007, Google had not stated if it planned to participate in the bandwidth auction.

Sources:
"Breaking News: FCC Adopts 'Open Access,' Disses Google." *TelecomWeb News Digest* (July 31, 2007).
"Duopoly, Meet Google-Opoly." *CT Reports* 2.61 (August 3, 2007).
Helft, Miguel. "Congress to Examine Google-DoubleClick Deal. (Business/Financial Desk)." *The New York Times* (July 19, 2007): C2(L).
"Google Eyes Joining in FCC Spectrum Auction. (Federal Communications Commission)." *eWeek* (July 17, 2007).
Google, Inc. Corporate Information, Google Milestones. http://www.google.com/corporate/history.html
"Google, Others Mull Next Steps in Race for 700 MHz; The Rules, Which are Expected to be Published Within a Few Weeks, Immediately Drew Praise from Some Quarters and Scorn from Others." *Information Week* (July 31, 2007).
"Google Will Bid in 700 MHz Wireless Auction if it's 'Open'; Google CEO Eric Schmidt Said His Company Will Commit $4.6 Billion to the Auction if Certain 'Open' Measures Are Included in the Plan." *Information Week* (July 20, 2007).
NetRatings, Inc, Nielsen//NetRatings. "Nielsen//NetRatings Announces June U.S. Search Share Rankings." www.nielsen-netratings.com
Spanbauer, Scott. "Is Google too Big? With its Empire Expanding, the Search Giant Can Have an Unprecented Breadth of Knowledge of You. Can We Trust it With so Much Data? (News & Trends)." *PC World* 25.8 (August 2007): 18(3).

"Strong Google Revenue Disappoints Investors But May Ease Antitrust Scrutiny." *Information Week* (July 19, 2007).

U.S. Federal Communications Commission. "NEWS: FCC Revises 700 MHz Rules to Advance Interoperable Public
    Safety Communications and Promote Wireless Broadband Deployment." http://hraunfoss.fcc.gov/edocs_public/
    attachmatch/DOC-275669A1.pdf

Ulanoff, Lance. "Google? A Monopoly? (Dominance in Online Search Market)." *PC Magazine* 26.14 (July 17,2007):
    56(1).

Percent

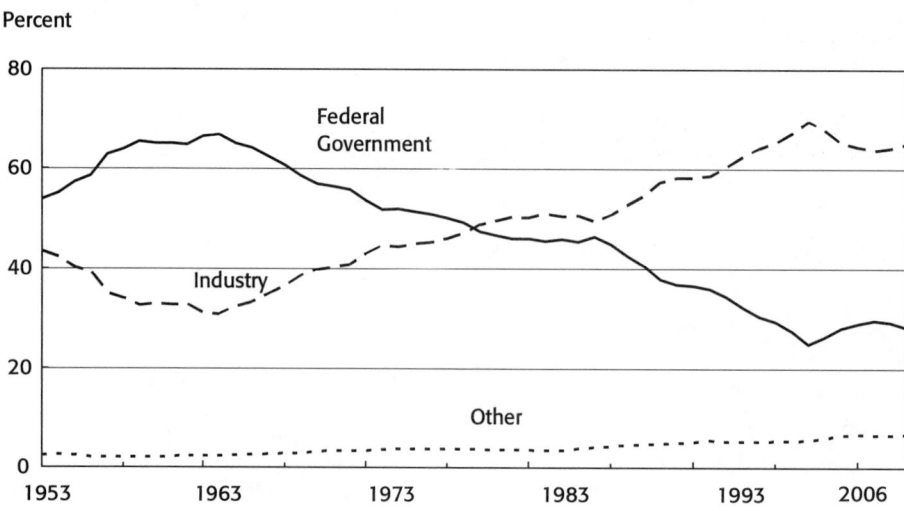

U.S. R&D Expenditures, by Source of Funds, 1953–2006

Note: Data for 2005 and 2006 are projections.
Source: National Science Foundation, Division of Science Resources Statistics, National Patterns of R&D Resources (annual series).

CHAPTER **15**

Productivity and Technological Development

HIGHLIGHTS

1 Productivity is the ratio of output to input expressed in a number of ways. The most common is output per unit of labor. Work in the field of productivity is carried on by many organizations, particularly the Bureau of Labor Statistics and the National Bureau of Economic Research. Labor productivity also reflects the state of the technology, availability of capital and physical resources, efficiency of management, quality of training, and other factors. Productivity may be affected by the specific year chosen as the weight base, because items that increase most in volume output are those with price declines or lower price increases. Productivity series also suffer from certain statistical limitations, because they do not measure the quality of the output.

2 Copyright, or that body of exclusive rights granted to authors by law, is the oldest of such protective statutes for intellectual property. The first U.S. copyright law of 1790 applied only to maps, charts, and books. Amendments extended the protection to prints (1802); musical compositions (1831); dramatic compositions (1856); photographs (1865); paintings, drawings, sculpture, and models or designs for works of fine arts (1870); performed music (1897); motion pictures and photoplays (1912); performance rights in nondramatic literary works (1952); and electronic books (1978). The original term of copyright was 15 years, with the privilege of renewal for another 14. In 1831, the first term was increased to 28 years, and in 1909, the second term was also increased to 28 years. Under current copyright law, works are protected for the author's life plus 70 years after the author's death; for works made for hire, the duration of the copyright is 95 years from publication or 120 years from creation, whichever is shorter. Before 1891, only residents or citizens of the United States could obtain copyrights. The Act of 1891 extended the privilege to citizens of other countries with whom the United States had reciprocal copyright agreements, as well as to countries which adhered to international copyright conventions (such as the Universal Copyright Convention of 1952) to which the United States was also a party.

3 A patent is a grant by the government to an inventor and his or her heirs and assigns the right to exclude others from making, using, or selling the invention without proper authorization. Patents may be obtained for any new and "useful" machine, composition of matter, or process, subject to the requirements of law. Since 1946, inventions used solely in the utilization of fissionable materials have been unpatentable. Patents have been issued by the federal government since 1790. The first body in charge of issuing patents (known as the Patent Board, or the Patent Commission, or the Commission for the Promotion of Useful Arts) had three members: Thomas Jefferson, Henry Knox, and Edmund Randolph. The responsibility for administering patent laws was vested in the Department of State. The first U.S. patent was issued to Samuel Hopkins of Vermont on July 31, 1790, for a process for making potash and pearl ashes. The patent bore the signatures of George Washington, Thomas Jefferson, and Edmund Randolph. Only three patents were issued in the first year. In 1833, the head of the Patent Office recommended to President Andrew Jackson that his office be abolished because "everything that could possibly be invented has already been invented." From 1790 to 1861, the term of a patent was 14 years. After 1861, it could be extended for an additional seven years. Since 1861, the term of a patent on an invention has been fixed at 17 years, with extensions possible only by a special act of Congress. Patents are numbered serially, beginning with the first patent issued after the Act of July 4, 1836.

4 The Federal Trademark Law of 1870 was based on the patent and copyright clause of the Constitution, instead of the interstate and foreign commerce clause, and was found unconstitutional in 1879. The Trademark Law of 1881 was limited to marks used in foreign commerce, but it was extended to interstate commerce by the Act of 1905. The Act of 1920 permitted the registration of a secondary class of marks not previously registrable. It was superseded by the Act of 1946, which granted registrations for a term of 20 years with a possible renewal for successive 20-year terms.

5 National estimates of funds for research and development (R&D) for the four major sectors of the economy have been made by the National Science Foundation since 1953. The data cover basic and applied research as well as development. The most recent estimates include processes, materials, methods, and prototypes. The federal budget provides data on expenditures and/or obligations for research and development on an agency basis.

6 Total R&D expenditures in 2004 amounted to $312.068 billion, compared with $13.711 billion in 1960. Of current expenditures, the federal government share is $93.384 billion, industry share is $199.025 billion, universities' share is $8.205 billion, and other nonprofits' share is $8.565 billion. Seventeen percent of the expenditure is defense related.

7 The John Hopkins University ranks number one in receipt of federal funds for R&D, a position it has occupied for many decades. The University of Washington, the University of Pennsylvania, the University of Michigan, and the University of California—Los Angeles are the runners up.

8 In 2004, United States spent 2.68 percent of its gross domestic product on R&D, down from 2.76 percent in 2001.

9 In 2004 there were 6,834,800 scientists, engineers, and technicians, of whom scientists numbered 1,080,800, computer specialists 3,045,800, engineers 1,448,900, drafters, engineering and drafting technicians 850,900, and surveyors 66,500.

10 Of the 42,155 persons who received doctorates in scientific fields in 2004, 29.3 percent were foreign nationals and 45.3 percent were female.

11 Total NASA appropriations in 2006 were $16.623 billion, of which space operations accounted for $6.870 billion and aeronautics research and technology $884.1 million.

12 Between 1995 and 2003, the United States has had 250 successful space shuttle launches, more than any other country in the world.

13 The United States has a commanding lead in the number of Nobel scientists. Of the total of 502 Nobel prizes awarded since 1901, the United States has 225, almost three times that of the United Kingdom.

14 Satellite manufacturing is down sharply from $7.9 billion in 1998 to $3.9 billion in 2004, however, satellite services are up from $7.4 billion to $20.8 billion in the same time frame.

Table 15-1. Copyright Registrations, by Type, 1870–2005

(Number.)

Year	Total copyright registrations[1]	Total books and pamphlets[2]	Periodicals	Musical compositions[3]	Renewals, all classes[4]
2005	515 200	191 400	57 700	133 700	15 800
2004	642 000	227 500	68 200	170 500	18 900
2003	514 100	188 000	56 300	129 400	19 500
2002	501 000	199 200	60 800	124 000	19 100
2001	580 800	212 100	62 200	156 300	19 700
2000	497 600	169 700	69 000	138 900	16 800
1999	569 900	207 500	75 600	155 200	23 800
1998	531 900	189 300	72 600	142 400	25 400
1997	539 400	176 400	83 300	154 400	28 600
1996	525 800	187 200	83 400	133 500	23 700
1995	577 800	196 000	88 700	163 600	30 600
1994	496 100	163 000	75 100	136 100	33 300
1993	526 600	185 800	82 600	152 300	37 700
1992	556 300	190 200	92 900	162 100	49 100
1991	610 200	193 800	109 200	191 200	52 300
1990	590 700	179 700	111 500	185 300	51 800
1989	618 300	153 800	133 900	197 200	38 600
1988	565 300	158 100	114 000	159 500	43 800
1987	582 200	153 900	131 000	161 600	45 500
1986	561 000	148 200	130 000	. . .	45 300
1985	495 100	154 500	120 000	147 900	43 800
1984	502 700	147 200	113 600	. . .	37 300
1983	488 200	135 300	106 100	127 800	39 100
1982	468 100	116 300	112 400	125 400	36 300
1981	471 100	119 000	118 500	125 000	34 200
1980	464 700	119 200	117 900	120 200	33 000
1979	429 000	122 800	109 600	108 300	27 000
1978	415 700	112 900	110 900	114 800	21 200
1977	452 700	122 100	106 500	131 200	31 000
1976	411 000	113 200	96 000	118 500	27 700
1975	401 300	111 900	95 100	114 800	28 200
1974	372 800	104 800	92 200	104 500	25 500
1973	353 600	104 500	88 600	95 300	23 100
1972	344 600	103 200	84 700	97 500	23 200
1971	329 696	96 124	84 491	95 202	20 835
1970	316 466	88 432	83 862	88 949	23 316
1969	301 258	83 603	80 706	83 608	25 667
1968	303 451	85 189	81 773	80 479	25 774
1967	294 406	80 910	81 647	79 291	23 499
1966	286 866	77 300	77 963	76 805	25 464
1965	293 617	76 098	78 307	80 881	23 520
1964	278 987	71 618	74 611	75 256	22 574
1963	264 845	68 445	69 682	72 583	20 164
1962	254 776	66 571	67 523	67 612	19 274
1961	247 014	62 415	66 251	65 500	18 194
1960	243 926	60 034	64 204	65 558	21 393
1959	241 735	55 967	62 246	70 707	21 533
1958	238 935	57 242	60 691	66 515	22 593
1957	225 807	53 503	59 724	59 614	21 473
1956	224 908	53 942	58 576	58 330	20 926
1955	224 732	54 414	59 448	57 527	19 519
1954	222 665	51 763	60 667	58 213	18 508
1953	218 506	49 059	59 371	59 302	17 101
1952	203 705	46 083	56 509	51 538	16 690
1951	200 354	47 125	55 129	48 319	16 372
1950	210 564	50 456	55 436	52 309	14 531
1949	201 190	47 422	54 163	48 210	13 675
1948	238 121	48 811	59 699	72 339	15 816
1947	230 215	49 525	58 340	68 709	13 201
1946	202 144	42 356	48 289	63 367	12 516
1945	178 848	35 688	45 763	57 835	11 367
1944	169 269	35 952	44 364	52 087	10 247
1943	160 795	36 889	42 995	48 348	9 650
1942	182 232	45 157	45 145	50 023	11 488
1941	180 647	46 040	42 207	49 135	10 342

[1]Prior to 1941, commercial prints and labels not included in the total; jurisdiction moved to copyright office in 1940.
[2]Prior to 1927, contributions to periodicals included with books and pamphlets. Includes computer software and machine readable works.
[3]Includes dramatic works, accompanying music, choreography, pantomimes, motion pictures, and filmstrips.
[4]Prior to 1941, excludes renewals of commercial prints and labels.
. . . = Not available.

Table 15-1. Copyright Registrations, by Type, 1870–2005—*Continued*

(Number.)

Year	Total copyright registrations[1]	Total books and pamphlets[2]	Periodicals	Musical compositions[3]	Renewals, all classes[4]
1940	176 997	50 125	40 173	37 975	10 207
1939	173 135	49 901	38 307	40 961	10 177
1938	166 248	49 156	39 249	35 334	9 940
1937	154 424	45 504	38 053	31 821	8 589
1936	156 962	47 667	38 418	33 250	8 180
1935	142 031	43 134	36 351	27 459	6 661
1934	139 047	40 658	35 819	27 001	6 989
1933	137 424	40 694	35 464	26 846	6 411
1932	151 735	46 576	39 177	29 264	5 888
1931	164 642	46 855	42 415	31 488	5 998
1930	172 792	47 248	43 939	32 129	5 937
1929	161 959	44 040	44 161	27 023	4 948
1928	193 914	50 095	47 364	26 897	5 447
1927	184 000	47 801	41 475	25 282	4 686
1926	177 635	73 455	41 169	25 484	4 029
1925	165 848	65 670	40 880	25 548	3 309
1924	162 694	61 982	39 806	26 734	3 433
1923	148 946	55 561	37 104	24 900	2 689
1922	138 633	46 307	35 471	27 381	2 726
1921	135 280	41 245	34 074	31 054	2 206
1920	126 562	39 090	28 935	29 151	2 112
1919	113 003	37 710	25 083	26 209	1 906
1918	106 728	33 617	25 822	21 849	1 857
1917	111 438	33 552	26 467	20 115	1 992
1916	115 967	32 897	26 553	20 644	1 628
1915	115 193	31 926	24 938	21 406	1 326
1914	123 154	31 891	24 134	28 493	1 231
1913	119 495	29 572	23 002	26 292	1 065
1912	120 931	29 286	22 580	26 777	1 349
1911	115 198	26 970	23 393	25 525	928
1910	109 074	24 740	21 608	24 345	1 007
1909	120 131	32 533	21 195	26 306	...
1908	119 742	30 191	22 409	28 427	...
1907	123 829	30 879	23 078	31 401	...
1906	117 704	29 261	23 163	26 435	...
1905	113 374	29 860	22 591	24 595	...
1904	103 130	27 824	21 496	23 110	...
1903	97 979	27 466	22 625	21 161	...
1902	92 978	24 272	21 071	19 706	...
1901	92 351	...	...	...	...
1900	94 798	...	...	...	...
1899	80 968	...	...	...	...
1898	75 545	...	...	...	...
1897	75 000	...	...	...	...
1896	72 470	...	12 892	20 951	...
1895	67 572	...	12 155	18 563	...
1894	62 762	...	12 149	18 460	...
1893	58 956	...	11 094	16 273	...
1892	54 735	...	10 327	14 649	...
1891	48 908	...	9 477	11 688	...
1890	42 794	...	8 164	9 132	...
1889	40 985	...	7 646	8 958	...
1888	38 225	...	7 086	8 066	...
1887	35 083	...	6 708	7 744	...
1886	31 241	...	6 089	7 514	...
1885	28 411	...	6 060	6 808	...
1884	26 893	...	5 570	6 241	...
1883	25 274	...	5 489	6 280	...
1882	22 918	...	4 612	6 143	...
1881	21 075	...	4 339	5 578	...
1880	20 686	...	4 369	5 628	...
1879	18 125	...	3 608	4 688	...
1878	15 798	...	3 242	3 772	...
1877	15 758	...	...	...	...
1876	14 882	...	...	...	...
1875	15 927	...	...	...	...
1874	16 283	...	...	...	...
1873	15 352	...	...	...	...
1872	14 164	...	...	...	...
1871	12 688	...	...	...	...
1870[5]	5 600	...	...	...	...

Source: U.S. Census Bureau. Library of Congress, Copyright Office.
[1]Prior to 1941, commercial prints and labels not included in the total; jurisdiction moved to copyright office in 1940.
[2]Prior to 1927, contributions to periodicals included with books and pamphlets. Includes computer software and machine readable works.
[3]Includes dramatic works, accompanying music, choreography, pantomimes, motion pictures, and filmstrips.
[4]Prior to 1941, excludes renewals of commercial prints and labels.
[5]July–December.
. . . = Not available.

Table 15-2. Patent Applications Filed and Patents Issued, 1879–2005

(Number.)

Year	Patent applications filed			Patents issued						
				Inventions						
					Corporations					
	Inventions	Design	Botanical plants	Individuals	U.S.	Foreign[1]	U.S. Government[2]	Designs	Botanical plants	Residents of foreign countries[3]
2005	390 700	25 600	1 200	14 700	65 200	63 200	700	13 000	700	75 200
2004	356 900	24 000	1 200	17 600	73 000	72 900	800	15 700	1 000	87 200
2003	342 400	22 600	1 000	19 600	75 300	73 200	900	16 600	1 000	88 500
2002	334 400	20 900	1 100	20 500	74 200	71 800	900	15 500	1 100	87 300
2001	326 500	18 300	900	21 700	74 300	69 000	1 000	16 900	600	85 400
2000	295 900	18 300	800	22 400	70 900	63 300	900	17 400	500	79 100
1999	270 200	17 800	900	22 800	69 400	60 300	1 000	14 700	400	75 100
1998	243 000	17 100	700	22 500	66 100	57 900	1 000	14 800	600	72 500
1997	215 300	16 500	600	17 600	50 200	42 900	900	11 400	400	54 200
1996	195 200	15 200	700	18 200	48 700	41 500	900	11 400	400	52 400
1995	212 400	15 400	500	17 400	44 000	39 100	1 000	11 700	400	49 400
1994	189 900	15 800	500	17 300	44 000	38 800	1 300	11 100	500	49 300
1993	174 700	13 600	400	16 500	41 800	38 800	1 200	10 600	400	48 700
1992	173 100	13 100	400	17 300	40 300	38 700	1 200	9 300	300	48 700
1991	164 300	13 100	400	18 100	39 200	38 100	1 200	9 600	400	49 000
1990	164 600	11 300	400	17 300	36 100	36 000	1 000	8 000	300	46 200
1989	152 800	12 600	400	18 000	38 700	38 000	900	6 100	600	47 900
1988	139 800	11 300	400	14 300	31 500	31 400	700	5 700	400	39 700
1987	127 900	11 200	400	15 300	33 800	32 900	1 000	6 000	200	41 700
1986	122 400	9 900	300	13 300	29 500	27 000	1 000	5 500	200	34 900
1985	117 000	9 600	200	12 900	31 200	26 400	1 100	5 100	200	33 900
1984	111 300	8 700	300	12 300	30 000	23 700	1 200	4 900	200	30 500
1983	103 700	8 100	300	10 500	25 700	19 600	1 000	4 600	200	25 400
1982	109 600	8 200	200	11 900	25 800	19 200	1 000	4 900	200	25 600
1981	106 400	7 400	200	14 200	29 500	21 000	1 100	4 700	200	27 900
1980	104 300	7 800	200	13 800	27 700	19 100	1 200	3 900	100	25 400
1979	100 500	7 500	200	9 300	23 800	14 800	900	3 100	100	18 200
1978	100 900	7 500	200	14 300	31 300	19 300	1 200	3 900	200	25 100
1977	100 900	7 300	200	14 000	31 500	18 200	1 500	3 900	200	23 900
1976	102 300	7 100	200	14 100	34 400	19 900	1 800	4 600	200	26 100
1975	101 014	6 292	150	17 192	34 577	18 344	1 881	4 282	150	25 391
1974	102 206	4 780	130	18 083	37 807	18 686	1 699	4 303	261	25 632
1973	103 695	5 425	118	16 929	38 615	16 513	2 082	4 033	132	22 638
1972	98 928	5 867	135	17 729	38 890	16 414	1 775	2 901	199	23 293
1971	104 566	6 211	155	17 299	43 022	16 048	1 947	3 156	71	22 850
1970	102 868	5 996	188	13 511	36 896	12 294	1 726	3 214	52	17 872
1969	98 386	5 496	111	14 772	38 847	12 188	1 750	3 335	103	17 573
1968	93 136	5 171	95	13 555	34 886	9 172	1 489	3 352	72	13 722
1967	87 872	4 744	103	15 647	38 353	9 895	1 757	3 165	85	14 711
1966	88 293	4 853	104	16 018	41 634	9 222	1 532	3 188	114	14 008
1965	94 632	5 413	105	16 063	37 158	8 096	1 540	3 424	120	12 782
1964	87 597	5 259	120	12 504	27 836	5 854	1 182	2 686	128	9 168
1963	85 724	4 968	145	12 525	26 632	5 501	1 021	2 965	129	8 736
1962	85 029	4 897	151	15 470	32 560	6 380	1 281	2 300	91	10 255
1961	83 100	4 714	107	13 383	28 351	5 161	1 473	2 487	108	8 384
1960	79 590	4 525	131	13 069	28 187	4 670	1 244	2 543	116	7 850
1959	78 594	4 879	114	16 017	29 888	5 081	1 422	2 768	101	8 340
1958	77 495	4 923	134	15 706	27 116	4 230	1 278	2 374	120	7 395
1957	74 197	4 714	101	15 154	23 255	3 372	963	2 362	129	6 282
1956	74 906	4 824	104	16 643	25 560	3 690	982	2 977	101	6 646
1955	77 188	5 764	118	11 914	16 084	1 744	689	2 713	103	4 065
1954	77 185	5 465	95	12 531	18 319	2 301	658	2 536	101	4 433
1953	72 284	5 450	99	16 284	21 230	2 294	658	2 713	78	4 331
1952	64 554	4 993	84	18 538	22 340	2 035	695	2 959	101	5 635
1951	60 438	4 279	71	19 192	22 305	2 163	659	4 163	58	4 888
1950	67 264	6 739	105	18 960	21 782	1 660	622	4 718	89	4 408
1949	67 592	6 998	70	14 957	18 536	1 127	485	4 450	93	3 105
1948	68 740	7 048	59	9 812	13 124	628	652	3 968	44	1 984
1947	75 443	7 644	92	7 784	11 448	669	155	2 102	52	1 617
1946	81 056	10 698	72	7 444	13 486	585	147	2 778	56	1 656
1945	67 846	8 066	52	8 981	15 665	580	87	3 524	17	2 112
1944	54 190	5 063	42	9 636	16 769	645	106	2 914	38	2 564
1943	45 493	2 986	41	11 654	18 022	524	48	2 228	47	2 625
1942	45 549	4 218	60	14 534	22 019	1 286	62	3 728	65	3 943
1941	52 339	7 203	67	16 322	22 632	2 112	43	6 486	62	5 311
1940	60 863	8 530	91	17 627	22 165	2 406	40	6 145	85	6 148
1939	64 093	7 137	76	18 583	21 800	2 640	50	5 592	45	6 338
1938	66 874	8 084	48	16 304	19 635	2 063	59	5 026	41	5 776
1937	65 324	7 207	45	15 995	19 831	1 824	33	5 136	55	5 638
1936	62 599	6 478	66	16 639	21 207	1 903	33	4 556	49	5 734

[1]Includes patents to foreign governments.
[2]Excludes patents issued to Alien Property Custodian.
[3]Includes patents for inventions, designs, botanical plants, and reissues.

Table 15-2. Patent Applications Filed and Patents Issued, 1879–2005—*Continued*

(Number.)

Year	Patent applications filed			Patents issued						
	Inventions	Design	Botanical plants	Inventions				Designs	Botanical plants	Residents of foreign countries[3]
				Individuals	Corporations		U.S. Government[2]			
					U.S.	Foreign[1]				
1935	58 117	5 728	72	17 757	20 821	2 018	22	3 864	45	5 980
1934	56 643	4 399	28	19 731	22 529	2 131	29	2 919	32	6 489
1933	56 558	3 600	27	22 713	23 667	2 343	51	2 411	33	7 170
1932	67 006	4 345	46	26 274	24 822	2 325	37	2 942	46	7 376
1931	79 740	4 190	37	26 618	23 149	1 961	28	2 438	5	6 897
1930	89 554	4 182	16	23 726	19 700	1 800	...	2 710	...	6 085
1929	89 752	4 520	...	25 367	18 500	1 400	...	2 905	...	5 921
1928	87 603	4 761	...	23 357	17 800	1 200	...	3 182	...	5 218
1927	87 219	4 473	...	25 417	15 100	1 200	...	2 387	...	4 918
1926	81 365	4 343	...	28 633	15 200	900	...	2 897	...	5 103
1925	80 208	4 082	...	30 332	14 800	1 300	...	2 819	...	5 347
1924	87 987	3 635	...	29 174	12 400	1 000	...	2 670	...	4 723
1923	76 783	3 550	...	27 016	10 800	800	...	1 927	...	4 133
1922	83 962	4 763	...	27 369	10 300	700	...	1 609	...	4 455
1921	87 467	5 596	...	27 098	9 860	840	...	3 265	...	3 963
1920	81 915	4 660	...	...	...	...	...	2 481	...	3 762
1919	76 710	3 627	...	...	...	...	...	1 521	...	3 687
1918	57 347	2 234	...	...	...	...	...	1 206	...	2 883
1917	67 590	3 545	...	...	...	...	...	1 505	...	3 209
1916	68 075	2 684	...	31 742	11 540	610	...	1 745	...	3 767
1915	67 138	2 734	...	...	...	...	...	1 538	...	4 334
1914	67 774	2 454	...	...	...	...	...	1 711	...	4 595
1913	68 117	2 060	...	...	...	...	...	1 677	...	4 212
1912	68 968	1 850	...	...	...	...	...	1 341	...	4 498
1911	67 370	1 534	...	24 756	7 580	520	...	1 004	...	4 058
1910	63 293	1 155	...	...	...	...	...	636	...	3 719
1909	64 408	1 234	...	...	...	...	...	679	...	3 812
1908	60 142	1 131	...	...	...	...	...	755	...	3 338
1907	57 679	896	...	...	...	...	...	589	...	3 866
1906	55 471	806	...	24 750	6 040	380	...	620	...	3 471
1905	54 034	781	...	...	...	...	...	486	...	3 292
1904	51 168	818	...	...	...	...	...	553	...	3 285
1903	49 289	770	...	...	...	...	...	536	...	3 763
1902	48 320	1 170	...	...	...	...	...	639	...	3 499
1901	43 973	2 361	...	20 896	4 370	280	...	1 729	...	3 402
1900	39 673	2 225	...	...	...	...	...	1 754	...	3 483
1899	38 937	2 400	...	...	...	...	...	2 137	...	2 311
1898	33 915	1 843	...	...	...	...	...	1 799	...	2 752
1897	45 661	2 150	...	...	...	...	...	1 620	...	2 221
1896	42 077	1 828	...	...	...	...	...	1 441	...	2 027
1895	39 145	1 463	...	...	...	...	...	1 108	...	2 049
1894	36 987	1 357	...	...	...	...	...	927	...	2 166
1893	37 293	1 060	...	...	...	...	...	899	...	2 473
1892	29 514	1 130	...	...	...	...	...	816	...	2 051
1891	39 418	1 025	...	...	...	...	...	835	...	1 928
1890	39 884	1 046	...	...	...	...	...	886	...	2 105
1889	39 607	857	...	...	...	...	...	723	...	2 003
1888	34 713	971	...	...	...	...	...	832	...	1 536
1887	37 420	1 041	...	...	...	...	...	948	...	1 466
1886	35 161	645	...	...	...	...	...	594	...	1 489
1885	34 697	862	...	...	...	...	...	769	...	1 549
1884	34 192	1 230	...	...	...	...	...	1 150	...	1 284
1883	33 073	1 238	...	...	...	...	...	1 017	...	1 259
1882	30 270	948	...	...	...	...	...	858	...	1 135
1881	24 878	678	...	...	...	...	...	565	...	995
1880	21 761	634	...	...	...	...	...	514	...	786
1879	20 059	...	...	...	...	...	...	591	...	648

Source: U.S. Census Bureau. U.S. Patent and Trademark Office.
[1]Includes patents to foreign governments.
[2]Excludes patents issued to Alien Property Custodian.
[3]Includes patents for inventions, designs, botanical plants, and reissues.
. . . = Not available.

Table 15-3. Trademarks Registered and Renewed, 1914–2005

(Number.)

Year	Registered	Renewed
2005	121 600	33 300
2004	113 700	32 300
2003	130 900	35 600
2002	146 900	29 200
2001	109 600	33 300
2000	106 400	8 800
1999	184 900	7 000
1998	129 900	6 200
1997	138 200	7 000
1996	93 700	8 800
1995	85 600	6 900
1994	63 900	6 200
1993	80 600	6 300
1992	80 200	5 600
1991	46 600	5 800
1990	53 600	7 200
1989	55 300	7 800
1988	47 400	6 900
1987	47 300	4 100
1986	46 700	5 100
1985	65 800	5 900
1984	48 600	5 400
1983	40 500	6 200
1982	42 400	6 000
1981	42 700	5 900
1980	18 900	5 900
1979	20 500	5 400
1978	29 600	5 500
1977	25 900	6 100
1976	26 300	6 800
1975	30 931	6 132
1974	28 099	5 513
1973	26 112	5 397
1972	23 252	5 637
1971	21 019	6 213
1970	21 745	6 076
1969	20 613	6 176
1968	21 528	4 646
1967	20 036	3 801
1966	20 259	3 585
1965	18 501	3 165
1964	20 087	2 702
1963	19 740	2 655
1962	17 023	2 809
1961	16 595	3 358
1960	18 434	3 933
1959	18 709	3 272
1958	15 351	3 070
1957	17 480	3 488
1956	20 753	3 756
1955	18 207	4 268
1954	15 946	3 491
1953	15 610	3 103
1952	16 172	3 419
1951	17 376	3 350
1950	16 817	3 564
1949	15 968	3 788
1948	11 472	5 056
1947	8 976	6 139
1946	8 106	5 725
1945	7 490	4 210
1944	6 025	4 052
1943	5 595	3 835
1942	6 795	2 894
1941	8 530	2 765
1940	9 974	2 547
1939	10 521	1 398
1938	10 204	1 051
1937	11 242	1 524
1936	10 722	1 888
1935	10 886	1 874
1934	11 362	2 445
1933	9 130	1 671
1932	9 603	1 587
1931	11 400	1 643

Table 15-3. Trademarks Registered and Renewed, 1914–2005—*Continued*

(Number.)

Year	Registered	Renewed
1930	13 246	1 661
1929	14 514	1 750
1928	14 133	2 049
1927	14 579	3 063
1926	14 955	4 273
1925	13 815	2 278
1924	15 727	227
1923	14 834	251
1922	12 793	254
1921	11 363	117
1920	10 268	73
1919	4 208	64
1918	4 061	38
1917	5 339	52
1916	6 791	55
1915	6 262	57
1914	6 817	48

Source: U.S. Census Bureau. U.S. Patent and Trademark Office.

Table 15.4 Funds Expended for Performance of Research and Development, by Sector, 1953–2004

(Millions of dollars.)

| | | | By performance sector | | | | | | | | |
| | | | Industry | | Universities and colleges | | | | | Other nonprofit institutions | |
Year	Total funds	Federal government	Federal funds	Industry funds[1]	Federal funds	Industry funds	University and college funds	Other nonprofit institutions funds	FFRIDC's[2]	Federal funds	Industry funds
2004[P]	312 068	24 742	23 535	195 691	26 115	2 135	8 205	3 087	7 500	6 072	1 199
2003[P]	291 864	23 326	20 699	183 305	24 580	2 142	7 820	2 913	7 275	5 807	1 121
2002	275 797	21 499	16 401	177 467	22 370	2 158	7 350	2 746	7 102	5 731	1 084
2001	277 326	20 426	16 899	185 118	19 767	2 188	6 820	2 540	6 225	5 289	1 132
2000	267 207	17 917	17 163	182 844	17 710	2 175	6 227	2 326	5 742	4 447	1 118
1999	244 970	17 851	20 586	161 594	16 252	2 082	5 617	2 111	5 652	3 761	984
1998	227 651	17 362	22 086	146 323	15 164	1 949	5 161	1 921	5 559	3 281	888
1997	212 140	16 819	21 798	133 611	14 522	1 807	4 837	1 786	5 463	3 014	809
1996	197 336	16 585	21 356	121 015	14 077	1 671	4 434	1 666	5 395	2 906	730
1995	183 616	16 904	21 178	108 652	13 586	1 547	4 109	1 616	5 367	2 847	671
1994	169 198	16 355	20 261	97 131	12 991	1 456	3 937	1 594	5 294	2 911	617
1993	165 188	16 532	20 844	94 591	12 133	1 374	3 654	1 509	5 289	2 839	737
1992	166 697	15 690	24 660	96 654	11 090	1 291	5 018	1 395	5 249	3 550	750
1991	160 096	15 238	26 372	90 580	10 230	1 205	4 835	1 307	5 079	3 300	700
1990	145 450	16 100	31 200	73 000	9 250	1 100	4 450	1 200	4 800	2 850	600
1989	140 486	15 121	31 366	70 233	8 972	984	3 948	1 083	4 729	2 500	550
1988	133 741	14 281	32 306	65 583	8 181	870	3 473	941	4 531	2 200	500
1987	125 352	13 413	30 752	61 403	7 333	789	3 200	831	4 206	2 200	450
1986	119 529	13 535	27 891	59 932	6 702	699	2 790	735	3 895	2 250	425
1985	113 818	12 945	27 196	57 043	6 056	559	2 376	695	3 523	2 400	375
1984	101 139	11 572	23 396	51 404	5 423	475	2 104	615	3 150	2 100	325
1983	89 139	10 582	20 680	44 588	4 983	388	1 929	577	2 737	1 850	275
1982	80 317	9 141	19 059	39 952	4 749	326	1 683	503	2 479	1 625	250
1981	71 912	8 425	16 382	35 476	4 559	288	1 523	448	2 486	1 550	225
1980	62 610	7 632	14 029	30 476	4 104	236	1 334	403	2 246	1 450	200
1979	54 933	7 417	12 518	25 708	3 595	193	1 200	373	1 935	1 350	180
1978	48 129	6 811	11 189	22 115	3 059	170	1 037	359	1 717	1 100	165
1977	42 783	6 012	10 485	19 340	2 726	139	888	314	1 384	987	150
1976	38 581	5 710	9 285	17 392	2 501	123	815	285	1 147	925	120
1975	35 196	5 397	8 605	15 559	2 291	113	743	258	987	875	115
1974	32 677	4 815	8 199	14 617	2 032	96	671	218	865	822	111
1973	30 581	4 619	8 131	13 068	2 041	86	613	200	817	690	105
1972	28 296	4 482	8 010	11 512	1 839	75	576	186	764	653	101
1971	27 336	4 156	7 685	10 647	1 724	70	1 099	177	716	732	100
1970	26 545	3 853	7 779	10 283	1 648	61	961	166	737	748	90
1969	26 169	3 501	8 451	9 867	1 595	60	895	145	725	640	81
1968	25 119	3 493	8 560	8 869	1 572	55	841	131	719	608	73
1967	23 613	3 396	8 365	8 020	1 409	48	753	119	673	577	66
1966	22 264	3 220	8 332	7 216	1 262	42	673	108	630	546	59
1965	20 439	3 093	7 740	6 445	1 073	41	615	93	629	498	53
1964	19 214	2 838	7 720	5 792	916	41	555	83	629	450	47
1963	17 371	2 279	7 270	5 360	760	41	485	73	530	380	48
1962	15 665	2 098	6 435	5 029	613	40	424	66	470	310	45
1961	14 552	1 874	6 240	4 668	500	40	371	58	410	240	41
1960	13 730	1 726	6 081	4 428	405	40	328	52	360	180	40
1959	12 540	1 640	5 635	3 983	306	39	290	47	338	140	35
1958	10 870	1 374	4 759	3 630	254	39	257	42	293	111	31
1957	9 912	1 220	4 335	3 396	229	34	230	38	240	95	30
1956	8 483	1 040	3 328	3 277	213	29	204	34	194	84	30
1955	6 279	905	2 180	2 460	169	25	185	30	180	75	28
1954	5 738	1 020	1 750	2 320	160	22	167	28	141	67	25
1953[3]	5 207	1 010	1 430	2 200	138	19	151	26	121	60	20

Source: U.S. Census Bureau. U.S. National Science Foundation.
[1]Includes all non-federal sources of industry R&D expenditures.
[2]Includes all R&D expenditures of federally funded research and development centers (FFRDCs) administered by academic institutions and funded by the federal government.
[3]Calendar year data for industry and nonprofit institutions combined with federal and university data for fiscal year 1953 (July 1952–July 1953).

Table 15-5. World Wide Successful Space Launches, 1957 to 2005

(Number. Criterion of success is attainment of Earth orbit or Earth escape.)

Country	Total, 1957–05	1957–64	1965–1969	1970–1974	1975–1979	1980–1984	1985–1989	1990–1994	1995–2001	1985	1990	1995	1996	1997	1998	1999	2000	2001	2002	2003	2004	2005
Total	4 410	289	586	555	607	605	550	466	524	120	116	75	73	86	77	73	82	58	62	61	53	52
Soviet Union/Russia[1]	2 746	82	302	405	461	483	447	283	193	97	75	32	25	28	24	26	35	23	24	21	22	23
United States	1 305	207	279	139	126	93	61	122	210	17	27	27	33	37	34	30	28	21	17	23	16	12
Japan	62	0	0	5	10	12	11	9	8	2	3	2	1	2	2	0	0	1	3	2	0	2
ESA[2]	160	0	0	0	1	8	21	33	74	3	5	11	10	12	11	10	12	8	11	4	3	5
China	88	0	0	2	6	6	9	15	27	1	5	2	3	6	6	4	5	1	4	6	8	5
France	10	0	4	3	3	0	0	0	0	0	0	0	0	0	0	0	0	0	0	0	0	0
India	16	0	0	0	0	3	0	3	5	0	0	0	1	1	0	1	0	2	1	2	1	1
Israel	4	0	0	0	0	0	1	1	1	0	1	1	0	0	0	0	0	1	0	0	0	0
Ukraine[1]	17	0	0	0	0	0	0	0	6	. . .	. . .	. . .	. . .	. . .	. . .	2	2	2	1	3	3	4
Australia	1	0	1	0	0	0	0	0	0	0	0	0	0	0	0	0	0	0	0	0	0	0
United Kingdom	1	0	0	1	0	0	0	0	0	0	0	0	0	0	0	0	0	0	0	0	0	0

Source: U.S. Census Bureau. *Statistical Abstract of the United States: 2007.* Library of Congress, Congressional Research Service, Science Policy Research Division.
[1]Includes launches conducted by the former Soviet Union, and, since its collapse in 1991, by Russia. Commercial launches of the Ukrainian-built Zenit vehicle after 1991 are listed under Ukraine, including launches by the U.S.-Ukrainian-Russian-Norwegian Sea Launch consortium.
[2]European Space Agency. Includes launches by Arianespace.
. . . = Not available.

Table 15-6. Federal Budget Authority for Research and Development (R&D), by Selected Budget Function in Current and Constant (2000) Dollars, 2002–2006

(Millions of dollars. For year ending September 30.)

Function	Current Dollars					Constant 2000 Dollars[1]				
	2002	2003	2004	2005[P]	2006[P]	2002	2003	2004	2005	2006
Total[2]	97 624	112 544	121 867	127 336	127 621	93 581	105 794	111 876	113 764	111 217
National defense	53 016	63 048	69 593	74 668	74 759	50 821	59 267	63 888	66 710	65 149
Health	23 560	26 517	28 251	28 746	28 984	22 584	24 927	25 935	25 682	25 258
Space research and technology	6 270	7 355	7 612	7 686	8 089	6 010	6 914	6 988	6 867	7 049
Energy	1 327	1 403	1 343	1 194	1 210	1 272	1 319	1 233	1 067	1 054
General science	5 753	6 129	6 466	6 482	6 423	5 515	5 761	5 936	5 791	5 597
Natural resources and environment	2 160	2 151	2 168	2 108	1 990	2 071	2 022	1 990	1 883	1 734
Transportation	1 838	1 869	1 863	1 828	1 640	1 762	1 757	1 710	1 633	1 429
Agriculture	1 606	1 708	1 750	1 803	1 575	1 539	1 606	1 607	1 611	1 373

Source: U.S. Census Bureau. *Statistical Abstract of the United States: 2007.* U.S. National Science Foundation.
Note: Excludes Research & Development plant (R&D). Represents budget authority. Functions shown are those for which $1 billion or more was authorized since 1995.)
[1]Based on gross domestic product implicit price deflator.
[2]Includes other functions, not shown separately.
P = Preliminary.

Table 15-7. Research and Development (R&D) Expenditures by Source and Objective, 1960–2004

(Millions of dollars, except as indicated. Calendar years.)

Year	Total	Sources of funds					Objective (percent of total)			Character of work		
		Federal government	Industry	Universities and colleges	Non-profit	Non-federal government[1]	Defense related[2]	Space related[3]	Other	Basic research	Applied research	Development
2004[P]	312 068	93 384	199 025	8 205	8 565	2 890	17	3	80	58 356	66 364	187 349
2003[P]	291 864	86 742	186 568	7 820	8 016	2 717	17	3	81	55 104	62 084	174 677
2002	275 797	77 685	180 709	7 350	7 492	2 560	15	2	82	51 033	50 787	173 977
2001	277 326	72 819	188 438	6 820	6 853	2 397	14	2	84	47 553	64 605	165 168
2000	267 207	66 400	186 136	6 227	6 198	2 247	13	2	84	42 567	56 844	167 792
1999	244 970	67 043	164 660	5 617	5 552	2 098	15	3	82	38 830	52 083	154 055
1998	227 651	66 373	149 160	5 161	4 986	1 971	16	4	80	35 268	46 361	146 023
1997	212 140	64 566	136 227	4 837	4 590	1 921	17	4	79	36 910	46 553	128 677
1996	197 336	63 387	123 416	4 434	4 240	1 860	18	4	78	32 796	43 165	121 375
1995	183 616	62 963	110 870	4 109	3 924	1 750	19	4	77	29 607	40 931	113 077
1994	169 198	60 772	99 203	3 937	3 665	1 622	20	5	76	29 648	36 614	102 936
1993	165 724	60 524	96 549	3 708	3 387	1 557	21	4	74	28 741	37 279	99 704
1992	165 347	60 912	96 229	3 568	3 114	1 525	22	4	74	27 604	37 933	99 810
1991	160 872	60 780	92 300	3 457	2 852	1 483	22	4	73	27 139	38 629	95 104
1990	151 990	61 607	83 208	3 187	2 589	1 399	25	4	71	23 028	34 896	94 067
1989	141 889	60 463	74 966	2 852	2 333	1 274	28	4	69	21 889	32 277	87 723
1988	133 880	60 130	67 977	2 527	2 081	1 165	30	4	66	19 786	29 528	84 566
1987	126 344	58 593	62 576	2 262	1 849	1 065	32	3	65	18 498	27 915	79 804
1986	120 259	54 633	60 991	2 019	1 647	969	31	3	66	17 247	27 259	75 754
1985	114 685	52 655	57 962	1 743	1 491	834	30	3	67	14 857	25 410	74 417
1984	102 251	46 477	52 187	1 514	1 352	721	29	3	68	13 484	22 505	66 261
1983	89 971	41 472	45 264	1 357	1 221	658	28	4	68	12 059	20 373	57 540
1982	80 783	37 168	40 692	1 207	1 095	621	26	5	69	10 824	18 280	51 679
1981	72 269	33 715	35 948	1 058	967	581	24	5	70	9 830	16 391	46 047
1980	63 213	29 975	30 929	920	871	519	24	5	70	8 790	13 745	40 678
1979	55 379	27 225	26 097	785	791	482	25	6	70	7 836	12 097	35 445
1978	48 719	24 414	22 457	679	727	443	26	6	68	6 959	10 704	31 056
1977	43 338	22 071	19 642	569	663	394	27	7	66	6 008	9 662	27 667
1976	39 435	20 292	17 702	480	592	369	27	8	65	5 373	8 976	25 085
1975	35 671	18 533	15 824	432	534	348	28	8	65	4 875	8 091	22 706
1974	33 359	17 287	14 885	393	474	320	29	7	64	4 511	7 344	21 504
1973	30 952	16 587	13 299	343	422	302	32	7	61	4 099	6 655	20 197
1972	28 740	16 039	11 715	312	393	282	33	8	59	3 850	6 147	18 743
1971	26 952	15 210	10 824	290	366	262	33	10	58	3 720	5 833	17 399
1970	26 271	14 984	10 449	259	343	237	33	10	56	3 594	5 752	16 925
1969	25 996	15 228	10 011	233	316	208	35	11	54	3 491	5 454	17 051
1968	24 666	14 964	9 008	221	290	185	35	14	52	3 376	5 137	16 154
1967	23 346	14 563	8 146	200	271	168	35	14	50	3 168	4 848	15 332
1966	22 072	14 165	7 331	165	252	160	32	20	48	2 930	4 653	14 490
1965	20 252	13 194	6 549	136	225	150	33	21	46	2 664	4 374	13 215
1964	19 103	12 764	5 888	114	200	138	37	19	44	2 396	4 201	12 506
1963	17 519	11 645	5 456	96	197	125	42	14	45	2 115	3 865	11 540
1962	15 636	10 138	5 124	84	179	112	49	7	44	1 824	3 698	10 115
1961	14 564	9 484	4 757	75	148	101	48	7	45	1 512	3 123	9 930
1960	13 711	8 915	4 516	67	123	90	51	4	44	1 286	3 065	9 360

Source: U.S. Census Bureau. *Statistical Abstract of the United States: 2007.* U.S. National Science Foundation.
[1]Nonfederal Research & Development (R&D) expenditures to university and college performers.
[2]R&D spending by the Department of Defense, including space activities, and a portion of the Department of Energy funds.
[3]For the National Aeronautics and Space Administration only.
P = Preliminary.

Table 15-8. Federally Funded Research and Development Centers' R&D Expenditures, 2003

(Thousands of current dollars. Fiscal year.)

FFRDC	Total	Federal	Sponsoring agency	Location
All FFRDCs	**12 126 881**	**11 681 288**		
University-administered FFRDCs	7 200 056	6 948 179		
Ames Laboratory	25 213	25 213	Department of Energy	Ames, IA
Argonne National Laboratory	500 828	466 340	Department of Energy	Argonne, IL
Ernest Orlando Lawrence Berkeley National Laboratory	441 500	381 264	Department of Energy	Berkeley, CA
Fermi National Accelerator Laboratory	303 340	303 041	Department of Energy	Batavia, IL
Jet Propulsion Laboratory	1 390 560	1 390 560	NASA	Pasadena, CA
Lawrence Livermore National Laboratory	1 286 215	1 258 505	Department of Energy	Livermore, CA
Lincoln Laboratory	522 851	516 112	DOD, Department of the Air Force	Lexington, MA
Los Alamos National Laboratory	2 106 145	1 990 573	Department of Energy	Los Alamos, NM
National Astronomy and Ionosphere Center	11 508	10 644	NSF	Arecibo, PR
National Center for Atmospheric Research	140 756	137 993	NSF	Boulder, CO
National Optical Astronomy Observatory	44 409	44 409	NSF	Tucson, AZ
National Radio Astronomy Observatory	42 842	42 644	NSF	Green Bank, WV
Princeton Plasma Physics Laboratory	66 764	66 345	Department of Energy	Princeton, NJ
Software Engineering Institute	45 412	43 470	DOD, Office of the Secretary of Defense	Pittsburgh, PA
Stanford Linear Accel Center	164 747	164 747	Department of Energy	Stanford, CA
Thomas Jefferson National Accelerator Facility	106 966	106 319	Department of Energy	Newport News, VA
Industry-administered FFRDCs	2 463 439	2 405 585		
Idaho National Engineering and Environmental Laboratory	330 154	318 363	Department of Energy	Idaho Falls, ID
National Cancer Institute at Frederick	296 000	296 000	NIH	Frederick, MD
Sandia National Laboratory	1 742 862	1 696 799	Department of Energy	Albuquerque, NM
Savannah River Technology	94 423	94 423	Department of Energy	Aiken, SC
Nonprofit-administered FFRDC	2 463 386	2 327 524		
Aerospace FFRDC	32 745	13 619	DOD, Department of the Air Force	El Segundo, CA
Arroyo Center	27 889	27 889	DOD, Department of the Army	Santa Monica, CA
Brookhaven National Laboratory	452 728	436 969	Department of Energy	Upton, NY
C3I FFRDC	32 696	32 696	DOD, Office of the Secretary of Defense	Bedford, MA/McLean, VA
Center for Advanced Aviation System Development	6 633	3 180	FAA	McLean, VA
Center for Naval Analyses	75 869	71 895	DOD, Department of the Navy	Alexandria, VA
Center for Nuclear Waste Regulatory Analyses	17 625	16 884	Nuclear Regulatory Commission	San Antonio, TX
Institute for Defense Analyses Communications and Computing	45 960	45 960	National Security Agency	Alexandria, VA
Institute for Defense Analysis Studies	110 200	110 200	DOD, Office of the Secretary of Defense	Alexandria, VA
Internal Revenue Service FFRDC	2 834	2 834	IRS	McLean, VA
National Defense Research Institute	26 908	26 908	DOD, Office of the Secretary of Defense	Santa Monica, CA
National Renewable Energy Laboratory	221 496	219 015	Department of Energy	Golden, CO
Oak Ridge National Laboratory	690 538	664 210	Department of Energy	Oak Ridge, TN
Pacific Northwest National Laboratory	679 000	615 000	Department of Energy	Richland, WA
Project Air Force	33 555	33 555	DOD, Department of the Air Force	Santa Monica, CA
Science and Technology Policy Institute	6 710	6 710	NSF	Washington, DC

Source: National Science Foundation, Division of Science Resources Statistics. *Academic Research and Development Expenditures: Fiscal Year 2003 (2005).*
DOD = Department of Defense.
FAA = Federal Aviation Administration.
FFRDC = Federally funded research and development center.
IRS = Internal Revenue Service.
NASA = National Air and Space Administration.
NIH = National Institutes of Health.
NSF = National Science Foundation.

Table 15-9. Federal Research and Development (R&D) Obligations to Selected Universities and Colleges, 1981–2002

(Millions of dollars, except rank. For years ending September 30.)

Major institution ranked by total 2002 federal research and development obligations.	1981 Obligation	1981 Rank	1985 Obligation	1985 Rank	1990 Obligation	1990 Rank	1995 Obligation	1995 Rank
Total, all institutions[1]	4 410.9	(X)	6 246.2	(X)	9 016.7	(X)	12 180.9	(X)
45 institutions, percent of total	60.2	(X)	58.4	(X)	58.2	(X)	57.6	(X)
Johns Hopkins University	363.4	1	297.4	1	469.5	1	569.3	1
University of Washington	100.0	4	146.2	4	217.2	4	299.7	2
University of Pennsylvania	76.1	10	103.1	15	142.5	13	202.3	10
University of Michigan	74.0	11	108.0	11	176.4	6	243.6	5
University of California—Los Angeles	94.9	5	128.2	5	176.7	5	216.4	7
Stanford University	106.1	3	175.0	3	248.0	2	266.7	4
University of California—San Diego	91.4	6	103.6	13	164.8	8	239.2	6
University of California—San Francisco	64.8	15	98.5	16	167.3	7	201.8	12
Washington University	54.2	17	72.0	22	117.9	19	165.4	18
University of Pittsburgh	38.5	29	58.6	28	116.6	20	166.3	16
Columbia University—City of New York	83.7	9	127.3	6	153.2	10	185.7	14
University of Wisconsin—Madison	86.9	8	124.6	7	155.2	9	207.7	8
Duke University	44.3	23	69.2	26	116.1	22	155.0	20
Harvard University	87.8	7	109.4	9	148.1	11	191.5	13
University of Colorado	46.1	22	71.4	23	116.4	21	165.4	17
Yale University	73.5	12	109.2	10	142.5	14	179.5	15
University of North Carolina at Chapel Hill	38.4	30	63.1	27	100.2	24	156.3	19
University of Minnesota	72.0	14	103.3	14	137.5	15	202.8	9
Pennsylvania State University	47.1	21	76.7	19	136.4	16	152.5	21
Cornell University	72.7	13	120.0	8	144.7	12	202.2	11
Massachusetts Institute of Technology	146.0	2	189.6	2	218.3	3	280.3	3
Baylor College of Medicine	35.1	35	45.8	45	72.3	33	84.1	43
University Southern California	49.2	20	89.7	17	122.7	17	152.2	22
University of Alabama—Birmingham	30.0	44	44.1	46	74.5	32	120.2	26
Vanderbilt University	27.4	49	39.9	48	70.6	35	94.4	35
Case Western Reserve University	33.7	38	48.0	40	71.3	34	127.4	25
University of Illinois—Urbana Champaign	53.6	19	83.1	18	99.7	25	115.7	28
The Scripps Research Institute	...	...	...	...	...	...	83.2	44
University of Rochester	43.0	25	70.4	25	102.5	23	107.6	30
University of California—Berkeley	64.1	16	106.7	12	121.7	18	142.4	23
University of California—Davis	31.8	42	43.2	47	68.9	37	98.9	33
Boston University	27.0	51	46.2	43	59.4	47	86.1	41
Emory University	17.4	72	27.0	70	49.6	57	75.8	49
Ohio State University	42.9	26	56.1	30	80.1	29	96.5	34
Northwestern University	32.4	47	48.3	39	61.1	45	101.9	32
University of Iowa	35.3	34	55.1	31	76.8	30	93.9	36
University of Arizona	36.3	33	49.7	37	92.8	26	137.1	24
University of Florida	30.8	43	47.7	41	55.5	49	82.5	45
University of Texas Southwester Medical Center Dallas	23.9	53	37.4	51	50.5	54	75.6	50
University of Chicago	54.0	18	71.2	24	88.5	28	106.7	31
University of Virginia	24.3	52	37.4	52	60.8	46	79.0	48
University of Utah	38.2	31	50.9	36	65.3	40	93.8	37
Oregon Health and Science University	8.5	112	12.1	113	25.3	93	48.1	75
California Institute of Technology	33.0	40	55.1	32	69.2	36	113.7	29
Mount Sinai School of Medicine	19.9	65	28.1	67	44.0	64	54.4	65
University of Texas at Austin	43.8	24	72.4	21	91.8	27	115.9	27
Indiana University	29.3	45	39.1	49	61.4	44	89.0	39
New York University	40.6	28	74.6	20	75.7	31	85.5	42
Carnegie Mellon University	21.9	57	48.9	38	50.0	56	80.3	47
University of Miami	29.0	46	33.7	59	63.7	42	80.7	46
University of Maryland—College Park	27.3	50	51.1	35	64.7	41	92.8	38

Source: U.S. Census Bureau. *Statistical Abstract of the United States: 2007.* U.S. National Science Foundation.
Note: For the top 51 institutions receiving Federal Research and Development (R&D) funds in fiscal year 2002. Awards to the administrative offices of university systems are excluded from totals for individual institutions because that allocation of funds is unknown, but those awards are included in "total all institutions".
[1]Includes other institutions, not shown separately.
X = Not applicable.
. . . = Not available.

Table 15-9. Federal Research and Development (R&D) Obligations to Selected Universities and Colleges, 1981–2002—*Continued*

(Millions of dollars, except rank. For years ending September 30.)

1996 Obligation	Rank	1997 Obligation	Rank	1998 Obligation	Rank	1999 Obligation	Rank	2000 Obligation	Rank	2001 Obligation	Rank	2002 Obligation	Rank
12 345.7	(X)	**13 019.4**	(X)	**13 875.8**	(X)	**15 569.1**	(X)	**17 289.8**	(X)	**19 390.2**	(X)	**21 117.9**	(X)
58.2	(X)	58.5	(X)	58.8	(X)	59.2	(X)	58.7	(X)	58.2	(X)	58.5	(X)
611.7	1	587.5	1	618.4	1	777.9	1	795.5	1	838.0	1	974.7	1
309.9	2	314.9	3	335.5	2	385.7	2	396.1	2	474.5	2	525.6	2
216.7	8	242.0	6	273.6	6	319.6	4	348.5	5	412.0	3	447.2	3
261.3	4	270.9	4	288.6	4	315.9	5	346.7	6	403.4	4	419.7	4
208.4	9	217.0	10	246.4	7	275.2	7	372.4	3	363.9	5	415.7	5
294.9	3	315.7	2	329.7	3	321.3	3	355.0	4	351.1	6	381.0	6
226.3	6	246.2	5	262.2	6	296.4	6	314.4	7	333.9	8	373.6	7
218.9	7	222.0	9	221.4	10	251.9	11	289.2	9	344.9	7	361.0	8
186.6	15	194.6	17	212.8	14	258.5	9	287.3	10	314.7	10	348.0	9
154.1	22	176.7	20	193.5	19	221.0	17	246.2	17	300.8	12	335.8	10
190.2	14	209.6	12	220.6	11	251.6	12	282.2	11	305.8	11	330.2	11
208.3	10	195.3	16	212.3	15	236.0	15	263.4	14	290.2	14	327.9	12
164.9	18	186.9	18	198.8	16	210.7	18	232.2	20	274.1	17	327.5	13
205.4	11	215.9	11	229.5	9	265.6	8	299.9	8	321.7	9	313.4	14
169.0	17	203.7	15	214.9	13	247.1	13	272.3	13	290.7	13	308.3	15
197.0	12	205.3	13	216.1	12	246.0	14	260.0	15	276.2	15	306.9	16
164.6	19	165.4	21	182.7	20	199.3	21	232.7	19	275.9	16	297.9	17
192.6	13	225.5	8	198.8	17	228.7	16	276.8	12	273.1	18	291.9	18
155.5	21	176.9	19	176.5	21	207.8	19	230.1	21	253.6	20	287.1	19
178.2	16	204.5	14	196.0	18	203.8	20	240.1	18	271.9	19	283.1	20
229.2	5	228.3	7	242.7	8	253.2	10	248.9	16	252.5	21	268.8	21
92.2	38	94.6	41	115.2	34	149.4	28	172.3	26	231.7	23	266.8	22
164.0	20	156.1	22	168.3	23	189.9	23	203.9	22	232.5	22	254.3	23
134.1	25	151.2	23	160.7	24	171.0	24	182.9	24	201.6	25	224.2	24
92.1	39	106.7	33	108.3	38	118.2	39	138.4	38	166.1	31	215.5	25
136.5	24	143.2	25	151.1	25	167.0	25	179.4	25	200.0	26	213.4	26
116.7	28	125.8	26	130.8	27	145.5	29	156.1	28	186.9	27	194.0	27
94.5	35	103.4	35	113.2	36	124.8	37	141.8	35	157.4	38	193.6	28
111.0	30	119.4	28	129.8	28	135.7	32	153.2	29	171.2	28	189.2	29
139.0	23	150.1	24	173.3	22	189.9	22	196.2	23	210.6	24	187.3	30
96.0	34	105.9	34	126.6	30	128.4	36	148.5	32	166.2	30	185.3	31
92.9	37	97.0	39	125.0	31	131.2	33	139.4	37	154.4	40	182.9	32
80.2	48	92.3	45	109.6	37	128.5	35	145.6	31	161.9	35	180.6	33
90.9	40	107.3	32	101.3	42	115.5	40	140.7	36	156.6	39	174.7	34
109.3	31	108.2	30	119.7	33	138.6	31	151.5	30	164.0	33	174.0	35
93.5	36	100.5	36	113.8	35	129.3	34	138.2	39	163.9	34	172.7	36
120.8	26	117.1	29	129.8	29	151.7	27	162.7	27	166.9	29	168.5	37
81.5	47	89.7	48	98.5	44	111.1	43	129.2	41	157.4	37	167.1	38
84.3	44	92.5	44	92.4	48	101.7	48	119.8	47	146.9	43	162.3	39
118.1	27	119.4	27	121.6	32	155.6	26	144.5	33	160.1	36	161.5	40
84.1	46	90.3	47	101.0	43	109.8	45	122.5	45	153.0	41	159.1	41
88.6	42	93.2	43	97.3	45	114.7	41	125.0	44	149.7	42	157.9	42
46.8	78	67.2	58	83.6	51	87.7	57	113.1	50	138.4	45	154.4	43
112.2	29	107.6	31	133.8	26	143.5	30	143.1	34	127.6	49	152.2	44
62.4	60	68.8	55	83.1	52	105.0	47	119.5	48	133.1	48	146.3	45
104.5	32	94.6	42	107.4	39	121.1	38	135.0	40	164.5	32	146.0	46
90.2	41	99.2	37	105.9	40	110.5	44	128.3	42	143.7	44	143.1	47
84.2	45	95.2	40	104.3	41	113.3	42	127.0	43	134.4	46	142.5	48
97.1	33	98.3	38	86.4	50	91.9	54	88.3	60	95.7	61	131.4	50
76.8	49	82.4	49	90.1	49	93.6	51	113.7	49	111.2	52	127.0	53
88.5	43	90.5	46	95.9	46	108.0	46	120.7	46	133.9	47	126.7	54

Table 15-10. Nobel Prize Laureates in Selected Sciences, 1901–2004

(Number. By location of award-winning research and by date of award.)

| Country | 1901–2004 | | | 1901–1930 | 1931–1945 | 1946–1960 | 1961–1975 | 1976–1990 | 1991–2003 | 2002 | 2003 | 2004 |
	Total	Physics	Chemistry	Physiology/ Medicine									
Total	**502**	**174**	**146**	**182**	**93**	**49**	**74**	**92**	**98**	**82**	**9**	**7**	**8**
United States	225	80	54	91	6	14	38	41	63	59	5	5	6
United Kingdom	76	21	27	28	15	11	14	20	9	6	1	1	0
Germany[1]	63	19	29	15	27	11	4	8	7	4	0	0	0
France	25	11	7	7	13	2	0	5	2	3	0	0	0
Soviet Union or Russia	12	9	1	2	2	0	4	3	1	2	0	1	0
Japan	8	4	4	0	0	0	1	2	1	4	2	0	0
Other countries	93	30	24	39	30	11	13	13	15	4	1	0	2

Source: U.S. Census Bureau. *Statistical Abstract of the United States: 2007*. U.S. National Science Foundation.
[1]Between 1946 and 1991, data are for the former West Germany only.

BOX 15 ■ Labor Productivity

Labor productivity, or the average output, adjusted for inflation, per hour of labor, is a key indicator of the health of the U.S. economy. Labor productivity is determined using gross domestic product (GDP) data and employment figures. Because GDP and employment figures are often revised, labor productivity numbers are not static. In addition, labor productivity growth figures can vary widely from quarter to quarter, making it difficult to see a trend in the figures until it is well established.

Labor productivity figures showed slow growth from 1974 to 1995, with an average annual growth of 1.4%. In the ten years from 1996 to 2006, productivity growth rebounded to 2.9%, more than double the 1974 to 1995 figures.

The upswing in quarterly productivity growth figures in the latter half of the 1990s was only recognized late in the decade partly because of inaccuracies in employment figures, which were revised several times. For instance, data available in 1997 indicated that for fourth quarter 1995 through third quarter 1996, productivity growth was 0.3%, but data available in 2007 indicated that the growth for that period was actually 3.1%.

The sources of this rapid change in productivity growth are not easily identifiable, but many analysts attribute it to the rapid and far-reaching advances in computer technology and its use in business during the 1990s.

Since 2003, labor productivity growth has slowed to 1.8% annually. In the second half of 2006, it averaged 0.5% at an annual rate. Once again, however, because these are relatively recent data, definitive conclusions cannot yet be drawn to determine if this slowdown is a trend. Further, as in the late 1990s, the underlying data may yet be revised. This, in turn, may result in productivity growth numbers that diverge sharply from those currently available.

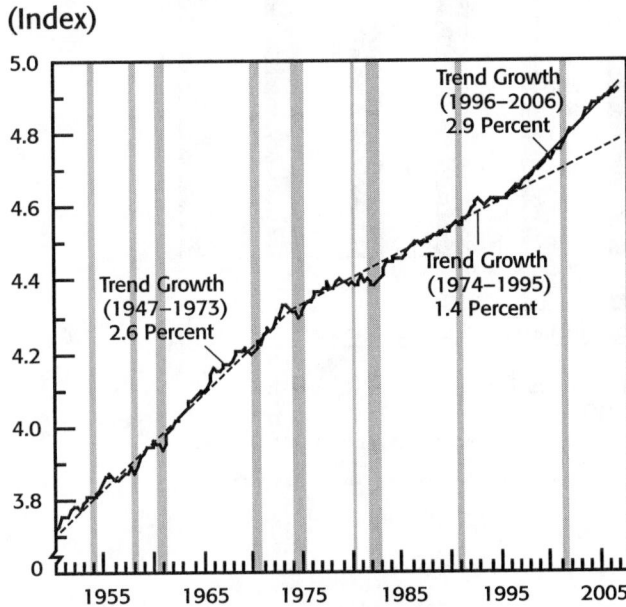

Labor Productivity and Trend Growth, 1950 to 2006

Note: Index (1996 = 1.0); data expressed in logarithmic form.
Sources: Congressional Budget Office; Department of Labor, Bureau of Labor Statistics.

Sources:
Congress of the United States, Congressional Budget Office. "Labor Productivity: Developments Since 1995."
        http://www.cbo.gov/ftpdocs/79xx/doc7910/03–26-Labor.pdf
Congress of the United States, Joint Economic Committee. Research Report #109–39, "Productivity: The Path to Prosperity," June 2006. http://www.house.gov/jec/news/news2006/rr109–39%20Productivity%20Expanded.pdf

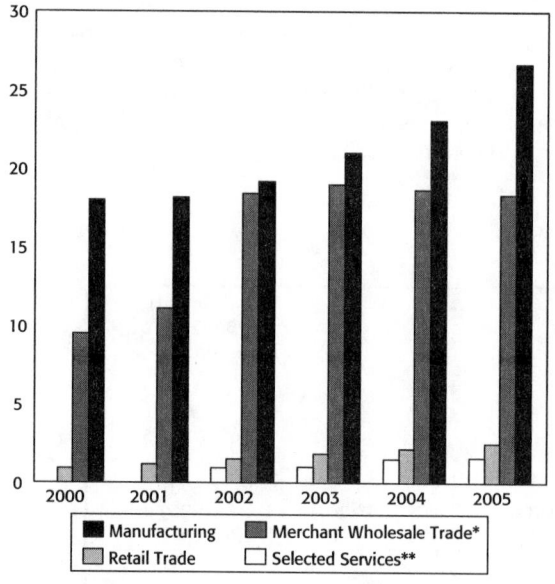

E-commerce as Percent of Total Value,
2000–2005

* Merchant Wholesale Trade data include MSBOs in 2002–2005, and exclude
MSBOs in 2000–2001.
** Selected Services data in 2000–2001 are not comparable due to the 2002
NAICS change.

CHAPTER **16**

Distribution and Services

HIGHLIGHTS

1 The *Survey of Current Business,* issued by the Bureau of Economic Analysis, is the principal source of data on domestic trade and services. Financial data relating to this sector appears in the *Statistics of Income* published by the Internal Revenue Service. Censuses of retail and wholesale trade have been taken at various intervals since 1929. Limited coverage of service industries started in 1933. Beginning with the 1967 Census, legislation provided that a census of each area be conducted every five years, in years ending with 2 or 7. The industries covered in the censuses and surveys are classified in the three divisions defined in the *Standard Industrial Classification Manual:* retail trade, wholesale trade, and services. The purview of the censuses has varied over the years so that some of the data is incomparable over time. Since 1954, data for nonemployer establishments have been published separately, and establishments with no paid employees are excluded from wholesale trade. Since 1977, sales taxes and finance charges have been excluded from sales figures. After 1987, the num-

ber of establishments was defined as those in business at any time during the year, rather than at the end of the year as defined previously. Starting in 1987, hospitals are included among services, but government operated services are excluded. In 1982 and 1987, data were not collected from educational institutions nor from services run by labor unions or political organizations. Beginning in 1982, each leased department in a store was classified separately, rather than consolidated with the store as before. Current retail and wholesale trade data appear in the *Monthly Retail Trade Report* and the *Monthly Wholesale Trade Report* respectively.

2 In 1990, the share of GDP of retail and wholesale trade was 15.2 percent, by 2001 it had reached 16 percent. The share of services has gone up slightly from 18.5 percent to 22.1 percent. Among services, the largest sectors in dollar value are health services ($589.8 billion), business services ($544.1 billion), and legal services ($145.6 billion).

361

3 Retail trade is the most visible and ubiquitous of all businesses. In 2003, there were 1,115,900 of them divided as follows:

Motor vehicles and parts dealers	127,000
Furniture and home furnishing stores	65,400
Electronics and appliance stores	47,700
Building material and garden equipment and supply dealers	87,700
Food and beverage stores	152,600
Health and personal care stores	82,400
Gasoline stations	119,500
Clothing and clothing accessories stores	148,000
Sporting goods, hobby, book and music stores	61,800
General music stores	42,000
Miscellaneous store retailers	127,600
Non-store retailers	54,100

Retail trade employed 14.868 million people with a payroll of $319.5 billion. Wholesale trade had 432,537 establishments, 5.864 million employees, and a payroll of $272.156 billion.

4 In terms of estimated per capita sales, motor vehicle and parts dealers led with $3,020 in 2005, followed by general merchandise stores ($1,774), food and beverage stores ($1,752), and gasoline stations ($1,310).

5 The 21,000 supermarkets in the United States have sales of $318 billion and account for 68.7 percent of all food sales.

6 Of the $142.978 billion worth of alcoholic beverages sold in 2004, 43 percent was bought in liquor, food, and other stores.

7 U.S. mail order sales reached $147.123 billion in 2004, of which e-commerce accounted for 35.5 percent.

8 According to projections, retail e-commerce will almost double from $172.4 billion in 2005 to $328.6 billion in 2010.

9 In 2005, there were 48,695 shopping centers in the United States, with 6,060 million square feet of gross leasable area and retail sales of $1.530 trillion. California has the most gross leasable area, with 755 million square feet, followed by Florida with 488 and Texas with 410.

10 In 2001, there were 4,386,000 service-related establishments. Health services are the most numerous with 671,000 firms.

11 The growth of the computer industry is reflected in the number of information technology establishments. In 2000, there were 5,596,000 establishments with nearly $800 billion in gross domestic income.

12 Sale of durable goods, such as furniture and lumber, and non-durable goods, such as drugs and petroleum, have almost equal sales of $1.761 trillion and $1.798 trillion respectively. However, the inventory for durable goods is much greater than that of non-durable goods at $228.9 billion and $133.1 billion respectively.

Table 16-1. Persons Engaged in Distribution and Selected Service Industries (NAICS Basis), 1939–2006

(Total employees in thousands.)

Year	Wholesale trade	Retail trade	Hotels and other lodging places	Professional and business services	Nursing and residential care facilities	Child day care services	Repair and maintenance services	Personal and laundry services
2006	5 897.6	15 319.3	1 833.4	17 552	2900.9	806.7	1 248.5	1 284.2
2005	5 764.4	15 279.6	1 818.6	16 954	2855	789.7	1 236.0	1 276.6
2004	5 662.9	15 058.2	1 789.5	16 395	2818.4	764.7	1 228.8	1 272.9
2003	5 607.5	14 917.3	1 775.4	15 987	2786.2	755.3	1 233.6	1 263.5
2002	5 652.3	15 025.1	1 778.6	15 976	2743.3	744.1	1 246.9	1 257.2
2001	5 772.7	15 238.6	1 852.2	16 476	2675.8	714.6	1 256.5	1 255.0
2000	5 933.2	15 279.8	1 884.4	16 666	2583.2	695.8	1 241.5	1 242.9
1999	5 892.5	14 970.1	1 831.7	15 957	2528.8	673.7	1 222.0	1 220.3
1998	5 795.2	14 609.3	1 773.5	15 147	2487.3	615.1	1 189.2	1 205.6
1997	5 663.9	14 388.9	1 729.5	4 335	2443.4	570.4	1 169.3	1 180.4
1996	5 522.0	14 142.5	1 698.9	13 462	2379.9	559.2	1 135.5	1 165.7
1995	5 433.1	13 896.7	1 652.5	12 844	2307.7	557.1	1 078.9	1 143.9
1994	5 247.3	13 490.8	1 615.3	12 174	2227	510	1 023.5	1 120.3
1993	5 093.2	13 020.5	1 580.5	11 495	2128.1	468.9	998.0	1 116.0
1992	5 109.7	12 827.9	1 561.5	10 970	2043.5	446.5	964.0	1 098.9
1991	5 185.3	12 896.4	1 574.3	10 714	1972	413.2	960.0	1 109.2
1990	5 268.4	13 182.3	1 616.0	10 848	1 856.4	387.8	1 009.0	1 119.9
1989	5 283.7	13 107.9	1 578.3	10 555	...	374.2	...	...
1988	5 152.8	12 808.2	1 523.2	10 090	...	352.4	...	...
1987	5 003.0	12 418.8	1 448.1	9 608	...	329.7	...	...
1986	4 935.0	12 078.1	1 362.7	9 211	...	318.4	...	...
1985	4 914.7	11 733.1	1 316.7	8 871	...	306.6	...	...
1984	4 788.1	11 222.6	1 249.0	8 464	...	...	...	...
1983	4 558.9	10 634.8	1 158.7	8 039	...	...	...	...
1982	4 574.5	10 371.7	1 120.6	7 848	...	...	...	...
1981	4 633.8	10 364.3	1 106.5	7 782	...	...	...	...
1980	4 557.4	10 244.1	1 064.1	7 544	...	...	...	...
1979	4 485.4	10 180.4	1 048.2	7 312	...	...	...	...
1978	4 280.0	9 878.7	977.3	6 972	...	...	...	...
1977	4 054.7	9 359.2	945.7	6 587	...	...	...	...
1976	3 919.5	8 966.2	919.3	6 287	...	...	...	...
1975	3 810.4	8 600.3	888.8	6 034	...	...	...	...
1974	3 823.1	8 535.5	868.3	5 974	...	...	...	...
1973	3 688.4	8 371.2	845.0	5 774	...	...	...	...
1972	3 547.0	8 037.7	804.3	5 523	...	...	...	...
1971	3 423.7	7 656.8	...	5 328	...	...	...	...
1970	3 417.5	7 463.3	...	5 267	...	...	...	...
1969	3 344.4	7 294.9	...	5 156	...	...	...	...
1968	3 235.6	6 977.2	...	4 918	...	...	...	...
1967	3 157.8	6 711.4	...	4 720	...	...	...	...
1966	3 079.5	6 530.0	...	4 517	...	...	...	...
1965	2 967.0	6 262.1	...	4 306	...	...	...	...
1964	2 856.1	5 976.6	...	4 137	...	...	...	...
1963	2 780.2	5 780.7	...	3 990	...	...	...	...
1962	2 736.8	5 672.2	...	3 885	...	...	...	...
1961	2 680.8	5 560.3	...	3 744	...	...	...	...
1960	2 690.4	5 588.7	...	3 694	...	...	...	...
1959	2 638.3	5 452.7	...	3 591	...	...	...	...
1958	2 550.5	5 266.5	...	3 449	...	...	...	...
1957	2 592.5	5 327.5	...	3 504	...	...	...	...
1956	2 583.4	5 314.9	...	3 437	...	...	...	...
1955	2 504.6	5 158.4	...	3 320	...	...	...	...
1954	2 453.8	4 998.5	...	3 197	...	...	...	...
1953	2 443.9	5 012.4	...	3 215	...	...	...	...
1952	2 407.7	4 880.2	...	3 128	...	...	...	...
1951	2 334.8	4 758.4	...	3 061	...	...	...	...
1950	2 255.3	4 580.1	...	2 928	...	...	...	...
1949	2 226.9	4 520.1	...	2 853	...	...	...	...
1948	2 229.7	4 523.6	...	2 893	...	...	...	...
1947	2 115.7	4 392.7	...	2 828	...	...	...	...
1946	1 962.4	4 118.3	...	2 666	...	...	...	...
1945	1 671.9	3 623.5	...	2 495	...	...	...	...
1944	1 585.0	3 515.5	...	2 523	...	...	...	...
1943	1 565.8	3 479.2	...	2 518	...	...	...	...
1942	1 635.0	3 521.5	...	2 410	...	...	...	...
1941	1 678.7	3 551.7	...	2 265	...	...	...	...
1940	1 570.9	3 324.4	...	2 073	...	...	...	...
1939	1 507.6	3 157.5	...	1 976	...	...	...	...

Source: U.S. Department of Labor, Bureau of Labor Statistics. *Current Employment Statistics* survey.
Note: The North American Industry Classification System (NAICS) replaced the Standard Industrial Classification (SIC) system. The Current Employment Statistics (CES) survey published National data on a NAICS 2002 basis with the release of May 2003 data on June 6, 2003. SIC-based data is no longer produced or published; 2002 was the last year for which annual SIC based data was published. Historical time series were reconstructed as part of the NAICS conversion process. The NAICS-based reconstruction effort covered all CES published data types. All NAICS series have history back to at least 1990. Other series that were highly interchangeable with an SIC series have history going farther back in time.
... = Not available.

Table 16-2. Persons Engaged in Distribution and Selected Service Industries (SIC Basis), 1939–2002

(Number in thousands.)

Year	Wholesale trade	Retail trade	Hotels and other lodging places	Personal services	Miscellaneous business services	Automobile repair, services, and parking	Miscellaneous repair services
2002	6 671	23 306	1 798	1 286	1 732	1 263	377
2001	6 776	23 522	1 870	1 269	1 764	1 257	374
2000	6 947	23 337	1 900	1 250	1 800	1 234	369
1999	6 911	22 848	1 848	1 226	1 797	1 196	372
1998	6 800	22 295	1 789	1 201	1 787	1 145	376
1997	6 648	21 966	1 746	1 186	1 718	1 120	374
1996	6 482	21 597	1 715	1 180	1 602	1 080	372
1995	6 378	21 187	1 668	1 163	1 508	1 020	359
1994	6 162	20 507	1 631	1 140	1 385	968	338
1993	5 981	19 773	1 596	1 137	1 322	925	349
1992	5 997	19 356	1 576	1 116	1 265	881	347
1991	6 081	19 284	1 589	1 112	1 242	882	341
1990	6 173	19 601	1 631	1 104	1 244	914	374
1989	6 187	19 475	1 596	1 086	1 198	884	374
1988	6 030	19 023	1 540	1 056	1 125	834	350
1987	5 848	18 422	1 464	1 027	. . .	794	321
1986	5 761	17 880	1 378	991	. . .	762	322
1985	5 727	17 315	1 331	957	. . .	730	319
1984	5 568	16 512	1 263	918	. . .	682	310
1983	5 283	15 587	1 172	869	. . .	619	287
1982	5 295	15 158	1 133	844	. . .	589	287
1981	5 375	15 171	1 119	828	. . .	574	293
1980	5 292	15 018	1 076	818	. . .	571	289
1979	5 221	14 972	1 060	821	. . .	575	282
1978	4 985	14 556	988	827	. . .	549	261
1977	4 723	13 792	956	806	. . .	498	241
1976	4 562	13 193	929	790	. . .	466	227
1975	4 430	12 630	898	782	. . .	439	218
1974	4 447	12 539	878	807	. . .	430	217
1973	4 291	12 315	854	823	. . .	422	205
1972	4 127	11 822	813	828	. . .	399	199
1971	4 014	11 338	722	848	. . .	. . .	193
1970	4 006	11 034	706	898	. . .	. . .	189
1969	3 919	10 785	691	931	. . .	. . .	184
1968	3 791	10 308	659	937	. . .	. . .	174
1967	3 700	9 906	635	933	. . .	. . .	168
1966	3 608	9 637	604	924	. . .	. . .	161
1965	3 477	9 239	569	895	. . .	. . .	155
1964	3 347	8 812	538	866	. . .	. . .	149
1963	3 258	8 520	509	845	. . .	. . .	. . .
1962	3 207	8 359	484	831	. . .	. . .	. . .
1961	3 142	8 195	472	816	. . .	. . .	. . .
1960	3 153	8 238	474	812	. . .	. . .	. . .
1959	3 092	8 035	459	809	. . .	. . .	. . .
1958	2 989	7 761	450	796	. . .	. . .	. . .
1957	3 037	7 848	459	459	. . .	. . .	. . .
1956	3 027	7 831	449	. . .	. . .	. . .	. . .
1955	2 934	7 601	442	. . .	. . .	. . .	. . .
1954	2 875	7 360	440	. . .	. . .	. . .	. . .
1953	2 862	7 385	451	. . .	. . .	. . .	. . .
1952	2 821	7 184	444	. . .	. . .	. . .	. . .
1951	2 735	7 007	438	. . .	. . .	. . .	. . .
1950	2 643	6 743	428	. . .	. . .	. . .	. . .
1949	2 610	6 654	434	. . .	. . .	. . .	. . .
1948	2 612	6 659	451	. . .	. . .	. . .	. . .
1947	2 478	6 477	461	. . .	. . .	. . .	. . .
1946	2 298	6 077	462	. . .	. . .	. . .	. . .
1945	1 955	5 359	417	. . .	. . .	. . .	. . .
1944	1 851	5 208	420	. . .	. . .	. . .	. . .
1943	1 828	5 154	412	. . .	. . .	. . .	. . .
1942	1 912	5 206	404	. . .	. . .	. . .	. . .
1941	1 966	5 244	404	. . .	. . .	. . .	. . .
1940	1 841	4 909	388	. . .	. . .	. . .	. . .
1939	1 767	4 659	377	. . .	. . .	. . .	. . .

Source: U.S. Bureau of Labor Statistics.
. . . = Not available.

Table 16-3. Retail Trade Corporations—Sales, Net Profit, and Profit Per Dollar of Sales, 2002–2005

Item	Total retail trade			Food and beverage stores (NAICS 445)			Clothing and general merchandise stores (NAICS 448, 452)			All other retail stores		
	2002	2004	2005	2002	2004	2005	2002	2004	2005	2002	2004	2005
Sales (Billions of dollars.)	1 415.5	1 666.5	1 779.8	311.9	360.0	373.6	586.1	637.1	638.2	517.5	669.4	768.1
Net profit (Billions of dollars.):												
Before income taxes	58.7	80.5	82.5	10.3	7.4	8.5	25.8	39.2	36.6	22.6	33.9	37.4
After income taxes	37.0	53.2	55.5	6.6	4.7	5.4	16.2	25.6	24.8	14.3	22.9	25.3
Profits per dollar of sales (Cents):												
Before income taxes	4.2	4.8	4.6	3.3	2.1	2.3	4.3	6.1	5.7	4.4	5.1	4.9
After income taxes	2.6	3.2	3.1	2.1	1.3	1.5	2.7	4.0	3.9	2.8	3.4	3.3
Profits on stockholders' equity (Percent):												
Before income taxes	22.5	25.5	23.8	26.4	18.4	19.6	20.2	26.6	22.9	23.8	26.5	26.1
After income taxes	14.2	16.8	16.0	16.9	11.7	12.5	12.6	17.4	15.5	15.1	17.8	17.6

Source: U.S. Census Bureau.
Note: Represents North American Industry Classification System, 1997 (NAICS) groups 44 and 45. Profit rates are averages of quarterly figures at annual rates. Covers corporations with assets of $50,000,000 or more.

Table 16-4. Retail Trade and Food Services—Sales, by Kind of Business (NAICS Basis), 1995–2005

(Millions of dollars.)

Kind of Business	1995	2000	2001	2002	2003	2004	2005
Retail sales and food services, total	**2 456 129**	**3 294 217**	**3 385 577**	**3 466 136**	**3 615 170**	**3 849 748**	**4 115 815**
Total (excluding motor vehicle and parts dealers)	1 875 287	2 496 649	2 568 636	2 645 867	2 773 955	2 984 900	3 220 565
Retail sales, total	**2 222 504**	**2 988 756**	**3 067 725**	**3 134 322**	**3 265 477**	**3 477 308**	**3 719 178**
Retail sales, total (excluding motor vehicle and parts dealers)	1 641 662	2 191 188	2 250 784	2 314 053	2 424 262	2 612 460	2 823 928
General merchandise, Apparel, Furniture, and Office Supplies (GAFO)[1]	651 071	863 903	883 866	913 925	948 246	1 007 937	1 061 836
Motor vehicle and parts dealers	580 842	797 568	816 941	820 269	841 215	864 848	895 250
Automobile and other motor vehicle dealers	528 722	733 875	755 592	757 354	776 620	797 484	822 276
Automobile dealers	502 482	688 733	708 623	707 675	721 032	735 130	747 156
New car dealers	464 642	630 123	649 413	645 759	656 885	665 894	669 985
Used car dealers	37 840	58 610	59 210	61 916	64 147	69 236	77 171
Auto parts, accessories, and tire stores	52 120	63 693	61 349	62 915	64 595	67 364	72 974
Furniture, home furnishings, electronics and appliance stores	128 520	173 691	172 039	178 507	184 485	200 466	211 733
Furniture and home furnishings stores	63 601	91 328	91 644	94 610	97 528	105 477	111 293
Furniture stores	37 034	50 689	50 646	51 342	52 070	56 575	58 867
Home furnishings stores	26 567	40 639	40 998	43 268	45 458	48 902	52 426
Electronics and appliance stores[2]	64 919	82 363	80 395	83 897	86 957	94 989	100 440
Appliances, T.V., and other electronics stores	42 142	58 260	60 245	63 343	66 129	72 302	77 231
Household appliance stores	9 986	12 636	13 485	14 211	14 524	15 749	17 392
Radio, T.V., and other electronics stores	32 156	45 624	46 760	49 132	51 605	56 553	59 839
Computer and software stores	20 502	20 713	16 930	17 311	17 512	19 209	19 702
Building materials, garden equipment, and supply stores	164 831	229 320	239 707	248 888	265 052	298 935	326 993
Building materials and supply dealers	141 218	197 890	207 263	217 445	231 984	263 714	288 746
Hardware stores	13 764	16 224	16 584	17 009	17 610	18 119	18 915
Food and beverage stores[2]	391 312	445 666	463 330	465 794	477 130	495 717	519 292
Grocery stores	356 932	402 988	418 596	420 288	429 962	445 104	463 905
Beer, wine and liquor stores	22 145	28 668	29 783	30 061	30 676	32 576	34 967
Health and personal care stores	101 719	155 372	166 678	180 143	192 224	198 588	208 376
Pharmacies and drug stores	85 851	130 867	141 781	153 946	164 588	167 234	174 173
Gasoline stations	181 294	249 975	251 537	250 770	273 566	320 793	388 261
Clothing and clothing access. stores[2]	131 593	167 968	167 583	172 617	178 778	190 204	201 682
Clothing stores[2]	90 809	118 210	119 323	122 954	128 303	137 131	146 950
Men's clothing stores	9 322	9 515	8 632	8 119	8 488	9 060	9 437
Women's clothing stores	28 723	31 480	31 487	31 280	32 525	34 718	36 735
Family clothing stores	40 014	58 928	60 165	64 305	67 272	71 991	77 268
Shoe stores	20 354	22 888	22 897	23 215	23 219	23 751	24 628
Jewelry stores	19 152	24 988	23 728	24 816	25 543	27 593	28 328
Sporting goods, hobby, book and music stores[2]	60 922	76 112	77 138	76 988	77 335	80 211	81 853
Sporting goods stores	19 986	25 436	26 286	26 347	27 168	28 925	31 032
Book stores	11 208	14 892	15 110	15 450	16 179	16 765	16 596
General merchandise stores	300 589	404 344	427 586	446 648	468 734	497 231	525 726
Department stores (excluding leased departments)	205 920	232 475	228 377	220 743	214 427	215 657	214 658
Department stores (except discount department stores)	89 300	96 282	90 782	86 857	85 982	86 110	84 053
Discount department stores	116 620	136 193	137 595	133 886	128 445	129 547	130 605
Department stores (including leased departments)	210 919	239 921	235 579	227 773	221 030	221 972	220 305
Department stores (except discount department stores)	92 258	100 284	93 871	90 228	89 298	89 274	86 660
Discount department stores	118 661	139 637	141 708	137 545	131 732	132 698	133 645
Other general merchandise stores	94 669	171 869	199 209	225 905	254 307	281 574	311 068
Warehouse clubs and superstores	65 101	139 614	164 716	191 252	216 327	242 423	270 771
All other general merchandise stores	29 568	32 255	34 493	34 653	37 980	39 151	40 297
Miscellaneous stores retail	77 177	108 052	104 381	104 163	103 056	105 616	111 001
Nonstore retailers[2]	103 705	180 688	180 805	189 535	203 902	224 699	249 011
Electronic shopping and mail-order houses	52 741	113 877	114 844	122 313	131 171	147 123	161 578
Fuel dealers	19 824	26 699	26 100	23 988	28 961	31 969	38 276
Food services and drinking places[2]	**233 625**	**305 461**	**317 852**	**331 814**	**349 693**	**372 440**	**396 637**
Full service restaurants	99 430	134 204	140 682	148 211	155 085	164 074	175 587
Limited service eating places	103 143	127 879	132 924	138 302	147 087	158 898	168 234
Drinking places	12 515	15 415	15 769	16 417	17 580	18 229	18 832

Source: U.S. Census Bureau. *Statistical Abstract of the United States: 2007.*
Note: Sales and inventories for leased departments and concessions are tabulated in the kind-of-business category of the leased department or concession.
[1] GAFO (General Merchandise, Apparel, Furniture, and Office Supplies) represents store classified in the following NAICS codes: 442,443,448,451,452, and 4532.
[2] Includes other kinds of business not shown separately.

Table 16.5. Wholesale Trade—Establishments, Employees, and Payroll, by Kind of Business, 2001–2003

(Number in thousands, millions of dollars).

Kind of business	Establishments (1,000)			Employees (1,000)			Annual payroll (billion dollars)		
	2001	2002	2003	2001	2002	2003	2001	2002	2003
Wholesale trade, total	**438.9**	**436.9**	**432.5**	**6,142**	**5,860**	**5,864**	**275.9**	**262.5**	**272.2**
Merchant wholesalers, durable goods	283.4	283.0	254.0	3,633	3,444	3,313	173.2	162.4	162.0
Motor vehicle/motor vehicle parts and supply merchant wholesalers	27.6	27.4	26.0	387	390	364	14.1	14.0	14.1
Furniture and home furnishing merchant wholesalers	14.5	14.5	13.8	166	155	162	606.0	6.4	6.6
Lumber and other construction materials merchant wholesalers	15.5	16.1	18.0	185	183	236	7.5	7.5	10.0
Professional and commercial equipment and supplies merchant wholesalers	43.1	41.6	36.4	777	723	703	45.1	41.8	42.6
Metal and mineral (except petroleum) merchant wholesalers	11.9	11.6	10.7	166	154	147	7.2	6.9	6.7
Electrical goods merchant wholesalers	37.8	36.6	31.4	559	512	469	34.8	30.2	29.1
Hardware, and plumbing and heating equipment and supplies merchant wholesalers	21.3	21.6	19.0	248	237	212	10.7	10.1	9.3
Machinery, equipment, and supplies merchant wholesalers	72.1	71.3	62.2	797	748	688	34.3	32.4	30.8
Miscellaneous durable goods merchant wholesalers	39.6	42.2	36.6	347	341	330	12.9	13.0	12.8
Merchant wholesalers, nondurable goods	155.5	153.9	138.9	2,509	2,417	2,288	10.3	100.1	99.3
Paper and paper product merchant wholesalers	14.4	13.7	12.9	226	209	215	8.9	8.2	8.8
Drugs and druggists' sundries merchant wholesalers	7.2	7.2	7.2	235	218	252	13.7	12.8	16.6
Apparel, piece goods and notions merchant wholesalers	19.5	19.0	17.3	212	201	197	9.0	9.3	9.1
Grocery and related product merchant wholesalers	39.2	38.6	35.2	871	861	757	33.0	32.7	29.3
Farm product raw material merchant wholesalers	9.3	8.8	7.3	91	84	65	2.6	2.4	2.2
Chemical and allied products merchant wholesalers	15.8	15.6	13.1	164	157	146	8.3	8.0	7.6
Petroleum and petroleum products merchant wholesalers	10.4	9.8	7.7	129	122	105	5.6	5.2	4.7
Beer/wine/distilled alcoholic beverage merchant wholesalers	4.6	4.4	4.3	161	163	169	7.1	7.3	7.7
Miscellaneous nondurable goods merchant wholesalers	35.1	36.9	33.4	420	401	383	14.6	14.2	13.4
Wholesale electronic markets and agents and brokers	...	...	39.7	...	...	264	...	...	10.8

Source: U.S. Census Bureau.
Note: Covers establishments with payroll. Employees are for the week including March 12. Most government employees are excluded. Kind-of-business classification based on North American Industry Classification System (NAICS) 2002.

Table 16-6. Estimated U.S. Merchant Wholesale Trade Sales[1], Excluding Manufacturers' Sales Branches and Offices—Total and E-commerce, 1998–2003

(Millions of dollars.)

Description	1998		1999		2000	
	Total	E-commerce	Total	E-commerce	Total	E-commerce
Total Merchant Wholesale Trade Excluding MSBOs[2]	**2 427 120**	**187 323**	**2 599 159**	**230 208**	**2 814 554**	**271 578**
Durable goods	**1 306 545**	**95 592**	**1 406 371**	**116 414**	**1 486 673**	**131 971**
Motor vehicles and automotive equipment	183 741	38 514	212 357	41 970	222 243	46 291
Furniture and home furnishings	43 020	2 431	46 925	2 930	52 697	3 215
Lumber and other construction material	79 784	2 515	88 505	2 549	87 179	2 893
Professional and commercial equipment and supplies	257 518	21 196	281 843	28 335	282 230	32 965
Computer equipment and supplies	157 836	11 680	175 779	19 434	174 848	22 079
Metals and minerals, excluding Petroleum	88 514	(S)	86 514	(S)	93 806	(S)
Electrical goods	201 145	8 412	224 125	13 200	260 041	16 983
Hardware, plumbing and heating equipment	65 540	6 473	68 505	7 111	72 056	7 185
Machinery, equipment and supplies	243 698	5 426	247 993	7 232	256 089	8 012
Miscellaneous durable goods	143 585	10 148	149 604	12 351	160 332	13 591
Nondurable goods	**1 120 575**	**91 731**	**1 192 788**	**113 794**	**1 327 881**	**139 607**
Paper and paper products	69 102	2 861	73 158	3 278	77 774	3 670
Drugs, drug proprietaries and druggists' sundries	125 599	55 822	151 527	68 615	175 979	83 495
Apparel, piece goods and notions	86 821	7 648	90 369	10 475	96 501	13 103
Groceries and related products	341 626	10 957	356 093	12 805	374 725	15 230
Farm-products raw materials	110 042	2 570	100 411	3 114	102 666	3 094
Chemicals and allied products	56 300	(D)	57 713	(D)	62 259	(D)
Petroleum and petroleum products	119 015	5 472	139 739	8 959	195 766	13 623
Beer, wine, and distilled beverages	61 759	(D)	67 330	(D)	71 337	(D)
Miscellaneous nondurable goods	150 311	4 388	156 448	4 247	170 874	4 637

[1]Estimates include data only for businesses with paid employees.
[2]Manufacturers' Sales Branches and Offices.
S = Estimate does not meet publication standards because of high sampling variability or poor response quality.
D = Estimate is withheld to avoid disclosing data of individual companies; these data are included in broader industry totals.

Table 16-6. Estimated U.S. Merchant Wholesale Trade Sales[1], Excluding Manufacturers' Sales Branches and Offices—Total and E-commerce, 1998–2003—*Continued*

(Millions of dollars.)

Description	2001 Total	2001 E-commerce	2002 Total	2002 E-commerce	2003 Total	2003 E-commerce
Total Merchant Wholesale Trade Excluding MSBOs[2]	**2 785 152**	**315 701**	**2 835 528**	**355 010**	**2 962 284**	**410 123**
Durable goods	**1 422 195**	**147 121**	**1 421 503**	**165 037**	**1 448 944**	**179 080**
Motor vehicles and automotive equipment	234 902	55 544	251 947	64 487	257 317	67 354
Furniture and home furnishings	52 433	4 605	53 484	6 425	54 758	6 883
Lumber and other construction material	89 730	3 483	95 091	4 020	105 672	4 939
Professional and commercial equipment and supplies	267 795	33 489	272 462	35 016	272 609	38 982
Computer equipment and supplies	153 845	19 609	150 618	19 680	144 319	20 907
Metals and minerals, excluding Petroleum	84 847	(S)	81 746	(S)	81 393	(S)
Electrical goods	231 864	19 510	222 957	21 218	227 129	22 516
Hardware, plumbing and heating equipment	69 047	7 747	70 431	8 398	71 235	9 165
Machinery, equipment and supplies	247 226	8 477	227 758	9 070	230 838	10 785
Miscellaneous durable goods	144 351	13 137	145 627	15 222	147 993	17 252
Nondurable goods	**1 362 957**	**168 580**	**1 414 025**	**189 973**	**1 513 340**	**231 043**
Paper and paper products	76 232	3 986	72 646	4 594	73 895	5 836
Drugs, drug proprietaries and druggists' sundries	210 672	105 718	245 625	120 657	273 546	140 480
Apparel, piece goods and notions	98 961	15 958	105 803	18 429	104 392	21 758
Groceries and related products	377 179	19 670	385 881	23 361	405 322	34 932
Farm-products raw materials	100 886	3 048	103 403	3 353	115 129	3 493
Chemicals and allied products	64 183	(D)	67 721	(D)	69 736	(D)
Petroleum and petroleum products	191 529	12 021	192 666	10 226	225 707	11 449
Beer, wine, and distilled beverages	74 854	(D)	79 189	(D)	82 215	(D)
Miscellaneous nondurable goods	168 461	4 628	161 091	5 129	163 398	7 763

Source: U.S. Census Bureau. *2004 E-Commerce Multi-Sector Data Tables.*
Note: Estimates are based on data from the Annual Trade Survey and are not adjusted for price changes. Totals may not equal the sum of the components due to independent rounding.
[1]Estimates include data only for businesses with paid employees.
[2]Manufacturers' Sales Branches and Offices.
S = Estimate does not meet publication standards because of high sampling variability or poor response quality.
D = Estimate is withheld to avoid disclosing data of individual companies; these data are included in broader industry totals.

Table 16-7. Service-Related Industries—Establishments, Employees, and Payroll, by Industry, 2001–2004

Industry	Establishments (1,000)			Employees[1] (1,000)			Annual payroll (billions of dollars)		
	2001	2003	2004	2001	2003	2004	2001	2003	2004
All industries, total	**7 095**	**7 255**	**7 388**	**115 061**	**113 398**	**115 075**	**3 989**	**4 041**	**4 254**
Professional, scientific, and technical services	**4 386**	**781**	**805**	**62 887**	**7 340**	**7 570**	**2 032**	**398**	**427**
Professional, scientific, and technical services	191	781	805	3 751	7 340	7 570	130	398	427
Legal services	5	182	185	609	1 183	1 218	29	74	78
Accounting/tax prep/bookkeeping/payroll services	2	114	117	70	1 325	1 390	3	43	47
Architectural, engineering and related services	110	106	109	1 398	1 235	1 265	46	71	76
Specialized design services	16	30	32	392	117	119	8	5	5
Computer systems design and related services	3	102	106	51	1 059	1 105	4	72	78
Management, science and technical consulting services	2	123	129	23	838	880	557	49	56
Scientific Research and Development services	32	15	16	485	616	641	17	47	51
Advertising and related services	13	37	39	578	419	390	18	21	20
Other professional, scientific, and technical services	7	71	72	145	547	562	4	16	17
Management of companies and enterprises	**48**	**47**	**46**	**2 879**	**2 879**	**2 825**	**213**	**212**	**222**
Administrative support, waste management and remediation services..	**363**	**349**	**359**	**9 062**	**8 511**	**8 708**	**221**	**219**	**236**
Administrative and support services	346	330	340	8 761	8 171	8 364	210	206	222
Employment services	45	41	41	4 364	3 902	4 028	101	97	107
Temporary help services	30	27	27	2 676	2 188	2 326	57	49	55
Business support services	34	35	35	711	760	774	18	19	20
Travel arrangement and reservation services	32	26	24	313	284	270	10	10	10
Waste management and remediation services	17	18	19	301	340	344	11	13	13
Accommodation and food services	**549**	**575**	**591**	**9 972**	**10 440**	**10 750**	**129**	**139**	**147**
Accommodation	60	61	62	1 753	1 804	1 845	34	37	39
Traveler accommodation	50	51	52	1 698	1 754	1 794	33	36	38
Recreational Vehicle (RV) parks and recreational camps	7	7	7	39	37	38	901	1	1
Food services and drinking places	488	514	529	8 220	8 636	8 905	95	102	108
Full-service restaurants	193	200	206	3 963	4 091	4 263	49	52	55
Limited-service eating places	216	234	242	3 407	3 641	3 772	35	38	40
Special foodservices	29	31	32	514	553	508	8	9	8
Drinking places (alcoholic beverages)	50	48	48	335	351	361	3	4	4
Other services (except public administration)	**719**	**732**	**735**	**5 370**	**5 367**	**5 416**	**115**	**118**	**123**
Repair and maintenance	231	229	229	1 343	1 305	1 320	38	37	38
Automotive Repair and Maintenance	164	165	166	871	892	905	21	23	23
Electronic and precision equipment Repair and Maintenance	15	14	14	141	130	127	6	6	6
Personal and Laundry services	197	205	208	1 312	1 310	1 333	24	24	25
Religious/grantmaking/professional/like organizations	292	299	297	2 716	2 753	2 763	53	57	59

Source: U.S. Census Bureau.
Note: Covers only those establishments with payroll. Excludes most government employees, railroad employees, and self-employed persons. Kind-of-business classification based on North American Industry Classification System (NAICS).
[1]Includes employees on the payroll for the pay period including March 12.

Table 16-8. Electronic Shopping and Mail-Order Houses—Total and E-commerce by Merchandise Line, 2001–2004

(Millions of dollars, except as indicated.)

	2001				
	Value of sales		E-commerce as percent of total sales	Percent distribution	
Merchandise lines	Total	E-commerce		Total sales	E-commerce sales
Total	**109,463**	**25,690**	**24.0**	**100.0**	**100.0**
Books and magazines	3,872	1,739	45.0	4.0	7.0
Clothing and clothing accessories[1]	15,351	3,250	21.0	14.0	13.0
Computer hardware	21,968	5,655	26.0	20.0	22.0
Computer software	3,955	1,203	30.0	4.0	5.0
Drugs, health aids, beauty aids	16,203	950	6.0	15.0	4.0
Electronics and appliances	3,739	1,470	39.0	3.0	6.0
Food, beer and wine	1,832	444	24.2	1.7	1.7
Furniture and home furnishings	6,530	1,658	25.4	6.0	6.5
Music and videos	3,971	1,306	32.9	3.6	5.1
Office equipment and supplies	6,605	1,981	30.0	6.0	7.7
Sporting goods	1,640	464	28.3	1.5	1.8
Toys, hobby goods, and games	3,008	931	31.0	2.7	3.6
Other merchandise[2]	16,710	3,082	18.4	15.3	12.0
Nonmerchandise receipts[3]	4,079	1,557	38.2	3.7	6.1

Source: U.S. Census Bureau.
Note: Represents North American Industry Classification System code 454110 which comprises establishments primarily engaged in retailing all types of merchandise using non-store means, such as catalogs, toll free telephone numbers, or electronic media, such as interactive television or computer. Included in this industry are establishments primarily engaged in retailing from catalog showrooms of mail-order houses. Covers businesses with or without paid employees. Based on the Annual Retail Survey.
[1]Includes footwear.
[2]Includes other merchandise such as jewelry, collectibles, souvenirs, auto parts and accessories, hardware, and lawn and garden equipment and supplies.
[3]Includes nonmerchandise receipts such as auction commissions, shipping and handling, customer training, customer support, and advertising.

Table 16-8. Electronic Shopping and Mail-Order Houses—Total and E-commerce by Merchandise Line, 2001–2004—*Continued*

(Millions of dollars, except as indicated.)

2003					2004				
Value of sales		E-commerce as percent of total sales	Percent distribution		Value of sales		E-commerce as percent of total sales	Percent distribution	
Total	E-commerce		Total sales	E-commerce sales	Total	E-commerce		Total	E-commerce
131,171	**42,022**	**32.0**	**100.0**	**100.0**	**147,123**	**52,217**	**35.5**	**100.0**	**100.0**
4,106	2,143	52.2	3.1	5.1	4,457	2,466	55.3	3.0	4.7
15,064	5,571	37.0	11.5	13.3	16,364	7,152	43.7	11.1	13.7
23,423	7,566	32.3	17.9	18.0	26,854	9,410	35.0	18.3	18.0
3,878	1,239	31.9	3.0	2.9	4,332	1,515	35.0	2.9	2.9
27,250	1,877	6.9	20.8	4.5	31,663	2,266	7.2	21.5	4.3
6,274	3,309	52.7	4.8	7.9	7,857	4,653	59.2	5.3	8.9
2,199	879	40.0	1.7	2.1	2,549	1,114	43.7	1.7	2.1
8,251	3,431	41.6	6.3	8.2	8,752	4,289	49.0	5.9	8.2
3,730	1,727	46.3	2.8	4.1	3,901	1,960	50.2	2.7	3.8
7,001	3,488	49.8	5.3	8.3	7,634	4,084	53.5	5.2	7.8
2,615	1,149	43.9	2.0	2.7	2,914	1,415	48.6	2.0	2.7
3,870	1,606	41.5	3.0	3.8	3,889	1,753	45.1	2.6	3.4
17,659	5,245	29.7	13.5	12.5	19,170	6,572	34.3	13.0	12.6
5,851	2,792	47.7	4.5	6.6	6,783	3,568	52.6	4.6	6.8

Table 16-9. Retail Trade and Food Services—Estimated Per Capita Sales by Selected Kinds of Business (NAICS Basis), 1992–2005

(Dollars.)

Kind of Business	1992	1995	2000	2001	2002	2003	2004	2005
Retail and food service sales	**7 918**	**9 346**	**11 673**	**11 875**	**12 036**	**12 429**	**13 109**	**13 885**
Retail sales, total	**7 120**	**8 457**	**10 591**	**10 760**	**10 884**	**11 227**	**11 841**	**12 547**
Total (excluding motor vehicle and parts dealers)	*5 475*	*6 247*	*7 765*	*7 894*	*8 035*	*8 335*	*8 896*	*9 527*
Furniture and home furnishings stores	206	242	324	321	329	335	359	375
Electronics and appliance stores	168	247	292	282	291	299	323	339
Building material and garden equipment and supplies dealers	515	627	813	841	864	911	1 018	1 103
Food and beverage stores	1 456	1 489	1 579	1 625	1 617	1 640	1 688	1 752
Health and personal care stores	352	387	551	585	626	661	676	703
Gasoline stations	614	690	886	882	871	941	1 092	1 310
Clothing and clothing accessories stores	472	501	595	588	599	615	648	680
Sporting goods, hobby, book, and music stores	193	232	270	271	267	266	273	276
General merchandise stores	972	1 144	1 433	1 500	1 551	1 612	1 693	1 774
Miscellaneous store retailers	219	294	383	366	362	354	360	374
Nonstore retailers	308	395	640	634	658	701	765	840
Food services and drinking places	798	889	1 082	1 115	1 152	1 202	1 268	1 338

Source: U.S. Census Bureau. *Statistical Abstract of the United States: 2007.*
Note: Based on estimated population estimates as of July 1. Based on the Annual Retail Trade Survey.

Table 16-10. Retail Foodstores—Number and Sales, by Type, 1990–2004

Type of foodstore	Number[1] (thousands)						
	1990	1995	2000	2001	2002	2003	2004
Total	**133.6**	**118.5**	**119.6**	**119.8**	**120.0**	**120.2**	**120.5**
Grocery stores	109.1	97.0	95.9	95.7	95.5	95.3	95.1
Supermarkets[3]	24.5	25.3	21.9	24.0	20.3	21.1	21.0
Conventional	13.2	12.3	7.2	8.8	4.4	4.1	3.6
Superstore[4]	5.8	6.8	7.9	7.9	7.9	8.1	8.2
Warehouse[5]	3.4	2.7	2.4	2.7	2.7	3.2	3.2
Combination food and drug[6]	1.6	2.7	3.7	3.9	4.5	5.0	5.2
Superwarehouse[7]	0.3	0.6	0.5	0.5	0.5	0.5	0.5
Hypermarket[8]	0.1	0.2	0.2	0.2	0.3	0.2	0.3
Convenience stores[9]	28.0	27.2	28.2	28.2	29.4	29.4	30.4
Superette[10]	56.6	44.4	45.8	43.5	45.8	44.8	43.8
Specialized food stores[11]	24.5	21.5	23.7	24.1	24.5	24.9	25.4

[1]Estimated.
[2]Includes nonfood items.
[3]A grocery store, primarily self-service in operation, providing a full range of departments, and having at least $2.5 million in annual sales in 1985 dollars.
[4]Contains greater variety of products than conventional supermarkets, including specialty and service departments, and considerable nonfood (general merchandise) products.
[5]Contains limited product variety and fewer services provided, incorporating case lot stocking and shelving practices.
[6]Contains a pharmacy, a nonprescription drug department, and a greater variety of health and beauty aids than that carried by conventional supermarkets.
[7]A larger warehouse store that offers expanded product variety and often service meat, deli, or seafood departments.
[8]A very large store offering a greater variety of general merchandise—like clothes, hardware, and seasonal goods—and personal care products than other grocery stores.
[9]A small grocery store selling a limited variety of food and nonfood products, typically open extended hours.
[10]A grocery store, primarily self-service in operation, selling a wide variety of food and nonfood products with annual sales below $2.5 million (1985 dollars).
[11]Primarily engaged in the retail sale of a single food category such as meat and seafood stores and retail bakeries.

Table 16-10. Retail Foodstores—Number and Sales, by Type, 1990–2004—
Continued

Type of foodstore	Sales[2] (billions of dollars)						
	1990	1995	2000	2001	2002	2003	2004
Total	**335.8**	**369.2**	**417.3**	**433.9**	**435.7**	**446.4**	**463.1**
Grocery stores	324.6	356.9	403.1	420.4	420.3	430.0	445.1
Supermarkets[3]	261.7	300.4	310.3	322.3	336.3	310.4	318.0
Conventional	92.3	76.4	58.3	59.8	62.4	57.6	59.0
Superstore[4]	87.6	116.7	131.0	138.2	144.2	133.1	136.3
Warehouse[5]	33.1	20.7	20.2	22.0	23.0	21.2	21.7
Combination food and drug[6]	29.3	59.3	75.3	76.2	79.5	73.4	75.2
Superwarehouse[7]	12.6	17.8	16.0	16.1	16.8	15.5	15.9
Hypermarket[8]	6.8	9.5	9.5	10.0	10.4	9.6	9.9
Convenience stores[9]	20.3	17.0	19.2	20.1	20.9	21.0	22.6
Superette[10]	42.5	39.5	73.6	78.0	63.1	98.6	104.5
Specialized food stores[11]	11.2	12.2	14.2	13.5	15.4	16.4	18.0

Source: U.S. Census Bureau. *Statistical Abstract of the United States: 2007.* U.S. Department of Agriculture, Economic Research Service.
Note: Beginning 2000, data based on North American Industry Classification System (NAICS), 2002. 1990 and 1995 based on Standard Industry Classification (SIC) codes.
[1]Estimated.
[2]Includes nonfood items.
[3]A grocery store, primarily self-service in operation, providing a full range of departments, and having at least $2.5 million in annual sales in 1985 dollars.
[4]Contains greater variety of products than conventional supermarkets, including specialty and service departments, and considerable nonfood (general merchandise) products.
[5]Contains limited product variety and fewer services provided, incorporating case lot stocking and shelving practices.
[6]Contains a pharmacy, a nonprescription drug department, and a greater variety of health and beauty aids than that carried by conventional supermarkets.
[7]A larger warehouse store that offers expanded product variety and often service meat, deli, or seafood departments.
[8]A very large store offering a greater variety of general merchandise—like clothes, hardware, and seasonal goods—and personal care products than other grocery stores.
[9]A small grocery store selling a limited variety of food and nonfood products, typically open extended hours.
[10]A grocery store, primarily self-service in operation, selling a wide variety of food and nonfood products with annual sales below $2.5 million (1985 dollars).
[11]Primarily engaged in the retail sale of a single food category such as meat and seafood stores and retail bakeries.

Table 16-10. Retail Foodstores—Number and Sales, by Type, 1990–2004—*Continued*

Percent distribution					
Number			Sales		
1990	2000	2004	1990	2000	2004
100.0	**100.0**	**100.0**	**100.0**	**100.0**	**100.0**
81.7	80.2	78.9	96.7	96.6	96.1
18.3	18.3	17.4	77.9	74.4	68.7
9.9	6.0	3.0	27.5	14.0	12.7
4.3	6.6	6.8	26.1	31.4	29.4
2.5	2.0	2.6	9.9	4.8	4.7
1.2	3.1	4.3	8.7	18.0	16.2
0.2	0.4	0.4	3.8	3.8	3.4
0.1	0.2	0.2	2.0	2.3	2.1
21.0	23.6	25.2	6.0	4.6	4.9
42.4	38.3	36.3	12.7	17.6	22.6
18.3	19.8	21.1	3.3	3.4	3.9

Table 16-11. General Merchandise Stores, by Number and Sales by Product Lines, 2002

Product line	Establishments with the product line		
	Number	Total sales (millions of dollars)	Product line sales (millions of dollars)
General merchandise stores	40 907	(X)	44 664
Groceries and other food items for human consumption off the premises, including bottled, canned or packaged soft drinks, candy, gum, packaged snacks, etc.	35 520	396 097	82 677
Drugs, health aids, beauty aids, including cosmetics	38 249	440 384	46 820
Soaps, detergents, and household cleaners	32 936	338 914	12 023
Men's wear	36 219	438 996	24 224
Women's, junior's, and misses' wear	37 041	439 187	46 557
Children's wear, including boys' (sizes 2 to 7 and 8 to 20), girls' (sizes 4 to 6x and 7 to 14), and infants' and toddlers' clothing and accessories	35 574	406 992	19 400
Footwear, including accessories	31 553	369 315	10 483
Curtains, draperies, blinds, slipcovers, bed and table coverings	35 981	432 009	12 082
Small electric appliances, including: mixers, blenders, can openers, toasters, coffee makers, fry pans, and personal care appliances, such as hair dryers, curling irons, shavers, etc.	33 335	398 088	5 903
Audio equipment, musical instruments, radios, stereos, compact discs, records, tapes, audio tape books, sheet music, accessories	27 222	375 195	9 992
Furniture, sleep equipment and outdoor/patio furniture	27 222	406 328	8 047
Kitchenware and home furniture, including cookware, cooking accessories, dinnerware, glassware, giftware, decorative accessories and lighting, clocks, mirrors, closet and bathroom accessories, outdoor charcoal grills, planters, etc.	38 507	440 381	14 298
Toys, hobby goods, and games including: stuffed animals, video and electronic games, electronic game devices and wheel goods, except bicycles	37 052	409 960	14 519

Source: U.S. Census Bureau. *Statistical Abstract of the United States: 2006.*
X = Not applicable.

BOX 16 ■ E-commerce

For most people, the term "e-commerce" brings to mind business-to-consumer retail sales. In actuality, the vast majority of e-commerce shipments are business-to-business (B-to-B) transactions involving either manufacturers or merchant whole-salers. In 2005, B-to-B activity accounted for 92% of e-commerce, or $2,211 billion.

E-commerce transactions in the manufacturing sector in 2005 accounted for 26.7% of all shipments, or $1,266 bil-lion. Since the U.S. Census Bureau began keeping e-commerce statistics in the late 1990s, manufacturing has consistently been the industry within which e-commerce conducts the largest share of its business. In 1999, e-commerce shipments in manufacturing accounted for 12.0% of all shipments or $485 billion. The share of e-commerce shipments has steadily grown, even when total manufacturing shipments were declining in 2001 and 2002.

Merchant wholesalers conducted 18.3% of their total sales electronically in 2005 for a value of $945 billion. The share of e-commerce sales in the merchant wholesale trade showed a slow but steady decline from 19.0% in 2003, although the value of those sales increased 14.1% from $828 billion in 2003. Among merchant wholesalers, 69% of e-commerce sales were attributable to four industry segments: drugs and druggists' sundries, motor vehicles and automotive equipment, pro-fessional equipment, and grocery products.

In comparison, e-commerce only made up 2.5% of retail sales in 2005, or $93.3 billion. Preliminary estimates indi-cate 2.9% of all retail sales, with a value of $114.6 billion, were electronically transacted in 2006. While this is only a small percent of total retail business, it is up appreciably since 1999 when e-commerce accounted for 0.5% of total sales. The two retail industry groups with the vast majority of sales in this segment are non-store retailers/mail-order houses ($68 billion) and motor vehicles and parts dealers ($17 billion) which together account for 91% of total retail e-commerce sales.

The Census Bureau suggests that one reason for retail's lagging e-commerce sales is likely the industry's relatively re-cent adoption of Internet systems coupled with the manufacturing and merchant wholesaling industries' long-standing use of electronic data interchange (EDI) systems for electronic sales.

Sources:
U.S. Census Bureau. *E-Stats,* May 25, 2007. http://www.census.gov/eos/www/2005/2005reportfinal.pdf
U.S. Census Bureau. *E-Stats,* March 1, 2002. http://www.census.gov/eos/www/1999/manu_final/finalv7text.pdf
U.S. Census Bureau. *E-Stats,* March 7, 2001. http://www.census.gov/eos/www/1999/manu_final/finalv7text.pdf

Health, Social Welfare, and Law Enforcement

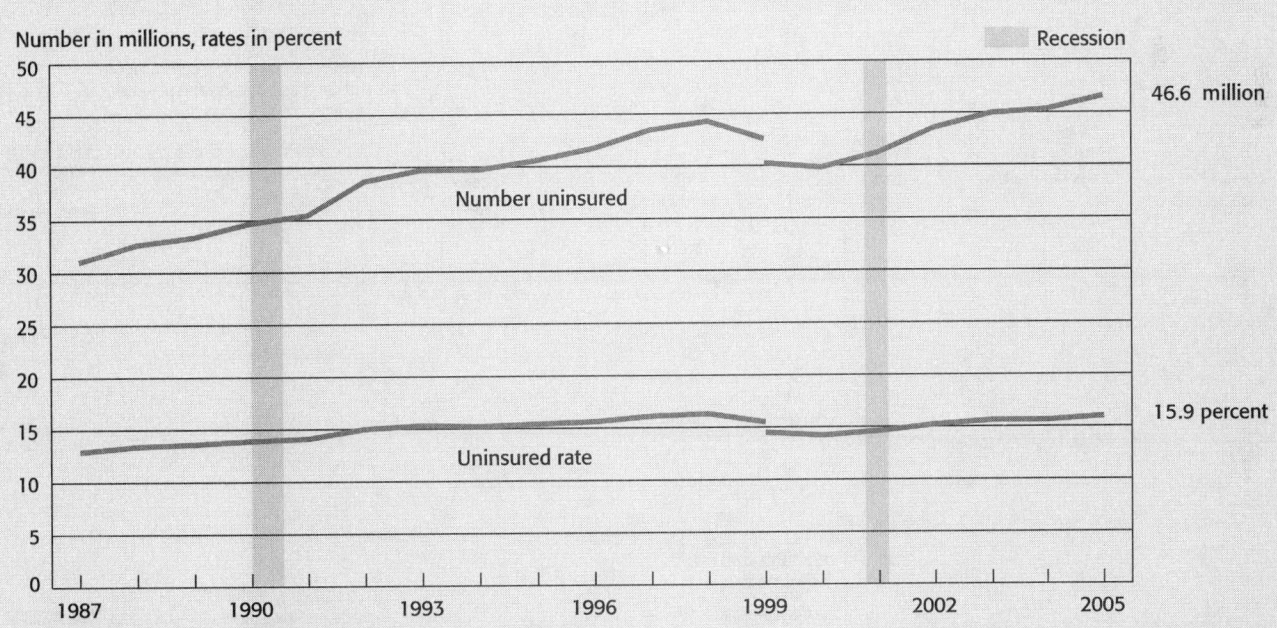

Number in millions, rates in percent

Recession

46.6 million

Number uninsured

15.9 percent

Uninsured rate

1987   1990   1993   1996   1999   2002   2005

Number Uninsured and Uninsured Rate: 1987 to 2005

Notes: Respondents were not asked detailed health insurance questions before the 1988 CPS. Implementation of Census 2000-based population controls occurred for the 2000 ASEC, which collected data for 1999. These estimates also reflect the results of follow-up verification questions that were asked of people who responded "no" to all questions about specific types of health insurance coverage in order to verify whether they were actually uninsured. This change increased the number and percentage of people covered by health insurance, bringing the CPS more in line with estimates from other national surveys.

The 20004 data have been revised to reflect a correction to the weights in the 2005 ASEC. The estimates also reflect improvements to the algorithm that assigns coverage to dependents. The data points are placed at the midpoints of the respective years.

Source: U.S. Census Bureau, Current Population Survey, 1988 to 2006 Annual Social and Economic Supplements.

Health

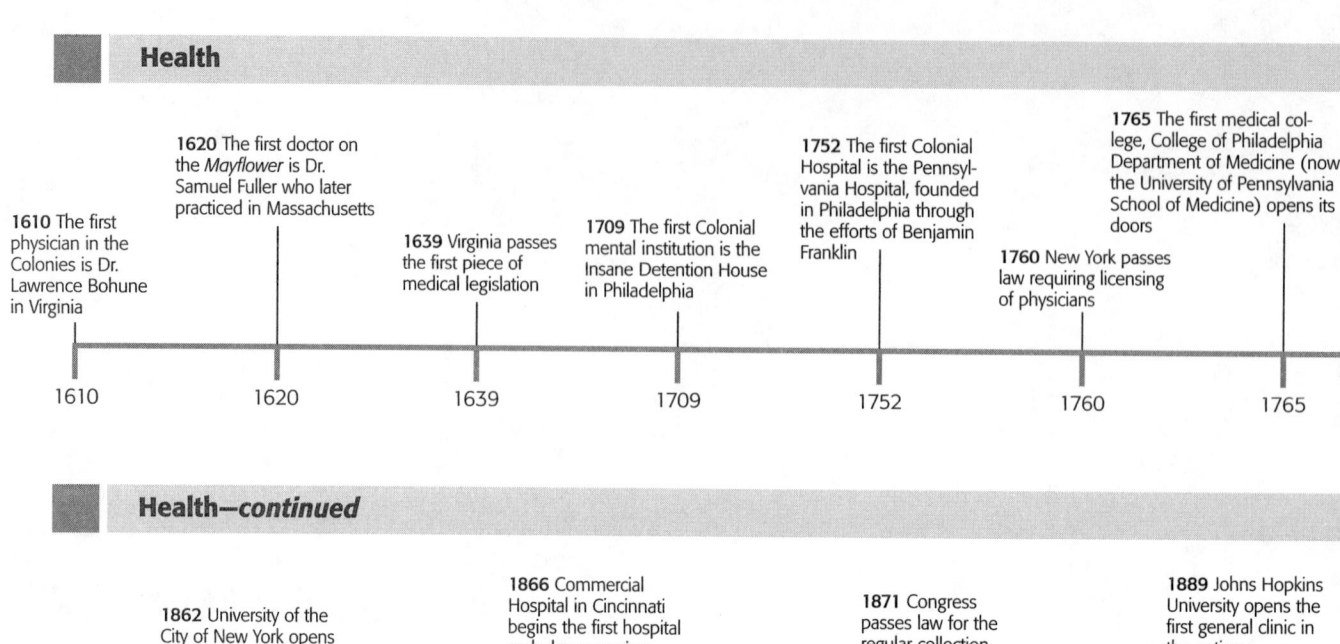

1610 The first physician in the Colonies is Dr. Lawrence Bohune in Virginia

1620 The first doctor on the *Mayflower* is Dr. Samuel Fuller who later practiced in Massachusetts

1639 Virginia passes the first piece of medical legislation

1709 The first Colonial mental institution is the Insane Detention House in Philadelphia

1752 The first Colonial Hospital is the Pennsylvania Hospital, founded in Philadelphia through the efforts of Benjamin Franklin

1760 New York passes law requiring licensing of physicians

1765 The first medical college, College of Philadelphia Department of Medicine (now the University of Pennsylvania School of Medicine) opens its doors

1610   1620   1639   1709   1752   1760   1765

Health—*continued*

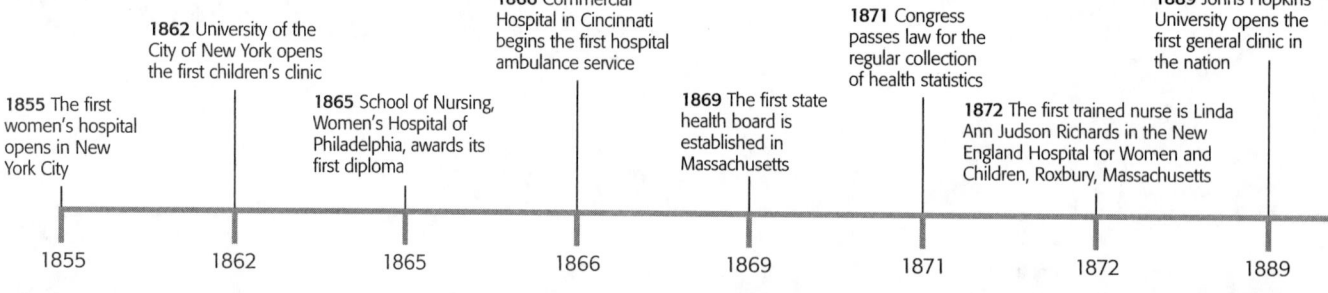

1855 The first women's hospital opens in New York City

1862 University of the City of New York opens the first children's clinic

1865 School of Nursing, Women's Hospital of Philadelphia, awards its first diploma

1866 Commercial Hospital in Cincinnati begins the first hospital ambulance service

1869 The first state health board is established in Massachusetts

1871 Congress passes law for the regular collection of health statistics

1872 The first trained nurse is Linda Ann Judson Richards in the New England Hospital for Women and Children, Roxbury, Massachusetts

1889 Johns Hopkins University opens the first general clinic in the nation

1855   1862   1865   1866   1869   1871   1872   1889

Food and Nutrition

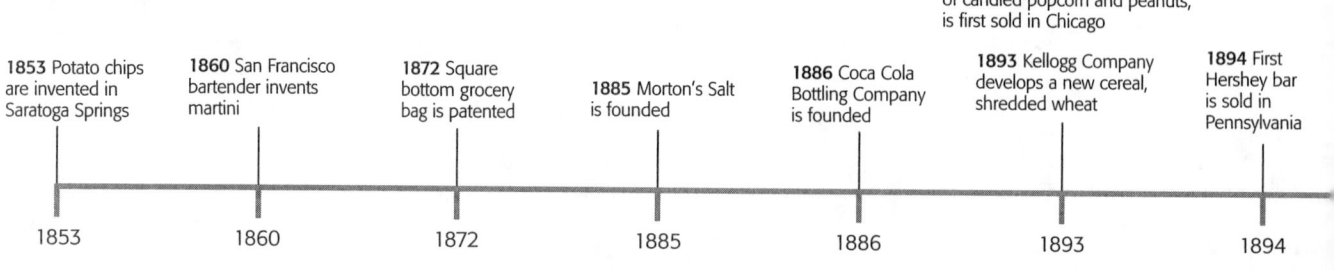

1853 Potato chips are invented in Saratoga Springs

1860 San Francisco bartender invents martini

1872 Square bottom grocery bag is patented

1885 Morton's Salt is founded

1886 Coca Cola Bottling Company is founded

1893 Cracker Jack, a combination of candied popcorn and peanuts, is first sold in Chicago

1893 Kellogg Company develops a new cereal, shredded wheat

1894 First Hershey bar is sold in Pennsylvania

1853   1860   1872   1885   1886   1893   1894

Food and Nutrition—*continued*

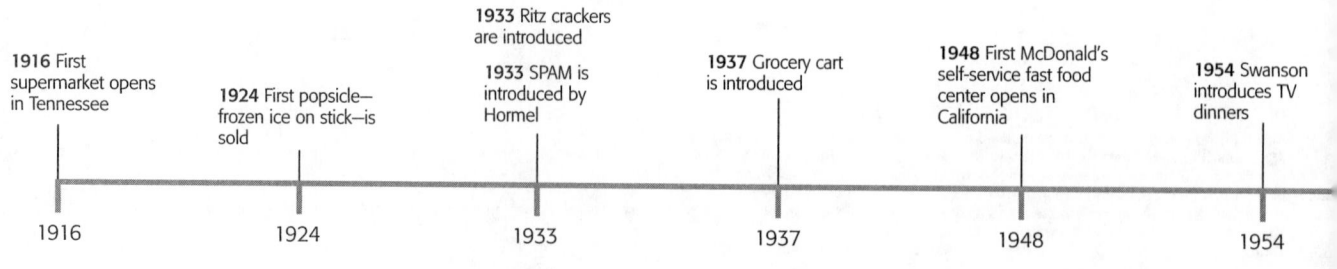

1916 First supermarket opens in Tennessee

1924 First popsicle—frozen ice on stick—is sold

1933 Ritz crackers are introduced

1933 SPAM is introduced by Hormel

1937 Grocery cart is introduced

1948 First McDonald's self-service fast food center opens in California

1954 Swanson introduces TV dinners

1916   1924   1933   1937   1948   1954

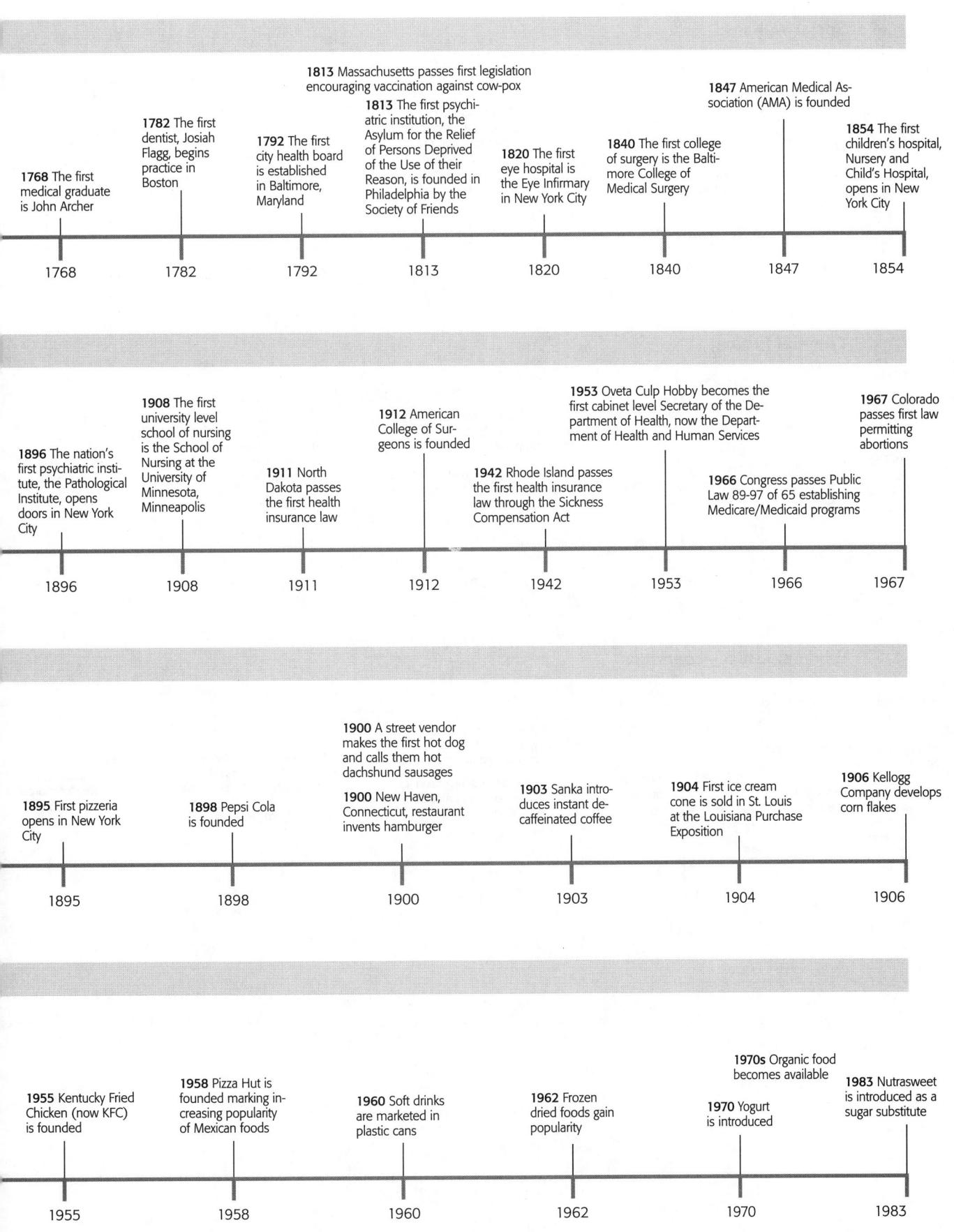

1768 The first medical graduate is John Archer

1782 The first dentist, Josiah Flagg, begins practice in Boston

1792 The first city health board is established in Baltimore, Maryland

1813 Massachusetts passes first legislation encouraging vaccination against cow-pox

1813 The first psychiatric institution, the Asylum for the Relief of Persons Deprived of the Use of their Reason, is founded in Philadelphia by the Society of Friends

1820 The first eye hospital is the Eye Infirmary in New York City

1840 The first college of surgery is the Baltimore College of Medical Surgery

1847 American Medical Association (AMA) is founded

1854 The first children's hospital, Nursery and Child's Hospital, opens in New York City

1768   1782   1792   1813   1820   1840   1847   1854

1896 The nation's first psychiatric institute, the Pathological Institute, opens doors in New York City

1908 The first university level school of nursing is the School of Nursing at the University of Minnesota, Minneapolis

1911 North Dakota passes the first health insurance law

1912 American College of Surgeons is founded

1942 Rhode Island passes the first health insurance law through the Sickness Compensation Act

1953 Oveta Culp Hobby becomes the first cabinet level Secretary of the Department of Health, now the Department of Health and Human Services

1966 Congress passes Public Law 89-97 of 65 establishing Medicare/Medicaid programs

1967 Colorado passes first law permitting abortions

1896   1908   1911   1912   1942   1953   1966   1967

1895 First pizzeria opens in New York City

1898 Pepsi Cola is founded

1900 A street vendor makes the first hot dog and calls them hot dachshund sausages

1900 New Haven, Connecticut, restaurant invents hamburger

1903 Sanka introduces instant decaffeinated coffee

1904 First ice cream cone is sold in St. Louis at the Louisiana Purchase Exposition

1906 Kellogg Company develops corn flakes

1895   1898   1900   1903   1904   1906

1955 Kentucky Fried Chicken (now KFC) is founded

1958 Pizza Hut is founded marking increasing popularity of Mexican foods

1960 Soft drinks are marketed in plastic cans

1962 Frozen dried foods gain popularity

1970s Organic food becomes available

1970 Yogurt is introduced

1983 Nutrasweet is introduced as a sugar substitute

1955   1958   1960   1962   1970   1983

Social Welfare

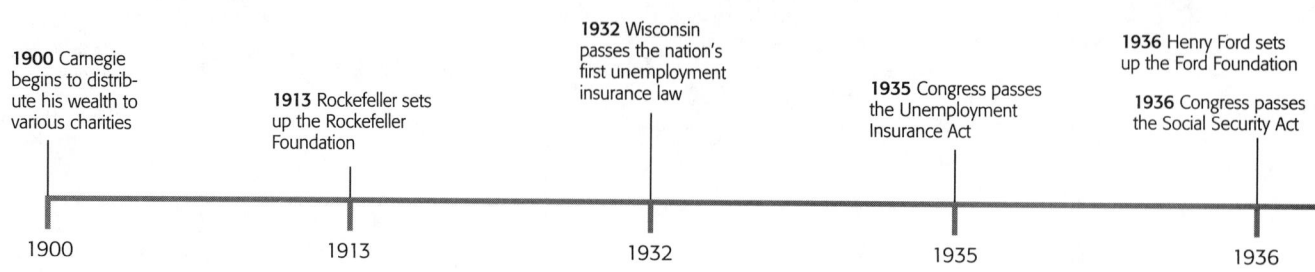

1900 Carnegie begins to distribute his wealth to various charities

1913 Rockefeller sets up the Rockefeller Foundation

1932 Wisconsin passes the nation's first unemployment insurance law

1935 Congress passes the Unemployment Insurance Act

1936 Henry Ford sets up the Ford Foundation

1936 Congress passes the Social Security Act

1900   1913   1932   1935   1936

Criminal Justice

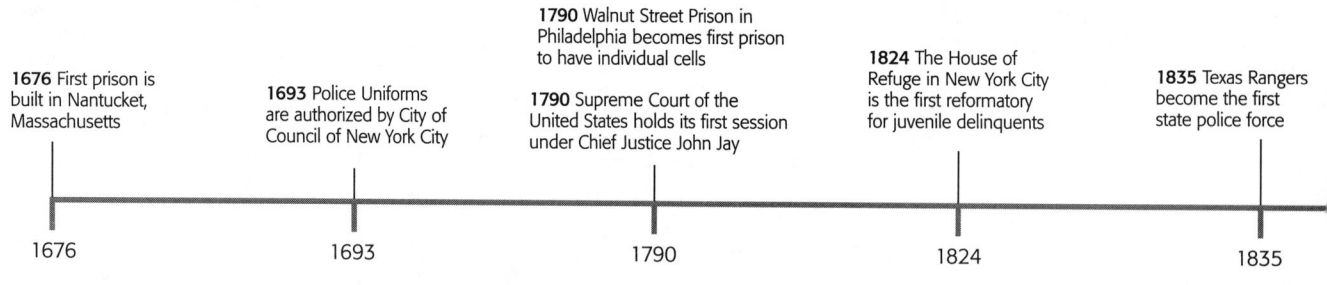

1676 First prison is built in Nantucket, Massachusetts

1693 Police Uniforms are authorized by City of Council of New York City

1790 Walnut Street Prison in Philadelphia becomes first prison to have individual cells

1790 Supreme Court of the United States holds its first session under Chief Justice John Jay

1824 The House of Refuge in New York City is the first reformatory for juvenile delinquents

1835 Texas Rangers become the first state police force

1676   1693   1790   1824   1835

Criminal Justice—*continued*

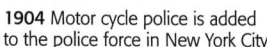

1904 Motor cycle police is added to the police force in New York City

1904 Police Bureau of Identification opens in Chicago

1904 First police department to adopt regular fingerprinting of all suspects is St. Louis, Missouri

1908 Federal Bureau of Investigation is founded as the nation's top investigative agency

1926 Department of Justice begins first nationwide collection of law enforcement data

1926 First federal prison for women opens at Alderson, West Virginia

1930 International Association of Chiefs of Police initiates the Uniform Crime Reporting Program, the forerunner of the *Uniform Crime Reports*

1934 Congress makes capital punishment mandatory for murder of police officers

1904   1908   1926   1930   1934

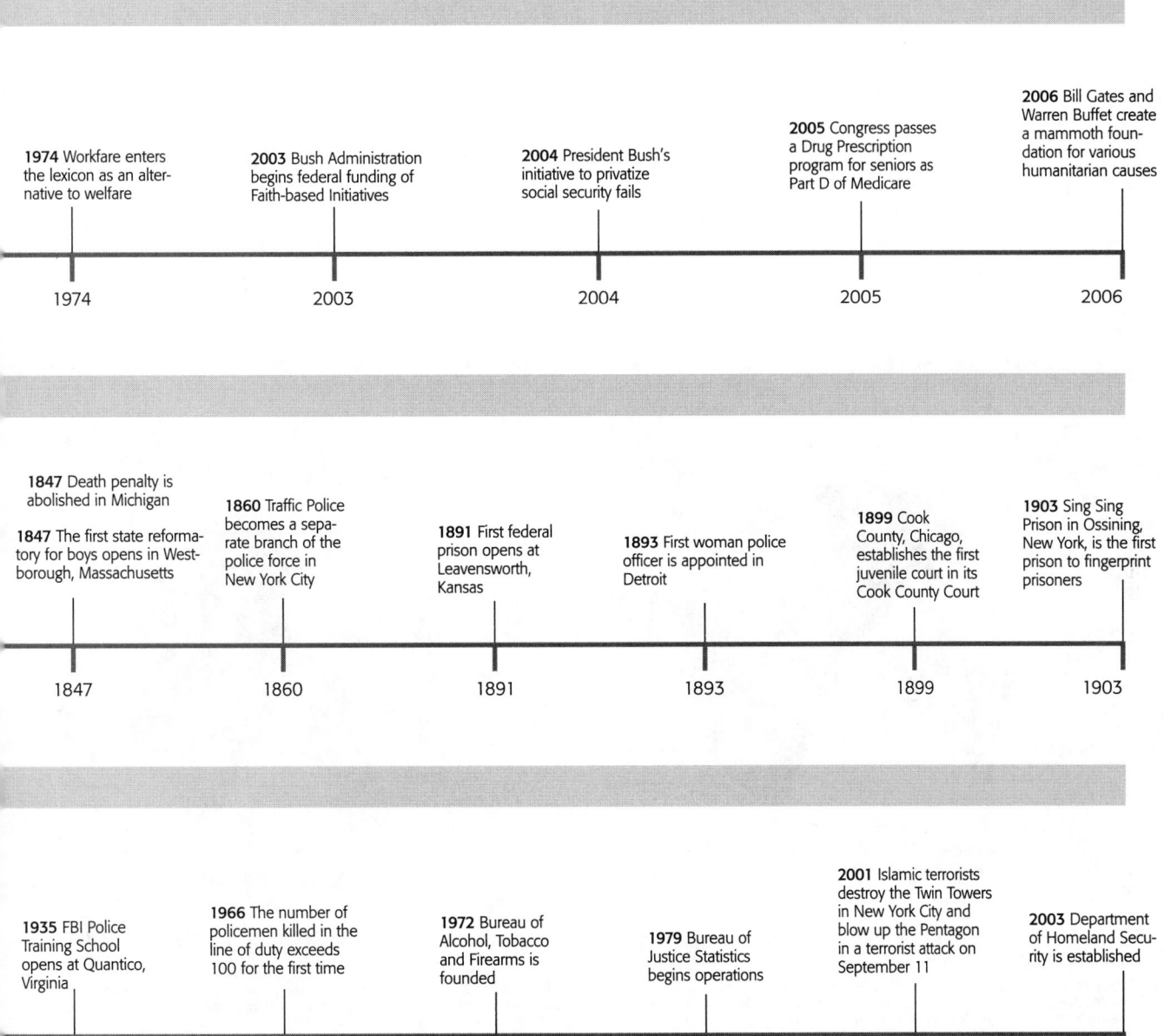

1974 Workfare enters the lexicon as an alternative to welfare

2003 Bush Administration begins federal funding of Faith-based Initiatives

2004 President Bush's initiative to privatize social security fails

2005 Congress passes a Drug Prescription program for seniors as Part D of Medicare

2006 Bill Gates and Warren Buffet create a mammoth foundation for various humanitarian causes

1974   2003   2004   2005   2006

1847 Death penalty is abolished in Michigan

1847 The first state reformatory for boys opens in Westborough, Massachusetts

1860 Traffic Police becomes a separate branch of the police force in New York City

1891 First federal prison opens at Leavensworth, Kansas

1893 First woman police officer is appointed in Detroit

1899 Cook County, Chicago, establishes the first juvenile court in its Cook County Court

1903 Sing Sing Prison in Ossining, New York, is the first prison to fingerprint prisoners

1847   1860   1891   1893   1899   1903

1935 FBI Police Training School opens at Quantico, Virginia

1966 The number of policemen killed in the line of duty exceeds 100 for the first time

1972 Bureau of Alcohol, Tobacco and Firearms is founded

1979 Bureau of Justice Statistics begins operations

2001 Islamic terrorists destroy the Twin Towers in New York City and blow up the Pentagon in a terrorist attack on September 11

2003 Department of Homeland Security is established

1935   1966   1972   1979   2001   2003

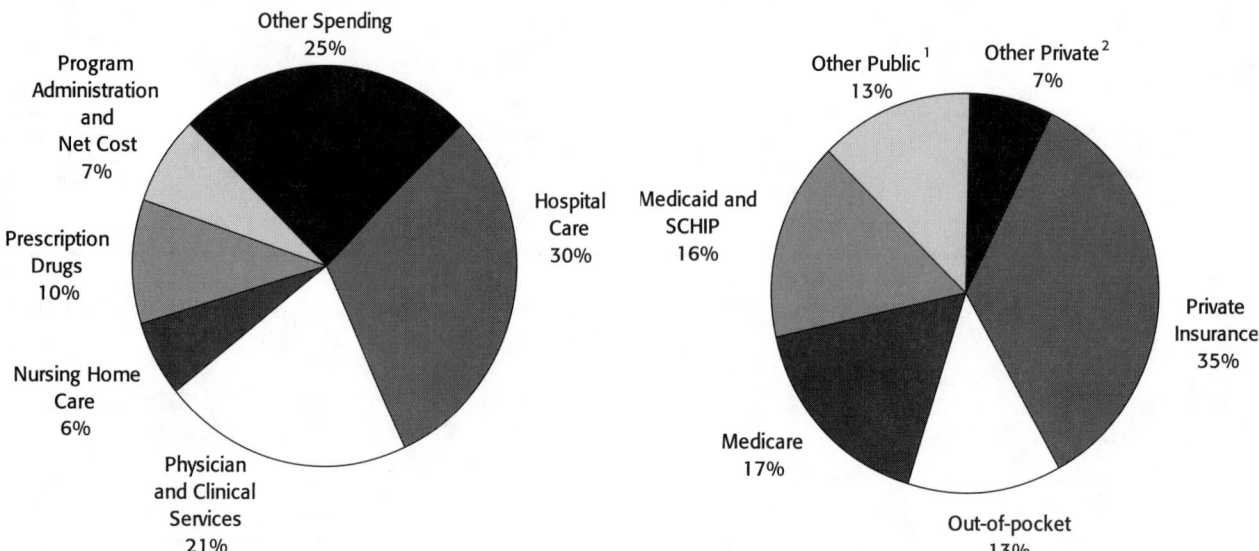

The Nation's Health Dollar, Calendar Year 2005:
Where It Went

Note: Other Spending includes dentist services, other professional services, home health, durable medical products, over-the-counter medicines and sundries, public health, other personal health care, research and structures and equipment.
Source: Centers for Medicare & Medicaid Services, Office of the Actuary, National Health Statistics Group.

The Nation's Health Dollar, Calendar Year 2005:
Where It Came From

[1]Other Public includes programs such as workers' compensation, public health activity, Department of Defense, Department of Veterans Affairs, Indian Health Service, State and local hospital subsidies and school health.
[2]Other Private includes industrial in-plant, privately funded construction, and non-patient revenues, including philanthropy.
Note: Numbers shown may not add to 100.0 because of rounding.
Source: Centers for Medicare & Medicaid Services, Office of the Actuary, National Health Statistics Group.

CHAPTER **17**

Health

HIGHLIGHTS

1 The federal government has provided hospital and medical care directly to specified groups of beneficiaries since 1798 when President John Adams signed into law the Act for the Relief of Sick and Disabled Seamen. Since that time, federally sponsored and financed medical care has been expanded to include such groups as Native Americans, Alaskan natives, veterans, narcotics addicts, and owners of commercial fishing boats. State, local, and county governments also provide hospital and medical care for their residents.

2 Beginning in 1966, the Medicaid Program which was enacted as Title XIX of the Social Security Act, enabled states to provide a single health program for the indigent with federal financial participation. Medicaid offers five basic services: inpatient hospital care; outpatient hospital services; laboratory and X-ray services; nursing home services; and physicians' services. In addition, states may offer other services, such as prescription plans or dental care, for which they receive matching federal funds.

3 Federal health insurance for the aged (Medicare) became effective July 1, 1966, providing hospital and medical protection to an enrolled population aged 65 and over. It includes Part A (hospital program) and Part B (a supplementary program covering physicians' services, outpatient hospital services, therapy, tests, ambulance services, and certain medical supplies). The Part A program is financed on a self-supporting basis through a federal tax, the proceeds of which are placed in a trust fund. Part B is financed through monthly premium payments paid by enrollees and matched by the federal government.

4 The first medical school in the United States, the College of Philadelphia Department of Medicine (now the University of Pennsylvania School of Medicine) was founded in 1765. The number of medical schools increased to three by 1800, 52 in 1850, and 162 in 1906. From 1906 to 1929, the number declined sharply because of tougher accreditation procedures by the American Medical Association's Council on Medical Education.

5 The first dental school, Baltimore College of Dental Surgery, was founded in 1840. Before that date physicians also practiced dentistry. From 1840 to 1880, dental practitioners learned their trade as apprentices, and it was not until 1880 that most states enacted laws requiring graduation from an accredited dental school.

6 Nursing education began in 1873 with the opening of three schools and by 1893 70 were in operation. By 1923, all states had licensing bodies for the nursing profession.

7 The first physician in the American Colonies was Dr. Lawrence Bohune, physician of the London Company, who arrived in Virginia in 1610. The first physician in New England was Dr. Samuel Fuller, one of the signers of the Compact on board the *Mayflower* on November 21, 1620. The first American medical graduate was Dr. John Archer, who graduated with nine others from the University of Pennsylvania in 1768.

8 The first American dentist was Josiah Flagg, who, at the age of 18, began practicing dentistry in Boston in 1782.

9 The first trained nurse in the United States was Linda Ann Judson Richards, who graduated from the training school of the New England Hospital for Women and Children in 1873.

10 Disease notification began in the Colonial period on a local basis, particularly in the port cities. It was limited to epidemics of pestilential diseases. Statewide notification was not required until 1883, when Michigan passed a law under which physicians were asked to report certain diseases to health officers or boards of health. Over the next three decades all states made similar requirements. In 1871, the federal government passed a law providing for the collection of such statistics. By 1912, the data were supplied by 19 states and the District of Columbia on diphtheria, measles, poliomyelitis, scarlet fever, tuberculosis, typhoid, and smallpox. None of these is now considered an important threat to public health. General statistics on health are collected and published by the National Center for Health Statistics in its *National Health Interview Survey* and *National Health and Nutrition Examination Surveys*. Data on diseases are compiled by the Public Health Service through its Centers for Disease Control in Atlanta and published in *Morbidity and Mortality Report*.

11 In 2004, 37.270 million Americans were enrolled in the Medicaid program. Of these, 15.398 million live below the poverty level.

12 In 2004, $39 billion was spent on medical research by the United States government, compared with $5.4 billion in 1980.

13 In 2004, 15.7 percent of the population, or 45.820 million people, carried no medical insurance coverage of any kind and had no safety net. Texas leads the country with 25 percent of its residents lacking health coverage, followed by New Mexico (21 percent), and Florida and Oklahoma (19.9 percent each).

14 There were 411 health maintenance organizations (HMOs) in the United States in 2005, compared with 235 in 1980. An HMO is a prepaid health plan offering comprehensive care to members through designated providers, with a fixed periodic payment for healthcare services and a requirement that members be in a plan for a specific period of time. A Group HMO contracts directly with physicians, associations of independent physicians, or multispecialty group practices. The total enrollment of these HMOs reached 68.8 million in 2004, compared with 33 million in 1990.

15 The number of doctors of medicine in the United States in 2004 was 885,000, of which 224,000 were foreign medical graduates, 649,300 were males, 235,600 were females, and 538,500 were in an office-based practice. The number of registered nurses in 2004 was 2.421 million, or 824 per 100,000.

16 The number of medical schools in the United States has remained steady since 1980 at between 125 and 127. These schools have a total enrollment of 67,013, a figure slightly bigger than in the previous years. In 2001, 15,778 students graduated from these schools.

17 The mean net income of physicians has grown from $5,224 in 1929 to $12,324 in 1950, $97,000 in 1982, $155,800 in 1989, and $205,700 in 2001. Surgeons report the highest income, earning an average of $274,700 annually, while pediatricians were among the lowest with an average annual income at $137,800. Physicians carry a large malpractice insurance premium load, which, in the case of obstetricians and gynecologists averages $39,200 a year.

18 In 2004, there were 5,759 hospitals in the United States (down from 6,965 in 1980), of which only 2,972 had 100 beds or more. Of the total, community hospitals numbered 4,919, for-profits 835, psychiatric hospitals 466, and federal hospitals 239. Hospital beds numbered 956,000, or 3.3 per 1,000 persons. Of these beds, only 685,000 are in use on any given day.

19 The average length of stay in a hospital in 2004 was 5.6 days, down from 15.3 days in 1931, 10.1 days in 1953, and 7.6 days in 1980. Because of pressure from HMOs, patients are allowed to remain in hospital care for fewer days than before. For the same reason, more cases are treated on an outpatient or ambulatory basis.

20 The average cost per day of a hospital stay rose from $5.21 in 1946 to $10.67 in 1954, $21.00 in 1963, $45.01 in 1969, $53.95 in 1970, $134 in 1975, $245 in 1980, $460 in 1985, $687 in 1990, $1,149 in 2000, and $1,450 in 2004.

21 Organ transplants and grafts have become relatively common since the 1970s. In 2005 there were 2,127 heart transplants, 6,444 liver transplants, 16,477 kidney transplants, 1,408 lung transplants, and 44,329 cornea grafts.

22 In 2004, there were 16,081 nursing homes (down from 19,100 in 1985), with 1,730,000 beds. Of these, 87.6 percent are Medicare and Medicaid certified and only 1.5 percent is not certified by either one.

23 Unintentional injuries caused a loss of $574.8 billion in 2004, including wage and productivity loses, medical and administrative expenses, and damages. Of this amount, motor vehicle accidents accounted for $240.6 billion.

24 Marijuana and hashish remain the most popular substances among 12-to-17-year olds, with 19 percent of persons in that age group acknowledging their use in 2004. There were 13,367 substance abuse treatment facilities in the United States in 2005, which treated 499,928 clients in 2005.

25 In 2005, 14,523,000 people were employed in the healthcare industry, up from 11,278,000 in 1995.

26 The average rate of physicians per 100,000 population in the United States is 266. Massachusetts has the highest rate with 450, followed by Maryland (411), and New York (389). Idaho has the lowest ratio of physicians to the general population at 169 per 100,000, followed by Oklahoma (171), Mississippi (181), and Nevada (186).

Table 17-1. Total National Health Expenditures and Projections, by Type of Service, 1929–2015

(Number.)

| Year | Total | Health services and supplies | | | | | | | | | | Research and medical-facilities construction | | |
		Total	Hospital care	Physicians' services	Dentists' services	Other professional services[1]	Drugs and drug sundries[1]	Eye-glasses and appliances	Nursing home care	Government public health activities	Other health services	Research[2]	Construction	Medical structures and equipment[3]
2015[4]	4 031 700	3 762 800	1 230 900	849 800	167 300	109 400	446 200	36 200	216 800	130 900	134 800	81 000	...	187 900
2014[4]	3 776 200	3 524 600	1 153 700	795 500	158 600	102 500	411 700	34 800	203 900	121 700	124 500	76 600	...	175 000
2013[4]	3 533 100	3 298 000	1 081 600	744 600	150 100	95 900	379 900	33 500	191 900	113 200	114 800	72 300	...	162 900
2012[4]	3 297 600	3 077 800	1 012 900	695 500	141 700	89 700	350 500	32 100	180 700	105 200	105 800	68 100	...	151 600
2011[4]	3 078 100	2 873 000	946 500	650 600	133 200	83 900	323 800	30 800	170 300	97 700	97 700	64 100	...	141 000
2010[4]	2 879 400	2 688 100	882 400	610 700	124 900	78 500	299 200	29 500	160 500	90 700	89 200	60 200	...	131 100
2009[4]	2 689 000	2 510 600	821 000	571 700	116 900	73 500	276 600	28 200	151 200	84 100	81 500	56 400	...	122 000
2008[4]	2 498 100	2 332 200	763 200	533 800	109 000	68 700	255 800	27 300	142 700	78 000	74 300	52 600	...	113 300
2007[4]	2 319 600	2 165 200	709 100	469 500	101 300	64 000	236 800	26 000	134 800	72 300	67 800	48 900	...	105 500
2006[4]	2 163 900	2 020 300	662 500	463 300	94 300	59 700	219 200	24 900	128 400	67 000	62 700	45 200	...	98 400
2005[4]	2 016 000	1 882 200	616 100	429 900	87 400	55 800	203 500	23 700	121 700	62 000	58 100	42 000	...	91 800
2004	1 877 600	1 753 000	570 800	399 900	81 500	52 700	188 500	23 000	115 200	56 100	53 300	39 000	...	85 700
2003	1 740 600	1 624 500	525 500	367 000	76 900	49 100	174 100	22 100	110 400	54 000	50 400	35 600	23 667	80 500
2002	1 607 900	1 499 200	488 600	337 900	73 300	45 700	157 900	20 800	105 700	51 700	46 300	32 500	22 366	76 200
2001	1 474 200	1 375 500	451 400	313 100	67 500	42 800	138 600	19 600	101 500	46 800	41 900	28 800	19 153	69 900
2000	1 358 500	1 264 500	417 000	288 600	62 000	39 100	120 800	19 300	95 300	43 400	37 100	25 600	19 218	68 400
1999	1 270 300	1 180 000	395 000	269 600	57 100	37 100	104 700	19 000	90 500	40 700	34 000	23 400	17 555	66 800
1998	1 195 600	1 111 800	376 300	256 400	53 500	35 700	88 600	18 700	89 500	37 600	30 300	21 500	17 716	62 300
1997	1 129 700	1 054 400	364 800	240 900	50 200	33 400	77 700	18 100	84 500	34 900	28 100	19 400	18 522	55 900
1996	1 072 600	1 002 900	352 200	229 400	46 800	30 900	68 500	16 600	79 600	32 500	25 800	17 800	16 396	52 000
1995	1 020 400	953 000	340 700	220 500	44 500	28 500	60 900	15 300	74 100	31 000	23 000	18 300	15 484	49 100
1994	966 000	900 500	329 600	210 500	41 400	25 700	54 300	14 200	67 900	29 600	19 800	17 700	16 218	47 800
1993	916 500	853 500	317 200	201 200	38 900	24 500	51 000	13 500	65 400	26 800	16 200	16 400	16 202	46 600
1992	852 500	793 800	299 800	189 700	37 000	22 200	47 600	12 600	62 000	24 400	13 600	15 100	14 870	43 700
1991	785 000	731 500	277 100	175 000	33 300	19 700	44 400	11 800	58 000	22 200	11 800	13 800	13 395	39 700
1990	717 300	666 700	251 600	157 500	31 500	18 200	40 300	11 200	52 600	20 000	9 600	12 700	13 728	38 000
1989	641 800	595 900	227 000	141 900	29 300	15 200	34 800	10 300	45 500	17 800	8 500	11 700	12 210	34 200
1988	576 600	534 700	207 400	127 400	27 300	14 300	30 600	9 600	40 500	15 300	7 200	10 800	11 903	31 100
1987	515 300	477 800	190 500	111 700	25 300	11 900	26 900	8 800	36 300	13 600	6 500	10 000	10 187	27 500
1986	473 900	439 800	176 500	99 600	23 100	9 700	24 300	7 600	34 500	12 300	5 900	9 000	9 073	25 000
1985	441 900	409 100	165 400	89 800	21 700	8 500	21 800	6 600	31 600	11 200	5 300	8 300	9 440	24 500
1984	404 000	371 800	155 100	76 500	19 800	7 700	19 600	5 700	28 800	9 900	4 700	7 600	10 304	24 600
1983	366 800	336 300	145 400	67 800	18 300	5 900	17 300	4 800	26 500	9 200	4 200	6 500	10 607	24 000
1982	332 100	304 700	134 300	60 800	17 000	5 100	15 000	4 300	23 200	8 600	3 800	6 000	9 583	21 300
1981	295 300	271 400	118 000	54 900	15 700	4 400	13 400	4 000	21 300	7 600	3 500	5 700	8 312	18 200
1980	254 900	234 000	101 000	47 100	13 300	3 600	12 000	3 800	19 000	6 400	3 300	5 400	6 814	15 500
1979	213 935	203 115	87 067	40 630	11 893	12 066	10 744	3 617	15 304	5 635	2 853	4 776	6 045	...
1978	189 412	179 037	76 336	35 293	10 957	11 233	9 891	3 284	13 439	4 895	2 527	4 457	5 917	...
1977	169 403	159 657	67 947	32 595	10 055	9 532	9 196	3 020	11 499	4 106	2 348	3 891	5 855	...
1976	148 826	138 976	60 054	28 183	8 972	8 980	8 722	2 817	9 905	3 332	2 177	3 728	6 122	...
1975	129 841	120 962	51 910	24 814	7 956	5 056	8 052	2 626	8 664	2 939	1 989	3 326	5 553	...
1974	113 730	105 963	44 812	21 738	7 076	4 663	7 422	2 334	7 397	2 591	1 814	2 745	5 022	...
1973	100 540	93 318	38 586	19 107	6 323	4 964	6 817	2 138	6 352	2 124	1 598	2 506	4 715	...
1972	90 674	83 567	34 385	17 269	5 516	4 488	6 324	1 919	5 515	1 854	1 489	2 375	4 732	...
1971	80 952	74 533	30 691	15 534	5 181	3 367	5 877	1 675	4 761	1 674	1 296	2 097	4 322	...
1970	73 056	67 324	27 630	13 980	4 669	2 773	5 497	1 649	4 216	1 356	1 266	1 956	3 776	...
1969	64 587	59 362	23 799	12 370	4 174	2 551	5 149	1 437	3 567	1 175	1 209	1 921	3 304	...
1968	57 460	53 061	20 943	11 002	3 664	2 769	4 742	1 238	2 981	969	1 110	1 884	2 514	...
1967	50 691	46 751	18 144	10 084	3 409	2 297	4 227	1 062	2 337	861	1 021	1 771	2 169	...
1966	45 128	41 357	15 566	8 980	2 961	2 215	3 985	1 128	1 811	732	919	1 623	2 148	...
1965	41 012	37 365	13 816	8 328	2 793	2 006	3 715	1 004	1 471	621	778	1 523	2 123	...
1964	37 461	34 375	12 697	8 056	2 648	940	4 446	1 072	1 214	610	1 511	1 324	1 762	...
1963	33 530	30 890	11 709	6 891	2 277	921	4 235	952	891	540	1 380	1 184	1 456	...
1962	31 295	28 857	10 658	6 498	2 234	902	4 095	908	695	505	1 277	1 032	1 406	...
1961	28 783	26 766	9 921	5 895	2 067	882	3 824	804	606	452	1 320	844	1 174	...
1960	26 895	25 185	9 092	5 684	1 977	862	3 657	776	526	414	1 336	662	1 048	...
1959	24 878	23 354	8 177	5 481	1 894	801	3 525	722	434	428	1 138	526	998	...
1958	22 848	21 442	7 548	4 910	1 850	729	3 242	678	383	424	1 045	416	990	...
1957	21 108	19 885	6 892	4 419	1 737	673	3 010	678	368	415	1 011	344	879	...
1956	19 246	18 348	6 347	4 067	1 625	610	2 686	668	358	402	965	270	628	...
1955	17 745	16 884	5 900	3 689	1 508	562	2 384	604	312	377	924	210	651	...
1954	16 799	15 946	5 502	3 574	1 406	541	2 181	606	270	374	904	183	670	...
1953	15 745	14 895	5 085	3 278	1 234	499	2 152	612	248	378	911	164	686	...
1952	14 988	13 949	4 685	3 042	1 098	459	2 071	586	228	427	952	150	889	...
1951	13 992	12 912	4 254	2 868	997	426	1 989	551	207	416	883	134	946	...
1950	12 662	11 702	3 851	2 747	961	396	1 726	491	187	361	666	117	843	...
1949	11 576	10 811	3 557	2 633	920	371	1 557	458	168	338	539	105	660	...
1948	10 612	10 184	3 203	2 611	900	354	1 466	436	150	306	470	89	339	...
1940	3 987	3 868	1 011	973	419	174	637	189	33	153	112	3	116	...
1935	2 936	2 875	763	773	302	153	475	133	...	117	64	...	61	...
1929	3 649	3 436	663	1 004	482	252	606	133	...	96	91	...	213	...

Source: U.S. Census Bureau. U.S. Centers for Medicare and Medicaid Services, Office of the Actuary.

[1] Includes services of registered and practical nurses in private duty, podiatrists, optometrists, physical therapists, clinical psychologists, chiropractors, naturopaths, and Christian Science practitioners.

[2] Research and development expenditures of drug companies and other manufacturers and providers of medical equipment and supplies are excluded from research expenditures, but are included in the expenditure class in which the product falls.

[3] Represents expenditures for total medical sector acquisitions of structures and equipment including structures that house medical professionals' offices.

[4] Beginning 2005, figures are projections.

... = Not available.

Table 17-2. National and Personal Health Care Expenditures and Projections, by Source of Funds, 1929–2015

(Billions of dollars, percent.)

	National health expenditures		Personal health care expenditures	
Year	Amount	Percent of gross national product	Private insurance benefits	Public expenditures
2015[1]	4 031.7	...	1 196.4	1 583.6
2014[1]	3 776.2	...	1 127.6	1 468.5
2013[1]	3 533.1	...	1,061.2	1,363
2012[1]	3 297.6	...	997.4	1,264
2011[1]	3 078.1	...	934.2	1,175
2010[1]	2 879.4	...	870.3	1,097
2009[1]	2 689.0	...	808.8	1,023
2008[1]	2 498.1	...	749.6	954
2007[1]	2 319.6	...	693.3	889
2006[1]	2 163.9	...	641.7	835
2005[1]	2 016.0	...	608.1	747
2004	1 877.6	16.0	563.5	692.4
2003	1 740.6	15.9	519.9	638.6
2002	1 607.9	15.4	481.8	590.6
2001	1 474.2	14.6	441.0	542.0
2000	1 358.5	13.8	402.7	487.7
1999	1 270.3	13.7	371.8	455.3
1998	1 195.6	13.7	344.6	435.4
1997	1 129.7	13.6	319.7	426.1
1996	1 072.6	13.7	301.6	409.5
1995	1 020.4	13.8	288.2	384.8
1994	966.0	13.7	270.7	360.7
1993	916.5	13.8	258.8	331.2
1992	852.5	13.5	243.6	303.2
1991	785.0	13.1	225.1	270.8
1990	717.3	12.4	204.6	236.2
1989	641.8	11.7	179.2	210.2
1988	576.6	11.3	157.0	188.6
1987	515.3	10.9	135.2	174.7
1986	473.9	10.6	119.7	160.0
1985	441.9	10.5	111.8	145.9
1984	404.0	10.3	100.3	134.9
1983	366.8	10.4	91.4	123.5
1982	332.1	10.2	82.5	111.7
1981	295.3	9.4	72.2	100.3
1980	254.9	9.1	61.2	86.2
1979	217.2	8.7	51.7	74.3
1978	193.7	8.6	43.9	65.1
1977	172.0	8.6	38.6	57.7
1976	152.2	8.5	32.9	50.8
1975	132.9	8.3	32.9	50.2
1974	116.1	7.9	27.8	42.8
1973	102.5	7.5	24.6	35.9
1972	92.3	7.6	21.9	31.8
1971	82.3	7.5	19.1	28.2
1970	71.6	7.3	15.7	21.9
1969	64.1	6.9	13.1	19.7
1968	56.6	6.5	11.3	17.5
1967	50.7	6.4	9.5	14.6
1966	44.9	6.0	9.1	9.5
1965	40.5	5.9	8.7	7.3
1964	37.5	5.9	7.8	6.9
1963	33.5	5.7	7.0	6.4
1962	31.3	5.6	6.3	6.0
1961	28.8	5.5	5.7	5.6
1960	26.9	5.3	5.0	5.2
1959	24.9	5.1	4.4	4.8
1958	22.8	5.1	3.9	4.5
1957	21.1	4.8	3.5	4.2
1956	19.2	4.6	3.0	3.9
1955	17.7	4.4	2.5	3.6
1954	16.8	4.6	2.2	3.4
1953	15.7	4.3	1.9	3.3
1952	15.0	4.3	1.6	3.3
1951	14.0	4.3	1.3	3.0
1950	12.7	4.5	1.0	2.4
1949	11.6	4.5	0.8	2.0
1948	10.6	4.1	0.6	1.8
1940	4.0	4.0	...	0.6
1935	3.0	4.0	...	0.4
1929	3.6	3.5	...	0.3

Source: U.S. Census Bureau. U.S. Centers for Medicare and Medicaid Services, Office of the Actuary.
Note: Excludes Puerto Rico and island areas. The most recent release by the U.S. Centers for Medicare and Medicaid Services of the National Health Expenditure Accounts (NHEA) 2004 was a benchmark (comprehensive) revision. The data for all NHEA tables have been completely revised.
[1]Beginning 2005, figures are projections.
... = Not available.

Table 17-3. Physicians, Dentists, and Nurses; and Medical, Dental, and Nursing Schools, 1810–2004

(Number, rate per 100,000.)

Year	Physicians[1] Amount	Rate	Medical schools[2] Number[3]	Students	Graduates	Dentists[4] Number	Rate
2004	...	...	...	78 870	...	...	...
2003	...	...	...	...	...	...	...
2002	772 296	278	125	77 354	...	...	...
2001	794 000	...	125	76 977	15 778	168 000	60
2000	783 000	...	125	76 765	15 704	168 000	...
1999	753 176	277	125	66 539	15 996	...	...
1998	...	...	125	...	16 314	164 700	61
1997	756 700	282	125	...	15 923	...	...
1996	737 800	278	125	...	15 907	196 000	61
1995	682 000	...	125	74 934	15 888	159 000	...
1994	684 000	262	126	...	15 555	191 000	61
1993	670 300	260	126	...	15 466	187 000	60
1992	653 100	255	126	...	16 365	183 000	60
1990	601 000	...	126	71 631	15 398	148 000	...
1989	645 000	261	142	71 600	17 200	168 000	59
1988	629 000	257	142	71 900	17 500	164 000	58
1987	612 000	253	142	72 300	17 400	161 000	58
1986	595 000	248	142	72 800	17 700	158 000	58
1985	577 000	243	142	73 200	17 800	156 000	58
1984	...	...	142	73 600	17 600	153 000	57
1983	542 000	232	142	73 500	17 100	150 000	56
1982	523 000	222	142	72 600	17 000	147 000	55
1981	505 000	217	142	71 600	16 800	144 000	54
1980	487 000	214	141	70 100	16 200	141 000	54
1979	472 000	207	138	66 500	16 000	138 000	53
1978	454 000	201	124	64 300	15 400	136 000	52
1977	438 000	196	126	61 900	14 500	133 000	52
1976	426 000	194	123	59 600	14 300	...	52
1975	409 000	190	123	59 300	13 900	127 000	50
1974	394 000	182	121	53 700	12 200	...	...
1973	382 000	178	114	50 100	11 000	122 000	48
1972	371 000	174	115	46 000	10 000	120 000	47
1971	359 000	174	110	42 600	9 400	118 000	47
1970	348 328	166	107	39 666	8 799	118 175	58
1969	338 942	163	104	37 712	8 486	115 610	57
1968	330 732	161	100	36 368	8 400	113 636	57
1967	322 045	158	95	35 212	8 148	112 152	56
1966	313 559	156	93	34 516	7 934	111 130	56
1965	305 115	153	93	34 089	7 803	109 301	56
1964	297 089	159	92	33 595	7 691	107 820	56
1963	289 188	149	92	33 072	7 631	106 230	56
1962	270 136	145	92	32 633	7 530	105 252	56
1961	...	...	92	32 232	7 500	103 596	56
1960	274 833	148	[8]91	[8]31 999	[8]7 508	101 947	56
1959	[8]236 818	[8]133.0	85	29 614	6 860	[8]100 615	[8]57
1958	...	...	85	29 473	6 861	98 540	57
1957	226 625	132	85	29 130	6 796	100 534	59
1956	...	...	82	28 639	6 845	99 227	59
1955	218 061	132	81	28 583	6 977	97 529	59
1954	214 200	132	80	28 227	6 861	95 883	59
1953	210 900	132	79	27 688	6 668	93 726	59
1952	207 900	132	79	27 076	6 080	91 638	58
1951	205 500	133	79	26 186	6 135	...	...
1950[10]	203 400	134	79	25 103	5 553	89 441	59
1950	191 947	128	...	...	...	74 855	50
1949	201 277	135	78	23 670	5 094	...	...
1948	...	...	77	22 739	5 543	...	...
1947	...	...	77	23 900	6 389	82 990	58
1946	...	...	77	23 216	5 826	...	...
1945	...	...	77	24 028	5 136	...	...
1944	...	...	77	48 195	10 303	...	...
1943	...	...	76	22 631	5 223	...	...
1942	180 496	134	77	22 031	5 163	...	...
1941	...	...	77	21 379	5 275	...	...

[1]Beginning 1960, includes osteopaths.
[2]Beginning 1954, includes Puerto Rico; beginning 1960, includes osteopaths and their schools.
[3]Approved medical and basic science schools.
[4]Beginning 1958, excludes graduates of the year stated. Personnel data exclude dentists in military service, U.S. Public Health Service, and U.S. Department of Veterans Affairs.
[5]For 1840 and 1926–1931, schools offering courses in dentistry; for 1850–1925, schools conferring degrees; for other years, schools in operation. Includes Puerto Rico.
[6]Includes nurses with advanced degrees.
[7]Some nursing schools offer more than one type of program. Numbers shown for nursing are number of nursing programs. Includes Hawaii and Puerto Rico beginning 1950 for number and students and 1952 for graduates.
[8]First year for which figures include Alaska and Hawaii.
[9]Census estimate adjusted to exclude student nurses enumerated as graduates.
[10]Census data.
. . . = Not available.

Table 17-3. Physicians, Dentists, and Nurses; and Medical, Dental, and Nursing Schools, 1810–2004—Continued

(Number, rate per 100,000.)

| Dental schools | | | Active professional graduate nurses | | Professional nursing schools[7] | | |
Number[5]	Students	Graduates	Number[6]	Rate	Number	Students	Graduates
...	...	...	...	...	...	244 769	...
...	...	...	...	...	...	221 698	...
54	17 487	...	...	...	1 459	...	...
54	17 349	...	2 262 000	...	...	...	68 709
55	17 242	4 367	2 249 000	...	...	192 202	71 392
55	17 033	4 171	2 271 300	833	...	211 694	76 523
55	...	4 095	...	...	...	...	83 165
55	...	4 041	...	...	1 508	...	...
54	...	3 810	2 162 000	815	1 516	...	94 757
54	16 353	3 908	2 116 000	805	1 516	268 350	97 052
54	...	3 875	2 044 000	785	1 493	...	94 870
55	...	3 778	1 976 000	767	1 484	...	88 149
55	...	3 918	1 907 000	748	1 484	...	80 839
56	16 412	4 233	1 790 000	714	1 470	201 458	66 088
58	16 200	4 300	1 666 000	675	1 457	201 000	62 000
58	17 100	4 600	1 648 000	674	1 442	185 000	65 000
58	17 900	4 700	1 627 000	671	1 465	183 000	71 000
59	18 700	5 000	1 589 000	662	1 469	194 000	77 000
60	19 600	5 400	1 544 000	649	1 473	218 000	82 000
60	20 600	5 300	1 486 000	630	1 477	237 000	80 000
60	21 400	5 800	1 439 000	616	1 466	251 000	77 000
60	22 200	5 400	1 380 111	595	1 432	242 000	74 000
60	22 600	5 600	1 327 000	578	1 401	235 000	74 000
60	22 800	5 300	1 273 000	560	1 385	231 000	76 000
60	22 200	5 400	1 200 000	534	1 374	235 000	77 000
59	21 500	5 300	...	...	1 340	239 000	78 000
59	21 000	5 200	1 028 000	468	1 339	245 000	78 000
59	20 800	5 300	961 000	449	1 349	250 000	78 000
59	20 800	5 000	961 000	446	1 360	250 000	75 000
58	19 400	4 500	857 000	404	1 359	233 000	68 000
56	18 400	4 200	815 000	390	1 363	213 000	59 000
52	17 300	4 000	780 000	376	1 350	188 000	52 000
53	16 600	3 800	723 000	353	1 343	165 000	47 000
53	16 008	3 700	700 000	345	1 328	150 795	43 639
52	15 408	3 433	680 000	338	1 287	145 588	42 196
50	14 955	3 457	659 000	331	2 262	141 948	41 555
49	14 421	3 360	640 000	325	1 219	139 070	38 237
49	14 020	3 198	621 000	319	1 191	135 702	35 125
49	13 876	3 181	613 188	319	1 153	129 629	24 686
48	13 691	3 213	582 000	306	1 142	124 744	35 259
48	13 576	3 233	...	...	1 128	123 861	32 398
47	13 513	3 207	550 000	297	1 118	123 012	31 186
47	13 580	3 290	...	...	1 123	118 849	30 267
[8]47	[8]13 581	[8]3 253	[8]504 000	[8]282	[8]1 119	[8]115 057	[8]30 113
47	13 509	3 156	...	...	1 126	113 518	30 312
47	13 279	3 083	460 000	268	1 118	112 989	30 410
45	13 004	3 050	...	...	1 115	114 674	29 933
43	12 730	3 038	430 000	262	1 125	114 423	30 236
43	12 601	3 081	[9]430 000	259	1 139	107 572	28 729
43	12 516	3 084	[9]389 600	244	1 141	103 019	28 539
42	12 370	2 945	...	...	1 148	102 019	29 308
42	12 169	2 975	...	...	1 167	102 550	29 016
42	11 891	2 830	...	...	1 183	103 433	28 794
41	11 460	2 565	[9]375 000	249	1 203	98 712	25 790
...	...	...	...	...	...	...	...
41	10 132	1 574	...	...	1 215	88 817	21 379
40	8 996	1 755	...	...	1 245	91 643	34 268
40	8 287	2 225	...	...	1 253	106 900	40 744
39	7 274	2 666	...	...	1 271	128 828	36 195
39	8 590	3 212	...	...	1 295	126 576	31 721
39	9 014	2 470	...	...	1 307	112 249	28 276
39	8 847	1 926	...	...	1 297	100 486	26 816
39	8 355	1 784	...	...	1 299	91 457	25 613
39	7 720	1 568	...	...	1 303	87 588	24 889

Table 17-3. Physicians, Dentists, and Nurses; and Medical, Dental, and Nursing Schools, 1810–2004—*Continued*

(Number, rate per 100,000.)

Year	Physicians[1] Amount	Physicians[1] Rate	Medical schools[2] Number[3]	Medical schools[2] Students	Medical schools[2] Graduates	Dentists[4] Number	Dentists[4] Rate
1940[9]	175 163	133	77	21 271	5 097	...	...
1940	165 989	126	...	...	...	69 921	53
1939	...	...	77	21 302	5 089	...	...
1938	169 628	131	77	21 587	5 194	...	...
1937	...	...	77	22 095	5 377	...	...
1936	165 163	129	77	22 564	5 183	...	...
1935	...	...	77	22 888	5 101	...	...
1934	161 359	128	77	22 799	5 035	...	...
1933	...	...	77	22 466	4 895	...	...
1932	...	...	76	22 135	4 936	...	...
1931	156 406	126	76	21 982	4 735	...	...
1930[9]	...	...	76	21 597	4 565	...	...
1930	153 803	125	...	...	...	71 055	58
1929	152 503	125	76	20 878	4 446	...	...
1928	...	...	80	20 545	4 262	67 334	56
1927	149 521	126	80	19 662	4 035	...	...
1926	...	...	79	18 840	3 962	...	...
1925	147 010	127	80	18 200	3 974	64 481	56
1924	...	...	79	17 728	3 562	...	...
1923	145 966	130	80	16 960	3 120	...	...
1922	...	...	81	15 635	2 520	...	...
1921	145 404	134	83	14 466	3 186	...	...
1920[9]	...	...	85	13 798	3 047	...	...
1920	144 977	137	...	...	...	56 152	53
1919	...	...	85	13 052	2 656	...	...
1918	147 812	141	90	13 630	2 670	...	...
1917	...	...	96	13 764	3 379	45 988	44
1916	145 241	142	95	14 012	3 518	...	...
1915	...	...	96	14 891	3 536	...	...
1914	142 332	144	102	16 502	3 594	42 606	43
1913	...	...	107	17 015	3 981	...	...
1912	137 199	144	118	18 412	4 483	38 866	41
1911	...	...	122	19 786	4 273	...	...
1910[9]	135 000	146	131	21 526	4 440	37 684	41
1910	151 132	164	...	...	...	39 997	43
1909	134 402	149	140	22 145	4 515	...	...
1908	...	...	151	22 602	4 741	36 670	41
1907	...	...	159	24 276	4 980	...	...
1906	134 688	158	162	25 204	5 364	35 238	41
1905	...	...	158	26 147	5 600	...	...
1904	128 950	157	160	28 142	5 747	32 204	39
1903	...	...	160	27 615	5 698	...	...
1902	123 196	156	160	27 501	5 009	28 109	36
1901	...	...	160	26 417	5 444	...	...
1900[9]	119 749	157	160	25 171	5 214	25 189	33
1900	132 002	173	...	...	...	29 665	39
1898	115 524	157	...	...	...	23 911	33
1896	104 554	147	...	...	...	20 063	28
1893	103 090	154	...	...	...	...	...
1890[9]	100 180	159	133	15 404	4 454	...	...
1890	104 805	166	...	...	...	17 498	28
1886	87 521	151	...	...	...	...	...
1880[9]	82 000	163	100	11 826	3 241	...	...
1880	85 671	171	...	...	...	12 314	25
1870[9]	60 000	150	75	...	...	...	...
1870	64 414	162	...	...	...	7 988	20
1860	55 055	175	65	...	...	5 606	18
1850	40 755	176	52	...	...	2 923	13
1840	...	...	35	...	...	1 000	6
1830	...	...	20	...	...	300	2
1820	...	...	10	...	...	100	1
1810	...	...	5	...	...	50	1

Source: U.S. Census Bureau. U.S. Department of Health and Human Services, Bureau of Health Professions. American Medical Association. *Physician Characteristics and Distribution in the U.S.* American Association of Colleges of Osteopathic Medicine. *Annual Statistical Report* June 1981 and unpublished data. American Osteopathic Association. *1980–81 Yearbook* and *Directory of Osteopathic Physicians, 1980.*

[1]Beginning 1960, includes osteopaths.
[2]Beginning 1954, includes Puerto Rico; beginning 1960, includes osteopaths and their schools.
[3]Approved medical and basic science schools.
[4]Beginning 1958, excludes graduates of the year stated. Personnel data exclude dentists in military service, U.S. Public Health Service, and U.S. Department of Veterans Affairs.
[5]For 1840 and 1926–1931, schools offering courses in dentistry; for 1850–1925, schools conferring degrees; for other years, schools in operation. Includes Puerto Rico.
[6]Includes nurses with advanced degrees.
[7]Some nursing schools offer more than one type of program. Numbers shown for nursing are number of nursing programs. Includes Hawaii and Puerto Rico beginning 1950 for number and students and 1952 for graduates.
[8]First year for which figures include Alaska and Hawaii.
[9]Census estimate adjusted to exclude student nurses enumerated as graduates.
. . . = Not available.

Table 17-3. Physicians, Dentists, and Nurses; and Medical, Dental, and Nursing Schools, 1810–2004—*Continued*

(Number, rate per 100,000.)

Dental schools			Active professional graduate nurses		Professional nursing schools[7]		
Number[5]	Students	Graduates	Number[6]	Rate	Number	Students	Graduates
39	7 407	1 757	[8]284 200	216	1 311	85 156	23 600
...	...	...	...	...	...	...	...
39	7 331	1 794			1 328	82 095	22 485
39	7 184	1 704			1 349	74 305	20 655
39	7 397	1 739			1 389	73 286	20 400
39	7 306	1 736			1 417	69 589	18 600
39	7 175	1 840			1 472	67 533	19 600
39	7 160	1 864			...	...	...
39	7 508	1 986			...	...	...
38	8 031	1 840			1 781	84 290	25 312
38	8 129	1 842			1 844	100 419	25 971
38	7 813	1 561	[8]214 300	174	...	...	...
...	...	...			...	...	...
40	8 200	2 442			1 885	78 771	23 810
40	...	2 563			...	...	...
40	10 333	2 642			1 797	77 768	18 623
44	...	2 610			...	...	...
43	11 863	2 590			...	...	...
43	...	3 422			...	...	...
45	13 099	3 271			...	...	...
45	...	1 765			...	...	...
45	11 745	1 795			...	...	...
46	...	906	[8]103 900	98	1 755	54 953	14 980
...	...	...			...	...	...
46	...	3 587			...	...	...
46	...	3 345			...	...	...
46	...	3 010			...	...	...
49	...	2 835			...	...	...
49	...	2 388			1 509	46 141	11 118
48	...	2 254			...	...	...
51	...	2 022			...	...	...
52	...	1 940			...	...	...
54	...	1 742			...	...	...
54	...	1 646	[8]50 500	55	1 129	32 636	8 140
...	...	...			...	...	...
56	...	1 761			...	...	...
55	...	2 005			...	...	...
55	...	1 724			...	...	...
55	...	1 519			...	...	...
55	...	2 621			862	19 824	5 795
56	...	2 168			...	...	...
55	...	2 198			...	...	...
56	...	2 294			...	...	...
57	...	2 304			...	...	...
57	...	2 091			432	11 164	3 456
...	...	...			...	...	...
54	...	1 894			...	...	...
48	...	1 432			...	...	...
37	...	...			...	...	...
31	...	960			35	1 552	471
...	...	...			...	...	...
23	...	473			...	...	...
14	...	315			15	323	157
...	...	...			...	...	...
10	...	147			...	...	...
...	...	...			...	...	...
3	...	64			...	...	...
2	...	17			...	...	...
1	...	...			...	...	...
...	...	...			...	...	...
...	...	...			...	...	...
...	...	...			...	...	...

Table 17-4. Medicare Enrollees, 1980–2005

(Number in Millions. As of July 1.)

Item	1980	1990	1995	1996	1997	1998	1999	2000	2001	2002	2003	2004	2005
Total	**28.4**	**34.3**	**37.6**	**38.1**	**38.5**	**38.9**	**39.2**	**39.7**	**40.1**	**40.5**	**41.2**	**41.9**	**42.5**
Aged	25.5	31.0	33.2	33.4	33.7	33.8	33.9	34.3	34.5	34.7	35.0	35.4	35.8
Disabled	3.0	3.3	4.4	4.7	4.9	5.1	5.2	5.4	5.6	5.8	6.2	6.4	6.7
Hospital insurance	28.0	33.7	37.2	37.7	38.1	38.5	38.8	39.3	39.7	40.1	40.7	41.4	42.0
Aged	25.0	30.5	32.7	33.0	33.2	33.4	33.5	33.8	34.0	34.2	34.6	35.0	35.4
Disabled	3.0	3.3	4.4	4.7	4.9	5.1	5.2	5.4	5.6	5.8	6.2	6.4	6.7
Supplementary medical insurance	27.3	32.6	35.6	36.1	36.4	36.8	37.0	37.3	37.7	38.0	38.6	39.1	39.6
Aged	24.6	29.6	31.7	32.0	32.1	32.3	32.4	32.6	32.7	32.9	33.2	33.4	33.7
Disabled	2.7	2.9	3.9	4.1	4.3	4.5	4.6	4.8	4.9	5.1	5.4	5.7	5.9

Source: U.S. Census Bureau. *Statistical Abstract of the United States: 2007.* U.S. Centers for Medicare and Medicaid Services.
Note: Includes Puerto Rico and island areas and enrollees in foreign countries and unknown place of residence.

Table 17-5. Medicare Insurance Trust Funds, 1990–2005

(Billions of dollars. Minus sign (–) indicates a decrease.)

Type of trust fund	1990	1995	1999	2000	2001	2002	2003	2004	2005
Total Medicare:									
Total income	126.3	175.3	232.5	257.1	273.3	284.8	291.6	317.7	357.5
Total expenditures	111.0	184.2	213.0	221.8	244.8	265.7	280.8	308.9	336.4
Assets, end of year	114.4	143.4	186.2	221.5	250.0	269.1	280.0	288.8	309.8
Net change in assets	15.3	-8.9	19.5	35.3	28.5	19.1	10.8	8.8	21.0
Hospital Insurance (HI):									
Net contribution income[1]	72.1	103.3	140.3	154.5	160.9	162.7	159.2	167.2	182.6
Interest received[2]	8.5	10.8	10.1	11.7	14.0	15.1	15.8	16.0	16.1
Benefit payments[3]	66.2	116.4	128.8	126.8	138.1	148.8	154.3	167.6	180.0
Assets, end of year	98.9	130.3	141.4	177.5	208.7	234.8	256.0	269.3	285.8
Supplementary Medical Insurance (SMI), Parts B and D:									
Net premium income	11.3	[4]19.7	19.0	20.6	22.8	25.1	27.4	31.4	37.5
Transfers from general revenue[5]	33.0	[4]39.0	59.1	65.9	72.8	78.3	86.4	100.4	119.2
Interest received[2]	1.6	1.6	2.8	3.5	3.1	2.8	2.0	1.5	1.4
Benefit payments[3,6]	42.5	65.0	80.7	88.9	99.7	111.0	123.8	135.0	150.3
Assets, end of year	15.5	13.1	44.8	44.0	41.3	34.3	24.0	19.4	24.0

Source: U.S. Census Bureau. *Statistical Abstract of the United States: 2007.* U.S. Centers for Medicare and Medicaid Services.
[1]Includes income from taxation of benefits beginning in 1994. Includes premiums from aged ineligibles enrolled in hospital insurance.
[2]Includes recoveries of amounts reimbursed from the trust fund.
[3]Beginning 1998 monies transferred to the SMI trust fund for home health agency costs, as provided for by P.L. 105-33, are included in HI benefit payments but excluded from SMI benefit payments.
[4]Premiums withheld from check and associated general revenue contributions that were to occur on Jan. 3, 1999, actually occurred on December 31, 1998. These amounts are therefore excluded from 1999 data.
[5]These amounts for 2004 and 2005 include amounts transferred for transitional assistance for Part D of Medicare.
[6]These amounts for 2004 and 2005 include transitional assistance for Part D of Medicare.

Table 17-6. People Without Health Insurance, 2000–2004

(Thousands, percent.)

Characteristic	2000			2001			2004		
		Uninsured Persons			Uninsured Persons			Uninsured Persons	
	Total persons	Number	Percent distribution	Total persons	Number	Percent distribution	Total persons	Number	Percent distribution
Total[1]	279 517	**39 804**	100.0	282 082	**41 207**	100.0	291 155	**45 820**	100.0
Under 18 years	72 314	8 617	21.6	72 628	8 509	20.6	73 821	8 269	18.0
18 to 24 years	26 815	7 406	18.6	27 312	7 673	18.6	27 972	8 772	19.1
25 to 34 years	38 865	8 507	21.4	38 670	9 051	22.0	39 307	10 177	22.2
35 to 44 years	44 566	6 898	17.3	44 284	7 131	17.3	43 350	8 110	17.7
45 to 64 years	63 391	8 124	20.4	65 419	8 571	20.8	71 492	10 196	22.3
65 years and over	33 566	251	0.6	33 769	272	0.7	35 213	297	0.6
Male	136 559	20 791	52.2	137 871	21 722	52.7	142 750	24 528	53.5
Female	142 958	19 013	47.8	144 211	19 485	47.3	148 405	21 293	46.5
White	228 208	30 075	75.6	23 071	31 193	75.7	...	...	...
Non-Hispanic	193 931	18 683	46.9	194 822	19 409	47.1	...	...	...
Black	35 597	6 683	16.8	36 023	6 833	16.6	...	...	...
Asian and Pacific Islander	12 693	2 287	5.7	12 500	2 278	5.5	...	...	...
White alone[2]	...	...	...	...	...	...	234 077	34 788	75.9
Black alone[2]	...	...	...	...	...	...	36 546	7 186	15.7
Asian alone[2]	...	...	...	...	...	...	12 311	2 070	4.5
Hispanic[3]	36 093	11 883	29.9	37 438	12 417	30.1	41 839	13 678	29.9

Source: U.S. Census Bureau.
Note: Based on the Current Population Survey; Annual Demographic Survey and subject to sampling error.
[1]Includes other races not shown separately.
[2]Refers to people who reported specified race and did not report any other race category.
[3]Persons of Hispanic origin may be of any race.
. . . = Not available.

Table 17-7. Average Daily Census and Admissions to Hospitals, 1946–2004

(Number.)

Year	Average daily census	Admissions during year
2004	658	. . .
2003	657	. . .
2002	662	. . .
2001	658	35 644
2000	650	34 891
1999	657	34 181
1998	662	33 766
1997	673	33 624
1996	685	33 307
1995	710	33 282
1994	745	33 125
1993	783	33 201
1992	807	33 536
1991	827	33 567
1990	844	33 774
1989	. . .	. . .
1988	863	34 100
1987	873	34 400
1986	883	35 200
1985	910	36 300
1984	970	37 900
1983	1 028	38 900
1982	1 053	39 100
1981	1 061	39 200
1980	1 060	38 900
1979	1 043	37 800
1978	1 042	37 200
1977	1 066	37 100
1976	1 090	36 800
1975	1 125	36 200
1974	1 187	35 500
1973	1 189	34 400
1972	1 209	33 300
1971	1 237	32 700
1970	1 298	31 759
1969	1 346	30 729
1968	1 378	29 766
1967	1 380	29 361
1966	1 398	29 151
1965	1 403	28 812
1964	1 421	28 266
1963	1 430	27 502
1962	1 407	26 531
1961	1 393	25 474
1960	1 402	25 027
1959[1]	1 363	23 605
1958	1 323	23 697
1957	1 320	22 993
1956	1 356	22 090
1955	1 363	21 073
1954	1 343	20 345
1953	1 342	20 184
1952	1 336	19 624
1951	1 298	18 783
1950	1 253	18 483
1949	1 240	17 224
1948	1 241	16 821
1947	1 190	17 689
1946	1 142	15 675

Source: U.S. Census Bureau. Health Forum, an American Hospital Association Company. *Hospital Statistics©*, 2006 Edition, and prior years.
[1]First year for which figures include Alaska and Hawaii.
. . . = Not available.

Table 17-8. Hospital Expenses per Patient Day, 1946–2004

(Dollars.)

Year	Average cost per day
2004	1 450
2003	1 379
2002	1 290
2001	1 217
2000	1 149
1999	1 103
1998	1 067
1997	1 033
1996	1 006
1995	968
1994	931
1993	881
1992	820
1991	752
1990	687
1989	637
1988	586
1987	539
1986	501
1985	460
1984	411
1983	369
1982	327
1981	284
1980	245
1979	217
1978	194
1977	174
1976	153
1975	134
1974	114
1973	84
1972	74
1971	64
1970	54
1969	45
1968	38
1967	33
1966	28
1965	25
1964	23
1963	21
1962	20
1961	18
1960	16
1959[1]	16
1958[2]	15
1957	13
1956	12
1955	11
1954	11
1953	10
1952	9
1951	8
1950	8
1949	8
1948	6
1947	5
1946	5

Source: U.S. Census Bureau. Health Forum, an American Hospital Company. *Hospital Statistics©,* 2006 Edition, and prior years.
[1]First year for which figures include Alaska and Hawaii.
[2]Includes Alaska.

Table 17-9. Hospital Expenses and Personnel, 1946–2004

(Dollars in millions, number.)

Yar	Expenses (millions of dollars)		Personnel (thousands)	
	Total	Federal	Total	Federal
2004	533 800	34 800	4 695	315
2003	498 100	30 900	4 650	300
2002	462 200	29 700	4 610	299
2001	426 800	27 500	4 535	299
2000	395 400	23 900	4 454	297
1999	372 900	23 700	4 369	295
1998	355 500	22 600	5 116	. . .
1997	342 300	22 700	5 130	296
1996	330 500	22 300	5 041	265
1995	320 300	20 200	4 273	301
1994	310 800	20 000	5 009	301
1993	301 500	19 600	5 032	320
1992	282 500	18 200	4 915	306
1991	258 500	16 800	4 839	301
1990	234 900	15 200	4 063	303
1989	214 900	15 100	4 568	288
1988	196 700	14 600	4 520	295
1987	178 700	13 700	4 444	297
1986	165 200	13 100	4 368	296
1985	153 300	12 300	4 269	299
1984	144 100	11 200	4 288	290
1983	136 300	10 700	4 348	286
1982	123 200	9 500	3 959	302
1981	107 100	8 600	3 661	283
1980	91 900	7 900	3 492	279
1979	79 800	7 300	3 382	273
1978	70 900	6 700	3 280	277
1977	63 600	6 200	3 213	278
1976	56 000	5 300	3 108	269
1975	48 700	4 500	3 023	256
1974	41 406	3 971	2 919	244
1973	36 290	3 524	2 769	238
1972	32 700	3 100	2 671	232
1971	28 812	2 821	2 589	225
1970	25 556	2 483	2 537	216
1969	22 103	2 350	2 426	213
1968	19 061	2 032	2 309	210
1967	16 395	1 795	2 203	214
1966	14 198	1 633	2 106	206
1965	12 948	1 568	1 952	199
1964	12 031	1 503	1 887	193
1963	10 956	1 458	1 840	206
1962	10 129	1 408	1 763	207
1961	9 387	1 308	1 696	202
1960	8 421	1 134	1 598	186
1959[1]	7 789	1 119	1 520	179
1958	7 133	1 051	1 465	181
1957	6 496	1 013	1 401	186
1956	6 017	968	1 375	198
1955	5 594	837	1 301	192
1954	5 229	927	1 246	195
1953	4 765	853	1 169	198
1952	4 456	925	1 119	206
1951	3 913	743	1 075	197
1950	3 651	712	1 058	169
1949	3 486	764	963	161
1948	2 875	480	939	154
1947	2 354	405	883	161
1946	1 963	373	830	162

Source: U.S. Census Bureau. Health Forum, an American Hospital Company. *Hospital Statistics*©, 2006 Edition, and prior years.
[1]First year for which figures include Alaska and Hawaii.
. . . = Not available.

Table 17-10. Mental Health Organizations, Number and Type, 1976–2002

Type of Organization[1]	1976	1980	1986	1990	1992	1994	1998	2000	2002
All organizations	3 480	3 727	4 747	5 284	5 498	5 392	5 722	4 541	4 301
State and county mental hospitals	303	280	285	273	273	256	229	223	222
Private psychiatric hospitals	182	184	314	462	475	430	348	269	253
Non-federal general hospitals with separate psychiatric services	870	923	1 351	1 674	1 616	1 612	1 707	1 373	1 285
VA medical centers[2]	126	136	139	141	162	161	145	142	140
Federally funded community health centers	517	691	-	-	-	-	-	-	-
Residential treatment centers for emotionally disturbed children	331	368	437	501	497	459	461	475	508
All other mental health organizations[3]	1 151	1 145	2 221	2 233	2 475	2 474	2 832	2 059	1 893

Source: U.S. Department of Health and Human Services, Substance Abuse and Mental Health Services Administration. *Mental Health, United States, 2004.*
[1]Some organizations were reclassified as a result of changes in reporting procedures and definitions. For 1979-1980, comparable data were not available for certain organization types and data for either an earlier or later period were substituted. These factors influence the comparability of 1980-1998 data with those of earlier years.
[2]Includes Department of Veterans Affairs (formerly Veterans Administration) neuropsychiatric hospitals, VA general hospital psychiatric services, and VA psychiatric outpatient clinics.
[3]Includes freestanding psychiatric outpatient clinics, partial care organizations, and multiservice mental health organizations. Multiservice mental health organizations were redefined in 1984.

Table 17-11. Cigarette Smoking Among Men, Women, High School Students, and Mothers During Pregnancy, 1965–2005

(Percent.)

Year	Men	Women	High school students	Mothers during pregnancy
2005	. . .	. . .	23.0	. . .
2004	23.0	18.7	. . .	10.2
2003	23.7	19.4	21.9	10.7
2002	24.6	20.0	. . .	11.4
2001	24.6	20.7	28.5	12.0
2000	25.2	21.1	. . .	12.2
1999	25.2	21.6	34.8	12.6
1998	25.9	22.1	. . .	12.9
1997	27.1	22.2	36.4	13.2
1996	. . .	. . .	. . .	13.6
1995	26.5	22.7	34.8	13.9
1994	27.6	23.1	. . .	14.6
1993	27.3	22.6	30.5	15.8
1992	28.1	24.6	. . .	16.9
1991	27.6	23.5	27.5	17.8
1990	28.0	22.9	. . .	18.4
1989	. . .	. . .	. . .	19.5
1988	30.3	25.7	. . .	. . .
1987	30.9	26.5	. . .	. . .
1985	32.2	27.9	. . .	. . .
1983	34.8	29.4	. . .	. . .
1979	37.0	30.1	. . .	. . .
1974	42.8	32.2	. . .	. . .
1965	51.2	33.7	. . .	. . .

Source: U.S. Centers for Disease Control and Prevention, National Center for Health Statistics. *Health, United States 2006.*
Note: Data for men and women are for the civilian noninstitutionalized population. Estimates for men and women are age adjusted to the 2000 standard population using five age groups: 18–24 years, 25–34 years, 35–44 years, 45–64 years, and 65 years and over. Age-adjusted estimates in this table may differ from other age-adjusted estimates based on the same data and presented elsewhere if different age groups are used in the adjustment procedure.
Cigarette smoking is defined as follows: among men and women 18 years and over, those who ever smoked 100 cigarettes in their lifetime and now smoke every day or some days; among high school students in grades 9-12, those who smoked cigarettes on 1 or more of the 30 days preceding the survey; and among mothers with a live birth, those who smoked during pregnancy.
Data for mothers who smoked during pregnancy are based on the 1989 Revision of the U.S. Certificate of Live Birth. Some states did not require the reporting of mother's tobacco use during pregnancy on the birth certificate and are not included in this analysis. Reporting of tobacco use during pregnancy increased from 43 states and the District of Columbia (DC) in 1989 to 49 states and DC in 2000–2002. Starting with 2003 data, some reporting areas adopted the 2003 Revision of the U.S. Standard Certificate of Live Birth and 1 state continued to not report data.
Tobacco use during pregnancy data based on the 2003 Revision are not comparable with data based on the 1989 Revision of the U.S. Standard Certificate of Live Birth and are excluded from this analysis.
. . . = Not available.

Table 17-12. Current Cigarette Smoking Among Adults 18 Years of Age and Over, by Sex, Race, and Age, 1974–2004

Sex, race, and age	Percent of persons who are current cigarette smokers[3]												
	1974[1]	1979[1]	1985[1]	1990[1]	1995[1]	1997	1998	1999	2000	2001	2002	2003	2004
18 years and over, age adjusted[2]													
All persons	37.0	33.3	29.9	25.3	24.6	24.6	24.0	23.3	23.1	22.6	22.3	21.5	20.8
Male	42.8	37.0	32.2	28.0	26.5	27.1	25.9	25.2	25.2	24.6	24.6	23.7	23.0
Female	32.2	30.1	27.9	22.9	22.7	22.2	22.1	21.6	21.1	20.7	20.0	19.4	18.7
White male[4]	41.7	36.4	31.3	27.6	26.2	26.8	26.0	25.0	25.4	24.8	24.9	23.8	23.0
Black or African American male[4]	53.6	43.9	40.2	32.8	29.4	32.4	29.0	28.4	25.7	27.5	26.6	25.3	23.5
White female[4]	32.0	30.3	27.9	23.5	23.4	22.8	23.0	22.5	22.0	22.0	21.0	20.1	19.5
Black or African American female[4]	35.6	30.5	30.9	20.8	23.5	22.5	21.1	20.5	20.7	18.0	18.3	17.9	16.9
18 years and over, crude													
All persons	37.1	33.5	30.1	25.5	24.7	24.7	24.1	23.5	23.2	22.7	22.4	21.6	20.9
Male	43.1	37.5	32.6	28.4	27.0	27.6	26.4	25.7	25.6	25.1	25.1	24.1	23.4
Female	32.1	29.9	27.9	22.8	22.6	22.1	22.0	21.5	20.9	20.6	19.8	19.2	18.5
White male[4]	41.9	36.8	31.7	28.0	26.6	27.2	26.3	25.3	25.7	25.0	25.0	24.0	23.2
Black or African American male[4]	54.3	44.1	39.9	32.5	28.5	32.2	29.0	28.6	26.2	27.6	27.0	25.7	23.9
White female[4]	31.7	30.1	27.7	23.4	23.1	22.5	22.6	22.1	21.4	21.5	20.6	19.7	19.1
Black or African American female[4]	36.4	31.1	31.0	21.2	23.5	22.5	21.1	20.6	20.8	18.1	18.5	18.1	17.3
All males													
18–24 years	42.1	35.0	28.0	26.6	27.8	31.7	31.3	29.5	28.1	30.2	32.1	26.3	25.6
25–34 years	50.5	43.9	38.2	31.6	29.5	30.3	28.5	29.1	28.9	26.9	27.2	28.7	26.1
35–44 years	51.0	41.8	37.6	34.5	31.5	32.1	30.2	30.0	30.2	27.3	29.7	28.1	26.5
45–64 years	42.6	39.3	33.4	29.3	27.1	27.6	27.7	25.8	26.4	26.4	24.5	23.9	25.0
65 years and over	24.8	20.9	19.6	14.6	14.9	12.8	10.4	10.5	10.2	11.5	10.1	10.1	9.8
White male[4]													
18–24 years	40.8	34.3	28.4	27.4	28.4	34.0	34.1	30.5	30.4	32.3	34.3	27.7	26.7
25–34 years	49.5	43.6	37.3	31.6	29.9	30.4	29.2	30.8	29.7	28.7	27.7	28.8	26.3
35–44 years	50.1	41.3	36.6	33.5	31.2	32.1	29.6	29.5	30.6	27.8	29.7	28.8	26.6
45–64 years	41.2	38.3	32.1	28.7	26.3	26.5	27.0	24.5	25.8	25.1	24.4	23.3	24.4
65 years and over	24.3	20.5	18.9	13.7	14.1	11.5	10.0	10.0	9.8	10.7	9.3	9.6	9.4
Black or African American male[4]													
18–24 years	54.9	40.2	27.2	21.3	*14.6	23.5	19.7	23.6	20.9	21.6	22.7	18.6	18.0
25–34 years	58.5	47.5	45.6	33.8	25.1	31.6	25.2	22.7	23.2	23.8	28.9	31.0	21.2
35–44 years	61.5	48.6	45.0	42.0	36.3	33.9	36.1	34.8	30.7	29.9	28.3	23.6	28.4
45–64 years	57.8	50.0	46.1	36.7	33.9	39.4	37.3	35.7	32.2	34.3	29.8	30.1	29.2
65 years and over	29.7	26.2	27.7	21.5	28.5	26.0	16.3	17.3	14.2	21.1	19.4	18.0	14.1
All females													
18–24 years	34.1	33.8	30.4	22.5	21.8	25.7	24.5	26.3	24.9	23.2	24.5	21.5	21.5
25–34 years	38.8	33.7	32.0	28.2	26.4	24.8	24.6	23.5	22.3	22.7	21.3	21.3	21.0
35–44 years	39.8	37.0	31.5	24.8	27.1	27.2	26.4	26.5	26.2	25.7	23.7	24.2	21.6
45–64 years	33.4	30.7	29.9	24.8	24.0	21.5	22.5	21.0	21.7	21.4	21.1	20.2	19.8
65 years and over	12.0	13.2	13.5	11.5	11.5	11.5	11.2	10.7	9.3	9.1	8.6	8.3	8.1
White female[4]													
18–24 years	34.0	34.5	31.8	25.4	24.9	29.4	28.1	29.6	28.5	27.1	26.7	23.6	22.9
25–34 years	38.6	34.1	32.0	28.5	27.3	26.1	26.9	25.5	24.9	25.2	23.8	22.5	22.6
35–44 years	39.3	37.2	31.0	25.0	27.0	27.5	26.6	26.9	26.6	26.9	24.4	25.2	22.7
45–64 years	33.0	30.6	29.7	25.4	24.3	20.9	22.5	21.2	21.4	21.6	21.5	20.1	20.1
65 years and over	12.3	13.8	13.3	11.5	11.7	11.7	11.2	10.5	9.1	9.4	8.5	8.4	8.2
Black or African American female[4]													
18–24 years	35.6	31.8	23.7	10.0	*8.8	11.5	*8.1	14.8	14.2	10.0	17.1	10.8	15.6
25–34 years	42.2	35.2	36.2	29.1	26.7	22.5	21.5	18.2	15.5	16.8	13.9	17.0	18.3
35–44 years	46.4	37.7	40.2	25.5	31.9	30.1	30.0	28.8	30.2	24.0	24.0	23.2	18.9
45–64 years	38.9	34.2	33.4	22.6	27.5	28.4	25.4	22.3	25.6	22.6	22.2	23.3	20.9
65 years and over	*8.9	*8.5	14.5	11.1	13.3	10.7	11.5	13.5	10.2	9.3	9.4	8.0	6.7

Source: U.S. Centers for Disease Control and Prevention, National Center for Health Statistics. *Health, United States 2006.*
Note: Data are based on household interviews of a sample of the civilian noninstitutionalized population.
[1]Data prior to 1997 are not strictly comparable with data for later years due to the 1997 questionnaire redesign.
[2]Estimates are age adjusted to the year 2000 standard population using five age groups: 18–24 years, 25–34 years, 35–44 years, 45–64 years, 65 years and over. Age-adjusted estimates in this table may differ from other age-adjusted estimates based on the same data and presented elsewhere if different age groups are used in the adjustment procedure.
[3]Starting with 1993 data, current cigarette smokers were defined as ever smoking 100 cigarettes in their lifetime and smoking now on every day or some days.
[4]The race groups, white and black, include persons of Hispanic and non-Hispanic origin. Starting with 1999 data, race-specific estimates are tabulated according to 1997 Revisions to the Standards for the Classification of Federal Data on Race and Ethnicity and are not strictly comparable with estimates for earlier years. The single race categories shown in the table conform to the 1997 Standards. Starting with 1999 data, race-specific estimates are for persons who reported only one racial group. Prior to 1999, data were tabulated according to 1977 Standards. Estimates for single race categories prior to 1999 included persons who reported one race or, if they reported more than one race, identified one race as best representing their race. Starting with 2003 data, race responses of other race and unspecified multiple race were treated as missing, and then race was imputed if these were the only race responses. Almost all persons with a race response of other race were of Hispanic origin.
* = Estimates are considered unreliable. Data preceded by an asterisk have a relative standard error of 20%–30%.

Table 17-13. Drug Use, by Type of Drug and Age, 1990–2004

(Percent.)

Age and type of drug	Ever used							Current User						
	1990	1995	2000	2001	2002	2003	2004	1990	1995	2000	2001	2002	2003	2004
12 Years and over														
Any illicit drug	34.2	34.2	38.9	41.7	46.0	46.4	45.8	6.7	6.1	6.3	7.1	8.3	8.2	7.9
Marijuana and hashish	30.5	31.0	34.2	36.9	40.4	40.6	40.2	5.4	4.7	4.8	5.4	6.2	6.2	6.1
Cocaine	11.2	10.3	11.2	12.3	14.4	14.7	14.2	0.9	0.7	0.5	0.7	0.9	1.0	0.8
Crack	1.5	1.8	2.4	2.8	3.6	3.3	3.3	0.3	0.2	0.1	0.2	0.2	0.3	0.2
Inhalants	5.7	5.7	7.5	8.1	9.7	9.7	9.5	0.4	0.4	0.3	0.2	0.3	0.2	0.3
Hallucinogens	7.9	9.5	11.7	12.5	14.6	14.5	14.3	0.4	0.7	0.4	0.6	0.5	0.4	0.4
PCP	2.0	3.2	2.6	2.7	3.2	3.0	2.8	...	-	-	-	0.0	-	0
LSD	5.8	7.5	8.8	9.0	10.4	10.3	9.7	...	0.3	0.2	0.1	0.0	0.1	0.1
Heroin	0.8	1.2	1.2	1.4	1.6	1.6	1.3	-	0.1	0.1	0.1	0.1	0.1	0.1
Any psychotherapeutic [1] ..	...	...	14.5	16.0	19.8	20.1	20.0	...	...	1.7	2.1	2.6	2.7	2.5
Pain relievers	6.3	6.1	8.6	9.8	12.6	13.1	13.2	0.9	0.6	1.2	1.6	1.9	2.0	1.8
Tranquilizers	4.0	3.9	5.8	6.2	8.2	8.5	8.3	0.6	0.4	0.4	0.6	0.8	0.8	0.7
Stimulants	5.5	4.9	6.6	7.1	9.0	8.8	8.3	0.6	0.4	0.4	0.5	0.5	0.5	0.5
Methamphetamine ..	...	...	4.0	4.3	5.3	5.2	4.9	...	...	0.2	0.3	0.3	0.3	0.2
Sedatives	2.8	2.7	3.2	3.3	4.2	4.0	4.1	0.2	0.2	0.1	0.1	0.2	0.1	0.1
Alcohol	82.2	82.3	81.0	81.7	83.1	83.1	82.4	52.6	52.2	46.6	48.3	51.0	50.1	50.3
"Binge" alcohol use [2]	...	...	...	...	...	...	...	14.4	15.8	20.6	20.5	22.9	22.6	22.8
Cigarettes	75.4	71.8	66.5	67.2	69.1	68.7	67.3	32.6	28.8	24.9	24.9	26.0	25.4	24.9
Smokeless tobacco	17.5	17.0	18.5	19.1	19.9	19.4	18.6	3.9	3.3	3.4	3.2	3.3	3.3	3.0
Cigars	...	...	34.2	35.4	37.4	37.1	36.3	...	...	4.8	5.4	5.4	5.4	5.7
Pipes	...	...	16.4	17.0	17.0	16.9	16.4	...	...	1.0	1.0	0.8	0.7	0.8
12 to 17 Years of age														
Any illicit drug	...	...	26.9	28.4	30.9	30.5	30.0	...	...	9.7	10.8	11.6	11.2	10.6
Marijuana and hashish	12.7	16.2	18.3	19.7	20.6	19.6	19.0	4.4	8.2	7.2	8.0	8.2	7.9	7.6
Cocaine	2.6	2.0	2.4	2.3	2.7	2.6	2.4	0.6	0.8	0.6	0.4	0.6	0.6	0.5
Hallucinogens	...	...	5.8	5.7	5.7	5.0	4.6	...	...	1.2	1.2	1.0	1.0	0.8
Inhalants	...	...	8.9	8.6	10.5	10.7	11.0	...	...	1.0	1.0	1.2	1.3	1.2
Any psychotherapeutic [1] ..	...	...	10.9	11.6	13.7	13.4	13.5	...	...	3.0	3.2	4.0	4.0	3.6
Alcohol	48.8	40.6	41.7	42.9	43.4	42.9	42.0	32.5	21.1	16.4	17.3	17.6	17.7	17.6
"Binge" alcohol use [2]	...	...	...	...	...	...	...	...	7.9	10.4	10.6	10.7	10.6	11.1
Cigarettes	45.1	38.1	34.6	33.6	33.3	31.0	29.2	22.4	20.2	13.4	13.0	13.0	12.2	11.9
Smokeless tobacco	...	...	8.6	8.3	8.0	7.6	7.1	...	...	2.1	2.1	2.0	2.0	2.3
Cigars	...	...	17.1	16.4	16.3	15.1	14.8	...	...	4.5	4.3	4.5	4.5	4.8
18 to 25 Years of age														
Any illicit drug	...	...	51.2	55.6	59.8	60.5	59.2	...	...	15.9	18.8	20.2	20.3	19.4
Marijuana and hashish	50.4	41.4	45.7	50.0	53.8	53.9	52.8	12.7	12.0	13.6	16.0	17.3	17.0	16.1
Cocaine	19.3	9.8	10.9	13.0	15.4	15.0	15.2	2.3	1.3	1.4	1.9	2.0	2.2	2.1
Hallucinogens	...	...	19.3	22.1	24.2	23.3	21.3	...	...	1.8	2.7	1.9	1.7	1.5
Inhalants	...	...	12.8	13.4	15.7	14.9	14.0	...	...	0.6	0.6	0.5	0.4	0.4
Any psychotherapeutic [1] ..	...	...	19.5	23.3	27.7	29.0	29.2	...	...	3.6	4.8	5.4	6.0	6.1
Alcohol	87.6	84.4	84.0	85.0	86.7	87.1	86.2	62.8	61.3	56.8	58.8	60.5	61.4	60.5
"Binge" alcohol use [2]	...	...	...	...	...	...	...	...	29.9	37.8	38.7	40.9	41.6	41.2
Cigarettes	70.7	67.7	67.3	69.0	71.2	70.2	68.7	40.9	35.3	38.3	39.1	40.8	40.2	39.5
Smokeless tobacco	...	...	23.6	23.7	23.7	22.0	21.4	...	...	5.0	5.4	4.8	4.7	4.9
Cigars	...	...	42.3	43.8	45.6	45.2	44.1	...	...	10.4	10.4	11.0	11.4	12.7
26 to 34 Years of age														
Any illicit drug	...	...	50.9	53.3	58.3	57.3	56.9	...	...	7.8	8.8	10.5	10.7	11.1
Marijuana and hashish	56.5	51.8	46.0	47.9	52.2	51.0	50.5	9.5	6.7	5.9	6.8	7.7	8.4	8.3
Cocaine	25.4	21.6	15.1	15.9	17.6	18.1	16.3	1.9	1.2	0.8	1.1	1.2	1.5	1.4
Hallucinogens	...	...	15.8	17.5	20.6	20.3	20.9	...	...	0.4	0.4	0.5	0.5	0.5
Inhalants	...	...	11.0	12.0	14.1	13.6	13.1	...	...	0.2	0.2	0.1	-	0.2
Any psychotherapeutic [1] ..	...	...	16.9	18.0	24.4	24.7	23.9	...	...	2.1	2.4	3.6	3.4	3.6
35 Years and over														
Any illicit drug	...	...	35.5	38.4	42.7	43.4	42.9	...	...	3.3	3.5	4.6	4.4	4.2
Marijuana and hashish	19.6	25.3	31.6	34.5	38.0	38.9	38.7	2.4	1.8	2.3	2.4	3.1	3.0	3.1
Cocaine	5.9	8.6	11.8	13.0	15.4	15.9	15.5	0.2	0.4	0.3	0.5	0.6	0.6	0.5
Hallucinogens	...	...	10.1	10.5	12.6	12.8	12.8	...	...	-	-	0.1	0.1	0
Inhalants	...	...	5.3	5.9	7.2	7.4	7.4	...	...	0.1	-	0.1	0.1	0.1
Any psychotherapeutic [1] ..	...	...	13.5	14.7	18.0	18.3	18.1	...	...	1.0	1.3	1.6	1.5	1.3
Alcohol	...	...	85.8	86.5	88.0	88.0	87.3	...	...	49.0	50.8	53.9	52.5	53.0
"Binge" alcohol use [2]	...	...	...	...	...	...	...	...	...	19.1	18.8	21.4	21.0	21.1
Cigarettes	...	...	70.7	71.5	73.7	73.6	72.3	...	...	24.2	24.2	25.2	24.7	24.1
Smokeless tobacco	...	...	19.1	19.8	20.9	20.6	19.6	...	...	3.3	3.0	3.2	3.2	2.7
Cigars	...	...	35.2	36.6	39.0	38.7	37.9	...	...	3.9	4.7	4.6	4.5	4.6

Source: U.S. Census Bureau. U.S. Substance Abuse and Mental Health Services Administration.
Note: The 2002 Survey changed names from the National Household Survey on Drug Abuse to National Household Survey on Drug Use and Health (NSDUH). Due to the impact of Survey improvements, 2002 data should not be compared with data collected in 2001 or earlier years. Current users are those who used drugs at least once within month prior to this study. Based on a representative sample of the U.S. population age 12 and older, including persons living in households and in some group quarters such as dormitories and homeless shelters. Estimates are based on computer-assisted interviews of about 68,000 respondents. Subject to sampling variability.
[1] Illicit drugs include marijuana/hashish, cocaine (including crack), heroin, hallucinogens, inhalants, or prescription-type psychotherapeutics used nonmedically.
[2] Nonmedical use of any prescription-type pain relievers, tranquilizers, stimulants, or sedatives; does not include over-the-counter drugs.
[3] Binge alcohol use is defined as drinking five or more drinks on the same occasion (i.e., at the same time or within a couple of hours of each other) on at least 1 day in the past 30 days. Heavy alcohol use is defined as drinking five or more drinks on the same occasion on each of 5 or more days in the past 30 days; all heavy alcohol users are also binge alcohol users.
. . . = Not available.
- = Quantity zero or rounds to zero.

Table 17-14. AIDS Cases Reported, by Patient Characteristic, 1981–2004

(Number.)

Characteristic	Cumulative total to 2004[1]	1990	1995	1996	1997
Total[2]	...	41 529	70 864	66 497	58 443
Age					
Under 5 years old	...	583	554	482	306
5 to 12 years old	...	137	189	168	145
13 to 19 years old	...	167	380	375	354
20 to 29 years old	...	7 854	10 866	9 655	8 130
30 to 39 years old	...	18 798	31 731	29 647	25 693
40 to 49 years old	...	9 725	19 446	18 818	16 957
50 to 59 years old	...	2 926	5 560	5 290	4 951
60 years old and over	...	1 253	1 924	1 858	1 733
Sex					
Male	...	36 667	57 451	52 969	45 696
Female	...	4 862	13 413	13 528	12 747
Race and Hispanic Origin					
Non-Hispanic White	...	22 258	29 386	26 172	20 170
Non-Hispanic Black	...	13 199	29 060	28 639	26 995
Hispanic	...	5 657	11 544	10 796	10 387
Other/unknown	...	415	874	890	891
Cases Reported by Characteristic					
Males, 13 years and over	737 300	36 277	57 082	52 630	45 440
Men who have sex with men	402 722	23 797	30 953	27 460	20 894
Injecting drug use	155 872	6 957	13 329	11 801	9 737
Men who have sex with men and injecting drug use	60 038	2 809	3 805	3 153	2 262
Hemophilia/coagulation disorder	5 096	332	426	304	180
Heterosexual contact[3]	43 347	260	1 930	2 348	2 087
Heterosexual contact with injecting drug user	11 048	457	874	827	703
Transfusion[4]	5 163	449	341	270	217
Undetermined[5]	65 062	1 216	5 424	6 467	9 360
Females, 13 years and over	171 603	4 529	13 017	13 195	12 530
Injecting drug use	63 181	2 325	5 290	4 728	4 044
Hemophilia/coagulation disorder	331	16	26	22	16
Heterosexual contact[3]	74 540	506	3 518	3 781	3 293
Heterosexual contact with injecting drug user	24 568	1 035	1 873	1 870	1 349
Transfusion[4]	4 111	335	271	266	181
Undetermined[5]	29 440	312	2 039	2 528	3 647

Source: U.S. Census Bureau. U.S. Centers for Disease Control and Prevention.

Note: Data are provisional. For cases reported in the year shown. Includes Puerto Rico, Virgin Islands, Guam, and U.S. Pacific Islands. Acquired immunodeficiency syndrome (AIDS) is a specific group of diseases or conditions which are indicative of severe immunosuppression related to infection with the human immunodeficiency virus (HIV). Data are subject to retrospective changes.

[1]Includes persons with a diagnosis of AIDS, reported from the beginning of the epidemic through 2004. Cumulative total includes persons with characteristics unknown.
[2]Includes unknown, not shown separately.
[3]Includes persons who have had heterosexual contact with a person with human immunodeficiency virus (HIV) infection or at risk of HIV infection.
[4]Receipt of blood transfusion, blood components, or tissue.
[5]Includes persons for whom risk information is incomplete (because of death, refusal to be interviewed, or loss to followup), persons still under investigation, men reported only to have had heterosexual contact with prostitutes, and interviewed persons for whom no risk is specified.
. . . = Not available.

Table 17-14. AIDS Cases Reported, by Patient Characteristic, 1981–2004—*Continued*

(Number.)

1998	1999	2000	2001	2002	2003	2004
48 269	44 580	40 282	41 450	42 745	...	...
...	...	...	...	...	...	...
...	255	189	170	150	...	...
...	297	315	355	402	...	...
...	5 858	5 077	5 008	5 252	...	...
...	18 644	16 516	16 227	16 092	...	...
...	13 625	12 505	13 408	14 035	...	...
...	4 395	4 254	4 632	5 109	...	...
...	1 506	1 426	1 650	1 705	...	...
37 076	34 013	30 135	30 663	31 644	...	...
11 190	10 312	9 958	10 617	10 951	...	...
13 553	14 587	13 173	13 047	13 151	...	...
20 672	21 541	19 571	20 727	21 649	...	...
8 460	175	206	191	197	...	...
503	356	365	415	449	...	...
36 886	...	...	31 901	32 513	32 250	32 756
16 642	15 464	13 562	13 265	14 545	15 859	15 607
7 869	7 207	5 922	5 261	5 121	4 866	4 564
1 984	1 806	1 548	1 502	1 510	1 695	1 696
145	139	93	97	79	74	71
1 979	2 858	2 549	2 213	3 213	3 371	3 373
631	635	519	549	519	477	435
156	137	144	105	147	111	90
7 480	7 746	7 683	8 909	7 898	7 274	7 355
10 998	...	...	11 082	11 279	11 561	11 859
3 201	2 931	2 609	2 212	2 381	2 262	2 355
17	12	3	9	11	11	21
2 913	4 281	3 981	3 205	4 740	5 234	5 278
1 212	1 155	977	937	985	985	871
137	119	138	113	118	108	106
3 518	3 437	3 728	4 606	4 029	3 946	...

Table 17-15. Abortions—Number, Rate, and Ratio, by Race, 1975–2002

Year	All races				White				Black and other			
		Abortions				Abortions				Abortions		
	Women 15 to 44 years old (1,000)	Number (1,000)	Rate per 1,000 women	Ratio per 1,000 live births[1]	Women 15 to 44 years old (1,000)	Number (1,000)	Rate per 1,000 women	Ratio per 1,000 live births[1]	Women 15 to 44 years old (1,000)	Number (1,000)	Rate per 1,000 women	Ratio per 1,000 live births[1]
2002[2]	62 044	1 293	20.8	319	48 998	719	14.7	225	13 046	574	44.0	672
2001[2]	61 673	1 303	21.1	325	48 868	723	14.8	229	12 805	579	45.3	686
1998[2]	61 326	1 319	21.5	334	49 012	762	15.5	244	12 313	557	45.2	678
1997[2]	61 041	1 335	21.9	341	48 942	777	15.9	251	12 099	558	46.1	684
1994[2]	60 020	1 423	23.7	362	48 592	856	17.6	275	11 429	567	49.6	696
1993[2]	59 712	1 495	25.0	376	48 497	908	18.7	290	11 215	587	52.4	698
1990[2]	58 700	1 609	27.4	389	48 224	1 039	21.5	318	10 476	570	54.4	655
1989[2]	58 365	1 567	26.8	380	48 104	1 006	20.9	309	10 261	561	54.7	650
1986[2]	57 483	1 574	27.4	416	48 010	1 045	21.8	350	9 473	529	55.9	661
1983[2]	55 340	1 575	28.5	436	46 506	1 084	23.3	376	8 834	491	55.5	670
2000	61 631	1 313	21.3	324	48 936	733	15.0	230	12 695	580	45.7	676
1999	61 475	1 315	21.4	327	48 974	743	15.2	234	12 501	572	45.8	674
1996	60 704	1 360	22.4	349	48 837	797	16.3	258	11 867	563	47.5	699
1995	60 368	1 359	22.5	350	48 719	817	16.8	265	11 648	542	46.6	684
1992	59 417	1 529	25.7	380	48 435	943	19.5	298	10 982	585	53.3	681
1991	59 305	1 557	26.2	379	48 560	982	20.2	303	10 745	574	53.5	661
1988	58 192	1 591	27.3	401	48 325	1 026	21.2	333	9 867	565	57.3	638
1987	57 964	1 559	27.1	405	48 288	1 017	21.1	338	9 676	542	56.0	648
1985	56 754	1 589	28.0	422	47 512	1 076	22.6	360	9 242	513	55.5	659
1984	56 061	1 577	28.1	423	47 023	1 087	23.1	366	9 038	491	54.3	646
1982	54 679	1 574	28.8	428	46 049	1 095	23.8	373	8 630	479	55.5	646
1981	53 901	1 577	29.3	430	45 494	1 108	24.3	377	8 407	470	55.9	645
1980	53 048	1 554	29.3	428	44 942	1 094	24.3	376	8 106	460	56.5	642
1979	52 016	1 498	28.8	420	44 266	1 062	24.0	373	7 750	435	56.2	625
1978	50 920	1 410	27.7	413	43 427	969	22.3	356	7 493	440	58.7	665
1977	49 814	1 317	26.4	400	42 567	889	20.9	333	7 247	428	59.0	679
1976	48 721	1 179	24.2	361	41 721	785	18.8	296	7 000	394	56.3	638
1975	47 606	1 034	21.7	331	40 857	701	17.2	276	6 749	333	49.3	565

Source: U.S. Census Bureau. *Statistical Abstract of the United States: 2007.* 1978–1988, S.K. Henshaw and J. Van Vort, eds., *Abortion Factbook,* 1992 Edition: Readings, Trends, and State and Local Data to 1988. The Alan Guttmacher Institute, 1992 ©. 1989–2000, L.B. Finer and S.K. Henshaw, "Abortion Incidence and Services in the United States in 2000." *Perspectives on Sexual and Reproductive Health,* 35:6. 2001–2002, L.B. Finer and S.K. Henshaw, "Estimates of U.S. abortion incidence in 2001 and 2002", New York: The Alan Guttmacher Institute, 2005; and unpublished data.

[1]Live births are those which occurred from July 1 of year shown through June 30 of the following year (to match time of conception with abortions). Births are classified by race of child 1972–1988, and by race of mother after 1988.

[2]Total numbers of abortions in 1983, 1986, 1989, 1990, 1993, 1994, 1997, and 1998 have been estimated by interpolation; 2001 and 2002 have been estimated using trends in CDC data.

Table 17-16. Organ Transplants and Grafts, 1990–2005

Procedure	Number of procedures								Number of centers		Number of people waiting	Patient survival rates
	1990	1995	2000	2001	2002	2003	2004	2005	1990	2005	2005	(percent)
Transplant:[1]												
Heart	2 095	2 342	2 172	2 202	2 153	2 057	2 016	2 127	148	135	2 993	87.7
Heart and lung	52	69	47	27	33	29	39	33	79	60	143	56.4
Lung	203	869	955	1 054	1 042	1 085	1 173	1 408	70	67	3 038	82.8
Liver	2 631	3 818	4 816	5 177	5 326	5 671	6 168	6 444	85	126	17 250	86.3
Kidney	9 358	10 957	13 258	14 152	14 741	15 129	16 000	16 477	232	247	66 701	98.0
Kidney and pancreas	459	915	910	884	903	871	880	903	. . .	. . .	2 506	95.5
Pancreas	60	103	420	468	546	502	604	540	84	145	1 747	94.2
Intestine	1	21	29	112	107	116	152	178	. . .	48	220	82.4
Multi organ	71	124	213	228	320	350	441	518	. . .	. . .	. . .	. . .
Cornea grafts[2]	40 631	44 652	46 949	46 532	46 625	46 436	46 841	44 329	[3]107	388	. . .	. . .
Bone grafts (1,000)	350	450	800	875	1 050	1 200	1 500	1 620	30	65	(X)	. . .
Skin grafts[4]	5 500	5 500	13 000	13 000	15 000	16 000	19 000	20 000	25	45	(X)	. . .

Source: U.S. Census Bureau. *Statistical Abstract of the United States: 2007.* U.S. Department of Health and Human Services, Health Resources and Services Administration, Office of Special Programs, Division of Transplantation. United Network for Organ Sharing (UNOS). University Renal Research and Education Association. American Association of Tissue Banks. Eye Bank Association of America.
Note: As of end of year. Based on reports of procurement programs and transplant centers in the United States, except as noted.
[1]Kidney-pancreas and heart-lung transplants are each counted as one organ. All other multi-organ transplants, excluding kidney-pancreas and heart-lung, are included in the multi-organ row. Based on the Organ Procurement and Transplant Network (OPTN) as of July 28, 2006. The data have been supplied by United Network for Organ Sharing (UNOS) under contract with the U.S. Department of Health and Human Services (HHS). This work was supported in part by Health Resources and Services Administration contract 231-00-0015. The authors alone are responsible for the reporting and interpretation of these data. Data subject to change based on future data submission or correction.
[2]1990–1992, number of procedures and eye banks include Canada. From 1993 on, the data is for the U.S. only.
[3]Eye banks.
[4]Procedure data are shown in terms of square feet.
. . . = Not available.
X = Not applicable.

Table 17-17. Asthma Incidence Among Children Under 18 Years of Age, by Selected Characteristics, 2004

(Thousands, percent.)

Characteristic	Total	Ever told had asthma		Had asthma attack in past 12 months	
		Number	Percent	Number	Percent
Total[1] (age-adjusted)	73 067	8 890	12.2	3 975	5.5
Total[1] (crude)	73 067	8 890	12.2	3 975	5.4
Sex:					
Male	37 351	5 524	14.8	2 497	6.7
Female	35 715	3 366	9.4	1 478	4.1
Age:[2]					
0 to 4 years	19 983	1 454	7.3	781	3.9
5 to 11 years	28 110	3 653	13.0	1 710	6.1
12 to 17 years	24 974	3 782	15.2	1 484	5.9
Race:					
Race alone:[3]	71 024	8 477	12.0	3 816	5.4
White	56 340	6 328	11.3	2 844	5.1
Black or African American	11 166	1 910	17.2	882	8.0
American Indian or Alaska Native	653	68	9.9	[4]29	(B)
Asian	2 726	171	6.2	[4]61	[4]2.2
Native Hawaiian or other Pacific Islander	139	0	0	–	0
2 or more races[5]	2 043	413	21.1	159	8.0
Hispanic origin and race:[6]					
Hispanic or Latino	13 956	1 423	10.4	568	4.2
Mexican or Mexican American	9 673	851	9.1	277	3.0
Not Hispanic or Latino	59 111	7 467	12.6	3 407	5.8
White, single race	43 405	5 059	11.6	2 329	5.3
Black or African American, single race	10 751	1 834	17.1	838	7.9

Source: U.S. Census Bureau. *Statistical Abstract of the United States: 2007.* U.S. National Center for Health Statistics.
Note: Based on the U.S. National Center for Health Statistics' National Health Interview Survey, a sample survey of the civilian noninstitutionalized population.
[1]Includes other races not shown separately.
[2]Estimates for age groups are not age adjusted.
[3]Refers to persons who indicated only a single race group.
[4]Figures do not meet standard of reliability or precision.
[5]Refers to all persons who indicated more than one race group.
[6]Persons of Hispanic or Latino origin may be of any race or combination of races.
B = Figure too small to meet statistical standards for reliability of a derived figure.

Table 17-18. Selected Respiratory Diseases Among Persons 18 Years of Age and Over, by Selected Characteristics, 2004

(Thousands.)

Selected characteristic	Total Persons	Selected respiratory conditions[1]					
			Asthma				
		Emphysema	Ever	Still	Hay fever	Sinusitis	Chronic bronchitis
Total[2]	**215 191**	**3 576**	**21 300**	**14 358**	**18 629**	**30 789**	**9 047**
Sex:							
Male	103 552	1 871	8 796	5 148	8 161	10 597	2 757
Female	111 640	1 704	12 503	9 210	10 468	20 192	6 291
Age:							
18 to 44 years	110 417	309	10 959	7 058	8 777	13 976	3 483
45 to 64 years	70 182	1 393	6 973	4 871	7 252	11 769	3 413
65 to 74 years	18 360	904	1 893	1 368	1 475	2 780	1 126
75 years and over	16 232	970	1 474	1 061	1 126	2 265	1 026
Race:							
1 race[3]	212 861	3 541	20 945	14 106	18 331	30 368	8 904
White	178 552	3 207	17 376	11 750	15 948	26 352	7 842
Black or African American	24 602	237	2 755	1 890	1 667	3 278	878
American Indian or Alaska Native	1 501	[4]30	251	147	84	203	[4]45
Asian	7 853	[4]59	541	302	606	521	131
Native Hawaiian or other Pacific Islander ..	352	(B)	(B)	(B)	(B)	(B)	(B)
2 or more races[5]	2 330	[4]35	355	252	298	421	143
Hispanic origin and race:[6]							
Hispanic or Latino	26 798	155	2 013	1 163	1 561	1 979	669
Mexican or Mexican American	17 139	82	997	604	873	1 064	354
Not Hispanic or Latino	188 393	3 420	19 287	13 195	17 068	28 810	8 378
White, single race	153 365	3 061	15 635	10 740	14 499	24 525	7 233
Black or African American, single race	23 806	235	2 648	1 831	1 615	3 184	865

Source: U.S. Census Bureau. *Statistical Abstract of the United States: 2007.* U.S. National Center for Health Statistics.

Note: Respondents were asked in two separate questions if they had ever been told by a doctor or other health professional that they had emphysema or asthma. Respondents who had been told they had asthma were asked if they still had asthma. Respondents were asked in three separate questions if they had been told by a doctor or other health professional in the past 12 months that they had hay fever, sinusitis, or bronchitis. Based on the National Center for Health Statistics' National Health Interview Survey, a sample survey of the civilian noninstitutionalized population.

[1]A person may be represented in more than one column.
[2]Total includes other races not shown separately.
[3]Refers to persons who indicated only a single race group.
[4]Figure does not meet standard of reliability or precision.
[5]Refers to all persons who indicated more than one race group.
[6]Persons of Hispanic or Latino origin may be of any race or combination of races.
B = Figure too small to meet statistical standards for reliability of a derived figure.

Table 17-19. Adults 18 Years and Over Who Used Complementary and Alternative Medicine (CAM), by Type of Therapy, 2002

(Thousands, percent.)

Therapy	Ever used	Used during past 12 months
Any CAM[1] use	**149 271**	**123 606**
Alternative medical systems:		
Acupuncture	8 188	2 136
Ayurveda	751	154
Homeopathic treatment	7 379	3 433
Naturopathy	1 795	498
Biologically based therapies:		
Chelation therapy	270	(B)
Folk medicine	1 393	233
Nonvitamin, nonmineral, natural products	50 613	38 183
Diet-based therapies[2]	13 799	7 099
Vegetarian diet	5 324	3 184
Macrobiotic diet	1 368	317
Atkins diet	7 312	3 417
Pritikin diet	580	137
Ornish diet	290	(B)
Zone diet	1 062	430
Megavitamin therapy	7 935	5 739
Manipulative and body-based therapies:		
Chiropractic care	40 242	15 226
Massage	18 899	10 052
Mind-body therapies:		
Biofeedback	1 986	278
Meditation	20 698	15 336
Guided imagery	6 067	4 194
Progressive relaxation	8 518	6 185
Deep breathing exercises	29 658	23 457
Hypnosis	3 733	505
Yoga	15 232	10 386
Tai chi	5 056	2 565
Qi gong	950	527
Prayer for health reasons[3]	110 012	89 624
Prayed for own health	103 662	85 432
Others ever prayed for your health	62 348	48 467
Participate in prayer group	25 167	18 984
Healing ritual for own health	9 230	4 045
Energy healing therapy/Reiki	2 264	1 080

Source: U.S. Census Bureau. *Statistical Abstract of the United States: 2007.* U.S. National Center for Health Statistics.
Note: The denominators for statistics shown exclude persons with unknown CAM information. Estimates were age adjusted to the year 2000 U.S. standard population using four age groups: 18 to 24 years, 25 to 44 years, 45 to 64 years, and 65 years and over.
[1]Respondents may have reported using more than one type of therapy.
[2]The totals of the numbers and percents of the categories listed under "Diet-based therapies" are greater than the number and percent of "Diet-based therapies" because respondents could choose more than one diet-based therapy.
[3]The sum of the categories listed under "Prayer for health reasons" are greater than the number and percent of "Prayer for health reasons" because respondents could choose more than one method of prayer.
B = Base figure too small to meet statistical standards for reliability of derived figures.

| BOX 17 ▪ Health Insurance |

Until the development of modern medicine in the twentieth century, health costs were comparatively low. During the Civil War, private insurance was offered for accidents incurred while traveling. This was followed in the 1890s with the first disability and illness policies. In 1932, Blue Cross/Blue Shield offered health insurance plans based on contracts with doctors and hospitals. During the height of the strength of organized labor in the 1940s and 1950s, unions negotiated group rates for members. Employees also began to offer group policies to attract workers. As the cost of health insurance began to rise significantly in the 1980s, many employees switched to managed-care plans, which were less expensive but subject to criticisms of rushed and inadequate health care, required increased contributions from employees to defray the premiums, or, in the case of many small businesses, simply canceled the benefit.

The U.S. government provides some health insurance benefits through social security and through the Medicare and Medicaid programs, but the issue of National Health Insurance, particularly insurance for children, has been the subject of heated debate. During Bill Clinton's first administration, Congress defeated legislation that would have provided universal health coverage, charging it was too expensive and gave the federal government too much control over the health care industry. Since then, many proposals have been introduced but none have received sufficient bipartisan support.

A proposal under debate in Congress concerns the State Children's Health Insurance Program (SCHIP), a joint federal/state program that is set to expire on September 30, 2007. SCHIP provides health insurance to children whose family's earnings are too high to qualify for Medicaid and yet too low to afford private coverage. The Democratic Congress proposed an increase in funding for the program that, in 2005, covered more than 6.1 million children at a cost of $7.3 billion. The proposed increase of $35-50 billion, spread over five years, would allow the program to include approximately 5 million middle class children whose parents cannot afford private health insurance. By and large Republican congress members and President George W. Bush asserted that the measure would, in effect, establish socialized medicine to the detriment of private insurers. In general, they favor much smaller increases in the program; President Bush proposed a $5 billion increase over five years.

According to the Centers for Disease Control and Prevention (CDC), in 2006 13% of children under 18 years of age in the U.S. (9.5 million) were uninsured for at least part of the year; up from the two years prior but lower than the seven previous years. Additionally, in 2006, 5.2% of children under 18 (3.8 million) were uninsured for more than one year. The Census Bureau states that in 2005 while 11.2% of all children (8.3 million) were uninsured, for children living in poverty, the percentage rises precipitously to 19%.

Medicare which covered approximately 19 million people in 1966 when it was first established, covered almost 43 million people in 2006. In 2003 Medicaid served more than 52.0 million people and in 2005 had total expenditures on

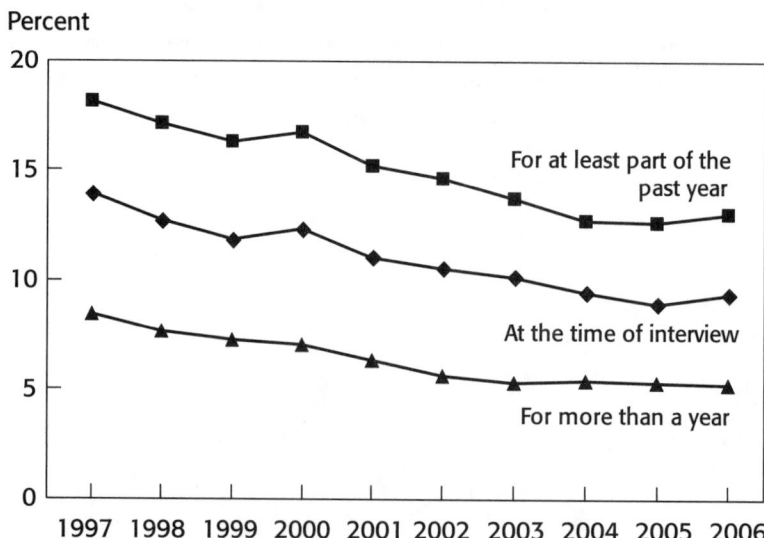

Percentage of Children Under 18 Years of Age Who Lacked Health Insurance Coverage at the Time of Interview, for at Least Part of the Past Year, or for More Than a Year: United States, 1997–2006

Source: Family Core component of the 1997–2006 National Health Interview Surveys. Data are based on household interviews of a sample of the civilian noninstitutionalized population.

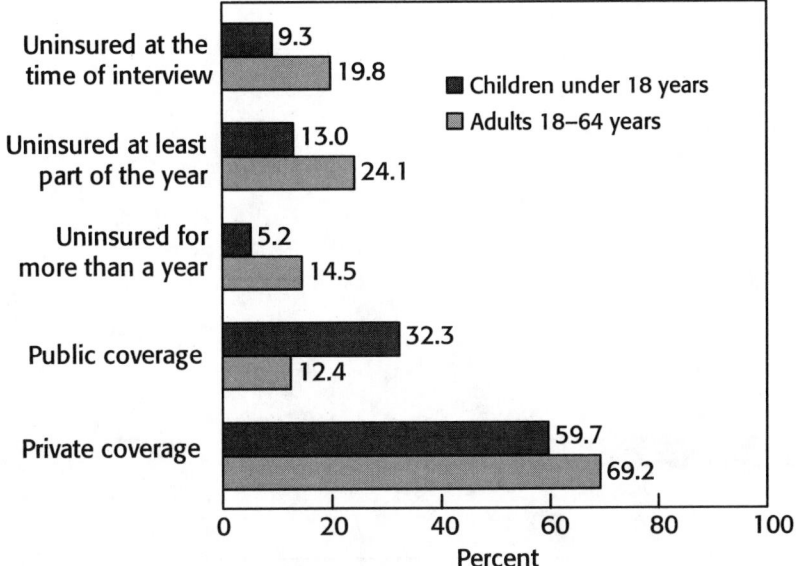

Percentage of Persons without Health Insurance, by Three Measurements and Age Group, and Percentage of Persons with Health Insurance, by Coverage Type and Age Group: United States, 2006

Source: Family Core component of the 2006 National Health Interview Survey. Data are based on household interviews of a sample of the civilian noninstitutionalized population.

both federal and state levels of $317.7 billion. In addition, the Centers for Medicare and Medicaid Services estimated that in 2005 Medicaid provided supplemental coverage to approximately 6.8 million Medicare beneficiaries.

In the eighteen years between 1987 and 2005 there were only four years in which the percentage of uninsured people in the U.S. did not increase. In 2006, at the time of the CDC's National Health Interview Survey, 43.6 million people in the U.S. were without health insurance; almost 15% of the population. The number of people who were without insurance for at least part of 2006 increases to 54.5 million while 30.7 million people had been without insurance for more than one year.

Sources:
"Bush Says He'll Veto Children's Health Funding." *Knight Ridder Washington Bureau (Washington D.C.)* (August 8, 2007).
"House Triples SCHIP Funding; GOP Can't Cap Eligibility, Cost. (Page One)." *The Washington Times* (August 2, 2007).
"House Vote Cuts $157 Billion from Medicare Advantage." *A.M. Best Newswire* (August 2, 2007).
U.S. Census Bureau. *Income, Poverty, and Health Insurance Coverage in the United States: 2005,* August 2006. http://www.census.gov/prod/2006pubs/p60-231.pdf
U.S. Department of Health and Human Services, Centers for Disease Control and Prevention. "Health Insurance Coverage: Early Release of Estimates from the National Interview Survey, 2006." http://www.cdc.gov/nchs/data/nhis/earlyrelease/insur200706.pdf
U.S. Department of Health and Human Services, Centers for Medicare and Medicaid Services. *Brief Summaries of Medicare and Medicaid,* November 1, 2006
U.S. Department of Health and Human Services, Centers for Medicare and Medicaid Services. The State Childrens Health Insurance Program, Mark McClellan, M.D., Ph.D., Administrator, Centers for Medicare and Medicaid Services, Testimony Before the Senate Subcommittee on Health, of the Committee on Finance. http://www.cms.hhs.gov/apps/media/press/testimony.asp?Counter=1913

Gallons per person

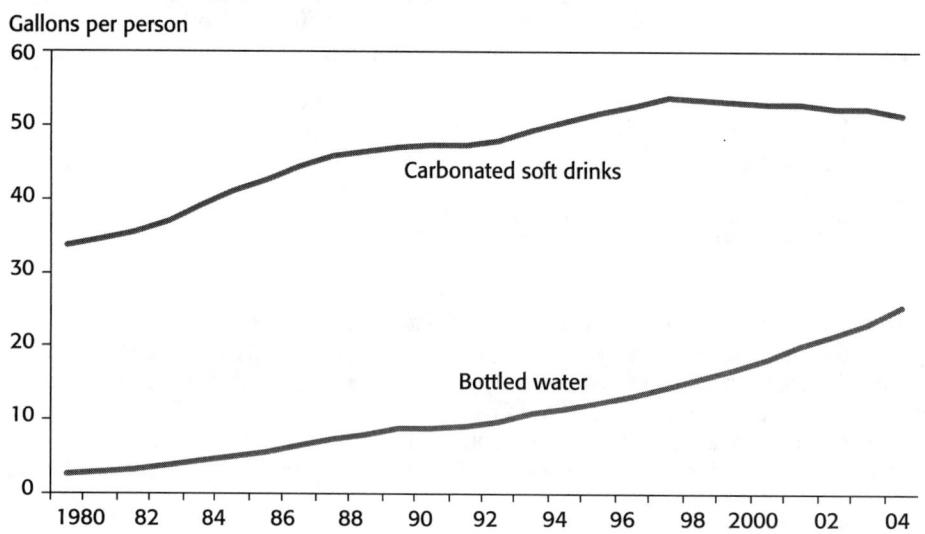

U.S. Bottled Water Consumption Continues to Set New Records
Sources: USDA, Economic Research Service, Food Availability (Per Capita) Data System; Beverage Marketing Corporation.

CHAPTER 18

Food and Nutrition

HIGHLIGHTS

1 The annual consumption of red meat has declined from 126.4 pounds per capita in 1980 to 112 pounds in 2004. Poultry has gained over the same period, its consumption rising from 40.8 pounds to 72.7 pounds. Fish and shellfish have also increased, from 12.4 pounds to 16.5 pounds.

2 Carbonated soft drinks remain the most popular beverage, with annual consumption increasing from 33.6 gallons per capita to 52.3 gallons between 1980 and 2004. Bottled water has also become popular, with annual per capita consumption soaring from 2.7 gallons to 23.2 gallons. With smaller gains are fruit juices from 7.6 gallons to 8.9 gallons and wine from 2.1 gallons to 2.3 gallons. All other beverages have declined during this period: coffee from 26.7 gallons to 24.6 gallons; milk from 27.1 gallons to 21 gallons; beer from 24.3 gallons to 21.6 gallons; and distilled spirits from 2.0 gallons to 1.4 gallons.

3 Although fresh fruits are being consumed in greater quantities than ever before, there are some exceptions. Apple consumption decreased from 19.4 pounds per capita in 1980 to 18.8 pounds in 2004, peaches and nectarines from 7.1 pounds to 5.1 pounds, plums and prunes from 1.5 pounds to 1.1 pounds, oranges from 14.3 to 10.8, and grapefruits from 7.3 pounds to 4.1 pounds.

4 Potatoes are still the most consumed vegetables with 46.5 pounds consumed per capita, but consumption is down from 51.1 pounds in 1980.

Table 18-1. Nutrients and Other Food Components of U.S. Food Supply, per Capita per Day,[1] 1909–2004

Year	Food energy	Carbohydrates	Protein	Total fat	Saturated	Monounsaturate	Polyunsaturate	Cholesterol	Dietary fiber
	Kilocalorie				Grams			Milligrams	Grams
2004	3 900	481	113	179	56	79	37	430	25
2003	3 900	482	112	178	56	78	37	420	25
2002	3 900	484	112	180	57	79	37	420	24
2001	4 000	508	115	174	54	77	36	420	27
2000	3 900	497	113	173	54	77	36	420	25
1999	3 800	498	112	155	50	66	32	420	25
1998	3 700	495	110	149	48	64	31	410	25
1997	3 700	495	109	147	46	63	31	400	25
1996	3 700	492	110	149	47	64	31	400	25
1995	3 600	481	109	148	47	64	31	400	24
1994	3 700	483	110	151	48	65	31	400	24
1993	3 700	477	109	155	49	67	32	400	24
1992	3 600	468	109	152	49	65	32	400	24
1991	3 500	459	107	149	48	63	31	400	24
1990	3 500	457	106	151	49	62	31	400	24
1989	3 500	444	105	150	49	61	31	410	23
1988	3 500	448	106	155	51	63	32	410	23
1987	3 500	441	104	154	51	63	31	420	22
1986	3 500	429	104	157	52	64	31	420	22
1985	3 500	424	102	158	52	64	32	420	22
1984	3 300	409	99	153	51	62	31	420	21
1983	3 300	404	98	150	50	60	31	420	21
1982	3 200	400	96	146	48	59	30	410	20
1981	3 200	399	97	146	49	59	30	420	20
1980	3 200	401	97	146	49	59	29	420	20
1979	3 200	401	97	145	48	58	29	430	20
1978	3 200	395	97	144	48	58	29	420	20
1977	3 200	403	98	143	48	57	28	420	20
1976	3 300	402	98	145	49	58	29	430	20
1975	3 100	389	95	140	47	55	27	420	20
1974	3 200	389	97	144	49	57	27	440	19
1973	3 200	399	97	142	49	56	27	430	20
1972	3 200	393	99	146	51	58	26	460	19
1971	3 300	395	99	149	53	59	26	480	19
1970	3 200	394	98	145	51	58	25	460	19
1969	3 200	391	95	150	55	60	24	460	19
1968	3 200	388	95	150	56	59	24	470	19
1967	3 200	385	94	146	55	57	23	470	19
1966	3 200	382	93	145	54	57	23	460	18
1965	3 100	379	92	142	54	56	22	460	18
1964	3 100	379	93	143	54	56	22	470	18
1963	3 100	380	92	141	54	55	22	470	18
1962	3 100	381	91	140	54	55	21	470	19
1961	3 100	381	92	138	53	54	20	470	19
1960	3 100	382	92	138	53	54	21	470	19
1959	3 100	382	92	141	55	56	20	490	19
1958	3 100	382	91	137	53	54	19	480	19
1957	3 100	379	92	137	54	54	19	490	19
1956	3 100	385	94	142	56	56	20	510	20
1955	3 100	385	92	141	55	56	19	500	19
1954	3 100	386	92	137	54	54	19	500	20
1953	3 100	395	93	137	54	54	18	510	20
1952	3 200	399	93	137	54	54	19	510	20
1951	3 100	401	92	134	54	53	18	510	21
1950	3 200	412	93	140	56	55	18	510	22
1949	3 200	411	93	135	54	53	18	510	22
1948	3 200	409	94	136	55	53	18	510	22
1947	3 300	430	97	139	56	54	18	520	23
1946	3 300	422	102	138	56	54	18	520	24
1945	3 300	430	104	138	55	54	18	540	26
1944	3 400	438	102	142	57	56	18	520	25
1943	3 400	439	101	140	56	55	18	500	25
1942	3 300	435	97	139	57	54	18	490	25
1941	3 400	453	93	140	58	54	17	470	25

[1]Data are based on U.S. Department of Agriculture's Economic Research Service (ERS) estimates of per capita quantities of food available for consumption, on imputed consumption data for foods no longer reported by ERS, and on estimates from USDA's Center for Nutrition Policy and Promotion (CNPP) of quantities of produce from home gardens.

**Table 18-1. Nutrients and Other Food Components of U.S. Food Supply, per Capita per Day,[1]
1909–2004—*Continued***

				Fat					
	Food energy	Carbohydrates	Protein	Total fat	Saturated	Monounsaturate	Polyunsaturate	Cholesterol	Dietary fiber
Year	Kilocalorie	Grams						Milligrams	Grams
1940	3 300	438	92	138	58	53	17	470	25
1939	3 300	448	91	134	56	52	16	460	26
1938	3 200	440	89	129	54	50	15	450	25
1937	3 200	441	88	129	54	50	15	450	25
1936	3 300	447	90	130	54	50	15	440	25
1935	3 200	444	86	124	52	47	14	420	26
1934	3 200	438	89	130	56	50	15	450	25
1933	3 300	447	88	129	55	49	15	450	25
1932	3 300	458	89	128	55	49	15	460	25
1931	3 400	471	90	130	55	50	15	470	26
1930	3 400	485	91	130	55	50	15	470	26
1929	3 400	483	93	132	55	51	16	470	27
1928	3 500	494	93	131	55	51	15	470	26
1927	3 500	489	94	130	55	50	15	480	26
1926	3 400	488	93	130	55	50	15	480	26
1925	3 400	483	93	130	55	50	15	470	26
1924	3 400	482	94	130	55	50	15	480	26
1923	3 400	474	94	129	54	50	15	470	27
1922	3 400	486	91	123	52	47	14	460	26
1921	3 100	445	88	115	49	44	13	440	25
1920	3 200	461	91	117	49	46	13	440	26
1919	3 400	481	93	122	50	49	14	440	27
1918	3 300	469	94	123	51	49	14	430	28
1917	3 300	473	93	115	48	46	12	420	28
1916	3 300	474	93	119	50	47	13	440	27
1915	3 400	485	94	119	49	47	13	440	28
1914	3 400	488	95	121	50	47	14	430	28
1913	3 400	493	97	119	50	46	13	440	28
1912	3 400	495	98	118	50	46	12	450	29
1911	3 400	494	98	121	51	47	13	470	28
1910	3 400	500	99	120	51	47	13	450	29
1909	3 500	502	101	122	52	47	13	450	29

[1]Data are based on U.S. Department of Agriculture's Economic Research Service (ERS) estimates of per capita quantities of food available for consumption, on imputed consumption data for foods no longer reported by ERS, and on estimates from USDA's Center for Nutrition Policy and Promotion (CNPP) of quantities of produce from home gardens.

Table 18-1. Nutrients and Other Food Components of U.S. Food Supply, per Capita per Day,[1] 1909–2004—*Continued*

Year	Vitamin A (RE)	Vitamin A (RAE) Micrograms RAE	Carotene Micrograms	Vitamin E Milligrams Alpha-TE	Vitamin C	Thiamin	Riboflavin	Niacin	Vitamin B6	Folate (DFE)	Vitamin B12
							Milligrams			Micrograms	
2004	1 470	1 080	680	21.0	119.0	2.9	2.9	33.0	2.4	898	8.2
2003	1 480	1 080	690	20.9	118.0	2.9	2.8	33.0	2.4	899	8.2
2002	1 450	1 070	650	21.0	114.0	2.9	2.8	32.0	2.4	889	8.2
2001	1 480	1 080	680	20.4	119.0	3.1	2.9	34.0	2.5	918	8.2
2000	1 670	1 250	720	20.0	130.0	3.0	2.9	33.0	2.5	925	8.2
1999	1 670	1 250	710	17.4	130.0	3.0	2.9	33.0	2.5	920	8.0
1998	1 660	1 250	730	16.5	131.0	3.0	2.9	32.0	2.4	911	8.0
1997	1 800	1 310	870	16.6	130.0	3.0	2.9	32.0	2.4	412	7.8
1996	1 770	1 300	820	16.7	131.0	3.0	2.9	32.0	2.4	414	8.0
1995	1 730	1 280	770	16.4	125.0	2.9	2.9	31.0	2.4	411	8.0
1994	1 800	1 320	830	16.8	129.0	3.0	3.0	32.0	2.5	421	7.9
1993	1 730	1 280	750	17.6	129.0	3.0	2.9	32.0	2.5	422	7.7
1992	1 680	1 250	680	17.1	125.0	3.0	3.0	32.0	2.5	432	7.9
1991	1 620	1 220	640	16.9	122.0	2.9	2.9	31.0	2.4	421	7.9
1990	1 650	1 240	670	16.4	118.0	2.9	3.0	31.0	2.4	410	8.0
1989	1 620	1 230	650	16.2	122.0	2.8	2.9	30.0	2.3	400	8.0
1988	1 570	1 200	610	16.6	121.0	2.8	2.9	30.0	2.3	406	8.0
1987	1 620	1 240	640	16.0	120.0	2.7	2.9	30.0	2.3	390	8.2
1986	1 590	1 230	610	16.0	123.0	2.7	2.8	29.0	2.3	398	8.2
1985	1 600	1 230	630	16.1	119.0	2.6	2.8	29.0	2.2	393	8.3
1984	1 620	1 240	640	15.6	118.0	2.5	2.7	28.0	2.2	376	8.2
1983	1 580	1 220	600	15.2	121.0	2.5	2.7	28.0	2.2	382	8.1
1982	1 590	1 220	630	14.8	116.0	2.5	2.6	27.0	2.1	377	7.9
1981	1 600	1 240	610	14.6	115.0	2.5	2.7	28.0	2.1	371	8.2
1980	1 600	1 240	600	14.4	117.0	2.5	2.7	27.0	2.1	373	8.2
1979	1 620	1 250	620	14.5	114.0	2.5	2.7	28.0	2.1	377	8.2
1978	1 580	1 240	580	14.4	113.0	2.4	2.7	27.0	2.1	365	8.5
1977	1 600	1 260	590	14.1	117.0	2.5	2.7	27.0	2.1	377	8.8
1976	1 650	1 300	630	14.5	118.0	2.5	2.7	27.0	2.1	376	8.9
1975	1 630	1 270	630	14.1	117.0	2.4	2.7	26.0	2.0	370	8.6
1974	1 640	1 280	610	13.9	112.0	2.4	2.7	26.0	2.1	358	9.1
1973	1 510	1 220	590	14.0	107.0	2.0	2.3	22.0	1.9	308	8.9
1972	1 520	1 240	560	13.5	108.0	2.0	2.3	23.0	2.0	302	9.4
1971	1 540	1 280	520	13.1	108.0	2.1	2.4	22.0	2.0	303	9.5
1970	1 490	1 240	510	13.3	106.0	2.0	2.3	22.0	2.0	300	9.5
1969	1 430	1 230	430	12.5	98.0	1.9	2.2	21.0	1.9	284	9.3
1968	1 440	1 200	450	12.2	98.0	1.9	2.2	21.0	1.9	284	9.2
1967	1 360	1 180	400	12.1	93.0	1.9	2.2	21.0	1.8	284	9.1
1966	1 330	1 160	390	12.2	90.0	1.8	2.2	21.0	1.8	278	8.9
1965	1 250	1 090	370	12.0	88.0	1.8	2.1	20.0	1.8	277	8.7
1964	1 270	1 120	350	11.7	86.0	1.8	2.2	20.0	1.8	284	9.0
1963	1 280	1 120	370	11.3	88.0	1.8	2.2	20.0	1.8	286	8.7
1962	1 270	1 110	380	11.0	94.0	1.8	2.2	20.0	1.7	291	8.6
1961	1 280	1 120	370	11.0	95.0	1.8	2.2	20.0	1.8	291	8.6
1960	1 300	1 130	390	11.1	96.0	1.8	2.2	20.0	1.8	293	8.6
1959	1 320	1 150	400	10.9	95.0	1.9	2.2	20.0	1.8	296	8.7
1958	1 290	1 130	390	10.5	92.0	1.8	2.2	20.0	1.8	294	8.5
1957	1 300	1 140	400	10.5	97.0	1.8	2.3	20.0	1.8	299	8.8
1956	1 330	1 160	410	10.6	96.0	1.9	2.3	20.0	1.8	301	9.1
1955	1 320	1 150	410	10.7	98.0	1.8	2.3	19.0	1.8	297	8.9
1954	1 300	1 140	400	10.8	98.0	1.8	2.3	19.0	1.8	300	8.7
1953	1 320	1 150	410	10.6	100.0	1.8	2.3	20.0	1.8	294	8.8
1952	1 300	1 130	400	10.6	99.0	1.9	2.4	19.0	1.8	300	8.4
1951	1 290	1 110	400	10.0	101.0	1.9	2.3	20.0	1.8	304	8.2
1950	1 340	1 150	450	10.6	99.0	1.9	2.3	19.0	1.8	307	8.3
1949	1 350	1 160	450	10.3	103.0	1.9	2.3	20.0	1.9	301	8.3
1948	1 360	1 170	460	10.2	106.0	1.9	2.3	20.0	1.9	306	8.4
1947	1 420	1 220	490	10.3	114.0	1.9	2.4	21.0	2.0	314	8.9
1946	1 480	1 250	540	10.5	117.0	2.1	2.5	22.0	2.0	338	8.9
1945	1 540	1 300	560	10.6	119.0	2.1	2.6	22.0	2.0	350	9.3
1944	1 520	1 290	550	10.4	121.0	2.1	2.5	22.0	2.1	342	9.5
1943	1 480	1 250	540	10.2	111.0	2.1	2.2	20.0	2.0	341	8.9
1942	1 430	1 210	520	10.4	112.0	1.8	2.0	18.0	1.9	344	8.5
1941	1 350	1 140	510	10.2	111.0	1.6	1.9	17.0	1.9	323	8.0

[1]Data are based on U.S. Department of Agriculture's Economic Research Service (ERS) estimates of per capita quantities of food available for consumption, on imputed consumption data for foods no longer reported by ERS, and on estimates from USDA's Center for Nutrition Policy and Promotion (CNPP) of quantities of produce from home gardens.

Table 18-1. Nutrients and Other Food Components of U.S. Food Supply, per Capita per Day,[1] 1909–2004—*Continued*

Year	Vitamin A (RE)	Vitamin A (RAE) Micrograms RAE	Carotene Micrograms	Vitamin E Milligrams Alpha-TE	Vitamin C	Thiamin	Riboflavin	Niacin	Vitamin B6	Folate (DFE) Micrograms	Vitamin B12
1940	1 310	1 110	490	9.7	110.0	1.5	1.9	17.0	1.9	320	7.6
1939	1 310	1 100	520	9.8	112.0	1.4	1.9	16.0	1.9	322	7.4
1938	1 280	1 070	510	9.8	108.0	1.4	1.8	16.0	1.9	319	7.2
1937	1 280	1 070	510	9.8	104.0	1.4	1.8	16.0	1.9	308	7.3
1936	1 240	1 040	500	9.5	103.0	1.4	1.8	16.0	1.9	315	7.3
1935	1 250	1 040	520	9.3	107.0	1.3	1.8	16.0	1.8	309	6.8
1934	1 300	1 090	510	8.9	102.0	1.4	1.8	16.0	1.9	310	7.5
1933	1 280	1 080	490	8.5	100.0	1.5	1.8	16.0	1.9	300	7.1
1932	1 310	1 100	520	8.5	101.0	1.5	1.8	17.0	1.9	307	7.0
1931	1 270	1 080	490	9.0	103.0	1.5	1.9	17.0	1.9	319	7.1
1930	1 260	1 080	480	9.2	97.0	1.5	1.9	17.0	1.9	316	7.1
1929	1 290	1 090	510	9.3	106.0	1.5	1.9	17.0	2.0	318	7.3
1928	1 250	1 070	470	9.2	99.0	1.5	1.9	17.0	2.0	314	7.3
1927	1 290	1 100	490	8.9	99.0	1.5	1.9	17.0	2.0	316	7.5
1926	1 270	1 100	460	9.3	98.0	1.4	1.9	17.0	1.9	310	7.6
1925	1 250	1 100	430	9.0	99.0	1.5	1.9	17.0	2.0	309	7.7
1924	1 260	1 100	440	8.2	102.0	1.5	1.9	18.0	2.0	313	7.8
1923	1 290	1 110	470	8.1	103.0	1.5	1.9	18.0	2.1	310	7.9
1922	1 280	1 090	500	8.1	97.0	1.5	1.8	17.0	2.0	298	7.7
1921	1 220	1 050	470	7.3	97.0	1.5	1.8	17.0	1.9	290	7.4
1920	1 240	1 060	470	7.5	97.0	1.5	1.8	17.0	2.0	299	7.7
1919	1 240	1 070	460	8.5	94.0	1.5	1.8	18.0	2.0	298	7.9
1918	1 220	1 050	450	8.5	95.0	1.5	1.8	18.0	2.1	314	8.0
1917	1 190	1 030	450	7.6	92.0	1.5	1.7	18.0	2.0	312	7.6
1916	1 190	1 030	420	7.5	90.0	1.5	1.7	17.0	1.9	297	7.5
1915	1 180	1 020	430	8.1	99.0	1.5	1.7	18.0	2.0	308	7.4
1914	1 150	1 000	400	8.4	95.0	1.5	1.8	18.0	2.0	307	7.5
1913	1 170	1 020	400	7.5	95.0	1.5	1.8	18.0	2.1	314	7.8
1912	1 200	1 050	420	7.2	98.0	1.6	1.9	18.0	2.1	323	8.0
1911	1 220	1 070	410	7.2	93.0	1.5	1.8	18.0	2.1	318	8.1
1910	1 210	1 060	430	7.3	99.0	1.6	1.8	19.0	2.2	325	8.0
1909	1 240	1 080	430	7.2	98.0	1.6	1.9	19.0	2.2	327	8.4

[1]Data are based on U.S. Department of Agriculture's Economic Research Service (ERS) estimates of per capita quantities of food available for consumption, on imputed consumption data for foods no longer reported by ERS, and on estimates from USDA's Center for Nutrition Policy and Promotion (CNPP) of quantities of produce from home gardens.

Table 18-1. Nutrients and Other Food Components of U.S. Food Supply, per Capita per Day,[1] 1909–2004—*Continued*

Year	Minerals								
	Calcium	Phosphorus	Magnesium	Iron	Zinc	Copper	Potassium	Selenium	Sodium
	Milligrams							Micrograms	Milligrams
2004	970	1 710	400	23.4	15.4	2.1	3 820	189.7	1 240
2003	950	1 690	400	23.3	15.3	2.0	3 810	186.0	1 240
2002	950	1 680	390	23.1	15.2	2.0	3 750	182.5	1 250
2001	970	1 770	430	24.3	15.9	2.1	3 900	197.0	1 240
2000	980	1 720	400	23.7	15.4	2.1	3 920	178.9	1 280
1999	980	1 710	400	23.6	15.4	2.1	3 910	177.2	1 270
1998	980	1 690	390	23.1	15.1	2.0	3 860	176.2	1 270
1997	980	1 680	390	23.0	14.8	2.0	3 850	162.9	1 280
1996	980	1 690	390	23.2	15.1	2.0	3 870	162.9	1 280
1995	970	1 680	390	22.8	15.2	2.0	3 800	158.5	1 290
1994	1 000	1 700	400	23.2	15.4	2.0	3 890	161.6	1 310
1993	970	1 690	400	23.3	15.5	2.0	3 850	161.1	1 310
1992	990	1 700	400	23.4	15.8	2.0	3 860	160.7	1 320
1991	970	1 670	400	23.0	15.4	2.0	3 810	156.9	1 300
1990	980	1 670	390	22.7	15.3	2.0	3 760	147.9	1 300
1989	950	1 640	380	22.0	14.9	1.9	3 730	146.0	1 270
1988	960	1 650	380	21.9	14.9	1.9	3 740	145.0	1 260
1987	960	1 630	380	21.4	14.6	1.9	3 700	143.6	1 290
1986	970	1 620	380	21.1	14.8	1.9	3 760	143.0	1 300
1985	960	1 600	370	20.9	14.5	1.9	3 700	140.7	1 290
1984	930	1 560	360	20.0	14.2	1.8	3 610	137.3	1 270
1983	920	1 530	350	19.9	14.0	1.8	3 590	137.1	1 240
1982	910	1 510	350	17.5	13.8	1.8	3 520	134.5	1 230
1981	900	1 510	340	17.3	13.8	1.8	3 510	132.0	1 220
1980	910	1 510	340	17.2	13.7	1.7	3 550	131.9	1 240
1979	920	1 530	350	17.3	13.8	1.8	3 590	134.0	1 270
1978	920	1 510	340	16.8	13.7	1.7	3 510	135.0	1 270
1977	930	1 530	350	17.3	14.0	1.8	3 590	133.5	1 280
1976	930	1 540	350	17.4	14.0	1.8	3 650	139.5	1 290
1975	920	1 490	340	16.9	13.6	1.7	3 580	136.2	1 240
1974	940	1 540	340	16.7	13.8	1.7	3 590	117.4	1 260
1973	970	1 540	350	16.4	12.4	1.7	3 650	122.8	1 260
1972	960	1 560	350	16.2	12.7	1.7	3 660	126.3	1 280
1971	970	1 560	340	16.1	12.8	1.7	3 670	125.4	1 280
1970	960	1 550	340	15.9	12.7	1.7	3 670	124.4	1 260
1969	910	1 490	330	15.6	12.2	1.6	3 480	128.1	1 320
1968	900	1 480	330	15.5	12.3	1.6	3 510	130.1	1 310
1967	900	1 470	330	15.3	12.2	1.6	3 450	128.8	1 280
1966	910	1 470	330	14.7	11.9	1.6	3 470	126.4	1 250
1965	910	1 460	320	14.6	11.8	1.6	3 440	126.0	1 250
1964	920	1 470	330	14.8	11.9	1.6	3 490	127.2	1 270
1963	920	1 460	330	14.8	11.8	1.6	3 520	125.4	1 250
1962	920	1 460	330	14.8	11.6	1.6	3 530	129.6	1 270
1961	920	1 460	330	14.7	11.7	1.6	3 560	129.4	1 230
1960	930	1 470	330	14.6	11.6	1.6	3 570	128.8	1 240
1959	930	1 480	330	14.5	11.7	1.6	3 590	130.2	1 250
1958	940	1 460	330	14.5	11.6	1.6	3 560	129.7	1 230
1957	940	1 480	330	14.5	11.8	1.6	3 640	132.0	1 220
1956	950	1 510	340	14.8	12.2	1.7	3 660	133.6	1 240
1955	950	1 490	330	14.6	12.0	1.7	3 670	135.0	1 230
1954	940	1 480	330	14.6	11.9	1.6	3 640	134.4	1 160
1953	950	1 480	340	14.5	12.0	1.7	3 710	136.9	1 160
1952	980	1 500	340	14.5	11.7	1.7	3 710	138.6	1 190
1951	970	1 490	350	14.6	11.7	1.7	3 770	138.7	1 170
1950	980	1 510	350	15.0	11.9	1.8	3 760	141.0	1 170
1949	970	1 500	360	14.9	11.8	1.8	3 820	138.7	1 150
1948	980	1 510	360	14.8	12.0	1.7	3 820	139.6	1 140
1947	1 030	1 580	380	15.4	12.6	1.9	4 050	142.9	1 200
1946	1 080	1 670	390	16.3	12.9	1.9	4 220	151.7	1 220
1945	1 070	1 670	400	16.4	13.3	1.9	4 280	150.3	1 170
1944	1 020	1 630	400	16.2	13.2	2.0	4 270	141.6	1 170
1943	990	1 610	390	14.8	12.8	1.9	4 070	145.4	1 140
1942	970	1 540	390	14.2	12.5	1.9	4 040	140.6	1 140
1941	920	1 480	370	13.3	12.0	1.9	3 940	141.7	1 110

[1]Data are based on U.S. Department of Agriculture's Economic Research Service (ERS) estimates of per capita quantities of food available for consumption, on imputed consumption data for foods no longer reported by ERS, and on estimates from USDA's Center for Nutrition Policy and Promotion (CNPP) of quantities of produce from home gardens.

Table 18-1. Nutrients and Other Food Components of U.S. Food Supply, per Capita per Day,[1] 1909–2004—*Continued*

Year	Minerals								
	Calcium	Phosphorus	Magnesium	Iron	Zinc	Copper	Potassium	Selenium	Sodium
	Milligrams							Micrograms	Milligrams
1940	900	1 460	370	12.9	11.8	1.8	3 870	145.0	1 110
1939	890	1 440	370	13.0	11.8	1.8	3 860	142.7	1 070
1938	880	1 410	360	12.7	11.5	1.8	3 820	142.1	1 040
1937	870	1 410	360	12.5	11.5	1.8	3 760	142.2	1 020
1936	860	1 420	370	13.0	11.6	1.8	3 800	142.8	1 010
1935	850	1 380	360	12.6	11.2	1.8	3 790	138.7	970
1934	830	1 390	360	12.7	11.6	1.8	3 740	138.0	1 010
1933	820	1 400	350	12.4	11.2	1.8	3 670	139.6	1 010
1932	830	1 420	360	12.5	11.4	1.8	3 710	144.7	1 010
1931	830	1 430	370	12.9	11.5	1.9	3 790	145.4	1 030
1930	840	1 430	370	12.9	11.7	1.8	3 750	147.2	1 040
1929	850	1 470	380	13.1	11.9	1.9	3 910	148.5	1 050
1928	830	1 450	370	13.0	11.8	1.9	3 820	151.6	1 030
1927	830	1 460	370	13.2	12.0	1.9	3 790	151.0	1 030
1926	820	1 440	360	13.0	12.0	1.9	3 750	151.1	1 030
1925	810	1 440	360	13.0	12.0	1.9	3 820	149.8	1 030
1924	810	1 450	370	13.2	12.3	1.9	3 860	150.6	1 030
1923	790	1 450	370	13.3	12.4	1.9	3 930	152.8	1 020
1922	790	1 410	360	12.9	12.1	1.8	3 750	149.9	960
1921	770	1 370	350	12.6	11.9	1.8	3 700	144.3	940
1920	790	1 410	360	12.9	12.2	1.8	3 750	150.9	960
1919	750	1 420	370	13.6	12.5	2.0	3 780	152.7	970
1918	790	1 460	390	14.2	12.9	2.0	3 980	149.2	910
1917	720	1 400	380	13.7	12.4	1.9	3 770	151.1	860
1916	690	1 370	360	13.0	12.2	1.8	3 610	154.2	900
1915	710	1 400	370	13.3	12.3	1.9	3 860	157.4	900
1914	730	1 410	360	13.2	12.5	1.9	3 770	158.8	910
1913	760	1 450	370	13.5	12.9	1.9	3 940	163.4	930
1912	780	1 480	390	13.8	13.1	2.0	4 040	164.2	940
1911	730	1 450	370	13.7	13.0	1.9	3 830	166.4	940
1910	750	1 470	390	14.1	13.3	2.0	4 040	164.4	930
1909	760	1 500	390	14.2	13.7	2.0	4 060	168.5	940

Source: U.S. Department of Agriculture, Economic Research Service and Center for Nutrition Policy Promotion.

[1]Data are based on U.S. Department of Agriculture's Economic Research Service (ERS) estimates of per capita quantities of food available for consumption, on imputed consumption data for foods no longer reported by ERS, and on estimates from USDA's Center for Nutrition Policy and Promotion (CNPP) of quantities of produce from home gardens.

Table 18-2. Per Capita Consumption of Selected Beverages, by Type, 1966–2004

(Gallons)

								Non-alcoholic		
		Milk						Carbonated soft drinks		
Year	Total	Total	Whole	Other	Tea	Coffee	Bottled water	Total	Diet	Regular
2004	137.5	21.0	7.3	13.7	7.3	24.6	23.2	52.3	15.8	36.5
2003	135.8	21.3	7.6	13.7	7.5	24.2	21.6	52.5	15.0	37.5
2002	134.2	21.7	7.7	13.9	7.8	23.6	20.1	52.8	14.4	38.4
2001	134.5	21.8	7.8	14.0	8.2	24.2	18.2	52.9	13.9	39.0
2000	135.4	22.2	8.1	14.2	7.8	26.3	16.7	53.2	13.8	39.4
1999	139.6	22.9	8.2	14.8	8.2	25.1	16.4	49.7	11.4	38.2
1998	135.4	23.0	8.1	14.9	8.3	23.9	15.0	47.9	11.0	36.8
1997	133.0	23.4	8.3	15.2	7.2	23.3	13.9	46.8	10.6	36.2
1996	130.6	23.8	8.5	15.3	7.6	22.1	13.0	46.6	10.6	36.0
1995	130.6	23.6	8.6	15.0	7.9	20.2	11.6	50.6	13.8	36.8
1994	129.2	24.3	9.0	15.3	8.1	20.8	11.3	48.4	11.3	37.1
1993	131.1	24.4	9.2	15.2	8.3	23.3	10.3	48.6	11.4	37.2
1992	132.3	25.1	9.7	15.4	8.0	25.8	9.7	48.2	11.5	36.7
1991	130.0	25.5	10.1	15.4	7.4	26.7	8.0	47.8	11.6	36.2
1990	128.2	25.3	10.5	14.8	6.9	26.8	8.8	47.1	14.0	33.1
1989	124.9	26.0	11.4	14.7	6.9	26.2	7.4	45.4	10.7	34.7
1988	124.0	26.1	12.4	13.7	7.0	25.6	6.5	44.7	10.1	34.5
1987	121.0	26.1	13.0	13.1	6.9	26.7	5.7	41.9	9.4	32.4
1986	. . .	26.5	13.5	13.0	7.1	27.5	5.0	35.8	7.6	28.2
1985	114.6	26.1	14.3	11.8	7.1	27.4	5.1	41.2	10.4	30.8
1984	. . .	26.4	14.8	11.6	7.1	26.8	4.0	35.9	6.6	29.3
1983	. . .	26.3	15.2	11.1	7.0	26.3	3.4	35.2	6.0	29.3
1982	. . .	26.4	15.5	10.9	6.9	25.9	3.0	35.3	5.5	29.8
1981	. . .	27.1	16.3	10.8	7.2	26.0	2.7	35.4	5.3	30.0
1980	104.9	27.1	17.0	10.1	7.3	26.7	2.7	33.6	5.1	29.9
1979	. . .	28.2	18.0	10.2	6.9	29.3	2.2	34.7	4.9	29.8
1978	. . .	28.6	18.7	9.8	7.2	27.3	1.9	34.2	4.6	29.5
1977	. . .	29.0	19.5	9.5	7.5	24.5	1.3	33.0	4.3	28.7
1976	. . .	29.3	20.4	9.0	7.7	32.5	1.2	30.8	3.8	27.0
1975	. . .	29.5	21.1	8.4	7.5	31.4	. . .	28.2	3.2	25.0
1974	. . .	29.5	21.7	7.7	7.5	33.2	. . .	27.6	2.9	24.7
1973	. . .	30.5	23.0	7.5	7.4	33.3	. . .	27.6	2.7	25.0
1972	. . .	31.0	24.1	6.9	7.3	33.6	. . .	26.2	2.3	23.9
1971	. . .	31.3	25.0	6.3	7.2	32.2	. . .	25.5	2.2	23.3
1970	. . .	31.3	25.5	5.8	6.8	33.4	. . .	24.3	2.1	22.2
1969	. . .	31.1	25.6	5.5	6.8	34.6	. . .	23.5	2.1	21.5
1968	. . .	31.3	26.4	4.9	6.8	36.5	. . .	23.0	2.0	21.0
1967	. . .	31.4	27.1	4.2	6.6	36.3	. . .	21.0	1.8	19.2
1966	. . .	33.0	29.1	3.9	6.5	35.7	. . .	20.3	1.6	18.7

Source: U.S. Department of Agriculture, Economic Research Service. U.S. Census Bureau.
Note: Consumption represents the residual after exports; non-food use and ending stocks are subtracted from the sum of beginning stocks, domestic production, and imports. Per capita consumption uses U.S. resident population, July 1 for all beverages except coffee, tea, and fruit juices which use U.S. total population, July 1.
[1]Beginning in 1983, includes wine coolers.
. . . = Not available.

Table 18-2. Per Capita Consumption of Selected Beverages, by Type, 1966–2004—*Continued*

(Gallons)

Fruit juices	Fruit drinks, cocktails, and ades	Canned iced tea	Vegetable juices	Alcoholic			
				Total	Beer	Wine[1]	Distilled spirits
8.9	...	...	0.2	25.2	21.6	2.3	1.4
8.5	...	...	0.2	25.1	21.6	2.2	1.3
7.9	...	...	0.2	25.2	21.8	2.1	1.3
9.0	...	...	0.2	25.0	21.8	2.0	1.3
8.9	...	...	0.2	24.9	21.7	2.0	1.3
8.5	7.7	0.7	0.3	25.0	21.8	2.0	1.2
8.8	7.7	0.7	0.3	24.8	21.7	1.9	1.2
9.0	8.2	0.8	0.3	24.7	21.6	1.9	1.2
8.6	7.9	0.7	0.3	24.8	21.7	1.9	1.2
8.1	7.7	0.7	0.3	24.7	21.8	1.7	1.2
8.1	7.3	0.6	0.3	25.3	22.3	1.7	1.3
8.6	6.9	0.4	0.3	25.5	22.4	1.7	1.3
8.5	6.5	0.2	0.3	25.9	22.7	1.9	1.4
7.4	6.9	0.2	0.3	26.3	23.1	1.8	1.4
6.6	6.3	0.1	0.3	27.5	23.9	2.0	1.5
6.6	5.9	0.1	0.3	27.2	23.6	2.1	1.5
8.2	5.7	0.1	0.3	27.6	23.8	2.3	1.5
7.9	5.4	0.1	0.2	28.0	24.0	2.4	1.6
8.3	...	...	...	28.2	24.1	2.4	1.6
7.6	...	...	...	28.0	23.8	2.4	1.8
7.7	...	...	...	28.1	24.0	2.4	1.8
7.3	...	...	...	28.3	24.2	2.3	1.8
8.4	...	...	...	28.5	24.4	2.2	1.9
6.7	...	...	...	28.8	24.6	2.2	2.0
7.6	...	...	...	28.3	24.3	2.1	2.0
7.2	...	...	...	27.8	23.8	2.0	2.0
6.8	...	...	...	26.9	23.0	2.0	2.0
6.5	...	...	...	26.1	22.4	1.8	2.0
7.0	...	...	...	25.2	21.5	1.7	2.0
6.9	...	...	...	25.0	21.3	1.7	2.0
6.6	...	...	...	24.5	20.9	1.6	2.0
6.0	...	...	...	23.6	20.1	1.6	1.9
6.1	...	...	...	22.8	19.3	1.6	1.9
6.2	...	...	...	22.3	18.9	1.5	1.8
5.7	...	...	...	21.6	18.5	1.3	1.8
...	...	...	...	20.8	17.8	1.2	1.8
...	...	...	...	20.1	17.3	1.1	1.7
...	...	...	...	19.4	16.8	1.0	1.6
...	...	...	...	19.0	16.5	1.0	1.6

Table 18-3. Per Capita Consumption of Major Food Commodities, 1985–2004

(Pounds, retail weight, except as indicated.)

Commodity	1985	1990	1995	2000	2001	2002	2003	2003	2004
Red meat, total (boneless, trimmed weight)[1,2]	124.9	112.2	113.6	113.7	111.4	114.0	111.9	111.6	112.0
Beef	74.6	63.9	63.5	64.5	63.1	64.5	62.0	61.9	62.9
Veal	1.5	0.9	0.8	0.5	0.5	0.5	0.5	0.5	0.4
Lamb and mutton	1.1	1.0	0.9	0.8	0.8	0.9	0.8	0.8	0.8
Pork	47.7	46.4	48.4	47.8	46.9	48.2	48.5	48.4	47.8
Poultry (boneless, trimmed weight)[2]	45.6	56.2	62.1	67.9	67.8	70.7	71.2	71.2	72.7
Chicken	36.4	42.4	48.2	54.2	54.0	56.8	57.5	57.5	59.2
Turkey	9.1	13.8	13.9	13.7	13.8	14.0	13.7	13.7	13.4
Fish and shellfish (boneless, trimmed weight)	15.0	14.9	14.8	15.2	14.7	15.6	16.3	16.3	16.5
Eggs (number)	255	234	232	251	252	255	253	254	256
Shell (number)	216	186	172	178	180	180	181	182	180
Processed (number)	39	48	60	73	72	75	72	72	76
Dairy products, total[3]	593.6	568.0	576.2	592.2	586.5	585.4	593.9	588.8	591.8
Fluid milk products[4] (gallons)	27.1	26.2	24.6	23.2	22.8	22.7	22.5	22.5	22.3
Beverage milks (gallons)	26.7	25.7	23.9	22.5	22.0	21.9	21.6	21.6	21.2
Plain whole milk (gallons)	13.9	10.2	8.3	7.7	7.4	7.3	7.2	7.2	6.9
Plain reduced fat milk (2%) (gallons)	7.9	9.1	8.0	7.1	7.0	7.0	6.9	6.9	6.9
Reduced fat milk (1%) and skim milk (gallons)	3.2	4.9	6.1	6.1	5.9	5.8	5.6	5.6	5.5
Flavored whole milk (gallons)	0.4	0.3	0.3	0.4	0.4	0.4	0.4	0.4	0.3
Flavored milks other than whole (gallons)	0.7	0.8	0.8	1.0	1.0	1.2	1.2	1.2	1.4
Buttermilk (gallons)	0.5	0.4	0.3	0.3	0.2	0.2	0.2	0.2	0.2
Yogurt (excluding frozen) (1/2 pints)	7.3	7.8	11.4	12.0	13.0	13.7	15.2	15.2	17.0
Fluid cream products[5] (1/2 pints)	13.5	14.3	15.6	18.3	20.0	19.7	22.2	22.2	23.5
Cream[6] (1/2 pints)	8.2	8.7	9.4	11.6	12.8	12.1	13.9	13.9	14.8
Sour cream and dips (1/2 pints)	4.3	4.7	5.4	6.1	6.5	6.7	7.5	7.5	7.9
Condensed and evaporated milks	7.5	7.9	6.8	5.8	5.4	6.0	5.6	5.9	5.5
Whole milk	3.7	3.1	2.3	2.0	2.0	2.3	2.5	2.6	2.2
Skim milk	3.8	4.8	4.5	3.8	3.5	3.7	3.1	3.3	3.2
Cheese[7]	22.5	24.6	26.9	29.8	30.0	30.5	30.6	30.4	31.3
American[8]	12.2	11.1	11.7	12.7	12.8	12.8	12.7	12.5	12.9
Cheddar	9.8	9.0	9.0	9.7	9.9	9.6	9.5	9.2	10.3
Italian[8]	6.5	9.0	10.3	12.1	12.4	12.5	12.3	12.6	12.9
Mozzarella	4.6	6.9	8.0	9.3	9.7	9.7	9.6	9.6	9.9
Other[8]	3.9	4.3	5.0	4.8	5.0	4.8	5.2	5.1	5.3
Swiss	1.3	1.4	1.1	1.0	1.2	1.1	1.1	1.2	1.2
Cream and Neufchatel	1.2	1.6	2.2	2.3	2.4	2.3	2.4	2.4	2.3
Cottage cheese, total	4.0	3.4	2.7	2.6	2.6	2.6	2.7	2.7	2.6
Lowfat	1.0	1.2	1.2	1.3	1.3	1.3	1.3	1.3	1.4
Frozen dairy products	27.9	28.5	29.0	28.0	27.0	26.6	26.7	27.1	26.4
Ice cream	18.1	15.8	15.5	16.7	16.3	16.7	16.7	16.4	15.4
Lowfat ice cream	6.9	7.7	7.4	7.3	7.3	6.5	6.7	7.5	7.8
Sherbet	1.3	1.2	1.3	1.2	1.2	1.3	1.3	1.2	1.2
Frozen yogurt	...	2.8	3.4	2.0	1.5	1.5	1.4	1.4	1.8
Fats and oils:									
Total, fat content only	64.1	62.3	64.2	82.3	84.0	88.6	85.8	88.0	87.5
Butter (product weight)	4.9	4.4	4.4	4.5	4.4	4.4	4.2	4.5	4.6
Margarine (product weight)	10.8	10.9	9.1	7.5	7.0	6.5	6.2	5.3	5.3
Lard (direct use)	1.6	0.9	0.4	0.8	1.1	1.3	2.4	1.3	0.7
Edible beef tallow (direct use)	2.0	0.6	2.7	4.0	3.1	3.4	3.8	3.8	4.0
Shortening	22.9	22.2	22.2	31.6	32.6	33.3	32.5	32.8	32.6
Salad and cooking oils	23.5	25.2	26.5	34.8	36.5	40.3	37.3	40.8	40.8
Other edible fats and oils	1.6	1.2	1.6	1.5	1.5	1.5	1.5	1.5	1.5
Flour and cereal products[9]	156.7	181.0	188.7	199.2	195.0	191.7	194.0	193.1	191.5
Wheat flour	124.6	135.9	140.0	146.3	141.0	136.8	137.9	136.7	134.3
Rice, milled	9.2	15.8	17.1	18.9	19.3	19.5	20.1	20.3	20.4
Corn products	17.2	21.4	24.9	28.4	29.0	29.7	30.3	30.3	30.9
Oat products	4.0	6.5	5.5	4.4	4.5	4.5	4.6	4.7	4.7
Caloric sweeteners, total[10]	126.2	132.4	144.1	148.8	147.0	146.1	141.7	141.4	141.0
Sugar, refined cane and beet	62.7	64.4	64.9	65.5	64.5	63.2	61.1	60.9	61.5
Corn sweeteners[11]	62.2	66.8	77.9	81.8	81.3	81.5	79.2	79.1	78.1
High fructose corn syrup	45.2	49.6	57.6	62.6	62.5	62.8	60.9	60.8	59.2
Other:									
Cocoa beans	4.6	5.4	4.5	5.9	5.6	4.8	5.7	5.3	6.0
Coffee (green beans)	10.5	10.3	7.9	10.3	9.5	9.2	9.5	9.5	9.6
Peanuts (shelled)	6.5	6.1	5.7	5.9	5.9	5.9	6.3	6.4	6.7
Tree nuts (shelled)	2.5	2.5	1.9	2.6	2.9	3.2	2.9	3.5	3.6

Source: U.S. Census Bureau. *Statistical Abstract of the United States: 2007.* U.S. Department of Agriculture, Economic Research Service.
Note: Consumption represents the residual after exports, nonfood use and ending stocks are subtracted from the sum of beginning stocks, domestic production, and imports. Based on Census Bureau estimated population.
[1]Excludes edible offals.
[2]Excludes shipments to Puerto Rico and the other U.S. possessions.
[3]Milk-equivalent, milkfat basis. Includes butter.
[4]Fluid milk figures are aggregates of commercial sales and milk produced and consumed on farms.
[5]Includes eggnog, not shown separately.
[6]Heavy cream, light cream, and half and half.
[7]Excludes full skim American, cottage, pot, and baker's cheese.
[8]Includes other cheeses not shown separately.
[9]Includes rye flour and barley products not shown separately. Excludes quantities used in alcoholic beverages.
[10]Dry weight. Includes edible syrups (maple, molasses, etc.) and honey not shown separately.
[11]Includes glucose and dextrose not shown separately.
. . . = Not available.

Table 18-4. Per Capita Utilization of Selected Commercially Produced Fruits and Vegetables, 1985–2004

(Pounds, farm weight.)

Commodity	1985	1990	1995	2000	2001	2002	2003	2004
Fruits and vegetables, total[1]	632.2	660.2	692.5	711.7	685.3	685.4	704.0	694.3
Fruits, total	271.8	274.2	284.8	288.7	273.0	273.7	282.2	271.4
Fresh fruits	110.7	117.0	123.5	128.7	126.1	127.0	128.3	127.1
Noncitrus	89.2	95.6	99.6	105.2	102.1	103.7	104.4	104.4
Apples	17.4	19.8	18.9	17.6	15.8	16.2	17.1	18.8
Bananas	23.5	24.3	27.1	28.4	26.6	26.8	26.2	25.8
Cantaloupes	8.5	9.2	9.0	11.1	11.2	11.1	10.8	9.5
Grapes	6.9	7.9	7.5	7.5	7.5	8.5	7.7	7.9
Peaches and nectarines	5.5	5.5	5.3	5.3	5.2	5.2	5.2	5.1
Pears	2.8	3.3	3.4	3.4	3.3	3.1	3.1	3.1
Pineapples	1.5	2.0	1.9	3.2	3.2	3.8	4.4	4.4
Plums and prunes	1.4	1.5	0.9	1.2	1.3	1.3	1.2	1.1
Strawberries	3.0	3.2	4.1	4.9	4.2	4.6	5.3	5.5
Watermelons	13.5	13.3	15.2	13.8	15.0	14.0	13.6	13.0
Other[2]	5.3	5.4	6.3	8.7	9.0	9.1	9.8	10.3
Fresh citrus	21.5	21.4	23.8	23.5	23.9	23.4	23.9	22.7
Oranges	11.6	12.4	11.8	11.7	11.9	11.7	11.9	10.8
Grapefruit	5.5	4.4	6.0	5.1	4.8	4.6	4.1	4.1
Other[3]	4.4	4.6	6.0	6.7	7.2	7.0	8.0	7.8
Processed fruits	161.1	157.2	161.4	160.0	146.9	146.6	153.9	144.3
Frozen fruits[4]	3.5	4.3	5.2	4.2	7.0	4.1	5.4	5.0
Dried fruits[5]	12.9	12.2	12.8	10.5	10.3	10.5	10.2	9.8
Canned fruits[6]	21.1	21.2	17.5	17.7	17.8	16.9	17.4	15.8
Fruit juices[7]	123.3	119.3	125.7	127.2	111.5	114.9	120.4	113.4
Vegetables, total	360.4	386.0	407.6	423.0	412.3	411.8	421.8	422.8
Fresh vegetables	158.6	170.2	180.9	198.7	195.7	194.7	199.8	204.6
Asparagus (all uses)	0.5	0.6	0.6	1.0	0.9	1.0	1.0	1.0
Broccoli	2.6	3.4	4.3	5.9	5.4	5.4	5.5	5.9
Cabbage	8.7	8.3	8.1	8.9	8.8	8.3	7.5	8.3
Carrots	6.5	8.3	11.2	9.2	9.4	8.4	8.8	8.9
Cauliflower	1.8	2.2	1.6	1.7	1.5	1.4	1.6	1.8
Celery (all uses)	6.9	7.2	6.9	6.3	6.4	6.3	6.3	6.0
Corn	6.4	6.7	7.8	9.0	9.2	9.0	9.5	9.6
Cucumbers	4.4	4.7	5.6	6.4	6.3	6.5	6.1	6.3
Head lettuce	23.7	27.7	22.2	23.5	23.0	22.5	22.2	22.5
Mushrooms	1.8	2.0	2.0	2.6	2.6	2.6	2.6	2.6
Onions	13.6	15.1	17.8	18.9	18.5	19.3	19.5	21.7
Snap beans	1.3	1.1	1.6	2.0	2.2	2.1	2.0	1.9
Bell peppers (all uses)	3.8	4.5	6.2	7.0	6.9	6.8	6.9	7.1
Potatoes	46.3	46.7	49.2	47.1	46.6	44.3	47.2	46.5
Sweet potatoes (all uses)	5.3	4.4	4.2	4.2	4.4	3.8	4.7	4.7
Tomatoes	14.9	15.5	16.8	19.0	19.2	20.3	19.5	19.3
Other fresh vegetables[8]	10.2	11.8	14.7	26.1	24.6	26.8	29.0	30.6
Processed vegetables	201.9	215.8	226.7	224.3	216.6	217.0	222.0	218.2
Vegetables for freezing[9]	64.5	66.8	78.8	79.3	78.6	76.7	78.3	77.6
Vegetables for canning[10]	99.4	110.8	108.5	103.4	96.9	100.5	101.7	102.4
Vegetables for dehydrating[11]	12.8	14.6	14.5	17.3	15.8	15.8	17.3	14.9
Potatoes for chips	17.6	16.4	16.4	15.9	17.6	16.5	17.3	16.5
Pulses[12]	7.6	7.2	8.4	8.5	7.8	7.5	7.3	6.7

Source: U.S. Census Bureau. *Statistical Abstract of the United States: 2007.* U.S. Department of Agriculture, Economic Research Service.
Note: Domestic food use of fresh fruits and vegetables reflects the fresh-market share of commodity production plus imports and minus exports.
[1]Excludes wine grapes.
[2]Apricots, avocados, cherries, cranberries, kiwifruit, mangoes, papayas, and honeydew melons.
[3]Lemons, limes, tangerines, and tangelos.
[4]Apples, apricots, blackberries, blueberries, boysenberries, cherries, loganberries, peaches, plums, prunes, raspberries, and strawberries.
[5]Apples, apricots, dates, figs, peaches, pears, prunes, and raisins.
[6]Apples, apricots, cherries, olives, peaches, pears, pineapples, plums, and prunes.
[7]Apple, cranberry, grape, grapefruit, lemon, lime, orange, pineapple, and prunes.
[8]Artichokes, Brussels sprouts, eggplant, escarole, endive, garlic, romaine, leaf lettuce, radishes, spinach, and squash. Beginning 2000 includes collard greens, kale, mustard greens, okra, pumpkin, and turnip greens.
[9]Asparagus, snap beans, lima beans, broccoli, carrots, cauliflower, sweet corn, green peas, potatoes, spinach, and miscellaneous vegetables.
[10]Asparagus, snap beans, beets, cabbage, carrots, chili peppers, sweet corn, cucumbers for pickling, green peas, lima beans, mushrooms, spinach, and tomatoes.
[11]Onions and potatoes.
[12]Dry peas, lentils, and dry edible beans.

BOX 18 ▪ Food Insecurity in the United States

In 2005, 12 million U.S. households (11.0%) had trouble providing adequate food for all its members at some point during the year. Of these food-insecure households, 4.4 million experienced very low food security at some point during the year, meaning that at least one member of the household had to reduce the amount of food in his or her diet because of a lack of resources. The U.S. Department of Agriculture (USDA) estimates that on any given day in 2005, between 531,000 and 797,000 households experienced very low food security.

Food insecurity was below the national average for the elderly population at 6.0%, but well above the average for households with annual incomes below the national poverty line (36%), which in 2005 was set at $19,806 for a family of four, and single parent families headed by a woman (30.8%) or a man (17.9%).

Approximately 56% of food-insecure households participated in one of the three largest federal food assistance programs during the USDA's one-month food security survey. These programs are the Federal Food Stamp Program, the National School Lunch Program and the Special Supplemental Nutrition Program for Women, Infants, and Children.

Of the 38 million people who were eligible to participate in the food stamp program in an average month of 2005, only 25 million received benefits. The National School Lunch Program provided free or low cost lunches to 30.1 million children in 2006. In 1998 Congress allocated additional monies to subsidize an after-school snack program. The Special Supplemental Nutrition Program from Women, Infants, and Children served 7.9 million people each month in 2004, including four million children, 2 million infants, and 1.9 million women who were pregnant or postpartum.

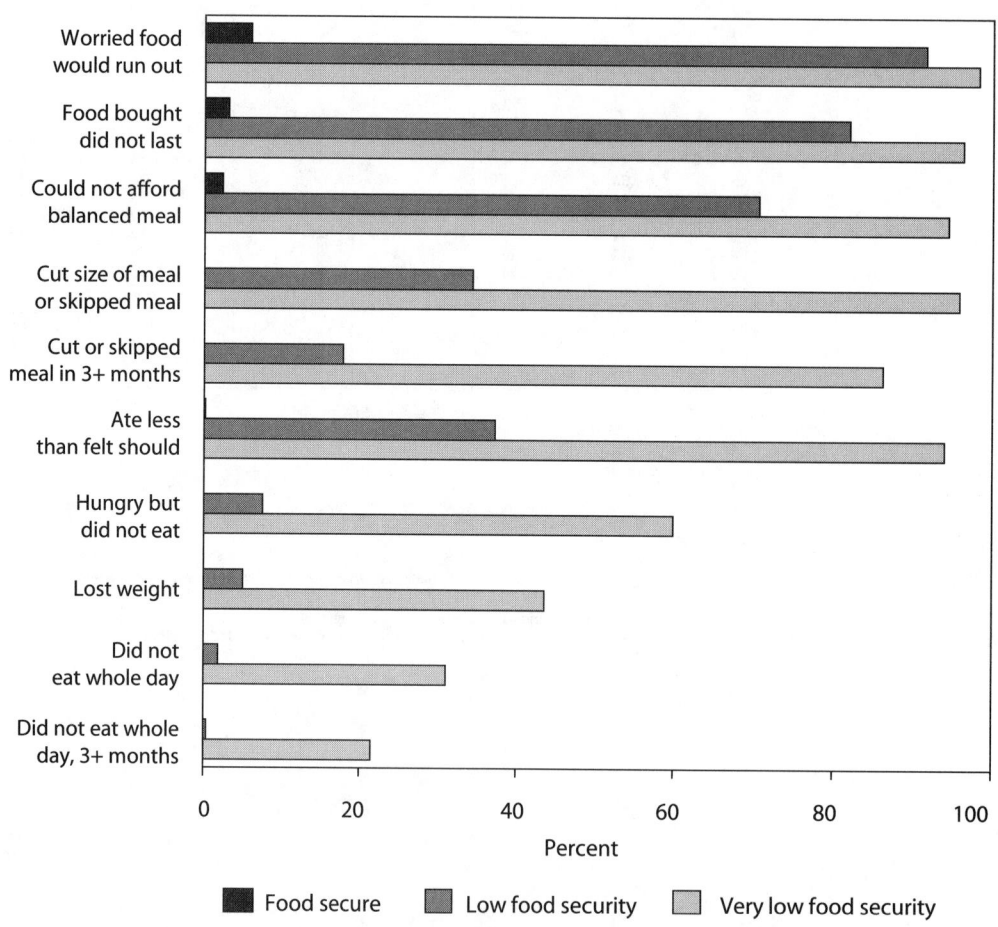

Percentage of Households Reporting Indicators of Adult Food Insecurity, by Food Security Status, 2005

Source: Calculated by ERS using data from the December 2005 Current Population Survey food Security Supplement.

Sources:

U.S. Department of Agriculture, Economic Research Service. *Household Food Security in the United States, 2005.* November 2006. www.ers.usda.gov/publications/err29

U.S. Department of Agriculture, Food and Nutrition Service. Food Stamp Program Participation Rates: 2005 Summary. June 2007. http://www.fns.usda.gov/oane/MENU/Published/FSP/FILES/Participation/Trends1999-2005Sum.pdf

U.S. Department of Agriculture, Food and Nutrition Service. National School Lunch Program Fact Sheet. http://www.fns.usda.gov/cnd/Lunch/AboutLunch/NSLPFactSheet.pdf

U.S. Department of Agriculture, Food and Nutrition Service. The Special Supplemental Nutrition Program for Women, Infants, and Children Program Fact Sheet.

U.S. Department of Agriculture, Food and Nutrition Service. The School Breakfast Program Fact Sheet. http://www.fns.usda.gov/cnd/breakfast/AboutBFast/SBPFactSheet.pdf

Food Research and Action Center. *Hunger Doesn't Take a Summer Vacation: Summer Nutrition Status Report 2007.* July 2007. http://www.frac.org/pdf/2007summer.pdf

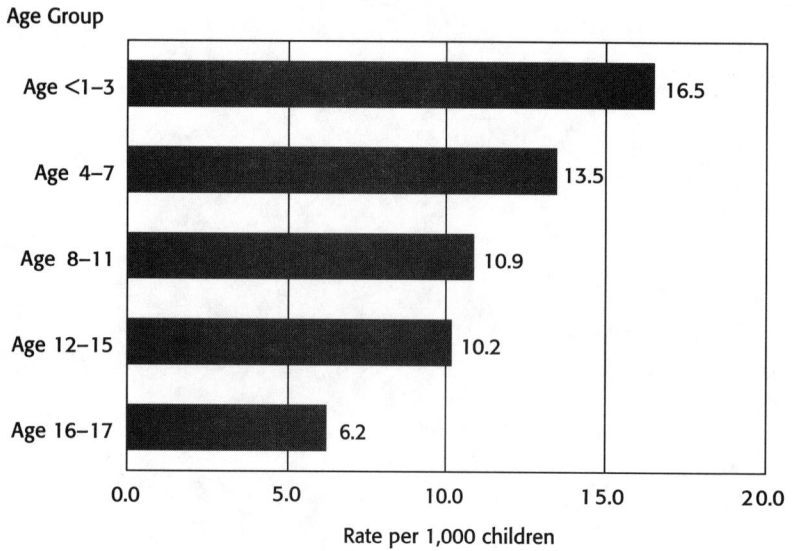

Victimization Rates by Age Group, 2005

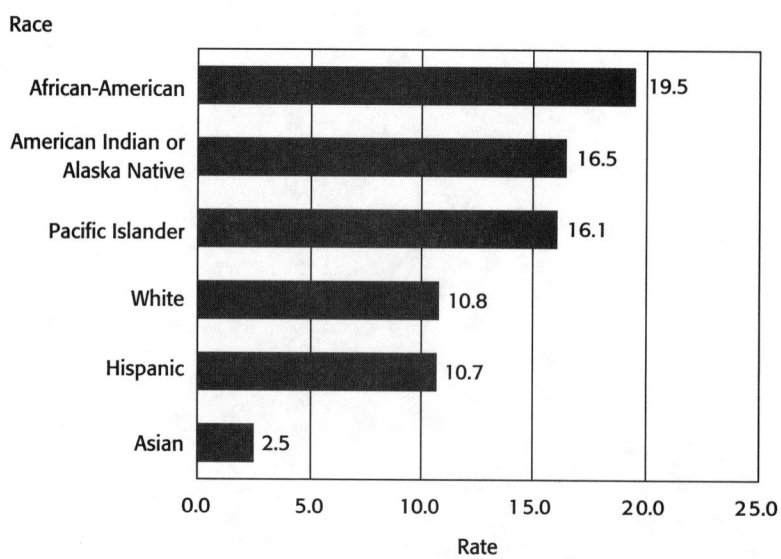

Race and Ethnicity of Victims, 2005

CHAPTER **19**

Social Welfare

HIGHLIGHTS

1 The United States adopted the concepts of Social Security and Welfare much later than other Western democracies. Throughout the nineteenth century, social welfare activities remained a local responsibility. Following public support of education in Massachusetts and other states, state intervention was extended to health programs, care of blind and orphaned people, worker's compensation, and retirement pensions. It was not until the Social Security Act of 1935 that the federal government participated in any major way in permanent welfare programs for the general population. The act established a national system of old age insurance and provided federal grants-in-aid to the states for public assistance, maternal and child health and welfare services, general public health services, and vocational rehabilitation services. The Social Security Administration administers many of these programs, and its annual and monthly reports carry an enormous volume of statistical data.

2 Of 111.3 million households in the United States in 2002, 6.3 million received food stamps, 7.9 million received school lunches, 5.1 million received public housing, and 16.8 million received Medicaid.

3 In 2005, 195.8 million people were covered by Social Security, of which 30.1 million were over the age of 65. The annual maximum taxable earnings were $90,000.

4 In 2001 there were 733,500 pension plans, of which 686,600 were defined contribution plans and 46,900 defined benefit plans. The total number of participants was 106.6 million.

5 In 2005, 19.656 million people received work disability benefits, representing approximately 10 percent of the labor force.

6 In 2005, 25.682 million people participated in federal food stamp programs.

7 Of the 13,383,000 custodial parents who were awarded child support in 2001, 1,804,000 did not receive any payments, and 3,131,000 custodial parents live below poverty level.

8 In 2005, 28.8 percent of the population did some volunteer work. More women volunteer than men (32.4 percent vs. 25.0 percent), and more Whites volunteer than Blacks (30.4 percent vs. 22.1 percent). Slightly more than one-third of voluntary work is church related.

9 In 2004, Americans donated $248.5 billion to charity, of which $187.9 billion came from individuals. The majority of philanthropy is earmarked for religion, health, education, human service and arts, culture, and humanities. The Census Bureau does not distinguish between religious organizations and religion affiliated charities. Religion itself is considered a charity, even if it does not engage in what is generally considered charitable work.

10 There were 67,736 foundations in the United States in 2004 of which 233 had assets of more than $250 million, 394 had assets between $100 million and $250 million, and 603 had assets between $50 million and $100 million.

11 In 2005, only 26.3 percent of America's children between 3 and 5 years of age were in childcare arrangements in the parental home: 22.6 percent were in the care of relatives; 11.6 percent in the care of babysitters other than relatives; and 57.2 percent in organized childcare facilities.

12 In 2005, there were 105,444 licensed childcare centers and 213,966 licensed family childcare providers.

13 In 2003, there were 523,000 children in foster care. Of these 119,000 are waiting to be adopted. That same year, 50,000 children were adopted from foster care. There are slightly more boys than girls at 274,820 and 248,150 respectively.

14 The five largest private foundations are the Bill and Melinda Gates Foundation at $31 billion, which is set to increase dramatically with the donation of Warren Buffet, The Ford Foundation ($11.6 billion), J. Paul Getty Trust ($9.6 billion), The Robert Wood Johnson Foundation ($9 billion), and the Lilly Endowment ($8.6 billion).

Table 19-1. Government Transfer Payments to Individuals—Summary, 1958–2004

(Billions of dollars.)

Year	Transfer payments, total	Retirement and disability insurance benefits	Medical payments	Income maintenance benefits	Unemployment insurance benefits	Veterans benefits	Federal education and training payments[1]	Other[2]
2004	1 361.7	517.8	609.0	141.5	37.1	33.8	14.8	7.5
2003	1 282.5	493.9	555.3	131.2	53.6	31.6	13.9	3.0
2002	1 220.0	474.9	525.4	119.7	53.7	29.3	14.5	2.4
2001	1 117.2	450.4	482.5	109.4	32.2	26.5	13.1	3.1
2000	1 018.1	424.8	427.7	106.6	20.7	24.9	11.0	2.4
1999	966.5	402.5	401.1	104.8	20.8	24.1	11.4	1.9
1998	932.6	391.8	383.7	101.1	19.9	23.2	11.2	1.8
1997	912.8	379.3	377.3	100.5	20.3	22.2	11.5	1.6
1996	883.1	364.9	361.7	102.6	22.4	21.4	8.6	1.6
1995	840.0	350.3	336.5	100.4	21.8	20.5	9.0	1.4
1994	795.2	335.1	310.7	95.6	24.0	19.7	8.6	1.5
1993	759.9	321.2	283.6	90.3	34.9	19.4	9.1	1.5
1992	715.5	305.0	257.7	84.6	39.7	18.6	8.0	2.0
1991	635.3	286.0	222.8	72.5	26.9	18.1	7.3	1.8
1990	561.5	264.2	188.8	63.5	18.2	17.7	7.3	1.8
1989	508.6	245.9	165.8	56.5	14.5	17.2	7.5	1.1
1988	465.6	231.2	145.5	52.0	13.4	16.7	5.9	0.8
1987	437.3	216.9	135.1	48.1	14.8	16.5	5.3	0.7
1986	418.4	208.4	124.2	46.9	16.6	16.6	5.1	0.6
1985	394.3	197.2	114.1	44.4	15.9	16.6	5.5	0.6
1984	372.4	186.3	105.6	42.8	16.0	16.3	5.2	0.4
1983	362.8	177.1	95.6	41.4	26.4	16.4	5.3	0.6
1982	335.5	165.8	84.6	38.3	25.3	16.3	4.7	0.5
1981	299.7	149.8	74.4	37.6	17.0	15.8	4.9	0.2
1980	263.4	128.8	62.6	34.3	18.7	14.7	4.1	0.2
1979	220.4	111.9	53.2	27.8	10.3	14.2	2.8	0.3
1978	196.7	99.2	46.1	25.0	10.3	13.6	2.3	0.2
1977	184.2	90.5	40.5	24.4	13.3	13.3	1.9	0.2
1976	172.5	81.3	35.7	23.6	16.6	13.8	1.4	0.2
1975	159.4	72.0	30.8	21.5	18.2	14.0	1.0	1.9
1974	125.4	63.0	25.1	17.9	7.0	11.6	0.6	0.2
1973	106.0	55.8	20.7	13.9	4.6	10.2	0.5	0.2
1972	92.1	45.0	17.8	13.4	6.1	9.4	0.5	0.1
1971	82.9	40.2	15.4	12.2	6.2	8.4	0.4	0.1
1970	69.5	34.3	13.2	9.9	4.2	7.5	0.4	0.1
1969	57.1	28.9	11.6	7.3	2.3	6.6	0.3	0.0
1968	51.7	27.0	10.1	6.2	2.2	5.9	0.3	0.0
1967	44.3	23.3	7.6	5.4	2.2	5.5	0.3	0.0
1966	36.5	21.8	3.0	4.7	1.9	4.8	0.2	0.0
1965	33.1	19.9	1.5	4.3	2.4	4.8	0.2	0.0
1964	30.7	17.8	1.3	4.1	2.8	4.6	0.1	0.0
1963	29.8	17.0	1.1	3.9	3.1	4.7	0.1	0.0
1962	28.4	15.9	.9	3.7	3.2	4.6	0.1	0.0
1961	27.7	14.2	.7	3.6	4.4	4.9	0.0	0.0
1960	24.1	12.6	.5	3.4	3.1	4.5	0.0	0.0
1959	22.7	11.5	.5	3.3	2.9	4.5	0.0	0.0
1958	22.0	9.7	.4	3.2	4.3	4.6	0.0	0.0

Source: U.S. Census Bureau. *Statistical Abstract of the United States: 2007.* U.S. Bureau of Economic Analysis.
[1]Consists largely of federal fellowship payments (National Science Foundation, fellowships and traineeships, subsistence payments to State maritime academy cadets, and other federal fellowships), interest subsidy on higher education loans, basic educational opportunity grants, and Job Corps payments.
[2]Excludes Veterans. Consists largely of Bureau of Indian Affairs payments, education exchange payments, Alaska Permanent Fund dividend payments, compensation of survivors of public safety officers, compensation of victims of crime, disaster relief payments, compensation for Japanese internment, and other special payments to individuals.

Table 19-2. Social Security Trust Funds, 1937–2005

(Millions of dollars.)

Year	Old Age Survivors Insurance (OASI)				Disability Insurance (DI)			
	Net contribution income[1]	Net interest[2]	Benefit payments[3]	Assets, end of year	Net contribution income[1]	Net interest[2]	Benefit payments[3]	Assets, end of year
2005	506 863	83 979	435 383	1 663 037	86 077	10 273	85 365	195 623
2004	472 758	78 986	415 034	1 500 622	80 281	9 988	78 229	186 217
2003	456 077	75 237	399 845	1 355 330	77 442	6 989	70 933	175 434
2002	455 199	71 184	388 119	1 217 497	77 272	9 178	65 702	160 468
2001	441 460	64 737	372 312	1 071 540	74 933	8 158	59 618	140 993
2000	421 391	57 529	352 652	930 986	71 093	6 942	54 983	118 459
1999	396 352	49 788	334 383	798 812	63 203	5 677	51 381	97 321
1998	371 207	44 491	326 762	681 645	58 966	4 832	48 207	80 815
1997	349 946	39 795	316 257	589 121	56 037	3 992	45 695	66 389
1996	321 557	35 706	302 861	514 026	57 325	3 012	44 189	52 924
1995	304 620	32 820	291 640	458 502	54 401	2 158	40 923	37 566
1994	293 323	29 946	279 068	413 460	51 373	1 157	37 744	22 925
1993	290 905	27 027	267 755	369 322	31 185	835	34 613	8 963
1992	280 992	24 303	254 883	319 150	30 136	1 062	31 112	12 324
1991	272 574	20 829	240 467	267 849	29 137	1 063	27 695	12 898
1990	267 530	16 363	222 987	214 197	28 539	883	24 829	11 079
1989	250 195	11 985	207 971	155 063	23 993	707	22 911	7 905
1988	229 775	7 568	195 454	102 899	22 039	600	21 695	6 864
1987	202 735	4 690	183 587	62 149	19 691	648	20 519	6 658
1986	190 741	3 069	176 813	39 081	18 399	803	19 853	7 780
1985	176 958	1 871	167 248	35 842	17 191	870	18 827	6 321
1984	164 122	2 266	157 841	27 117	15 945	1 174	17 898	3 959
1983	138 337	6 706	149 221	19 672	17 991	1 569	17 524	5 195
1982	123 673	845	138 806	22 088	21 995	546	17 376	2 691
1981	122 627	2 060	123 803	21 490	16 738	172	17 192	3 049
1980	103 456	1 845	105 083	22 823	13 255	485	15 515	3 629
1979	87 919	1 797	90 573	24 660	15 114	358	13 786	5 630
1978	75 471	2 008	80 361	27 520	13 413	256	12 599	4 226
1977	69 572	2 227	73 121	32 491	9 138	304	11 547	3 370
1976	63 362	2 301	65 705	35 388	8 233	422	10 055	5 745
1975	56 816	2 364	58 517	36 987	7 444	502	8 505	7 354
1974	52 081	2 159	51 623	37 777	6 826	500	6 957	8 109
1973	45 975	1 928	45 745	36 487	5 932	458	5 764	7 927
1972	37 781	1 794	37 124	35 318	5 107	414	4 502	7 457
1971	33 723	1 667	33 414	33 789	4 620	361	3 783	6 645
1970	30 256	1 515	28 798	32 454	4 481	277	3 085	5 614
1969	27 947	1 165	24 210	30 082	3 599	177	2 557	4 100
1968	23 719	939	22 643	25 704	3 316	106	2 311	3 025
1967	23 138	818	19 468	24 222	2 286	78	1 950	2 029
1966	20 580	644	18 267	20 570	2 006	58	1 784	1 739
1965	16 017	593	16 737	18 235	1 188	59	1 573	1 606
1964	...	...	...	...	1 154	64	1 309	2 047
1963	...	...	...	...	1 099	66	1 210	2 235
1962	...	...	...	...	1 046	68	1 105	2 368
1961	...	...	...	...	1 038	66	887	2 437
1960	10 866	516	10 677	20 324	1 010	53	468	2 289
1959	...	...	...	...	891	40	457	1 825
1958	...	...	...	...	966	25	249	1 379
1957	...	...	...	...	702	7	57	649
1955	5 713	454	4 968	21 663	...	...	...	...
1950	2 667	257	961	13 721	...	...	...	...
1945	1 285	134	274	7 121	...	...	...	...
1940	325	43	35	2 031	...	...	...	...
1939	580	27	14	1 724	...	...	...	...
1938	360	15	10	1 132	...	...	...	...
1937	765	2	1	766	...	...	...	...

Source: U.S. Social Security Administration. *Annual Statistical Supplement, 2006.*
[1]Beginning in 1983, includes transfers from the general fund of the Treasury representing contributions that would have been paid on deemed wage credits for military service in 1957–2001, if such credits were considered to be covered wages.
[2]Net interest includes net profits or losses on marketable investments. Beginning in 1967, administrative expenses are charged to the trust fund on an estimated basis, with a final adjustment, including interest, made in the following fiscal year. The amounts of these interest adjustments are included in net interest. Beginning in July 1974, the figures shown include relatively small amounts of gifts to the fund. Figures for 1983–1986 reflect payments from a borrowing trust fund to a lending trust fund for interest on amounts owed under the interfund borrowing provisions. During 1983–1990, interest paid from the trust fund to the general fund of the Treasury on advance tax transfers is reflected. The amount shown for 1985 includes an interest adjustment of $14.8 million on unnegotiated checks issued before April 1985.
[3]Beginning in 1966, includes payments for vocational rehabilitation services furnished to disabled persons receiving benefits because of their disabilities. Beginning in 1983, amounts are reduced by amount of reimbursement for unnegotiated benefit checks.

Table 19-3. Social Security—Covered Employment, Earnings, and Contribution Rates, 1970–2005

(Millions, unless otherwise indicated.)

Item	1970	1980	1985	1990	1995	2000	2001	2002	2003	2004	2005
Workers with insured status[1]	108.4	140.5	151.0	164.0	173.2	185.5	187.7	189.6	191.5	193.7	195.8
Male	62.9	76.6	80.7	86.5	90.2	95.6	96.6	97.4	98.4	99.4	100.4
Female	45.5	63.8	70.2	77.5	83.0	89.8	91.1	92.2	93.1	94.3	95.4
Under 25 years old	19.1	25.7	22.0	21.3	18.8	20.8	21.1	21.0	20.8	20.7	20.5
25 to 34 years old	22.9	36.5	40.1	41.6	39.4	36.6	36.4	36.3	36.2	36.2	36.2
35 to 44 years old	18.9	23.0	29.9	36.5	40.6	42.5	42.3	41.8	41.5	41.2	40.8
45 to 54 years old	19.2	18.6	19.3	22.8	29.5	35.9	36.8	37.6	38.5	39.3	40.2
55 to 59 years old	7.9	9.3	9.0	8.8	9.7	12.2	13.0	13.8	14.5	15.4	16.1
60 to 64 years old	6.7	8.2	8.8	8.7	8.5	9.5	10.0	10.5	11.1	11.5	12.0
65 to 69 years old	5.3	7.0	7.5	8.2	8.1	8.1	8.2	8.3	8.6	8.9	9.2
70 years old and over	8.5	12.2	14.3	16.3	18.5	19.9	20.0	20.2	20.4	20.7	20.9
Workers reported with—											
Taxable earnings[2]	93	113	120	134	141	155	155	155	155	157	159
Maximum earnings[2]	24	10	8	8	8	10	9	8	8	9	10
Earnings in covered employment[2] (billion dollars)	532	1 329	1 937	2 704	3 402	4 839	4 939	4 950	5 082	5 378	5 693
Reported taxable[2] (billion dollars)	416	1 181	1 723	2 358	2 919	4 009	4 168	4 248	4 364	4 543	4 770
Percent of total	78.2	88.9	88.9	87.2	85.8	82.8	84.4	85.8	85.9	84.5	83.8
Average per worker:											
Total earnings[2] (dollars)	5 711	11 759	16 167	20 238	24 126	31 209	31 781	31 976	32 799	34 256	35 772
Taxable earnings[2] (dollars)	4 464	10 449	14 379	17 650	20 703	25 854	26 818	27 441	28 164	28 940	29 973
Annual maximum taxable earnings[3] (dollars)	7 800	25 900	39 600	51 300	61 200	76 200	80 400	84 900	87 000	87 900	90 000
Contribution rates for old age, survivors, disability and health insurance (OASDHI):[4]											
Each employer and employee (percent)	4.80	6.13	7.05	7.65	7.65	7.65	7.65	7.65	7.65	7.65	7.65
Old age, survivors, disability and health insurance (OASDI) (percent)	4.20	5.08	5.70	6.20	6.20	6.20	6.20	6.20	6.20	6.20	6.20
Hospital insurance (HI) (percent)	0.60	1.05	1.35	1.45	1.45	1.45	1.45	1.45	1.45	1.45	1.45
Self-employed[5] (percent)	6.90	8.10	14.10	15.30	15.30	15.30	15.30	15.30	15.30	15.30	15.30
Old age, survivors, disability & health insurance (OASDI) (percent)	6.30	7.05	11.40	12.40	12.40	12.40	12.40	12.40	12.40	12.40	12.40
Hospital insurance (percent)	0.60	1.05	2.70	2.90	2.90	2.90	2.90	2.90	2.90	2.90	2.90
Supplementary medical insurance (SMI), monthly premium[6] (dollars)	5.30	9.60	15.50	28.60	46.10	45.50	50.00	54.00	58.70	66.60	78.20

Source: U.S. Census Bureau. *Statistical Abstract of the United States: 2007.* U.S. Social Security Administration.
Note: Includes Puerto Rico, Virgin Islands, American Samoa, and Guam. Represents all reported employment. Data are estimated.
[1]Estimated number fully insured for retirement and/or survivor benefits as of end of year, except 1970 as of beginning of year.
[2]Includes self-employment.
[3]The maximum taxable earnings for Hospital Insurance (HI) was $125,000 in 1991, $130,200 in 1992, and 135,000 in 1993. Beginning 1994 upper limit on earnings subject to HI taxes was repealed.
[4]As of January 1, 2006, each employee and employer pays 7.65 percent and the self-employed pay 15.3 percent.
[5]Self-employed paid 11.3 percent in 1984, 11.8 percent in 1985, 12.3 percent in 1986 and 1987, and 13.02 percent in 1988 and 1989. The additional amount is supplied from general revenues. Beginning 1990, self-employed pay 15.3 percent, and half of the tax is deductible for income tax purposes and for computing self-employment income subject to social security tax.
[6]1970–1982, as of July 1; beginning 1983, as of January 1.
OASDI = Old-age, survivors, disability, and health insurance.
SMI = Supplementary medical insurance.

Table 19-4. Private Pension Plans—Summary by Type of Plan, 1985–2001

Item	Unit	1985	1990	1991	1992	1993	1994	1995	1996	1997	1998	1999	2000	2001
Total														
Number of plans[1]	Thous.	632.1	712.3	699.3	708.3	702.1	690.3	693.4	696.2	720.0	730.0	733.0	736.0	733.5
Total participants[2,3]	Million	74.7	76.9	77.7	81.9	83.9	85.1	87.5	91.7	95.0	99.5	101.8	103.3	106.6
Active participants[2,4]	Million	62.3	61.8	61.5	64.2	64.7	65.0	66.2	67.9	70.7	73.3	73.0	73.1	74.4
Assets[5]	Bil. dol.	1 252.7	1 674.1	1 936.3	2 094.1	2 316.3	2 298.6	2 723.7	3 136.3	3 553.8	4 021.8	4 407.8	4 203.0	3 941.0
Contributions[6]	Bil. dol.	95.1	98.8	111.1	128.8	153.6	144.4	158.8	169.5	177.9	201.9	215.8	231.9	253.8
Benefits[7]	Bil. dol.	101.9	129.4	135.6	152.4	156.3	163.9	183.0	213.4	232.5	273.1	314.5	341.0	311.6
Defined Contribution Plan														
Number of plans[1]	Thous.	462.0	599.2	597.5	619.7	618.5	615.9	623.9	632.6	660.5	673.6	683.1	686.9	686.6
Total participants[2,3]	Million	35.0	38.1	38.6	42.4	43.6	44.8	47.7	50.6	54.6	57.9	60.4	61.7	64.5
Active participants[2,4]	Million	33.2	35.5	35.8	38.9	39.6	40.4	42.7	44.6	48.0	50.3	50.4	50.9	52.3
Assets[5]	Bil. dol.	426.6	712.2	834.3	947.3	1 068.1	1 087.7	1 321.7	1 550.9	1 818.2	2 085.3	2 350.3	2 216.0	2 116.0
Contributions[6]	Bil. dol.	53.1	75.8	80.9	93.6	101.5	105.3	117.4	133.7	148.1	166.9	185.9	198.5	204.0
Benefits[7]	Bil. dol.	47.4	63.0	64.0	74.6	77.2	81.3	97.9	116.5	135.3	161.9	195.1	213.5	182.2
Defined Benefit Plan														
Number of plans[1]	Thous.	170.2	113.1	101.8	88.6	83.6	74.4	69.5	63.7	59.5	56.4	49.9	48.7	46.9
Total participants[2,3]	Million	39.7	38.8	39.0	39.5	40.3	40.3	39.7	41.1	40.4	41.6	41.4	41.6	42.1
Active participants[2,4]	Million	29.0	26.3	25.7	25.4	25.1	24.6	23.5	23.3	22.7	23.0	22.6	22.2	22.1
Assets[5]	Bil. dol.	826.1	961.9	1 102.0	1 146.8	1 248.2	1 210.9	1 402.1	1 585.4	1 735.6	1 936.6	2 057.5	1 986.0	1 825.0
Contributions[6]	Bil. dol.	42.0	23.0	30.1	35.2	52.1	39.0	41.4	35.8	29.9	35.0	30.0	33.4	49.7
Benefits[7]	Bil. dol.	54.5	66.4	71.5	77.9	79.1	82.6	85.1	96.9	97.2	111.2	119.4	127.5	129.4

Source: U.S. Census Bureau. *Statistical Abstract of the United States: 2007.* U.S. Department of Labor, Employee Benefits Security Administration.
Note: "Pension plan" is defined by the Employee Retirement Income Security Act (ERISA) as "any plan, fund, or program which was heretofore or is hereafter established or maintained by an employer or an employee organization, or by both, to the extent that such plan (a) provides retirement income to employees, or (b) results in a deferral of income by employees for periods extending to the termination of covered employment or beyond, regardless of the method of calculating the contributions made to the plan, the method of calculating the benefits under the plan, or the method of distributing benefits from the plan." A defined benefit plan provides a definite benefit formula for calculating benefit amounts—such as a flat amount per year of service or a percentage of salary times years of service. A defined contribution plan is a pension plan in which the contributions are made to an individual account for each employee. The retirement benefit is dependent upon the account balance at retirement. The balance depends upon amounts contributed, investment experience, and, in the case of profit sharing plans, amounts which may be allocated to the account due to forfeitures by terminating employees. Employee Stock Ownership Plans (ESOP) and 401(k) plans are included among defined contribution plans. Data are based on Form 5500 series reports filed with the Department of Labor.
[1]Excludes all plans covering only one participant.
[2]Includes double counting of workers in more than one plan.
[3]Total participants include active participants, vested separated workers, and retirees.
[4]Any workers currently in employment covered by a plan and who are earning or retaining credited service under a plan. Includes any nonvested former employees who have not yet incurred breaks in service.
[5]Asset amounts shown exclude funds held by life insurance companies under allocated group insurance contracts for payment of retirement benefits. These excluded funds make up roughly 10 to 15 percent of total private fund assets.
[6]Includes both employer and employee contributions.
[7]Benefits paid directly from trust and premium payments made from plan to insurance carriers. Excludes benefits paid directly by insurance carriers.
. . . = Not available.

Table 19-5. State Unemployment Insurance—Summary, 1980–2005

(Thousand.)

Item	Unit	1980	1985	1990	1995	1996	1997	1998	1999	2000	2001	2002	2003	2004	2005
Insured unemployment, average weekly	Thousand	3 356	2 617	2 522	2 572	2 596	2 323	2 222	2 188	2 110	2 974	3 585	3 531	2 950	2 662
Percent of covered employment[1]	Percent	3.9	2.9	2.4	2.3	2.3	2.0	1.9	1.8	1.7	2.3	2.8	2.8	2.3	2.1
Percent of civilian unemployed	Percent	43.9	31.5	35.8	34.7	35.9	34.5	35.8	38.0	37.6	44.2	43.2	40.7	36.8	35.7
Unemployment benefits, average weekly	Dollars	100	128	161	187	189	193	200	212	221	238	257	262	263	267
Percent of weekly wage	Percent	36.6	35.3	36.0	35.5	34.5	33.5	32.9	33.1	32.9	34.6	36.8	36.5	35.2	35.5
Weeks compensated	Million	149.0	119.3	116.2	118.3	119.0	106.6	101.4	100.6	96.0	136.3	166.3	163.2	135.1	121.1
Beneficiaries, first payments	Thousand	9 992	8 372	8 629	8 035	7 990	7 325	7 332	6 951	7 033	9 877	10 088	9 935	8 369	7 922
Average duration of benefits[2]	Weeks	14.9	14.2	13.4	14.7	14.9	14.6	13.8	14.5	13.7	13.8	16.5	16.4	16.1	15.3
Claimants exhausting benefits	Thousand	3 072	2 572	2 323	2 662	2 739	2 485	2 266	2 300	2 144	2 827	4 416	4 417	3 532	2 856
Percent of first payment[3]	Percent	33.2	31.2	29.4	34.3	33.4	32.8	31.8	31.4	31.8	34.1	42.5	43.4	39.0	35.9
Contributions collected[4]	Billion dollars	11.4	19.3	15.2	22.0	21.6	21.2	19.8	19.2	19.9	19.7	19.7	25.3	31.2	34.8
Benefits paid	Billion dollars	14.2	14.7	18.1	21.2	21.8	19.7	19.4	20.3	20.5	31.6	42.0	41.4	34.4	31.2
Funds available for benefits[5]	Billion dollars	6.6	10.1	37.9	35.4	38.6	43.8	48.0	50.3	53.4	45.6	35.2	23.4	23.0	28.6
Average employer contribution rate[6]	Percent	2.37	3.13	1.95	2.44	2.28	2.13	1.92	1.77	1.75	1.71	1.80	2.20	2.68	2.92

Source: U.S. Census Bureau. *Statistical Abstract of the United States: 2007.* U.S. Employment and Training Administration.
Note: Includes unemployment compensation for state and local government employees where covered by state law.
[1]Insured unemployment as percent of average covered employment in preceding year.
[2]Weeks compensated divided by first payment.
[3]Based on first payments for 12-month period ending June 30.
[4]Contributions from employers; also employees in states which tax workers.
[5]End of year. Sum of balances in state clearing accounts, benefit-payment accounts, and state accounts in Federal unemployment trust funds.
[6]As percent of taxable wages.

Table 19-6. Nonprofit Charitable Organizations—Information Returns, 1990–2002

(Billions of dollars, except as indicated.)

Year and category	Number of returns (thousands)	Total assets	Total liabilities	Total fund balance or net worth	Revenue Total	Program service revenue[1]	Contributions, gifts, and grants	Membership dues and assessments	Other	Total expenses	Excess of revenue over expenses (net)
2002, Total	**251.7**	**1 733.9**	**693.6**	**1 040.3**	**955.3**	**691.8**	**214.5**	**7.9**	**41.1**	**934.7**	**20.6**
Arts, culture, and humanities	27.1	68.8	12.8	56.1	22.3	6.3	12.8	1.0	2.2	21.6	0.7
Education	45.2	563.8	171.6	392.2	170.7	101.8	54.7	1.2	13.0	164.3	6.4
Environment, animals	9.7	25.5	4.6	20.9	8.7	2.1	5.6	0.4	0.7	7.8	0.9
Health	34.1	678.5	337.0	341.6	550.5	492.6	40.6	1.2	16.0	541.2	9.3
Human services	94.7	201.1	105.2	95.9	141.7	74.0	58.8	3.0	5.9	140.0	1.7
International, foreign affairs ..	3.5	12.3	2.9	9.4	12.6	1.0	11.4	0.1	0.2	12.2	0.4
Mutual, membership benefit	0.6	10.8	2.4	8.4	1.7	1.5	0.2	(Z)	(Z)	1.9	-0.2
Public, societal benefit	21.4	156.8	54.1	102.7	40.4	11.6	25.3	1.0	2.5	39.0	1.3
Religion related	15.3	16.1	3.0	13.1	6.7	1.1	5.0	(Z)	0.6	6.7	0.1
2001, Total	**240.6**	**1 631.7**	**611.4**	**1 020.3**	**897.0**	**630.8**	**212.4**	**7.2**	**46.5**	**862.7**	**34.3**
Arts, culture, and humanities	26.0	65.7	11.7	54.0	22.7	6.2	12.9	1.0	2.6	20.5	2.3
Education	41.2	518.7	141.0	377.8	157.3	90.8	52.5	0.9	13.1	148.4	8.9
Environment, animals	9.4	24.2	4.0	20.2	9.0	1.9	6.0	0.4	0.8	7.5	1.6
Health	32.2	647.0	307.6	339.4	509.0	450.0	39.6	0.9	18.5	497.1	11.9
Human services	91.1	189.4	95.0	94.5	135.8	67.2	59.1	2.9	6.6	131.2	4.7
International, foreign affairs ..	3.4	10.8	2.6	8.2	10.5	0.9	9.3	(Z)	0.2	9.9	0.6
Mutual, membership benefit	0.6	10.3	2.0	8.3	1.7	1.2	0.3	(Z)	0.1	1.6	0.1
Public, societal benefit	21.5	149.6	44.5	105.1	43.7	11.4	27.4	1.0	3.8	39.8	3.8
Religion related	15.0	15.9	3.1	12.8	7.2	1.1	5.3	(Z)	0.7	6.7	0.4
Unknown, unclassified[2]	0.2	0.2	(Z)	0.1	0.1	0.0	(Z)	(Z)	(Z)	0.1	0.0
2000	230.2	1 562.5	539.4	1 023.2	866.2	579.1	199.1	6.7	81.4	796.4	69.8
1999	211.6	1 453.7	481.4	972.2	800.7	518.1	175.0	6.3	101.2	714.5	86.2
1998	207.3	1 351.5	459.2	892.4	752.0	502.8	161.8	7.0	80.5	684.6	67.5
1997	199.0	1 439.0	625.0	814.0	754.6	486.4	146.2	6.8	115.2	677.1	77.5
1996	192.1	1 293.4	564.6	728.9	704.3	467.6	137.7	6.3	92.8	637.9	66.4
1995	180.9	1 143.1	512.4	630.7	663.4	443.1	127.7	6.1	86.4	604.6	58.7
1994	174.9	993.4	464.0	529.3	589.1	422.4	110.7	6.4	49.5	548.2	40.9
1993	165.6	926.8	438.5	488.4	566.1	402.8	103.1	5.8	54.4	530.2	35.9
1992	157.9	849.3	398.2	451.1	523.8	374.8	95.0	5.7	48.3	490.2	33.5
1991	149.5	777.5	365.7	411.9	491.1	344.4	87.5	5.2	54.0	458.7	32.4
1990	141.8	697.3	322.0	375.3	435.6	306.9	85.3	5.0	38.3	409.4	26.1

Source: U.S. Census Bureau. *Statistical Abstract of the United States: 2007.*
Note: Categories based on The National Taxonomy of Exempt Entities (NTEE), a classification system that uses 26 major field areas that are aggregated into 10 categories. Includes data reported by organizations described in Internal Revenue Code section 501(3), excluding private foundations and most religious organizations. Organizations with receipts under $25,000 were not required to file.
[1]Represents fees collected by organizations in support of their tax-exempt purposes, and income such as tuition and fees at educational institutions, hospital patient charges, and admission and activity fees collected by museums and other nonprofit organizations or institutions.
[2]Estimates in this row should be used with caution because of the small number of sample returns on which they are based.
Z = Less than 50 million.

Table 19-7. Child Abuse and Neglect Cases Substantiated and Indicated Victim Characteristics, 1990–2004

	1990		2000		2003		2004	
	Number	Percent	Number	Percent	Number	Percent	Number	Percent
Types of Substantiated Maltreatment[1]								
Victims, total[2]	**690 658**	(X)	**864 837**	(X)	**893 296**	113.3	**872 088**	113.4
Neglect	338 770	49.1	517 118	59.8	550 178	61.6	544 050	62.4
Physical abuse	186 801	27.0	167 713	19.4	164 689	18.4	152 250	17.5
Sexual abuse	119 506	17.3	87 770	10.2	87 078	9.8	84 398	9.7
Emotional maltreatment	45 621	6.6	66 965	7.7	57 391	6.4	61 272	7.0
Medical neglect	...	...	25 498	3.0	17 945	2.0	17 968	2.1
Sex of Victim								
Victims, total	**742 519**	**100.0**	**864 837**	**100.0**	**893 296**	**100.0**	**872 088**	**100.0**
Male	323 339	43.5	413 744	47.8	428 948	48.0	419 743	48.1
Female	369 919	49.8	446 230	51.6	461 068	51.6	449 416	51.5
Age of Victim								
Victims, total	**731 282**	**100.0**	**864 837**	**100.0**	**893 296**	**100.0**	**872 088**	**100.0**
1 year and younger	97 101	13.3	133 094	15.4	144 508	16.2	145 773	16.7
2 to 5 years old	172 791	23.6	205 790	23.8	219 725	24.6	217 297	24.9
6 to 9 years old	157 681	21.6	212 186	24.5	202 070	22.6	192 941	22.1
10 to 13 years old	135 130	18.5	176 071	20.4	185 995	20.8	176 485	20.2
14 to 17 years old	103 383	14.1	126 207	14.6	135 998	15.2	135 858	15.6
18 and over	4 880	0.7	992	0.1	589	0.1	475	0.1

Source: U.S. Census Bureau. *Statistical Abstract of the United States: 2007.* U.S. Department of Health and Human Services, Administration for Children and Families.
Note: Based on reports alleging child abuse and neglect that were referred for investigation/assessment by the respective child protective services agency in each state. The reporting period may be either calendar or fiscal year. Children are counted each time they were subjects of an investigation report. Victims are children whose alleged maltreatments have been substantiated, indicated, or assessed as maltreatments. A substantiated case represents a type of investigation disposition that determines that there is sufficient evidence under state law to conclude that maltreatment occurred or that the child is at risk of maltreatment. An indicated case represents a type of disposition that concludes that there was a reason to suspect maltreatment had occurred. An alternative response-victim case represents a type of disposition that identifies a child as a victim within the alternative response system.
[1]Not all types of maltreatment are shown.
[2]A child may be a victim of more than one maltreatment. Therefore, the total for this item adds up to more than 100%.
. . . = Not available.
X = Not applicable.

BOX 19 ■ Cost of Fraudulent Activity

The history of social service programs in the United States is rife with fraudulent activity. The complexity of the programs, the large number of claims, the high percentage of Americans receiving benefits, and the lack of sufficient oversight staff are among the causes. Although many programs are state run, the examples below illustrate the scope of the problem at the federal level.

For example, inspections by the U.S. Department of Agriculture's (USDA) Office of the Inspector General (OIG) determined that from 2000 to 2005, fraudulent activity on some of the department's largest programs, such as food stamps, crop insurance, and rural development programs, resulted in overpayments of at least $635 million. The USDA's Food and Nutrition Service (FNS) estimates that the rate of trafficking in food stamps has decreased from 3.8 cents on every dollar in benefits redeemed in 1993 to only one cent on the dollar for the years averaged from 2002 to 2005. Nonetheless, one cent for each dollar of benefits redeemed adds up to a $241 million annual average expenditure, down from $811 million in 1993. In 1999, the program provided benefits to approximately 18 million food stamp recipients in 1999, with annual expenditures of $15.8 billion. This number rose to 26 million in 2005, with annual expenditures of $28.6 billion. Trafficking in food stamps decreased at the same time that the number of participants and expenditures increased. In part, the FNS credits the decrease in fraudulent activity to the program's switch to an electronic benefits transfer system (EBT) that allows the agency to track transactions much more efficiently and effectively than the old paper coupon system.

The Department of Health and Human Services' (HHS) Office of the Inspector General (OIG) announced that their investigations for 2006 were responsible for the recovery of $1.6 billion relative to criminal and fraudulent activity. Between 2002 and 2006 Medicare and Medicaid investigations of durable medical equipment, prosthetics, orthotics, and supplies companies (DMEPOS) resulted in $796 million in restitution, fines, and penalties.

Because so much money is spent on prescription drugs in the Medicare and Medicaid programs, $10 billion and $41 billion respectively in 2005, some pharmaceutical companies have engaged in fraudulent activity. In 2005 GlaxoSmithKline was accused of illegal pricing and marketing; the company settled for $149 million. Two corporations settled with the U.S. government amid charges of false pricing that affected the Medicaid prescription drug program: In 2002 Pfizer settled for $49 million and in 2004 Schering-Plough settled for $293 million. In another scam, a patient receives a generic drug while the government is charged for a higher priced drug. As a result of this activity, the U.S. government has concluded a series of settlements with several national pharmacy chains for more than $30 million. Additionally, Omnicare, Inc., an institutional pharmacy, settled for $49.5 million.

Both federal and state law enforcement agencies are continuing extensive investigations of the pharmaceutical industry given the expansion of Medicaid's drug coverage with the 2006 Part D drug benefit which will greatly increase the program's drug spending and, therefore, its susceptibility to fraud.

Sources:

U.S. Department of Agriculture, Food and Nutrition Service, Office of Analysis, Nutrition and Evaluation. "The Extent of Trafficking in the Food Stamp Program: 2002-2005, Final Report," December 2006. http://www.fns.usda.gov/oane/menu/Published/FSP/FILES/ProgramIntegrity/Trafficking2005.pdf

U.S. Department of Agriculture, Office of the Inspector General. "Management Challenges," August 2007. http://www.usda.gov/oig/webdocs/MgmtChallenges2007.pdf

U.S. Department of Health and Human Services, Office of the Inspector General. *OIG News,*" OIG Reports More than $38 Billion in Savings and Recoveries for FY 2006," December 5, 2006.

U.S. Department of Agriculture, Food and Nutrition Service. Testimony before the U.S. House of Representatives, Committee on Agriculture, Subcommittee on Department Operations, Oversight, Nutrition and Forestry, by Eric M. Bost, Under Secretary, Food, Nutrition and Consumer Services, June 27, 2001. http://www.fns.usda.gov/cga/Speeches/CT062701.html

U.S. Department of Health and Human Services, Office of the Inspector General. "Suspected Medicaid Fraud Referrals," January 2007. http://oig.hhs.gov/oei/reports/oei-07-04-00181.pdf

U.S. Department of Health and Human Services, Office of the Inspector General. Testimony before the U.S. House of Representatives, Committee on Energy and Commerce, Subcommittee on Health, by Stuart Wright, Deputy Inspector General for Evaluation and Inspections, April 18, 2007. http://www.oig.hhs.gov/testimony.html

U.S. Department of Health and Human Services, Office of the Inspector General. Testimony before the U.S. House of Representatives, Oversight and Government Reform Committee, by Lewis Morris, Chief Counsel to the Inspector General, "Allegations of Waste, Fraud and Abuse in Pharmaceutical Pricing: Financial Impacts on Federal Health Programs and the Federal Taxpayer," February 9, 2007. http://www.oig.hhs.gov/testimony.html

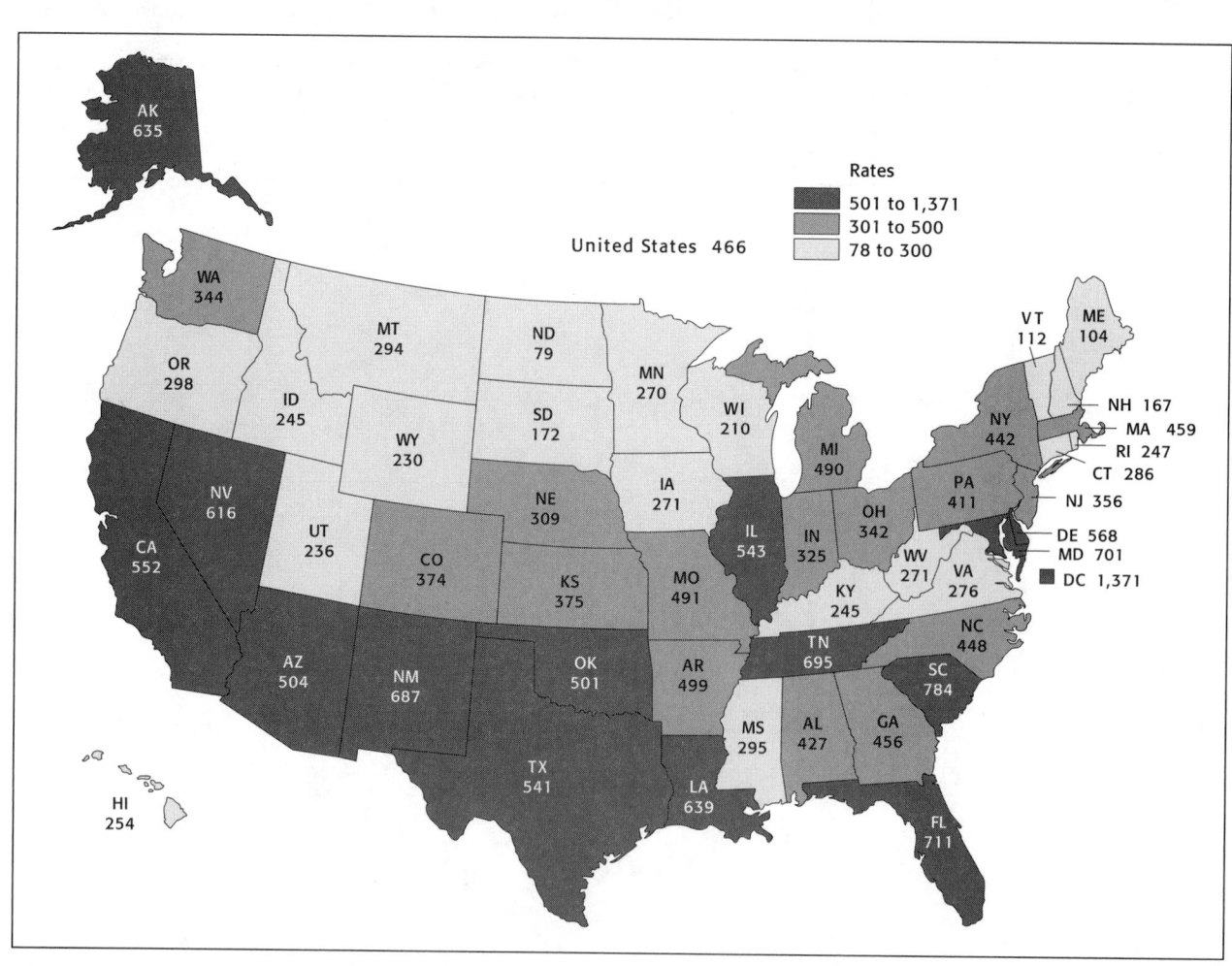

Violent Crime Rates per 100,000 Population by State: 2004
Source: Chart prepared by U.S. Census Bureau.

CHAPTER **20**

Criminal Justice

HIGHLIGHTS

1 Under the U.S. Constitution, law enforcement is a function of state and municipal governments. Crimes under federal jurisdiction include offenses against the U.S. government and against or by its employees while engaged on official duties, as well as offenses that involve the crossing of state lines or interference with interstate commerce. Excluding the military and federal jurisdictions, there are 51 separate criminal law jurisdictions, one in each of the 50 states and one in the District of Columbia. Each of these has its own criminal law and procedure and its own law enforcement agencies with substantial differences in penalties for like offenses. While almost all of them follow the Anglo-Saxon Common Law, Louisiana's legal heritage, for example, is largely French and Continental.

2 The major sources of law enforcement and criminal justice data are the Federal Bureau of Investigation (FBI) and the Bureau of Justice Statistics. The latter has emerged in recent years as an incomparable data provider, publishing such reports as *Sourcebook of Criminal Justice Statistics, Criminal Victimization in the United States, Prisoners in State and Federal Institutions, Children in Custody, National Surveys of Courts, Census of State Correctional Facilities, Survey of Prison Inmates, Parole in the United States, Capital Punishment,* and *Expenditure and Employment Data for the Criminal Justice System.* The FBI's major publication is *Crime in the United*

States, which grew out of the Uniform Crime Reporting Program initiated in 1930 by the International Association of Chiefs of Police. In 1958, a special committee was appointed to study the program. Their report made 22 recommendations that were incorporated in the *Uniform Crime Reports,* beginning with the 1958 issue. Its major innovations were the Crime Index and the Crime Rates per 100,000. Offenses are divided into two groups, designated Part I and Part II. Part I offenses make up the Crime Index. The original eight FBI Index offenses are murder, nonnegligent manslaughter, forcible rape, robbery, aggravated assault, burglary, larceny, and motor vehicle theft. Arson was added as the eighth Index offense in 1979. The FBI Reports are complemented by the National Crime Survey (NCS) of the Bureau of Justice Statistics. NCS data come directly from the victims and include offenses reported to the police as well as those not reported. When an offense involves more than one criminal act, it is counted only once under the more serious category.

3 The earliest statistics on the courts were collected and published by the Bureau of the Census from 1932 to 1945. There are several types of courts with varying degrees of jurisdiction: original, appellate, general, and limited or special. The 94 federal courts of original jurisdiction are known as the District Courts.

4 Statistics on prisoners were collected by the Bureau of the Census in connection with each decennial census of population from 1850 to 1890. Independent enumerations of prisoners were made in 1904, 1910, 1923, and 1933. The first nationwide collection of data was made in 1926 by the Bureau of the Census, which published an annual summary until 1950. From 1950 to 1971, the data were published by the FBI, from 1971 to 1979 by the Law Enforcement Assistance Administration, and since 1979 by the Bureau of Justice Statistics.

5 Violent and property crime rates have declined since the early 1990s. Since 1991, the rate of violent crimes dropped 29 percent from 1.912 million offenses to 1.367 million in 2004, while property crime rates dropped 20 percent from 12.961 million to 10.328 million in the same time period.

6 The states with the highest violent crime rate per 100,000 as of 2004 are South Carolina (784), Florida (711), Maryland (701), and Tennessee (695). The states with the lowest violent crime rates are North Dakota (79), Maine (104), Vermont (112), and New Hampshire (167). The District of Columbia tops all states on this basis, with the highest rate at 1,371, but this figure is more comparable with city data because the District of Columbia is effectively a single city.

7 Among cities, the highest violent crime rate per 100,000 population in 2004 are Saint Louis, MO (2,076), Atlanta, GA (1,842), Baltimore, MD (1,839), and Detroit, MI (1,740). Among the cities with the lowest violent crime rates are Virginia Beach, VA (227), and Honolulu, HI (277).

8 Beginning in 1988, more Black males become homicide victims than White males. In 2003, 7,803 Black males were murdered compared with 6,337 White males. The Black male homicide rate is 38.9 per 100,000 compared with 5.4 for White males. Black females also have a higher homicide rate than White females (6.6 vs. 2.0).

9 In 2004, there were 7,679 hate crimes reported by 12,723 law enforcement agencies. Of these, 2,751 were directed against Blacks, 963 against Jews, and 738 against male homosexuals.

10 In 2004, there were 68,247 arrests of juveniles under 18 years of age for violent crimes, 30,530 juvenile arrests for weapon law violations, and 135,056 juvenile arrests for substance abuse.

11 In 2004 there were 10,047,300 arrests. Of these, 7,067,400 were of Whites and 2,714,000 were of Blacks. Males made up 76.2 percent of the arrestees. Of the serious crimes, the most common arrests were for larceny/theft (866,200) and aggravated assault (316,600). The most common nonserious crimes were substance abuse violation (1,251,100), driving under the influence (1,014,100), and other assaults (923,100).

12 In 2005, 2,821,890 pounds of drugs were seized by the Drug Enforcement Administration, compared with 1,574,890 in 1995. Drug arrest rates for substance use violation rose to 555 per 100,000 in 2004, compared with 435.3 in 1990, down from a high of 587.1 in 2000.

13 In 2000, 1.815 million illegal aliens were apprehended by the Border Patrol, compared with 1.170 in 1990. From these, $1.945 billion worth of narcotics were seized.

14 In 2000, there were 15,785 general purpose law enforcement agencies in the United States, of which 12,666 were local agencies.

15 The number of police officers killed in the line of duty was 139 in 2004, which is about average for the past ten years. In 2001, the number was 220, including 72 officers killed during the terrorist attack on September 11, 2001. Other than in 2001, more police officers are killed in the South than in any other region.

16 In 2004, the Supreme Court docket consisted of 8,588 cases, up from 5,144 cases in 1980 but down from a high of 9,406 in 2002. Appellate cases made up 2,041 of those cases, compared with 2,749 in 1980. Although the total cases on the Supreme Court docket has dramatically increased since 1980, the total cases available for argument have dropped to 128 from 264. The number of signed options also dropped to 74 in 2004 from 123 in 1980.

17 In 2004, a total of 1,213 public officials were indicted for corruption, 1,029 were convicted, and 419 were awaiting trial. Of these 424 federal officials, 111 state officials, and 268 local officials were indicted.

18 In 2004, 872,088 children were reported as victims of abuse and neglect. Of these, neglect was involved in 544,050 cases (62.4 percent), physical abuse in 152,250 cases (17.5 percent), sexual abuse in 84,398 cases (9.7 percent), emotional maltreatment in 61,272 cases (7.0 percent), and medical neglect in 17,968 cases (2.1 percent).

19 In 2004, there were 1.497 million prisoners in state and federal prisons in the United States. The total of all persons on probation or parole and in jails and prisons was 6.997 million or 3.2 percent of the resident adult population.

20 At the start of 2007, there were more than 190,000 prisoners in federal prisons. Of these, citizens of the United States made up 73.2 percent, followed by citizens of Mexico (16.9 percent), Colombia (1.6 percent), Cuba (0.8 percent), Dominican Republic (1.6 percent), and other countries (5.7 percent).

21 In 2005, there were 60 prisoners executed in the United States. Of these, 59 were male and 1 was female; 68.3 percent were White and 31.7 were Black.

22 The largest number of child abuse and neglect victims in 2004 was in Florida with 129,914, making up almost 15 percent of all victims nationwide.

Table 20-1. Crimes and Crime Rates by Type, 1960–2004

(Number in thousands, rate per 100,000 inhabitants.)

Year	Total	Violent crime					Property crime			
		Total	Murder and non-negligent manslaughter	Forcible rape	Robbery	Aggravated assault	Total	Burglary	Larceny $50 and over	Auto theft
Number of Offenses										
2004	...	1 367	16	95	401	855	10 328	2 143	6 948	1 237
2003	...	1 384	17	94	414	859	10 443	2 155	7 027	1 261
2002	11 877	1 424	16	95	421	891	10 455	2 151	7 057	1 247
2001[1]	11 877	1 439	16	91	424	909	10 437	2 117	7 092	1 228
2000	11 608	1 425	16	90	408	912	10 183	2 051	6 972	1 160
1999	11 634	1 426	16	89	409	912	10 208	2 101	6 956	1 152
1998	12 486	1 534	17	93	447	977	10 952	2 333	7 376	1 243
1997	13 195	1 636	18	96	499	1 023	11 558	2 461	7 744	1 354
1996	13 494	1 689	20	96	536	1 037	11 805	2 506	7 905	1 394
1995	13 863	1 799	22	97	581	1 099	12 064	2 594	7 998	1 472
1994	13 990	1 858	23	102	619	1 113	12 132	2 713	7 880	1 539
1993	14 145	1 926	25	106	660	1 136	12 219	2 835	7 821	1 563
1992	14 438	1 932	24	109	672	1 127	12 506	2 980	7 915	1 611
1991	14 873	1 912	25	107	688	1 093	12 961	3 157	8 142	1 662
1990	14 476	1 820	23	103	639	1 055	12 655	3 074	7 946	1 636
1989	14 251	1 646	22	95	578	952	12 605	3 168	7 872	1 565
1988	13 923	1 566	21	92	543	910	12 357	3 218	7 706	1 433
1987	13 509	1 484	20	91	518	855	12 025	3 236	7 500	1 289
1986	13 212	1 489	21	91	543	834	11 723	3 241	7 257	1 224
1985	12 430	1 328	19	88	498	723	11 103	3 073	6 926	1 103
1984	11 882	1 273	19	84	485	685	10 608	2 984	6 592	1 032
1983	12 109	1 258	19	79	507	653	10 851	3 130	6 713	1 008
1982	12 974	1 322	21	79	553	669	11 652	3 447	7 143	1 062
1981	13 424	1 362	23	83	593	664	12 062	3 780	7 194	1 088
1980	13 408	1 345	23	83	566	673	12 064	3 795	7 137	1 132
1979	12 250	1 208	21	76	481	629	11 042	3 328	6 601	1 113
1978	11 209	1 086	20	68	427	571	10 123	3 128	5 991	1 004
1977	10 985	1 030	19	64	413	534	9 955	3 072	5 906	978
1976	11 350	1 004	19	57	428	501	10 346	3 109	6 271	966
1975	11 292	1 040	21	56	471	493	10 253	3 265	5 978	1 010
1974	10 253	975	21	55	442	456	9 279	3 039	5 263	977
1973	8 718	876	20	51	384	421	7 842	2 566	4 348	929
1972	8 249	835	19	47	376	393	7 414	2 376	4 151	887
1971	8 588	817	18	42	388	369	7 772	2 399	4 424	948
1970	8 098	739	16	38	350	335	7 359	2 205	4 226	928
1969	7 411	662	15	37	299	311	6 749	1 982	3 889	879
1968	6 720	595	14	32	263	287	6 125	1 859	3 483	784
1967	5 903	500	12	28	203	257	5 404	1 632	3 112	660
1966	5 224	430	11	26	158	235	4 793	1 410	2 822	561
1965	4 739	387	10	23	139	215	4 352	1 283	2 573	497
1964	4 565	364	9	21	130	203	4 200	1 213	2 514	473
1963	4 109	317	9	18	116	174	3 793	1 086	2 298	408
1962	3 752	302	9	18	111	165	3 451	994	2 090	367
1961	3 488	289	9	17	107	157	3 199	950	1 913	336
1960	3 384	288	9	17	108	154	3 096	912	1 855	328

Note: Data refer to offenses known to the police. Rates are based on Census Bureau estimated resident population.

Table 20-1. **Crimes and Crime Rates by Type, 1960–2004—***Continued*

(Number in thousands, rate per 100,000 inhabitants.)

Year	Total	Violent crime					Property crime			
		Total	Murder and non-negligent manslaughter	Forcible rape	Robbery	Aggravated assault	Total	Burglary	Larceny $50 and over	Auto theft
Rate per 100,000 Inhabitants										
2004	. . .	465.5	5.5	32.2	136.7	291.1	3 517.1	729.9	2 365.9	421.3
2003	. . .	475.8	5.7	32.3	142.5	295.4	3 591.2	741.0	2 416.5	433.7
2002	4 118.8	494.4	5.6	33.1	146.1	309.5	3 630.6	747.0	2 450.7	432.9
2001[1]	4 162.6	504.5	5.6	31.8	148.5	318.6	3 658.1	741.8	2 485.7	430.5
2000	4 124.8	506.5	5.5	32.0	145.0	324.0	3 618.3	728.8	2 477.3	412.2
1999	4 266.5	523.0	5.7	32.8	150.1	334.3	3 743.6	770.4	2 550.7	422.5
1998	4 619.3	567.6	6.3	34.5	165.5	361.4	4 052.5	863.2	2 729.5	459.9
1997	4 930.0	611.0	6.8	35.9	186.2	382.1	4 316.3	918.8	2 891.8	505.7
1996	5 086.6	636.6	7.4	36.3	201.9	391.0	4 451.0	945.0	2 980.3	525.7
1995	5 275.9	684.5	8.2	37.1	220.9	418.3	4 590.5	987.0	3 043.2	560.3
1994	5 373.8	713.6	9.0	39.3	237.8	427.6	4 660.2	1 042.1	3 026.9	591.3
1993	5 487.1	747.1	9.5	41.1	256.0	440.5	4 740.0	1 099.7	3 033.9	606.3
1992	5 661.4	757.5	9.3	42.8	263.7	441.9	4 903.7	1 168.4	3 103.6	631.6
1991	5 898.4	758.2	9.8	42.3	272.7	433.4	5 140.2	1 252.1	3 229.1	659.0
1990	5 802.7	729.6	9.4	41.1	256.3	422.9	5 073.1	1 232.2	3 185.1	655.8
1989	5 774.0	666.9	8.7	38.3	234.3	385.6	5 107.1	1 283.6	3 189.6	634.0
1988	5 694.5	640.6	8.5	37.8	222.1	372.2	5 054.0	1 316.2	3 151.7	586.1
1987	5 575.5	612.5	8.3	37.6	213.7	352.9	4 963.0	1 335.7	3 095.4	531.9
1986	5 501.9	620.1	8.6	38.1	226.0	347.4	4 881.8	1 349.8	3 022.1	509.8
1985	5 224.5	558.1	8.0	36.8	209.3	304.0	4 666.4	1 291.7	2 911.2	463.5
1984	5 031.3	539.2	7.9	35.7	205.4	290.2	4 492.1	1 265.5	2 795.2	437.7
1983	5 175.0	537.7	8.3	33.7	216.5	279.2	4 637.4	1 338.7	2 871.3	431.1
1982	5 603.6	571.1	9.1	34.0	238.9	289.2	5 032.5	1 488.0	3 083.1	458.6
1981	5 858.2	594.3	9.8	36.0	258.7	289.7	5 263.9	1 647.2	3 135.3	474.1
1980	5 950.0	596.6	10.2	36.8	251.1	298.5	5 353.3	1 684.1	3 167.0	502.2
1979	5 565.5	548.9	9.7	34.7	218.4	286.0	5 016.6	1 511.9	2 999.1	505.6
1978	5 140.3	497.8	9.0	31.0	195.8	262.1	4 642.5	1 434.6	2 747.4	460.5
1977	5 077.6	475.9	8.8	29.4	190.7	240.0	4 601.7	1 419.8	2 729.9	451.9
1976	5 287.3	467.8	8.8	26.6	199.3	233.2	4 819.5	1 448.2	2 921.3	450.0
1975	5 298.5	487.8	9.6	26.3	220.8	231.1	4 810.7	1 532.1	2 804.8	473.7
1974	4 850.4	461.1	9.8	26.2	209.3	215.8	4 389.3	1 437.7	2 489.5	462.2
1973	4 154.4	417.4	9.4	24.5	183.1	200.5	3 737.0	1 222.5	2 071.9	442.6
1972	3 961.4	401.0	9.0	22.5	180.7	188.8	3 560.4	1 140.8	1 993.6	426.1
1971	4 164.7	396.0	8.6	20.5	188.0	178.8	3 768.8	1 163.5	2 145.5	459.8
1970	3 984.5	363.5	7.9	18.7	172.1	164.8	3 621.0	1 084.9	2 079.3	456.8
1969	3 680.0	328.7	7.3	18.5	148.4	154.5	3 351.3	984.1	1 930.9	436.2
1968	3 370.2	298.4	6.9	15.9	131.8	143.8	3 071.8	932.3	1 746.6	393.0
1967	2 989.7	253.2	6.2	14.0	102.8	130.2	2 736.5	826.6	1 575.8	334.1
1966	2 670.8	220.0	5.6	13.2	80.8	120.3	2 450.9	721.0	1 442.9	286.9
1965	2 449.0	200.2	5.1	12.1	71.7	111.3	2 248.8	662.7	1 329.3	256.8
1964	2 388.1	190.6	4.9	11.2	68.2	106.2	2 197.5	634.7	1 315.5	247.4
1963	2 180.3	168.2	4.6	9.4	61.8	92.4	2 012.1	576.4	1 219.1	216.6
1962	2 019.8	162.3	4.6	9.4	59.7	88.6	1 857.5	535.2	1 124.8	197.4
1961	1 906.1	158.1	4.8	9.4	58.3	85.7	1 747.9	518.9	1 045.4	183.6
1960	1 887.2	160.9	5.1	9.6	60.1	86.1	1 726.3	508.6	1 034.7	183.0

Source: U.S. Census Bureau. U.S. Department of Justice, Federal Bureau of Investigation.
Note: Data refer to offenses known to the police. Rates are based on Census Bureau estimated resident population.

Table 20-2. Federal Drug Seizures, by Type of Drug, 1990–2005

(Pounds. For fiscal years ending in year shown.)

Year	Total	Heroin	Cocaine	Cannabis Total	Marijuana	Hashish
2005	2 821 890	4 294	398 842	2 418 754	2 417 936	818
2004	3 047 047	4 078	336 365	2 706 604	2 706 031	573
2003	2 956 580	5 920	245 623	2 705 037	2 703 664	1 373
2002	2 649 756	6 859	225 368	2 417 529	2 417 343	186
2001	2 922 543	4 358	237 857	2 680 328	2 679 898	430
2000	2 888 169	3 341	248 894	2 635 934	2 611 947	23 987
1999	2 568 899	2 727	282 207	2 283 965	2 282 287	1 678
1998	2 084 882	3 214	259 895	1 821 773	1 821 241	532
1997	1 762 806	3 592	221 375	1 537 839	1 536 170	1 669
1996	1 737 647	3 014	283 490	1 451 142	1 397 976	53 167
1995	1 574 890	2 971	234 342	1 337 577	1 305 701	31 876
1994	1 336 561	2 830	285 230	1 048 502	1 047 284	1 218
1993	1 046 914	3 516	244 315	799 083	773 004	26 080
1992	1 094 165	2 552	304 086	787 527	783 479	4 048
1991	920 331	3 067	246 318	670 946	499 097	171 849
1990	464 583	1 704	235 891	226 988	219 249	7 739

Source: U.S. Census Bureau. U.S. Drug Enforcement Administration.
Note: Reflects the combined drug seizure effort of the Drug Enforcement Administration, the Federal Bureau of Investigation, the U.S. Customs Services, and beginning October 1995, the U.S. Border Patrol within the jurisdiction of the United States as well as maritime seizures by the U.S. Coast Guard. Based on reports to the Federal-wide Drug Seizure System, which eliminates duplicate reporting of a seizure involving more than one federal agency. Data have been revised for 1990, 1995, and 1999–2004.

Table 20-3. Suicides, 1900–2003

(Number, rate per 100,000 resident population; refers only to deaths occurring within the United States.)

Year	Suicides	
	Number	Rate
2003	31 484	10.8
2002	31 655	11.0
2001	30 622	10.8
2000	29 350	10.4
1999	29 199	10.5
1998	30 600	11.1
1997	30 500	11.2
1996	30 900	11.5
1995	31 300	11.7
1994[1]	32 400	12.4
1993[1]	31 100	12.1
1992[1]	29 800	11.7
1991	30 200	12.0
1990	30 900	12.4
1989	30 200	12.2
1988	30 407	12.4
1987	30 796	12.7
1986	30 904	12.8
1985	29 500	12.4
1984	29 286	11.9
1983	28 295	12.1
1982	28 242	12.2
1981	27 596	12.0
1980	26 900	11.9
1979	27 206	12.1
1978	27 300	12.5
1977	28 681	13.3
1976	26 934	12.5
1975	27 100	12.7
1974	25 683	12.1
1973	25 118	12.0
1972	25 004	12.6
1971	24 092	11.7
1970	23 480	11.6
1969	22 364	11.1
1968	21 372	10.7
1967	21 325	10.8
1966	21 281	10.9
1965	21 507	11.1
1964	20 588	10.8
1963	20 825	11.0
1962	20 207	10.9
1961	18 999	10.4
1960	19 041	10.6
1959	18 633	10.6
1958	18 519	10.7
1957	16 632	9.8
1956	16 727	10.0
1955	16 760	10.2
1954	16 356	10.1
1953	15 947	10.1
1952	15 567	10.0
1951	15 909	10.4
1950	17 145	11.4
1949	16 993	11.4
1948	16 354	11.2
1947	16 538	11.5
1946	16 152	11.5
1945	14 782	11.2
1944	13 231	10.0
1943	13 725	10.2
1942	16 117	12.0
1941	17 102	12.8
1940	18 907	14.4
1939	18 511	14.1
1938	19 802	15.3
1937	19 294	15.0
1936	18 294	14.3
1935	18 214	14.3
1934	18 828	14.9
1933	19 993	15.9
1932	20 646	17.4
1931	19 807	16.8

[1]Based on a 10 percent sample of deaths. Includes deaths of nonresidents.

Table 20-3. Suicides, 1900–2003—*Continued*

(Number, rate per 100,000 resident population; refers only to deaths occurring within the United States.)

Year	Suicides	
	Number	Rate
1930	18 323	15.6
1929	16 045	13.9
1928	15 390	13.5
1927	14 096	13.2
1926	13 082	12.6
1925	12 209	12.0
1924	11 846	11.9
1923	11 096	11.5
1922	10 876	11.7
1921	10 906	12.4
1920	8 790	10.2
1919	9 543	11.5
1918	9 685	12.3
1917	9 157	13.0
1916	9 181	13.7
1915	10 011	16.2
1914	9 802	16.1
1913	8 932	15.4
1912	8 549	15.6
1911	8 612	16.0
1910	7 283	15.3
1909	7 061	16.0
1908	6 506	16.8
1907	5 027	14.5
1906	4 323	12.8
1905	2 940	13.5
1904	2 611	12.2
1903	2 371	11.3
1902	2 124	10.3
1901	2 105	10.4
1900	2 036	10.2

Source: U.S. Census Bureau. U.S. Centers for Disease Control and Prevention, National Center for Health Statistics.
[1]Based on a 10 percent sample of deaths. Includes deaths of nonresidents.

Table 20-4. Police Officers Killed, 1945–2004

(Covers law enforcement officers killed feloniously and accidentally in the line of duty; includes federal offices.)

Year	Total killed
2004	139
2003	133
2002	132
2001[1]	218
2000	134
1999	107
1998	142
1997	132
1996	112
1995	133
1994	141
1993	129
1992	130
1991	124
1990	132
1989	145
1988	155
1987	148
1986	133
1985	148
1984	147
1983	152
1982	164
1981	157
1980	165
1979	165
1978	146
1977	123
1976	140
1975	185
1974	179
1973	176
1972	157
1971	181
1970	146
1969	125
1968	123
1967	123
1966	99
1965	83
1964	88
1963	88
1962	78
1961	71
1960	48
1959	49
1958	49
1957	45
1956	46
1955	55
1954	61
1953	63
1952	63
1951	64
1950	36
1949	55
1948	64
1947	67
1946	82
1945	59

Source: U.S. Census Bureau. U.S. Federal Bureau of Investigation.
[1]The 72 officers feloniously slain during the events of September 11, 2001 are included in data for 2001.

Table 20-5. Criminal Justice System—Public Expenditures, by Level of Government, 1902–2003

(Millions of dollars.)

Year	All government				Federal government			
	Total¹	Police protection	Judicial activities	Correction	Total¹	Police protection	Judicial actitivies	Correction
2003	185 490	83 089	41 545	60 855	35 323	20 422	9 356	5 545
2002	...	...	...	...	34 346	17 626	11 013	5 707
2001	167 113	72 406	37 751	56 956	30 443	15 014	10 230	5 199
2000	155 722	68 911	34 298	52 512	27 820	13 999	9 353	4 467
1999	146 556	65 364	32 185	49 007	27 392	14 797	8 515	4 080
1998	135 899	60 828	29 901	45 170	22 834	12 208	7 462	3 165
1997	...	...	...	...	27 065	12 518	10 651	3 896
1996	120 194	53 007	26 158	41 029	23 344	10 115	9 459	3 766
1995	112 868	48 645	24 472	39 752	22 651	9 298	9 184	4 169
1994	103 471	46 005	22 602	34 864	19 084	8 059	8 184	2 841
1993	97 542	44 037	21 558	31 947	18 591	8 069	7 832	2 690
1992	93 777	41 327	20 989	31 461	17 423	7 400	7 377	2 646
1991	87 567	38 971	19 298	29 297	15 231	6 725	6 384	2 122
1990	79 434	35 923	17 357	26 154	12 798	5 666	5 398	1 734
1989	70 949	32 794	15 589	22 567	9 674	5 307	2 949	1 418
1988	65 231	30 961	13 971	20 299	8 851	4 954	2 639	1 258
1987	58 871	28 768	12 555	17 549	7 496	4 231	2 271	994
1986	53 500	26 255	11 485	15 759	6 595	3 643	2 090	862
1985	48 563	24 399	10 629	13 535	6 416	3 495	2 129	792
1984	43 943	22 686	9 463	11 794	5 868	3 396	1 785	687
1983	39 680	20 648	8 621	10 411	4 844	2 815	1 523	606
1982	35 842	19 022	7 771	9 048	4 458	2 527	1 390	541
1981	24 691	16 822	...	7 869	2 317	1 904	...	413
1980	22 064	15 163	...	6 901	2 126	1 739	...	387
1979	26 028	13 917	5 628	6 040	3 379	2 053	876	354
1978	24 132	13 120	5 051	5 523	3 122	1 952	746	337
1977	21 574	11 865	4 267	4 934	2 779	1 765	616	299
1976	19 681	11 028	3 807	4 386	2 450	1 612	472	256
1975	17 249	9 786	3 281	3 843	2 189	1 461	429	217
1974	14 954	8 512	1 708	3 240	1 961	1 222	136	215
1973	12 985	7 624	1 579	2 740	1 629	1 089	118	171
1972	11 721	6 903	1 491	2 422	1 492	962	179	133
1971	10 517	6 165	1 358	2 291	1 448	805	134	121
1970	8 571	5 081	1 190	1 706	978	589	129	83
1969	7 340	4 430	1 002	1 462	800	492	106	71
1968	6 070	3 725	976	1 369	445	290	90	65
1967	5 424	3 331	894	1 199	429	282	87	60
1966	4 903	3 033	793	1 077	393	257	79	57
1965	4 574	2 792	748	1 034	377	243	75	59
1964	4 222	2 586	697	939	342	220	66	56
1963	4 009	2 440	693	876	358	209	94	55
1962	3 795	2 326	628	841	304	196	57	51
1961	3 613	2 210	593	810	298	193	58	47
1960	3 349	2 030	597	722	291	173	74	44
1959	3 149	1 880	561	708	275	170	68	37
1958	2 861	1 769	519	573	261	159	63	39
1957	2 655	1 624	481	550	252	155	62	35
1956	2 434	1 487	447	500	250	156	61	33
1955	2 231	1 359	409	463	206	129	49	28
1954	2 080	1 254	399	427	210	124	56	30
1953	...	1 160	...	...	...	122	...	...
1952	...	1 080	...	365	...	141	...	28
1951	...	...	...	...	...	104	...	...
1950	...	864	...	...	...	88	...	...
1948	...	724	...	...	...	80	...	...
1947	...	...	...	...	...	...	...	...
1946	...	549	...	...	...	70	...	...
1945	...	...	...	...	...	...	...	...
1944	...	497	...	...	...	83	...	...
1942	...	444	...	...	...	50	...	...
1940	...	386	...	...	...	21	...	...
1938	...	378	...	...	...	19	...	...
1936	...	331	...	...	...	17	...	...
1932	...	349	...	...	...	31	...	...
1927	...	290	...	...	...	20	...	...
1922	...	204	...	...	...	14	...	...
1913	...	92	...	...	...	3	...	...
1902	...	50	...	...	...	0	...	...

Source: U.S. Census Bureau. U.S. Department of Justice, Bureau of Justice Statistics.
¹Beginning 1969, legal services and prosecution and indigent defense included in totals.
. . . = Not available.

Table 20-5. Criminal Justice System—Public Expenditures, by Level of Government, 1902–2003—*Continued*

(Millions of dollars.)

State government				Local government			
Total¹	Police protection	Judicial actitivies	Correction	Total¹	Police protection	Judicial actitivies	Correction
66 114	11 144	15 782	39 187	93 877	57 503	17 718	18 656
65 508	11 081	15 365	39 062	90 485	55 086	17 042	18 358
63 372	10 497	14 444	38 432	83 377	50 718	15 938	16 721
58 165	9 787	13 249	35 129	78 995	48 219	14 842	15 934
57 186	9 632	12 875	34 680	74 830	45 593	14 142	15 098
49 454	7 996	10 858	30 599	70 831	43 312	13 559	13 960
46 444	7 501	9 803	29 141	67 083	40 976	13 101	13 007
39 903	6 499	8 110	25 294	62 811	38 227	12 355	12 229
41 196	6 451	8 676	26 069	58 933	35 364	11 674	11 895
37 161	6 000	8 026	23 135	55 517	33 365	11 023	11 130
34 227	5 603	7 820	20 803	52 562	31 733	10 283	10 546
33 755	5 593	7 723	20 439	50 115	29 659	10 052	10 404
31 484	5 507	6 754	19 223	47 075	28 017	9 418	9 640
28 345	5 163	5 971	17 211	43 559	26 097	8 676	8 786
25 269	4 780	5 442	15 047	38 825	23 672	7 682	7 471
22 837	4 531	4 886	13 420	36 098	22 371	6 826	6 901
20 157	4 067	4 339	11 691	33 265	21 089	6 230	5 947
18 556	3 749	4 005	10 802	30 178	19 356	5 691	5 132
16 252	3 469	3 636	9 148	27 462	17 847	5 090	4 524
14 213	3 173	3 271	7 768	25 154	16 516	4 627	4 011
12 785	2 963	2 950	6 873	23 186	15 276	4 361	3 548
11 602	2 833	2 748	6 020	20 968	14 172	3 784	3 011
7 085	2 241	...	4 844	15 289	12 677	...	2 612
6 285	2 027	...	4 258	13 653	11 397	...	2 256
8 463	2 150	1 318	3 824	15 401	9 882	1 903	2 197
6 888	1 892	1 497	3 177	14 322	9 276	2 809	2 009
5 812	1 800	1 026	2 847	12 983	8 300	2 626	1 788
5 204	1 696	903	2 475	12 027	7 720	2 432	1 654
4 612	1 512	779	2 193	10 449	6 813	2 073	1 434
3 906	1 308	439	1 813	9 092	5 982	1 223	1 213
3 304	1 132	386	1 534	8 052	5 403	1 075	1 035
2 948	903	346	1 378	7 281	4 948	965	911
2 291	932	327	1 387	6 663	4 489	912	895
2 134	689	282	1 051	5 454	3 803	779	572
1 849	621	236	914	4 691	3 317	660	477
1 622	541	209	872	4 003	2 894	677	432
1 381	441	193	747	3 615	2 609	614	392
1 224	385	175	664	3 286	2 391	539	356
1 135	348	155	632	3 062	2 201	518	343
1 042	315	141	586	2 838	2 051	490	297
960	297	127	536	2 691	1 934	472	285
902	276	118	508	2 589	1 854	453	282
849	261	109	479	2 466	1 756	426	284
769	245	99	425	2 289	1 612	424	253
733	228	92	413	2 141	1 482	401	258
671	214	87	370	1 929	1 396	369	164
584	179	77	328	1 819	1 290	342	187
526	159	72	295	1 658	1 172	314	172
475	139	68	268	1 550	1 091	292	167
446	130	66	250	1 424	1 000	277	147
418	119	61	238	...	919	...	...
386	106	57	223	...	833	...	114
365	97	53	215	...	...	...	...
332	85	49	198	...	691	...	...
...	65	...	153	...	579	...	...
...	...	...	107	...	...	...	...
...	45	...	97	...	434	...	...
...	...	...	82	...	...	...	...
159	41	35	83	...	373	...	...
...	40	...	80	...	354	...	...
...	34	...	86	...	331	...	...
...	30	...	85	...	329	...	...
...	19	...	73	...	295	...	...
...	15	...	87	...	303	...	...
...	7	...	64	...	263	...	...
...	4	...	64	...	186	...	...
...	1	...	28	...	88	...	...
...	0	...	14	...	50	...	...

Table 20-6. U.S. Supreme Court—Cases Filed and Disposed of During October Terms, 1940–2004

Year	Total cases	
	Filed	Available for argument
2004	8 588	128
2003	8 882	140
2002	9 406	139
2001	9 176	137
2000	8 965	138
1999	8 445	124
1998	8 083	124
1997	7 692	138
1996	7 602	140
1995	7 565	145
1994	8 100	136
1993	7 786	145
1992	7 245	166
1991	6 770	196
1990	6 316	201
1989	5 746	275
1988	5 657	301
1987	5 268	239
1986	5 123	319
1985	5 158	317
1984	5 006	309
1983	5 100	331
1982	5 079	331
1981	5 311	321
1980	5 144	264
1979	4 781	285
1978	4 731	291
1977	4 704	290
1976	4 731	302
1975	4 761	314
1974	4 688	287
1973	5 079	309
1972	4 640	308
1971	4 533	296
1969	3 405	347
1968	3 271	346
1967	3 106	462
1966	2 752	402
1965	2 774	338
1964	2 288	275
1963	2 294	393
1962	2 373	388
1961	2 185	264
1960	1 940	282
1959	1 862	249
1958	1 819	275
1957	1 639	323
1956	1 802	266
1955	1 644	246
1954	1 397	196
1953	1 302	170
1952	1 283	193
1951	1 234	197
1950	1 181	191
1949	1 270	202
1948	1 465	238
1947	1 295	208
1946	1 510	256
1945	1 316	215
1944	1 237	274
1943	997	210
1942	984	259
1941	1 178	376
1940	977	281

Source: U.S. Census Bureau. Supreme Court of the United States, Office of the Clerk.
Note: Statutory term of court begins the first Monday in October.

Table 20-7. U.S. District Courts—Civil and Criminal Cases, 1941–2006

(Number, for years ending June 30.)

Year	Civil cases		Criminal cases				
	Total cases commenced	Total cases terminated	Cases commenced[1]	Not convicted	Defendants disposed of		
					Total	Imprisonment	Probation[2]
2006	244 068	281 220	68 670	8 429	88 061	...	...
2005	253 273	271 753	69 575	8 661	86 000	...	...
2004	281 338	252 761	71 022	8 101	81 717	...	...
2003	252 962	253 015	70 642	8 680	83 530	...	...
2002	274 841	259 537	67 000	7 953	78 835	...	...
2001	250 907	248 174	62 708	7 919	75 650	...	...
2000	259 517	259 637	62 745	8 035	75 071	...	...
1999	251 511	...	...	...	...	...	...
1998	261 262	...	...	...	...	...	...
1997	265 200	249 000	48 700	7 500	54 500	39 900	11 900
1996	272 700	246 400	47 100	8 500	51 000	36 500	11 600
1995	248 335	229 820	45 788	8 207	54 980	...	...
1994	236 000	228 900	44 900	10 000	51 100	34 500	12 800
1993	228 600	225 200	45 700	9 200	50 400	34 200	12 600
1992	226 900	239 600	47 500	10 000	48 400	31 100	13 100
1991	207 700	211 700	45 100	10 000	46 800	29 200	13 800
1990	217 013	214 435	48 035	9 747	55 267	...	...
1989	233 500	234 600	44 900	10 100	44 500	24 900	15 000
1988	239 600	238 100	43 500	9 900	42 900	22 500	16 100
1987	239 000	237 500	42 200	10 200	43 900	23 300	16 000
1986	254 800	265 800	40 400	9 300	40 700	20 600	15 200
1985	273 700	268 600	38 500	8 800	38 500	18 700	14 400
1984	261 500	241 800	35 900	8 400	36 100	17 700	13 900
1983	241 800	213 600	34 900	7 700	35 600	17 900	14 100
1982	206 200	185 500	31 600	8 200	32 300	15 900	12 700
1981	180 600	172 900	30 400	8 300	29 900	13 700	12 200
1980	168 800	155 000	28 000	8 000	28 600	13 200	11 100
1979	154 700	140 000	31 500	8 300	32 900	14 600	13 500
1978	138 800	123 200	34 600	9 400	36 500	17 400	14 500
1977	130 600	115 500	39 800	11 700	41 500	19 600	16 100
1976	130 600	108 600	39 100	11 500	40 100	18 500	18 200
1975	117 300	103 800	41 100	11 800	37 400	17 300	17 900
1974	103 500	96 700	37 700	11 800	36 200	17 200	16 600
1973	98 560	97 402	40 367	11 741	34 983	17 540	15 026
1972	96 173	94 256	47 043	12 296	37 220	16 832	15 395
1971	93 396	85 368	41 290	12 512	32 103	14 378	13 243
1970	87 321	80 435	39 959	8 178	28 178	12 415	11 387
1969	77 193	73 354	35 413	5 993	26 803	12 847	9 991
1968	71 449	68 873	32 571	6 169	25 674	12 610	9 820
1967	70 961	70 172	32 207	5 191	26 344	13 085	9 435
1966	70 906	66 184	31 494	4 661	27 314	13 282	10 256
1965	67 678	65 478	33 334	4 961	28 757	13 668	10 779
1964	66 930	63 954	30 268	4 211	29 170	13 273	11 634
1963	63 630	62 379	39 920	5 042	29 803	13 639	12 047
1962	61 836	57 996	37 665	4 599	28 511	14 042	11 071
1961	58 293	55 416	28 460	4 046	28 625	14 162	10 714
1960	59 284	61 829	28 137	3 784	26 728	13 433	10 391
1959	57 800	62 172	28 729	3 696	27 033	13 648	10 726
1958	67 115	61 285	28 897	3 661	26 808	13 288	10 903
1957	62 380	63 568	28 120	3 471	26 254	12 986	10 760
1956	62 394	67 700	28 739	4 244	27 567	12 854	11 759
1955	59 375	58 974	35 310	5 135	33 855	16 889	14 021
1954	59 461	59 903	41 808	4 848	38 141	18 483	16 856
1953	64 001	57 490	37 291	4 289	33 473	15 637	15 118
1952	58 428	53 150	37 950	3 834	34 788	15 379	17 018
1951	51 600	52 119	38 670	4 066	37 000	14 963	19 271
1950	54 622	53 259	36 383	4 173	33 502	14 435	16 046
1949	53 421	48 396	34 432	4 190	32 074	14 204	14 690
1948	46 725	48 791	32 097	4 862	29 380	12 961	13 422
1947	58 956	54 515	33 652	5 527	31 108	14 375	12 612
1946	67 835	61 000	33 203	6 597	29 885	14 353	11 446
1945	60 965	52 300	39 429	7 536	34 117	16 311	13 153
1944	38 499	37 086	39 621	...	...	...	...
1943	36 789	36 044	36 588	...	...	...	...
1942	38 140	38 352	33 294	...	...	...	...
1941	38 477	38 561	31 823	...	...	...	...

Source: U.S. Census Bureau. Administrative Office of the U.S. Courts.
[1] Excludes transfers.
[2] Includes probation and suspended sentence.
... = Not available.

Table 20-8. Juvenile Court—Cases Handled, 1940–2002

(Number in thousands, rate per 100,000 population.)

Year	Delinquency cases, 10 to 17 years old	
	Total[1]	Rate
2002	1 615	51.6
2001	1 621	52.2
2000	1 624	52.9
1999	1 670	55.3
1998	1 755	58.9
1997	1 822	61.8
1996	1 807	62.2
1995	1 763	61.5
1994	1 667	59.3
1993	1 521	55.2
1992	1 482	55.2
1991	1 414	54.0
1990	1 318	51.4
1989	1 189	47.0
1988	1 151	45.2
1987	1 145	44.5
1986	1 150	44.2
1985	1 112	42.2
1984	1 034	38.7
1983	1 030	38.3
1982	1 073	39.1
1981	1 100	39.1
1980	1 093	38.3
1979	1 048	36.2
1978	1 023	34.6
1977	1 076	35.8
1976	1 077	35.1
1975	1 050	33.8
1974	1 252	37.5
1973	1 143	34.2
1972	1 112	33.6
1971	1 125	34.1
1970	1 052	32.3
1969	989	30.7
1968	900	28.5
1967	811	26.3
1966	745	24.7
1965	697	23.6
1964	686	23.5
1963	601	21.4
1962	555	20.6
1961	503	19.3
1960	510	20.1
1959	483	19.6
1958	470	20.0
1957	440	19.8
1956	520	25.2
1955	431	21.4
1954	395	20.2
1953	374	19.7
1952	332	18.2
1951	298	16.8
1950	280	16.1
1949	272	15.6
1948	254	14.9
1947	262	15.1
1946	295	16.9
1945	344	19.6
1944	330	18.6
1943	344	18.7
1942	250	13.4
1941	224	11.8
1940	200	10.5

Source: U.S. Census Bureau. National Center for Juvenile Justice. *Juvenile Court Statistics.*
Note: A delinquency offense is an act committed by a juvenile for which an adult could be prosecuted in a criminal court.
[1]For 1940–1956, includes traffic cases.

Table 20-9. Crimes Occurring in Public Schools, by Selected School Characteristics, 2003–2004

School characteristic	Number of schools	Violent incidents[1]			Serious violent incidents[2]			Theft[3]			Other incidents[4]		
		Percent of schools	Number of incidents	Rate per 1,000 students	Percent of schools	Number of incidents	Rate per 1,000 students	Percent of schools	Number of incidents	Rate per 1,000 students	Percent of schools	Number of incidents	Rate per 1,000 students
Total	80 500	81.4	1 553 300	33.3	18.3	55 200	1.2	46.0	199 800	4.3	64.0	380 100	8.1
School level[5]													
Primary	48 800	74.2	638 500	28.2	13.3	18 900	0.8	29.8	35 500	1.6	50.8	78 300	3.5
Middle	14 500	93.6	515 800	52.7	24.4	15 700	1.6	63.3	54 100	5.5	82.9	104 700	10.7
High school	10 800	95.9	320 100	27.5	29.4	16 700	1.4	83.5	93 900	8.1	93.0	168 200	14.5
Combined	6 400	84.7	78 800	29.7	23.9	3 800*	1.4*	67.1	16 300	6.2	72.5	29 000	10.9
Enrollment size													
Less than 300	19 000	68.8	142 600	36.4	15.3	8 100	2.1	40.5	18 500	4.7	50.7	27 800	7.1
300–499	23 500	80.2	330 600	33.9	14.8	8 400	0.9	33.8	24 700	2.5	59.6	51 200	5.2
500–999	29 000	85.8	656 100	33.5	17.5	18 700	1.0	48.9	68 300	3.5	67.2	130 900	6.7
1,000 or more	8 900	97.5	424 100	31.6	36.3	20 000	1.5	80.7	88 300	6.6	93.3	170 200	12.7
Urbanicity													
City	20 100	87.7	487 100	35.9	21.5	20 400	1.5	46.6	54 800	4.0	68.7	128 900	9.5
Urban fringe	26 600	80.2	565 100	30.7	18.5	18 300	1.0	46.0	80 000	4.3	65.2	139 500	7.6
Town	9 600	86.9	159 300	32.1	19.2	8 100	1.6	45.0	19 900	4.0	67.8	39 700	8.0
Rural	24 200	75.4	341 800	35.1	15.1	8 400	0.9	46.0	45 100	4.6	57.2	72 100	7.4
Percent minority enrollment[6]													
Less than 5 percent	17 100	74.1	192 500	27.1	15.6	6 200	0.9	43.1	31 500	4.4	58.3	51 500	7.2
5 to 20 percent	19 700	76.9	278 900	24.7	13.9	9 100	0.8	45.8	50 900	4.5	63.3	83 100	7.4
20 to 50 percent	17 700	84.5	354 200	32.0	19.3	10 900	1.0	45.3	49 200	4.4	64.6	85 200	7.7
50 percent or more	24 300	88.0	699 500	43.4	23.6	28 300	1.8	49.3	66 100	4.1	68.0	152 900	9.5
Percent of students eligible for free lunch or reduced price lunch													
0–20 percent	18 900	71.3	247 800	19.0	15.4	10 000	0.8	46.3	56 700	4.4	64.4	93 100	7.2
21–50 percent	28 600	82.0	527 200	32.5	16.2	17 100	1.1	46.6	78 800	4.9	65.3	134 600	8.3
More than 50 percent ..	32 900	86.7	778 300	44.5	21.8	28 200	1.6	45.4	64 400	3.7	62.6	152 300	8.7
Student/teacher ratio[7]													
Less than 12	35 800	77.1	528 000	34.8	17.9	19 000	1.3	45.5	66 300	4.4	61.2	118 000	7.8
12–16	29 800	84.1	629 400	32.3	15.6	22 000	1.1	45.2	81 900	4.2	64.9	152 000	7.8
More than 16	14 800	86.7	395 900	32.9	24.7	14 100	1.2	49.2	51 600	4.3	68.7	110 100	9.1

Source: U.S. Department of Education, National Center for Education Statistics and U.S. Department of Justice, Bureau of Justice Statistics. *Indicators of School Crime and Safety 2006.*
Note: Either school principals or the person most knowledgeable about discipline issues at school completed the National Center for Education Statistics' School Survey on Crime and Safety (SSOCS) questionnaire. "At school" is defined to include activities that happen in school buildings, on school grounds, on school buses, and at places that hold school-sponsored events or activities. Respondents were instructed to respond only for those times that were during normal school hours or when school activities or events were in session, unless the survey specified otherwise. Totals may not equal sum of the components due to independent rounding. Estimates of number of incidents are rounded to the nearest 100.
[1]Violent incidents include rape, sexual battery other than rape, physical attack or fight with or without a weapon, threat of physical attack with or without a weapon, and robbery with or without a weapon. Serious violent incidents are also included in violent incidents.
[2]Serious violent incidents include rape, sexual battery other than rape, physical attack or fight with a weapon, threat of physical attack with a weapon, and robbery with or without a weapon.
[3]Theft/larceny (taking things over $10 without personal confrontation) was defined for respondents as "the unlawful taking of another person's property without personal confrontation, threat, violence, or bodily harm. Included are pocket picking, stealing purse or backpack (if left unattended or no force was used to take it from owner), theft from a building, theft from a motor vehicle or motor vehicle parts or accessories, theft of bicycles, theft from vending machines, and all other types of thefts."
[4]Other incidents include possession of a firearm or explosive device, possession of a knife or sharp object, distribution of illegal drugs, possession or use of alcohol or illegal drug, or vandalism.
[5]Primary schools are defined as schools in which the lowest grade is not higher than grade 3 and the highest grade is not higher than grade 8. Middle schools are defined as schools in which the lowest grade is not lower than grade 4 and the highest grade is not higher than grade 9. High schools are defined as schools in which the lowest grade is not lower than grade 9. Combined schools include all other combinations of grades, including K-12 schools.
[6]These estimates exclude data from Tennessee because schools in this state did not report estimates of student race/ethnicity.
[7]Student/teacher ratio was calculated by dividing the total number of students enrolled in the school by the total number of full-time-equivalent (FTE) teachers and aides. The total number of FTE teachers and aides is a combination of the full-time and part-time teachers and aides, including special education teachers and aides, with an adjustment for part-time status.
* = Interpret data with caution.

Table 20-10. Federal and State Prisoners by Jurisdiction and Sex, 1925–2004

(Prisoners under jurisdiction of state and federal authorities; inmates sentenced to maximum term of more than one year.)

Year	Prisoners present (at end of year)					
	Total	Rate[1]	Federal institutions	State institutions	Male	Female
2004	1 433 793	486	159 137	1 274 656	1 337 668	96 125
2003	1 408 361	482	151 919	1 256 442	1 315 790	92 571
2002	1 380 516	476	143 040	1 237 476	1 291 450	89 066
2001	1 345 217	470	136 509	1 208 708	1 260 033	85 184
2000[2]	1 331 278	470	126 955	1 204 323	1 246 234	85 044
1999	1 304 074	476	114 275	1 189 799	1 221 611	82 463
1998	1 245 402	461	103 682	1 141 720	1 167 802	77 600
1997	1 195 498	445	94 987	1 100 511	1 121 663	73 835
1996	1 137 722	427	88 815	1 048 907	1 068 123	69 599
1995	1 085 022	411	83 663	1 001 359	1 021 059	63 963
1994	1 016 691	389	79 795	936 896	956 566	60 125
1993	932 074	359	74 399	857 675	878 037	54 037
1992	846 277	332	65 706	780 571	799 776	46 501
1991	789 610	313	56 696	732 914	745 808	43 802
1990	739 980	297	50 403	689 577	699 416	40 564
1989	680 907	276	47 168	633 739	643 643	37 264
1988	603 732	247	42 738	560 994	573 587	30 145
1987	560 812	231	39 523	521 289	533 990	26 822
1986	522 084	217	36 531	485 553	497 540	24 544
1985	480 568	202	32 695	447 873	459 223	21 345
1984	443 398	188	27 602	415 796	424 193	19 205
1983	419 346	179	26 331	393 015	401 870	17 476
1982	395 516	171	23 652	371 864	379 075	16 441
1981	353 673	154	22 169	331 504	339 375	14 298
1980	315 974	139	20 611	295 363	303 643	12 331
1979	301 470	133	22 588	278 882	289 465	12 005
1978	294 396	132	26 391	268 005	282 813	11 583
1977[3]	285 456	129	28 650	256 806	274 244	11 212
1977[4]	278 141	126	28 650	249 491	267 097	11 044
1976	262 833	120	26 980	235 853	252 794	10 039
1975	240 593	111	24 131	216 462	231 918	8 675
1974	218 466	102	22 361	196 105	211 077	7 389
1973	204 211	96	22 815	181 396	197 523	6 004
1972	196 092	93	21 713	174 470	189 823	6 269
1971	198 061	95	20 948	177 113	191 732	6 329
1970	196 429	96	20 038	176 391	190 794	5 635
1969	196 007	97	19 623	176 384	189 413	6 594
1968	187 914	94	19 703	168 211	182 102	5 812
1967	194 896	98	19 579	175 317	188 661	6 235
1966	199 654	102	19 245	180 409	192 703	6 951
1965	210 895	108	21 040	189 855	203 327	7 568
1964	214 336	111	21 709	192 627	206 632	7 704
1963	217 283	114	23 128	194 155	209 538	7 745
1962	218 830	117	23 944	194 886	210 823	8 007
1961	220 149	119	23 696	196 453	212 268	7 881
1960	212 953	117	23 218	189 739	205 265	7 688
1959	208 105	117	22 492	184 954	200 469	7 636
1958	205 643	117	21 549	183 944	198 208	7 435
1957	195 414	113	20 420	174 836	188 113	7 301
1956	189 565	112	20 134	169 287	182 190	7 375
1955	185 780	112	20 088	165 692	178 655	7 125
1954	182 901	112	20 003	162 845	175 907	6 994
1953	173 579	108	19 363	154 184	166 909	6 670
1952	168 233	107	18 014	150 186	161 994	6 239
1951	165 680	107	17 395	148 245	159 610	6 070
1950	166 123	109	17 134	148 989	160 309	5 814
1949	163 749	109	16 868	146 881	157 663	6 086
1948	155 977	106	16 328	139 649	149 739	6 238
1947	151 304	105	17 146	134 158	144 961	6 343
1946	140 079	99	17 622	122 457	134 075	6 004
1945	133 649	98	18 638	115 011	127 609	6 040
1944	132 456	100	18 139	114 317	126 350	6 106
1943	137 220	103	16 113	121 107	131 054	6 166
1942	150 384	112	16 623	133 761	144 167	6 217
1941	165 439	124	18 465	146 974	159 228	6 211

[1]Rate per 100,000 estimated population.
[2]Decrease in incarceration rate from 1999 to 2000 is due to the use of new census numbers.
[3]Jurisdiction counts.
[4]Custody counts.

Table 20-10. Federal and State Prisoners by Jurisdiction and Sex, 1925–2004—*Continued*

(Prisoners under jurisdiction of state and federal authorities; inmates sentenced to maximum term of more than one year.)

| Year | Prisoners present (at end of year) | | | | | |
	Total	Rate[1]	Federal institutions	State institutions	Male	Female
1940	173 706	131	19 260	154 446	167 345	6 361
1939	179 818	137	19 730	160 088	173 143	6 675
1938	160 285	123	17 083	142 299	154 826	5 459
1937	152 741	118	15 309	134 048	147 375	5 366
1936	145 038	113	15 373	128 200	139 990	5 048
1935	144 180	113	14 777	129 888	139 278	4 902
1934	138 316	109	12 080	126 140	133 769	4 547
1933	136 810	109	10 851	126 096	132 520	4 290
1932	137 997	110	12 282	124 901	133 573	4 424
1931	137 082	110	12 964	124 118	132 638	4 444
1930	129 453	104	12 181	115 314	124 785	4 668
1929	120 496	98	12 964	107 532	115 876	4 620
1928	116 390	96	8 204	108 422	111 836	4 554
1927	109 983	91	7 722	98 795	104 983	4 363
1926	97 991	83	6 803	89 322	94 287	3 704
1925	91 669	79	. . .	. . .	88 231	3 438

Source: U.S. Census Bureau. U.S. Department of Justice, Office of Justice Programs, Bureau of Justice Statistics.
[1]Rate per 100,000 estimated population.
. . . = Not available.

Table 20-11. Adults on Probation, in Jail or Prison, or on Parole, 1980–2004

(As of December 31, except jail counts as of June 30.)

Year	Total[1]	Percent of adult population	Probation	Jail	Prison	Parole	Male	Female
2004[P]	6 996 500	3.2	4 151 125	713 990	1 421 911	765 355	. . .	. . .
2003	6 936 600	3.2	4 144 782	691 301	1 392 796	745 125	. . .	. . .
2002	6 758 800	3.1	4 024 067	665 475	1 367 547	750 934	. . .	. . .
2001	6 581 700	3.1	3 931 731	631 240	1 330 007	732 333	. . .	. . .
2000	6 445 100	3.1	3 826 209	621 149	1 316 333	723 898	. . .	. . .
1999	6 331 400	3.1	3 779 922	596 485	1 287 172	714 457	. . .	. . .
1998	6 126 100	3.1	3 670 441	584 372	1 224 469	696 385	. . .	. . .
1997	5 725 800	2.9	3 296 513	557 974	1 176 564	694 787	4 825 300	900 500
1996	5 482 700	2.8	3 164 996	510 400	1 127 528	679 733	4 629 900	852 800
1995	5 342 900	2.8	3 077 861	507 044	1 078 542	679 421	4 513 000	822 100
1994	5 141 300	2.7	2 981 022	479 800	990 147	690 371	4 377 400	763 900
1993	4 944 000	2.6	2 903 061	455 500	909 381	676 100	4 215 800	728 200
1992	4 762 600	2.5	2 811 611	441 781	850 566	658 601	4 050 300	712 300
1991	4 535 600	2.4	2 728 472	424 129	792 535	590 442	3 913 000	622 600
1990	4 348 000	2.3	2 670 234	403 019	743 382	531 407	3 746 300	601 700
1989	4 055 600	2.2	2 522 125	393 303	683 367	456 803	3 501 600	554 000
1988	3 714 100	2.0	2 356 483	341 893	607 766	407 977	3 223 000	491 100
1987	3 459 600	1.9	2 247 158	294 092	562 814	355 505	3 021 000	438 600
1986	3 239 400	1.8	2 114 621	272 735	526 436	325 638	2 829 100	410 300
1985	3 011 500	1.7	1 968 712	254 986	487 593	300 203	2 606 000	405 500
1984	2 689 200	. . .	1 740 948	233 018	448 264	266 992	. . .	. . .
1983	2 475 100	. . .	1 582 947	221 815	423 898	246 440	. . .	. . .
1982	2 192 600	. . .	1 357 264	207 853	402 914	224 604	. . .	. . .
1981	2 006 600	. . .	1 225 934	[2]195 085	360 029	225 539	. . .	. . .
1980	1 840 400	. . .	1 118 097	[2]182 288	319 598	220 438	. . .	. . .

Source: U.S. Census Bureau. *Statistical Abstract of the United States: 2007.* U.S. Department of Justice, Office of Justice Programs, Bureau of Justice Statistics.
[1]Totals may not add due to individuals having multiple correctional statuses.
[2]Estimated.
. . . = Not available.
P = Preliminary.

Table 20-12. Prisoners Executed Under Civil Authority, by Race, 1930–2005

(Prior to 1960, excludes Alaska and Hawaii except for three federal executions in Alaska: 1939, 1948, and 1950.)

Year	All offenses Total[1]	White	Black
2005	60	41	19
2004	59	39	19
2003	65	44	20
2002	71	53	18
2001	66	48	17
2000	85	49	35
1999	98	61	33
1998	68	48	18
1997	74	45	27
1996	45	31	14
1995	56	33	22
1994	31	20	11
1993	38	23	14
1992	31	19	11
1991	14	7	7
1990	23	16	7
1989	16	8	8
1988	11	6	5
1987	25	13	12
1986	18	11	7
1985	18	11	7
1984	21	13	8
1983	5	4	1
1982	2	1	1
1981	1	1	-
1971–1980	3	3	-
1970	-	-	-
1969	-	-	-
1968	-	-	-
1967	2	1	1
1966	1	1	-
1965	7	6	1
1964	15	8	7
1963	21	13	8
1962	47	28	19
1961	42	20	22
1960	56	21	35
1959	49	16	33
1958	49	20	28
1957	65	34	31
1956	65	21	43
1955	76	44	32
1954	81	38	42
1953	62	30	31
1952	83	36	47
1951	105	57	47
1950	82	40	42
1949	119	50	67
1948	119	35	82
1947	153	42	111
1946	131	46	84
1945	117	41	75
1944	120	47	70
1943	131	54	74
1942	147	67	80
1941	123	59	63
1940	124	49	75
1939	160	80	77
1938	190	96	92
1937	147	69	74
1936	195	92	101
1935	199	119	77
1934	168	65	102
1933	160	77	81
1932	140	62	75
1931	153	77	72
1930	155	90	65

Source: U.S. Census Bureau. *Statistical Abstract of the United States: 2003.* U.S. Department of Justice, Office of Justice Programs, Bureau of Justice Statistics.
[1]Includes races other than white or black.
- = Quantity zero.

Table 20-13. Federal Prosecutions of Public Corruption, 1985–2004

(As of December 31. Prosecution of persons who have corrupted public office in violation of Federal Criminal Statutes.)

Prosecution Status	1985	1990	1995	1996	1997	1998	1999	2000	2001	2002	2003	2004
Total: Charged[1]	1 157	1 176	1 051	984	1 057	1 174	1 134	1 000	1 087	1 136	1 150	1 213
Convicted	997	1 084	878	902	853	1 014	1 065	938	920	1 011	868	1 020
Awaiting trial	256	300	323	244	327	340	329	327	437	413	412	419
Federal officials: Charged	563	615	527	456	459	442	480	441	502	478	479	424
Convicted	470	583	438	459	392	414	460	422	414	429	421	381
Awaiting trial	90	103	120	64	83	85	101	92	131	119	129	98
State officials: Charged	79	96	61	109	51	91	115	92	95	110	94	111
Convicted	66	79	61	83	49	58	80	91	61	132	87	81
Awaiting trial	20	28	23	40	20	37	44	37	75	50	38	48
Local officials: Charged	248	257	236	219	255	277	237	211	224	299	259	268
Convicted	221	225	191	190	169	264	219	183	184	262	119	252
Awaiting trial	49	98	89	60	118	90	95	89	110	118	106	105
Others involved: Charged	267	208	227	200	292	364	302	256	266	249	318	410
Convicted	240	197	188	170	243	278	306	242	261	188	241	306
Awaiting trial	97	71	91	80	106	128	89	109	121	126	139	168

Source: U.S. Census Bureau. *Statistical Abstract of the United States: 2007.* U.S. Department of Justice.
[1]Includes individuals who are neither public officials nor employees but who were involved with public officials or employees in violating the law, not shown separately.

Table 20-14. Criminal Victimizations by Age of Victim, 1993–2002

(Percent. Covers period 1993 to 2002.)

Characteristic	12–64 years old	65 years old or older
Nonfatal Violent Victimizations		
Victims facing weapons	25.7	30.2
Firearm	9.4	12.7
Victims resisting	71.0	55.5
Threatened/attacked without weapon	27.9	15.3
Victims not resisting	29.0	44.5
Victims injured	25.9	21.8
Characteristic of Offender		
Relationship to victim:		
Known to victim	31.7	23.6
Well known person	15.8	13.9
Casual acquaintance	18.2	15.7
Stranger	46.3	52.5
Don't know relationship	3.7	8.2
Age 30 or older	30.2	48.3
Male	78.8	75.6
Characteristics of Violent Crimes		
Occurring at night:	45.8	27.2
Occurring at/near home:	27.0	45.5
Crime reported to police:	43.9	53.0

Source: U.S. Census Bureau. *Statistical Abstract of the United States: 2007.* U.S. Department of Justice, Office of Justice Programs, Bureau of Justice Statistics.
Note: Offender characteristics are based on victim's perception.

Table 20-15. Demographic Characteristics of Family Violence Offenders Compared to Nonfamily Violence Offenders, by Relationship, 1998–2002

(Percent, unless otherwise indicated. Covers period between 1998 and 2002.)

| Offender characteristic | All non-fatal violent crimes | Percent of crimes in which the victim was the offender's — | | | | | | | |
| | | Family member | | | | Nonfamily member | | | |
		Total	Spouse	Son or daughter	Other family	Total	Boyfriend or girlfriend	Friend or acquaintance	Stranger
All offenses	100.0	100.0	100.0	100.0	100.0	100.0	100.0	100.0	100.0
Gender									
Male	79.9	75.6	86.1	68.2	64.9	80.4	82.4	73.1	86.0
Female	17.0	22.6	13.0	29.6	32.4	16.4	15.6	24.0	10.4
Both	3.1	1.8	0.9	2.2	2.6	3.2	2.0	2.9	3.6
Race									
White	62.0	78.5	82.5	82.0	72.8	59.9	67.5	67.0	53.1
Black	25.0	15.0	12.0	14.0	19.0	26.0	22.0	21.0	30.0
Other[1]	13.4	6.6	6.0	3.8	8.0	14.3	10.9	11.9	16.7
Age									
Under 18	22.4	10.7	[2]0.8	[2]2.2	25.2	23.8	5.8	36.2	16.2
18–29	34.3	25.5	25.5	2.5	31.5	35.4	56.2	26.3	39.9
30 or older	34.2	62.4	73.0	93.9	40.9	30.7	36.6	30.0	30.4
Mixed age group	9.1	1.4	[2]0.6	[2]1.4	2.4	10.1	[2]1.4	7.5	13.5
Total offenses (number)	32 116 920	3 534 150	1 729 360	369 220	1 435 570	28 582 770	2 034 160	11 753 660	14 794 960
Percent of all offenses	100.0	11.0	5.4	1.1	4.5	89.0	6.3	36.6	46.1

Source: U.S. Department of Justice, Bureau of Justice Statistics. *Family Violence Statistics: Including Statistics on Strangers and Acquaintances.*
Note: Data identifying the victim's relationship to the offender were reported for 95.9% of 33,501,120 nonfatal violent crimes. Of the 32,116,920 crimes with known relationships, offender gender was reported for 99.2%; race for 97.6%; age for 95.3%. Totals may not equal sum of the components due to independent rounding.
[1]Includes 2.8% of violent victimizations involving multiple offenders of mixed races.
[2]Estimate based on 10 or fewer sample cases.

Table 20-16. Demographic Characteristics of Family Violence Victims Compared to Nonfamily Violence Victims, by Relationship, 1998–2002

(Percent, unless otherwise indicated. Covers period between 1998 and 2002.)

| Victim characteristic | All violent crimes | Percent of crimes in which the victim was the offender's — | | | | | | | |
| | | Family member | | | | Nonfamily member | | | |
		Total	Spouse	Son or daughter	Other family	Total	Boyfriend or girlfriend	Friend or acquaintance	Stranger
All offenses	100.0	100.0	100.0	100.0	100.0	100.0	100.0	100.0	100.0
Gender									
Male	54.9	26.6	15.7	37.1	37.1	58.4	14.1	53.6	68.3
Female	45.1	73.4	84.3	62.9	62.9	41.6	85.9	46.4	31.7
Race/Hispanic origin									
White	72.3	74.0	76.8	78.5	69.5	72.1	71.0	74.5	70.3
Black	14.3	13.6	10.9	12.6	17.1	14.3	17.2	14.6	13.7
Hispanic	10.5	10.1	9.8	8.0	11.1	10.6	9.0	8.9	12.2
Other	2.9	2.3	2.6	0.9	2.3	2.9	2.8	2.0	3.7
American Indian/Alaska Native	1.1	1.6	2.1	¹0.0	¹1.4	1.0	1.5	1.0	0.9
Asian/Pacific Islander	1.7	¹0.5	¹0.4	¹0.8	¹0.5	1.9	¹1.0	0.9	2.7
Age									
Under 18	23.3	10.8	¹0.8	50.1	12.6	24.8	9.4	35.4	18.5
18–24	24.5	17.6	14.7	27.2	18.6	25.3	42.0	20.8	26.6
25–34	19.7	24.5	33.5	13.6	16.6	19.1	25.3	15.7	21.0
35–54	27.4	41.2	47.8	7.9	41.7	25.7	21.4	23.8	27.9
55 or older	5.1	6.0	3.2	¹1.3	10.6	5.0	2.0	4.3	6.0
Total offenses (number)	32 163 870	3 544 900	1 733 960	371 890	1 439 060	28 618 970	2 037 800	11 775 660	14 805 510
Percent of all offenses	100.0	11.0	5.4	1.2	4.5	89.0	6.3	36.6	46.0

Source: U.S. Department of Justice, Bureau of Justice Statistics. *Family Violence Statistics: Including Statistics on Strangers and Acquaintances.*
Note: Data identifying the victim's relationship to the offender were reported for 95.9% of 33,501,120 nonfatal violent crimes and for 58.4% of 80,319 murders. Of the 32,163,870 crimes with known relationships, victim characteristics were reported for virtually all victims. Totals may not equal sum of the components due to independent rounding.
¹Estimate based on 10 or fewer sample cases.

Table 20-17. Child Abuse Victim Maltreatment Types, by Perpetrator Relationship, 2005

(Number, percent.)

Perpetrator's relationship to the victim	Total	Maltreatment Type				
		Physical abuse	Neglect	Sexual abuse	Psychological maltreatment, other, or unknown	Multiple maltreatments
Parent	678 406	70 877	450 470	17 543	66 839	72 677
Percent	79.4	76.5	86.6	26.3	80.0	79.4
Other relative	58 346	67 744	23 607	19 171	3 726	5 098
Percent	6.8	7.3	4.5	28.7	4.5	5.6
Foster parent	3 805	654	2 188	253	286	424
Percent	0.4	0.7	0.4	0.4	0.3	0.5
Residential facility staff ...	1 622	308	798	137	128	251
Percent	0.2	0.3	0.2	0.2	0.2	0.3
Child daycare provider	5 056	751	2 673	1 186	162	284
Percent	0.6	0.8	0.5	1.8	0.2	0.3
Unmarried partner of parent	32 802	5 830	13 606	4 125	5 930	3 311
Percent	3.8	6.3	2.6	6.2	7.1	3.6
Legal guardian	2 192	268	1 359	87	172	306
Percent	0.3	0.3	0.3	0.1	0.2	0.3
Other professionals	1 095	301	338	319	60	77
Percent	0.1	0.3	0.1	0.5	0.1	0.1
Friends or neighbors	4 886	598	593	3 255	133	307
Percent	0.6	0.6	0.1	4.9	0.2	0.3
Other	35 006	3 246	9 583	15 521	2 876	3 780
Percent	4.1	3.5	1.8	23.3	3.4	4.1
Perpetrator's relationship unknown or missing	31 158	3 086	14 741	5 139	3 224	4 968
Percent	3.6	3.3	2.8	7.7	3.9	5.4
Total perpetrators	854 374	92 663	519 956	66 736	83 536	91 483
Percent	100.0	100.0	100.0	100.0	100.0	100.0

Source: U.S. Department of Health and Human Services, Administration for Children and Families, Administration on Children, Youth and Families. *Child Maltreatment 2005.*
Note: Based on data from 42 states. National estimates for Federal Fiscal Year (FFY) 2005 are based on child populations for the 50 States, the District of Columbia, and Puerto Rico. FFY 2005 is the first year that Puerto Rico's data have been included in *Child Maltreatment.* During FFY 2005: An estimated 899,000 children were victims of maltreatment with a rate of victimization of 12.1 per 1,000 children in the population; nearly 3.6 million children received a Children's Protective Services investigation or assessment.

BOX 20 ■ Personal Identity Theft

Identity theft includes all crimes in which an individual or organization steals personal information about someone to commit fraud. This fraud most commonly involves the victim's current accounts, whether those accounts are credit card, bank, cell phone, or government benefits. In a less common but more costly form of identity theft, the criminal uses the victim's personal information to open new fraudulent accounts. A newer form of identity theft involves the theft of a corporate identity and/or corporate personnel records, including pension information, to commit fraud.

In 1998, the U.S. Congress enacted legislation that made identity theft a federal crime. Since then, law enforcement agencies, private industry, consumers, and government agencies whose databases hold key identifying information have been struggling to stem the tide of crime. According to the Bureau of Justice Statistics, in 2004 at least one person in each of 3.6 million households had been a victim of identity theft in the previous 6 months. This translates into one in every 33 households, with a victim of identity theft every six months and an estimated annual loss of $3.2 billion.

The Bureau of Justice Statistics states that credit card theft is the most common form of identity theft at 48.4% of all cases, or 1.7 million households. It is followed by the theft of other existing accounts in 25.0% of all cases, or 900,000 households. Victims in approximately 500,000 households had their identities stolen and used to open new fraudulent accounts. In 11.6% of cases, multiple forms of theft were involved in the same incident.

These crimes are difficult to solve. One difficulty is that many victims do not report these crimes. This becomes evident when comparing the Bureau of Justice Statistics National Crime Victimization Survey results with the number of identity thefts reported to the Federal Trade Commission (FTC) and the results of Gartner Research's Survey. Gartner states that the incidence of identity theft increased more than 50% between 2003 and 2006 to approximately 15 million incidences annually. However, only 246,035 cases were reported to the Federal Trade Commission for 2006. The statistics from the Bureau of Justice for 2004 (the last year for which data are available) fall in the middle, with 3.6 million cases. Even with an increase of 50%, this figure is a far cry from Gartner's 15 million.

Phishing, an online form of identity theft, entails the theft of both consumer and corporate identities. The perpetrators send E-mails purportedly from a corporation, usually a financial firm, directing a consumer to a bogus Web site where they are asked to provide their account information. Once armed with this information, the thieves have unfettered access to the consumer's accounts and usually enough information to open new accounts in that person's name.

According to the Anti-Phishing Working Group, in May 2007 there were 37,438 unique phishing URLs, which was a decrease from 55,643 in April. However, the Group believes this is just a cyclical fluctuation. A twist on phishing scams are phishing-based Trojans. Instead of sending a consumer an E-mail with a link to a bogus Web site, this scam redirects a consumer's browser from the site he or she intended to access to a fraudulent site. Because the consumer entered the url himself or herself, there is little reason to suspect the site that pops up is not legitimate.

In 2006 President George W. Bush formed the President's Identity Theft Task Force, co-chaired by the Attorney General and the Chair of the Federal Trade Commission, to learn more about the crime and ways it might be avoided. The task force recommended limiting the use of Social Security numbers at government agencies; establishing a National Identity

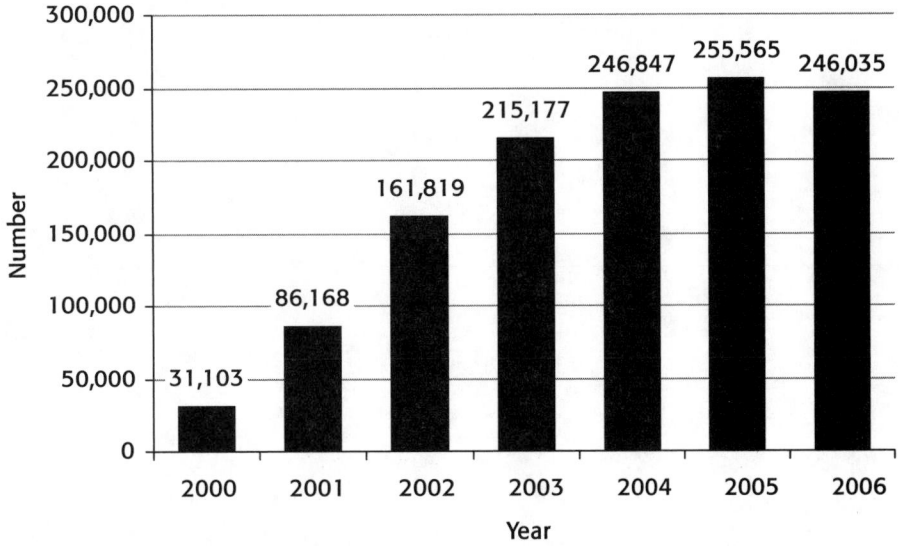

Number of Reported Identity Thefts, 2000 to 2006
Source: Federal Trade Commission.

Theft Law Enforcement Center to encourage the sharing of information among different law enforcement agencies; a government campaign to raise awareness both with consumers and in private industry with an emphasis on prevention; and establishing national standards for the safeguarding of personal information by private industry.

Critics, however, say that the guidelines are too general and do not account for the dramatic changes in technology. They say that both the government and private industry are operating under the aegis of legislation such as the Privacy Law of 1974 that are outmoded and insufficient for today's technologically based crimes.

Sources:

Anti-Phishing Working Group, San Francisco, CA. *Phishing Activity Trends: Report for the Month of May, 2007.* http://www.antiphishing.org/reports/apwg_report_may_2007.pdf

Chen, Michelle. "White House ID Theft Soft on Industry, Critics Say." *The New Standard,* April 27, 2007. http://newstandardnews.net/content/index.cfm/items/4756

Gartner Research, Stamford, CT. "The Truth Behind Identity Theft Numbers," Avivah Litan, February 28, 2007.

U.S. Department of Justice, Office of the Attorney General. *Bureau of Justice Statistics Bulletin,* "Identity Theft, 2004," April 2006. http://www.ojp.usdoj.gov/bjs/abstract/it04.htm

U.S. Department of Justice, Office of the Attorney General and the Federal Trade Commission, The President's Identity Theft Task Force. "Combating Identity Theft: A Strategic Plan," April 2007. http://www.idtheft.gov/reports/StrategicPlan.pdf

U.S. Department of Justice, Office of the Attorney General, National Drug Intelligence Center. *Intelligence Bulletin: Methamphetamine-Related Identity Theft,* May 2007. http://www.usdoj.gov/ndic/pubs22/22972/22972p.pdf

Education, Society, and Leisure

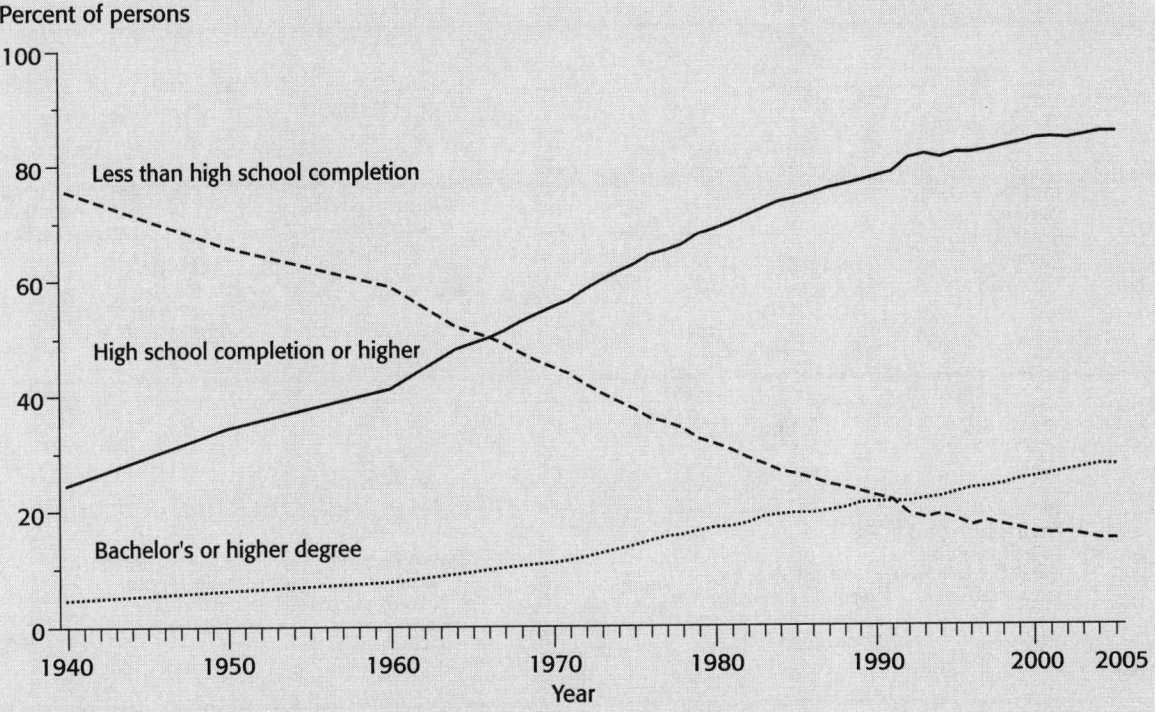

Percent of persons

Less than high school completion

High school completion or higher

Bachelor's or higher degree

Year

Percentage of Persons 25 Years Old and Over, by Highest Level of Educational Attainment: 1940 through 2005

Source: U.S. Department of Commerce, Census Bureau, *U.S. Census of Population, 1960, Volume 1, Part 1;* Current Population Reports, Series P0210; Current Population Survey (CPS), March 1961 through March 2005; and *1960 Census Monograph, Education of the American Population,* by John K. Folger and Charles B. Nam.

Education and Learning

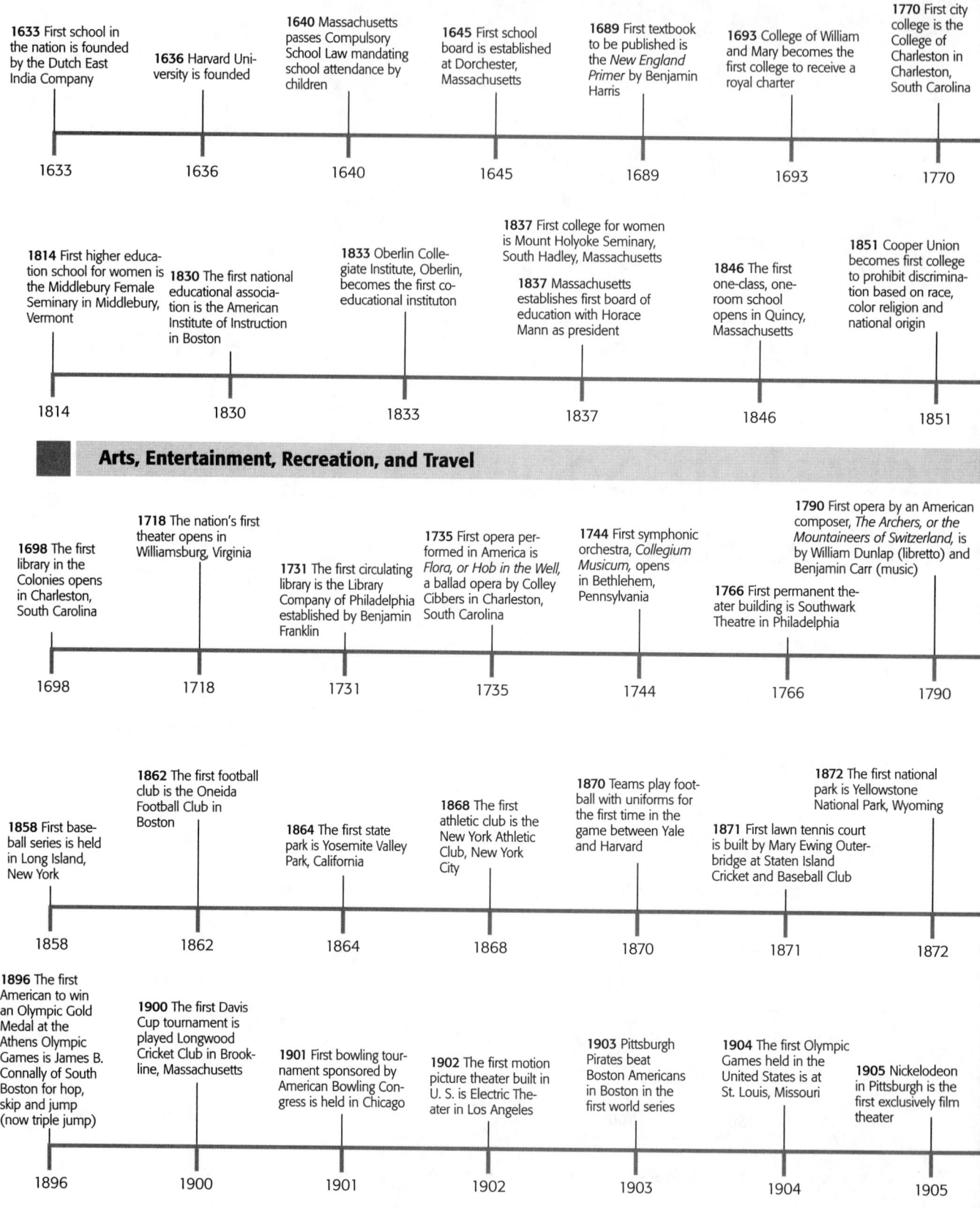

1633 First school in the nation is founded by the Dutch East India Company

1636 Harvard University is founded

1640 Massachusetts passes Compulsory School Law mandating school attendance by children

1645 First school board is established at Dorchester, Massachusetts

1689 First textbook to be published is the *New England Primer* by Benjamin Harris

1693 College of William and Mary becomes the first college to receive a royal charter

1770 First city college is the College of Charleston in Charleston, South Carolina

1633   1636   1640   1645   1689   1693   1770

1814 First higher education school for women is the Middlebury Female Seminary in Middlebury, Vermont

1830 The first national educational association is the American Institute of Instruction in Boston

1833 Oberlin Collegiate Institute, Oberlin, becomes the first coeducational instituton

1837 First college for women is Mount Holyoke Seminary, South Hadley, Massachusetts

1837 Massachusetts establishes first board of education with Horace Mann as president

1846 The first one-class, one-room school opens in Quincy, Massachusetts

1851 Cooper Union becomes first college to prohibit discrimination based on race, color religion and national origin

1814   1830   1833   1837   1846   1851

Arts, Entertainment, Recreation, and Travel

1698 The first library in the Colonies opens in Charleston, South Carolina

1718 The nation's first theater opens in Williamsburg, Virginia

1731 The first circulating library is the Library Company of Philadelphia established by Benjamin Franklin

1735 First opera performed in America is *Flora, or Hob in the Well,* a ballad opera by Colley Cibbers in Charleston, South Carolina

1744 First symphonic orchestra, *Collegium Musicum,* opens in Bethlehem, Pennsylvania

1766 First permanent theater building is Southwark Theatre in Philadelphia

1790 First opera by an American composer, *The Archers, or the Mountaineers of Switzerland,* is by William Dunlap (libretto) and Benjamin Carr (music)

1698   1718   1731   1735   1744   1766   1790

1858 First baseball series is held in Long Island, New York

1862 The first football club is the Oneida Football Club in Boston

1864 The first state park is Yosemite Valley Park, California

1868 The first athletic club is the New York Athletic Club, New York City

1870 Teams play football with uniforms for the first time in the game between Yale and Harvard

1871 First lawn tennis court is built by Mary Ewing Outerbridge at Staten Island Cricket and Baseball Club

1872 The first national park is Yellowstone National Park, Wyoming

1858   1862   1864   1868   1870   1871   1872

1896 The first American to win an Olympic Gold Medal at the Athens Olympic Games is James B. Connally of South Boston for hop, skip and jump (now triple jump)

1900 The first Davis Cup tournament is played Longwood Cricket Club in Brookline, Massachusetts

1901 First bowling tournament sponsored by American Bowling Congress is held in Chicago

1902 The first motion picture theater built in U. S. is Electric Theater in Los Angeles

1903 Pittsburgh Pirates beat Boston Americans in Boston in the first world series

1904 The first Olympic Games held in the United States is at St. Louis, Missouri

1905 Nickelodeon in Pittsburgh is the first exclusively film theater

1896   1900   1901   1902   1903   1904   1905

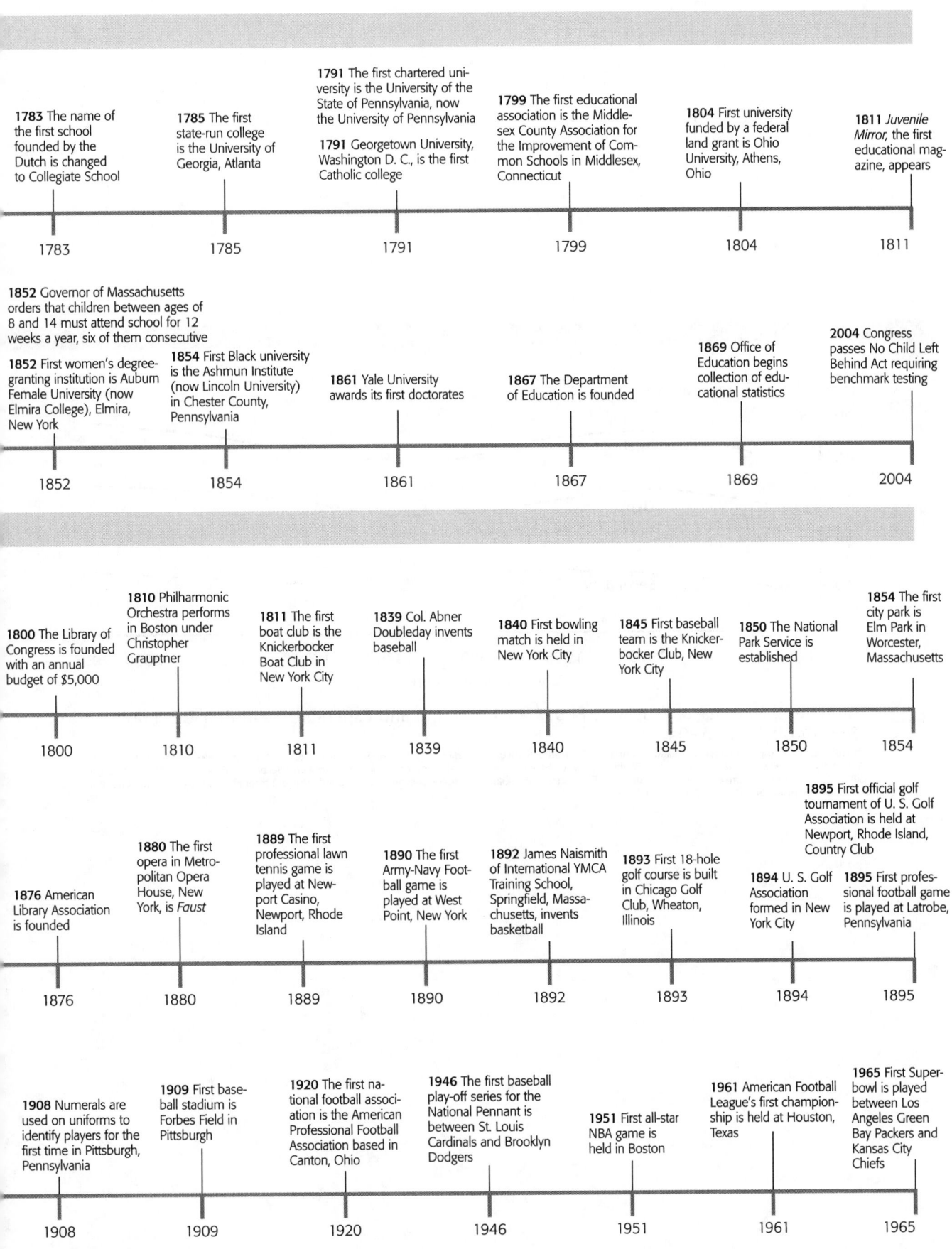

1783 The name of the first school founded by the Dutch is changed to Collegiate School

1785 The first state-run college is the University of Georgia, Atlanta

1791 The first chartered university is the University of the State of Pennsylvania, now the University of Pennsylvania

1791 Georgetown University, Washington D. C., is the first Catholic college

1799 The first educational association is the Middlesex County Association for the Improvement of Common Schools in Middlesex, Connecticut

1804 First university funded by a federal land grant is Ohio University, Athens, Ohio

1811 *Juvenile Mirror*, the first educational magazine, appears

1783   1785   1791   1799   1804   1811

1852 Governor of Massachusetts orders that children between ages of 8 and 14 must attend school for 12 weeks a year, six of them consecutive

1852 First women's degree-granting institution is Auburn Female University (now Elmira College), Elmira, New York

1854 First Black university is the Ashmun Institute (now Lincoln University) in Chester County, Pennsylvania

1861 Yale University awards its first doctorates

1867 The Department of Education is founded

1869 Office of Education begins collection of educational statistics

2004 Congress passes No Child Left Behind Act requiring benchmark testing

1852   1854   1861   1867   1869   2004

1800 The Library of Congress is founded with an annual budget of $5,000

1810 Philharmonic Orchestra performs in Boston under Christopher Grauptner

1811 The first boat club is the Knickerbocker Boat Club in New York City

1839 Col. Abner Doubleday invents baseball

1840 First bowling match is held in New York City

1845 First baseball team is the Knickerbocker Club, New York City

1850 The National Park Service is established

1854 The first city park is Elm Park in Worcester, Massachusetts

1800   1810   1811   1839   1840   1845   1850   1854

1876 American Library Association is founded

1880 The first opera in Metropolitan Opera House, New York, is *Faust*

1889 The first professional lawn tennis game is played at Newport Casino, Newport, Rhode Island

1890 The first Army-Navy Football game is played at West Point, New York

1892 James Naismith of International YMCA Training School, Springfield, Massachusetts, invents basketball

1893 First 18-hole golf course is built in Chicago Golf Club, Wheaton, Illinois

1894 U. S. Golf Association formed in New York City

1895 First official golf tournament of U. S. Golf Association is held at Newport, Rhode Island, Country Club

1895 First professional football game is played at Latrobe, Pennsylvania

1876   1880   1889   1890   1892   1893   1894   1895

1908 Numerals are used on uniforms to identify players for the first time in Pittsburgh, Pennsylvania

1909 First baseball stadium is Forbes Field in Pittsburgh

1920 The first national football association is the American Professional Football Association based in Canton, Ohio

1946 The first baseball play-off series for the National Pennant is between St. Louis Cardinals and Brooklyn Dodgers

1951 First all-star NBA game is held in Boston

1961 American Football League's first championship is held at Houston, Texas

1965 First Super-bowl is played between Los Angeles Green Bay Packers and Kansas City Chiefs

1908   1909   1920   1946   1951   1961   1965

Fall enrollment, in millions

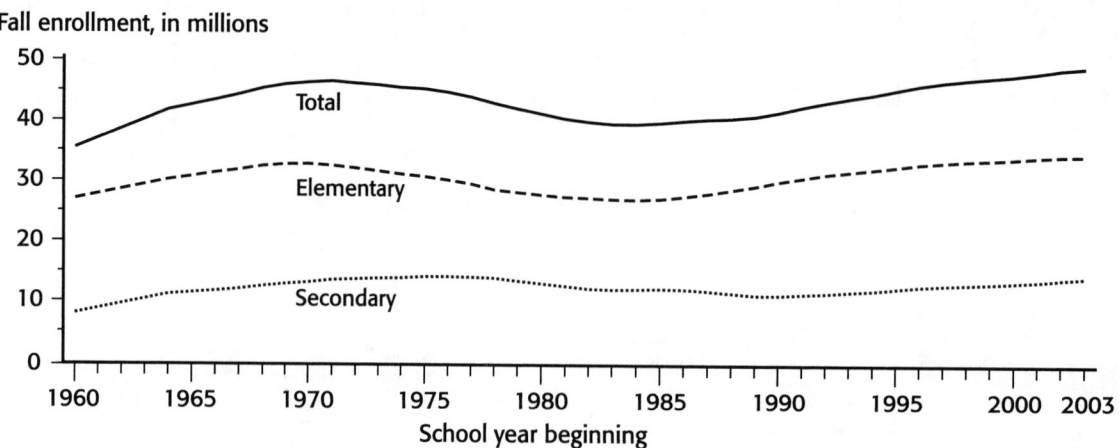

Enrollment, Number of Teachers, Pupil/Teacher Ratio, and Expenditures in Public Schools:
1960 through 2003–04

Source: U.S. Department of Education, National Center for Education Statistics, *Statistics of State School Systems,* 1959–60 through 1969–70; *Statistics of Public Elementary and Secondary School Systems,* 1970 through 1980; *Revenues and Expenditures for Public Elementary and Secondary Education,* 1970–71 through 1980–81; and Common Core of Data (CCD), "State Nonfiscal Survey of Public Elementary/Secondary Education," 1981–82 through 2003–04, and "National Public Education Financial Survey," 1989–90 through 2002–03.

CHAPTER 21

Education and Learning

HIGHLIGHTS

1 Educational statistics have been collected and issued by the Office of Education from 1870 to 1953, by the Department of Health, Education, and Welfare from 1953 to 1979, and by the Department of Education from 1979 to the present. From 1870 to 1917, these statistics were included in the *Annual Report of the United States Commissioner of Education* and from 1918 to 1958 in the *Biennial Survey of Education*. Since 1962, the National Center for Educational Statistics has published summary data on education in two annual publications: *Digest of Educational Statistics* and *Condition of Education*. Two problems that arise in the study of educational statistics are inconsistencies in the definitions of terms and procedures and a lack of timeliness. School authorities are not compelled by law to report to the Office of Education, but the vast majority of them do so voluntarily. Nonpublic schools under the operational control of private individuals and groups have reported their data in a slightly different format over the years, making this data incomparable with public school data. Enrollment information is collected on a state-by-state basis and represents a cumulative count of the total number of pupils registered at any time during the school year in each state. Pupils enrolled in more than one state in a school year are counted more than once, resulting in inflated totals.

2 The first school in the United States was established by the Dutch West India Company on Manhattan Island in 1633, with Adam Roelantsen as its first master. In 1783, the school's name was changed to Collegiate School. The first school committee or board was elected in Dorchester, Massachusetts, in 1645. The first school to operate on a one class to one room basis was set up in Quincy, Massachusetts, in 1846. The first school superintendent, Roswell William Haskins, was appointed in 1836 in Buffalo, New York. The Compulsory School Law, the first piece of educational legislation, was passed on June 14, 1642, by Massachusetts. According to the records of the Governor and Company of Massachusetts Bay, the legislation stated that "This Court, taking into consideration the great neglect of many parents and masters in training up their children in learning and labor and other employments which may be profitable to the Commonwealth, so hereupon order and decree that in every town the chosen men appointed for managing the prudential affairs of the same shall henceforth stand charged with the care of the redress of this evil." On November 11, 1647, Massachusetts ordered that "every town in this jurisdiction, after the Lord has increased them to the number of 50 householders, shall then forthwith appoint one within their town to teach all such children as shall resort to him to write and read, whose wages shall be paid either by the parents or masters of such children, or by the inhabitants in general." In 1852, the governor of Massachusetts ordered that children between the ages of 8 and 14 must attend school for 12 weeks in the year, six of which must be consecutive."

The first public school tax was an act providing "for the establishment of free schools," enacted January 15, 1825 by the state of Illinois. The tax was levied at the rate of 2 percent. The first schoolbook was the *New England Primer* (1689–90) printed by R. Pierce and sold by Benjamin Harris at the London Coffee House in Boston. Middlesex County Association for the Improvement of Common Schools was the first local education association organized in Middlesex, Connecticut, in May 1799. The first national education association, the American Institute of Instruction, was founded in Boston in 1830. The oldest educational magazine, the *Juvenile Mirror,* first appeared in New York City in 1811.

3 The Department of Education was founded by the Act of Congress on March 2, 1867, as an agency for the "purpose of collecting such statistics and facts as shall show the condition and progress of education in the several states and territories, and of diffusing such information respecting the organization and management of school systems and methods of teaching as shall aid the people of the United States in the establishment and maintenance of efficient school systems and otherwise promote the cause of education." The first commissioner was Henry Barnard. The Act of July 28, 1868 abolished the Department of Education and created in its stead the Office of Education in the Department of Interior.

4 The first college in the United States was Harvard College, founded in 1636. The first commencement, held in 1642, was presided over by Henry Dunster, the college's first president, who served from 1640 to 1654. Georgetown College, the first Catholic college, was established in Washington, D.C., in 1791. The first city college, the College of Charleston in Charleston, South Carolina, was founded in 1770, chartered in 1785, and opened in 1790. Oberlin Collegiate Institute, the first coeducational college, opened in 1833. The first college to receive a royal charter was the Royal College of William and Mary in 1693. The first college for women was Mount Holyoke Seminary in South Hadley, Massachusetts, founded in 1837. The Cooper Union in New York City was the first college to prohibit discrimination on account of race, religion, or color in 1851. The first state university was the University of Georgia in Athens, Georgia, chartered in 1785 and opened in 1801. Lincoln University, the first Black university, was chartered in 1854 as Ashmun Institute in Chester County, Pennsylvania. The first educational institution legally designated as a university was the University of the State of Pennsylvania in 1791, known now as the University of Pennsylvania. The first university founded by a federal land grant was Ohio University in Athens, Ohio, chartered in 1804 and opened in 1808. The first college alumni association was the Society of Alumni of Williams College, Williamstown, Massachusetts, founded in 1821. Yale University awarded the first doctorates in 1861 to Eugene Schuyler, James Morris Whiton, and Arthur Williams Wright.

5 In 2003, there were 71.890 million pupils enrolled at all levels of education, of which 61.398 million were enrolled in public schools; 48.540 million pupils were enrolled in public school K through 12; 6.448 million in private schools K through 12; 12.857 million in public colleges; and 4.043 million in private colleges. Total enrollment in schools and colleges is expected to reach 77.981 million in 2015. Between 1975 and 1980, total school and college enrollment dropped from 61 million to 58.3 million, but then picked up again in the 1990s and into 2000.

6 Education ranks among the largest expenditure items in national and state budgets. In 2004, public elementary and secondary education cost $475.5 billion, and public college and university education cost $200.1 billion, for a total of $675.6 billion, compared with $118.712 billion in 1960.

7 The number of high school graduates in 2003 was 2.720 million, slightly more than the previous years but less than in 1980 when 2.758 million people graduated from high school.

8 Higher education had a healthy growth rate through 2004. Of the total enrollment of 17.272 million in 2004, males made up 7.387 million (42.8 percent) and females 9.885 million (57.2 percent). Females were in minority in higher education until 1980. In 1960 male enrollment was 2.3 million compared with female enrollment of 1.2 million. Female majority status in college enrollment began in the 1980s and has continued ever since. Of total enrollment, 12.980 million (75.2 percent) are enrolled in public institutions and 4.292 million (24.8 percent) are enrolled in private institutions; 14,781 million are in undergraduate programs, 2.157 in graduate programs, and 335,000 in first-time professional programs.

9 In terms of college graduates in 2005, Asians have the highest level with 50.1 percent, followed by Whites with 28.0 percent, Blacks with 17.6 percent, and Hispanics with 12.0 percent.

10 Blacks have made dramatic gains in education as a result of federal programs. In 1960, only 20.1 percent of Blacks over 25 were high school graduates and only 3.1 percent held college degrees. By 2005, the relative numbers increased to 81.1 percent and 17.6 percent.

11 Southern states are much less successful in the educational attainment of their citizens than Northern states. In terms of the percentage of persons with high school diplomas in 2005, Texas is at the bottom with 78.2 percent. Other Southern states with less than the national average of 85.2 are Alabama (80.9 percent), Arkansas (81.4 percent), Kentucky (78.9 percent), Louisiana (80.2 percent), Mississippi (79.9 percent), New Mexico (81.0 percent), South Carolina (83.0 percent), Tennessee (78.2 percent), and West Virginia (82.4 percent). The states leading in educational attainment at the high school level are Minnesota and Utah (92.7 percent each). The states that have the highest percentage of people with bachelor's degrees or more are Connecticut (36.9 percent), Massachusetts (36.8 percent), and Maryland and New Jersey (36.3 percent each).

12 In 2000, 1,946,400 nonfatal crimes against students were reported. Of these, 128.4 were considered serious. These include, rape, sexual assault, robbery, and aggravated assault.

13 Preprimary school enrollment in 2004 was 7.968 million, of which 4.672 million were in nursery schools and 3.298 million in kindergarten. Black enrollment rate is higher than that of Whites at this level (67.0 percent vs. 63.8 percent). Only slightly more children are enrolled in public nursery schools than private ones (2.429 million vs. 2.244 million). However, many more children are enrolled in public kindergartens than private ones (2,813,000 vs. 485,000).

14 The annual salary of a classroom teacher has risen from $23,587 in 1985 to $45,884 in 2005. The highest salaries in 2004 were in Connecticut ($57,300), California ($56,400), New Jersey ($55,600), and New York ($55,200). They were lowest in South Dakota ($33,200), Oklahoma ($35,100), and North Dakota ($35,400).

15 One of the determinants of the quality of education is the student-teacher ratio. This ratio has usually been higher in private schools at all levels, but the federal government is now engaged in an effort to reduce overcrowding in public schools and to appoint more teachers. Since 1960, the student–teacher ratio has improved in public elementary and secondary schools from 25.8 to 15.9 in 2003.

16 Schools are among the largest users of computers in the United States. During the 2005-2006 school year, there were 14.165 million computers in school, or 3.9 students per computer, and 84.3 percent of schools with computers have high-speed Internet access.

17 Catholic school systems in the United States have been downsizing since the 1960s. In 2003-2004, there were 6,539 Catholic elementary schools enrolling 1,659,000 students and 1,096 Catholic secondary schools enrolling 610,000 students, compared with 10,133 elementary schools enrolling 3,860 students and 1,227 secondary schools enrolling 636,000 students in 1967.

18 Average Scholastic Assessment Test (SAT) scores have been declining. In 1967, average SAT scores were 543 for verbal (540 for males and 545 for females) and 516 for math (535 for males and 495 for females). The relative scores in 2005 were 508 for verbal (513 for males and 505 for females) and 520 for math (538 for males and 504 for females). Only 22.5 percent scored 600 or above in verbal and 26.5 percent in math, while 15.5 percent scored below 400 in verbal and 13.8 percent in math.

19 Average American College Testing (ACT) scores inched higher from 20.6 in 1990 to 20.9 in 2005, but males did better than females (21.1 for males vs. 20.9 for females). Males did better in math and science reasoning while females did better in English and reading.

20 Spanish and French are the most popular foreign languages in schools, preferred by 68 percent and 18 percent respectively. German is a distant third at 4.8 percent.

21 Hispanic students lead in the proportion of status dropouts, that is, the percentage of the population who have not completed high school and are not enrolled. While the White dropout rate was 11.9 percent in 2004 (13.7 percent for males and 10.0 percent for females) and the Black dropout rate was 15.1 percent (17.9 percent for males and 12.7 percent for females), the Hispanic rate was 28.0 percent (33.5 percent for males and 21.7 percent for females).

22 More high school graduates enroll in higher education institutions compared with the 1960s. In 2004, 66.7 percent of high school graduates went on to college (61.4 percent male, 71.5 percent female, 68.8 percent White, and 62.5 percent Black), compared with 50.7 percent of high school graduates in 1975 (52.6 percent males, 49.0 percent females, 51.1 percent White, and 41.7 percent Black).

23 In 2005, 565,000 foreign (nonimmigrant) students were enrolled in U.S. colleges and universities. Of these, 36,000 were from Africa, 356,000 from Asia, 72,000 from Europe, and 68,000 from Latin America. Of the large number of Asian, 80,000 came from India, 53,000 from South Korea, 42,000 from Japan, and 26,000 from China (Taiwan). Engineering, science, and business remain popular majors for foreign students.

24 Of the 4,182 institutions of higher education in the United States in 2000, 2,450 were four-year institutions and 1,732 two-year institutions.

25 With 1983 = 100, the Higher Education Price Index increased from 39.5 in 1970 to 251.9 in 2006. During the same time period, fringe benefits of the personnel compensation component of the price index grew from 24.7 to 343.7.

26 Federal financial assistance for college and university students in the form of loans and grants totaled $72.112 billion in 2005.

27 Charges in 2004, including tuition, room, and board, were $9,249 (compared with $3,408 in 1985) in public institutions and $24,636 in private institutions (compared with $8,203 in 1985).

28 Voluntary financial support for higher education rose to $25.6 billion annually in 2005 from $6.3 billion in 1985. The increase includes $19.2 billion from individuals and alumnae, $4.4 billion from business corporations, and $7.0 billion from foundations.

29 During the 2003-2004 academic year, 63.0 percent of all undergraduates received some sort of financial aid with the average amount of $7,400.

30 In 2002, the 12 most popular languages on campuses were Spanish (746,300), French (202,000), German (91,100), Italian (63,900), American Sign Language (60,800), Japanese (52,200), Chinese (34,200), Latin (29,800), Russian (23,900), Hebrew (22,800), Ancient Greek (20,400), and Arabic (10,600).

31 Of college freshmen in 2001, 46.6 percent were A- to A+ in high school, 48.0 percent were B- to B+ students, and 5.4 percent were C to C+ students. By political orientation, 27.1 percent were liberal, 45.0 percent middle of the road, and 22.6 percent conservative.

32 In 2004, 2.755 million students earned degrees from colleges and universities. Of that total, 41.8 percent were men (compared with 65.8 percent male in 1960). More women than men received associate's, bachelor's, and master's degrees, but men earned more first professional and doctoral degrees.

33 The most popular fields of study in 2004, at the baccalaureate level by the number of degrees earned were business (22.0 percent), social sciences and history (10.8 percent), and education (7.6 percent).

34 In 2004, 15,442 medical degrees (46.4 percent female) were conferred by medical schools, 4,335 dental degrees (41.6 percent female) by dental schools, and 5,332 theological degrees (34.2 percent female) by seminaries.

35 Nonresident aliens earned 26.4 percent of all doctoral degrees and 13.4 percent of all master's degrees. Their doctoral share is highest in engineering, mathematics, and computer and information science.

36 California has the greatest number of institutions of higher learning at 399, followed by New York (307), Texas (208), and Ohio (194).

Table 21-1. School Enrollment, with Projections, 1965–2015

(Thousands. As of fall.)

Year	All levels			Pre-kindergarten through grade 8		Grades 9 through 12		College[1]	
	Total	Public	Private	Public	Private	Public	Private	Public	Private
2015, projection	77 981	66 193	11 787	36 439	5 448	14 780	1 440	14 974	4 900
2014, projection	77 243	65 570	11 673	36 142	5 401	14 593	1 425	14 835	4 847
2013, projection	76 497	64 953	11 545	35 724	5 341	14 569	1 424	14 659	4 780
2012, projection	75 830	64 411	11 418	35 297	5 280	14 641	1 429	14 473	4 709
2011, projection	75 252	63 948	11 304	34 907	5 224	14 730	1 435	14 311	4 645
2010, projection	74 779	63 574	11 205	34 618	5 181	14 797	1 437	14 159	4 587
2009, projection	74 332	63 235	11 097	34 350	5 139	14 917	1 446	13 968	4 511
2008, projection	73 928	62 931	10 997	34 154	5 105	15 013	1 454	13 765	4 437
2007, projection	73 544	62 647	10 897	33 990	5 074	15 101	1 463	13 555	4 361
2006, projection	73 107	62 308	10 800	33 906	5 055	15 042	1 456	13 360	4 288
2005, projection	72 576	61 912	10 664	33 823	4 997	14 887	1 441	13 202	4 226
2004[2], projection	72 236	61 540	10 696	33 925	4 990	14 634	1 414	12 980	4 292
2003	71 890	61 398	10 492	34 202	5 065	14 338	1 383	12 857	4 043
2002	71 188	60 935	10 253	34 116	5 034	14 067	1 359	12 752	3 860
2001	69 920	59 905	10 014	33 938	4 993	13 734	1 326	12 233	3 695
2000	68 670	58 956	9 713	33 688	4 867	13 515	1 287	11 753	3 560
1999	67 667	58 166	9 501	33 488	4 765	13 369	1 254	11 309	3 482
1998	66 983	57 677	9 306	33 346	4 702	13 193	1 235	11 138	3 369
1997	66 470	57 323	9 147	33 073	4 623	13 054	1 218	11 196	3 306
1996	65 744	56 733	9 011	32 764	4 551	12 847	1 213	11 121	3 247
1995	64 764	55 933	8 831	32 341	4 465	12 500	1 197	11 092	3 169
1994	63 888	55 245	8 643	31 898	4 335	12 213	1 163	11 134	3 145
1993	63 118	54 654	8 464	31 504	4 215	11 961	1 132	11 189	3 116
1992	62 633	54 208	8 425	31 088	4 175	11 735	1 147	11 385	3 103
1991	61 681	53 357	8 324	30 506	4 113	11 541	1 162	11 310	3 049
1990	60 269	52 061	8 208	29 878	4 084	11 338	1 150	10 845	2 974
1989	59 279	51 120	8 159	29 152	4 035	11 390	1 163	10 578	2 961
1988	58 485	50 349	8 136	28 501	4 036	11 687	1 206	10 161	2 894
1987	58 253	49 982	8 272	27 933	4 232	12 076	1 247	9 973	2 793
1986	57 709	49 467	8 242	27 420	4 116	12 333	1 336	9 714	2 790
1985	57 226	48 901	8 325	27 034	4 195	12 388	1 362	9 479	2 768
1984	57 150	48 686	8 465	26 905	4 300	12 304	1 400	9 477	2 765
1983	57 432	48 935	8 497	26 981	4 315	12 271	1 400	9 683	2 782
1982	57 591	49 262	8 330	27 161	4 200	12 405	1 400	9 696	2 730
1981	57 916	49 691	8 225	27 280	4 100	12 764	1 400	9 647	2 725
1980	58 305	50 335	7 971	27 647	3 992	13 231	1 339	9 457	2 640
1979	58 221	50 687	7 533	28 034	3 700	13 616	1 300	9 037	2 533
1978	58 897	51 337	7 559	28 463	3 732	14 088	1 353	8 786	2 474
1977	60 003	52 425	7 579	29 375	3 797	14 203	1 343	8 847	2 439
1976	60 490	52 964	7 526	29 997	3 825	14 314	1 342	8 653	2 359
1975	61 004	53 654	7 350	30 515	3 700	14 304	1 300	8 835	2 350
1974	60 297	53 063	7 235	30 971	3 700	14 103	1 300	7 989	2 235
1973	60 047	52 865	7 183	31 401	3 700	14 044	1 300	7 420	2 183
1972	59 941	52 798	7 144	31 879	3 700	13 848	1 300	7 071	2 144
1971	60 220	52 875	7 344	32 318	3 900	13 753	1 300	6 804	2 144
1970	59 838	52 322	7 516	32 558	4 052	13 336	1 311	6 428	2 153
1969	59 055	51 447	7 608	32 513	4 200	13 037	1 300	5 897	2 108
1968	58 257	50 375	7 882	32 226	4 400	12 718	1 400	5 431	2 082
1967	56 803	48 707	8 096	31 641	4 600	12 250	1 400	4 816	2 096
1966	55 629	47 388	8 241	31 145	4 800	11 894	1 400	4 349	2 041
1965	54 394	46 143	8 251	30 563	4 900	11 610	1 400	3 970	1 951

Source: U.S. Census Bureau. *Statistical Abstract of the United States: 2007.* U.S. National Center for Education Statistics.
Note: Based on surveys of state education agencies and private schools.
[1]Data beginning 1996 based on new classification system; this classification includes some additional, primarily 2-year, colleges and excludes a few institutions that did not award degrees. Includes institutions that were eligible to participate in Title IV federal financial aid programs.
[2]Pre-Kindergarten through grade 12 are projections, college data are actual.

Table 21-2. School Expenditures, by Type of Control and Level of Instruction in Constant (2003–2004) Dollars, 1960–2004

(Millions of dollars. For school years ending in year shown.)

Year	Total	Elementary and secondary schools			Colleges and universities[2]		
		Total	Public	Private[1]	Total	Public	Private
2004	826 600	511 200	475 500	35 700	315 400	200 100	115 300
2003	801 403	499 397	464 858	34 539	302 006	193 819	108 187
2002	781 663	488 502	454 666	33 836	293 161	191 568	101 592
2001	746 333	469 780	436 620	33 160	276 553	181 047	95 506
2000	712 660	452 378	419 731	32 647	260 282	167 441	92 841
1999	682 254	434 335	402 442	31 893	247 919	158 945	88 974
1998	656 124	415 825	384 646	31 180	240 299	152 846	87 453
1997	631 268	397 169	366 721	30 448	234 100	147 529	86 571
1996	612 746	383 321	353 691	29 630	229 425	143 965	85 460
1995	600 522	374 144	345 193	28 952	226 378	142 859	83 519
1994	586 538	365 913	337 659	28 254	220 625	139 119	81 506
1993	573 945	358 193	330 252	27 942	215 752	136 535	79 217
1992	562 073	351 770	324 571	27 199	210 303	133 094	77 209
1991	548 919	345 914	318 817	27 097	203 005	129 179	73 825
1990	535 853	338 504	311 831	26 674	197 348	125 704	71 645
1985	421 127	262 862	241 045	21 817	158 265	102 602	55 663
1980	383 712	247 286	230 027	17 259	136 426	90 533	45 893
1975	373 332	247 368	232 995	14 372	125 964	84 401	41 563
1970	316 401	212 736	200 420	12 316	103 665	65 272	38 394
1960	141 322	105 850	98 884	6 967	35 471	19 828	15 643

Source: U.S. Census Bureau. *Statistical Abstract of the United States: 2007.* U.S. National Center for Education Statistics.
Note: Data shown reflect historical revisions. Total expenditures for public elementary and secondary schools include current expenditures, interest on school debt and capital outlay. Data deflated by the Consumer Price Index, wage earners, and clerical workers through 1977; thereafter, all urban consumers, on a school year basis (supplied by the National Center for Education Statistics). Based on survey of state education agencies.
[1]Estimated.
[2]Data beginning 1996 based on new classification system; this classification includes some additional, primarily 2-year, colleges and excludes a few institutions that did not award degrees. Includes institutions that were eligible to participate in Title IV federal financial aid programs.

Table 21-3. School Enrollment by Sex and Level, 1960–2004

(Millions. As of October.)

Year	All levels[1]			Elementary			High school			College		
	Total	Male	Female	Total	Male	Female	Total	Male	Female	Total	Male	Female
2004	75.5	37.4	38.0	36.5	19.0	17.6	16.8	8.4	8.4	17.4	7.6	9.8
2003	74.9	37.3	37.6	36.3	18.7	17.6	17.1	8.6	8.4	16.6	7.3	9.3
2002	74.0	36.8	37.3	36.7	18.9	17.8	16.4	8.3	8.0	16.5	7.2	9.3
2001	73.1	36.3	36.9	36.9	19.0	17.9	16.1	8.2	7.8	15.9	6.9	9.0
2000	72.2	35.8	36.4	36.7	18.9	17.9	15.8	8.1	7.7	15.3	6.7	8.6
1999	72.4	36.3	36.1	36.7	18.8	17.9	15.9	8.2	7.7	15.2	7.0	8.2
1998	72.1	36.0	36.1	36.4	18.7	17.7	15.6	7.9	7.6	15.5	6.9	8.6
1997	72.0	35.9	36.2	36.3	18.7	17.6	15.8	8.0	7.7	15.4	6.8	8.6
1996	70.3	35.1	35.2	35.5	18.3	17.3	15.3	7.9	7.4	15.2	6.8	8.4
1995	69.8	35.0	34.8	35.7	18.3	17.4	15.0	7.7	7.3	14.7	6.7	8.0
1994	69.3	34.6	34.6	35.4	18.2	17.2	14.6	7.4	7.2	15.0	6.8	8.2
1993	65.4	32.9	32.5	34.8	17.9	16.9	13.6	7.0	6.6	13.9	6.3	7.6
1992	64.6	32.2	32.3	34.3	17.7	16.6	13.3	6.8	6.5	14.0	6.2	7.8
1991	63.9	32.1	31.8	33.8	17.3	16.4	13.1	6.8	6.4	14.1	6.4	7.6
1990	63.0	31.5	31.5	33.2	17.1	16.0	12.8	6.5	6.4	13.6	6.2	7.4
1989	61.5	30.8	30.7	32.5	16.7	15.8	12.9	6.6	6.3	13.2	6.0	7.2
1988	61.1	30.7	30.5	32.2	16.6	15.6	13.2	6.7	6.4	13.1	5.9	7.2
1987	60.6	30.7	29.9	31.6	16.3	15.3	13.8	7.0	6.8	12.7	6.0	6.7
1986[2]	60.5	30.6	30.0	31.1	16.1	15.0	14.2	7.2	7.0	12.7	6.0	6.7
1985	59.8	30.0	29.7	30.7	15.7	15.0	14.1	7.2	6.9	12.5	5.9	6.6
1980	58.6	29.6	29.1	30.6	15.8	14.9	14.6	7.3	7.3	11.4	5.4	6.0
1975	61.0	31.6	29.4	33.8	17.3	16.5	15.7	8.0	7.7	9.7	5.3	4.4
1970	60.4	31.4	28.9	37.1	19.0	18.1	14.7	7.4	7.3	7.4	4.4	3.0
1960	46.3	24.2	22.0	32.4	16.7	15.7	10.2	5.2	5.1	3.6	2.3	1.2

Source: U.S. Census Bureau. *Statistical Abstract of the United States: 2007.*
Note: For the civilian noninstitutional population. 1970–1979 for persons 3 to 34 years old; beginning 1980, 3 years old and over. Elementary includes kindergarten and grades 1–8; high school, grades 9–12; and college, 2-year and 4-year colleges, universities, and graduate and professional schools. Data for college represent degree-credit enrollment. Based on U.S. Census Bureau's Current Population Survey.
[1] Beginning 1970, includes nursery schools, not shown separately.
[2] Revised. Data beginning 1986, based on a revised edit and tabulation package.

Table 21-4. Educational Attainment, by Race, Hispanic Origin, and Sex, 1940–2005

(Percent.)

Year	All races[1]		White[2]		Black[3]		Asian and Pacific Islander[3]		Hispanic[3]	
	Male	Female	Male	Female	Male	Female	Male	Female	Male	Female
High School Graduate or More[4]										
2005	84.9	85.4	85.2	86.2	81.1	81.2	90.4	85.1	58.0	58.9
2004	84.8	85.4	85.3	86.3	80.4	80.8	88.7	85.0	57.3	59.5
2003	84.1	85.0	84.5	85.7	79.6	80.3	[5]89.5	[5]86.0	56.3	57.8
2002	83.8	84.4	84.3	85.2	78.5	78.9	89.5	85.5	56.1	57.9
2001	84.1	84.2	84.4	85.1	79.2	78.5	90.3	85.1	55.5	58.0
2000	84.2	84.0	84.8	85.0	78.7	78.3	88.2	83.4	56.6	57.5
1995	81.7	81.6	83.0	83.0	73.4	74.1	...	...	52.9	53.8
1990	77.7	77.5	79.1	79.0	65.8	66.5	84.0	77.2	50.3	51.3
1985	74.4	73.5	76.0	75.1	58.4	60.8	...	...	48.5	47.4
1980	67.3	65.8	69.6	68.1	50.8	51.5	...	...	67.3	65.8
1975	63.1	62.1	65.0	64.1	41.6	43.3	...	...	39.5	36.7
1970	51.9	52.8	54.0	55.0	30.1	32.5	...	...	37.9	34.2
1965	48.0	49.9	50.2	52.2	25.8	28.4	...	...	...	...
1960	39.5	42.5	41.6	44.7	18.2	21.8	...	...	...	...
1950	32.6	36.0	34.6	38.2	12.6	14.7	...	...	...	...
1940	22.7	26.3	24.2	28.1	6.9	8.4	...	...	...	...
College Graduate or More[4]										
2005	28.9	26.5	29.4	26.7	16.1	18.8	54.0	46.7	11.8	12.1
2004	29.4	26.1	30.0	26.4	16.6	18.5	53.7	45.6	11.8	12.3
2003	28.9	25.7	29.4	25.9	16.7	17.8	53.9	46.1	11.2	11.6
2002	28.5	25.1	29.1	25.4	16.4	17.5	50.9	43.8	11.0	11.2
2001	28.2	24.3	28.7	24.0	15.3	16.1	52.3	43.2	10.8	11.4
2000	27.8	23.6	28.5	23.9	16.3	16.7	47.6	40.7	10.7	10.6
1995	26.0	20.2	27.2	21.0	13.6	12.9	...	...	10.1	8.4
1990	24.4	18.4	25.3	19.0	11.9	10.8	44.9	35.4	9.8	8.7
1985	23.1	16.0	24.0	16.3	11.2	11.0	...	...	9.7	7.3
1980	20.1	12.8	21.3	13.3	8.4	8.3	...	...	9.4	6.0
1975	17.6	10.6	18.4	11.0	6.7	6.2	...	...	8.3	4.6
1970	13.5	8.1	14.4	8.4	4.2	4.6	...	...	7.8	4.3
1965	12.0	7.1	12.7	7.3	4.9	4.5	...	...	...	...
1960	9.7	5.8	10.3	6.0	2.8	3.3	...	...	...	...
1950	7.3	5.2	7.9	5.4	2.1	2.4	...	...	...	...
1940	5.5	3.8	5.9	4.0	1.4	1.2	...	...	...	...

Source: U.S. Census Bureau.
Note: For persons 25 years old and over. 1960, 1970, and 1980 as of April 1 and based on sample data from the censuses of population. Other years as of March and based on the Current Population Survey.
[1]Includes other races, not shown separately.
[2]Beginning 2003, for persons who selected this race group only. The 2003 Current Population Survey (CPS) allowed respondents to choose more than one race. Beginning 2003 data represent persons who selected this race group only and exclude persons reporting more than one race. The CPS in prior years only allowed respondents to report one race group.
[3]Persons of Hispanic origin may be of any race.
[4]Through 1991, completed 4 years of high school or more and 4 years of college or more.
[5]Starting in 2003, data are for Asians only, excludes Pacific Islanders.
. . . = Not available.

Table 21-5. Preprimary School Enrollment—Summary, 1980–2004

(Thousands, percent. As of October.)

Item	1980	1985	1990	1995	2000	2001	2002	2003	2004
Number of Children									
Population, 3 to 5 years old ..	**9 284**	**10 733**	**11 207**	**12 518**	**11 858**	**11 653**	**11 481**	**12 204**	**12 362**
Total enrolled[1]	**4 878**	**5 865**	**6 659**	**7 739**	**7 592**	**7 441**	**7 504**	**7 921**	**7 968**
Nursery	1 981	2 477	3 378	4 331	4 326	4 250	4 423	4 859	4 672
Public	628	846	1 202	1 950	2 146	2 126	2 205	2 512	2 429
Private	1 353	1 631	2 177	2 381	2 180	2 124	2 218	2 347	2 244
Kindergarten	2 897	3 388	3 281	3 408	3 266	3 191	3 081	3 062	3 296
Public	2 438	2 847	2 767	2 799	2 701	2 690	2 551	2 539	2 813
Private	459	541	513	608	565	501	530	523	485
White[2]	3 994	4 757	5 389	6 144	5 861	5 678	5 799	6 204	5 976
Black[2]	725	919	964	1 236	1 265	1 323	1 239	1 156	1 332
Hispanic[3]	370	496	642	1 040	1 155	1 218	1 263	1 320	1 438
3 years old	857	1 035	1 205	1 489	1 540	1 504	1 619	1 806	1 583
4 years old	1 423	1 765	2 086	2 553	2 556	2 526	2 568	2 785	2 969
5 years old	2 598	3 065	3 367	3 697	3 496	3 411	3 317	3 331	3 417
Enrollment Rate									
Total enrolled[1]	**52.5**	**54.6**	**59.4**	**61.8**	**64.0**	**63.9**	**65.4**	**64.9**	**64.4**
White[2]	52.7	54.7	59.7	63.0	63.2	63.2	65.0	65.8	63.8
Black[2]	51.8	55.8	57.8	58.9	68.5	69.2	67.7	62.7	67.0
Hispanic[3]	43.3	43.3	49.0	51.1	52.6	53.9	56.1	54.2	55.6
3 years old	27.3	28.8	32.6	35.9	39.2	38.4	42.4	42.4	38.7
4 years old	46.3	49.1	56.0	61.6	64.9	66.4	66.6	68.3	68.4
5 years old	84.7	86.5	88.8	87.5	87.6	86.7	87.2	86.1	86.9

Source: U.S. Census Bureau. *Statistical Abstract of the United States: 2007.*
Note: Civilian noninstitutional population. Includes public and nonpublic nursery school and kindergarten programs. Excludes 5-year olds enrolled in elementary school. Based on Current Population Survey.
[1]Includes races not shown separately.
[2]Beginning 2003 for this race group only. The 2003 Current Population Survey (CPS) allowed respondents to choose more than one race. Beginning 2003 data represent persons who selected this race group only and exclude persons reporting more than one race. The CPS in prior years only allowed respondents to report one race group.
[3]Persons of Hispanic origin may be of any race. The method of identifying Hispanic children was changed in 1980 from allocation based on status of mother to status reported for each child. The number of Hispanic children using the new method is larger.
. . . = Not available.

Table 21-6. Elementary and Secondary Schools—Teachers, Enrollment, and Pupil-Teacher Ratio, 1955–2004

(Thousands, percent. As of fall. Data are for full-time equivalent teachers.)

Year	Teachers			Enrollment			Pupil-teacher ratio		
	Total	Public	Private	Total	Public	Private	Total	Public	Private
2004, projection	3 504	3 111	393	54 964	48 560	6 404	15.7	15.6	16.3
2003	3 444	3 049	396	54 989	48 541	6 448	16.0	15.9	16.3
2002	3 428	3 034	394	54 576	48 183	6 393	15.9	15.9	16.2
2001	3 390	3 000	390	53 992	47 672	6 320	15.9	15.9	16.2
2000	3 331	2 941	390	53 358	47 204	6 155	16.0	16.0	15.8
1999	3 306	2 911	395	52 876	46 857	6 018	16.0	16.1	15.2
1998	3 221	2 830	391	52 475	46 539	5 937	16.3	16.4	15.2
1997	3 134	2 746	388	51 968	46 127	5 841	16.6	16.8	15.1
1996	3 054	2 667	387	51 375	45 611	5 764	16.8	17.1	14.9
1995	2 978	2 598	380	50 502	44 840	5 662	17.0	17.3	14.9
1994	2 926	2 552	374	49 609	44 111	5 498	17.0	17.3	14.7
1993	2 870	2 504	366	48 813	43 465	5 348	17.0	17.4	14.6
1992	2 822	2 459	363	48 145	42 823	5 322	17.1	17.4	14.7
1991	2 787	2 432	355	47 322	42 047	5 275	17.0	17.3	14.9
1990	2 753	2 398	355	46 451	41 217	5 234	16.9	17.2	14.7
1989	2 734	2 357	377	45 741	40 543	5 198	16.7	17.2	13.8
1988	2 668	2 323	345	45 430	40 189	5 242	17.0	17.3	15.2
1987	2 631	2 279	352	45 487	40 008	5 479	17.3	17.6	15.6
1986	2 592	2 244	348	45 205	39 753	5 452	17.4	17.7	15.7
1985	2 549	2 206	343	44 979	39 422	5 557	17.6	17.9	16.2
1984	2 508	2 168	340	44 908	39 208	5 700	17.9	18.1	16.8
1983	2 476	2 139	337	44 967	39 252	5 715	18.2	18.4	17.0
1982	2 458	2 133	325	45 166	39 566	5 600	18.4	18.6	17.2
1981	2 440	2 127	313	45 544	40 044	5 500	18.7	18.8	17.6
1980	2 485	2 184	301	46 208	40 877	5 331	18.6	18.7	17.7
1979	2 461	2 185	276	46 651	41 651	5 000	19.0	19.1	18.1
1978	2 479	2 207	272	47 637	42 551	5 086	19.2	19.3	18.7
1977	2 488	2 209	279	48 717	43 577	5 140	19.6	19.7	18.4
1976	2 457	2 189	268	49 478	44 311	5 167	20.1	20.2	19.3
1975	2 453	2 198	255	49 819	44 819	5 000	20.3	20.4	19.6
1974	2 410	2 165	245	50 073	45 073	5 000	20.8	20.8	20.4
1973	2 372	2 136	236	50 446	45 446	5 000	21.3	21.3	21.2
1972	2 337	2 106	231	50 726	45 726	5 000	21.7	21.7	21.6
1971	2 293	2 063	230	51 271	46 071	5 200	22.4	22.3	22.6
1970	2 292	2 059	233	51 257	45 894	5 363	22.4	22.3	23.0
1965	1 933	1 710	223	48 473	42 173	6 300	25.1	24.7	28.3
1960	1 600	1 408	192	42 181	36 281	5 900	26.4	25.8	30.7
1955	1 286	1 141	145	35 280	30 680	4 600	27.4	26.9	31.7

Source: U.S. Census Bureau. *Statistical Abstract of the United States: 2007.* U.S. National Center for Education Statistics.
Note: Based on surveys of state education agencies and private schools.

Table 21-7. High School Graduates, 1870–2005

(Number in thousands.)

Year of graduation	Total
2005[P]	3 089
2004[P]	3 063
2003	3 021
2002	2 908
2001	2 848
2000	2 833
1999	2 759
1998	2 704
1997	2 612
1996	2 518
1995	2 520
1994	2 464
1993	2 480
1992	2 478
1991	2 493
1990	2 589
1989	2 744
1988	2 773
1987	2 694
1986	2 643
1985	2 677
1984	2 767
1983	2 888
1982	2 995
1981	3 020
1980	3 043
1979	3 101
1978	3 127
1977	3 152
1976	3 148
1975	3 133
1974	3 073
1973	3 035
1972	3 002
1971	2 938
1970	2 889
1969	2 822
1968	2 695
1967	2 672
1966	2 665
1965	2 658
1964	2 283
1963	1 943
1962	1 918
1961	1 964
1960	1 858
1959	1 627
1958	1 506
1957	1 434
1956	1 415
1954	1 276
1952	1 197
1950	1 200
1948	1 190
1946	1 080
1944	1 019
1942	1 242
1940	1 221
1938	1 120
1937	1 068
1936	1 015
1935	965
1934	915
1933	871
1932	827
1931	747

P = Preliminary.

Table 21-7. High School Graduates, 1870–2005—
Continued

(Number in thousands.)

Year of graduation	Total
1930	667
1929	632
1928	597
1927	579
1926	561
1925	528
1924	494
1923	426
1922	357
1921	334
1920	311
1919	298
1918	285
1917	272
1916	259
1915	240
1914	219
1913	200
1912	181
1911	168
1910	156
1909	142
1908	129
1907	127
1906	126
1905	119
1904	112
1903	105
1902	99
1901	97
1900	95
1899	90
1898	84
1897	80
1896	76
1895	72
1894	65
1893	59
1892	53
1891	48
1890	44
1889	39
1888	33
1887	32
1886	33
1885	32
1884	31
1883	28
1882	27
1881	25
1880	24
1879	23
1878	22
1877	21
1876	20
1875	20
1874	19
1873	18
1872	17
1871	17
1870	16

Source: U.S. Department of Education, National Center for Education Statistics.

Table 21-8. High School Dropouts by Race and Hispanic Origin, 1980–2004

(Percent. As of October.)

Item	1980	1985	1990	1995	1998	1999	2000	2001	2002	2003	2004
EVENT DROPOUTS[2]											
Total[3]	**6.0**	**5.2**	**4.5**	**5.4**	**4.4**	**4.7**	**4.5**	**4.7**	**3.3**	**3.8**	**4.4**
White[4]	5.6	4.8	3.9	5.1	4.4	4.4	4.3	4.6	3.0	3.7	4.2
Male	6.4	4.9	4.1	5.4	4.4	4.1	4.7	5.3	3.0	3.9	4.9
Female	4.9	4.7	3.8	4.8	4.4	4.7	4.0	3.8	3.0	3.4	3.5
Black[4]	8.3	7.7	7.7	6.1	5.0	6.0	5.6	5.7	4.4	4.5	5.2
Male	8.0	8.3	6.9	7.9	4.6	5.2	7.6	6.1	5.1	4.1	4.8
Female	8.5	7.2	8.6	4.4	5.5	6.8	3.8	5.4	3.8	4.9	5.7
Hispanic[5]	11.5	9.7	7.7	11.6	8.4	7.1	6.8	8.1	5.3	6.5	8.0
Male	16.9	9.3	7.6	10.9	8.6	6.9	7.1	7.6	6.2	7.7	11.5
Female	6.9	9.8	7.7	12.5	8.2	7.3	6.5	8.7	4.4	5.4	4.6
STATUS DROPOUTS[6]											
Total[3]	**15.6**	**13.9**	**14.4**	**13.9**	**13.9**	**13.1**	**12.4**	**13.0**	**12.3**	**11.8**	**12.1**
White[4]	14.4	13.5	14.1	13.6	13.7	12.8	12.2	13.4	12.2	11.6	11.9
Male	15.7	14.7	15.4	14.3	15.7	13.9	13.5	15.3	13.7	13.3	13.7
Female	13.2	12.3	12.8	13.0	11.7	11.8	10.9	11.4	10.6	9.8	10.0
Black[4]	23.5	17.6	16.4	14.4	17.1	16.0	15.3	13.8	14.6	14.2	15.1
Male	26.0	18.8	18.6	14.2	20.5	16.3	17.4	16.9	16.9	16.7	17.9
Female	21.5	16.6	14.5	14.6	14.3	15.7	13.5	11.0	12.5	12.0	12.7
Hispanic[5]	40.3	31.5	37.7	34.7	34.4	33.9	32.3	31.7	30.1	28.4	28.0
Male	42.6	35.8	40.3	34.2	39.7	36.4	36.8	37.1	33.8	31.7	33.5
Female	38.1	27.0	35.0	35.4	28.6	31.1	27.3	25.5	25.6	24.7	21.7

Source: U.S. Census Bureau. *Statistical Abstract of the United States: 2007.*
[1]Beginning 1990, reflects new editing procedures for cases with missing data on school enrollment.
[2]Percent of students who drop out in a single year without completing high school. For grades 10 to 12.
[3]Includes other races, not shown separately.
[4]Beginning 2003, for persons who selected this race group only. The 2003 Current Population Survey (CPS) allowed respondents to choose more than one race. Beginning 2003 data represent persons who selected this race group only and exclude persons reporting more than one race. The CPS in prior years only allowed respondents to report one race group.
[5]Persons of Hispanic origin may be of any race.
[6]Percent of the population who have not completed high school and are not enrolled, regardless of when they dropped out. For persons 18 to 24 years old.

Table 21-9. Higher Education—Summary, 1985–2004

(Institutions, staff, and enrollment as of fall. Finances for fiscal year ending in the following year.)

Item	1985	1990	1995	2000	2001	2002	2003	2004
ALL INSTITUTIONS								
Number of institutions[1]	3 340	3 559	3 706	4 182	4 197	4 168	4 236	4 216
4-year	2 029	2 141	2 244	2 450	2 487	2 466	2 530	2 533
2-year	1 311	1 418	1 462	1 732	1 710	1 702	1 706	1 683
Instructional staff (Lecturer or above)[2]								
(thousands)	715	817	932	...	1 113	...	1 175	...
Percent full-time	64	61	59	...	56	...	54	...
Total enrollment[3,4] (thousands)	12 247	13 819	14 262	15 312	15 928	16 612	16 900	17 272
Male	5 818	6 284	6 343	6 722	6 961	7 202	7 256	7 387
Female	6 429	7 535	7 919	8 591	8 967	9 410	9 645	9 885
4-year institutions	7 716	8 579	8 769	9 364	9 677	10 082	10 408	10 726
2-year institutions	4 531	5 240	5 493	5 948	6 251	6 529	6 493	6 546
Full-time	7 075	7 821	8 129	9 010	9 448	9 946	10 312	10 610
Part-time	5 172	5 998	6 133	6 303	6 480	6 665	6 589	6 662
Public	9 479	10 845	11 092	11 753	12 233	12 752	12 857	12 980
Private	2 768	2 974	3 169	3 560	3 695	3 860	4 043	4 292
Not-for-profit	2 572	2 760	2 929	3 109	3 167	3 265	3 341	3 412
For profit	196	213	240	450	528	594	703	880
Undergraduate[4]	10 597	11 959	12 232	13 155	13 716	14 257	14 474	14 781
Men	4 962	5 380	5 401	5 778	6 004	6 192	6 224	6 340
Women	5 635	6 579	6 831	7 377	7 711	8 065	8 250	8 441
First-time freshmen	2 292	2 257	2 169	2 428	2 497	2 571	2 605	...
First professional	274	273	298	307	309	319	329	335
Men	180	167	174	164	161	163	166	168
Women	94	107	124	143	148	156	163	166
Graduate[4]	1 376	1 586	1 732	1 850	1 904	2 036	2 098	2 157
Men	677	737	768	780	796	847	865	879
Women	700	849	965	1 071	1 108	1 189	1 233	1 278
Public institutions: (millions of dollars)								
Current funds revenues[5]	65 005	94 905	123 501	176 645	174 503	...	...	...
Tuition and fees	9 439	15 258	23 257	31 919	31 464	...	...	...
Federal government	6 852	9 763	13 672	19 744	18 668	...	...	...
State government	29 221	38 240	44 243	62 895	62 543	...	...	...
Auxiliary enterprises	6 685	9 059	11 595	16 501	16 379	...	...	...
Public institutions: (millions of dollars)								
Current funds expenditures[5]	63 194	92 961	119 525	170 345	168 296	...	...	...
Educational and general	50 873	74 395	96 086	136 613	135 549	...	...	...
Auxiliary enterprises	6 830	9 050	11 309	16 377	16 245	...	...	...
2-YEAR INSTITUTIONS								
Number of institutions[1,6]	1 311	1 418	1 462	1 732	1 710	1 702	1 706	1 683
Public	932	972	1 047	1 076	1 085	1 081	1 086	1 061
Private	379	446	415	656	625	621	620	622
Instructional staff (thousands)								
(Lecturer or above)[2]	211	...	285	...	349	...	359	...
Enrollment[3,4] (thousands)	4 531	5 240	5 493	5 948	6 251	6 529	6 493	6 546
Public	4 270	4 996	5 278	5 697	5 997	6 270	6 208	6 244
Private	261	244	215	251	254	259	285	302
Male	2 002	2 233	2 329	2 559	2 675	2 753	2 689	2 698
Female	2 529	3 007	3 164	3 390	3 575	3 776	3 804	3 848

Source: U.S. Census Bureau. *Statistical Abstract of the United States: 2007.* U.S. National Center for Education Statistics.
Note: Covers universities, colleges, professional schools, junior and teachers colleges, both publicly and privately controlled, regular session. Includes estimates for institutions not reporting.
[1]Number of institutions includes count of branch campuses. Due to revised survey procedures, data beginning 1990 are not comparable with previous years. Beginning 1996 (2000 for this table), data reflect a new classification of institutions; this classification includes some additional, primarily 2-year, colleges and excludes a few institutions that did not award degrees. Includes institutions that were eligible to participate in Title IV federal financial aid programs.
[2]Due to revised survey methods, data beginning 1990 not comparable with previous years.
[3]Branch campuses counted according to actual status, e.g., 2-year branch in 2-year category.
[4]Includes unclassified students (students taking courses for credit, but are not candidates for degrees).
[5]Includes items not shown separately.
[6]Includes schools accredited by the National Association of Trade and Technical Schools. See footnote 1 for information pertaining to data beginning 2000.
... = Not available.

Table 21-10. Degrees Conferred by Degree-granting Institutions, by Level of Degree and Sex of Student, 1870–2014

Year (projection)	Associate's degrees Total	Males	Females	Bachelor's degrees Total	Males	Females	Master's degrees Total	Males	Females	First-professional degrees Total	Males	Females	Doctor's degrees[1] Total	Males	Females
2014	735 000	275 000	460 000	1 582 000	633 000	949 000	693 000	275 000	418 000	99 000	47 300	53 700	54 900	27 300	27 600
2013	733 000	275 000	458 000	1 578 000	632 000	946 000	680 000	269 000	411 000	99 600	46 700	52 900	53 800	26 900	26 900
2012	731 000	274 000	457 000	1 570 000	629 000	941 000	671 000	264 000	407 000	98 500	46 200	52 300	52 700	26 400	26 200
2011	728 000	273 000	454 000	1 558 000	625 000	933 000	661 000	260 000	402 000	97 200	45 700	51 500	51 800	26 100	25 700
2010	719 000	271 000	448 000	1 538 000	618 000	920 000	650 000	255 000	395 000	95 700	45 200	50 500	51 100	25 900	25 200
2009	705 000	266 000	438 000	1 507 000	608 000	898 000	634 000	249 000	384 000	93 700	44 500	49 200	50 600	25 800	24 800
2008	689 000	262 000	427 000	1 475 000	598 000	877 000	615 000	243 000	373 000	91 600	43 800	47 800	50 200	25 700	24 400
2007	676 000	258 000	418 000	1 449 000	590 000	859 000	596 000	236 000	361 000	89 600	43 300	46 400	49 500	25 600	24 000
2006	668 000	256 000	412 000	1 431 000	586 000	845 000	580 000	229 000	350 000	87 600	42 700	44 900	48 500	25 100	23 300
2005	668 000	257 000	411 000	1 416 000	584 000	832 000	562 000	224 000	338 000	85 000	42 000	43 000	47 200	24 600	22 600
2004	665 301	260 033	405 268	1 399 542	595 425	804 117	558 940	229 545	329 395	83 041	42 169	40 872	48 378	25 323	23 055
2003	632 912	253 060	379 852	1 348 503	573 079	775 424	512 645	211 381	301 264	80 810	41 834	38 976	46 024	24 341	21 683
2002	595 133	238 109	357 024	1 291 900	549 816	742 084	482 118	199 120	282 998	80 698	42 507	38 191	44 160	23 708	20 452
2001	578 865	231 645	347 220	1 244 171	531 840	712 331	468 476	194 351	274 125	79 707	42 862	36 845	44 904	24 728	20 176
2000	564 933	224 721	340 212	1 237 875	530 367	707 508	457 056	191 792	265 264	80 057	44 239	35 818	44 808	25 028	19 780
1999[2]	559 954	218 417	341 537	1 200 303	518 746	681 557	439 986	186 148	253 838	78 439	44 339	34 100	44 077	25 146	18 931
1998	558 555	217 613	340 942	1 184 406	519 956	664 450	430 164	184 375	245 789	78 598	44 911	33 687	46 010	26 664	19 346
1997	571 226	223 948	347 278	1 172 879	520 515	652 364	419 401	180 947	238 454	78 730	45 564	33 166	45 876	27 146	18 730
1996	555 216	219 514	335 702	1 164 792	522 454	642 338	406 301	179 081	227 220	76 734	44 748	31 986	44 652	26 841	17 811
1995	539 691	218 352	321 339	1 160 134	526 131	634 003	397 629	178 598	219 031	75 800	44 853	30 947	44 446	26 916	17 530
1994	530 632	215 261	315 371	1 169 275	532 422	636 853	387 070	176 085	210 985	75 418	44 707	30 711	43 185	26 552	16 633
1993	514 756	211 964	302 792	1 165 178	532 881	632 297	369 585	169 258	200 327	75 387	45 153	30 234	42 132	26 073	16 059
1992	504 231	207 481	296 750	1 136 553	520 811	615 742	352 838	161 842	190 996	74 146	45 071	29 075	40 659	25 557	15 102
1991	481 720	198 634	283 086	1 094 538	504 045	590 493	337 168	156 482	180 686	71 948	43 846	28 102	39 294	24 756	14 538
1990	455 102	191 195	263 907	1 051 344	491 696	559 648	324 301	153 653	170 648	70 988	43 961	27 027	38 371	24 401	13 970
1989	436 764	186 316	250 448	1 018 755	483 346	535 409	310 621	149 354	161 267	70 856	45 046	25 810	35 720	22 648	13 072
1988	435 085	190 047	245 038	994 829	477 203	517 626	299 317	145 163	154 154	70 735	45 484	25 251	34 870	22 615	12 255
1987	436 304	190 839	245 465	991 264	480 782	510 482	289 349	141 269	148 080	71 617	46 523	25 094	34 041	22 061	11 980
1986	446 047	196 166	249 881	987 823	485 923	501 900	288 567	143 508	145 059	73 910	49 261	24 649	33 653	21 819	11 834
1985	454 712	202 932	251 780	979 477	482 528	496 949	286 251	143 390	142 861	75 063	50 455	24 608	32 943	21 700	11 243
1984	452 240	202 704	249 536	974 309	482 319	491 990	284 263	143 595	140 668	74 468	51 378	23 090	33 209	22 064	11 145
1983	449 620	203 991	245 629	969 510	479 140	490 370	289 921	144 697	145 224	73 054	51 250	21 804	32 775	21 902	10 873
1982	434 526	196 944	237 582	952 998	473 364	479 634	295 546	145 532	150 014	72 032	52 223	19 809	32 707	22 224	10 483
1981	416 377	188 638	227 739	935 140	469 883	465 257	295 739	147 043	148 696	71 956	52 792	19 164	32 958	22 711	10 247
1980	400 910	183 737	217 173	929 417	473 611	455 806	298 081	150 749	147 332	70 131	52 716	17 415	32 615	22 943	9 672
1979	402 702	192 091	210 611	921 390	477 344	444 046	301 079	153 370	147 709	68 848	52 652	16 196	32 730	23 541	9 189
1978	412 246	204 718	207 528	921 204	487 347	433 857	311 620	161 212	150 408	66 581	52 270	14 311	32 131	23 658	8 473
1977	406 377	210 842	195 535	919 549	495 545	424 004	317 164	167 783	149 381	64 359	52 374	11 985	33 232	25 142	8 090
1976	391 454	209 996	181 458	925 746	504 925	420 821	311 771	167 248	144 523	62 649	52 892	9 757	34 064	26 267	7 797
1975	360 171	191 017	169 154	922 933	504 841	418 092	292 450	161 570	130 880	55 916	48 956	6 960	34 083	26 817	7 266
1974	343 924	188 591	155 333	945 776	527 313	418 463	277 033	157 842	119 191	53 816	48 530	5 286	33 816	27 365	6 451
1973	316 174	175 413	140 761	922 362	518 191	404 171	263 371	154 468	108 903	50 018	46 489	3 529	34 777	28 571	6 206
1972	292 014	166 227	125 787	887 273	500 590	386 683	251 633	149 550	102 083	43 411	40 723	2 688	33 363	28 090	5 273
1971	252 311	144 144	108 167	839 730	475 594	364 136	230 509	138 146	92 363	37 946	35 544	2 402	32 107	27 530	4 577
1970	206 023	117 432	88 591	792 316	451 097	341 219	208 291	125 624	82 667	34 918	33 077	1 841	29 866	25 890	3 976
1969	183 279	105 661	77 618	728 845	410 595	318 250	193 756	121 531	72 225	35 114	33 595	1 519	26 158	22 722	3 436
1968	159 441	90 317	69 124	632 289	357 682	274 607	176 749	113 552	63 197	33 939	32 402	1 537	23 089	20 183	2 906
1967	139 183	78 356	60 827	558 534	322 711	235 823	157 726	103 109	54 617	31 695	30 401	1 294	20 617	18 163	2 454
1966	111 607	63 779	47 828	520 115	299 287	220 828	140 602	93 081	47 521	30 124	28 982	1 142	18 237	16 121	2 116
1965	...	...	...	493 757	282 173	211 584	121 167	81 319	39 848	28 290	27 283	1 007	16 467	14 692	1 775
1964	...	...	...	461 266	265 349	195 917	109 183	73 850	35 333	27 209	26 357	852	14 490	12 955	1 535
1963	...	...	...	411 420	241 309	170 111	98 684	67 302	31 382	26 590	25 753	837	12 822	11 448	1 374
1962	...	...	...	383 961	230 456	153 505	91 418	62 603	28 815	25 607	24 836	771	11 622	10 377	1 245
1961	...	...	...	365 174	224 538	140 636	84 609	57 830	26 779	25 253	24 577	676	10 575	9 463	1 112
1960	...	...	...	[3]392 440	[3]254 063	[3]138 377	74 435	50 898	23 537	[4]	[4]	[4]	9 829	8 801	1 028
1950	...	...	...	[3]432 058	[3]328 841	[3]103 217	58 183	41 220	16 963	[4]	[4]	[4]	6 420	5 804	616
1940	...	...	...	[3]186 500	[3]109 546	[3]76 954	26 731	16 508	10 223	[4]	[4]	[4]	3 290	2 861	429
1930	...	...	...	[3]122 484	[3]73 615	[3]48 869	14 969	8 925	6 044	[4]	[4]	[4]	2 299	1 946	353
1920	...	...	...	[3]48 622	[3]31 980	[3]16 642	4 279	2 985	1 294	[4]	[4]	[4]	615	522	93
1910	...	...	...	[3]37 199	[3]28 762	[3]8 437	2 113	1 555	558	[4]	[4]	[4]	443	399	44
1900	...	...	...	[3]27 410	[3]22 173	[3]5 237	1 583	1 280	303	[4]	[4]	[4]	382	359	23
1890	...	...	...	[3]15 539	[3]12 857	[3]2 682	1 015	821	194	[4]	[4]	[4]	149	147	2
1880	...	...	...	[3]12 896	[3]10 411	[3]2 485	879	868	11	[4]	[4]	[4]	54	51	3
1870	...	...	...	[3]9 371	[3]7 993	[3]1 378	0	0	0	[4]	[4]	[4]	1	1	0

Source: U.S. Department of Education, National Center for Education Statistics. *Digest of Education Statistics 2005.*
Note: Data for 1869–70 to 1994–95 are for institutions of higher education. Institutions of higher education were accredited by an agency or association that was recognized by the U.S. Department of Education, or recognized directly by the Secretary of Education. The new degree-granting classification is very similar to the earlier higher education classification, except that it includes some additional institutions, primarily 2-year colleges, and excludes a few higher education institutions that did not award associate's or higher degrees. Some data have been revised from previously published figures. Totals may not equal sum of the components due to independent rounding.
[1]Includes Ph.D., Ed.D., and comparable degrees at the doctoral level. Excludes first-professional, such as M.D., D.D.S., and law degrees.
[2]Data for 1998–99 were imputed using alternative procedures.
[3]Includes first-professional degrees.
[4]First-professional degrees are included with bachelor's degrees.
. . . = Not available.

Table 21-11. Institutions of Higher Education—Charges, 1970–2005

(Dollars. Estimated. For the entire academic year ending in year shown.)

Academic control and year	Tuition and required fees[1]				Board rates[2]				Dormitory charges			
	All institutions	2-year colleges	4-year universities	Other 4-year schools	All institutions	2-year colleges	4-year universities	Other 4-year schools	All institutions	2-year colleges	4-year universities	Other 4-year schools
Public:												
2005[P]	3 638	1 847	5 948	4 520	2 935	2 333	3 226	2 813	3 304	2 154	3 431	3 409
2004	3 319	1 702	5 363	4 141	2 823	2 233	3 084	2 724	3 107	2 086	3 232	3 198
2003	2 903	1 483	4 686	3 668	2 669	2 164	2 895	2 580	2 930	1 954	3 023	3 032
2002	2 700	1 380	4 273	3 409	2 598	2 036	2 835	2 504	2 723	1 722	2 838	2 801
2001	2 562	1 333	3 979	3 208	2 455	1 906	2 686	2 358	2 569	1 600	2 657	2 652
2000	2 506	1 338	3 768	3 091	2 364	1 834	2 628	2 239	2 440	1 549	2 516	2 521
1999	2 430	1 327	3 640	2 974	2 347	1 828	2 576	2 247	2 330	1 450	2 408	2 410
1998	2 360	1 314	3 486	2 877	2 228	1 795	2 438	2 130	2 225	1 401	2 285	2 312
1997	2 271	1 276	3 323	2 778	2 111	1 789	2 282	2 025	2 148	1 339	2 187	2 232
1996	2 179	1 239	3 151	2 660	2 020	1 681	2 192	1 937	2 057	1 297	2 104	2 133
1995	2 057	1 192	2 977	2 499	1 949	1 712	2 108	1 866	1 959	1 232	1 992	2 044
1994	1 942	1 125	2 820	2 360	1 880	1 681	1 993	1 828	1 873	1 190	1 897	1 958
1993	1 782	1 025	2 604	2 192	1 841	1 668	1 982	1 761	1 756	1 106	1 856	1 787
1992	1 624	937	2 410	1 933	1 780	1 612	1 852	1 745	1 731	1 074	1 789	1 782
1991	1 454	824	2 159	1 707	1 691	1 594	1 767	1 641	1 612	1 050	1 658	1 655
1990	1 356	756	2 035	1 608	1 635	1 581	1 728	1 561	1 513	962	1 561	1 554
1985	971	584	1 386	1 117	1 241	1 302	1 276	1 201	1 196	921	1 237	1 200
1980	583	355	840	662	867	893	898	833	715	574	750	703
1975	432	277	599	448	625	638	634	613	506	424	527	497
1970	323	178	427	306	511	465	540	483	369	308	395	346
Private:												
2005[P]	18 374	12 182	25 600	17 261	3 486	3 556	3 854	3 371	4 165	4 162	5 244	3 849
2004	17 327	11 546	24 128	16 298	3 364	4 432	3 778	3 222	3 945	3 581	4 979	3 647
2003	16 383	10 651	22 716	15 416	3 206	3 870	3 602	3 071	3 752	3 232	4 724	3 478
2002	15 742	10 076	21 176	14 923	3 104	2 633	3 462	2 996	3 567	3 116	4 478	3 301
2001	15 000	9 067	20 106	14 233	2 993	3 000	3 300	2 893	3 374	2 722	4 270	3 121
2000	14 081	8 235	19 307	13 361	2 882	2 922	3 157	2 790	3 224	2 808	4 070	2 976
1999	13 428	7 854	18 340	12 815	2 865	2 884	3 188	2 765	3 075	2 581	3 914	2 850
1998	12 801	7 464	17 229	12 338	2 762	2 785	3 132	2 648	2 954	2 672	3 756	2 731
1997	12 498	7 236	16 552	11 871	2 663	2 181	3 142	2 520	2 878	2 537	3 826	2 602
1996	11 864	7 094	15 605	11 297	2 606	2 098	3 218	2 429	2 738	2 371	3 680	2 473
1995	11 111	6 914	14 537	10 653	2 509	2 023	3 035	2 362	2 587	2 233	3 469	2 347
1994	10 572	6 370	13 874	10 100	2 434	1 970	2 946	2 278	2 490	2 067	3 277	2 261
1993	9 942	6 059	13 055	9 533	2 344	1 875	2 825	2 197	2 348	1 970	3 018	2 151
1992	9 434	5 752	12 192	9 053	2 252	2 090	2 727	2 098	2 221	1 789	2 860	2 038
1991	8 772	5 570	11 379	8 389	2 074	1 989	2 470	1 943	2 063	1 744	2 654	1 889
1990	8 147	5 196	10 348	7 778	1 948	1 811	2 339	1 823	1 923	1 663	2 411	1 774
1985	5 315	3 485	6 843	5 135	1 462	1 294	1 647	1 405	1 426	1 424	1 753	1 309
1980	3 130	2 062	3 811	3 020	955	923	1 078	912	827	766	1 001	768
1975	2 117	1 367	2 614	1 954	700	660	771	666	586	564	691	536
1970	1 533	1 034	1 809	1 468	561	546	608	543	436	413	503	409

Source: U.S. Census Bureau. *Statistical Abstract of the United States: 2007.* U.S. National Center for Education Statistics.
Note: Figures are average charges per full-time equivalent student. Room and board are based on full-time students.
[1]For in-state students.
[2]Beginning 1987, rates reflect 20 meals per week, rather than meals served 7 days a week.
P = Preliminary.

Table 21-12. Type of School Attended by Student and Household Characteristics, 1993–2003

(Percent, except total in thousands. For students in grades 1 to 12. Includes home-schooled students enrolled in public or private school 9 or more hours per week.)

Characteristic	Public								Private							
	Assigned				Chosen				Church-related				Not church related			
	1993	1996	1999	2003	1993	1996	1999	2003	1993	1996	1999	2003	1993	1996	1999	2003
Total students	33 900	34 600	35 800	35 300	4 700	6 200	6 800	7 400	3 200	3 700	3 400	4 000	700	1 000	1 100	1 100
Percent distribution	79.9	76.0	75.9	73.9	11.0	13.7	14.5	15.4	7.5	8.0	7.3	8.4	1.6	2.3	2.3	2.4
Grade level:																
1 to 5	78.6	74.1	73.7	71.6	11.6	14.8	15.3	16.6	8.3	8.9	8.6	9.7	1.5	2.2	2.5	2.1
6 to 8	81.3	79.4	78.6	75.0	9.9	11.2	11.7	14.5	7.4	7.4	7.5	7.9	1.5	2.0	2.2	2.5
9 to 12	80.6	75.9	76.9	76.0	11.2	14.1	15.6	14.4	6.5	7.3	5.3	6.9	1.8	2.7	2.3	2.6
Race/ethnicity:																
White, non-Hispanic	81.0	77.1	77.1	74.7	8.6	11.1	11.5	12.9	8.6	9.2	8.7	9.7	1.8	2.7	2.7	2.7
Black, non-Hispanic	77.2	72.9	71.5	68.1	18.6	21.5	22.6	24.0	3.4	4.2	4.4	5.7	0.8	1.4	1.6	2.2
Other, non-Hispanic	73.0	69.3	72.6	70.1	14.9	19.0	17.4	19.3	9.0	9.5	6.9	7.2	3.1	2.2	3.1	3.4
Hispanic[1]	79.2	76.4	77.0	77.9	13.7	16.1	18.0	15.1	6.4	6.3	3.9	6.2	0.7	1.3	1.1	0.8
Family type:																
Two-parent household	80.1	76.3	76.8	73.6	9.3	11.7	12.2	14.1	8.8	9.5	8.4	9.7	1.8	2.4	2.5	2.6
One-parent household	78.9	74.6	74.4	74.5	15.2	18.4	18.4	18.3	4.8	5.0	5.2	5.3	1.1	1.9	2.1	1.9
Nonparent guardians	83.7	80.2	72.9	74.7	13.5	14.6	21.7	20.0	2.1	2.3	4.1	3.7	0.7	2.9	1.2	1.5
Parents' education:																
Less than high school	83.6	78.8	79.6	77.6	13.7	17.4	17.8	19.7	2.4	2.0	1.7	2.1	0.2	1.8	0.9	0.6
High school diploma or equivalent	83.5	82.1	80.3	79.3	11.4	12.3	14.3	15.8	4.6	5.0	4.1	3.7	0.5	0.7	1.3	1.2
Some college, including vocational/																
technical	79.8	76.4	77.4	75.8	11.1	14.7	15.2	15.8	7.7	7.1	6.0	6.7	1.4	1.8	1.4	1.7
Bachelor's degree	75.8	70.7	71.5	69.0	9.2	13.1	13.1	13.7	12.5	13.0	12.5	14.5	2.6	3.3	2.9	2.8
Graduate/professional degree	72.7	66.1	68.1	66.2	9.8	12.6	13.1	14.1	13.1	15.3	12.8	14.1	4.4	6.0	6.1	5.6
Region:[2]																
Northeast	77.8	74.3	74.1	73.5	9.3	12.9	13.7	11.6	10.5	9.2	8.7	11.0	2.4	3.6	3.6	3.9
South	82.0	78.7	77.6	75.9	10.9	12.5	13.5	15.8	5.4	6.4	6.4	6.1	1.7	2.4	2.5	2.1
Midwest	79.6	75.4	76.0	71.6	10.4	12.4	13.5	14.4	9.2	10.9	9.3	12.1	0.8	1.3	1.2	1.9
West	78.7	74.0	74.8	73.6	13.4	17.7	18.1	18.6	6.5	6.3	4.9	5.8	1.5	2.0	2.3	2.0

Source: U.S. Census Bureau. *Statistical Abstract of the United States: 2007.* U.S. National Center for Education Statistics.
Note: Based on the Parent and Family Involvement Survey of the National Household Education Survey Program of the U.S. Department of Education, National Center for Education Statistics.
[1]Persons of Hispanic origin may be of any race.
[2]Composition of regions:
NORTHEAST: Maine, New Hampshire, Vermont, Massachusetts, Rhode Island, Connecticut, New York, New Jersey, and Pennsylvania.
MIDWEST: Ohio, Indiana, Illinois, Michigan, Wisconsin, Minnesota, Iowa, Missouri, North Dakota, South Dakota, Nebraska, and Kansas.
SOUTH: Delaware, Maryland, District of Columbia, Virginia, West Virginia, North Carolina, South Carolina, Georgia, Florida, Kentucky, Tennessee, Alabama, Mississippi, Arkansas, Louisiana, Oklahoma, and Texas.
WEST: Montana, Idaho, Wyoming, Colorado, New Mexico, Arizona, Utah, Nevada, Washington, Oregon, California, Alaska, and Hawaii.

Table 21-13. Public Charter and Traditional Schools—Selected Characteristics, 2003–2004

Characteristics	All schools			Elementary schools			Secondary schools			Combined schools		
	Total	Traditional	Public charter	Total	Traditional	Public charter	Total	Traditional	Public charter	Total	Traditional	Public charter
Number of schools	88 113	85 934	2 179	61 572	60 419	1 152	19 886	19 365	521	6 655	6 150	505
Enrollment (1,000)	47 316	46 689	627	29 639	29 588	51	15 301	15 186	116	2 060	1 915	145
PERCENT DISTRIBUTION OF STUDENTS												
Race/ethnicity	100.0	100.0	100.0	100.0	100.0	100.0	100.0	100.0	100.0	100.0	100.0	100.0
White, non-Hispanic	60.3	60.6	43.4	57.8	58.0	42.9	63.6	63.6	34	74.2	75.9	51.8
Black, non-Hispanic	16.8	16.6	29.7	17.7	17.5	31.3	15.6	15.6	28	11.6	10.5	26.8
Hispanic[1]	17.7	17.6	21.7	19.6	19.6	20.6	14.9	14.9	33	9.0	8.5	15.8
Asian/Pacific Islander ..	3.9	3.9	3.8	3.8	3.7	4.5	4.7	4.7	1	1.6	1.4	4.0
American Indian/ Alaska Native	1.3	1.3	1.4	1.2	1.2	0.7	1.2	1.2	3	3.6	3.7	1.7
PERCENT DISTRIBUTION OF SCHOOLS												
Size of enrollment	100.0	100.0	100.0	100.0	100.0	100.0	100.0	100.0	100.0	100.0	100.0	100.0
Less than 300	29.2	28.2	67.9	25.6	25.0	60.3	29.0	27.6	81.4	62.5	61.8	71.4
300 to 599	38.9	39.4	19.2	46.1	46.5	23.7	22.2	22.5	12.0	22.8	23.4	16.4
600 to 999	21.6	21.9	9.9	23.6	23.8	13.4	19.4	19.8	4.4	9.7	9.9	7.3
1,000 or more	10.3	10.5	3.0	4.7	4.8	2.6	29.3	30.0	2.1	4.9	4.9	4.9
Percent minority enrollment	100.0	100.0	100.0	100.0	100.0	100.0	100.0	100.0	100.0	100.0	100.0	100.0
Less than 10.0	32.1	32.5	14.8	30.0	30.3	13.8	35.6	36.3	12	40.7	42.4	20.1
10.0 to 24.9	18.5	18.5	19.7	19.3	19.3	19.5	17.8	17.9	16	13.4	12.5	24.2
25.0 to 49.9	17.0	17.0	16.1	17.2	17.2	17.3	17.2	17.3	13	14.3	14.1	16.4
50.0 to 74.9	13.1	13.1	12.3	12.4	12.3	13.0	13.7	13.8	11	17.6	18.1	11.6
75.0 or more	19.4	18.9	37.1	21.2	20.9	36.4	15.6	14.7	48	14.0	12.9	27.7
Percent of students eligible for free or reduced-price lunch[2]	100.0	100.0	100.0	100.0	100.0	100.0	100.0	100.0	100.0	100.0	100.0	100.0
Less than 15.0	17.3	17.1	28.3	16.4	16.3	20.8	22.5	22.1	(3)	10.4	8.3	37.3
15.0 to 29.9	18.1	18.2	14.3	16.3	16.2	22.2	25.4	26.0	(3)	13.8	14.2	8.1
30.0 to 49.9	23.5	23.7	16.4	23.4	23.5	19.5	22.8	23.1	(3)	27.5	28.4	16.2
50.0 to 74.9	22.2	22.3	18.6	23.5	23.6	16.7	16.8	16.4	(3)	26.5	27.6	12.3
75.0 or more	18.8	18.7	22.3	20.4	20.4	20.8	12.5	12.3	(3)	21.8	21.5	26.1

Source: U.S. Census Bureau. *Statistical Abstract of the United States: 2007.* U.S. National Center for Education Statistics.
Note: A public charter school is a public school that, in accordance with an enabling state statue, has been granted a charter exempting it from selected state and local rules and regulations. Schools open as public charter schools during 2002–03 and still open in the 2003–04 school year were surveyed. Based on the National Center for Education Statistics' 2003–2004 School and Staffing Survey and subject to sampling error.
[1]Persons of Hispanic origin may be of any race.
[2]Excludes data for schools not providing information on eligibility for free or reduced-price lunch.
[3]Does not meet standard of reliability or precision.

Table 21-14. Public Schools with Broadband and Wireless Connections, 2000–2003

(Percent. As of fall. Excludes special education, vocational education, and alternative schools.)

School characteristic	Percent of schools with Internet access using broadband connections				Percent using any type of wireless Internet connection		Percent of instructional rooms with wireless Internet connections	
	2000	2001	2002	2003	2002	2003	2002	2003
Total[1]	**80**	**85**	**94**	**95**	**23**	**32**	**15**	**11**
Instructional level:								
Elementary	77	83	93	94	20	29	13	11
Secondary	89	94	98	97	33	42	19	11
Size of enrollment:								
Less than 300	67	72	90	90	17	28	12	15
300 to 999	83	89	94	96	23	30	14	10
1,000 or more	90	96	100	100	37	51	19	11
Percent minority enrollment:								
Less than 6 percent	76	81	92	90	21	31	14	14
6 to 20 percent	82	85	91	96	23	36	13	12
21 to 49 percent	84	85	96	98	25	35	15	10
50 percent or more	81	93	95	97	23	28	16	9
Percent of students eligible for free or reduced-price lunch:								
Less than 35 percent	81	84	93	95	24	36	15	13
35 to 49 percent	82	86	96	96	25	33	15	12
50 to 74 percent	79	84	93	96	23	28	17	9
75 percent or more	75	90	95	93	20	25	11	9

Source: U.S. Census Bureau. *Statistical Abstract of the United States: 2007.* U.S. National Center for Education Statistics.
Note: Based on the Fast Response Survey System of the National Center for Education Statistics and subject to sampling error.
[1]Includes combined schools.

BOX 21 ■ Distance Learning

Distance learning, or virtual education, is a rapidly growing phenomenon in U.S. public schools. In the 2002–2003 academic year, 36% of public school districts had more than 328,000 students enrolled in distance education courses. This rate was highest for large school districts (50%) and rural districts (46%). While fewer small school districts had students enrolled in distance learning (37%), those that did had a greater rate of school participation (15%) in comparison to large or small school districts (both 6%). In addition, 72% of these school districts intend to expand these programs.

Virtual education is instruction in which student and teacher are separated by time and/or location and technology is used to bridge that gap. The majority of school districts use two-way video technology (55%), although the rate increases for small (60%) and rural school districts (64%). Almost half the districts (47%) use asynchronous Internet for courses, allowing students to proceed at their own pace and on their own schedules, while approximately one-fifth of the districts use synchronous Internet, with students and instructors interacting in real time.

Eighty percent of all school districts use distance learning to expand their course offerings; this rate increases to 93% for small school districts and to 95% for rural districts. Other reasons cited for the implementation of virtual education were to meet the needs of specific groups of students (59%), to offer advance placement or college level courses (50%). As a result of distance learning, school districts can offer courses that require instructors with specialized education or for which they do not have a sufficiently large enrollment to justify offering a class. Such programs also provide educational possibilities for Americans with disabilities, who are homebound or have difficulty traveling, and for individuals who cannot attend classes during regular school hours. There were approximately 45,300 enrollments in advanced placement or college level courses, which accounted for 14% of total enrollments. Social studies/social science comprised 23% of enrollments (47,600) for the largest area of study while the smallest area, at only 3%, was general elementary curriculum (8,200).

Of the total distance learning enrollments in the 2002–2003 academic year, 68% were in high school and 29% were in combined or ungraded schools, while a very small minority were in middle or elementary school (2% and 1% respectively).

Sources:

U.S. Department of Education, National Center for Education Statistics, National Forum on Education Statistics. "Forum Guide to Elementary/Secondary Virtual Education," July 2006. http://nces.ed.gov/pubsearch/pubsinfo.asp?pubid=2006803

U.S. Department of Education, National Center for Education Statistics. "Distance Education Courses for Public Elementary and Secondary School Students: 2002–03," March 2005. http://nces.ed.gov/pubs2005/2005010.pdf

U.S. Department of Education, National Center for Education Statistics. "Homeschooling in the United States: 2003," February 2006. http://nces.ed.gov/pubs2006/2006042.pdf

Thousands of visits

Travel Between the United States and Foreign Countries
Source: U.S. Department of Transportation, Research and Innovative Technology Administration, Bureau of Transportation Statistics, *U.S. International Travel and Transportation Trends, 2006 Update,* Table 1.1 (Washington, DC: 2006) and *U.S. International Travel and Transportation Trends,* Table 1 (Washington, DC: 2002).

CHAPTER **22**

Arts, Entertainment, Recreation, and Travel

HIGHLIGHTS

1 Statistics on recreation have not been generally compiled and published systematically. One major difficulty is in defining the term "recreation." Another difficulty is that even the compiled data remain in the files of the collecting agency. The National Park Service is the most dependable source. Since 1850, it has administered the large areas set aside for recreational purposes by Congress or by executive order. These include National Parks, National Seashores, National Monuments, National Historical and Military Areas, and National Parkways. Data on municipal parks and state parks come from the National Recreation and Park Association and data on national forests from the Forest Service.

2 In 2005, the National Park System included 79,048,000 acres, of which national parks accounted for 49,892,000. The system had 273.5 million visitors who stayed an average of 13.5 nights.

3 In 2004, per capita annual expenditure was $2,218 on entertainment of all kinds. An additional $130 was spent on reading materials, which is substantially lower than in the 1990s.

4 The expenditures on reading materials have been steadily dropping for the last couple of years. In 1985, the average amount spent on reading was $141, rising to a high of $166 in 1993 and dropping to a low of $130 in 2004.

5 In 2000, there were 37,024 libraries of all kinds in the United States, including 9,480 public libraries, 4,777 academic libraries, 9,948 special libraries, and 1,411 government libraries. With over 14 million volumes, Harvard University has the largest university library.

6 In 2002, consumers spent $12.6 billion on sound recordings (compared with $7.5 billion in 1990). Rock was the most popular genre, accounting for $24.7 billion, followed by rap ($13.8 billion), rhythm and blues ($11.7 billion), country ($10.7 billion), pop ($9.0 billion), religious ($6.7 billion), jazz ($3.2 billion), and classical ($3.1 billion).

7 In 2001, there were 34.1 million anglers, 13.0 million hunters, and 66.1 wildlife watchers.

8 Attendance at major league baseball in 2005 was 76.3 million, with more than 7 million attending at National League games compared with the American league. The average salary of a major league baseball player was $2.476 million compared with $371,000 in 1985.

9 In 2005, there were 983 NCAA men's and 1,036 NCAA women's college teams. A total of 3.202 million people attended professional basketball games at least once a month and 9.168 million attended less than once a month.

10 In 2005, there were 32 professional football teams and 615 college teams. The average professional player's salary was $1.4 million in 2005 compared with $354,000 in 1990.

11 In 2001, there were 15,689 golf courses in the United States catering to 27.4 million golfers. Of the total number of golf courses, 4,313 were private.

12 In 2005, there were 24.72 million tennis players, up from 17.82 million in 1995.

13 In 2005, there were 5,818 tenpin bowling establishments with a membership of 2.9 million people.

14 In 2005, there were 39,000 motion picture theaters in the United States attended by 1.403 billion people. Total box-office receipts were $8.991 billion.

15 In 2005, there were 18 million boats, and retail expenditures on boating were $37.317 billion.

16 Sales of sporting goods reached $73.485 billion in 2004. Of this, athletic and sport clothing accounted for $11.201 billion, and athletic and sport footwear accounted for $14.752 billion.

17 Sales of bicycles and related supplies increased from $2.4 billion in 1990 to $4.9 billion in 2004.

18 The most popular participatory arts and crafts activity as of 2002 are weaving (16 percent), photography (12 percent), drawing (9 percent), pottery (7 percent), and creative writing (7 percent).

19 In 2004, there were 39 new theatrical productions attended by 11.6 million persons that grossed $771 million in ticket sales. Broadway road tours were attended by 12.9 million people and grossed $714 million. There were 1,477 nonprofit professional theaters whose 11,000 productions and 169,000 performances were attended by 32.1 million people.

20 In 2004, there were 95 professional opera companies whose 1,946 performances were attended by 5.1 million people.

21 In 2004, symphony orchestras staged 37,263 performances attended by 27.7 million people and grossing $826.8 million in revenues.

22 As of 2004, the 10 most popular sports activities are exercise walking (84.7 million), camping (55.3 million), swimming (53.5 million), exercising with equipment (52.2 million), bowling (43.8 million), net fishing (41.2 million), bicycle riding (40.3 million), fresh water fishing (36.3 million), billiards/pool (34.2 million), and aerobic exercise (29.5 million).

23 Information on travel is compiled annually by the Bureau of Economic Analysis and published periodically in the *Survey of Current Business*. Statistics on arrivals in the United States are reported by the U.S. Travel and Tourism Administration, while those on departures are reported in *International Air Travel Statistics*. Data on domestic travel are published by the Travel Data Center.

24 In 2005, there were 42.402 million foreign visitors to the United States generating $81.680 billion. That year 63.866 million Americans visited foreign countries, spending $69.529 billion abroad.

25 Of Americans visiting foreign countries, 14.416 million went to Canada, 20.663 million to Mexico, and 11.976 million to Europe.

26 Domestic travel generated $532.355 billion in 2004. The states with the largest internal tourism revenues were California ($65.7 billion or 12.3 percent), Florida ($46.672 billion), Texas ($33.818 billion), New York ($30.458 billon), and Nevada ($26.250 billion).

27 In 2004, there were 192 cruise ships with berth capacity for 240,401 people. More than 4.8 million passengers embarked from Florida, a number greater than from all other ports in the United States combined.

Table 22-1. Arts and Humanities—Selected Federal Aid Programs, 1991–2004

(Millions of dollars, except as indicated. For fiscal year ending September 30.)

Type of fund and program	1991	1992	1993	1994	1995	1996	1997	1998	1999	2000	2001	2002	2003	2004
National Endowment for the Arts:														
Funds available[1]	166.5	163.0	159.7	158.1	152.1	86.9	98.4	85.3	85.0	85.2	94.0	98.6	101.0	105.5
Program appropriation	124.6	123.0	120.0	116.3	109.0	63.5	65.8	64.3	66.0	66.0	86.7	95.8	95.1	99.3
Grants awarded (number)	4 239	4 229	4 096	3 843	3 685	1 751	1 098	1 459	1 675	1 882	2 093	2 138	1 925	2 150
Funds obligated[2,3]	158.0	154.6	148.4	145.2	147.9	75.3	94.4	82.3	82.6	83.5	92.5	96.2	99.3	102.6
National Endowment for the Humanities:														
Funds available[1]	152.1	156.5	158.5	157.9	152.3	93.9	94.8	94.0	95.5	102.6	106.8	110.1	111.6	127.1
Program appropriation	125.1	131.2	131.9	131.4	125.7	77.2	80.0	80.0	80.0	82.7	86.4	89.9	89.3	98.7
Matching funds[4]	27.0	25.2	26.5	26.5	25.7	15.9	13.9	13.9	13.9	15.1	15.6	16.1	16.0	15.9
Grants awarded (number)	2 171	2 199	2 197	1 881	1 871	815	900	852	874	1 230	1 290	1 252	963	1 246
Funds obligated[2]	149.8	159.1	160.3	159.0	151.8	93.4	94.8	92.7	92.1	100.0	105.7	106.1	100.1	125.1
Education programs	18.5	20.0	20.8	19.6	19.2	13.5	10.5	10.8	10.3	13.0	12.1	12.1	11.3	17.4
State partnership	30.8	31.8	32.4	32.2	32.0	29.0	29.5	29.1	29.3	30.6	32.1	32.8	33.0	36.3
Research grants	24.0	25.3	23.7	23.4	22.2	5.1	8.5	7.7	6.6	6.9	7.0	7.0	7.9	8.4
Fellowships	16.2	17.4	18.9	17.7	16.5	5.1	5.6	5.7	5.6	6.1	7.0	7.7	6.9	8.1
Challenge[5]	15.1	12.4	14.2	14.4	13.8	9.9	9.9	9.9	9.9	10.8	11.9	13.4	8.3	12.6
Public programs	25.3	27.0	26.7	27.5	25.8	12.5	12.6	11.1	12.2	11.8	16.3	13.2	12.7	18.3
Preservation and access ..	19.9	25.1	23.5	24.1	22.2	18.3	18.2	18.4	18.2	20.7	19.2	19.8	20.7	23.7

Source: U.S. Census Bureau. *Statistical Abstract of the United States: 2007.* U.S. National Endowment for the Arts. U.S. National Endowment for the Humanities.
[1]Includes other funds, not shown separately. Excludes administrative funds.
[2]Includes obligations for new grants, supplemental awards on previous years' grants, and program contracts.
[3]Beginning with 1997 data, the grantmaking structure changed from discipline-based categories to thematic ones.
[4]Represents federal funds obligated only upon receipt or certification by Endowment of matching nonfederal gifts.
[5]Program designed to stimulate new sources and higher levels of giving to institutions for the purpose of guaranteeing long-term stability and financial independence. Program usually requires a match of at least 3 private dollars to each federal dollar. Funds for challenge grants are not allocated by program area because they are awarded on a grant-by-grant basis.

Table 22-2. Performing Arts—Selected Data, 1990–2004

(Sales, receipts and expenditures in millions of dollars. For season ending in year shown, except as indicated.)

Item	1990	1995	1996	1997	1998	1999	2000	2001	2002	2003	2004
Legitimate theater:[1]											
Broadway shows:											
New productions	40	33	38	37	33	39	37	28	37	36	39
Attendance (millions)	8.0	9.0	9.5	10.6	11.5	11.7	11.4	11.9	11.0	11.4	11.6
Playing weeks[2,3]	1 070	1 120	1 146	1 349	1 442	1 441	1 464	1 484	1 434	1 544	1 451
Gross ticket sales	282	406	436	499	558	588	603	666	643	721	771
Broadway road tours:[4]											
Attendance (millions)	11.1	15.6	18.1	17.6	15.2	14.6	11.7	11.0	11.7	12.4	12.9
Playing weeks	944	1 242	1 345	1 334	1 127	1 082	888	823	863	877	1 060
Gross ticket sales	367	701	796	782	721	707	572	541	593	642	714
Nonprofit professional theatres:[5]											
Companies reporting[6]	185	215	228	197	189	313	262	363	1 146	1 274	1 477
Gross income	307.6	444.4	450.7	565.0	570.0	740.0	791.0	961.1	1 436.0	1 481.0	1 570.8
Earned income	188.4	281.2	274.0	349.9	342.0	442.0	466.0	554.5	761.0	787.0	856.2
Contributed income	119.2	163.1	176.7	215.1	228.0	298.0	325.0	406.6	675.0	694.0	714.6
Gross expenses	306.3	444.9	439.5	526.6	518.5	701.0	708.0	923.6	1 405.0	1 476.0	1 464.4
Productions	2 265	2 646	3 074	2 295	2 135	3 921	3 241	4 787	10 000	13 000	11 000
Performances	46 131	56 608	56 954	51 453	46 628	64 556	66 123	81 828	157 000	170 000	169 000
Total attendance (millions)	15.2	18.6	17.1	17.2	14.6	18.0	22.0	21.1	32.2	34.3	32.1
OPERA America professional member companies:[7]											
Number of companies reporting[7]	98	88	83	91	89	95	98	96	86	89	95
Expenses[8]	321.2	435.0	466.7	534.1	556.3	591.1	636.7	685.1	684.4	691.6	677.9
Performances[9]	2 336	2 251	2 019	2 137	2 222	2 200	2 153	2 031	1 868	1 730	1 946
Total attendance (millions)[9,10]	7.5	6.5	6.5	6.9	6.6	6.6	6.7	6.5	4.9	5.9	5.1
Main season attendance (millions)[9,11]	4.1	3.9	3.9	4.0	3.7	4.0	4.3	4.2	3.2	3.1	3.4
Symphony orchestras:[1,2]											
Concerts	18 931	29 328	28 887	26 906	31 766	31 549	33 154	36 437	37 118	38 182	37 263
Attendance (millions)	24.7	30.9	31.1	31.9	32.2	30.8	31.7	31.5	30.3	27.8	27.7
Gross revenue	377.5	536.2	558.9	575.5	627.6	671.8	734.0	774.7	763.6	781.2	826.8
Operating expenses	621.7	858.8	892.4	937.1	1 012.0	1 088.0	1 126.3	1 285.9	1 311.9	1 314.8	1 482.6
Support	257.8	351.0	382.8	401.1	459.7	486.0	521.0	559.6	580.0	575.7	639.4

Source: U.S. Census Bureau. *Statistical Abstract of the United States: 2007.*
[1]Source: The League of American Theaters and Producers, Inc, New York, NY. For season ending in year shown.
[2]All shows (new productions and holdovers from previous seasons).
[3]Eight performances constitute one playing week.
[4]North American Tours include U.S. and Canadian companies.
[5]Source: Theatre Communications Group, New York, NY. For years ending on or prior to August 31.
[6]Beginning in 2002, nonprofit theatre data is based on survey responses and extrapolated data from IRS Form 990.
[7]Source: OPERA America, Washington, DC. For years ending on or prior to August 31.
[8]U.S. companies.
[9]Prior to 1993, and for 1999, United States and Canadian companies; 1993 to 1998, U.S. companies only; 2000–2004 U.S. only excluding Canada.
[10]Includes educational performances, outreach, etc.
[11]For paid performances.
[12]Source: American Symphony Orchestra League, Inc., New York, NY. For years ending August 31. Prior to 1995, represents 254 U.S. orchestras; beginning 1995, represents all U.S. orchestras, excluding college/university and youth orchestras. Also, beginning 1995, data based on 1,200 orchestras.

Table 22-3. Attendance Rates for Various Arts Activities, 2002

(Percent.)

Item	Jazz	Classical music	Musicals	Non-musical plays	Ballet	Art museums/ galleries	Art/craft fairs and festivals	Historic sites[1]	Literature[2]
Total, 2002	**10.8**	**11.6**	**17.1**	**12.3**	**3.9**	**26.5**	**33.4**	**31.6**	**46.7**
Sex:									
Male	10.7	10.3	14.0	10.3	2.5	24.6	27.0	30.5	37.6
Female	10.8	12.7	20.0	14.2	5.1	28.2	39.2	32.5	55.1
Race:									
White	11.4	13.7	20.1	14.2	4.7	29.5	38.0	36.0	51.4
African American	12.7	4.5	10.3	7.1	1.5	14.8	9.7	17.8	37.1
Other	7.3	10.3	11.9	10.0	2.3	32.7	25.8	30.4	43.7
Hispanic	6.2	5.5	6.9	6.2	1.6	16.1	20.3	17.2	26.5
Age:									
18 to 24 years old	10.5	7.8	14.8	11.4	2.6	23.7	29.2	28.3	42.8
25 to 34 years old	10.8	9.0	15.4	10.7	3.5	26.7	33.5	33.3	47.7
35 to 44 years old	13.0	10.7	19.1	13.0	4.9	27.4	37.2	35.8	46.6
45 to 54 years old	13.9	15.2	19.3	15.2	5.1	32.9	38.8	38.0	51.6
55 to 64 years old	8.8	15.6	19.7	13.8	3.3	27.8	35.1	31.6	48.9
65 to 74 years old	7.6	12.5	16.6	13.0	3.3	23.4	31.1	24.2	45.3
75 years old and older	3.9	9.5	10.1	5.4	2.2	13.4	15.7	12.8	36.7
Education:									
Grade school	0.9	1.5	1.6	1.1	-	4.5	8.4	6.3	14.0
Some high school	2.7	1.9	4.1	3.7	0.8	7.7	14.0	11.4	23.4
High school graduate	5.3	4.5	9.1	5.7	1.2	14.2	25.7	20.2	37.7
Some college	12.2	11.5	19.4	12.7	3.9	29.0	38.2	36.5	52.9
College graduate	19.4	21.9	30.2	22.5	7.2	46.6	49.3	51.2	63.1
Graduate school	24.0	34.1	37.6	31.8	12.9	58.6	51.9	56.8	74.3
Income:									
Less than $10,000	5.1	6.7	7.6	5.3	1.5	12.4	19.7	14.1	32.1
$10,000 to $19,999	5.4	5.2	8.2	5.4	1.9	14.0	21.4	14.9	37.5
$20,000 to $29,999	6.3	6.3	8.6	6.0	2.4	16.2	24.5	20.8	37.5
$30,000 to $39,999	10.9	10.3	13.6	10.0	2.8	23.3	33.2	28.6	44.1
$40,000 to $49,999	10.3	12.9	16.1	12.2	3.6	25.3	34.6	32.7	47.9
$50,000 to $74,999	11.2	12.4	21.5	14.0	4.3	30.4	40.3	39.1	52.3
$75,000 or More	18.2	19.9	29.3	21.8	7.2	44.6	46.5	50.9	60.8

Source: U.S. Census Bureau. *Statistical Abstract of the United States: 2007.* U.S. National Endowment for the Arts.
Note: For persons 18 years old and over. Represents attendance at least once in the prior 12 months. Excludes elementary and high school performances. Based on the National Endowment for the Arts' 2002 household surveys of Public Participation in the Arts. Data are subject to sampling error.
[1]Parks, historic buildings, and neighborhoods.
[2]Read a book (literature) during the previous twelve months. Includes novels, short stories, poetry, and/or plays.
- = Quantity zero or rounds to zero.

Table 22-4. Participation in Various Leisure Activities, 2002

(Percent, except as indicated. Covers activities engaged in at least once in the prior 12 months.)

Item	Adult population (million)	Attendance at—			Participation in—					
		Movies	Sports events	Amusement park	Exercise program	Playing sports	Outdoor activities[1]	Charity work	Home improvement repair	Gardening
Total, 2002	**205.9**	**60.0**	**35.0**	**41.7**	**55.1**	**30.4**	**30.9**	**29.0**	**42.4**	**47.3**
Sex: Male	98.7	59.5	41.4	40.4	55.0	38.8	34.3	25.6	46.3	37.1
Female	107.2	60.5	29.2	42.9	55.1	22.7	27.7	32.1	38.9	56.7
Race and Ethnicity										
White alone	150.1	63.0	38.4	42.8	59.1	33.0	37.3	32.5	47.7	52.3
African American alone ...	23.7	49.2	27.0	36.6	46.1	23.1	8.2	22.7	26.3	30.3
Other alone	9.5	58.1	22.3	43.9	50.4	26.9	23.9	22.5	33.8	41.3
Hispanic	22.7	52.5	26.4	38.9	40.1	22.3	14.9	15.3	28.0	34.8
Age:										
18 to 24 years old	26.8	82.8	46.0	57.6	61.3	49.4	37.7	25.3	21.1	20.7
25 to 34 years old	36.9	73.3	41.8	56.2	60.2	39.6	38.8	26.0	41.1	41.4
35 to 44 years old	44.2	68.0	42.2	53.3	59.5	36.6	39.0	33.2	53.0	51.8
45 to 54 years old	39.0	60.4	35.8	37.1	58.6	28.6	33.0	33.4	54.9	55.4
55 to 64 years old	25.9	46.6	25.5	27.1	48.4	16.0	21.7	28.1	44.8	56.6
65 to 74 years old	17.6	32.2	19.7	18.4	47.0	13.7	14.9	28.8	38.4	57.2
75 years old and over	15.5	19.5	11.1	9.6	31.3	6.0	5.8	21.3	22.1	47.9
Education:										
Grade school	11.6	19.5	9.4	17.2	21.0	6.9	6.0	8.2	19.5	32.5
Some high school	20.1	39.4	17.4	30.6	32.7	17.2	15.7	12.5	24.9	31.2
High school graduate ..	63.8	51.7	28.3	37.9	45.6	22.6	24.8	20.2	35.6	43.8
Some college	56.9	68.7	39.9	48.9	62.3	35.2	36.1	33.1	46.5	49.6
College graduate	36.1	77.1	51.0	50.1	73.2	45.2	43.0	42.6	56.0	56.1
Graduate school	17.4	77.5	48.3	44.0	77.3	43.6	45.3	53.1	61.6	63.3
Income:										
Less than $10,000	14.4	38.7	16.5	30.4	36.5	15.0	15.2	16.2	19.7	32.2
$10,000 to $19,999	22.7	41.8	20.1	30.7	42.0	18.5	17.4	18.8	23.5	38.8
$20,000 to $29,999	25.0	48.3	23.0	34.7	45.2	21.4	21.2	20.7	28.4	40.9
$30,000 to $39,999	24.2	57.5	30.0	39.3	53.3	26.6	29.8	27.4	42.0	46.6
$40,000 to $49,999	17.6	63.1	34.8	42.6	55.0	29.3	33.7	29.1	46.0	49.1
$50,000 to $74,999	34.7	69.3	44.8	50.2	63.0	36.0	38.2	35.3	53.6	54.4
$75,000 or More	45.8	79.4	53.3	54.0	72.5	48.0	45.3	41.5	61.2	56.3

Source: U.S. Census Bureau. *Statistical Abstract of the United States: 2007.* U.S. National Endowment for the Arts.

Table 22-5. Selected Spectator Sports, 1990–2005

(Thousands, except as indicated.)

Sport	1990	1995	2000	2001	2002	2003	2004	2005
Baseball, major leagues:[1]								
Attendance	55 512	51 288	74 339	73 881	69 428	69 501	74 822	76 286
Regular season	54 824	50 469	72 748	72 267	67 859	67 568	73 023	74 926
National League	24 492	25 110	39 851	39 558	36 949	36 661	40 221	41 644
American League	30 332	25 359	32 898	32 709	30 910	30 908	32 802	33 282
Playoffs[2]	479	533	1 314	1 247	1 262	1 568	1 625	1 191
World Series	209	286	277	366	306	365	174	168
Players' salaries:[3]								
Average (thousand dollars)	598	1 111	1 896	2 139	2 296	2 372	2 313	2 476
Basketball:[4,5]								
NCAA Men's college:								
Teams (number)	767	868	932	937	936	967	981	983
Attendance	28 741	28 548	29 025	28 949	29 395	30 124	30 761	30 569
NCAA Women's college:								
Teams (number)	782	864	956	958	975	1 009	1 008	1 036
Attendance	2 777	4 962	8 698	8 825	9 533	10 164	10 016	9 940
National Hockey League:[6]								
Regular season attendance	12 580	9 234	18 800	20 373	20 615	20 409	22 065	(7)
Playoffs attendance	1 356	1 329	1 525	1 584	1 691	1 636	1 709	(7)
Professional rodeo:[8]								
Rodeos (number)	754	739	688	668	666	657	671	662
Performances (number)	2 159	2 217	2 081	2 015	2 207	1 949	1 982	1 940
Members (number)	5 693	6 894	6 255	5 913	6 209	6 158	6 247	6 127
Permit holders (rookies) (number)	3 290	3 835	3 249	2 544	2 543	3 121	2 990	2 701
Total prize money (million dollars)	18.2	24.5	32.3	33.1	33.3	34.3	35.5	36.6

Source: U.S. Census Bureau. *Statistical Abstract of the United States: 2007.*
[1]Source: Major League Baseball (previously, The National League of Professional Baseball Clubs), New York, NY, National League Green Book; and The American League of Professional Baseball Clubs, New York, NY, American League Red Book.
[2]Beginning 1997, two rounds of playoffs were played. Prior years had one round.
[3]Source: Major League Baseball Players Association, New York, NY.
[4]Season ending in year shown.
[5]Source: National Collegiate Athletic Association, Indianapolis, IN ©. For women's attendance total, excludes double-headers with men's teams.
[6]For season ending in year shown. Source: National Hockey League, Montreal, Quebec.
[7]In September 2004, franchise owners locked out their players upon the expiration of the collective bargaining agreement. The entire season was cancelled in February 2005.
[8]Source: Professional Rodeo Cowboys Association, Colorado Springs, CO, Official Professional Rodeo Media Guide, annual ©.

Table 22-6. Adult Attendance at Sports Events by Frequency, 2005

(Thousands, percent. For fall 2005.)

Event	Attend one or more times a month		Attend less than once a month	
	Number	Percent	Number	Percent
Auto racing - NASCAR	2 664	1.2	8 518	4.0
Auto racing - Other	2 440	1.1	6 083	2.8
Baseball	8 502	3.9	18 575	8.6
Basketball:				
College games	4 383	2.0	7 485	3.5
Professional games	3 202	1.5	9 168	4.3
Bowling	1 749	0.8	3 533	1.6
Boxing	1 175	0.5	3 240	1.5
Equestrian events	574	0.3	3 534	1.6
Figure skating	696	0.3	3 330	1.5
Fishing tournaments	716	0.3	3 132	1.5
Football:				
College games	6 308	2.9	9 513	4.4
Monday night professional games	1 958	0.9	4 493	2.1
Weekend professional games	3 809	1.8	9 591	4.4
Golf	1 587	0.7	4 636	2.2
High school sports	12 087	5.6	8 363	3.9
Horse racing:				
Flats, runners	1 281	0.6	3 842	1.8
Trotters and harness	745	0.4	2 747	1.3
Ice hockey	1 973	0.9	6 754	3.1
Motorcycle racing	980	0.5	3 554	1.7
Pro beach volleyball	254	0.1	2 731	1.3
Rodeo/Bull Riding	1 190	0.6	4 267	2.0
Soccer	3 389	1.6	4 429	2.1
Tennis	903	0.4	3 655	1.7
Truck and tractor pull/mud racing	655	0.3	3 638	1.7
Wrestling professional	1 243	0.6	3 604	1.7

Source: U.S. Census Bureau. *Statistical Abstract of the United States: 2007.* Mediamark Research, Inc. *Top-line Reports©.*
Note: Based on survey and subject to sampling error.

Table 22-7. Participation in NCAA Sports by Sex, 2004–2005

Sport	Males			Females		
	Teams	Athletes	Average squad	Teams	Athletes	Average squad
Total[1]	**8 135**	**222 838**	**(X)**	**9 074**	**166 728**	**(X)**
Baseball	873	28 009	32.1	(X)	(X)	(X)
Basketball	1 000	16 271	16.3	1 025	14 686	14.3
Bowling[2]	1	22	22.0	45	393	8.7
Cross country	865	11 638	13.5	940	12 901	13.7
Equestrian[2]	3	28	9.3	39	1 103	28.3
Fencing[3]	36	623	17.3	45	696	15.5
Field hockey	(X)	(X)	(X)	257	5 505	21.4
Football	614	60 117	97.9	(X)	(X)	(X)
Golf	762	7 953	10.4	483	3 828	7.9
Gymnastics	19	329	17.3	85	1 402	16.5
Ice hockey[4]	133	3 843	28.9	74	1 679	22.7
Lacrosse	214	7 313	34.2	264	5 746	21.8
Rifle[3]	35	241	6.9	36	229	6.4
Rowing[5]	59	2 254	38.2	141	6 987	49.6
Rugby	1	25	25.0	3	76	25.3
Sailing[2]	33	385	11.7	(X)	(X)	(X)
Skiing[3]	35	489	14.0	39	474	12.2
Soccer	737	19 291	26.2	913	21 126	23.1
Softball	(X)	(X)	(X)	911	16 324	17.9
Squash[2]	21	369	17.6	27	380	14.1
Swimming/diving	381	7 650	20.1	489	10 845	22.2
Synchronized swimming[4]	(X)	(X)	(X)	8	104	13.0
Tennis	742	7 386	10.0	876	8 429	9.6
Track, indoor	565	18 866	33.4	621	18 533	29.8
Track, outdoor	656	21 686	33.1	704	20 388	29.0
Volleyball	79	1 161	14.7	982	13 634	13.9
Water polo	46	939	20.4	61	1 193	19.6
Wrestling	224	5 939	26.5	(X)	(X)	(X)

Source: U.S. Census Bureau. *Statistical Abstract of the United States: 2007.* The National Collegiate Athletic Association. *2004–05 participation Study©.*
[1]Includes other sports, not shown separately.
[2]Sport recognized by the NCAA but does not have an NCAA championship.
[3]Co-ed championship sport.
[4]Sport recognized by the NCAA but does not have an NCAA championship for women.
[5]Sport recognized by the NCAA but does not have an NCAA championship for men.
X = Not applicable.

Table 22-8. Personal Consumption Expenditures for Recreation, 1929–2005

(Billions of dollars.)

Year	Total	Non-durable toys and sport supplies	Wheel goods, sports and photographic equipment, boats, and pleasure aircraft	Video and audio goods, computer equipment, and musical instruments	Radio and television repair	Admissions to specified spectator amusements				Clubs and fraternal organizations	Commercial participant amusements	Pari-mutuel net receipts	Books and maps	Magazines, newspapers, and sheet music	Flowers, seeds, and potted plants
						Total	Motion picture theaters	Legitimate theaters and opera, and entertainments of nonprofit institutions	Spectator sports						
2005	756.3	67.2	81.5	141.2	4.8	38.3	9.7	12.7	15.9	23.5	107.3	6.2	42.2	43.8	19.7
2004	708.4	63.5	71.4	133.4	4.6	37.4	9.9	12.4	15.1	22.3	100.7	5.6	40.6	39.6	18.3
2003	659.9	60.6	65.6	123.1	4.1	36.0	9.9	11.9	14.3	22.2	91.2	5.2	38.7	36.3	17.9
2002	629.9	59.2	61.4	120.0	4.1	34.8	9.6	11.7	13.5	21.1	83.7	5.3	37.1	35.1	18.0
2001	604.0	57.6	59.2	115.5	4.0	32.2	9.0	10.9	12.4	20.0	79.6	5.1	34.6	35.0	18.0
2000	585.7	56.6	57.6	116.6	4.2	30.4	8.6	10.3	11.5	19.0	75.8	5.0	33.7	35.0	18.0
1999	546.1	54.7	52.6	108.1	4.1	28.4	7.9	9.9	10.6	18.0	68.8	4.9	31.5	33.5	17.1
1998	505.8	51.3	48.3	99.7	4.1	26.2	7.2	9.2	9.8	17.1	63.1	4.4	28.8	32.1	16.4
1997	474.5	48.4	44.8	92.3	3.9	25.0	6.6	9.2	9.2	16.3	59.4	4.0	27.0	31.2	15.7
1996	448.4	46.5	42.2	87.6	3.7	23.5	6.1	8.6	8.9	17.1	54.2	3.9	25.1	29.5	15.0
1995	418.1	44.4	39.7	81.5	3.6	21.1	5.6	8.1	7.4	17.4	48.8	3.7	23.2	27.5	14.0
1994	383.4	42.0	36.3	73.7	3.3	19.7	5.3	7.6	6.8	17.3	42.3	3.5	21.1	25.6	13.3
1993	351.0	38.8	33.1	63.9	3.2	18.5	5.1	7.1	6.4	17.3	36.1	3.4	18.8	23.4	12.6
1992	321.3	36.5	30.1	57.0	3.0	16.6	4.9	6.0	5.6	16.6	30.9	3.4	17.1	22.0	12.0
1991	302.0	34.6	29.5	55.4	2.9	16.0	5.2	5.4	5.3	15.3	26.5	3.4	16.4	22.1	11.0
1990	290.2	32.8	29.7	53.0	3.2	15.1	5.1	5.2	4.8	13.5	25.2	3.5	16.2	21.6	10.9
1989	268.2	30.7	29.3	52.4	3.7	13.3	4.6	4.4	4.3	8.0	21.8	3.3	15.0	20.1	10.5
1988	248.4	27.7	27.7	50.8	3.8	11.9	3.9	4.4	3.6	7.1	19.8	3.4	14.2	19.2	9.7
1987	224.5	25.3	25.6	46.2	3.5	10.8	3.4	4.0	3.4	6.7	17.3	3.0	13.0	17.6	9.2
1986	204.7	22.9	23.0	41.8	3.2	10.5	3.3	3.9	3.3	6.1	16.0	2.9	11.4	16.5	7.7
1985	187.6	21.4	21.2	35.9	3.2	9.7	3.2	3.2	3.3	5.5	15.1	2.8	10.6	15.9	6.9
1984	172.9	20.5	20.4	32.0	2.8	9.7	3.4	2.8	3.5	4.7	13.8	2.8	10.0	15.7	6.5
1983	155.0	18.4	16.9	28.5	2.8	8.7	3.2	2.4	3.1	4.4	12.9	2.6	9.0	14.6	6.0
1982	138.9	17.1	16.3	23.0	2.6	8.0	3.1	2.1	2.7	4.1	11.6	2.6	8.0	13.8	5.7
1981	129.5	16.0	16.4	22.2	2.5	7.1	2.7	2.0	2.4	3.4	10.8	2.5	7.3	13.0	5.3
1980	116.7	14.6	15.6	20.6	2.5	6.6	2.6	1.8	2.3	2.9	9.1	2.3	6.5	12.0	4.7
1979	108.4	13.6	16.2	19.4	2.4	6.4	2.8	1.5	2.1	2.5	8.0	2.1	5.7	10.9	4.2
1978	95.9	12.3	14.1	17.3	2.4	5.9	2.8	1.3	1.8	2.1	7.2	2.0	5.0	9.1	3.6
1977	85.5	10.8	12.8	15.8	2.5	5.0	2.4	1.1	1.6	2.2	6.4	1.9	4.1	7.7	2.9
1976	78.2	10.0	11.4	14.8	2.3	4.4	2.1	0.9	1.4	2.1	5.6	1.8	3.6	7.0	2.9
1975	70.5	9.0	10.1	13.5	2.2	4.3	2.2	0.8	1.3	2.0	4.9	1.7	3.6	6.4	2.7
1974	63.4	8.2	9.0	12.1	2.0	4.0	2.0	0.7	1.2	1.8	4.2	1.6	3.2	5.9	2.6
1973	57.6	7.4	8.5	11.3	1.9	3.5	1.6	0.6	1.2	1.6	3.5	1.4	3.1	5.3	2.3
1972	51.5	6.6	7.4	10.1	1.7	3.5	1.7	0.6	1.2	1.5	3.0	1.3	2.9	4.8	2.2
1971	46.0	5.8	5.6	8.9	1.5	3.5	1.7	0.5	1.2	1.5	2.6	1.2	3.0	4.4	1.9
1970	43.1	5.5	5.2	8.5	1.4	3.3	1.6	0.5	1.1	1.5	2.4	1.1	2.9	4.1	1.8
1969	40.0	5.2	5.2	8.0	1.3	3.1	1.5	0.5	1.1	1.5	2.1	1.0	2.3	3.7	1.7
1968	36.7	4.8	4.8	7.6	1.2	2.9	1.4	0.5	1.0	1.4	1.9	0.9	2.0	3.4	1.7
1967	33.1	4.3	4.1	7.0	1.1	2.5	1.2	0.5	0.8	1.3	1.8	0.9	1.9	3.3	1.5
1966	30.9	4.0	3.6	6.3	1.0	2.4	1.2	0.4	0.7	1.3	1.7	0.8	1.8	3.2	1.4
1965	26.9	3.6	2.9	5.1	1.0	2.2	1.2	0.4	0.7	1.2	1.6	0.8	1.7	2.7	1.3
1964	24.6	3.4	2.5	4.3	1.0	2.0	1.0	0.4	0.6	1.1	1.6	0.8	1.6	2.5	1.1
1963	22.5	3.1	2.2	3.7	1.0	1.9	1.0	0.4	0.5	1.1	1.5	0.7	1.4	2.5	1.0
1962	20.8	2.9	2.0	3.4	1.0	1.9	1.0	0.4	0.5	1.0	1.4	0.7	1.3	2.3	0.9
1961	19.3	2.7	2.0	3.2	0.9	1.8	1.0	0.3	0.4	1.0	1.2	0.6	1.2	2.0	0.7
1960	18.5	2.5	2.0	3.0	0.9	1.8	1.0	0.3	0.4	0.9	1.1	0.5	1.1	2.2	0.7
1959	17.7	2.4	2.0	3.1	0.8	1.7	1.0	0.3	0.3	0.9	0.9	0.5	1.1	2.1	0.6
1958	16.3	2.1	1.9	2.8	0.8	1.7	1.1	0.3	0.3	0.8	0.7	0.5	1.0	2.1	0.6
1957	15.9	2.0	1.7	2.9	0.7	1.8	1.2	0.3	0.3	0.8	0.6	0.4	1.0	2.0	0.6
1956	15.5	2.0	1.6	3.0	0.6	2.1	1.5	0.3	0.2	0.7	0.6	0.4	1.0	1.9	0.6
1955	14.6	1.8	1.4	2.9	0.6	2.0	1.5	0.2	0.2	0.7	0.5	0.4	0.9	1.9	0.6
1954	13.6	1.6	1.2	2.8	0.5	1.8	1.4	0.2	0.2	0.6	0.5	0.4	0.8	1.8	0.6
1953	13.1	1.7	1.1	2.6	0.5	1.7	1.3	0.2	0.2	0.6	0.4	0.4	0.8	1.8	0.6
1952	12.3	1.7	1.0	2.4	0.4	1.7	1.3	0.2	0.2	0.6	0.4	0.3	0.8	1.7	0.5
1951	11.7	1.7	0.9	2.2	0.4	1.8	1.3	0.2	0.2	0.6	0.4	0.3	0.8	1.6	0.5

. . . = Not available.

Table 22-8. Personal Consumption Expenditures for Recreation, 1929–2005—*Continued*

(Billions of dollars.)

| Year | Total | Non-durable toys and sport supplies | Wheel goods, sports and photo-graphic equipment, boats, and pleasure aircraft | Video and audio goods, computer equipment, and musical instruments | Radio and television repair | Admissions to specified spectator amusements | | | | Clubs and fraternal organi-zations | Commercial participant amuse-ments | Pari-mutuel net receipts | Books and maps | Magazines, news-papers, and sheet music | Flowers, seeds, and potted plants |
						Total	Motion picture theaters	Legitimate theaters and opera, and entertain-ments of nonprofit institutions	Spectator sports						
1950	11.2	1.4	0.9	2.4	0.3	1.8	1.4	0.2	0.2	0.5	0.4	0.2	0.7	1.5	0.5
1949	10.0	1.2	0.8	1.7	0.2	1.9	1.5	0.2	0.2	0.5	0.4	0.2	0.6	1.5	0.5
1948	9.7	1.1	1.0	1.5	0.2	1.9	1.5	0.2	0.2	0.5	0.3	0.3	0.6	1.4	0.4
1947	9.3	0.9	1.0	1.4	0.1	2.0	1.6	0.2	0.2	0.5	0.3	0.3	0.5	1.2	0.4
1946	8.6	0.8	0.8	1.1	0.1	2.1	1.7	0.2	0.2	0.4	0.3	0.2	0.6	1.1	0.4
1945	6.2	0.6	0.4	0.3	0.1	1.7	1.5	0.1	0.1	0.3	0.2	0.2	0.5	1.0	0.4
1944	5.4	0.5	0.3	0.3	0.1	1.6	1.3	0.1	0.1	0.3	0.2	0.1	0.5	0.9	0.3
1943	5.0	0.4	0.3	0.4	0.1	1.5	1.3	0.1	0.1	0.3	0.2	0.1	0.4	0.8	0.3
1942	4.7	0.4	0.3	0.6	. . .	1.2	1.0	0.1	0.1	0.2	0.2	0.1	0.3	0.7	0.2
1941	4.3	0.4	0.3	0.6	. . .	1.0	0.8	0.1	0.1	0.2	0.2	0.1	0.3	0.6	0.2
1940	3.8	0.3	0.3	0.5	. . .	0.9	0.7	0.1	0.1	0.2	0.2	0.1	0.2	0.6	0.2
1939	3.5	0.3	0.2	0.4	. . .	0.8	0.7	0.1	0.1	0.2	0.2	. . .	0.2	0.6	0.2
1938	3.3	0.3	0.2	0.3	. . .	0.8	0.7	0.1	0.1	0.2	0.1	. . .	0.2	0.5	0.2
1937	3.4	0.3	0.2	0.4	. . .	0.8	0.7	0.1	0.1	0.2	0.2	. . .	0.2	0.5	0.2
1936	3.0	0.2	0.2	0.3	. . .	0.8	0.6	0.1	0.1	0.2	0.1	. . .	0.2	0.5	0.2
1935	2.6	0.2	0.1	0.2	. . .	0.7	0.6	. . .	0.1	0.2	0.1	. . .	0.2	0.5	0.1
1934	2.5	0.2	0.1	0.2	. . .	0.6	0.5	. . .	0.1	0.2	0.1	. . .	0.2	0.4	0.1
1933	2.2	0.2	0.1	0.2	. . .	0.6	0.5	. . .	0.1	0.2	0.1	. . .	0.2	0.4	0.1
1932	2.5	0.2	0.1	0.3	. . .	0.6	0.5	0.1	. . .	0.3	0.1	. . .	0.2	0.4	0.1
1931	3.3	0.3	0.2	0.5	. . .	0.9	0.7	0.1	0.1	0.3	0.1	. . .	0.3	0.5	0.1
1930	4.0	0.3	0.2	0.9	. . .	0.9	0.7	0.1	0.1	0.3	0.2	. . .	0.3	0.5	0.2
1929	4.4	0.3	0.2	1.0	. . .	0.9	0.7	0.1	0.1	0.3	0.2	. . .	0.3	0.5	0.2

Source: U.S. Census Bureau. U.S. Bureau of Economic Analysis.
. . . = Not available.

Table 22-9. Selected Recreational Activities, 1990–2005

(Million, except as indicated.)

Sport	1990	1995	2000	2001	2002	2003	2004	2005
Softball, amateur:[1]								
Total participants[2]	41	42	31	31	31	30	28	27
Youth participants (thousand)	1 100	1 350	1 370	1 355	1 365	1 351	1 356	1 447
Adult teams[3] (thousand)	188	187	155	149	143	119	132	128
Youth teams[3] (thousand)	46	74	81	80	80	79	80	85
Golf facilities[4] (number)	12 846	14 074	15 489	15 689	15 827	15 899	16 057	16 052
Tennis players:[5] (thousand)	21 000	17 820	22 900	22 000	23 200	24 100	24 000	24 720
Tenpin bowling:[6]								
Establishments (number)	7 611	7 049	6 247	6 022	5 973	5 811	5 761	5 818
Membership, total[7] (thousand)	6 588	4 925	3 756	3 553	3 382	3 246	3 112	2 896
Skiing:[8]								
Skier visits[9]	50.0	52.7	52.2	57.3	54.4	57.6	57.1	56.9
Operating resorts (number)	591	520	503	490	493	490	494	492
Motion picture screens[10] (thousand)	24	28	38	37	36	37	37	39
Receipts, box office (mil. dol.)	5 022	5 494	7 661	8 413	9 520	9 489	9 539	8 991
Attendance	1 189	1 263	1 421	1 487	1 639	1 574	1 536	1 403
Boating:[11]								
People participating in recreational boating	73.4	76.8	68.9	68.0	71.6	68.7	69.0	71.3
Retail expenditures on boating[12] (mil. dol.)	13 731	17 226	27 065	29 710	31 563	30 283	32 953	37 317
Recreational boats in use by boat type[13]	16.0	15.4	16.8	17.0	17.4	17.4	17.6	18.0
Outboard	...	...	8.3	8.3	8.4	8.4	8.5	8.6
Inboard	...	...	1.7	1.7	1.7	1.7	1.8	1.8
Sterndrive	...	...	1.7	1.7	1.8	1.8	1.8	1.9
Personal Watercraft	...	...	1.2	1.3	1.4	1.4	1.5	1.6
Sailboard	...	...	1.6	1.6	1.6	1.6	1.6	1.6
Other	...	...	2.3	2.4	2.5	2.5	2.5	2.7

Source: U.S. Census Bureau. *Statistical Abstract of the United States: 2007.*
[1]Source: Amateur Softball Association, Oklahoma City, OK.
[2]Amateur Softball Association teams and other amateur softball teams.
[3]Amateur Softball Association teams only.
[4]Source: National Golf Foundation, Jupiter, FL.
[5]Source: Tennis Industry Association, Hilton Head, SC. Players for persons 12 years old and over who played at least once.
[6]Source: Bowling Headquarters, Greendale, WI.
[7]Membership totals are for U.S., Canada, and for U.S. military personnel worldwide.
[8]Source: National Ski Areas Association, Kottke National End of Season Survey 2004/05-final report (copyright).
[9]Represents one person visiting a ski area for all or any part of a day or night, and includes full-and half-day, night, complimentary, adult, child, season, and other types of tickets. Data are estimated and are for the season ending in the year shown.
[10]Source: Motion Picture Association of America, Inc., Encino, CA.
[11]Source: National Marine Manufacturers Association, Chicago, IL ©.
[12]Represents estimated expenditures for new and used boats, motors and engines, accessories, safety equipment, fuel, insurance, docking, maintenance, launching, storage, repairs, and other expenses.
[13]2005 data are estimated.
. . . = Not available.

Table 22-10. National Parks, Monuments, and Allied Areas—Area and Visits, 1850–2005

(Thousands of acres, number in thousands; for years ending Sept. 30 prior to 1941; thereafter, for years ending Dec. 31, or as of Jan. 1 of the following year. Includes data for five areas in Puerto Rico and the Virgin Islands, one area in American Samoa, and one area in Guam.)

Year	Total, enumerated areas[1]		National parks		National monuments visits	National historical and military areas[4] visits	Naitional parkways visits
	Area (thousand visits)	Visits[2,3]	Area (thousand acres)	Visits[3]			
2005	79 048	273 500	49 892	63 500	20 900	74 900	31 700
2004	79 023	276 900	49 892	63 800	19 800	77 000	31 700
2003	79 006	266 100	49 823	63 400	20 000	66 600	31 100
2002	78 811	277 300	49 639	64 500	20 300	70 200	35 700
2001	78 943	279 900	49 862	64 100	21 800	66 700	34 400
2000	78 153	285 900	49 785	66 100	23 800	72 200	34 000
1999	78 166	287 100	49 859	64 300	24 300	72 600	34 600
1998	77 654	286 700	49 416	64 500	23 600	74 200	32 800
1997	77 457	275 500	49 384	65 300	24 100	63 000	31 600
1996	77 458	265 800	49 315	63 100	23 600	59 000	30 900
1995	77 355	269 600	49 307	64 800	23 500	56 900	31 300
1994	74 905	268 600	48 111	63 000	23 600	59 500	29 300
1993	75 515	273 100	45 521	59 800	26 500	61 900	30 400
1992	76 492	274 700	46 208	58 700	26 600	63 300	30 700
1991	76 607	267 800	46 135	57 400	25 800	61 000	28 800
1990	76 362	258 700	46 089	57 700	23 900	57 500	29 100
1989	76 331	269 400	46 081	57 400	23 700	63 900	31 200
1988	76 176	282 500	45 985	56 400	23 200	61 200	42 000
1987	75 970	287 200	45 875	56 600	23 500	68 600	39 300
1986	75 863	281 100	45 791	53 500	21 200	65 500	41 600
1985	75 749	263 400	45 739	50 000	15 900	61 900	40 000
1984	74 913	248 600	45 454	49 700	15 800	63 600	37 900
1983	74 846	243 600	45 427	50 000	16 200	57 300	37 700
1982	74 800	244 100	45 414	49 600	16 200	62 300	36 100
1981	73 665	329 700	44 470	63 300	17 100	95 000	43 800
1980	70 936	300 300	15 801	60 200	16 300	88 500	40 200
1979	70 797	282 400	15 684	57 500	16 800	83 900	35 000
1978	70 541	283 100	15 679	62 900	19 100	88 400	37 700
1977	29 571	262 600	15 374	62 000	18 500	85 500	36 200
1976	29 389	267 700	15 365	60 600	19 300	82 800	30 900
1975	29 091	238 800	15 344	58 800	17 300	75 700	36 000
1974	29 031	217 400	14 777	53 100	15 200	72 900	18 100
1973	29 117	215 600	14 740	54 700	16 300	71 600	13 000
1972	28 878	211 600	14 730	54 400	16 300	72 600	30 900
1971	28 731	200 543	14 470	49 115	15 913	75 182	27 671
1970	28 543	172 005	14 307	[5]45 879	17 304	46 593	27 818
1969	28 460	163 990	14 275	42 519	14 610	47 052	26 678
1968	27 971	150 836	14 212	42 515	14 206	43 838	23 919
1967	27 187	139 676	13 664	39 641	13 741	40 403	21 130
1966	26 551	133 081	13 628	38 556	13 144	43 030	15 925
1965	26 549	121 312	13 619	36 566	12 286	39 022	12 977
1964	26 102	111 386	13 566	34 047	12 164	34 847	11 478
1963	25 869	102 711	13 338	33 438	11 676	30 786	12 523
1962	26 003	97 045	13 333	32 191	11 752	27 958	11 835
1961	25 958	86 663	13 211	27 906	10 922	26 356	9 733
1960	25 704	79 229	13 208	26 630	10 738	21 820	8 983
1959	24 497	68 901	13 205	22 392	10 696	15 437	8 952
1958	24 398	65 461	13 106	21 672	9 734	14 076	8 131
1957	24 410	68 016	13 136	20 903	9 351	15 582	7 890
1956	24 398	61 602	13 131	20 055	8 769	13 543	7 438
1955	23 924	56 573	12 670	18 830	7 953	12 605	6 700
1954	23 908	54 210	12 641	17 969	7 805	12 587	6 067
1953	23 902	52 268	12 640	17 372	7 540	12 593	5 693
1952	23 840	47 379	12 589	17 143	6 807	11 979	3 558
1951	23 702	37 106	12 557	15 079	6 187	10 590	2 449
1950	23 836	33 253	12 222	13 919	5 310	9 476	1 996
1949	22 976	31 736	11 420	12 968	4 923	8 778	1 422
1948	22 955	29 859	11 347	11 849	4 438	7 849	1 510
1947	22 824	25 534	11 347	10 674	4 027	7 575	1 247
1946	22 424	21 752	11 062	8 991	3 603	6 734	1 262
1945	22 126	11 714	11 061	4 538	2 512	3 694	383
1944	22 107	8 340	11 055	2 646	1 851	3 310	268
1943	21 061	6 828	10 303	2 054	1 578	2 851	131
1942	20 886	9 371	10 300	3 815	1 832	3 130	256
1941	20 817	21 237	10 285	8 459	3 745	7 292	896

[1]Not the same as the "national park system." Definition of the national park system has changed from time to time. For 1850–1962, "total enumerated areas" are merely totals of the other items listed; thereafter, totals include other national parks and allied areas not shown separately, as follows (as of year end or Jan. 1 of the following year): 1970, 16 areas, 100 thousand acres and 4,742 visits; 1969, 13 areas, 94 thousand acres, and 2,415 thousand visits; 1968, 14 areas, 128 thousand acres and 1,790 thousand visits; 1967, 10 areas, 48 thousand acres and 2,393 thousand visits; 1966, 10 areas, 23 thousand acres and 2,296 thousand visits; 1965, 1 area, 18 acres and 1,673 thousand visits; 1964, 1 area, 18 acres and 1,840 thousand visits; 1963, 1 area, 18 acres and no reported visits.
[2]Includes others areas not shown separately.
[3]Beginning 1964, includes visits to the White House.
[4]Includes national historical parks, national military parks, national battlefields, national battlefield parks, national battlefield sites, national cemeteries, national historic sites, national memorials, and one national memorial park. Does not include historical areas established under the Antiquities Act of 1906 and designated national monuments, nor the White House.
[5]Includes visits to two National Recreation Areas adjacent to North Cascades National Park.

Table 22-10. National Parks, Monuments, and Allied Areas—Area and Visits, 1850–2005—*Continued*

(Thousands of acres, number in thousands; for years ending Sept. 30 prior to 1941; thereafter, for years ending Dec. 31, or as of Jan. 1 of the following year. Includes data for five areas in Puerto Rico and the Virgin Islands, one area in American Samoa, and one area in Guam.)

Year	Total, enumerated areas[1]		National parks		National monuments visits	National historical and military areas[4] visits	Naitional parkways visits
	Area (thousand visits)	Visits[2,3]	Area (thousand acres)	Visits[3]			
1940	20 762	16 755	10 258	7 358	2 817	5 924	...
1939	19 892	15 531	9 459	6 854	2 592	5 472	...
1938	18 647	16 331	9 409	6 619	2 364	6 784	...
1937	16 537	15 133	8 750	6 705	1 966	6 073	...
1936	15 433	11 990	8 692	5 791	1 681	4 518	...
1935	15 115	7 676	8 486	4 056	1 332	2 288	...
1934	15 244	6 337	8 532	3 517	1 386	1 434	...
1933	15 140	3 482	8 435	2 867	523	91	...
1932	12 968	3 755	8 417	2 949	406	400	...
1931	12 523	3 545	8 027	3 153	392	...	...
1930	10 581	3 247	7 797	2 775	472	...	...
1929	10 538	3 248	7 755	2 757	491	...	...
1928	10 359	3 025	7 581	2 569	456	...	...
1927	10 320	2 798	7 570	2 381	417	...	...
1926	10 249	2 315	7 501	1 942	373	...	...
1925	9 987	2 055	7 286	1 762	292	...	...
1924	8 813	1 671	7 278	1 424	247	...	...
1923	8 790	1 494	7 278	1 281	213	...	...
1922	8 781	1 216	7 278	1 045	172	...	...
1921	8 452	1 172	6 950	1 007	164	...	...
1920	8 452	1 058	6 950	920	139	...	...
1919	8 372	811	6 873	757	54	...	...
1918	7 554	455	6 255	452	3	...	...
1917	7 491	491	6 254	488	2	...	...
1916	5 984	358	4 742	356	2	...	...
1915	5 880	335	4 666	335	1	...	...
1914	5 986	240	4 437	240	1	...	...
1913	5 984	252	4 437	252	(Z)	...	...
1912	5 977	230	4 431	229	(Z)	...	...
1911	5 978	224	4 431	224	(Z)	...	...
1910	5 998	199	4 431	199	...	...	...
1909	5 013	86	3 449	86	...	...	...
1908	4 363	69	3 449	69	...	...	...
1907	3 547	61	3 444	61	...	...	...
1906	3 265	31	3 251	31	...	...	...
1905	3 471	141	3 457	141	...	...	...
1904	3 471	121	3 457	121	...	...	...
1903	3 470	...	3 456	...	...	...	...
1902	3 459	...	3 445	...	...	...	...
1901	3 300	...	3 286	...	...	...	...
1900	3 300	...	3 286	...	...	...	...
1899	3 300	...	3 286	...	...	...	...
1898	3 287	...	3 274	...	...	...	...
1897	3 287	...	3 274	...	...	...	...
1896	3 287	...	3 274	...	...	...	...
1895	3 287	...	3 274	...	...	...	...
1894	3 058	...	3 052	...	...	...	...
1893	3 058	...	3 052	...	...	...	...
1892	3 058	...	3 052	...	...	...	...
1891	3 058	...	3 051	...	...	...	...
1890	2 889	...	2 889	...	...	...	...
1872–1889[6]	1 921	...	1 921	...	...	...	...
1850–1871[7]	1	...	1	...	...	...	...

Source: U.S. Census Bureau. U.S. National Park Service.

[1]Not the same as the "national park system." Definition of the national park system has changed from time to time. For 1850–1962, "total enumerated areas" are merely totals of the other items listed; thereafter, totals include other national parks and allied areas not shown separately, as follows (as of year end or Jan. 1 of the following year): 1970, 16 areas, 100 thousand acres and 4,742 visits; 1969, 13 areas, 94 thousand acres, and 2,415 thousand visits; 1968, 14 areas, 128 thousand acres and 1,790 thousand visits; 1967, 10 areas, 48 thousand acres and 2,393 thousand visits; 1966, 10 areas, 23 thousand acres and 2,296 thousand visits; 1965, 1 area, 18 acres and 1,673 thousand visits; 1964, 1 area, 18 acres and 1,840 thousand visits; 1963, 1 area, 18 acres and no reported visits.
[2]Includes others areas not shown separately.
[3]Beginning 1964, includes visits to the White House.
[4]Includes national historical parks, national military parks, national battlefields, national battlefield parks, national battlefield sites, national cemeteries, national historic sites, national memorials, and one national memorial park. Does not include historical areas established under the Antiquities Act of 1906 and designated national monuments, nor the White House.
[6]Yellowstone National Park, the first national park, established 1872.
[7]Hot Springs Reservation set aside by the federal government in 1832 and established as a national park in 1921. Initial federal acreage was much greater than indicated, but over a period of years was subdivided into tracts and sold, some 900-odd acres being permanently reserved to the federal government. These series begin with 1850, the first year following the establishment of the Department of the Interior.
... = Not available.
Z = Less than 500.

Table 22-11. State Parks—Acreage, Expenditures, and Attendance, 1939–2004

Year	Acreage[1] (thousand acres)	Expenditures (thousand dollars)	Attendance (thousand visitors)
2004	14 180	1 812 228	697 831
2003	13 571	...	734 990
2002	13 162	1 886 201	758 216
2001	13 030	1 774 085	766 021
2000	12 807	1 629 594	786 610
1999	12 916	1 499 687	766 842
1998	...	...	...
1997	12 484	1 322 991	783 400
1996	12 318	1 283 839	747 812
1995	11 807	1 245 779	745 602
1994	...	...	...
1993	...	...	...
1992	11 831	1 086 631	724 805
1991	11 148	1 094 573	736 897
1990	11 238	1 060 158	722 819
1989	11 061	981 760	762 842
1988	10 820	903 426	710 342
1987	13 752	848 290	694 432
1986	13 726	799 851	675 465
1985	10 128	101 500	661 916
1984	10 148	892 000	665 524
1983	9 936	838 000	644 843
1982	9 912	888 000	631 031
1981	9 326	968 000	618 080
1980	9 468	993 000	548 912
1979	9 411	1 078 000	609 010
1975	9 838	649 000	566 000
1970	8 555	386 752	482 536
1967	7 352	279 520	391 063
1962	5 763	108 881	284 795
1961	5 799	110 101	273 484
1960	5 602	87 373	259 001
1959	5 681	88 268	255 310
1958	5 406	73 222	237 329
1957	5 248	74 008	216 780
1956	5 165	65 844	200 705
1955	5 086	55 093	183 188
1954	5 005	49 134	166 427
1953	4 876	49 565	159 116
1952	4 928	40 469	149 255
1951	4 877	38 545	120 722
1950	4 657	36 399	114 291
1949	...	31 921	106 792
1948	...	32 059	105 248
1947	...	25 991	109 995
1946	4 634	15 445	92 507
1945	...	10 564	57 649
1944	...	6 466	39 668
1943	...	6 570	38 306
1942	...	9 373	70 359
1941	4 260	10 022	97 489
1940	...	9 443	...
1939	...	7 429	...

Source: U.S. Census Bureau. National Association of State Park Directors. *2006 Annual Information Exchange.*
[1]Excludes state forests, wildlife refuges and waysides not administered by state park agencies.
... = Not available.

Table 22-12. Domestic Travel by U.S. Resident Households—Summary, 1998–2004

(Millions.)

Type of trip	1998	1999	2000	2001	2002	2003	2004
All travel:[1]							
Household trips	656.3	640.8	637.7	645.6	637.0	643.5	663.5
Person-trips	1 108.0	1 089.5	1 100.8	1 123.1	1 127.0	1 140.0	1 163.9
All overnight travel:							
Household trips	479.4	475.5	477.5	483.7	482.7	491.2	508.4
Person-trips	800.0	804.9	822.4	839.2	855.4	871.6	893.1
Business travel:							
Household trips	195.8	192.9	184.9	179.0	166.6	163.5	168.2
Person-trips	245.4	240.9	235.1	227.6	214.7	210.5	219.0
Leisure travel:[2]							
Household trips	460.5	447.9	452.8	466.6	470.4	480.0	490.1
Person-trips	862.6	848.6	865.7	895.5	912.3	929.5	944.3

Source: U.S. Census Bureau. *Statistical Abstract of the United States: 2007.* Travel Industry Association of America. Travel Scope©.
[1]Includes personal and other trips (e.g., medical, funerals, weddings), not shown separately. All domestic travel included. 95% of U.S. resident person-trips are domestic.
[2]Includes visiting friends/relatives, outdoor recreation, entertainment and travel for other pleasure/personal reasons, etc.

Table 22-13. Travel to Foreign Countries—Travelers and Expenditures, 1919–2005

(Travelers in thousands, expenditures in millions of dollars.)

Year	Total overseas travelers[1]	Total expenditures abroad[2]
2005	28 787	69 529
2004	27 351	65 635
2003	24 452	57 444
2002	23 397	58 715
2001	25 249	60 200
2000	26 853	64 705
1999	24 579	58 963
1998	23 069	56 483
1997	21 634	52 051
1996	19 786	48 076
1995	19 059	44 916
1994	18 149	43 782
1993	17 102	40 713
1992	15 965	38 552
1991	14 521	35 322
1990	15 990	37 349
1989	14 791	33 416
1988	14 443	32 114
1987	13 616	30 022
1986	12 038	26 746
1985	12 696	25 155
1984	11 690	23 305
1983	9 628	13 149
1982	8 510	12 394
1981	8 040	11 479
1980	8 163	10 397
1979	7 835	9 413
1978	7 790	8 475
1977	7 390	7 451
1976	6 897	6 856
1975	6 354	6 417
1974	6 467	5 980
1973	6 933	5 371
1972	6 790	4 944
1971	5 667	4 311
1970	5 260	3 973
1969	4 623	3 407
1968	3 885	3 030
1967	3 425	3 207
1966	2 975	2 657
1965	2 623	2 438
1964	2 220	2 211
1963	1 990	2 114
1962	1 767	1 939
1961	1 575	1 785
1960	1 634	1 750
1959	1 516	1 610
1958	1 398	1 460
1957	1 369	1 372
1956	1 239	1 275
1955	1 075	1 153
1954	912	1 009
1953	827	929
1952	772	840
1951	684	757
1950	676	754
1949	573	700
1948	495	631
1947	435	573
1946	329	457
1945	117	298
1944	75	225
1943	57	173
1942	71	155
1941	170	212

[1]Excludes the following: travel to Canada and Mexico; travel between conterminous United States and Alaska, Hawaii, Puerto Rico and Virgin Islands; cruise travelers; military personnel and other government employees and their dependents stationed abroad and U.S. citizens residing abroad.
[2]Includes shore expenditures of cruise travelers; excludes travel expenditures of military personnel and other government employees and their dependents stationed abroad and U.S. citizens residing abroad.

Table 22-13. Travel to Foreign Countries—Travelers and Expenditures, 1919–2005—*Continued*

(Travelers in thousands, expenditures in millions of dollars.)

Year	Total overseas travelers[1]	Total expenditures abroad[2]
1940	156	190
1939	282	290
1938	370	303
1937	435	348
1936	381	297
1935	314	245
1934	302	218
1933	300	199
1932	393	259
1931	438	341
1930	538	463
1929	517	483
1928	518	448
1927	471	400
1926	433	372
1925	408	347
1924	351	303
1923	291	260
1922	320	243
1921	294	200
1920	302	190
1919	152	123

Source: U.S. Census Bureau. U.S. Office of Travel and Tourism Industries. U.S. Bureau of Economic Analysis.
[1]Excludes the following: travel to Canada and Mexico; travel between conterminous United States and Alaska, Hawaii, Puerto Rico and Virgin Islands; cruise travelers; military personnel and other government employees and their dependents stationed abroad and U.S. citizens residing abroad.
[2]Includes shore expenditures of cruise travelers; excludes travel expenditures of military personnel and other government employees and their dependents stationed abroad and U.S. citizens residing abroad.

Table 22-14. Foreign Visitors to the United States—Number and Receipts, 1919–2005

(Travelers in thousands, expenditures in millions of dollars.)

Year	Total visitors[1]	Total receipts[2]
2005	19 117	81 680
2004	18 026	74 547
2003	20 322	64 348
2002	21 679	66 605
2001	21 833	71 893
2000	25 975	82 400
1999	24 466	74 801
1998	23 698	71 325
1997	24 194	73 426
1996	22 658	69 809
1995	20 639	63 395
1994	18 458	58 417
1993	18 662	57 875
1992	17 791	54 742
1991	16 155	48 384
1990	15 059	43 007
1989	13 999	36 205
1988	12 512	29 434
1987	10 434	23 563
1986	8 860	20 385
1985	7 537	17 762
1984	7 528	17 177
1983	7 873	11 408
1982	8 761	12 393
1981	9 069	12 913
1980	8 200	10 588
1979	7 230	8 441
1978	5 764	7 183
1977	4 509	6 150
1976	4 456	5 742
1975	3 674	4 697
1974	3 700	4 032
1973	3 554	...
1972	2 861	2 706
1971	2 490	2 464
1970	2 193	2 330
1969	1 894	2 058
1968	1 825	1 775
1967	1 431	1 646
1966	1 274	1 590
1965	1 130	1 380
1964	937	1 207
1963	780	1 015
1962	671	957
1961	602	885
1960	572	919
1959	520	902
1958	447	825
1957	419	785
1956	345	705
1955	328	654
1954	307	595
1953	287	574
1952	296	550
1951	255	473
1950	242	419
1949	258	392
1948	282	334
1947	229	342
1946	117	257
1945	102	162
1944	70	117
1943	50	84
1942	42	82
1941	46	70

[1]Excludes Canada and Mexico, except for 1933 and 1934. For years ending June.
[2]Excludes trans-ocean fares.

Table 22-14. Foreign Visitors to the United States—Number and Receipts, 1919–2005—*Continued*

(Travelers in thousands, expenditures in millions of dollars.)

Year	Total visitors[1]	Total receipts[2]
1940	81	95
1939	100	135
1938	98	130
1937	96	135
1936	81	117
1935	69	101
1934	75	81
1933	60	66
1932	49	65
1931	66	94
1930	83	129
1929	78	139
1928	78	121
1927	73	114
1926	70	110
1925	65	83
1924	79	77
1923	65	71
1922	53	61
1921	75	76
1920	81	67
1919	47	56

Source: U.S. Census Bureau. U.S. Office of Travel and Tourism Industries. U.S. Bureau of Economic Analysis.
[1]Excludes Canada and Mexico, except for 1933 and 1934. For years ending June.
[2]Excludes trans-ocean fares.
. . . = Not available.

BOX 22 ■ Copyright Issues and Music on the Internet

Since the mid-1990s, the spread of the Internet and digital technology have changed the distribution of entertainment content. In turn, this digital revolution has raised issues concerning the rights to reproduce, share, and download music.

The conflict between traditional entertainment corporations and digital providers officially began with the 2001 Recording Industry Association of America (RIAA) suit against peer-to-peer (P2P) file-sharing service pioneer, Napster. Napster created a phenomenon by enabling users to upload and download digital music without paying the traditional fees for copyright material. The success of the Web site attracted the attention of the music industry, whose concerns over copyright issues led to a series of lawsuits and a judgment by the Ninth Circuit Court of Appeals that Napster was illegally facilitating in the trade of copyrighted materials. As a result of this decision, Napster declared bankruptcy, but it was later bought and reincarnated by media giant Bertelsmann.

An unexpected twist in the litigation, which was based on the 1998 Digital Millennium Copyright Act, was the judge's determination that the record companies did not provide adequate proof that they were indeed the copyright holders of the music on Napster's site. Although the judge agreed that the record companies probably did own the rights, the judge concluded that their evidence did not meet the burden of proof required by law necessary to fine Napster the billions of dollars in restitution the record labels were seeking.

Subsequently several P2P sites have flourished, drawn litigation, and settled with copyright holders. The last large P2P is LimeWire which, according to NPD Group was responsible for 62% of P2P downloads in 2006. RIAA spokesperson Jonathan Lamy stated that 466 million tunes were downloaded illegally in December 2006, which was six times more than the number of legal downloads. The RIAA has settled approximately 5,700 of its 18,000 lawsuits, each for approximately $4000.

The RIAA has continued litigation against P2P sites, but it has also turned its attention to the individual user, especially students in colleges and universities. In the 2004–2005 academic year, the RIAA started sending subpoenas threatening to sue students involved in illegal file sharing. In 2007, the Association changed tactics and began sending pre-litigation letters offering students an opportunity to settle for reduced fees averaging more than $3,000, if they identified themselves within 20 days. According to RIAA officials, almost 3,000 of these letters were sent in the first six months of the campaign. In 2006–2007, the RIAA sent three times as many letters than in the previous year. According to an RIAA press release in 2007, more than half of all college students download music illegally. The NPD Group, a market research firm, has stated that students alone accounted for more than 1.3 billion illegal music downloads in 2006. Thus, while college students represented only 10% of the sample in the study, they accounted for 26% of all music downloading on P2P networks and 21% of all P2P users.

The proliferation of illegal downloads over college and university networks led the music industry to seek the assistance of the U.S. Congress. In May 2007, a bipartisan group of congressional representatives sent a letter and survey to the 20 universities that the RIAA cited as the schools with the largest number of illegal file downloads. The letter requested information on how the universities planned to deal with the problem. Until then, a safe harbor clause in the Digital Millennium Copyright Act had protected universities from liability for illegal activities that occur on their networks, if officials were unaware of the problem. Members of Congress have stated that this immunity will be reconsidered unless the extent of file sharing on campuses is reduced.

Some schools have responded by changing the technology of their networks to trace the content of P2P files, or even to make P2P file transfers impossible altogether. Others have refused to forward the pre-litigation letters to students whose identities are otherwise unknown to the RIAA.

These and similar issues in the entertainment industry will continue to evolve as litigation and legislation continue to shape the legal environment surrounding the recording industry and the means of delivery of digital music files. Because of the nature of the theft, it is difficult to quantify its financial impact.

Sources:
Albanese, Andrew. "Cyberexperts: Fight the RIAA! Harvard Academics Warn Against Fosters Student Settlements. (lj News)(Recording Industry Association of America)(Brief article)." *Library Journal* 132.10 (June 1, 2007): 15(2).
Bonisteel, Steven. "Latest Napster Ruling Turns Tables on Record Labels." *Newsbytes* (Feb. 25, 2002).
Bray, Hiawatha. "Record Firms Crack Down on Campuses." *Boston Globe* (March 8, 2007).
Butler, Susan. "Class(room) Action: One University Refuses to Pass on RIAA File-Sharing Letters, But the Rest Play Ball.(LEGAL)." *Billboard* 119.16 (April 21, 2007): 8(1).
"Could Napster Rise from the Ashes in Wireless?" *Wireless Data News* 10.24 (Nov. 20, 2002): 0.
"Google: Viacom Suit Threat to Internet Use." *PC Magazine Online* (May 1, 2007).
NPD Group, Port Washington, NY. "The NPD Group: Legal Music Downloads Were Fastest Growing Digital Music Category in 2006," March14, 2007. http://www.npd.com/press/releases/press_0703141.html
Recording Industry Association of America, Washington, D.C. *Newsroom,* "23 New Schools to Receive Latest Round of RIAA Pre-Lawsuit Letters," July 18, 2007. http://riaa.org/newsitem.php?news_year_filter=&resultpage=&id=780E8751-0E03-4258-D651-F991B66E1708

Recording Industry Association of America, Washington, D.C. "Piracy Online." http://riaa.org/physicalpiracy.php?content_selector=piracy_details _online

Recording Industry Association of America, Washington, D.C. "For Students Doing Reports." http://riaa.org/faq.php

Richtel, Matt. "Napster Wins One Round in Music Case; Judge Questions Tactics of Major Record Labels." *The New York Times* (Feb. 23, 2002 pC1(N) pC1(L) col 5 (35 col): C1(L).

Richtel, Matt. "Judge Grants a Suspension of Lawsuit on Napster." *The New York Times* (Jan. 24, 2002 pC4 (N) pC4(L) col 6 (16 col): C4(L).

Triplett, William. "Pols Scold Schools Over File Sharing." *Daily Variety* 295.23 (May 3, 2007): 5(2).

U.S. House of Representatives, Committee on Education and the Workforce. Testimony of Professor Cheryl Asper Elzy before the Subcommittee on 21st Century Competitiveness Committee on Education and the Workforce, September 26, 2006. http://republicans.edlabor.house .gov/archive/hearings/109th/21st/piracy092606/elzy.htm

Economics

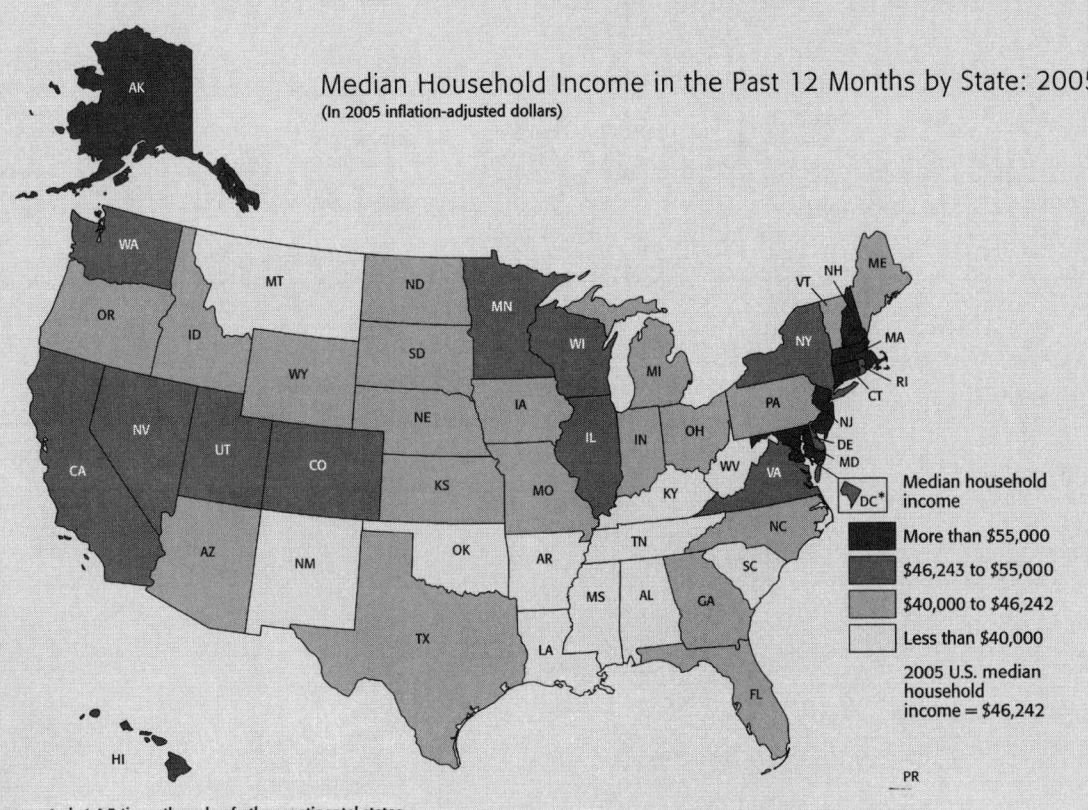

Median Household Income in the Past 12 Months by State: 2005
(In 2005 inflation-adjusted dollars)

Median household income

- More than $55,000
- $46,243 to $55,000
- $40,000 to $46,242
- Less than $40,000

2005 U.S. median household income = $46,242

* DC is represented at 4.5 times the sale of other continental states.
Source: U.S. Census Bureau, 2005 American Community Survey.

National Income and Wealth

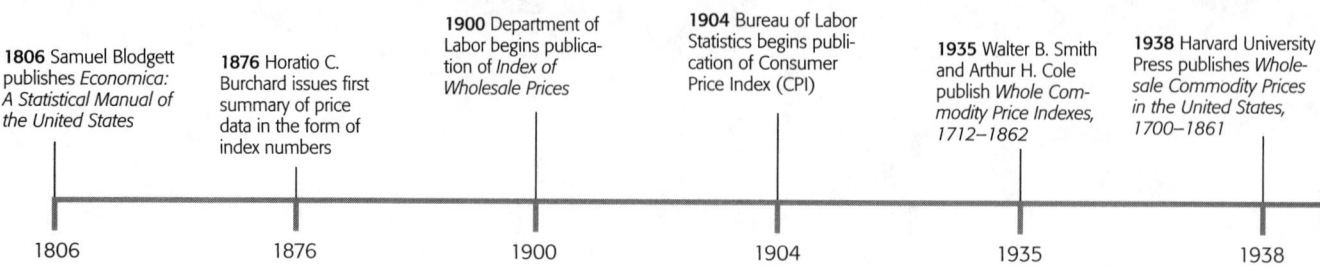

1806 Samuel Blodgett publishes *Economica: A Statistical Manual of the United States*

1876 Horatio C. Burchard issues first summary of price data in the form of index numbers

1900 Department of Labor begins publication of *Index of Wholesale Prices*

1904 Bureau of Labor Statistics begins publication of Consumer Price Index (CPI)

1935 Walter B. Smith and Arthur H. Cole publish *Whole Commodity Price Indexes, 1712–1862*

1938 Harvard University Press publishes *Wholesale Commodity Prices in the United States, 1700–1861*

1806   1876   1900   1904   1935   1938

Consumer Income and Expenditures

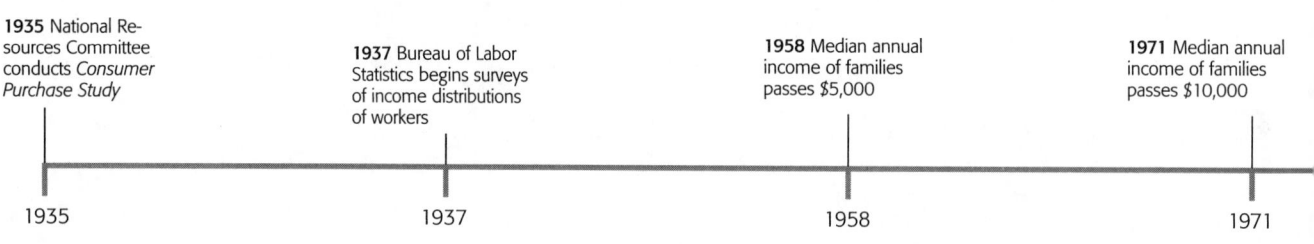

1935 National Resources Committee conducts *Consumer Purchase Study*

1937 Bureau of Labor Statistics begins surveys of income distributions of workers

1958 Median annual income of families passes $5,000

1971 Median annual income of families passes $10,000

1935   1937   1958   1971

Business Enterprise

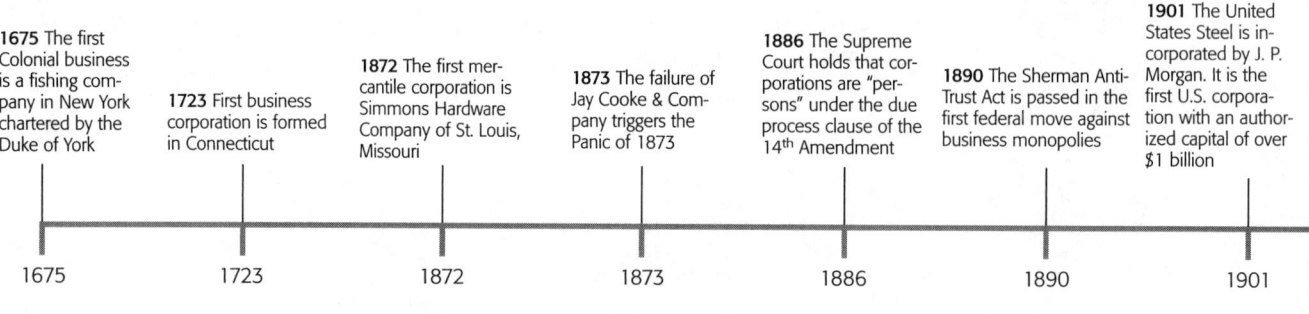

1675 The first Colonial business is a fishing company in New York chartered by the Duke of York

1723 First business corporation is formed in Connecticut

1872 The first mercantile corporation is Simmons Hardware Company of St. Louis, Missouri

1873 The failure of Jay Cooke & Company triggers the Panic of 1873

1886 The Supreme Court holds that corporations are "persons" under the due process clause of the 14th Amendment

1890 The Sherman Anti-Trust Act is passed in the first federal move against business monopolies

1901 The United States Steel is incorporated by J. P. Morgan. It is the first U.S. corporation with an authorized capital of over $1 billion

1675   1723   1872   1873   1886   1890   1901

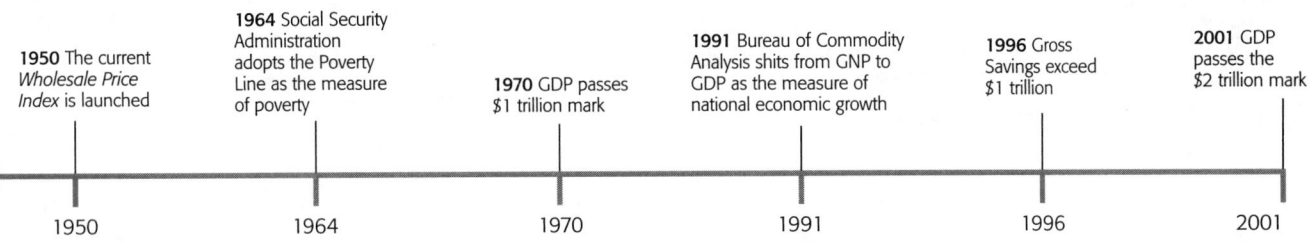

1950 The current *Wholesale Price Index* is launched

1964 Social Security Administration adopts the Poverty Line as the measure of poverty

1970 GDP passes $1 trillion mark

1991 Bureau of Commodity Analysis shits from GNP to GDP as the measure of national economic growth

1996 Gross Savings exceed $1 trillion

2001 GDP passes the $2 trillion mark

1950   1964   1970   1991   1996   2001

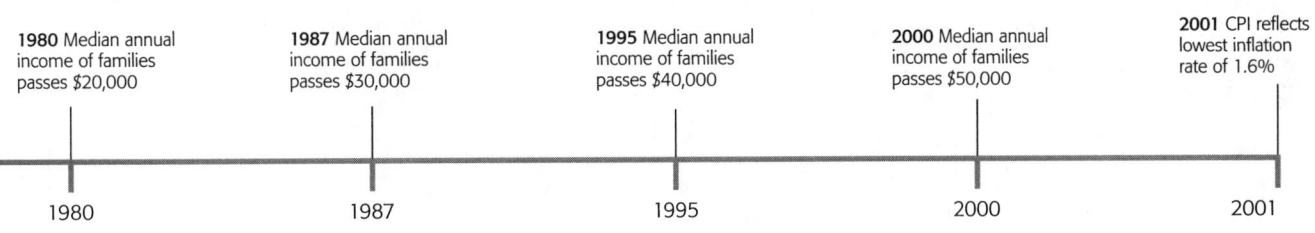

1980 Median annual income of families passes $20,000

1987 Median annual income of families passes $30,000

1995 Median annual income of families passes $40,000

2000 Median annual income of families passes $50,000

2001 CPI reflects lowest inflation rate of 1.6%

1980   1987   1995   2000   2001

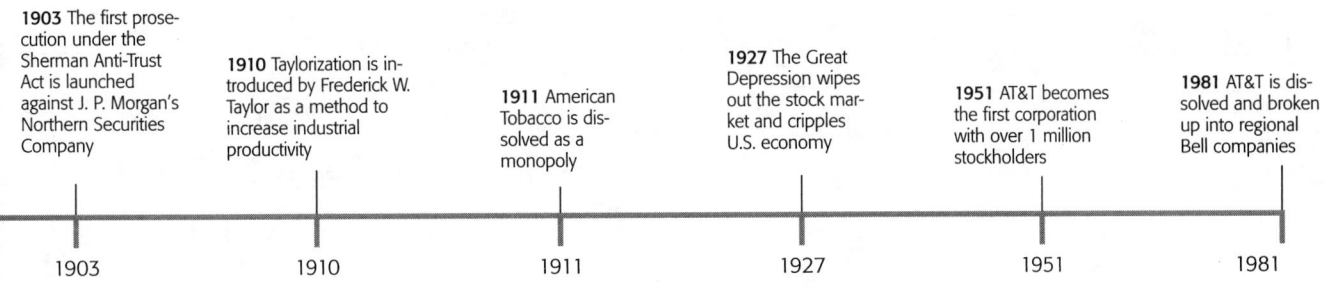

1903 The first prosecution under the Sherman Anti-Trust Act is launched against J. P. Morgan's Northern Securities Company

1910 Taylorization is introduced by Frederick W. Taylor as a method to increase industrial productivity

1911 American Tobacco is dissolved as a monopoly

1927 The Great Depression wipes out the stock market and cripples U.S. economy

1951 AT&T becomes the first corporation with over 1 million stockholders

1981 AT&T is dissolved and broken up into regional Bell companies

1903   1910   1911   1927   1951   1981

Financial Markets and Institutions

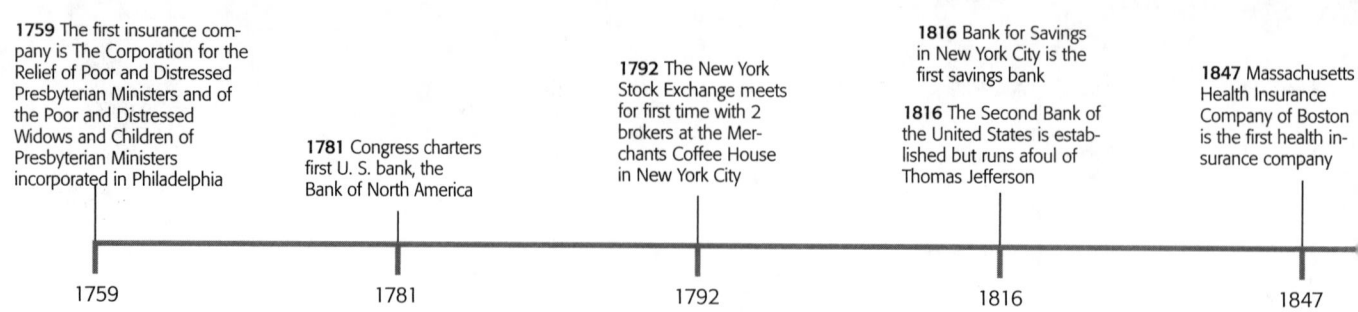

1759 The first insurance company is The Corporation for the Relief of Poor and Distressed Presbyterian Ministers and of the Poor and Distressed Widows and Children of Presbyterian Ministers incorporated in Philadelphia

1781 Congress charters first U. S. bank, the Bank of North America

1792 The New York Stock Exchange meets for first time with 2 brokers at the Merchants Coffee House in New York City

1816 Bank for Savings in New York City is the first savings bank

1816 The Second Bank of the United States is established but runs afoul of Thomas Jefferson

1847 Massachusetts Health Insurance Company of Boston is the first health insurance company

1759　1781　1792　1816　1847

Financial Markets and Institutions—*continued*

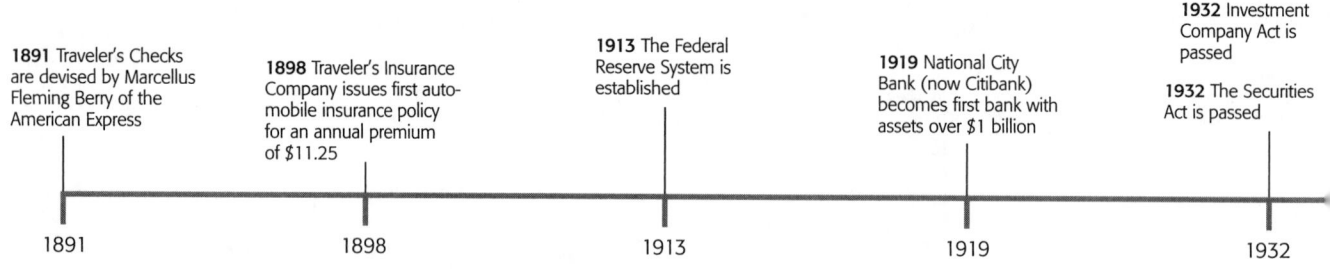

1891 Traveler's Checks are devised by Marcellus Fleming Berry of the American Express

1898 Traveler's Insurance Company issues first automobile insurance policy for an annual premium of $11.25

1913 The Federal Reserve System is established

1919 National City Bank (now Citibank) becomes first bank with assets over $1 billion

1932 Investment Company Act is passed

1932 The Securities Act is passed

1891　1898　1913　1919　1932

Public Finance

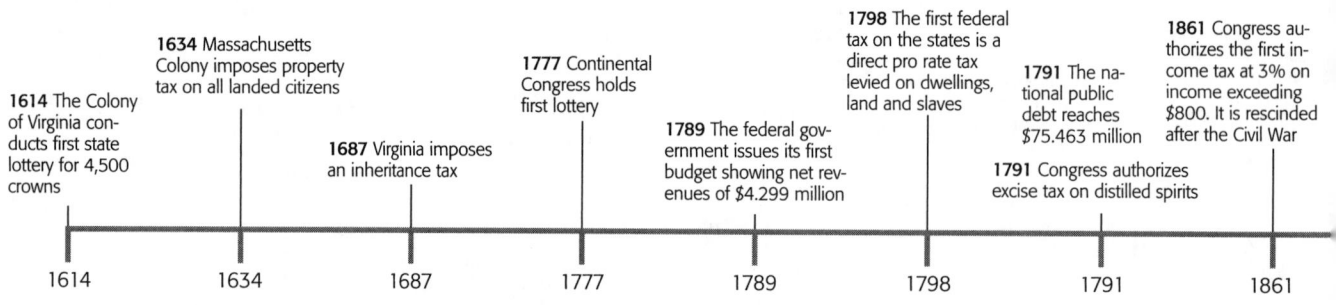

1614 The Colony of Virginia conducts first state lottery for 4,500 crowns

1634 Massachusetts Colony imposes property tax on all landed citizens

1687 Virginia imposes an inheritance tax

1777 Continental Congress holds first lottery

1789 The federal government issues its first budget showing net revenues of $4.299 million

1798 The first federal tax on the states is a direct pro rate tax levied on dwellings, land and slaves

1791 The national public debt reaches $75.463 million

1791 Congress authorizes excise tax on distilled spirits

1861 Congress authorizes the first income tax at 3% on income exceeding $800. It is rescinded after the Civil War

1614　1634　1687　1777　1789　1798　1791　1861

International Transactions and Foreign Commerce

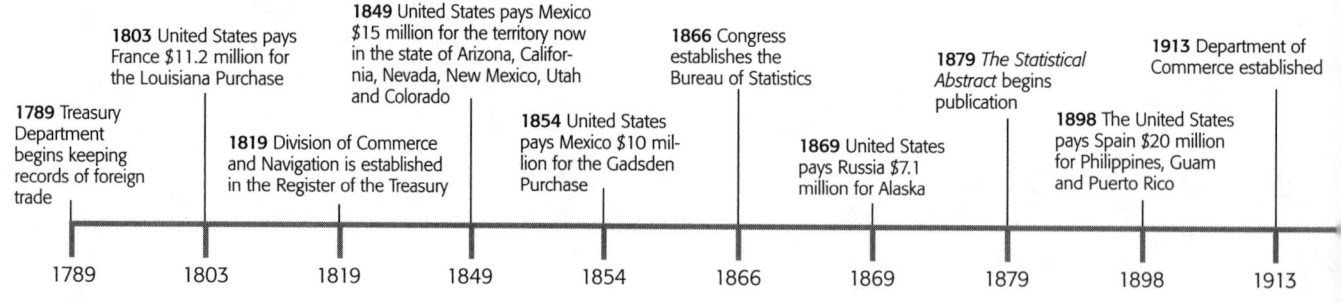

1789 Treasury Department begins keeping records of foreign trade

1803 United States pays France $11.2 million for the Louisiana Purchase

1819 Division of Commerce and Navigation is established in the Register of the Treasury

1849 United States pays Mexico $15 million for the territory now in the state of Arizona, California, Nevada, New Mexico, Utah and Colorado

1854 United States pays Mexico $10 million for the Gadsden Purchase

1866 Congress establishes the Bureau of Statistics

1869 United States pays Russia $7.1 million for Alaska

1879 *The Statistical Abstract* begins publication

1898 The United States pays Spain $20 million for Philippines, Guam and Puerto Rico

1913 Department of Commerce established

1789　1803　1819　1849　1854　1866　1869　1879　1898　1913

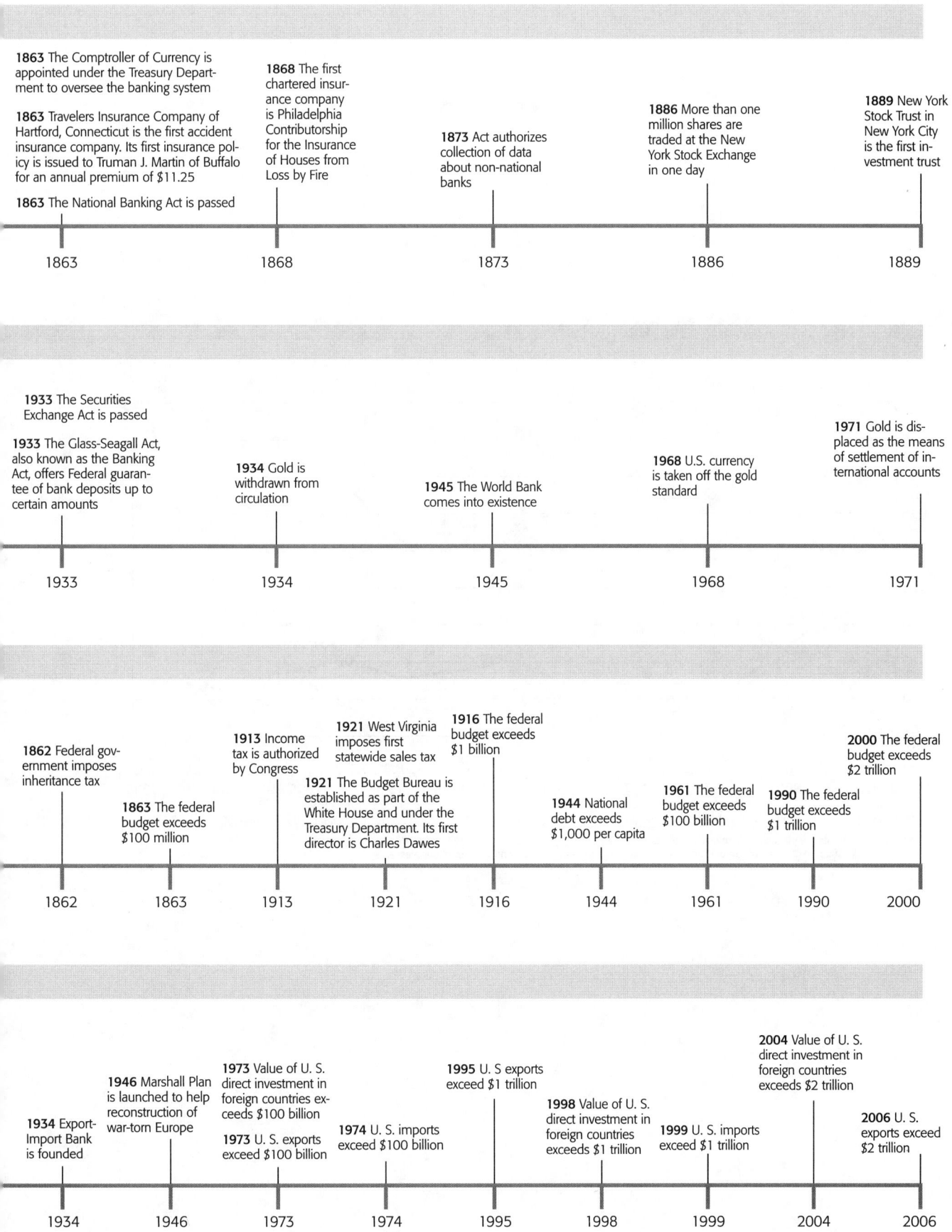

1863 The Comptroller of Currency is appointed under the Treasury Department to oversee the banking system

1863 Travelers Insurance Company of Hartford, Connecticut is the first accident insurance company. Its first insurance policy is issued to Truman J. Martin of Buffalo for an annual premium of $11.25

1863 The National Banking Act is passed

1868 The first chartered insurance company is Philadelphia Contributorship for the Insurance of Houses from Loss by Fire

1873 Act authorizes collection of data about non-national banks

1886 More than one million shares are traded at the New York Stock Exchange in one day

1889 New York Stock Trust in New York City is the first investment trust

1863　1868　1873　1886　1889

1933 The Securities Exchange Act is passed

1933 The Glass-Seagall Act, also known as the Banking Act, offers Federal guarantee of bank deposits up to certain amounts

1934 Gold is withdrawn from circulation

1945 The World Bank comes into existence

1968 U.S. currency is taken off the gold standard

1971 Gold is displaced as the means of settlement of international accounts

1933　1934　1945　1968　1971

1862 Federal government imposes inheritance tax

1863 The federal budget exceeds $100 million

1913 Income tax is authorized by Congress

1921 West Virginia imposes first statewide sales tax

1921 The Budget Bureau is established as part of the White House and under the Treasury Department. Its first director is Charles Dawes

1916 The federal budget exceeds $1 billion

1944 National debt exceeds $1,000 per capita

1961 The federal budget exceeds $100 billion

1990 The federal budget exceeds $1 trillion

2000 The federal budget exceeds $2 trillion

1862　1863　1913　1921　1916　1944　1961　1990　2000

1934 Export-Import Bank is founded

1946 Marshall Plan is launched to help reconstruction of war-torn Europe

1973 Value of U. S. direct investment in foreign countries exceeds $100 billion

1973 U. S. exports exceed $100 billion

1974 U. S. imports exceed $100 billion

1995 U. S exports exceed $1 trillion

1998 Value of U. S. direct investment in foreign countries exceeds $1 trillion

1999 U. S. imports exceed $1 trillion

2004 Value of U. S. direct investment in foreign countries exceeds $2 trillion

2006 U. S. exports exceed $2 trillion

1934　1946　1973　1974　1995　1998　1999　2004　2006

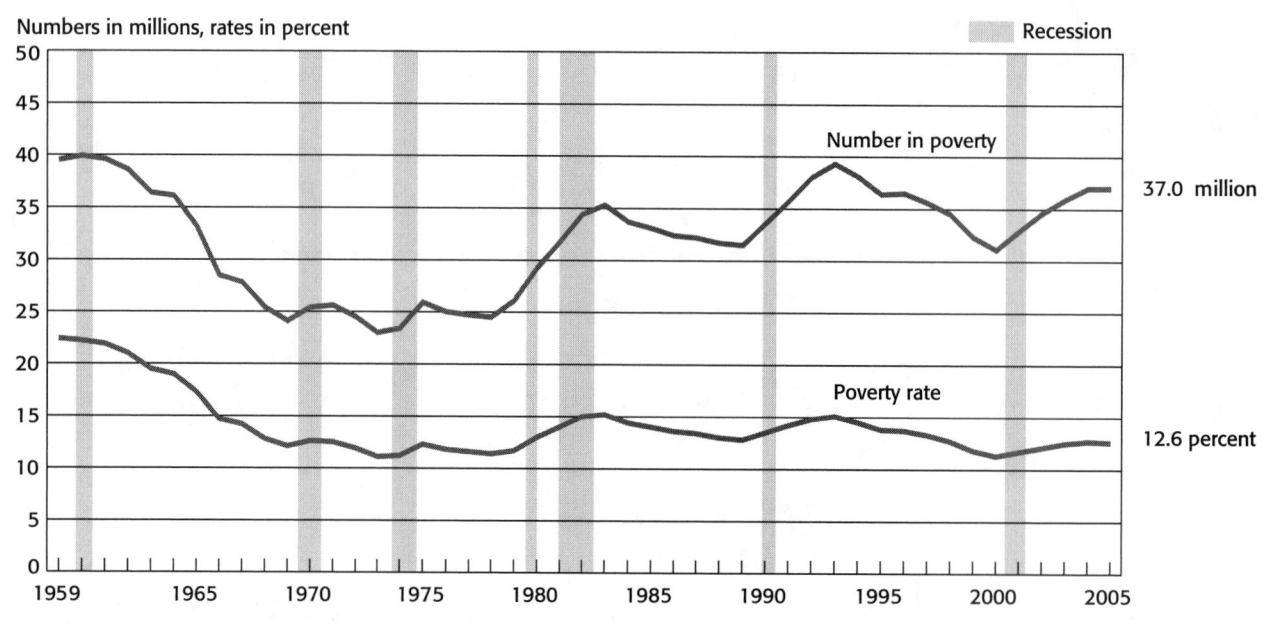

Number in Poverty and Poverty Rate: 1959 to 2005

Note: The data points are placed at the midpoints of the respective years.
Source: U.S. Census Bureau, Current Population Survey, 1960 to 2006 Annual Social and Economic Supplements.

CHAPTER **23**

National Income and Wealth

HIGHLIGHTS

1 The earliest statistics of prices were compiled by Samuel Blodgett Jr. in *Economica: A Statistical Manual of the United States of America,* published in 1806. It includes a collection of prices for 16 important commodities in five markets for the years 1785 to 1805. The first serious attempt to summarize price data in the form of index numbers was made by Horatio C. Burchard, Director of the Mint, in his report to the Secretary of the Treasury in 1881. In 1886, a special report containing retail prices for about 60 "necessaries of life," was included in volume 20 of the Tenth Census. In 1891, a Senate Resolution led Roland P. Falkner to collect a voluminous body of data covering wholesale prices from 1840–1891, and retail prices for the 28-month period ending September 1891. This information was published in the Aldrich Reports. In 1900, Falkner extended his indexes to 1899 with quotations for 142 articles, collected by the Department of Labor.

In 1902 the Department of Labor began publishing its *Index of Wholesale Prices,* which has published continuously to the present day (though in 1978 the main index was renamed as the Producer Price Index). In addition to this series, John R. Commons published an *Index of Wholesale Prices* for 1878 to 1900 in his *Quarterly Bulletin of the Bureau of Economic Research.* Bradstreet's Index of Wholesale Prices for about 96 commodities was established in 1897 and included data beginning with 1890.

Dun's Index numbers of Wholesale Prices for about 350 commodities was published in *Dun's Review* beginning in 1901 and extending back to 1860. Walter B. Smith and Arthur H. Cole computed wholesale commodity price indexes covering 1792 to 1862 for *Fluctuations in American Business, 1790–1860,* published by Harvard University Press in 1935. It covered Boston, New York, and Philadelphia.

The most extensive historical price investigations, however, were undertaken under the auspices of the International Scientific Committee on Price History. They were summarized in *Wholesale Commodity Prices in the United States, 1700–1861,* published by Harvard University Press in 1938. Wholesale price indexes were compiled by Frederick C. Mills for economically significant commodities. Part of this series was first published by the National Bureau of Economic Research for 1830 to 1931 in *Economic Tendencies in the United States.* (Wholesale prices are compiled from prices in primary markets and pertain to the first major commercial transaction for each commodity. The quotations are generally selling prices of manufacturers or producers or the selling price on an organized exchange or at a central market.) The current price index was begun in 1952 and spliced to the former series. While the 1952 revision did not alter the conceptual definition of the index, it did adopt major changes in coverage and methods. The list of priced commodities was expanded from 947 to 1,800 in 1952, 2,450 in 1970, and 10,000 in 1998. The index is currently known as the Producer Price Index, as of 1978. The base years changed from 1890 to 1899 to 1913, 1926, 1967, and 1982. The weighting factors for each commodity represent the value of shipments for the specific commodity priced and for all others in the same group known to have similar price movements. The indexes are calculated as averages of relatives weighted by value of shipments. Changes in quality are factored into the index.

2 The volume of information available for wholesale prices is not matched at the retail level, especially for the early years. The official Consumer Price Index (CPI) was initiated by the Bureau of Labor Statistics (BLS) in 1904 with a food index covering the years 1890 to 1893. The Food Index was continued until the end of World War I when it became one component group of a comprehensive Cost of Living Index. Since then, the index has been expanded in scope, resulting in an improvement in the quality of data. At present the index is issued monthly. From 1918 to 1958, the National Industrial Conference Board also compiled a consumer price index. Consumer price data before 1913 are extremely patchy. The only cost of living indexes computed from retail price data before 1913 are Wesley C. Mitchell's *Relative Cost of Living for 1860 to 1880,* Ethel Hoover's *Consumer Price Index for 1851 to 1880,* and Rees' *Cost of Living Index, 1890–1914.* These indexes were compiled from newspapers and other sources, and their reliability is affected by changes in quality, incomplete files, nominal prices, changes in consumer tastes, and demographic and other changes. In 1919, the BLS began the publication of complete indexes at semiannual intervals. The first major revision of the Consumer Price Index occurred in 1940, with subsequent revisions in 1953, 1964, 1978, 1987, and 1998. The last revision changed the base year to 1982–1984. The BLS publishes CPIs for two population groups: CPI-W covering urban wage-earners and clerical workers who comprise about 32 percent of the population and CPI-U for all urban consumers, including groups excluded from CPI-W, such as the unemployed, self-employed, retirees, professionals, and managers. The current CPI is based on a market basket of goods and services, including food, clothing, shelter, fuels, transportation, healthcare, and so on. It is based on data collected from 85 areas across the country (up from 40 in 1952, 46 in 1953, 50 in 1964, and 56 in 1966), and from more than 50,000 housing units and 23,000 establishments. The BLS publishes a national index as well as separate indexes for regions, area-size classes, and 26 local areas or MSAs. In calculating the index, each item is assigned a weight to account for its relative importance in consumer budgets. Price changes for the various items in each location are then averaged. Local data are then combined to obtain a city average.

The percent change in the CPI from month to month or relative to the same month in the previous year is known as the inflation rate. PPI and CPI show the same general pattern of inflation but the latter is more volatile. The PPI is generally the leading indicator and often tends to foreshadow trends that later occur in the CPI. Other measures of inflation include the Index of Industrial Materials Prices, the Dow Jones Commodity Spot Price Index, Futures Price Index, Employment Cost Index, Hourly Compensation Index, and the Unit Labor Cost Index.

3 Income and expenditures represent two facets of an economy and are commonly measured by the Gross National Product (GNP) and the Gross Domestic Product (GDP). In 1991, the Bureau of Economic Analysis began featuring GDP rather than GNP as the measure of national production because it is the more appropriate measure for short-term monitoring of the economy and also because it facilitates international comparisons. GDP is the primary measure of production in the System of National Accounts and is the total national output of goods and services valued at market prices. It includes purchases of goods and services by consumers and government, gross private domestic investment, and net exports of goods and services. GDP measures the output attributable to all labor and property supplied by U.S. residents. It differs from national income mainly in that GNP includes allowances for depreciation and for indirect business taxes. The dollar levels of GDP and GNP differ little but percentage changes may differ more significantly. The annual rates of growth of real GNP have been slightly less than the annual rates of growth of real GDP for most years. The short-term differences are greater and tend to fluctuate more. National income is the aggregate of labor and property earnings which arise in the current production of goods and services. It is the sum of employee compensation, proprietors' income, rental income of persons, corporate profits, and net interest. It measures the total factor cost of the goods and services produced by the economy. Capital consumption adjustment for corporations, sole proprietorships, and partnerships is the difference between capital consumption claimed on income tax returns and capital consumption allowances measured at straight-line depreciation, consistent service lives, and replacement cost. Personal income is the current income received by persons from all sources minus their contributions for social insurance (including transfers from government, such as Social Security, but excluding interpersonal transfers). Disposable personal income (income available for spending or saving) is personal income less personal tax and nontax payments.

4 In recent years, discussion has focused on the limitations of the standard measurements of national income and wealth. First, national product is primarily a measure of the output of the market economy. No account is taken of the value of homemakers' services, home repairs, or noncommercial recreation. Second, there is no agreement on what goods should be properly considered the end products of the economy. As ordinarily constituted, national product includes all items of consumer expenditure, including expenditures on commuting and labor union dues, which are not end products in themselves. It also overstates the growth of the economy because it includes defense expenditures, as well as police and fire protection. Third, because of the techniques used in adjusting for price changes, national product fails to reflect fully the changes in the quality of goods. The limitation tends to understate economic growth. Fourth, aggregate figures on national product mask changes in the distribution of income between rich and poor, the age-composition of the population, and people-hours spent in economic activity.

5 As part of a comprehensive revision in 1996, BEA replaced its fixed-weight (1987 dollars) index as the featured measure of real GDP with an index based on chain-type annual weights. Under the new system, changes in real output and prices are calculated as the average of changes based on weights for the current and preceding years. (Components of real output are weighted by price, and components of price are weighted by output.) These annual changes are "chained" (multiplied) together to form a time series that allows for the effects of changes in relative prices and changes in the composition of output over time. As of the 1999 comprehensive revision, the new output indexes and new price indexes are expressed as 1996 = 100. The most recent comprehensive revision was in December of 2003, which expresses indexes as 2000 = 100.

6 The primary source of national income and product data is the *Survey of Current Business,* published monthly by the Department of Commerce. Detailed historical data appear in the two-volume *National Income and Product Accounts of the United States.* For earlier periods, the classic sources are Simon Kuznets' *National Income and Its Composition, 1919–1983; Capital in the American Economy: Its Formation and Financing; National Product Since 1869;* and *Enterprise and Social Progress;* Willford I. King's *The Wealth and Income of the People of the United States;* and Robert F. Martin's *National Income in the United States, 1799-1938.*

7 Generally speaking, national saving equals national income minus national consumption and is identical to net national investment. Although data on saving are imperfect for statistical and conceptual reasons, they throw important light on the nature of the different groups of savers and the various forms of savings.

8 The Poverty Index was devised by the Social Security Administration in 1964 and revised by the Federal Inter-Agency Committee in 1969 and 1980. It is based solely on money income and does not include non-cash benefits, such as food stamps, Medicaid, and public housing. The Poverty Threshold is updated every year to reflect changes in the Consumer Price Index. In 1980, it was $4,290 for one person under 65 years, $3,949 for one person 65 years or over, $11,269 for six persons, and $16,896 for nine or more persons. In 2004, the Poverty Threshold was $9,645 for one person ($9,827 for a person under 65 years and $9,060 for a person 65 years and over), going up to $39,048 for nine or more persons.

9 The GDP passed the $1 trillion mark in 1970 and the $10 trillion mark in 2001. In 2005, it was $12.487 trillion, the largest national GDP in the world.

10 The annual growth rate of GDP remained fairly consistent throughout the 1990s, growing by between 3.2 percent (1991) and 6.5 percent (1997). The growth rate was buttressed by strong showing by consumption expenditures on services and gross private domestic investment.

11 The Gross State Product is the gross market value of goods and services and is the state counterpart of the GDP. The states with the highest GSP in 2005 were California ($1.622 trillion), Texas ($982.403 billion), and New York ($963.466 billion). The states with the lowest GSP were Vermont ($23.134 billion), North Dakota ($24.178 billion), and Wyoming ($27.422 billion).

12 Manufacturing is strongest in California ($145.216 billion), Texas ($110.172 billion), and Ohio ($83.766 billion), as of 2004. California leads across the board in most sectors and accounts for more than 13 percent of the national GDP.

13 Of personal consumption expenditures totaling $8.214 trillion in 2004, the largest item was for medical care ($1.677 trillion), followed by food and tobacco ($1.222 trillion), housing ($1.221 trillion), transportation ($979.1 billion), household operation ($821.0 billion), recreation ($702.4 billion), personal business ($612.2 billion), clothing, accessories and jewelry ($445.5 billion), religious and welfare activities ($219.0 billion), and education and research ($211.3 billion).

14 In 2005, gross saving reached $1.680 trillion, of which gross government saving was $73.0 billion ($224.7 federal and $151.7 billion state and local).

15 In 2005, total personal income in the United States was $10.248 trillion, of which wage and salary disbursements accounted for $5.724 billion, personal interest income $945.7 billion, proprietors' income $938.7 billion, personal dividend income $511.7 billion, and rental income $72.9 billion.

16 Personal income per capita, one of the key indicators of prosperity, was $34,586 in 2005. In constant 2000 dollars, personal income per capita is up from $24,196 in 1990 to $31,071 in 2005. Connecticut was the top state in this category with a per capita income of $42,959, followed by Massachusetts ($39,778), New Jersey ($39,322), New York ($36,390), Maryland ($37,516), New Hampshire ($34,505), Colorado ($34,089), Minnesota ($33,575), and Delaware ($33,298). The three states with the lowest per capita income are Louisiana ($22,297), Mississippi ($22,745), and Arkansas ($24,143).

17 In 2004, an average family spent $43,395 on housing needs. Of these, the largest items were housing ($13,918), transportation ($7,801), food ($5,781), personal insurance and pensions ($4,823), healthcare ($2,574), entertainment ($2,218), apparel and services ($1,816), alcoholic beverages ($459), tobacco products and smoking supplies ($288), and reading ($130).

18 Asian households receive the highest median money income ($57,518), as of 2004. Whites are next ($48,977), Hispanics third ($34,241), and Blacks last ($30,134). The gap between Blacks and Hispanics on the one hand, and Asians and Whites on the other, has not improved since the 1970s.

19 The gap between the rich and the poor widened in recent decades. In 1980, the share of aggregate income received by the lowest fifth of families was 5.3 percent while that of the highest fifth was 41.1 percent. In 2004, the share of aggregate income received by the lowest fifth of families was 4.0 percent and that of the highest fifth was 47.9 percent. The top 5 percent of families received 14.6 percent and 20.9 percent in 1980 and 2004, respectively, of the aggregate income.

20 As of 2004, 22.8 percent of Black families and 20.5 percent of Hispanic families live below poverty level, compared with 8.4 percent of White families and 7.4 percent of Asian families. Overall, 10.2 percent of families live below the poverty level. The states with the largest percentage of individuals below the poverty level are Mississippi (21.6 percent), Louisiana (19.4 percent), and New Mexico (19.3 percent).

21 The mean net worth, measured in constant 2004 dollars, of an American family has increased from $421,500 in 2001 to $448,200 in 2004.

22 The net stock of fixed tangible personal and institutional wealth in 2004 was $37.610 trillion, of which the private sector accounted for $27.043 trillion.

23 Vehicles were the number one nonfinancial asset held by families in 2004, with 86.3 percent, followed by primary residence (69.1 percent) and other residential property (12.5 percent).

Table 23-1. Gross Domestic Product and GDP Growth Rate, in Current and Chained (2000) Dollars, 1929–2006

Year	Current dollars		Chained (2000) dollars	
	Gross domestic product (billion dollars)	GDP percent change	Gross domestic product (billion dollars)	GDP percent change
2006	13 247	6.3	11 415	3.3
2005	12 456	6.3	11 049	3.2
2004	11 713	6.9	10 704	3.9
2003	10 961	4.7	10 301	2.5
2002	10 470	3.4	10 049	1.6
2001	10 128	3.2	9 891	0.8
2000	9 817	5.9	9 817	3.7
1999	9 268	6.0	9 470	4.5
1998	8 747	5.3	9 067	4.2
1997	8 304	6.2	8 704	4.5
1996	7 817	5.7	8 329	3.7
1995	7 398	4.6	8 032	2.5
1994	7 072	6.2	7 836	4.0
1993	6 657	5.0	7 533	2.7
1992	6 338	5.7	7 337	3.3
1991	5 996	3.3	7 101	−0.2
1990	5 803	5.8	7 113	1.9
1989	5 484	7.5	6 981	3.5
1988	5 104	7.7	6 743	4.1
1987	4 740	6.2	6 475	3.4
1986	4 463	5.7	6 264	3.5
1985	4 220	7.3	6 054	4.1
1984	3 933	11.2	5 814	7.2
1983	3 537	8.7	5 424	4.5
1982	3 255	4.0	5 189	−1.9
1981	3 128	12.2	5 292	2.5
1980	2 790	8.8	5 162	−0.2
1979	2 563	11.7	5 173	3.2
1978	2 295	13.0	5 015	5.6
1977	2 031	11.3	4 751	4.6
1976	1 825	11.4	4 541	5.3
1975	1 638	9.2	4 311	−0.2
1974	1 500	8.5	4 320	−0.5
1973	1 383	11.7	4 342	5.8
1972	1 238	9.9	4 105	5.3
1971	1 127	8.5	3 899	3.4
1970	1 039	5.5	3 772	0.2
1969	985	8.2	3 765	3.1
1968	910	9.3	3 653	4.8
1967	833	5.7	3 485	2.5
1966	788	9.5	3 399	6.5
1965	719	8.4	3 191	6.4
1964	664	7.4	2 999	5.8
1963	618	5.5	2 834	4.4
1962	586	7.5	2 715	6.1
1961	545	3.5	2 560	2.3
1960	526	3.9	2 502	2.5
1959	507	8.4	2 441	7.1
1958	467	1.3	2 279	−1.0
1957	461	5.4	2 301	2.0
1956	438	5.5	2 256	1.9
1955	415	9.0	2 213	7.1
1954	380	0.3	2 065	−0.7
1953	379	5.9	2 080	4.6
1952	358	5.6	1 988	3.8
1951	339	15.5	1 915	7.7
1950	294	9.9	1 777	8.7
1949	267	−0.7	1 635	−0.5
1948	269	10.2	1 643	4.4
1947	244	9.8	1 575	−0.9
1946	222	−0.4	1 589	−11.0
1945	223	1.5	1 786	−1.1
1944	220	10.7	1 807	8.1
1943	199	22.7	1 671	16.4
1942	162	27.7	1 435	18.5
1941	127	25.0	1 211	17.1
1940	101	10.0	1 034	8.8
1939	92	7.0	951	8.1
1938	86	−6.2	880	−3.4
1937	92	9.7	911	5.1
1936	84	14.3	867	13.0
1935	73	11.1	767	8.9
1934	66	17.0	704	10.8
1933	56	−4.0	636	−1.3
1932	59	−23.2	644	−13.0
1931	77	−16.1	740	−6.4
1930	91	−12.0	791	−8.6
1929	104	X	865	X

Source: U.S. Department of Commerce, Bureau of Economic Analysis. National Income and Products Accounts Tables.
X = Not applicable.

Table 23-2. Gross Domestic Product (GDP) Components in Current and Chained (2000) Dollars, 1929–2005

(Billions of dollars.)

		Current dollars															
		Personal consumption expenditures				Gross private domestic investment					Net exports of goods			Government consumption			
															Federal		
Year	Gross domestic product	Total	Durable goods	Non-durable goods	Services	Total	Fixed investment	Non-residential	Residential	Change in private inventories	Total	Exports	Imports	Total	Total	National defense	State and local
2005	12 487.1	8 745.7	1 026.5	2 564.4	5 154.9	2 105.0	2 086.1	1 329.8	756.3	18.9	−726.5	1 301.2	2 027.7	2 362.9	877.7	587.1	1 485.2
2004	11 734.3	8 214.3	987.8	2 368.3	4 858.2	1 928.1	1 872.6	1 198.8	673.8	55.4	−624.0	1 173.8	1 797.8	2 215.9	827.6	552.7	1 388.3
2003	10 971.2	7 709.9	950.1	2 189.0	4 570.8	1 670.4	1 654.9	1 082.4	572.5	15.4	−500.9	1 045.6	1 546.5	2 091.9	754.8	496.7	1 337.1
2002	10 469.6	7 350.7	923.9	2 079.6	4 347.2	1 582.1	1 570.2	1 066.3	503.9	11.9	−424.4	1 005.9	1 430.3	1 961.1	679.7	437.1	1 281.5
2001	10 128.0	7 055.0	883.7	2 017.1	4 154.3	1 614.3	1 646.1	1 176.8	469.3	−31.7	−367.0	1 032.8	1 399.8	1 825.6	612.9	392.6	1 212.8
2000	9 817.0	6 739.4	863.3	1 947.2	3 928.8	1 735.5	1 679.0	1 232.1	446.9	56.5	−379.5	1 096.3	1 475.8	1 721.6	578.8	370.3	1 142.8
1999	9 268.4	6 282.5	817.6	1 804.8	3 660.0	1 625.7	1 558.8	1 133.9	424.9	66.9	−260.5	991.2	1 251.7	1 620.8	555.8	360.6	1 065.0
1998	8 747.0	5 879.5	750.2	1 683.6	3 445.7	1 509.1	1 438.4	1 052.6	385.8	70.8	−159.9	955.9	1 115.9	1 518.3	530.4	345.7	987.9
1997	8 304.3	5 547.4	692.7	1 619.0	3 235.8	1 389.8	1 317.8	968.7	349.1	72.0	−101.6	955.3	1 056.9	1 468.7	530.9	349.6	937.8
1996	7 816.9	5 256.8	652.6	1 555.5	3 048.7	1 240.3	1 209.5	875.4	334.1	30.8	−96.2	868.6	964.8	1 416.0	527.4	354.6	888.6
1995	7 397.7	4 975.8	611.6	1 485.1	2 879.1	1 144.0	1 112.9	810.0	302.8	31.1	−91.4	812.2	903.6	1 369.2	519.2	348.7	850.0
1994	7 072.2	4 743.3	582.2	1 437.2	2 723.9	1 097.1	1 033.3	731.4	301.9	63.8	−93.6	720.9	814.5	1 325.5	519.1	353.7	806.3
1993	6 657.4	4 477.9	526.7	1 379.4	2 571.8	953.4	932.5	666.6	266.0	20.8	−65.0	655.8	720.9	1 291.2	525.2	362.9	766.0
1992	6 337.7	4 235.3	483.6	1 330.5	2 421.2	864.8	848.5	612.1	236.3	16.3	−33.2	635.3	668.6	1 271.0	533.9	376.9	737.0
1991	5 995.9	3 986.1	453.9	1 284.8	2 247.4	802.9	803.3	598.2	205.1	−0.4	−27.5	596.8	624.3	1 234.4	527.7	383.2	706.7
1990	5 803.1	3 839.9	474.2	1 249.9	2 115.9	861.0	846.4	622.4	224.0	14.5	−78.0	552.4	630.3	1 180.2	508.3	374.0	671.9
1989	5 484.4	3 598.5	471.8	1 166.7	1 960.0	874.9	847.3	607.7	239.5	27.7	−88.2	503.3	591.5	1 099.1	482.2	362.2	616.9
1988	5 103.8	3 353.6	453.6	1 083.5	1 816.5	821.6	803.1	563.8	239.3	18.5	−110.4	444.1	554.5	1 039.0	462.3	354.9	576.7
1987	4 739.5	3 100.2	421.7	1 015.3	1 663.3	785.0	757.8	524.1	233.7	27.1	−145.2	363.9	509.1	999.5	460.1	350.0	539.4
1986	4 462.8	2 899.7	403.0	958.4	1 538.3	746.5	739.9	519.8	220.1	6.6	−132.7	320.5	453.3	949.3	438.6	330.9	510.7
1985	4 220.3	2 720.3	363.5	928.7	1 428.1	736.2	714.4	526.2	188.2	21.8	−115.2	302.0	417.2	879.0	412.8	311.2	466.2
1984	3 933.2	2 503.3	326.5	884.6	1 292.2	735.6	670.2	489.6	180.6	65.4	−102.7	302.4	405.1	797.0	374.4	281.6	422.6
1983	3 536.7	2 290.6	280.8	831.2	1 178.6	564.3	570.1	417.2	152.9	−5.8	−51.7	277.0	328.6	733.5	342.9	250.7	390.5
1982	3 255.0	2 077.3	240.2	787.6	1 049.4	517.2	532.1	426.5	105.7	−14.9	−20.0	283.2	303.2	680.5	310.8	225.9	369.7
1981	3 128.4	1 941.1	231.3	758.9	950.8	572.4	542.6	420.0	122.6	29.8	−12.5	305.2	317.8	627.5	280.2	196.3	347.3
1980	2 789.5	1 757.1	214.2	696.1	846.9	479.3	485.6	362.4	123.2	−6.3	−13.1	280.8	293.8	566.2	243.8	168.0	322.4
1979	2 563.3	1 592.2	214.4	624.5	753.3	492.9	474.9	333.9	141.0	18.0	−22.5	230.1	252.7	500.8	210.6	145.2	290.2
1978	2 294.7	1 428.5	201.7	550.2	676.6	438.0	412.2	280.6	131.6	25.8	−25.4	186.9	212.3	453.6	190.9	130.5	262.6
1977	2 030.9	1 278.6	181.2	497.1	600.2	361.3	339.0	228.7	110.3	22.3	−23.1	159.4	182.4	414.1	175.4	120.9	238.7
1976	1 825.3	1 151.9	158.9	458.3	534.7	292.0	274.8	192.4	82.5	17.1	−1.6	149.5	151.1	383.0	159.7	111.1	223.3
1975	1 638.3	1 034.4	133.5	420.7	480.2	230.2	236.5	173.7	62.7	−6.3	16.0	138.7	122.7	357.7	149.1	103.9	208.7
1974	1 500.0	933.4	122.3	384.5	426.6	249.4	235.4	169.5	66.0	14.0	−0.8	126.7	127.5	317.9	134.6	95.6	183.4
1973	1 382.7	852.4	123.5	343.1	385.8	244.5	228.6	153.3	75.3	15.9	4.1	95.3	91.2	281.7	122.5	88.2	159.2
1972	1 238.3	770.6	110.4	308.0	352.2	207.6	198.5	128.8	69.7	9.1	−3.4	70.8	74.2	263.5	119.7	87.0	143.8
1971	1 127.1	701.9	96.9	285.5	319.5	178.2	169.9	114.1	55.8	8.3	0.6	63.0	62.3	246.5	113.7	84.6	132.8
1970	1 038.5	648.5	85.0	272.0	291.5	152.4	150.4	109.0	41.4	2.0	4.0	59.7	55.8	233.8	113.5	87.6	120.3
1969	984.6	605.2	85.9	253.1	266.1	156.4	147.3	104.7	42.6	9.2	1.4	51.9	50.5	221.5	113.4	89.5	108.2
1968	910.0	558.0	80.8	235.7	241.6	141.2	132.1	93.4	38.7	9.1	1.4	47.9	46.6	209.4	111.4	89.3	98.0
1967	832.6	507.8	70.4	217.1	220.3	128.6	118.7	86.4	32.4	9.9	3.6	43.5	39.9	192.7	104.8	83.5	87.9
1966	787.8	480.9	68.3	208.7	203.8	131.3	117.7	85.4	32.3	13.6	3.9	40.9	37.1	171.8	92.5	71.7	79.2
1965	719.1	443.8	63.3	191.5	189.0	118.2	109.0	74.8	34.2	9.2	5.6	37.1	31.5	151.5	80.4	60.6	71.0
1964	663.6	411.4	56.7	178.6	176.1	102.1	97.2	63.0	34.3	4.8	6.9	35.0	28.1	143.2	78.5	60.3	64.8
1963	617.7	382.7	51.6	168.2	162.9	93.8	88.1	56.0	32.1	5.6	4.9	31.1	26.1	136.4	76.9	61.0	59.5
1962	585.6	363.3	46.9	162.8	153.6	88.1	82.0	53.1	29.0	6.1	4.1	29.1	25.0	130.1	75.3	61.1	54.9
1961	544.7	342.1	41.8	156.6	143.8	78.2	75.2	48.8	26.4	3.0	4.9	27.6	22.7	119.5	67.9	56.5	51.6
1960	526.4	331.7	43.3	152.8	135.6	78.9	75.7	49.4	26.3	3.2	4.2	27.0	22.8	111.6	64.1	53.4	47.5
1959	506.6	317.6	42.7	148.5	126.5	78.5	74.6	46.5	28.1	3.9	0.4	22.7	22.3	110.0	65.4	53.8	44.7
1958	467.2	296.2	37.4	141.7	117.0	64.5	64.9	42.5	22.3	−0.4	0.5	20.6	20.0	106.0	63.8	55.4	42.2
1957	461.1	286.9	40.0	137.1	109.8	70.5	69.7	47.5	22.2	0.8	4.1	24.0	19.9	99.7	61.3	53.6	38.3
1956	437.5	271.7	38.1	130.8	102.8	72.0	68.1	44.5	23.6	4.0	2.4	21.3	18.9	91.4	56.7	49.2	34.7
1955	414.8	258.8	38.8	124.7	95.2	69.0	64.0	39.0	25.0	5.0	0.5	17.7	17.2	86.5	54.9	47.0	31.6
1954	380.4	240.0	31.9	119.7	88.4	53.8	55.8	34.7	21.1	−1.9	0.4	15.8	15.4	86.2	57.3	49.2	28.9
1953	379.4	233.1	32.7	117.8	82.5	56.4	54.5	35.1	19.4	1.9	−0.7	15.3	16.0	90.6	64.4	55.9	26.1
1952	358.3	219.5	29.3	114.7	75.4	54.0	50.5	31.9	18.6	3.5	1.2	16.5	15.3	83.6	59.2	52.4	24.4
1951	339.3	208.5	29.9	109.2	69.5	60.2	50.3	31.8	18.4	9.9	2.5	17.1	14.6	68.1	45.1	39.3	23.0
1950	293.8	192.2	30.7	98.2	63.3	54.1	48.3	27.8	20.5	5.8	0.7	12.4	11.6	46.8	26.0	19.6	20.7
1949	267.3	178.5	25.1	94.9	58.6	36.9	39.6	24.9	14.6	−2.7	5.2	14.5	9.2	46.7	27.7	19.8	19.0
1948	269.2	175.0	22.9	96.6	55.6	48.1	42.4	26.8	15.6	5.7	5.5	15.5	10.1	40.6	24.2	18.3	16.3
1947	244.2	162.0	20.4	90.9	50.7	35.0	35.5	23.5	12.1	−0.6	10.8	18.7	7.9	36.4	22.7	18.2	13.7
1946	222.3	144.3	15.8	82.7	45.8	31.1	25.1	17.3	7.8	6.0	7.2	14.2	7.0	39.6	28.9	25.2	10.8
1945	223.1	120.0	8.0	71.9	40.1	10.8	12.3	10.6	1.7	−1.5	−0.8	6.8	7.5	93.0	84.1	82.0	9.0
1944	219.8	108.7	6.7	64.3	37.6	7.8	8.7	7.4	1.4	−0.9	−2.0	4.9	6.9	105.3	97.0	94.5	8.4
1943	198.6	99.9	6.5	58.6	34.8	6.1	6.9	5.4	1.4	−0.7	−2.2	4.0	6.3	94.8	86.5	84.2	8.4
1942	161.9	89.0	6.9	50.8	31.4	10.4	8.5	6.3	2.2	1.9	−0.3	4.4	4.6	62.7	54.1	51.1	8.6
1941	126.7	81.1	9.7	42.9	28.5	18.1	13.8	9.7	4.1	4.3	1.0	5.5	4.4	26.5	18.0	14.3	8.6

Table 23-2. Gross Domestic Product (GDP) Components in Current and Chained (2000) Dollars, 1929–2005—*Continued*

(Billions of dollars.)

		Current dollars															
		Personal consumption expenditures				Gross private domestic investment					Net exports of goods			Government consumption			
															Federal		
Year	Gross domestic product	Total	Durable goods	Non-durable goods	Services	Total	Fixed invest-ment	Non-residential	Resi-dential	Change in private in-ventories	Total	Exports	Imports	Total	Total	National defense	State and local
1940	101.4	71.3	7.8	37.0	26.5	13.6	11.2	7.7	3.5	2.4	1.5	4.9	3.4	15.0	6.5	2.5	8.6
1939	92.2	67.2	6.7	35.1	25.4	9.3	9.1	6.1	3.0	0.2	0.8	4.0	3.1	14.8	6.0	1.5	8.8
1938	86.1	64.3	5.7	34.0	24.6	7.1	7.7	5.5	2.1	−0.6	1.0	3.8	2.8	13.8	5.7	1.4	8.1
1937	91.9	66.8	6.9	35.2	24.7	12.2	9.5	7.5	2.1	2.6	0.1	4.0	4.0	12.8	5.1	1.3	7.7
1936	83.8	62.2	6.3	32.9	23.0	8.6	7.5	5.8	1.7	1.2	−0.1	3.0	3.2	13.1	5.6	1.2	7.5
1935	73.3	55.9	5.1	29.3	21.5	6.7	5.6	4.3	1.3	1.1	−0.2	2.8	3.0	10.9	3.4	1.0	7.5
1934	66.0	51.5	4.2	26.7	20.5	3.7	4.3	3.3	0.9	−0.6	0.3	2.6	2.2	10.5	3.3	0.8	7.2
1933	56.4	45.9	3.5	22.3	20.2	1.7	3.1	2.5	0.6	−1.4	0.1	2.0	1.9	8.7	2.3	0.9	6.4
1932	58.7	48.7	3.6	22.7	22.3	1.3	3.6	2.9	0.8	−2.4	0.0	2.0	1.9	8.7	1.8	0.9	6.9
1931	76.5	60.7	5.5	29.0	26.2	5.9	7.0	5.3	1.8	−1.1	0.0	2.9	2.9	9.9	1.9	0.9	8.0
1930	91.2	70.1	7.2	34.0	29.0	10.8	11.0	8.6	2.4	−0.2	0.3	4.4	4.1	10.0	1.8	0.9	8.2
1929	103.6	77.4	9.2	37.7	30.5	16.5	14.9	11.0	4.0	1.5	0.4	5.9	5.6	9.4	1.7	0.9	7.6

Table 23-2. Gross Domestic Product (GDP) Components in Current and Chained (2000) Dollars, 1929–2005—*Continued*

(Billions of dollars.)

Year	Gross domestic product	Personal consumption expenditures				Gross private domestic investment					Net exports of goods			Government consumption			
															Federal		
		Total	Durable goods	Non-durable goods	Services	Total	Fixed invest-ment	Non-residential	Resi-dential	Change in private in-ventories	Total	Exports	Imports	Total	Total	National defense	State and local
2005	11 134.8	7 856.9	1 138.4	2 297.9	4 436.4	1 919.8	1 897.1	1 289.0	601.9	20.3	−633.1	1 195.3	1 828.3	1 987.1	740.5	493.6	1 246.3
2004	10 755.7	7 588.6	1 089.9	2 200.4	4 310.9	1 809.8	1 755.1	1 186.7	561.8	52.0	−601.3	1 117.9	1 719.2	1 952.3	723.7	481.3	1 228.4
2003	10 320.6	7 306.6	1 028.5	2 101.8	4 183.9	1 617.4	1 600.0	1 085.0	509.4	15.5	−521.4	1 031.2	1 552.6	1 911.1	687.8	449.7	1 223.3
2002	10 048.8	7 099.3	964.8	2 037.1	4 100.4	1 557.1	1 544.6	1 071.5	469.9	12.5	−471.3	1 013.3	1 484.6	1 858.8	643.4	413.2	1 215.4
2001	9 890.7	6 910.4	900.7	1 986.7	4 023.2	1 598.4	1 629.4	1 180.5	448.5	−31.7	−399.1	1 036.7	1 435.8	1 780.3	601.4	384.9	1 179.0
2000	9 817.0	6 739.4	863.3	1 947.2	3 928.8	1 735.5	1 679.0	1 232.1	446.9	56.5	−379.5	1 096.3	1 475.8	1 721.6	578.8	370.3	1 142.8
1999	9 470.3	6 438.6	804.6	1 876.6	3 758.0	1 642.6	1 576.3	1 133.3	443.6	68.9	−296.2	1 008.2	1 304.4	1 686.9	573.7	372.2	1 113.2
1998	9 066.9	6 125.8	720.3	1 794.4	3 615.0	1 524.1	1 455.0	1 037.8	418.3	72.6	−203.7	966.5	1 170.3	1 624.4	561.2	365.3	1 063.0
1997	8 703.5	5 831.8	646.9	1 725.3	3 468.0	1 387.7	1 320.6	934.2	388.6	71.2	−104.6	943.7	1 048.3	1 594.0	567.6	373.0	1 025.9
1996	8 328.9	5 619.4	595.9	1 680.4	3 356.0	1 234.3	1 209.2	833.6	381.3	28.7	−79.6	843.4	923.0	1 564.9	573.5	383.8	990.5
1995	8 031.7	5 433.5	552.6	1 638.6	3 259.9	1 134.0	1 109.6	762.5	353.1	29.9	−71.0	778.2	849.1	1 549.7	580.3	389.2	968.3
1994	7 835.5	5 290.7	529.4	1 603.9	3 176.6	1 099.6	1 042.3	689.9	364.8	63.6	−79.4	706.5	785.9	1 541.3	596.4	404.6	943.3
1993	7 532.7	5 099.8	488.4	1 550.4	3 085.7	968.3	953.5	631.9	332.7	20.6	−52.1	650.0	702.1	1 541.1	619.6	425.3	919.5
1992	7 336.6	4 934.8	453.0	1 510.1	3 000.8	889.0	878.3	581.3	307.6	16.5	−15.9	629.7	645.6	1 555.3	646.6	450.7	906.5
1991	7 100.5	4 778.4	427.9	1 480.5	2 900.0	822.2	829.1	563.2	270.2	−0.5	−14.6	589.1	603.7	1 547.2	658.0	474.2	886.8
1990	7 112.5	4 770.3	453.5	1 484.0	2 851.7	895.1	886.6	595.1	298.9	15.4	−54.7	552.5	607.1	1 530.0	659.1	479.4	868.4
1989	6 981.4	4 675.0	...	...	...	926.2	...	...	...	...	...	506.8	586.0	1 482.5	...	...	...
1988	6 742.7	4 546.9	...	...	...	890.5	...	...	...	...	...	454.6	561.4	1 445.1	...	...	...
1987	6 475.1	4 369.8	...	...	...	870.0	...	...	...	...	...	391.8	540.2	1 426.7	...	...	...
1986	6 263.6	4 228.9	...	...	...	843.9	...	...	...	...	...	353.7	510.0	1 392.5	...	...	...
1985	6 053.7	4 064.0	...	...	...	849.7	...	...	...	...	...	328.3	469.8	1 312.5	...	...	...
1984	5 813.6	3 863.3	...	...	...	857.7	...	...	...	...	...	318.7	441.1	1 227.0	...	...	...
1983	5 423.8	3 668.6	...	...	...	662.5	...	...	...	...	...	294.6	354.8	1 187.3	...	...	...
1982	5 189.3	3 470.3	...	...	...	606.0	...	...	...	...	...	302.4	315.0	1 145.4	...	...	...
1981	5 291.7	3 422.2	...	...	...	704.9	...	...	...	...	...	327.4	319.1	1 125.6	...	...	...
1980	5 161.7	3 374.1	...	...	...	645.3	...	...	...	...	...	323.5	310.9	1 115.4	...	...	...
1979	5 173.4	3 383.4	...	...	...	725.0	...	...	...	...	...	292.0	333.0	1 094.1	...	...	...
1978	5 015.0	3 303.1	...	...	...	702.6	...	...	...	...	...	265.7	327.6	1 074.0	...	...	...
1977	4 750.5	3 164.1	...	...	...	627.0	...	...	...	...	...	240.3	301.4	1 043.3	...	...	...
1976	4 540.9	3 035.5	...	...	...	544.7	...	...	...	...	...	234.7	271.7	1 031.9	...	...	...
1975	4 311.2	2 876.9	...	...	...	453.1	...	...	...	...	...	224.9	227.3	1 027.4	...	...	...
1974	4 319.6	2 812.3	...	...	...	550.6	...	...	...	...	...	226.3	255.7	1 004.7	...	...	...
1973	4 341.5	2 833.8	...	...	...	594.4	...	...	...	...	...	209.7	261.6	980.0	...	...	...
1972	4 105.0	2 701.3	...	...	...	532.1	...	...	...	...	...	176.5	250.0	983.5	...	...	...
1971	3 898.6	2 545.5	...	...	...	475.7	...	...	...	...	...	164.1	224.7	990.8	...	...	...
1970	3 771.9	2 451.9	...	...	...	427.1	...	...	...	...	...	161.4	213.4	1 012.9	...	...	...
1969	3 765.4	2 396.4	...	...	...	457.1	...	...	...	...	...	145.7	204.6	1 038.0	...	...	...
1968	3 652.7	2 310.5	...	...	...	431.9	...	...	...	...	...	139.0	193.6	1 040.5	...	...	...
1967	3 484.6	2 185.0	...	...	...	408.1	...	...	...	...	...	128.9	168.5	1 008.9	...	...	...
1966	3 399.1	2 121.8	...	...	...	427.7	...	...	...	...	...	126.0	157.1	937.1	...	...	...
1965	3 191.1	2 007.7	...	...	...	393.1	...	...	...	...	...	117.8	136.7	861.3	...	...	...
1964	2 998.6	1 888.4	...	...	...	344.7	...	...	...	...	...	114.6	123.6	836.1	...	...	...
1963	2 834.0	1 781.6	...	...	...	318.5	...	...	...	...	...	102.5	117.3	818.1	...	...	...
1962	2 715.2	1 711.1	...	...	...	298.4	...	...	...	...	...	95.7	114.3	797.6	...	...	...
1961	2 560.0	1 630.3	...	...	...	264.9	...	...	...	...	...	91.1	102.6	751.3	...	...	...
1960	2 501.8	1 597.4	...	...	...	266.6	...	...	...	...	...	90.6	103.3	715.4	...	...	...
1959	2 441.3	1 554.6	...	...	...	266.7	...	...	...	...	...	77.2	101.9	714.3	...	...	...
1958	2 279.2	1 472.3	...	...	...	221.7	...	...	...	...	...	70.0	92.3	690.9	...	...	...
1957	2 301.1	1 460.7	...	...	...	241.7	...	...	...	...	...	80.9	88.1	669.5	...	...	...
1956	2 255.8	1 425.4	...	...	...	252.7	...	...	...	...	...	74.4	84.5	641.0	...	...	...
1955	2 212.8	1 385.5	...	...	...	256.2	...	...	...	...	...	63.9	78.2	640.7	...	...	...
1954	2 065.4	1 291.4	...	...	...	206.1	...	...	...	...	...	57.7	69.8	665.1	...	...	...
1953	2 079.5	1 265.7	...	...	...	216.2	...	...	...	...	...	55.1	73.4	713.9	...	...	...
1952	1 988.3	1 208.2	...	...	...	206.5	...	...	...	...	...	59.0	67.1	666.3	...	...	...
1951	1 915.0	1 171.2	...	...	...	228.3	...	...	...	...	...	61.7	61.7	553.5	...	...	...
1950	1 777.3	1 152.8	...	...	...	227.7	...	...	...	...	...	50.3	59.3	405.3	...	...	...
1949	1 634.6	1 083.5	...	...	...	161.2	...	...	...	...	...	57.5	50.2	404.9	...	...	...
1948	1 643.2	1 054.4	...	...	...	211.2	...	...	...	...	...	58.0	52.0	361.7	...	...	...
1947	1 574.5	1 031.6	...	...	...	165.3	...	...	...	...	...	73.7	44.6	337.2	...	...	...
1946	1 589.4	1 012.9	...	...	...	172.1	...	...	...	...	...	64.6	47.0	396.8	...	...	...
1945	1 786.3	902.7	...	...	...	67.0	...	...	...	...	...	29.9	56.7	1 152.9	...	...	...
1944	1 806.5	850.2	...	...	...	50.8	...	...	...	...	...	21.4	53.3	1 320.5	...	...	...
1943	1 670.9	826.1	...	...	...	41.1	...	...	...	...	...	19.9	50.9	1 173.3	...	...	...
1942	1 435.4	803.1	...	...	...	69.6	...	...	...	...	...	23.6	40.4	788.6	...	...	...
1941	1 211.1	821.9	...	...	...	131.7	...	...	...	...	...	35.7	44.5	335.1	...	...	...

. . . = Not available.

Table 23-2. Gross Domestic Product (GDP) Components in Current and Chained (2000) Dollars, 1929–2005—*Continued*

(Billions of dollars.)

		Current dollars															
		Personal consumption expenditures				Gross private domestic investment					Net exports of goods			Government consumption			
															Federal		
Year	Gross domestic product	Total	Durable goods	Non-durable goods	Services	Total	Fixed invest-ment	Non-residential	Resi-dential	Change in private in-ventories	Total	Exports	Imports	Total	Total	National defense	State and local
1940	1 034.1	767.1	...	...	...	107.9	...	...	...	...	...	34.8	36.2	201.5	...	...	...
1939	950.7	729.1	...	...	...	77.4	...	...	...	...	...	30.6	35.3	196.0	...	...	...
1938	879.7	690.7	...	...	...	60.2	...	...	...	...	...	29.0	33.6	180.2	...	...	...
1937	911.1	702.0	...	...	...	91.1	...	...	...	...	...	29.3	43.3	167.3	...	...	...
1936	866.6	677.0	...	...	...	72.9	...	...	...	...	...	23.3	38.4	174.7	...	...	...
1935	766.9	614.8	...	...	...	56.9	...	...	...	...	...	22.2	38.9	149.7	...	...	...
1934	704.2	579.3	...	...	...	30.7	...	...	...	...	...	21.0	29.7	145.7	...	...	...
1933	635.5	541.0	...	...	...	17.0	...	...	...	...	...	18.9	29.1	129.2	...	...	...
1932	643.7	553.0	...	...	...	11.5	...	...	...	...	...	18.8	27.9	133.8	...	...	...
1931	739.9	606.9	...	...	...	38.3	...	...	...	...	...	24.0	33.6	138.5	...	...	...
1930	790.7	626.1	...	...	...	60.9	...	...	...	...	...	28.9	38.5	132.9	...	...	...
1929	865.2	661.4	...	...	...	91.3	...	...	...	...	...	34.9	44.3	120.6	...	...	...

Source: U.S. Census Bureau. U.S. Bureau of Economic Analysis.
. . . = Not available.

Table 23.3. Gross Domestic Product (GDP) by State in Current and Chained (2000) Dollars, 1963–2005

(Millions.)

Year	United States	Alabama	Alaska	Arizona	Arkansas	California	Colorado	Connecticut	Delaware	District of Columbia	Florida	Georgia	Hawaii
Current dollars													
NAICS													
2005	12 409 555	151 610	39 314	216 528	86 752	1 622 116	216 537	193 745	56 483	81 830	673 274	363 839	54 019
2004	11 655 335	141 366	35 988	194 246	82 712	1 519 202	201 392	182 468	52 298	77 510	609 372	339 730	50 238
2003	10 896 356	130 526	31 488	182 414	75 564	1 410 539	188 873	170 235	48 109	71 280	556 748	317 490	46 386
2002	10 398 402	123 805	29 186	171 942	72 203	1 340 446	182 154	166 073	45 324	67 717	522 719	306 680	43 476
2001	10 058 168	118 682	26 609	165 358	68 927	1 301 050	178 078	165 025	44 206	63 730	497 423	299 442	41 822
2000	9 749 103	114 576	27 034	158 533	66 801	1 287 145	171 862	160 436	41 472	58 699	471 316	290 887	40 202
1999	9 201 138	111 923	24 322	148 518	65 615	1 180 590	156 284	150 303	39 439	56 407	442 582	277 082	38 625
1998	8 679 657	106 656	23 165	137 581	61 861	1 085 884	143 160	145 373	36 831	51 682	417 169	255 612	37 549
1997	8 237 994	102 433	25 028	127 370	59 182	1 019 150	132 881	137 698	35 488	50 368	391 451	237 468	37 546
SIC Basis													
1997	8 170 994	102 533	26 884	122 889	58 746	1 028 645	127 946	137 452	31 269	49 427	383 980	230 370	37 923
1996	7 659 651	97 941	26 083	113 138	56 455	958 476	116 045	126 744	28 885	47 560	362 950	215 128	36 959
1995	7 232 722	94 021	24 805	104 036	53 303	908 963	108 043	120 800	27 507	47 123	340 501	199 138	36 572
1994	6 865 513	88 581	23 110	95 292	50 179	862 481	100 434	111 171	25 128	46 842	322 073	184 256	36 256
1993	6 453 455	83 453	22 965	85 157	46 599	833 656	92 540	106 319	23 590	45 713	302 063	168 959	35 929
1992	6 174 369	80 450	22 591	79 695	44 312	819 389	85 110	104 171	23 031	43 757	283 800	158 265	35 204
1991	5 857 335	75 293	22 164	72 263	40 950	801 193	78 624	100 229	21 925	41 806	267 851	146 334	33 579
1990	5 674 013	71 085	24 987	69 322	38 109	788 322	74 206	98 976	20 118	40 056	257 242	139 526	31 898
1989	5 385 776	67 875	23 357	66 390	36 647	734 406	69 618	94 578	19 008	37 735	243 320	133 070	28 423
1988	5 067 453	65 435	21 307	63 639	34 508	678 774	66 265	89 328	16 989	35 345	226 571	126 149	25 733
1987	4 663 282	60 586	22 258	59 171	32 190	620 177	62 873	81 251	15 553	32 240	206 894	116 822	23 321
1986	4 364 279	56 046	18 849	55 191	30 415	568 365	60 055	73 490	14 217	30 051	188 134	108 412	21 547
1985	4 155 029	53 688	26 219	50 080	29 086	528 012	59 265	67 434	13 222	28 483	173 754	98 689	19 985
1984	3 872 847	49 713	23 829	45 235	28 183	483 246	55 949	62 067	12 011	26 436	158 808	88 641	18 554
1983	3 451 340	45 248	22 548	38 835	25 035	423 883	50 447	54 424	10 671	24 308	139 474	76 599	16 843
1982	3 217 617	41 478	23 348	34 994	23 278	389 932	47 424	49 392	9 578	22 782	124 779	68 257	15 396
1981	3 064 552	40 084	21 665	33 703	22 688	365 182	43 785	45 065	8 870	21 444	115 287	63 715	14 456
1980	2 719 134	36 006	15 138	30 431	20 100	324 407	38 151	40 257	7 889	19 502	100 627	56 314	13 337
1979	2 491 428	33 535	10 863	27 306	18 942	291 892	33 696	36 383	7 278	17 999	88 247	51 643	11 905
1978	2 243 638	30 377	9 088	23 000	17 337	261 456	29 192	32 756	6 717	16 523	77 117	46 264	10 473
1977	1 986 138	26 546	7 492	19 397	14 953	228 519	25 131	29 278	6 037	15 118	66 261	40 853	9 373
1976	1 779 570	24 206	7 433	16 722	13 643	197 872	21 765	26 198	5 504	13 541	58 832	36 489	8 502
1975	1 601 506	21 295	6 195	15 081	11 836	178 827	19 776	23 742	5 055	12 368	55 350	32 036	8 155
1974	1 471 593	19 438	3 982	14 472	10 668	162 261	17 669	22 412	4 759	11 163	52 246	30 464	7 125
1973	1 356 315	17 416	3 028	13 202	9 836	147 718	16 113	20 769	4 537	10 141	47 120	28 305	6 342
1972	1 210 471	15 336	2 729	11 179	8 491	133 609	13 770	18 874	4 002	9 659	39 830	24 681	5 613
1971	1 096 810	13 599	2 522	9 541	7 432	120 696	11 975	17 174	3 635	8 952	34 236	21 620	5 163
1970	1 011 966	12 455	2 347	8 470	6 657	112 298	10 409	16 423	3 174	8 323	30 757	19 410	4 802
1969	962 647	11 839	2 059	7 442	6 219	106 955	9 454	15 785	3 077	7 831	27 488	18 135	4 248
1968	887 304	10 949	1 886	6 482	5 692	99 037	8 516	14 427	2 891	7 495	23 841	16 475	3 707
1967	811 632	10 034	1 631	5 680	5 120	89 897	7 646	13 696	2 612	6 955	21 175	14 767	3 293
1966	766 961	9 831	1 483	5 428	4 856	84 925	7 255	12 894	2 490	6 230	19 225	13 859	3 097
1965	704 545	8 978	1 364	4 931	4 434	78 495	6 612	11 518	2 320	5 820	17 478	12 558	2 841
1964	650 382	8 201	1 221	4 729	4 138	73 727	6 211	10 586	2 074	5 342	16 049	11 283	2 568
1963	606 913	7 328	1 076	4 403	3 781	68 039	5 914	9 943	1 891	4 941	14 708	10 345	2 366
Chained (2000) dollars													
NAICS													
2005	11 041 471	133 982	29 571	198 510	76 792	1 469 459	192 992	172 259	49 509	69 763	595 385	327 453	47 067
2004	10 662 196	128 267	29 710	181 995	74 988	1 409 228	184 948	166 850	46 981	67 313	552 665	313 144	44 683
2003	10 237 201	121 998	27 713	174 693	70 737	1 340 162	177 945	159 751	44 655	64 270	518 753	299 504	42 575
2002	9 981 850	118 185	28 022	166 860	68 901	1 298 750	175 484	158 628	42 939	62 825	497 343	294 105	41 093
2001	9 836 576	115 599	25 763	163 448	66 982	1 281 733	174 763	161 197	42 966	61 569	484 886	292 832	40 626
2000	9 749 103	114 576	27 034	158 533	66 801	1 287 145	171 862	160 436	41 472	58 699	471 316	290 887	40 202
1999	9 404 251	114 430	27 070	149 717	67 071	1 196 642	159 365	153 298	40 779	58 351	453 277	282 849	39 747
1998	9 004 670	110 703	26 774	138 668	64 274	1 108 722	147 938	150 823	38 846	55 090	435 601	266 020	39 568
1997	8 620 955	107 563	28 121	127 439	62 474	1 043 477	137 900	144 921	38 274	54 686	414 710	250 758	40 412
SIC													
1997	8 521 597	106 762	29 852	124 771	60 460	1 065 590	133 826	143 707	33 685	52 777	403 393	242 354	40 469
1996	8 106 740	103 233	29 521	116 083	58 448	1 007 350	123 408	135 091	32 345	52 221	387 723	229 685	40 387
1995	7 784 237	100 205	29 922	107 538	56 062	971 314	117 221	131 296	31 729	53 218	369 554	215 527	40 768
1994	7 538 478	97 120	28 517	100 206	53 859	937 893	111 150	123 956	30 100	54 899	357 367	204 141	41 311
1993	7 240 810	93 722	28 572	91 709	51 140	927 133	104 714	121 635	29 133	55 199	343 546	191 094	41 936
1992	7 114 708	92 625	28 860	88 059	49 840	936 275	98 884	122 710	29 168	54 644	332 167	183 598	42 275
1991	6 917 680	88 786	28 550	81 771	47 088	937 429	93 550	121 446	28 988	54 042	321 623	174 017	41 397
1990	6 939 733	86 582	31 904	81 143	45 066	955 881	91 346	124 587	28 059	55 080	320 500	172 127	41 020

Note: There is a discontinuity in the GDP by state time series at 1997, where the data change from SIC industry definitions to NAICS industry definitions. This discontinuity results from many sources, including differences in source data and different estimation methodologies. In addition, the NAICS-based GDP by state estimates are consistent with U.S. gross domestic product (GDP) while the SIC-based GDP by state estimates are consistent with U.S. gross domestic income (GDI). This data discontinuity may affect both the levels and the growth rates of the GDP by state estimates. Users of the GDP by state estimates are strongly cautioned against appending the two data series in an attempt to construct a single time series of GDP by state estimates for 1963 to 2005.

NAICS industry detail is based on the 1997 NAICS. SIC industry detail 1987–1997 is based on the 1987 SIC. SIC industry detail 1963 to 1986 is based on the 1972 SIC.

Table 23.3. Gross Domestic Product (GDP) by State in Current and Chained (2000) Dollars, 1963–2005—*Continued*

(Millions.)

Year	Idaho	Illinois	Indiana	Iowa	Kansas	Kentucky	Louisiana	Maine	Maryland	Massachusetts	Michigan	Minnesota	Mississippi
Current dollars													
NAICS													
2005	47 189	560 032	238 568	113 552	105 574	140 501	168 204	44 971	246 234	325 917	376 243	234 552	81 290
2004	43 509	533 735	229 449	110 210	98 927	133 003	160 186	43 258	230 698	312 700	366 601	224 620	77 107
2003	38 468	509 161	216 650	102 358	93 076	125 832	146 105	40 197	214 488	295 938	362 805	209 335	72 532
2002	36 651	487 129	205 015	97 356	89 573	120 726	134 308	38 625	204 120	284 386	349 837	198 558	68 144
2001	35 631	476 461	195 196	91 920	86 430	115 113	133 689	37 129	192 659	280 509	334 419	190 231	65 961
2000	34 989	464 194	194 419	90 186	82 812	111 900	131 520	35 542	180 367	274 949	337 235	185 093	64 266
1999	32 653	443 751	185 737	86 113	78 664	113 480	124 047	33 361	171 373	252 617	326 153	172 874	63 036
1998	29 800	423 855	178 909	83 665	76 005	108 813	118 085	31 731	161 954	236 079	309 431	164 897	60 513
1997	28 510	403 982	168 115	81 923	72 071	105 725	113 261	30 873	154 139	221 827	298 994	155 938	57 954
SIC Basis													
1997	29 388	401 068	164 207	81 881	72 509	101 845	121 743	29 945	152 259	223 025	278 815	152 235	58 278
1996	28 152	377 271	155 512	77 244	67 965	94 987	114 967	28 636	142 910	208 288	263 871	141 664	55 997
1995	27 099	359 723	147 984	71 905	63 699	90 459	109 153	27 648	137 391	195 277	251 017	131 357	53 816
1994	24 817	343 363	141 157	69 150	61 805	86 283	101 943	26 204	132 052	185 335	246 064	124 733	50 642
1993	22 696	317 216	130 561	62 709	57 925	80 361	93 243	25 013	124 745	173 234	221 261	114 946	46 717
1992	20 332	303 989	123 570	61 313	56 091	76 572	88 912	24 239	119 454	166 585	207 379	111 919	43 676
1991	18 601	286 582	113 831	57 677	53 345	70 536	94 298	23 398	116 226	160 193	194 253	103 791	40 839
1990	17 769	277 241	110 084	55 876	51 274	67 508	93 591	23 343	113 723	158 903	189 748	100 327	38 768
1989	16 753	265 152	106 498	52 771	48 335	64 718	86 196	22 836	108 470	157 701	186 693	96 165	37 309
1988	15 127	251 086	98 740	48 891	46 268	60 727	82 320	21 552	102 026	151 213	177 353	89 991	35 699
1987	13 826	230 594	91 170	45 055	43 883	56 565	76 501	19 316	92 102	138 536	166 855	83 947	33 626
1986	13 104	218 492	86 148	43 111	41 716	53 348	75 858	17 501	84 402	126 413	161 499	78 194	31 296
1985	12 999	206 509	81 781	42 381	40 763	51 547	84 771	16 112	77 318	115 579	151 822	74 808	30 579
1984	12 483	194 740	78 559	41 031	38 441	48 829	83 043	14 853	69 915	104 948	141 474	70 296	29 068
1983	11 686	173 528	68 982	36 957	35 213	43 374	77 297	13 133	61 797	91 442	125 503	61 029	26 234
1982	10 587	165 181	64 681	36 910	33 528	41 723	78 484	12 037	55 913	82 292	113 401	56 952	24 860
1981	10 584	160 806	64 550	37 866	32 007	40 659	77 638	11 145	52 654	76 205	113 048	54 966	24 273
1980	9 826	146 414	58 687	34 032	28 247	36 593	64 007	10 136	46 983	68 011	102 414	49 717	21 535
1979	9 193	139 925	57 831	32 765	26 285	35 164	51 768	9 223	43 193	61 354	103 822	46 353	20 162
1978	8 373	128 794	53 713	30 121	22 792	32 054	45 226	8 345	39 266	55 476	97 995	41 126	17 894
1977	7 108	115 683	47 840	26 385	20 501	28 595	39 601	7 552	35 432	49 557	88 300	36 380	16 026
1976	6 576	105 052	43 739	24 339	19 262	25 760	34 450	6 976	32 825	44 400	78 738	32 610	14 544
1975	5 821	96 032	37 639	21 768	17 035	22 564	30 743	5 980	29 790	41 399	67 051	29 527	12 280
1974	5 179	88 297	35 612	19 047	15 119	21 000	26 808	5 604	27 545	39 000	63 060	27 345	11 306
1973	4 478	81 521	33 982	18 195	14 048	18 729	22 612	5 204	25 274	36 333	62 945	25 739	10 582
1972	3 768	73 756	29 977	15 022	12 131	16 814	20 107	4 604	22 802	33 350	56 612	21 714	9 205
1971	3 260	67 567	26 907	13 416	10 816	15 494	18 396	4 197	20 631	30 666	51 716	19 841	7 937
1970	3 011	62 931	24 583	12 754	9 740	13 852	16 998	3 956	18 836	28 831	46 194	18 513	7 269
1969	2 744	61 036	24 295	12 194	9 152	13 137	16 156	3 696	17 502	27 302	47 893	17 515	6 819
1968	2 491	56 521	22 740	11 135	8 502	12 159	14 956	3 416	15 963	25 076	44 717	15 970	6 283
1967	2 331	53 000	21 052	10 468	7 768	10 995	13 934	3 171	14 428	23 186	40 025	14 480	5 669
1966	2 268	50 600	20 183	10 028	7 407	10 327	12 730	3 006	13 661	21 771	39 259	13 627	5 339
1965	2 192	46 124	18 578	9 024	6 851	9 484	11 389	2 803	12 342	19 948	36 991	12 386	4 942
1964	1 942	42 602	16 787	8 214	6 438	8 754	10 435	2 606	11 237	18 608	32 556	11 307	4 537
1963	1 836	39 619	15 699	7 789	6 149	8 330	9 637	2 424	10 319	17 452	30 445	10 740	4 444
Chained (2000) dollars													
NAICS													
2005	43 485	499 245	214 463	100 760	92 597	125 353	135 474	39 696	217 314	297 489	343 210	211 194	70 562
2004	40 508	489 042	211 745	99 780	89 092	121 738	137 524	39 184	208 534	292 423	342 371	207 196	68 830
2003	36 792	478 391	204 837	95 562	86 360	118 246	131 625	37 426	199 143	282 375	344 942	198 041	66 914
2002	35 696	466 150	196 828	92 821	85 259	115 492	129 740	36 719	193 490	274 997	336 862	191 116	64 569
2001	35 220	464 910	190 327	89 360	83 898	112 166	129 233	36 176	187 483	276 634	326 869	186 336	63 963
2000	34 989	464 194	194 419	90 186	82 812	111 900	131 520	35 542	180 367	274 949	337 235	185 093	64 266
1999	32 754	452 859	189 327	87 579	80 798	115 708	137 042	34 268	175 403	255 189	332 986	176 253	64 667
1998	30 003	439 980	185 174	86 409	79 417	113 151	134 686	33 364	168 915	240 617	323 089	170 581	63 307
1997	28 781	425 023	176 853	85 692	76 095	111 576	128 936	33 355	162 706	227 074	317 263	163 072	61 648
SIC													
1997	28 908	416 041	169 260	83 536	75 419	107 152	136 547	31 576	160 875	231 960	289 890	157 690	60 583
1996	27 684	397 327	161 947	78 809	71 415	101 066	131 810	30 572	154 000	220 373	277 568	148 404	58 959
1995	26 864	384 226	155 815	74 834	68 538	97 565	130 679	29 780	150 788	209 796	268 323	139 631	57 520
1994	24 774	373 636	151 239	72 960	67 767	94 320	124 373	29 212	148 820	203 326	267 872	135 841	54 939
1993	23 130	353 296	143 295	67 594	64 936	88 926	115 024	28 648	144 433	194 471	247 453	128 346	51 790
1992	21 311	347 482	139 133	67 624	64 632	86 551	113 067	28 553	142 440	192 099	238 759	128 325	49 874
1991	19 964	335 599	131 022	64 842	62 993	81 760	121 350	28 322	142 395	189 882	230 061	121 701	47 653
1990	19 550	336 301	131 012	64 503	62 391	81 317	121 745	29 255	145 184	195 734	234 181	121 527	46 664

Note: There is a discontinuity in the GDP by state time series at 1997, where the data change from SIC industry definitions to NAICS industry definitions. This discontinuity results from many sources, including differences in source data and different estimation methodologies. In addition, the NAICS-based GDP by state estimates are consistent with U.S. gross domestic product (GDP) while the SIC-based GDP by state estimates are consistent with U.S. gross domestic income (GDI). This data discontinuity may affect both the levels and the growth rates of the GDP by state estimates. Users of the GDP by state estimates are strongly cautioned against appending the two data series in an attempt to construct a single time series of GDP by state estimates for 1963 to 2005.

NAICS industry detail is based on the 1997 NAICS. SIC industry detail 1987–1997 is based on the 1987 SIC. SIC industry detail 1963 to 1986 is based on the 1972 SIC.

Table 23-3. Gross Domestic Product (GDP) by State in Current and Chained (2000) Dollars, 1963–2005—Continued

(Millions.)

Year	Missouri	Montana	Nebraska	Nevada	New Hampshire	New Jersey	New Mexico	New York	North Carolina	North Dakota	Ohio	Oklahoma	Oregon
Current dollars													
NAICS													
2005	216 065	29 885	70 676	111 342	55 061	431 079	68 870	957 873	346 640	24 397	440 923	121 490	144 278
2004	205 847	27 583	67 989	99 143	52 084	410 306	63 645	906 783	323 962	22 692	425 173	111 838	134 615
2003	195 615	25 477	64 789	89 035	48 380	388 645	57 453	847 123	307 871	21 703	402 607	103 824	120 480
2002	188 351	23 560	59 934	81 274	46 188	372 754	52 510	821 577	296 435	19 880	389 773	97 170	117 131
2001	182 362	22 471	57 438	77 291	44 279	362 987	51 359	808 537	285 651	18 527	374 719	94 329	110 916
2000	176 708	21 366	55 478	73 719	43 518	344 824	50 725	777 157	273 698	17 752	372 006	89 757	112 438
1999	168 980	20 405	53 404	68 841	40 212	327 263	48 999	730 293	262 676	16 853	360 614	83 220	104 270
1998	164 267	19 884	52 076	63 635	39 102	314 117	45 918	686 906	242 904	16 936	348 723	79 341	100 951
1997	158 203	19 142	50 542	59 917	36 569	300 910	47 442	654 750	228 864	16 316	332 124	78 019	96 591
SIC Basis													
1997	154 459	18 769	49 820	58 949	37 136	296 141	47 559	668 092	218 357	16 067	325 359	79 456	97 499
1996	145 044	17 998	48 317	54 085	34 823	281 806	43 658	630 003	201 329	16 075	305 413	74 936	91 166
1995	137 528	17 393	44 505	48 974	32 149	266 724	41 459	594 444	191 579	14 515	293 260	69 580	80 099
1994	128 473	16 961	42 838	44 855	29 456	254 546	41 143	569 398	179 574	14 036	278 508	67 137	74 435
1993	118 323	16 112	39 098	40 038	27 612	243 396	36 545	549 229	167 200	12 907	258 288	65 000	69 160
1992	115 209	15 043	37 950	36 503	26 555	233 153	32 581	532 616	159 245	12 788	250 164	61 953	63 712
1991	109 548	14 057	35 619	33 599	24 778	221 678	30 454	508 889	146 502	11 664	234 736	59 468	60 078
1990	104 097	13 417	33 776	31 820	23 784	214 845	26 871	503 608	140 272	11 480	228 343	57 709	57 275
1989	102 004	12 849	31 409	28 587	23 885	206 442	25 303	481 344	134 644	10 702	218 483	54 844	53 259
1988	96 489	11 875	29 270	25 468	23 171	196 353	23 780	462 765	125 205	9 743	206 251	52 711	49 641
1987	89 836	11 653	26 801	22 367	21 463	175 651	22 981	423 760	114 126	10 308	192 809	48 904	44 963
1986	84 744	11 241	26 105	20 246	18 773	160 458	22 439	394 133	106 209	9 803	184 482	49 199	42 256
1985	79 389	11 218	25 840	18 548	16 867	147 575	23 318	366 828	98 016	10 740	175 989	53 565	40 064
1984	75 872	11 219	24 609	17 023	14 947	134 933	22 052	342 054	89 299	10 739	165 379	52 035	37 892
1983	66 515	10 721	21 727	15 420	12 714	118 993	20 394	305 226	78 202	10 102	146 052	48 286	34 036
1982	61 625	10 379	21 193	14 250	11 463	106 847	19 697	282 616	69 384	10 027	135 922	49 799	31 923
1981	58 672	10 317	20 762	13 598	10 562	99 921	18 868	261 322	66 372	10 024	134 245	45 828	32 025
1980	53 361	9 021	18 143	12 007	9 365	89 656	16 016	234 974	59 303	7 697	122 691	37 820	30 544
1979	51 449	8 250	17 285	10 607	8 429	82 070	13 380	215 699	54 929	7 267	118 304	31 686	28 958
1978	46 866	7 511	15 709	9 105	7 452	73 760	11 736	198 456	50 170	6 460	108 557	27 194	25 863
1977	41 710	6 390	13 716	7 521	6 340	66 607	10 260	179 233	44 046	5 274	97 863	24 041	22 348
1976	37 170	6 006	12 945	6 268	5 519	60 556	9 253	163 578	40 370	5 090	87 443	20 700	19 742
1975	32 975	5 209	11 790	5 531	4 859	56 109	8 107	155 494	35 932	4 897	78 131	18 090	16 811
1974	30 474	4 646	10 392	4 972	4 489	53 075	7 120	145 665	33 588	4 514	74 329	16 151	15 427
1973	29 279	4 329	9 917	4 540	4 193	49 398	6 199	136 669	31 736	4 395	69 965	14 436	14 184
1972	26 414	3 645	8 449	3 999	3 645	45 480	5 410	127 515	27 991	3 064	63 064	12 679	12 225
1971	24 236	3 131	7 618	3 619	3 349	41 370	4 826	119 338	25 009	2 617	58 073	11 224	10 860
1970	22 232	2 911	6 881	3 268	3 065	38 549	4 436	112 514	22 814	2 282	53 804	10 327	9 795
1969	21 096	2 751	6 519	2 951	2 830	35 904	4 088	107 170	20 853	2 164	52 912	9 573	9 351
1968	19 716	2 524	5 807	2 553	2 607	33 706	3 804	99 955	18 931	1 944	48 785	8 789	8 525
1967	17 857	2 359	5 471	2 251	2 382	31 026	3 514	92 218	17 130	1 862	44 510	8 054	7 636
1966	16 854	2 339	5 182	2 132	2 179	29 075	3 447	86 683	15 942	1 834	42 763	7 432	7 263
1965	15 625	2 168	4 728	2 032	1 971	26 692	3 306	80 455	14 518	1 814	39 143	6 924	6 719
1964	14 451	2 014	4 379	1 933	1 821	24 802	3 153	75 624	13 453	1 580	35 702	6 503	6 156
1963	13 610	1 963	4 241	1 818	1 659	23 408	3 026	70 723	12 611	1 612	33 318	6 111	5 698
Chained (2000) dollars													
NAICS													
2005	192 491	25 445	61 887	97 296	50 086	385 605	59 325	863 828	310 596	21 015	394 465	101 164	135 615
2004	188 193	24 182	60 751	89 264	48 533	377 564	57 227	839 286	296 725	19 964	390 882	97 907	128 085
2003	183 500	23 287	60 089	82 771	46 063	366 325	53 681	802 823	288 561	19 905	379 439	94 781	116 894
2002	179 918	22 248	56 942	77 081	44 573	357 923	51 633	791 689	282 389	18 818	373 457	92 933	115 000
2001	177 810	21 670	55 819	75 131	43 584	355 106	50 926	794 392	278 277	17 907	365 735	91 793	110 513
2000	176 708	21 366	55 478	73 719	43 518	344 824	50 725	777 157	273 698	17 752	372 006	89 757	112 438
1999	172 930	20 923	54 376	70 657	40 611	334 104	50 052	736 540	267 001	17 244	368 482	86 863	104 345
1998	171 653	20 633	53 722	66 885	39 551	325 775	46 278	698 883	251 022	17 527	362 724	84 496	100 858
1997	168 205	20 098	52 781	64 480	36 607	316 128	45 762	670 980	239 698	17 032	350 603	82 858	95 568
SIC													
1997	160 945	19 507	51 319	63 140	37 713	310 383	47 209	693 878	233 522	16 569	336 157	83 116	94 041
1996	153 203	18 930	50 035	59 372	35 675	300 908	43 396	665 717	218 384	16 588	319 426	79 580	88 064
1995	147 661	18 608	47 334	54 470	33 173	288 385	41 711	640 084	210 680	15 460	310 416	75 865	77 499
1994	140 704	18 551	46 483	51 290	30 858	281 689	41 143	627 133	200 793	15 226	300 451	74 454	73 136
1993	132 946	18 047	43 397	47 072	29 605	276 229	36 819	616 896	187 725	14 263	285 610	73 322	69 619
1992	132 978	17 344	43 221	43 930	29 198	272 318	33 478	614 332	182 648	14 491	283 793	71 820	66 288
1991	129 706	16 555	41 481	41 333	27 867	264 954	31 833	606 041	173 294	13 493	272 686	70 245	64 169
1990	127 995	16 157	40 271	40 507	27 711	266 565	28 724	624 344	173 593	13 533	274 921	69 977	63 203

Note: There is a discontinuity in the GDP by state time series at 1997, where the data change from SIC industry definitions to NAICS industry definitions. This discontinuity results from many sources, including differences in source data and different estimation methodologies. In addition, the NAICS-based GDP by state estimates are consistent with U.S. gross domestic product (GDP) while the SIC-based GDP by state estimates are consistent with U.S. gross domestic income (GDI). This data discontinuity may affect both the levels and the growth rates of the GDP by state estimates. Users of the GDP by state estimates are strongly cautioned against appending the two data series in an attempt to construct a single time series of GDP by state estimates for 1963 to 2005.

NAICS industry detail is based on the 1997 NAICS. SIC industry detail 1987–1997 is based on the 1987 SIC. SIC industry detail 1963 to 1986 is based on the 1972 SIC.

Table 23-3. Gross Domestic Product (GDP) by State in Current and Chained (2000) Dollars, 1963–2005—*Continued*

(Millions.)

Year	Pennsylvania	Rhode Island	South Carolina	South Dakota	Tennessee	Texas	Utah	Vermont	Virginia	Washington	West Virginia	Wisconsin	Wyoming
Current dollars													
NAICS													
2005	489 025	43 787	140 019	30 919	229 215	989 443	90 778	23 065	351 903	267 308	53 050	216 322	27 269
2004	463 752	41 844	131 492	29 699	216 769	903 208	82 546	21 992	327 032	253 085	49 903	207 739	24 092
2003	439 241	39 260	127 459	27 399	201 522	828 456	76 180	20 580	301 867	240 025	46 645	196 316	21 806
2002	423 110	36 909	121 582	26 416	191 525	783 480	72 665	19 553	285 759	231 463	45 032	188 600	19 619
2001	406 713	35 149	117 296	23 910	180 582	762 247	70 109	18 828	276 762	225 765	43 365	181 936	18 941
2000	389 619	33 609	112 514	23 099	174 851	727 233	67 568	17 782	260 743	221 961	41 476	175 737	17 331
1999	376 111	30 843	108 663	21 575	169 648	668 996	63 834	16 788	242 679	214 375	41 105	169 012	15 931
1998	361 800	29 537	102 945	20 771	160 872	629 209	60 168	15 935	226 569	195 794	39 500	160 681	14 859
1997	343 368	28 506	97 397	19 804	153 405	599 492	56 590	15 167	211 921	178 334	38 795	151 549	14 904
SIC Basis													
1997	341 982	28 950	94 898	19 498	150 999	605 302	54 584	15 459	208 597	174 412	38 517	148 831	16 041
1996	325 515	26 665	89 260	19 073	141 335	550 014	51 442	14 632	196 638	161 760	37 346	141 755	15 732
1995	314 504	25 666	86 053	17 807	135 655	507 441	46 303	13 892	185 490	151 338	36 362	134 096	14 567
1994	298 329	24 375	81 033	17 014	128 905	478 143	42 218	13 717	177 008	146 726	34 855	128 394	14 082
1993	285 007	23 591	75 528	16 020	118 870	449 185	38 397	13 070	168 583	138 834	32 404	119 592	13 897
1992	273 513	22 611	71 584	14 894	111 341	422 097	35 671	12 590	160 534	131 148	30 977	112 795	13 337
1991	258 127	21 607	68 380	13 832	101 378	398 935	33 691	11 722	152 673	122 657	29 352	104 859	13 271
1990	248 307	21 537	65 710	12 825	94 553	384 136	31 444	11 727	147 026	115 650	28 336	100 313	13 150
1989	236 685	20 921	62 001	11 861	91 921	354 671	28 872	11 259	140 173	105 057	27 280	95 412	11 882
1988	223 774	19 656	57 963	11 243	87 533	331 595	27 401	10 429	130 443	96 240	26 163	89 936	11 324
1987	206 507	17 854	53 238	10 731	81 235	302 359	25 289	9 286	120 101	87 712	24 713	82 365	10 963
1986	191 652	16 673	48 522	10 150	74 103	298 781	24 584	8 324	109 973	81 932	24 013	78 536	11 090
1985	181 155	15 304	44 850	9 706	69 280	312 564	24 401	7 676	100 366	75 870	23 609	74 607	12 796
1984	171 205	13 923	41 944	9 290	64 610	293 459	22 394	7 006	91 840	72 596	22 848	70 652	12 674
1983	155 246	12 375	36 345	8 196	57 468	268 188	19 913	6 354	80 988	66 765	20 963	63 664	11 995
1982	145 236	11 496	32 794	7 814	52 436	262 519	18 547	5 826	72 905	61 572	21 285	60 008	12 864
1981	141 438	10 820	31 503	7 758	50 685	247 344	17 490	5 514	67 586	58 003	20 503	58 031	13 019
1980	129 625	9 718	28 010	6 853	45 392	204 612	15 436	4 925	59 973	52 158	19 031	53 401	10 641
1979	122 322	8 880	25 829	6 776	42 442	172 593	13 806	4 450	54 448	48 389	17 732	50 572	8 150
1978	111 680	8 010	23 227	6 022	38 364	149 698	12 077	3 985	49 224	42 229	16 254	45 820	6 736
1977	100 402	7 284	20 300	5 152	33 687	130 755	10 424	3 376	43 952	36 276	14 718	41 007	5 536
1976	92 324	6 543	18 189	4 639	30 412	113 842	9 294	3 242	39 671	31 679	13 405	37 013	4 700
1975	85 563	6 020	16 040	4 398	26 521	98 926	8 183	2 821	35 147	28 246	12 125	32 270	3 967
1974	78 976	5 609	15 337	3 968	25 054	85 519	7 359	2 594	32 543	25 245	10 795	28 713	3 458
1973	72 399	5 430	13 779	3 959	23 101	73 986	6 482	2 499	29 561	22 520	9 308	27 047	2 836
1972	65 914	5 123	11 913	3 048	20 282	64 161	5 613	2 311	26 163	19 804	8 504	24 078	2 347
1971	60 744	4 606	10 558	2 656	17 814	57 457	4 942	2 137	23 225	18 134	7 704	22 083	2 094
1970	57 075	4 317	9 561	2 438	16 052	52 449	4 454	1 992	21 100	17 352	7 173	20 193	1 941
1969	54 904	4 115	8 880	2 274	15 118	48 713	4 040	1 810	19 690	17 183	6 457	19 527	1 799
1968	50 354	3 913	8 175	2 093	13 928	44 613	3 729	1 639	17 740	16 079	6 158	18 234	1 672
1967	46 893	3 634	7 386	1 961	12 558	40 032	3 495	1 515	15 973	14 623	5 887	16 849	1 545
1966	44 465	3 475	6 945	1 919	11 945	36 875	3 416	1 446	14 950	13 340	5 636	16 141	1 505
1965	40 888	3 161	6 214	1 763	10 783	33 937	3 213	1 218	13 706	11 657	5 272	14 793	1 444
1964	37 700	2 883	5 545	1 596	9 723	31 426	3 086	1 098	12 746	10 777	4 957	13 722	1 400
1963	34 838	2 689	5 058	1 609	9 023	29 317	3 008	1 001	11 712	10 472	4 683	12 741	1 345
Chained (2000) dollars													
NAICS													
2005	431 459	38 537	124 746	27 522	206 052	848 968	79 891	21 043	313 531	238 072	45 190	193 538	20 444
2004	421 443	37 792	120 110	26 735	199 816	810 510	74 814	20 482	297 471	230 722	44 280	190 597	19 695
2003	410 364	36 439	119 337	25 722	189 752	771 082	70 945	19 606	281 083	224 443	42 880	184 777	18 985
2002	402 978	34 918	115 713	25 312	183 153	760 588	69 091	18 909	271 184	221 115	42 453	180 330	18 395
2001	395 633	34 176	114 055	23 351	176 253	745 325	68 275	18 543	269 620	220 190	41 922	177 434	18 114
2000	389 619	33 609	112 514	23 099	174 851	727 233	67 568	17 782	260 743	221 961	41 476	175 737	17 331
1999	384 378	31 608	110 902	21 832	173 574	699 101	65 596	16 953	248 630	219 569	42 032	172 445	16 990
1998	376 189	30 905	107 126	21 066	168 184	666 590	62 974	16 204	237 601	204 314	40 832	166 943	16 095
1997	362 900	30 438	103 331	20 155	163 038	627 501	60 081	15 501	226 029	188 481	40 605	160 193	16 001
SIC													
1997	356 751	30 522	98 700	19 700	157 459	634 428	57 375	15 844	223 755	183 719	39 962	153 329	17 183
1996	345 158	28 704	93 815	19 252	149 447	585 843	55 016	15 170	215 092	173 119	39 273	147 152	17 082
1995	337 534	28 142	91 324	18 450	145 234	554 850	50 238	14 564	206 573	164 783	38 490	140 831	16 595
1994	327 100	27 322	88 177	17 986	140 929	530 387	46 904	14 579	201 554	163 769	37 551	138 075	16 167
1993	320 424	27 111	83 909	17 286	133 056	505 783	43 741	14 189	194 750	159 045	35 649	131 738	15 929
1992	315 991	26 711	81 327	16 445	127 942	488 348	41 715	14 010	190 063	154 831	34 715	127 035	15 506
1991	305 712	26 256	79 447	15 673	119 236	469 373	40 267	13 317	186 530	148 912	33 477	120 680	15 460
1990	305 168	27 243	78 975	14 910	115 483	462 032	38 799	13 762	187 926	145 628	33 210	119 126	15 181

Source: U.S. Department of Commerce, Bureau of Economic Analysis.
Note: There is a discontinuity in the GDP by state time series at 1997, where the data change from SIC industry definitions to NAICS industry definitions. This discontinuity results from many sources, including differences in source data and different estimation methodologies. In addition, the NAICS-based GDP by state estimates are consistent with U.S. gross domestic product (GDP) while the SIC-based GDP by state estimates are consistent with U.S. gross domestic income (GDI). This data discontinuity may affect both the levels and the growth rates of the GDP by state estimates. Users of the GDP by state estimates are strongly cautioned against appending the two data series in an attempt to construct a single time series of GDP by state estimates for 1963 to 2005.

NAICS industry detail is based on the 1997 NAICS. SIC industry detail 1987–1997 is based on the 1987 SIC. SIC industry detail 1963 to 1986 is based on the 1972 SIC.

Table 23-4. Selected Per Capita Income and Product Items in Current and Chained (2000) Dollars, 1929–2005

(Dollars.)

Year	Current dollars				Chained (2000) dollars		
	Gross domestic product	Personal income	Disposable personal income	Personal consumption expenditures, total	Gross domestic product	Disposable personal income	Personal consumption expenditures, total
2005	42 090	34 544	30 466	29 479	37 532	27 370	26 483
2004	39 922	33 046	29 477	27 946	36 592	27 232	25 817
2003	37 687	31 497	28 062	26 484	35 452	26 594	25 099
2002	36 321	30 813	27 164	25 501	34 861	26 235	24 629
2001	35 491	30 571	26 235	24 722	34 659	25 697	24 215
2000	34 759	29 847	25 472	23 862	34 759	25 472	23 862
1999	33 181	27 933	23 968	22 491	33 904	24 564	23 050
1998	31 674	26 880	23 161	21 291	32 833	24 131	22 183
1997	30 424	25 334	21 940	20 323	31 886	23 065	21 365
1996	28 982	24 176	21 091	19 490	30 881	22 546	20 835
1995	27 749	23 078	20 287	18 665	30 128	22 153	20 382
1994	26 844	22 176	19 555	18 004	29 741	21 812	20 082
1993	25 578	21 356	18 872	17 204	28 940	21 493	19 593
1992	24 668	20 870	18 494	16 485	28 556	21 548	19 208
1991	23 650	19 923	17 609	15 722	28 007	21 109	18 848
1990	23 195	19 500	17 131	15 349	28 429	21 281	19 067
1989	22 169	18 545	16 257	14 546	28 221	21 120	18 898
1988	20 827	17 358	15 297	13 685	27 514	20 740	18 554
1987	19 517	16 255	14 241	12 766	26 664	20 072	17 994
1986	18 542	15 466	13 649	12 048	26 024	19 906	17 570
1985	17 695	14 787	13 037	11 406	25 382	19 476	17 040
1984	16 638	13 915	12 319	10 589	24 593	19 011	16 343
1983	15 092	12 635	11 131	9 775	23 146	17 828	15 656
1982	14 017	11 951	10 426	8 945	22 346	17 418	14 944
1981	13 601	11 266	9 765	8 439	23 007	17 217	14 879
1980	12 249	10 134	8 822	7 716	22 666	16 940	14 816
1979	11 387	9 161	7 967	7 073	22 982	16 931	15 030
1978	10 307	8 255	7 224	6 417	22 526	16 704	14 837
1977	9 219	7 414	6 517	5 804	21 565	16 128	14 364
1976	8 369	6 762	5 972	5 282	20 822	15 738	13 919
1975	7 586	6 181	5 498	4 789	19 961	15 291	13 320
1974	7 013	5 716	5 010	4 364	20 195	15 094	13 148
1973	6 524	5 241	4 616	4 022	20 484	15 345	13 371
1972	5 899	4 729	4 140	3 671	19 555	14 512	12 868
1971	5 427	4 350	3 860	3 379	18 771	14 001	12 256
1970	5 064	4 090	3 587	3 162	18 391	13 563	11 955
1969	4 857	3 840	3 324	2 985	18 573	13 163	11 820
1968	4 533	3 547	3 114	2 780	18 196	12 892	11 510
1967	4 189	3 262	2 895	2 555	17 533	12 457	10 994
1966	4 007	3 072	2 734	2 446	17 290	12 065	10 793
1965	3 700	2 860	2 563	2 283	16 420	11 594	10 331
1964	3 458	2 681	2 410	2 144	15 624	11 061	9 839
1963	3 263	2 534	2 246	2 022	14 971	10 455	9 412
1962	3 139	2 448	2 171	1 947	14 552	10 227	9 170
1961	2 965	2 335	2 078	1 862	13 932	9 901	8 873
1960	2 912	2 277	2 022	1 835	13 840	9 735	8 837
1959	2 865	2 224	1 983	1 796	13 092	9 167	8 303
1958	2 687	2 125	1 899	1 703	12 420	8 922	7 999
1957	2 694	2 098	1 867	1 675	12 751	8 988	8 068
1956	2 603	2 021	1 800	1 616	12 728	8 930	8 018
1955	2 512	1 917	1 715	1 567	12 703	8 675	7 928
1954	2 347	1 818	1 629	1 481	12 073	8 276	7 524
1953	2 381	1 834	1 622	1 463	12 371	8 319	7 503
1952	2 285	1 759	1 552	1 400	12 024	8 071	7 279
1951	2 201	1 677	1 499	1 352	11 764	7 953	7 176
1950	1 940	1 516	1 388	1 270	11 119	7 863	7 192
1949	1 794	1 396	1 281	1 199	10 396	7 343	6 872
1948	1 838	1 440	1 307	1 196	10 639	7 433	6 807
1947	1 696	1 333	1 194	1 126	10 374	7 183	6 775
1946	1 572	1 269	1 145	1 020	10 648	7 599	6 768
1945	1 594	1 229	1 087	856	12 101	7 729	6 088
1944	1 587	1 201	1 072	784	12 386	7 920	5 793
1943	1 451	1 114	990	729	11 582	7 737	5 698
1942	1 199	918	880	659	10 084	7 507	5 623
1941	950	722	703	607	8 612	6 739	5 822

Table 23-4. Selected Per Capita Income and Product Items in Current and Chained (2000) Dollars, 1929–2005—*Continued*

(Dollars.)

Year	Current dollars				Chained (2000) dollars		
	Gross domestic product	Personal income	Disposable personal income	Personal consumption expenditures, total	Gross domestic product	Disposable personal income	Personal consumption expenditures, total
1940	767	595	581	539	7 423	5 912	5 486
1939	702	558	545	513	6 896	5 589	5 259
1938	662	528	512	494	6 429	5 201	5 022
1937	712	576	560	518	6 713	5 556	5 145
1936	653	537	525	485	6 417	5 400	4 990
1935	576	475	465	439	5 718	4 827	4 558
1934	522	425	417	407	5 284	4 430	4 324
1933	449	373	365	366	4 800	4 063	4 065
1932	471	400	393	390	4 897	4 214	4 186
1931	617	528	517	489	5 667	4 896	4 626
1930	741	621	605	570	6 101	5 109	4 808
1929	851	700	683	635	6 746	5 516	5 134

Source: U.S. Census Bureau. *Statistical Abstract of the United States: 2007.* U.S. Bureau of Economic Analysis.
Note: Based on U.S. Census Bureau estimated population including Armed Forces abroad; based on quarterly averages. Prior to 1960, excludes Alaska and Hawaii.

Table 23-5. National Income by Sector, Legal Form of Organization, and Type of Income, 1929–2005

(Billions of dollars.)

Year	Total	Domestic industries	Corporate business				Sole proprietorships and partnerships			
		Total	Total	Compensation of employees	Corporate profits[1]	Net interest	Total	Compensation of employees	Proprietors' income[1]	Net interest
2005	10 811.8	8 438.1	6 500.2	4 612.5	1 133.7	56.3	1 669.2	498.5	969.1	100.8
2004	10 255.9	7 933.3	6 077.1	4 354.6	1 006.3	78.3	1 577.5	462.2	909.6	101.1
2003	9 632.3	7 411.2	5 697.1	4 156.9	827.7	120.8	1 439.0	430.5	810.0	102.0
2002	9 229.3	7 134.6	5 483.7	4 044.5	730.5	135.9	1 375.3	411.3	767.1	104.6
2001	8 979.8	6 993.8	5 346.9	4 016.7	597.6	171.3	1 374.9	398.5	770.5	129.8
2000	8 795.2	6 924.5	5 361.8	3 957.7	672.2	178.1	1 299.2	374.8	726.9	124.4
1999	8 236.7	6 478.2	5 023.0	3 645.2	729.8	142.3	1 203.1	346.9	676.7	106.3
1998	7 752.8	6 094.0	4 724.6	3 397.6	698.7	143.3	1 126.7	316.8	625.7	111.9
1997	7 292.2	5 697.8	4 430.0	3 125.0	757.5	95.4	1 031.4	291.7	573.3	98.1
1996	6 840.1	5 305.4	4 112.9	2 916.1	684.3	70.0	965.7	274.7	540.8	89.6
1995	6 453.9	4 973.3	3 867.6	2 774.1	603.9	66.4	888.0	259.1	489.5	84.7
1994	6 122.3	4 708.6	3 646.9	2 633.0	523.2	74.9	853.2	244.9	470.8	86.6
1993	5 773.4	4 408.7	3 403.5	2 489.2	465.0	72.1	806.3	232.0	451.8	80.2
1992	5 512.8	4 205.2	3 234.4	2 377.0	406.2	79.3	773.6	218.4	425.6	82.9
1991	5 227.9	3 978.4	3 073.2	2 253.0	374.7	101.7	721.0	207.9	375.2	92.3
1990	5 089.1	3 909.9	3 014.5	2 208.1	361.7	125.3	725.6	204.8	379.0	98.1
1989	4 826.6	3 744.0	2 890.4	2 097.6	359.5	129.4	692.5	192.0	361.3	101.3
1988	4 549.4	3 541.5	2 752.3	1 988.9	375.7	108.7	637.3	179.2	339.7	85.1
1987	4 173.7	3 246.0	2 537.9	1 849.8	320.8	108.3	565.3	159.6	300.5	76.6
1986	3 902.3	3 039.3	2 365.4	1 728.6	280.0	107.0	536.9	152.7	274.6	81.3
1985	3 723.4	2 906.5	2 261.3	1 630.9	292.2	96.9	511.7	145.2	261.2	76.2
1984	3 482.3	2 715.5	2 125.1	1 520.3	282.0	98.8	472.1	134.6	242.0	68.6
1983	3 084.2	2 381.0	1 885.0	1 371.2	229.2	86.6	389.5	121.9	191.4	54.1
1982	2 864.3	2 210.8	1 743.9	1 297.5	177.1	90.0	368.1	116.2	175.6	50.8
1981	2 742.4	2 148.2	1 688.0	1 243.9	196.4	77.7	370.0	110.5	182.3	44.0
1980	2 439.3	1 902.7	1 485.8	1 122.6	165.7	55.9	340.0	103.3	173.5	34.5
1979	2 249.1	1 771.2	1 373.4	1 023.4	188.6	34.9	328.5	95.9	179.4	28.1
1978	2 027.4	1 599.9	1 240.4	901.9	193.8	27.5	295.5	85.4	166.0	22.1
1977	1 798.9	1 409.0	1 087.8	784.8	173.3	23.3	262.5	76.8	145.0	19.3
1976	1 611.8	1 255.3	960.1	695.2	146.8	18.8	241.6	71.6	131.5	17.1
1975	1 445.9	1 120.5	851.6	614.9	120.2	23.4	220.2	65.8	118.9	15.5
1974	1 342.1	1 045.2	791.7	587.4	98.3	20.7	207.7	62.3	112.5	14.0
1973	1 247.4	976.8	736.6	533.9	110.6	13.0	197.5	58.1	112.8	11.2
1972	1 111.2	865.4	657.7	472.5	102.6	11.3	168.7	51.6	95.3	8.4
1971	1 008.1	782.5	593.2	425.3	90.2	11.5	154.4	49.6	84.3	7.2
1970	930.9	726.2	548.9	400.2	76.5	11.3	144.7	49.2	77.9	6.0
1969	889.7	703.4	532.5	378.6	88.8	7.8	140.4	48.1	76.9	5.1
1968	823.2	653.2	490.1	341.3	93.2	3.9	134.3	46.4	73.8	4.2
1967	751.9	597.8	443.6	308.4	86.6	4.0	127.5	44.5	69.3	3.8
1966	711.0	570.6	421.4	288.5	88.7	2.3	123.8	43.9	67.6	3.5
1965	653.4	526.1	385.0	259.9	82.8	1.2	116.8	41.3	63.4	2.9
1964	602.7	484.1	350.4	239.2	72.0	0.8	110.6	40.1	58.9	2.5
1963	560.6	450.4	323.5	222.7	64.9	0.4	104.9	38.1	56.0	2.0
1962	530.1	427.1	304.4	211.0	59.5	0.7	102.5	37.2	54.9	1.7
1961	491.6	396.5	278.2	195.6	51.5	0.4	99.2	36.5	52.8	1.5
1960	474.9	386.2	270.6	190.7	50.6	− 0.2	97.4	37.0	50.4	1.4
1959	455.8	374.3	260.1	180.3	53.0	−0.2	96.9	37.1	50.3	1.3
1958	416.8	340.1	230.2	164.0	41.0	0.6	...	35.2	50.2	1.3
1957	414.3	342.9	236.4	166.5	45.3	0.2	...	35.2	47.9	1.1
1956	395.6	329.4	226.9	158.2	45.7	0.0	...	34.1	45.9	1.0
1955	372.7	311.3	212.9	144.6	47.2	0.2	...	32.2	44.3	0.9
1954	339.4	282.4	188.0	132.2	36.9	0.2	...	31.2	42.4	0.8
1953	339.5	285.3	191.4	134.0	37.9	0.0	...	31.4	42.2	0.8
1952	321.8	270.6	178.6	123.0	37.4	−0.2	...	29.9	43.2	0.8
1951	304.3	258.9	170.7	114.6	39.5	−0.2	...	28.2	42.7	0.7
1950	264.4	227.5	148.8	98.7	34.7	−0.1	...	25.3	37.6	0.6
1949	238.0	203.9	130.7	88.8	27.9	0.0	...	23.6	34.7	0.5
1948	243.0	211.9	134.4	91.1	29.9	0.0	...	24.0	39.3	0.5
1947	198.6	174.6	104.7	82.1	22.5	0.0	58.4	22.4	35.6	0.4
1946	182.3	154.7	86.3	69.9	16.7	−0.2	57.2	20.4	36.6	0.3
1945	183.3	143.5	84.1	64.1	19.8	0.2	49.6	17.6	31.7	0.3
1944	184.3	147.9	91.6	67.1	24.2	0.3	46.8	16.2	30.3	0.3
1943	171.4	142.1	88.8	64.1	24.1	0.5	44.1	14.6	29.1	0.4
1942	137.6	119.0	73.2	52.8	19.7	0.7	37.3	12.7	24.1	0.5
1941	104.3	91.8	56.9	41.6	14.6	0.7	27.6	9.8	17.3	0.5

[1]Includes inventory valuation and capital consumption adjustments.

Table 23-5. National Income by Sector, Legal Form of Organization, and Type of Income, 1929–2005—*Continued*

(Billions of dollars.)

Year	Total	Domestic business								
		Total	Corporate business				Sole proprietorships and partnerships			
			Total	Compensation of employees	Corporate profits[1]	Net interest	Total	Compensation of employees	Proprietors' income[1]	Net interest
1940	81.1	70.5	42.8	32.9	9.2	0.8	21.1	7.8	12.9	0.5
1939	72.9	62.5	36.7	29.8	5.9	1.0	19.4	7.2	11.7	0.5
1938	67.4	57.1	32.6	27.3	4.3	1.1	18.5	6.8	11.2	0.5
1937	74.0	64.4	38.1	30.5	6.5	1.1	20.7	7.1	13.1	0.5
1936	65.8	56.2	33.3	26.3	5.8	1.1	17.7	6.2	11.0	0.5
1935	57.9	49.7	28.0	23.1	3.6	1.3	16.7	5.5	10.7	0.5
1934	50.2	42.5	24.5	21.0	2.2	1.3	13.1	5.0	7.6	0.6
1933	41.4	34.7	18.7	18.0	−0.3	1.0	10.8	4.4	5.8	0.6
1932	43.9	37.2	19.9	19.0	−0.4	1.3	11.2	4.8	5.6	0.7
1931	60.4	52.9	29.6	25.4	2.8	1.4	16.3	6.4	9.1	0.8
1930	75.6	67.6	39.4	30.8	7.1	1.4	20.3	7.8	11.7	0.8
1929	86.8	78.8	45.9	34.2	10.4	1.3	24.2	8.6	14.9	0.6

[1]Includes inventory valuation and capital consumption adjustments.

Table 23-5. National Income by Sector, Legal Form of Organization, and Type of Income, 1929–2005—*Continued*

(Billions of dollars.)

Year	Domestic industries—*Continued*					Government enterprises	Households and institutions	General government	Rest of the world
	Other private business								
	Total	Total Compensation of employees	Proprietors' income[1]	Rental income of persons[2]	Net interest				
2005	158.3	31.6	1.5	45.4	63.7	110.5	1 126.1	1 215.7	31.9
2004	159.7	29.9	1.4	52.0	57.8	119.1	1 120.6	1 155.7	46.3
2003	157.9	27.9	1.2	57.3	54.1	117.2	1 067.5	1 096.9	56.8
2002	159.2	26.3	1.3	65.7	53.6	116.4	1 040.5	1 023.6	30.6
2001	162.4	23.7	1.4	59.6	52.1	109.7	988.6	953.7	43.6
2000	150.6	22.5	1.5	58.7	48.2	113.0	928.6	903.2	38.9
1999	141.1	20.7	1.5	58.1	43.7	111.0	870.3	854.3	33.8
1998	134.5	19.0	2.0	58.8	40.8	108.2	819.1	818.4	21.3
1997	129.3	16.5	2.7	57.4	39.2	107.1	773.0	788.5	32.9
1996	122.6	15.4	2.4	54.4	37.9	104.1	736.4	763.3	35.0
1995	117.5	14.8	2.6	50.5	37.4	100.2	704.5	740.3	35.8
1994	113.4	14.4	2.5	44.8	36.8	95.1	666.4	721.1	26.2
1993	108.8	14.1	2.0	41.0	38.0	90.0	634.1	698.6	31.9
1992	107.9	13.7	2.0	32.7	41.7	89.2	603.2	674.6	29.7
1991	101.5	13.2	1.9	27.8	44.1	82.8	573.4	645.6	30.4
1990	94.8	13.0	1.6	24.1	43.3	75.0	536.0	608.5	34.8
1989	88.9	12.5	2.0	24.6	41.6	72.1	490.2	566.2	26.2
1988	85.3	11.8	1.9	25.2	38.6	66.5	452.6	531.7	23.6
1987	82.7	11.6	1.7	27.3	36.1	60.0	410.8	499.1	17.9
1986	80.1	11.1	1.1	31.9	33.9	56.8	374.8	470.4	17.8
1985	79.1	10.7	1.1	28.1	30.0	54.3	346.7	443.7	26.5
1984	70.7	10.0	1.3	25.4	26.4	47.4	320.1	410.4	36.3
1983	63.6	9.2	1.1	24.7	23.8	42.8	290.9	375.3	37.1
1982	59.8	8.6	0.8	21.3	22.1	38.8	264.3	352.7	36.5
1981	54.3	8.2	0.7	15.7	20.2	35.7	236.1	325.2	32.9
1980	45.9	7.5	0.6	12.7	18.1	31.0	206.9	295.5	34.2
1979	40.5	6.9	0.7	11.3	16.0	28.7	179.8	266.1	31.9
1978	37.4	6.2	0.7	10.4	14.4	26.5	161.3	244.7	21.6
1977	35.2	5.7	0.7	8.7	13.1	23.3	144.7	225.0	20.3
1976	31.4	5.1	0.6	8.7	11.8	22.2	133.3	206.4	16.8
1975	29.7	4.7	0.6	8.6	10.9	19.0	122.8	189.6	13.0
1974	27.3	4.4	0.6	8.8	9.4	18.4	111.7	169.7	15.5
1973	26.2	4.1	0.6	7.6	8.3	16.4	102.6	155.4	12.6
1972	23.3	3.8	0.6	6.5	7.3	15.7	94.2	143.1	8.6
1971	21.0	3.4	0.5	6.5	6.6	13.8	87.1	130.9	7.6
1970	19.8	3.2	0.5	6.3	5.9	12.8	79.0	119.4	6.4
1969	18.5	3.0	0.5	6.4	5.3	12.0	72.7	107.5	6.1
1968	17.7	2.8	0.5	6.3	4.9	11.1	66.1	97.8	6.1
1967	16.8	2.6	0.5	6.4	4.6	9.7	61.3	87.4	5.4
1966	16.1	2.3	0.5	6.3	4.3	9.3	56.9	78.4	5.1
1965	15.4	2.1	0.5	6.1	4.0	9.0	52.8	69.3	5.3
1964	14.6	2.0	0.5	6.1	3.7	8.4	49.3	64.4	4.9
1963	14.0	1.9	0.5	5.9	3.4	7.9	46.3	59.3	4.5
1962	13.2	1.8	0.5	5.8	3.1	7.0	43.4	55.5	4.1
1961	12.6	1.7	0.5	5.7	2.8	6.5	40.0	51.6	3.5
1960	11.9	1.5	0.4	5.7	2.6	6.4	37.5	48.1	3.1
1959	11.4	1.4	0.4	5.8	2.4	6.0	33.9	44.9	2.8
1958	...	1.4	0.0	5.6	2.2	...	31.1	42.9	2.6
1957	...	1.3	−0.1	5.6	2.0	...	28.5	39.8	3.1
1956	...	1.3	0.0	5.6	1.8	...	26.2	37.2	2.8
1955	...	1.3	0.0	5.6	1.6	...	24.1	34.8	2.4
1954	...	1.2	0.0	5.5	1.5	...	21.8	33.0	2.1
1953	...	1.2	0.0	5.4	1.3	...	19.9	32.4	1.9
1952	...	1.1	0.0	5.3	1.2	...	17.7	31.5	2.0
1951	...	1.1	0.0	5.0	1.1	...	15.8	27.7	1.9
1950	...	1.0	0.0	4.6	0.9	...	14.2	21.2	1.4
1949	...	0.8	0.0	4.7	0.8	...	12.7	20.1	1.3
1948	...	0.8	0.0	4.7	0.7	...	11.6	18.1	1.5
1947	9.5	0.7	0.0	7.0	1.8	2.0	17.6	5.1	1.2
1946	9.3	0.6	0.0	7.0	1.6	1.9	22.4	4.5	0.7
1945	8.2	0.5	0.0	6.1	1.6	1.6	35.3	4.1	0.4
1944	8.0	0.5	0.0	5.9	1.6	1.5	32.3	3.7	0.5
1943	7.8	0.5	0.0	5.6	1.7	1.5	25.6	3.2	0.4
1942	7.3	0.4	0.0	5.0	1.8	1.2	15.2	2.9	0.5
1941	6.2	0.4	0.0	4.0	1.9	1.1	9.5	2.5	0.5

[1]Includes inventory valuation and capital consumption adjustments.
[2]Includes capital consumption adjustment.

Table 23-5. National Income by Sector, Legal Form of Organization, and Type of Income, 1929–2005—*Continued*

(Billions of dollars.)

Year	Domestic industries—*Continued*					Government enterprises	Households and institutions	General government	Rest of the world
	Other private business								
	Total	Total Compensation of employees	Proprietors' income[1]	Rental income of persons[2]	Net interest				
1940	5.5	0.3	0.0	3.4	1.8	1.0	7.8	2.4	0.4
1939	5.4	0.3	0.0	3.3	1.8	0.9	7.6	2.3	0.4
1938	5.2	0.3	0.0	3.1	1.8	0.9	7.7	2.2	0.4
1937	4.7	0.3	0.0	2.6	1.9	0.9	6.9	2.3	0.4
1936	4.4	0.2	0.0	2.3	1.9	0.8	7.3	2.0	0.3
1935	4.3	0.2	0.0	2.2	1.9	0.8	6.0	1.9	0.3
1934	4.2	0.2	0.0	2.1	1.9	0.7	5.6	1.8	0.3
1933	4.5	0.2	0.0	2.5	1.9	0.6	4.7	1.7	0.3
1932	5.4	0.2	0.0	3.2	2.0	0.7	4.5	1.9	0.4
1931	6.3	0.2	0.0	4.0	2.1	0.8	4.7	2.3	0.5
1930	7.2	0.3	0.0	4.9	2.0	0.8	4.6	2.7	0.7
1929	8.0	0.3	0.0	5.6	2.1	0.8	4.4	2.9	0.8

Source: U.S. Department of Commerce, Bureau of Economic Analysis.
[1]Includes inventory valuation and capital consumption adjustments.
[2]Includes capital consumption adjustment.

Table 23-6. National Income Without Capital Consumption Adjustment by Industry Group, 1929–2006

(Billions of dollars.)

Year	Total	Domestic industries											Government	Rest of the world
		Total	Private industries											
			Total	Agriculture, forestry, and fishing	Mining	Construction	Manufacturing	Wholesale and retail trade	Finance, insurance, and real estate	Transportation	Communication and public utilities	Services		
2006	11 786.6	11 756.7	10 383.4	89.2	193.7	635.7	1 480.8	1 621.4	2 013.8	338.8	650.3	3 359.7	1 373.3	29.9
2005	10 917.9	10 886.0	9 574.6	87.6	158.9	604.2	1 365.8	1 514.6	1 832.9	306.3	593.8	3 110.4	1 311.4	31.9
2004	10 069.5	10 023.2	8 763.1	95.3	123.7	522.8	1 211.0	1 391.0	1 797.4	280.8	515.5	2 825.6	1 260.2	46.3
2003	9 425.3	9 368.5	8 168.2	80.7	104.0	478.3	1 112.3	1 313.4	1 690.7	258.8	462.5	2 667.7	1 200.2	56.8
2002	9 013.5	8 982.9	7 854.7	65.9	81.4	470.8	1 071.6	1 263.5	1 644.7	250.3	451.1	2 555.6	1 128.2	30.6
2001	8 854.9	8 811.2	7 758.4	69.3	101.0	463.3	1 094.1	1 246.7	1 643.7	251.9	454.8	2 433.5	1 052.8	43.6
2000	8 687.4	8 648.5	7 642.8	70.1	93.8	440.6	1 228.5	1 229.1	1 529.3	261.2	452.6	2 337.5	1 005.7	38.9
1999	8 122.9	8 089.2	7 134.9	73.6	69.3	408.7	1 150.3	1 163.9	1 396.3	247.4	445.4	2 180.0	954.3	33.8
1998	7 661.4	7 640.1	6 724.6	78.5	72.6	366.6	1 112.1	1 096.5	1 328.5	235.3	412.3	2 022.3	915.5	21.3
1997	6 599.6	6 592.6	5 709.9	101.6	58.2	309.3	1 119.3	933.6	1 197.1	207.2	266.5	1 517.2	882.6	7.1
1996	6 206.4	6 188.3	5 338.7	101.9	50.7	290.3	1 073.9	864.5	1 088.0	194.7	266.9	1 407.8	849.6	18.1
1995	5 884.4	5 864.0	5 039.9	86.9	45.7	266.7	1 058.5	810.0	1 013.5	183.9	256.7	1 318.1	824.2	20.3
1994	5 576.4	5 559.6	4 756.6	93.7	43.9	252.8	1 006.0	774.7	932.7	176.6	246.6	1 229.5	803.0	16.8
1993	5 267.9	5 243.5	4 466.0	91.9	40.5	228.3	929.1	721.5	897.1	163.2	229.1	1 165.4	777.5	24.4
1992	5 018.2	4 994.8	4 241.8	90.7	39.7	215.6	886.0	698.7	841.5	152.9	213.2	1 103.6	753.0	23.4
1991	4 769.1	4 744.4	4 022.6	83.6	40.2	214.6	863.9	667.3	786.4	146.1	205.0	1 015.6	721.8	24.7
1990	4 640.5	4 611.6	3 929.0	89.0	40.8	230.5	879.0	651.3	738.5	138.7	191.8	969.5	682.6	29.0
1989	4 366.9	4 346.5	3 712.1	85.5	36.2	227.1	853.4	630.6	691.6	133.7	180.0	873.8	634.5	20.4
1988	4 112.1	4 093.6	3 497.1	78.2	35.9	218.9	822.2	591.4	651.5	132.7	170.9	795.3	596.5	18.4
1987	3 760.3	3 746.6	3 187.9	78.9	28.6	202.9	739.8	546.0	599.7	123.4	162.8	705.9	558.8	13.7
1986	3 475.8	3 460.3	2 933.6	70.7	28.4	191.8	686.8	522.4	528.8	115.5	152.4	636.8	526.7	15.5
1985	3 318.1	3 292.8	2 795.0	69.0	40.1	171.8	691.3	499.5	484.9	107.3	148.0	583.0	497.8	25.4
1984	3 126.5	3 091.1	2 630.8	70.2	43.8	153.0	672.5	470.7	439.6	106.6	143.4	531.1	460.3	35.3
1983	2 788.1	2 751.2	2 329.4	54.7	40.3	128.2	598.0	416.1	397.6	93.3	130.5	470.6	421.8	36.9
1982	2 620.2	2 583.7	2 187.9	61.2	50.2	119.2	576.7	386.8	355.2	86.5	126.0	426.2	395.8	36.4
1981	2 523.4	2 488.7	2 122.6	63.5	51.7	121.3	594.1	371.8	334.1	88.4	110.3	387.5	366.1	34.7
1980	2 282.9	2 247.6	1 916.0	52.2	45.7	120.9	536.6	336.4	300.9	83.5	94.7	345.1	331.6	35.3
1979	2 107.5	2 074.6	1 776.9	58.6	33.1	117.9	518.4	317.1	266.3	78.7	81.7	304.9	297.7	32.9
1978	1 885.0	1 862.9	1 589.7	51.1	27.5	104.6	471.7	285.0	232.2	71.3	77.1	269.1	273.2	22.1
1977	1 656.0	1 635.4	1 384.4	42.9	25.2	88.4	416.7	252.0	194.7	62.9	67.7	233.8	251.0	20.7
1976	1 476.2	1 459.0	1 228.6	42.7	21.5	79.8	366.6	227.9	168.7	56.1	60.7	204.6	230.4	17.1
1975	1 317.9	1 304.7	1 092.9	44.4	20.9	69.7	318.0	205.0	152.0	48.0	53.5	181.5	211.8	13.2
1974	1 217.6	1 201.9	1 012.9	43.4	16.7	69.5	302.3	184.7	140.2	47.6	45.2	163.3	189.0	15.7
1973	1 127.2	1 114.5	942.3	46.6	11.2	65.1	286.1	169.7	129.9	42.8	42.4	148.5	172.2	12.7
1972	999.4	990.7	832.5	32.2	9.3	57.3	253.2	152.5	118.4	38.2	39.1	132.2	158.3	8.7
1971	904.0	896.3	751.4	27.0	8.4	51.8	227.4	138.9	108.6	34.4	35.7	119.1	144.9	7.7
1970	836.1	829.7	697.5	25.6	8.3	47.2	215.9	128.3	97.8	31.2	33.1	110.1	132.2	6.4
1969	799.7	793.5	675.1	24.8	7.3	44.9	222.7	121.2	91.8	29.9	31.2	101.3	118.4	6.2
1968	740.4	734.2	626.5	22.5	7.1	40.1	211.9	111.7	85.2	28.0	28.8	91.2	107.7	6.2
1967	677.7	672.2	575.9	21.7	6.4	36.7	194.7	101.8	78.7	26.0	26.6	83.3	96.3	5.5
1966	642.5	637.3	550.6	22.7	6.3	35.1	190.7	95.2	74.1	25.5	25.4	75.7	86.7	5.2
1965	585.2	579.8	502.9	21.2	6.1	32.1	172.0	88.2	68.2	23.7	23.3	68.0	76.9	5.4
1964	538.1	533.1	461.5	18.4	6.0	29.3	154.9	82.5	63.7	21.8	22.0	62.9	71.5	5.0
1963	501.1	496.6	430.6	19.0	5.8	26.7	144.4	75.8	60.0	20.6	20.5	57.6	66.0	4.6
1962	475.1	470.9	409.3	19.0	5.5	25.0	136.5	72.7	57.6	19.6	19.3	54.0	61.6	4.2
1961	443.5	439.8	382.5	18.6	5.6	23.3	125.3	68.3	54.4	18.7	18.2	50.2	57.3	3.6
1960	429.2	425.9	372.4	17.7	5.6	22.3	125.5	66.7	51.6	18.5	17.4	47.0	53.5	3.2
1959	413.6	410.8	360.9	16.9	5.5	21.8	124.6	65.4	48.3	18.2	16.0	44.1	49.9	2.9
1958	380.1	377.4	329.8	18.9	5.7	20.0	108.2	60.1	45.1	16.9	14.7	40.2	47.6	2.7
1957	378.0	374.8	330.8	16.7	6.6	20.5	116.6	59.0	41.9	17.8	13.8	38.1	44.0	3.2
1956	361.4	358.5	317.3	16.5	6.6	19.6	113.4	56.3	39.3	17.3	12.9	35.3	41.2	2.9
1955	340.4	337.9	299.3	16.5	5.9	17.6	108.2	53.5	37.1	16.2	12.0	32.3	38.6	2.5
1954	311.6	309.4	272.8	17.5	5.3	16.5	94.9	49.4	34.5	14.8	11.1	28.8	36.6	2.2
1953	312.5	310.5	274.6	18.1	5.5	16.4	100.6	48.3	31.7	16.0	10.3	27.7	35.9	2.0
1952	298.5	296.3	261.3	20.3	5.5	15.9	92.7	47.5	28.8	15.6	9.4	25.7	35.0	2.1
1951	284.3	282.3	251.5	21.2	5.8	14.7	90.5	45.8	26.1	15.1	8.5	24.0	30.7	2.0
1950	245.8	244.2	220.3	18.3	5.3	12.4	76.4	41.4	23.8	13.4	7.3	22.0	23.9	1.5
1949	221.5	220.1	197.5	17.3	4.5	10.9	64.9	39.2	21.4	12.1	6.7	20.4	22.7	1.3
1948	228.3	226.8	206.4	22.2	5.4	11.0	68.8	40.1	20.1	12.8	6.0	20.0	20.4	1.5
1947	202.9	201.7	182.1	19.3	4.3	8.5	59.6	37.7	18.0	11.6	5.1	18.1	19.6	1.2
1946	185.9	185.2	160.9	18.5	3.0	6.5	49.2	34.7	17.1	10.4	4.8	16.6	24.3	0.7
1945	183.7	183.4	146.4	15.7	2.8	4.3	52.2	28.1	14.5	10.5	4.2	14.1	36.9	0.4
1944	184.8	184.4	150.6	15.2	3.0	4.1	60.3	25.9	13.7	11.2	4.0	13.1	33.8	0.5
1943	172.5	172.1	145.0	15.0	2.8	5.5	58.3	24.0	13.0	10.8	4.0	11.8	27.1	0.4
1942	139.2	138.7	122.4	12.7	2.6	6.5	45.5	20.6	12.0	8.6	3.7	10.2	16.4	0.5
1941	105.9	105.4	94.9	8.5	2.4	4.2	33.2	17.5	10.6	6.3	3.3	8.8	10.6	0.5

Table 23-6. National Income Without Capital Consumption Adjustment by Industry Group, 1929–2006—*Continued*

(Billions of dollars.)

Year	Total	Domestic industries											Govern-ment	Rest of the world
		Total	Private industries											
			Total	Agriculture, forestry, and fishing	Mining	Con-struction	Manu-facturing	Wholesale and retail trade	Finance, insurance, and real estate	Trans-portation	Commu-nication and public utilities	Services		
1940	82.5	82.2	73.4	6.2	1.9	2.6	22.5	14.7	9.5	5.0	3.0	8.0	8.8	0.4
1939	74.1	73.7	65.1	6.1	1.6	2.3	18.1	12.7	9.2	4.6	2.9	7.5	8.6	0.4
1938	68.8	68.4	59.8	6.1	1.6	2.0	15.1	12.3	8.9	4.1	2.7	7.2	8.6	0.4
1937	75.2	74.8	67.0	7.7	2.0	2.1	19.5	12.5	8.3	4.6	2.7	7.5	7.8	0.4
1936	66.4	66.1	58.0	5.9	1.6	2.0	16.3	11.0	7.7	4.3	2.5	6.8	8.2	0.3
1935	58.5	58.2	51.4	6.7	1.2	1.3	13.3	9.6	7.1	3.7	2.3	6.1	6.8	0.3
1934	50.8	50.6	44.3	4.3	1.2	1.1	11.0	8.5	6.7	3.4	2.2	5.7	6.3	0.3
1933	41.6	41.3	36.0	3.9	0.6	0.8	7.7	5.9	6.9	3.1	2.0	5.1	5.4	0.3
1932	44.2	43.8	38.6	3.6	0.7	1.1	7.3	6.9	8.0	3.2	2.3	5.6	5.2	0.4
1931	61.0	60.5	55.1	5.3	1.0	2.2	12.5	10.2	9.7	4.4	2.6	7.2	5.5	0.5
1930	76.7	76.0	70.7	6.6	1.7	3.2	18.3	12.7	11.6	5.6	2.8	8.3	5.3	0.7
1929	88.2	87.4	82.3	8.7	2.1	3.8	22.0	13.9	13.7	6.6	2.8	8.8	5.1	0.8

Source: U.S. Department of Commerce, Bureau of Economic Analysis.

Table 23-7. Personal Income by States, 1929–2005

Year		Total income (millions of dollars)											
	Alabama	Alaska	Arizona	Arkansas	California	Colorado	Connecticut	Delaware	District of Columbia	Florida	Georgia	Hawaii	Idaho
2005	132 796	23 634	179 765	74 687	1 338 181	177 025	167 858	31 265	30 270	590 954	282 347	44 044	40 241
2004	125 330	22 363	164 495	70 988	1 262 306	166 188	158 566	29 657	28 352	547 107	265 599	41 176	37 497
2003	118 516	21 416	151 708	66 325	1 184 265	157 035	148 822	27 620	26 619	511 977	250 735	38 115	34 654
2002	113 835	20 722	144 150	63 234	1 147 716	153 066	146 997	26 530	25 786	495 489	244 957	36 370	33 849
2001	110 421	20 050	138 854	61 967	1 135 304	152 700	147 356	25 537	25 525	478 637	240 616	35 126	33 054
2000	105 807	18 741	132 558	58 726	1 103 842	144 394	141 570	24 277	23 102	457 539	230 356	34 451	31 290
1999	100 662	17 557	120 857	56 052	999 228	128 860	129 807	22 416	21 115	423 834	212 081	32 646	29 068
1998	97 012	17 085	113 370	53 810	936 009	118 493	123 918	21 565	20 562	402 454	198 782	31 757	27 287
1997	91 419	16 402	103 557	50 955	860 545	107 873	115 134	19 895	19 580	372 094	182 868	31 002	25 367
1996	86 972	15 704	95 514	48 679	810 448	100 233	108 189	19 063	18 766	351 355	172 113	30 122	24 360
1995	83 534	15 415	88 333	45 829	765 806	92 704	103 199	17 811	18 151	329 885	158 858	29 926	22 871
1994	79 265	15 113	81 555	43 272	730 529	85 671	98 467	16 884	18 169	308 508	148 234	29 424	21 422
1993	74 863	14 709	74 370	40 822	707 906	79 697	95 882	16 224	17 857	293 167	137 607	28 799	20 073
1992	71 977	14 004	69 609	39 162	696 670	73 794	93 615	15 754	17 279	278 700	130 041	27 910	18 318
1991	67 250	13 207	65 390	36 043	662 728	68 283	87 567	15 089	16 564	264 449	120 222	26 026	16 692
1990	63 679	12 617	62 649	34 076	648 263	64 748	87 251	14 343	16 025	254 984	114 643	24 704	15 918
1989	59 911	11 834	59 413	32 334	601 456	60 652	84 330	13 655	15 063	238 049	107 069	22 462	14 647
1988	55 120	10 789	55 246	30 223	557 867	55 884	77 821	12 308	14 042	213 834	99 402	20 161	13 300
1987	51 502	10 440	51 506	28 308	515 252	53 063	70 599	11 293	12 829	194 991	91 395	18 386	12 366
1986	48 553	10 780	47 730	27 307	478 832	51 108	64 552	10 484	12 135	180 125	85 000	17 225	11 833
1985	45 944	10 821	43 833	26 203	448 335	49 537	59 962	9 884	11 516	166 837	78 332	16 311	11 572
1984	42 692	10 019	39 524	24 523	413 355	46 846	55 880	9 046	10 829	152 157	71 237	15 352	10 973
1983	38 491	9 365	34 656	21 884	369 132	42 631	49 978	8 172	9 796	136 037	62 289	14 087	10 143
1982	35 988	8 335	31 598	20 511	341 593	39 663	46 731	7 593	9 352	122 669	56 834	12 715	9 368
1981	34 004	6 934	29 889	19 545	319 962	36 126	43 267	7 051	8 610	113 537	52 395	12 015	9 032
1980	30 564	6 025	26 073	17 221	284 455	31 259	38 470	6 394	7 845	97 741	46 192	11 073	8 198
1979	27 855	5 328	22 702	16 084	252 213	27 342	34 008	5 718	7 432	84 094	41 633	9 679	7 363
1978	24 923	5 013	19 100	14 587	219 674	23 625	30 081	5 179	7 001	72 332	36 945	8 497	6 668
1977	22 005	4 906	16 122	12 514	191 536	20 400	26 909	4 707	6 615	62 309	32 423	7 652	5 751
1976	19 893	4 736	14 262	11 179	171 412	18 144	24 334	4 356	6 110	55 438	29 189	7 032	5 241
1975	17 537	3 932	12 640	10 047	152 721	16 347	22 329	3 962	5 731	50 353	26 061	6 465	4 635
1974	15 786	2 795	11 854	9 191	138 734	14 901	20 955	3 701	5 266	46 712	24 312	5 965	4 349
1973	14 181	2 266	10 476	8 203	124 102	13 252	19 154	3 400	4 785	41 495	22 064	5 178	3 683
1972	12 544	1 939	9 013	6 893	112 211	11 520	17 488	3 043	4 517	35 365	19 411	4 660	3 168
1971	11 279	1 766	7 860	6 105	102 416	10 166	16 227	2 765	4 162	30 701	17 268	4 221	2 778
1970	10 276	1 595	6 897	5 500	96 421	9 018	15 468	2 536	3 789	27 419	15 630	3 888	2 552
1969	9 453	1 406	6 061	5 010	89 485	7 983	14 540	2 387	3 450	24 297	14 390	3 379	2 311
1968	8 669	1 214	5 200	4 581	81 589	7 168	13 170	2 178	3 378	20 898	12 956	2 950	2 023
1967	7 933	1 114	4 533	4 219	74 368	6 451	12 314	1 987	3 178	18 155	11 703	2 620	1 896
1966	7 512	1 006	4 175	3 976	69 086	5 986	11 247	1 863	2 961	16 389	10 779	2 412	1 785
1965	6 990	931	3 821	3 573	63 503	5 559	10 237	1 758	2 837	14 873	9 780	2 205	1 752
1964	6 417	862	3 594	3 370	59 422	5 197	9 517	1 595	2 683	13 573	8 866	2 012	1 530
1963	5 905	762	3 352	3 104	54 811	4 915	8 863	1 473	2 556	12 380	8 180	1 850	1 481
1962	5 539	700	3 188	2 916	51 276	4 692	8 405	1 375	2 440	11 535	7 533	1 735	1 448
1961	5 263	665	2 959	2 729	47 512	4 457	7 866	1 298	2 327	10 692	7 001	1 620	1 351
1960	5 100	666	2 719	2 514	44 794	4 139	7 444	1 259	2 237	10 123	6 716	1 497	1 273
1959	4 889	564	2 489	2 480	42 383	3 866	7 145	1 201	2 151	9 664	6 421	1 307	1 243
1958	4 643	528	2 249	2 268	38 627	3 595	6 679	1 148	2 086	8 736	6 021	1 168	1 174
1957	4 416	539	2 130	2 156	36 781	3 501	6 629	1 127	1 995	8 028	5 736	1 107	1 145
1956	4 164	551	1 948	2 095	34 210	3 185	6 217	1 121	1 941	7 248	5 547	1 039	1 085
1955	3 882	506	1 729	2 029	31 248	2 890	5 696	975	1 857	6 269	5 175	983	986
1954	3 432	495	1 583	1 862	28 384	2 646	5 286	849	1 859	5 476	4 690	934	935
1953	3 544	514	1 534	1 897	27 550	2 594	5 188	822	1 904	5 186	4 717	921	924
1952	3 394	488	1 445	1 887	25 682	2 567	4 781	765	1 968	4 654	4 587	892	965
1951	3 198	446	1 274	1 820	23 154	2 381	4 377	713	1 885	4 135	4 253	816	882
1950	2 778	324	1 033	1 616	20 036	2 015	3 813	666	1 796	3 664	3 683	713	784
1949	2 499	. . .	932	1 500	18 026	1 852	3 380	570	1 710	3 222	3 223	. . .	728
1948	2 616	. . .	914	1 617	17 740	1 836	3 464	526	1 652	3 097	3 220	. . .	741
1947	2 369	. . .	773	1 360	16 785	1 679	3 351	509	1 554	2 962	2 901	. . .	667
1946	2 191	. . .	690	1 364	16 258	1 449	3 020	470	1 541	2 891	2 748	. . .	612
1945	2 173	. . .	664	1 301	15 223	1 324	2 789	436	1 432	2 954	2 715	. . .	556
1944	2 067	. . .	649	1 217	14 664	1 197	2 880	430	1 359	2 831	2 627	. . .	563
1943	1 899	. . .	664	1 028	13 355	1 196	2 863	411	1 355	2 520	2 353	. . .	511
1942	1 528	. . .	486	954	10 050	1 014	2 549	363	1 171	1 723	1 824	. . .	440
1941	1 087	. . .	314	673	7 364	729	2 004	321	930	1 236	1 334	. . .	299
1940	800	. . .	252	508	5 868	616	1 568	276	813	1 000	1 050	. . .	242
1939	708	. . .	237	486	5 302	578	1 418	236	741	910	964	. . .	228
1938	679	. . .	223	446	5 134	563	1 294	204	706	816	896	. . .	219
1937	738	. . .	228	488	5 189	587	1 443	241	722	832	951	. . .	215
1936	690	. . .	205	468	4 887	590	1 347	220	695	743	899	. . .	235
1935	591	. . .	180	391	4 073	478	1 177	177	599	606	793	. . .	192
1934	567	. . .	155	350	3 652	396	1 078	161	525	552	725	. . .	191
1933	443	. . .	131	291	3 258	378	958	140	478	447	602	. . .	105
1932	431	. . .	137	289	3 417	377	1 015	145	541	485	586	. . .	126
1931	593	. . .	184	397	4 360	498	1 303	187	603	595	749	. . .	170
1930	707	. . .	226	424	5 066	601	1 486	205	613	691	892	. . .	225
1929	855	. . .	258	575	5 482	639	1 633	243	613	749	1 007	. . .	227

. . . = Not available.

Table 23-7. Personal Income by States, 1929–2005—*Continued*

Year	Alabama	Alaska	Arizona	Arkansas	California	Colorado	Connecticut	Delaware	District of Columbia	Florida	Georgia	Hawaii	Idaho
2005	29 136	35 612	30 267	26 874	37 036	37 946	47 819	37 065	54 985	33 219	31 121	34 539	28 158
2004	27 695	34 000	28 658	25 814	35 219	36 113	45 318	35 728	51 155	31 469	29 782	32 625	26 877
2003	26 326	33 023	27 199	24 329	33 400	34 528	42 693	33 772	47 718	30 128	28 666	30 536	25 330
2002	25 409	32 343	26 507	23 363	32 803	34 027	42 505	32 925	45 670	29 709	28 544	29 464	25 185
2001	24 717	31 711	26 219	23 023	32 882	34 493	42 930	32 105	44 834	29 273	28 592	28 748	25 019
2000	23 764	29 867	25 660	21 925	32 463	33 371	41 489	30 869	40 456	28 509	27 989	28 422	24 075
1999	22 722	28 100	24 057	21 137	29 828	30 492	38 332	28 925	37 030	26 894	26 359	26 973	22 786
1998	22 025	27 560	23 216	20 489	28 374	28 784	36 822	28 252	36 379	25 987	25 279	26 132	21 789
1997	20 930	26 759	21 861	19 590	26 490	26 846	34 375	26 475	34 488	24 502	23 795	25 587	20 648
1996	20 081	25 805	20 823	18 926	25 570	25 312	32 424	25 727	32 786	23 655	22 945	25 024	20 248
1995	19 441	25 504	19 929	18 076	24 161	24 226	31 045	24 407	31 266	22 691	21 677	25 004	19 426
1994	18 606	25 050	19 212	17 350	23 203	23 004	29 693	23 530	30 835	21 666	20 711	24 777	18 707
1993	17 764	24 538	18 293	16 619	22 635	22 054	28 975	22 967	29 996	21 050	19 719	24 555	18 103
1992	17 327	23 786	17 777	16 209	22 492	21 109	28 362	22 670	28 916	20 417	19 075	24 089	17 093
1991	16 406	23 161	17 260	15 124	21 750	20 160	26 512	22 090	27 567	19 780	18 070	22 895	16 030
1990	15 723	22 804	17 005	14 460	21 638	19 575	26 504	21 422	26 473	19 564	17 603	22 186	15 724
1989	14 865	21 628	16 403	13 781	20 585	18 515	25 684	20 743	24 133	18 836	16 701	20 521	14 729
1988	13 698	19 907	15 627	12 901	19 599	17 130	23 784	19 006	22 273	17 376	15 738	18 671	13 493
1987	12 826	19 357	14 985	12 085	18 549	16 275	21 741	17 730	20 141	16 253	14 721	17 217	12 554
1986	12 164	19 807	14 427	11 710	17 668	15 786	20 024	16 706	19 013	15 438	13 970	16 377	11 949
1985	11 566	20 321	13 769	11 260	16 956	15 438	18 731	15 987	18 148	14 698	13 137	15 688	11 641
1984	10 803	19 503	12 886	10 571	15 994	14 778	17 572	14 792	17 098	13 782	12 209	14 935	11 074
1983	9 784	19 174	11 673	9 491	14 556	13 604	15 804	13 498	15 490	12 655	10 874	13 910	10 330
1982	9 168	18 538	10 934	8 940	13 763	12 955	14 887	12 673	14 747	11 715	10 059	12 794	9 621
1981	8 678	16 569	10 636	8 523	13 175	12 131	13 828	11 831	13 519	11 139	9 409	12 283	9 387
1980	7 836	14 866	9 524	7 524	11 951	10 746	12 357	10 748	12 291	9 933	8 420	11 443	8 648
1979	7 199	13 204	8 604	7 088	10 846	9 596	10 971	9 549	11 336	8 879	7 722	10 188	7 894
1978	6 500	12 464	7 586	6 509	9 618	8 539	9 720	8 658	10 448	7 921	6 989	9 148	7 319
1977	5 817	12 346	6 642	5 670	8 570	7 567	8 712	7 913	9 702	7 010	6 221	8 356	6 510
1976	5 323	12 048	6 074	5 155	7 815	6 895	7 885	7 349	8 775	6 376	5 694	7 880	6 116
1975	4 765	10 600	5 528	4 655	7 091	6 321	7 239	6 729	8 068	5 895	5 152	7 388	5 571
1974	4 351	8 108	5 329	4 376	6 553	5 864	6 813	6 347	7 306	5 616	4 867	6 952	5 382
1973	3 960	6 801	4 929	3 985	5 947	5 310	6 241	5 871	6 522	5 235	4 497	6 151	4 709
1972	3 544	5 939	4 487	3 415	5 451	4 791	5 697	5 303	6 073	4 703	4 038	5 697	4 150
1971	3 225	5 581	4 145	3 096	5 034	4 413	5 300	4 892	5 545	4 286	3 666	5 332	3 761
1970	2 979	5 243	3 843	2 849	4 815	4 055	5 090	4 608	5 018	4 006	3 394	5 096	3 558
1969	2 748	4 749	3 489	2 619	4 540	3 686	4 847	4 421	4 528	3 659	3 162	4 548	3 269
1968	2 516	4 258	3 092	2 409	4 207	3 381	4 443	4 079	4 342	3 249	2 891	4 019	2 910
1967	2 294	4 009	2 754	2 219	3 878	3 142	4 195	3 785	4 017	2 909	2 655	3 624	2 755
1966	2 169	3 713	2 587	2 094	3 663	2 982	3 874	3 610	3 744	2 685	2 462	3 397	2 591
1965	2 030	3 435	2 412	1 886	3 417	2 800	3 583	3 468	3 559	2 498	2 258	3 132	2 554
1964	1 890	3 276	2 310	1 777	3 274	2 638	3 401	3 210	3 363	2 348	2 082	2 874	2 250
1963	1 758	2 978	2 204	1 656	3 102	2 539	3 250	3 049	3 203	2 200	1 961	2 712	2 168
1962	1 667	2 846	2 167	1 574	3 004	2 471	3 175	2 933	3 097	2 113	1 844	2 536	2 092
1961	1 587	2 795	2 103	1 511	2 880	2 417	3 042	2 815	2 991	2 039	1 744	2 458	1 975
1960	1 558	2 907	2 059	1 405	2 823	2 340	2 926	2 805	2 924	2 023	1 698	2 332	1 898
1959	1 526	2 520	1 974	1 412	2 740	2 261	2 832	2 724	2 827	2 010	1 660	2 101	1 891
1958	1 468	2 357	1 885	1 314	2 596	2 157	2 731	2 651	2 756	1 887	1 583	1 931	1 817
1957	1 421	2 332	1 893	1 244	2 579	2 104	2 810	2 645	2 615	1 836	1 523	1 931	1 783
1956	1 356	2 460	1 850	1 230	2 495	1 960	2 684	2 749	2 558	1 791	1 499	1 895	1 728
1955	1 273	2 280	1 752	1 176	2 379	1 869	2 477	2 507	2 365	1 673	1 423	1 859	1 596
1954	1 139	2 304	1 696	1 074	2 227	1 773	2 350	2 306	2 350	1 562	1 302	1 853	1 559
1953	1 161	2 509	1 716	1 066	2 249	1 813	2 393	2 341	2 350	1 567	1 326	1 846	1 550
1952	1 106	2 584	1 716	1 027	2 207	1 880	2 298	2 244	2 445	1 474	1 280	1 802	1 644
1951	1 045	2 823	1 623	957	2 080	1 796	2 158	2 155	2 332	1 388	1 204	1 626	1 497
1950	909	2 400	1 367	847	1 877	1 521	1 891	2 075	2 228	1 304	1 065	1 429	1 329
1949	833	...	1 305	813	1 744	1 430	1 663	1 805	2 118	1 208	969	...	1 277
1948	881	...	1 324	886	1 763	1 454	1 720	1 685	1 967	1 201	988	...	1 345
1947	805	...	1 186	741	1 693	1 359	1 702	1 664	1 780	1 167	887	...	1 278
1946	754	...	1 117	756	1 671	1 211	1 580	1 565	1 725	1 169	845	...	1 203
1945	784	...	1 124	740	1 583	1 189	1 565	1 526	1 656	1 174	879	...	1 135
1944	738	...	1 050	687	1 583	1 065	1 599	1 504	1 577	1 114	831	...	1 095
1943	658	...	1 004	559	1 549	1 039	1 593	1 464	1 526	1 009	725	...	1 025
1942	518	...	917	481	1 286	895	1 418	1 291	1 384	787	567	...	914
1941	375	...	638	342	1 013	649	1 145	1 164	1 217	609	419	...	596
1940	281	...	505	260	844	545	918	1 027	1 178	522	337	...	463
1939	252	...	490	249	781	516	836	899	1 127	495	309	...	437
1938	244	...	478	231	771	506	769	795	1 106	460	290	...	426
1937	267	...	504	256	795	532	860	949	1 172	487	313	...	423
1936	251	...	462	247	771	542	806	868	1 105	450	302	...	475
1935	217	...	416	207	660	444	706	701	985	376	268	...	399
1934	211	...	362	187	603	368	653	645	925	348	244	...	403
1933	166	...	308	157	546	353	583	564	903	288	204	...	227
1932	162	...	321	157	580	354	620	590	1 054	319	200	...	274
1931	224	...	429	215	749	471	801	775	1 196	398	256	...	374
1930	267	...	520	228	887	578	921	857	1 256	470	307	...	503
1929	323	...	600	310	991	634	1 024	1 032	1 269	518	347	...	507

... = Not available.

Table 23-7. Personal Income by States, 1929–2005—*Continued*

Year						Total income (millions of dollars)							
	Illinois	Indiana	Iowa	Kansas	Kentucky	Louisiana	Maine	Maryland	Massa-chusetts	Michigan	Minnesota	Mississippi	Missouri
2005	461 014	196 160	95 858	90 126	118 998	112 275	41 300	233 874	283 391	335 164	191 830	73 955	185 026
2004	441 373	188 065	91 712	84 957	112 925	123 021	39 510	220 402	270 236	324 134	184 414	71 122	175 524
2003	427 003	178 929	84 051	80 904	106 836	116 196	37 281	206 292	255 403	318 283	173 394	67 038	167 042
2002	413 711	172 474	82 398	78 606	103 866	112 744	35 998	198 824	249 954	303 465	166 968	63 979	161 104
2001	407 254	167 881	79 456	77 564	101 346	110 256	35 107	191 657	249 095	299 542	162 578	62 739	156 937
2000	400 373	165 285	77 763	74 570	98 845	103 151	33 173	181 957	240 209	294 227	157 964	59 837	152 722
1999	373 385	154 842	73 285	70 158	91 462	98 200	31 016	167 075	216 221	278 062	146 722	56 719	142 925
1998	360 095	149 336	71 704	67 800	87 851	96 677	29 710	157 784	203 987	265 098	139 553	54 820	137 619
1997	337 897	138 794	68 297	63 356	82 436	91 432	27 830	147 843	189 885	248 821	128 388	51 514	129 992
1996	320 081	132 103	64 862	59 729	77 819	87 036	26 484	140 035	178 797	237 193	121 195	48 646	122 469
1995	301 688	125 269	60 012	56 073	73 389	83 535	25 044	133 814	168 623	227 466	112 209	45 973	115 948
1994	285 537	120 278	57 873	54 164	70 148	80 043	24 092	128 523	160 322	217 812	105 971	43 805	111 005
1993	271 174	113 428	53 098	51 729	66 791	75 161	23 156	122 906	152 578	201 574	98 571	40 596	104 699
1992	263 702	108 029	53 082	49 867	64 671	72 000	22 606	118 847	147 930	192 788	96 401	38 199	100 945
1991	245 434	100 361	49 808	46 541	60 160	67 628	21 681	113 436	141 024	181 655	90 050	35 607	94 900
1990	238 499	97 213	48 358	44 876	57 026	64 052	21 402	109 686	138 782	176 189	87 318	33 754	90 407
1989	225 574	92 341	45 981	42 157	53 733	59 437	20 499	103 528	134 399	168 637	82 088	32 164	86 570
1988	212 011	84 969	42 415	40 070	49 914	55 908	18 912	95 867	127 622	156 961	75 230	29 832	81 340
1987	197 603	79 846	41 242	38 146	47 171	53 052	17 231	87 696	116 181	147 486	71 516	27 962	77 057
1986	187 025	75 378	39 389	36 501	44 492	52 905	15 789	81 069	107 119	142 459	67 102	26 440	73 310
1985	178 529	71 838	38 171	35 078	42 974	53 398	14 602	75 325	99 445	134 083	63 458	25 602	69 812
1984	169 736	68 027	36 836	33 274	41 139	51 348	13 506	68 984	91 835	123 531	59 664	24 278	65 162
1983	153 546	61 123	33 153	30 221	36 630	47 894	12 108	61 841	81 246	111 468	52 586	22 021	58 534
1982	147 604	58 448	32 477	28 988	35 477	45 962	11 282	57 330	74 684	105 189	49 807	21 064	54 839
1981	139 569	56 488	31 569	26 764	33 296	42 887	10 415	52 794	68 062	102 206	46 460	19 928	51 359
1980	125 838	51 469	27 930	23 578	29 965	37 067	9 406	47 296	60 920	95 460	41 898	17 695	45 893
1979	117 000	48 256	26 584	21 690	27 838	32 342	8 434	42 381	54 427	89 727	37 996	16 425	42 601
1978	106 079	43 602	24 630	18 853	24 501	28 314	7 531	38 168	48 698	81 287	33 924	14 445	37 933
1977	95 637	38 910	21 225	16 937	21 788	24 636	6 789	34 360	43 863	72 863	30 085	12 937	33 874
1976	86 598	35 002	19 106	15 448	19 283	21 960	6 222	31 442	40 208	64 588	26 623	11 562	30 416
1975	78 990	31 197	17 841	14 097	17 113	19 263	5 386	28 592	37 100	57 191	24 404	10 093	27 494
1974	72 877	29 103	16 050	12 965	15 741	17 233	5 050	26 378	34 802	53 984	22 757	9 362	25 277
1973	66 471	27 177	15 460	11 943	13 974	15 132	4 520	23 923	32 108	50 370	21 099	8 489	23 574
1972	59 280	23 593	12 796	10 405	12 394	13 515	3 999	21 593	29 420	44 815	17 898	7 403	21 120
1971	54 617	21 549	11 421	9 309	11 185	12 348	3 650	19 684	27 244	40 381	16 467	6 495	19 396
1970	50 948	19 827	10 924	8 577	10 287	11 336	3 412	18 010	25 589	37 310	15 463	5 866	18 003
1969	48 062	19 099	10 244	7 934	9 503	10 498	3 115	16 281	23 770	36 400	14 201	5 345	16 522
1968	44 470	17 321	9 285	7 242	8 684	9 904	2 854	14 616	21 928	33 970	12 824	4 876	15 396
1967	41 436	15 932	8 638	6 662	7 934	9 049	2 669	13 210	20 043	30 675	11 644	4 459	13 920
1966	38 998	15 204	8 470	6 366	7 330	8 423	2 536	12 133	18 439	29 364	10 839	4 129	13 096
1965	35 930	14 059	7 769	5 932	6 701	7 477	2 376	10 998	17 060	26 865	9 988	3 792	12 229
1964	33 130	12 710	6 999	5 557	6 171	6 904	2 197	10 062	15 972	24 142	9 038	3 490	11 253
1963	31 012	11 930	6 680	5 285	5 900	6 446	2 035	9 216	14 956	21 983	8 685	3 363	10 660
1962	29 832	11 361	6 280	5 143	5 611	6 041	1 971	8 608	14 390	20 559	8 190	3 054	10 154
1961	28 251	10 622	6 008	4 934	5 288	5 723	1 894	7 962	13 595	19 156	7 758	2 917	9 635
1960	27 236	10 324	5 679	4 726	4 967	5 510	1 871	7 492	12 957	19 096	7 382	2 698	9 326
1959	26 387	9 832	5 528	4 548	4 812	5 406	1 771	7 127	12 434	18 315	6 950	2 661	9 054
1958	24 827	9 233	5 388	4 495	4 569	5 159	1 696	6 734	11 627	17 223	6 680	2 412	8 556
1957	24 383	9 250	5 265	4 066	4 367	5 034	1 622	6 512	11 319	17 480	6 318	2 219	8 162
1956	23 369	8 951	4 751	3 858	4 166	4 554	1 565	6 138	10 731	16 989	5 954	2 192	7 930
1955	21 418	8 319	4 475	3 668	3 918	4 115	1 477	5 613	10 109	16 303	5 676	2 153	7 515
1954	20 144	7 699	4 694	3 658	3 741	3 861	1 342	5 203	9 476	14 671	5 367	1 916	7 019
1953	20 020	8 126	4 357	3 468	3 789	3 849	1 323	5 179	9 356	15 021	5 217	1 978	6 983
1952	18 725	7 377	4 530	3 612	3 612	3 631	1 316	4 859	8 813	13 203	4 949	1 949	6 589
1951	17 808	7 009	4 286	3 124	3 390	3 350	1 209	4 430	8 459	12 320	4 762	1 841	6 241
1950	16 003	6 047	4 021	2 803	2 906	3 012	1 095	3 867	7 758	11 009	4 306	1 675	5 658
1949	14 609	5 388	3 496	2 501	2 672	2 828	1 068	3 484	7 016	9 669	3 898	1 470	5 151
1948	15 532	5 643	4 177	2 558	2 804	2 644	1 088	3 407	7 065	9 710	4 161	1 666	5 288
1947	13 672	4 963	3 054	2 426	2 423	2 282	999	3 057	6 584	8 903	3 551	1 412	4 709
1946	12 523	4 458	3 071	2 048	2 279	2 116	947	2 928	6 333	7 808	3 256	1 266	4 477
1945	11 151	4 284	2 513	2 003	2 091	2 146	865	2 815	5 811	7 246	2 812	1 308	3 968
1944	10 697	4 116	2 300	2 061	2 005	2 170	887	2 854	5 667	7 593	2 537	1 333	3 799
1943	9 766	3 918	2 388	1 883	1 885	2 012	889	2 698	5 397	7 309	2 435	1 202	3 558
1942	8 341	3 211	2 038	1 506	1 512	1 505	718	2 247	4 708	5 830	2 122	967	3 085
1941	7 130	2 521	1 517	976	1 125	1 123	537	1 669	3 963	4 530	1 673	672	2 441
1940	5 937	1 890	1 272	760	916	862	447	1 306	3 364	3 616	1 461	467	1 964
1939	5 557	1 764	1 197	696	862	839	419	1 188	3 146	3 224	1 434	445	1 906
1938	5 096	1 598	1 143	706	831	795	397	1 119	2 933	2 893	1 359	427	1 797
1937	5 744	1 847	1 306	794	949	796	429	1 167	3 192	3 405	1 482	468	1 927
1936	5 092	1 610	986	723	813	742	425	1 078	3 110	3 027	1 291	474	1 771
1935	4 471	1 401	1 073	677	727	646	359	948	2 793	2 564	1 224	365	1 597
1934	3 921	1 190	675	536	635	584	345	895	2 622	2 175	964	356	1 387
1933	3 392	971	630	469	553	494	304	790	2 395	1 659	824	266	1 260
1932	3 761	1 016	740	501	565	518	308	859	2 613	1 885	961	254	1 368
1931	5 155	1 425	994	754	772	675	396	1 058	3 223	2 592	1 196	349	1 823
1930	6 169	1 667	1 263	879	852	748	461	1 164	3 551	3 174	1 423	405	2 046
1929	7 211	1 958	1 429	994	1 023	863	479	1 245	3 832	3 788	1 541	571	2 250

Table 23-7. Personal Income by States, 1929–2005—*Continued*

	Total income (millions of dollars)												
Year	Illinois	Indiana	Iowa	Kansas	Kentucky	Louisiana	Maine	Maryland	Massa-chusetts	Michigan	Minnesota	Mississippi	Missouri
2005	36 120	31 276	32 315	32 836	28 513	24 820	31 252	41 760	44 289	33 116	37 373	25 318	31 899
2004	34 721	30 204	31 058	31 078	27 265	27 297	30 046	39 631	42 176	32 079	36 184	24 518	30 475
2003	33 755	28 877	28 576	29 698	25 951	25 877	28 497	37 423	39 798	31 582	34 256	23 271	29 210
2002	32 869	28 023	28 081	28 980	25 404	25 194	27 756	36 533	38 985	30 227	33 237	22 321	28 358
2001	32 532	27 406	27 106	28 718	24 920	24 692	27 292	35 627	38 953	29 946	32 616	21 955	27 809
2000	32 185	27 132	26 554	27 694	24 412	23 079	25 969	34 257	37 756	29 552	32 017	21 005	27 241
1999	30 212	25 615	25 118	26 195	22 763	22 014	24 484	31 796	34 227	28 095	30 106	20 053	25 697
1998	29 343	24 894	24 701	25 483	22 043	21 772	23 596	30 317	32 524	26 919	28 993	19 545	24 923
1997	27 729	23 306	23 623	24 041	20 855	20 681	22 179	28 666	30 498	25 367	26 953	18 550	23 716
1996	26 449	22 368	22 521	22 845	19 854	19 786	21 203	27 393	28 933	24 306	25 716	17 702	22 548
1995	25 123	21 408	20 929	21 558	18 879	19 077	20 140	26 393	27 457	23 508	24 078	16 885	21 559
1994	23 969	20 761	20 301	20 990	18 225	18 411	19 387	25 587	26 303	22 694	22 985	16 291	20 848
1993	22 962	19 764	18 716	20 234	17 520	17 413	18 869	24 720	25 176	21 129	21 636	15 290	19 862
1992	22 550	19 037	18 834	19 692	17 175	16 771	18 253	24 139	24 538	20 338	21 443	14 559	19 349
1991	21 215	17 869	17 804	18 626	16 162	15 900	17 526	23 304	23 432	19 324	20 278	13 702	18 353
1990	20 824	17 491	17 389	18 085	15 437	15 173	17 376	22 852	23 043	18 922	19 891	13 089	17 627
1989	19 770	16 717	16 596	17 048	14 612	13 976	16 803	21 900	22 342	18 225	18 923	12 495	16 988
1988	18 613	15 472	15 321	16 275	13 564	13 036	15 710	20 582	21 341	17 028	17 511	11 561	16 006
1987	17 347	14 589	14 905	15 599	12 807	12 212	14 546	19 208	19 575	16 053	16 886	10 802	15 239
1986	16 424	13 820	14 108	15 005	12 065	12 005	13 494	18 068	18 148	15 607	15 957	10 194	14 595
1985	15 661	13 159	13 490	14 451	11 631	12 113	12 556	17 069	16 910	14 773	15 166	9 892	13 962
1984	14 873	12 463	12 886	13 726	11 132	11 669	11 687	15 803	15 723	13 651	14 350	9 417	13 097
1983	13 459	11 214	11 550	12 511	9 915	10 897	10 577	14 337	14 009	12 320	12 698	8 576	11 840
1982	12 921	10 689	11 245	12 072	9 631	10 560	9 925	13 386	12 941	11 540	12 056	8 238	11 125
1981	12 196	10 307	10 856	11 223	9 072	10 013	9 193	12 388	11 798	11 098	11 299	7 849	10 413
1980	11 005	9 374	9 585	9 953	8 178	8 777	8 347	11 187	10 602	10 314	10 256	7 007	9 324
1979	10 243	8 814	9 114	9 240	7 640	7 813	7 497	10 035	9 472	9 701	9 409	6 549	8 713
1978	9 277	8 006	8 438	8 082	6 784	6 951	6 751	9 062	8 480	8 834	8 471	5 806	7 787
1977	8 385	7 199	7 283	7 307	6 095	6 135	6 142	8 191	7 636	7 957	7 559	5 259	6 991
1976	7 623	6 516	6 580	6 721	5 462	5 557	5 708	7 536	6 994	7 084	6 729	4 757	6 306
1975	6 986	5 830	6 192	6 186	4 933	4 956	5 019	6 878	6 439	6 279	6 216	4 205	5 733
1974	6 464	5 440	5 596	5 717	4 607	4 510	4 764	6 382	6 024	5 926	5 838	3 936	5 282
1973	5 903	5 100	5 398	5 274	4 145	3 994	4 319	5 822	5 551	5 552	5 431	3 613	4 937
1972	5 266	4 455	4 473	4 613	3 715	3 593	3 864	5 291	5 106	4 966	4 628	3 208	4 443
1971	4 874	4 105	4 005	4 145	3 391	3 328	3 594	4 894	4 748	4 501	4 275	2 867	4 107
1970	4 580	3 810	3 862	3 816	3 184	3 106	3 423	4 573	4 486	4 194	4 053	2 641	3 843
1969	4 354	3 714	3 652	3 548	2 971	2 901	3 140	4 209	4 207	4 145	3 779	2 408	3 561
1968	4 045	3 401	3 312	3 268	2 718	2 749	2 872	3 831	3 903	3 906	3 463	2 197	3 370
1967	3 785	3 153	3 093	3 032	2 501	2 527	2 658	3 516	3 583	3 554	3 182	2 001	3 067
1966	3 599	3 041	3 067	2 894	2 329	2 331	2 539	3 284	3 331	3 450	2 997	1 839	2 895
1965	3 360	2 856	2 833	2 689	2 134	2 139	2 383	3 055	3 101	3 215	2 781	1 688	2 738
1964	3 131	2 617	2 549	2 516	1 972	2 003	2 212	2 881	2 932	2 949	2 540	1 557	2 533
1963	2 981	2 486	2 432	2 384	1 906	1 909	2 049	2 722	2 799	2 728	2 460	1 499	2 427
1962	2 902	2 399	2 284	2 305	1 822	1 806	1 983	2 638	2 734	2 592	2 331	1 362	2 330
1961	2 789	2 246	2 180	2 227	1 731	1 741	1 903	2 507	2 605	2 427	2 236	1 322	2 215
1960	2 700	2 209	2 061	2 165	1 633	1 690	1 919	2 407	2 511	2 438	2 155	1 237	2 156
1959	2 642	2 131	2 026	2 106	1 604	1 685	1 850	2 324	2 430	2 358	2 065	1 245	2 126
1958	2 511	2 015	1 990	2 098	1 543	1 635	1 797	2 258	2 321	2 246	2 016	1 156	2 044
1957	2 522	2 042	1 939	1 911	1 491	1 616	1 720	2 267	2 296	2 309	1 930	1 063	1 949
1956	2 452	2 008	1 758	1 821	1 437	1 502	1 669	2 184	2 194	2 275	1 838	1 051	1 905
1955	2 270	1 907	1 670	1 753	1 346	1 397	1 581	2 047	2 071	2 238	1 790	1 045	1 818
1954	2 177	1 805	1 788	1 791	1 289	1 339	1 448	1 938	1 930	2 076	1 724	928	1 726
1953	2 209	1 943	1 657	1 739	1 305	1 343	1 449	2 017	1 947	2 202	1 711	940	1 737
1952	2 091	1 778	1 725	1 827	1 237	1 278	1 438	1 944	1 895	1 985	1 633	906	1 659
1951	2 026	1 711	1 638	1 602	1 153	1 210	1 319	1 815	1 817	1 896	1 582	851	1 554
1950	1 831	1 524	1 532	1 463	990	1 117	1 195	1 642	1 656	1 718	1 437	770	1 427
1949	1 685	1 361	1 356	1 299	938	1 074	1 183	1 496	1 480	1 527	1 328	705	1 327
1948	1 816	1 456	1 642	1 352	995	1 019	1 240	1 500	1 512	1 563	1 451	802	1 376
1947	1 639	1 313	1 217	1 310	865	885	1 169	1 355	1 435	1 466	1 270	670	1 224
1946	1 534	1 204	1 245	1 136	826	833	1 134	1 315	1 396	1 329	1 190	611	1 191
1945	1 465	1 251	1 092	1 165	803	889	1 079	1 312	1 348	1 325	1 110	629	1 130
1944	1 386	1 198	1 003	1 169	767	876	1 102	1 324	1 299	1 391	1 006	629	1 068
1943	1 258	1 138	1 024	1 045	701	786	1 102	1 287	1 262	1 354	947	533	963
1942	1 036	913	835	851	538	592	857	1 117	1 073	1 050	797	439	806
1941	892	724	609	552	395	449	631	870	901	829	615	307	640
1940	751	551	501	425	320	364	526	710	779	680	524	215	519
1939	704	518	475	382	305	360	495	663	724	625	517	205	504
1938	648	472	458	383	297	348	471	633	672	572	494	201	475
1937	731	547	523	428	341	353	510	665	732	685	540	224	508
1936	650	481	393	387	294	330	506	618	714	619	472	229	466
1935	573	421	425	362	265	290	430	548	643	530	451	177	420
1934	505	359	269	287	233	265	416	523	609	453	358	174	367
1933	437	294	253	250	205	227	371	466	559	347	308	131	334
1932	486	310	297	266	211	241	377	512	613	394	363	127	365
1931	671	438	400	401	291	318	491	638	759	540	457	175	491
1930	807	514	510	467	325	355	576	712	836	657	552	202	561
1929	948	607	581	532	393	414	601	768	906	790	599	286	621

Table 23-7. Personal Income by States, 1929–2005—*Continued*

Year	Montana	Nebraska	Nevada	New Hampshire	New Jersey	New Mexico	New York	North Carolina	North Dakota	Ohio	Oklahoma	Oregon	Pennsylvania
							Total income (millions of dollars)						
2005	27 497	59 124	86 650	50 312	381 595	53 308	779 941	265 296	19 988	372 332	104 060	116 889	433 752
2004	25 635	56 523	78 822	47 570	361 524	49 828	737 756	250 427	18 768	356 796	98 095	109 757	412 890
2003	24 028	53 438	71 606	44 422	342 362	46 779	691 123	234 638	18 250	342 425	93 092	103 890	392 792
2002	22 819	50 390	66 632	43 393	337 009	44 987	677 604	228 684	16 743	333 158	90 178	101 882	382 251
2001	22 359	49 303	64 367	42 624	332 951	44 138	679 886	225 395	16 465	325 623	90 161	99 020	372 339
2000	20 716	47 329	61 428	41 429	323 554	40 318	663 005	218 668	16 097	320 538	84 310	96 402	364 838
1999	19 373	45 116	56 462	37 125	294 385	38 046	619 659	203 187	14 934	304 464	77 565	89 873	342 611
1998	18 857	43 314	52 371	35 149	282 721	37 046	591 847	193 223	14 810	294 292	74 118	85 629	330 161
1997	17 688	40 576	47 388	32 420	263 420	34 961	557 024	180 163	13 440	278 049	69 720	80 854	311 509
1996	16 880	39 382	43 466	31 045	248 320	33 345	528 363	167 416	13 702	262 201	65 944	75 975	297 494
1995	16 084	36 006	39 250	28 647	233 937	31 701	501 667	156 407	12 221	252 003	62 395	70 990	283 764
1994	15 384	34 012	35 641	26 972	220 859	29 662	475 979	146 620	12 255	242 146	60 283	65 735	272 695
1993	15 012	32 105	32 143	25 273	213 222	27 753	462 008	137 865	11 351	229 065	57 937	61 349	263 462
1992	13 928	31 184	29 844	24 594	207 904	25 963	453 737	129 957	11 277	221 277	55 958	57 547	255 874
1991	13 213	29 563	26 910	23 518	194 174	24 302	434 304	119 927	10 351	209 066	52 565	54 256	242 822
1990	12 361	28 444	24 837	22 817	190 753	22 708	423 897	114 926	10 166	203 630	50 971	51 515	234 334
1989	11 707	26 497	22 019	22 615	181 461	21 173	400 769	108 309	9 338	192 358	48 111	47 580	220 748
1988	10 640	25 095	19 531	21 178	169 577	19 816	372 771	99 786	8 343	179 628	45 023	43 446	203 661
1987	10 448	23 549	17 260	19 252	154 440	18 769	341 560	91 611	9 057	167 984	43 171	39 999	189 585
1986	10 148	22 565	15 856	17 407	143 017	17 993	320 223	85 223	8 796	160 469	43 291	37 965	178 939
1985	9 793	21 978	14 723	15 763	133 915	17 376	300 275	79 417	8 710	153 758	43 614	36 197	170 050
1984	9 609	20 826	13 521	14 211	124 744	16 030	281 237	72 997	8 410	144 833	41 833	34 350	160 164
1983	9 009	18 630	12 317	12 517	112 659	14 594	252 521	63 973	7 734	131 008	38 747	31 490	147 915
1982	8 566	17 984	11 594	11 382	104 313	13 559	235 868	58 508	7 383	123 709	37 938	29 672	141 241
1981	8 124	16 722	10 809	10 323	96 485	12 415	216 592	54 553	6 819	118 192	33 952	28 882	132 196
1980	7 144	14 403	9 480	9 104	86 355	10 929	193 492	48 344	5 174	108 500	28 906	26 710	119 692
1979	6 549	13 742	8 237	8 007	77 188	9 756	175 040	43 288	5 477	99 899	25 200	24 275	109 533
1978	6 053	12 674	7 035	6 960	69 206	8 571	159 114	38 921	5 294	89 887	21 518	21 272	98 539
1977	5 119	10 870	5 798	6 009	62 130	7 459	145 544	34 339	4 172	80 906	18 874	18 431	89 035
1976	4 703	9 996	4 993	5 301	56 572	6 606	134 395	31 233	3 990	72 611	16 867	16 398	80 837
1975	4 341	9 507	4 345	4 642	51 658	5 866	125 420	27 889	4 044	65 556	15 176	14 367	73 412
1974	3 966	8 404	3 873	4 313	48 236	5 160	117 323	25 904	3 881	61 722	13 623	13 062	67 674
1973	3 646	8 054	3 478	3 913	44 327	4 568	108 803	23 492	3 903	56 188	12 188	11 497	61 420
1972	3 132	6 873	3 038	3 457	40 507	4 054	101 636	20 647	2 761	50 410	10 682	10 153	55 755
1971	2 694	6 200	2 718	3 126	37 335	3 613	95 115	18 255	2 299	46 461	9 716	9 056	51 036
1970	2 527	5 648	2 440	2 890	34 763	3 271	89 292	16 748	1 989	43 748	8 925	8 276	48 153
1969	2 279	5 266	2 170	2 711	32 106	2 953	83 346	15 351	1 895	41 555	8 108	7 582	44 796
1968	2 068	4 646	1 909	2 440	29 679	2 693	77 536	13 782	1 689	38 026	7 380	6 910	41 175
1967	1 967	4 357	1 643	2 204	26 965	2 490	70 368	12 504	1 622	34 463	6 726	6 335	37 912
1966	1 930	4 208	1 548	2 018	25 019	2 402	65 248	11 568	1 622	32 865	6 178	5 971	35 457
1965	1 799	3 907	1 465	1 831	23 104	2 277	60 686	10 419	1 598	30 070	5 760	5 524	32 880
1964	1 670	3 546	1 367	1 692	21 473	2 146	57 227	9 646	1 371	27 757	5 372	5 069	30 668
1963	1 638	3 456	1 260	1 575	20 009	2 032	53 604	8 903	1 380	26 001	5 013	4 708	28 684
1962	1 649	3 355	1 121	1 512	19 064	1 964	51 553	8 459	1 478	24 972	4 839	4 467	27 691
1961	1 410	3 085	931	1 409	17 730	1 883	48 899	7 874	1 060	23 697	4 633	4 197	26 592
1960	1 409	3 011	841	1 338	16 870	1 797	46 937	7 447	1 155	23 278	4 475	4 046	26 067
1959	1 354	2 825	767	1 266	16 001	1 741	44 974	7 046	1 038	22 378	4 251	3 917	25 169
1958	1 377	2 800	698	1 164	14 872	1 617	42 383	6 585	1 119	20 902	4 067	3 618	23 926
1957	1 323	2 699	666	1 148	14 633	1 468	41 289	6 219	978	21 111	3 780	3 518	23 817
1956	1 266	2 341	622	1 075	13 745	1 310	38 919	6 186	954	20 088	3 620	3 515	22 633
1955	1 204	2 267	599	1 019	12 656	1 211	36 640	5 803	916	18 819	3 411	3 282	20 945
1954	1 105	2 349	514	943	11 894	1 116	34 401	5 343	833	17 432	3 221	3 036	19 767
1953	1 115	2 209	477	904	11 670	1 091	33 283	5 248	813	17 386	3 217	3 067	20 195
1952	1 097	2 309	434	844	10 832	1 046	31 247	5 054	801	15 854	3 108	3 024	18 785
1951	1 076	2 160	371	798	10 014	965	29 817	4 909	872	14 789	2 850	2 848	17 915
1950	981	2 070	323	717	8 781	830	27 614	4 380	842	12 834	2 550	2 539	16 306
1949	803	1 753	282	679	7 942	738	25 748	3 791	723	11 608	2 455	2 295	14 596
1948	890	1 971	274	671	7 867	679	25 677	3 848	860	12 124	2 389	2 313	14 768
1947	787	1 612	264	619	7 271	589	24 144	3 394	864	10 798	2 192	2 051	13 915
1946	672	1 490	255	569	6 873	522	22 794	3 228	620	9 850	2 028	1 851	12 731
1945	575	1 435	237	516	6 521	499	20 607	2 899	569	9 268	1 963	1 709	11 749
1944	557	1 325	230	485	6 483	463	19 502	2 782	551	9 090	1 947	1 734	11 563
1943	555	1 259	230	450	6 012	412	17 808	2 524	527	8 605	1 722	1 696	10 796
1942	470	1 023	217	410	5 034	323	15 211	2 053	388	7 115	1 395	1 261	9 235
1941	387	701	120	348	4 070	239	13 212	1 517	326	5 712	978	875	7 692
1940	318	582	101	285	3 425	201	11 693	1 158	227	4 560	869	662	6 436
1939	296	527	92	275	3 094	187	11 154	1 108	206	4 234	814	617	5 952
1938	285	536	82	258	2 859	173	10 665	1 013	183	3 833	805	567	5 599
1937	284	556	79	272	3 054	182	11 316	1 098	214	4 409	876	582	6 229
1936	263	538	85	258	2 896	168	10 898	995	155	4 035	760	561	5 867
1935	262	562	66	240	2 554	139	9 659	900	182	3 502	711	458	5 057
1934	198	357	54	228	2 344	114	9 006	837	121	3 069	603	433	4 717
1933	161	381	48	198	2 148	95	8 214	680	99	2 592	531	350	4 084
1932	183	425	53	202	2 418	92	8 790	604	119	2 689	518	369	4 388
1931	206	572	61	262	3 033	126	11 314	789	127	3 766	722	488	5 823
1930	270	719	77	301	3 444	143	13 091	924	212	4 406	884	580	6 873
1929	310	819	78	320	3 662	172	14 020	1 039	258	5 106	1 079	633	7 508

Table 23-7. Personal Income by States, 1929–2005—*Continued*

Year						Total income (millions of dollars)							
	Montana	Nebraska	Nevada	New Hampshire	New Jersey	New Mexico	New York	North Carolina	North Dakota	Ohio	Oklahoma	Oregon	Pennsylvania
2005	29 387	33 616	35 883	38 408	43 771	27 644	40 507	30 553	31 395	32 478	29 330	32 103	34 897
2004	27 657	32 341	33 787	36 616	41 626	26 184	38 264	29 322	29 494	31 161	27 840	30 561	33 312
2003	26 177	30 747	31 943	34 500	39 625	24 892	35 944	27 859	28 828	29 954	26 560	29 161	31 767
2002	25 065	29 182	30 736	34 043	39 296	24 246	35 357	27 510	26 427	29 212	25 861	28 924	31 016
2001	24 676	28 682	30 727	33 868	39 148	24 085	35 612	27 493	25 879	28 601	26 015	28 507	30 281
2000	22 929	27 625	30 437	33 396	38 364	22 134	34 897	27 068	25 106	28 207	24 407	28 097	29 695
1999	21 585	26 465	29 184	30 380	35 215	21 042	32 816	25 560	23 180	26 859	22 567	26 480	27 937
1998	21 130	25 542	28 260	29 147	34 115	20 656	31 555	24 743	22 872	26 017	21 766	25 542	26 961
1997	19 877	24 061	26 862	27 257	32 051	19 698	29 857	23 530	20 686	24 656	20 671	24 469	25 475
1996	19 047	23 530	26 085	26 427	30 470	19 029	28 424	22 320	21 068	23 322	19 743	23 398	24 344
1995	18 349	21 730	24 817	24 748	28 941	18 426	27 082	21 295	18 865	22 495	18 861	22 293	23 262
1994	17 861	20 751	23 772	23 607	27 558	17 631	25 785	20 400	19 006	21 712	18 374	21 060	22 414
1993	17 770	19 750	22 777	22 376	26 824	16 959	25 143	19 575	17 703	20 634	17 814	20 046	21 738
1992	16 867	19 349	22 084	22 002	26 382	16 273	24 867	18 842	17 669	20 062	17 376	19 235	21 235
1991	16 318	18 524	20 761	21 189	24 847	15 625	23 965	17 677	16 282	19 100	16 554	18 527	20 265
1990	15 448	17 983	20 346	20 512	24 572	14 924	23 523	17 246	15 943	18 743	16 187	18 010	19 687
1989	14 641	16 825	19 360	20 475	23 487	14 078	22 286	16 497	14 447	17 763	15 272	17 050	18 603
1988	13 296	15 969	18 168	19 563	21 988	13 296	20 777	15 398	12 731	16 634	14 216	15 849	17 193
1987	12 978	15 032	16 865	18 261	20 134	12 695	19 115	14 306	13 699	15 612	13 448	14 809	16 052
1986	12 470	14 333	16 170	16 981	18 763	12 301	17 956	13 481	13 137	14 955	13 309	14 148	15 187
1985	11 909	13 869	15 481	15 815	17 701	12 080	16 877	12 699	12 866	14 323	13 332	13 543	14 447
1984	11 706	13 109	14 618	14 547	16 598	11 315	15 848	11 842	12 358	13 488	12 732	12 882	13 556
1983	11 067	11 759	13 656	13 064	15 086	10 467	14 277	10 527	11 430	12 201	11 776	11 869	12 495
1982	10 654	11 370	13 152	12 010	14 038	9 942	13 409	9 720	11 036	11 500	11 833	11 134	11 924
1981	10 214	10 593	12 752	11 021	13 025	9 316	12 329	9 158	10 340	10 956	10 966	10 825	11 148
1980	9 058	9 160	11 700	9 850	11 707	8 346	11 015	8 195	7 907	10 046	9 506	10 113	10 085
1979	8 299	8 784	10 765	8 781	10 469	7 619	9 927	7 461	8 398	9 251	8 485	9 415	9 225
1978	7 721	8 120	9 780	7 786	9 408	6 847	8 979	6 780	8 136	8 326	7 387	8 476	8 305
1977	6 636	6 993	8 550	6 892	8 462	6 087	8 153	6 058	6 427	7 511	6 586	7 556	7 493
1976	6 200	6 453	7 719	6 258	7 703	5 527	7 477	5 584	6 184	6 753	5 974	6 913	6 800
1975	5 794	6 168	7 009	5 592	7 037	5 045	6 955	5 039	6 334	6 087	5 475	6 181	6 170
1974	5 380	5 465	6 490	5 279	6 576	4 568	6 492	4 743	6 120	5 733	4 986	5 726	5 704
1973	5 012	5 269	6 114	4 880	6 043	4 137	5 980	4 365	6 172	5 218	4 524	5 135	5 168
1972	4 355	4 527	5 557	4 423	5 521	3 761	5 538	3 899	4 377	4 691	4 020	4 625	4 683
1971	3 789	4 121	5 227	4 102	5 127	3 431	5 179	3 510	3 669	4 328	3 711	4 212	4 294
1970	3 625	3 796	4 946	3 896	4 835	3 197	4 887	3 285	3 214	4 101	3 477	3 940	4 077
1969	3 284	3 572	4 520	3 744	4 525	2 921	4 603	3 051	3 052	3 934	3 198	3 677	3 815
1968	2 955	3 167	4 114	3 441	4 237	2 709	4 295	2 754	2 719	3 616	2 948	3 448	3 507
1967	2 805	2 990	3 660	3 162	3 892	2 490	3 923	2 525	2 592	3 309	2 702	3 201	3 246
1966	2 730	2 890	3 471	2 963	3 652	2 386	3 657	2 363	2 507	3 181	2 517	3 033	3 040
1965	2 548	2 656	3 299	2 708	3 414	2 250	3 422	2 143	2 463	2 948	2 361	2 852	2 830
1964	2 366	2 392	3 209	2 552	3 224	2 134	3 254	2 009	2 112	2 754	2 196	2 685	2 662
1963	2 330	2 341	3 174	2 427	3 064	2 054	3 070	1 877	2 142	2 604	2 055	2 541	2 511
1962	2 363	2 292	3 184	2 392	2 990	2 006	2 980	1 797	2 320	2 515	1 994	2 457	2 439
1961	2 025	2 134	2 957	2 281	2 830	1 952	2 866	1 689	1 653	2 405	1 947	2 349	2 334
1960	2 075	2 125	2 890	2 197	2 764	1 884	2 788	1 629	1 821	2 391	1 916	2 283	2 301
1959	2 023	2 022	2 749	2 124	2 660	1 895	2 695	1 581	1 679	2 314	1 857	2 244	2 240
1958	2 068	2 025	2 594	2 004	2 525	1 825	2 553	1 505	1 847	2 177	1 794	2 106	2 164
1957	1 983	1 936	2 562	2 007	2 551	1 733	2 522	1 424	1 598	2 243	1 657	2 055	2 174
1956	1 929	1 675	2 488	1 900	2 448	1 626	2 416	1 436	1 556	2 182	1 593	2 070	2 063
1955	1 894	1 650	2 527	1 829	2 300	1 543	2 295	1 368	1 490	2 087	1 516	1 978	1 915
1954	1 771	1 753	2 415	1 703	2 219	1 462	2 175	1 293	1 364	1 965	1 458	1 867	1 827
1953	1 810	1 676	2 447	1 653	2 232	1 444	2 144	1 274	1 336	2 024	1 475	1 916	1 894
1952	1 823	1 761	2 397	1 577	2 114	1 423	2 057	1 230	1 318	1 916	1 401	1 912	1 789
1951	1 806	1 641	2 211	1 508	2 000	1 346	2 002	1 192	1 444	1 835	1 290	1 830	1 713
1950	1 654	1 560	1 991	1 348	1 802	1 204	1 858	1 077	1 360	1 608	1 144	1 657	1 552
1949	1 412	1 346	1 795	1 274	1 624	1 145	1 729	969	1 211	1 456	1 166	1 604	1 405
1948	1 642	1 558	1 758	1 291	1 648	1 124	1 771	1 003	1 483	1 539	1 143	1 646	1 436
1947	1 484	1 274	1 770	1 217	1 571	1 013	1 725	900	1 494	1 401	1 028	1 504	1 364
1946	1 308	1 186	1 757	1 150	1 526	929	1 697	866	1 088	1 310	952	1 379	1 289
1945	1 206	1 186	1 611	1 111	1 582	942	1 644	823	1 046	1 340	970	1 357	1 280
1944	1 183	1 091	1 483	1 054	1 554	881	1 538	766	1 031	1 312	947	1 389	1 250
1943	1 150	1 019	1 511	976	1 429	773	1 384	693	966	1 253	782	1 381	1 146
1942	901	822	1 558	851	1 167	636	1 169	572	665	1 021	626	1 118	951
1941	713	551	982	708	957	474	996	422	529	821	432	818	776
1940	569	442	895	579	820	378	869	324	355	658	374	609	650
1939	533	400	861	561	749	357	825	315	319	615	349	571	601
1938	517	405	780	533	697	338	789	295	282	561	346	531	563
1937	512	415	762	565	747	362	838	324	326	648	376	556	636
1936	475	396	843	537	709	343	808	297	234	593	321	548	601
1935	476	409	658	498	625	292	722	271	272	516	298	458	517
1934	364	259	546	476	573	247	680	253	180	455	252	439	482
1933	298	275	495	416	523	211	626	208	146	385	222	358	417
1932	339	307	550	427	587	208	676	187	176	400	216	379	449
1931	382	413	652	558	736	289	881	248	187	563	301	505	600
1930	501	521	833	647	847	334	1 035	292	311	661	368	607	712
1929	592	596	868	686	918	410	1 152	332	382	771	455	668	772

Table 23-7. Personal Income by States, 1929–2005—*Continued*

Year	Rhode Island	South Carolina	South Dakota	Tennessee	Texas	Utah	Vermont	Virginia	Washington	West Virginia	Wisconsin	Wyoming
											Total income (millions of dollars)	
2005	38 907	120 639	24 530	185 488	742 074	69 299	20 764	290 511	222 643	49 445	185 821	18 731
2004	36 940	114 121	23 280	175 880	690 588	64 399	19 743	270 522	217 503	46 750	177 026	17 341
2003	34 917	107 701	22 251	166 135	650 875	60 298	18 663	251 139	201 607	44 381	167 786	16 202
2002	33 635	104 046	20 596	159 173	626 604	58 172	18 051	240 534	197 452	43 312	163 309	15 463
2001	32 478	101 468	20 429	154 416	619 642	56 594	17 742	233 770	193 498	41 902	158 888	14 972
2000	30 697	98 270	19 438	148 833	593 139	53 561	16 883	220 845	187 853	39 582	153 548	14 063
1999	28 568	91 716	18 367	140 395	539 661	49 343	15 650	204 586	175 491	37 557	144 702	13 050
1998	27 501	86 854	17 523	133 620	507 681	47 019	14 788	191 711	163 762	36 722	138 667	12 189
1997	25 983	81 004	16 335	124 699	466 182	43 667	13 738	179 654	150 119	35 005	129 099	11 459
1996	24 609	76 144	15 948	118 374	427 810	40 386	13 040	169 001	139 650	33 622	121 718	10 678
1995	23 620	71 688	14 390	112 793	398 192	37 218	12 370	160 470	129 845	32 328	115 180	10 207
1994	22 450	68 050	14 172	105 846	374 791	34 437	11 809	153 654	123 294	31 301	109 927	9 845
1993	21 913	64 220	13 207	99 074	354 213	31 810	11 257	146 273	117 266	30 077	103 379	9 450
1992	21 129	61 377	12 687	93 807	335 941	29 601	10 919	139 901	112 035	29 105	98 917	9 020
1991	20 262	57 987	11 803	85 914	311 926	27 573	10 227	131 913	103 974	27 152	92 124	8 579
1990	20 126	55 647	11 273	81 700	297 146	25 817	10 096	127 129	97 399	25 980	88 635	8 167
1989	19 559	51 381	10 267	76 859	274 145	23 891	9 685	120 816	88 084	24 305	83 936	7 536
1988	17 980	47 510	9 577	71 640	255 422	22 287	8 792	111 768	79 648	22 922	77 433	6 938
1987	16 310	43 838	9 223	66 412	240 661	21 361	8 037	102 769	73 461	22 010	73 006	6 762
1986	15 174	40 900	8 755	61 771	235 416	20 663	7 388	94 892	69 203	21 444	69 089	6 971
1985	14 161	38 534	8 401	57 984	232 242	19 794	6 873	87 821	64 924	20 777	65 709	7 154
1984	13 183	35 810	8 159	53 966	215 633	18 546	6 341	81 186	61 086	20 063	62 462	6 854
1983	11 890	31 715	7 142	48 130	194 872	16 803	5 735	72 551	56 666	18 700	57 004	6 528
1982	11 036	29 155	6 887	45 249	183 782	15 541	5 359	66 758	53 328	18 325	54 851	6 794
1981	10 263	27 402	6 507	42 404	167 287	14 206	4 983	61 447	50 295	17 249	51 994	6 335
1980	9 181	24 270	5 577	37 994	141 659	12 519	4 414	54 457	45 004	15 841	47 623	5 556
1979	8 222	21 744	5 621	34 535	124 003	11 026	3 972	47 894	39 987	14 411	43 302	4 777
1978	7 364	19 264	5 064	30 761	106 800	9 606	3 506	42 483	34 536	12 872	38 408	4 044
1977	6 690	16 990	4 376	26 887	92 059	8 331	3 041	37 439	29 544	11 535	34 218	3 355
1976	6 093	15 462	3 840	24 132	82 087	7 302	2 791	33 538	26 502	10 287	30 578	2 852
1975	5 531	13 689	3 862	21 378	72 117	6 355	2 492	30 005	23 641	9 154	27 697	2 550
1974	5 154	12 678	3 520	19 732	63 719	5 686	2 304	27 300	20 999	8 085	25 512	2 250
1973	4 863	11 181	3 505	17 786	56 283	5 057	2 131	24 396	18 473	7 268	23 182	1 912
1972	4 515	9 795	2 754	15 569	49 287	4 514	1 934	21 657	16 307	6 617	20 670	1 633
1971	4 140	8 715	2 376	13 839	44 434	4 026	1 752	19 448	15 100	5 981	18 901	1 451
1970	3 910	7 961	2 171	12 557	40 969	3 614	1 622	17 685	14 372	5 444	17 629	1 308
1969	3 602	7 264	2 001	11 563	37 257	3 249	1 481	16 418	13 696	4 886	16 421	1 179
1968	3 315	6 577	1 855	10 631	33 590	2 984	1 345	14 820	12 590	4 536	14 949	1 074
1967	3 032	5 927	1 729	9 544	30 105	2 773	1 220	13 373	11 318	4 276	13 685	1 005
1966	2 798	5 485	1 707	8 915	27 590	2 629	1 127	12 236	10 348	4 031	12 928	939
1965	2 563	4 882	1 577	8 082	25 249	2 472	992	11 303	9 131	3 796	11 803	911
1964	2 381	4 423	1 402	7 412	23 460	2 334	904	10 468	8 462	3 548	10 894	877
1963	2 235	4 106	1 430	6 896	21 893	2 221	845	9 482	8 082	3 328	10 106	852
1962	2 140	3 881	1 475	6 503	20 896	2 137	814	8 867	7 886	3 188	9 767	833
1961	1 998	3 609	1 291	6 123	19 845	1 958	778	8 212	7 307	3 054	9 235	804
1960	1 910	3 438	1 277	5 785	18 815	1 832	748	7 717	6 955	3 011	8 948	765
1959	1 871	3 267	1 043	5 629	18 325	1 714	709	7 446	6 713	2 962	8 656	729
1958	1 774	3 033	1 142	5 249	17 311	1 595	658	6 981	6 325	2 862	7 974	684
1957	1 723	2 924	1 112	5 069	16 837	1 538	647	6 680	6 162	2 937	7 810	669
1956	1 678	2 809	951	4 855	15 752	1 422	624	6 371	5 796	2 743	7 448	627
1955	1 611	2 703	890	4 530	14 696	1 305	572	5 872	5 509	2 478	6 899	587
1954	1 507	2 536	954	4 278	13 661	1 180	549	5 525	5 225	2 334	6 402	544
1953	1 512	2 689	931	4 235	13 322	1 185	543	5 452	5 095	2 462	6 448	560
1952	1 415	2 604	864	3 950	13 000	1 156	518	5 291	4 831	2 441	6 242	560
1951	1 346	2 417	980	3 783	12 068	1 090	504	4 876	4 542	2 346	5 969	569
1950	1 220	1 954	840	3 407	10 602	938	443	4 167	4 109	2 118	5 178	498
1949	1 104	1 770	704	3 078	9 912	847	415	3 725	3 659	1 975	4 702	456
1948	1 128	1 818	934	3 102	9 257	821	428	3 680	3 663	2 109	4 751	433
1947	1 144	1 584	762	2 825	8 472	751	399	3 322	3 347	1 942	4 213	386
1946	1 081	1 516	666	2 683	7 535	698	373	3 379	3 222	1 691	3 836	345
1945	1 076	1 447	622	2 621	7 219	668	326	3 387	3 176	1 516	3 499	302
1944	1 078	1 428	550	2 486	7 172	646	300	3 278	3 265	1 400	3 295	294
1943	1 042	1 279	497	2 141	6 552	706	303	2 957	2 970	1 287	3 165	283
1942	894	1 099	452	1 658	4 867	512	267	2 598	2 277	1 122	2 654	235
1941	695	774	291	1 298	3 484	327	224	1 731	1 549	938	2 110	194
1940	540	589	232	998	2 811	265	187	1 270	1 146	776	1 720	151
1939	505	517	223	894	2 654	249	176	1 136	1 053	725	1 602	146
1938	467	459	208	847	2 544	237	163	1 028	987	676	1 572	138
1937	508	491	212	935	2 614	235	173	1 095	1 006	758	1 703	147
1936	487	460	162	849	2 303	244	168	996	941	705	1 596	132
1935	437	406	208	737	1 993	204	148	882	798	604	1 416	118
1934	405	371	126	681	1 779	162	137	796	714	554	1 160	96
1933	377	307	89	560	1 543	155	121	701	598	454	1 011	85
1932	389	278	131	536	1 587	158	131	696	637	450	1 094	86
1931	484	360	167	736	2 055	190	170	904	845	619	1 403	109
1930	540	424	254	850	2 410	253	208	932	1 032	707	1 733	132
1929	598	471	294	984	2 763	280	227	1 053	1 153	789	1 975	150

Table 23-7. Personal Income by States, 1929–2005—*Continued*

Year		Total income (millions of dollars)										
	Rhode Island	South Carolina	South Dakota	Tennessee	Texas	Utah	Vermont	Virginia	Washington	West Virginia	Wisconsin	Wyoming
2005	36 153	28 352	31 614	31 107	32 462	28 061	33 327	38 390	35 409	27 215	33 565	36 778
2004	34 207	27 185	30 209	29 844	30 732	26 603	31 780	36 160	35 041	25 792	32 166	34 279
2003	32 459	25 972	29 102	28 440	29 452	25 349	30 146	34 014	32 882	24 515	30 664	32 279
2002	31 478	25 361	27 087	27 490	28 846	24 895	29 291	33 013	32 549	24 002	30 025	30 986
2001	30 687	24 994	26 949	26 870	29 045	24 738	28 951	32 505	32 291	23 261	29 400	30 305
2000	29 214	24 424	25 720	26 097	28 313	23 878	27 680	31 087	31 779	21 899	28 570	28 460
1999	27 459	23 075	24 475	24 898	26 250	22 393	25 881	29 226	30 037	20 729	27 135	26 536
1998	26 670	22 161	23 488	23 989	25 186	21 708	24 629	27 780	28 384	20 226	26 175	24 836
1997	25 341	20 987	21 949	22 676	23 616	20 600	23 002	26 307	26 454	19 243	24 514	23 412
1996	24 106	20 058	21 488	21 854	22 120	19 529	21 964	25 034	25 073	18 445	23 273	21 875
1995	23 225	19 124	19 501	21 174	21 003	18 478	21 002	24 056	23 690	17 727	22 215	21 039
1994	22 097	18 365	19 392	20 233	20 189	17 566	20 226	23 305	22 938	17 194	21 413	20 498
1993	21 586	17 531	18 289	19 284	19 503	16 756	19 485	22 470	22 214	16 548	20 331	19 976
1992	20 867	16 953	17 799	18 577	18 916	16 115	19 065	21 811	21 709	16 112	19 683	19 346
1991	20 049	16 241	16 774	17 298	17 929	15 492	17 985	20 934	20 689	15 095	18 557	18 680
1990	20 006	15 894	16 172	16 692	17 421	14 913	17 876	20 449	19 865	14 493	18 072	18 002
1989	19 546	14 864	14 737	15 833	16 312	14 005	17 365	19 740	18 558	13 454	17 283	16 440
1988	18 045	13 924	13 717	14 856	15 325	13 192	15 992	18 514	17 166	12 524	16 057	14 918
1987	16 482	12 968	13 251	13 885	14 479	12 729	14 875	17 324	16 210	11 849	15 280	14 177
1986	15 526	12 235	12 578	13 035	14 215	12 426	13 834	16 328	15 542	11 392	14 528	14 064
1985	14 615	11 666	12 029	12 297	14 272	12 048	12 968	15 366	14 755	10 896	13 840	14 317
1984	13 705	10 945	11 701	11 515	13 471	11 431	12 040	14 385	14 063	10 408	13 190	13 576
1983	12 432	9 806	10 306	10 329	12 372	10 535	10 959	13 038	13 177	9 614	12 073	12 791
1982	11 566	9 089	9 972	9 739	11 987	9 973	10 324	12 154	12 470	9 399	11 599	13 417
1981	10 769	8 619	9 437	9 163	11 344	9 374	9 664	11 287	11 874	8 827	11 001	12 883
1980	9 677	7 743	8 073	8 259	9 880	8 501	8 613	10 144	10 832	8 118	10 107	11 718
1979	8 595	7 044	8 158	7 618	8 929	7 786	7 853	8 995	9 965	7 432	9 281	10 572
1978	7 693	6 334	7 347	6 895	7 912	7 041	7 036	8 040	8 887	6 703	8 292	9 384
1977	7 004	5 684	6 351	6 108	6 979	6 328	6 179	7 192	7 832	6 053	7 417	8 152
1976	6 411	5 257	5 591	5 574	6 362	5 739	5 753	6 534	7 181	5 479	6 670	7 212
1975	5 844	4 720	5 667	5 017	5 738	5 150	5 192	5 934	6 533	4 974	6 061	6 701
1974	5 405	4 459	5 178	4 696	5 194	4 743	4 869	5 484	5 919	4 457	5 622	6 172
1973	4 972	4 029	5 163	4 298	4 683	4 326	4 548	4 972	5 312	4 026	5 130	5 410
1972	4 625	3 603	4 065	3 808	4 192	3 979	4 176	4 486	4 731	3 682	4 595	4 709
1971	4 295	3 274	3 538	3 451	3 861	3 658	3 856	4 092	4 381	3 378	4 238	4 269
1970	4 114	3 064	3 256	3 189	3 646	3 391	3 634	3 795	4 205	3 117	3 983	3 919
1969	3 865	2 827	2 995	2 967	3 373	3 103	3 388	3 558	4 097	2 798	3 751	3 584
1968	3 595	2 570	2 773	2 741	3 105	2 900	3 128	3 252	3 850	2 573	3 441	3 315
1967	3 336	2 340	2 577	2 473	2 840	2 721	2 885	2 967	3 566	2 417	3 180	3 121
1966	3 113	2 176	2 500	2 332	2 630	2 605	2 729	2 746	3 385	2 271	3 025	2 906
1965	2 870	1 958	2 278	2 128	2 433	2 494	2 456	2 563	3 078	2 126	2 789	2 743
1964	2 691	1 787	2 000	1 965	2 284	2 386	2 266	2 403	2 858	1 974	2 616	2 588
1963	2 552	1 669	2 020	1 855	2 155	2 281	2 128	2 218	2 735	1 853	2 458	2 535
1962	2 457	1 602	2 092	1 771	2 079	2 230	2 072	2 121	2 680	1 762	2 412	2 502
1961	2 329	1 498	1 863	1 690	2 021	2 091	1 994	2 005	2 535	1 671	2 304	2 387
1960	2 234	1 437	1 870	1 618	1 955	2 035	1 923	1 936	2 436	1 625	2 258	2 312
1959	2 183	1 392	1 564	1 598	1 948	1 970	1 832	1 885	2 380	1 597	2 225	2 278
1958	2 067	1 316	1 740	1 512	1 871	1 888	1 732	1 784	2 281	1 551	2 075	2 172
1957	2 024	1 286	1 669	1 476	1 856	1 862	1 720	1 738	2 262	1 594	2 060	2 132
1956	1 998	1 260	1 419	1 422	1 784	1 758	1 655	1 712	2 172	1 477	1 990	2 011
1955	1 958	1 229	1 342	1 327	1 697	1 666	1 524	1 637	2 116	1 318	1 875	1 913
1954	1 847	1 166	1 457	1 274	1 630	1 573	1 456	1 554	2 077	1 225	1 774	1 858
1953	1 855	1 233	1 436	1 276	1 598	1 604	1 432	1 533	2 066	1 276	1 839	1 932
1952	1 765	1 196	1 327	1 178	1 564	1 596	1 380	1 510	1 973	1 247	1 799	1 912
1951	1 717	1 115	1 497	1 122	1 488	1 544	1 334	1 420	1 874	1 182	1 736	1 955
1950	1 553	925	1 283	1 028	1 363	1 348	1 169	1 257	1 721	1 056	1 506	1 719
1949	1 378	873	1 116	951	1 300	1 262	1 125	1 132	1 595	1 023	1 387	1 647
1948	1 433	911	1 526	965	1 214	1 257	1 192	1 148	1 624	1 110	1 434	1 610
1947	1 459	793	1 270	892	1 147	1 180	1 127	1 015	1 504	1 032	1 296	1 506
1946	1 369	780	1 132	872	1 047	1 094	1 090	1 002	1 401	925	1 211	1 362
1945	1 278	753	1 086	912	1 058	1 121	1 035	950	1 419	888	1 182	1 258
1944	1 274	732	979	864	1 045	1 049	953	900	1 527	820	1 109	1 224
1943	1 201	648	846	728	944	1 126	932	843	1 469	739	1 053	1 150
1942	1 149	545	757	561	719	880	775	785	1 196	613	866	944
1941	934	394	475	436	528	594	643	582	864	498	672	779
1940	750	310	361	340	438	480	516	467	658	407	547	602
1939	720	276	345	311	417	458	491	426	614	388	513	587
1938	672	250	320	300	404	444	457	390	582	370	507	561
1937	731	273	323	334	418	444	485	423	599	418	551	607
1936	711	258	244	304	372	463	471	390	569	390	518	551
1935	645	229	309	264	326	389	414	350	490	337	461	496
1934	600	211	184	245	294	310	383	320	443	313	380	411
1933	559	175	129	204	257	298	338	285	376	259	333	371
1932	575	159	189	198	266	305	365	284	402	257	362	374
1931	711	205	241	277	348	369	474	370	534	356	469	476
1930	788	243	366	325	412	498	576	384	658	408	588	585
1929	874	271	426	378	479	551	634	434	741	460	673	675

Source: U.S. Department of Commerce, Bureau of Economic Analysis.

Table 23-8. Saving and Investment, 1929–2006

(Billions of dollars.)

Year	Gross saving						Gross investment		Statistical discrepancy	Gross saving as a percentage of gross national income
	Total	Personal saving	Undistributed corporate profits[1]	Consumption of fixed capital	Government saving		Private domestic	Government		
					Federal	State and local				
2006	1 834.2	−102.8	498.6	1 576.9	104.3	161.4	2 212.5	431.3	−2.5	13.8
2005	1 612.0	−34.8	354.5	1 604.8	99.0	153.2	2 057.4	397.1	71.0	13.0
2004	1 543.7	174.3	343.0	1 436.2	94.1	136.7	1 888.0	371.4	66.7	13.2
2003	1 459.0	174.9	325.1	1 336.5	90.4	127.8	1 664.1	356.0	48.8	13.3
2002	1 489.1	184.7	294.5	1 292.0	88.9	122.7	1 582.1	344.3	−21.0	14.2
2001	1 657.6	132.3	192.3	1 281.5	88.2	117.8	1 614.3	324.0	−89.6	16.2
2000	1 770.5	168.5	174.8	1 187.8	87.2	109.8	1 735.5	304.5	−127.2	17.7
1999	1 674.3	158.6	255.3	1 101.3	84.8	102.1	1 625.7	286.8	−35.7	17.9
1998	1 598.7	276.8	201.7	1 030.2	82.8	96.2	1 509.1	262.4	−14.6	18.2
1997	1 461.1	218.3	287.9	974.4	82.5	91.6	1 389.8	252.2	70.7	17.7
1996	1 291.1	228.4	256.9	918.1	82.0	87.2	1 240.3	244.9	93.7	16.6
1995	1 184.5	250.9	223.8	878.4	81.9	83.1	1 144.0	232.7	101.2	16.2
1994	1 070.7	249.5	171.8	833.7	80.2	78.5	1 097.1	221.4	142.5	15.4
1993	962.4	284.0	168.1	776.4	77.9	73.8	953.4	219.0	139.5	14.7
1992	948.2	366.0	142.7	751.9	74.7	69.9	864.8	223.1	102.7	15.1
1991	964.1	324.2	131.9	725.9	72.2	66.9	802.9	220.3	72.5	16.2
1990	940.4	299.4	123.3	682.5	67.9	63.0	861.0	215.7	66.2	16.3
1989	944.7	287.1	122.6	644.3	63.5	58.7	874.9	197.7	39.7	17.3
1988	915.0	272.9	161.1	597.6	59.3	54.8	821.6	186.1	−19.5	17.8
1987	796.8	241.4	126.1	561.9	55.2	51.4	785.0	184.3	21.7	16.8
1986	733.5	268.4	103.7	531.3	51.6	47.9	746.5	173.2	47.0	16.5
1985	767.5	280.0	133.4	506.7	48.1	44.6	736.2	158.8	16.7	18.1
1984	773.4	314.8	130.3	472.6	44.6	42.3	735.6	139.4	14.6	19.6
1983	609.4	233.6	100.1	443.8	40.8	40.9	564.3	122.9	45.7	17.3
1982	629.1	270.8	65.4	426.9	37.6	39.5	517.2	112.3	0.3	19.1
1981	654.7	244.3	68.0	388.1	33.8	36.3	572.4	106.9	30.9	20.9
1980	549.4	201.4	49.9	343.0	30.1	31.8	479.3	100.3	41.4	19.7
1979	536.7	159.1	75.7	300.1	27.0	27.5	492.9	88.5	46.0	21.1
1978	478.0	142.5	81.0	262.3	25.0	24.5	438.0	77.1	26.6	20.9
1977	397.5	125.3	73.2	230.0	23.1	22.6	361.3	67.5	22.3	19.6
1976	342.1	122.3	59.0	205.2	21.4	21.3	292.0	66.4	25.1	18.8
1975	297.0	125.6	50.2	187.7	19.7	20.2	230.2	63.1	17.7	18.2
1974	301.5	113.6	29.8	162.5	18.2	17.7	249.4	56.3	10.9	20.0
1973	292.0	102.7	45.6	139.3	17.1	14.3	244.5	46.8	8.6	21.1
1972	237.5	77.2	42.9	126.5	16.6	12.8	207.6	42.6	9.1	19.2
1971	208.9	80.6	34.8	115.0	16.5	11.8	178.2	41.8	11.6	18.6
1970	192.7	69.5	24.6	106.7	16.1	10.6	152.4	43.6	7.3	18.6
1969	198.3	52.5	31.2	97.9	15.5	9.3	156.4	43.3	3.2	20.1
1968	182.0	52.8	35.6	88.4	14.8	8.3	141.2	43.6	4.6	20.0
1967	170.5	54.4	36.9	81.5	14.0	7.5	128.6	43.0	4.6	20.5
1966	168.7	44.4	38.7	75.6	13.2	6.9	131.3	39.8	6.3	21.4
1965	158.5	43.0	36.2	69.4	12.7	6.2	118.2	35.6	1.6	21.9
1964	143.4	40.8	30.1	65.0	12.3	5.7	102.1	34.6	0.8	21.5
1963	133.2	33.3	26.4	62.4	12.1	5.4	93.8	33.6	−0.8	21.4
1962	124.9	33.8	24.1	59.3	11.5	5.0	88.1	33.3	0.4	21.2
1961	114.3	32.2	18.1	57.2	10.9	4.7	78.2	31.3	−0.6	20.8
1960	111.3	26.7	17.6	55.6	10.6	4.4	78.9	28.3	−0.9	21.0
1959	106.2	26.7	19.4	53.0	10.2	4.2	78.5	29.3	0.5	20.9
1958	90.8	28.3	13.0	52.0	9.9	4.0	64.5	26.5	1.0	19.4
1957	99.6	27.0	15.2	49.9	9.8	3.9	70.5	24.4	0.0	21.5
1956	99.4	25.8	15.3	46.4	9.3	3.5	72.0	22.9	−1.7	22.5
1955	88.0	19.7	17.0	42.1	8.7	3.1	69.0	21.0	2.5	21.2
1954	73.4	20.0	11.9	39.9	8.3	2.9	53.8	22.5	3.2	19.3
1953	75.1	21.5	10.6	37.8	7.6	2.8	56.4	24.0	4.0	19.9
1952	74.2	20.5	11.3	35.7	6.8	2.7	54.0	22.3	2.8	20.7
1951	75.0	19.5	10.1	33.2	6.1	2.6	60.2	17.6	3.6	22.2
1950	60.6	15.1	9.3	29.4	5.8	2.1	54.1	9.8	1.4	20.6
1949	45.6	9.5	11.6	28.7	6.6	2.1	36.9	9.7	1.8	17.1
1948	58.0	13.4	11.7	28.1	7.6	2.1	48.1	7.0	−0.5	21.4
1947	46.6	7.4	6.1	26.4	8.8	1.8	35.0	4.6	2.3	19.2
1946	38.4	15.5	3.2	23.3	9.3	1.5	31.1	3.5	1.2	17.3
1945	29.8	31.1	5.0	21.1	8.7	1.4	10.8	24.1	3.9	13.6
1944	39.9	38.7	7.4	19.4	7.5	1.4	7.8	36.6	2.6	18.3
1943	44.9	34.6	6.4	16.3	4.8	1.5	6.1	39.1	−1.8	22.4
1942	39.8	28.6	5.0	13.4	2.1	1.4	10.4	28.5	−0.9	24.4
1941	29.8	11.5	3.4	10.8	0.8	1.2	18.1	10.8	0.3	23.5

[1]Includes inventory valuation and capital consumption adjustments.

Table 23-8. Saving and Investment, 1929–2006—*Continued*

(Billions of dollars.)

Year	Gross saving						Gross investment		Statistical discrepancy	Gross saving as a percentage of gross national income
	Total	Personal saving	Undistributed corporate profits[1]	Consumption of fixed capital	Government saving		Private domestic	Government		
					Federal	State and local				
1940	18.5	4.4	3.0	9.4	0.5	1.1	13.6	4.4	1.1	18.4
1939	13.6	3.2	1.4	9.0	0.4	1.0	9.3	4.5	1.3	14.9
1938	11.7	1.3	0.8	9.0	0.4	1.0	7.1	4.2	0.7	13.7
1937	16.2	4.3	0.9	8.7	0.4	1.0	12.2	3.8	0.0	17.5
1936	11.5	4.3	0.3	7.8	0.3	0.9	8.6	4.1	1.2	13.9
1935	9.6	2.6	0.2	7.6	0.3	0.8	6.7	2.8	−0.2	13.0
1934	6.4	0.5	−0.8	7.6	0.2	0.8	3.7	2.7	0.4	9.7
1933	3.3	−0.7	−2.7	7.2	0.2	0.7	1.7	1.9	0.6	5.8
1932	3.3	−0.5	−3.1	7.5	0.2	0.6	1.3	2.1	0.3	5.6
1931	8.3	2.5	−1.6	8.6	0.2	0.7	5.9	3.0	0.8	10.9
1930	15.0	3.1	1.1	9.2	0.2	0.7	10.8	3.2	−0.4	16.3
1929	19.3	3.8	3.6	9.4	0.2	0.7	16.5	2.8	0.8	18.6

Source: U.S. Department of Commerce, Bureau of Economic Analysis. *National Income and Product Accounts.*
[1]Includes inventory valuation and capital consumption adjustments.

Table 23-9. Persons Below Poverty Level and Below 125 Percent of Poverty Level by Race and Hispanic Origin, 1960–2004

(Persons as of March of the following year.)

Year	Number of persons below poverty (1,000)											
	All races[1]	White	White alone[2]	Black	Black alone[3]	Black alone or in combination	Asian and Pacific Islander	Asian alone[4]	Asian alone or in combination	Hispanic[5]	White non-Hispanic	White alone, not Hispanic[6]
2004	36 997	...	25 301	...	9 000	9 393	...	1 209	1 303	9 132	...	16 870
2003	35 861	...	24 272	...	8 781	9 108	...	1 401	1 527	9 051	...	15 902
2002[8]	34 570	...	23 466	...	8 602	8 884	...	1 161	1 243	8 555	...	15 567
2001	32 907	22 739	...	8 136	...	...	1 275	...	...	7 997	15 271	...
2000[7]	31 581	21 645	...	7 982	...	...	1 258	...	...	7 747	14 366	...
1999	32 791	22 169	...	8 441	...	...	1 285	...	...	7 876	14 735	...
1998	34 476	23 454	...	9 091	...	...	1 360	...	...	8 070	15 799	...
1997	35 574	24 396	...	9 116	...	...	1 468	...	...	8 308	16 491	...
1996	36 529	24 650	...	9 694	...	...	1 454	...	...	8 697	16 462	...
1995	36 425	24 423	...	9 872	...	...	1 411	...	...	8 574	16 267	...
1994	38 059	25 379	...	10 196	...	...	974	...	...	8 416	18 110	...
1993	39 265	26 226	...	10 877	...	...	1 134	...	...	8 126	18 882	...
1992	38 014	25 259	...	10 827	...	...	985	...	...	7 592	18 202	...
1991	35 708	23 747	...	10 242	...	...	996	...	...	6 339	17 741	...
1990	33 585	22 326	...	9 837	...	...	858	...	...	6 006	16 622	...
1989	31 528	20 785	...	9 302	...	...	939	...	...	5 430	15 599	...
1988	31 745	20 715	...	9 356	...	...	1 117	...	...	5 357	15 565	...
1987	32 221	21 195	...	9 520	...	...	1 021	...	...	5 422	16 029	...
1986	32 370	22 183	...	8 983	...	...	...	...	...	5 117	17 244	...
1985	33 064	22 860	...	8 926	...	...	...	...	...	5 236	17 839	...
1984	33 700	22 955	...	9 490	...	...	...	...	...	4 806	18 300	...
1983	35 303	23 984	...	9 882	...	...	...	...	...	4 633	19 538	...
1982	34 398	23 517	...	9 697	...	...	...	...	...	4 301	19 362	...
1981	31 822	21 553	...	9 173	...	...	...	...	...	3 713	17 987	...
1980	29 272	19 699	...	8 579	...	...	...	...	...	3 491	16 365	...
1979	26 072	17 214	...	8 050	...	...	...	...	...	2 921	14 419	...
1978	24 497	16 259	...	7 625	...	...	...	...	...	2 607	13 755	...
1977	24 720	16 416	...	7 726	...	...	...	...	...	2 700	13 802	...
1976	24 975	16 713	...	7 595	...	...	...	...	...	2 783	14 025	...
1975	25 877	17 770	...	7 545	...	...	...	...	...	2 991	14 883	...
1974	23 370	15 736	...	7 182	...	...	...	...	...	2 575	13 217	...
1973	22 973	15 142	...	7 388	...	...	...	...	...	2 366	12 864	...
1972	24 460	16 203	...	7 710	...	...	...	...	...	2 414	...	...
1971	25 559	17 780	...	7 396	...	...	...	...	...	...	...	...
1970	25 420	17 484	...	7 548	...	...	...	...	...	...	...	...
1969	24 147	16 659	...	7 095	...	...	...	...	...	...	...	...
1968	25 389	17 395	...	7 616	...	...	...	...	...	...	...	...
1967	27 769	18 983	...	8 486	...	...	...	...	...	...	...	...
1966	28 510	19 290	...	8 867	...	...	...	...	...	...	...	...
1965	33 185	22 496	...	...	...	...	...	...	...	...	...	...
1964	36 055	24 957	...	...	...	...	...	...	...	...	...	...
1963	36 436	25 238	...	...	...	...	...	...	...	...	...	...
1962	38 625	26 672	...	...	...	...	...	...	...	...	...	...
1961	39 628	27 890	...	...	...	...	...	...	...	...	...	...
1960	39 851	28 309	...	...	...	...	...	...	...	...	...	...

Note: Based on the Current Population Survey of the U.S. Census Bureau.
[1] Includes other races not shown separately.
[2] Data represents White alone, which refers to people who reported White and did not report any other race category.
[3] Data represents Black alone, which refers to people who reported Black and did not report any other race category.
[4] Data represents Asian alone, which refers to people who reported Asian and did not report any other race category.
[5] People of Hispanic origin may be of any race.
[6] Data represents White alone, not Hispanic, which refers to people who reported White, not Hispanic and did not report any other race category.
[7] Reflects implementation of Census 2000 based population controls and a 28,000 household sample expansion to 78,000 households.
[8] Beginning with the 2003 Current Population Survey (CPS), the questionnaire allowed respondents to choose more than one race. For 2002 and later, data represent persons who selected this race group only and excludes persons reporting more than one race. The CPS in prior years allowed respondents to report only one race group.
. . . = Not available.

Table 23-9. Persons Below Poverty Level and Below 125 Percent of Poverty Level by Race and Hispanic Origin, 1960–2004—*Continued*

(Persons as of March of the following year.)

Year	All races[1]	White	White alone[2]	Black	Black alone[3]	Black alone or in combination	Asian and Pacific Islander	Asian alone[4]	Asian alone or in combination	Hispanic[5]	White non-Hispanic	White alone, not Hispanic[6]	Number	Percent of total population
					Percent of persons below poverty								Below 125 percent of poverty level	
2004	12.7	...	10.8	...	24.7	24.7	...	9.8	9.8	21.9	...	8.6	49,666	17.1
2003	12.5	...	10.5	...	24.4	24.3	...	11.8	11.8	22.5	...	8.2	48,687	16.9
2002[8]	12.1	...	10.2	...	24.1	23.9	...	10.1	10.0	21.8	...	8.0	47,084	16.5
2001	11.7	9.9	...	22.7	...	...	10.2	...	...	21.4	7.8	...	45,320	16.1
2000[7]	11.3	9.5	...	22.5	...	...	9.9	...	...	21.5	7.4	...	43,612	15.6
1999	11.9	9.8	...	23.6	...	...	10.7	...	...	22.7	7.7	...	44,286	16.2
1998	12.7	10.5	...	26.1	...	...	12.5	...	...	25.6	8.2	...	46,036	17.0
1997	13.3	11.0	...	26.5	...	...	14.0	...	...	27.1	8.6	...	47,853	17.8
1996	13.7	11.2	...	28.4	...	...	14.5	...	...	29.4	8.6	...	49,310	18.5
1995	13.8	11.2	...	29.3	...	...	14.6	...	...	30.3	8.5	...	48,761	18.5
1994	14.5	11.7	...	30.6	...	...	14.6	...	...	30.7	9.4	...	50,401	19.3
1993	15.1	12.2	...	33.1	...	...	15.3	...	...	30.6	9.9	...	51,801	20.0
1992	14.8	11.9	...	33.4	...	...	12.7	...	...	29.6	9.6	...	50,592	19.7
1991	14.2	11.3	...	32.7	...	...	13.8	...	...	28.7	9.4	...	47,527	18.9
1990	13.5	10.7	...	31.9	...	...	12.2	...	...	28.1	8.8	...	44,837	18.0
1989	12.8	10.0	...	30.7	...	...	14.1	...	...	26.2	8.3	...	42,653	17.3
1988	13.0	10.1	...	31.3	...	...	17.3	...	...	26.7	8.4	...	42,551	17.5
1987	13.4	10.4	...	32.4	...	...	16.1	...	...	28.0	8.7	...	43,032	17.9
1986	13.6	11.0	...	31.1	...	...	...	...	...	27.3	9.4	...	43,486	18.2
1985	14.0	11.4	...	31.3	...	...	...	...	...	29.0	9.7	...	44,166	18.7
1984	14.4	11.5	...	33.8	...	...	...	...	...	28.4	10.0	...	45,288	19.4
1983	15.2	12.1	...	35.7	...	...	...	...	...	28.0	10.8	...	47,150	20.3
1982	15.0	12.0	...	35.6	...	...	...	...	...	29.9	10.6	...	46,520	20.3
1981	14.0	11.1	...	34.2	...	...	...	...	...	26.5	9.9	...	43,748	19.3
1980	13.0	10.2	...	32.5	...	...	...	...	...	25.7	9.1	...	40,658	18.1
1979	11.7	9.0	...	31.0	...	...	...	...	...	21.8	8.1	...	36,616	16.4
1978	11.4	8.7	...	30.6	...	...	...	...	...	21.6	7.9	...	34,155	15.8
1977	11.6	8.9	...	31.3	...	...	...	...	...	22.4	8.0	...	35,659	16.7
1976	11.8	9.1	...	31.1	...	...	...	...	...	24.7	8.1	...	35,509	16.7
1975	12.3	9.7	...	31.3	...	...	...	...	...	26.9	8.6	...	37,182	17.6
1974	11.2	8.6	...	30.3	...	...	...	...	...	23.0	7.7	...	33,666	16.1
1973	11.1	8.4	...	31.4	...	...	...	...	...	21.9	7.5	...	32,828	15.8
1972	11.9	9.0	...	33.3	...	...	...	...	...	22.8	...	...	34,653	16.8
1971	12.5	9.9	...	32.5	...	...	...	...	...	...	...	...	36,501	17.8
1970	12.6	9.9	...	33.5	...	...	...	...	...	...	...	...	35,624	17.6
1969	12.1	9.5	...	32.2	...	...	...	...	...	...	...	...	34,665	17.4
1968	12.8	10.0	...	34.7	...	...	...	...	...	...	...	...	35,905	18.2
1967	14.2	11.0	...	39.3	...	...	...	...	...	...	...	...	39,206	20.0
1966	14.7	11.3	...	41.8	...	...	...	...	...	...	...	...	41,267	21.3
1965	17.3	13.3	...	...	...	...	...	...	...	...	...	...	46,163	24.1
1964	19.0	14.9	...	...	...	...	...	...	...	...	...	...	49,819	26.3
1963	19.5	15.3	...	...	...	...	...	...	...	...	...	...	50,778	27.1
1962	21.0	16.4	...	...	...	...	...	...	...	...	...	...	53,119	28.8
1961	21.9	17.4	...	...	...	...	...	...	...	...	...	...	54,280	30.0
1960	22.2	17.8	...	...	...	...	...	...	...	...	...	...	54,560	30.4

Source: U.S. Census Bureau. *Statistical Abstract of the United States: 2007.*
Note: Based on the Current Population Survey of the U.S. Census Bureau.
[1]Includes other races not shown separately.
[2]Data represents White alone, which refers to people who reported White and did not report any other race category.
[3]Data represents Black alone, which refers to people who reported Black and did not report any other race category.
[4]Data represents Asian alone, which refers to people who reported Asian and did not report any other race category.
[5]People of Hispanic origin may be of any race.
[6]Data represents White alone, not Hispanic, which refers to people who reported White, not Hispanic and did not report any other race category.
[7]Reflects implementation of Census 2000 based population controls and a 28,000 household sample expansion to 78,000 households.
[8]Beginning with the 2003 Current Population Survey (CPS), the questionnaire allowed respondents to choose more than one race. For 2002 and later, data represent persons who selected this race group only and excludes persons reporting more than one race. The CPS in prior years allowed respondents to report only one race group.
... = Not available.

Table 23-10. Individuals and Families Below the Poverty Level, Number and Rate, by State, 2000 and 2003

(Thousands, percent.)

Year	Number below poverty level (thousands)				Percent below poverty level			
	Individuals		Families		Individuals		Families	
	2000	2003	2000	2003	2000	2003	2000	2003
United States	33 311	35 846	6 615	7 143	12.2	12.7	9.3	9.8
Alabama	672	748	146	164	15.6	17.1	12.4	13.7
Alaska	55	61	11	13	9.1	9.7	6.8	8.0
Arizona	780	839	150	166	15.6	15.4	11.6	11.9
Arkansas	439	421	96	89	17.0	16.0	13.0	12.1
California	4 520	4 610	832	849	13.7	13.4	10.7	10.5
Colorado	363	433	64	88	8.7	9.8	5.7	7.3
Connecticut	254	273	51	58	7.7	8.1	5.8	6.4
Delaware	70	69	14	12	9.3	8.7	6.7	5.8
District of Columbia	94	105	17	21	17.5	19.9	15.4	18.5
Florida	1 987	2 174	387	422	12.8	13.1	9.3	9.7
Georgia	999	1 125	206	234	12.6	13.4	10.0	10.8
Hawaii	103	132	19	21	8.8	10.9	6.8	7.4
Idaho	144	183	26	35	11.4	13.8	7.7	9.8
Illinois	1 335	1 389	262	265	11.1	11.3	8.6	8.5
Indiana	592	633	113	119	10.1	10.6	7.1	7.5
Iowa	281	286	53	53	10.0	10.1	7.0	6.9
Kansas	247	284	43	51	9.5	10.8	6.2	7.1
Kentucky	640	696	148	159	16.4	17.4	13.5	14.2
Louisiana	862	882	182	191	20.0	20.3	16.0	16.6
Maine	124	133	22	26	10.1	10.5	6.6	7.6
Maryland	477	439	89	86	9.3	8.2	6.6	6.1
Massachusetts	586	582	110	118	9.6	9.4	7.1	7.5
Michigan	975	1 118	196	224	10.1	11.4	7.7	8.6
Minnesota	328	383	66	75	6.9	7.8	5.1	5.6
Mississippi	498	553	104	121	18.2	19.9	14.2	16.4
Missouri	606	646	118	133	11.2	11.7	7.7	8.6
Montana	117	126	23	24	13.4	14.2	9.5	9.9
Nebraska	158	182	28	36	9.6	10.8	6.5	8.2
Nevada	194	252	34	47	9.9	11.5	6.9	8.7
New Hampshire	63	96	11	17	5.3	7.7	3.5	5.1
New Jersey	651	704	126	145	7.9	8.4	6.0	6.6
New Mexico	320	340	64	70	18.0	18.6	14.2	14.8
New York	2 391	2 501	491	499	13.1	13.5	10.7	10.7
North Carolina	1 018	1 136	203	239	13.1	14.0	9.6	10.7
North Dakota	71	71	14	13	11.6	11.7	8.1	8.4
Ohio	1 216	1 343	246	280	11.1	12.1	8.4	9.4
Oklahoma	459	546	100	112	13.8	16.1	11.0	12.4
Oregon	439	481	84	88	13.2	13.9	9.5	9.7
Pennsylvania	1 240	1 296	247	260	10.5	10.9	7.8	8.2
Rhode Island	108	117	23	22	10.7	11.3	8.5	8.2
South Carolina	557	563	123	121	14.4	14.1	11.7	11.3
South Dakota	83	81	16	14	11.5	11.1	8.4	7.2
Tennessee	745	780	158	164	13.5	13.8	10.5	10.6
Texas	3 056	3 508	639	712	15.1	16.3	12.3	13.1
Utah	192	244	40	43	8.8	10.6	7.2	7.6
Vermont	63	57	12	10	10.7	9.7	7.5	6.4
Virginia	630	642	124	126	9.2	9.0	6.8	6.6
Washington	667	654	127	121	11.6	11.0	8.6	7.9
West Virginia	327	326	72	76	18.6	18.5	14.7	15.5
Wisconsin	461	554	75	101	8.9	10.5	5.6	7.2
Wyoming	55	47	10	10	11.4	9.7	7.9	7.3

Source: U.S. Census Bureau. *Statistical Abstract of the United States: 2006.*
Note: Represents number and percent below poverty in the past 12 months. The American Community Survey universe is limited to the household population and excludes the population living in institutions, college dormitories, and other group quarters. Based on a sample and subject to sampling variability.

Table 23-11. Children Below Poverty Level by Race and Hispanic Origin, 1960–2004

(Thousands. Persons as of March of the following year. Covers only related children in families, under 18 years old.)

Year	All races[1]	White	White alone[2]	Black	Black alone[3]	Black alone or in combination	Asian and Pacific Islander	Asian alone[4]	Asian alone or in combination	Hispanic[5]	White non-Hispanic	White alone, not Hispanic[6]
							Number of children below poevery level (thousands)					
2004	12 460	...	7 868	...	3 694	3 952	...	269	316	3 989	...	4 179
2003	12 340	...	7 624	...	3 750	3 977	...	331	406	3 982	...	3 957
2002[7]	11 646	...	7 203	...	3 570	3 733	...	302	338	3 653	...	3 848
2001	11 175	7 086	...	3 423	...	...	353	...	...	3 433	3 887	...
2000[8]	11 005	6 834	...	3 495	...	...	407	...	...	3 342	3 715	...
1999	11 678	7 194	...	3 698	...	...	367	...	...	3 561	3 832	...
1998	12 845	7 935	...	4 073	...	...	542	...	...	3 670	4 458	...
1997	13 422	8 441	...	4 116	...	...	608	...	...	3 865	4 759	...
1996	13 764	8 488	...	4 411	...	...	553	...	...	4 090	4 656	...
1995	13 999	8 474	...	4 644	...	...	532	...	...	3 938	4 745	...
1994	14 610	8 826	...	4 787	...	...	308	...	...	3 956	5 404	...
1993	14 961	9 123	...	5 030	...	...	358	...	...	3 666	5 819	...
1992	14 521	8 752	...	5 015	...	...	352	...	...	3 440	5 558	...
1991	13 658	8 316	...	4 637	...	...	348	...	...	2 977	5 497	...
1990	12 715	7 696	...	4 412	...	...	356	...	...	2 750	5 106	...
1989	12 001	7 164	...	4 257	...	...	368	...	...	2 496	4 779	...
1988	11 935	7 095	...	4 148	...	...	458	...	...	2 576	4 594	...
1987	12 275	7 398	...	4 234	...	...	432	...	...	2 606	4 901	...
1986	12 257	7 714	...	4 037	...	...	...	...	...	2 413	5 388	...
1985	12 483	7 838	...	4 057	...	...	...	...	...	2 512	5 421	...
1984	12 929	8 086	...	4 320	...	...	...	...	...	2 317	5 828	...
1983	13 427	8 534	...	4 273	...	...	...	...	...	2 251	6 381	...
1982	13 139	8 282	...	4 388	...	...	...	...	...	2 117	6 229	...
1981	12 068	7 429	...	4 170	...	...	...	...	...	1 874	5 639	...
1980	11 114	6 817	...	3 906	...	...	...	...	...	1 718	5 174	...
1979	9 993	5 909	...	3 745	...	...	...	...	...	1 505	4 476	...
1978	9 722	5 674	...	3 781	...	...	...	...	...	1 354	4 383	...
1977	10 028	5 943	...	3 850	...	...	...	...	...	1 402	4 582	...
1976	10 081	6 034	...	3 758	...	...	...	...	...	1 424	4 664	...
1975	10 882	6 748	...	3 884	...	...	...	...	...	1 619	5 185	...
1974	9 967	6 079	...	3 713	...	...	...	...	...	1 414	4 697	...
1973	9 453	5 462	...	3 822	...	...	...	...	...	1 364	...	...
1972	10 082	5 784	...	4 025	...	...	...	...	...	...	...	...
1971	10 344	6 341	...	3 836	...	...	...	...	...	...	...	...
1970	10 235	6 138	...	3 922	...	...	...	...	...	...	...	...
1969	9 501	5 667	...	3 677	...	...	...	...	...	...	...	...
1968	10 739	6 373	...	4 188	...	...	...	...	...	...	...	...
1967	11 427	6 729	...	4 558	...	...	...	...	...	...	...	...
1966	12 146	7 204	...	4 774	...	...	...	...	...	...	...	...
1965	14 388	8 595	...	5 022	...	...	...	...	...	...	...	...
1964	15 736	...	...	...	...	...	...	...	...	...	...	...
1963	15 691	...	...	...	...	...	...	...	...	...	...	...
1962	16 630	...	...	...	...	...	...	...	...	...	...	...
1961	16 577	...	...	...	...	...	...	...	...	...	...	...
1960	17 288	11 229	...	...	...	...	...	...	...	...	...	...

[1]Includes other races not shown separately.
[2]Data represents White alone, which refers to people who reported White and did not report any other race category.
[3]Data represents Black alone, which refers to people who reported Black and did not report any other race category.
[4]Data represents Asian alone, which refers to people who reported Asian and did not report any other race category.
[5]People of Hispanic origin may be of any race.
[6]Data represents White alone, not Hispanic, which refers to people who reported White, not Hispanic and did not report any other race category.
[7]Beginning with the 2003 Current Population Survey (CPS), the questionnaire allowed respondents to choose more than one race. For 2002 and later, data represent persons who selected this race group only and excludes persons reporting more than one race. The CPS in prior years allowed respondents to report only one race group.
[8]Implementation of Census 2000 based population controls and a 28,000 household sample expansion to 78,000 households.
. . . = Not available.

Table 23-11. Children Below Poverty Level by Race and Hispanic Origin, 1960–2004—*Continued*

(Thousands. Persons as of March of the following year. Covers only related children in families, under 18 years old.)

Year						Percent of children below poverty level							
	All races[1]	White	White alone[2]	Black	Black alone[3]	Black alone or in combination	Asian and Pacific Islander	Asian alone[4]	Asian alone or in combination	Hispanic[5]	White non-Hispanic	White alone, not Hispanic[6]
2004	17.3	...	14.2	...	33.3	32.9	...	9.5	9.3	28.6	...	9.9
2003	17.2	...	13.9	...	33.6	33.2	...	12.1	12.4	29.5	...	9.3
2002[7]	16.3	...	13.1	...	32.1	31.3	...	11.4	10.7	28.2	...	8.9
2001	15.8	12.8	...	30.0	...	...	11.1	...	...	27.4	8.9	...
2000[8]	15.6	12.4	...	30.9	...	...	12.5	...	...	27.6	8.5	...
1999	16.6	13.1	...	32.8	...	...	11.5	...	...	29.9	8.8	...
1998	18.3	14.4	...	36.4	...	...	17.5	...	...	33.6	10.0	...
1997	19.2	15.4	...	36.8	...	...	19.9	...	...	36.4	10.7	...
1996	19.8	15.5	...	39.5	...	...	19.1	...	...	39.9	10.4	...
1995	20.2	15.5	...	41.5	...	...	18.6	...	...	39.3	10.6	...
1994	21.2	16.3	...	43.3	...	...	17.9	...	...	41.1	11.8	...
1993	22.0	17.0	...	45.9	...	...	17.6	...	...	39.9	12.8	...
1992	21.6	16.5	...	46.3	...	...	16.0	...	...	39.0	12.4	...
1991	21.1	16.1	...	45.6	...	...	17.1	...	...	39.8	12.4	...
1990	19.9	15.1	...	44.2	...	...	17.0	...	...	37.7	11.6	...
1989	19.0	14.1	...	43.2	...	...	18.9	...	...	35.5	10.9	...
1988	19.0	14.0	...	42.8	...	...	23.5	...	...	37.3	10.5	...
1987	19.7	14.7	...	44.4	...	...	22.7	...	...	38.9	11.2	...
1986	19.8	15.3	...	42.7	...	...	...	...	...	37.1	12.2	...
1985	20.1	15.6	...	43.1	...	...	...	...	...	39.6	12.3	...
1984	21.0	16.1	...	46.2	...	...	...	...	...	38.7	13.1	...
1983	21.8	17.0	...	46.2	...	...	...	...	...	37.7	14.4	...
1982	21.3	16.5	...	47.3	...	...	...	...	...	38.9	13.8	...
1981	19.5	14.7	...	44.9	...	...	...	...	...	35.4	12.4	...
1980	17.9	13.4	...	42.1	...	...	...	...	...	33.0	11.3	...
1979	16.0	11.4	...	40.8	...	...	...	...	...	27.7	9.6	...
1978	15.7	11.0	...	41.2	...	...	...	...	...	27.2	9.4	...
1977	16.0	11.4	...	41.6	...	...	...	...	...	28.0	9.7	...
1976	15.8	11.3	...	40.4	...	...	...	...	...	30.1	9.6	...
1975	16.8	12.5	...	41.4	...	...	...	...	...	33.1	10.5	...
1974	15.1	11.0	...	39.6	...	...	...	...	...	28.6	9.3	...
1973	14.2	9.7	...	40.6	...	...	...	...	...	27.8	...	...
1972	14.9	10.1	...	42.7	...	...	...	...	...	...	...	...
1971	15.1	10.9	...	40.4	...	...	...	...	...	...	...	...
1970	14.9	10.5	...	41.5	...	...	...	...	...	...	...	...
1969	13.8	9.7	...	39.6	...	...	...	...	...	...	...	...
1968	15.3	10.7	...	43.1	...	...	...	...	...	...	...	...
1967	16.3	11.3	...	47.4	...	...	...	...	...	...	...	...
1966	17.4	12.1	...	50.6	...	...	...	...	...	...	...	...
1965	20.7	14.4	...	65.6	...	...	...	...	...	...	...	...
1964	22.7	...	...	...	...	...	...	...	...	...	...	...
1963	22.8	...	...	...	...	...	...	...	...	...	...	...
1962	24.7	...	...	...	...	...	...	...	...	...	...	...
1961	25.2	...	...	...	...	...	...	...	...	...	...	...
	26.5	20.0	...	...	...	...	...	...	...	...	...	...

Source: U.S. Census Bureau. *Statistical Abstract of the United States: 2007.*
Note: Based on the Current Population Survey of the U.S. Census Bureau.
[1]Includes other races not shown separately.
[2]Data represents White alone, which refers to people who reported White and did not report any other race category.
[3]Data represents Black alone, which refers to people who reported Black and did not report any other race category.
[4]Data represents Asian alone, which refers to people who reported Asian and did not report any other race category.
[5]People of Hispanic origin may be of any race.
[6]Data represents White alone, not Hispanic, which refers to people who reported White, not Hispanic and did not report any other race category.
[7]Beginning with the 2003 Current Population Survey (CPS), the questionnaire allowed respondents to choose more than one race. For 2002 and later, data represent persons who selected this race group only and excludes persons reporting more than one race. The CPS in prior years allowed respondents to report only one race group.
[8]Implementation of Census 2000 based population controls and a 28,000 household sample expansion to 78,000 households.
. . . = Not available.

Table 23-12. Current-Cost Net Stock of Fixed Assets and Consumer Durable Goods, 1925–2005

(Billions of dollars, year-end estimates.)

Year	Total	Private fixed assets					Government fixed assets			Consumer durable goods
		Total	Nonresidential			Residential	Total	Federal	State and local	
			Total	Equipment and software	Structures					
2005	40 988.6	29 343.8	13 543.8	4 742.5	8 801.3	15 800.1	7 906.7	1 681.0	6 225.7	3 738.0
2004	37 988.0	27 192.8	12 533.0	4 553.6	7 979.4	14 659.8	7 228.3	1 593.2	5 635.1	3 566.8
2003	34 804.7	24 916.9	11 692.2	4 380.8	7 311.3	13 224.7	6 507.5	1 498.9	5 008.6	3 380.3
2002	33 061.3	23 522.7	11 329.6	4 270.8	7 058.8	12 193.1	6 265.6	1 469.9	4 795.7	3 273.0
2001	31 608.9	22 484.8	11 020.0	4 203.2	6 816.8	11 464.8	5 979.9	1 446.8	4 533.1	3 144.2
2000	29 917.1	21 189.5	10 513.8	4 077.3	6 436.5	10 675.7	5 712.7	1 424.6	4 288.1	3 014.9
1999	28 081.1	19 847.2	9 860.4	3 822.1	6 038.4	9 986.7	5 398.9	1 398.9	4 000.0	2 835.0
1998	26 404.5	18 620.5	9 320.4	3 583.8	5 736.6	9 300.1	5 101.1	1 355.8	3 745.3	2 682.9
1997	25 012.1	17 549.3	8 818.7	3 394.6	5 424.1	8 730.6	4 901.2	1 334.7	3 566.5	2 561.7
1996	23 768.2	16 618.1	8 347.4	3 233.1	5 114.3	8 270.6	4 681.8	1 315.5	3 366.3	2 468.3
1995	22 669.6	15 794.3	7 954.4	3 067.4	4 887.1	7 839.8	4 504.7	1 291.3	3 213.4	2 370.7
1994	21 621.5	15 056.7	7 551.3	2 880.6	4 670.7	7 505.4	4 295.2	1 260.7	3 034.5	2 269.6
1993	20 380.0	14 166.8	7 161.9	2 728.2	4 433.7	7 004.9	4 064.3	1 209.0	2 855.2	2 148.9
1992	19 368.0	13 438.8	6 838.8	2 613.9	4 224.9	6 599.9	3 885.1	1 169.4	2 715.7	2 044.1
1991	18 574.8	12 880.7	6 632.4	2 541.1	4 091.4	6 248.3	3 722.1	1 122.5	2 599.6	1 972.0
1990	18 110.7	12 610.9	6 499.9	2 469.1	4 030.8	6 111.0	3 600.7	1 078.9	2 521.8	1 899.2
1989	17 275.3	12 051.7	6 168.1	2 335.2	3 832.9	5 883.6	3 428.5	1 031.2	2 397.4	1 795.1
1988	16 319.2	11 391.6	5 817.2	2 198.7	3 618.5	5 574.3	3 251.3	977.3	2 274.0	1 676.3
1987	15 346.3	10 710.8	5 462.3	2 071.2	3 391.1	5 248.5	3 092.6	921.5	2 171.1	1 542.8
1986	14 468.8	10 110.1	5 180.2	1 970.1	3 210.1	4 929.9	2 936.2	885.2	2 051.0	1 422.6
1985	13 560.4	9 509.0	4 944.3	1 865.6	3 078.6	4 564.7	2 766.5	842.4	1 924.1	1 284.9
1984	12 842.4	9 011.2	4 680.1	1 760.7	2 919.4	4 331.1	2 650.3	810.6	1 839.7	1 180.9
1983	12 156.2	8 516.4	4 416.7	1 669.4	2 747.3	4 099.7	2 550.9	772.4	1 778.5	1 088.9
1982	11 739.8	8 229.0	4 288.4	1 615.8	2 672.6	3 940.6	2 491.3	735.5	1 755.8	1 019.5
1981	11 141.6	7 802.6	4 032.9	1 525.1	2 507.8	3 769.7	2 360.7	697.1	1 663.6	978.3
1980	10 126.9	7 067.8	3 563.2	1 367.4	2 195.8	3 504.6	2 148.9	648.0	1 501.0	910.2
1979	8 912.4	6 210.7	3 102.4	1 178.5	1 924.0	3 108.2	1 877.0	583.9	1 293.1	824.7
1978	7 746.3	5 364.2	2 687.2	1 014.2	1 673.0	2 677.0	1 648.0	524.0	1 124.0	734.1
1977	6 844.3	4 686.9	2 365.7	887.7	1 477.9	2 321.2	1 507.1	485.7	1 021.4	650.3
1976	6 119.2	4 115.7	2 126.9	790.4	1 336.5	1 988.9	1 418.1	462.8	955.3	585.4
1975	5 610.2	3 734.7	1 942.9	713.9	1 228.9	1 791.8	1 341.1	426.6	914.5	534.4
1974	5 177.5	3 415.8	1 763.0	623.4	1 139.6	1 652.7	1 276.6	403.3	873.3	485.1
1973	4 359.4	2 899.6	1 447.3	505.4	941.9	1 452.3	1 038.8	349.5	689.3	421.1
1972	3 854.7	2 550.6	1 283.2	452.8	830.4	1 267.4	923.4	322.5	600.9	380.7
1971	3 510.4	2 311.6	1 178.4	419.8	758.6	1 133.2	847.5	299.5	548.0	351.3
1970	3 190.9	2 078.4	1 070.3	392.2	678.0	1 008.2	782.4	285.3	497.1	330.1
1969	2 934.7	1 924.5	972.1	357.4	614.7	952.3	703.2	267.4	435.8	307.1
1968	2 693.0	1 772.7	882.5	323.9	558.7	890.2	638.9	253.0	385.9	281.3
1967	2 450.0	1 608.5	802.8	293.8	509.0	805.7	588.6	240.9	347.7	253.0
1966	2 273.2	1 496.9	742.5	268.2	474.4	754.4	544.9	226.7	318.2	231.4
1965	2 095.0	1 379.4	681.9	240.7	441.1	697.6	504.0	216.0	288.0	211.5
1964	1 967.4	1 293.6	636.6	223.4	413.3	657.0	473.7	209.0	264.7	200.2
1963	1 850.8	1 209.0	601.0	210.7	390.3	608.0	451.6	203.5	248.1	190.3
1962	1 784.5	1 173.3	579.9	202.2	377.7	593.4	430.7	197.9	232.8	180.4
1961	1 711.0	1 132.0	559.7	194.8	364.8	572.3	404.4	187.0	217.4	174.6
1960	1 653.9	1 096.8	544.6	191.6	353.0	552.2	385.1	180.0	205.1	172.0
1959	1 603.7	1 064.8	533.5	185.7	347.7	531.3	371.6	175.9	195.7	167.4
1958	1 542.1	1 020.6	511.5	176.7	334.8	509.2	361.3	171.7	189.5	160.2
1957	1 496.1	996.5	502.2	171.3	331.0	494.2	343.2	165.7	177.4	156.5
1956	1 425.3	948.4	470.2	157.3	312.9	478.2	329.1	159.8	169.3	147.7
1955	1 315.0	881.4	425.2	140.3	284.9	456.2	296.9	147.5	149.4	136.7
1954	1 211.8	809.2	385.8	127.7	258.0	423.4	275.2	140.7	134.5	127.4
1953	1 161.3	777.7	375.9	124.2	251.7	401.9	259.3	130.5	128.8	124.3
1952	1 118.2	747.6	360.2	114.8	245.3	387.4	254.1	123.9	130.2	116.6
1951	1 056.8	710.5	341.8	109.3	232.4	368.7	236.7	113.9	122.9	109.6
1950	963.9	653.2	313.6	99.4	214.1	339.6	211.5	102.3	109.3	99.2
1949	861.0	579.4	276.9	86.0	190.9	302.5	199.8	102.8	96.9	81.9
1948	848.5	560.0	272.0	82.2	189.8	288.0	214.6	113.0	101.6	73.9
1947	794.9	515.4	248.0	68.0	180.0	267.4	214.4	121.1	93.3	65.1
1946	687.9	433.4	206.3	56.3	150.0	227.1	200.3	122.4	77.9	54.1
1945	586.0	351.5	167.2	46.8	120.4	184.3	188.4	118.9	69.5	46.2
1944	543.1	326.7	152.0	40.5	111.5	174.7	169.9	103.0	66.9	46.5
1943	507.6	314.0	150.5	40.3	110.3	163.5	149.3	80.8	68.5	44.3
1942	456.2	299.1	148.5	39.8	108.7	150.6	117.0	49.7	67.4	40.1
1941	400.1	279.3	139.5	38.7	100.8	139.9	84.5	24.4	60.2	36.2
1940	350.4	251.7	123.6	33.6	90.0	128.1	67.6	15.7	51.9	31.0
1939	323.0	233.0	116.2	31.1	85.2	116.7	61.6	14.0	47.6	28.5
1938	315.6	228.7	115.5	30.3	85.2	113.1	59.2	13.3	45.9	27.8
1937	313.2	228.1	116.8	30.2	86.6	111.3	57.2	12.6	44.6	27.9
1936	297.4	216.5	111.8	27.9	83.9	104.7	54.2	11.4	42.8	26.7
1935	269.1	195.5	101.3	25.9	75.4	94.2	48.7	9.8	38.8	24.9
1934	265.1	194.2	101.6	26.4	75.2	92.7	45.9	8.6	37.2	25.1
1933	259.2	192.0	100.3	26.2	74.0	91.7	41.8	7.6	34.2	25.5
1932	244.0	182.6	98.7	26.5	72.2	83.9	35.7	6.7	29.0	25.7
1931	265.1	200.1	106.6	29.4	77.2	93.5	36.1	6.8	29.3	28.9
1930	306.9	233.7	119.4	32.1	87.3	114.3	39.7	7.4	32.2	33.5
1929	321.5	245.0	125.2	33.4	91.8	119.8	40.8	7.9	32.9	35.8
1928	316.6	240.8	125.1	32.8	92.3	115.7	40.6	8.3	32.3	35.2
1927	303.8	229.0	121.8	32.4	89.4	107.2	40.0	8.7	31.3	34.8
1926	296.3	223.7	119.3	32.0	87.2	104.4	39.2	9.0	30.2	33.4
1925	285.8	215.5	114.8	30.5	84.3	100.7	38.3	9.2	29.1	32.0

Source: U.S. Department of Commerce, Bureau of Economic Analysis.

Table 23-13. Chain-Type Quantity Indexes for Net Stock of Fixed Assets and Consumer Durable Goods, 1925–2005

(Index numbers, 2000 = 100.)

Year	Total	Private fixed assets					Government fixed assets			Consumer durable goods
		Total	Nonresidential			Residential	Total	Federal	State and local	
			Total	Equipment and software	Structures					
2005	114.288	112.470	109.078	113.995	106.223	115.620	110.706	100.482	114.036	135.886
2004	111.324	109.780	107.250	110.535	105.282	112.155	108.728	99.912	111.617	128.296
2003	108.387	107.204	105.625	107.919	104.225	108.711	106.522	99.451	108.849	120.833
2002	105.624	104.892	104.229	105.998	103.139	105.531	104.266	99.358	105.886	113.563
2001	102.929	102.674	102.665	103.882	101.912	102.682	102.026	99.460	102.876	106.517
2000	100.000	100.000	100.000	100.000	100.000	100.000	100.000	100.000	100.000	100.000
1999	96.600	96.694	96.096	93.465	97.801	97.288	98.085	100.543	97.261	93.202
1998	93.311	93.499	92.422	87.197	95.884	94.579	96.235	100.845	94.680	86.764
1997	90.310	90.474	88.930	81.600	93.886	92.039	94.634	101.348	92.363	81.589
1996	87.650	87.755	85.805	76.724	92.076	89.750	93.109	102.024	90.081	77.473
1995	85.193	85.268	83.120	72.656	90.480	87.474	91.451	101.562	88.008	73.985
1994	83.045	83.080	80.789	69.089	89.149	85.442	90.029	101.705	86.036	70.996
1993	81.087	81.119	78.985	66.225	88.227	83.315	88.736	101.918	84.214	68.112
1992	79.330	79.389	77.417	64.084	87.164	81.412	87.275	101.570	82.362	65.818
1991	77.844	78.032	76.330	62.867	86.210	79.761	85.517	100.453	80.381	64.056
1990	76.471	76.766	75.144	61.909	84.854	78.408	83.670	99.096	78.367	62.811
1989	74.590	75.040	73.356	60.398	82.868	76.753	81.696	97.237	76.355	60.276
1988	72.538	73.134	71.491	58.496	81.070	74.806	79.905	95.427	74.574	57.123
1987	70.414	71.183	69.663	56.768	79.195	72.724	78.130	93.454	72.868	53.665
1986	68.270	69.244	67.935	55.373	77.219	70.557	76.165	90.423	71.263	50.283
1985	66.033	67.236	66.039	53.688	75.184	68.429	74.239	87.536	69.669	46.522
1984	63.815	65.122	63.645	51.627	72.556	66.637	72.478	84.906	68.211	43.233
1983	61.780	63.109	61.425	49.520	70.288	64.863	71.052	82.891	66.990	40.355
1982	60.335	61.680	60.004	48.468	68.580	63.431	69.923	81.282	66.027	38.458
1981	59.207	60.439	58.318	47.517	66.303	62.704	68.930	80.208	65.062	37.765
1980	57.739	58.739	56.109	45.657	63.843	61.589	67.832	79.308	63.895	37.024
1979	56.228	57.011	54.030	43.746	61.669	60.256	66.592	78.699	62.431	36.302
1978	54.277	54.835	51.679	41.053	59.679	58.281	65.374	78.256	60.930	34.648
1977	52.357	52.743	49.606	38.581	58.028	56.174	64.295	78.062	59.526	32.656
1976	50.704	50.980	48.034	36.735	56.760	54.196	63.382	77.954	58.318	30.736
1975	49.345	49.615	46.781	35.466	55.566	52.703	62.330	77.871	56.923	29.149
1974	48.224	48.471	45.585	34.331	54.349	51.631	61.271	78.032	55.460	28.132
1973	46.773	46.865	43.788	32.300	52.801	50.256	60.217	78.407	53.924	26.971
1972	44.965	44.893	41.819	30.088	51.114	48.290	59.294	79.334	52.349	25.047
1971	43.350	43.127	40.269	28.565	49.605	46.277	58.427	80.589	50.741	23.451
1970	41.973	41.630	38.912	27.427	48.108	44.622	57.529	82.157	48.998	22.245
1969	40.684	40.269	37.408	26.101	46.524	43.440	56.297	82.789	47.121	21.365
1968	39.160	38.743	35.714	24.470	44.890	42.121	54.820	83.163	44.990	20.083
1967	37.618	37.309	34.160	23.001	43.372	40.836	53.084	83.059	42.667	18.648
1966	36.169	35.979	32.630	21.590	41.847	39.754	51.149	81.951	40.432	17.506
1965	34.603	34.502	30.897	19.897	40.227	38.599	49.295	80.787	38.327	16.210
1964	33.126	33.068	29.409	18.568	38.704	37.243	47.640	79.993	36.356	15.059
1963	31.827	31.805	28.303	17.667	37.491	35.801	45.964	78.723	34.521	14.225
1962	30.679	30.709	27.426	16.991	36.466	34.444	44.310	77.167	32.819	13.561
1961	29.629	29.723	26.603	16.438	35.420	33.268	42.570	74.842	31.276	13.073
1960	28.753	28.879	25.935	16.100	34.446	32.217	40.908	72.700	29.775	12.873
1959	27.857	28.000	25.215	15.661	33.478	31.151	39.504	71.202	28.395	12.504
1958	26.895	27.103	24.577	15.275	32.620	29.944	37.944	69.141	27.007	12.013
1957	26.200	26.413	24.054	15.073	31.791	29.055	36.607	67.899	25.633	11.928
1956	25.330	25.559	23.238	14.471	30.811	28.162	35.470	67.042	24.401	11.410
1955	24.438	24.646	22.400	13.864	29.789	27.165	34.340	65.963	23.257	10.958
1954	23.443	23.715	21.657	13.286	28.929	26.024	33.197	64.784	22.125	10.138
1953	22.606	22.949	21.058	12.900	28.147	25.073	31.832	62.458	21.097	9.679
1952	21.671	22.168	20.353	12.298	27.386	24.206	30.234	58.562	20.293	9.019
1951	20.847	21.450	19.746	11.786	26.722	23.365	28.725	54.757	19.573	8.579
1950	20.028	20.677	19.067	11.171	26.030	22.486	27.641	52.620	18.858	8.036
1949	19.277	19.806	18.431	10.559	25.421	21.359	28.083	56.400	18.163	7.067
1948	18.760	19.156	17.886	10.036	24.898	20.595	28.630	60.292	17.586	6.359
1947	18.342	18.345	17.118	9.126	24.330	19.733	30.288	67.929	17.248	5.721
1946	18.056	17.624	16.383	8.173	23.875	19.026	32.536	77.358	17.047	5.038
1945	17.997	17.082	15.793	7.607	23.327	18.531	35.164	87.703	17.035	4.563
1944	17.672	16.961	15.496	7.120	23.298	18.595	33.495	80.633	17.187	4.645
1943	16.896	16.993	15.497	6.998	23.446	18.661	28.637	60.898	17.374	4.732
1942	15.972	17.125	15.694	7.113	23.713	18.718	22.682	37.260	17.528	4.907
1941	15.101	17.157	15.796	7.174	23.848	18.666	17.734	18.748	17.494	4.923

Table 23-13. Chain-Type Quantity Indexes for Net Stock of Fixed Assets and Consumer Durable Goods, 1925–2005—*Continued*

(Index numbers, 2000 = 100.)

Year	Total	Private fixed assets					Government fixed assets			Consumer durable goods
		Total	Nonresidential			Residential	Total	Federal	State and local	
			Total	Equipment and software	Structures					
1940	14.537	16.839	15.485	6.783	23.698	18.343	15.847	12.833	17.169	4.808
1939	14.193	16.590	15.276	6.501	23.625	18.047	15.151	11.862	16.581	4.567
1938	13.933	16.451	15.223	6.419	23.621	17.808	14.392	11.228	15.766	4.425
1937	13.780	16.413	15.236	6.420	23.647	17.707	13.719	10.530	15.099	4.402
1936	13.525	16.235	15.000	6.118	23.537	17.605	13.130	9.801	14.561	4.267
1935	13.302	16.147	14.904	5.944	23.562	17.526	12.418	9.001	13.878	4.151
1934	13.253	16.195	15.000	5.974	23.724	17.513	11.977	8.154	13.589	4.174
1933	13.298	16.342	15.216	6.156	23.935	17.571	11.570	7.542	13.258	4.285
1932	13.458	16.579	15.551	6.491	24.198	17.677	11.264	7.103	13.004	4.516
1931	13.563	16.790	15.861	6.865	24.358	17.755	10.812	6.880	12.457	4.690
1930	13.487	16.784	15.900	7.042	24.214	17.696	10.248	6.744	11.715	4.762
1929	13.224	16.544	15.559	6.945	23.631	17.575	9.704	6.694	10.972	4.690
1928	12.790	16.080	15.005	6.629	22.871	17.224	9.274	6.718	10.359	4.445
1927	12.379	15.611	14.603	6.520	22.178	16.677	8.865	6.780	9.759	4.277
1926	11.954	15.117	14.205	6.445	21.451	16.066	8.488	6.875	9.191	4.096
1925	11.489	14.557	13.736	6.261	20.708	15.396	8.177	6.985	8.711	3.876

Source: U.S. Department of Commerce, Bureau of Economic Analysis. *National Income Product Accounts.*

BOX 23 ■ Subprime Mortgages

Owning a home has always been a cornerstone of the American dream. In the years following September 11, 2001, Federal Reserve Chairman Alan Greenspan, in an attempt to avoid an economic slowdown, lowered interest rates and encouraged lenders to create alternatives to the standard 30-year fixed rate mortgage that required a 20% down payment. Nonstandard mortgages with smaller down payments, initial interest only payments, or adjustable rates with very low initial payments enabled many people, who had not previously qualified, to purchase a home. This included borrowers with no cash for a down payment, borrowers with no credit history or a poor credit rating, and borrowers who could not provide documentation of their income or savings. These mortgagees received loans that generally carry a higher interest rate than standard market loans and are referred to as subprime loans.

The expanded availability of mortgage loans did increase homeownership. From 2004 to 2006, 14 million families purchased homes. As a result, real estate prices increased throughout the country, as did jobs in such related industries as construction, real estate sales, banking, and retail home furnishings. Five years after 9/11, the White House reported a record high in homeownership in the fourth quarter of 2006, with more than 75 million owner-occupied households, which was almost 69% of all households. The subprime market, estimated at $120 billion in 2001, reached $600 billion in 2006. By 2007, the subprime market was estimated at $1.5 trillion in home loans.

When Alan Greenspan retired as Chairman of the Federal Reserve in 2005, he cautioned that the large number of mortgages with very low introductory interest rates could lead to economic trouble if housing prices dropped. In that year, interest rates were rising. This was coupled with the fact that the grace period ended for many subprime mortgages, which meant that these loans were now subject to an adjustable interest rate. As a result, many subprime borrowers experienced a significant increase in monthly mortgage payments. It is estimated that during 2007, an additional $1 trillion in mortgages will change from a fixed to an adjustable rate.

In the first quarter of 2007, almost 14% of subprime borrowers were delinquent in their mortgage payments. In the first half of that year, there were 925,986 foreclosure filings, which was an increase of 58% from the same period in 2006. Studies estimate the number of foreclosures for 2007 could surpass two million. The highest delinquency rates occurred with second mortgages that were taken out to cover increased costs on what were originally subprime loans.

On Wall Street, the value of bonds backed by bundled mortgages began to drop in the summer of 2007; one of Goldman Sachs' hedge funds dropped 30% in just weeks. The S&P 500 Homebuilding Index dropped 20% in less than two months. By late summer of 2007, the lenders responsible for approximately 40% of subprime loans in 2006 were out of business, sold, in bankruptcy, or in the process of being sold. In just the first eight months of 2007, almost 16,000 financial services jobs directly related to real estate were eliminated, while financial services overall lost almost 90,000 jobs in the same period. Lehman Brothers, one of the biggest underwriters of mortgage debt on Wall Street, announced the closing of its subprime mortgage unit, thereby incurring a loss of $52 million in August 2007.

Members of Congress introduced legislation to change personal bankruptcy laws, to allocate emergency funds to bail out homeowners in danger of losing their homes, to reduce predatory lending, and to change lending laws to increase disclosure to the consumer. The Federal Reserve Bank shocked financial markets by reducing the discount rate at which banks borrow from the central bank by half a percentage point in one day. Fannie Mae modified underwriting standards for adjustable rate mortgages of three years or less to help consumers understand the possible impact associated with some subprime loans after the expiration of any introductory interest rate period.

Sources:

Cramer, James J. "Bloody and Bloodier: The Subprime-Lending Crisis is Worse than You Think, and Could Crush Financial and Real-Estate Markets for Years." *New York Magazine* (August 20, 2007).

"Financial Job Cuts Soar on Housing Woes." Reuters (August 21, 2007).

"Foreclosures Jump, Trending Higher: RealtyTrac." Reuters (July 30, 2007).

Giannone, Joseph, D. Wilchins, T. McLaughlin, R. Leong and A. Yoon. "Lehman Closes Subprime Unit and Cut 1,200 Jobs." Reuters (August 22, 2007).

"Greenspan Still Worried by IOs." *Mortgage Line* 30.1 (Oct. 11, 2005):6.

"July Foreclosures Up 9 Percent from June." The Associated Press (August 21, 2007).

Kogut, David. "Berson's Weekly Commentary." Fannie Mae (August 20, 2007).

Krugman, Paul. "Greenspan and the Bubble." *The New York Times* (August 29, 2005): A15(L).

Leonhardt and Motoko Rich. "The Trillion Dollar Bet." *The New York Times* (June 16, 2005).

Liedtke, Michael. "High-Risk Mortgages Become Toxic Mess." Associated Press (August 11, 2007).

Lohr, Steve. "Loan by Loan, the Making of a Credit Squeeze." *The New York Times* (August 19, 2007).

Morgenson, Gretchen. "More Home Foreclosures Loom as Owners Face Mortgage Maze.(Business/Financial Desk)." *The New York Times* (August 6, 2007): A1(L).

Schwartz, Nelson D., and Vikas Bajaj. "Credit Time Bomb Ticked, but Few Heard. (Business/Financial Desk)." *The New York Times* (August 9, 2007): A1(L).

Veiga, Alex. "July Foreclosures Up 9 Percent from June." Associated Press, August 21, 2007.

U.S. Census Bureau. American Community Survey. http://www.census.gov/acs/www/

U.S. Federal Housing Finance Board of the United States. Terms on Conventional Single Family Mortgages, Annual National Averages, All Homes. http://www.fhfb.gov/Default.aspx?Page=53

The White House. Homeownership. http://www.whitehouse.gov/infocus/homeownership/

Wilchins, Dan. "Top Banks Tap Fed Discount Window." Reuters (August 22, 2007).

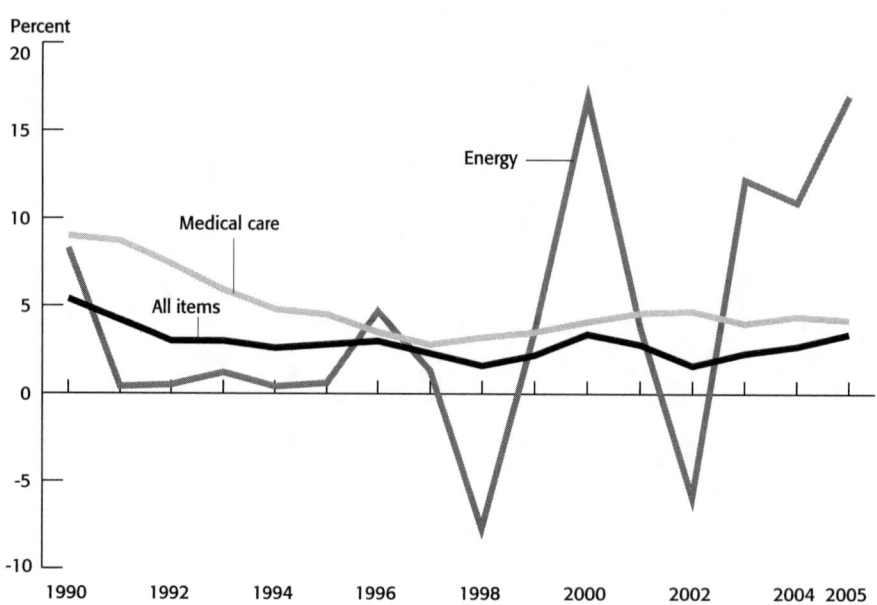

Annual Percent Change in Consumer Price Indexes: 1990 to 2005
Source: Chart prepared by U.S. Census Bureau.

CHAPTER **24**

Consumer Income and Expenditures

HIGHLIGHTS

1 Reasonably reliable nationwide estimates of income distribution are available only from the 1940s when the minimum income requirement for filing income tax returns was substantially lowered to cover the vast majority of the population. Annual tabulations of tax-return data began during World War I but initially covered only a small fraction of the upper-income population. Sample field surveys of family incomes covering all income and occupation groups were introduced in the 1930s. Estimates of income distribution before the 1940s were pieced together from sample surveys in *American Studies of the Distribution of Wealth and Income by Size* (1939) by C. L. Merwin, *The Present Distribution of Wealth in the United States* (1896) by Charles B. Spahr, *Wealth and Income of the People of the United States* (1915) by Willford I. King, *Income in the United States* (1921–1922) by W. C. Mitchell, W. I. King, F. R. Maucaulay, and O. W. Knauth, and *America's Capacity to Consume* (1934) by Maurice Leven, H. H. Moulton, and Clark Warburton. *The Consumer Purchase Study* (1935–1936) conducted by the National Resources Committee under Hildegarde Kneeland was the first sample field survey in which income data were collected from all types of families. Based largely on 300,000 family income schedules, it represented a marked improvement over earlier estimates by providing data for numerous subgroups classified by occupation, community, region, color, and family size. *The Survey of Spending and Saving in Wartime* is the only other pre–World War II source on

the distribution of family income nationwide. The 1940 decennial census was the first to include income questions, making it possible to compare prewar and postwar income levels. For the post–World War II years, income data are available from two sources: the annual Current Population Surveys of the Census Bureau and the annual surveys of consumer finances conducted by the Survey Research Center of the University of Michigan. In addition, all censuses since 1950 provide detailed information on the level of total money income, as well as wage and salary income, classified by demographic and socioeconomic characteristics and cross-classified by sex, race and occupation, and industry groups. Complementing these sources are income and expenditure surveys conducted by the Bureau of Labor Statistics for selected population groups, studies of farm family income by the Department of Agriculture, and, since 1937, surveys of income distributions of workers covered under the Old Age, Survivors, Disability and Health Insurance (OASDHI) program. The much broader coverage of Federal Individual Income Tax Returns since World War II has made it possible to measure changes in relative income distribution over time. As part of its national income work, the Bureau of Economic Analysis, formerly the Office of Business Economics, publishes a personal income series by combining census and income tax data. To derive meaningful comparisons over time, the data for the prewar period have been adjusted to make them compatible with the postwar data. Direct compatibility among income distribution series has not been fully achieved because of variations in definitions and coverage. Definitional differences apply to the basic unit of classification, the income measure, the time period, and the family unit.

2 Collection of data on consumer expenditures began in the United States in the 1870s. The most substantial of these studies was made for Massachusetts by Carroll D. Wright in 1875. The usefulness of the data gathered in this study led Congress to request that further studies of this type on a broader base be conducted by the newly formed U.S. Bureau of Labor (of which Wright was made commissioner). The data on food expenditures obtained in the 1901 survey were used to devise an index of food prices purchased by workers. During that period, the need for a more inclusive index of retail prices became clearer because food prices rose much faster than those of many other commodities and rent. A nationwide study of the expenditures of wage earners and clerical workers was undertaken in 1918. The survey was first undertaken in seacoast cities (because of the number of wage disputes in shipbuilding centers) but later was expanded to other industrial centers. The first study of overall consumer expenditures of farm families was made in Livingstone County in New York State in 1909. Dramatic increases in industrial and agricultural productivity and the collapse of the economy in 1929 led a number of economists to study the factors affecting consumer expenditures and to estimate changes in consumption patterns over time. The pioneer investigation in this field was presented in Simon Kuznets' *Commodity Flow and Capital Formation* (1938). It showed national aggregates for four types of consumer goods and services. The Brookings Institution published estimates of expenditure patterns at different income levels for farm and nonfarm families in 1934 and for single individuals in 1929. In the middle 1930s, two national cross-section studies of consumer expenditure patterns were undertaken. The first, conducted by the Bureau of Labor Statistics, covered employed city wage and clerical workers and was initiated to provide a new list of items and weights for the Consumer Price Index. The second, the Study of Consumer Purchases, was conducted jointly by the Bureau of Labor Statistics and the Bureau of Home Economics of the Department of Agriculture. The results of the second study were used by the National Resources Planning Board as the basis for a national estimate of consumer expenditures. The first detailed estimates and aggregate consumer expenditures in goods and services appeared in *High-Level Consumption* by William H. Lough in 1935 and covered the period from 1909 to 1931. Data for later years were revised and extended in *Outlay and Income in the United States, 1921–1938,* by Harold Barger and in *America's Needs and Resources* (1947) by J. Frederic Dewhurst. The first detailed estimates by the Department of Commerce of consumer expenditures for commodities and services were published in the *Survey of Current Business* in June 1944. As defined by the Department of Commerce, consumer expenditures represent the market value of purchases of goods and services by individuals and nonprofit institutions as well as the value of food, clothing, housing, and financial services received by them as income in kind. Rental value of owner-occupied houses is included, but purchases of dwellings, which are classified as capital goods, are not. Other national sample surveys include the Surveys of Consumer Finances, conducted for the Board of Governors of the Federal Reserve System by the Consumer Research Center of the University of Michigan, and the Household Food Consumption Surveys of the Department of Agriculture.

3 Based on 1982-1984 = 100, the Consumer Price Index in 2005 was 195.3. The rise was highest in energy (17 percent to 177.1), transportation (6.6 percent to 173.9), and medical care (4.2 percent to 323.2). It was lowest in apparel (down 0.7 percent to 119.5) and education and communication (1.9 percent to 113.7). The U.S. city average CPI was 195.3, with wide rational variations. It was highest in San Diego (220.6) and Boston (216.4), and lowest in Phoenix-Mesa, Arizona (108.3).

4 The weekly moderate cost plan food cost of a family of two people of twenty to fifty years of age has increased from $96.40 in 1990 to $111.00 in 2005. The cost for a family of four, with children between the ages of one and two and three and four, has increased in the same period from $137.60 to $158.30.

5 From 2000 to 2005, the price of whole wheat bread has actually declined in price from $1.36 a pound to $1.29. At the same time, the price of white bread has gone up from $0.99 in 2000 to $1.05 in 2005.

6 Although the annual percentage rise in consumer prices in the United States was only 3.4 in 2005, it has one of the highest rates in the OECD. For example, Japan had an annual percentage decline 0.3 percent and Switzerland had a rise of 1.2 percent.

7 Based on the 1980 index, 1st quarter of 100, the most expensive housing in 2005 was in Massachusetts (732), New York (635), and California (618). The least expensive housing was in Oklahoma (193), Texas (205), and Louisiana (221).

8 The purchasing power of the dollar has declined substantially since 1950. With 1982 = $1.00, the purchasing power of the dollar was $3.546 measured by producer prices and $4.151 measured by consumer prices in 1950. In 2005, the relative values were $0.642 and $0.512.

Table 24-2. Families by Total Money Income, Race, and Hispanic Origin of Householder, 1967–2005—*Continued*

(Income in 2005 Consumer Price Index Research Series Using Current Methods (CPI-U-RS[1]) adjusted dollars. Families as of March of the following year.)

Race and Hispanic origin of house-holder and year	Number (thou-sands)	Percent distribution										Median income		Mean income	
		Total	Under $5,000	$5,000–$9,999	$10,000–$14,999	$15,000–$24,999	$25,000–$34,999	$35,000–$49,999	$50,000–$74,999	$75,000–$99,999	$100,000 and over	Value (dollars)	Standard error (dollars)	Value (dollars)	Standard error (dollars)
Asian alone or in combination															
2005	3 358	100.0	2.7	1.9	3.3	7.6	7.0	11.9	19.4	14.7	31.5	69,282	1 552	88 120	1 607
2004[2]	3 283	100.0	1.9	1.9	2.4	7.7	8.3	13.2	20.4	13.8	30.5	67,426	1 340	87 837	1 786
2003	3 194	100.0	3.6	2.3	3.1	8.4	6.8	12.8	19.7	14.2	29.1	66,297	1 424	81 567	1 515
2002	2 939	100.0	2.4	1.1	2.6	8.2	9.4	13.1	19.3	14.7	29.1	66,223	917	85 318	1 832
Asian alone															
2005	3 208	100.0	2.6	1.9	3.3	7.7	7.0	11.8	19.7	14.4	31.6	68 957	1 589	88 372	1 662
2004[2]	3 142	100.0	1.8	2.0	2.4	7.5	8.3	13.1	20.4	13.7	30.8	67 608	1 331	88 133	1 821
2003	3 064	100.0	3.6	2.3	3.1	8.4	6.5	12.6	19.7	14.2	29.6	67 123	1 634	82 258	1 564
2002	2 845	100.0	2.4	1.1	2.6	8.2	9.6	13.0	19.2	14.6	29.3	66 200	909	85 700	1 883
Asian and Pacific Islander															
2001	2 980	100.0	2.5	1.5	2.5	9.0	9.2	12.5	19.0	13.8	29.9	66 342	1 392	87 682	2 227
2000[3]	2 982	100.0	2.3	1.2	3.4	6.9	8.1	12.6	18.9	16.0	30.6	70 981	1 249	89 814	1 736
1995[4]	2 125	100.0	2.5	2.6	6.0	8.8	8.5	13.1	21.6	15.1	21.7	58 966	1 367	76 820	3 347
1990	1 536	100.0	3.1	2.4	3.2	9.0	8.0	12.8	23.4	15.2	22.7	61 185	2 275	72 351	2 157
1988	1 481	100.0	1.7	3.2	4.3	11.1	9.3	14.6	19.8	12.9	23.1	57 970	1 903	70 081	2 294
Hispanic of any race															
2005	9 868	100.0	3.9	4.3	6.5	16.3	15.2	17.4	18.2	8.9	9.3	37 867	483	48 847	521
2004[2]	9 521	100.0	4.1	4.4	6.9	17.6	15.0	16.7	17.5	8.3	9.5	36 625	418	49 430	693
2003	9 274	100.0	4.2	4.0	7.3	16.8	16.1	17.1	16.7	8.7	9.2	36 370	532	48 818	594
2002	9 094	100.0	3.9	4.2	6.5	17.2	16.0	16.8	17.2	9.0	9.0	37 109	576	50 166	759
2001	8 516	100.0	3.9	4.1	6.7	16.5	15.0	17.8	17.0	9.6	9.4	38 035	515	49 878	637
2000[3]	8 017	100.0	3.6	3.9	7.0	16.1	14.3	17.8	18.8	9.5	8.9	39 043	574	51 932	866
1995[4]	6 287	100.0	4.1	7.3	9.2	19.4	15.5	16.7	14.8	7.1	5.9	31 254	706	41 537	962
1990	4 981	100.0	3.6	6.6	9.7	17.0	14.8	17.3	17.4	7.3	6.2	33 935	820	42 451	762
1985[5]	4 206	100.0	3.4	7.4	10.0	18.0	14.7	17.8	16.7	7.2	4.9	32 924	848	40 062	703
1980	3 235	100.0	3.2	6.6	8.7	18.9	16.1	18.6	18.3	6.2	3.6	33 021	882	39 526	828
1975[6]	2 499	100.0	2.7	7.7	9.7	20.3	17.3	20.6	15.6	4.1	2.0	30 544	732	35 485	659
1972[8]	2 312	100.0	2.2	5.6	9.1	19.1	19.4	23.0	15.8	3.8	2.1	33 093	...	37 642	...

Source: U.S. Census Bureau. *Current Population Survey, Annual Social and Economic Supplement.*
[1]The CPI-U-RS is a price index of inflation that incorporates most of the improvements in methodology made to the current CPI-U since 1978 into a single, uniform series.
[2]Data have been revised to reflect a correction to the weights in the 2005 Annual Social and Economic Supplement.
[3]Reflects implementation of a 28,000 household sample expansion.
[4]Data reflect full implementation of the 1990 census-based sample design and metropolitan definitions, 7,000 household sample reduction, and revised race edits.
[5]Data reflect full implementation of 1980 census-based sample design.
[6]Some of these estimates were derived using Pareto interpolation and may differ from published data which were derived using linear interpolation.
[8]Data reflect full implementation of 1970 census-based sample design.
. . . = Not available.

Table 24-3. Percent Distribution of Aggregate Income Received by Each Fifth and Top 5 Percent of Families, 1947–2004

(Constant dollars based on Consumer Price Index Research Series Using Current Methods[1] (CPI-U-RS) deflator. Families as of March of the following year.)

Year	Number of families (1,000)	Lowest fifth	Second fifth	Third fifth	Fourth fifth	Highest fifth	Top 5 percent
2004	77 019	4.0	9.6	15.4	23.0	47.9	20.9
2003	76 232	4.1	9.6	15.5	23.2	47.6	20.5
2002	75 616	4.2	9.7	15.5	23.0	47.6	20.8
2001	74 340	4.2	9.7	15.4	22.9	47.7	21.0
2000[2,3]	73 778	4.3	9.8	15.4	22.7	47.7	21.1
1999[4]	73 206	4.3	9.9	15.6	23.0	47.2	20.3
1998	71 551	4.2	9.9	15.7	23.0	47.3	20.7
1997	70 884	4.2	9.9	15.7	23.0	47.2	20.7
1996	70 241	4.2	10.0	15.8	23.1	46.8	20.3
1995[5]	69 597	4.4	10.1	15.8	23.2	46.5	20.0
1994[6]	69 313	4.2	10.0	15.7	23.3	46.9	20.1
1993[7]	68 506	4.1	9.9	15.7	23.3	47.0	20.3
1992[8]	68 216	4.3	10.5	16.5	24.0	44.7	17.6
1991	67 173	4.5	10.7	16.6	24.1	44.2	17.1
1990	66 322	4.6	10.8	16.6	23.8	44.3	17.4
1989	66 090	4.6	10.6	16.5	23.7	44.6	17.9
1988	65 837	4.6	10.7	16.7	24.0	44.0	17.2
1987[9]	65 204	4.6	10.7	16.8	24.0	43.8	17.2
1986	64 491	4.7	10.9	16.9	24.1	43.4	16.5
1985[10]	63 558	4.8	11.0	16.9	24.3	43.1	16.1
1984	62 706	4.8	11.1	17.1	24.5	42.5	15.4
1983[11]	62 015	4.9	11.2	17.2	24.5	42.4	15.3
1982	61 393	5.0	11.3	17.2	24.4	42.2	15.3
1981	61 019	5.3	11.4	17.5	24.6	41.2	14.4
1980	60 309	5.3	11.6	17.6	24.4	41.1	14.6
1979[12]	59 550	5.4	11.6	17.5	24.1	41.4	15.3
1978	57 804	5.4	11.7	17.6	24.2	41.1	15.1
1977	57 215	5.5	11.7	17.6	24.3	40.9	14.9
1976[13]	56 710	5.6	11.9	17.7	24.2	40.7	14.9
1975[14]	56 245	5.6	11.9	17.7	24.2	40.7	14.9
1974[14,15]	55 698	5.7	12.0	17.6	24.1	40.6	14.8
1973	55 053	5.5	11.9	17.5	24.0	41.1	15.5
1972[16]	54 373	5.5	11.9	17.5	23.9	41.4	15.9
1971[17]	53 296	5.5	12.0	17.6	23.8	41.1	15.7
1970	52 227	5.4	12.2	17.6	23.8	40.9	15.6
1969	51 586	5.6	12.4	17.7	23.7	40.6	15.6
1968	50 823	5.6	12.4	17.7	23.7	40.5	15.6
1967[18]	50 111	5.4	12.2	17.5	23.5	41.4	16.4
1966[19]	49 214	5.6	12.4	17.8	23.8	40.5	15.6
1965[20]	48 509	5.2	12.2	17.8	23.9	40.9	15.5
1964	47 956	5.1	12.0	17.7	24.0	41.2	15.9
1963	47 540	5.0	12.1	17.7	24.0	41.2	15.8
1962[21]	47 059	5.0	12.1	17.6	24.0	41.3	15.7
1961[22]	46 418	4.7	11.9	17.5	23.8	42.2	16.6
1960	45 539	4.8	12.2	17.8	24.0	41.3	15.9
1959	45 111	4.9	12.3	17.9	23.8	41.1	15.9
1958	44 232	5.0	12.5	18.0	23.9	40.6	15.4
1957	43 696	5.1	12.7	18.1	23.8	40.4	15.6
1956	43 497	5.0	12.5	17.9	23.7	41.0	16.1
1955	42 889	4.8	12.3	17.8	23.7	41.3	16.4
1954	41 951	4.5	12.1	17.7	23.9	41.8	16.3
1953	41 202	4.7	12.5	18.0	23.9	40.9	15.7
1952[23]	40 832	4.9	12.3	17.4	23.4	41.9	17.4
1951	40 578	5.0	12.4	17.6	23.4	41.6	16.8
1950	39 929	4.5	12.0	17.4	23.4	42.7	17.3
1949[24]	39 303	4.5	11.9	17.3	23.5	42.7	16.9
1948	38 624	4.9	12.1	17.3	23.2	42.4	17.1
1947[25]	37 237	5.0	11.9	17.0	23.1	43.0	17.5

Source: U.S. Census Bureau. *Statistical Abstract of the United States: 2007.*

[1]The CPI-U-RS is a price index of inflation that incorporates most of the improvements in methodology made to the current CPI-U since 1978 into a single, uniform series. Before 1977 the CPI-U-RS is extrapolated.

[2]Reflects implementation of 2000 census-based population controls and a 28,000 household sample expansion to 78,000 households.

[3]Starting in 1999, 50th percentile is based on micro-sorted data.

[4]Starting in 1999, alternative income definition 7 includes federal Earned Income Credit (EIC) and EIC for the states that use federal eligibility rules to compute the state credit as a percentage of the federal EIC. The nine states are: Iowa, Kansas, Massachusetts, Maryland, New York, Oregon, Rhode Island, Vermont, and Wisconsin.

[5]Data reflect full implementation of the 1990 census-based sample design and metropolitan definitions, 7,000 household sample reduction, and revised race edits.

[6]Data reflect introduction of 1990 census-based sample design.

[7]Data collection method changed from paper and pencil to computer-assisted interviewing. In addition, the March 1994 income supplement was revised to allow for the coding of different income amounts on selected questionnaire items. Child support and alimony limits decreased to $49,999. Limits increased in the following categories: earnings to $999,999; social security to $49,999; supplemental security income and public assistance income to $24,999; and veterans' benefits to $99,999.

[8]Data reflect implementation of 1990 census population controls.

[9]Data reflect implementation of a new March CPS processing system.

[10]Recording of amounts for earnings from longest job were increased to $299,999. Data reflect full implementation of 1980 census-based sample design.

[11]Data reflect implementation of Hispanic population weighting controls and introduction of 1980 census-based sample design.

[12]Data reflect implementation of 1980 census population controls. Questionnaire expanded to show 27 possible values from 51 possible sources of income.

[13]First year medians were derived using both Pareto and linear interpolation. Before this year, all medians were derived using linear interpolation.

[14]Some of these estimates were derived using Pareto interpolation and may differ from published data which were derived using linear interpolation.

[15]Data reflect implementation of a new March CPS processing system. Questionnaire expanded to ask 11 income questions.

[16]Data reflect full implementation of 1970 census-based sample design.

[17]Data reflect introduction of 1970 census-based sample design and population controls.

[18]Data reflect implementation of a new March CPS processing system.

[19]Questionnaire expanded to ask eight income questions.

[20]Data reflect implementation of new procedures to impute missing data only.

[21]Data reflect full implementation of 1960 census-based sample design and population controls.

[22]Data reflect implementation of first hotdeck procedure to impute missing income entries (all income data imputed if any missing). Data also reflect introduction of 1960 census-based sample design.

[23]Data reflect implementation of 1950 census population controls.

[24]Data reflect implementation of expanded income questions to show wage and salary, farm self-employment, nonfarm self-employment, and all other nonearned income separately.

[25]Data based on 1940 census population controls.

Table 24-4. Purchasing Power of the Dollar, 1950–2005

(Indexes: Producer Price Index (PPI), 1982=$1.00; Consumer Price Index (CPI), 1982–84=$1.00.)

Year	Annual average as measured by—	
	Producer prices	Consumer prices
2005	0.642	0.512
2004	0.673	0.530
2003	0.698	0.544
2002	0.720	0.556
2001	0.711	0.565
2000	0.725	0.581
1999	0.752	0.600
1998	0.765	0.614
1997	0.759	0.623
1996	0.762	0.638
1995	0.782	0.656
1994	0.797	0.675
1993	0.802	0.692
1992	0.812	0.713
1991	0.822	0.734
1990	0.839	0.766
1989	0.880	0.807
1988	0.926	0.846
1987	0.949	0.880
1986	0.969	0.913
1985	0.955	0.928
1984	0.964	0.961
1983	0.984	1.003
1982	1.000	1.035
1981	1.041	1.098
1980	1.136	1.215
1979	1.289	1.380
1978	1.433	1.532
1977	1.546	1.649
1976	1.645	1.757
1975	1.718	1.859
1974	1.901	2.029
1973	2.193	2.251
1972	2.392	2.391
1971	2.469	2.466
1970	2.545	2.574
1969	2.632	2.726
1968	2.732	2.873
1967	2.809	2.993
1966	2.841	3.080
1965	2.933	3.166
1964	2.985	3.220
1963	2.994	3.265
1962	2.985	3.304
1961	2.994	3.340
1960	2.994	3.373
1959	3.021	3.427
1958	3.012	3.457
1957	3.077	3.549
1956	3.195	3.678
1955	3.279	3.732
1954	3.289	3.717
1953	3.300	3.735
1952	3.268	3.765
1951	3.247	3.846
1950	3.546	4.151

Source: U.S. Census Bureau. *Statistical Abstract of the United States: 2007.* U.S. Bureau of Labor Statistics.
Note: Producer prices prior to 1961, and consumer prices prior to 1964, exclude Alaska and Hawaii. Producer prices based on finished goods index, obtained by dividing the average price index for the 1982=100, PPI; 1982 to 1984=100, CPI base periods (100.0) by the price index for a given period and expressing the result in dollars and cents. Annual figures are based on average of monthly data.

Table 24-5. Consumer Price Indexes (CPI-U) by Major Groups, 1990–2005

(Annual averages of monthly figures. Reflects buying patterns of all urban consumers. Minus sign (–) indicates a decrease.)

Year	All items	Commodities, total	Services	Food	Energy	All items less food and energy	Food and beverages	Shelter	Transportation	Medical care	Apparel	Education and communication[1]
Index (1982–1984 =100)												
2005	195.3	160.2	230.1	190.7	177.1	200.9	191.2	224.4	173.9	323.2	119.5	113.7
2004	188.9	154.7	222.8	186.2	151.4	196.6	186.6	218.8	163.1	310.1	120.4	111.6
2003	184.0	151.2	216.5	180.0	136.5	193.2	180.5	213.1	157.6	297.1	120.9	109.8
2002	179.9	149.7	209.8	176.2	121.7	190.5	176.8	208.1	152.9	285.6	124.0	107.9
2001	177.1	150.7	203.4	173.1	129.3	186.1	173.6	200.6	154.3	272.8	127.3	105.2
2000	172.2	149.2	195.3	167.8	124.6	181.3	168.4	193.4	153.3	260.8	129.6	102.5
1999	166.6	144.4	188.8	164.1	106.6	177.0	164.6	187.3	144.4	250.6	131.3	101.2
1998	163.0	141.9	184.2	160.7	102.9	173.4	161.1	182.1	141.6	242.1	133.0	100.3
1997	160.5	141.8	179.4	157.3	111.5	169.5	157.7	176.3	144.3	234.6	132.9	98.4
1996	156.9	139.9	174.1	153.3	110.1	165.6	153.7	171.0	143.0	228.2	131.7	95.3
1995	152.4	136.4	168.7	148.4	105.2	161.2	148.9	165.7	139.1	220.5	132.0	92.2
1994	148.2	133.8	163.1	144.3	104.6	156.5	144.9	160.5	134.3	211.0	133.4	88.8
1993	144.5	131.5	157.9	140.9	104.2	152.2	141.6	155.7	130.4	201.4	133.7	85.5
1992	140.3	129.1	152.0	137.9	103.0	147.3	138.7	151.2	126.5	190.1	131.9	...
1991	136.2	126.6	146.3	136.3	102.5	142.1	136.8	146.3	123.8	177.0	128.7	...
1990	130.7	122.8	139.2	132.4	102.1	135.5	132.1	140.0	120.5	162.8	124.1	...
Percent change from prior year shown[2]												
2005	3.4	3.6	3.3	2.4	17.0	2.2	2.5	2.6	6.6	4.2	–0.7	1.9
2004	2.7	2.3	2.9	3.4	10.9	1.8	3.4	2.7	3.5	4.4	–0.4	1.6
2003	2.3	1.0	3.2	2.2	12.2	1.4	2.1	2.4	3.1	4.0	–2.5	1.8
2002	1.6	–0.7	3.1	1.8	–5.9	2.4	1.8	3.7	–0.9	4.7	–2.6	2.6
2001	2.8	1.0	4.1	3.2	3.8	2.6	3.1	3.7	0.7	4.6	–1.8	2.6
2000	3.4	3.3	3.4	2.3	16.9	2.4	2.3	3.3	6.2	4.1	–1.3	1.3
1999	2.2	1.8	2.5	2.1	3.6	2.1	2.2	2.9	2.0	3.5	–1.3	0.9
1998	1.6	0.1	2.7	2.2	–7.7	2.3	2.2	3.3	–1.9	3.2	0.1	1.9
1997	2.3	1.4	3.0	2.6	1.3	2.4	2.6	3.1	0.9	2.8	0.9	3.3
1996	3.0	2.6	3.2	3.3	4.7	2.7	3.2	3.2	2.8	3.5	–0.2	3.4
1995	2.8	1.9	3.4	2.8	0.6	3.0	2.8	3.2	3.6	4.5	–1.0	3.8
1994	2.6	1.7	3.3	2.4	0.4	2.8	2.3	3.1	3.0	4.8	–0.2	3.9
1993	3.0	1.9	3.9	2.2	1.2	3.3	2.1	3.0	3.1	5.9	1.4	...
1992	3.0	2.0	3.9	1.2	0.5	3.7	1.4	3.3	2.2	7.4	2.5	...
1991	4.2	3.1	5.1	2.9	0.4	4.9	3.6	4.5	2.7	8.7	3.7	...
1990	5.4	5.2	5.5	5.8	8.3	5.0	5.8	5.4	5.6	9.0	4.6	...

Source: U.S. Census Bureau. *Statistical Abstract of the United States: 2007.* U.S. Bureau of Labor Statistics.
[1]December 1997 = 100.
[2]Change from immediate prior year. 1990 change from 1989.
. . . = Not available.

Table 24-6. Personal Consumption Expenditures, by Major Type of Product, 1929–2006

(Millions of dollars.)

	Total	Durable goods	Motor vehicles and parts	Furniture and household equipment	Other	Nondurable goods	Food	Clothing and shoes
2006	9 268 922	1 070 312	444 726	404 554	221 035	2 714 867	1 281 141	358 623
2005	8 742 350	1 033 072	448 217	377 195	207 659	2 539 295	1 201 390	341 808
2004	8 211 504	986 260	437 940	356 500	191 821	2 345 180	1 114 783	325 138
2003	7 703 630	942 662	431 709	331 505	179 447	2 190 200	1 045 972	310 921
2002	7 350 722	923 940	429 264	323 094	171 582	2 079 632	1 001 902	303 500
2001	7 055 038	883 689	407 885	312 087	163 717	2 017 095	967 911	297 706
2000	6 739 378	863 326	386 517	312 906	163 900	1 947 216	925 164	297 711
1999	6 282 474	817 628	370 787	293 867	152 974	1 804 806	873 119	286 317
1998	5 879 482	750 198	336 103	273 119	140 977	1 683 567	829 789	270 875
1997	5 547 400	692 658	305 120	256 165	131 375	1 618 963	796 201	258 084
1996	5 256 832	652 563	284 887	242 922	124 755	1 555 528	768 680	250 225
1995	4 975 787	611 600	266 691	228 625	116 284	1 485 065	740 851	241 722
1994	4 743 287	582 221	260 517	213 372	108 332	1 437 175	720 586	238 091
1993	4 477 887	526 737	234 005	193 389	99 342	1 379 390	691 851	229 856
1992	4 235 265	483 588	213 048	178 654	91 886	1 330 505	669 325	221 851
1991	3 986 066	453 915	193 476	171 718	88 722	1 284 784	657 503	208 656
1990	3 839 937	474 204	212 773	171 612	89 819	1 249 882	636 776	204 088
1989	3 598 496	471 764	215 299	171 553	84 911	1 166 701	591 639	198 921
1988	3 353 615	453 589	209 358	163 704	80 528	1 083 484	553 498	185 525
1987	3 100 234	421 667	195 043	153 399	73 225	1 015 262	515 205	174 363
1986	2 899 724	402 988	194 054	142 971	65 964	958 444	492 008	163 114
1985	2 720 305	363 498	175 918	128 531	59 049	928 702	467 579	152 143
1984	2 503 287	326 477	152 120	118 980	55 375	884 641	447 398	142 526
1983	2 290 556	280 798	126 503	106 622	47 672	831 164	423 762	130 853
1982	2 077 268	240 227	102 919	93 424	43 884	787 594	403 353	120 481
1981	1 941 060	231 334	95 825	92 101	43 409	758 887	383 515	117 186
1980	1 757 133	214 161	87 018	86 692	40 451	696 088	355 977	107 337
1979	1 592 215	214 409	93 478	82 726	38 205	624 459	324 670	101 193
1978	1 428 535	201 721	93 134	74 286	34 301	550 245	289 562	94 318
1977	1 278 609	181 213	83 521	67 213	30 479	497 147	262 642	84 113
1976	1 151 914	158 850	71 258	60 224	27 368	458 320	242 523	76 639
1975	1 034 394	133 457	54 801	54 504	24 152	420 729	223 211	70 833
1974	933 426	122 327	49 527	51 502	21 298	384 497	201 808	65 988
1973	852 417	123 549	56 139	47 887	19 523	343 082	179 613	62 501
1972	770 603	110 365	51 092	42 406	16 867	308 026	161 389	56 379
1971	701 868	96 892	44 520	37 806	14 566	285 493	149 686	51 699
1970	648 465	84 991	35 508	35 740	13 743	271 981	143 774	47 788
1969	605 218	85 946	38 360	34 711	12 875	253 141	131 483	46 476
1968	558 033	80 772	36 103	32 899	11 770	235 670	122 216	43 151
1967	507 753	70 434	29 994	30 009	10 431	217 065	112 439	39 196
1966	480 859	68 284	30 282	28 244	9 758	208 747	109 310	37 380
1965	443 779	63 254	29 925	25 116	8 213	191 546	100 710	34 068
1964	411 416	56 654	25 987	23 214	7 453	178 638	93 537	32 378
1963	382 670	51 599	24 370	20 650	6 579	168 150	88 247	29 795
1962	363 283	46 870	21 485	19 252	6 133	162 793	86 081	28 984
1961	342 122	41 770	17 812	18 251	5 707	156 581	83 985	27 645
1960	331 726	43 319	19 664	17 964	5 691	152 833	82 329	26 963
1959	317 628	42 660	18 871	18 083	5 706	148 459	80 643	26 374
1958	296 187	37 447	15 085	16 931	5 431	141 747	77 886	24 879
1957	286 864	39 964	17 554	17 165	5 245	137 089	75 052	24 538
1956	271 671	38 142	15 786	17 313	5 043	130 763	71 354	24 351
1955	258 764	38 798	17 727	16 434	4 637	124 724	68 589	23 292
1954	240 002	31 874	12 799	14 823	4 252	119 687	66 774	22 270
1953	233 078	32 717	13 901	14 699	4 117	117 822	65 383	22 197
1952	219 528	29 349	11 406	14 042	3 901	114 748	64 113	22 029
1951	208 531	29 873	12 177	14 056	3 640	109 171	60 674	21 258
1950	192 227	30 748	13 712	13 689	3 347	98 226	53 869	19 647
1949	178 496	25 056	10 580	11 261	3 215	94 855	52 484	19 328
1948	175 026	22 885	7 997	11 534	3 354	96 582	54 177	20 100
1947	161 988	20 435	6 570	10 584	3 281	90 879	52 345	18 759
1946	144 309	15 756	4 130	8 421	3 205	82 728	47 368	18 208
1945	119 982	7 961	970	4 540	2 451	71 903	40 649	16 459
1944	108 651	6 694	771	3 813	2 110	64 348	36 667	14 646
1943	99 904	6 537	776	3 882	1 879	58 597	33 220	13 389
1942	89 001	6 865	718	4 570	1 577	50 753	28 358	10 987
1941	81 069	9 669	3 514	4 809	1 346	42 853	23 358	8 797
1940	71 284	7 774	2 842	3 849	1 083	37 017	20 162	7 450
1939	67 205	6 684	2 254	3 449	981	35 116	19 149	7 135
1938	64 268	5 683	1 693	3 079	911	33 953	18 857	6 766
1937	66 834	6 938	2 517	3 470	951	35 224	19 919	6 838
1936	62 183	6 325	2 416	3 125	784	32 857	18 441	6 560
1935	55 928	5 122	1 947	2 492	683	29 322	16 190	6 022
1934	51 459	4 219	1 427	2 187	605	26 691	14 217	5 664
1933	45 944	3 464	1 094	1 861	509	22 257	11 530	4 629
1932	48 715	3 641	979	2 054	608	22 741	11 365	5 054
1931	60 674	5 483	1 632	2 994	857	28 956	14 741	6 929
1930	70 139	7 166	2 243	3 841	1 082	34 022	17 976	8 045
1929	77 387	9 243	3 345	4 679	1 219	37 686	19 544	9 369

Table 24-6. Personal Consumption Expenditures, by Major Type of Product, 1929–2006—*Continued*

(Millions of dollars.)

Total	Gasoline, fuel oil, and other energy goods	Other	Services	Housing	Transportation	Medical care	Recreation	Other
2006	338 317	736 789	5 483 743	1 382 223	337 128	1 588 498	379 351	1 290 190
2005	302 138	693 957	5 169 983	1 304 067	320 430	1 493 413	360 631	1 208 446
2004	248 792	656 470	4 880 064	1 236 062	307 782	1 395 746	341 553	1 148 915
2003	209 606	623 700	4 570 768	1 161 808	297 308	1 300 530	317 707	1 064 039
2002	178 767	595 462	4 347 150	1 123 113	288 431	1 206 197	299 055	1 022 678
2001	187 062	564 417	4 154 254	1 073 711	292 840	1 113 829	284 136	980 713
2000	191 482	532 858	3 928 836	1 006 457	291 254	1 026 812	268 265	945 938
1999	149 780	495 589	3 660 040	948 412	276 399	961 143	248 592	860 707
1998	133 899	449 004	3 445 717	894 612	259 481	921 389	229 267	790 487
1997	147 738	416 941	3 235 779	842 613	245 667	873 033	215 064	722 408
1996	144 762	391 861	3 048 741	800 092	226 503	833 534	202 471	667 597
1995	133 287	369 204	2 879 122	764 385	207 674	797 851	187 920	622 545
1994	128 997	349 499	2 723 891	726 143	190 597	752 946	171 389	596 658
1993	126 552	331 132	2 571 760	683 886	172 677	715 106	160 373	569 841
1992	124 639	314 690	2 421 172	658 466	157 663	672 213	146 595	535 489
1991	120 848	297 779	2 247 367	631 115	145 296	608 876	132 908	490 567
1990	124 065	284 954	2 115 851	597 939	147 722	556 026	125 907	460 995
1989	110 443	265 700	1 960 031	557 354	142 034	492 486	114 257	432 830
1988	99 995	244 464	1 816 542	521 501	133 415	442 848	102 126	409 364
1987	96 556	229 137	1 663 305	483 663	120 853	392 169	89 963	381 242
1986	91 390	211 934	1 538 292	448 369	111 071	357 538	83 676	349 893
1985	110 761	198 218	1 428 105	412 710	104 544	331 517	77 708	319 802
1984	108 442	186 275	1 292 169	374 543	93 213	303 203	69 734	282 100
1983	106 701	169 849	1 178 594	340 998	81 098	274 272	63 638	261 575
1982	108 596	155 164	1 049 447	315 163	72 928	243 301	56 843	218 752
1981	113 699	144 487	950 839	289 727	70 273	216 706	50 609	196 748
1980	102 137	130 636	846 884	256 171	65 232	184 367	43 602	183 780
1979	80 598	117 998	753 347	227 279	59 903	160 974	38 777	166 156
1978	61 634	104 731	676 569	202 361	53 422	143 082	34 732	151 786
1977	57 991	92 400	600 249	180 235	48 674	125 299	31 428	132 819
1976	53 169	85 989	534 744	162 220	42 480	109 084	28 358	120 074
1975	48 142	78 544	480 208	147 710	37 860	95 557	25 387	109 693
1974	43 974	72 728	426 602	134 754	34 068	82 348	22 513	97 087
1973	34 411	66 558	385 786	123 313	31 555	73 308	19 728	87 950
1972	29 461	60 797	352 212	112 602	29 552	65 623	17 606	81 381
1971	27 710	56 398	319 483	102 794	26 818	58 425	16 329	74 016
1970	26 344	54 075	291 493	94 075	24 033	51 697	15 058	68 836
1969	25 021	50 161	266 131	86 932	21 621	45 833	13 784	62 916
1968	23 265	47 038	241 591	79 782	19 276	40 148	12 463	57 666
1967	21 923	43 508	220 254	74 056	17 440	34 663	11 081	52 982
1966	20 705	41 353	203 828	69 460	15 928	31 467	10 422	48 447
1965	19 182	37 586	188 979	65 426	14 699	28 568	9 617	44 184
1964	17 708	35 015	176 124	61 365	13 769	26 427	9 117	40 427
1963	16 968	33 140	162 921	57 960	12 902	23 043	8 523	36 866
1962	16 354	31 374	153 620	54 732	12 291	21 173	7 997	35 003
1961	15 760	29 191	143 771	51 179	11 634	18 972	7 444	33 324
1960	15 848	27 693	135 574	48 151	11 175	17 683	6 937	31 334
1959	15 328	26 114	126 509	45 032	10 568	16 373	6 358	29 446
1958	14 758	24 224	116 993	42 002	9 852	14 804	5 834	27 031
1957	14 284	23 215	109 811	39 331	9 669	13 382	5 645	25 423
1956	13 327	21 731	102 766	36 713	9 176	12 130	5 594	23 762
1955	12 395	20 448	95 242	34 380	8 647	11 181	5 179	21 681
1954	11 361	19 282	88 441	32 261	8 156	10 519	4 790	20 005
1953	10 876	19 366	82 539	29 865	8 046	9 485	4 499	18 536
1952	10 217	18 389	75 431	26 977	7 428	8 523	4 254	17 055
1951	9 628	17 611	69 487	24 308	6 996	7 689	4 042	16 020
1950	8 896	15 814	63 253	21 697	5 997	7 185	3 872	14 971
1949	8 372	14 671	58 585	19 636	5 837	6 712	3 832	14 006
1948	8 235	14 070	55 559	17 895	5 658	6 502	3 833	13 583
1947	6 965	12 810	50 674	15 992	5 241	5 678	3 797	12 499
1946	5 850	11 302	45 825	14 186	4 949	4 895	3 706	11 319
1945	3 998	10 797	40 118	12 769	4 052	3 922	2 999	9 943
1944	3 427	9 608	37 609	12 327	3 717	3 661	2 691	9 352
1943	3 334	8 654	34 770	11 755	3 448	3 225	2 434	8 673
1942	3 941	7 467	31 383	11 218	2 779	2 960	2 116	7 497
1941	4 323	6 375	28 547	10 419	2 422	2 632	1 854	6 962
1940	3 822	5 583	26 493	9 690	2 137	2 448	1 700	6 478
1939	3 579	5 253	25 405	9 374	2 036	2 306	1 565	6 335
1938	3 456	4 874	24 632	9 162	1 877	2 194	1 531	6 299
1937	3 560	4 907	24 672	8 750	1 950	2 185	1 588	6 510
1936	3 356	4 500	23 001	8 219	1 855	2 052	1 434	6 040
1935	3 024	4 086	21 484	7 902	1 671	1 874	1 279	5 582
1934	2 903	3 907	20 549	7 792	1 594	1 754	1 190	5 197
1933	2 618	3 480	20 223	8 088	1 477	1 629	1 090	5 116
1932	2 614	3 708	22 333	9 182	1 560	1 779	1 208	5 550
1931	2 858	4 428	26 235	10 452	1 900	2 152	1 557	6 650
1930	3 291	4 710	28 951	11 201	2 243	2 377	1 675	7 564
1929	3 422	5 351	30 458	11 672	2 559	2 421	1 721	8 039

Source: U.S. Department of Commerce, Bureau of Economic Analysis. *National Income and Product Accounts.*
Note: Cautionary note on the use of data in millions of dollars—this table includes estimates in the millions of dollars for National Income and Product Accounts (NIPA) series that regularly appear in the tables published in the Survey of Current Business. The Bureau of Economic Analysis (BEA) generally does not include estimates at this level of precision in the published tables because the associated sampling and nonsampling errors are larger than this implied level of precision. Compared with the published aggregates, the million-dollar estimates are generally not any more accurate.

Table 24-7. Apparent Civilian Per Capita Consumption of Foods, 1849—2005

(Pounds, except eggs. Calendar years, except as noted.)

Year	Meats Total (carcass weight)	Beef and veal (boneless weight)	Pork, excluding lard (boneless weight)	Fish (edible weight)	Edible fats and oils Total[1] (fat content)	Margarine[2] (actual weight)	Butter, farm and factory weight (actual weight)	Fruits Fresh (farm weight) Total[3]	Citrus[4]	Apples
2005	158.8	62.7	46.5	16.1	85.5	4.0	4.6	127.8	21.6	17.1
2004	161.5	63.3	47.8	16.5	86.4	5.2	4.5	127.9	22.7	19.0
2003	160.9	62.4	48.4	16.3	87.3	5.2	4.5	128.2	23.9	17.1
2002	164.5	65.0	48.2	15.6	87.9	6.5	4.4	127.0	23.4	16.2
2001	160.7	63.6	46.9	14.7	83.0	7.0	4.4	126.0	23.9	15.8
2000	164.0	65.1	47.8	15.2	81.8	8.2	4.5	128.7	23.5	17.6
1999	166.0	64.9	49.3	14.8	65.6	7.9	4.7	130.4	20.4	18.7
1998	163.4	64.2	48.2	14.5	63.0	8.2	4.4	129.3	26.6	19.2
1997	157.4	63.5	44.7	14.3	62.6	8.4	4.1	130.1	26.5	18.3
1996	160.4	65.0	45.2	14.5	63.0	9.0	4.2	126.7	24.6	18.9
1995	164.4	64.4	48.4	14.8	64.4	9.1	4.7	123.5	23.8	18.9
1994	164.8	63.7	49.0	15.0	66.4	9.8	4.9	125.3	24.7	19.6
1993	161.1	61.8	48.5	14.8	68.4	11.0	4.8	123.3	25.8	19.2
1992	164.3	63.2	49.1	14.6	66.1	10.9	4.7	124.1	24.2	19.4
1991	161.8	63.7	46.8	14.8	64.1	10.5	4.5	113.1	19.0	18.3
1990	162.3	64.8	46.4	14.9	61.9	10.9	4.0	117.0	21.4	19.8
1989	167.1	66.1	48.4	15.6	61.8	10.2	4.7	122.9	23.6	21.4
1988	173.1	69.7	48.8	15.1	64.7	10.3	4.6	121.4	25.4	20.0
1987	169.8	70.8	45.6	16.1	63.9	10.5	4.7	121.3	23.9	21.0
1986	174.0	75.9	45.2	15.4	65.3	11.4	5.0	118.6	24.2	18.0
1985	176.7	76.1	47.7	15.0	64.9	10.8	5.3	110.7	21.5	17.4
1984	175.1	75.3	47.2	14.1	61.5	10.4	5.0	112.7	22.5	18.5
1983	175.7	75.4	47.4	13.3	59.8	10.4	4.9	110.7	28.0	18.4
1982	170.1	73.9	44.9	12.4	57.7	11.0	4.4	108.1	23.4	17.7
1981	177.6	74.1	49.9	12.6	57.1	11.1	4.2	103.5	23.5	17.0
1980	179.9	73.3	52.1	12.4	57.0	11.3	4.5	106.5	26.1	19.4
1979	177.5	74.9	48.6	13.0	56.1	11.2	4.5	99.9	23.0	17.3
1978	182.4	84.2	42.3	13.4	54.8	11.3	4.4	103.8	26.2	18.1
1977	189.7	89.0	42.3	12.6	53.2	11.4	4.3	99.9	26.1	16.7
1976	191.5	91.5	40.7	12.9	54.9	11.9	4.3	102.2	28.5	17.2
1975	181.0	86.0	38.4	12.1	52.4	11.1	4.7	101.5	29.0	19.7
1974	188.9	82.4	47.0	12.1	52.4	11.1	4.5	96.3	27.1	16.6
1973	176.8	77.2	43.2	12.7	53.3	11.1	4.8	96.9	27.2	16.3
1972	192.2	82.0	48.1	12.5	53.4	11.1	5.0	94.6	27.2	15.7
1971	198.4	81.0	53.0	11.5	51.8	10.9	5.2	101.0	29.0	16.6
1970	192.7	81.7	48.1	11.7	52.6	10.8	5.4	101.1	28.8	17.2
1969	189.5	80.1	46.9	11.2	54.8	10.7	5.6	79.0	28.3	14.9
1968	191.9	79.9	48.3	11.0	54.1	10.7	5.8	78.3	26.3	15.7
1967	188.0	78.1	47.0	10.6	52.3	10.5	5.5	80.9	31.6	16.2
1966	180.3	76.9	42.8	10.9	52.8	10.6	5.8	81.4	29.1	16.1
1965	177.8	74.1	43.6	10.9	50.9	9.8	6.6	81.1	29.1	16.3
1964	186.9	74.3	48.8	10.5	50.8	9.6	7.1	78.7	26.2	17.9
1963	181.2	68.8	48.5	10.5	49.5	9.4	7.1	74.5	22.1	16.7
1962	175.3	65.5	47.4	10.6	48.8	9.2	7.5	83.4	29.5	17.4
1961	173.8	65.0	46.8	10.7	48.4	9.3	7.5	88.6	30.8	16.4
1960*	174.5	63.3	48.6	10.3	48.5	9.3	7.7	93.4	33.7	18.3
1959	174.7	60.6	51.0	10.9	49.6	9.1	8.0	95.7	34.0	21.1
1958	165.4	60.6	45.3	10.6	48.6	8.9	8.4	94.0	31.0	22.5
1957	173.6	64.8	46.4	10.2	47.6	8.5	8.5	96.7	37.1	19.3
1956	183.4	66.1	51.0	10.4	48.6	8.1	9.0	98.9	39.1	18.9
1955	179.2	63.7	50.4	10.4	49.3	8.0	9.3	99.4	41.8	19.6
1954	156.4	62.9	37.2	11.1	48.8	8.3	9.1	105.1	42.0	20.0
1953	157.4	61.1	39.2	11.3	47.3	8.1	8.6	109.4	44.1	20.9
1952	148.6	49.0	45.0	11.1	47.3	8.1	8.6	114.4	45.1	21.6
1951	143.6	45.9	45.2	11.3	45.4	6.7	9.7	118.0	45.8	25.7
1950	146.9	50.2	43.0	11.9	49.3	6.1	10.9	108.8	41.7	22.7
1949	146.3	50.9	41.9	10.9	45.9	5.7	10.6	122.9	47.9	24.7
1948	147.2	50.9	42.0	11.2	46.0	6.1	10.1	131.6	54.4	26.3
1947	158.3	56.7	43.2	10.3	45.2	5.0	11.3	143.7	62.2	25.4
1946	157.4	51.1	46.8	10.8	42.7	3.8	10.7	133.9	59.1	23.0
1945	159.4	56.1	43.4	9.8	43.9	3.9	11.7	139.9	66.6	22.9
1944	174.2	55.0	53.6	8.7	46.2	3.6	13.4	140.1	68.2	25.5
1943	161.9	48.7	51.7	8.0	46.0	3.7	13.1	118.4	60.3	24.9
1942	151.4	51.7	42.2	8.8	49.4	2.9	16.4	130.0	57.7	28.1
1941	145.3	47.9	42.3	11.1	51.6	2.7	16.4	146.0	57.7	31.7
1940	142.4	42.9	45.1	11.0	50.1	2.4	17.0	139.1	56.7	29.7
1939	133.5	42.8	39.7	10.8	50.2	2.3	17.4	148.2	61.4	30.7
1938	127.0	42.6	35.7	10.8	49.1	3.0	16.6	131.7	49.1	28.2
1937	126.1	43.9	34.2	11.7	49.3	3.1	16.7	138.6	44.5	33.6
1936	130.5	47.3	33.8	11.6	49.4	3.1	16.8	125.6	46.2	27.6
1935	117.3	42.4	29.7	10.5	48.0	3.0	17.5	133.2	44.6	32.9
1934	143.8	50.3	39.5	9.2	48.4	2.1	18.5	116.3	39.8	25.3
1933	136.0	40.4	43.4	8.6	46.9	1.9	18.1	124.8	39.4	40.0
1932	130.9	36.6	43.4	8.4	46.8	1.6	18.5	125.9	36.7	39.2
1931	130.6	37.9	41.9	8.8	48.2	1.9	18.3	160.3	42.3	51.7

[1] Computed from unrounded numbers.
[2] Prior to 1909, data are for year beginning in July.
[3] Beginning 1934, excludes apples from non-commercial areas. Citrus fruit on crop year basis, 1941 to date.
[4] Beginning 1941, year begins October or November prior to year indicated.
. . . = Not available.
* = First year for which figures include Alaska and Hawaii.

Table 24-7. Apparent Civilian Per Capita Consumption of Foods, 1849–2005—*Continued*

(Pounds, except eggs. Calendar years, except as noted.)

Year	Meats — Total (carcass weight)	Beef and veal (boneless weight)	Pork, excluding lard (boneless weight)	Fish (edible weight)	Edible fats and oils — Total[1] (fat content)	Margarine[2] (actual weight)	Butter, farm and factory weight (actual weight)	Fruits — Fresh (farm weight) Total[3]	Citrus[4]	Apples
1930	128.9	38.1	41.1	10.2	48.8	2.6	17.6	129.9	31.2	42.1
1929	131.3	38.5	42.8	11.8	48.7	2.9	17.6	139.2	39.8	39.7
1928	131.6	38.0	43.5	12.1	47.7	2.6	17.6	146.1	29.5	48.9
1927	134.8	42.5	41.6	12.2	47.9	2.3	18.3	126.0	32.2	37.4
1926	138.0	47.1	39.4	11.4	47.7	2.0	18.3	160.8	31.4	62.3
1925	140.0	46.9	41.0	11.1	46.8	2.0	18.1	132.2	28.9	46.3
1924	147.3	46.9	45.5	11.0	45.4	2.0	17.9	148.0	33.9	54.1
1923	147.3	46.7	45.6	10.7	44.7	2.0	17.9	144.5	32.5	54.7
1922	137.8	46.0	40.4	11.3	43.2	1.7	17.1	144.8	24.6	57.5
1921	134.0	43.4	39.8	10.5	39.5	2.0	16.3	112.8	30.5	36.1
1920	136.1	46.2	39.0	11.8	39.7	3.4	14.9	142.6	26.0	63.0
1919	138.9	47.8	39.2	11.6	43.4	3.4	15.3	122.3	23.5	45.2
1918	141.7	52.2	37.5	10.9	43.5	3.3	14.2	119.6	16.5	56.9
1917	135.3	49.5	36.2	10.9	40.2	2.7	15.8	129.8	22.0	56.1
1916	140.2	45.0	42.4	11.0	42.2	1.8	17.3	133.7	22.0	63.9
1915	134.9	42.8	40.9	11.2	43.2	1.4	17.2	154.5	23.1	69.0
1914	140.0	46.7	40.0	11.7	43.6	1.4	17.0	160.4	24.1	71.8
1913	143.7	47.9	41.1	11.5	40.2	1.5	16.5	130.2	16.6	59.3
1912	145.8	49.3	40.9	11.3	38.8	1.5	16.6	156.5	18.5	74.6
1911	152.0	52.1	42.4	11.3	34.9	1.1	18.7	152.6	19.8	73.5
1910	146.4	53.4	38.2	11.2	37.7	1.6	18.4	134.7	17.8	59.4
1909	155.2	56.1	41.2	11.0	35.5	1.2	17.9	135.0	16.2	62.2
1908	163.3	79.3	77.7	...	...	1.0	19.7	...	...	...
1907	158.2	77.8	74.1	...	...	0.9	17.6	...	...	...
1906	155.6	78.3	71.0	...	...	0.8	17.8	...	...	...
1905	155.2	77.9	71.0	...	...	0.6	19.9	...	...	...
1904	152.7	75.6	70.6	...	...	0.6	18.5	...	...	...
1903	152.1	77.0	68.2	...	...	0.6	18.3	...	...	...
1902	144.8	71.0	66.7	...	...	0.9	17.6	...	...	...
1901	151.1	73.3	70.8	...	...	1.6	20.0	...	...	...
1900	150.7	72.3	71.9	...	...	1.3	20.1	...	...	...
1899	150.7	72.4	71.8	...	...	1.4	19.6	...	...	...
1898	...	...	...	...	...	...	19.8	...	...	...
1897	...	...	...	...	...	...	20.8	...	...	...
1896	...	...	...	...	...	...	22.2	...	...	...
1895	...	...	...	...	...	...	18.4	...	...	...
1894	...	...	...	...	...	...	15.4	...	...	...
1893	...	...	...	...	...	...	15.5	...	...	...
1892	...	...	...	...	...	...	15.9	...	...	...
1891	...	...	...	...	...	...	16.7	...	...	...
1890	...	...	...	...	...	...	18.2	...	...	...
1889	...	...	...	...	...	...	20.5	...	...	...
1888	...	...	...	...	...	...	16.0	...	...	...
1887	...	...	...	...	...	...	16.3	...	...	...
1886	...	...	...	...	...	...	16.8	...	...	...
1885	...	...	...	...	...	...	16.1	...	...	...
1884	...	...	...	...	...	...	15.3	...	...	...
1883	...	...	...	...	...	...	15.2	...	...	...
1882	...	...	...	...	...	...	13.9	...	...	...
1881	...	...	...	...	...	...	15.2	...	...	...
1880	...	...	...	...	...	...	15.5	...	...	...
1879	...	...	...	...	...	...	15.6	...	...	...
1878	...	...	...	...	...	...	14.6	...	...	...
1877	...	...	...	...	...	...	14.4	...	...	...
1876	...	...	...	...	...	...	14.5	...	...	...
1875	...	...	...	...	...	...	12.4	...	...	...
1874	...	...	...	...	...	...	13.4	...	...	...
1873	...	...	...	...	...	...	13.4	...	...	...
1872	...	...	...	...	...	...	10.6	...	...	...
1871	...	...	...	...	...	...	11.7	...	...	...
1870	...	...	...	...	...	...	10.7	...	...	...
1869	...	...	...	...	...	...	13.6	...	...	...
1859	...	...	...	...	...	...	14.8	...	...	...
1849	...	...	...	...	...	...	13.7	...	...	...

[1]Computed from unrounded numbers.
[2]Prior to 1909, data are for year beginning in July.
[3]Beginning 1934, excludes apples from non-commercial areas. Citrus fruit on crop year basis, 1941 to date.
[4]Beginning 1941, year begins October or November prior to year indicated.
. . . = Not available.

Table 24-7. Apparent Civilian Per Capita Consumption of Foods, 1849–2005—*Continued*

(Pounds, except eggs. Calendar years, except as noted.)

Year	Potatoes (farm weight)	Fresh vegetables	Dairy products Fluid milk and cream[5]	Cheese	Ice cream product (weight)	Eggs (number)	Chicken and turkey[6] (boneless)	Wheat flour	Peanuts (shelled)[7]	Coffee (greenbean basis)
2005	127.3	198.6	202.5	31.4	15.4	253.9	73.6	134.1	6.6	9.5
2004	134.6	202.4	204.9	31.2	15.0	256.0	72.7	134.3	6.6	9.6
2003	138.2	199.1	205.9	30.5	16.4	254.3	71.2	136.6	6.3	9.5
2002	132.1	194.7	206.7	30.5	16.7	254.6	70.7	136.7	5.8	9.2
2001	138.6	195.7	207.6	30.0	16.3	252.4	67.8	141.0	5.8	9.5
2000	138.0	198.7	210.1	29.8	16.7	251.0	67.9	146.3	5.8	10.3
1999	136.2	192.3	213.1	29.0	16.7	249.7	67.4	144.0	6.0	9.8
1998	137.7	185.7	213.3	27.8	16.3	239.2	64.3	143.0	5.8	9.3
1997	137.9	190.4	216.4	27.5	16.1	234.3	63.6	146.8	5.7	9.1
1996	145.0	185.9	219.8	27.3	15.6	233.4	63.1	146.4	5.6	8.7
1995	136.9	180.9	220.7	26.9	15.5	232.3	62.1	140.0	5.6	7.9
1994	136.8	186.5	222.5	26.6	16.0	235.1	62.6	143.0	5.7	8.1
1993	136.7	180.7	223.7	26.0	16.0	233.7	62.0	142.2	6.0	9.0
1992	130.0	173.9	228.7	25.8	16.2	233.6	60.4	138.1	6.2	10.0
1991	134.1	170.3	231.6	25.0	16.3	232.9	58.1	136.5	6.5	10.3
1990	123.9	170.2	233.3	24.6	15.8	234.1	56.2	135.9	6.0	10.3
1989	127.0	175.6	236.9	23.8	16.1	237.0	53.6	129.8	7.0	10.1
1988	122.4	170.3	237.1	23.7	17.3	246.6	51.9	131.7	6.9	9.8
1987	125.9	165.2	237.3	24.1	18.4	253.8	51.0	129.8	6.4	10.2
1986	126.0	158.6	240.3	23.1	18.4	253.5	47.1	125.6	6.4	10.5
1985	122.4	158.6	240.8	22.5	18.1	255.2	45.6	124.6	6.3	10.5
1984	122.1	156.6	237.6	21.5	18.2	260.1	44.0	119.1	6.1	10.2
1983	118.6	151.3	235.9	20.6	18.1	260.2	42.7	117.7	5.9	10.1
1982	115.0	150.9	235.6	19.9	17.6	264.1	42.2	116.9	6.0	9.9
1981	116.5	145.1	241.7	18.2	17.4	264.4	42.0	115.9	5.5	10.0
1980	114.7	151.4	245.5	17.5	17.5	271.1	40.8	116.9	4.8	10.3
1979	117.8	148.5	250.6	17.2	17.3	276.6	40.2	116.4	5.9	11.3
1978	119.4	143.4	253.9	16.8	17.6	271.5	37.2	115.2	5.9	10.5
1977	122.1	148.6	257.5	16.0	17.6	267.0	35.9	115.5	5.7	9.4
1976	125.3	148.1	260.2	15.5	18.0	269.8	35.6	119.1	5.6	12.5
1975	122.0	148.8	261.4	14.3	18.6	276.0	32.8	114.5	6.0	12.2
1974	117.2	145.9	260.4	14.4	17.5	283.0	33.9	111.0	5.8	12.8
1973	118.3	148.0	269.0	13.5	17.5	288.4	33.8	112.8	6.0	13.5
1972	119.4	151.3	273.6	13.0	17.6	303.0	35.4	109.8	5.7	13.7
1971	117.8	148.0	275.7	12.0	17.7	309.9	34.0	110.5	5.5	13.1
1970	121.7	154.3	275.3	11.4	17.8	308.9	33.8	110.9	5.5	13.6
1969	92.0	98.9	273.7	10.8	18.1	309.7	32.9	112.5	5.5	14.1
1968	94.0	98.7	275.8	10.5	18.5	316.5	31.6	112.8	5.5	14.9
1967	92.0	98.1	276.6	10.0	18.0	321.6	31.9	113.0	5.3	14.8
1966	96.0	96.0	291.0	9.7	18.3	313.6	30.7	112.0	5.5	14.6
1965	93.0	98.6	290.7	9.5	18.7	314.5	28.9	113.0	5.6	15.0
1964	96.0	98.6	291.5	9.4	18.5	317.9	27.2	114.0	5.3	15.4
1963	100.0	101.4	292.0	9.2	18.2	316.9	26.6	114.0	5.0	15.7
1962	98.0	101.4	291.2	9.1	18.1	325.8	26.2	115.0	4.9	16.0
1961	102.0	103.8	292.9	8.5	18.3	328.0	26.5	118.0	4.9	16.0
1960*	101.0	105.9	300.3	8.3	18.6	333.8	24.1	118.0	4.9	15.9
1959	101.0	102.3	305.1	8.0	18.9	351.7	24.8	120.0	4.7	16.0
1958	101.0	103.7	311.5	8.1	18.1	353.9	24.1	121.0	4.5	15.5
1957	106.0	106.4	318.0	7.6	18.2	361.5	22.3	119.0	4.5	15.6
1956	99.0	107.0	321.6	8.0	18.3	368.6	21.0	121.0	4.4	15.9
1955	106.0	105.2	321.1	7.8	18.3	371.2	18.8	123.0	4.1	15.4
1954	106.0	107.2	320.9	7.9	17.6	375.9	20.0	126.0	4.2	14.7
1953	106.0	109.1	328.3	7.4	18.2	379.4	19.1	128.0	4.4	17.0
1952	101.0	111.6	333.5	7.6	18.1	390.1	19.1	131.0	4.4	16.9
1951	113.0	111.9	333.6	7.2	17.6	396.4	18.7	133.0	4.6	17.4
1950	106.0	115.2	331.5	7.7	17.4	391.4	17.6	135.0	4.5	16.3
1949	110.0	116.2	334.5	7.3	17.8	384.6	16.1	136.0	4.1	19.1
1948	105.0	123.0	339.5	7.0	18.6	395.8	15.1	137.0	4.6	18.4
1947	125.0	122.4	355.9	6.9	20.1	385.6	15.5	139.0	4.5	17.3
1946	123.0	129.9	374.8	6.6	23.1	385.2	17.1	156.0	5.3	19.6
1945	122.0	134.3	397.1	6.4	15.5	421.4	18.7	161.0	6.6	18.8
1944	136.0	123.9	388.5	6.0	14.6	373.5	18.4	149.0	6.0	17.7
1943	125.0	116.7	367.5	5.6	14.0	360.3	18.5	163.0	5.7	14.0
1942	127.0	119.0	332.6	6.7	16.2	324.6	15.3	157.0	6.2	15.3
1941	128.0	113.8	309.5	5.9	13.8	313.1	13.4	156.0	4.8	16.1
1940	123.0	116.9	306.1	6.0	11.4	318.8	12.3	155.0	5.0	15.5
1939	122.0	116.6	305.9	5.9	11.0	312.8	11.9	158.0	4.4	14.9
1938	129.0	114.5	300.9	5.8	10.4	310.0	10.8	160.0	4.3	14.9
1937	126.0	111.0	301.5	5.6	10.6	307.7	11.5	159.0	4.4	13.3
1936	130.0	112.5	299.4	5.4	9.5	288.4	11.4	163.0	4.6	13.7
1935	142.0	111.2	296.6	5.3	8.1	279.3	10.7	158.0	4.0	13.4
1934	135.0	115.2	292.4	4.9	7.1	288.4	11.0	157.0	3.3	12.3
1933	132.0	104.5	302.6	4.5	6.0	296.3	12.0	162.0	3.6	12.8
1932	134.0	108.8	303.9	4.4	6.3	312.9	11.6	170.0	4.1	12.4
1931	136.0	108.3	298.1	4.5	8.6	332.4	11.1	169.0	4.4	13.0

[5]Fluid milk figures are aggregates of commercial sales and milk produced and consumed on farms. Cream included on whole-milk equivalent basis.
[6]Chicken only, 1909–1928, but turkey consumption very small during that time.
[7]September–August year through 1939; August–July year, thereafter.
* = First year for which figures include Alaska and Hawaii.

Table 24-7. Apparent Civilian Per Capita Consumption of Foods, 1849–2005—*Continued*

(Pounds, except eggs. Calendar years, except as noted.)

Year	Potatoes (farm weight)	Fresh vegetables	Dairy products Fluid milk and cream[5]	Cheese	Ice cream product (weight)	Eggs (number)	Chicken and turkey[6] (boneless)	Wheat flour	Peanuts (shelled)[7]	Coffee (greenbean basis)
1930	132.0	111.9	298.1	4.7	9.7	331.0	12.3	171.0	3.2	12.5
1929	159.0	112.6	300.3	4.7	10.7	334.4	11.3	177.0	4.1	12.2
1928	147.0	104.2	298.4	4.4	9.9	338.3	11.5	179.0	3.8	11.9
1927	141.0	106.0	298.1	4.6	9.9	341.9	11.9	181.0	3.9	12.2
1926	128.0	100.6	301.2	4.6	9.5	338.5	11.1	182.0	3.4	12.4
1925	157.0	101.3	301.7	4.7	9.7	318.1	11.2	180.0	3.6	10.6
1924	154.0	100.9	293.9	4.6	8.8	324.2	10.7	180.0	3.5	12.2
1923	174.0	90.1	292.2	4.5	9.0	326.5	11.4	180.0	3.2	12.6
1922	143.0	92.8	300.6	4.3	8.2	315.9	11.1	180.0	2.7	11.8
1921	156.0	82.2	298.6	4.2	7.6	299.5	10.5	167.0	2.7	12.0
1920	140.0	95.0	305.8	4.0	7.6	299.5	10.8	179.0	3.0	11.7
1919	152.0	76.6	273.1	4.2	6.8	303.1	11.2	192.0	4.6	11.8
1918	174.0	...	305.6	4.0	6.4	284.3	10.3	179.0	2.8	10.1
1917	146.0	...	266.8	3.7	4.8	281.3	10.3	191.0	4.2	12.1
1916	143.0	...	250.9	3.8	4.3	299.2	10.6	204.0	2.8	11.5
1915	185.0	...	260.5	4.1	3.9	312.9	11.2	205.0	2.8	10.6
1914	157.0	...	279.3	4.2	3.4	295.3	11.1	207.0	2.5	9.2
1913	189.0	...	297.2	4.2	3.0	303.3	11.2	209.0	2.5	9.0
1912	179.0	...	309.1	3.9	2.7	311.4	11.5	211.0	2.3	10.8
1911	157.0	...	280.4	4.0	2.3	329.2	12.0	213.0	2.3	8.4
1910	198.0	...	289.1	4.3	1.9	306.0	11.8	214.0	2.5	9.2
1909	187.0	...	306.3	3.8	1.6	292.8	11.2	217.0	2.4	...
1908	...	...	...	3.8	...	...	...	...	...	...
1907	...	...	...	3.5	...	...	...	...	...	...
1906	...	...	...	3.5	...	...	...	...	...	...
1905	...	...	...	4.1	...	...	...	...	...	...
1904	...	...	...	4.1	...	...	...	...	...	...
1903	...	...	...	4.0	...	...	...	...	...	...
1902	...	...	...	4.0	...	...	...	...	...	...
1901	...	...	...	4.5	...	...	...	...	...	...
1900	...	...	...	3.7	...	...	...	...	...	...
1899	...	...	...	3.7	...	...	...	...	...	...
1898	...	...	...	3.4	...	...	...	...	...	...
1897	...	...	...	3.6	...	...	...	...	...	...
1896	...	...	...	2.9	...	...	...	...	...	...
1895	...	...	...	2.9	...	...	...	...	...	...
1894	...	...	...	2.9	...	...	...	...	...	...
1893	...	...	...	2.9	...	...	...	...	...	...
1892	...	...	...	3.7	...	...	...	...	...	...
1891	...	...	...	3.5	...	...	...	...	...	...
1890	...	...	...	3.8	...	...	...	...	...	...
1889	...	...	...	3.5	...	...	...	...	...	...
1888	...	...	...	3.5	...	...	...	...	...	...
1887	...	...	...	3.2	...	...	...	...	...	...
1886	...	...	...	2.8	...	...	...	...	...	...
1885	...	...	...	3.0	...	...	...	...	...	...
1884	...	...	...	3.1	...	...	...	...	...	...
1883	...	...	...	3.3	...	...	...	...	...	...
1882	...	...	...	3.1	...	...	...	...	...	...
1881	...	...	...	3.2	...	...	...	...	...	...
1880	...	...	...	2.7	...	...	...	...	...	...
1879	...	...	...	2.2	...	...	...	...	...	...
1878	...	...	...	3.5	...	...	...	...	...	...
1877	...	...	...	2.7	...	...	...	...	...	...
1876	...	...	...	2.6	...	...	...	...	...	...
1875	...	...	...	3.1	...	...	...	...	...	...
1874	...	...	...	2.6	...	...	...	...	...	...
1873	...	...	...	2.9	...	...	...	...	...	...
1872	...	...	...	3.0	...	...	...	...	...	...
1871	...	...	...	2.4	...	...	...	...	...	...
1870	...	...	...	3.2	...	...	...	...	...	...
1869	...	...	...	3.0	...	...	...	...	...	...
1859	...	...	...	2.9	...	...	...	...	...	...
1849	...	...	...	4.1	...	...	...	...	...	...

Source: U.S. Department of Agriculture. Economic Research Service.
Fluid milk figures are aggregates of commercial sales and milk produced and consumed on farms. Cream included on whole-milke equivalent basis.
[6]Chicken only, 1909–1928, but turkey consumption very small during that time.
[7]September–August year through 1939; August–July year, thereafter.
. . . = Not available.

Table 24-8. Retail Gasoline Prices, by Selected Areas, 2003–2006

(Prices are annual averages.)

Year	Boston, MA	Chicago, IL	Cleveland, OH	Denver, CO	Houston, TX	Los Angeles, CA	Miami, FL	New York, NY	San Francisco, CA	Seattle, WA
Regular										
2006	261.2	271.4	254.2	257.9	251.4	288.8	272.2	268.2	284.5	273.5
2005	225.7	231.8	222.0	223.9	216.8	249.0	238.9	230.0	248.1	236.3
2004	185.8	190.0	180.2	180.4	171.2	214.7	191.3	190.4	214.8	194.9
2003	158.9	161.9	151.8	151.9	143.3	181.9	219.3	163.1	189.8	162.5
Midgrade										
2006	268.2	276.6	259.7	264.7	256.7	293.4	277.9	275.8	291.0	278.9
2005	236.3	241.9	232.2	235.4	226.8	258.6	249.3	241.5	259.4	247.3
2004	195.8	200.1	190.2	191.9	181.0	224.8	202.0	201.0	225.9	205.9
2003	168.9	171.9	161.7	163.4	153.3	192.6	234.7	173.1	200.7	173.1
Premium										
2006	278.7	286.8	270.6	274.5	266.6	303.3	286.9	286.4	301.1	289.1
2005	246.4	251.9	243.0	245.4	236.5	268.1	258.5	251.3	269.4	257.6
2004	205.6	209.9	200.4	201.8	190.7	234.6	210.5	209.2	235.7	216.0
2003	178.5	181.8	172.1	173.7	163.3	202.3	246.1	181.2	210.5	183.1

Source: U.S. Department of Energy, Energy Information Administration. U.S. Census Bureau.

Table 24-9. Total Nonbusiness Bankruptcy Cases Filed, 1995–2006

(Calendar year.)

	1995	2000	2005	2006
Total	874 642	1 217 972	2 039 214	597 965
District of Columbia	1 402	2 288	2 386	523
1st Circuit	29 760	41 494	56 696	17 913
Maine	1 918	3 880	6 470	1 238
Massachusetts	13 796	15 208	26 308	8 147
New Hampshire	3 115	3 313	5 511	1 707
Rhode Island	3 173	4 383	5 703	1 573
Puerto Rico	7 758	14 710	12 704	5 248
2nd Circuit	57 807	69 135	125 149	34 484
Connecticut	8 942	10 504	15 116	4 806
New York	47 976	57 210	107 489	29 059
Vermont	889	1 421	2 544	619
3rd Circuit	50 703	81 584	130 626	38 035
Delaware	1 402	2 375	4 150	1 284
New Jersey	26 593	36 645	48 832	13 548
Pennsylvania	22 669	42 515	77 587	23 190
U.S. Virgin Islands	39	49	57	13
4th Circuit	69 662	111 869	154 435	47 721
Maryland	16 432	29 658	34 585	9 016
North Carolina	15 208	26 646	42 402	16 838
South Carolina	7 120	11 820	15 352	6 047
Virginia	27 014	35 376	44 621	12 901
West Virginia	3 888	8 369	17 475	2 919
5th Circuit	70 606	100 300	177 117	53 939
Louisiana	14 176	22 516	36 024	10 750
Mississippi	11 541	18 255	23 481	8 639
Texas	44 889	59 529	117 612	34 550
6th Circuit	108 627	157 806	327 168	110 792
Kentucky	13 915	20 663	39 865	12 174
Michigan	23 556	35 835	88 402	32 746
Ohio	33 376	52 713	133 541	34 466
Tennessee	37 780	48 595	65 360	31 406
7th Circuit	75 456	114 182	221 585	62 642
Illinois	41 147	59 892	105 964	29 774
Indiana	22 681	37 126	78 201	21 858
Wisconsin	11 628	17 164	37 420	11 010
8th Circuit	50 213	73 402	143 760	42 622
Arkansas	8 956	16 523	30 142	9 288
Iowa	6 038	8 079	18 254	4 683
Minnesota	12 934	13 822	24 068	7 658
Missouri	16 236	25 651	52 060	15 423
Nebraska	3 577	5 514	11 817	3 959
North Dakota	1 193	1 841	3 444	711
South Dakota	1 279	1 972	3 975	900
9th Circuit	199 081	235 145	327 969	75 090
Alaska	787	1 301	2 214	577
Arizona	14 967	20 190	39 689	7 532
California	134 905	138 124	162 532	37 107
Hawaii	1 877	4 486	4 408	940
Idaho	3 730	6 850	11 826	2 875
Montana	2 125	3 195	5 770	1 806
Nevada	7 522	13 678	23 453	5 339
Oregon	13 317	16 774	31 527	7 284
Washington	19 809	30 414	46 144	11 510
Guam	36	124	375	106
Northern Mariana Islands	6	9	31	14
10th Circuit	47 135	68 025	139 287	30 933
Colorado	13 095	15 185	42 173	9 544
Kansas	8 732	11 146	22 376	6 189
New Mexico	4 012	6 519	11 592	2 426
Oklahoma	13 086	18 403	38 487	6 909
Utah	7 083	14 741	21 476	5 215
Wyoming	1 127	2 031	3 183	650
11th Circuit	114 190	162 742	233 036	83 271
Alabama	25 966	32 543	47 513	19 420
Florida	43 856	71 284	106 250	24 709
Georgia	44 368	58 915	79 273	39 142

Source: U.S. Courts.

> ## BOX 24 ■ Postal Rates, 1863–2007

An interesting exercise in assessing inflation, the purchasing power of the dollar, and the overall quality of life is the change in the cost of a basic good or service. Some costs, such as food, housing, and clothes, can differ by region, neighborhood, income level, and other variables. One constant measure that holds steady for all Americans is the cost of mailing a first-class letter or postcard, as shown in the table below.

Postal Rates for First-Class Mail, Letters and Postal Cards, 1863–2006

(Dollars. First-class mail as a mail category not officially established until 1863. Ship and steamboat letters, 1792–1863, carried special rates.)

Year of rate change	Letters, nonlocal	Postal cards
2007 (May 14)	0.41	0.26
2006 (Jan. 8)	0.39	0.24
2002 (June 30)	0.37	0.23
2001 (Jan. 7)	0.34	0.20
1999 (Jan. 10)	0.33	0.20
1995 (Jan. 1)	0.32	0.20
1991 (Feb. 3)	0.29	0.19
1988 (April 3)	0.25	0.15
1985 (Feb. 17)	0.22	0.14
1981 (Nov. 1)	0.20	0.13
1981 (March 22)	0.18	0.12
1978 (May 29)	0.15	0.10
1975 (Dec. 31)[2]	0.13	0.09
1975 (Sept. 14)	0.10	0.07
1974 (March 2)	0.10 per oz.	0.08
1971 (May 16)	0.08 per oz.	0.06
1968 (Jan. 7)	0.06 per oz.	0.05
1963 (Jan. 7)	0.05 per oz.	0.04
1958 (Aug. 1)	0.04 per oz.	0.03
1952 (Jan. 1)	0.03 peroz.	0.02
1940	(3)	(3)
1932	0.03 per oz.	0.01
1932	0.02 per oz.	0.01
1917	0.03 per oz.	0.02
1885	0.02 per oz.	0.01
1883	0.02 per 1/2 oz.	0.01
1872	0.03 per 1/2 oz.	0.01
1863[5]	0.03 per 1/2 oz	[4]0.01

Source: U.S. Census Bureau. U.S. Postal Service.
[1]Beginning 1975, rates are for domestic letters weighing up to one ounce; prior years rate per ounce or 1/2 ounce as indicated.
[2]As of October 11, 1975, surface mail service upgraded to level of airmail.
[3]The 1940 rate change provided that the three-cent letter rate was not to apply to first-class matter for local delivery or for delivery within a county with a population of more than 1 million people if it was entirely within a corporate city.
[4]Government postal cards first authorized in 1872.
[5]A uniform rate regardless of distance, a free city delivery service, and a letter unit of 1/2 ounce instead of the former "single letter" were inaugurated.

Billions of dollars

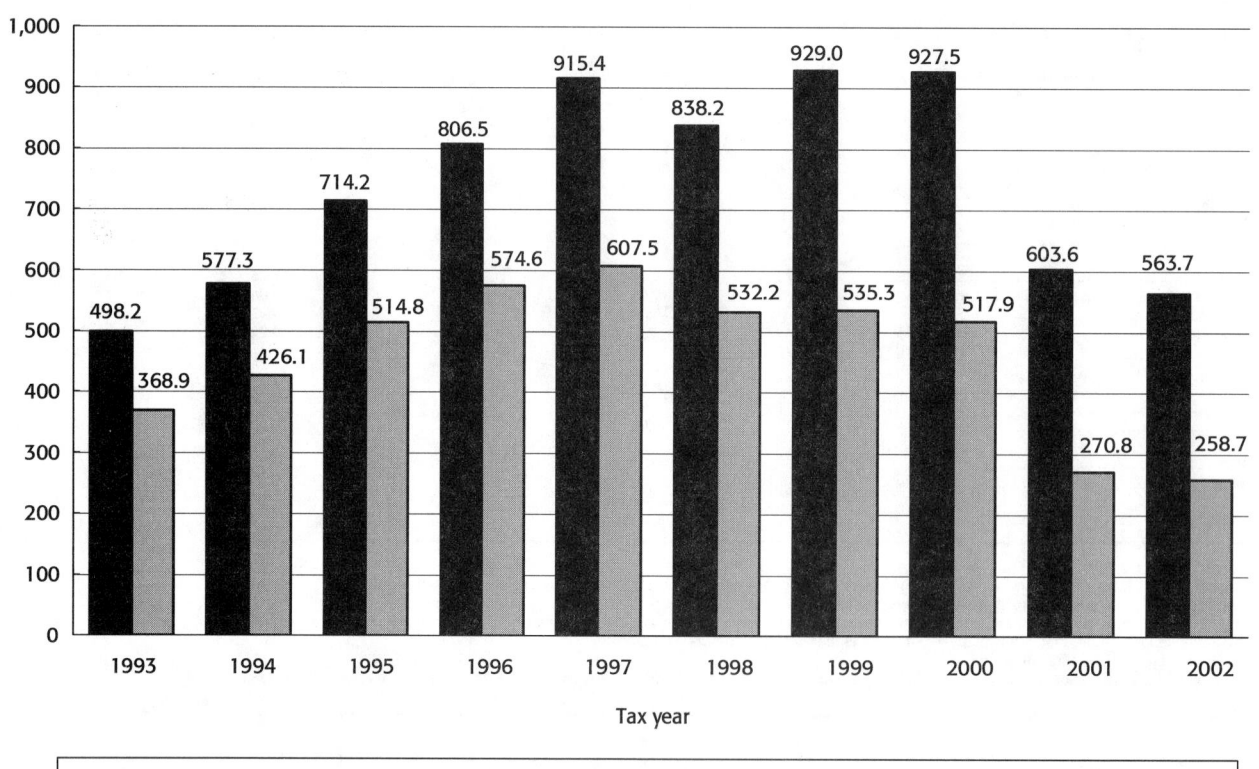

Corporate Pretax Profits, Tax Years 1993–2002

[1]Excludes net long-term capital gain reduced by net short-term capital loss of regulated investment companies and investment, rental, and portfolio income (including capital gains) of S corporations (qualifying corporations electing to be taxed through their shareholders).
Note: Pretax profits are net income (less deficit) in the statistics.

CHAPTER **25**

Business Enterprise

HIGHLIGHTS

1 As President Coolidge allegedly said, "The business of America is business." This business is conducted by more than 20 million firms, but data on the total number and size distribution of firms must be used with caution. There has never been a satisfactory definition of a firm, and the boundary between self-employment and a firm is tenuous at best. In addition, there are problems with inactive or partly active firms and seasonal firms. This problem is compounded when an effort is made to group firms into industrial categories whose boundaries are arbitrary and too tidy for real life. There are activities that defy known categories. Because small firms dominate the business landscape and because many small firms are on the boundary line, a slight difference in method may generate a considerable change in the total. If, however, the focus is on activity and output rather than number, then the unequal size distribution of firms becomes a statistical advantage because it permits a more efficient sample design at lower cost. Similarly, mergers and acquisitions, changes in public taste, and cyclical economic fluctuations all help to distort the structural profile of American business in ways of which statisticians may not be aware.

2 The principal sources of business data are official and nonofficial. Official sources include the *Survey of Current Business* published by the Bureau of Economic Analysis and the *Statistics of Income* produced by the Internal Revenue Service. Unofficial sources include publications of Dun & Bradstreet, including *Business Failure Record*.

3 Business firms are conventionally divided into the categories of corporation, partnership, and nonfarm proprietorship. Of the total 27.486 million business firms in the United States in 2003, nonfarm proprietorships were the most numerous (19.710 million), partnerships the least numerous (2.375 million), and corporations in the middle (5.401 million). However, in terms of receipts and income, corporations accounted for the lion's share with $19.755 trillion, followed by partnerships ($2.818 trillion) and nonfarm proprietorships ($1.050 trillion). The order was slightly different in net income. Corporations had a net income of $780 billion, nonfarm proprietorships $230 billion and partnerships $301 billion.

4 In 2003, U.S. corporations had assets of $53.645 trillion, of which $2.120 trillion was in cash and $4.073 in mortgage and real estate. In the same year, they had liabilities of $53.645 trillion, of which $11.386 trillion was in short-term and long-term debt. Net worth of all corporations was $18.819 trillion and net income of $780 billion.

5 In terms of private fixed assets by an industry, real estate, rental and leasing leads with $15.412 trillion, followed by manufacturing ($1.892 trillion), and utilities ($1.308 trillion).

6 In terms of assets of more than $250 million finance and insurance has 6,365 corporations, manufacturing has 1,483, wholesale and retail has 741, and transportation and warehousing 137. Agriculture is near the bottom with 21.

7 The business sector employed 113,398,000 people, and its annual payroll is $4.041 trillion. Retail trade has the most number of establishments (1,115,900), the second highest number of employees (14.890 million), and a payroll of $315 billion. Manufacturing is tenth in terms of establishments (352,600), the highest in the number of employees (15.950 million), and has the largest payroll at $576 billion.

8 Between 1990 and 2003, 7,514,700 new firms were born in the United States and 6,912,700 firms died.

9 In 2002, the 6,489,259 firms owned by women had annual sales of $939.538 billion. Of these firms, 16 percent are in health care and social assistance and 14 percent are in professional, scientific, and technical services.

10 Asian Americans received more in minority loans than African Americans, Hispanic Americans, and native Americans combined in 2005 ($4.056 billion vs. $627 million, $1.325 billion, and $125 million respectively).

11 There were 1.637 million bankruptcies in the United States in 2005, compared with 0.725 million in 1990, 1.042 million in 1996, and 1.277 million in 2000.

12 The Small Business Administration extended loans valued at $6.133 billion to 29,717 small minority firms. Minority business loans accounted for 28.3 percent of all loans.

13 Reflecting the changes in the economy, there were 11,169 mergers and acquisitions in 2000 valued at $3.440 trillion. Foreign interests acquired 336 U.S. companies valued at $68 billion, and U.S. companies acquired 378 overseas companies valued at $56 billion. Domestic mergers and acquisitions activity was most prominent in business services where 271 companies were acquired for $23.461 billion, followed by prepackaged software (126 companies for $8.481 billion) and real estate, mortgage bankers, and brokers (109 companies for $16.958 billion).

14 In 2005, 418,400 patent applications were filed, and 157,700 were granted. Of the patents issued, 143,800 were for inventions. The same year, 334,700 trademark applications were filed, and 154,800 new trademarks were issued.

15 Almost one-fourth of all patents granted in the United States in 2005 went to people living in California.

16 Gross private domestic investment increased from $861 billion in 1990 to $1.928 trillion in 2005.

17 In 2001, 549 corporations with assets of more than $1 billion had assets of more than $3.018 trillion and a net profit of $184.707 billion. The 500 largest corporations gave a 30.5 percent return to investors.

18 In 2003, U.S. multinational companies had assets of $15.911 trillion, gross product of $1.983 billion, and a work force of 21.701 million.

Table 25-1. Number of Tax Returns, Receipts, and Net Income by Type of Business, 1970–2003

(Covers active enterprises only. Figures are estimates based on sample of unaudited tax returns. Minus sign (–) indicates a net loss.)

Year	Number of returns (1,000)			Business receipts[2] (billions of dollars)			Net income (less loss)[3] (billions of dollars)		
	Nonfarm proprietorships[1]	Partnerships	Corporations	Nonfarm proprietorships[1]	Partnerships	Corporations	Nonfarm proprietorships[1]	Partnerships	Corporations
2003	19 710	2 375	5 401	1 050	2 818	19 755	230	301	780
2002	18 926	2 242	5 267	1 030	2 669	18 849	221	271	564
2001	18 338	2 132	5 136	1 017	2 569	19 308	217	276	604
2000	17 905	2 058	5 045	1 021	2 316	19 593	215	269	928
1999	17 576	1 937	4 936	969	1 829	18 009	208	228	929
1998	17 409	1 855	4 849	918	1 534	16 543	202	187	838
1997	17 176	1 759	4 710	870	1 297	15 890	187	168	915
1996	16 955	1 654	4 631	843	1 042	14 890	177	145	806
1995	16 424	1 581	4 474	807	854	13 969	169	107	714
1994	16 154	1 494	4 342	791	732	12 858	167	82	577
1993	15 848	1 468	3 965	757	627	11 814	156	67	498
1992	15 495	1 485	3 869	737	571	11 272	154	43	402
1991	15 181	1 515	3 803	713	539	10 963	142	21	345
1990	14 783	1 554	3 717	731	541	10 914	141	17	371
1989	14 298	1 635	3 628	693	524	10 440	133	14	389
1988	13 679	1 654	3 563	672	516	9 804	126	15	413
1987	13 091	1 648	3 612	611	428	9 186	106	–5	328
1986	12 394	1 703	3 429	559	379	8 282	90	–17	270
1985	11 929	1 714	3 277	540	349	8 050	79	–9	240
1984	11 262	1 644	3 171	515	358	7 551	71	–4	233
1980	8 932	1 380	2 711	411	286	6 172	55	8	239
1975	7 221	1 073	2 024	274	146	3 120	40	8	143
1970	5 770	936	1 665	199	92	1 706	31	10	66

Source: U.S. Census Bureau. Statistical Abstract of the United States: 2007. U.S. Internal Revenue Service.
[1]Through 1980, represents individually-owned businesses, including farms; thereafter, represents only nonfarm proprietors, i.e., business owners.
[2]Excludes investment income except for partnerships and corporations in finance, insurance, and real estate before 1998. Beginning 1998 finance and insurance, real estate, and management of companies included investment income for partnerships and corporations. Starting 1985, investment income no longer included for S corporations. S corporations are certain small qualifying corporations that elected to be taxed at the shareholder level. These corporations could have no more than 75 shareholders (mostly individuals), starting with Income Year 1997; no more than 35 for Income Years 1983–1996; no more than 25 for Income Year 1982; no more than 15 for Income Years 1977–1981; and no more than 10 for Income Years 1970–1976.
[3]Net income (less loss) is defined differently by form of organization, basically as follows: (a) Proprietorships: Total taxable receipts less total business deductions, including cost of sales and operations, depletion, and certain capital expensing, excluding charitable contributions and owners' salaries; (b) Partnerships: Total taxable receipts (including investment income except capital gains) less deductions, including cost of sales and operations and certain payments to partners, excluding charitable contributions, oil and gas depletion, and certain capital expensing; (c) Corporations: Total taxable receipts (including investment income, capital gains, and income from foreign subsidiaries deemed received for tax purposes, except for S corporations beginning 1985) less business deductions, including cost of sales and operations, depletion, certain capital expensing, and officers' compensation excluding S corporation charitable contributions and investment expenses starting 1985; net income is before income tax.

Table 25-2. Proprietorships, Partnerships, and Corporations—Number, Receipts, and Profit, 1939–2004

(Number in thousands; money figures in billions of dollars; based on sample of unaudited tax returns filed for accounting periods ending between July 1 of year shown and June 30 of following year.)

Year	Proprietorships[1]		Partnerships		Corporations	
	Number	Business receipts[2]	Number	Total receipts[2]	Number	Total receipts[2]
2004	20 591	1 140	2 547	3 260	5 558	22 712
2003	19 710	1 050	2 375	2 923	5 401	20 690
2002	18 926	1 030	2 242	2 773	5 267	19 749
2001	18 338	1 017	2 132	2 665	5 136	20 273
2000	17 905	1 021	2 058	2 405	5 045	20 606
1999	17 576	969	1 937	1 907	4 936	18 892
1998	17 409	918	1 855	1 603	4 849	17 324
1997	17 176	870	1 759	1 354	4 710	16 610
1996	16 955	843	1 654	1 042	4 631	15 526
1995	16 424	807	1 581	854	4 474	14 539
1994	16 154	791	1 493	731	4 342	13 360
1993	15 848	757	1 468	627	3 965	12 270
1992	15 495	737	1 485	571	3 869	11 742
1991	15 181	713	1 515	539	3 803	11 436
1990	14 783	731	1 554	541	3 717	11 410
1989	14 298	693	1 635	524	3 628	10 935
1988	13 679	672	1 654	464	3 563	9 804
1987	13 091	611	1 648	411	3 612	9 186
1986	12 394	559	1 703	379	3 429	8 282
1985	11 929	540	1 714	349	3 277	8 050
1984	11 262	516	1 644	375	3 171	7 861
1983	10 704	465	1 542	291	2 999	7 135
1982	10 106	434	1 514	297	2 926	7 024
1981	9 585	427	1 461	272	2 812	7 026
1980	8 932	411	1 380	286	2 711	6 172
1979	...	...	1 300	258	2 557	5 599
1978	...	...	1 234	219	2 377	4 715
1977	...	...	1 153	177	2 242	4 128
1976	...	...	1 096	160	2 082	3 635
1975	7 221	274	1 073	147	2 024	3 199
1974	...	...	1 062	139	1 966	3 090
1973	...	...	1 039	124	1 905	2 558
1972	...	...	992	104	1 813	2 171
1971	...	...	959	100	1 733	1 906
1970	9 399	238	936	93	1 665	1 751
1969	9 429	234	920	87	1 659	1 680
1968	9 212	222	918	83	1 542	1 508
1967	9 126	211	906	80	1 534	1 375
1966	9 087	207	923	80	1 469	1 307
1965	9 078	199	914	75	1 424	1 195
1964	9 193	189	922	75	1 374	1 087
1963	9 136	182	924	73	1 323	1 009
1962	9 193	178	932	74	1 268	949
1961	9 242	171	939	75	1 190	873
1960	9 090	171	941	74	1 141	849
1959	9 142	176	949	78	1 074	817
1958	8 800	163	954	78	990	735
1957	8 738	163	971	82	940	720
1956	8 973	...	...	...	886	680
1955	8 239	139	...	.	807	642
1954	7 786	...	...	...	723	555
1953	7 715	144	959	79	698	558
1952	6 873	...	...	...	672	531
1951	7 340	132	...	...	652	517
1950	6 865	...	...	...	629	458
1949	6 901	110	....	...	615	393
1948	7 208	...	...	...	594	411
1947	6 624	101	889	60	552	368
1946	6 944	...	...	...	491	289
1945	5 689	79	627	47	421	255
1944	6 134	66	...	...	412	262
1943	5 121	58	....	...	421	250
1942	...	...	...	...	443	218
1941	3 169	38	...	...	469	190
1940	2 018	31	...	...	473	148
1939	1 052	24	271	13	470	133

Source: U.S. Census Bureau. U.S. Internal Revenue Service.
Note: Most of the data are subject to sampling error; tax law and tax form changes affect the year-to-year comparability of the data.
[1]Through 1970, includes individually owned businesses and farms; thereafter, nonfarm businesses only. Represents the number of returns, even if there was more than one business per return.
[2]Excludes investment income except for partnerships and corporations in finance, insurance, and real estate before 1998. Beginning 1998 finance and insurance, and management of companies included investment income for corporations. Starting 1983 investment income no longer included for S corporations. S corporations are certain small qualifying corporations that elected to be taxed at the shareholder level. These corporations could have no more than 75 shareholders (mostly individuals), starting with Income Year 1997; no more than 35 for Income Years 1983–1996; no more than 25 for Income Year 1982; no more than 15 for Income Years 1977–1981; and no more than 10 for Income Years 1970–1976.
... = Not available.

Table 25-3. Establishments, Employees, and Payroll, by Employment-Size Class, 1980–2003

(Thousands.)

Employment-size class	1980	1985	1990	1995	1996	1997	1998	1999	2000	2001	2002	2003
Establishments, total												
(thousands)	...	...	6 176	6 613	6 739	6 895	6 942	7 008	7 070	7 095	7 201	7 255
Under 20 employees	...	...	5 354	5 733	5 843	5 968	5 991	6 036	6 069	6 083	6 199	6 240
20–99 employees	...	...	684	730	741	767	786	802	826	836	835	845
100–499 employees	...	...	122	135	138	143	147	152	157	157	149	151
500–999 employees	...	...	10	10	11	11	11	12	12	12	11	11
1 000 or more employees	...	...	6	6	6	6	6	7	7	7	7	7
Employees, total[1]												
(thousands)	74 844	81 111	93 476	100 335	102 199	105 299	108 118	110 706	114 065	115 061	112 401	113 398
Under 20 employees	19 423	21 810	24 373	25 785	26 115	26 883	27 131	27 289	27 569	27 681	28 116	28 313
20–99 employees	21 168	23 539	27 414	29 202	29 697	30 631	31 464	32 193	33 147	33 555	33 335	33 760
100–499 employees	17 840	19 410	22 926	25 364	26 086	26 993	27 842	28 707	29 736	29 692	28 101	28 549
500–999 employees	5 689	5 716	6 551	7 021	7 274	7 422	7 689	7 923	8 291	8 357	7 743	7 638
1 000 or more employees	10 716	10 645	12 212	12 962	13 026	13 370	13 991	14 594	15 322	15 776	15 105	15 138
Annual payroll, total[1]												
(billions of dollars)	1 035	1 514	2 104	2 666	2 849	3 048	3 309	3 555	3 879	3 989	3 943	4 041
Under 20 employees	231	352	485	608	647	688	734	773	818	839	866	885
20–99 employees	261	388	547	696	747	796	866	925	1 006	1 037	1 041	1 068
100–499 employees	249	362	518	675	730	786	858	931	1 031	1 052	1 021	1 054
500–999 employees	91	126	174	219	240	254	277	298	336	342	329	334
1 000 or more employees	208	286	381	467	485	524	575	628	690	719	685	700

Source: U.S. Census Bureau. *Statistical Abstract of the United States: 2007.*
Note: Excludes most government employees, railroad employees, and self-employed persons. Employees are for the week including March 12. Covers establishments with payroll. An establishment is a single physical location where business is conducted or where services or industrial operations are performed.
[1]Prior to 1987, totals for employees and annual payroll have been revised. Detail may not add to totals because revisions for size class are not available.
. . . = Not available.

Table 25-4. Firm Births and Deaths by Employment Size of Enterprise, 1990–2003

(Thousands. Represents activity from March of the beginning year to March of the ending year.)

	Births (initial locations)				Deaths (initial locations)			
Year	Total	Less than 20	Less than 500	500 or more	Total	Less than 20	Less than 500	500 or more
Firms								
2002 to 2003	612.3	585.6	612.0	0.3	540.7	514.6	540.3	0.3
2001 to 2002[1]	569.8	541.5	568.3	1.5	586.9	557.1	586.5	0.4
2000 to 2001	585.1	558.0	584.8	0.3	553.3	524.0	552.8	0.5
1999 to 2000	574.3	548.0	574.0	0.3	542.8	514.2	542.4	0.5
1998 to 1999	579.6	554.3	579.3	0.3	544.5	514.3	544.0	0.4
1997 to 1998	590.0	564.8	589.7	0.3	540.6	511.6	540.1	0.5
1996 to 1997	590.6	564.2	590.3	0.3	530.0	500.0	529.5	0.5
1995 to 1996	597.8	572.4	597.5	0.3	512.4	485.5	512.0	0.4
1994 to 1995	594.4	568.9	594.1	0.3	497.2	472.4	496.9	0.4
1993 to 1994	570.6	546.4	570.3	0.3	503.6	476.7	503.1	0.4
1992 to 1993	564.5	539.6	564.1	0.4	492.7	466.6	492.3	0.4
1991 to 1992	544.6	519.0	544.3	0.3	521.6	492.7	521.2	0.4
1990 to 1991	541.1	515.9	540.9	0.3	546.5	517.0	546.1	0.4
Employment								
2002 to 2003	3 667	1 856	3 174	493	3 324	1 608	2 880	445
2001 to 2002	3 370	1 748	3 034	336	3 660	1 755	3 257	403
2000 to 2001	3 418	1 821	3 109	310	3 262	1 701	3 050	212
1999 to 2000	3 229	1 793	3 031	198	3 177	1 654	2 946	230
1998 to 1999	3 225	1 670	2 991	235	3 180	1 645	2 969	210
1997 to 1998	3 205	1 812	3 002	203	3 233	1 662	2 992	242
1996 to 1997	3 228	1 814	3 030	198	3 275	1 621	2 961	314
1995 to 1996	3 256	1 845	3 056	200	3 100	1 560	2 808	291
1994 to 1995	3 322	1 836	3 049	273	2 823	1 517	2 634	189
1993 to 1994	3 106	1 760	2 890	216	3 077	1 549	2 801	276
1992 to 1993	3 438	1 751	3 054	384	2 906	1 516	2 698	209
1991 to 1992	3 201	1 703	2 864	337	3 126	1 603	2 894	232
1990 to 1991	3 105	1 713	2 907	198	3 208	1 723	3 044	164

Source: U.S. Census Bureau. *Statistical Abstract of the United States: 2007.* U.S. Small Business Administration, Office of Advocacy.
Note: Establishments with no employment in the first quarter of the beginning year were excluded. This table provides the number of births and deaths of initial establishments (based on plant number) as an approximation of firm births and deaths.
[1]A change in methodology has affected the allocation of firms by employment size.

Table 25-5. Business Bankruptcies by State, 2000–2005

(Number.)

State	2000	2001	2002	2003	2004	2005
United States[1]	35 161	40 099	38 540	34 710	33 978	38 711
District of Columbia	58	49	52	55	41	46
Alabama	445	428	381	287	325	331
Alaska	118	104	120	121	64	83
Arizona	765	753	756	701	480	525
Arkansas	261	290	282	429	376	426
California	4 595	5 238	5 141	4 501	3 748	4 236
Colorado	373	467	590	552	786	1 120
Connecticut	139	156	181	187	132	156
Delaware	2 320	1 374	649	505	276	218
Florida	1 447	1 896	1 803	1 534	1 183	1 622
Georgia	1 012	1 162	1 359	1 585	2 090	2 232
Hawaii	63	68	53	72	47	81
Idaho	269	303	260	225	160	141
Illinois	1 270	1 547	1 240	991	912	1 042
Indiana	398	604	661	640	524	758
Iowa	214	289	354	323	360	455
Kansas	169	220	238	303	268	410
Kentucky	355	474	445	327	319	409
Louisiana	619	716	672	499	622	718
Maine	162	151	101	105	138	144
Maryland	677	758	873	523	417	760
Massachusetts	393	427	380	396	315	406
Michigan	577	688	802	684	681	1 071
Minnesota	1 492	1 887	1 729	1 379	1 374	1 721
Mississippi	203	289	309	282	170	200
Missouri	369	505	394	378	354	438
Montana	141	149	120	98	109	129
Nebraska	115	144	152	238	207	296
Nevada	332	419	462	321	257	333
New Hampshire	302	334	212	178	158	586
New Jersey	660	730	689	734	684	765
New Mexico	513	620	693	774	727	828
New York	1 960	2 432	2 585	1 987	4 070	2 112
North Carolina	445	613	576	528	486	612
North Dakota	92	115	116	105	85	95
Ohio	1 471	1 794	1 538	1 426	1 432	2 099
Oklahoma	876	941	607	612	659	944
Oregon	1 453	1 389	1 606	1 591	852	1 160
Pennsylvania	1 455	1 541	1 263	1 193	1 138	1 356
Rhode Island	74	64	65	48	74	136
South Carolina	138	147	178	142	175	176
South Dakota	133	164	119	110	108	196
Tennessee	641	886	735	597	548	574
Texas	2 592	3 155	2 994	3 153	3 094	3 590
Utah	451	475	602	519	440	449
Vermont	71	97	91	78	85	78
Virginia	815	924	969	956	750	476
Washington	717	642	698	737	665	786
West Virginia	277	322	357	290	247	282
Wisconsin	685	734	856	722	742	820
Wyoming	47	45	47	44	65	84

Source: U.S. Census Bureau. *Statistical Abstract of the United States: 2007.* U.S. Small Business Administration, Office of Advocacy.

Table 25-6. Recorded Mergers and Acquisitions, 1895–2003

(Merger values in millions of dollars.)

Year	Recorded mergers (FTC)	Value of recorded mergers (Eis)
2003	7 743	1 318 000
2002	7 032	1 185 000
2001	7 713	1 688 000
2000	11 169	3 440 000
1999	9 599	3 402 000
1998	9 634	2 480 200
1997	8 770	1 610 300
1996	5 639	1 059 300
1995	4 981	895 800
1994	4 383	524 900
1993	3 722	420 400
1992	3 502	125 300
1991	3 446	141 500
1990	4 239	205 600
1989	3 752	316 800
1988	2 970	218 800
1987	2 479	198 800
1986	2 497	223 100
1985	1 719	149 600
1984	. . .	126 000
1983	. . .	53 000
1982	. . .	61 000
1981	. . .	70 000
1980	. . .	33 000
1979	519	12 867
1978	610	10 724
1977	590	8 670
1976	559	6 279
1975	439	4 950
1974	602	4 466
1973	874	3 149
1972	911	1 885
1971	1 011	2 480
1970	1 351	5 904
1969	2 307	. . .
1968	2 407	. . .
1967	1 496	. . .
1966	995	. . .
1965	1 008	3 254
1964	854	. . .
1963	861	. . .
1962	853	. . .
1961	954	. . .
1960	844	1 535
1959	835	. . .
1958	589	. . .
1957	585	. . .
1956	673	. . .
1955	683	. . .
1954	387	. . .
1953	295	. . .
1952	288	. . .
1951	235	. . .
1950	219	. . .
1949	126	. . .
1948	223	. . .
1947	404	. . .
1946	419	. . .
1945	333	. . .
1944	324	. . .
1943	213	. . .
1942	118	. . .
1941	111	. . .
1940	140	. . .
1939	87	. . .
1938	110	. . .
1937	124	. . .
1936	126	. . .
1935	130	. . .
1934	101	. . .
1933	120	. . .
1932	203	. . .
1931	464	. . .
1930	799	1 757
1929	1 245	1 993
1928	1 058	1 653
1927	870	727
1926	856	1 135
1925	554	721
1924	368	466

. . . = Not available.

Table 25-6. Recorded Mergers and Acquisitions, 1895–2003—*Continued*

(Merger values in millions of dollars.)

Year	Recorded mergers (FTC)	Value of recorded mergers (Eis)
1923	311	1 171
1922	309	502
1921	487	430
1920	760	809
1919	438	777
1918	. . .	254
1917	. . .	679
1916	. . .	470
1915	. . .	158
1914	. . .	160
1913	. . .	176
1912	. . .	322
1911	. . .	210
1910	. . .	257
1909	. . .	89
1908	. . .	188
1907	. . .	185
1906	. . .	378
1905	. . .	243
1904	. . .	110
1903	. . .	298
1902	. . .	911
1901	. . .	2 053
1900	. . .	442
1899	. . .	2 263
1898	. . .	651
1897	. . .	120
1896	. . .	25
1895	. . .	41

Source: U.S. Census Bureau. Thomson Financial. *Mergers & Corporate Transactions Database©.*
. . . = Not available.

Table 25-7. Corporate Asset, Liability, Income, Deduction, Tax and Profit Items, and Dividends Paid for All Industries, 1926–2003

(Millions of dollars, except number of tax returns.)

Year	Number of corporate tax returns	Total assets	Total liabilities	Total receipts[1]	Total compiled deductions[1]	Net income[1,2]
2003	5 401 000	53 645 000	53 645 000	20 690 000	19 941 000	780 000
2002	5 267 000	50 414 000	50 414 000	19 749 000	19 199 000	564 000
2001	5 136 000	49 154 000	49 154 000	20 273 000	19 683 000	604 000
2000	5 045 000	47 027 000	47 027 000	20 606 000	19 692 000	928 000
1999	4 936 000	41 464 000	41 464 000	18 892 000	17 967 000	929 000
1998	4 849 000	37 347 000	37 347 000	17 324 000	16 489 000	838 000
1997	4 710 000	33 030 000	33 030 000	16 610 000	15 704 000	915 000
1996	4 631 000	28 642 000	28 642 000	15 526 000	14 728 000	806 000
1995	4 474 000	26 014 000	26 014 000	14 539 000	13 821 000	714 000
1994	4 342 000	23 446 000	23 446 000	13 360 000	12 775 000	577 000
1993	3 965 000	21 816 000	21 816 000	12 270 000	11 765 000	498 000
1992	3 869 000	20 002 000	20 002 000	11 742 000	11 330 000	402 000
1991	3 803 000	19 030 000	19 030 000	11 436 000	11 087 000	345 000
1990	3 717 000	18 190 000	18 190 000	11 410 000	11 033 000	371 000
1989	3 628 000	17 647 000	17 647 000	10 935 000	10 545 000	389 000
1988	3 563 000	16 568 000	16 568 000	10 265 000	9 853 000	413 000
1987	3 612 000	15 311 000	15 311 000	9 582 000	9 244 000	328 000
1986	3 429 000	14 163 000	14 163 000	8 669 000	8 395 000	270 000
1985	3 277 000	12 773 000	12 773 000	8 398 000	8 158 000	240 000
1984	3 171 000	11 107 000	11 107 000	7 861 000	7 629 000	233 000
1983	2 999 000	10 201 000	10 201 000	7 135 000	6 945 000	188 000
1982	2 926 000	9 358 000	9 358 000	7 024 000	6 869 000	154 000
1981	2 812 000	8 547 000	8 547 000	7 026 000	6 814 000	214 000
1980	2 711 000	7 617 000	7 617 000	6 361 000	6 125 000	239 000
1979	2 557 000	6 835 000	6 835 000	5 598 700	5 315 700	283 000
1978	2 377 000	6 014 000	6 014 000	4 714 600	4 467 000	247 400
1977	2 242 000	5 326 000	5 326 000	4 128 300	3 908 900	219 500
1976	2 082 000	4 721 000	4 721 000	3 635 500	3 448 900	186 600
1975	2 024 000	4 287 000	4 287 000	3 198 600	3 052 700	143 000
1974	1 966 000	4 016 000	4 016 000	3 089 700	2 941 500	148 200
1973	1 905 000	3 649 000	3 649 000	2 557 700	2 435 000	122 600
1972	1 813 000	3 257 000	3 257 000	2 171 200	2 071 700	99 500
1971	1 733 300	2 889 000	2 889 000	1 906 000	1 824 000	81 900
1970	1 665 477	2 634 707	2 634 707	1 750 728	1 682 779	67 949
1969	1 658 820	2 445 328	2 445 628	1 680 482	1 598 348	82 135
1968	1 541 670	2 215 625	2 215 625	1 507 786	1 420 309	87 477
1967	1 534 360	2 010 443	2 010 443	1 374 599	1 295 348	79 520
1966	1 468 725	1 844 775	1 844 775	1 306 518	1 225 225	81 293
1965	1 423 980	1 723 524	1 723 524	1 194 601	1 119 860	74 742
1964	1 373 517	1 585 619	1 585 619	1 086 739	1 023 680	63 059
1963	1 323 187	1 481 236	1 481 236	1 008 743	953 006	55 737
1962	1 268 042	1 388 127	1 388 127	949 305	898 463	50 842
1961	1 190 286	1 289 516	1 289 516	873 178	826 144	47 034
1960	1 140 574	1 206 662	1 206 662	849 132	804 633	44 499
1959	1 074 120	1 136 668	1 136 668	816 800	769 145	47 655
1958	990 381	1 064 481	1 064 481	735 338	696 114	39 224
1957	940 147	996 400	996 400	720 414	675 340	45 073
1956	827 916	948 951	948 951	673 493	626 309	47 184
1955	746 962	888 621	888 621	634 508	586 907	47 601
1954	667 856	805 300	805 300	547 001	510 515	36 486
1953	640 073	761 877	[3]761 877	551 984	512 402	39 582
1952	615 698	721 864	721 864	525 011	486 504	38 507
1951	596 385	647 524	647 524	511 849	468 354	43 495
1950	569 961	598 369	598 369	452 523	409 988	42 535
1949	554 573	543 562	543 562	387 636	359 505	28 130
1948	536 833	525 136	525 136	405 430	371 182	34 248
1947	496 821	494 615	494 625	361 521	330 314	31 207
1946	440 750	454 705	454 705	283 917	258 893	25 025
1945	374 950	441 461	441 461	252 636	231 417	21 220
1944	363 056	418 324	418 324	258 880	232 426	26 454
1943	366 870	389 524	389 524	245 796	217 863	27 933
1942	383 534	360 018	360 018	213 777	190 497	23 280
1941	407 053	340 452	340 452	186 137	169 546	16 592

[1]Beginning 1987, receipts, deductions and net income of S corporations are limited to those from trade or business; those from investments are excluded.
[2]Excludes regulated investment companies.
[3]Includes deficit of $7,655 million.

Table 25-7. Corporate Asset, Liability, Income, Deduction, Tax and Profit Items, and Dividends Paid for All Industries, 1926–2003—*Continued*

(Millions of dollars, except number of tax returns.)

Year	Number of corporate tax returns	Total assets	Total liabilities	Total receipts[1]	Total compiled deductions[1]	Net income[1,2]
1940	413 716	320 478	320 478	145 427	135 955	9 472
1939	412 759	306 801	306 801	130 365	123 129	7 236
1938	411 941	300 022	300 022	117 596	113 452	4 144
1937	416 902	303 357	303 357	138 907	131 130	7 777
1936	415 654	303 180	303 180	126 269	118 651	7 618
1935	415 205	303 150	303 150	112 098	106 599	5 500
1934	410 626	301 307	301 307	99 095	96 058	3 037
1933	388 564	268 206	268 206	82 148	82 787	[3]–639
1932	392 021	280 083	280 083	79 701	83 211	[3]–3 511
1931	381 088	296 497	296 497	105 238	105 725	[3]–487
1930	403 173	334 002	334 002	[4]	[4]	[4]
1929	398 815	335 775	335 778	[4]	[4]	[4]
1928	384 548	307 218	307 218	[4]	[4]	[4]
1927	379 156	287 542	287 542	[4]	[4]	[4]
1926	359 449	262 179	262 179	[4]	[4]	[4]

Source: U.S. Census Bureau. U.S. Internal Revenue Service.
[1]Beginning 1987, receipts, deductions and net income of S corporations are limited to those from trade or business; those from investments are excluded.
[2]Excludes regulated investment companies.
[3]Includes deficit of $7,655 million.
[4]Loss.
[5]Not available separately for returns with balance sheets.

Table 25-8. Business Cycle Expansions and Contractions—Months of Duration, 1854–2001

Business cycle reference dates				Contraction (peak to trough)	Expansion (previous trough to this peak)	Length of cycle	
Peak		Trough				Trough from previous trough	Peak from previous peak
Month	Year	Month	Year				
March	2001	November	2001	8	120	128	128
July	1990	March	1991	8	92	100	108
July	1981	November	1982	16	12	28	18
January	1980	July	1980	6	58	64	74
November	1973	March	1975	16	36	52	47
December	1969	November	1970	11	106	117	116
April	1960	February	1961	10	24	34	32
August	1957	April	1958	8	39	47	49
July	1953	May	1954	10	45	55	56
November	1948	October	1949	11	37	48	45
February	1945	October	1945	8	80	88	93
May	1937	June	1938	13	50	63	93
August	1929	March	1933	43	21	64	34
October	1926	November	1927	13	27	40	41
May	1923	July	1924	14	22	36	40
January	1920	July	1921	18	10	28	17
August	1918	March	1919	7	44	51	67
January	1913	December	1914	23	12	35	36
January	1910	January	1912	24	19	43	32
May	1907	June	1908	13	33	46	56
September	1902	August	1904	23	21	44	39
June	1899	December	1900	18	24	42	42
December	1895	June	1897	18	18	36	35
January	1893	June	1894	17	20	37	30
July	1890	May	1891	10	27	37	40
March	1887	April	1888	13	22	35	60
March	1882	May	1885	38	36	74	101
October	1873	March	1879	65	34	99	52
June	1869	December	1870	18	18	36	50
April	1865	December	1867	32	46	78	54
October	1860	June	1861	8	22	30	40
June	1857	December	1858	18	30	48	-
		December	1854	-	-	-	-
Average, all cycles:							
1854 to 2001 (32 cycles)				17	38	55	[1]56
1854 to 1919 (16 cycles)				22	27	48	[2]49
1919 to 1945 (6 cycles)				18	35	53	53
1945 to 2001 (10 cycles)				10	57	67	67
Average, peacetime cycles:							
1854 to 2001 (27 cycles)				18	33	51	52
1854 to 1919 (14 cycles)				22	24	46	47
1919 to 1945 (5 cycles)				20	26	46	45
1945 to 2001 (8 cycles)				10	52	63	63

Source: U.S. Census Bureau. Statistical Abstract of the United States: 2007. National Bureau of Economic Research, Inc. Business Cycle Expansions and Contractions.
Note: A trough is the low point of a business cycle; a peak is the high point. Contraction, or recession, is the period from peak to subsequent trough; expansion is the period from trough to subsequent peak. Business cycle reference dates are determined by the National Bureau of Economic Research, Incorporated.
[1]31 cycles.
[2]15 cycles.

Table 25-9. Small Business Administration Loans to Minority-Owned Small Businesses, 1980–2005

(Number, percent, millions of dollars. For year ending September 30.)

Year	Number of loans to minorities						Value of loans to minority owned businesses (millions of dollars)				
	Total	Percent of all loans	African American	Asian American	Hispanic American	Native American	Total	African American	Asian American	Hispanic American	Native American
2005	29 717	28.3	6 632	13 455	8 795	835	6 133	627	4 056	1 325	125
2004	25 413	28.4	4 827	12 100	7 686	800	5 144	481	3 400	1 151	113
2003	20 183	27.2	3 769	9 507	6 112	795	4 215	399	2 756	942	118
2002	14 304	25.0	2 148	7 248	4 272	636	4 228	419	2 799	885	126
2001	11 855	24.6	1 936	5 720	3 627	572	3 456	374	2 247	733	102
2000	11 999	24.8	2 120	5 838	3 500	541	3 634	388	2 383	761	101
1999	12 051	24.6	2 181	5 581	3 752	537	3 377	390	2 148	755	84
1998	10 869	23.0	1 925	5 201	3 280	463	2 709	304	1 696	633	77
1997	10 225	20.7	1 908	4 532	3 378	407	2 499	292	1 501	626	81
1996	9 955	18.9	2 325	3 831	3 357	442	2 084	298	1 174	530	83
1995	10 877	18.1	2 770	3 767	3 940	400	1 838	293	945	539	61
1994	7 048	17.6	1 470	2 809	2 530	239	1 732	224	965	490	53
1993	4 285	14.7	843	1 763	1 533	146	1 149	154	635	324	37
1992	3 602	13.8	700	1 550	1 230	122	1 002	130	565	278	28
1991	2 813	13.9	538	1 313	865	97	735	99	438	179	19
1990	2 367	12.0	513	1 075	694	85	576	96	317	149	14
1989	2 092	11.9	585	861	556	90	441	94	220	109	18
1988	1 850	11.2	501	776	490	83	362	80	175	91	15
1987	1 752	10.7	413	732	533	74	313	63	151	87	12
1986	1 538	10.2	380	608	496	54	254	56	116	73	8
1985	2 027	11.8	606	657	690	74	291	64	115	102	10
1984	2 339	12.4	780	632	853	74	299	84	96	110	9
1983	2 030	11.9	641	492	818	79	237	67	69	90	10
1982	1 987	14.0	620	448	840	79	200	55	55	81	9
1981	3 781	14.5	1 379	669	1 574	159	377	123	84	151	20
1980	4 276	14.9	1 732	659	1 715	170	381	146	70	149	15

Source: U.S. Census Bureau. *Statistical Abstract of the United States: 2007.* U.S. Small Business Administration.
Note: A small business must be independently owned and operated, must not be dominant in its particular industry, and must meet standards set by the Small Business Administration as to its annual receipts or number of employees. Loans include both direct and guaranteed loans to small business establishments. Does not include Disaster Assistance Loans.

Table 25-10. Selected Characteristics of Employer Business Owners, 2002

Characteristic	Percent of employer business owners	Characteristic	Percent of employer business owners
Owner's age		Ethnicity	
Under 25 years old	1	Hispanic[2]	4
25–34 years old	8	Non-Hispanic	93
35–44 years old	24	Not reported	3
45–64 years old	53		
65 years old and over	10	Owner's educational level	
Not reported	4	High school or less	24
		Some college	28
Sex		Undergraduate	24
Male	71	Post graduate	19
Female	27	Not reported	4
Not reported	3		
		Average number of hours owner spent managing or working in the business	
Race[1]		None	7
White	88	Less than 20	13
Black or African American	2	20–39	12
American Indian or Alaska Native	1	40	14
Asian	6	41–59	30
Native Hawaiian or Other Pacific Islander	Z	60 or more	19
Not reported	4	Not reported	4

Source: U.S. Census Bureau. *Statistical Abstract of the United States: 2006.*
Note: The preliminary estimates in this report are based on responses from owners of businesses with paid employees operating in the United States. Data were collected on the 2002 Survey of Business Owners (SBO). Businesses were asked to report information about the characteristics of up to 3 individuals with the largest share of ownership. If a business had more than 3 owners, no characteristic information was requested from the additional owners. The data represent the characteristics of approximately 7.7 million owners. The estimates in this report are subject to sampling variability as well as nonsampling errors. Sources of nonsampling error include errors of response, nonreporting and coverage.
[1] Owners reporting more than one race are counted in each race group reported.
[2] Persons of Hispanic origin may be of any race.
Z = Less than 0.5 percent.

BOX 25 ■ Corporate Accounting Scandals

From late 2001 to 2003, the United States experienced a wave of corporate accounting scandals that were unprecedented in numbers and magnitude. In December 2001, the Enron Corporation entered the largest bankruptcy filing to date, as officers admitted overstating earnings since 1997 in the amount of $586 million. The eventual cost to investors was $60 billion; the cost to employees in lost retirement benefits was estimated at $1 billion.

Then, in July 2002, WorldCom declared bankruptcy as a result of an accounting scandal that involved overstated earnings of $11 billion and a cost to shareholders of $180 billion. Investigators uncovered a series of accounting irregularities in the books of Tyco International and, eventually, its CEO, Dennis Kozlowski, was convicted of fraud for $400 million dollars and grand larceny for $150 million. Subsequently, large-scale fraud was uncovered at other corporations, including Health-South and Adelphia.

Some theorists postulate that this series of accounting irregularities was the product of increasing demands placed on corporations and their executive staffs by shareholders and Wall Street to meet analysts' earnings estimates. Others suggest it was more a matter of executive arrogance that began in the economic well being of the 1990s and the technology boom that drove stock prices higher and higher. In short, these executives believed that the only thing that mattered was rising share prices.

In response to these scandals and to plunging investor confidence, the U.S. Congress revamped regulations of corporate governance with the 2002 Sarbanes-Oxley Act, considered the most significant modification in securities law since the formation of the Securities and Exchange Commission (SEC) in 1934. It sought to increase the accountability of executive staffs, remove boards of directors from the influence of executive staffs, and increase the influence of shareholders. The Sarbanes-Oxley Act requires that company executives certify their companies' finances to prevent executives from claiming ignorance of rampant fraud, as occurred in the cases of Enron, WorldCom, and HealthSouth. Section 404 specifically requires management of corporations to establish internal controls and procedures for financial reporting and to attest to the effectiveness of these controls in their companies' annual reports. Building on these changes, individual stock exchanges have increased requirements from listed companies. For example, the New York Stock Exchange and the Nasdaq require that the majority of members of any company's board must be independent and not have any relationship to the firm or its executive staff.

The corporate sector has consistently lobbied for changes in Sarbanes-Oxley, claiming that the increased costs of accounting are prohibitive to smaller corporations and that the onerous regulations prevent U.S. firms from being competitive in the global market. However, in the five years since Sarbanes-Oxley was passed, Japan, France, China, Canada, and other countries have begun to adopt similar requirements for internal controls. U.S. companies spent $6 billion in 2006 on accounting costs to comply with the requirements of Sarbanes-Oxley, but this number pales in comparison to the amount of money lost by stockholders in the scandals of 2002 and 2003. Corporate boards have indeed become more independent.

In 2005, 83% of boards had a majority of independent directors, as compared with 54% in 2000. In 2007, the SEC eased outside audit requirements for corporations with a market cap below $75 million, instituted fewer and smaller fines, gave legal protection to auditors who fail to catch fraud, and made it encourage investors to settle disagreements through arbitration by making it harder to sue companies.

Despite all the regulatory changes intended to stop fraud and corruption, an academic study in 2006 found that almost 10% of publicly listed companies had executives who backdated stock options to a time when the stock price was low, providing them with an artificially low purchase price.

Sources:

"CEOs & Scandal.(News)(Brief Article)." *Crain's Chicago Business* (March 5, 2007): 30.10.
"Forget a Rollback of Sarbanes-Oxley." *The Kiplinger Letter* (April 27, 2007): 84.17.
Healy, Thomas J. "Sarbox Was the Right Medicine." *Wall Street Journal* (Eastern Edition) New York, NY (August 9, 2007): A13.
"Hot Topic: Why Corporate Boardrooms Are in Turmoil." *Wall Street Journal* (Eastern Edition) New York, NY (September 16, 2006): A7.
Iwata, Edward. "Enron's Legacy: Scandal Marked Turning Point for Business World." *USA Today* (January 30, 2006): 04B.
"Seeds of Scandal.(Enron Bankruptcy)(Brief Article)(Company Profile)." *U.S. News & World Report* (March 18, 2002):28.
Van, Jon. "Newborn MCI Still Has Debt, Lawsuit Problems." *Knight Ridder/Tribune News Service* (April 20, 2004): K1451.
"WorldCom Out of Bankruptcy, MCI New Name." *UPI NewsTrack* (April 20, 2004).

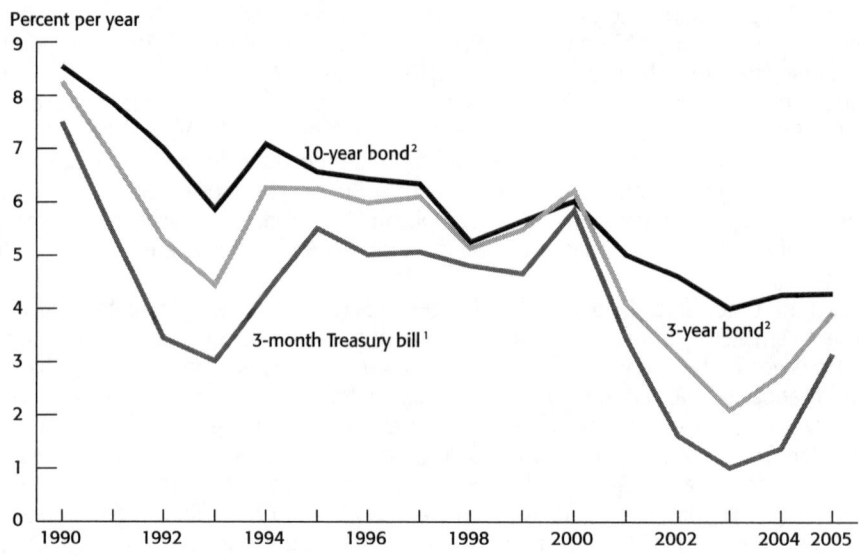

Percent per year

10-year bond[2]

3-month Treasury bill[1]

3-year bond[2]

Interest Rates and Bond Yields: 1990 to 2005
(Percent per year. Annual averages)
[1] New issues.
[2] U.S. Treasury, constant maturities.
Source: Chart prepared by U.S.Census Bureau.

CHAPTER **26**

Financial Markets and Institutions

HIGHLIGHTS

1 Financial markets and institutions not only influence but also drive the U.S. economy. Financial data summarize the types of claims, liabilities, and assets, and also illustrate how lending and borrowing are related to income and expenditure flows. They are derived from banking statistics, Treasury accounts, census data, tax returns, balance of payments reports, and security market reports. The data present a picture of the distribution of wealth ownership and of the major components of national wealth. Financial data also provide information on the structure of debt—who owes what to whom—which has a bearing on corporate and private spending decisions. Other types of data cover savings, investments, money supplies, U.S. government securities, bonds and mortgages, and corporate equities.

2 Money supply, broadly defined, includes both bank deposits and currency. Before 1934, gold was also a part of means of payments, but in January of that year it was withdrawn from circulation. Until 1971, gold served as a means of settlement of international accounts, and until 1968, as domestic reserve money. At present, gold is held solely by the Treasury Department. Private gold holdings are forbidden except

in limited amounts for licensed purposes. U.S. residents may purchase, hold, or sell foreign and domestic gold coins minted before April 5, 1933, but those minted after that date may be held only by collectors. From 1873 to 1907, gold coins in circulation in the United States were included in the estimates of the Annual Report of the Director of the Mint. In 1934, gold coins worth $287 million were still in circulation, but they disappeared from circulation immediately after the U.S. dollar was taken off the gold standard. Following the enactment of the Old Series Currency Adjustment Act of 1961, both gold and silver certificates were retired.

3 The chief money market in the country is New York City. The New York money market comprises a number of markets with differences in rates corresponding to differences in the supply of funds relative to demand. These markets are called "open" markets because transactions on them are usually made on an impersonal basis with the borrower and lender dealing through agents. In contrast, in a "customer" market, borrower and lender deal directly with each other, and transactions are often made on a personal basis.

4 Although investment companies date back to the nineteenth century, they became popular only after the rise of mutual funds. A mutual fund is a company that combines the funds of many investors whose investment goals are similar, and which invests those funds in a wide variety of securities. Different mutual funds have different investment objectives, management policies, and degrees of risk. Some emphasize capital growth, others, current income; still others are highly speculative. Mutual funds are technically known as open-end investment companies because they are always ready to redeem outstanding shares at the request of the investor. Mutual funds are regulated by both federal and state governments; the major federal statutes governing them are the Securities Act of 1933, the Securities Exchange Act of 1934, and the Investment Company Act of 1940.

5 The banking system of the United States has evolved over two centuries. Banks are in part regulated by state governments and in part by the federal government. Supervision and regulation of banks are the primary responsibility of the chartering authorities—the Comptroller of Currency in the case of national banks organized under the federal law of 1863 and state officials in the case of state banks. Two other federal entities with additional supervisory authority have been superimposed on the banking system: the Federal Reserve System, which was established in 1914 to exercise central banking functions, and the Federal Deposit Insurance Corporation, created in 1933 to insure bank deposits. The Federal Reserve System includes all national banks and those state banks that choose to join voluntarily. Insurance of bank deposits is obligatory for all banks belonging to the Federal Reserve System and is optional for others. Before the National Banking Act of 1863, the only official banking statistics were compiled by the Treasury Department and were based on reports submitted voluntarily by the banks. No data on state banks were included in these reports, but the Act of 1873 authorized the Comptroller to obtain data about nonnational banks from state authorities. Although coverage was improved, it was far from complete because many banks operated outside the state system, and some states had no departments to collect the information. Efforts to promote uniformity in bank statistics culminated in 1947, when a standardized balance-sheet form was approved and adopted by the federal and state banking agencies. To provide more adequate historical banking statistics comparable to those available beginning 1947, a revised retrospective series was published in 1959 under the title *All-Bank Statistics 1896–1955*. This series covered number of banks, principal assets and liabilities for major classes of banks, and data for individual states and outlying territories.

6 The first bank chartered by Congress was the Bank of North America in Philadelphia founded in 1781. The Bank of the United States was sponsored by the Federalist Party and chartered in 1791 in Philadelphia. Secretary of the Treasury, Alexander Hamilton, used it as a fiscal agent—a depository bank for government funds. Its charter expired in 1811 and was not renewed by Congress. The Second Bank of the United States was authorized in 1816 and opened in 1817. Its 20-year charter was not renewed either. It failed in 1841 and was liquidated in 1856.

7 There are three sources of primary data about life insurance: reports of the state insurance departments; commercial publishers, such as A. M. Best Company; and trade associations, such as the American Life Insurance Association.

8 The first life insurance company was the Corporation for the Relief of Poor and Distressed Presbyterian Ministers and of the Poor and Distressed Widows and Children of Presbyterian Ministers, incorporated in 1759 in Philadelphia. The first health insurance company was the Massachusetts Health Insurance Company of Boston, founded in 1847. The first accident insurance company was Travelers Insurance Company of Hartford, chartered in 1863. It issued the first automobile insurance policy in 1898 to Dr. Truman J. Martin of Buffalo—the one-year premium was $11.25. The first fire insurance company to receive a charter was the Philadelphia Contributorship for the Insurance of Houses from Loss by Fire in 1868.

9 Savings institutions are primarily involved in credit extension in the form of mortgage loans. Statistics on savings institutions are collected by the U.S. Office of Thrift Supervision. The Financial Institutions Reform, Recovery, and Enforcement Act of 1989 authorized the establishment of the Resolution Trust Corporation (RTC), which is responsible for the disposal of assets from failed savings institutions.

10 In 2001, the Finance, Insurance and Real Estate (FIRE) sector contributed 20.6 percent to the GDP, or $2.077 trillion. Of the total 425,000 establishments in this sector, 75,800 were commercial banks, 15,700 were savings institutions, 76,900 were personal credit institutions, 12,200 were mortgage and nonmortgage brokers, 76,900 were securities and commodities dealers, and 30,900 were life insurance carriers.

11 In 2005, American households had total liabilities of $11.916 trillion, of which mortgages made up $8.660 trillion and consumer credit $2.189 trillion. Home mortgages made up 72.7 percent of all debt. More than 7 out of every 10 Americans carried some debt, of which 47.9 percent had a mortgage, 46.0 percent had installment debt, and 46.2 percent had credit card debt.

12 In 2005, mortgage delinquency rates on loans were 4.5 percent, slightly less than the average of the last five years. The highest delinquency rate is for credit cards, at 3.70 percent in 2005.

13 Foreign banks have increased their share of the U.S. financial market since 1980 from 11.9 percent of assets to 19.8 percent in 2005, and from 6.6 percent of deposits in 1980 to 16.2 percent in 2005.

14 Although the number of federal and state credit unions fell from 17,350 in 1980 to 8,695 in 2005, they had more members in 2005 and more assets. Credit union membership was 84.810 million and total assets of $678.698 billion.

15 In 2004, there were 1.422 billion credit cards in use held by 164 million cardholders, or an average of nearly nine cards per cardholder. Bank cards are the most numerous at 567 million, followed by store cards (503 million), and oil company cards (81 million). The number of debit cards reached 278 million in 2004.

16 The total volume of trading on the New York Stock exchange rose from 11.562 billion in 1980 to 410.832 billion in 2005. The value of shares traded in 2005 was $14.441 trillion.

17 In 2005, there were 7,977 mutual funds with assets of $8.905 trillion, and 277.7 million shareholder accounts.

18 Individual Retirement Account (IRA) plans had a total value of $3.667 trillion in 2005, of which $1.668 trillion was held by mutual funds.

19 In 2004, 373 million life insurance policies were in effect, with a value of $17.580 trillion. The number of life insurance companies decreased from 2,195 in 1990 to 1,179 in 2004.

20 In 2005, there were 8,832 FDIC insured financial institutions, such as banks in the United States. Of these, the greatest number are located in Illinois (707), Texas (661), and Minnesota (466).

21 In 2003, there were 460,600 finance and insurance businesses that employed 6.464 million people and had a payroll of $392.9 billion.

Table 26-1. Household Assets, Financial Obligations, and Delinquency Rates, 1945–2005

(Billions of dollars, except as noted; end of period; not seasonally adjusted, except as noted.)

Year	Total	Foreign deposits	Checkable deposits and currency	Time and savings deposits	Money market fund shares	Open market paper	U.S. savings bonds	Other Treasury securities	Agency securities	Municipal securities	Corporate and foreign bonds	Corporate equities[2]	Mutual fund shares	Mortgages
2005	38 465	64	219	4 654	951	164	205	196	656	845	492	6 089	4 207	174
2004	36 429	58	242	4 251	903	136	204	291	455	762	672	6 406	3 726	161
2003	33 692	51	286	3 905	960	106	204	248	378	725	749	6 216	3 188	148
2002	29 255	50	342	3 564	1 070	110	195	109	206	690	774	4 997	2 500	136
2001	31 582	49	348	3 250	1 113	97	190	280	398	589	494	6 721	2 835	125
2000	33 151	48	280	3 024	960	97	185	434	508	539	518	8 091	3 041	117
1999	34 408	41	371	2 803	816	85	186	661	481	536	491	9 596	3 226	106
1998	30 110	38	416	2 697	707	80	187	572	406	506	627	7 481	2 611	98
1997	27 286	37	405	2 602	610	77	186	616	344	504	559	6 635	2 150	101
1996	23 894	35	456	2 458	534	76	187	707	298	498	581	5 112	1 705	109
1995	21 483	23	525	2 310	478	72	185	649	199	537	527	4 347	1 344	116
1994	18 859	19	582	2 167	377	70	180	695	175	597	404	3 249	1 138	124
1993	18 234	16	616	2 193	367	65	172	506	57	644	383	3 404	1 127	133
1992	16 971	16	571	2 302	368	53	157	475	113	675	337	3 074	817	140
1991	16 169	15	462	2 410	410	59	138	401	117	704	330	2 751	651	146
1990	14 602	13	413	2 485	392	94	126	382	119	656	272	1 960	512	143
1989	14 213	12	425	2 454	361	88	118	281	77	621	212	2 147	513	135
1988	12 865	11	426	2 374	283	94	110	288	54	590	156	1 757	439	126
1987	11 715	10	428	2 194	265	55	101	207	34	517	162	1 463	425	124
1986	11 091	9	425	2 072	243	56	93	181	27	412	140	1 494	379	116
1985	9 962	8	312	1 981	205	56	80	206	26	396	97	1 229	214	120
1984	8 824	7	296	1 849	199	66	75	206	30	291	39	1 009	118	103
1983	8 299	7	284	1 623	155	44	71	161	16	248	38	1 089	98	111
1982	7 539	2	278	1 424	188	49	68	117	15	202	36	966	65	111
1981	6 943	0	263	1 314	155	42	68	101	15	161	39	905	53	101
1980	6 555	0	221	1 245	64	52	73	101	19	131	42	1 010	52	87
1979	5 690	0	208	1 127	39	56	80	76	12	124	55	775	45	72
1978	4 964	0	190	1 057	9	46	81	30	10	104	65	646	41	62
1977	4 434	0	176	956	3	32	77	28	8	79	73	636	40	55
1976	4 162	0	162	854	3	17	72	31	12	73	72	739	41	53
1975	3 668	0	152	752	4	20	67	42	8	67	64	585	39	50
1974	3 208	0	152	675	2	22	63	31	14	62	54	445	32	51
1973	3 232	0	147	620	0	14	60	27	8	55	41	694	44	47
1972	3 223	0	139	558	0	9	58	19	9	48	39	921	56	48
1971	2 816	0	128	486	0	14	54	20	15	46	37	744	53	47
1970	2 529	0	114	422	0	17	52	31	16	47	30	650	45	50
1969	2 437	0	107	380	0	19	52	41	11	47	22	667	46	49
1968	2 492	0	109	371	0	12	52	30	6	36	18	815	50	49
1967	2 227	0	99	340	0	10	51	28	6	38	15	682	43	46
1966	1 977	0	89	306	0	8	50	29	6	41	11	548	34	45
1965	1 954	0	87	287	0	6	50	25	1	37	9	616	34	43
1964	1 788	0	80	259	0	5	49	25	0	35	10	544	28	42
1963	1 633	0	77	233	0	4	48	25	0	32	10	470	25	40
1962	1 534	0	73	207	0	3	47	27	0	32	10	431	21	39
1961	1 492	0	73	182	0	2	46	25	1	33	11	443	23	37
1960	1 348	0	74	163	0	3	46	27	1	31	11	360	17	34
1959	1 299	0	72	151	0	2	46	26	2	28	8	357	16	31
1958	1 224	0	70	140	0	2	48	21	1	25	8	322	13	29
1957	1 096	0	68	127	0	2	48	23	1	24	7	244	9	26
1956	1 083	0	69	115	0	1	50	20	1	22	6	271	9	24
1955	1 015	0	67	105	0	1	50	19	1	19	5	248	8	23
1954	925	0	66	97	0	1	50	16	0	16	5	199	6	21
1953	847	0	64	88	0	1	49	19	0	14	6	146	4	20
1952	829	0	63	80	0	1	49	18	0	11	6	151	4	19
1951	805	0	61	72	0	1	49	16	0	6	6	151	4	19
1950	739	0	57	67	0	0	50	17	0	6	6	129	3	18
1949	688	0	54	65	0	0	49	18	0	4	6	105	3	17
1948	667	0	56	62	0	0	48	18	0	5	7	98	2	16
1947	643	0	59	60	0	0	46	19	0	5	7	99	1	15
1946	603	0	59	57	0	0	44	21	0	4	8	101	1	14
1945	563	0	54	50	0	0	43	24	0	4	8	110	1	12

[1]Includes nonprofit organizations.
[2]Only those directly held and those in closed-end and exchange-traded funds. Other equities are included in mutual funds and life insurance and pension reserves.

Table 26-1. Household Assets, Financial Obligations, and Delinquency Rates, 1945–2005—*Continued*

(Billions of dollars, except as noted; end of period; not seasonally adjusted, except as noted.)

Year	Security credit	Life insurance reserves	Pension fund reserves	Equity in non-corporate business	Miscel-laneous assets	Total[1]	Household real estate[3]	Household debt service	Total	Home-owners	Renters	Delinquency rate on credit card accounts held at banks (percent of loans serviced)
2005	567	1 121	10 647	6 677	535	25 558	19 817	13.86	18.62	16.77	28.43	3.70
2004	578	1 060	10 150	5 869	503	22 556	17 221	13.17	17.97	15.87	29.22	4.11
2003	475	1 013	9 214	5 365	462	20 040	15 061	13.17	18.18	15.83	30.76	4.47
2002	413	921	7 815	4 943	420	18 424	13 674	13.27	18.53	16.10	30.81	4.87
2001	454	880	8 572	4 797	389	17 028	12 490	13.20	18.68	16.06	31.73	4.86
2000	412	819	9 000	4 705	371	15 793	11 399	12.77	18.14	15.64	30.54	4.50
1999	324	784	9 192	4 344	364	14 488	10 394	12.35	17.83	15.41	29.39	4.54
1998	277	718	8 185	4 152	352	13 405	9 548	12.04	17.47	15.14	28.23	4.73
1997	215	665	7 301	3 939	339	12 391	8 779	12.09	17.66	15.44	27.38	4.72
1996	163	611	6 340	3 696	327	11 729	8 321	12.06	17.65	15.38	27.32	4.34
1995	128	566	5 695	3 465	316	11 248	7 991	11.84	17.45	15.14	27.00	3.74
1994	109	520	4 886	3 267	300	10 644	7 524	11.14	16.64	14.50	25.24	3.35
1993	102	485	4 603	3 076	285	10 310	7 358	10.77	16.18	14.20	23.91	4.25
1992	76	448	4 128	2 951	271	9 962	7 122	10.78	16.14	14.27	23.36	5.00
1991	87	419	3 822	2 994	253	9 617	6 809	11.52	16.96	15.19	23.63	5.33
1990	62	392	3 306	3 032	243	9 351	6 576	11.98	17.37	15.50	24.69	...
1989	53	365	3 167	2 960	224	9 139	6 474	12.04	17.35	15.50	24.76	...
1988	41	336	2 736	2 838	208	8 473	5 976	11.75	17.07	15.04	25.29	...
1987	39	310	2 502	2 690	189	7 813	5 501	11.98	17.43	15.26	26.23	...
1986	44	283	2 325	2 630	163	7 135	5 001	12.26	17.65	15.44	26.44	...
1985	35	264	2 088	2 500	144	6 531	4 574	11.84	17.09	14.91	25.69	...
1984	22	253	1 707	2 441	115	5 846	4 027	10.98	15.95	13.94	23.78	...
1983	21	247	1 536	2 440	113	5 210	3 522	10.62	15.60	13.69	22.77	...
1982	18	238	1 289	2 377	96	4 957	3 367	10.62	15.64	13.80	22.35	...
1981	15	230	1 063	2 331	87	4 729	3 214	10.64	15.56	13.45	24.17	...
1980	16	221	970	2 172	79	4 272	2 867	10.58	15.37	13.31	23.70	...
1979	10	210	801	1 928	72	3 803	2 534	...	...	...	...	...
1978	9	199	691	1 660	64	3 269	2 149	...	...	...	...	...
1977	6	188	590	1 429	57	2 823	1 832	...	...	...	...	...
1976	6	178	535	1 265	50	2 432	1 542	...	...	...	...	...
1975	4	169	467	1 134	44	2 187	1 369	...	...	...	...	...
1974	4	158	367	1 035	40	1 972	1 219	...	...	...	...	...
1973	5	151	358	923	37	1 864	1 214	...	...	...	...	...
1972	5	144	349	786	34	1 644	1 065	...	...	...	...	...
1971	5	137	293	706	31	1 453	926	...	...	...	...	...
1970	4	131	254	639	29	1 332	846	...	...	...	...	...
1969	5	125	231	609	26	1 253	804	...	...	...	...	...
1968	7	120	219	574	24	1 149	741	...	...	...	...	...
1967	5	116	196	529	22	1 026	660	...	...	...	...	...
1966	3	111	172	505	20	960	624	...	...	...	...	...
1965	3	106	162	471	19	889	582	...	...	...	...	...
1964	2	101	145	445	17	844	557	...	...	...	...	...
1963	1	97	128	426	16	801	531	...	...	...	...	...
1962	1	92	114	421	16	765	511	...	...	...	...	...
1961	1	89	107	405	15	732	489	...	...	...	...	...
1960	1	85	94	388	14	700	464	...	...	...	...	...
1959	1	82	85	378	14	669	441	...	...	...	...	...
1958	1	79	75	377	13	634	416	...	...	...	...	...
1957	1	75	65	362	13	608	394	...	...	...	...	...
1956	1	73	58	351	13	573	371	...	...	...	...	...
1955	1	69	52	334	12	531	345	...	...	...	...	...
1954	1	66	44	325	12	487	315	...	...	...	...	...
1953	1	64	39	321	11	460	293	...	...	...	...	...
1952	1	61	33	321	11	431	273	...	...	...	...	...
1951	1	58	28	325	9	425	272	...	...	...	...	...
1950	1	55	24	297	9	382	244	...	...	...	...	...
1949	1	52	21	284	8	336	218	...	...	...	...	...
1948	1	49	18	279	8	309	200	...	...	...	...	...
1947	1	47	16	262	8	275	178	...	...	...	...	...
1946	1	43	14	230	7	231	150	...	...	...	...	...
1945	1	40	12	198	6	199	131	...	...	...	...	...

Source: U.S. Census Bureau. Board of Governors of the Federal Reserve System. Federal Financial Institutions Examination Council. *Consolidated Reports of Condition and Income.*
[1]Includes nonprofit organizations.
[2]Excludes nonprofit organizations.
. . . = Not available.

Table 26-2. Money Stock—Currency, Deposits, Bank Vault Cash, and Gold, 1867–2005

(Billions of dollars, December data.)

Year	Currency held by the public[1]	Demand deposits adjusted, commercial[2]	M1 Money Supply[3]	M2 Money Supply (M1 plus time[4] deposits)
2005	724.0	321	1 369	6 676
2004	697.0	340	1 372	6 422
2003	662.0	325	1 304	6 080
2002	626.0	306	1 219	5 801
2001	581.0	336	1 182	5 451
2000	531.0	310	1 088	4 931
1999	518.0	353	1 123	4 649
1998	460.0	377	1 095	4 384
1997	424.0	394	1 072	4 032
1996	394.0	402	1 080	3 815
1995	372.0	389	1 127	3 641
1994	354.0	384	1 150	3 498
1993	322.0	385	1 130	3 484
1992	292.0	340	1 025	3 433
1991	267.0	290	897	3 380
1990	246.0	277	825	3 279
1989	222.0	279	793	3 158
1988	212.0	287	787	2 994
1987	197.0	288	750	2 831
1986	180.0	303	725	2 732
1985	168.0	267	620	2 496
1984	156.0	243	551	2 312
1983	146.0	238	521	2 128
1982	133.0	234	474	1 911
1981	123.0	231	436	1 756
1980	115.4	261	408	1 600
1979	104.8	258	383	1 476
1978	96.0	251	358	1 368
1977	87.4	237	331	1 272
1976	72.8	212	287	1 017
1975	72.8	212	287	1 017
1974	67.0	205	274	902
1973	60.8	200	263	856
1972	56.2	192	249	802
1971	52.0	175	228	710
1970	48.6	165	214	627
1969	45.7	157	209	590
1968	43.0	154	203	570
1967	40.0	143	188	528
1966	38.0	133	177	484
1965	36.0	131	173	463
1964	33.9	126	165	428
1963	32.2	121	158	396
1962	30.3	117	152	366
1961	29.3	116	149	339
1960	28.7	112	145	315
1959	28.8	111	144	301
1958	28.4	110	138	201
1957	28.3	108	137	192
1956	28.0	108	136	187
1955	27.6	107	134	184
1954	27.5	103	130	177
1953	27.8	101	128	171
1952	26.7	99	125	165
1951	25.5	94	119	156
1950	25.0	89	114	151
1949	25.5	86	111	147
1948	26.1	86	112	148
1947	26.6	85	112	146
1946	28.5	80	103	139
1945	25.3	74	99	127
1944	21.2	64	85	107
1943	16.4	56	72	90
1942	11.5	44	55	71
1941	8.4	38	47	63

[1]Currency outside U.S. Treasury, Federal Reserve Banks and the vaults of depository institutions.
[2]Demand deposits at domestically chartered commercial banks, U.S. branches and agencies of foreign banks, and Edge Act corporations (excluding those amounts held by depository institutions, the U.S. government, and foreign banks and official institutions) less cash items in the process of collection and Federal Reserve float.
[3]Currency, demand deposits, other checkable deposits, and travelers' checks.
[4]Includes M1 plus household savings and time deposits, and retail money market funds. Prior to 1948, it does not include deposits at saving and loan associations. From 1882 to 1906, M2 shows June data; from 1867 to 1881, January or February data.

Table 26-2. Money Stock—Currency, Deposits, Bank Vault Cash, and Gold, 1867–2005—*Continued*

(Billions of dollars, December data.)

Year	Currency held by the public[1]	Demand deposits adjusted, commercial[2]	M1 Money Supply[3]	M2 Money Supply (M1 plus time[4] deposits)
1940	6.8	33	40	55
1939	6.0	28	34	49
1938	5.6	25	31	46
1937	5.6	25	31	46
1936	5.2	24	30	43
1935	4.8	21	26	39
1934	4.6	17	22	34
1933	5.1	15	20	32
1932	4.9	16	21	36
1931	4.2	20	24	43
1930	3.7	22	26	46
1929	3.9	23	27	47
1928	3.9	22	26	46
1927	4.0	22	26	45
1926	4.0	22	26	44
1925	4.0	22	26	42
1924	4.0	20	24	39
1923	4.0	19	23	37
1922	3.7	18	22	34
1921	4.0	17	22	33
1920	4.5	19	24	35
1919	4.0	18	22	31
1918	2.8	16	19	27
1917	2.2	15	17	24
1916	2.2	13	15	21
1915	1.9	11	12	18
1914	1.9	...	...	16
1913	1.9	...	...	16
1912	1.8	...	...	15
1911	1.8	...	...	14
1910	1.7	...	...	13
1909	1.7	...	...	13
1908	1.8	...	...	11
1907	1.7	...	...	11
1906	1.6	...	...	11
1905	1.5	...	...	10
1904	1.4	...	...	9
1903	1.4	...	...	9
1902	1.3	...	...	8
1901	1.3	...	...	7
1900	1.2	...	...	7
1899	1.1	...	...	6
1898	1.0	...	...	5
1897	0.9	...	...	5
1896	0.9	...	...	4
1895	0.9	...	...	4
1894	0.9	...	...	4
1893	1.0	...	...	4
1892	1.0	...	...	4
1891	1.0	...	...	4
1890	0.9	...	...	4
1889	0.9	...	...	4
1888	0.8	...	...	3
1887	0.8	...	...	3
1886	0.8	...	...	3
1885	0.8	...	...	3
1884	0.8	...	...	3
1883	0.9	...	...	3
1882	0.8	...	...	3
1881	0.8	...	...	2
1880	0.7	...	...	2
1879	0.6	...	...	2
1878	0.5	...	...	2
1877	0.5	...	...	2
1876	0.5	...	...	2
1875	0.5	...	...	2
1874	0.5	...	...	2
1873	0.6	...	...	2
1872	0.6	...	...	2
1871	0.5	...	...	2
1870	0.5	...	...	1
1869	0.6	...	...	1
1868	0.5	...	...	1
1867	0.6	...	...	1

Source: The Federal Reserve Board. U.S. Census Bureau. Board of Governors of the Federal Reserve System.
[1]Currency outside U.S. Treasury, Federal Reserve Banks and the vaults of depository institutions.
[2]Demand deposits at domestically chartered commercial banks, U.S. branches and agencies of foreign banks, and Edge Act corporations (excluding those amounts held by depository institutions, the U.S. government, and foreign banks and official institutions) less cash items in the process of collection and Federal Reserve float.
[3]Currency, demand deposits, other checkable deposits, and travelers' checks.
[4]Includes M1 plus household savings and time deposits, and retail money market funds. Prior to 1948, it does not include deposits at saving and loan associations. From 1882 to 1906, M2 shows June data; from 1867 to 1881, January or February data.
. . . = Not available.

Table 26-3. Money Market Rates, 1890–2003

Year	Prime commercial paper, 4 to 6 months[1,2]	Finance company paper, place directly, 3 to 6 months[3]	Prime bankers acceptances, 3 month[1]	U.S. government securities[4], 3-month bills[5], rate on new issues	Federal Reserve Bank of New York discount rate	
					Low	High
2003	1.13	...	...	...	...	...
2002	1.70	...	...	...	0.75	1.25
2001	3.65	...	...	...	1.25	6.00
2000	6.33	...	6.23	5.66	5.00	...
1999	5.22	...	5.24	4.66	4.50	5.00
1998	5.37	...	5.39	4.81	4.50	5.00
1997	5.60	5.48	5.54	5.07	5.00	5.00
1996	5.42	5.29	5.31	5.02	5.00	5.25
1995	5.93	5.78	5.81	5.51	4.75	5.25
1994	4.93	4.53	4.56	4.29	3.00	4.75
1993	3.30	3.16	3.13	3.02	3.00	3.00
1992	3.80	3.65	3.62	3.45	3.00	3.50
1991	5.85	5.71	5.70	5.42	3.50	6.50
1990	7.95	7.87	7.93	7.51	3.50	7.00
1989	8.80	8.72	8.87	8.12	6.50	7.00
1988	7.68	7.38	7.56	6.69	7.00	6.50
1987	6.85	6.54	6.75	5.82	6.50	6.00
1986	6.39	6.38	6.38	5.98	6.00	7.00
1985	8.00	7.77	7.91	7.47	5.50	7.50
1984	10.18	9.75	10.17	9.53	7.50	9.00
1983	8.90	8.71	8.91	8.63	8.50	8.00
1982	11.89	11.24	11.89	10.69	8.50	11.50
1981	14.77	14.09	15.34	14.03	12.00	14.00
1980	12.24	11.45	12.67	11.51	10.00	13.00
1979	10.90	10.45	10.97	10.05	10.50	12.00
1978	7.99	7.79	8.05	7.22	10.00	12.00
1977	5.61	5.48	5.53	5.27	7.00	9.50
1976	5.35	5.20	5.08	4.99	5.75	6.00
1975	6.33	6.16	6.33	5.84	6.25	7.25
1974	9.88	8.67	9.74	7.89	7.75	8.00
1973	8.15	7.41	8.27	7.04	5.00	8.50
1972	4.72	4.54	4.33	4.07	...	...
1971	5.11	4.89	4.67	4.35	4.25	5.25
1970	7.72	7.18	7.23	6.43	5.50	6.00
1969	7.83	7.11	7.75	6.68	5.50	6.00
1968	5.90	5.69	5.79	5.34	4.50	5.50
1967	5.10	4.89	4.82	4.32	4.00	4.50
1966	5.55	5.43	5.42	4.88	4.50	4.50
1965	4.38	4.27	4.34	3.95	4.00	4.50
1964	3.97	3.84	3.77	3.56	3.50	4.00
1963	3.55	3.39	3.36	3.16	3.00	3.50
1962	3.26	3.06	3.01	2.78	3.00	3.00
1961	2.97	2.65	2.81	2.38	3.00	3.00
1960	3.85	3.50	3.51	2.93	3.00	4.00
1959	3.97	3.75	3.49	3.41	2.50	4.00
1958	2.46	2.12	2.04	1.84	1.75	3.00
1957	3.81	3.56	3.45	3.27	3.00	3.50
1956	3.31	3.02	2.64	2.66	2.50	3.00
1955	2.18	1.85	1.71	1.75	1.50	2.50
1954	1.58	1.29	1.35	0.95	1.50	2.00
1953	2.52	2.33	1.87	1.93	1.75	2.00
1952	2.33	2.16	1.75	1.77	1.75	1.75
1951	2.16	1.87	1.60	1.55	1.75	1.75
1950	1.45	1.41	1.15	1.22	1.50	1.75
1949	1.49	1.46	1.13	1.10	1.50	1.50
1948	1.44	1.34	1.11	1.04	1.00	1.50
1947	1.03	0.94	0.87	0.59	1.00	1.00
1946	0.81	...	0.61	0.38	50.50	1.00
1945	0.75	...	0.44	0.38	50.50	1.00
1944	0.73	...	0.44	0.38	50.50	1.00
1943	0.69	...	0.44	0.37	50.50	1.00
1942	0.66	...	0.44	0.33	50.50	1.00
1941	0.53	...	0.44	0.10	1.00	1.00

[1]Averages of weekly prevailing rates through 1934; average of the most representative daily offering rate quoted by dealers thereafter.
[2]From 1996 financial commercial paper.
[3]Averages of the most representative daily offering rates published by finance companies, for varying maturities in the 90–170 day range.
[4]Yields are averages computed from daily closing bid prices.
[5]Bills quoted on bank discount rate basis.
. . . = Not available.

Table 26-3. Money Market Rates, 1890–2003—*Continued*

Year	Prime commercial paper, 4 to 6 months[1,2]	Finance company paper, place directly, 3 to 6 months[3]	Prime bankers acceptances, 3 month[1]	U.S. government securities[4], 3-month bills[5], rate on new issues	Federal Reserve Bank of New York discount rate Low	High
1940	0.56	...	0.44	0.01	1.00	1.00
1939	0.59	...	0.44	0.02	1.00	1.00
1938	0.81	...	0.44	0.05	1.00	1.00
1937	0.94	...	0.43	0.45	1.00	1.50
1936	0.75	...	0.15	0.14	1.15	1.50
1935	0.75	...	0.13	0.14	1.50	1.50
1934	1.02	...	0.25	0.26	1.50	2.00
1933	1.73	...	0.63	0.25	2.00	3.50
1932	2.73	...	1.28	0.88	2.50	3.50
1931	2.64	...	1.57	1.40	1.50	3.50
1930	3.59	...	2.48	...	2.00	4.50
1929	5.85	...	5.03	...	4.50	6.00
1928	4.85	...	4.09	...	3.50	5.00
1927	4.11	...	3.45	...	3.50	4.00
1926	4.34	...	3.59	...	3.50	4.00
1925	4.02	...	3.29	...	3.00	3.50
1924	3.98	...	2.98	...	3.00	4.50
1923	5.07	...	4.09	...	4.00	4.50
1922	4.52	...	3.51	...	4.00	4.50
1921	6.62	...	5.28	...	4.50	7.00
1920	7.50	...	6.06	...	4.75	7.00
1919	5.37	...	4.37	...	4.00	4.75
1918	6.02	...	4.19	...	3.50	4.00
1917	5.07	...	...	...	3.00	3.50
1916	3.84	...	...	...	3.00	4.00
1915	4.01	...	...	...	4.00	5.00
1914	5.47	...	...	...	5.00	6.00
1913	6.20	...	...	...	...	...
1912	5.41	...	...	...	...	...
1911	4.75	...	...	...	...	...
1910	5.72	...	...	...	...	...
1909	64.67	...	...	...	...	...
1908	65.00	...	...	...	...	...
1907	66.66	...	...	...	...	...
1906	6.25	...	...	...	...	...
1905	5.18	...	...	...	...	...
1904	5.14	...	...	...	...	...
1903	6.16	...	...	...	...	...
1902	5.81	...	...	...	...	...
1901	5.40	...	...	...	...	...
1900	5.71	...	...	...	...	...
1899	5.50	...	...	...	...	...
1898	5.34	...	...	...	...	...
1897	4.72	...	...	...	...	...
1896	7.02	...	...	...	...	...
1895	5.80	...	...	...	...	...
1894	5.22	...	...	...	...	...
1893	7.64	...	...	...	...	...
1892	5.40	...	...	...	...	...
1891	6.48	...	...	...	...	...
1890	6.91	...	...	...	...	...

Source: Board of Governors of the Federal Reserve System.
[1]Averages of weekly prevailing rates through 1934; average of the most representative daily offering rate quoted by dealers thereafter.
[2]From 1996 financial commercial paper.
[3]Averages of the most representative daily offering rates published by finance companies, for varying maturities in the 90–170 day range.
[4]Yields are averages computed from daily closing bid prices.
[5]Bills quoted on bank discount rate basis.
... = Not available.

Table 26-4. Money Market Interest Rates, 1970–2005

(Percent per year. Annual averages of monthly data, except as indicated.)

Year	Federal funds, effective rate	Prime rate charged by banks	Discount rate[1]	Large negotiable certificates of deposit (secondary market)		Taxable money market funds[2]	Tax exempt money market funds[2]	Certificates of deposit[3]				U.S. Government securities (secondary market)[4]		Auction average:[5] 3-month Treasury bill
				3-month	6-month			6-month	1-year	2 1/2-year	5-year	3-month Treasury bill	6-month Treasury bill	
2005	3.22	6.19	4.19	3.51	3.73	2.66	1.87	2.37	2.77	3.18	3.75	3.15	3.39	3.16
2004	1.35	4.34	2.34	1.57	1.74	0.82	0.66	1.14	1.45	2.21	3.34	1.37	1.58	1.38
2003	1.13	4.12	2.12	1.15	1.17	0.64	0.53	1.02	1.20	1.77	2.93	1.01	1.05	1.02
2002	1.67	4.67	1.17	1.73	1.81	1.29	0.94	1.67	1.98	2.74	3.96	1.61	1.68	1.62
2001	3.88	6.91	3.40	3.71	3.66	3.67	2.24	3.43	3.60	3.97	4.58	3.40	3.34	3.45
2000	6.24	9.23	5.73	6.46	6.59	5.89	3.54	5.09	5.46	5.64	5.97	5.82	5.90	5.85
1999	4.97	8.00	4.62	5.33	5.46	4.64	2.72	4.27	4.55	4.73	4.93	4.64	4.75	4.66
1998	5.35	8.35	4.92	5.47	5.44	5.04	2.94	4.58	4.81	4.93	5.08	4.78	4.83	4.81
1997	5.46	8.44	5.00	5.62	5.73	5.10	3.14	4.86	5.15	5.40	5.66	5.06	5.18	5.07
1996	5.30	8.27	5.02	5.39	5.47	4.95	2.99	4.68	4.95	5.14	6.46	5.01	5.08	5.02
1995	5.83	8.83	5.21	5.92	5.98	5.48	3.39	4.92	5.39	5.69	6.00	5.49	5.56	5.51
1994	4.21	7.15	3.60	4.63	4.96	3.75	2.38	3.42	4.01	4.58	5.42	4.25	4.64	4.29
1993	3.02	6.00	3.00	3.17	3.28	2.70	1.97	2.88	3.16	3.80	4.98	3.00	3.12	3.02
1992	3.52	6.25	3.25	3.68	3.76	3.36	2.58	3.51	3.78	4.56	5.76	3.43	3.54	3.45
1991	5.69	8.46	5.45	5.83	5.91	5.71	4.13	5.80	6.03	6.46	7.02	5.38	5.44	5.42
1990	8.10	10.01	6.98	8.15	8.17	7.82	5.45	7.79	7.92	7.96	8.06	7.50	7.46	7.51
1989	9.21	10.87	6.93	9.09	9.08	8.87	5.90	8.55	8.65	8.58	8.56	8.11	8.03	8.12
1988	7.57	9.32	6.20	7.73	7.91	7.11	4.79	7.34	7.66	7.99	8.35	6.67	6.91	6.68
1987	6.66	8.21	5.66	6.87	7.01	6.12	4.14	6.60	6.92	7.35	7.87	5.78	6.03	5.82
1986	6.80	8.33	6.32	6.51	6.50	6.26	4.31	6.51	6.75	7.13	7.60	5.97	6.02	5.98
1985	8.10	9.93	7.69	8.04	8.24	7.71	4.90	8.05	8.53	9.32	9.99	7.47	7.65	7.48
1984	10.23	12.04	8.80	10.39	10.71	10.04	5.61	9.99	10.37	10.82	11.25	9.54	9.78	9.35
1983	9.09	10.79	8.50	9.07	9.28	8.58	4.82	...	...	10.06	...	8.62	8.74	8.63
1982	12.24	14.85	11.01	12.27	12.57	12.23	6.86	...	...	...	...	10.60	11.06	10.69
1981	16.39	18.87	13.42	15.93	15.79	16.82	...	...	...	...	...	14.04	13.81	14.03
1980	13.35	15.26	11.77	13.02	12.94	12.68	...	...	...	...	...	11.39	11.32	11.51
1975	5.82	7.86	6.25	6.44	6.90	6.36	...	...	...	...	...	5.79	6.10	5.84
1970	7.17	7.91	5.95	7.55	7.64	...	...	...	...	...	...	6.39	6.51	6.46

Source: U.S. Census Bureau. U.S. Council of Economic Advisors. Board of Governors of the Federal Reserve System.
[1] Rate for the Federal Reserve Bank of New York. Beginning 2003, the rate charged for discounts made and advances extended under the Federal Reserve's primary credit discount window program, which became effective January 9, 2003. The rate replaced that for adjustment credit, which was discontinued after January 8, 2003.
[2] 12 month return for period ending December 31. Source: iMoneyNet, Inc., Westborough, MA. Money Market Insight, monthly, http://www.imoneynet.com (copyright).
[3] Annual averages. Source: Bankrate, Inc., North Palm Beach, FL. Bank Rate Monitor, weekly (copyright).
[4] Averages based on daily closing bid yields, bank discount basis.
[5] Averages computed on an issue-date basis; bank discount basis.
. . . = Not available.

Table 26-5. Bond and Stock Yields, 1901–2005

Year	Federal funds	Municipal high grade[1]	Corporate Aaa (Moody's)[2]	Corporate Baa (Moody's)[2]	Common stocks, Dividend-price ratio[1,3,4]
2005	3.22	4.29	5.23	6.06	1.83
2004	1.35	4.63	5.63	6.39	1.72
2003	1.13	4.73	5.66	6.76	1.77
2002	1.67	5.05	6.49	7.80	1.61
2001	3.88	5.19	7.08	7.95	1.32
2000	6.24	5.77	7.62	8.37	1.15
1999	4.97	5.43	7.05	7.88	1.25
1998	5.35	5.12	6.53	7.22	1.49
1997	5.46	5.55	7.27	7.87	1.77
1996	5.30	5.75	7.37	8.05	2.19
1995	5.83	5.95	7.59	8.20	2.56
1994	4.21	6.19	7.97	8.63	2.82
1993	3.02	5.63	7.22	7.93	2.78
1992	3.52	6.41	8.14	8.98	2.99
1991	5.69	6.89	8.77	9.80	3.24
1990	8.10	7.25	9.32	10.36	3.61
1989	9.21	7.24	9.26	10.18	3.45
1988	7.57	7.76	9.71	10.83	3.64
1987	6.66	7.73	9.38	10.58	3.08
1986	6.80	7.38	9.02	10.39	3.48
1985	8.10	9.18	11.37	12.72	4.25
1984	10.23	10.15	12.71	14.19	4.64
1983	9.09	9.47	12.04	13.55	4.40
1982	12.24	11.57	13.79	16.11	5.81
1981	16.39	11.23	14.17	16.04	5.20
1980	13.35	8.51	11.94	13.67	5.26
1979	11.19	6.39	9.63	10.69	5.47
1978	7.93	5.90	8.73	9.49	5.28
1977	5.54	5.56	8.02	8.97	4.62
1976	5.04	6.49	8.43	9.75	3.77
1975	5.82	6.89	8.83	10.61	4.31
1974	10.50	6.09	8.57	9.50	4.47
1973	8.73	5.18	7.44	8.24	3.06
1972	4.43	5.27	7.21	8.16	2.84
1971	4.66	5.70	7.39	8.56	3.14
1970	7.17	6.51	8.04	9.11	3.83
1969	8.20	5.81	7.03	7.81	3.42
1968	5.66	4.51	6.18	6.94	3.22
1967	4.22	3.98	5.51	6.23	3.35
1966	5.11	3.82	5.13	5.67	3.57
1965	4.07	3.27	4.49	4.87	3.06
1964	3.50	3.22	4.40	4.83	3.00
1963	3.18	3.23	4.26	4.86	3.17
1962	2.68	3.18	4.33	5.02	3.37
1961	1.96	3.46	4.35	5.08	3.07
1960	3.22	3.73	4.41	5.19	3.60
1959	3.30	3.95	4.38	5.05	3.31
1958	1.57	3.56	3.79	4.73	4.01
1957	3.11	3.60	3.89	4.71	4.33
1956	2.73	2.93	3.36	3.88	4.07
1955	1.78	2.53	3.06	3.53	4.05
1954	...	2.37	2.90	3.51	4.75
1953	...	2.72	3.20	3.74	5.49
1952	...	2.19	2.96	3.52	5.49
1951	...	2.00	2.86	3.41	6.11
1950	...	1.98	2.62	3.24	6.28
1949	...	2.21	2.66	3.42	6.62
1948	...	2.40	2.82	3.47	5.77
1947	...	2.01	2.61	3.24	5.12
1946	...	1.64	2.53	3.05	3.93
1945	...	1.67	2.62	3.29	4.17
1944	...	1.86	2.72	3.61	4.83
1943	...	2.06	2.73	3.91	4.89
1942	...	2.36	2.83	4.28	6.64
1941	...	2.10	2.77	4.33	6.23

[1] Source of data; U.S. Council of Economic Advisors. *Economic Indicators.*
[2] Source of data: Moody's Investor Service.
[3] Aggregate cash dividends (based on latest known annual rate) divided by aggregate market value based on Wednesday closing prices. Averages of monthly figures.
[4] From 1970 to 2005: Standard and Poor's composite. Prior to 1971, Moody's composite. In 1970, the yield according to Standard and Poor's was 3.83 percent.
. . . = Not available.

Table 26-5. Bond and Stock Yields, 1901–2005—*Continued*

Year	Federal funds	Municipal high grade[1]	Corporate Aaa (Moody's)[2]	Corporate Baa (Moody's)[2]	Common stocks, Dividend-price ratio[1,3,4]
1940	...	2.50	2.84	4.75	5.26
1939	...	2.76	3.01	4.96	...
1938	...	2.91	3.19	...	4.30
1937	...	3.10	3.26	...	4.63
1936	...	3.07	3.24	...	3.50
1935	...	3.40	3.60	...	4.01
1934	...	4.03	4.00	...	4.07
1933	...	4.71	4.49	7.76	4.22
1932	...	4.65	5.01	...	7.13
1931	...	4.01	4.58	...	5.93
1930	...	4.07	4.55	...	4.45
1929	...	4.27	4.73	5.90	3.36
1928	...	4.05	4.55	...	...
1927	...	3.98	4.57	...	...
1926	...	4.08	4.73	...	...
1925	...	4.09	4.88	...	...
1924	...	4.20	5.00	...	...
1923	...	4.25	5.12	...	...
1922	...	4.23	5.10	...	...
1921	...	5.09	5.97	...	...
1920	...	4.98	6.12	...	...
1919	...	4.46	5.49	...	...
1918	...	4.50	...	...	...
1917	...	4.20	...	...	...
1916	...	3.94	...	...	...
1915	...	4.16	...	...	...
1914	...	4.12	...	...	...
1913	...	4.22	...	...	...
1912	...	4.02	...	...	...
1911	...	3.98	...	...	...
1910	...	3.97	...	...	...
1909	...	3.78	...	...	...
1908	...	3.93	...	...	...
1907	...	3.86	...	...	...
1906	...	3.57	...	...	...
1905	...	3.40	...	...	...
1904	...	3.45	...	...	...
1903	...	3.38	...	...	...
1902	...	3.20	...	...	...
1901	...	3.13	...	...	...

Source: U.S. Census Bureau. Board of Governors of the Federal Reserve System.
[1]Source of data; U.S. Council of Economic Advisors. *Economic Indicators.*
[2]Source of data: Moody's Investor Service.
[3]Aggregate cash dividends (based on latest known annual rate) divided by aggregate market value based on Wednesday closing prices. Averages of monthly figures.
[4]From 1970 to 2005: Standard and Poor's composite. Prior to 1971, Moody's composite. In 1970, the yield according to Standard and Poor's was 3.83 percent.
... = Not available.

Table 26-6. Market Value and Volume of Sales of Stocks and Bonds on Registered Securities Exchanges, 1935–2005

(Millions of dollars in millions.)

Year	All exchanges		New York Stock Exchange[1]	
	Market value, all sales	Shares of stocks sold	Market value, all sales	Shares of stocks sold
2005	. . .	. . .	14 441 416	410 832
2004	. . .	. . .	11 841 142	372 718
2003	. . .	. . .	9 846 509	356 767
2002	13 662 000	480 200	10 491 000	369 069
2001	13 315 000	371 100	10 644 500	311 290
2000	14 552 000	317 700	11 205 000	265 499
1999	11 220 000	244 100	9 073 000	206 299
1998	8 698 000	206 400	7 395 000	171 188
1997	6 879 000	159 700	5 833 469	134 404
1996	4 735 000	125 700	4 102 061	105 477
1995	3 690 000	106 400	3 110 162	87 873
1994	2 966 000	90 500	2 476 592	74 003
1993	2 734 000	82 800	2 305 166	67 461
1992	2 149 000	65 500	1 764 590	51 826
1991	1 903 000	58 000	1 533 578	45 599
1990	1 752 000	53 338	1 336 229	39 946
1989	2 010 000	54 239	1 556 008	42 022
1988	1 702 000	52 533	1 365 892	41 118
1987	2 492 000	63 771	1 888 707	48 143
1986	1 868 000	48 338	1 388 819	36 009
1985	1 260 000	37 046	980 772	27 774
1984	1 004 000	30 456	773 426	23 309
1983	1 023 000	30 146	775 337	21 846
1982	658 000	22 423	495 130	16 669
1981	533 000	15 910	396 070	12 049
1980	522 000	15 480	382 447	11 562
1979	323 000	10 850	252 000	8 675
1978	269 000	9 483	211 000	7 617
1977	198 000	7 023	157 000	5 613
1976	207 000	7 036	165 000	5 649
1975	167 000	6 231	143 000	5 051
1974	125 000	4 846	106 000	3 822
1973	187 000	5 732	155 000	4 337
1972	215 000	6 310	169 000	4 496
1971	195 000	5 916	155 000	4 265
1970	136 465	4 539	107 649	3 213
1969	180 877	4 963	133 173	3 174
1968	202 772	5 312	149 395	3 299
1967	168 258	4 504	160 791	2 886
1966	127 914	3 188	102 754	2 205
1965	93 325	2 587	76 878	1 809
1964	75 328	2 045	63 284	1 482
1963	66 157	1 838	56 564	1 351
1962	56 564	1 664	49 019	1 187
1961	66 068	2 010	54 785	1 292
1960	46 901	1 389	39 552	958
1959	53 877	1 605	45 368	1 039
1958	39 962	1 400	34 351	999
1957	33 360	1 292	28 686	914
1956	36 360	1 182	31 064	784
1955	39 261	1 212	34 038	820
1954	29 156	1 053	25 267	749
1953	17 488	716	15 010	520
1952	18 179	732	15 531	522
1951	22 127	863	19 013	643
1950	22 840	857	19 735	655
1949	11 443	516	9 674	380
1948	13 749	570	11 731	413
1947	12 541	512	10 617	358
1946	20 001	802	16 675	531
1945	18 112	744	15 190	496
1944	11 780	464	10 089	342
1943	10 986	485	9 457	362
1942	5 570	220	4 796	169
1941	7 603	310	6 408	230
1940	9 726	372	8 223	283
1939	13 347	467	11 488	366
1938	13 927	542	12 306	424
1937	23 709	837	20 769	614
1936	27 283	956	23 323	702
1935[2]	19 115	662	16 138	499

[1] *Source:* U.S. Census Bureau. New York Stock Exchange, Inc. *Fact Book*©.
[2] Stock and bond sales for New York Stock Exchange and New York Curb Exchange, January to March, exclude stopped sales; stock sales for these exchanges also exclude odd-lot sales.

Table 26-7. Net Assets, Sales, and Redemptions of Mutual Funds, 1940–2005

(Millions of dollars, except where noted.)

Year	Number of funds	Net assets	Sales	Redemptions
2005	7 977	8 905 000	14 042 000	13 649 000
2004	8 041	8 107 000	12 270 000	12 118 000
2003	8 126	7 414 080	12 452 868	12 416 000
2002	8 244	6 390 000	13 196 000	13 039 000
2001	8 305	6 975 000	12 867 000	12 242 000
2000	8 155	6 965 000	11 109 000	10 586 000
1999	7 791	6 846 000	9 044 000	8 562 000
1998	7 314	5 525 000	7 231 000	6 649 000
1997	6 684	4 468 000	5 801 000	5 325 000
1996	6 248	3 526 000	4 672 000	4 265 000
1995	5 725	2 811 000	3 600 000	3 315 000
1994	5 325	2 155 000	3 075 000	2 928 000
1993	4 534	2 070 000	3 188 000	2 905 000
1992	3 824	1 643 000	2 750 000	2 548 000
1991	3 403	1 393 000	2 037 000	1 881 000
1990	3 079	1 065 000	1 565 000	1 471 000
1989	2 935	981 000	1 445 000	1 327 000
1988	2 737	809 000	1 176 000	1 166 000
1987	2 312	769 000	1 251 000	1 179 000
1986	1 835	716 000	1 204 000	1 015 000
1985	1 528	495 000	954 000	865 000
1984	1 243	371 000	680 000	607 000
1983	1 026	293 000	548 000	566 000
1982	857	297 000	627 000	589 000
1981	665	241 000	473 000	362 000
1980	564	135 000	247 000	216 000
1979	526	95 000	119 000	86 000
1978	505	56 000	37 000	31 000
1977	477	49 000	17 000	17 000
1976	452	51 000	13 000	17 000
1975	426	46 000	10 000	10 000
1974	431	36 000	3 000	3 000
1973	421	47 000	4 000	6 000
1972	410	60 000	5 000	7 000
1971	392	55 000	5 000	5 000
1970	361	48 000	5 000	3 000
1969	269	48 291	1 503	847
1968	240	52 677	1 994	1 028
1967	204	44 701	1 378	743
1966	182	34 829	924	427
1965	170	35 220	1 228	512
1964	160	29 116	958	411
1963	165	25 214	649	388
1962	169	21 271	511	286
1961	170	22 789	813	263
1960	161	17 026	481	193
1959	155	15 818	541	172
1958	151	13 242	482	175
1957	143	8 714	332	96
1956	135	9 046	343	91
1955	125	7 838	290	93
1954	115	6 109	271	99
1953	110	4 146	160	57
1952	110	3 931	214	49
1951	103	3 130	194	62
1950	98	2 531	135	83
1949	91	1 974	126	41
1948	87	1 506	75	34
1947	80	1 409	67	28
1946	74	1 311	83	32
1945	73	1 284	93	30
1944	68	882	53	17
1943	68	654	116	51
1942	68	487	73	25
1941	68	402	53	45
1940	. . .	448	. . .	. . .

Source: U.S. Census Bureau. Investment Company Institute. *Mutual Fund Fact Book©.*
. . . = Not available.

Table 26-8. Mortgage Debt Outstanding, 1945–2005

(Billions of dollars; end of period; not seasonally adjusted.)

Year	Total	By type of property				By type of holder						
		Home	Multi-family residences	Commercial	Farm	Commercial Banks	Savings Institutions[1]	Life insurance companies	Federal and related agencies	Mortgage pools or trusts		
										Total[2]	Federally related agencies	ABS issuers
2005	11 942	9 149	674	1 968	151	2 958	1 152	283	551	5 822	3 678	2 144
2004	10 472	8 016	612	1 702	142	2 595	1 057	273	554	4 970	3 542	1 428
2003	9 234	7 024	557	1 520	133	2 256	870	261	537	4 456	3 489	967
2002	8 244	6 244	487	1 388	125	2 058	781	250	434	3 956	3 159	797
2001	7 423	5 571	448	1 286	118	1 790	758	243	373	3 544	2 832	712
2000	6 761	5 075	406	1 170	110	1 660	723	236	341	3 104	2 493	611
1999	6 216	4 674	376	1 063	103	1 495	668	231	320	2 846	2 294	552
1998	5 614	4 259	334	923	97	1 337	644	214	292	2 498	2 019	479
1997	5 133	3 910	300	833	91	1 245	632	207	285	2 176	1 826	349
1996	4 819	3 675	288	769	87	1 145	628	208	294	1 997	1 712	286
1995	4 550	3 451	276	739	85	1 090	597	213	308	1 819	1 571	248
1994	4 363	3 283	270	727	83	1 013	596	216	316	1 703	1 472	231
1993	4 196	3 106	269	740	81	948	598	224	326	1 565	1 357	208
1992	4 063	2 947	272	763	80	901	628	242	286	1 442	1 272	170
1991	3 953	2 782	285	807	79	881	705	260	266	1 271	1 156	115
1990	3 803	2 615	288	821	79	849	802	268	239	1 088	1 020	68
1989	3 548	2 379	288	801	80	771	873	254	198	923	870	53
1988	3 278	2 154	275	766	83	677	888	233	192	787	745	41
1987	2 961	1 921	259	694	88	595	824	212	189	702	669	32
1986	2 659	1 722	239	603	95	505	785	194	202	550	532	19
1985	2 372	1 519	206	542	106	431	766	172	213	393	368	25
1984	2 092	1 321	186	472	112	381	710	157	202	300	289	11
1983	1 850	1 186	161	389	114	331	627	151	188	245	245	0
1982	1 661	1 070	146	334	111	301	576	142	177	179	179	0
1981	1 579	1 030	142	300	107	284	612	138	160	129	129	0
1980	1 458	958	143	260	97	263	594	131	143	114	114	0
1979	1 317	856	135	239	87	245	565	118	121	95	95	0
1978	1 151	738	125	215	73	214	517	106	100	70	70	0
1977	999	628	114	193	64	179	459	97	84	57	57	0
1976	870	535	106	174	55	151	398	92	76	41	41	0
1975	786	474	101	161	50	136	351	89	73	29	29	0
1974	728	435	100	148	45	132	321	86	61	21	21	0
1973	666	400	93	134	40	119	300	81	47	18	18	0
1972	590	357	83	114	35	99	268	77	40	14	14	0
1971	518	318	70	97	32	83	231	75	37	10	10	0
1970	469	292	60	87	30	73	205	74	34	5	5	0
1969	439	278	53	79	29	71	194	72	28	3	3	0
1968	411	262	48	73	27	65	182	70	23	3	3	0
1967	381	245	45	66	25	59	170	68	19	2	2	0
1966	358	232	41	61	23	54	160	65	16	1	1	0
1965	334	219	38	56	21	50	153	60	13	1	1	0
1964	306	201	35	51	19	44	140	55	12	1	1	0
1963	278	184	30	47	17	39	125	51	11	1	1	0
1962	252	167	27	42	15	34	109	47	12	0	0	0
1961	228	153	24	37	14	30	96	44	12	0	0	0
1960	208	141	21	33	13	29	86	42	11	0	0	0
1959	191	130	19	30	12	28	77	39	10	0	0	0
1958	172	117	17	27	11	26	68	37	8	0	0	0
1957	156	107	15	24	10	23	60	35	7	0	0	0
1956	144	98	14	22	10	23	55	33	6	0	0	0
1955	129	88	13	19	9	21	48	29	5	0	0	0
1954	113	75	13	17	8	19	40	26	5	0	0	0
1953	101	66	12	16	8	17	34	23	5	0	0	0
1952	91	58	11	14	7	16	29	21	4	0	0	0
1951	82	51	11	14	7	15	25	19	3	0	0	0
1950	73	45	9	13	6	14	22	16	3	0	0	0
1949	63	37	8	12	6	12	18	13	2	0	0	0
1948	56	33	7	11	5	11	16	11	2	0	0	0
1947	49	28	6	10	5	9	14	9	2	0	0	0
1946	42	23	5	9	5	7	12	7	2	0	0	0
1945	36	19	5	8	5	5	10	7	2	0	0	0

Source: U.S. Census Bureau. Board of Governors of the Federal Reserve System.
[1]Federal Home Loan Bank loans to savings institutions are included in other loans and advances.
[2]Outstanding principal balances of mortgage-backed securities issued or guaranteed by the holder indicated.

Table 26-9. Consumer Credit Outstanding and Finance Rates, 1970–2005

	Credit (billions of dollars)			Finance rates (percent)				
				Commercial banks			Finance companies	
Year	Total	Revolving	Nonrevolving[1]	New automobiles (48 months)[2]	Other consumer goods (24 months)	Credit-card plans	New automobiles	Used automobiles
2005	2 158.0	802.0	1 356.0	7.08	12.02	12.50	5.46	9.03
2004	2 097.0	781.0	1 316.0	6.60	11.89	12.71	4.36	8.96
2003	2 010.0	753.0	1 257.0	6.93	11.95	12.30	3.40	9.72
2002	1 922.0	733.0	1 189.0	7.62	12.54	13.40	4.29	10.74
2001	1 836.0	713.0	1 122.0	8.50	13.22	14.87	5.65	12.18
2000	1 705.1	676.0	1 029.0	9.34	13.90	15.78	6.61	13.55
1999	1 528.0	604.0	924.0	8.44	13.39	15.19	6.66	12.60
1998	1 416.0	576.0	839.0	8.73	13.76	15.70	6.30	12.64
1997	1 320.0	537.0	783.4	9.02	13.90	15.80	7.12	13.27
1996	1 242.9	499.6	743.2	9.05	13.54	15.63	9.84	13.53
1995	1 140.6	443.1	697.5	9.57	13.94	15.99	11.19	14.48
1994	997.1	365.6	631.6	8.12	13.19	16.06	9.79	13.49
1993	865.7	309.9	555.7	8.09	13.47	16.82	9.48	12.79
1992	806.1	278.4	527.7	9.29	14.04	17.78	9.93	13.80
1991	798.0	263.8	534.3	11.14	15.18	18.24	12.41	15.60
1990	808.2	238.6	569.6	11.78	15.46	18.17	12.54	15.99
1989	794.6	211.2	583.4	12.07	15.44	17.99	12.62	16.18
1988	731.9	184.6	547.3	10.85	14.68	17.79	12.60	15.11
1987	686.3	160.9	525.5	10.45	14.22	17.92	10.73	14.61
1986	654.8	141.1	513.7	11.33	14.82	18.27	9.44	15.95
1985	599.7	124.5	475.2	12.91	15.94	18.70	11.98	17.59
1984	517.3	100.4	416.9	13.71	16.47	18.77	14.62	17.85
1983	437.1	79.0	358.0	13.92	16.68	18.79	12.58	18.74
1982	389.8	66.3	323.5	16.82	18.64	18.51	16.15	20.75
1981	371.3	60.9	310.4	16.54	18.09	17.78	16.17	20.00
1980	351.9	55.0	297.0	14.30	15.47	17.31	14.82	19.10
1979	348.6	53.6	295.0	12.01	13.85	17.03	13.51	17.98
1978	306.1	45.7	260.4	11.02	13.19	17.03	13.15	17.67
1977	260.6	37.4	223.1	10.92	12.97	16.88	13.14	17.62
1976	225.7	16.5	209.2	11.07	13.01	17.05	13.17	17.63
1975	204.0	14.5	189.5	11.36	13.08	17.16	13.12	17.63
1974	198.9	13.2	185.7	10.97	12.99	17.20	12.61	17.18
1973	190.1	11.3	178.7	10.21	12.60	17.21	12.08	16.70
1972	166.2	9.4	156.8	10.05	12.46	17.21	11.90	16.53
1971	146.9	8.2	138.7	. . .	. . .	. . .	. . .	. . .
1970	131.6	5.0	126.6	. . .	. . .	. . .	. . .	. . .

Source: U.S. Census Bureau. *Statistical Abstract of the United States: 2007.* Board of Governors of the Federal Reserve System.
[1] Comprises automobile loans and all other loans not included in revolving credit, such as loans for mobile homes, education, boats, trailers, or vacations. These loans may be secured or unsecured.
[2] Prior to 1983, maturities were 36 months for new car loans.
. . . = Not available.

Table 26-10. Life Insurance Companies and Life Insurance in Force, by Type, 1815–2004

(As of December 31.)

Year	Policies (millions)	Life insurance in force, value (millions of dollars)					Average size of policy in force (dollars)	
		Total	Ordinary	Group[1]	Industrial[2]	Credit[3]	Ordinary	Group
2004	373	17 508 000	9 717 000	7 631 000	...	160 000	...	...
2003	379	17 044 000	9 655 000	7 236 000	...	153 000	...	...
2002	375	16 346 338	9 311 729	6 876 075	...	158 534	...	...
2001	377	16 289 648	9 345 723	6 765 074	...	178 851	...	...
2000	369	15 953 267	9 376 370	6 376 127	...	200 770	...	...
1999	367	15 496 069	9 172 397	6 110 218	...	213 453	...	...
1998	358	14 471 449	8 523 259	5 735 273	...	212 917	...	...
1997	351	13 363 858	7 872 561	5 279 042	18 000	212 255	56 044	32 221
1996	355	12 704 296	7 425 746	5 067 804	18 000	210 746	52 285	32 577
1995	370	11 696 325	6 890 386	4 604 856	18 000	201 083	45 090	27 051
1994	366	11 081 335	6 448 758	4 443 179	19 000	189 398	45 870	26 338
1993	363	11 104 741	6 448 885	4 456 338	20 000	199 518	45 770	31 430
1992	366	10 405 792	5 962 783	4 240 919	21 000	202 090	42 960	29 930
1991	375	9 986 336	5 700 252	4 057 606	22 000	228 478	41 450	28 760
1990	389	9 392 597	5 391 053	3 753 506	24 000	248 038	37 910	26 630
1989	394	8 694 015	4 964 410	3 469 498	24 000	260 107	34 410	24 510
1988	391	8 020 159	4 537 064	3 232 080	26 000	251 015	31 390	23 410
1987	395	7 452 498	4 165 739	3 043 782	27 000	242 977	28 510	22 380
1986	391	6 720 279	3 685 371	2 801 049	27 000	233 859	25 540	20 720
1985	386	6 053 107	3 275 539	2 561 595	28 000	215 973	22 780	19 720
1984	385	5 499 987	2 917 678	2 392 358	30 000	189 951	19 970	18 780
1983	387	4 965 861	2 575 629	2 219 573	31 000	170 659	17 380	17 530
1982	389	4 476 659	2 249 154	2 066 361	33 000	161 144	15 140	16 630
1981	400	4 063 595	2 012 627	1 888 612	35 000	162 356	13 310	15 400
1980	402	3 541 038	1 796 468	1 579 355	38 000	165 215	11 920	13 410
1979	407	3 222 340	1 623 672	1 419 418	37 800	179 250	10 890	12 350
1978	401	2 870 250	1 463 175	1 243 994	38 100	163 081	10 010	11 260
1977	390	2 582 815	1 328 366	1 115 047	39 000	139 402	9 240	10 550
1976	382	2 343 063	1 216 847	1 002 647	39 200	123 569	8 610	10 010
1975	380	2 139 571	1 122 844	904 695	39 400	112 032	8 090	9 360
1974	380	1 985 000	1 048 000	827 000	39 400	110 000	7 690	8 840
1973	369	1 778 000	969 000	708 000	40 600	101 000	7 230	8 010
1972	365	1 628 000	894 000	641 000	40 000	93 000	6 790	7 730
1971	357	1 503 000	831 000	590 000	39 200	82 000	6 440	7 170
1970	355	1 402 123	773 374	551 357	38 644	77 392	6 105	6 905
1969	351	1 284 529	682 453	488 864	38 614	74 598	5 773	6 473
1968	346	1 183 354	633 392	442 778	38 827	68 357	5 453	6 074
1967	336	1 079 821	584 570	394 501	39 215	61 535	5 150	5 733
1966	331	984 689	541 022	345 945	39 663	58 059	4 938	5 356
1965	320	900 554	499 638	308 078	39 818	53 020	4 662	5 056
1964	308	797 808	457 868	253 620	39 833	46 487	4 382	4 637
1963	299	730 623	420 808	229 477	39 672	40 666	4 136	4 494
1962	290	675 977	391 048	209 950	39 638	35 341	3 932	4 323
1961	286	629 493	366 141	192 794	39 451	31 107	3 766	4 167
1960*	282	586 448	341 881	175 903	39 563	29 101	3 597	4 034
1959	275	542 128	317 158	160 163	39 809	24 998	3 424	3 875
1958	267	493 561	288 607	144 772	39 646	20 536	3 227	3 736
1957	266	458 359	264 949	133 905	40 139	19 366	3 041	3 580
1956	261	412 630	238 348	117 399	40 109	16 774	2 853	3 361
1955	251	372 332	216 812	101 345	39 682	14 493	2 721	3 202
1954	237	333 719	198 599	86 410	38 664	10 046	2 619	3 018
1953	229	304 259	185 007	72 913	37 781	8 558	2 530	2 755
1952	219	276 591	170 875	62 913	36 448	6 355	2 452	2 667
1951	210	253 140	159 109	54 398	34 870	4 763	2 378	2 535
1950	202	234 168	149 116	47 793	33 415	3 844	2 319	2 478
1949	194	213 672	138 862	40 207	32 087	2 516	2 264	2 330
1948	187	201 208	131 158	37 068	31 253	1 729	2 240	2 280
1947	182	186 035	122 393	32 026	30 406	1 210	2 200	2 050
1946	173	170 066	112 818	27 206	29 313	729	2 150	2 060
1945	163	151 762	101 550	22 172	27 675	365	2 100	1 930
1944	159	145 771	95 085	23 922	26 474	290	2 080	1 860
1943	151	137 158	89 596	22 413	24 874	275	2 080	1 760
1942	144	127 721	85 139	19 316	22 911	355	2 090	1 740
1941	140	122 178	82 525	17 359	21 825	469	2 100	1 710

[1]Initial Year 1911.
[2]First weekly premium policy issued 1873; industrial agency system introduced 1975.
[3]Initial year 1917. Insures borrower to cover consumer loan in case of death.
... = Not available.

Table 26-10. Life Insurance Companies and Life Insurance in Force, by Type, 1815–2004—*Continued*

(As of December 31.)

Year	Policies (millions)	Life insurance in force, value (millions of dollars)					Average size of policy in force (dollars)	
		Total	Ordinary	Group[1]	Industrial[2]	Credit[3]	Ordinary	Group
1940	134	115 530	79 346	14 938	20 866	380	2 130	1 700
1939	131	111 569	77 121	13 641	20 500	307	2 130	1 790
1938	129	108 927	75 772	12 503	20 396	256	2 150	1 890
1937	128	107 794	74 836	12 638	20 104	216	2 180	1 710
1936	124	102 653	72 361	11 291	18 863	138	2 160	1 670
1935	121	98 464	70 684	10 208	17 471	101	2 160	1 590
1934	117	96 677	70 094	9 472	17 036	75	2 210	1 710
1933	115	96 246	70 872	8 681	16 630	63	2 260	1 780
1932	116	101 559	75 898	8 923	16 669	69	2 380	1 860
1931	124	106 970	79 514	9 736	17 635	85	2 420	1 730
1930	124	106 413	78 576	8 901	17 963	73	2 460	1 700
1929	123	102 086	75 686	8 994	17 349	57	2 470	1 590
1928	116	92 590	68 430	7 889	16 231	40	2 410	1 580
1927	110	84 775	63 334	6 333	15 078	30	2 400	1 450
1926	104	77 642	58 453	5 362	13 803	24	2 350	1 400
1925	97	69 475	52 892	4 247	12 318	18	2 270	1 340
1924	90	61 327	47 283	3 127	10 905	12	2 200	1 280
1923	83	55 097	43 077	2 393	9 618	9	2 160	1 180
1922	76	48 342	38 053	1 795	8 486	8	2 090	1 150
1921	70	43 944	34 777	1 527	7 633	7	2 040	1 070
1920	65	40 540	32 018	1 570	6 948	4	1 990	960
1919	60	32 971	25 783	1 092	6 092	4	1 860	920
1918	53	27 924	21 818	630	5 474	2	1 840	840
1917	49	25 243	19 868	349	5 026	–3	1 830	780
1916	45	22 853	18 081	155	4 617	...	1 800	780
1915	41	21 029	16 650	100	4 279	...	1 800	830
1914	39	19 737	15 661	65	4 011	...	1 810	970
1913	37	18 683	14 827	31	3 825	...	1 810	910
1912	34	17 301	13 709	13	3 579	...	1 800	1 080
1911	31	16 125	12 772	(Z)	3 353	...	1 790	...
1910	29	14 908	11 783	...	3 125	...	1 830	...
1909	27	13 878	10 960	...	2 918	...	1 830	...
1908	25	13 085	10 450	...	2 635	...	1 850	...
1907	24	12 639	10 103	...	2 536	...	1 860	...
1906	23	12 285	9 871	...	2 414	...	1 870	...
1905	22	11 863	9 585	...	2 278	...	1 880	...
1904	20	11 165	9 059	...	2 106	...	1 930	...
1903	19	10 217	8 264	...	1 953	...	1 970	...
1902	17	9 369	7 594	...	1 775	...	2 020	...
1901	16	8 369	6 766	...	1 603	...	2 040	...
1900	14	7 573	6 124	...	1 449	...	2 160	...
1899	12	6 822	5 547	...	1 275	...	2 210	...
1898	11	6 053	4 952	...	1 101	...	2 310	...
1897	10	5 555	4 563	...	992	...	2 340	...
1896	9	5 207	4 323	...	884	...	2 420	...
1895	9	4 988	4 170	...	818	...	2 440	...
1894	...	4 847	4 048	...	799	...	...	...
1893	...	4 609	3 948	...	661	...	...	...
1892	...	4 267	3 685	...	582	...	...	...
1891	...	3 868	3 388	...	481	...	...	...
1890	...	3 522	3 095	...	428	...	...	...
1889	...	3 123	2 758	...	364	...	...	...
1888	...	2 742	2 438	...	304	...	...	...
1887	...	2 456	2 202	...	254	...	...	...
1886	...	2 097	1 899	...	198	...	...	...
1885	...	2 007	1 861	...	146	...	...	...
1884	...	1 996	1 885	...	111	...	...	...
1883	...	1 872	1 785	...	87	...	...	...
1882	...	1 721	1 665	...	56	...	...	...
1881	...	1 606	1 573	...	34	...	...	...
1880	...	1 523	1 502	...	20	...	...	...
1879	...	1 475	1 470	...	5.4	...	...	...
1878	...	1 520	1 518	...	2.0	...	...	...
1877	...	1 512	1 511	...	1.0	...	...	...
1876	...	1 691	1 690	...	0.4	...	...	...
1875	...	1 874	1 874	...	...	...	...	...
1874	...	1 948	1 948	...	...	...	...	...
1873	...	2 041	2 041	...	...	...	...	...
1872	...	2 079	2 079	...	...	...	...	...
1871	...	2 083	2 083	...	...	...	...	...

[1]Initial Year 1911.
[2]First weekly premium policy issued 1873; industrial agency system introduced 1975.
[3]Initial year 1917. Insures borrower to cover consumer loan in case of death.
. . . = Not available.
Z = Less than $50,000 or less than $500,000.

Table 26-10. Life Insurance Companies and Life Insurance in Force, by Type, 1815–2004—*Continued*

(As of December 31.)

| Year | Policies (millions) | Life insurance in force, value (millions of dollars) | | | | | Average size of policy in force (dollars) | |
		Total	Ordinary	Group[1]	Industrial[2]	Credit[3]	Ordinary	Group
1870	...	2 006	2 006	...	...	...	...	...
1869	...	1 825	1 825	...	...	...	...	...
1868	...	1 535	1 535	...	...	...	...	...
1867	...	1 168	1 168	...	...	...	...	...
1866	...	874	...	...	...	...	...	...
1865	...	590	590	...	...	...	...	...
1864	...	404	404	...	...	...	...	...
1863	...	276	...	...	...	...	...	...
1862	...	192	192	...	...	...	...	...
1861	...	173	173	...	...	...	...	...
1860	...	173	173	...	...	...	...	...
1859	...	152	152	...	...	...	...	...
1858	...	130	130	...	...	...	...	...
1857	...	121	121	...	...	...	...	...
1856	...	106	106	...	...	...	...	...
1855	...	106	106	...	...	...	...	...
1854	...	94	94	...	...	...	...	...
1850	...	97	97	...	...	...	...	...
1845	...	14	14	...	...	...	...	...
1840	...	4.7	4.7	...	...	...	...	...
1835	...	2.8	2.8	...	...	...	...	...
1830	...	0.6	0.6	...	...	...	...	...
1825	...	0.2	0.2	...	...	...	...	...
1820	...	0.1	0.1	...	...	...	...	...
1815	...	(Z)	...	...	...	...	...	...

Source: U.S. Census Bureau. Board of Governors of the Federal Reserve System. American Council of Life Insurers. *Life Insurers Fact Book,* annual (copyright).
[1]Initial Year 1911.
[2]First weekly premium policy issued 1873; industrial agency system introduced 1975.
[3]Initial year 1917. Insures borrower to cover consumer loan in case of death.
. . . = Not available.
Z = Less than $50,000 or less than $500,000.

BOX 26 ■ Online Banking

In November 1993, the Stanford Federal Credit Union became the first financial institution to provide customers with online banking services; it was more than a year ahead of its competitors. However, these early versions of online banking programs were cumbersome and slow, requiring users to dial in directly to a secure banking database. As a result, consumer acceptance was less enthusiastic than originally anticipated. But by 1996, the technology had moved to the Internet. There, customers could use any browser, and the processes became easier and faster. According to independent research firm Gartner, Inc., nine million people in the United States were doing at least some of their banking online in 1999. That number jumped to 27.5 million, or 22% of Internet users, by 2000. By 2007, approximately 90 million people banked online, but the rate of growth was slowing. In 2004, online banking customers increased by 47.3%, but by only 27.1% in 2005 and 9.5% in 2006.

One reason for the decline may be customers' security concerns. In 2007, Gartner, Inc. estimated that nine million adults in the United States stopped banking online because of such concerns and that almost 24 million have not begun online banking for the same reasons. This attitude prevailed despite the fact that federal regulators with the Federal Financial Examination Council required that banks adopt a two-factor authentication system by the end of 2006. This system involves two layers of security clearance. The first is that users sign in with their user name and pin number. This is in addition to a smart-card that users insert into their computers or an image customers have chosen and must identify each time they log on to the bank's site. However, many industry watchdogs find these safeguards insufficient because the smart-card allows the bank to identify the customer but does not guarantee that the customer has not been diverted to a pharming site that looks like the bank's own site. In addition, banks using a customer-chosen image deposit a cookie on each computer that hackers can intercept.

Despite a slowdown in growth, online banking is still a growing trend and one that banks want to encourage. Online transactions cost banks far less than both ATM and teller transactions. Further, online banking customers tend to maintain larger balances, buy more additional banking products, and, according to an executive at the Bank of America, bring the bank a 27% greater profit than other customers.

To increase online customers, some banks are now offering faster bill and loan payments; the ability to open accounts online within one day; the ability to track frequent flyer accounts from your banking site; account aggregation tools that allow customers to view all accounts on one site regardless of where the accounts are held; and the ability to bank by mobile phone browser or text message. Although mobile banking is currently only of interest to a quarter of those who currently bank online. it is thought to be the next trend in electronic banking.

Sources:

"Birthday of First Online Banking Site Marketed by SFCU." *Banking Wire* 16.12 (December 23, 2003): 24.

Hechinger, John. "E-Commerce (A Special Report): Industry by Industry—Banking—Check it Out: Online Banking is Finally Succeeding Thanks to an Added Ingredient: People." *Wall Street Journal* (Eastern Edition) New York, NY (February 12, 2001): R28.

Klein, Andrea. "Viewpoint: 2-Way Authentication Needed for Safety. (Online Banking)(Column)." *American Banker* 172.149 (August 3, 2007): 11.

Matthews, Robert Guy. "How Safe is Your Online Bank?" *Wall Street Journal* (Eastern Edition) New York, NY (January 2, 2007): D2.

Mazur, Michael. "Online Banking Starts to Slow Down.(Surveys & Trends)." *Community Banker* 16.6 (June 2007): 72(1).

"U.S. to Require More Security for Banks' Internet Customers." *Wall Street Journal* (Eastern Edition) New York, NY (October 18, 2005): B13.

Vara, Vauhini. "Lockdown: Banks Make Online Services More Secure; Measures Address Fraud Fears But Can Confuse Customers; Typing Your First Pet's Name." *Wall Street Journal* (Eastern Edition) New York, NY (August 23, 2006): D1.

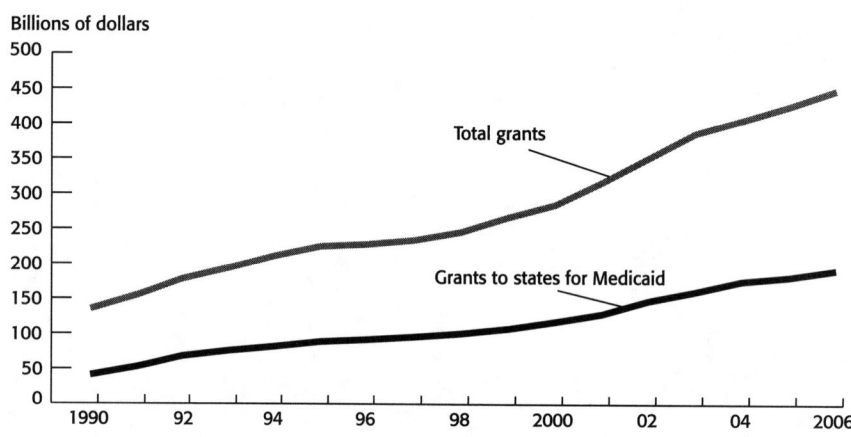

Billions of dollars

Total grants

Grants to states for Medicaid

Federal Aid to State and Local Governments: 1990 to 2006
Source: Figure prepared by U.S. Census Bureau.

CHAPTER **27**

Public Finance

HIGHLIGHTS

1 The first federal budget of 1789–1791 showed net revenues of $4.399 million, of which all but $20,000 were derived from customs duties. The budget remained under $100 million until 1863 when, under the financial strains of the Civil War, it rose to $112 million. It crossed the $1 billion mark in 1917, again during wartime; the $100 billion mark in 1963, as the Vietnam War was escalating; and the $2 trillion mark in 2000. As a percentage of GDP, it inched up from 16 percent in 1950 to 18.4 percent in 2000. In 1998 through 2001, it showed a surplus for the first time since 1960, but by 2002, budget deficits had returned. The Unified Federal Budget concept was introduced in 1968 to incorporate reforms recommended by the Presidential Commission on Budget Concepts. Under the Unified Budget, trust funds were included in the federal budget to show the total impact of government spending on the economy.

2 When income tax was introduced in 1913, the effective rate was 0.4 percent for a family in the $5,000 annual earnings range and only 6 percent for a family earning over $1 million (in 1912 dollars). The total number of returns in 1913 was 357,598. Before the introduction of income tax, 54 percent of internal revenue collections was from alcohol and 20 percent from tobacco.

3 For a number of years there were two categories of public debt: public debt and the debt subject to the debt limit. The public debt originates from the Treasury Department, but excludes debt incurred by public agencies, such as the Tennessee Valley Authority. Gross Public Debt (GPD) is a new concept that includes both public and agency debt. Approximately three-fourths of the GPD is owed to the public; the rest is a paper debt consisting of surpluses of trust funds invested by the government in public debt securities. Interest payments on this part of the debt are paid from one account within the budget to another account also within the budget, and therefore, do not affect the budget surplus or deficit. Because the Federal Reserve System is an independent body outside the federal budget, the U.S. government pays the Federal Reserve interest on money borrowed from it for budgetary purposes. Debt held by the system is shown as debt held by the public, and interest paid to the system affects budget surplus or deficit. In years of heavy borrowing, the government has to pay billions of dollars in interest, thus adding to the deficit, and vice versa. However, since 1947, the Federal Reserve has made annual payments to the Treasury from its surplus, which, in turn, arises primarily as a result of interest payments made by the Treasury. The public debt in 1791 was $75.463 million or $19.21 per capita. By the time of the Civil War, it had been reduced to $2.85 per capita. The Civil War and the half century following saw growth in public debt, but it decreased to the very low level of $11.99 per capita by the start of World War I. Thereafter it rose steadily, crossing the $1,000 per capita mark in 1944. In 2002, the GPD was $6.198 trillion, or $21,885 per capita.

4 Seven states do not have state individual income tax: Alaska, Florida, Nevada, South Dakota, Texas, Washington, and Wyoming. Six states have flat rates: Colorado, Illinois, Indiana, Massachusetts, Michigan, and Pennsylvania. Rhode Island has taxes calculated as a percentage of federal tax liability.

5 In 2004, lottery revenue was $45.466 billion. Only 12 states do not have lotteries: Alabama, Alaska, Arkansas, Hawaii, Mississippi, Nevada, North Carolina, North Dakota, Oklahoma, Tennessee, Utah, and Wyoming.

6 State and local governments generate less revenue than the federal government: $1.689 trillion for the former compared with $2.154 trillion for the latter in 2005. State and local revenues rely more on sales taxes and less on direct income taxes than the federal government. Patterns of expenditure are also different, with state and local governments spending more on education, highways, and similar services, and less on national defense, environment, and general interest on public debt than the federal government.

7 Total federal grants in aid to state and local governments increased from $135.325 billion in 1990 to $426.243 billion in 2005. This figure represents 17.2 percent of federal outlay and 3.5 percent of the GDP.

8 Delaware received the least amount of government aid at only $1.113 billion, followed by Vermont ($1.274 billion), and North Dakota ($1.316 billion). The states that received the greatest amount are California ($47.283 billion) and New York ($42.576 billion).

9 In 2005, Americans paid $341.4 billion in property taxes and $392.1 billion in sales taxes. State and local expenditures reached $1.686 trillion, most of which was consumer expenditures at $1.193 trillion.

10 Honolulu, Hawaii is the lowest taxed city in the nation with an effective property rate per $100 of 0.38. Houston, Texas is the highest, with an effective property tax rate per $100 of 2.99.

11 New York City has the largest city budget in the United States, with revenues of $60.897 billion and expenditures of $69.430 billion in 2002. Los Angeles county has the largest county budget, with revenues of $17.263 billion and expenditures of $16.069 billion.

12 Americans paid a total of $927.2 billion in individual income taxes to the federal government in 2005, making up more than 40 percent of all revenue. Social insurance and retirement receipts made up another $794.1 billion.

13 By agencies and units of administration, the largest segment of the federal budget in 2005 was $581.5 billion spent by Health and Human Services, followed by $474.4 billion by Department of Defense, and $408.7 billion by Treasury.

14 Federal spending on Homeland Security has tripled from $13.1 billion in 2000 to $39.9 billion in 2005.

Table 27-1. Summary of Federal Government Finances—Administrative Budget, 1789–1939

(Thousands of dollars; for 1789–1842, years ending December 31; 1844–1939, June 30; 1843 figures are for January 1–June 30.)

Year	Budget receipts[1]	Budget expenditures[2]	Surplus or deficit (−)[3]	Total public debt[4]
1939	4 979 066	8 841 224	−3 862 158	40 439 532
1938	5 588 012	6 764 628	−1 176 617	37 164 740
1937	4 955 613	7 733 033	−2 777 421	36 424 614
1936	3 997 059	8 421 608	−4 424 549	33 778 543
1935	3 705 956	6 497 008	−2 791 052	28 700 893
1934	3 014 970	6 644 602	−3 629 632	27 053 141
1933	1 996 844	4 958 496	−2 601 652	22 538 673
1932	1 923 892	4 659 182	−2 735 290	19 487 002
1931	3 115 557	3 577 434	−461 877	16 801 281
1930	4 057 884	3 320 211	737 673	16 185 310
1929	3 861 589	3 127 199	734 391	16 931 088
1928	3 900 329	2 961 245	939 083	17 604 293
1927	4 012 794	2 857 429	1 155 365	18 511 907
1926	3 795 108	2 929 964	865 144	19 643 216
1925	3 640 805	2 923 762	717 043	20 516 194
1924	3 871 214	2 907 847	963 367	21 250 813
1923	3 852 795	3 140 287	712 508	22 349 707
1922	4 025 901	3 289 404	736 496	22 963 382
1921	5 570 790	5 061 785	509 005	23 977 451
1920	6 648 898	6 357 677	291 222	24 299 321
1919	5 130 042	18 492 665	−13 362 623	25 484 506
1918	3 645 240	12 677 359	−9 032 120	12 455 225
1917	1 100 500	1 953 857	−853 357	2 975 619
1916	761 445	712 967	48 478	1 225 146
1915	683 417	746 093	−62 676	1 191 264
1914	725 117	725 525	−408	1 188 235
1913	714 463	714 864	−401	1 193 048
1912	692 609	689 881	2 728	1 193 839
1911	701 833	691 202	10 631	1 153 985
1910	675 512	693 617	−18 105	1 146 940
1909	604 320	693 744	−89 423	1 148 315
1908	601 862	659 196	−57 334	1 177 690
1907	665 860	579 129	86 732	1 147 178
1906	594 984	570 202	24 782	1 142 523
1905	544 275	567 279	−23 004	1 132 357
1904	541 087	583 660	−42 573	1 136 259
1903	561 881	517 006	44 875	1 159 406
1902	562 478	485 234	77 244	1 178 031
1901	587 685	524 617	63 068	1 221 572
1900	567 241	520 861	46 380	1 263 417
1899	515 961	605 072	−89 112	1 436 701
1898	405 321	443 369	−38 047	1 232 743
1897	347 722	365 774	−18 052	1 226 794
1896	338 142	352 179	−14 037	1 222 729
1895	324 729	356 195	−31 466	1 096 913
1894	306 355	367 525	−61 170	1 016 898
1893	385 820	383 478	2 342	961 432
1892	354 938	345 023	9 914	968 219
1891	392 612	365 774	26 839	1 005 807
1890	403 081	318 041	85 040	1 122 397
1889	387 050	299 289	87 761	1 249 471
1888	379 266	267 925	111 341	1 384 632
1887	371 403	267 932	103 471	1 465 485
1886	336 440	242 483	93 957	1 555 660
1885	323 691	260 227	63 464	1 578 551
1884	348 520	244 126	104 394	1 625 307
1883	398 288	265 408	132 879	1 721 959
1882	403 525	257 981	145 544	1 856 916
1881	360 782	260 713	100 069	2 019 286
1880	333 527	267 643	65 884	2 090 909
1879	273 827	266 948	6 879	2 298 913
1878	257 764	236 964	20 800	2 159 418
1877	281 406	241 334	40 072	2 107 760
1876	294 096	265 101	28 995	2 130 846
1875	288 000	274 623	13 377	2 156 277
1874	304 979	302 634	2 345	2 159 933
1873	333 738	290 345	43 393	2 151 210
1872	374 107	277 518	96 589	2 209 991
1871	383 324	292 177	91 147	2 322 052

[1]Excludes receipts from borrowing. Prior to 1913, total receipts; thereafter, net receipts.
[2]Excludes debt repayment. Prior to 1913, total expenditures; thereafter, net expenditures.
[3]Receipts compared with expenditures.
[4]As of end of period.

Table 27-1. Summary of Federal Government Finances—Administrative Budget, 1789–1939—*Continued*

(Thousands of dollars; for 1789–1842, years ending December 31; 1844–1939, June 30; 1843 figures are for January 1–June 30.)

Year	Budget receipts[1]	Budget expenditures[2]	Surplus or deficit (–)[3]	Total public debt[4]
1870	411 255	309 654	101 602	2 436 453
1869	370 944	322 865	48 078	2 545 111
1868	405 638	377 640	28 298	2 583 446
1867	490 634	357 543	133 091	2 650 168
1866	558 033	520 809	37 223	2 755 764
1865	333 715	1 297 555	–963 841	2 677 929
1864	264 627	865 323	–600 696	1 815 831
1863	112 697	714 741	–602 043	1 119 774
1862	51 987	474 762	–422 774	524 178
1861	41 510	66 547	–25 037	90 582
1860	56 065	63 131	–7 066	64 844
1859	53 486	69 071	–15 585	58 498
1858	46 655	74 185	–27 530	44 913
1857	68 965	67 796	1 170	28 701
1856	74 057	69 571	4 486	31 974
1855	65 351	59 743	5 608	35 588
1854	73 800	58 045	15 755	42 244
1853	61 587	48 184	13 403	59 805
1852	49 847	44 195	5 652	66 199
1851	52 559	47 709	4 850	68 305
1850	43 603	39 543	4 060	63 453
1849	31 208	45 052	–13 844	63 062
1848	35 736	45 377	–9 641	47 045
1847	26 496	57 281	–30 786	38 827
1846	29 700	27 767	1 933	15 550
1845	29 970	22 937	7 033	15 925
1844	29 321	22 338	6 984	23 462
1843	8 303	11 858	–3 555	32 743
1842	19 976	25 206	–5 230	20 201
1841	16 860	26 522	–9 706	13 594
1840	19 480	24 318	–4 837	5 351
1839	31 483	26 899	4 584	3 573
1838	26 303	33 865	–7 562	10 434
1837	24 954	37 243	–12 289	3 308
1836	50 827	30 868	–19 959	337
1835	35 430	17 573	17 857	38
1834	21 792	18 628	3 164	38
1833	33 948	23 018	10 931	4 760
1832	31 866	17 289	14 577	7 012
1831	28 527	15 248	13 279	24 322
1830	24 844	15 143	9 701	39 123
1829	24 828	15 203	9 624	48 565
1828	24 764	16 395	8 369	58 421
1827	22 966	16 139	6 827	67 475
1826	25 260	17 036	8 225	73 987
1825	21 841	15 857	5 984	81 054
1824	19 381	20 327	–945	83 788
1823	20 541	14 707	5 834	90 270
1822	20 232	15 000	5 232	90 876
1821	14 573	15 811	–1 237	93 547
1820	17 881	18 261	–380	89 987
1819	24 603	21 464	3 140	91 016
1818	21 585	19 825	1 760	95 530
1817	33 099	21 844	11 255	103 467
1816	47 678	30 587	17 091	123 492
1815	15 729	32 709	–16 979	127 335
1814	11 182	34 721	–23 539	99 834
1813	14 340	31 682	–17 341	81 488
1812	9 801	20 281	–10 480	55 963
1811	14 424	8 058	6 365	45 210
1810	9 384	8 157	1 228	48 006
1809	7 773	10 281	–2 507	53 173
1808	17 061	9 932	7 128	57 023
1807	16 398	8 354	8 044	65 196
1806	15 560	9 804	5 756	69 218
1805	13 561	10 506	3 054	75 723
1804	11 826	8 719	3 107	82 312
1803	11 064	7 852	3 212	86 427
1802	14 996	7 862	7 134	77 055
1801	12 935	9 395	3 541	80 713

[1]Excludes receipts from borrowing. Prior to 1913, total receipts; thereafter, net receipts.
[2]Excludes debt repayment. Prior to 1913, total expenditures; thereafter, net expenditures.
[3]Receipts compared with expenditures.
[4]As of end of period.

Table 27-1. Summary of Federal Government Finances—Administrative Budget, 1789–1939—
Continued

(Thousands of dollars; for 1789–1842, years ending December 31; 1844–1939, June 30; 1843 figures are for January 1–June 30.)

Year	Budget receipts[1]	Budget expenditures[2]	Surplus or deficit (–)[3]	Total public debt[4]
1800	10 849	10 786	63	83 038
1799	7 547	9 666	–2 120	82 976
1798	7 900	7 677	224	78 409
1797	5 689	6 134	2 555	79 229
1796	8 378	5 727	2 651	82 064
1795	6 115	7 540	–1 425	83 762
1794	5 432	6 991	–1 559	80 748
1793	4 653	4 482	171	78 427
1792	3 670	5 080	–1 410	80 359
1789–1791	4 419	4 269	150	77 228

Source: U.S. Census Bureau.
[1]Excludes receipts from borrowing. Prior to 1913, total receipts; thereafter, net receipts.
[2]Excludes debt repayment. Prior to 1913, total expenditures; thereafter, net expenditures.
[3]Receipts compared with expenditures.
[4]As of end of period.

Table 27-2. Federal Budget—Receipts and Outlays, 1940–2011

(Billions of dollars, percent.)

Fiscal Year[1]	In current dollars			In constant (FY 2000 Dollars)			As percentage of GDP		
	Receipts	Outlays	Surplus or deficit (−)	Receipts	Outlays	Surplus or deficit (−)	Receipts	Outlays	Surplus or deficit (−)
2011 estimate	3 034.9	3 239.8	−204.9	2 314.2	2 470.5	−156.3	17.9	19.1	−1.2
2010 estimate	2 878.2	3 060.9	−182.7	2 245.4	2 388.0	−142.5	17.9	19.0	−1.1
2009 estimate	2 714.2	2 921.8	−207.6	2 166.3	2 332.0	−165.7	17.7	19.1	−1.4
2008 estimate	2 590.3	2 813.6	−223.3	2 115.5	2 297.9	−182.4	17.8	19.4	−1.5
2007 estimate	2 415.9	2 770.1	−354.2	2 018.1	2 314.0	−295.9	17.6	20.1	−2.6
2006 estimate	2 285.5	2 708.7	−423.2	1 951.1	2 312.3	−361.3	17.5	20.8	−3.2
2005	2 153.9	2 472.2	−318.3	1 898.3	2 178.9	−280.6	17.5	20.1	−2.6
2004	1 880.3	2 293.0	−412.7	1 712.5	2 088.3	−375.9	16.3	19.9	−3.6
2003	1 782.5	2 160.1	−377.6	1 667.0	2 020.1	−353.1	16.5	20.0	−3.5
2002	1 853.4	2 011.2	−157.8	1 777.8	1 929.2	−151.3	17.9	19.4	−1.5
2001	1 991.4	1 863.2	128.2	1 946.1	1 820.8	125.3	19.8	18.5	1.3
2000	2 025.5	1 789.2	236.2	2 025.5	1 789.2	236.2	20.9	18.4	2.4
1999	1 827.6	1 702.0	125.6	1 874.9	1 746.0	128.9	20.0	18.7	1.4
1998	1 722.0	1 652.7	69.3	1 793.1	1 721.0	72.1	20.0	19.2	0.8
1997	1 579.4	1 601.3	−21.9	1 661.2	1 684.2	−23.0	19.3	19.6	−0.3
1996	1 453.2	1 560.6	−107.4	1 557.9	1 673.0	−115.2	18.9	20.3	−1.4
1995	1 351.9	1 515.9	−164.0	1 482.4	1 662.2	−179.8	18.5	20.7	−2.2
1994	1 258.7	1 461.9	−203.2	1 414.0	1 642.2	−228.2	18.1	21.0	−2.9
1993	1 154.5	1 409.5	−255.1	1 323.2	1 615.5	−292.3	17.6	21.4	−3.9
1992	1 091.3	1 381.6	−290.3	1 282.7	1 623.9	−341.2	17.5	22.1	−4.7
1991	1 055.1	1 324.3	−269.2	1 282.6	1 609.9	−327.3	17.8	22.3	−4.5
1990	1 032.1	1 253.1	−221.0	1 309.4	1 589.9	−280.4	18.0	21.8	−3.9
1989	991.2	1 143.8	−152.6	1 298.9	1 498.9	−200.0	18.4	21.2	−2.8
1988	909.3	1 064.5	−155.2	1 235.6	1 446.5	−210.9	18.2	21.3	−3.1
1987	854.4	1 004.1	−149.7	1 196.1	1 405.7	−209.6	18.4	21.6	−3.2
1986	769.2	990.4	−221.2	1 107.3	1 425.7	−318.4	17.4	22.4	−5.0
1985	734.1	946.4	−212.3	1 082.6	1 395.7	−313.1	17.7	22.9	−5.1
1984	666.5	851.9	−185.4	1 016.8	1 299.5	−282.8	17.4	22.2	−4.8
1983	600.6	808.4	−207.8	961.7	1 294.4	−332.7	17.5	23.5	−6.0
1982	617.8	745.7	−128.0	1 036.9	1 251.7	−214.8	19.1	23.1	−4.0
1981	599.3	678.2	−79.0	1 077.4	1 219.4	−142.0	19.6	22.2	−2.6
1980	517.1	590.9	−73.8	1 028.3	1 175.1	−146.8	19.0	21.7	−2.7
1979	463.3	504.0	−40.7	1 017.8	1 107.3	−89.5	18.5	20.2	−1.6
1978	399.6	458.7	−59.2	952.5	1 093.6	−141.1	18.0	20.7	−2.7
1977	355.6	409.2	−53.7	903.8	1 040.2	−136.4	18.0	20.7	−2.7
1976, TQ	81.2	96.0	−14.7	216.5	255.8	−39.3	17.8	21.0	−3.2
1976	298.1	371.8	−73.7	818.8	1 021.4	−202.6	17.2	21.4	−4.2
1975	279.1	332.3	−53.2	824.7	982.1	−157.3	17.9	21.3	−3.4
1974	263.2	269.4	−6.1	857.4	877.4	−20.0	18.3	18.7	−0.4
1973	230.8	245.7	−14.9	814.7	867.3	−52.6	17.7	18.8	−1.1
1972	207.3	230.7	−23.4	770.7	857.6	−86.9	17.6	19.6	−2.0
1971	187.1	210.2	−23.0	742.9	834.3	−91.4	17.3	19.5	−2.1
1970	192.8	195.6	−2.8	815.9	828.0	−12.0	19.0	19.3	−0.3
1969	186.9	183.6	3.2	838.0	823.5	14.5	19.7	19.4	0.3
1968	153.0	178.1	−25.2	727.4	847.0	−119.6	17.7	20.6	−2.9
1967	148.8	157.5	−8.6	734.6	777.2	−42.7	18.3	19.4	−1.1
1966	130.8	134.5	−3.7	662.8	681.5	−18.7	17.4	17.9	−0.5
1965	116.8	118.2	−1.4	605.9	613.2	−7.3	17.0	17.2	−0.2
1964	112.6	118.5	−5.9	592.7	623.8	−31.1	17.6	18.5	−0.9
1963	106.6	111.3	−4.8	568.9	594.3	−25.4	17.8	18.6	−0.8
1962	99.7	106.8	−7.1	552.8	592.5	−39.6	17.6	18.8	−1.3
1961	94.4	97.7	−3.3	525.8	544.4	−18.6	17.8	18.4	−0.6
1960	92.5	92.2	0.3	528.5	526.8	1.7	17.9	17.8	0.1
1959	79.2	92.1	−12.8	453.9	527.5	−73.6	16.1	18.7	−2.6
1958	79.6	82.4	−2.8	472.1	488.5	−16.4	17.3	17.9	−0.6
1957	80.0	76.6	3.4	499.6	478.3	21.3	17.8	17.0	0.8
1956	74.6	70.6	3.9	488.8	462.9	25.9	17.5	16.5	0.9
1955	65.5	68.4	−3.0	449.8	470.4	−20.6	16.6	17.3	−0.8
1954	69.7	70.9	−1.2	494.7	502.9	−8.2	18.5	18.8	−0.3
1953	69.6	76.1	−6.5	508.8	556.3	−47.5	18.7	20.4	−1.7
1952	66.2	67.7	−1.5	516.9	528.8	−11.9	19.0	19.4	−0.4
1951	51.6	45.5	6.1	403.6	355.9	47.7	16.1	14.2	1.9
1950	39.4	42.6	−3.1	306.5	330.7	−24.2	14.4	15.6	−1.1
1949	39.4	38.8	0.6	316.3	311.7	4.7	14.5	14.3	0.2
1948	41.6	29.8	11.8	326.5	233.8	92.7	16.2	11.6	4.6
1947	38.5	34.5	4.0	331.4	296.9	34.6	16.5	14.8	1.7
1946	39.3	55.2	−15.9	366.9	515.7	−148.8	17.6	24.8	−7.2
1945	45.2	92.7	−47.6	433.8	890.6	−456.8	20.4	41.9	−21.5
1944	43.7	91.3	−47.6	412.3	860.5	−448.2	20.9	43.6	−22.7
1943	24.0	78.6	−54.6	213.9	700.1	−486.2	13.3	43.6	−30.3
1942	14.6	35.1	−20.5	142.4	341.8	−199.4	10.1	24.3	−14.2
1941	8.7	13.7	−4.9	93.9	147.1	−53.2	7.6	12.0	−4.3
1940	6.5	9.5	−2.9	75.3	108.8	−33.6	6.8	9.8	−3.0

Source: U.S. Census Bureau. U.S. Office of Management and Budget.
[1]Fiscal years through 1976, ended June 30. Beginning with October 1976 (fiscal year 1977), fiscal years ended September 30. The period from July 1 through September 30, 1976 is a separate fiscal period known as the transition quarter (TQ) and is not included in any fiscal year.

Table 27-3. Individual Income Tax Returns, 1913–1943

Income year	Total number of returns with net income[1]
1943	43 506 553
1942	36 456 110
1941	26 770 089
1940	14 598 074
1939	7 570 320
1938	6 150 776
1937	6 301 833
1936	5 418 499
1935	4 575 012
1934	4 049 420
1933	3 723 558
1932	3 877 430
1931	3 225 924
1930	3 707 509
1929	4 044 327
1928	4 070 851
1927	4 101 547
1926	4 138 092
1925	4 171 051
1924	7 369 788
1923	7 698 321
1922	6 787 481
1921	6 662 176
1920	7 259 944
1919	5 332 760
1918	4 425 114
1917	3 472 890
1916	437 036
1915	336 652
1914	357 515
1913[2]	357 598

Source: U.S. Census Bureau.
[1]Includes fiduciary returns with net income filed on Form 1040, 1913–1936.
[2]Data pertain to last 10 months of year.

Table 27-4. Individual Income Tax Returns, 1944–2003

(Thousands of dollars, except number of returns.)

Income year	Total number of returns	Returns with adjusted gross income	
		Taxable income	Income tax (after credits)
2003	130 424 000	4 200 218 000	748 010 000
2002	130 076 000	4 096 128 000	796 980 000
2001	130 255 000	4 268 506 000	887 936 000
2000	129 374 000	4 544 242 000	980 497 000
1999	127 075 000	4 136 120 000	870 919 000
1998	124 772 000	3 780 838 000	783 513 000
1997	122 422 000	3 429 109 000	727 303 000
1996	120 351 000	3 089 667 000	655 420 000
1995	118 218 000	2 813 826 000	588 419 000
1994	115 943 000	2 597 980 000	534 856 000
1993	114 602 000	2 453 543 000	502 788 000
1992	113 605 000	2 395 696 000	476 239 000
1991	114 730 000	2 284 088 000	448 430 000
1990	113 717 000	2 263 661 000	446 296 000
1989	112 136 000	2 173 346 000	432 940 000
1988	109 708 000	2 069 967 000	412 870 000
1987	106 996 000	1 850 597 000	369 203 000
1986	103 045 000	1 947 025 000	367 287 000
1985	101 660 000	1 820 741 000	325 710 000
1984	99 400 000	1 701 400 000	301 900 000
1983	96 300 000	1 544 900 000	274 200 000
1982	95 300 000	1 473 300 000	277 600 000
1981	95 400 000	1 410 900 000	284 100 000
1980	93 902 000	1 279 985 000	250 341 000
1979	92 700 000	1 157 200 000	213 300 000
1978	89 800 000	1 062 200 000	186 700 000
1977	86 600 000	939 000 000	158 500 000
1976	84 700 000	674 900 000	140 800 000
1975	82 200 000	595 500 000	124 500 000
1974	83 300 000	573 600 000	123 500 000
1973	80 700 000	511 900 000	107 900 000
1972	77 570 000	444 600 000	93 354 000
1971	74 573 000	413 400 000	85 253 000
1970	74 279 831	400 859 064	83 909 314
1969	75 834 388	388 153 971	86 568 215
1968	73 728 708	352 799 662	76 637 902
1967	71 651 909	315 108 212	62 919 958
1966	70 160 425	286 296 994	56 087 084
1965	67 596 300	255 082 124	49 529 695
1964	65 375 601	229 875 078	47 152 855
1963	63 943 236	209 090 323	48 203 580
1962	62 712 386	195 320 479	44 902 840
1961	61 499 420	181 779 732	42 224 498
1960	61 027 931	171 627 771	39 464 156
1959	60 271 297	166 540 616	38 645 299
1958	59 085 182	149 337 414	34 335 652
1957	59 825 121	149 363 077	34 393 639
1956	59 197 004	141 532 061	32 732 132
1955	58 250 188	128 020 111	29 613 722
1954	56 747 008	115 331 301	26 665 753
1953	57 838 184	...	29 430 659
1952	56 528 817	...	27 802 831
1951	55 447 009	...	24 227 780
1950	53 060 098	...	18 374 922
1949	51 814 124	...	14 538 141
1948	52 072 006	...	15 441 529
1947	55 099 008	...	18 076 281
1946	52 816 547	...	16 075 913
1945	49 932 783	...	17 050 378
1944	47 111 495	...	16 216 401

Source: U.S. Census Bureau. U.S. Internal Revenue Service.
. . . = Not available.

Table 27-5. Public Debt Outstanding, 1791–2006

(Millions of dollars. Represents the face amount or principal amount of marketable and non-marketable securities outstanding as of the end of fiscal year indicated.)

Fiscal year[1]	Total	Fiscal year[1]	Total	Fiscal year[1]	Total
2006	8 506 973.9	1930	16 185.3	1860	64.8
2005	7 932 709.7	1929	16 931.1	1859	58.5
2004	7 379 052.7	1928	17 604.3	1858	44.9
2003	6 783 231.1	1927	18 511.9	1857	28.7
2002	6 228 236.0	1926	19 643.2	1856	32.0
2001	5 807 463.4	1925	20 516.2	1855	35.6
		1924	21 250.8	1854	42.2
2000	5 674 178.2	1923	22 349.7	1853	59.8
1999	5 656 270.9	1922	22 963.4	1852	66.2
1998	5 526 193.0	1921	23 977.5	1851	68.3
1997	5 413 146.0				
1996	5 224 810.9	1920	25 952.5	1850	63.5
1995	4 973 982.9	1919	27 391.0	1849	63.1
1994	4 692 749.9	1918	14 592.2	1848	47.0
1993	4 411 488.9	1917	5 717.8	1847	38.8
1992	4 064 620.7	1916	3 609.2	1846	15.6
1991	3 665 303.4	1915	3 058.1	1845	15.9
		1914	2 912.5	1844	23.5
1990	3 233 313.5	1913	2 916.2	1843[2]	32.7
1989	2 857 431.0	1912	2 868.4	1843[3]	20.2
1988	2 602 337.7	1911	2 765.6	1842	13.6
1987	2 350 276.9			1841	5.3
1986	2 125 302.6	1910	2 652.7		
1985	1 823 103.0	1909	2 639.5	1840	3.6
1984	1 572 266.0	1908	2 626.8	1839	10.4
1983	1 377 210.0	1907	2 457.2	1838	3.3
1982	1 142 034.0	1906	2 337.2	1837	0.3
1981	997 855.0	1905	2 274.6	1836	-
		1904	2 264.0	1835	-
1980	907 701.0	1903	2 202.5	1834	4.8
1979	826 519.0	1902	2 158.6	1833	7.0
1978	771 544.0	1901	2 143.3	1832	24.3
1977	698 840.0			1831	39.1
1976	620 433.0	1900	2 137.0		
1975	533 189.0	1899	1 991.9	1830	48.6
1974	475 059.8	1898	1 796.5	1829	58.4
1973	458 141.6	1897	1 817.7	1828	67.5
1972	427 260.5	1896	1 769.8	1827	74.0
1971	398 129.7	1895	1 676.1	1826	81.1
		1894	1 632.3	1825	83.8
1970	370 918.7	1893	1 546.0	1824	90.3
1969	353 720.3	1892	1 588.5	1823	90.9
1968	347 578.4	1891	1 546.0	1822	93.5
1967	326 220.9			1821	90.0
1966	319 907.1	1890	1 552.1		
1965	317 273.9	1889	1 619.1	1820	91.0
1964	311 712.9	1888	1 692.9	1819	95.5
1963	305 859.6	1887	1 657.6	1818	103.5
1962	298 200.8	1886	1 775.1	1817	123.5
1961	288 970.9	1885	1 864.0	1816	127.3
		1884	1 830.5	1815	99.8
1960	286 330.8	1883	1 884.2	1814	81.5
1959	284 705.9	1882	1 918.3	1813	56.0
1958	276 343.2	1881	2 069.0	1812	45.2
1957	270 527.2			1811	48.0
1956	272 750.8	1880	2 120.4		
1955	274 374.2	1879	2 349.6	1810	53.2
1954	271 259.6	1878	2 256.2	1809	57.0
1953	266 071.1	1877	2 205.3	1808	65.2
1952	259 105.2	1876	2 180.4	1807	69.2
1951	255 222.0	1875	2 232.3	1806	75.7
		1874	2 251.7	1805	82.3
1950	257 357.4	1873	2 234.5	1804	86.4
1949	252 770.4	1872	2 253.3	1803	77.1
1948	252 292.2	1871	2 353.2	1802	80.7
1947	258 286.4			1801	83.0
1946	269 422.1	1870	2 480.7		
1945	258 682.2	1869	2 588.5	1800	83.0
1944	201 003.4	1868	2 611.7	1799	78.4
1943	136 696.1	1867	2 678.1	1798	78.2
1942	72 422.4	1866	2 773.2	1797	82.1
1941	48 961.4	1865	2 680.6	1796	83.8
		1864	1 815.8	1795	80.7
1940	42 967.5	1863	1 119.8	1794	78.4
1939	40 439.5	1862	524.2	1793	80.4
1938	37 164.7	1861	90.6	1792	77.2
1937	36 424.6			1791	75.5
1936	33 778.5				
1935	28 700.9				
1934	27 053.1				
1933	22 538.7				
1932	19 487.0				
1931	16 801.3				

Source: U.S. Department of the Treasury, Bureau of the Public Debt.
[1]The first fiscal year for the U.S. Government started January 1, 1789. Congress changed the beginning of the fiscal year from January 1 to July 1 in 1842 and finally, from July 1 to October 1 in 1977 where it remains today.
[2]Fiscal year starting July 1, 1843.
[3]Fiscal year starting January 1, 1843.
- = Less than $50,000.

Table 27-6. Federal Budget Debt, 1940–2011

(Billions of dollars, percent. As of the end of the fiscal year.)

Fiscal Year[1]	Total					Percent of GDP				
		Less: Held by federal government accounts	Equals: Held by the public				Less: Held by federal government accounts	Equals: Held by the public		
	Gross federal debt		Total	Federal Reserve System	Other	Gross federal debt		Total	Federal Reserve System	Other
2011 estimate	11 536.7	5 250.8	6 285.9	...	...	68.0	31.0	37.1	...	...
2010 estimate	10 982.7	4 921.8	6 060.8	...	...	68.2	30.6	37.6	...	...
2009 estimate	10 436.9	4 577.5	5 859.4	...	...	68.2	29.9	38.3	...	...
2008 estimate	9 865.3	4 231.9	5 633.4	...	...	67.9	29.1	38.8	...	...
2007 estimate	9 295.4	3 904.0	5 391.5	...	...	67.5	28.4	39.2	...	...
2006 estimate	8 611.5	3 592.6	5 018.9	...	...	66.1	27.6	38.5	...	...
2005	7 905.3	3 313.1	4 592.2	736.4	3 855.9	64.3	27.0	37.4	6.0	31.4
2004	7 354.7	3 059.1	4 295.5	700.3	3 595.2	3.7	26.5	37.2	6.1	31.1
2003	6 760.0	2 846.6	3 913.4	656.1	3 257.3	62.6	26.3	36.2	6.1	30.1
2002	6 198.4	2 658.0	3 540.4	604.2	2 936.2	59.7	25.6	34.1	5.8	28.3
2001	5 769.9	2 450.3	3 319.6	534.1	2 785.5	57.4	24.4	33.0	5.3	27.7
2000	5 628.7	2 218.9	3 409.8	511.4	2 898.4	58.0	22.9	35.1	5.3	29.9
1999	5 605.5	1 973.2	3 632.4	496.6	3 135.7	61.4	21.6	39.8	5.4	34.4
1998	5 478.2	1 757.1	3 721.1	458.2	3 262.9	63.5	20.4	43.1	5.3	37.8
1997	5 369.2	1 596.9	3 772.3	424.5	3 347.8	65.6	19.5	46.1	5.2	40.9
1996	5 181.5	1 447.4	3 734.1	390.9	3 343.1	67.3	18.8	48.5	5.1	43.5
1995	4 920.6	1 316.2	3 604.4	374.1	3 230.3	67.2	18.0	49.2	5.1	44.1
1994	4 643.3	1 210.2	3 433.1	355.2	3 077.9	66.7	17.4	49.3	5.1	44.2
1993	4 351.0	1 102.6	3 248.4	325.7	2 922.7	66.2	16.8	49.4	5.0	44.4
1992	4 001.8	1 002.1	2 999.7	296.4	2 703.3	64.1	16.1	48.1	4.8	43.3
1991	3 598.2	909.2	2 689.0	258.6	2 430.4	60.6	15.3	45.3	4.4	40.9
1990	3 206.3	794.7	2 411.6	234.4	2 177.1	55.9	13.9	42.0	4.1	38.0
1989	2 867.8	677.1	2 190.7	220.1	1 970.6	53.1	12.5	40.6	4.1	36.5
1988	2 601.1	549.5	2 051.6	229.2	1 822.4	51.9	11.0	41.0	4.6	36.4
1987	2 346.0	456.2	1 889.8	212.0	1 677.7	50.5	9.8	40.7	4.6	36.1
1986	2 120.5	379.9	1 740.6	190.9	1 549.8	48.1	8.6	39.4	4.3	35.1
1985	1 817.4	310.2	1 507.3	169.8	1 337.5	43.9	7.5	36.4	4.1	32.3
1984	1 564.6	257.6	1 307.0	155.1	1 151.9	40.7	6.7	34.0	4.0	30.0
1983	1 371.7	234.4	1 137.3	155.5	981.7	39.9	6.8	33.1	4.5	28.5
1982	1 137.3	212.7	924.6	134.5	790.1	35.2	6.6	28.6	4.2	24.5
1981	994.8	205.4	789.4	124.5	664.9	32.6	6.7	25.8	4.1	21.8
1980	909.0	197.1	711.9	120.8	591.1	33.3	7.2	26.1	4.4	21.7
1979	829.5	189.2	640.3	115.6	524.7	33.2	7.6	25.6	4.6	21.0
1978	776.6	169.5	607.1	115.5	491.6	35.0	7.6	27.4	5.2	22.2
1977	706.4	157.3	549.1	105.0	444.1	35.8	8.0	27.8	5.3	22.5
1976, TQ	643.6	148.1	495.5	96.7	398.8	35.2	8.1	27.1	5.3	21.8
1976	629.0	151.6	477.4	94.7	382.7	36.2	8.7	27.5	5.5	22.0
1975	541.9	147.2	394.7	85.0	309.7	34.7	9.4	25.3	5.4	19.8
1974	483.9	140.2	343.7	80.6	263.1	33.6	9.7	23.9	5.6	18.3
1973	466.3	125.4	340.9	75.2	265.7	35.7	9.6	26.1	5.7	20.3
1972	435.9	113.6	322.4	71.4	251.0	37.0	9.6	27.4	6.1	21.3
1971	408.2	105.1	303.0	65.5	237.5	37.8	9.7	28.1	6.1	22.0
1970	380.9	97.7	283.2	57.7	225.5	37.6	9.7	28.0	5.7	22.3
1969	365.8	87.7	278.1	54.1	224.0	38.6	9.2	29.3	5.7	23.6
1968	368.7	79.1	289.5	52.2	237.3	42.5	9.1	33.4	6.0	27.4
1967	340.4	73.8	266.6	46.7	219.9	41.9	9.1	32.8	5.8	27.1
1966	328.5	64.8	263.7	42.2	221.5	43.6	8.6	35.0	5.6	29.4
1965	322.3	61.5	260.8	39.1	221.7	46.9	9.0	38.0	5.7	32.3
1964	316.1	59.2	256.8	34.8	222.1	49.4	9.2	40.1	5.4	34.7
1963	310.3	56.3	254.0	32.0	222.0	51.8	9.4	42.4	5.3	37.1
1962	302.9	54.9	248.0	29.7	218.3	53.4	9.7	43.7	5.2	38.5
1961	292.6	54.3	238.4	27.3	211.1	55.1	10.2	44.9	5.1	39.8
1960	290.5	53.7	236.8	26.5	210.3	56.1	10.4	45.7	5.1	40.6
1959	287.5	52.8	234.7	26.0	208.7	58.5	10.7	47.8	5.3	42.5
1958	279.7	53.3	226.3	25.4	200.9	60.7	11.6	49.2	5.5	43.6
1957	272.3	52.9	219.3	23.0	196.3	60.5	11.8	48.7	5.1	43.6
1956	272.7	50.5	222.2	23.8	198.4	63.8	11.8	52.0	5.6	46.4
1955	274.4	47.8	226.6	23.6	203.0	69.5	12.1	57.4	6.0	51.4
1954	270.8	46.3	224.5	25.0	199.5	71.8	12.3	59.5	6.6	52.9
1953	266.0	47.6	218.4	24.7	193.6	71.3	12.8	58.6	6.6	51.9
1952	259.1	44.3	214.8	22.9	191.9	74.3	12.7	61.6	6.6	55.0
1951	255.3	41.0	214.3	23.0	191.3	79.6	12.8	66.9	7.2	59.7

[1] Fiscal years through 1976, ended June 30. Beginning with October 1976 (fiscal year 1977), fiscal years ended September 30. The period from July 1 through September 30, 1976 is a separate fiscal period known as the transition quarter (TQ) and is not included in any fiscal year.
. . . = Not available.

Table 27-6. Federal Budget Debt, 1940–2011—*Continued*

(Billions of dollars, percent. As of the end of the fiscal year.)

Fiscal Year[1]	Total					Percent of GDP				
	Gross federal debt	Less: Held by federal government accounts	Equals: Held by the public			Gross federal debt	Less: Held by federal government accounts	Equals: Held by the public		
			Total	Federal Reserve System	Other			Total	Federal Reserve System	Other
1950	256.9	37.8	219.0	18.3	200.7	94.1	13.9	80.2	6.7	73.5
1949	252.6	38.3	214.3	19.3	195.0	93.2	14.1	79.1	7.1	71.9
1948	252.0	35.8	216.3	21.4	194.9	98.4	14.0	84.5	8.3	76.1
1947	257.1	32.8	224.3	21.9	202.5	110.3	14.1	96.2	9.4	86.8
1946	271.0	29.1	241.9	23.8	218.1	121.7	13.1	108.6	10.7	97.9
1945	260.1	24.9	235.2	21.8	213.4	117.5	11.3	106.2	9.8	96.4
1944	204.1	19.3	184.8	14.9	169.9	97.6	9.2	88.3	7.1	81.2
1943	142.6	14.9	127.8	7.1	120.6	79.1	8.3	70.9	4.0	66.9
1942	79.2	11.4	67.8	2.6	65.1	54.9	7.9	47.0	1.8	45.1
1941	57.5	9.3	48.2	2.2	46.0	50.4	8.2	42.3	1.9	40.4
1940	50.7	7.9	42.8	2.5	40.3	52.4	8.2	44.2	2.5	41.6

Source: U.S. Census Bureau. U.S. Office of Management and Budget.
[1]Fiscal years through 1976, ended June 30. Beginning with October 1976 (fiscal year 1977), fiscal years ended September 30. The period from July 1 through September 30, 1976 is a separate fiscal period known as the transition quarter (TQ) and is not included in any fiscal year.

Table 27-7. Government Consumption Expenditures and Gross Investment, by Type, 1929–2006

(Billions of dollars.)

		Federal										
			National defense									
				Consumption expenditures[1]							Gross investment[2]		
								Services					
Year	Total government	Total	Total	Total	Durable goods	Nondurable goods	Compensation of employees	Consumption of fixed capital[3]	Other services	Total	Structures	Equipment and software
2006	2 527.7	926.6	621.0	542.0	32.3	19.7	219.8	71.7	204.2	79.0	5.8	73.3
2005	2 372.8	878.3	589.3	516.9	30.0	20.3	215.4	68.0	188.5	72.4	5.2	67.2
2004	2 226.2	825.9	551.2	483.7	28.8	16.9	200.2	64.5	177.9	67.5	5.1	62.4
2003	2 092.5	756.4	497.2	436.8	25.9	13.4	183.3	61.6	157.0	60.4	5.3	55.2
2002	1 961.1	679.7	437.1	381.7	23.4	11.5	163.1	60.5	127.4	55.4	4.4	51.0
2001	1 825.6	612.9	392.6	342.4	22.5	10.3	145.7	60.4	107.2	50.2	4.6	45.6
2000	1 721.6	578.8	370.3	321.5	22.3	10.4	138.9	60.2	92.7	48.8	5.0	43.8
1999	1 620.8	555.8	360.6	312.9	22.3	8.2	133.5	59.8	92.2	47.7	5.0	42.8
1998	1 518.3	530.4	345.7	300.7	21.0	7.0	131.6	59.6	84.7	45.0	5.1	39.9
1997	1 468.7	530.9	349.6	304.7	20.9	7.6	132.8	60.4	86.5	44.9	5.7	39.2
1996	1 416.0	527.4	354.6	302.5	20.8	7.6	133.3	61.2	83.6	52.1	6.7	45.4
1995	1 369.2	519.2	348.7	297.3	20.9	6.3	130.8	61.8	81.1	51.4	6.3	45.1
1994	1 325.5	519.1	353.7	300.7	22.9	7.6	134.7	61.0	80.5	52.9	5.7	47.2
1993	1 291.2	525.2	362.9	307.6	26.4	8.5	138.7	59.5	78.8	55.2	5.1	50.1
1992	1 271.0	533.9	376.9	315.3	28.4	9.4	143.0	57.3	81.3	61.6	5.2	56.3
1991	1 234.4	527.7	383.2	319.8	31.0	10.7	141.8	55.5	84.3	63.4	4.6	58.8
1990	1 180.2	508.3	374.0	308.1	31.6	11.0	134.5	52.4	81.8	65.9	6.1	59.8
1989	1 099.1	482.2	362.2	299.5	32.0	10.8	131.7	49.1	78.3	62.7	6.4	56.3
1988	1 039.0	462.3	354.9	293.6	33.5	10.6	126.9	46.0	79.0	61.3	7.4	53.9
1987	999.5	460.1	350.0	283.6	33.8	10.3	123.5	43.0	75.1	66.4	7.7	58.8
1986	949.3	438.6	330.9	268.0	31.9	10.2	118.8	40.2	68.7	62.9	6.8	56.1
1985	879.0	412.8	311.2	253.7	29.3	10.0	115.3	37.5	63.4	57.5	6.2	51.3
1984	797.0	374.4	281.6	232.9	27.1	10.4	107.5	34.8	54.7	48.7	4.9	43.8
1983	733.5	342.9	250.7	208.8	25.1	11.3	92.4	31.7	49.5	41.9	4.8	37.1
1982	680.5	310.8	225.9	191.2	19.6	11.5	87.4	29.2	45.4	34.7	4.0	30.8
1981	627.5	280.2	196.3	167.3	16.2	11.8	78.8	26.3	35.8	28.9	3.2	25.7
1980	566.2	243.8	168.0	143.7	12.8	10.0	68.6	23.5	30.2	24.3	3.2	21.1
1979	500.8	210.6	145.2	123.8	11.3	6.2	61.7	21.3	24.2	21.4	2.5	18.9
1978	453.6	190.9	130.5	112.7	9.6	4.9	57.5	20.0	21.7	17.8	2.5	15.3
1977	414.1	175.4	120.9	104.2	8.0	4.5	53.6	18.4	20.4	16.7	2.4	14.4
1976	383.0	159.7	111.1	95.8	5.8	4.5	50.3	17.1	18.8	15.3	2.1	13.2
1975	357.7	149.1	103.9	90.9	6.0	5.1	47.9	15.7	17.4	13.0	2.3	10.7
1974	317.9	134.6	95.6	84.5	5.2	5.2	44.1	14.7	16.9	11.1	2.2	8.9
1973	281.7	122.5	88.2	79.4	5.5	4.3	41.4	14.0	15.3	8.7	2.1	6.6
1972	263.5	119.7	87.0	79.5	5.7	4.7	40.5	13.8	15.5	7.5	1.8	5.7
1971	246.5	113.7	84.6	77.1	4.6	4.4	38.2	13.8	16.3	7.5	1.8	5.7
1970	233.8	113.5	87.6	76.6	6.1	5.4	36.6	13.6	15.2	11.1	1.3	9.8
1969	221.5	113.4	89.5	78.2	6.5	7.6	34.7	13.2	16.5	11.3	1.5	9.9
1968	209.4	111.4	89.3	77.2	7.5	8.4	32.4	12.7	16.4	12.2	1.2	10.9
1967	192.7	104.8	83.5	70.0	6.2	7.3	29.3	12.1	15.5	13.5	1.2	12.3
1966	171.8	92.5	71.7	60.0	6.2	4.7	26.3	11.6	12.2	11.8	1.3	10.5
1965	151.5	80.4	60.6	50.6	4.2	3.2	22.6	11.3	9.9	10.0	1.1	8.9
1964	143.2	78.5	60.3	48.8	4.0	2.9	21.6	11.2	9.7	11.5	1.3	10.2
1963	136.4	76.9	61.0	48.3	4.7	2.7	20.1	11.1	10.2	12.6	1.6	11.0
1962	130.1	75.3	61.1	46.6	4.6	2.9	19.4	10.6	9.6	14.5	2.0	12.5
1961	119.5	67.9	56.5	42.7	3.6	2.3	18.3	10.0	8.8	13.9	2.4	11.5
1960	111.6	64.1	53.4	41.0	4.4	1.9	17.7	9.8	7.7	12.3	2.2	10.1
1959	110.0	65.4	53.8	40.1	5.1	1.8	17.3	9.5	6.9	13.7	2.5	11.2
1958	106.0	63.8	55.4	44.1	7.1	2.1	17.0	9.1	9.5	11.3	2.6	8.7
1957	99.7	61.3	53.6	43.2	6.7	2.2	16.5	9.0	9.3	10.5	2.3	8.2
1956	91.4	56.7	49.2	38.8	6.1	1.7	16.1	8.5	6.7	10.5	2.1	8.4
1955	86.5	54.9	47.0	36.9	6.0	1.7	15.8	8.0	5.9	10.1	2.1	8.0
1954	86.2	57.3	49.2	37.1	6.8	3.2	15.4	7.6	4.2	12.1	2.7	9.4
1953	90.6	64.4	55.9	41.2	9.1	4.2	16.0	6.9	5.1	14.7	3.3	11.4
1952	83.6	59.2	52.4	38.9	8.0	2.8	16.1	6.2	6.1	13.4	3.3	10.1
1951	68.1	45.1	39.3	30.1	4.4	2.3	13.5	5.4	5.0	9.1	2.0	7.1

[1]Government consumption expenditures are services (such as education and national defense) produced by government that are valued at their cost of production. Excludes government sales to other sectors and government own-account investment (construction and software).
[2]Gross government investment consists of general government and government enterprise expenditures for fixed assets; inventory investment is included in government consumption expenditures.
[3]Consumption of fixed capital, or depreciation, is included in government gross output as a partial measure of the services of general government fixed assets; the use of depreciation assumes a zero net return on these assets.

Table 27-7. Government Consumption Expenditures and Gross Investment, by Type, 1929–2006—*Continued*

(Billions of dollars.)

Year	Total government	Federal											
		Total	National defense										
			Consumption expenditures[1]							Gross investment[2]			
			Total	Total	Durable goods	Nondurable goods	Services			Total	Structures	Equipment and software	
							Compensation of employees	Consumption of fixed capital[3]	Other services				
1950	46.8	26.0	19.6	17.2	1.7	0.9	8.0	5.2	1.5	2.4	0.5	1.9	
1949	46.7	27.7	19.8	16.9	1.0	0.8	7.8	6.0	1.5	2.9	0.4	2.6	
1948	40.6	24.2	18.3	16.3	0.8	0.7	6.9	7.0	1.1	2.0	0.4	1.6	
1947	36.4	22.7	18.2	17.3	0.3	0.3	7.8	8.2	0.7	0.9	0.2	0.8	
1946	39.6	28.9	25.2	23.7	0.5	0.7	14.1	8.8	2.2	1.5	0.3	1.2	
1945	93.0	84.1	82.0	59.3	13.6	7.3	29.3	8.3	3.6	22.7	1.7	21.0	
1944	105.3	97.0	94.5	59.1	13.5	9.7	27.0	7.0	3.4	35.4	2.5	33.0	
1943	94.8	86.5	84.2	46.8	13.1	8.7	20.3	4.4	1.4	37.4	5.8	31.5	
1942	62.7	54.1	51.1	25.1	7.2	5.2	10.1	1.7	1.4	26.0	10.3	15.7	
1941	26.5	18.0	14.3	7.1	1.4	0.6	3.6	0.5	1.1	7.2	3.6	3.6	
1940	15.0	6.5	2.5	1.7	0.1	0.1	1.1	0.2	0.2	0.8	0.6	0.2	
1939	14.8	6.0	1.5	1.2	0.1	0.1	0.7	0.2	0.2	0.3	0.2	0.2	
1938	13.8	5.7	1.4	1.0	0.0	0.1	0.7	0.2	0.1	0.3	0.2	0.1	
1937	12.8	5.1	1.3	1.0	0.0	0.0	0.6	0.2	0.1	0.3	0.2	0.1	
1936	13.1	5.6	1.2	1.0	0.0	0.1	0.6	0.2	0.1	0.3	0.2	0.1	
1935	10.9	3.4	1.0	0.9	0.0	0.1	0.6	0.2	0.1	0.1	0.1	0.0	
1934	10.5	3.3	0.8	0.7	0.0	0.0	0.5	0.1	0.1	0.1	0.1	0.0	
1933	8.7	2.3	0.9	0.8	0.0	0.1	0.5	0.1	0.1	0.1	0.0	0.0	
1932	8.7	1.8	0.9	0.9	0.0	0.1	0.5	0.1	0.1	0.1	0.0	0.0	
1931	9.9	1.9	0.9	0.9	0.0	0.1	0.6	0.1	0.1	0.1	0.1	0.0	
1930	10.0	1.8	0.9	0.9	0.0	0.1	0.6	0.2	0.1	0.1	0.0	0.0	
1929	9.4	1.7	0.9	0.9	0.0	0.1	0.6	0.2	0.1	0.0	0.0	0.0	

[1]Government consumption expenditures are services (such as education and national defense) produced by government that are valued at their cost of production. Excludes government sales to other sectors and government own-account investment (construction and software).
[2]Gross government investment consists of general government and government enterprise expenditures for fixed assets; inventory investment is included in government consumption expenditures.
[3]Consumption of fixed capital, or depreciation, is included in government gross output as a partial measure of the services of general government fixed assets; the use of depreciation assumes a zero net return on these assets.

Table 27-7. Government Consumption Expenditures and Gross Investment, by Type, 1929–2006—*Continued*

(Billions of dollars.)

	Federal											
	Nondefense											
		Consumption expenditures[1]								Gross investment[2]		
				Nondurable goods			Services					
Year	Total	Total	Durable goods	Total	Commodity Credit Corporation Inventory change	Other nondurable goods	Compensation of employees	Consumption of fixed capital[3]	Other services	Total	Structures	Equipment and software
2006	305.6	266.1	2.7	16.4	−0.1	16.4	133.5	26.6	94.1	39.5	10.6	28.9
2005	289.0	251.7	2.6	15.7	−0.5	16.3	128.1	25.2	88.1	37.4	10.2	27.1
2004	274.7	240.7	2.4	13.9	−1.0	14.8	122.8	24.1	83.5	33.9	9.6	24.3
2003	259.2	226.0	2.1	12.6	−0.1	12.8	115.5	23.4	77.6	33.3	10.1	23.1
2002	242.5	209.9	2.2	11.3	0.1	11.2	106.3	22.9	72.2	32.7	9.9	22.8
2001	220.3	189.5	1.9	9.9	0.8	9.1	97.2	22.4	63.6	30.8	8.3	22.5
2000	208.5	177.8	1.8	8.5	0.8	7.7	94.8	21.4	58.1	30.7	8.3	22.3
1999	195.2	162.2	1.7	6.7	0.1	6.6	87.8	19.8	51.6	33.0	10.6	22.4
1998	184.7	153.9	1.7	8.2	0.2	8.0	83.5	18.4	49.0	30.8	10.6	20.2
1997	181.3	153.0	1.8	8.2	−0.1	8.2	80.1	17.6	51.0	28.3	9.8	18.5
1996	172.8	143.8	1.8	7.2	−0.3	7.5	77.3	16.7	47.8	29.1	11.2	17.9
1995	170.5	143.2	1.7	7.3	−0.2	7.5	76.0	16.1	49.1	27.3	10.8	16.5
1994	165.5	140.1	1.6	7.0	−0.5	7.4	75.1	15.3	48.1	25.4	10.5	14.9
1993	162.4	134.2	1.6	7.4	−0.2	7.6	73.3	14.8	43.9	28.1	11.2	16.9
1992	157.0	129.8	1.7	6.9	−0.6	7.5	67.7	14.2	46.7	27.2	10.3	16.9
1991	144.5	119.7	1.6	6.3	0.2	6.1	64.0	13.6	42.1	24.8	9.2	15.7
1990	134.3	111.7	1.5	5.7	−1.5	7.2	59.3	12.7	39.6	22.6	8.0	14.6
1989	120.0	99.7	1.3	5.7	−0.8	6.5	54.0	11.8	33.9	20.3	6.9	13.4
1988	107.4	88.9	1.2	−0.1	−7.1	7.0	51.1	10.9	32.2	18.6	6.8	11.7
1987	110.0	90.6	1.1	6.9	−0.2	7.1	46.8	10.1	31.6	19.4	9.0	10.4
1986	107.8	90.3	1.0	12.4	6.4	6.0	44.3	9.3	28.2	17.5	8.0	9.5
1985	101.6	84.7	1.0	9.5	2.2	7.2	43.6	8.7	27.1	16.9	7.3	9.6
1984	92.8	77.1	0.9	6.4	−1.8	8.2	41.8	7.9	24.9	15.7	7.0	8.7
1983	92.3	77.7	0.9	10.6	2.5	8.1	39.9	7.3	23.9	14.5	6.7	7.8
1982	84.9	72.1	0.6	9.1	1.7	7.5	37.9	6.7	22.1	12.7	6.8	6.0
1981	84.0	71.0	0.6	11.2	0.9	10.3	36.3	6.0	21.4	13.0	7.7	5.3
1980	75.8	63.8	0.7	7.4	1.5	6.0	34.0	5.2	21.3	12.0	7.1	4.9
1979	65.4	55.1	0.5	5.2	0.0	5.2	30.1	4.5	19.4	10.2	6.3	4.0
1978	60.4	50.6	0.4	4.9	0.0	4.8	28.3	4.0	16.7	9.8	6.1	3.7
1977	54.5	46.5	0.3	4.4	0.4	4.0	26.3	3.7	14.7	8.0	5.0	3.0
1976	48.6	41.4	0.3	3.5	0.2	3.3	23.1	3.4	13.3	7.3	4.6	2.7
1975	45.1	38.7	0.2	2.8	0.3	2.5	20.5	3.2	13.7	6.5	4.1	2.4
1974	39.0	33.4	0.2	2.6	− 0.5	3.1	18.0	2.8	11.7	5.6	3.4	2.2
1973	34.3	29.4	0.2	1.9	− 0.7	2.6	16.0	2.5	10.4	4.9	3.1	1.8
1972	32.7	28.2	0.3	2.4	− 0.4	2.8	14.8	2.4	9.9	4.5	2.7	1.8
1971	29.1	24.9	0.3	2.1	− 0.3	2.4	13.4	2.3	8.1	4.2	2.5	1.7
1970	25.8	22.1	0.3	2.0	− 0.4	2.4	11.7	2.1	7.1	3.8	2.1	1.7
1969	23.8	20.2	0.3	3.0	0.7	2.3	10.1	2.0	5.9	3.6	1.9	1.7
1968	22.1	18.3	0.4	1.9	0.2	1.8	9.5	1.8	5.7	3.8	2.1	1.7
1967	21.3	17.1	0.4	1.2	− 0.9	2.1	8.6	1.7	6.2	4.2	2.2	1.9
1966	20.8	15.9	0.5	0.4	− 1.5	1.9	8.0	1.5	6.4	4.9	2.8	2.1
1965	19.8	15.1	0.5	1.1	− 0.4	1.6	7.4	1.2	5.7	4.7	2.8	1.9
1964	18.2	14.0	0.4	1.1	− 0.4	1.5	7.0	1.0	5.3	4.2	2.5	1.6
1963	15.9	12.4	0.3	1.2	− 0.2	1.3	6.4	0.9	4.5	3.5	2.3	1.2
1962	14.2	11.3	0.2	1.5	0.3	1.2	5.8	0.8	3.6	2.9	2.1	0.8
1961	11.4	9.0	0.1	0.4	−0.8	1.2	5.4	0.7	3.0	2.4	1.9	0.6
1960	10.7	8.7	0.1	1.1	0.2	1.0	5.0	0.7	2.5	2.0	1.7	0.3
1959	11.5	9.8	0.0	3.3	2.1	1.2	4.4	0.7	2.1	1.7	1.5	0.2
1958	8.4	6.8	0.0	0.7	0.3	0.4	4.3	0.7	1.7	1.6	1.4	0.2
1957	7.7	6.3	0.1	0.8	−0.1	0.9	3.7	0.6	1.8	1.4	1.1	0.2
1956	7.5	6.3	0.1	0.8	0.2	0.6	3.5	0.6	1.7	1.2	0.9	0.3
1955	7.9	7.1	0.1	2.5	2.0	0.4	3.2	0.6	1.6	0.9	0.6	0.2
1954	8.1	6.9	0.1	2.2	1.9	0.4	2.9	0.6	1.4	1.2	0.9	0.3
1953	8.5	7.1	0.1	2.4	2.0	0.3	3.1	0.6	1.3	1.4	1.1	0.3
1952	6.8	5.3	0.1	0.5	0.2	0.3	3.2	0.6	1.3	1.6	1.1	0.5
1951	5.8	4.3	0.1	0.1	−0.4	0.5	3.1	0.6	0.7	1.5	1.1	0.4

[1]Government consumption expenditures are services (such as education and national defense) produced by government that are valued at their cost of production. Excludes government sales to other sectors and government own-account investment (construction and software).
[2]Gross government investment consists of general government and government enterprise expenditures for fixed assets; inventory investment is included in government consumption expenditures.
[3]Consumption of fixed capital, or depreciation, is included in government gross output as a partial measure of the services of general government fixed assets; the use of depreciation assumes a zero net return on these assets.

Table 27-7. Government Consumption Expenditures and Gross Investment, by Type, 1929–2006—*Continued*

(Billions of dollars.)

	Federal											
	Nondefense											
		Consumption expenditures[1]								Gross investment[2]		
				Nondurable goods			Services					
Year	Total	Total	Durable goods	Total	Commodity Credit Corporation Inventory change	Other nondurable goods	Compen-sation of employees	Consumption of fixed capital[3]	Other services	Total	Structures	Equipment and software
1950	6.5	4.9	0.1	0.5	0.3	0.3	3.1	0.6	0.9	1.6	1.2	0.4
1949	7.9	6.4	0.1	2.1	1.5	0.6	2.9	0.6	1.0	1.4	1.1	0.3
1948	5.9	4.9	0.1	0.8	0.3	0.5	2.6	0.6	1.1	1.0	0.7	0.4
1947	4.4	3.6	0.1	0.4	0.1	0.3	2.5	0.6	0.7	0.8	0.3	0.5
1946	3.7	3.3	0.1	0.4	−0.5	1.0	2.1	0.5	1.2	0.4	0.0	0.4
1945	2.1	1.5	0.1	0.2	−0.4	0.6	0.6	0.4	1.1	0.6	0.2	0.5
1944	2.4	1.9	0.1	0.8	0.5	0.3	0.3	0.4	0.7	0.5	0.2	0.3
1943	2.3	1.5	0.1	−0.2	−0.4	0.2	0.6	0.4	0.8	0.8	0.4	0.4
1942	3.0	2.0	0.1	0.8	0.6	0.2	0.6	0.4	0.4	1.0	0.5	0.6
1941	3.7	2.3	0.2	0.3	0.2	0.2	1.5	0.3	0.3	1.4	0.6	0.8
1940	4.0	3.2	0.1	0.5	0.3	0.2	2.4	0.2	0.4	0.8	0.6	0.2
1939	4.5	3.7	0.1	0.6	0.3	0.3	2.7	0.2	0.5	0.8	0.6	0.2
1938	4.4	3.5	0.1	0.3	0.0	0.3	2.9	0.2	0.4	0.9	0.7	0.2
1937	3.8	2.9	0.1	0.3	0.0	0.3	2.4	0.2	0.4	0.9	0.7	0.2
1936	4.3	3.3	0.1	0.3	0.0	0.3	3.0	0.1	0.4	1.0	0.8	0.2
1935	2.3	1.3	0.1	0.2	0.0	0.2	1.2	0.1	0.3	1.1	0.8	0.3
1934	2.5	1.7	0.1	0.3	0.0	0.3	1.3	0.1	0.4	0.8	0.6	0.2
1933	1.4	0.9	0.0	0.1	0.0	0.1	0.7	0.1	0.3	0.5	0.5	0.0
1932	0.9	0.6	0.0	0.0	0.0	0.0	0.4	0.0	0.2	0.3	0.3	0.0
1931	0.9	0.7	0.0	0.1	0.0	0.1	0.4	0.0	0.2	0.3	0.2	0.0
1930	0.9	0.7	0.0	0.1	0.0	0.1	0.4	0.0	0.2	0.2	0.2	0.0
1929	0.8	0.7	0.0	0.1	0.0	0.1	0.4	0.0	0.2	0.2	0.1	0.0

[1]Government consumption expenditures are services (such as education and national defense) produced by government that are valued at their cost of production. Excludes government sales to other sectors and government own-account investment (construction and software).
[2]Gross government investment consists of general government and government enterprise expenditures for fixed assets; inventory investment is included in government consumption expenditures.
[3]Consumption of fixed capital, or depreciation, is included in government gross output as a partial measure of the services of general government fixed assets; the use of depreciation assumes a zero net return on these assets.

Table 27-7. Government Consumption Expenditures and Gross Investment, by Type, 1929–2006—*Continued*

(Billions of dollars.)

		State and local								
		Consumption expenditures[1]						Gross investment[2]		
					Services					
Year	Total	Total	Durable goods	Nondurable goods	Compensation of employees	Consumption of fixed capital[3]	Other services	Total	Structures	Equipment and software
2006	1 601.1	1 288.3	24.5	210.0	915.8	123.2	360.8	312.8	257.2	55.6
2005	1 494.4	1 207.2	23.4	188.7	872.3	113.9	333.6	287.3	233.5	53.8
2004	1 400.3	1 130.3	22.4	162.9	832.7	104.1	314.9	270.0	218.4	51.6
2003	1 336.0	1 073.8	21.6	145.7	798.0	98.2	299.7	262.2	212.0	50.3
2002	1 281.5	1 025.3	21.8	137.2	754.2	94.8	293.9	256.1	205.9	50.2
2001	1 212.8	969.8	21.4	133.5	710.8	89.9	273.4	243.0	192.4	50.6
2000	1 142.8	917.8	20.1	126.4	669.4	84.8	252.5	225.0	176.0	49.0
1999	1 065.0	858.9	19.0	108.0	633.1	78.7	237.5	206.0	159.7	46.4
1998	987.9	801.4	18.1	96.9	603.3	73.9	216.4	186.5	143.6	43.0
1997	937.8	758.9	17.0	94.3	575.5	70.2	197.2	178.9	139.5	39.4
1996	888.6	724.8	16.0	90.6	552.7	66.7	183.0	163.8	126.8	36.9
1995	850.0	696.1	15.6	84.5	533.5	63.4	174.7	154.0	117.3	36.7
1994	806.3	663.3	14.5	77.4	511.2	59.5	164.1	143.0	108.7	34.3
1993	766.0	630.3	13.7	72.7	486.7	56.3	153.3	135.7	104.5	31.2
1992	737.0	602.7	13.3	69.1	463.9	53.4	141.6	134.3	104.2	30.1
1991	706.7	574.6	12.7	66.0	439.8	51.1	129.7	132.1	103.2	28.9
1990	671.9	544.6	12.0	63.8	414.6	48.0	118.2	127.2	98.5	28.7
1989	616.9	502.1	11.4	57.7	380.5	44.4	109.7	114.7	88.7	26.0
1988	576.7	470.4	10.5	51.8	353.7	41.5	103.7	106.3	84.8	21.5
1987	539.4	440.9	9.8	49.3	328.8	39.0	97.1	98.4	78.8	19.6
1986	510.7	417.9	9.2	45.6	307.3	36.2	96.7	92.8	74.2	18.6
1985	466.2	381.8	8.4	45.6	284.7	33.7	80.0	84.4	67.6	16.8
1984	422.6	347.7	7.8	42.8	261.1	32.0	68.5	75.0	60.5	14.4
1983	390.5	324.1	7.2	40.0	243.0	31.2	62.5	66.4	54.2	12.2
1982	369.7	304.9	6.7	38.4	227.4	30.3	55.5	64.8	54.2	10.6
1981	347.3	282.3	6.1	37.2	210.1	27.8	48.4	65.0	55.4	9.5
1980	322.4	258.4	5.3	33.8	193.0	24.3	42.9	64.0	55.1	8.9
1979	290.2	233.3	4.9	30.0	174.3	21.1	39.3	56.8	49.0	7.8
1978	262.6	213.2	4.4	26.3	158.9	18.9	36.2	49.5	42.8	6.6
1977	238.7	195.9	4.0	24.2	145.1	17.5	32.9	42.8	36.9	5.9
1976	223.3	179.5	3.6	21.3	133.0	16.6	30.2	43.8	38.1	5.7
1975	208.7	165.1	3.3	18.9	121.2	15.9	28.5	43.6	38.1	5.5
1974	183.4	143.7	2.9	15.5	107.7	14.1	24.3	39.6	34.7	4.9
1973	159.2	126.0	2.5	12.4	98.0	11.3	20.6	33.2	29.1	4.1
1972	143.8	113.2	2.2	11.0	87.7	10.2	19.0	30.6	27.1	3.5
1971	132.8	102.7	1.9	10.2	79.2	9.4	17.1	30.1	27.0	3.1
1970	120.3	91.5	1.6	9.0	71.1	8.4	14.9	28.7	25.8	3.0
1969	108.2	79.9	1.3	7.8	62.6	7.4	12.7	28.3	25.6	2.7
1968	98.0	70.4	1.1	6.9	55.9	6.6	10.7	27.7	25.2	2.4
1967	87.9	62.6	0.9	6.2	49.5	6.0	9.3	25.3	23.0	2.3
1966	79.2	56.1	0.8	5.8	44.1	5.5	8.3	23.1	21.0	2.1
1965	71.0	50.2	0.7	5.4	39.3	4.9	7.3	20.8	19.0	1.9
1964	64.8	45.8	0.6	4.9	35.9	4.5	6.4	19.0	17.2	1.8
1963	59.5	41.9	0.6	4.6	32.9	4.2	5.7	17.5	16.0	1.5
1962	54.9	39.0	0.5	4.3	30.2	3.9	5.2	15.9	14.5	1.3
1961	51.6	36.6	0.5	4.1	27.9	3.7	5.0	15.0	13.8	1.3
1960	47.5	33.5	0.5	3.9	25.5	3.5	4.6	13.9	12.7	1.2
1959	44.7	30.7	0.4	3.6	23.1	3.3	4.3	13.9	12.8	1.1
1958	42.2	28.6	0.4	3.1	21.6	3.1	4.1	13.5	12.5	1.1
1957	38.3	25.8	0.4	2.5	19.6	3.0	3.5	12.5	11.5	1.1
1956	34.7	23.4	0.3	2.4	17.6	2.8	3.2	11.3	10.4	0.9
1955	31.6	21.6	0.3	2.5	15.8	2.4	3.2	10.0	9.3	0.8
1954	28.9	19.7	0.3	2.1	14.7	2.2	2.8	9.2	8.5	0.7
1953	26.1	18.2	0.2	2.1	13.3	2.2	2.6	7.9	7.3	0.6
1952	24.4	17.1	0.2	2.1	12.3	2.2	2.5	7.3	6.7	0.6
1951	23.0	16.1	0.2	2.2	11.2	2.0	2.5	7.0	6.4	0.5

[1]Government consumption expenditures are services (such as education and national defense) produced by government that are valued at their cost of production. Excludes government sales to other sectors and government own-account investment (construction and software).

[2]Gross government investment consists of general government and government enterprise expenditures for fixed assets; inventory investment is included in government consumption expenditures.

[3]Consumption of fixed capital, or depreciation, is included in government gross output as a partial measure of the services of general government fixed assets; the use of depreciation assumes a zero net return on these assets.

Table 27-7. Government Consumption Expenditures and Gross Investment, by Type, 1929–2006— *Continued*

(Billions of dollars.)

Year	State and local									
		Consumption expenditures[1]						Gross investment[2]		
						Services				
	Total	Total	Durable goods	Nondurable goods	Compensation of employees	Consumption of fixed capital[3]	Other services	Total	Structures	Equipment and software
1950	20.7	14.9	0.2	2.3	10.1	1.7	2.5	5.9	5.4	0.5
1949	19.0	13.7	0.2	2.0	9.4	1.7	2.1	5.3	4.9	0.5
1948	16.3	12.3	0.2	1.7	8.5	1.7	1.8	4.0	3.6	0.4
1947	13.7	10.9	0.1	1.6	7.3	1.5	1.7	2.8	2.5	0.3
1946	10.8	9.2	0.1	1.3	6.2	1.2	1.4	1.6	1.4	0.2
1945	9.0	8.2	0.0	1.3	5.4	1.1	1.3	0.8	0.7	0.1
1944	8.4	7.7	0.0	1.3	4.9	1.1	1.2	0.7	0.6	0.1
1943	8.4	7.5	0.0	1.3	4.7	1.2	1.2	0.9	0.8	0.1
1942	8.6	7.0	0.1	1.4	4.5	1.1	1.3	1.5	1.4	0.1
1941	8.6	6.3	0.2	1.5	4.4	0.9	1.3	2.2	2.1	0.2
1940	8.6	5.8	0.2	1.4	4.3	0.8	1.2	2.8	2.6	0.2
1939	8.8	5.4	0.3	1.4	4.2	0.8	1.2	3.4	3.1	0.2
1938	8.1	5.1	0.3	1.5	4.1	0.8	1.3	3.0	2.8	0.2
1937	7.7	5.1	0.2	1.3	3.9	0.8	1.1	2.6	2.4	0.2
1936	7.5	4.6	0.2	1.3	3.7	0.7	1.1	2.9	2.8	0.1
1935	7.5	5.9	0.1	1.2	4.2	0.7	1.0	1.6	1.5	0.1
1934	7.2	5.5	0.1	1.2	3.9	0.7	1.0	1.8	1.6	0.1
1933	6.4	5.0	0.1	0.9	3.5	0.6	0.7	1.3	1.2	0.1
1932	6.9	5.1	0.1	0.8	3.6	0.5	0.7	1.8	1.6	0.2
1931	8.0	5.4	0.1	0.9	3.7	0.6	0.7	2.6	2.4	0.2
1930	8.2	5.2	0.1	0.8	3.6	0.6	0.7	2.9	2.7	0.2
1929	7.6	5.0	0.1	0.7	3.5	0.6	0.6	2.6	2.4	0.2

Source: U.S. Bureau of Economic Analysis. National Income and Product Accounts.
[1]Government consumption expenditures are services (such as education and national defense) produced by government that are valued at their cost of production. Excludes government sales to other sectors and government own-account investment (construction and software).
[2]Gross government investment consists of general government and government enterprise expenditures for fixed assets; inventory investment is included in government consumption expenditures.
[3]Consumption of fixed capital, or depreciation, is included in government gross output as a partial measure of the services of general government fixed assets; the use of depreciation assumes a zero net return on these assets.

Table 27-8. State and Local Government Revenue, by Source, 1902–2005

(Millions of dollars.)

Year	Total revenue from all sources	Total general revenue	Revenue from state and local sources, general revenue					Charges and miscellaneous
			Taxes					
			Total	Individual income	Corporation income	Sales and gross receipts	Property	
2005	2 020 926	1 582 770	1 096 385	240 930	43 138	383 264	335 678	486 386
2004	2 435 084	1 464 058	1 010 277	215 215	33 716	360 629	318 242	453 781
2003	2 047 337	1 373 948	938 972	199 407	31 369	337 787	296 683	434 976
2002	1 806 592	1 324 333	905 101	202 832	28 152	324 123	279 191	419 232
2001	1 890 891	1 323 128	914 119	226 334	35 296	320 217	263 689	409 009
2000	1 942 328	1 249 373	872 351	211 661	36 059	309 290	249 178	377 022
1999	1 794 557	1 163 836	815 777	189 309	33 922	290 993	240 107	348 060
1998	1 720 889	1 110 714	773 963	175 630	34 412	274 883	230 150	336 751
1997	1 616 495	1 044 391	728 304	159 042	33 820	261 418	218 877	316 087
1996	1 513 633	987 930	689 038	146 844	32 009	248 993	209 440	298 892
1995	1 417 925	940 733	660 577	137 931	31 406	237 268	203 451	280 156
1994	1 331 442	884 996	625 527	128 810	28 320	223 628	197 140	259 469
1993	1 270 748	842 977	594 300	123 235	26 417	209 649	189 743	248 677
1992	1 185 191	793 399	555 610	115 170	23 595	196 112	178 536	237 789
1991	1 080 862	748 108	525 355	109 341	22 242	185 570	167 999	222 753
1990	1 032 115	712 700	501 619	105 640	23 566	177 885	155 613	211 081
1980	451 537	299 293	223 463	42 080	13 321	79 927	68 499	75 830
1975	264 013	191 137	141 465	21 454	6 642	49 815	51 494	39 668
1970	150 106	108 898	86 795	10 812	3 738	30 322	34 054	22 103
1969	132 153	95 397	76 712	8 908	3 180	26 519	30 673	18 686
1968	117 581	84 083	67 572	7 308	2 518	22 911	27 747	16 511
1967	106 581	75 827	61 000	5 826	2 227	20 530	26 047	14 827
1966	97 619	69 822	56 647	4 760	2 038	19 085	24 670	13 175
1965	87 777	62 971	51 243	4 090	1 929	17 118	22 583	11 729
1964	81 455	58 440	47 785	3 791	1 695	15 762	21 241	10 655
1963	74 408	53 606	44 014	3 267	1 505	14 446	19 833	9 593
1962	69 492	50 381	41 554	3 037	1 308	13 494	19 054	8 827
1961	64 531	46 907	38 861	2 613	1 266	12 463	18 002	8 045
1960*	60 277	43 530	36 117	2 463	1 180	11 849	16 405	7 414
1959[1]	53 972	38 929	32 379	1 994	1 001	10 437	14 983	6 550
1958	49 262	36 354	30 380	1 759	1 018	9 829	14 047	5 974
1957	45 929	34 320	28 817	1 754	984	9 467	12 864	5 503
1956	41 692	31 332	26 368	1 538	890	8 691	11 749	4 964
1955	37 619	27 942	23 483	1 237	744	7 643	10 735	4 459
1954	35 386	26 046	22 067	1 127	778	7 276	9 967	3 979
1953	33 411	24 437	20 908	1 065	817	6 927	9 375	3 529
1952	31 013	22 615	19 323	998	846	6 357	8 652	3 292
1950	25 639	18 425	15 914	788	593	5 154	7 349	2 511
1948	21 613	15 389	13 342	543	592	4 442	6 126	2 047
1946	15 983	11 501	10 094	422	447	2 986	4 986	1 407
1944	14 333	9 954	8 774	342	451	2 289	4 604	1 180
1942	13 148	9 560	8 528	276	272	2 351	4 537	1 031
1940	11 749	8 664	7 810	224	156	1 982	4 430	854
1938	11 058	8 428	7 605	218	165	1 794	4 440	823
1936	9 360	7 447	6 701	153	113	1 484	4 093	746
1934	8 430	6 662	5 912	80	49	1 008	4 076	750
1932	7 887	7 035	6 164	74	79	752	4 487	871
1927	7 383	7 155	6 087	70	92	470	4 730	1 068
1922	5 169	4 673	4 016	43	58	154	3 321	657
1913	2 030	1 900	1 609	...	...	58	1 332	291
1902	1 048	979	860	...	...	28	706	119

Source: U.S. Census Bureau.
[1]Includes Alaska.
*First year for which figures include Alaska and Hawaii.
... = Not available.

Table 27-9. State Government Expenditure, by Character and Object and by Function, 1902–2005

(Millions of dollars.)

Year	Direct expenditure by character and object							Outstanding debt at end of fiscal year
	Total	Current operation	Capital outlay		Assistance and subsidies	Interest on debt	Insurance benefits and repayments	
			Total	Construction				
2005	1 066 989	738 063	94 550	77 220	30 308	36 094	167 975	797 561
2004	1 016 469	691 652	90 950	73 372	28 104	34 624	171 139	754 150
2003	976 852	656 989	91 943	72 374	25 901	33 040	168 979	697 929
2002	915 501	620 763	89 919	71 035	24 313	33 220	147 286	642 202
2001	835 782	580 374	81 881	64 668	23 496	31 198	118 833	576 494
2000	757 027	523 114	76 233	59 681	22 136	30 089	105 456	547 876
1999	693 432	476 958	68 509	53 857	22 229	28 582	97 144	510 486
1998	651 098	446 440	64 441	50 542	21 515	27 590	91 113	483 117
1997	629 620	425 898	59 658	46 991	21 867	27 025	95 171	455 698
1996	607 856	405 416	58 915	46 924	23 313	26 167	94 045	447 339
1995	595 916	396 035	57 829	48 113	23 511	25 259	93 282	427 239
1994	554 293	370 409	52 929	39 604	23 012	24 494	83 450	410 998
1993	528 999	345 397	49 776	39 220	21 976	24 800	87 050	389 721
1992	499 580	323 830	50 126	39 001	20 784	25 482	79 359	371 901
1991	442 264	287 079	47 937	37 647	18 876	24 189	64 182	345 554
1990	397 291	258 046	45 524	34 803	16 902	22 367	54 452	318 254
1980	173 307	108 131	23 325	19 736	9 818	7 052	24 981	121 958
1975	106 905	60 793	17 307	14 443	6 673	3 272	18 860	72 127
1970	56 163	30 971	13 295	11 185	4 387	1 499	6 010	42 008
1969	49 448	27 052	12 701	10 610	3 509	1 275	4 911	39 553
1968	44 304	23 379	12 210	10 053	2 960	1 128	4 626	35 666
1967	39 704	20 201	11 544	9 550	2 665	1 026	4 268	32 472
1966	34 195	16 855	10 193	8 287	2 301	894	3 952	29 564
1965	31 465	14 930	9 307	7 600	2 236	822	4 170	27 034
1964	29 616	13 492	8 820	7 263	2 175	765	4 364	25 041
1963	27 698	12 449	8 110	6 717	2 112	721	4 306	23 176
1962	25 495	11 290	7 214	5 960	2 118	635	4 238	22 023
1961	24 578	10 384	6 865	5 699	2 044	584	4 701	19 993
1960*	22 152	9 534	6 607	5 509	2 015	536	3 461	18 543
1959[1]	22 436	8 775	7 059	5 937	1 891	453	4 259	16 930
1958	19 991	8 161	5 946	5 022	1 813	396	3 675	15 394
1957	16 796	7 330	5 163	4 318	1 639	351	2 313	13 738
1956	15 148	6 758	4 564	3 872	1 531	311	1 984	12 890
1955	14 371	6 234	3 992	3 404	1 482	251	2 411	11 198
1954	13 008	5 886	3 347	2 831	1 486	193	2 096	9 600
1953	11 466	5 540	2 847	2 472	1 501	162	1 416	7 824
1952	10 790	5 173	2 658	2 323	1 402	144	1 413	6 874
1950	10 864	4 450	2 237	1 966	1 891	109	2 177	5 285
1948	7 897	3 837	1 456	1 268	1 499	86	1 020	3 676
1946	4 974	2 701	368	292	663	84	1 158	2 353
1944	3 319	2 134	330	288	527	101	226	2 776
1942	3 563	1 827	642	560	466	122	505	3 257
1940	3 555	1 570	737	643	517	130	601	3 590
1938	3 082	1 503	701	612	448	128	302	3 343
1936	2 445	1 192	634	553	416	124	79	3 413
1934	2 143	985	619	540	356	119	64	2 248
1932	2 028	982	786	686	83	114	63	2 832
1927	1 451	762	492	430	43	83	71	1 971
1922	1 085	562	302	263	122	45	54	1 131
1913	297	218	48	42	17	14	...	379
1902	136	114	2	2	10	10	...	230

[1]Includes Alaska.
*First year for which figures include Alaska and Hawaii.
. . . = Not available.

Table 27-9. State Government Expenditure, by Character and Object and by Function, 1902–2005—Continued

(Millions of dollars.)

| | Direct expenditure by function | | | | | | | | | | |
| Year | General expenditure[2] | | | | | | | | | Liquor stores expenditure | Total insurance expenditure |
	Total education	Highways	Total public welfare	Hospitals	Health	Police	Natural resources	Financial administration and general control	Interest on general debt		
2005	...	...	317 295	42 324	...	...	16 473	21 044	34 362	4 082	167 975
2004	...	...	291 968	40 011	...	...	17 226	21 387	32 953	3 924	171 139
2003	411 094	85 726	314 407	38 395	50 221	11 144	18 577	20 627	31 295	3 697	168 979
2002	389 390	84 198	287 016	37 393	50 293	10 706	17 821	18 940	31 407	3 498	147 286
2001	374 444	78 786	262 346	34 538	43 732	10 145	17 309	17 111	30 452	3 347	118 833
2000	346 465	74 415	238 890	32 578	42 066	9 788	15 967	16 141	30 089	3 195	105 456
1999	318 602	68 317	221 167	29 994	38 008	8 794	14 482	...	28 582	2 967	97 144
1998	294 814	63 620	207 926	28 928	35 067	8 038	13 541	...	27 590	2 820	91 113
1997	275 821	60 204	203 204	29 313	33 880	7 501	12 909	...	27 025	2 697	95 172
1996	263 519	58 255	195 731	29 421	32 612	7 173	12 862	...	26 167	2 593	94 045
1995	249 670	57 374	194 954	60 003	(3)	6 451	12 534	...	25 259	2 522	93 282
1994	230 791	53 849	185 186	56 577	(3)	6 000	11 878	...	24 494	2 495	83 450
1993	221 342	51 268	168 421	53 202	(3)	5 600	11 212	...	24 800	2 558	87 050
1992	211 570	48 747	156 364	48 123	(3)	5 489	10 521	19 771	25 482	2 577	79 359
1991	196 648	47 038	124 456	45 878	(3)	5 506	10 256	18 45	24 189	2 504	64 182
1990	181 935	44 249	104 971	22 637	20 029	5 166	9 909	17 000	22 367	2 452	54 452
1980	87 939	25 044	44 219	11 015	6 840	2 263	4 346	6 263	7 052	2 206	24 981
1975	54 012	17 483	25 559	6 891	3 267	1 423	3 554	3 288	3 272	1 719	18 860
1970	13 780	11 044	8 203	4 002	786	688	2 158	1 720	1 499	1 404	8 010
1969	12 304	10 414	6 464	3 582	676	585	2 035	1 496	1 275	1 293	4 911
1968	10 957	9 819	5 122	3 233	599	516	1 954	1 310	1 128	1 233	4 626
1967	9 384	9 423	4 291	2 857	501	441	1 801	1 175	1 026	1 187	4 268
1966	7 572	8 624	3 138	2 533	433	385	1 532	1 024	894	1 081	3 952
1965	6 181	8 214	2 998	2 317	384	348	1 343	948	822	1 022	4 170
1964	5 465	7 850	2 796	2 127	337	315	1 185	871	765	977	4 364
1963	4 718	7 425	2 712	2 006	324	297	1 097	830	721	900	4 306
1962	4 270	6 635	2 509	1 878	283	276	973	763	635	882	4 238
1961	3 792	6 230	2 311	1 799	260	261	906	726	584	873	4 701
1960*	3 396	6 070	2 221	1 664	232	245	842	654	536	907	3 461
1959[1]	3 093	6 414	2 124	1 627	223	228	813	619	453	860	4 259
1958	2 728	5 507	1 944	1 549	211	214	753	569	396	869	3 675
1957	2 342	4 875	1 826	1 373	198	179	688	531	351	836	2 313
1956	2 138	4 367	1 603	1 268	202	159	670	477	311	845	1 984
1955	1 905	3 899	1 600	1 145	193	139	597	447	251	770	2 411
1954	1 715	3 254	1 548	1 089	187	130	563	419	193	803	2 096
1953	1 634	2 781	1 534	1 014	170	119	531	399	162	757	1 416
1952	1 494	2 556	1 410	968	164	106	539	361	144	723	1 413
1950	1 358	2 058	1 566	788	159	85	468	317	109	654	2 177
1948	1 081	1 510	962	533	130	65	344	266	86	691	1 020
1946	518	613	680	308	116	45	207	192	84	663	1 158
1944	489	540	577	253	78	41	164	162	101	426	226
1942	391	790	523	235	64	40	159	164	122	288	505
1940	375	793	527	236	64	34	144	151	130	224	601
1938	347	815	453	209	59	30	128	146	128	204	302
1936	297	754	422	180	41	19	93	130	124	143	97
1934	228	738	363	167	36	15	85	108	119	70	64
1932	278	843	74	181	34	15	119	114	114	...	63
1927	218	514	40	146	24	7	94	96	83	...	71
1922	164	303	38	105	20	4	61	69	45	...	54
1913	55	26	16	47	6	1	14	38	14	...	...
1902	17	4	10	28	4	...	9	23	10	2	...

Source: U.S. Census Bureau.
[1]Includes Alaska.
[2]Through 1970, includes direct expenditure only; after 1970, includes intergovernmental and direct.
[3]Health is included with hospitals.
*First year for which figures include Alaska and Hawaii.
... = Not available.

Table 27-10. Governmental Payrolls, 1946–2004

(Millions of dollars, covers full-time and part-time employees, local government data are estimates subject to sampling variation.)

Year	Total	Federal (civilian)[1]	State and local		
			Total	State	Local
2004	68 760.0	12 845.0	55 915.0	15 478.0	40 437.0
2003	67 194.0	12 672.0	54 522.0	15 116.0	39 406.0
2002	63 922.5	11 599.0	52 323.5	14 837.8	37 485.7
2001	60 632.2	11 369.8	49 262.4	14 136.3	35 126.1
2000	58 166.0	11 485.0	46 681.4	13 279.1	33 402.3
1999	54 363.0	10 477.6	43 886.0	12 564.7	31 321.0
1998	51 568.0	10 115.0	41 453.0	11 845.0	29 608.0
1997	49 156.0	9 744.0	39 411.7	11 413.1	27 998.6
1996	...	...	...	...	...
1995	47 457.8	9 744.1	37 713.6	10 926.5	26 787.1
1994	46 236.4	9 691.8	36 544.6	10 666.1	25 878.4
1993	...	...	34 539.7	10 288.2	24 251.5
1992	43 120.0	9 937.0	33 183.0	9 828.0	23 355.0
1991	41 237.3	9 686.8	31 550.5	9 437.0	22 113.4
1990	39 228.1	8 998.8	30 229.2	9 083.0	22 146.2
1989	36 762.9	8 635.8	28 127.2	8 443.0	19 684.1
1988	34 202.8	7 975.8	26 227.0	7 842.0	18 384.6
1987	32 668.7	7 924.2	24 744.5	7 262.9	17 481.6
1986	30 669.6	7 560.8	23 108.8	6 810.4	16 298.4
1985	28 945.0	7 580.3	21 364.7	6 328.6	15 036.1
1984	26 904.2	7 137.3	19 766.8	5 814.9	13 951.9
1983	24 524.4	6 301.5	18 222.9	5 345.5	12 877.4
1982	23 173.3	5 959.0	17 214.3	5 022.1	12 192.2
1981	21 192.9	5 238.6	15 954.3	4 667.5	11 286.8
1980	19 935.2	5 205.1	14 730.1	4 284.7	10 445.4
1979	18 077.0	4 727.7	13 349.3	3 869.3	9 480.0
1978	16 483.0	4 343.9	12 139.1	3 483.0	8 656.1
1977	15 338.4	3 918.4	11 420.0	3 194.6	8 225.4
1976	13 923.7	3 564.6	10 359.1	2 893.7	7 465.4
1975	13 223.8	3 583.8	9 640.1	2 652.7	6 987.4
1974	12 085.8	3 294.3	8 791.5	2 409.5	6 382.0
1973	11 026.9	3 012.0	8 014.9	2 158.2	5 856.8
1972	9 949.6	2 709.6	7 240.0	1 936.6	5 303.4
1971	8 910.9	2 528.7	6 382.2	1 741.7	4 640.5
1970	8 334.2	2 427.9	5 906.4	1 612.2	4 294.2
1969	7 587.6	2 335.3	5 252.3	1 430.5	3 821.7
1968	6 889.2	2 137.3	4 751.9	1 256.6	3 495.2
1967	6 055.5	1 842.3	4 213.2	1 105.5	3 107.7
1966	5 463.0	1 664.8	3 798.2	975.2	2 823.0
1965	4 884.0	1 483.7	3 400.3	849.2	2 551.1
1964	4 572.4	1 475.2	3 097.2	761.1	2 336.1
1963	4 263.5	1 423.2	2 840.3	696.4	2 143.9
1962	3 966.2	1 346.9	2 619.3	634.6	1 984.7
1961	3 633.5	1 213.6	2 419.9	586.2	1 833.7
1960	3 332.8	1 117.8	2 215.0	524.1	1 690.9
1959	3 114.4	1 072.7	2 041.7	485.4	1 556.3
1958	2 977.2	1 091.4	1 885.8	446.5	1 439.3
1957	2 533.1	918.6	1 614.5	372.5	1 242.0
1956	2 509.4	943.7	1 565.7	366.5	1 199.2
1955	2 264.5	845.7	1 418.8	325.9	1 092.9
1954	2 103.1	784.8	1 318.3	300.7	1 017.5
1953	2 013.6	793.1	1 220.5	278.6	941.9
1952	1 979.6	855.9	1 123.7	260.3	863.4
1951	1 865.4	857.4	1 008.0	245.8	762.3
1950	1 527.9	613.4	914.6	218.4	696.2
1949	1 406.0	539.2	866.7	209.8	656.9
1948	1 329.0	533.9	795.1	184.9	610.1
1947	1 183.7	481.4	702.3	160.8	541.5
1946	1 155.5	571.5	584.0	128.0	456.0

Source: U.S. Census Bureau.
[1]Includes employees outside the United States.
... = Not available.

Table 27-11. State and Local Governments—Indebtedness, 1980–2003

(Billions of dollars, except as indicated. For fiscal year ending in year shown. Amounts are estimates and therefore, subject to sampling variation.)

Item	Debt outstanding						Long term		
			Long-term						
	Total	Per capita dollars[1]	Local schools[2]	Utilities	All other	Short-term	Net long term[3]	Debt issued	Debt retired
2003									
Total	1,812.7	6,234	272.7	238.4	1,261.1	40.5	1,242.7	345.8	215.2
State	697.9	2,405	24.0	36.1	621.7	16.1	366.2	148.8	85.9
Local	1,114.7	3,833	248.7	202.3	639.4	24.3	876.5	196.9	129.3
2002									
Total	1,686.1	5,855	250.2	218.5	1,174.2	43.2	1,126.6	262.3	162.5
State	642.2	2,234	23.8	26.1	573.6	18.6	317.8	103.7	65.3
Local	1,043.9	3,625	226.4	192.4	600.5	24.6	808.8	158.6	97.2
2001									
Total	1,554.0	5,447	225.3	210.4	1,096.2	22.1	1,038.6	199.6	130.6
State	576.5	2,025	21.5	18.7	532.6	3.7	287.4	81.3	50.7
Local	977.5	3,426	203.8	191.7	563.5	18.5	751.2	118.3	79.9
2000									
Total	1,451.8	5,159	197.7	200.1	1,029.8	24.3	959.6	184.8	121.9
State	547.9	1,951	18.7	17.9	505.0	6.4	266.9	75.0	44.4
Local	903.9	3,212	179.0	182.2	524.8	17.9	692.7	109.8	77.5
1999									
Total	1,369.3	5,021	180.7	194.9	975.7	17.8	907.3	229.4	153.1
State	510.5	1,876	15.4	16.7	475.8	2.7	249.4	83.2	55.6
Local	858.8	3,149	165.3	178.3	500.0	15.2	657.9	146.2	97.5
1998									
Total	1,283.6	4,750	159.2	182.8	924.3	17.3	842.6	204.4	144.6
State	483.1	1,791	13.6	16.7	450.6	2.2	237.2	83.4	58.1
Local	800.4	2,962	145.5	166.1	473.8	15.1	605.4	120.9	86.5
1997									
Total	1,224.5	4,573	139.0	179.1	889.8	16.6	797.7	151.3	109.3
State	456.7	1,709	11.7	16.0	426.8	2.1	222.7	54.4	41.1
Local	767.9	2,867	127.3	163.1	463.0	14.5	575.1	96.8	68.2
1996									
Total	1,169.7	4,410	130.7	170.3	844.7	24.0	751.6	141.1	106.5
State	452.4	1,709	11.2	16.3	419.1	5.8	220.3	60.2	42.4
Local	717.3	2,705	119.5	154.0	425.6	18.2	531.3	80.9	64.1
1995									
Total	1,115.4	4,244	118.2	163.9	806.2	27.0	697.3	129.3	95.1
State	427.2	1,629	11.3	17.0	392.8	6.1	205.3	52.6	37.5
Local	688.1	2,618	107.0	146.9	413.4	20.9	491.9	76.8	57.6
1994									
Total	1,074.7	4,128	94.3	164.9	788.8	26.7	672.8	207.8	166.6
State	411.0	1,582	10.4	16.7	379.0	4.9	200.8	78.5	61.3
Local	663.7	2,549	83.9	148.2	409.7	21.8	472.0	129.3	105.3
1993									
Total	1,017.7	3,943	89.8	157.6	747.5	22.7	617.1	195.6	147.0
State	389.7	1,515	9.4	14.8	361.7	3.9	176.9	77.1	60.7
Local	628.0	2,436	80.5	142.8	385.8	18.8	440.1	118.4	86.3
1992									
Total	970.5	3,806	78.4	150.4	720.4	21.3	561.6	155.1	99.2
State	372.3	1,463	7.6	13.7	348.1	2.9	125.4	70.2	45.0
Local	598.1	2,345	70.9	136.7	373.1	18.4	409.1	85.0	54.3
1991									
Total	915.8	3,632	71.0	141.2	681.8	21.7	509.9	118.1	65.7
State	345.6	1,374	5.9	12.5	323.7	3.4	139.9	50.5	25.4
Local	570.2	2,261	65.1	128.7	358.1	18.3	369.9	67.6	40.3
1990									
Total	858.0	3,449	60.4	134.8	643.5	19.3	474.4	108.5	64.8
State	318.3	1,282	4.4	12.3	298.7	2.8	125.5	43.5	22.9
Local	539.8	2,169	56.0	122.4	344.8	16.5	348.9	65.0	42.0
1980									
Total	335.6	1,481	32.3	55.2	235.0	13.1	262.9	42.4	17.4
State	122.0	540	3.8	4.6	111.5	2.1	79.8	16.4	5.7
Local	213.6	943	28.5	50.6	123.5	11.0	183.1	25.9	11.7

Source: U.S. Census Bureau.
[1] 1980, 1990 and 2000 based on enumerated resident population as of April 1; other years based on estimated resident population as of July 1.
[2] Includes debt for education activities other than higher education.
[3] Net long-term debt outstanding is the amount of long-term debt held by a government for which no funds have been set aside for its repayment.

Table 27-12. Federal Grants-in-Aid to State and Local Governments, 1990–2006

(Percent, except as indicated. For fiscal year ending in year shown. Minus sign(–) indicates decrease.)

Year	Current Dollars							Constant (2000) dollars	
			Grants to individuals		Grants as percent of				
	Total grants (million dollars)	Annual percent change[1]	Total (million dollars)	Percent of total grants	State/local government expenditures[2]	Federal outlays	Gross domestic product	Total grants (billion dollars)	Annual percent change[1]
2006, est.	449 277	5.4	287 634	64.0	. . .	16.6	3.4	379.3	1.4
2005	426 243	4.9	273 464	64.2	30.7	17.2	3.5	374.0	0.9
2004	406 330	4.9	262 177	64.5	31.3	17.7	3.5	370.6	2.1
2003	387 366	10.2	246 570	63.7	31.0	17.9	3.6	362.9	7.6
2002	351 550	10.8	227 373	64.7	29.3	17.5	3.4	337.2	9.0
2001	317 211	11.4	203 920	64.3	28.2	17.0	3.2	309.4	8.7
2000	284 659	6.6	182 592	64.1	27.2	15.9	2.9	284.7	3.6
1999	267 081	8.5	172 384	64.5	31.2	15.7	2.9	274.7	6.8
1998	246 128	5.1	160 305	65.1	30.3	14.9	2.9	257.3	3.9
1997	234 160	2.8	148 236	63.3	30.2	14.6	2.9	247.7	0.9
1996	227 811	1.3	146 493	64.3	30.8	14.6	3.0	245.5	-1.0
1995	224 991	6.8	144 427	64.2	31.5	14.8	3.1	247.9	4.1
1994	210 596	8.8	134 153	63.7	30.9	14.4	3.0	238.1	6.3
1993	193 612	8.7	124 155	64.1	29.6	13.7	3.0	223.9	5.9
1992	178 065	15.2	112 522	63.2	28.7	12.9	2.9	211.4	12.1
1991	154 519	14.2	92 865	60.1	26.6	11.7	2.6	188.6	9.6
1990	135 325	11.0	77 264	57.1	25.2	10.8	2.4	172.1	6.3

Source: U.S. Census Bureau. *Statistical Abstract of the United States: 2007.* U.S. Office of Management and Budget.
[1]Average annual percent change from prior year shown. For 1990, change from 1989.
[2]Expenditures from own sources as defined in the national income and product accounts.
. . . = Not available.

BOX 27 ■ The Cost of the War in Iraq

Tracking costs specific to the Iraq War and subsequent conflict, collectively named Operation Iraqi Freedom (OIF), can be difficult and confusing. Appropriations requests made by the administration on behalf of the Department of Defense (DOD) are not itemized by the area of the world for which they are intended nor are they listed by the area within the DOD to which they will be apportioned. Because of this lack of transparency, various government bodies have estimated allocations, and because of the nature of these approximations, numbers vary depending on the office that prepared the estimate.

Between fiscal year 2001 and May 25, 2007, Congress allocated $610 billion in war-related appropriations for military operations and other activities related to Operation Enduring Freedom (OEF) in Afghanistan and other counterterror operations, Operation Noble Eagle (ONE) to provide enhanced security at military bases, and Operation Iraqi Freedom. The Congressional Research Service (CRS) of the Library of Congress estimates that of the $610 billion total, approximately $450 billion went to Operation Iraqi Freedom and an estimated 93% of the total funds, of $567.3 billion, went to the DOD. The Congressional Budget Office (CBO) estimates this number to be approximately $533 billion.

In fiscal year 2007, the DOD received $165.8 billion for war costs, accounting for more than a quarter of its annual budget. This was a sharp increase of almost 40% from the year prior. CRS estimates that DOD's monthly expenses related to Iraq are "about $10 billion," while the CBO gives the figure as "more than $9 billion." CRS estimates the remaining DOD 2007 monthly expenses at $1.9 billion in Afghanistan and less than $100 million for enhanced security. Despite the increase in funds spent in Iraq in 2007, an opinion poll conducted by the *New York Times* and CBS in May 2007 found that 76% of Americans are of the opinion that "things are going badly" in Iraq. This includes 47% who feel "things are going very badly."

The allocations to the Veterans Administration (VA) to treat veterans of the conflicts in Iraq and Afghanistan in 2007 were approximately $1 billion, according to CRS estimates. The administration requested a reduced amount of $800 million for 2008 despite an increase in the number of troops deployed in Iraq in the second half of 2007. The total amount apportioned to the VA since 2001 to provide medical care and other associated services to veterans of operations related to the war on terror, was $3 billion. Criticism of the care provided by the VA and of the conditions in VA hospitals is a widening scandal.

The Congressional Budget Office estimated that the projected total war costs for all operations related to the Global War on Terror until 2017 to be between $1 trillion and $1.45 trillion. The lower

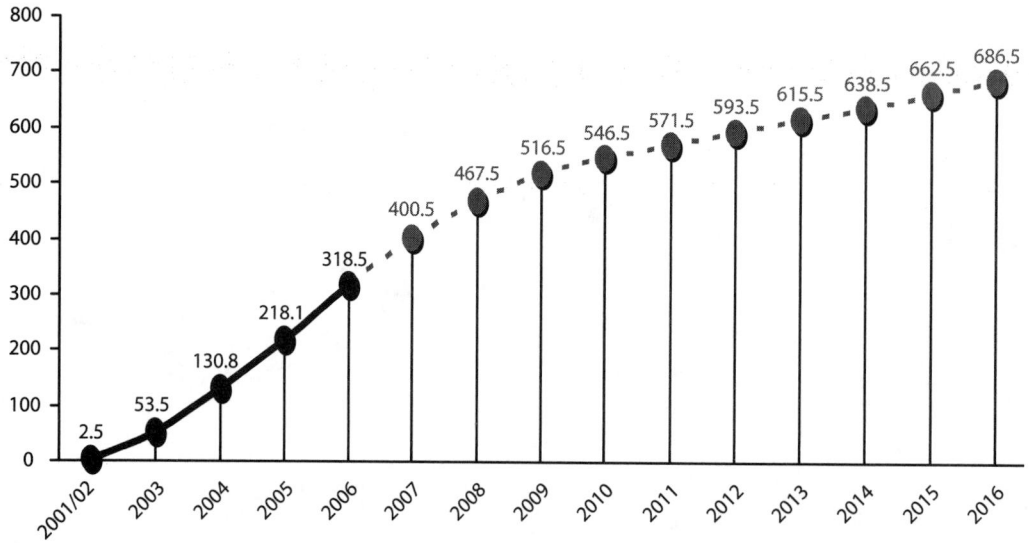

The Growing Cost of Iraq

All Costs in Billions
Sources: "Estimated Costs of U.S. Operations in Iraq Under Two Specified Scenarios," Congressional Budget Office, July 13, 2006; "The Cost of Iraq, Afghanistan, and Other Global War on Terror Operations Since 9/11," CRS RL33110. Prepared by the Office of Congressman John B. Larson (CT-1).

number is associated with an assumption that troop levels would fall to 30,000 by 2010; the higher number assumes a reduction in troop numbers to 75,000 by 2013.

Between September 30, 2001 and July 31, 2007 the U.S. debt rose from $5.8 trillion to $8.9 trillion.

Sources:

"As Democrats Collapse on Iraq, NYT/CBS Poll Finds Public More Antiwar than Ever." *Editor & Publisher* (May 25, 2007).

"The Harris Poll: Bush Regains Some Supporters on Handling of Iraq, Poll Shows; Online Edition." *Wall Street Journal* (Eastern Edition) New York, NY (May 22, 2007).

U.S. Congress, Congressional Budget Office. CBO Testimony: Statement of Robert A. Sunshine, Assistant Director for Budget Analysis, "Estimated Costs of U.S. Operations in Iraq and Afghanistan and Other Activities Related to the War on Terrorism" July 31, 2007. http://www.cbo.gov/ftpdocs/84xx/doc8497/07-30-WarCosts_Testimony.pdf

U.S. Library of Congress, Congressional Research Service. CRS Report for Congress: The Cost of Iraq, Afghanistan, and Other Global War on Terror Operations Since 9/11, Updated July 16, 2007. http://fpc.state.gov/documents/organization/89927.pdf

U.S. Treasury. Debt Position and Activity Report. http://www.treasurydirect.gov/govt/reports/pd/pd_debtposactrpt.htm

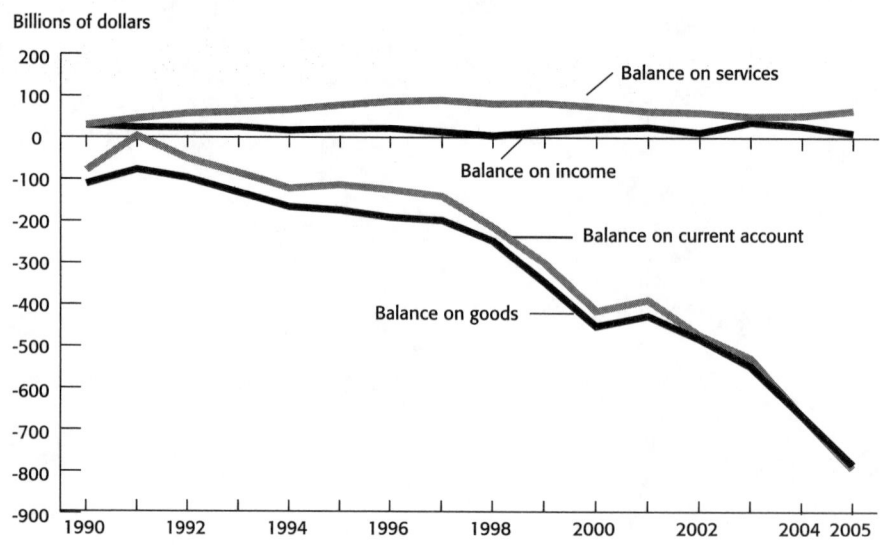

Billions of dollars

U.S. International Transaction Balances: 1990 to 2005
Source: Chart prepared by U.S. Census Bureau.

CHAPTER **28**

International Transactions and Foreign Commerce

HIGHLIGHTS

1 The first edition of the *Statistical Abstract of the United States,* published in 1879, was almost wholly devoted to foreign trade and shipping. Data on imports of gold, silver coins, and bullion took up 11 of its 154 pages and nearly 100 pages were devoted to imports and exports. The section on exports showed that the major U.S. exports were raw cotton and wheat, which together accounted for 38 percent of all exports. In the early years of the republic, international trade and transactions loomed large in the public economy and received considerable attention from statisticians, because at that time the United States was more heavily dependent on foreign markets than it has been in the twentieth century. Records of foreign trade have been kept by the Treasury Department since August 1, 1789 (in a more or less complete fashion), although they do not show the value of commerce with each country. However, Edward Ely, author of *International Trade Statistics,* observes that the United States may be said to have an adequate set of import and export statistics only since about 1821. No information was compiled on the amounts of articles that were imported free of duty or on imports subject to specific rates of duty. The total dollar value of imports from 1795 to 1801 was apparently estimated by the Secretary of the Treasury, and the figures for 1790 to 1794 and from 1802 to 1820 were apparently estimated many years later. The adequacy of these early records, of course, depends on the use made of them. Some of the earliest

records were not published officially, and scholars have had to rely on other sources, particularly, *A View of the United States of America* by Tench Coxe, *A Statistical Manual of the United States of America* by Samuel Blodgett Jr., *A Statistical View of Commerce of the United States of America* by Timothy Pitkin, and the *History of Domestic and Foreign Commerce of the United States* by Emory Johnson.

2 Foreign trade data are subject to a variety of special statistical problems. The record of gold movements, in particular, has been subject to considerable error because of smuggling. The Civil War introduced two special difficulties. Because the ports of the Southern States stopped furnishing reports to the Treasury in 1861, exports of cotton are based on estimates derived from records of recipient countries. A second difficulty was introduced in 1862 when the United States abandoned its specie backing (dollars of a fixed parity to gold) for money. The dollar fluctuated against foreign currencies and gold with each reverse or success of the Northern forces. While exports or re-exports continued to be valued in specie, domestic exports were recorded in mixed values from 1862 until the resumption of specie payment in 1879. A third problem affecting the comparability of trade statistics arose between 1934 and 1953, when the foreign exchange value of the dollar was allowed to depreciate as a result of the restriction placed on gold shipments to foreign countries.

World War II introduced such complications as Lend-Lease, surplus property disposal after the war, and economic and military aid.

3 In 1820, Congress established the Division of Commerce and Navigation in the Register of the Treasury. Collectors of Customs were required to compile and transmit annual reports to that office on trade and navigation with foreign countries. Beginning in 1821, these reports were consolidated and published annually in *Commerce and Navigation of the United States.* In 1866, Congress established the Bureau of Statistics and charged it with the collection of data on all articles imported, exported or re-exported classified by countries of destination. Since 1866, monthly trade statistics have been published in addition to annual data.

4 Balance of international payments data for the period from 1790 to 1918 are derived basically from private authors. They illustrate U.S. foreign relations, territorial expansion, immigration and the cost of wars and the Civil War. For example, $600,000 was paid between 1794 and 1796 to the Barbary pirates; $11.2 million was paid to France in 1803 for the Louisiana Purchase; $15 million was given to Mexico between 1849 and 1852 for territory now constituting Arizona, New Mexico, California, Nevada, Utah, and Colorado; $10 million was paid to Mexico between 1854 and 1856 for the Gadsden Purchase; $7.1 million was given to Russia in 1869 for Alaska; and $20 million was paid to Spain in 1898 for the Philippines, Guam, and Puerto Rico. Similarly, the United States received $5.5 million from France between 1836 and 1838 as indemnity for losses suffered during the Napoleonic Wars, as well as $15.5 million from Great Britain for losses suffered from British privateers during the Civil War. After World War II, the United States became a grantor, providing extensive grants and credits to its allies in the Cold War. Data for foreign aid programs are presented by the Agency for International Development.

5 Exports and imports constitute the backbone of foreign trade. The Bureau of the Census compiles export data primarily from the Shippers' Export Declarations that are required to be filed with customs officials for shipments leaving the United States. Import data are compiled from various required customs forms as well. The data suffer from serious under-reporting because of the exclusion of low-valued shipments exported and imported. For exports, the minimum is $2,500 and for imports it is $1,250. Data for shipments below these limits are estimated, and such estimates may have a wide margin of error. Low value shipments are believed to represent less than 2.5 percent of U.S. exports and 4 percent of U.S. imports. Since 1982, import prices have been based on customs values and export prices on f.a.s. (free alongside ship) values at the U.S. port of export.

6 Since 1983, foreign assets in the United States have exceeded U.S. assets abroad by a considerable margin. In 2005, foreign assets in the United States exceeded $13 trillion, and U.S. assets abroad were $11.079 trillion at market value. Similarly, the United States runs a deficit on current accounts in international transactions with exports worth $1.750 trillion and imports of $2.455 trillion. Generally, the United States has a negative balance in transactions with almost all countries and areas. Among the exceptions are Belgium-Luxembourg and the Netherlands.

7 Foreign direct investment in the United States rose from $394.911 billion in 1990 to $1.257 trillion in 2000 and $1.635 trillion in 2005. The United Kingdom is the largest single direct investor in the United States with $282.457 billion, followed by Japan ($190.279 billion), Germany ($184.213 billion), Netherlands ($170.770 billion), France ($143.378 billion), Switzerland ($122.399 billion), and Luxembourg ($116.736 billion).

8 Of U.S. direct foreign investment of $2.070 trillion in 2005, Europe accounted for over 51 percent. Latin America accounted for 17.1 percent, Africa for 1.2 percent, and Asia and the Pacific for 18.2 percent.

9 Between 1990 and 2005, the United States extended over $232 billion as grants and credits to foreign countries. Grants and credits to Western Europe, the Western hemisphere and the Pacific have tapered off since the 1980s, while those to Eastern Europe, Near East and South Asia, and Africa increased. In 2005, grants and credits to Western Europe were $139 million, Eastern Europe –$193 million, Near East and South Asia $20.158 billion, Africa $1.970 billion, Far East and Pacific –$18 million, and Western Hemisphere $1.392 billion.

10 Total economic and military aid in 2004 totaled $33.405 billion, of which economic aid accounted for $26.613 billion and military aid for $6.791 billion.

11 Iraq receives the most military and economic aid from the United States. In 2004, military aid totaled $6.421 billion and economic aid $1.842 billion. Israel also received heavy military and economic assistance: $2.147 billion for the former and $555 for the latter. Iraq received 27.1 percent of all military assistance and 24.1 percent of all economic assistance granted by the United States.

12 The United States has always maintained a healthy balance in services, unlike in merchandise trade. In 2004, it had a balance of $54.114 billion in services. For manufactured goods, it had a deficit of $464.4 billion and for mineral fuels it had a deficit of $187.6 billion.

13 Texas leads all states in exports with $128.761 billion, followed by California ($116.819 billion), New York ($50.492 billon), Washington ($37.948 billion), Michigan ($37.584 billion), Illinois ($35.868 billion), Ohio ($34.801 billion), Florida ($33.377 billion), Pennsylvania ($22.271 billion), and Massachusetts ($22.043 billion).

14 California leads with agricultural exports with $10.168 billion, followed by Iowa ($4.017 billion), Texas ($3.526 billion), Illinois ($3.282 billion), Minnesota ($2.869 billion), and Nebraska ($2.825 billion).

15 United States has a negative merchandise trade balance of $767.477 billion in 2005. The worst balance was with China ($201.545 billion) followed by Japan ($82.519 bullion), and Canada ($78.486 billion). The highest positive balance was with the Netherlands at $11.623 billion.

Table 28-1. U.S. Exports and Imports of Goods and Services and Income Receipts and Payments, 1960–2006

(Millions of dollars.)

Year	Exports of goods and services and income receipts				Imports of goods and services and income payments			
	Total	Goods balance of payments basis[1]	Travel	Income receipts on U.S.-owned assets abroad	Total	Goods, balance of payments basis[1]	Direct defense expenditures	Income payments on foreign-owned assets in the U.S.
2006ᴾ	2 058 836	1 023 689	85 697	619 085	−2 831 369	−1 859 655	−31 180	−619 862
2005	1 749 892	894 631	81 680	471 722	−2 455 328	−1 677 371	−30 062	−454 124
2004	1 526 855	807 516	74 547	372 035	−2 110 559	−1 472 926	−29 299	−338 400
2003	1 319 158	713 415	64 348	300 249	−1 777 462	−1 260 717	−25 296	−257 957
2002	1 245 373	682 422	66 605	267 841	−1 654 232	−1 164 720	−19 101	−250 063
2001	1 293 147	718 712	71 893	285 372	−1 630 811	−1 145 900	−14 835	−255 034
2000	1 421 515	771 994	82 400	348 083	−1 778 020	−1 224 408	−13 473	−322 345
1999	1 259 809	683 965	74 801	291 177	−1 509 207	−1 029 980	−13 335	−272 082
1998	1 194 993	670 416	71 325	259 382	−1 355 334	−917 103	−12 185	−250 560
1997	1 191 257	678 366	73 426	254 534	−1 286 597	−876 470	−11 707	−237 529
1996	1 077 731	612 113	69 809	223 948	−1 159 478	−803 113	−11 061	−197 511
1995	1 004 631	575 204	63 395	208 065	−1 080 124	−749 374	−10 043	−183 090
1994	869 775	502 859	58 417	164 578	−951 122	−668 690	−10 217	−143 423
1993	778 921	456 943	57 875	134 237	−823 914	−589 394	−12 087	−105 609
1992	750 648	439 631	54 742	131 971	−765 626	−536 528	−13 835	−104 780
1991	727 557	414 083	48 385	147 924	−734 564	−491 020	−16 409	−121 059
1990	706 975	387 401	43 007	170 570	−759 290	−498 438	−17 531	−139 728
1989	648 290	359 916	36 205	160 270	−721 607	−477 665	−15 313	−139 177
1988	567 862	320 230	29 434	135 718	−663 741	−447 189	−15 604	−116 179
1987	457 053	250 208	23 563	107 190	−594 443	−409 765	−14 950	−91 553
1986	407 098	223 344	20 385	96 156	−530 142	−368 425	−13 730	−78 893
1985	387 612	215 915	17 762	98 542	−483 769	−338 088	−13 108	−72 819
1984	399 913	219 926	217 177	108 819	−473 923	−332 418	−12 516	−73 756
1983	356 106	201 799	10 947	90 000	−377 488	−268 901	−13 087	−53 614
1982	366 983	211 157	12 393	91 747	−355 975	−247 642	−12 460	−56 583
1981	380 928	237 044	12 913	86 529	−364 196	−265 067	−11 564	−53 626
1980	344 440	224 250	10 588	72 606	−333 774	−249 750	−10 851	−42 532
1979	287 965	184 439	8 441	63 834	−281 657	−212 007	−8 294	−32 961
1978	220 516	142 075	7 183	42 088	−229 870	−176 002	−7 352	−21 680
1977	184 655	120 816	6 150	32 354	−193 764	−151 907	−5 823	−14 217
1976	172 090	114 745	5 742	29 375	−162 109	−124 228	−4 895	−13 311
1975	157 936	107 088	4 697	25 351	−132 745	−98 185	−4 795	−12 564
1974	148 484	98 306	4 032	27 587	−137 274	−103 811	−5 032	−12 084
1973	113 050	71 410	3 412	21 808	−98 997	−70 499	−4 629	−9 655
1972	81 986	49 381	2 817	14 765	−79 237	−55 797	−4 784	−6 572
1971	72 384	43 319	2 534	12 707	−66 414	−45 579	−4 819	−5 435
1970	68 387	42 469	2 331	11 748	−59 901	−39 866	−4 855	−5 515
1969	60 132	36 414	2 043	10 913	−53 998	−35 807	−4 856	−4 869
1968	54 911	33 626	1 775	9 367	−48 671	−32 991	−4 535	−3 378
1967	49 353	30 666	1 646	8 021	−41 476	−26 866	−4 378	−2 747
1966	46 454	29 310	1 590	7 528	−38 468	−25 493	−3 764	−2 481
1965	42 722	26 461	1 380	7 437	−32 708	−21 510	−2 952	−2 088
1964	40 165	25 501	1 207	6 824	−29 102	−18 700	−2 880	−1 783
1963	35 776	22 272	1 015	6 157	−26 970	−17 048	−2 961	−1 560
1962	33 340	20 781	957	5 618	−25 676	−16 260	−3 105	−1 324
1961	31 402	20 108	947	4 999	−23 453	−14 537	−2 998	−1 245
1960	30 556	19 650	919	4 616	−23 670	−14 758	−3 087	−1 238

Source: U.S. Bureau of Economic Analysis. *International Economic Accounts.*
[1]Excludes exports of goods under U.S. military agency sales contracts identified in Census export documents, excludes imports of goods under direct defense expenditures identified in Census import documents, and reflects various other adjustments (for valuation, coverage, and timing) of Census statistics to balance of payments basis.
[2]Break in series. The Bureau of Economic Analysis (BEA), in an effort to address gaps in the coverage of transactions and in response to a number of suggestions by working groups at the International Monetary Fund (IMF) and the National Academy of Sciences, greatly expanded the use of counterpart data. Because these counterpart data are much more comprehensive in coverage than the U.S. source data, they have been substituted into the U.S. accounts.
P = Preliminary.

Table 28-2. International Investment Position of the United States, 1843–2005

(Billions of dollars.)

| Year | U.S.-owned assets abroad[1] | | | Total foreign-owned assets in U.S.[1] |
	Total[2]	Private	U.S. government[2]	
2005[P]	10 009	9 743	266	12 702
2004[R]	9 187	8 914	273	11 547
2003[R]	7 649	7 381	268	9 780
2002[R]	6 652	6 408	244	8 740
2001	6 309	6 093	216	8 228
2000	6 239	6 025	214	7 620
1999	5 974	5 754	221	6 741
1998	5 096	4 863	233	5 991
1997	4 568	4 347	221	5 389
1996	4 032	3 785	247	4 527
1995	3 486	3 225	261	3 945
1994	2 987	2 740	247	3 311
1993	2 754	2 505	248	3 061
1992	2 332	2 101	230	2 763
1991	2 286	2 046	241	2 596
1990	2 179	1 920	259	2 424
1989	2 071	1 816	255	2 330
1988	1 830	1 598	232	2 008
1987	1 647	1 393	253	1 727
1986	1 469	1 238	232	1 506
1985	1 287	1 080	208	1 233
1984	1 205	1 013	192	1 044
1983	1 211	1 006	205	913
1982	1 108	888	220	779
1981	1 002	806	195	662
1980	930	693	237	569
1979	787	585	202	470
1978	621	499	123	415
1977	512	410	102	341
1976[3]	457	368	89.0	292
1976[4]	347	282	46.0	264
1975	295	237	41.8	221
1974	256	202	38.3	197
1973	226	165	38.8	163
1972	201	146	36.1	149
1971	181	130	34.2	123
1970	167	120	46.7	97.7
1969	158	110	47.7	90.8
1968	147	102	44.3	81.2
1967	135	93.6	41.1	69.7
1966	125	86.4	38.8	60.4
1965	120	81.5	38.8	58.8
1964	115	75.9	38.8	56.9
1963	104	66.6	37.4	51.5
1962	96.5	60.1	36.4	46.3
1961	92.0	55.6	36.4	46.0
1960	85.6	49.3	36.3	40.9
1959	82.2	44.8	37.4	39.1
1958	79.2	41.1	38.1	34.4
1957	76.4	36.9	39.5	30.7
1956	70.8	33.4	37.4	30.5
1955	65.1	29.1	35.9	27.8
1954	62.4	26.6	35.8	25.0
1953	60.2	23.8	36.4	21.9
1952	59.1	22.7	36.4	20.8
1951	56.4	20.8	35.6	18.7
1950	54.4	19.0	35.4	17.6
1949	53.9	16.9	37.0	14.8
1948	52.5	16.3	36.2	14.4
1947	48.3	14.9	33.4	13.8
1946	39.4	13.5	25.9	15.2
1945	36.9	14.7	22.2	17.0
1940	34.3	12.2	22.1	13.5
1935	23.6	13.5	10.1	6.4
1931	20.1	15.9	4.2	3.8
1930	21.5	17.2	4.3	8.4
1927	17.9	13.8	4.1	6.6
1924	15.1	10.9	4.2	3.9
1919	9.7	7.0	2.7	3.3
1914 (June 30)	5.0	3.5	1.5	7.2
1908	2.5	2.5	...	6.4
1897	0.7	0.7	...	3.4
1869	0.1	0.1	...	1.5
1843	...	...	...	0.2

Source: Bureau of Economic Analysis.
[1]From 1976 to the present, direct investment is valued at current (i.e., replacement) cost. Previously, it was valued at book value (historical cost).
[2]Beginning 1914, includes U.S. monetary gold stock.
[3]Comparable with later years.
[4]Comparable with earlier years.
. . . = Not available.
P = Preliminary.
R = Revised data.

Table 28-3. Value of Direct Investment in Foreign Countries, 1929–2005

(Millions of dollars. Historical cost basis.)

Year	Total, all areas	Canada	Latin America and other Western Hemisphere	Western Europe[1]
2005	2 069 983	234 831	353 011	1 048 582
2004	2 051 204	212 829	330 468	1 092 882
2003	1 769 613	187 953	297 222	965 999
2002	1 616 548	166 473	289 413	849 447
2001	1 460 352	152 601	279 611	762 684
2000	1 316 247	132 472	266 576	687 320
1999	1 215 960	119 590	253 928	627 754
1998	1 000 703	98 200	196 755	518 433
1997	871 316	96 626	180 818	425 139
1996	795 195	89 592	155 925	389 378
1995	699 015	83 498	131 377	344 596
1994	612 893	74 221	116 478	297 133
1993	564 283	69 922	59 302	285 735
1992	502 063	68 690	54 339	248 744
1991	467 844	70 711	48 546	235 163
1990	421 494	68 431	72 467	214 739
1989	370 091	65 548	62 727	175 213
1988	335 893	62 656	53 506	157 077
1987	314 307	57 783	47 551	150 439
1986	259 582	49 994	34 790	122 165
1985	230 250	46 909	28 261	105 171
1984	211 480	46 730	24 627	91 589
1983	207 203	44 339	24 133	92 178
1982	221 343	44 509	31 175	99 877
1981	226 359	45 129	30 020	101 514
1980	215 375	45 119	38 761	96 287
1979	187 658	40 662	22 792	85 056
1978	167 804	37 071	21 467	69 553
1977	149 848	35 200	18 882	60 930
1976	136 809	33 838	17 125	55 139
1975	124 050	31 038	16 394	49 305
1974	118 819	28 404	14 597	44 782
1973	103 675	25 541	13 527	38 255
1972	94 337	25 771	13 667	30 817
1971	86 198	24 105	12 982	27 740
1970	78 178	22 790	12 252	24 516
1969	71 016	21 127	11 694	21 650
1968	64 983	19 535	11 033	19 407
1967	59 491	18 102	10 270	17 926
1966	54 799	17 017	9 876	16 234
1965	49 474	15 318	9 441	13 985
1964	44 480	13 855	8 742	12 129
1963	40 736	13 044	8 712	10 340
1962	37 276	12 133	8 474	8 930
1961	34 717	11 602	8 286	7 742
1960	31 865	11 197	7 481	6 691
1959	29 827	10 310	8 120	5 323
1958	27 409	9 470	7 773	4 573
1957	25 394	8 769	7 434	4 151
1956	22 505	7 795	6 844	3 561
1955	19 395	6 761	6 031	3 002
1954	17 631	6 043	5 741	2 643
1953	16 253	5 349	5 589	2 375
1952	14 721	4 641	5 355	2 153
1951	12 979	3 969	4 818	1 989
1950	11 788	3 579	4 445	1 733
1940	7 000	2 103	2 771	1 420
1936	6 691	1 952	2 847	1 245
1929	7 528	2 010	3 519	1 353

Source: Bureau of Economic Analysis.
[1]Western Europe includes Eastern Europe for 1929, 1936, and 1940 but excludes Turkey for 1936 and 1940.

Table 28-4. Value of Foreign Direct Investment in the United States, by Area and Industry (SIC and NAICS Basis), 1937–2005

(Millions of dollars. Historical cost basis.)

Year	All areas				Canada			
	Total[1]	Petroleum	Manufacturing	Finance and Insurance[2]	Total[1]	Petroleum	Manufacturing	Finance and insurance[2]
NAICS Basis								
2005	1 635 291	128 879	538 122	207 552	144 033	...	30 588	43 735
2004	1 520 729	125 980	485 659	193 743	125 503	...	25 633	39 214
2003	1 395 159	106 753	465 401	182 951	95 707	...	23 419	23 584
2002	1 327 170	119 263	451 985	162 817	92 529	...	21 566	28 584
2001	1 355 114	102 743	484 042	174 109	102 127	...	26 854	25 289
2000	1 256 867	85 713	480 561	167 007	114 309	...	46 504	19 904
1999	955 726	50 550	406 415	132 203	90 559	2 399	29 524	16 982
1998	778 418	48 469	344 564	111 924	72 696	...	25 621	15 434
1997	681 842	40 674	278 431	103 683	65 175	...	24 830	12 576
SIC Basis								
1996	598 021	43 483	245 662	124 919	54 836	3 220	23 096	13 384
1995	535 553	34 907	214 504	119 333	45 618	3 240	20 320	10 900
1994	480 667	32 290	189 459	91 099	41 219	3 097	17 439	8 364
1993	467 412	32 214	168 147	74 733	40 373	2 455	15 303	8 168
1992	423 131	34 746	160 360	48 780	37 515	2 443	15 598	7 235
1991	419 108	40 051	157 115	44 748	36 834	2 468	15 716	7 354
1990	394 911	42 882	152 805	58 437	29 544	1 417	9 327	7 325
1989	368 924	40 345	150 949	58 215	30 370	1 233	9 934	7 227
1988	314 754	36 006	122 582	44 010	26 566	1 181	9 730	5 769
1987	263 394	37 815	93 865	39 455	24 684	1 088	8 085	5 797
1986	220 414	29 094	71 963	34 978	20 318	1 432	6 108	4 283
1985	184 615	28 270	59 584	27 429	17 131	1 589	4 607	4 008
1984	164 583	25 400	51 802	24 881	15 286	1 544	4 115	3 245
1983	137 061	18 209	47 665	10 934	11 434	1 391	3 313	1 061
1982	124 677	17 660	44 065	17 933	11 708	1 550	3 500	1 801
1981	90 421	18 005	29 976	12 574	9 883	1 387	3 519	818
1980	83 046	12 200	32 993	12 027	12 162	1 817	5 227	1 612
1979	54 462	9 906	20 876	7 575	7 154	943	3 615	505
1978	42 471	7 762	17 202	5 231	6 180	723	3 213	397
1977	34 595	6 573	14 030	4 544	5 650	710	3 077	367
1976	30 770	5 921	12 620	2 943	5 907	676	3 386	422
1975	27 662	6 213	11 386	3 152	5 352	596	3 061	341
1974	22 421	5 979	10 685	2 864	4 930	468	2 966	342
1973	18 284	4 649	8 559	2 854	4 044	296	2 430	320
1972	14 868	3 272	7 262	2 911	3 466	243	2 201	353
1971	13 914	3 139	6 722	2 553	3 335	207	2 013	330
1970	13 270	2 992	6 140	2 256	3 117	190	1 836	324
1969	11 818	2 493	5 344	2 189	2 834	132	1 644	352
1968	10 815	2 261	4 475	2 305	2 659	100	1 413	376
1967	9 923	1 885	4 181	2 193	2 575	99	1 397	354
1966	9 054	1 740	3 789	2 072	2 439	98	1 342	386
1965	8 797	1 710	3 478	2 169	2 388	208	1 219	370
1964	8 363	1 621	3 213	2 181	2 284	205	1 129	382
1963	7 944	1 513	3 018	2 045	2 183	213	1 063	337
1962	7 612	1 419	2 885	1 943	2 064	212	1 015	269
1961	7 392	1 325	2 754	2 025	1 989	194	975	274
1960	6 910	1 238	2 611	1 810	1 934	203	932	246
1959	6 604	1 184	2 471	1 734	1 896	207	907	227
1958	6 115	1 099	2 232	1 660	1 835	214	863	222
1957	5 710	1 043	2 083	1 496	1 773	211	816	208
1956	5 459	937	1 940	1 534	1 690	200	775	196
1955	5 076	853	1 759	1 499	1 542	196	711	179
1954	4 633	776	1 582	1 371	1 427	192	651	168
1953	4 251	706	1 451	1 219	1 350	168	611	162
1952	3 945	552	1 377	1 170	1 218	90	592	149
1951	3 658	466	1 274	1 105	1 119	62	525	150
1950	3 391	405	1 138	1 065	1 029	56	468	153
1941	2 312	222	714	521	530	...	...	...
1937	1 882	283	729	412	463	...	...	...

[1]Includes industries not shown separately: mining and smelting, transportation and utilities, trade and miscellaneous.
[2]Does not include depository institutions.
. . . = Not available.

Table 28-4. Value of Foreign Direct Investment in the United States, by Area and Industry (SIC and NAICS Basis), 1937–2005—*Continued*

(Millions of dollars. Historical cost basis.)

Year	Europe				United Kingdom			
	Total[1]	Petroleum	Manufacturing	Finance and insurance[2]	Total[1]	Petroleum	Manufacturing	Finance and insurance[2]
NAICS Basis								
2005	1 143 614	...	414 852	130 356	282 457	...	76 792	(D)
2004	1 066 908	...	372 484	119 341	251 422	...	61 678	(D)
2003	1 001 237	...	361 789	127 471	217 841	...	57 969	28 675
2002	958 330	...	356 341	105 808	211 699	...	63 575	8 795
2001	1 005 606	...	391 570	121 091	269 321	...	72 809	5 126
2000	887 014	...	363 494	117 671	277 613	...	81 602	12 163
1999	639 923	46 689	306 565	90 151	153 797	32 189	84 636	10 038
1998	518 576	...	265 376	76 472	137 489	...	80 350	13 394
1997	428 721	...	205 461	65 343	129 421	...	68 249	16 261
SIC Basis								
1996	370 843	29 194	176 309	71 960	121 582	11 060	58 675	21 021
1995	332 374	24 039	156 543	67 908	116 272	9 275	56 703	21 821
1994	294 035	23 947	138 751	53 074	98 732	9 489	47 334	14 615
1993	285 004	29 396	124 454	46 895	98 739	9 963	42 783	19 927
1992	249 904	29 167	115 215	28 550	86 587	11 080	40 818	12 436
1991	256 053	31 436	114 248	27 715	100 085	14 068	41 924	13 391
1990	247 320	31 197	125 568	30 329	98 676	15 310	52 955	13 139
1989	239 190	32 476	120 132	31 609	103 458	16 545	51 798	11 859
1988	208 942	33 499	95 641	27 121	95 698	19 522	41 708	11 256
1987	181 006	35 700	74 300	26 336	75 519	17 950	30 372	9 801
1986	144 181	26 139	56 016	21 787	55 935	11 758	16 500	10 163
1985	121 413	25 636	45 841	17 022	43 555	12 155	11 687	6 483
1984	108 211	23 142	39 083	15 945	38 387	10 991	9 179	5 485
1983	92 936	16 326	36 866	8 450	32 152	5 955	9 221	3 777
1982	83 193	15 071	33 032	12 601	28 447	5 444	8 504	5 661
1981	60 510	14 937	21 995	8 841	15 576	-165	6 109	4 330
1980	54 688	10 137	21 953	8 673	14 105	-257	6 159	3 350
1979	37 403	8 010	13 952	5 529	9 796	199	3 547	2 432
1978	29 180	6 569	11 717	3 575	7 638	492	3 014	1 596
1977	23 754	5 523	9 267	3 076	6 397	486	2 305	1 425
1976	20 162	4 999	7 426	2 637	5 802	602	1 963	1 211
1975	18 584	5 478	6 673	2 088	6 331	...	1 833	932
1974	14 627	3 871	7 143	2 181	6 188	1 650	2 476	1 363
1973	12 504	3 438	5 828	2 261	5 649	1 377	2 250	1 506
1972	11 087	3 011	4 836	2 335	4 987	1 297	1 719	1 567
1971	10 336	2 893	4 455	2 047	4 853	1 270	1 615	1 326
1970	9 554	2 777	4 091	1 805	4 127	1 220	1 391	1 141
1969	8 510	2 322	3 530	1 766	3 496	829	1 176	1 143
1968	7 750	2 146	2 941	1 855	3 409	749	1 076	1 239
1967	7 005	1 772	2 669	1 758	3 156	612	1 009	1 189
1966	6 273	1 620	2 335	1 611	2 864	558	906	1 075
1965	6 076	1 481	2 167	1 724	2 852	511	839	1 176
1964	5 819	1 404	2 005	1 723	2 796	498	812	1 154
1963	5 491	1 306	1 881	1 640	2 665	480	779	1 085
1962	5 245	1 203	1 797	1 611	2 474	416	762	1 023
1961	5 129	1 125	1 708	1 690	2 484	381	750	1 091
1960	4 707	1 028	1 611	1 504	2 248	339	722	953
1959	4 452	972	1 501	1 451	2 167	316	698	927
1958	4 070	885	1 332	1 384	2 024	283	640	889
1957	3 753	832	1 248	1 238	1 881	271	611	794
1956	3 598	737	1 155	1 289	1 833	227	566	841
1955	3 369	657	1 040	1 272	1 749	204	510	836
1954	3 049	584	925	1 158	1 590	180	460	751
1953	2 751	538	836	1 014	1 422	163	419	647
1952	2 575	462	782	977	1 345	137	395	626
1951	2 410	404	747	912	1 273	118	388	583
1950	2 228	349	669	870	1 168	95	337	554
1941	1 569	...	...	...	712	...	...	...
1937	1 337	...	...	...	833	...	...	...

Source: Bureau of Economic Analysis.
[1]Includes industries not shown separately: mining and smelting, transportation and utilities, trade and miscellaneous.
[2]Does not include depository institutions.
. . . = Not available.
D = Suppressed to avoid disclosure of data of individual companies.

Table 28-5. Value of Exports and Imports, 1790–2005

(Millions of dollars.)

Year	Merchandise[1]		Total general imports	Excess of exports (+) or imports (–)
	Exports and re-export			
	Total	Exports of U.S. merchandise		
2005	905 978	804 853	1 673 455	–767 477
2004	818 775	729 113	1 469 704	–650 929
2003	724 006	651 687	1 259 705	–535 699
2002	693 103	629 311	1 161 366	–468 263
2001	729 100	664 320	1 140 999	–411 899
2000	781 918	713 715	1 218 022	–436 104
1999	695 797	644 828	1 024 618	–328 821
1998	682 138	636 455	911 896	–229 758
1997	689 182	645 029	870 671	–181 489
1996	624 767	584 077	791 364	–166 597
1995	584 742	548 161	743 445	–158 703
1994	512 626	482 645	663 256	–150 630
1993	465 091	439 847	580 659	–115 568
1992	448 164	425 737	532 665	–84 501
1991	421 730	401 109	487 129	–65 399
1990	393 592	375 076	495 311	–101 718
1989	363 800	349 400	473 400	–109 600
1988	322 400	310 000	441 000	–118 600
1987	254 100	243 900	406 200	–152 100
1986	217 300	206 400	370 000	–152 700
1985	213 100	206 900	345 300	–132 100
1984	217 900	212 100	325 700	–107 900
1983	200 500	196 000	258 000	–57 500
1982	212 300	207 100	244 000	–31 800
1981	233 700	228 900	261 000	–27 300
1980	220 600	216 500	244 900	–24 200
1979	181 900	178 600	209 500	–27 600
1978	143 700	141 000	174 800	–31 100
1977	121 200	118 900	150 400	–29 200
1976	115 200	113 500	123 500	–8 300
1975	107 700	106 100	98 500	9 100
1974	98 100	96 500	102 600	–4 500
1973	70 800	69 700	69 500	1 300
1972	49 200	48 400	55 600	–6 400
1971	43 500	42 900	45 600	–2 000
1970	43 224	42 590	39 952	3 272
1969	38 006	37 462	36 043	1 964
1968	34 636	34 199	33 226	1 410
1967	31 526	31 142	26 812	4 714
1966	30 320	29 884	25 542	4 777
1965	27 470	27 127	21 364	6 105
1964	26 508	26 156	18 684	7 824
1963	23 347	23 062	17 138	6 209
1962	21 700	21 431	16 380	5 320
1961	20 999	20 755	14 714	6 286
1960	20 575	20 375	14 654	5 922
1959	17 634	17 451	15 207	2 427
1958	17 910	17 745	12 792	5 118
1957	20 850	20 671	12 982	7 868
1956	19 090	18 940	12 615	6 475
1955	15 547	15 419	11 384	4 163
1954	15 110	14 981	10 215	4 894
1953	15 774	15 652	10 873	4 900
1952	15 201	15 049	10 717	4 483
1951	15 032	14 879	10 967	4 065
1950	10 275	10 142	8 852	1 423
1949	12 051	11 936	6 622	5 429
1948	12 653	12 532	7 124	5 529
1947	14 430	14 252	5 756	8 673
1946	9 738	9 500	4 942	4 796
1945	9 806	9 585	4 159	5 646
1944	14 259	14 162	3 929	10 330
1943	12 965	12 842	3 381	9 583
1942	8 079	8 003	2 756	5 323
1941	5 147	5 020	3 345	1 802

[1]Includes gold and silver prior to 1921. Beginning 1961, includes exports and imports of uranium, thorium and related products; beginning 1968, includes silver ore and bullion.

Table 28-5. Value of Exports and Imports, 1790—2005—*Continued*
(Millions of dollars.)

| | Merchandise[1] | | | |
| | Exports and re-export | | | |
Year	Total	Exports of U.S. merchandise	Total general imports	Excess of exports (+) or imports (−)
1940	4 021	3 934	2 625	1 396
1939	3 177	3 123	2 318	859
1938	3 094	3 057	1 960	1 134
1937	3 349	3 299	3 084	265
1936	2 456	2 419	2 423	33
1935	2 283	2 243	2 047	235
1934	2 133	2 100	1 655	478
1933	1 675	1 647	1 450	225
1932	1 611	1 576	1 323	288
1931	2 424	2 378	2 091	334
1930	3 843	3 781	3 061	782
1929	5 241	5 157	4 399	842
1928	5 128	5 030	4 091	1 037
1927	4 865	4 759	4 185	681
1926	4 809	4 712	4 431	378
1925	4 910	4 819	4 227	683
1924	4 591	4 498	3 610	981
1923	4 167	4 091	3 792	375
1922	3 832	3 765	3 113	719
1921	4 485	4 379	2 509	1 976
1920	8 228	8 080	5 278	2 950
1919	7 920	7 750	3 904	4 016
1918	6 149	6 048	3 031	3 118
1917	6 234	6 170	2 952	3 281
1916	5 483	5 423	2 392	3 091
1915	2 769	2 716	1 674	1 094
1914	2 365	2 330	1 894	471
1913	2 466	2 429	1 813	653
1912	2 204	2 170	1 653	551
1911	2 049	2 014	1 527	522
1910	1 745	1 710	1 557	188
1909	1 663	1 638	1 312	351
1908	1 861	1 835	1 194	666
1907	1 881	1 854	1 434	446
1906	1 744	1 718	1 227	517
1905	1 519	1 492	1 118	401
1904	1 461	1 435	991	470
1903	1 420	1 392	1 026	394
1902	1 382	1 355	903	478
1901	1 488	1 460	823	665
1900	1 394	1 371	850	545
1899	1 227	1 204	697	530
1898	1 231	1 210	616	615
1897	1 051	1 032	765	286
1896	883	863	780	103
1895	808	793	732	76
1894	892	869	655	237
1893	848	831	866	−19
1892	1 030	1 016	827	203
1891	884	872	845	40
1890	858	845	789	69
1889	742	730	745	−3
1888	696	684	724	−28
1887	716	703	692	24
1886	680	666	635	44
1885	742	727	578	165
1884	741	725	668	73
1883	824	804	723	101
1882	751	733	725	26
1881	902	884	643	260
1880	836	824	668	168
1879	710	698	446	265
1878	695	681	437	258
1877	602	590	451	151
1876	540	526	461	80
1875	513	499	533	−20
1874	596	569	567	19
1873	522	505	642	−120
1872	444	428	627	−182
1871	443	428	520	−77

[1]Includes gold and silver prior to 1921. Beginning 1961, includes exports and imports of uranium, thorium and related products; beginning 1968, includes silver ore and bullion.

Table 28-5. Value of Exports and Imports, 1790–2005—*Continued*

(Millions of dollars.)

| Year | Merchandise[1] | | Total general imports | Excess of exports (+) or imports (−) |
| | Exports and re-export | | | |
	Total	Exports of U.S. merchandise		
1870	393	377	436	−43
1869	286	275	418	−131
1868	282	269	357	−75
1867	295	290	396	−101
1866	349	338	435	−86
1865	166	137	239	−73
1864	159	144	316	−158
1863	204	186	243	−39
1862	191	180	189	1
1861	220	205	289	−70
1860	334	316	354	−20
1859	293	278	331	−38
1858	272	251	263	9
1857	294	279	348	−55
1856	281	166	310	−29
1855	219	193	258	−39
1854	237	215	298	−61
1853	203	190	264	−60
1852	167	155	207	−40
1851	189	179	211	−22
1850	144	135	174	−29
1849	140	132	141	−1
1848	138	130	149	−10
1847	157	151	122	34
1846	110	102	118	−8
1845	106	98	113	−7
1844	106	100	103	3
1843	83	78	42	40
1842	100	92	96	4
1841	112	104	123	−11
1840	124	112	98	25
1839	112	102	156	−44
1838	105	96	96	9
1837	111	94	130	−19
1836	124	107	177	−52
1835	115	100	137	−22
1834	102	81	109	−6
1833	88	70	101	−14
1832	82	62	95	−14
1831	72	59	96	−24
1830	72	59	63	9
1829	67	55	67	(Z)
1828	64	50	81	−17
1827	74	58	71	3
1826	73	52	78	−5
1825	91	67	90	1
1824	69	51	72	−3
1823	68	47	72	−4
1822	61	50	80	−19
1821	55	41	55	(Z)
1820	70	52	74	−5
1819	70	51	87	−17
1818	93	74	122	−28
1817	88	68	99	−12
1816	82	65	147	−65
1815	53	46	113	−60
1814	7	7	13	−6
1813	28	25	22	6
1812	39	30	77	−39
1811	61	45	53	8
1810	67	42	85	−19
1809	52	31	59	−7
1808	22	9	57	−35
1807	108	49	139	−30
1806	102	41	129	−28
1805	96	42	121	−25
1804	78	41	85	−7
1803	56	42	65	−9
1802	72	36	76	−4
1801	93	46	111	−18

[1]Includes gold and silver prior to 1921. Beginning 1961, includes exports and imports of uranium, thorium and related products; beginning 1968, includes silver ore and bullion.
Z = Less than $500,000 or less than −$500,000.

Table 28-5. Value of Exports and Imports, 1790–2005—*Continued*

(Millions of dollars.)

Year	Merchandise[1]		Total general imports	Excess of exports (+) or imports (−)
	Exports and re-export			
	Total	Exports of U.S. merchandise		
1800	71	32	91	−20
1799	79	33	79	(Z)
1798	61	28	69	−7
1797	51	24	75	−24
1796	59	32	81	−23
1795	48	40	70	−22
1794	33	27	35	−2
1793	26	24	31	−5
1792	21	19	32	−11
1791	19	19	29	−10
1790	20	. . .	23	−3

Source: U.S. Census Bureau.
[1]Includes gold and silver prior to 1921. Beginning 1961, includes exports and imports of uranium, thorium and related products; beginning 1968, includes silver ore and bullion.
. . . = Not available.
Z = Less than $500,000 or less than −$500,000.

Table 28-6. U.S. Foreign Economic and Military Aid Programs, 1970–2004

(Millions of dollars. Prior to 1977, for years ending June 30; beginning 1977, years ending September 30.)

Year and region	Total economic and military aid	Economic aid			Military aid		
		Total	Loans	Grants	Total	Loans	Grants
2004, total	33 405	26 613	216	26 397	6 791	0	6 791
Asia	3 587	2 865	81	2 783	722	0	722
Central Asia	1 942	1 893	18	1 875	49	0	49
Eastern Europe	715	551	0	551	163	0	163
Latin America and Caribbean	2 362	2 228	37	2 191	134	0	134
Middle East and North Africa	14 118	8 514	58	8 456	5 604	0	5 604
Oceania	146	145	0	145	1	0	1
Sub-Saharan Africa	3 975	3 911	22	3 888	64	0	64
Western Europe	66	25	0	25	41	0	41
World not specified	6 473	6 461	0	6 461	12	0	12
2003, total	27 312	20 807	245	20 562	6 506	0	6 506
Asia	2 786	2 130	134	1 997	655	0	655
Central Asia	1 606	1 557	0	1 557	49	0	49
Eastern Europe	819	600	0	600	219	0	219
Latin America and Caribbean	2 118	2 070	21	2 048	49	0	49
Middle East and North Africa	11 711	6 371	47	6 324	5 340	0	5 340
Oceania	175	174	0	174	1	0	1
Sub-Saharan Africa	3 313	3 197	43	3 154	117	0	117
Western Europe	1 087	1 060	0	1 060	27	0	27
World not specified	3 674	3 624	0	3 624	50	0	50
2002, total	20 689	16 166	187	15 979	4 522	0	4 522
Asia	2 899	2 439	121	2 318	461	0	461
Central Asia	1 580	1 421	20	1 401	159	0	159
Eastern Europe	910	753	0	753	157	0	157
Latin America and Caribbean	1 865	1 840	36	1 804	25	0	25
Middle East and North Africa	5 952	2 402	0	2 402	3 550	0	3 550
Oceania	190	189	0	189	1	0	1
Sub-Saharan Africa	2 148	2 045	10	2 035	104	0	104
Western Europe	278	226	0	226	52	0	52
World not specified	4 867	4 852	0	4 852	15	0	15
2001, total	16 740	12 986	268	12 718	3 754	0	3 754
Asia	1 487	1 464	127	1 337	23	0	23
Central Asia	1 356	1 333	46	1 287	24	0	24
Eastern Europe	1 055	875	15	860	180	0	180
Latin America and Caribbean	1 481	1 463	43	1 421	17	0	17
Middle East and North Africa	5 525	2 145	10	2 135	3 380	0	3 380
Oceania	165	164	0	164	1	0	1
Sub-Saharan Africa	2 066	1 959	28	1 931	107	0	107
Western Europe	78	72	0	72	5	0	5
World not specified	3 529	3 512	0	3 512	17	0	17
2000	16 092	11 474	244	11 229	4 619	0	4 619
1999	15 787	12 023	900	11 123	3 764	0	3 764
1998	14 469	10 827	335	10 492	3 642	100	3 542
1997	13 544	9 588	244	9 344	3 956	298	3 658
1996	14 201	9 898	393	9 505	4 303	544	3 759
1995	15 823	11 894	277	11 617	3 930	558	3 372
1994	16 705	12 355	978	11 377	4 350	770	3 581
1993	17 434	12 611	545	12 066	4 823	855	3 968
1992	16 181	11 564	494	11 070	4 617	345	4 272
1991	17 268	12 099	345	11 754	5 169	478	4 692
1990	16 056	11 044	748	10 296	5 012	404	4 608
1989	14 846	10 018	687	9 331	4 828	410	4 418
1988	13 965	9 135	693	8 442	4 831	763	4 068
1987	14 797	9 705	892	8 813	5 092	953	4 139
1986	16 620	10 796	890	9 907	5 824	1 980	3 844
1985	18 128	12 327	984	11 343	5 801	2 365	3 436
1984	15 524	9 038	784	8 255	6 485	4 401	2 084
1983	19 314	8 602	773	7 830	10 711	9 044	1 667
1982	12 316	8 122	690	7 432	4 195	3 084	1 111
1981	10 539	7 294	775	6 519	3 245	2 546	699
1980	9 694	7 572	843	6 729	2 122	1 450	672
1979	13 845	7 120	747	6 374	6 725	5 173	1 552
1978	9 014	6 661	767	5 893	2 353	1 601	752
1977	7 785	5 594	735	4 859	2 191	1 411	780
1976, TQ[1]	2 703	1 931	109	1 823	772	494	278
1976	6 412	3 878	902	2 976	2 534	1 441	1 093
1975	6 907	4 899	869	4 030	2 008	749	1 259
1974	8 504	3 906	631	3 275	4 598	1 389	3 209
1973	9 453	4 117	728	3 389	5 337	531	4 806
1972	9 019	3 941	1 077	2 864	5 078	548	4 531
1971	7 835	3 442	797	2 645	4 393	741	3 652
1970	6 568	3 676	714	2 962	2 892	70	2 822

Source: U.S. Census Bureau. *Statistical Abstract of the United States: 2007.* U.S. Agency for International Development.
Note: Economic aid shown here represents U.S. economic aid, not just aid under Foreign Assistance Act. Major components in recent years include USAID, Food for Peace, Peace Corps, and paid-in subscriptions to international financial institutions, such as the World Bank's International Bank for Reconstruction and Development (IBRD), and the Inter-American Development Bank (IDB). Data are gross unadjusted program figures. Military aid includes Military Assistance Program (MAP) grants, foreign military credit sales, service-funded programs, and excess defense articles.
[1]Fiscal years through 1976, ended June 30. Beginning with October 1976 (fiscal year 1977), fiscal years ended September 30. The period from July 1 through September 30, 1976 is a separate fiscal period known as the transition quarter (TQ) and is not included in any fiscal year.

Table 28-7. U.S. Government Foreign Grants and Credits by Region, 1995–2005

(Millions of dollars.)

Area	1995	1996	1997	1998	1999	2000	2001	2002	2003	2004	2005
Total, net	12 666	16 689	12 833	14 029	18 659	17 878	12 602	17 213	22 973	22 108	29 993
Investment in financial institutions	1 517	1 833	1 588	1 580	1 451	1 500	1 704	1 486	1 434	1 994	1 263
African Development Bank	0	0	0	0	0	4	6	5	5	5	4
African Development Fund	38	71	90	94	96	40	89	99	46	139	106
Asian Development Bank	62	137	184	195	210	173	180	171	166	282	156
Inter-American Development Bank	116	101	77	83	42	42	37	15	10	0	0
Special Facility For Sub-Saharan Africa	0	0	0	0	0	0	0	0	0	0	0
International Bank for Reconstruction and Development (IBRD)	24	26	13	0	0	0	0	0	0	0	0
IBRD - Global Environmental Fund	0	9	46	49	53	62	171	99	161	148	139
International Development Association	1 130	1 187	1 100	1 087	976	1 098	1 099	974	902	1 328	789
International Finance Corporation	48	65	36	0	0	0	0	0	0	0	0
International Monetary Fund - Enhanced Structural Adjustment Facility	19	19	26	24	22	17	9	0	0	0	0
Inter-American Investment Corporation	0	0	0	0	0	7	15	18	19	18	0
Multilateral Investment Guarantee Agency	0	0	0	0	0	1	13	5	2	1	0
European Bank for Reconstruction and Development	61	76	16	21	23	27	43	47	36	36	36
Enterprise for the Americas Investment Fund	18	30	0	23	30	29	40	53	87	37	33
North American Development Bank	2	112	0	6	0	0	0	0	0	0	0
Western Europe	177	185	390	317	431	183	220	104	345	152	139
Eastern Europe	1 979	1 957	1 410	1 790	2 152	1 830	1 300	1 464	1 291	1 186	−193
Near East and South Asia	3 025	7 666	4 675	5 045	4 378	7 658	2 520	5 656	10 024	11 791	20 158
Africa	2 217	1 957	1 354	1 366	841	1 042	1 562	2 015	2 822	2 157	1 970
Far East and Pacific	753	783	137	759	1 145	550	725	331	689	−193	−18
Western Hemisphere	485	511	663	1 033	5 120	1 173	1 380	710	676	1 294	1 392
Other international organizations and unspecified areas	2 513	1 798	2 616	2 138	3 141	3 942	3 191	5 447	5 692	3 727	5 282

Source: U.S. Census Bureau. *Statistical Abstract of the United States: 2007.* U.S. Bureau of Economic Analysis.
Note: Negative figures (−) occur when the total of grant returns, principal repayments, and/or foreign currencies disbursed by the U.S. Government exceeds new grants and new credits utilized and/or acquisitions of foreign currencies through new sales of farm products.

BOX 28 ■ U.S. Trade in Goods and Services

U.S. trade in goods and services has changed dramatically over the last forty years. Although imports and exports in both goods and services have steadily increased, imports of goods have surpassed exports and exports of services have surpassed imports. The year 2006 experienced a record overall deficit in the balance of trade of $758.5 billion, a deficit in balance of payment of goods of $838.3 billion, and a surplus of services of $79.7 billion.

In the mid-1980s, the U.S. trade deficit began to rise dramatically. The Congressional Budget Office postulated that the reasons behind this growth included the nation's decline in federal and personal savings since World War II and the rising strength of the dollar in the 1980s that made imports less expensive for the U.S. consumer, while simultaneously making U.S. exports more expensive—and therefore less desirable—abroad.

The U.S. deficit in the balance of payment in international trade in goods increased sharply again in 2000, a year when the U.S. economy was in a pattern of strong growth, with a tight labor market and a very strong dollar. This combination made U.S. exports less attractive. However, that same year saw an increase in petroleum imports, with a sharply higher price paid for those imports.

U.S. Trade in Goods and Services—Balance of Payments (BOP) Basis

Value in millions of dollars 1960 thru 2006

Period	Balance			Exports			Imports		
	Total	Goods BOP	Services	Total	Goods BOP	Services	Total	Goods BOP	Services
1960	3,508	4,892	−1,384	25,940	19,650	6,290	22,432	14,758	7,674
1961	4,195	5,571	−1,376	26,403	20,108	6,295	22,208	14,537	7,671
1962	3,370	4,521	−1,151	27,722	20,781	6,941	24,352	16,260	8,092
1963	4,210	5,224	−1,014	29,620	22,272	7,348	25,410	17,048	8,362
1964	6,022	6,801	−779	33,341	25,501	7,840	27,319	18,700	8,619
1965	4,664	4,951	−287	35,285	26,461	8,824	30,621	21,510	9,111
1966	2,939	3,817	−878	38,926	29,310	9,616	35,987	25,493	10,494
1967	2,604	3,800	−1,196	41,333	30,666	10,667	38,729	26,866	11,863
1968	250	635	−385	45,543	33,626	11,917	45,293	32,991	12,302
1969	91	607	−516	49,220	36,414	12,806	49,129	35,807	13,322
1970	2,254	2,603	−349	56,640	42,469	14,171	54,386	39,866	14,520
1971	−1,302	−2,260	958	59,677	43,319	16,358	60,979	45,579	15,400
1972	−5,443	−6,416	973	67,222	49,381	17,841	72,665	55,797	16,868
1973	1,900	911	989	91,242	71,410	19,832	89,342	70,499	18,843
1974	−4,293	−5,505	1,212	120,897	98,306	22,591	125,190	103,811	21,379
1975	12,404	8,903	3,501	132,585	107,088	25,497	120,181	98,185	21,996
1976	−6,082	−9,483	3,401	142,716	114,745	27,971	148,798	124,228	24,570
1977	−27,246	−31,091	3,845	152,301	120,816	31,485	179,547	151,907	27,640
1978	−29,763	−33,927	4,164	178,428	142,075	36,353	208,191	176,002	32,189
1979	−24,565	−27,568	3,003	224,131	184,439	39,692	248,696	212,007	36,689
1980	−19,407	−25,500	6,093	271,834	224,250	47,584	291,241	249,750	41,491
1981	−16,172	−28,023	11,851	294,398	237,044	57,354	310,570	265,067	45,503
1982	−24,156	−36,485	12,329	275,236	211,157	64,079	299,391	247,642	51,749
1983	−57,767	−67,102	9,335	266,106	201,799	64,307	323,874	268,901	54,973
1984	−109,072	−112,492	3,420	291,094	219,926	71,168	400,166	332,418	67,748
1985	−121,880	−122,173	294	289,070	215,915	73,155	410,950	338,088	72,862
1986	−138,538	−145,081	6,543	310,033	223,344	86,689	448,572	368,425	80,147
1987	−151,684	−159,557	7,874	348,869	250,208	98,661	500,552	409,765	90,787
1988	−114,566	−126,959	12,393	431,149	320,230	110,919	545,715	447,189	98,526
1989	−93,141	−117,749	24,607	487,003	359,916	127,087	580,144	477,665	102,479
1990	−80,864	−111,037	30,173	535,233	387,401	147,832	616,097	498,438	117,659
1991	−31,135	−76,937	45,802	578,344	414,083	164,261	609,479	491,020	118,459
1992	−39,212	−96,897	57,685	616,882	439,631	177,251	656,094	536,528	119,566
1993	−70,311	−132,451	62,141	642,863	456,943	185,920	713,174	589,394	123,780
1994	−98,493	−165,831	67,338	703,254	502,859	200,395	801,747	668,690	133,057
1995	−96,384	−174,170	77,786	794,387	575,204	219,183	890,771	749,374	141,397
1996	−104,065	−191,000	86,935	851,602	612,113	239,489	955,667	803,113	152,554
1997	−108,273	−198,428	90,155	934,453	678,366	256,087	1,042,726	876,794	165,932
1998	−166,140	−248,221	82,081	933,174	670,416	262,758	1,099,314	918,637	180,677
1999	−265,090	−347,819	82,729	965,884	683,965	281,919	1,230,974	1,031,784	199,190
2000	−379,835	−454,690	74,855	1,070,597	771,994	298,603	1,450,432	1,226,684	223,748
2001	−365,126	−429,519	64,393	1,004,896	718,712	286,184	1,370,022	1,148,231	221,791
2002	−423,725	−484,955	61,230	974,721	682,422	292,299	1,398,446	1,167,377	231,069
2003	−496,915	−550,892	53,977	1,017,757	713,415	304,342	1,514,672	1,264,307	250,365
2004	−612,092	−669,579	57,487	1,157,250	807,516	349,734	1,769,341	1,477,094	292,247
2005	−714,371	−787,149	72,778	1,283,070	894,631	388,439	1,997,441	1,681,780	315,661
2006	−758,522	−838,271	79,749	1,445,703	1,023,109	422,594	2,204,225	1,861,380	342,845

Source: U.S. Census Bureau, Foreign Trade Division.
Note: (1) Data presented on a Balance of Payment (BOP) basis. Information on data sources and methodology are available at www.census.gov/foreign-trade/www/press.html.

Then, the U.S. Congress granted China Permanent Normal Trading Relations or most-favored-nation trading status, which opened trade with China at lower tariff rates. Since then, the U.S. trade deficit with China is the largest of any country, reaching $232.6 billion in 200. However, since 2005, China has been the fourth largest export market for U.S. goods and services.

In 2007, a weaker dollar combined with rising interest rates began to make U.S. exports more attractive to foreign markets, but although the trade deficit began to ease in early 2007, analysts predict a continuation of the trend.

Sources:

"A Much Needed Victory." *The Economist (US)* 355.8172 (May 27, 2000): 27.

Field, Alan M. "Climbing the Ladder." *The Journal of Commerce* (June 4, 2007): 34.

Levy, Mickey. "Global Investor: Don't Count America Out." *Newsweek International* (July 2, 2007).

U.S. Census Bureau, Foreign Trade Division. Trade in Goods (Imports, Exports and Trade Balance) with China. http://www.census.gov/foreign-trade/balance/c5700.html#2006

U.S. Census Bureau, Foreign Trade Division. U.S. Trade in Goods and Services—Balance of Payments (BOP) Basis. June 8, 2007. http://www.census.gov/foreign-trade/statistics/historical/gands.pdf

U.S. Congress, Congressional Budget Office. CBO Memorandum: Causes and Consequences of the Trade Deficit: An Overview. March 2000.

U.S. Department of Commerce, Bureau of Economic Analysis. U.S. International Transactions Fourth Quarter and Year 2000 (Balance of Trade). *Survey of Current Business* 81.4 (April 2001): 21.

Politics and Defense

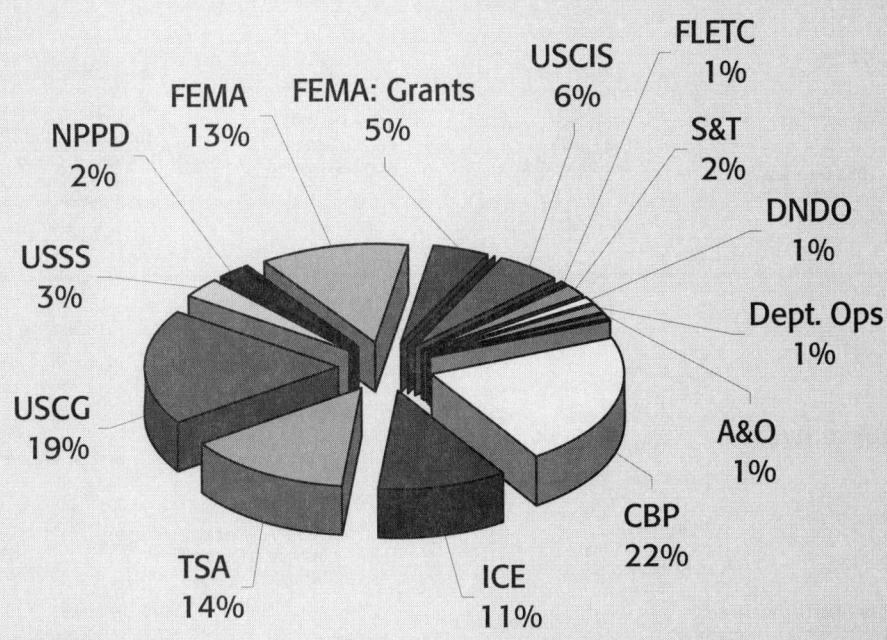

FLETC
1%

USCIS
6%

FEMA: Grants
5%

FEMA
13%

NPPD
2%

S&T
2%

DNDO
1%

USSS
3%

Dept. Ops
1%

USCG
19%

A&O
1%

TSA
14%

ICE
11%

CBP
22%

Department of Homeland Security FY 2008 Percent of Total Budget Authority by Organization
$46,399,702,000

Notes:

1. The following offices are less than one perent of the total budget authority and are not labeled in the chart above: Office of the Inspector General, Office of Health Affairs.
2. Departmental Operations is comprised of the Office of the Secretary & Executive Management, the Office of the Federal Coordinator for Gulf Coast Rebuilding, the Office of the Undersecretary for Management, the Office of the Chief Financial Officer, and the Office of the Chief Information Officer.

Politics and Elections

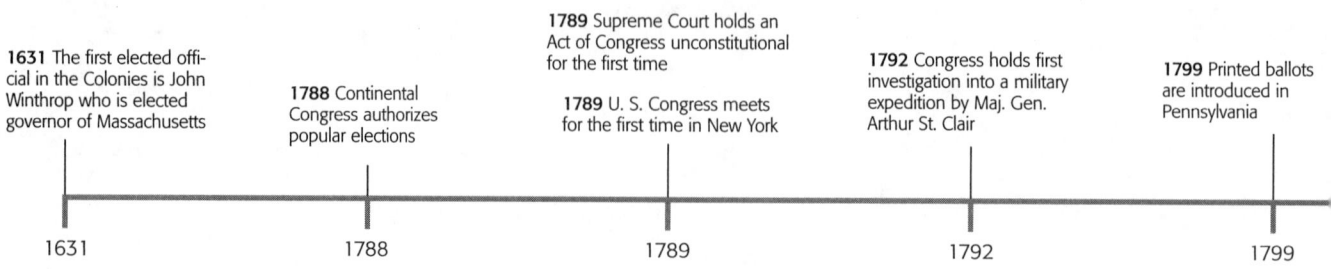

1631 The first elected official in the Colonies is John Winthrop who is elected governor of Massachusetts

1788 Continental Congress authorizes popular elections

1789 Supreme Court holds an Act of Congress unconstitutional for the first time

1789 U. S. Congress meets for the first time in New York

1792 Congress holds first investigation into a military expedition by Maj. Gen. Arthur St. Clair

1799 Printed ballots are introduced in Pennsylvania

1631   1788   1789   1792   1799

Politics and Elections—*continued*

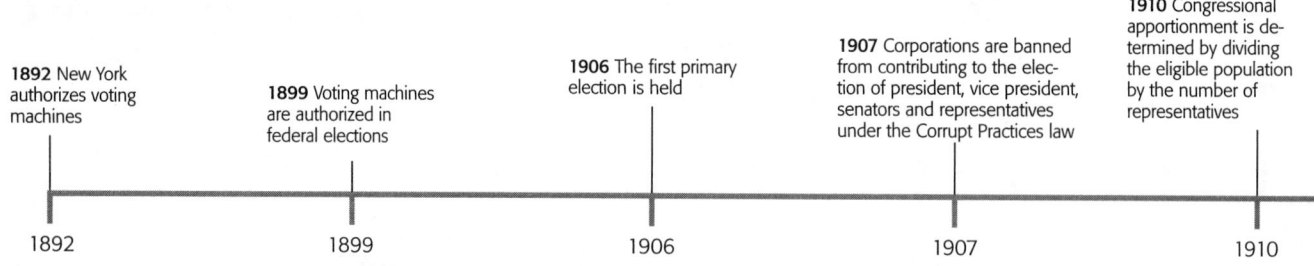

1892 New York authorizes voting machines

1899 Voting machines are authorized in federal elections

1906 The first primary election is held

1907 Corporations are banned from contributing to the election of president, vice president, senators and representatives under the Corrupt Practices law

1910 Congressional apportionment is determined by dividing the eligible population by the number of representatives

1892   1899   1906   1907   1910

Government: Federal, State, and Local

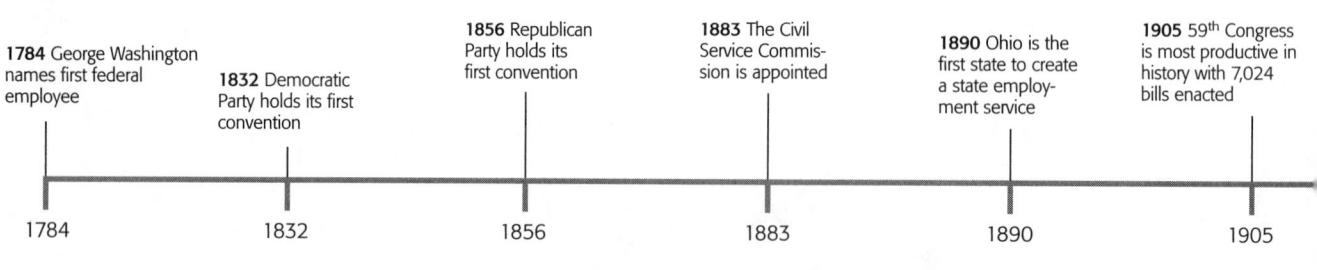

1784 George Washington names first federal employee

1832 Democratic Party holds its first convention

1856 Republican Party holds its first convention

1883 The Civil Service Commission is appointed

1890 Ohio is the first state to create a state employment service

1905 59th Congress is most productive in history with 7,024 bills enacted

1784   1832   1856   1883   1890   1905

National Security

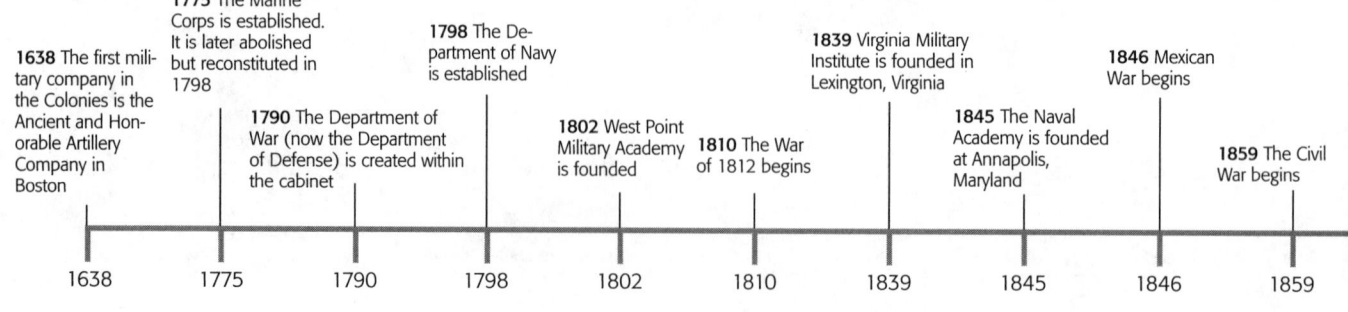

1638 The first military company in the Colonies is the Ancient and Honorable Artillery Company in Boston

1775 The Marine Corps is established. It is later abolished but reconstituted in 1798

1790 The Department of War (now the Department of Defense) is created within the cabinet

1798 The Department of Navy is established

1802 West Point Military Academy is founded

1810 The War of 1812 begins

1839 Virginia Military Institute is founded in Lexington, Virginia

1845 The Naval Academy is founded at Annapolis, Maryland

1846 Mexican War begins

1859 The Civil War begins

1638   1775   1790   1798   1802   1810   1839   1845   1846   1859

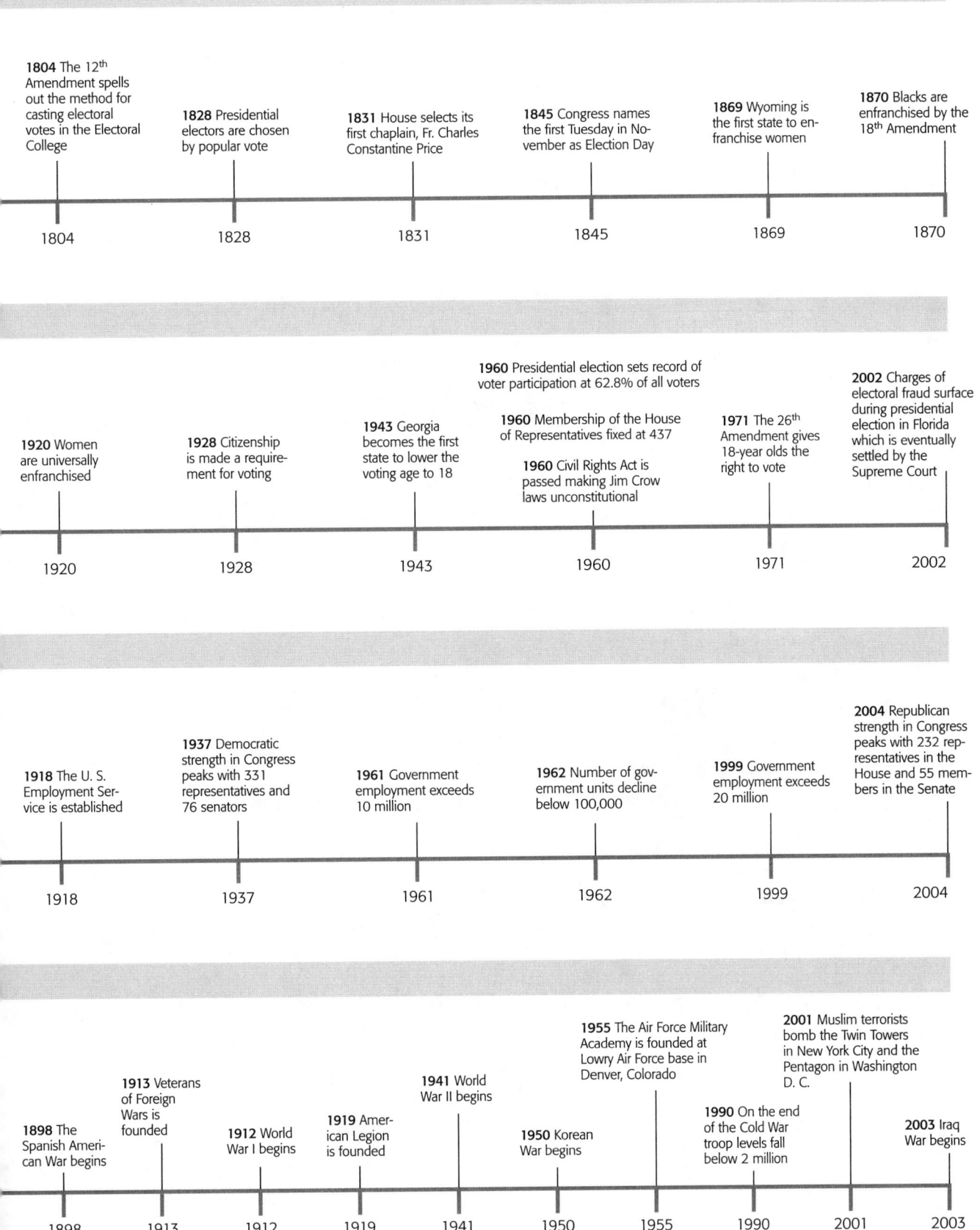

1804 The 12th Amendment spells out the method for casting electoral votes in the Electoral College

1828 Presidential electors are chosen by popular vote

1831 House selects its first chaplain, Fr. Charles Constantine Price

1845 Congress names the first Tuesday in November as Election Day

1869 Wyoming is the first state to enfranchise women

1870 Blacks are enfranchised by the 18th Amendment

1804   1828   1831   1845   1869   1870

1920 Women are universally enfranchised

1928 Citizenship is made a requirement for voting

1943 Georgia becomes the first state to lower the voting age to 18

1960 Presidential election sets record of voter participation at 62.8% of all voters

1960 Membership of the House of Representatives fixed at 437

1960 Civil Rights Act is passed making Jim Crow laws unconstitutional

1971 The 26th Amendment gives 18-year olds the right to vote

2002 Charges of electoral fraud surface during presidential election in Florida which is eventually settled by the Supreme Court

1920   1928   1943   1960   1971   2002

1918 The U. S. Employment Service is established

1937 Democratic strength in Congress peaks with 331 representatives and 76 senators

1961 Government employment exceeds 10 million

1962 Number of government units decline below 100,000

1999 Government employment exceeds 20 million

2004 Republican strength in Congress peaks with 232 representatives in the House and 55 members in the Senate

1918   1937   1961   1962   1999   2004

1898 The Spanish American War begins

1913 Veterans of Foreign Wars is founded

1912 World War I begins

1919 American Legion is founded

1941 World War II begins

1950 Korean War begins

1955 The Air Force Military Academy is founded at Lowry Air Force base in Denver, Colorado

1990 On the end of the Cold War troop levels fall below 2 million

2001 Muslim terrorists bomb the Twin Towers in New York City and the Pentagon in Washington D. C.

2003 Iraq War begins

1898   1913   1912   1919   1941   1950   1955   1990   2001   2003

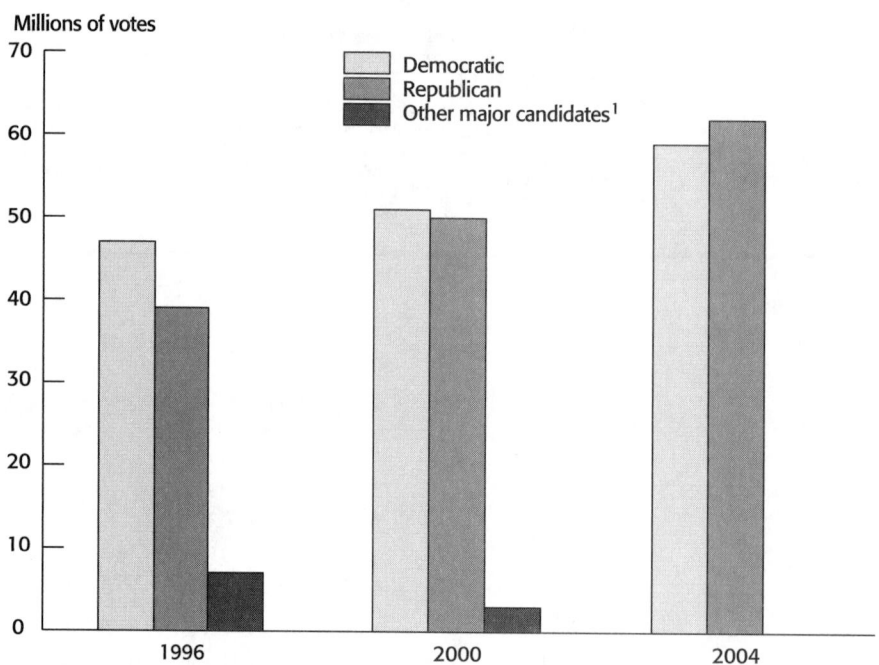

Millions of votes

Vote Cast for President by Major Political Party: 1996 to 2004

[1]Candidates with 1 million or more votes: 1996—Reform, Ross Perot;
2000—Green, Ralph Nadar.

Source: Chart prepared by U.S. Census Bureau.

CHAPTER **29**

Politics and Elections

HIGHLIGHTS

1 Although the United States was founded as a democracy, it took more than 200 years for its electoral mechanisms to evolve from a highly elite, non-democratic format to its present state. For the first 100 or so years, each state determined for itself who its voters were and how they should be enrolled and permitted to vote. Over the years, constitutional amendments, congressional legislation, and judicial decisions applied certain constraints to the states' discretion in specified areas of legal procedure pertaining to elections. In the South, for example, fraudulent stuffing of boxes, suppression of returns, and other irregularities were fairly common from after the Civil War until well into the twentieth century. As late as the 1940s, Lyndon Johnson's victory in his first Senate race was attributed to such practices. Originally, only free White males were enfranchised. Women were universally enfranchised in 1920, but a number of states gave women suffrage earlier: Wyoming, as a territory, in 1869; Colorado in 1893; Utah in 1896; Idaho in 1897; Washington and California in 1911; Oregon, Arizona, and Kansas in 1913; Montana and Nevada in 1914; Illinois in 1916; and Michigan and New York in 1918. Blacks were enfranchised in 1870 by the 15th Amendment to the U.S. Constitution, but were handicapped in the South by a number of procedural and technical restrictions designed to keep them away from the ballot box. In the 1960s, the Civil Rights Act made such restrictions unconstitutional. Until 1928, citizenship was not a requirement for voting and aliens voted freely in many states. Because of the difficulty in estimating the number of foreign-born males in the population, the electoral data for years before and after 1928 are not strictly comparable.

2 Article II, Section I of the U.S. Constitution delineates the method for the election of the president of the United States—the establishment of an electoral college in each state. The method of casting the electoral votes was modified in 1804 by the adoption of the 12th Amendment to the U.S. Constitution. With a few exceptions, presidential electors have been chosen by direct popular vote since 1828, although state legislators still have the right to choose the electors. On four occasions in U.S. history, the entire electoral vote of a state remained uncast for technical reasons.

3 The number of members of the U.S. House of Representatives is fixed by Congress at the time of each apportionment and is based on the population of each state as shown in the decennial censuses. No change in total house membership has been made since 1912, except to allot one representative each to Hawaii and Alaska when they attained statehood. Membership was increased to 437 in 1960, but reverted to 435 after 1962. Prior to the passage of the 14th Amendment, Native Americans were excluded from the census and only three out of five slaves were included. Before 1850, apportionment ratios were chosen arbitrarily. From 1850 to 1900, it was by dividing the total population by a predetermined number of representatives; from 1910 on, it was by dividing the eligible population by a fixed number of representatives.

4 The United States has one of the lowest rates of voter participation in elections and one of the highest rates of political apathy among all democracies (as measured by voter turnout for elections, number of citizens running for office, membership in political parties, and so on). Generally, presidential election years draw more voters to the polling booths than mid-term election years. Even so, only 54.7 percent of eligible voters turn out in average presidential years. The highest percentage of voting age population participating in a presidential election was 62.8 percent in 1960. In congressional elections, the percentage is much lower, for example 42.3 percent in 2002.

5 The power of incumbency on Congress is illustrated by the fact that 97.8 percent of all representatives and 79.3 percent of all senators in presidential election years, and 97.8 percent of all representatives and 89.7 percent of senators in mid-term election years, are re-elected.

6 The women and minorities share of both the House and Senate has increased since the 1980s. The number of women jumped from 19 in the House and 2 in the Senate in 1981 to 65 in the House and 14 in the Senate in 2005. Similarly, the number of Blacks grew from 18 in the House and none in the Senate to 42 in the House and one in the Senate in 2005. The members of both houses are now older than the members in 1981. There are 22 members in the House and no members of the Senate below age 40, compared with 94 and 9 respectively in 1981. Senators tend to be even older. There were 21 members over age 70 in 2001, compared with 6 in 1981.

7 The number of states with Democratic governors has grown in recent years, but remains less than those with Republican governors. The governor elected in 2004 with the highest percentage of popular votes was John Hoeven, a Republican from North Dakota, who received 71.3 percent of the vote.

8 Of the total voting-age citizen population of 197 million in 2004, 72.1 percent reported being registered and 63.8 percent reported to have voted. More White voters register and vote than Black voters and, as a result, the 3–5 percent gap between these two categories of voters has remained despite efforts to bring more Blacks into the political stream. By states, the highest percentage of voters was 79.2 percent in Minnesota and 50.8 percent in Hawaii.

9 In 2004, the federal government employed 2.734 million civilians and state and local governments employed 18.760 million. Monthly payroll was $12.845 billion for the federal government and $55.915 billion for state and local government.

10 Between 1789 and 2006, the various U.S. presidents have used their veto power a total of 2551 times. President Franklin Roosevelt used it the most with 635 times, almost a quarter of the total number.

Table 29-1. Electoral and Popular Vote Cast for President, by Political Party, 1789–2004

(Excludes unpledged tickets and minor candidates polling under 10,000 votes; various party labels may have been used by a candidate in different states, the more important of which are listed below.)

Year	Number of states	Presidential candidate	Political party	Vote cast	
				Electoral	Popular
2004	50	George W. Bush	Republican	286	61 872 711
		John Kerry	Democratic	251	58 894 584
		Ralph Nader	Green	-	115 670
		Michael Badnarik	Libertarian	-	369 000
2000	50	George W. Bush	Republican	271	50 465 169
		Al Gore	Democratic	266	50 996 062
		Ralph Nader	Green	-	2 529 871
		Pat Buchanan	Reform	-	323 930
1996	50	Bill Clinton	Democratic	379	47 401 989
		Robert Dole	Republican	159	39 198 482
		H. Ross Perot	Independent	-	7 137 235
		Ralph Nader	Green	-	526 794
1992	50	Bill Clinton	Democratic	370	44 909 326
		George Bush	Republican	168	38 798 913
		H. Ross Perot	Independent	-	19 722 042
		Andre Marrou	Libertarian	-	280 848
1988	50	George Bush	Republican	426	48 642 640
		Michael Dukakis	Democratic	111	41 716 679
		Ron Paul	Libertarian	-	409 608
		Lenora B. Fulani	New Alliance	-	128 678
1984	50	Ronald Regan	Republican	525	54 166 829
		Walter Mondale	Democratic	13	37 449 813
		David Bergland	Libertarian	-	227 204
		Lyndon H. LaRouche	Independent	-	78 773
1980	50	Ronald Regan	Republican	489	43 642 639
		Jimmy Carter	Democratic	49	35 480 948
		John Anderson	Independent	-	5 251 421
		Ed Clark	Libertarian	-	920 049
1976	50	Jimmy Carter	Democratic	297	40 825 839
		Gerald Ford	Republican	240	39 147 770
		Eugene McCarthy	Independent	-	680 390
		Roger McBride	Libertarian	-	171 627
1972	50	Richard Nixon	Republican	520	46 740 323
		George McGovern	Democratic	17	28 901 598
		John Schmitz	American	-	993 199
		Benjamin Spock	People's	-	79 328
1968	50	Richard Nixon	Republican	301	31 710 470
		Hubert Humphrey	Democratic	191	30 989 055
		George C. Wallace	American Independent	46	9 446 167
		Henning Blomen	Socialist Labor	-	51 962
		Dick Gregory	(¹)	-	47 133
		Fred Halstead	Socialist Workers	-	41 388
		Eldridge Cleaver	Peace and Freedom	-	36 563
		Eugene J. McCarthy	(²)	-	25 552
		E. Harold Munn	Prohibition	-	15 123
1964	50	Lyndon B. Johnson	Democratic	486	42 825 463
		Barry M. Goldwater	Republican	52	27 146 969
		Eric Hass	Socialist Labor	-	42 642
		Clifton DeBerry	Socialist Workers	-	22 249
		E. Harold Munn	Prohibition	-	23 267
1960	50	John F. Kennedy	Democratic	³303	34 227 096
		Richard Nixon	Republican	219	34 107 646
		Eric Hass	Socialist Labor	-	46 478
		Rutherford Decker	Prohibition	-	45 919
		Orval E. Faubus	National States' Rights	-	44 977
		Farrell Dobbs	Socialist Workers	-	40 165
		Charles L. Sullivan	Constitution	-	18 162
1956	48	Dwight D. Eisenhower	Republican	457	35 581 003
		Adlai E. Stevenson	Democratic	⁴73	26 738 765
		T. Coleman Andrews	States' Rights	-	91 471
		Eric Hass	Socialist Labor	-	41 309
		Enoch A. Holtwick	Prohibition	-	41 937

Note: Prior to 1964, excludes the District of Columbia.
¹Total vote for Gregory includes write-in votes as well as votes for the Freedom and Peace Party, the Peace Freedom Alternative, the Peace and Freedom Party and the New Party.
²Total vote for McCarthy includes write-in votes as well as votes for the Alternative in November Party and the New Party.
³Six Democratic electors in Alabama, all eight unpledged Democratic electors in Mississippi and one Republican elector in Oklahoma voted for Senator Harry F. Byrd.
⁴One Democratic elector in Alabama voted for Watler Jones.
- = Quantity zero.

Table 29-1. Electoral and Popular Vote Cast for President, by Political Party, 1789–2004—*Continued*

(Excludes unpledged tickets and minor candidates polling under 10,000 votes; various party labels may have been used by a candidate in different states, the more important of which are listed below.)

Year	Number of states	Presidential candidate	Political party	Vote cast	
				Electoral	Popular
1952	48	Dwight D. Eisenhower	Republican	442	33 778 963
		Adlai E. Stevenson	Democratic	89	27 314 992
		Vincent Hallinan	Progressive	-	135 007
		Stuart Hamblen	Prohibition	-	72 769
		Eric Hass	Socialist Labor	-	30 267
		Darlington Hoopes	Socialist	-	20 203
		Douglas A. MacArthur	Constitution	-	17 205
		Farrell Dobbs	Socialist Workers	-	10 312
1948	48	Harry S. Truman	Democratic	303	24 105 695
		Thomas E. Dewey	Republican	189	21 969 170
		Strom Thurmond	States' Rights	39	1 169 021
		Henry Wallace	Progressive	-	1 156 103
		Norman Thomas	Socialist	-	139 572
		Claude A. Watson	Prohibition	-	103 900
		Edward A. Teichert	Socialist Labor	-	29 241
		Farrell Dobbs	Socialist Workers	-	13 614
1944	48	Franklin D. Roosevelt	Democratic	432	25 606 585
		Thomas E. Dewey	Republican	99	22 014 745
		Norman Thomas	Socialist	-	80 518
		Claude A. Watson	Prohibition	-	74 758
		Edward A. Teichert	Socialist Labor	-	45 336
1940	48	Franklin D. Roosevelt	Democratic	449	27 307 819
		Wendell L. Willkie	Republican	82	22 321 018
		Norman Thomas	Socialist	-	99 557
		Roger Q. Babson	Prohibition	-	57 812
		Earl Browder	Communist	-	46 251
		John W. Aiken	Socialist Labor	-	14 892
1936	48	Franklin D. Roosevelt	Democratic	523	27 752 869
		Alfred M. Landon	Republican	8	16 674 665
		William Lemke	Union	-	882 479
		Norman Thomas	Socialist	-	187 720
		Earl Browder	Communist	-	80 159
		D. Leigh Colvin	Prohibition	-	37 847
		John W. Aiken	Socialist Labor	-	12 777
1932	48	Franklin D. Roosevelt	Democratic	472	22 809 638
		Herbert C. Hoover	Republican	59	15 758 901
		Norman Thomas	Socialist	-	881 951
		William Z. Foster	Communist	-	102 785
		William D. Upshaw	Prohibition	-	81 869
		Verne L. Reynolds	Socialist Labor	-	33 276
		William H. Harvey	Liberty	-	53 425
1928	48	Herbert C. Hoover	Republican	444	21 391 993
		Alfred E. Smith	Democratic	87	15 016 169
		Norman Thomas	Socialist	-	267 835
		Verne L. Reynolds	Socialist Labor	-	21 603
		William Z. Foster	Workers	-	21 181
		William F. Varney	Prohibition	-	20 106
1924	48	Calvin Coolidge	Republican	382	15 718 211
		John W. Davis	Democratic	136	8 385 283
		Robert M. LaFollette	Progressive	13	4 831 289
		Herman P. Faris	Prohibition	-	57 520
		Frank T. Johns	Socialist Labor	-	36 428
		William Z. Foster	Workers	-	36 386
		Gilbert O. Nations	American	-	23 967
1920	48	Warren G. Harding	Republican	404	16 143 407
		James M. Cox	Democratic	127	9 130 328
		Eugene V. Debs	Socialist	-	919 799
		P.P. Christensen	Farmer-Labor	-	265 411
		Aaron S. Watkins	Prohibition	-	189 408
		James E. Ferguson	American	-	48 000
		W.W. Cox	Socialist Labor	-	31 715
1916	48	Woodrow Wilson	Democratic	277	9 127 695
		Charles E. Hughes	Republican	254	8 533 507
		A.L. Benson	Socialist	-	585 113
		J. Frank Hanly	Prohibition	-	220 506
		Arthur E. Reimer	Socialist Labor	-	13 403

- = Quantity zero.

Table 29-1. Electoral and Popular Vote Cast for President, by Political Party, 1789–2004—*Continued*

(Excludes unpledged tickets and minor candidates polling under 10,000 votes; various party labels may have been used by a candidate in different states, the more important of which are listed below.)

Year	Number of states	Presidential candidate	Political party	Vote cast	
				Electoral	Popular
1912	48	Woodrow Wilson	Democratic	435	6 296 547
		Theodore Roosevelt	Progressive	88	4 118 571
		William H. Taft	Republican	8	3 486 720
		Eugene V. Debs	Socialist	-	900 672
		Eugene W. Chafin	Prohibition	-	206 275
		Arthur E. Reimer	Socialist Labor	-	28 750
1908	46	William H. Taft	Republican	321	7 675 320
		William J. Bryan	Democratic	162	6 412 294
		Eugene V. Debs	Socialist	-	420 793
		Eugene W. Chafin	Prohibition	-	253 840
		Thomas L Hisgen	Independence	-	82 872
		Thomas E. Watson	People's	-	29 100
		August Gillhaus	Socialist Labor	-	14 021
1904	45	Theodore Roosevelt	Republican	336	7 628 461
		Alton B. Parker	Democratic	140	5 084 223
		Eugene V. Debs	Socialist	-	402 283
		Silas C. Swallow	Prohibition	-	258 536
		Thomas E. Watson	People's	-	117 183
		Charles H. Corregan	Socialist Labor	-	31 249
1900	45	William McKinley	Republican	292	7 218 491
		William J. Bryan	Democratic[5]	155	6 356 734
		John C. Wooley	Prohibition	-	208 914
		Eugene V. Debs	Socialist	-	87 814
		Wharton Barker	People's	-	50 373
		Joseph F. Malloney	Socialist Labor	-	39 739
1896	45	William McKinley	Republican	271	7 102 246
		William J. Bryan	Democratic[5]	176	6 492 559
		John M. Palmer	National Democratic	-	133 148
		Joshua Levering	Prohibition	-	132 007
		Charles H. Matchett	Socialist Labor	-	36 274
		Charles E. Bentley	Nationalist	-	13 969
1892	44	Grover Cleveland	Democratic	277	5 555 426
		Benjamin Harrison	Republican	145	5 182 690
		James B. Weaver	People's	22	1 029 846
		John Bidwell	Prohibition	-	264 133
		Simon Wing	Socialist Labor	-	21 164
1888	38	Benjamin Harrison	Republican	233	5 447 129
		Grover Cleveland	Democratic	168	5 537 857
		Clinton B. Fisk	Prohibition	-	249 506
		Anson J. Streeter	Union Labor	-	146 935
1884	38	Grover Cleveland	Democratic	219	4 879 507
		James G. Blaine	Republican	182	4 850 293
		Benjamin F. Butler	Greenback-Labor	-	175 370
		John P. St. John	Prohibition	-	150 369
1880	38	James A. Garfield	Republican	214	4 453 295
		Winfield S. Hancock	Democratic	155	4 414 082
		James B. Weaver	Greenback-Labor	-	308 578
		Neal Dow	Prohibition	-	10 305
1876	38	Rutherford B. Hayes	Republican	185	4 036 572
		Samuel J. Tilden	Democratic	184	4 284 020
		Peter Cooper	Greenback		81 737
1872	37	Ulysses S. Grant	Republican	286	3 596 745
		Horace Greeley	Democratic	([6])	2 843 446
		Charles O'Connor	Straight Democratic	-	29 489
		Thomas A. Hendricks	Independent Democratic	42	...
		B. Gratz Brown	Democratic	18	...
		Charles J. Jenkins	Democratic	2	...
		David Davis	Democratic	1	...
		(Not voted)		7	...
1868	37	Ulysses S. Grant	Republican	214	3 013 421
		Horatio Seymour	Democratic	80	2 706 829
		(Not voted)		23	...
1864	36	Abraham Lincoln	Republican	212	2 206 938
		George B. McClellan	Democratic	21	1 803 787
		(Not voted)		81	...

[5]Includes a variety of joint tickets with People's Party electors committed to Bryan.
[6]Greeley died shortly after the election and presidential electors supporting him cast their votes as indicated, including three for Greeley, which were not counted.
- = Quantity zero.

Table 29-1. Electoral and Popular Vote Cast for President, by Political Party, 1789–2004—*Continued*

(Excludes unpledged tickets and minor candidates polling under 10,000 votes; various party labels may have been used by a candidate in different states, the more important of which are listed below.)

Year	Number of states	Presidential candidate	Political party	Vote cast	
				Electoral	Popular
1860	33	Abraham Lincoln	Republican	180	1 865 593
		J.C. Breckinridge	Democratic	(S)	72 848 356
		Stephen A. Douglas	Democratic	12	1 382 713
		John Bell	Constitutional Union	39	592 906
1856	31	James Buchanan	Democratic	174	1 832 955
		John C. Fremont	Republican	114	1 339 932
		Millard Fillmore	American	8	871 731
1852	31	Franklin Pierce	Democratic	254	1 601 117
		Winfield Scott	Whig	42	1 385 453
		John P. Hale	Free Soil	-	155 825
1848	30	Zachary Taylor	Whig	163	1 360 967
		Lewis Cass	Democratic	127	1 222 342
		Martin Van Buren	Free Soil	-	291 263
1844	26	James K. Polk	Democratic	170	1 338 464
		Henry Clay	Whig	105	1 300 097
		James G. Birney	Liberty	-	62 300
1840	26	William H. Harrison	Whig	234	1 274 624
		Martin Van Buren	Democratic	60	1 127 781
1836	26	Martin Van Buren	Democratic	170	765 483
		William H. Harrison	Whig	73	...
		Hugh L. White	Whig	26	[7]739 795
		Daniel Webster	Whig	14	...
		W.P. Mangum	Anti-Jackson	11	...
1832	24	Andrew Jackson	Democratic	219	687 502
		Henry Clay National	Republican	49	530 189
		William Wirt	Anti-Masonic	7	...
		John Floyd	Nullifiers	11	...
		(Not voted)		2	...
1828	24	Andrew Jackson	Democratic	178	647 286
		John Q. Adams	National Republican	83	508 064
1824	24	John Q. Adams	No distinct party designations	[8]84	108 740
		Andrew Jackson		[8]99	153 544
		Henry Clay		37	47 136
		W.H. Crawford		41	46 618
1820	24	James Monroe	Republican	231	...
		John Q. Adams	Independent-Republican	1	...
		(Not voted)		3	...
1816	19	James Monroe	Republican	183	...
		Rufus King	Federalist	34	...
		(Not voted)		4	...
1812	18	James Madison	Democratic-Republican	128	...
		DeWitt Clinton	Fusion	89	...
		(Not voted)		1	...
1808	17	James Madison	Democratic-Republican	122	...
		C.C. Pinckney	Federalist	47	...
		George Clinton	Independent-Republican	6	...
		(Not voted)		1	...
1804	17	Thomas Jefferson	Democratic-Republican	162	...
		C.C. Pinckney	Federalist	14	...
1800[9]	16	Thomas Jefferson	Democratic-Republican	73	...
		Aaron Burr	Democratic-Republican	73	...
		John Adams	Federalist	65	...
		C.C. Pinckney	Federalist	64	...
		John Jay	Federalist	1	...

[7]Whig tickets were pledged to various candidates in various states.
[8]No candidate having a majority in the electoral college, the election was decided in the House of Representatives.
[9]Prior to the election of 1804, each elector voted for two candidates for president; the one receiving the highest number of votes, if a majority, was declared elected president, the next highest, vice president. This provision was modified by adoption of the 12th amendment, which was declared ratified by the legislatures of three-fourths of the states in a proclamation of the Secretary of State, Sept. 25, 1804.
- = Quantity zero.
... = Not available.

Table 29-1. Electoral and Popular Vote Cast for President, by Political Party, 1789–2004—*Continued*

(Excludes unpledged tickets and minor candidates polling under 10,000 votes; various party labels may have been used by a candidate in different states, the more important of which are listed below.)

Year	Number of states	Presidential candidate	Political party	Vote cast	
				Electoral	Popular
1796[9]	16	John Adams	Federalist	71	...
		Thomas Jefferson	Democratic-Republican	68	...
		Thomas Pinckney	Federalist	59	...
		Aaron Burr	Anti-Federalist	30	...
		Samuel Adams	Democratic-Republican	15	...
		Oliver Ellsworth	Federalist	11	...
		George Clinton	Democratic-Republican	7	...
		John Jay	Independent-Federalist	5	...
		James Iredell	Federalist	3	...
		George Washington	Federalist	2	...
		John Henry	Independent	2	...
		S. Johnston	Independent-Federalist	2	...
		C.C. Pinckney	Independent-Federalist	1	...
1792[9]	15	George Washington	Federalist	132	...
		John Adams	Federalist	77	...
		George Clinton	Democratic-Republican	50	...
		Thomas Jefferson	...	4	...
		Aaron Burr	...	1	...
1789[9]	10	George Washington	...	69	...
		John Adams	...	34	...
		John Jay	...	9	...
		R.H. Harrison	...	6	...
		John Rutledge	...	6	...
		John Hancock	...	4	...
		George Clinton	...	3	...
		Samuel Huntington	...	2	...
		John Milton	...	2	...
		James Armstrong	...	1	...
		Benjamin Lincoln	...	1	...
		Edward Telfair	...	1	...
		(Not voted)	...	12	...

Source: U.S. Census Bureau. U.S. House of Representatives, Office of the Clerk.
Note: Prior to 1964, excludes the District of Columbia.
[9]Prior to the election of 1804, each elector voted for two candidates for president; the one receiving the highest number of votes, if a majority, was declared elected president, the next highest, vice president. This provision was modified by adoption of the 12th amendment, which was declared ratified by the legislatures of three-fourths of the states in a proclamation of the Secretary of State, Sept. 25, 1804.
... = Not available.

Table 29-2. Popular Vote Cast for President, by State and Political Party, 1960–2004

(Thousands; Rep. = Republican; Dem. = Democratic; vote listed is normally that of the highest candidate for presidential elector for each party; party totals generally include votes cast for the presidential candidate under other designations than that of the party itself; "Total" includes other parties.)

State	1960			1964			1968			1972		
	Total	Rep.	Dem.	Total	Rep.	Dem.	Total	Rep.	Dem.	Total	Rep.	Dem.
United States	68 838	34 108	34 277	70 645	27 178	43 130	73 212	31 785	31 275	77 719	47 170	29 170
Alabama	570	238	324	690	479	. . .	1 050	147	197	1 006	729	257
Alaska	61	31	30	67	23	44	83	38	35	95	55	33
Arizona	398	221	177	481	243	238	487	267	171	623	403	109
Arkansas	429	185	215	560	243	314	620	191	188	651	449	200
California	6 507	3 260	3 224	7 058	2 879	4 172	7 252	3 468	3 244	8 368	4 602	3 476
Colorado	736	402	331	777	297	476	811	409	335	954	597	330
Connecticut	1 223	566	657	1 219	391	826	1 256	557	622	1 384	811	555
Delaware	197	96	100	201	78	123	214	97	89	236	140	92
District of Columbia	X	X	X	199	29	170	171	31	140	163	35	128
Florida	1 544	795	749	1 854	906	949	2 188	887	677	2 583	1 858	718
Georgia	733	274	459	1 139	617	523	1 250	380	334	1 175	881	290
Hawaii	185	92	92	207	44	163	236	91	141	270	169	101
Idaho	300	162	139	292	144	149	291	165	89	310	199	81
Illinois	4 757	2 369	2 378	4 703	1 906	2 797	4 620	2 175	2 040	4 723	2 788	1 913
Indiana	2 135	1 175	952	2 092	911	1 171	2 124	1 068	807	2 126	1 405	709
Iowa	1 274	722	551	1 185	449	733	1 168	619	477	1 226	706	496
Kansas	929	561	363	858	387	464	873	479	303	916	620	270
Kentucky	1 124	603	522	1 046	373	670	1 056	462	398	1 067	676	371
Louisiana	808	231	407	896	509	387	1 097	258	310	1 051	687	298
Maine	422	241	181	381	119	262	393	169	217	417	256	161
Maryland	1 055	490	566	1 116	385	731	1 235	518	538	1 354	829	506
Massachusetts	2 469	977	1 487	2 345	550	1 786	2 332	767	1 469	2 459	1 112	1 333
Michigan	3 318	1 620	1 687	3 203	1 060	2 137	3 306	1 371	1 593	3 490	1 962	1 459
Minnesota	1 542	758	780	1 554	560	991	1 589	659	858	1 742	898	802
Mississippi	298	74	108	409	357	53	655	89	151	646	505	127
Missouri	1 934	962	972	1 818	654	1 164	1 810	812	791	1 856	1 154	697
Montana	278	142	135	279	113	164	274	139	114	318	184	120
Nebraska	613	381	233	584	277	307	537	321	171	576	406	170
Nevada	107	52	55	135	56	79	154	73	61	182	116	66
New Hampshire	296	158	138	288	104	184	297	155	131	334	214	116
New Jersey	2 773	1 363	1 385	2 848	964	1 868	2 875	1 325	1 264	2 997	1 846	1 102
New Mexico	311	154	156	329	133	194	327	170	130	386	236	141
New York	7 291	3 446	3 830	7 166	2 244	4 913	6 792	3 008	3 378	7 166	4 193	2 951
North Carolina	1 369	655	713	1 425	625	800	1 587	627	464	1 519	1 055	439
North Dakota	278	154	124	258	108	150	248	139	95	281	174	100
Ohio	4 162	2 218	1 944	3 969	1 471	2 498	3 960	1 791	1 701	4 095	2 442	1 559
Oklahoma	903	533	370	932	413	520	943	450	302	1 030	759	247
Oregon	776	408	367	786	283	501	820	408	359	928	487	393
Pennsylvania	5 007	2 440	2 556	4 823	1 674	3 131	4 748	2 090	2 259	4 592	2 715	1 797
Rhode Island	406	148	258	390	75	315	385	122	247	416	220	195
South Carolina	387	189	198	525	309	216	667	254	197	674	477	187
South Dakota	306	178	128	293	130	163	281	150	118	307	166	140
Tennessee	1 052	557	481	1 144	509	635	1 249	473	351	1 201	813	357
Texas	2 311	1 121	1 168	2 627	959	1 663	3 079	1 228	1 267	3 471	2 299	1 154
Utah	375	205	169	401	182	220	423	239	157	478	324	126
Vermont	167	98	69	163	55	108	161	85	70	187	117	68
Virginia	771	405	362	1 042	481	558	1 361	590	442	1 457	988	439
Washington	1 242	629	599	1 259	470	780	1 304	589	616	1 471	837	568
West Virginia	838	396	442	792	254	538	754	308	374	762	485	277
Wisconsin	1 729	895	831	1 692	638	1 050	1 692	810	749	1 853	989	810
Wyoming	141	77	63	143	62	81	127	71	45	146	100	44

. . . = Not available.
X = Not applicable.

Table 29-2. Popular Vote Cast for President, by State and Political Party, 1960–2004—*Continued*

(Thousands; Rep. = Republican; Dem. = Democratic; vote listed is normally that of the highest candidate for presidential elector for each party; party totals generally include votes cast for the presidential candidate under other designations than that of the party itself; "Total" includes other parties.)

State	1976			1980			1984			1988		
	Total	Rep.	Dem.	Total	Rep.	Dem.	Total	Rep.	Dem.	Total	Rep.	Dem.
United States	81 556	39 148	40 831	86 515	43 904	35 484	92 653	54 455	37 577	91 595	48 886	41 809
Alabama	1 183	504	659	1 342	654	637	1 442	873	552	1 378	816	550
Alaska	124	72	44	158	86	42	208	138	62	200	119	73
Arizona	743	419	296	874	530	247	1 026	681	334	1 172	703	454
Arkansas	768	268	499	838	403	398	884	535	339	828	467	349
California	7 867	3 882	3 742	8 587	4 525	3 084	9 505	5 467	3 923	9 887	5 055	4 702
Colorado	1 082	584	460	1 184	652	368	1 295	822	455	1 372	728	621
Connecticut	1 382	719	648	1 406	677	542	1 467	891	570	1 443	750	677
Delaware	236	110	123	236	111	106	255	152	102	250	140	109
District of Columbia	169	28	138	175	24	131	211	29	180	193	28	159
Florida	3 151	1 470	1 636	3 687	2 047	1 419	4 180	2 730	1 449	4 302	2 619	1 657
Georgia	1 467	484	979	1 597	654	891	1 776	1 069	707	1 810	1 081	715
Hawaii	291	140	147	303	130	136	336	185	147	354	159	192
Idaho	344	204	127	437	291	110	411	298	109	409	254	147
Illinois	4 719	2 364	2 271	4 750	1 981	2 358	4 819	2 707	2 086	4 559	2 311	2 216
Indiana	2 220	1 184	1 015	2 242	1 256	844	2 233	1 377	841	2 169	1 298	861
Iowa	1 279	633	620	1 318	676	509	1 320	703	606	1 226	545	671
Kansas	958	503	430	980	567	326	1 022	677	333	993	554	423
Kentucky	1 167	532	616	1 295	635	616	1 369	822	540	1 323	734	580
Louisiana	1 278	587	661	1 549	793	708	1 707	1 037	652	1 628	884	717
Maine	483	236	232	523	239	221	553	337	215	555	307	244
Maryland	1 440	673	760	1 540	681	726	1 676	880	788	1 714	876	826
Massachusetts	2 548	1 030	1 429	2 524	1 058	1 054	2 559	1 311	1 240	2 633	1 195	1 401
Michigan	3 654	1 894	1 697	3 910	1 915	1 662	3 802	2 252	1 530	3 669	1 965	1 676
Minnesota	1 950	819	1 070	2 052	873	954	2 084	1 033	1 036	2 007	962	1 109
Mississippi	769	367	381	893	441	429	941	852	352	932	558	364
Missouri	1 954	927	998	2 100	1 074	931	2 123	1 274	849	2 094	1 085	1 002
Montana	329	174	149	364	207	118	384	232	147	366	190	169
Nebraska	608	360	234	641	420	167	652	460	188	661	398	259
Nevada	202	101	92	248	155	67	287	189	92	350	206	133
New Hampshire	340	186	148	384	222	109	389	267	120	451	282	164
New Jersey	3 014	1 510	1 445	2 976	1 547	1 147	3 218	1 934	1 261	3 100	1 743	1 320
New Mexico	418	211	201	457	251	168	514	307	202	521	270	244
New York	6 534	3 101	3 390	6 202	2 894	2 728	6 807	3 665	3 120	6 486	3 082	3 348
North Carolina	1 679	742	927	1 856	915	876	2 175	1 346	824	2 134	1 237	890
North Dakota	297	153	136	302	194	79	309	200	104	297	167	128
Ohio	4 112	2 001	2 012	4 284	2 207	1 752	4 548	2 679	1 825	4 394	2 417	1 940
Oklahoma	1 092	546	532	1 150	696	402	1 256	862	385	1 171	678	483
Oregon	1 030	492	490	1 182	571	457	1 227	686	536	1 202	560	616
Pennsylvania	4 621	2 206	2 329	4 562	2 262	1 938	4 845	2 584	2 228	4 536	2 300	2 195
Rhode Island	411	181	228	416	155	198	410	212	197	405	178	225
South Carolina	803	346	451	894	442	430	969	616	344	986	606	371
South Dakota	301	152	147	328	198	104	318	200	116	313	165	146
Tennessee	1 476	634	826	1 618	788	783	1 712	990	712	1 636	947	680
Texas	4 072	1 953	2 082	4 542	2 511	1 881	5 398	3 433	1 949	5 427	3 037	2 353
Utah	541	338	182	604	440	124	630	469	155	647	428	207
Vermont	188	102	81	213	95	82	235	136	96	243	124	116
Virginia	1 697	837	814	1 866	990	752	2 147	1 337	796	2 192	1 309	860
Washington	1 556	778	717	1 742	865	650	1 884	1 052	807	1 865	904	934
West Virginia	751	315	436	738	334	367	736	405	328	653	341	310
Wisconsin	2 104	1 005	1 040	2 273	1 089	982	2 212	1 199	996	2 192	1 047	1 127
Wyoming	156	93	62	177	111	49	189	133	53	177	107	67

Table 29-2. Popular Vote Cast for President, by State and Political Party, 1960–2004—*Continued*

(Thousands; Rep. = Republican; Dem. = Democratic; vote listed is normally that of the highest candidate for presidential elector for each party; party totals generally include votes cast for the presidential candidate under other designations than that of the party itself; "Total" includes other parties.)

State	1992			1996			2000			2004		
	Total	Dem.	Rep.	Total	Dem.	Rep.	Total	Dem.	Rep.	Total	Dem.	Rep.
United States	104 425	44 909	39 104	96 278	47 402	39 199	105 594	50 996	50 465	122 349	58 895	61 873
Alabama	1 688	690	804	1 534	662	769	1 666	693	941	1 883	694	1 176
Alaska	259	78	102	242	80	123	286	79	167	313	111	191
Arizona	1 487	543	572	1 404	653	622	1 532	685	782	2 013	894	1 104
Arkansas	951	506	337	884	475	325	922	423	473	1 055	470	573
California	11 132	5 121	3 631	10	019	5 120	10 966	5 861	4 567	12 421	6 745	5 510
Colorado	1 569	630	563	1 511	671	692	1 741	738	884	2 130	1 002	1 101
Connecticut	1 616	682	578	1 393	736	483	1 460	816	561	1 579	857	694
Delaware	290	126	102	271	140	99	328	180	137	375	200	172
District of Columbia	228	193	21	186	158	17	202	172	18	228	203	21
Florida	5 314	2 073	2 173	5 304	2 547	2 245	5 963	2 912	2 913	7 610	3 584	3 965
Georgia	2 321	1 009	995	2 299	1 054	1 081	2 583	1 116	1 420	3 302	1 366	1 914
Hawaii	373	179	137	360	205	114	368	205	138	429	232	194
Idaho	482	137	203	492	165	257	502	139	337	598	181	409
Illinois	5 050	2 453	1 734	4 311	2 342	1 587	4 742	2 589	2 019	5 274	2 892	2 346
Indiana	2 306	848	989	2 136	887	1 007	2 199	902	1 246	2 468	969	1 479
Iowa	1 355	586	505	1 234	620	493	1 353	639	634	1 507	742	752
Kansas	1 157	390	450	1 074	388	583	1 072	399	622	1 188	435	736
Kentucky	1 493	665	617	1 389	637	623	1 544	639	873	1 796	713	1 069
Louisiana	1 790	816	733	1 784	928	713	1 766	792	928	1 943	820	1 102
Maine	679	263	207	606	313	186	652	320	287	741	397	330
Maryland	1 985	989	707	1 781	966	682	2 025	1 144	814	2 384	1 334	1 025
Massachusetts	2 774	1 319	805	2 557	1 572	718	2 734	1 616	879	2 927	1 804	1 071
Michigan	4 275	1 871	1 555	3 849	1 990	1 481	4 233	2 170	1 953	4 839	2 479	2 314
Minnesota	2 348	1 021	748	2 193	1 120	766	2 439	1 168	1 110	2 828	1 445	1 347
Mississippi	982	400	488	894	394	440	994	405	573	1 140	458	673
Missouri	2 392	1 054	811	2 158	1 026	890	2 360	1 111	1 190	2 731	1 259	1 456
Montana	411	155	144	407	168	180	411	137	240	450	174	266
Nebraska	738	217	344	677	237	363	697	232	434	778	254	513
Nevada	506	189	176	464	204	199	609	280	302	830	397	419
New Hampshire	538	209	202	499	246	196	569	266	274	678	341	331
New Jersey	3 344	1 436	1 357	3 076	1 652	1 103	3 187	1 789	1 284	3 612	1 911	1 670
New Mexico	570	262	213	556	273	233	599	287	286	756	371	377
New York	6 927	3 444	2 347	6 316	3 756	1 933	6 960	4 108	2 403	7 448	4 181	2 807
North Carolina	2 612	1 114	1 135	2 516	1 108	1 226	2 915	1 258	1 631	3 501	1 526	1 961
North Dakota	308	99	136	266	107	125	288	95	175	313	111	197
Ohio	4 940	1 985	1 894	4 534	2 148	1 860	4 702	2 184	2 350	5 628	2 741	2 860
Oklahoma	1 390	473	593	1 207	488	582	1 234	474	744	1 464	504	960
Oregon	1 463	621	476	1 378	650	538	1 534	720	714	1 837	943	867
Pennsylvania	4 960	2 239	1 792	4 506	2 216	1 801	4 912	2 486	2 281	5 770	2 938	2 794
Rhode Island	453	213	132	390	233	105	409	250	131	437	260	169
South Carolina	1 203	480	578	1 152	506	573	1 384	566	787	1 618	662	938
South Dakota	336	125	137	324	139	151	316	119	191	388	149	233
Tennessee	1 983	934	841	1 894	909	864	2 076	982	1 062	2 437	1 036	1 384
Texas	6 154	2 282	2 496	5 612	2 460	2 736	6 408	2 434	3 800	7 411	2 833	4 527
Utah	744	183	323	666	222	362	771	203	515	928	241	664
Vermont	290	134	88	258	138	80	294	149	120	312	184	121
Virginia	2 559	1 039	1 151	2 417	1 091	1 138	2 739	1 217	1 437	3 195	1 455	1 717
Washington	2 288	993	731	2 254	1 123	841	2 487	1 248	1 109	2 859	1 510	1 305
West Virginia	684	331	242	636	328	234	648	295	336	756	327	424
Wisconsin	2 531	1 041	931	2 196	1 072	845	2 599	1 243	1 237	2 997	1 490	1 478
Wyoming	201	68	79	212	78	105	214	60	148	244	71	168

Source: U.S. Census Bureau. U.S. House of Representatives, Office of the Clerk.

Table 29-3. Voting-Age Population, Percent Reporting Registered, and Voted, 1972–2004

(Millions, percent. As of November. Covers civilian noninstitutional population 18 years old and over. Includes aliens. Figures are based on Current Population Survey and differ from those based on population estimates and official vote counts.)

Characteristics	Voting-age population (millions)					Percent reporting they registered								
						Presidential election years					Congressional election years			
	1972	1982	1992	2002	2004	1972	1984	1996	2000	2004	1974	1986	1998	2002
Total[1]	136.2	165.5	185.7	210.4	215.7	72.3	68.3	65.9	63.9	65.9	62.2	64.3	62.1	60.9
18 to 20 years old	11.0	12.1	9.7	11.7	11.5	58.1	47.0	45.6	40.5	50.7	36.4	35.4	32.1	32.6
21 to 24 years old	13.6	16.7	14.6	15.6	16.4	59.5	54.3	51.2	49.3	52.1	45.3	46.6	35	42.5
25 to 34 years old	26.9	38.8	41.6	38.5	39.0	68.4	63.3	56.9	54.7	55.6	54.7	55.8	52.4	50.2
35 to 44 years old	22.2	28.1	39.7	43.7	43.1	74.8	70.9	66.5	63.8	64.2	66.7	67.9	62.4	60
45 to 64 years old	42.3	44.2	49.1	66.9	71.0	79.7	76.6	73.5	71.2	72.7	73.6	74.8	71.1	69.4
65 years old and over	20.1	25.6	30.8	33.9	34.7	75.6	76.9	77.0	76.1	76.9	70.2	76.9	75.4	75.8
Male	63.8	78.0	88.6	100.9	103.8	73.1	67.3	64.4	62.2	64.0	62.8	63.4	60.6	58.9
Female	72.4	87.4	97.1	109.5	111.9	71.6	69.3	67.3	65.6	67.6	61.7	65.0	63.5	62.8
White[2]	121.2	143.6	157.8	174.1	176.6	73.4	69.6	67.7	65.6	67.9	63.5	65.3	63.9	63.1
Black[2]	13.5	17.6	21.0	24.4	24.9	65.5	66.3	63.5	63.6	64.4	54.9	64.0	60.2	58.8
Asian[2,3]	...	...	...	9.6	9.3	...	...	...	30.7	34.9	...	...	...	30.7
Hispanic[4]	5.6	8.8	14.7	25.2	27.1	44.4	40.1	35.7	34.9	34.3	34.9	35.9	33.7	32.6
Region:														
Northeast	93.7	36.4	38.3	41.1	41.0	73.9	66.6	64.7	63.7	65.3	62.2	62.0	60.8	60.8
Midwest	...	41.9	44.4	48.8	48.4	...	74.6	71.6	70.2	72.8	66.6	70.7	68.2	66.5
South	42.6	55.4	63.7	74.2	77.2	68.7	66.9	65.9	64.5	65.5	59.8	63.0	62.7	61.6
West	...	31.9	39.3	46.3	49.1	...	64.7	60.8	56.9	60.1	59.8	60.8	56	54
School years completed:														
8 years or less	28.1	22.4	15.4	12.3	12.6	61.5	53.4	40.7	36.1	32.5	54.1	50.5	40.2	32.4
High school:														
Less than high school graduate	22.3	22.3	21.0	20.9	20.7	63.0	54.9	47.9	45.9	45.8	54.3	52.4	43.4	41.6
High school graduate or GED[5]	50.7	65.2	65.3	68.9	68.5	74.0	67.3	62.2	60.1	61.5	61.9	62.9	58.6	57.1
College:														
Some college or associate's degree	19.3	28.8	46.7	57.3	58.9	81.7	75.7	72.9	70.0	73.7	66.9	70.0	68.3	66.7
Bachelor's or advanced degree	15.9	26.9	37.4	51.0	54.9	87.8	83.8	80.4	77.3	78.1	76.0	77.8	75.1	74.4
Employed	80.2	97.2	116.3	134.9	138.8	74.3	69.4	67.0	64.7	67.1	63.8	64.4	62.6	61.7
Unemployed	3.7	10.8	8.3	7.7	7.3	58.7	54.3	52.5	46.1	56.3	44.4	50.6	48.5	48.1
Not in labor force	52.3	57.5	61.1	67.8	69.6	70.3	68.1	65.1	63.8	64.4	61.3	65.4	62.1	60.9

[1]Includes other races not shown separately.
[2]Beginning with the 2003 Current Population Survey (CPS), respondents could choose more than one race. 2004 data represent persons who selected this race group only and exclude persons reporting more than one race. The CPS in prior years only allowed respondents to report one race group.
[3]Prior to 2004, this category was 'Asian and Pacific Islanders,' therefore rates are not comparable with prior years.
[4]Hispanic persons may be any race.
[5]The General Educational Development (GED) Test measures how well a non-high school graduate has mastered the skills and general knowledge that are acquired in a four-year high school education. Successfully passing the exam is a credential generally considered to be equivalent to a high school diploma.
... = Not available.

Table 29-3. Voting-Age Population, Percent Reporting Registered, and Voted, 1972–2004—*Continued*

(Millions, percent. As of November. Covers civilian noninstitutional population 18 years old and over. Includes aliens. Figures are based on Current Population Survey and differ from those based on population estimates and official vote counts.)

Characteristics	Percent reporting they voted								
	Presidential election years					Congressional election years			
	1972	1984	1996	2000	2004	1974	1986	1998	2002
Total[1]	63	59.9	54.2	54.7	58.3	44.7	46.0	41.9	42.3
18 to 20 years old	48.3	36.7	31.2	28.4	41	20.8	18.6	13.5	15.1
21 to 24 years old	50.7	43.5	33.4	35.4	42.5	26.4	24.2	19.2	18.7
25 to 34 years old	59.7	54.5	43.1	43.7	46.9	37.0	35.1	28	27.1
35 to 44 years old	66.3	63.5	54.9	55.0	56.9	49.1	49.3	40.7	40.2
45 to 64 years old	70.8	69.8	64.4	64.1	66.6	56.9	58.7	53.6	53.1
65 years old and over	63.5	67.7	67	67.6	68.9	51.4	60.9	59.5	61
Male	64.1	59.0	52.8	53.1	56.3	46.2	45.8	41.4	41.4
Female	62	60.8	55.5	56.2	60.1	43.4	46.1	42.4	43
White[2]	64.5	61.4	56	56.4	60.3	46.3	47.0	43.3	44.1
Black[2]	52.1	55.8	50.6	53.5	56.3	33.8	43.2	39.6	39.7
Asian[2,3]	...	...	...	25.4	29.8	...	...	...	19.4
Hispanic[4]	37.5	32.6	26.7	27.5	28	22.9	24.2	20	18.9
Region:									
Northeast	66.4	59.7	54.5	55.2	58.6	48.7	44.4	41.2	41.4
Midwest	...	65.7	59.3	60.9	65	49.3	49.5	47.3	47.1
South	55.4	56.8	52.2	53.5	56.4	36.0	43.0	38.6	41.6
West	...	58.5	51.8	49.9	54.4	48.1	48.4	42.3	39
School years completed:									
8 years or less	47.4	42.9	28.1	26.8	23.6	34.4	32.7	24.6	19.4
High school:									
Less than high school graduate	52	44.4	33.8	33.6	34.6	35.9	33.8	25	23.3
High school graduate or GED[5]	65.4	58.7	49.1	49.4	52.4	44.7	44.1	37.1	37.1
College:									
Some college or associate's degree	74.9	67.5	60.5	60.3	66.1	49.6	49.9	46.2	45.8
Bachelor's or advanced degree	83.6	79.1	73	72.0	74.2	61.3	62.5	57.2	58.5
Employed	66	61.6	55.2	55.5	60	46.8	45.7	41.2	42.1
Unemployed	49.9	44.0	37.2	35.1	46.4	28.8	31.2	28.4	27.2
Not in labor force	59.3	58.9	54.1	54.5	56.2	43.0	48.2	44.5	44.2

Source: U.S. Census Bureau. *Statistical Abstract of the United States: 2007.*

[1] Includes other races not shown separately.

[2] Beginning with the 2003 Current Population Survey (CPS), respondents could choose more than one race. 2004 data represent persons who selected this race group only and exclude persons reporting more than one race. The CPS in prior years only allowed respondents to report one race group.

[3] Prior to 2004, this category was 'Asian and Pacific Islanders,' therefore rates are not comparable with prior years.

[4] Hispanic persons may be any race.

[5] The General Educational Development (GED) Test measures how well a non-high school graduate has mastered the skills and general knowledge that are acquired in a four-year high school education. Successfully passing the exam is a credential generally considered to be equivalent to a high school diploma.

. . . = Not available.

Table 29-4. Political Party Affiliation in Congress and the Presidency, 1789–2006

(Figures are for the beginning of the first session of each Congress except as noted; letter symbols for political parties: Ad = "Administration;" AM = Anti-Masonic; C = Coalition; D = Democratic; DR = Democratic-Republican; F = Federalist; J = Jacksonian; NR = National Republican; Op = "Opposition;" R = Republican; U = Unionist; W = Whig.)

Year	Congress	House of Representatives		Senate		President
		Majority party	Principal minority party	Majority party	Principal minority party	
2006[1,2,3]	109	R-231	D-201	R-55	D-44	R-George W. Bush
2005–2006[1]	109	R-232	D-202	R-55	D-44	R-George W. Bush
2003–2004[1,4]						
2001–2002[5]	108	R-229	D-204	R-51	D-48	R-George W. Bush
1999–2000[6]	107	R-221	D-212	D-50	R-50	R-George W. Bush
	106	R-223	D-211	R-55	D-45	D-Clinton
1997–1998[5]	105	R-226	D-207	R-55	D-45	D-Clinton
1995–1996[6]	104	R-230	D-204	R-52	D-48	D-Clinton
1993–1994[6]	103	D-258	R-176	D-57	R-43	D-Clinton
1991–1992[6]	102	D-267	R-167	D-56	R-44	R-George Bush
1989–1990	101	D-260	R-175	D-55	R-45	R-George Bush
1987–1988	100	D-258	R-177	D-55	R-45	R-Reagan
1985–1986	99	D-253	R-182	R-53	D-47	R-Reagan
1983–1984	98	D-269	R-166	R-54	D-46	R-Reagan
1981–1982[7]	97	D-242	R-192	R-53	D-46	R-Reagan
1979–1980[7]	96	D-277	R-155	D-58	R-41	D-Carter
1977–1978[7]	95	D-292	R-143	D-61	R-38	D-Carter
1975–1976[8]	94	D-291	R-144	D-61	R-37	R-Ford
1973–1974[9,10]	93	D-242	R-192	D-56	R-42	R-Nixon
1971–1972[9]	92	D-255	R-180	D-54	R-44	R-Nixon
1969–1970	91	D-243	R-192	D-58	R-42	R-Nixon
1967–1968	90	D-248	R-187	D-64	R-36	D-L. Johnson
1965–1966	89	D-295	R-140	D-68	R-32	D-L. Johnson
1963–1964[4]	88	D-258	R-176	D-67	R-33	D-L. Johnson D-Kennedy
1961–1962	87	D-262	R-175	D-64	R-36	D-Kennedy
1959–1960[11]	86	D-283	R-153	D-64	R-34	R-Eisenhower
1957–1958	85	D-233	R-200	D-49	R-47	R-Eisenhower
1955–1956	84	D-232	R-203	D-48	R-47	R-Eisenhower
1953–1954	83	R-221	D-211	R-48	D-47	R-Eisenhower
1951–1952	82	D-234	R-199	D-49	R-47	D-Truman
1949–1950	81	D-263	R-171	D-54	R-42	D-Truman
1947–1948	80	R-245	D-188	R-51	D-45	D-Truman
1945–1946	79	D-242	R-190	D-56	R-38	D-Truman
1943–1944	78	D-218	R-208	D-58	R-37	D-F. Roosevelt
1941–1942	77	D-268	R-162	D-66	R-28	D-F. Roosevelt
1939–1940	76	D-261	R-164	D-69	R-23	D-F. Roosevelt
1937–1938	75	D-331	R-89	D-76	R-16	D-F. Roosevelt
1935–1936	74	D-319	R-103	D-69	R-25	D-F. Roosevelt
1933–1934	73	D-310	R-117	D-60	R-35	D-F. Roosevelt
1931–1933	72	D-220	R-214	R-48	D-47	R-Hoover
1929–1931	71	R-267	D-167	R-56	D-39	R-Hoover
1927–1929	70	R-237	D-195	R-49	D-46	R-Coolidge
1925–1927	69	R-247	D-183	R-56	D-39	R-Coolidge
1923–1925	68	R-225	D-205	R-51	D-43	R-Coolidge
1921–1923	67	R-301	D-131	R-59	D-37	R-Harding
1919–1921	66	R-240	D-190	R-49	D-47	D-Wilson
1917–1919	65	D-216	R-210	D-53	R-42	D-Wilson
1915–1917	64	D-230	R-196	D-56	R-40	D-Wilson
1913–1915	63	D-291	R-127	D-51	R-44	D-Wilson
1911–1913	62	D-228	R-161	R-51	D-41	R-Taft
1909–1911	61	R-219	D-172	R-61	D-32	R-Taft
1907–1909	60	R-222	D-164	R-61	D-31	R-T. Roosevelt
1905–1907	59	R-250	D-136	R-57	D-33	R-T. Roosevelt
1903–1905	58	R-208	D-178	R-57	D-33	R-T. Roosevelt
1901–1903	57	R-197	D-151	R-55	D-31	R-T. Roosevelt R-McKinley

[1] House and Senate each had one Independent.
[2] As of beginning of second session.
[3] House had two vacancies.
[4] House had one vacancy.
[5] House had one Independent-Socialist and one Independent
[6] House had one Independent-Socialist.
[7] Senate had one Independent.
[8] Senate had one Independent and one Conservative-Republican.
[9] Senate had one Independent and one Conservative-Republican.
[10] House had one Independent-Democrat.
[11] Excludes Hawaii; two senators (1-R, 1-D) and one representative (D) seated August 1959.

Table 29-4. Political Party Affiliation in Congress and the Presidency, 1789–2006—*Continued*

(Figures are for the beginning of the first session of each Congress except as noted; letter symbols for political parties: Ad = "Administration;" AM = Anti-Masonic; C = Coalition; D = Democratic; DR = Democratic-Republican; F = Federalist; J = Jacksonian; NR = National Republican; Op = "Opposition;" R = Republican; U = Unionist; W = Whig.)

| Year | Congress | House of Representatives | | Senate | | President |
		Majority party	Principal minority party	Majority party	Principal minority party	
1899–1901	56	R-185	D-163	R-53	D-26	R-McKinley
1897–1899	55	R-204	D-113	R-47	D-34	R-McKinley
1895–1897	54	R-244	D-105	R-43	D-39	D-Cleveland
1893–1895	53	D-218	R-127	D-44	R-38	D-Cleveland
1891–1893	52	D-235	R-88	R-47	D-39	R-B. Harrison
1889–1891	51	R-166	D-159	R-39	D-37	R-B. Harrison
1887–1889	50	D-169	R-152	R-39	D-37	D-Cleveland
1885–1887	49	D-183	R-140	R-43	D-34	D-Cleveland
1883–1885	48	D-197	R-118	R-38	D-36	R-Arthur
1881–1883	47	R-147	D-135	R-37	D-37	R-Arthur R-Garfield
1879–1881	46	D-149	R-130	D-42	R-33	R-Hayes
1877–1879	45	D-153	R-140	R-39	D-36	R-Hayes
1875–1877	44	D-169	R-109	R-45	D-29	R-Grant
1873–1875	43	R-194	D-92	R-49	D-19	R-Grant
1871–1873	42	R-134	D-104	R-52	D-17	R-Grant
1869–1871	41	R-149	D-63	R-56	D-11	R-Grant
1867–1869	40	R-143	D-49	R-42	D-11	R-A. Johnson
1865–1867	39	U-149	D-42	U-42	D-10	R-A. Johnson R-Lincoln
1863–1865	38	R-102	D-75	R-36	D-9	R-Lincoln
1861–1863	37	R-105	D-43	R-31	D-10	R-Lincoln
1859–1861	36	R-114	D-92	D-36	R-26	D-Buchanan
1857–1859	35	D-118	R-92	D-36	R-20	D-Buchanan
1855–1857	34	R-108	D-83	D-40	R-15	D-Pierce
1853–1855	33	D-159	W-71	D-38	W-22	D-Pierce
1851–1853	32	D-140	W-88	D-35	W-24	W-Fillmore
1849–1851	31	D-112	W-109	D-35	W-25	W-Fillmore W-Taylor
1847–1849	30	W-115	D-108	D-36	W-21	D-Polk
1845–1847	29	D-143	W-77	D-31	W-25	D-Polk
1843–1845	28	D-142	W-79	W-28	D-25	W-Tyler
1841–1843	27	W-133	D-102	W-28	D-22	W-Tyler W-W. H. Harrison
1839–1841	26	D-124	W-118	D-28	W-22	D-Van Buren
1837–1839	25	D-108	W-107	D-30	W-18	D-Van Buren
1835–1837	24	D-145	W-98	D-27	W-25	D-Jackson
1833–1835	23	D-147	AM-53	D-20	NR-20	D-Jackson
1831–1833	22	D-141	NR-58	D-25	NR-21	D-Jackson
1829–1831	21	D-139	NR-74	D-26	NR-22	D-Jackson
1827–1829	20	J-119	Ad-94	J-28	Ad-20	C-J. Q. Adams
1825–1827	19	Ad-105	J-97	Ad-26	J-20	C-J. Q. Adams
1823–1825	18	DR-187	F-26	DR-44	F-4	DR-Monroe
1821–1823	17	DR-158	F-25	DR-44	F-4	DR-Monroe
1819–1821	16	DR-156	F-27	DR-35	F-7	DR-Monroe
1817–1819	15	DR-141	F-42	DR-34	F-10	DR-Monroe
1815–1817	14	DR-117	F-65	DR-25	F-11	DR-Madison
1813–1815	13	DR-112	F-68	DR-27	F-9	DR-Madison
1811–1813	12	DR-108	F-36	DR-30	F-6	DR-Madison
1809–1811	11	DR-94	F-48	DR-28	F-6	DR-Madison
1807–1809	10	DR-118	F-24	DR-28	F-6	DR-Jefferson
1805–1807	9	DR-116	F-25	DR-27	F-7	DR-Jefferson
1803–1805	8	DR-102	F-39	DR-25	F-9	DR-Jefferson
1801–1803	7	DR-69	F-36	DR-18	F-13	DR-Jefferson
1799–1801	6	F-64	DR-42	F-19	DR-13	F-John Adams
1797–1799	5	F-58	DR-48	F-20	DR-12	F-John Adams
1795–1797	4	F-54	DR-52	F-19	DR-13	F-Washington
1793–1795	3	DR-57	F-48	F-17	DR-13	F-Washington
1791–1793	2	F-37	DR-33	F-16	DR-13	F-Washington
1789–1791	1	Ad-38	Op-26	Ad-17	Op-9	F-Washington

Source: U.S. Census Bureau. U.S. House of Representatives, Office of the Clerk.

Table 29-5. Presidential Campaign Finances—Primary Campaign Receipts and Disbursements, 1979–2004

(Millions of dollars. Covers campaign finance activity during 2-year calendar period indicated. Covers candidates who received Federal matching funds or who had significant financial activity.)

Year	Total, all parties				Democratic party				Republican party			
	Receipts, total[1,2]			Disburse-ments	Receipts, total[1]			Disburse-ments	Receipts, total[1]			Disburse-ments
	Total	Individual contributions	Federal matching		Total	Individual contributions	Federal matching		Total	Individual contributions	Federal matching	
2003–2004	673.9	611.4	28.0	661.1	401.8	351.0	27.2	389.7	269.6	258.9	0	268.9
1999–2000	351.6	238.2	61.6	343.5	96.6	66.7	29.3	92.2	236.7	159.1	26.5	233.2
1995–1996	243.9	126.4	56.0	234.1	46.2	31.3	14.0	41.8	187.0	93.1	41.6	182.1
1991–1992	125.2	82.4	41.5	118.7	70.0	44.7	24.4	64.4	49.7	34.4	15.0	48.8
1987–1988[3]	213.8	141.1	65.7	210.7	91.9	59.4	30.1	90.2	116.0	76.8	34.7	114.6
1983–1984[4]	105.0	62.8	34.9	103.6	77.5	46.2	24.6	77.4	27.1	16.4	10.1	25.9
1979–1980	94.2	61.0	30.9	92.3	35.6	23.9	10.3	35.6	58.5	37.1	20.5	56.7

Source: U.S. Census Bureau. *Statistical Abstract of the United States: 2007.* U.S. Federal Election Commission.
[1]Includes other types of receipts, not shown separately.
[2]Includes other parties, not shown separately.
[3]Includes a minor party candidate who sought several party nominations and a Democratic candidate who did not receive Federal matching funds, but who had significant financial activity.
[4]Includes a Citizens Party candidate not shown separately.

Table 29-6. Presidential Campaign Finances—Federal Funds for General Election, 1980–2004

(Millions of dollars. Based on Federal Election Commission (FEC) certifications, audit reports, and U.S. Department of the Treasury reports.)

Year	Total	Democratic party		Republican party		Minor party	
		Candidate	Amount	Candidate	Amount	Candidate	Amount
2004	150.1	John Kerry	74.6	George W. Bush	74.6	Ralph Nader	0.9
2000	147.7	Al Gore	67.6	George W. Bush	67.6	Pat Buchanan	12.6
1996	152.6	Bill Clinton	61.8	Robert Dole	61.8	Ross H. Perot	29.0
1992	110.4	Bill Clinton	55.2	George Bush	55.2	Ross H. Perot	0.0
1988	92.2	Michael Dukakis	46.1	George Bush	46.1	X	X
1984	80.3	Walter Mondale	40.2	Ronald Reagan	40.1	X	X
1980	62.7	Jimmy Carter	29.4	Ronald Reagan	29.2	John Anderson[1]	4.2

Source: U.S. Census Bureau. *Statistical Abstract of the United States: 2007.* U.S. Federal Election Commission.
[1]John Anderson, as the candidate of a new party, was permitted to raise funds privately. Total receipts for the Anderson campaign, including Federal funds, were $17.6 million, and total expenditures were $15.6 million.
X = Not applicable.

Table 29-7. Political Party Control of State Legislatures, by Party, 1961–2006

(As of beginning of year. Until 1972 there were two nonpartisan legislatures in Minnesota and Nebraska. Since then only Nebraska has had a nonpartisan legislature.)

Year	Legislatures under—		
	Democratic control	Split control or tie	Republican control
2006	19	10	20
2005	19	10	20
2004	17	11	21
2003	16	12	21
2002	17	15	17
2001	16	15	18
2000	16	15	18
1998	20	12	17
1997	20	11	18
1996	16	15	18
1995	18	12	19
1994	24	17	8
1993	25	16	8
1992	29	14	6
1990	29	11	9
1989[1]	28	13	8
1987	28	12	9
1985	27	11	11
1983[2]	34	4	11
1981	28	6	15
1979	30	7	12
1977	36	8	5
1975	37	7	5
1973	27	6	16
1971	23	9	16
1969	20	8	20
1967	24	8	16
1965	32	10	6
1963	25	7	16
1961	27	6	15

Source: U.S. Census Bureau. *Statistical Abstract of the United States: 2007.* National Conference of State Legislatures. State Legislatures.
[1]A party change during the year by a Democratic representative broke the tie in the Indiana House of Representatives, giving the Republicans control of both chambers.
[2]Two 1984 midterm recall elections resulted in a change in control of the Michigan State Senate. At the time of the 1984 election, therefore, Democrats controlled 33 legislatures.

Table 29-8. Political Action Committees—Number, by Committee Type, 1975–2005

(As of December 31, except 1975 as of November 24.)

Year	Total	Committee type					
		Corporate	Labor	Trade/member-ship/health	Nonconnected	Cooperative	Corporation without stock
2005	4 343	1 638	296	912	1 357	37	103
2004	4 867	1 756	328	986	1 650	38	109
2003	4 023	1 552	308	877	1 147	36	103
2002	4 027	1 528	320	975	1 055	39	110
2001	3 907	1 545	317	860	1 026	41	118
2000	3 706	1 523	316	812	902	39	114
1999	3 835	1 548	318	844	972	38	115
1998	3 798	1 567	321	821	935	39	115
1997	3 844	1 597	332	825	931	42	117
1996	4 079	1 642	332	838	1 103	41	123
1995	4 016	1 674	334	815	1 020	44	129
1994	3 954	1 660	333	792	980	53	136
1993	4 210	1 789	337	761	1 121	56	146
1992	4 195	1 735	347	770	1 145	56	142
1991	4 094	1 738	338	742	1 083	57	136
1990	4 172	1 795	346	774	1 062	59	136
1989	4 178	1 796	349	777	1 060	59	137
1988	4 268	1 816	354	786	1 115	59	138
1987	4 165	1 775	364	865	957	59	145
1986	4 157	1 744	384	745	1 077	56	151
1985	3 992	1 710	388	695	1 003	54	142
1984	4 009	1 682	394	698	1 053	52	130
1983	3 525	1 538	378	643	793	51	122
1982	3 371	1 469	380	649	723	47	103
1981	2 901	1 329	318	614	531	41	68
1980	2 551	1 206	297	576	374	42	56
1979	2 000	950	240	514	247	17	32
1978	1 653	785	217	453	162	12	24
1977	1 360	550	234	438	110	8	20
1976	1 146	433	224	...	...	...	...
1975	722	139	226	...	...	...	...

Source: U.S. Census Bureau. *Statistical Abstract of the United States: 2007.* U.S. Federal Election Commission.
. . . = Not available.

Table 29-9. Congressional Campaign Finances—Receipts and Disbursements, 1983–2004

(Millions of dollars, percent. Covers all campaign finance activity during 2-year calendar period indicated for primary, general, run-off, and special elections. Data have been adjusted to eliminate transfers between all committees within a campaign.)

Year	Total	Individual contributions	Contributions from PACs	Candidate loans	Candidate contributions	Political party affiliation Democrats	Republicans	Others	Candidate status Incumbents	Challengers	Open seats[2]
House of Representatives											
2003–2004	708.5	396.7	225.4	47.4	7.8	307.4	399.2	1.9	452.6	118.2	137.8
Percent distribution	100	56.0	31.8	6.7	1.1	43.4	56.3	(Z)	63.9	16.7	19.4
2001–2002	643.3	322.5	214.1	72.0	9.2	314.2	326.3	2.8	369.8	107.0	166.5
Percent distribution	100	50.1	33.3	11.2	1.4	48.8	50.7	(Z)	57.5	16.6	25.9
1999–2000	610.4	315.6	193.4	61.9	6.3	286.7	317.7	6.0	361.8	127.4	121.1
Percent distribution	100	51.7	31.7	10.1	1.0	47.0	52.0	1.0	59.3	20.9	19.8
1997– 1998	493.7	253.2	158.5	46.8	5.3	233.4	255.8	4.5	293.6	92.8	102.7
Percent distribution	100	51.9	32.1	9.8	1.1	47.3	51.8	0.9	59.6	19.5	20.9
1995–1996	505.4	272.9	155.0	42.0	7.0	233.1	266.9	5.4	279.8	119.1	101.1
Percent distribution	100	54.7	30.8	8.4	1.4	46.1	52.8	1.1	55.7	24.1	14.3
1993–1994	418.5	214.9	132.1	43.7	9.2	216.7	201.8	2.8	223.3	99.0	96.2
Percent distribution	100	51.3	31.4	10.4	2.4	51.4	47.9	0.7	53.2	23.9	22.9
1991–1992	395.9	190.3	127.1	42.0	11.0	217.7	174.3	3.9	126.8	34.6	56.3
Percent distribution	100	48.6	32.2	10.9	2.9	55.0	44.0	1.0	51.4	23.1	25.5
1989–1990	285.4	129.3	108.5	20.9	4.6	163.4	120.9	1.1	111.9	20.1	31.5
Percent distribution	100	45.5	38.0	7.3	1.7	57.2	42.4	(Z)	63.7	16.7	19.6
1987–1988	278.3	128.7	102.4	22.7	5.1	159.9	116.0	1.0	102.5	29.5	28.0
Percent distribution	100	46.7	36.7	8.3	1.8	57.6	42.0	(Z)	63.1	18.9	18.0
1985–1986	257.7	127.6	87.4	20.9	4.8	139.9	117.7	0.1	149.7	49.2	58.8
Percent distribution	100	49.5	33.9	8.1	1.9	54.3	45.7	(Z)	58.1	19.1	22.8
1983–1984	222.5	108.0	75.7	18.0	3.4	121.4	100.5	0.5	132.4	55.5	34.6
Percent distribution	100	48.5	34.0	8.1	1.5	54.6	45.2	0.2	59.5	25.0	15.5
Senate											
2003–2004	497.6	324.1	63.7	39.8	38.2	250.6	246.1	0.9	171.7	79.5	246.4
Percent distribution	100	65.1	12.8	8.0	7.7	50.4	49.5	(Z)	34.5	16.0	49.5
2001–2002	326.1	214.3	60.2	28.1	0.8	162.9	162.7	0.6	145.0	109.7	71.4
Percent distribution	100	65.7	18.5	8.6	(Z)	49.9	49.9	(Z)	44.5	33.6	21.9
1999–2000	437.0	252.1	52.0	89.0	18.7	230.4	203.8	2.8	130.6	99.6	206.7
Percent distribution	100	57.7	11.9	20.4	4.3	52.7	46.6	0.6	29.9	22.8	47.3
1997–1998	287.5	166.5	48.1	52.2	1.3	134.1	153.0	0.4	135.5	113.9	37.7
Percent distribution	100	58.0	16.7	18.2	(Z)	46.6	53.2	(Z)	47.1	39.6	13.1
1995–1996	285.1	166.9	45.6	40.3	16.4	126.5	157.7	0.9	81.8	79.2	124.1
Percent distribution	100	58.8	16.0	14.1	5.8	44.4	55.3	(Z)	28.7	27.8	43.5
1993–1994	319.1	185.2	47.2	43.1	24.9	133.6	183.6	2.0	113.3	119.2	86.6
Percent distribution	100	58.4	14.8	13.6	7.8	41.8	57.5	0.6	35.5	37.4	27.1
1991–1992	263.4	162.4	51.2	28.1	6.5	143.8	118.4	1.3	99.7	95.6	68.2
Percent distribution	100	61.8	19.4	10.9	2.5	54.6	44.9	(Z)	37.9	36.3	25.9
1989–1990	186.3	119.6	41.2	10.0	2.4	89.5	96.8	(Z)	118.7	54.8	12.8
Percent distribution	100	64.2	22.1	5.4	1.3	48.0	52.0	(Z)	63.7	29.4	6.9
1987–1988	199.3	127.6	46.0	8.2	6.8	107.4	91.3	0.3	98.3	56.3	44.7
Percent distribution	100	64.3	22.9	4.1	3.4	54.0	45.8	(Z)	49.3	28.3	22.4
1985–1986	214.4	140.1	45.3	6.2	1.9	91.8	122.5	0.1	90.3	67.2	56.9
Percent distribution	100	65.3	21.1	2.9	0.9	42.8	57.1	(Z)	42.1	31.3	26.5
1983–1984	174.7	110.3	29.7	21.4	3.7	84.2	90.3	0.2	74.8	38.9	61.0
Percent distribution	100	63.1	17.0	12.2	2.1	48.2	51.7	0.1	42.8	22.3	34.9

Source: U.S. Census Bureau. *Statistical Abstract of the United States: 2007.* U.S. Federal Election Commission.
[1] Includes other types of receipts, not shown separately.
[2] Elections in which an incumbent did not seek re-election.
Z = Less than $50,000 or 0.5 percent.

Table 29-9. Congressional Campaign Finances—Receipts and Disbursements, 1983–2004—*Continued*

(Millions of dollars, percent. Covers all campaign finance activity during 2-year calendar period indicated for primary, general, run-off, and special elections. Data have been adjusted to eliminate transfers between all committees within a campaign.)

Year	Total disbursements						
		Political party affilitation			Candidate status		
	Total	Democrats	Republicans	Others	Incumbents	Challengers	Open seats[2]
House of Representatives							
2003–2004	660.3	288.5	370.0	1.8	410.1	116.6	133.6
Percent distribution	100	43.7	56.0	(Z)	62.1	17.7	20.2
2001–2002	613.9	301.1	310.0	2.9	343.9	103.9	166.1
Percent distribution	100	49.0	50.5	(Z)	56.0	16.9	27.1
1999–2000	572.3	266.8	299.7	5.7	327.0	125.6	119.7
Percent distribution	100	46.6	52.4	1.0	57.1	21.9	20.9
1997– 1998	452.5	211.1	237.2	4.2	257.2	94.7	100.6
Percent distribution	100	46.7	52.4	0.9	56.8	20.9	22.2
1995–1996	477.8	221.1	251.4	5.3	258.1	119.6	100.2
Percent distribution	95	43.7	49.7	1.0	51.1	23.7	19.8
1993–1994	404.4	213.4	191.0	2.8	213.5	99.1	94.6
Percent distribution	100	46.3	52.6	1.1	54.0	25.0	21.0
1991–1992	407.6	228.3	176.0	3.3	217.9	90.0	99.7
Percent distribution	100	56.0	43.2	0.8	53.5	22.1	24.5
1989–1990	265.8	151.0	113.7	1.1	163.4	47.0	55.4
Percent distribution	100	56.8	42.8	(Z)	61.5	17.7	20.8
1987–1988	257.6	145.6	111.0	1.0	156.6	51.7	49.3
Percent distribution	100	56.5	43.1	(Z)	60.8	20.1	19.1
1985–1986	239.3	128.7	110.5	0.1	132.5	48.8	58.0
Percent distribution	100	53.8	46.2	(Z)	55.4	20.4	24.2
1983–1984	203.6	111.0	91.8	0.7	114.9	54.7	33.9
Percent distribution	100	54.5	45.1	0.3	56.5	26.9	16.7
Senate							
2003–2004	496.4	254.6	241.0	0.8	171.7	76.6	248.1
Percent distribution	100	51.3	48.5	(Z)	34.6	15.4	50.0
2001–2002	322.4	162.9	158.9	0.6	145.6	108.4	68.5
Percent distribution	100	50.5	49.3	(Z)	45.1	33.6	21.2
1999–2000	434.7	226.3	205.7	2.7	130.2	99.3	205.1
Percent distribution	100	52.1	47.3	0.6	30.0	22.8	47.2
1997–1998	287.9	134.6	152.9	0.4	137.3	112.5	38.1
Percent distribution	100	46.7	53.1	(Z)	47.7	39.1	13.2
1995–1996	287.4	127.4	159.1	0.9	85.4	78.9	123.1
Percent distribution	100	44.3	55.4	(Z)	29.7	27.5	42.8
1993–1994	318.8	136.3	180.6	2.0	115.1	118.3	85.5
Percent distribution	100	42.7	56.6	0.6	36.1	37.1	26.8
1991–1992	272.1	147.6	123.2	1.2	107.2	95.3	69.6
Percent distribution	100	54.2	45.3	(Z)	39.4	35.0	25.6
1989–1990	180.4	87.6	92.9	(Z)	113.5	54.9	12.1
Percent distribution	100	48.5	51.5	(Z)	62.9	30.4	6.7
1987–1988	201.4	107.9	93.1	0.3	101.2	56.1	44.1
Percent distribution	100	53.6	46.3	(Z)	50.3	27.8	21.9
1985–1986	211.6	89.0	122.6	(Z)	89.3	66.2	56.1
Percent distribution	100	42.0	57.9	(Z)	42.2	31.3	26.5
1983–1984	170.5	82.0	88.3	0.2	72.1	38.3	60.1
Percent distribution	100	48.1	51.8	0.1	42.3	22.5	35.3

Source: U.S. Census Bureau. *Statistical Abstract of the United States: 2007.* U.S. Federal Election Commission.
[2]Elections in which an incumbent did not seek re-election.
Z = Less than $50,000 or 0.5 percent.

BOX 29 ■ Campaign Finance Reform

Throughout U.S. history, political campaigns have always presented the opportunity to peddle influence. As long as money is required to attain elected office, the opportunity to trade favors for cash always exists. At the turn of the twentieth century, campaign finance reform laws were passed to prohibit contributions from corporations and, later, trade unions. The first campaign fund disclosure law was passed in 1910. Legislation passed in 1925 remained U.S. basic campaign finance law until the 1970s.

The main issues in campaign finance in recent elections have been the high costs of running a campaign, the fear that candidates spend so much time raising money that they neglect their public office and constituents, and large contributions from special interest groups can influence future legislation. In 1976, $540 million was spent on all elections in the United States. By 2000, that number had risen to $3.9 billion, and estimates put 2004 spending at a substantially higher number.

Political action committees (PACs) are the most visible manifestation of special interests that donate money to specific candidates. The number of PACs in the United States grew from 608 in 1974 to a high of 4,268 in 1988, but then dipped slightly to 4,040 in 2004. The amount of money PACs contribute to congressional candidates rose from $12.5 million in 1974 to $289.1 million in 2004. However, the percentage of congressional candidates' campaign financing coming from PACs dropped from 34% in 1988 to 28% in 2004.

One of the main goals of the Bipartisan Campaign Reform Act of 2002, popularly know as McCain-Feingold, was the ban on unlimited contributions to political parties from special interest groups. Some candidates feared that these limits would cripple the political fundraising process, but in 2004 the two parties raised a record amount of more than $1 billion by mid-October. This number was higher than the amount raised by the same period in the 2000 election cycle despite the fact that in that election they could accept contributions for hundreds of thousands or even millions of dollars.

Lawsuits continue to change the provisions of McCain-Feingold. In June 2007, the Supreme Court of the United States ruled against a provision that required a blackout 30 days prior to a primary election and 60 days prior to a general election on corporate and union sponsored television advertisements that constitute "electioneering communications" according to the law. The suit was brought by Wisconsin Right to Life, Inc. The group argued that its first amendment rights were violated because it was not able to run a television advertisement in 2004 urging people to ask their senators to stop a filibuster and permit a vote on President Bush's judicial nominations. Of the states' two senators only one was up for reelection, Senator Russell D. Feingold (D).

Sources:

Greenhouse, Linda. "Justices Revisit Campaign Finance Issue." *The New York Times* (January 20, 2007): A9(L).

Greenhouse, Linda and David D. Kirkpatrick. "Justices Loosen Ad Restrictions in Campaign Law." *The New York Times* (June 26, 2007): A1(L).

Justice, Glen. "Despite New Financing Rules, Parties Collect Record $1 Billion." *The New York Times* (October 26, 2004): A22(L).

U.S. Department of State. *Issues of Democracy* "Financing Presidential Election Campaigns." Herbert E. Alexander, September 1996. http://usinfo.state.gov/journals/itdhr/0996/ijde/alex.htm

U.S. Library of Congress, Congressional Research Service. CRS Issue Brief for Congress: Campaign Finance, Updated May 4, 2006. http://fpc.state.gov/documents/organization/67152.pdf

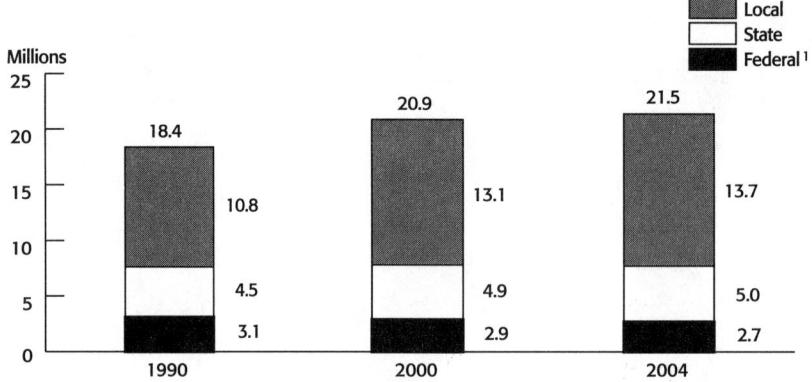

Government Employees: 1990 to 2004

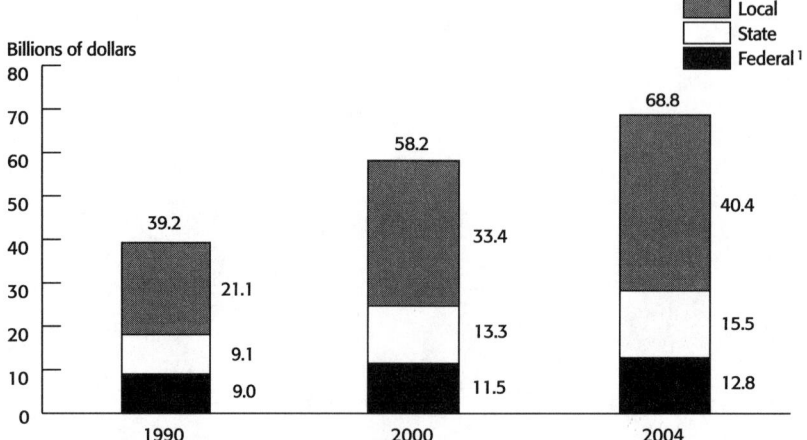

Government Payrolls: 1990 to 2004

[1]Civilian employees only. Includes employees outside the United States.
Source: Figures prepared by U.S. Census Bureau.

CHAPTER 30

Government: Federal, State, and Local

HIGHLIGHTS

1 In any given place, an American lives under at least five governments: federal, state, county, township, and school district. In addition, there are many offshoots, such as single-function and multiple-function districts, authorities, and commissions and boards with varying degrees of autonomy and budgetary powers. When William Anderson's monograph, *The Units of Government in the United States,* was published in 1934, there were 175,418 governments in the country. The number declined to 155,116 in 1942 and to 87,576 by 2002. This decrease was mainly a result of mergers or eliminations of school districts, which shrank in number from 108,579 in 1942 to 13,506 in 2002. Complete censuses of governments, covering structure, personnel, expenditure, revenues, and debt were conducted in 1932, 1942, and 1957, and at five-year intervals thereafter. Earlier censuses were held decennially, from 1850 to 1890, and for 1902, 1912, and 1922, but were much narrower in scope. These censuses differ not only in scope but also in basic concepts and classifications, thus affecting their comparability. Statistics on government employment and payroll have been published by the Bureau of Labor Statistics since 1955; from 1940 to 1955, they were published by the Bureau of the Census. Data for municipalities are for city, borough, village, and (except in New England, New York, and Wisconsin) town governments. Data for school districts are restricted to independent districts and do not include school systems operated by state, city, county, or township governments.

2 Under George Washington, the entire executive staff consisted of two assistants.

3 In 1975, Republicans controlled only five state legislatures and Democrats controlled 37. In 2006, control was fairly even, with Democrats controlling 19 and Republicans 20, with 10 states divided.

4 The number of Black elected officials nationwide grew from 1,469 in 1970 to 9,061 in 2001, and the number of Hispanic public officials also grew from 3,147 in 1985 to 4,651 in 2004. The number of women elected officials at state level grew to 1,755 in 2005, from 1,435 in 1992.

5 The number of measures enacted by Congress has declined since 1972, primarily because private bills are being bundled together as omnibus bills. The number of measures enacted in the 2003–2004 term was only 504, compared with 736 in 1979–1980. On average, in 2003–2004, a representative worked for 1,894 hours annually, or 7.8 hours per day, and a senator for 2,486 hours annually, or 8.3 hours per day.

Table 30-1. Congressional Bills, Acts, and Resolutions, 1789–2005

(Excludes simple and concurrent resolutions.)

Period of session	Congress	Measures introduced			Measures enacted		
		Total	Bills	Joint resolutions	Total	Total public	Total private
Jan. 2005–Dec. 2005[1]	109	6 924	6 822	102	147	147	0
Jan. 2003–Dec. 2004	108	8 625	8 468	157	504	498	6
Jan. 2001–Nov. 2002	107	9 130	8 953	177	337	331	6
Jan. 1999–Dec. 2000	106	9 158	8 968	190	604	580	24
Jan. 1997–Dec. 1998	105	7 732	7 532	200	404	394	10
Jan. 1995–Oct. 1996	104	6 808	6 545	263	337	333	4
Jan. 1993–Dec. 1994	103	8 544	7 883	661	473	465	8
Jan. 1991–Oct. 1992	102	6 775	6 212	563	609	589	20
Jan. 1989–Oct. 1990	101	6 664	5 977	687	666	650	16
Jan. 1987–Oct. 1988	100	9 588	8 515	1 073	761	713	48
Jan. 1985–Oct. 1986	99	9 885	8 697	1 188	483	466	17
Jan. 1983–Oct. 1984	98	11 156	10 134	1 022	677	623	54
Jan. 1981–Dec. 1982	97	11 490	10 582	908	529	473	56
Jan. 1979–Dec. 1980	96	12 583	11 722	861	736	613	123
Jan. 1977–Oct. 1978	95	19 387	18 045	1 342	803	633	170
Jan. 1975–Oct. 1976	94	21 096	19 762	1 334	729	588	141
Jan. 1973–Dec. 1974	93	23 396	21 950	1 446	774	651	123
Jan. 1971–Oct. 1972	92	22 969	21 363	1 606	768	607	161
Jan. 1969–Jan. 1971	91	26 303	24 631	1 672	941	695	246
Jan. 1967–Oct. 1968	90	26 460	24 786	1 674	1 002	640	362
Jan. 1965–Oct. 1966	89	24 003	22 483	1 520	1 283	810	473
Jan. 1963–Oct. 1964	88	17 480	16 079	1 401	1 026	666	360
Jan. 1961–Oct. 1962	87	18 376	17 230	1 146	1 569	885	684
Jan. 1959–Sept. 1960	86	18 261	17 230	1 031	1 292	800	492
Jan. 1957–Aug. 1958	85	19 112	18 205	907	1 720	936	784
Jan. 1955–July 1956	84	17 687	16 782	905	1 921	1 028	893
Jan. 1953–Dec. 1954	83	14 952	14 181	771	1 783	781	1 002
Jan. 1951–July 1952	82	12 730	12 062	668	1 617	594	1 023
Jan. 1949–Jan. 1951	81	14 988	14 219	769	2 024	921	1 103
Jan. 1947–Dec. 1948	80	10 797	10 108	689	1 363	906	457
Jan. 1945–Aug. 1946	79	10 330	9 748	582	1 625	733	892
Jan. 1943–Dec. 1944	78	8 334	7 845	489	1 157	568	589
Jan. 1941–Dec. 1942	77	11 334	10 793	541	1 485	850	635
Jan. 1939–Jan. 1941	76	16 105	15 174	931	1 662	1 005	657
Jan. 1937–June 1938	75	16 156	15 120	1 036	1 759	919	840
Jan. 1935–June 1936	74	18 754	17 819	935	1 724	987	737
March 1933–June 1934	73	14 370	13 774	596	975	539	436
Dec. 1931–March 1933	72	21 382	20 501	881	843	516	327
April 1929–March 1931	71	24 453	23 652	801	1 522	1 009	513
Dec. 1927–March 1929	70	23 897	23 238	659	1 722	1 145	577
Dec. 1925–March 1927	69	23 799	23 250	549	1 423	879	544
Dec. 1923–March 1925	68	17 462	16 884	578	996	707	289
April 1921–March 1923	67	19 889	19 133	756	930	654	276
May 1919–March 1921	66	21 967	21 222	745	594	470	124
May 1917–Dec. 1919	65	22 594	21 919	675	453	405	48
Dec. 1915–March 1917	64	30 052	29 438	614	684	458	226
March 1913–March 1915	63	30 053	29 367	686	700	417	283
April 1911–March 1913	62	38 032	37 459	573	716	530	186
March 1909–March 1911	61	44 363	43 921	442	884	595	289
Dec. 1907–March 1909	60	38 388	37 981	407	646	411	235
March 1905–March 1907	59	34 879	34 524	355	7 024	775	6 249
March 1903–March 1905	58	26 851	26 504	347	4 041	575	3 466
March 1901–March 1903	57	25 460	25 007	453	2 790	480	2 310
Dec. 1899–March 1901	56	20 893	20 409	484	1 942	443	1 499
March 1897–March 1899	55	18 463	17 817	646	1 437	552	885
Dec. 1895–March 1897	54	14 585	14 114	471	948	434	514
March 1893–March 1895	53	12 226	11 796	430	711	463	248
Dec. 1891–March 1893	52	14 893	14 518	375	722	398	324
March 1889–March 1891	51	19 630	19 163	467	2 251	611	1 640
Dec. 1887–March 1889	50	17 078	16 664	414	1 824	570	1 254
March 1885–March 1887	49	15 002	14 618	384	1 452	424	1 028
Dec. 1883–March 1885	48	11 443	10 961	482	969	284	685
March 1881–March 1883	47	10 704	10 194	510	761	419	342
March 1879–March 1881	46	10 067	9 481	586	650	372	278

[1]Includes only the first session of the 109th Congress.

Table 30-1. Congressional Bills, Acts, and Resolutions, 1789–2005—*Continued*

(Excludes simple and concurrent resolutions.)

Period of session	Congress	Measures introduced			Measures enacted		
		Total	Bills	Joint resolutions	Total	Total public	Total private
March 1877–March 1879	45	8 735	8 413	322	746	303	443
March 1875–March 1877	44	6 230	6 001	229	580	278	302
March 1873–March 1875	43	6 434	6 252	182	859	415	444
March 1871–March 1873	42	5 943	5 725	218	1 012	531	481
March 1869–March 1871	41	5 314	4 466	848	769	470	299
April 1867–March 1869	40	3 723	3 003	720	765	354	411
March 1865–March 1867	39	2 348	1 864	484	714	427	287
March 1863–March 1865	38	1 708	1 402	306	515	411	104
March 1861–March 1863	37	1 661	1 370	291	521	428	93
March 1859–March 1861	36	1 746	1 595	151	370	157	213
March 1857–March 1859	35	1 686	1 544	142	312	129	183
Dec. 1855–March 1857	34	1 608	1 515	93	433	157	276
March 1853–March 1855	33	1 660	1 552	108	540	188	352
March 1851–March 1853	32	1 167	1 011	156	306	137	169
March 1849–March 1851	31	1 080	978	102	167	109	58
Dec. 1847–March 1849	30	1 433	1 305	128	446	176	270
March 1845–March 1847	29	1 051	956	95	303	142	161
Dec. 1843–March 1845	28	1 085	979	106	279	142	137
March 1841–March 1843	27	1 210	1 146	64	524	201	323
Dec. 1839–March 1841	26	1 122	1 081	41	147	55	92
March 1837–March 1839	25	1 631	1 566	65	532	150	382
Dec. 1835–March 1837	24	1 107	1 055	52	459	144	315
Dec. 1833–March 1835	23	993	946	47	390	128	262
Dec. 1831–March 1833	22	1 000	976	24	462	191	271
March 1829–March 1831	21	856	842	14	369	152	217
Dec. 1827–March 1829	20	632	612	20	235	134	101
March 1825–March 1827	19	622	609	13	266	153	113
Dec. 1823–March 1825	18	498	481	17	335	141	194
Dec. 1821–March 1823	17	...	492	...	238	136	102
Dec. 1819–March 1821	16	...	480	...	208	117	91
March 1817–March 1819	15	...	507	...	257	156	101
Dec. 1815–March 1817	14	...	465	...	298	173	125
March 1813–March 1815	13	...	400	...	273	185	88
March 1811–March 1813	12	...	406	...	209	170	39
March 1809–March 1811	11	...	348	...	119	94	25
Oct. 1807–March 1809	10	...	266	...	105	88	17
March 1805–March 1807	9	...	219	...	106	90	16
Oct. 1803–March 1805	8	...	217	...	111	93	18
March 1801–March 1803	7	...	161	...	95	80	15
Dec. 1799–March 1801	6	...	157	...	112	100	12
March 1797–March 1799	5	...	234	...	155	137	18
June 1795–March 1797	4	...	132	...	85	75	10
March 1793–March 1795	3	...	122	...	127	103	24
March 1791–March 1793	2	...	105	...	77	65	12
March 1789–March 1791	1	...	144	...	118	108	10

Source: U.S. Census Bureau. U.S. Congress.
. . . = Not available.

Table 30-2. Congressional Bills Vetoed, 1789–2006

Period	President	Vetoed bills			Vetoes sustained	Bills passed over veto
		Total	Regular	Pocket		
2001–2006[1]	George W. Bush	0	0	0	0	0
1993–2001	William J. Clinton	38	37	1	36	2
1989–1993	George Bush	44	29	15	43	1
1981–1989	Ronald W. Reagan	78	39	39	69	9
1977–1981	Jimmy Carter	31	13	18	29	2
1974–1977	Gerald R. Ford	66	48	18	54	12
1969–1974	Richard M. Nixon	43	26	17	36	7
1963–1969	Lyndon B. Johnson	30	16	14	30	0
1961–1963	John F. Kennedy	21	12	9	21	0
1953–1961	Dwight D. Eisenhower	181	73	108	181	2
1945–1953	Harry S. Truman	250	180	70	248	12
1933–1945	Franklin D. Roosevelt	635	372	263	623	9
1929–1933	Herbert Hoover	37	21	16	28	3
1923–1929	Calvin Coolidge	50	20	30	47	4
1921–1923	Warren Harding	6	5	1	3	0
1913–1921	Woodrow Wilson	44	33	11	40	6
1909–1913	William H. Taft	39	30	9	33	1
1901–1909	Theodore Roosevelt	82	42	40	81	1
1897–1901	William McKinley	42	6	36	41	0
1893–1897	Grover Cleveland	170	42	128	170	5
1889–1893	Benjamin Harrison	44	19	25	43	1
1885–1889	Grover Cleveland	414	304	110	412	2
1881–1885	Chester A. Arthur	12	4	8	11	1
1881	James A. Garfield	0	0	0	0	0
1877–1881	Rutherford B. Hayes	13	12	1	12	1
1869–1877	Ulysses S. Grant	93	45	48	89	4
1865–1869	Andrew Johnson	29	21	8	14	15
1961–1865	Abraham Lincoln	7	2	5	7	0
1857–1861	James Buchanan	7	4	3	7	0
1853–1857	Franklin Pierce	9	9	0	4	5
1850–1853	Millard Fillmore	0	0	0	0	0
1849–1850	Zachary Taylor	0	0	0	0	0
1845–1849	James Polk	3	2	1	3	0
1841–1845	John Tyler	10	6	4	9	1
1841	William Henry Harrison	0	0	0	0	0
1837–1841	Martin Van Buren	1	0	1	1	0
1829–1837	Andrew Jackson	12	5	7	12	0
1825–1829	John Quincy Adams	0	0	0	0	0
1817–1825	James Monroe	1	1	0	1	0
1809–1817	James Madison	7	5	2	7	0
1801–1809	Thomas Jefferson	0	0	0	0	0
1797–1801	John Adams	0	0	0	0	0
1789–1797	George Washington	2	2	0	2	0

Source: U.S. Census Bureau. *Statistical Abstract of the United States: 2007.* U.S. Congress, Senate Library.
[1]Through April 10, 2006.

Table 30-3. Composition of Congress, by Political Party Affiliation—States, 1983–2005

(Figures are for the beginning of the first session [as of January 3], except as noted. Dem.=Democratic; Rep.=Republican.)

State	Representatives											
	98th Congress[1] 1983		102nd Congress[2] 1991		106th Congress[2] 1999		107th Congress[2,3,4] 2001		108th Congress[2] 2003		109th Congress[2,5,6] 2005	
	Dem.	Rep.	Dem.	Rep.	Dem.	Rep.	Dem.	Rep.	Dem.	Rep.	Dem.	Rep.
United States	**269**	**165**	**267**	**167**	**212**	**222**	**211**	**221**	**205**	**229**	**202**	**231**
Alabama	5	2	5	2	2	5	2	5	2	5	2	5
Alaska	0	1	0	1	0	1	0	1	0	1	0	1
Arizona	2	3	1	4	1	5	1	5	2	6	2	6
Arkansas	2	2	3	1	2	2	3	1	3	1	3	1
California	28	17	26	19	28	24	31	20	33	20	33	20
Colorado	3	2	3	3	2	4	2	4	2	5	3	4
Connecticut	4	2	3	3	4	2	3	3	2	3	2	3
Delaware	1	0	1	0	0	1	0	1	0	1	0	1
Florida	13	6	9	10	8	15	8	15	7	18	7	18
Georgia	9	1	9	1	3	8	3	8	5	8	6	7
Hawaii	2	0	2	0	2	0	2	0	2	0	2	0
Idaho	0	2	2	0	0	2	0	2	0	2	0	2
Illinois	12	10	15	7	10	10	10	10	9	10	10	9
Indiana	5	5	8	2	4	6	4	6	3	6	2	7
Iowa	3	3	2	4	1	4	1	4	1	4	1	4
Kansas	2	3	2	3	1	3	1	3	1	3	1	3
Kentucky	4	3	4	3	1	5	1	5	1	5	1	5
Louisiana	6	2	4	4	2	5	2	5	3	4	2	5
Maine	0	2	1	1	2	0	2	0	2	0	2	0
Maryland	7	1	5	3	4	4	4	4	6	2	6	2
Massachusetts	10	1	10	1	10	0	10	0	10	0	10	0
Michigan	12	6	11	7	10	6	9	7	6	9	6	9
Minnesota	5	3	6	2	6	2	5	3	4	4	4	4
Mississippi	3	2	5	0	3	2	3	2	2	2	2	2
Missouri	6	3	6	3	5	4	4	5	4	5	4	5
Montana	1	1	1	1	0	1	0	1	0	1	0	1
Nebraska	0	3	1	2	0	3	0	3	0	3	0	3
Nevada	1	1	1	1	1	1	1	1	1	2	1	2
New Hampshire ..	1	1	1	1	0	2	0	2	0	2	0	2
New Jersey	9	5	8	6	7	6	7	6	7	6	7	6
New Mexico	1	2	1	2	1	2	1	2	1	2	1	2
New York	20	14	21	13	19	12	19	12	19	10	20	9
North Carolina	9	2	7	4	5	7	5	7	6	7	6	7
North Dakota	1	0	1	0	1	0	1	0	1	0	1	0
Ohio	10	11	11	10	8	11	8	11	6	12	6	11
Oklahoma	5	1	4	2	0	6	1	5	1	4	1	4
Oregon	3	2	4	1	4	1	4	1	4	1	4	1
Pennsylvania	13	10	11	12	11	10	10	11	7	12	7	12
Rhode Island	1	1	1	1	2	0	2	0	2	0	2	0
South Carolina	3	3	4	2	2	4	2	4	2	4	2	4
South Dakota	1	0	1	0	0	1	0	1	0	1	1	0
Tennessee	6	3	6	3	4	5	4	5	5	4	5	4
Texas	22	5	19	8	17	13	17	13	17	15	11	21
Utah	0	3	2	1	0	3	1	2	1	2	1	2
Vermont	0	1	0	0	0	0	0	0	0	0	0	0
Virginia	4	6	6	4	6	5	4	6	3	8	3	8
Washington	5	3	5	3	5	4	6	3	6	3	6	3
West Virginia	4	0	4	0	3	0	2	1	2	1	2	1
Wisconsin	5	4	4	5	5	4	5	4	4	4	4	4
Wyoming	0	1	0	1	0	1	0	1	0	1	0	1

[1] Colorado had one vacancy.
[2] Vermont had one Independent-Socialist Representative.
[3] California had one vacancy.
[4] Virginia had one Independent Representative.
[5] Vacancy due to the resignation of Rob Portman (OH) April 29, 2005.
[6] As of June 28, 2005.

Table 30-3. Composition of Congress, by Political Party Affiliation—States, 1983–2005—*Continued*

(Figures are for the beginning of the first session [as of January 3], except as noted. Dem.=Democratic; Rep.=Republican.)

State	Senators											
	98th Congress 1983		102nd Congress 1991		106th Congress 1999		107th Congress[7] 2001		108th Congress[7] 2003		109th Congress[6,7] 2005	
	Dem.	Rep.	Dem.	Rep.	Dem.	Rep.	Dem.	Rep.	Dem.	Rep.	Dem.	Rep.
United States	**46**	**54**	**57**	**43**	**45**	**55**	**50**	**50**	**48**	**51**	**44**	**55**
Alabama	1	1	2	0	0	2	0	2	0	2	0	2
Alaska	0	2	0	2	0	2	0	2	0	2	0	2
Arizona	1	1	1	1	0	2	0	2	0	2	0	2
Arkansas	2	0	2	0	1	1	1	1	2	0	2	0
California	1	1	2	0	2	0	2	0	2	0	2	0
Colorado	1	1	1	1	0	2	0	2	0	2	1	1
Connecticut	1	1	2	0	2	0	2	0	2	0	2	0
Delaware	1	1	1	1	1	1	2	0	2	0	2	0
Florida	1	1	1	1	1	1	2	0	2	0	1	1
Georgia	1	1	1	1	1	1	2	0	1	1	0	2
Hawaii	2	0	2	0	2	0	2	0	2	0	2	0
Idaho	0	2	0	2	0	2	0	2	0	2	0	2
Illinois	1	1	2	0	1	1	1	1	1	1	2	0
Indiana	0	2	0	2	1	1	1	1	1	1	1	1
Iowa	0	2	1	1	1	1	1	1	1	1	1	1
Kansas	0	2	0	2	0	2	0	2	0	2	0	2
Kentucky	2	0	1	1	0	2	0	2	0	2	0	2
Louisiana	2	0	2	0	2	0	2	0	2	0	1	1
Maine	1	1	1	1	0	2	0	2	0	2	0	2
Maryland	1	1	2	0	2	0	2	0	2	0	2	0
Massachusetts	2	0	2	0	2	0	2	0	2	0	2	0
Michigan	2	0	2	0	1	1	2	0	2	0	2	0
Minnesota	0	2	1	1	1	1	2	0	1	1	1	1
Mississippi	1	1	0	2	0	2	0	2	0	2	0	2
Missouri	1	1	0	2	0	2	1	1	0	2	0	2
Montana	2	0	1	1	1	1	1	1	1	1	1	1
Nebraska	2	0	2	0	1	1	1	1	1	1	1	1
Nevada	0	2	2	0	2	0	1	1	1	1	1	1
New Hampshire	0	2	0	2	0	2	0	2	0	2	0	2
New Jersey	2	0	2	0	2	0	2	0	2	0	2	0
New Mexico	1	1	1	1	1	1	1	1	1	1	1	1
New York	1	1	1	1	2	0	2	0	2	0	2	0
North Carolina	0	2	0	2	1	1	1	1	1	1	0	2
North Dakota	1	1	2	0	2	0	2	0	2	0	2	0
Ohio	2	0	2	0	0	2	0	2	0	2	0	2
Oklahoma	1	1	1	1	0	2	0	2	0	2	0	2
Oregon	0	2	0	2	1	1	1	1	1	1	1	1
Pennsylvania	0	2	1	1	0	2	0	2	0	2	0	2
Rhode Island	1	1	1	1	1	1	1	1	1	1	1	1
South Carolina	1	1	1	1	1	1	1	1	1	1	0	2
South Dakota	0	2	1	1	2	0	2	0	2	0	1	1
Tennessee	1	1	2	0	0	2	0	2	0	2	0	2
Texas	1	1	1	1	0	2	0	2	0	2	0	2
Utah	0	2	0	2	0	2	0	2	0	2	0	2
Vermont	1	1	1	1	1	1	1	1	1	0	1	0
Virginia	0	2	1	1	1	1	0	2	0	2	0	2
Washington	1	1	1	1	1	1	2	0	2	0	2	0
West Virginia	2	0	2	0	2	0	2	0	2	0	2	0
Wisconsin	1	1	2	0	2	0	2	0	2	0	2	0
Wyoming	0	2	0	2	0	2	0	2	0	2	0	2

Source: U.S. Census Bureau. *Statistical Abstract of the United States: 2007.* U.S. Congress, Joint Committee on Printing.
[6]As of June 28, 2005.
[7]Vermont had one Independent Senator. (Jeffords was reelected in Vermont in 2000 as a Republican, but subsequently switched to Independent status in June 2001.)

Table 30-4. Members of Congress—Selected Characteristics, 1975–2005

(As of beginning of first session of each Congress, [January 3]. Figures for Representatives exclude vacancies.)

Members of Congress and year	Male	Female	Black[1]	Asian and Pacific Islanders[2]	Hispanic[3]	Age[4] (in years)					Seniority[5,6]				
						Under 40	40–49	50–59	60–69	70 and over	Less than 2 years	2–9 years	10–19 years	20–29 years	30 years or more
Representatives															
109th Congress, 2005	369	65	[7]42	4	23	22	96	175	113	28	37	173	158	48	18
108th Congress, 2003	376	59	[9]39	5	22	19	86	174	121	32	54	178	140	48	13
107th Congress, 2001	376	59	[9]39	7	19	14	97	167	117	35	44	155	158	63	14
106th Congress, 1999	379	56	[9]39	6	19	23	116	173	87	35	41	236	104	46	7
105th Congress, 1997	...	...	[9]39	6	...	...	...	...	...	...	...	...	...	...	...
104th Congress, 1995	388	47	[9]40	7	17	53	155	135	79	13	92	188	110	36	9
103d Congress, 1993[8]	388	47	[9]38	7	17	47	151	128	89	15	118	141	132	32	12
102d Congress, 1991	407	28	[9]26	5	11	39	152	134	86	24	55	178	147	44	11
101st Congress, 1989	408	25	[9]24	6	10	41	163	133	74	22	39	207	139	35	13
100th Congress, 1987	412	23	[9]23	6	11	63	153	137	56	26	51	221	114	37	12
99th Congress, 1985	412	22	[9]21	5	10	71	154	131	59	19	49	237	104	34	10
98th Congress, 1983	413	21	[9]21	5	8	86	145	132	57	14	83	224	88	28	11
97th Congress, 1981	416	19	[9]18	5	6	94	142	132	54	13	77	231	96	23	8
96th Congress, 1979	417	16	[9]17	4	5	86	125	145	63	14	80	206	105	32	10
95th Congress, 1977	417	18	[9]16	3	5	81	121	147	71	15	71	207	116	33	8
94th Congress, 1975	416	19	[9]17	4	7	69	138	137	75	16	96	162	125	42	10
Senators															
109th Congress, 2005	86	14	1	2	2	0	17	29	33	21	9	41	29	14	7
108th Congress, 2003	86	14	0	2	0	1	12	29	34	24	9	42	29	13	7
107th Congress, 2001	87	13	0	2	0	0	8	39	33	18	11	34	30	14	9
106th Congress, 1999	91	9	0	2	0	0	14	38	35	13	8	39	33	14	6
105th Congress, 1997	...	...	1	2	...	...	...	...	...	...	...	...	...	...	...
104th Congress, 1995	92	8	1	2	0	1	14	41	27	17	12	38	30	15	5
103d Congress, 1993[8]	93	7	1	2	0	1	16	48	22	12	15	30	39	11	5
102d Congress, 1991	98	2	0	2	0	0	23	46	24	7	5	34	47	10	4
101st Congress, 1989	98	2	0	3	0	0	30	40	22	8	23	22	43	10	2
100th Congress, 1987	98	2	0	2	0	5	30	36	22	7	14	41	36	7	2
99th Congress, 1985	98	2	0	2	0	4	27	38	25	6	8	56	27	7	2
98th Congress, 1983	98	2	0	2	0	7	28	39	20	6	5	61	21	10	3
97th Congress, 1981	98	2	0	3	0	9	35	36	14	6	19	51	17	11	2
96th Congress, 1979	99	1	0	3	0	10	31	33	17	9	20	41	23	12	4
95th Congress, 1977	100	0	1	3	0	6	26	35	21	12	18	41	24	12	5
94th Congress, 1975	100	0	1	2	0	5	21	35	24	15	11	41	34	10	4

Source: U.S. Census Bureau. *Statistical Abstract of the United States: 2007.* U.S. Congress, Joint Committee on Printing.
[1]Source: Joint Center for Political and Economic Studies, Washington, DC, *Black Elected Officials: A Statistical Summary,* annual (copyright).
[2]Source: Prior to 2005, Library of Congress, Congressional Research Service, *Asian Pacific Americans in the United States Congress,* Report 94-767 GOV; starting 2005, U.S. House of Representatives, *House Press Gallery,* <http:222.house.gov/daily/hpg.htm> (as of January 17, 2006) and U.S. Senate, *Minorities in the Senate,* <http://222.senate.gov/artandhistory/history/common/briefing/minority_senators.htm>.
[3]Source: National Association of Latino Elected and Appointed Officials, Washington, DC, *National Roster of Hispanic Elected Officials,* annual.
[4]Some members do not provide date of birth.
[5]Represents consecutive years of service.
[6]Some members do not provide years of service.
[7]Includes District of Columbia and Virgin Islands delegate.
[8]Includes members elected to fill vacant seats through June 14, 1993.
[9]Includes District of Columbia delegate but not Virgin Islands delegate.
. . . = Not available.

Table 30-5. Apportionment of Membership in House of Representatives, by State, 1790–2000

(Total membership includes Representatives assigned to newly admitted states after the apportionment acts; population figures used for apportionment purposes are those determined for states by each decennial census; no reapportionment based on 1920 population census; for method of calculating apportionment and a short history of apportionment, see House Report 91-1314, 91st Congress, 2nd session, the decennial population census, and Congressional Apportionment.)

State	Membership based on census of																				
	1790	1800	1810	1820	1830	1840	1850	1860	1870	1880	1890	1900	1910	1930	1940	1950	1960	1970	1980	1990	2000
United States	106	142	186	213	242	232	237	243	293	332	357	391	435	435	435	437	435	435	435	435	435
Alabama	X	X	1[1]	3	5	7	7	6	8	8	9	9	10	9	9	9	8	7	7	7	7
Alaska	X	X	X	X	X	X	X	X	X	X	X	X	X	X	X	1[1]	1	1	1	1	1
Arizona	X	X	X	X	X	X	X	X	X	X	X	X	1[2]	1	2	2	3	4	5	6	8
Arkansas	X	X	X	X	1[1]	1	2	3	4	5	6	7	7	7	7	6	4	4	4	4	4
California	X	X	X	X	X	2[1]	2	3	4	6	7	8	11	20	23	30	38	43	45	52	53
Colorado	X	X	X	X	X	X	X	X	1[1]	1	2	3	4	4	4	4	4	5	6	6	7
Connecticut	7	7	7	6	6	4	4	4	4	4	4	5	5	6	6	6	6	6	6	6	5
Delaware	1	1	2	1	1	1	1	1	1	1	1	1	1	1	1	1	1	1	1	1	1
Florida	X	X	X	X	X	1[1]	1	1	2	2	2	3	4	5	6	8	12	15	19	23	25
Georgia	2	4	6	7	9	8	8	7	9	10	11	11	12	10	10	10	10	10	10	11	13
Hawaii	X	X	X	X	X	X	X	X	X	X	X	X	X	X	X	1[1]	2	2	2	2	2
Idaho	X	X	X	X	X	X	X	X	X	1[1]	1	1	2	2	2	2	2	2	2	2	2
Illinois	X	X	1[1]	1	3	7	9	14	19	20	22	25	27	27	26	25	24	24	22	20	19
Indiana	X	X	1[1]	3	7	10	11	11	13	13	13	13	13	12	11	11	11	11	10	10	9
Iowa	X	X	X	X	X	2[1]	2	6	9	11	11	11	11	9	8	8	7	6	6	5	5
Kansas	X	X	X	X	X	X	X	1	3	7	8	8	8	7	6	6	5	5	5	4	4
Kentucky	2	6	10	12	13	10	10	9	10	11	11	11	11	9	9	8	7	7	7	6	6
Louisiana	X	X	1[1]	3	3	4	4	5	6	6	6	7	8	8	8	8	8	8	8	7	7
Maine	X	X	X	7	8	7	6	5	5	4	4	4	4	3	3	3	2	2	2	2	2
Maryland	8	9	9	9	8	6	6	5	6	6	6	6	6	6	6	7	8	8	8	8	8
Massachusetts	14	17	20	13	12	10	11	10	11	12	13	14	16	15	14	14	12	12	11	10	10
Michigan	X	X	X	X	1[1]	3	4	6	9	11	12	12	13	17	17	18	19	19	18	16	15
Minnesota	X	X	X	X	X	X	2[1]	2	3	5	7	9	10	9	9	9	8	8	8	8	8
Mississippi	X	X	1[1]	1	2	4	5	5	6	7	7	8	8	7	7	6	5	5	5	5	4
Missouri	X	X	X	1	2	5	7	9	13	14	15	16	16	13	13	11	10	10	9	9	9
Montana	X	X	X	X	X	X	X	X	X	1[1]	1	1	2	2	2	2	2	2	2	1	1
Nebraska	X	X	X	X	X	X	X	1[1]	1	3	6	6	6	5	4	4	3	3	3	3	3
Nevada	X	X	X	X	X	X	X	1[1]	1	1	1	1	1	1	1	1	1	1	2	2	3
New Hampshire ..	4	5	6	6	5	4	3	3	3	2	2	2	2	2	2	2	2	2	2	2	2
New Jersey	5	6	6	6	6	5	5	5	7	7	8	10	12	14	14	14	15	15	14	13	13
New Mexico	X	X	X	X	X	X	X	X	X	X	X	X	1[2]	1	2	2	2	2	3	3	3
New York	10	17	27	34	40	34	33	31	33	34	34	37	43	45	45	43	41	39	34	31	29
North Carolina	10	12	13	13	13	9	8	7	8	9	9	10	10	11	12	12	11	11	11	12	13
North Dakota	X	X	X	X	X	X	X	X	X	1[1]	1	2	3	2	2	2	2	1	1	1	1
Ohio	X	1[1]	6	14	19	21	21	19	20	21	21	21	22	24	23	23	24	23	21	19	18
Oklahoma	X	X	X	X	X	X	X	X	X	X	X	5[1]	8	9	8	6	6	6	6	6	5
Oregon	X	X	X	X	X	X	1[1]	1	1	1	2	2	3	3	4	4	4	4	5	5	5
Pennsylvania	13	18	23	26	28	24	25	24	27	28	30	32	36	34	33	30	27	25	23	21	19
Rhode Island	2	2	2	2	2	2	2	2	2	2	2	2	3	2	2	2	2	2	2	2	2
South Carolina	6	8	9	9	9	7	6	4	5	7	7	7	7	6	6	6	6	6	6	6	6
South Dakota	X	X	X	X	X	X	X	X	X	2[1]	2	2	3	2	2	2	2	2	1	1	1
Tennessee	1[1]	3	6	9	13	11	10	8	10	10	10	10	10	9	10	9	9	8	9	9	9
Texas	X	X	X	X	X	X	2	4	6	11	13	16	18	21	21	22	23	24	27	30	32
Utah	X	X	X	X	X	X	X	X	X	X	1[1]	1	2	2	2	2	2	2	3	3	3
Vermont	2	4	6	5	5	4	3	3	3	2	2	2	2	1	1	1	1	1	1	1	1
Virginia	19	22	23	22	21	15	13	11	9	10	10	10	10	9	9	10	10	10	10	11	11
Washington	X	X	X	X	X	X	X	X	X	1[1]	2	3	5	6	6	6	7	7	8	9	9
West Virginia	X	X	X	X	X	X	X	3[1]	3	4	4	5	6	6	6	6	5	4	4	3	3
Wisconsin	X	X	X	X	X	2[1]	3	6	8	9	10	11	11	10	10	10	10	9	9	9	8
Wyoming	X	X	X	X	X	X	X	X	X	1[1]	1	1	1	1	1	1	1	1	1	1	1

Source: U.S. Census Bureau.

[1] Assigned after apportionment.

[2] Included in apportionment in anticipation of statehood.

X = Not applicable.

Table 30-6. House of Representatives, Majority and Minority Leaders, 1899–2007

Congress	Majority Leader	Minority Leader	Years of Service
110th	Steny Hoyer (D-MD)	John Boehner (R-OH)	(2007–)
109th	John Boehner (R-OH)[1]	Nancy Pelosi (D-CA)	(2006–2007)
109th	Roy Blunt (R-MO)[2]	Nancy Pelosi (D-CA)	(2005–2006)
109th	Tom DeLay (R-TX)[3]	Nancy Pelosi (D-CA)	(2005)
108th	Tom DeLay (R-TX)	Nancy Pelosi (D-CA)	(2003–2005)
107th	Richard K. Armey (R-TX)	Richard A. Gephardt (D-MO)	(2001–2003)
106th	Richard K. Armey (R-TX)	Richard A. Gephardt (D-MO)	(1999–2001)
105th	Richard K. Armey (R-TX)	Richard A. Gephardt (D-MO)	(1997–1999)
104th	Richard K. Armey (R-TX)	Richard A. Gephardt (D-MO)	(1995–1997)
103rd	Richard A. Gephardt (D-MO)	Robert H. Michel (R-IL)	(1993–1995)
102nd	Richard A. Gephardt (D-MO)	Robert H. Michel (R-IL)	(1991–1993)
101st	Richard A. Gephardt (D-MO)[4]	Robert H. Michel (R-IL)	(1989–1991)
101st	Thomas S. Foley (D-WA)[5]	Robert H. Michel (R-IL)	(1989–1990)
100th	Thomas S. Foley (D-WA)	Robert H. Michel (R-IL)	(1987–1989)
99th	James C. Wright, Jr. (D-TX)	Robert H. Michel (R-IL)	(1985–1987)
98th	James C. Wright, Jr. (D-TX)	Robert H. Michel (R-IL)	(1983–1985)
97th	James C. Wright, Jr. (D-TX)	Robert H. Michel (R-IL)	(1981–1983)
96th	James C. Wright, Jr. (D-TX)	John J. Rhodes (R-AZ)	(1979–1981)
95th	James C. Wright, Jr. (D-TX)	John J. Rhodes (R-AZ)	(1977–1979)
94th	Thomas P. O'Neill Jr. (D-MA)	John J. Rhodes (R-AZ)	(1975–1977)
93rd	Thomas P. O'Neill Jr. (D-MA)	John J. Rhodes (R-AZ)	(1974–1975)
93rd	Thomas P. O'Neill Jr. (D-MA)	Gerald R. Ford (R-MI)[6]	(1973)
92nd	Hale Boggs (D-LA)[7]	Gerald R. Ford (R-MI)	(1971–1973)
91st	Carl B. Albert (D-OK)	Gerald R. Ford (R-MI)	(1969–1971)
90th	Carl B. Albert (D-OK)	Gerald R. Ford (R-MI)	(1967–1969)
89th	Carl B. Albert (D-OK)	Gerald R. Ford (R-MI)	(1965–1967)
88th	Carl B. Albert (D-OK)	Charles A. Halleck (R-IN)	(1963–1965)
87th	Carl B. Albert (D-OK)[8]	Charles A. Halleck (R-IN)	(1962–1963)
87th	John W. McCormack (D-MA)[9]	Charles A. Halleck (R-IN)	(1961–1962)
86th	John W. McCormack (D-MA)	Charles A. Halleck (R-IN)	(1959–1961)
85th	John W. McCormack (D-MA)	Joseph W. Martin, Jr. (R-MA)	(1957–1959)
84th	John W. McCormack (D-MA)	Joseph W. Martin, Jr. (R-MA)	(1955–1957)
83rd	Charles A. Halleck (R-IN)	Sam Rayburn (D-TX)	(1953–1955)
82nd	John W. McCormack (D-MA)	Joseph W. Martin, Jr. (R-MA)	(1951–1953)
81st	John W. McCormack (D-MA)	Joseph W. Martin, Jr. (R-MA)	(1949–1951)
80th	Charles A. Halleck (R-IN)	Sam Rayburn (D-TX)	(1947–1949)
79th	John W. McCormack (D-MA)	Joseph W. Martin, Jr. (R-MA)	(1945–1947)
78th	John W. McCormack (D-MA)	Joseph W. Martin, Jr. (R-MA)	(1943–1945)
77th	John W. McCormack (D-MA)	Joseph W. Martin, Jr. (R-MA)	(1941–1942)
76th	John W. McCormack (D-MA)[10]	Joseph W. Martin, Jr. (R-MA)	(1940–1941)
76th	Sam Rayburn (D-TX)[11]	Joseph W. Martin, Jr. (R-MA)	(1939–1940)
75th	Sam Rayburn (D-TX)	Bertrand H. Snell (R-NY)	(1937–1939)
74th	William B. Bankhead (D-AL)	Bertrand H. Snell (R-NY)	(1935–1937)
73rd	Joseph W. Byrns (D-TN)	Bertrand H. Snell (R-NY)	(1933–1935)
72nd	Henry T. Rainey (D-IL)	Bertrand H. Snell (R-NY)	(1931–1933)
71st	John Q. Tilson (R-CT)	John N. Garner (D-TX)	(1929–1931)
70th	John Q. Tilson (R-CT)	Finis J. Garrett (D-TN)	(1927–1929)
69th	John Q. Tilson (R-CT)	Finis J. Garrett (D-TN)	(1925–1927)
68th	Nicholas Longworth (R-OH)	Finis J. Garrett (D-TN)	(1923–1925)
67th	Frank W. Mondell (R-WY)	Claude Kitchin (D-NC)	(1921–1923)
66th	Frank W. Mondell (R-WY)	James Beauchamp Clark (D-MO)	(1919–1921)
65th	Claude Kitchin (D-NC)	James R. Mann (R-IL)	(1917–1919)
64th	Claude Kitchin (D-NC)	James R. Mann (R-IL)	(1915–1917)
63rd	Oscar W. Underwood (D-AL)	James R. Mann (R-IL)	(1913–1915)
62nd	Oscar W. Underwood (D-AL)	James R. Mann (R-IL)	(1911–1913)
61st	Sereno E. Payne (R-NY)	James Beauchamp Clark (D-MO)	(1909–1911)
60th	Sereno E. Payne (R-NY)	James Beauchamp Clark (D-MO)	(1908–1909)
60th	Sereno E. Payne (R-NY)	John Sharp Williams (D-MS)	(1907–1908)
59th	Sereno E. Payne (R-NY)	John Sharp Williams (D-MS)	(1905–1907)
58th	Sereno E. Payne (R-NY)	John Sharp Williams (D-MS)	(1903–1905)
57th	Sereno E. Payne (R-NY)	James D. Richardson (D-TN)	(1901–1903)
56th	Sereno E. Payne (R-NY)	James D. Richardson (D-TN)	(1899–1901)

Source: U.S. House of Representatives, Office of the Clerk. *Biographical Directory of the U.S. Congress.*

[1]Elected Majority Leader by the Republican Conference on February 2, 2006.
[2]Elected Majority Leader on an interim basis by the Republican Conference on September 28, 2005, to fill the vacancy created when Majority Leader Tom DeLay temporarily stepped aside.
[3]On September 28, 2005, Majority Leader Tom DeLay temporarily stepped aside as Majority Leader pursuant to Republican Conference rules.
[4]Elected Majority Leader on June 14, 1989, to fill the vacancy left when Majority Leader Thomas Foley was elected Speaker on June 6, 1989.
[5]Elected Speaker on June 6, 1989, following Speaker James Wright's resignation on the same date.
[6]Resigned from the House of Representatives on December 6, 1973, after having been confirmed by the Senate to become Vice President to fill the vacancy created by the resignation of Vice President Spiro Agnew.
[7]Disappeared on a flight from Anchorage to Juneau, Alaska, October 16, 1972. Presumed dead pursuant to House Resolution 1, at the commencement of the 93rd Congress.
[8]Elected Majority Leader on January 10, 1962, at the commencement of the 87th Congress, 2nd session, to fill the vacancy left when Majority Leader John McCormack was elected Speaker.
[9]Elected Speaker on January 10, 1962, at the commencement of the 87th Congress, 2nd session, filling the vacancy caused by the death of Sam Rayburn.
[10]Elected Majority Leader on September 16, 1940, to fill the vacancy left when Majority Leader Sam Rayburn was elected Speaker.
[11]Elected Speaker on September 16, 1940, filling the vacancy caused by the death of Speaker William Bankhead.

Table 30-7. Senate Legislative Activity, 1987–2006

	1987	1990	1995	2000	2001	2002	2003	2004	2005	2006
Senate convened	Jan. 6	Jan. 23	Jan. 4	Jan. 24	Jan. 3	Jan. 23	Jan. 7	Jan. 20	Jan. 4	Jan. 3
Senate adjourned	Dec. 22	Oct. 28	Jan. 23 ('96)	Dec. 15	Dec. 20	Nov. 20	Dec. 9	Dec. 8	Dec. 22	Dec. 9
Days in session	170	138	211	141	173	149	167	133	159	138
Hours in session	1,214'52_	1,250'14_	1,839'10_	1,017'51_	1,236'15_	1,043'23_	1,454'05_	1,031'31_	1,222'26_	1,027'48_
Average hours per day	7.1	9.1	8.7	7.2	7.1	7	8.7	7.7	7.7	7.4
Total measures passed	616	716	346	696	425	523	590	663	624	635
Roll call votes	420	326	613	298	380	253	459	216	366	279
Quorum calls	36	3	3	6	3	2	3	1	3	1
Public laws	240	244	88	410	136	241	198	300	169	248
Treaties ratified	3	15	10	39	3	17	11	15	6	14
Nominations confirmed	46 404	42 493	40 535	22 512	25 091	23 633	21 580	24 420	25 942	29 603
Average voting attendance	94.03	97.47	98.07	96.99	98.29	96.36	96.07	95.54	97.41	97.13
Sessions convened before 12 noon	131	116	184	107	140	119	133	104	121	110
Sessions convened at 12 noon	12	4	2	25	10	12	4	9	1	4
Sessions convened after 12 noon	25	17	12	24	21	23	23	21	36	24
Sessions continued after 6 p.m.	97	100	158	94	108	103	134	129	120	129
Sessions continued after 12 midnight	6	13	3	0	2	3	8	2	3	3
Saturday sessions	3	3	5	1	3	0	1	2	2	2
Sunday sessions	1	2	3	1	0	0	1	1	2	0

Source: U.S. Senate, Office of the Secretary.

Table 30-8. Number of Governmental Units, by Type, 1942–2002

Year	Total	U.S. government	State government	Local government					
				Total	County	Municipal	Township and town	School district	Special district
2002	87 576	1	50	87 525	3 034	19 429	16 504	13 506	35 052
1997	87 504	1	50	87 453	3 043	19 372	16 629	13 726	34 683
1992	85 006	1	50	84 955	3 043	19 279	16 656	14 422	31 555
1987	83 237	1	50	83 186	3 042	19 200	16 691	14 721	29 532
1982	81 831	1	50	81 780	3 041	19 076	16 734	14 851	28 078
1977	79 913	1	50	79 862	3 042	18 862	16 822	15 174	25 962
1972	78 269	1	50	78 218	3 044	18 517	16 991	15 781	23 885
1967	81 299	1	50	81 248	3 049	18 048	17 105	21 782	21 264
1962	91 237	1	50	91 186	3 043	18 000	17 142	34 678	18 323
1952[1]	116 807	1	50	116 756	3 052	16 807	17 202	67 355	12 340
1942	155 116	1	48	155 067	3 050	16 220	18 919	108 579	8 299

Source: U.S. Census Bureau.
[1]Adjusted to include units in Alaska and Hawaii, which adopted statehood in 1959.

Table 30-9. Number of Governors, by Political Party Affiliation, 1970–2006

(Reflects figures after inaugurations for each year.)

Year	Democratic	Republican	Independent or other party
2006	22	28	0
2005	22	28	0
2004	22	28	0
2003	23	27	0
2002	22	27	1
2001	19	29	2
2000	18	30	2
1999	17	31	1
1998	17	32	1
1997	17	32	1
1996[1]	18	31	1
1995	19	30	1
1994	29	19	2
1993[2]	30	18	2
1992	28	20	2
1991[3]	28	20	2
1990	29	21	0
1989	28	22	0
1988[4]	26	24	0
1987	26	24	0
1986	34	16	0
1985	34	16	0
1984	35	15	0
1983	34	16	0
1982	27	23	0
1981	27	23	0
1980	31	19	0
1979	32	18	0
1978	37	12	1
1977	37	12	1
1976	36	13	1
1975	36	13	1
1974	32	18	0
1973	31	19	0
1972	30	20	0
1971	29	21	0
1970	18	32	0

Source: U.S. Census Bureau. *Statistical Abstract of the United States: 2007.* National Governors Association. 1970–87 and 1991–2006, *Directory of Governors of the American States, Commonwealths & Territories* and 1988–90, *Directory of Governors* (Copyright).
[1]Arkansas's Democratic governor was succeeded midyear by a Republican.
[2]Alaska's Republican governor was succeeded midyear by a Democrat.
[3]In 1991, Arizona's Democratic governor was succeeded midyear by a Democrat and Vermont's Republican governor was succeeded midyear by a Democrat.
[4]In 1988, Arizona's Republican governor was succeeded midyear by a Democrat.

Table 30-10. Governmental Employment, 1946–2004

(Thousands of employees, covers full-time and part-time employees, local government data are estimates subject to sampling variation.)

Year	Total	Federal (civilian)[1]	State and local		
			Total	State	Local
2004	21 494	2 734	18 760	5 041	13 719
2003	21 336	2 717	18 649	5 042	13 606
2002	21 039	2 690	18 349	5 072	13 277
2001	20 970	2 698	18 272	4 985	13 288
2000	20 876	2 899	17 976	4 877	13 099
1999	20 306	2 799	17 506	4 818	12 689
1998	19 854	2 765	17 089	4 758	12 271
1997	19 540	2 807	16 733	4 733	12 000
1996	. . .	. . .	. . .	. . .	. . .
1995	19 521	2 895	16 626	4 719	11 906
1994	19 420	2 952	16 468	4 694	11 775
1993	18 823	2 999	15 824	4 673	11 151
1992	18 745	3 047	15 698	4 595	11 103
1991	18 554	3 103	15 452	4 521	10 390
1990	18 369	3 105	15 263	4 503	10 760
1989	17 897	3 114	14 765	4 365	10 400
1988	17 588	3 112	14 476	4 236	10 240
1987	17 212	3 091	14 121	4 116	10 005
1986	16 933	3 019	13 913	4 068	9 846
1985	16 690	3 021	13 669	3 984	9 685
1984	16 436	2 942	13 494	3 898	9 595
1983	16 033	2 874	13 159	3 816	9 344
1982	15 841	2 848	12 993	3 744	9 249
1981	15 968	2 865	13 103	3 726	9 377
1980	16 213	2 898	13 315	3 753	9 562
1979	15 971	2 869	13 102	3 699	9 403
1978	15 628	2 885	12 743	3 539	9 204
1977	15 459	2 848	12 611	3 491	9 120
1976	15 012	2 843	12 169	3 343	8 826
1975	14 973	2 890	12 084	3 271	8 813
1974	14 628	2 874	11 754	3 155	8 599
1973	14 139	2 786	11 353	3 013	8 339
1972	13 759	2 795	10 964	2 957	8 007
1971	13 316	2 872	10 444	2 832	7 612
1970	13 028	2 881	10 147	2 755	7 392
1969	12 685	2 969	9 716	2 614	7 102
1968	12 342	2 984	9 358	2 495	6 864
1967	11 867	2 993	8 874	2 335	6 539
1966	11 388	2 861	8 527	2 211	6 316
1965	10 589	2 588	8 001	2 028	5 973
1964	10 064	2 528	7 536	1 873	5 663
1963	9 736	2 548	7 188	1 775	5 413
1962	9 388	2 539	6 849	1 680	5 169
1961	9 100	2 484	6 616	1 625	4 992
1960	8 808	2 421	6 387	1 527	4 860
1959	8 487	2 399	6 088	1 454	4 634
1958	8 297	2 405	5 892	1 408	4 484
1957	8 047	2 439	5 608	1 300	4 307
1956	7 685	2 410	5 275	1 268	4 007
1955	7 432	2 378	5 054	1 199	3 855
1954	7 232	2 373	4 859	1 149	3 710
1953	7 048	2 385	4 663	1 082	3 580
1952	7 105	2 583	4 522	1 060	3 461
1951	6 802	2 515	4 287	1 070	3 218
1950	6 402	2 117	4 285	1 057	3 228
1949	6 203	2 047	4 156	1 037	3 119
1948	6 042	2 076	3 966	963	3 002
1947	5 791	2 002	3 789	909	2 880
1946	6 001	2 434	3 567	804	2 762

Source: U.S. Census Bureau.
[1]Includes employees outside the United States.
. . . = Not available.

Table 30-11. Caseload of the U.S. Supreme Court, 1970–2004

(Statutory term of court begins first Monday in October.)

Action	1970	1975	1980	1985	1990	1995	2000	2001	2002	2003	2004
Total Cases on Docket	4 212	4 761	5 144	5 158	6 316	7 565	8 965	9 176	9 406	8 882	8 588
Appellate cases on docket	1 903	2 352	2 749	2 571	2 351	2 456	2 305	2 210	2 190	2 058	2 041
From prior term	325	431	527	400	365	361	351	324	321	336	300
Docketed during present term	1 578	1 921	2 222	2 171	1 986	2 095	1 954	1 886	1 869	1 722	1 741
Cases acted upon[1]	1 613	1 900	2 324	2 185	2 042	2 130	2 024	1 932	1 899	1 798	1 727
Granted review	214	244	167	166	114	92	85	82	83	74	69
Denied, dismissed, or withdrawn	1 285	1 538	1 999	1 863	1 802	1 945	1 842	1 751	1 727	1 641	1 529
Summarily decided	114	118	90	78	81	62	63	57	46	37	89
Cases not acted upon	290	452	425	386	309	326	281	278	291	260	314
Pauper cases on docket	2 289	2 395	2 371	2 577	3 951	5 098	6 651	6 958	7 209	6 818	6 543
Cases acted upon	1 802	1 997	2 027	2 189	3 436	4 514	5 736	6 139	6 488	6 036	5 815
Granted review	41	28	17	20	27	13	14	6	8	13	11
Denied, dismissed, or withdrawn	1 683	1 903	1 968	2 136	3 369	4 439	5 658	6 114	6 459	6 005	5 061
Summarily decided	48	66	32	24	28	55	61	13	17	13	737
Cases not acted upon	487	398	344	388	515	584	915	819	721	782	728
Original cases on docket	20	14	24	10	14	11	9	8	7	6	4
Cases disposed of during term	7	7	7	2	3	5	2	1	1	2	0
Total Cases Available for Argument	267	280	264	276	201	145	138	137	139	140	128
Cases disposed of	160	181	162	175	131	93	89	90	87	93	87
Cases argued	151	179	154	171	125	90	86	88	84	91	87
Cases dismissed or remanded without argument	9	2	8	4	6	3	3	2	3	2	0
Cases remaining	107	99	102	101	70	52	49	47	52	47	41
Cases decided by signed opinion	126	160	144	161	121	87	83	85	79	89	85
Cases decided by per curiam opinion	22	16	8	10	4	3	4	3	5	2	2
Number of signed opinions	109	138	123	146	112	75	77	76	71	73	74

Source: U.S. Census Bureau. Supreme Court of the United States, Office of the Clerk.
[1] Includes cases granted review and carried over to next term, not shown separately.

BOX 30 ■ The Changing Makeup of Congress

The racial, ethnic, religious, and gender makeup of members of congress increasingly reflects the characteristics of the voting public. Until 1870, members of Congress were all white men. In that year of Reconstruction, two African American men were elected: Hiram Revels became a senator from Mississippi and Joseph Rainey became a representative from South Carolina. Revels served one year, but Rainey served five terms in the House. In 1875, another African-American, Blanche Bruce, was voted in as a senator from Mississippi. Another non-white was not elected to Congress until well into the twentieth century.

Of the 19 members of ethnic/racial minority groups who have served in the U.S. Senate, only one was a woman and six, or 31%, are currently in office, including one African American, two Asian Americans, and three Hispanic Americans. Of the thirty-five women who have served in the Senate, 16 are currently in office.

In 1917, Jeannette Rankin of Montana became the first woman elected to Congress. A woman was not elected to the Senate until 1938, when Hattie Wyatt Caraway who had been appointed to fill the remainder of her late husband's term, was then elected to a second term. She served until 1945.

By 1969, women accounted for 2% of Congress, African Americans, 1.9%, and all other racial and ethnic groups, only 0.7%. These members accounted for only 25 of 535 members of Congress. These numbers remained relatively stable until 1985, when voters elected 10 Hispanic Americans, 20 African Americans, and 24 women, representing 1.9%, 3.7%, and 4.5% of the membership, respectively. However, almost all diversity candidates were in the House; there were no racial or ethnic minorities and only two women in the Senate at this time.

Minority representation increased sharply in the 103rd Congress that first met in 1993. There were 39 African Americans (7.3%). This number was an increase of 50% from 26 members in the 102nd Congress in 1991. In 1993, Congress also included 9 Americans of Asian or Pacific Island descent (1.7%), up 28% from the prior term; 17 Hispanic American members (3.2%), up 55%. Fifty-four women (10.1%) was an increase of 80%.

By 2005, the 109th Congress had 43 African Americans (8.0%), 6 Americans of Asian or Pacific Island descent (1.1%), 25 Hispanic Americans (4.7%), and 79 women (14.8%). While these numbers, for the most part, are increasing, they are still not representative of the population at large. This is especially true for the Senate, where the 109th Congress had only 1 African American, 2 Asian or Pacific Island descent senators, and 2 Hispanic American senators.

Representation from diverse religious groups is also increasing. In 1969, there were 19 Jewish members of Congress (3.6%). By 2001, that number increased to 37 (6.9%), an 8% increase from the 1999 body. The current Congress welcomed 43 Jewish members (8.0%). In addition, in 2007 Congress for the first time included a Muslim and two Buddhists.

Sources:

Tilove, Jonathan. "Following Their Creeds; A Measure of Faith; Religious Makeup of New Congress is Groundbreaking." *The Houston Chronicle* (December 30, 2006): 1.

U.S. Census Bureau. *Statistical Abstract of the United States,* (1972, 1978, 1992, and 2007 editions).

U.S. Congress, House of Representatives. Women in Congress. http://womenincongress.house.gov/

U.S. Congress, House of Representatives, Office of the Clerk. House History. http://clerk.house.gov/art_history/house_history/index.html

U.S. Congress, Senate. Senators, Biographical Characteristics. http://www.senate.gov/pagelayout/reference/three_column_table/Senators.htm

Witham, Larry. "Catholics Still Top Religions on Hill." *The Washington Times* (December 31, 2000): 1.

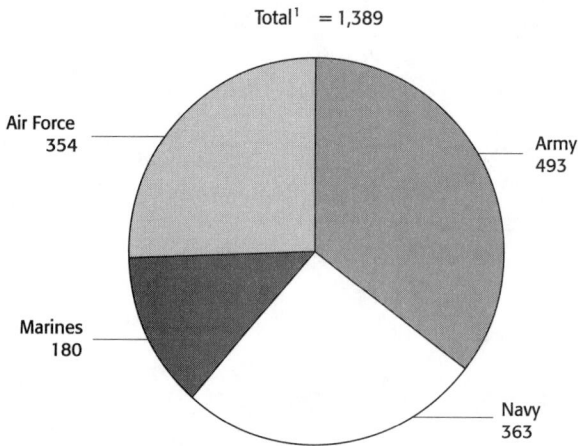

Total[1] = 1,389

Air Force
354

Army
493

Marines
180

Navy
363

Department of Defense Manpower: 2005

(In thousands)
[1]Includes National Guard, Reserve, and retired regular personnel on extended or
continuous active duty. Excludes Coast Goard.
Source: Chart prepared by U.S. Census Bureau.

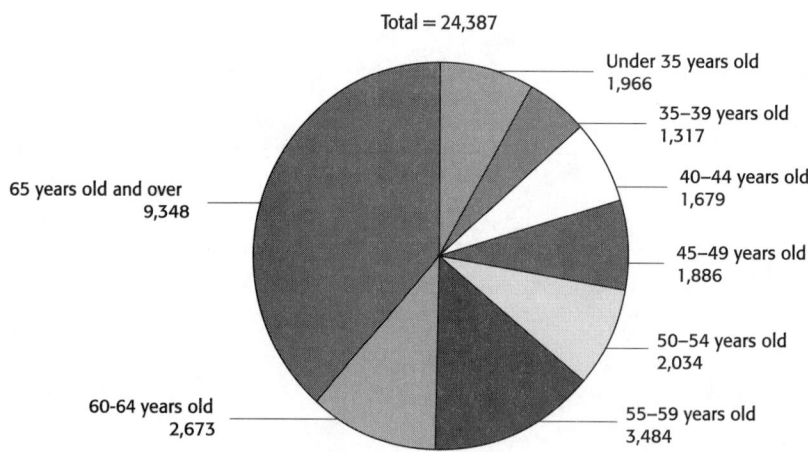

Total = 24,387

Under 35 years old
1,966

35–39 years old
1,317

40–44 years old
1,679

45–49 years old
1,886

50–54 years old
2,034

55–59 years old
3,484

60-64 years old
2,673

65 years old and over
9,348

Living Veterans by Age: 2005

(In thousands)
Source: Chart prepared by U.S. Census Bureau.

CHAPTER 31

National Security

HIGHLIGHTS

1 The Department of War (now the Department of Defense) was established in 1789. The Navy started functioning in 1794, and a separate Navy Department was authorized and organized in 1798. The Department of the Air Force was set up in 1947 under the National Security Act. The Marine Corps was founded in 1775, disbanded in 1783, and re-activated in 1794. In 1794, under George Washington, the defense force of the new republic consisted of an army of 3,813 persons (including 235 officers) and a Navy of 1,856 persons (including 150 officers). The total military budget was $2.639 million for the Army and $61,000 for the Navy.

2 The federal defense budget reached 495.3 billion in 2005, up from 48.1 billion in 1960. As a percentage of GDP, the defense budget declined from 9.3 percent in 1960 to 4.0 percent in 2005. The 2006 estimated budget was $535.9 billion. Military downsizing led to a substantial reduction in personnel, from 3,693,000 in 1990 to 2,764,000 in 2004. As of 2005, the United States accounts for 48 percent of military expenditures throughout the world.

3 The United States is a major arms exporter. Between 1998 and 2005 it has sold $107.222 billion worth of weaponry, more than double of its nearest rival.

4 In 2005, 290,997 U.S. military personnel were on active military duty abroad, including 11,841 in Italy, 30,983 in South Korea, 66,418 in Germany, and 35,571 in Japan.

5 The number of veterans in 2004 was 24.387 million, of which war veterans numbered 18.156 million.

6 There were 1,055,314 military and civilian personnel stationed in installations throughout the United States in 2004. Of those California had the most at 128,277. Other states with a high number of personnel include Texas (109,760) and North Carolina (101, 033). States with the smallest numbers of military and civilian personnel were Vermont (60), New Hampshire (218), and Iowa (364).

Table 31-1. Armed Forces Personnel—Summary of Major Conflicts

(Thousands, except as noted. For Revolutionary War, number of personnel serving not known, but estimates range from 184,000 to 250,000; for War of 1812, 286,730 served; for Mexican War, 78,718 served. Dates of the major conflicts may differ from those specified in various laws providing benefits for veterans.)

Item	Civil War[1]	Spanish-American War	World War I	World War II	Korean Conflict	Vietnam Conflict	Persian Gulf War
Personnel serving[2]	2 213	307	4 735	[3]16 113	[4]5 720	[5]8 744	2 233
Average duration of service (months)	20	8	12	33	19	23	...
Service abroad: Personnel serving (percent)	...	[6]29	53	73	[7]56	...	...
Average duration[8] (months)	...	1.5	6	16	13	...	...
Casualties:[9]							
Battle deaths[2]	140	(Z)	53	292	34	[10]47	(Z)
Other deaths	224	2	63	114	3	11	(Z)
Wounds not mortal[2]	282	2	204	671	103	[10]153	(Z)
Draftees: Classified	777	X	24 234	36 677	9 123	[5]75 717	X
Examined	522	X	3 764	17 955	3 685	[5]8 611	X
Rejected	160	X	803	6 420	1 189	[5]3 880	X
Inducted	46	X	2 820	10 022	1 560	[5]1 759	X

Source: U.S. Census Bureau. The President's Commission on Veterans' Pensions. U.S. Department of Defense.
[1]Union forces only. Estimates of the number serving in Confederate forces range from 600,000 to 1.5 million.
[2]Source: U.S. Department of Defense, Selected Manpower Statistics, annual.
[3]Covers Dec. 1, 1941, to Dec. 31, 1946.
[4]Covers June 25, 1950, to July 27, 1953.
[5]Covers Aug. 4, 1964, to Jan. 27, 1973.
[6]Army and Marines only.
[7]Excludes Navy. Covers July 1950 through Jan.1955. Far East area only.
[8]During hostilities only.
[9]For periods covered, see footnotes 3, 4, and 5.
[10]Covers Jan.1, 1961, to Jan. 27, 1973. Includes known military service personnel who have died from combat related wounds.
. . . = Not available.
X = Not applicable.
Z = Fewer than 500.

Table 31-2. Military Personnel on Active Duty, by Location, 1980–2005

(Thousands, as of September 30.)

Year	Total	Shore based[1]	Afloat[2]	United States[3]	Foreign countries
2005	1 389	1 262	127	1 098	291
2004	1 427	1 291	136	1 139	288
2003	1 434	1 287	148	1 182	253
2002	1 412	1 262	150	1 181	230
2001	1 385	1 244	141	1 130	255
2000	1 384	1 237	147	1 127	258
1999	1 386	1 241	145	1 133	253
1998	1 407	1 267	140	1 147	260
1997	1 439	1 294	145	1 211	227
1996	1 472	1 317	155	1 231	240
1995	1 518	1 351	167	1 280	238
1994	1 611	1 431	180	1 324	287
1993	1 705	1 505	200	1 397	308
1992	1 807	1 589	218	1 463	344
1991	1 986	1 743	243	1 539	448
1990	2 046	1 794	252	1 437	609
1989	2 130	1 884	246	1 620	510
1988	2 138	1 891	248	1 598	541
1987	2 174	1 928	246	1 650	524
1986	2 169	1 929	240	1 644	526
1985	2 151	1 920	231	1 636	515
1984	2 138	1 908	230	1 628	510
1983	2 123	1 889	234	1 604	519
1982	2 109	1 880	229	1 580	528
1981	2 083	1 869	214	1 581	502
1980	2 051	1 840	211	1 562	489

Source: U.S. Census Bureau. *Statistical Abstract of the United States: 2007.* U.S. Department of Defense.
[1]Includes Navy personnel temporarily on shore.
[2]Includes Marine Corps.
[3]Includes Puerto Rico and Island areas.

Table 31-3. Department of Defense Personnel, 1960–2005

(Thousands, as of end of fiscal year. Includes National Guard, Reserve, and retired regular personnel on extended or continuous active duty. Excludes Coast Guard. Other officer candidates are included under enlisted personnel.)

Year	Total[1,2]	Army					Navy[2]				
		Total[1]	Male		Female		Total[1]	Male		Female	
			Officers	Enlisted	Officers	Enlisted		Officers	Enlisted	Officers	Enlisted
2005	1 389	493	69	353	12.40	57.90	363	45	266	7.80	44.50
2004	1 427	500	69	358	12.30	61.00	373	46	273	8.10	46.10
2003	1 434	499	68	352	11.98	63.50	382	47	276	8.25	47.34
2002	1 414	487	66	341	11.54	63.22	385	47	279	8.19	47.33
2001	1 385	481	65	337	11.03	63.39	378	46	273	8.04	46.59
2000	1 384	482	66	339	10.81	62.89	373	46	272	7.85	43.76
1999	1 386	479	67	337	10.52	61.51	373	46	271	7.70	43.92
1998	1 407	484	68	340	10.37	61.41	382	47	280	7.78	42.92
1997	1 439	492	69	346	10.39	62.44	396	48	290	7.80	44.78
1996	1 472	491	70	347	10.58	59.04	417	50	308	7.83	46.87
1995	1 518	509	72	365	10.79	57.26	435	51	324	7.90	47.93
1994	1 610	541	74	394	10.88	58.99	469	54	355	7.97	47.86
1993	1 705	572	77	420	11.14	60.19	510	58	390	8.27	49.34
1992	1 807	610	83	449	11.74	61.69	542	61	417	8.29	51.01
1991	1 986	711	91	535	12.53	67.77	570	63	444	7.98	51.41
1990	2 044	732	92	553	12.40	71.22	579	64	451	7.81	52.10
1989	2 130	770	95	584	12.20	74.30	593	65	464	7.45	52.07
1988	2 138	772	95	588	11.75	72.02	593	65	466	7.34	49.67
1987	2 174	781	96	596	11.57	71.61	587	65	462	7.22	47.74
1986	2 169	781	99	597	11.26	69.67	581	65	457	7.26	47.20
1985	2 151	781	99	599	10.83	68.42	571	64	449	6.91	45.69
1984	2 138	780	98	601	10.23	67.13	565	62	448	6.55	42.58
1983	2 123	780	97	602	9.49	66.54	558	62	444	6.30	40.79
1982	2 109	780	94	609	9.03	64.07	553	61	444	5.74	37.32
1981	2 083	781	94	610	8.35	65.30	540	60	435	5.35	34.56
1980	2 051	777	91	612	7.61	61.73	527	58	430	4.88	30.10
1979	2 027	759	90	602	6.87	55.15	523	58	432	4.36	25.04
1978	2 062	772	92	619	6.29	50.55	530	59	442	3.98	21.31
1977	2 075	782	92	634	5.70	46.09	530	59	443	3.79	19.46
1976	2 082	779	94	634	4.84	43.81	525	60	439	3.54	19.29
1975	2 128	784	98	640	4.59	37.70	535	62	449	3.68	17.50
1974	2 162	783	102	648	4.39	26.33	546	63	462	3.65	13.38
1973	2 252	801	112	666	4.28	16.46	564	68	481	3.45	9.17
1972	2 322	811	117	675	4.42	12.35	587	70	505	3.19	6.26
1971	2 713	1 124	144	960	5.04	11.83	622	72	536	2.87	5.93
1970	3 065	1 323	162	1,142	5.25	11.48	691	78	600	2.89	5.80
1969	3 458	1 512	168	1,326	5.16	10.72	774	82	678	2.88	5.75
1968	3 546	1 570	161	1,391	5.10	10.71	764	82	668	3.03	5.66
1967	3 375	1 442	139	1,287	4.74	9.74	750	79	658	3.02	5.50
1966	3 092	1 200	114	1,071	4.14	9.18	743	77	654	2.81	5.39
1965	2 654	969	108	846	3.81	8.52	670	75	583	2.60	5.26
1964	2 686	973	107	853	3.77	7.96	666	73	580	2.68	5.06
1963	2 699	976	104	858	3.85	8.29	664	73	578	2.66	5.56
1962	2 806	1 066	112	940	4.35	8.72	664	72	579	2.74	5.93
1961	2 483	859	96	748	4.25	8.56	626	67	546	2.74	5.94
1960	2 475	873	97	762	4.26	8.28	617	67	540	2.71	5.36

Source: U.S. Census Bureau. *Statistical Abstract of the United States: 2007.* U.S. Department of Defense.
[1]Includes cadets, midshipmen and others not shown separately.
[2]Beginning 1980, excludes Navy Reserve personnel on active duty for Training and Administration of Reserves (TARS).

Table 31-3. Department of Defense Personnel, 1960–2005—*Continued*

(Thousands, as of end of fiscal year. Includes National Guard, Reserve, and retired regular personnel on extended or continuous active duty. Excludes Coast Guard. Other officer candidates are included under enlisted personnel.)

Marine Corps					Air Force				
	Male		Female			Male		Female	
Total[1]	Officers	Enlisted	Officers	Enlisted	Total[1]	Officers	Enlisted	Officers	Enlisted
180	18	151	1.00	9.80	354	60	225	13.40	55.60
178	18	149	1.10	9.70	377	61	242	13.60	60.20
178	18	149	1.09	9.58	375	61	237	13.48	60.03
174	17	146	1.00	9.48	368	59	233	12.91	58.60
173	17	145	0.98	9.57	354	57	224	12.03	55.55
173	17	146	0.93	9.53	356	57	227	11.82	55.01
173	17	145	0.89	9.28	361	58	232	11.84	54.63
173	17	146	0.85	8.93	368	60	237	11.97	54.20
174	17	148	0.79	8.50	377	62	246	12.01	53.83
175	17	149	0.75	7.81	389	64	256	12.05	52.77
175	17	150	0.69	7.40	400	66	266	12.07	52.08
174	17	149	0.64	7.03	426	69	287	12.32	53.99
178	17	153	0.64	7.21	444	72	302	12.25	54.48
185	18	157	0.65	7.88	470	77	320	12.68	56.11
194	19	166	0.69	8.32	510	84	350	13.32	59.11
197	19	168	0.68	8.68	535	87	370	13.33	60.80
197	19	168	0.70	9.01	571	91	399	13.40	63.70
197	19	168	0.65	8.96	576	92	405	12.90	61.55
200	19	170	0.65	9.14	607	94	432	12.64	63.24
200	19	170	0.64	9.25	608	97	434	12.38	61.23
198	19	169	0.65	9.04	602	96	431	11.93	58.13
196	19	167	0.65	8.58	597	95	430	11.23	55.88
194	19	166	0.62	8.27	592	94	428	10.56	55.31
192	18	165	0.56	7.88	583	92	421	9.94	54.51
191	17	165	0.53	7.09	570	90	413	9.11	54.37
189	18	164	0.49	6.22	558	90	404	8.49	51.90
185	18	161	0.46	5.50	560	89	413	7.28	46.43
191	18	167	0.43	4.65	570	89	429	6.01	41.08
192	19	169	0.42	3.51	571	91	435	5.38	34.61
192	19	171	0.39	3.06	585	95	452	4.97	29.24
196	19	174	0.35	2.84	613	100	478	4.98	25.23
189	19	168	0.34	2.40	644	105	510	4.77	19.47
196	19	175	0.32	1.97	691	110	557	4.73	15.02
198	20	176	0.26	2.07	726	117	588	4.77	11.73
212	22	189	0.28	1.98	755	121	615	4.72	10.13
260	25	233	0.30	2.12	791	125	648	4.67	8.99
310	26	282	0.28	2.44	862	130	716	4.86	7.41
307	25	280	0.23	2.56	905	135	756	4.99	6.12
285	24	260	0.19	2.12	897	130	754	4.67	5.19
262	21	239	0.15	1.68	887	127	748	4.19	5.05
190	17	172	0.14	1.44	825	128	685	4.10	4.74
190	17	172	0.13	1.32	857	129	716	4.03	4.85
190	17	171	0.14	1.56	869	130	728	3.91	4.80
191	17	172	0.12	1.58	884	131	741	3.95	4.82
177	16	160	0.12	1.50	821	125	685	3.68	5.30
171	16	153	0.12	1.49	815	126	677	3.68	5.65

Table 31-4. Veterans and Active Duty Military Personnel, 1900–2006

(Thousands, for fiscal year ending in year shown.)

Year	Veterans	Active duty military personnel				
		Total	Army	Navy	Marine Corps	Air Force
2006	23 977	1 385.0	505.4	350.2	180.4	349.0
2005	24 387	1 389.4	492.7	362.9	180.0	353.7
2004	24 793	1 426.8	499.5	373.2	177.5	376.6
2003	25 191	1 434.4	499.3	382.2	177.8	375.1
2002	25 582	1 414.0	487.0	385.0	174.0	368.0
2001	26 066	1 385.0	481.0	378.0	173.0	354.0
2000	26 542	1 384.3	482.2	373.2	173.3	355.7
1999	24 803	1 385.7	479.4	373.0	172.6	360.6
1998	25 188	1 406.8	483.8	382.3	173.1	367.5
1997	25 551	1 438.6	491.7	395.6	173.9	377.4
1996	25 881	1 471.7	491.1	416.7	174.9	389.0
1995	26 198	1 518.0	509.0	435.0	175.0	400.0
1994	26 503	1 610.0	541.0	469.0	174.0	426.0
1993	26 789	1 705.0	572.0	510.0	178.0	444.0
1992	26 980	1 807.0	610.0	542.0	185.0	470.0
1991	27 152	1 986.0	711.0	570.0	194.0	510.0
1990	27 320	2 044.0	732.0	579.0	197.0	535.0
1989	27 497	2 130.2	769.7	592.7	197.0	570.9
1988	27 650	2 138.2	771.8	592.6	197.4	576.4
1987	27 803	2 174.2	780.8	586.8	199.5	607.0
1986	27 946	2 169.1	781.0	581.1	198.8	608.2
1985	28 075	2 151.0	780.8	570.7	198.0	301.5
1984	28 207	2 138.2	780.2	564.6	196.2	597.1
1983	28 316	2 123.3	779.6	557.6	194.1	592.0
1982	28 432	2 108.6	780.4	553.0	192.4	582.8
1981	28 519	2 082.6	781.4	540.2	190.6	570.3
1980	28 640	2 050.6	777.0	527.2	188.5	558.0
1979	28 605	2 026.9	758.9	523.3	185.2	559.5
1978	28 546	2 061.7	771.6	529.6	190.8	569.7
1977	28 526	2 074.5	782.2	529.9	191.7	570.7
TQ[1]	28 447	. . .	. . .	. . .	. . .	. . .
1976	28 405	2 081.9	779.4	524.7	192.4	585.4
1975	28 281	2 128.1	784.3	535.1	196.0	612.8
1974	28 218	2 162.0	783.3	545.9	188.8	644.0
1973	28 125	2 251.9	801.0	563.7	196.1	691.2
1972	27 956	2 322.0	811.0	586.9	198.2	725.8
1971	27 523	2 713.0	1 123.8	621.6	212.4	755.3
1970	26 976	3 064.8	1 322.5	691.1	259.7	791.3
1969	26 925	3 458.1	1 512.2	773.8	309.8	862.4
1968	26 273	3 546.1	1 570.3	763.6	307.3	904.8
1967	25 805	3 375.5	1 442.5	750.2	285.3	897.5
1966	25 534	3 092.2	1 199.8	743.3	261.3	887.4
1965	21 834	2 653.9	969.1	670.0	190.2	824.7
1964	22 013	2 685.8	973.2	666.0	189.8	856.8
1963	22 166	2 698.9	975.9	663.9	189.7	869.4
1962	22 275	2 805.6	1 066.4	664.2	191.0	884.0
1961	22 403	2 482.9	858.6	626.2	176.9	821.2
1960	22 534	2 475.4	873.1	617.0	170.6	814.8
1959	22 666	2 503.6	862.0	625.7	175.6	840.4
1958	22 727	2 599.5	898.9	639.9	189.5	871.2
1957	22 634	2 794.8	998.0	676.1	200.9	919.8
1956	22 372	2 806.4	1 025.8	669.9	200.8	910.0
1955	21 861	2 935.1	1 109.3	660.7	205.2	959.9
1954	20 951	3 302.1	1 404.6	725.7	223.9	947.9
1953	20 196	3 555.1	1 533.8	794.4	249.2	977.6
1952	19 338	3 635.9	1 596.4	824.3	232.0	983.3
1951	18 919	3 249.4	1 531.8	736.6	192.6	788.4
1950	19 077	1 459.5	593.2	380.7	74.3	411.3
1949	18 945	1 613.7	660.5	447.9	86.0	419.3
1948	18 745	1 444.3	554.0	417.5	85.0	387.7
1947	18 262	1 582.1	685.5	497.8	93.1	305.8
1946	16 655	3 024.9	1 435.5	978.2	155.7	455.5
1945	6 498	12 055.9	8 266.4	3 319.6	469.9	X
1944	5 689	11 451.7	7 994.8	2 981.4	475.6	X
1943	5 002	9 044.7	6 994.5	1 741.8	308.5	X
1942	4 485	3 858.8	3 075.6	640.6	142.6	X
1941	4 337	1 801.1	1 462.3	284.4	54.4	X

[1]Fiscal years through 1976 are from July 1 through June 30. Beginning with October 1976 (fiscal year 1977), fiscal years are from October 1 through September 30. The period from July 1 through September 30, 1976 is a separate fiscal period known as the transition quarter (TQ) and not included in any fiscal year.
. . . = Not available.
X = Not applicable.

Table 31-4. Veterans and Active Duty Military Personnel, 1900–2006—*Continued*

(Thousands, for fiscal year ending in year shown.)

Year	Veterans	Active duty military personnel				
		Total	Army	Navy	Marine Corps	Air Force
1940	4 286	458.4	269.0	161.0	28.3	X
1939	...	334.5	189.8	152.2	19.4	X
1938	...	322.9	185.5	119.1	18.4	X
1937	...	311.8	180.0	113.6	18.2	X
1936	...	291.4	167.8	106.3	17.2	X
1935	4 494	251.8	139.5	95.1	17.3	X
1934	...	247.1	138.5	92.3	16.4	X
1933	...	243.8	136.5	91.2	16.1	X
1932	...	244.9	135.0	93.4	16.6	X
1931	...	252.6	140.5	93.3	18.8	X
1930	4 680	255.6	139.4	96.9	19.4	X
1929	...	255.0	139.1	97.1	18.8	X
1928	...	250.9	136.1	95.8	19.0	X
1927	...	248.9	134.8	94.9	19.2	X
1926	...	247.4	134.9	93.3	19.2	X
1925	4 894	251.8	137.0	95.2	19.5	X
1924	...	261.2	142.7	98.2	20.3	X
1923	...	247.0	133.2	94.1	19.7	X
1922	...	270.2	148.8	100.2	21.2	X
1921	...	386.5	230.7	132.8	23.0	X
1920	5 146	343.3	204.3	121.8	17.2	X
1919	...	1 172.6	851.6	272.1	48.8	X
1918	...	2 897.2	2 395.7	448.6	52.8	X
1917	...	643.8	421.5	194.6	27.7	X
1916	...	179.4	108.4	60.4	10.6	X
1915	773	174.1	106.8	57.1	10.3	X
1914	...	165.9	98.5	57.0	10.4	X
1913	...	154.9	92.8	52.2	10.0	X
1912	...	153.2	92.1	51.4	9.7	X
1911	...	144.8	84.0	51.2	9.6	X
1910	977	139.3	81.3	48.5	9.6	X
1909	...	142.2	85.0	47.5	9.7	X
1908	...	128.5	76.9	42.3	9.2	X
1907	...	108.4	64.2	36.1	8.1	X
1906	...	112.2	68.9	35.1	8.2	X
1905	1 192	108.3	67.5	33.8	7.0	X
1904	...	110.1	70.4	32.2	7.6	X
1903	...	106.0	69.6	29.8	6.7	X
1902	...	111.1	81.3	23.6	6.2	X
1901	...	112.3	85.6	20.9	5.9	X
1900	1 224	125.9	101.7	18.8	5.4	X

Source: U.S. Census Bureau. U.S. Department of Defense. U.S. Department of Veterans Affairs.
. . . = Not available.
X = Not applicable.

Table 31-5. National Defense Outlays and Veterans Benefits, 1900–2007

(For year ending September 30; includes outlays of Department of Defense, Department of Veterans' Affairs, and other agencies for activities primarily related to national defense and veterans programs; minus sign (–) indicates decline.)

Year	National defense and veterans outlays (billion dollars)				Annual percent change[1]			Defense outlays, percent of	
		Defense outlays							
	Total outlays	Current dollars	Constant (2000) dollars	Veterans outlays	Total outlays	Defense outlays	Veterans outlays	Federal outlays	Gross domestic product[2]
2007 estimate	601.4	527.4	427.4	73.5	−0.8	−1.6	4.4	19.0	3.8
2006 estimate	606.4	535.9	443.1	70.4	7.2	8.2	0.4	19.8	4.1
2005	565.5	495.3	419.8	70.2	9.7	8.6	17.4	20.0	4.0
2004	515.7	455.9	397.3	59.8	11.6	12.6	4.8	19.9	3.9
2003	461.9	404.9	365.3	57.0	15.6	16.2	11.8	18.7	3.7
2002	399.5	348.6	329.4	51.0	12.7	13.0	11.4	17.3	3.4
2001	354.4	308.5	297.2	45.8	3.7	4.8	−2.8	16.4	3.0
2000	341.6	294.5	294.5	47.1	6.7	7.1	9.0	16.6	3.0
1999	320.2	274.9	283.7	43.2	3.2	2.4	3.4	16.1	3.0
1998	310.2	268.5	282.6	41.8	0.1	−0.8	6.3	16.2	3.1
1997	309.8	270.5	288.4	39.3	2.3	1.8	6.3	16.9	3.3
1996	302.7	265.8	289.2	37.0	−2.3	−2.3	−2.4	17.0	3.5
1995	310.0	272.1	305.9	37.9	−2.9	−3.4	0.8	17.9	3.7
1994	319.2	281.6	322.8	37.6	−2.3	−3.2	5.4	19.3	4.1
1993	326.8	291.1	...	35.7	−1.7	−2.4	4.7	20.7	4.4
1992	332.4	298.4	...	34.1	9.1	9.2	8.8	21.6	4.8
1991	304.6	273.3	...	31.3	−7.2	−8.7	7.7	20.6	4.6
1990	328.4	299.3	382.7	29.1	−1.6	−1.4	−3.2	23.9	5.2
1989	333.6	303.6	...	30.0	4.3	4.5	2.2	26.5	5.6
1988	319.7	290.4	...	29.4	3.6	3.0	9.9	27.3	5.8
1987	308.7	282.0	...	26.8	3.0	3.2	1.6	28.1	6.1
1986	299.7	273.4	...	26.3	7.4	8.2	0.2	27.6	6.2
1985	279.0	252.7	356.5	26.3	10.3	11.1	2.6	26.7	6.2
1984	253.0	227.4	...	25.6	7.8	8.3	3.1	26.7	6.0
1983	234.7	209.9	...	24.8	12.2	13.3	3.7	26.0	6.1
1982	209.2	185.3	...	23.9	15.9	17.6	4.2	24.8	5.8
1981	180.5	157.5	...	23.0	16.3	17.6	8.5	23.2	5.2
1980	155.2	134.0	267.1	21.2	13.9	15.2	6.3	22.7	4.9
1979	136.3	116.3	...	19.9	10.4	11.3	5.0	23.1	4.7
1978	123.5	104.5	...	19.0	7.1	7.5	5.2	22.8	4.7
1977	115.3	97.2	...	18.0	339.4	336.7	355.1	23.8	4.9
TQ[3]	26.2	22.3	...	4.0	−75.7	−75.2	−78.5	23.2	4.9
1976	108.0	89.6	...	18.4	4.8	3.6	11.1	24.1	5.2
1975	103.1	86.5	...	16.6	11.2	9.0	24.0	26.0	5.5
1974	92.7	79.3	...	13.4	4.6	3.5	11.4	29.5	5.5
1973	88.7	76.7	...	12.0	−1.3	−3.1	12.0	31.2	5.9
1972	89.9	79.2	...	10.7	1.4	0.4	9.7	34.3	6.7
1971	88.6	78.9	...	9.8	−1.9	−3.5	12.7	37.5	7.3
1970	90.4	81.7	375.1	8.7	0.3	−1.0	13.6	41.8	8.1
1969	90.1	82.5	...	7.6	1.3	0.7	8.5	44.9	8.7
1968	89.0	81.9	...	7.0	13.8	14.7	4.4	46.0	9.4
1967	78.2	71.4	...	6.7	22.1	22.9	13.8	45.4	8.8
1966	64.0	58.1	...	5.9	13.7	14.8	3.5	43.2	7.7
1965	56.3	50.6	...	5.7	−6.8	−7.6	0.7	42.8	7.4
1964	60.4	54.8	...	5.7	2.6	2.5	2.9	46.2	8.6
1963	58.9	53.4	...	5.5	1.6	2.0	−1.9	48.0	8.9
1962	58.0	52.3	...	5.6	4.8	5.5	−1.5	49.0	9.2
1961	55.3	49.6	...	5.7	3.2	3.1	4.9	50.8	9.3
1960	53.6	48.1	300.2	5.4	−1.6	−1.8	0.0	52.2	9.3
1959	54.5	49.0	...	5.4	4.4	4.7	1.7	53.2	10.0
1958	52.2	46.8	...	5.4	3.4	3.0	6.9	56.8	10.2
1957	50.4	45.4	...	5.0	6.4	6.8	2.3	59.3	10.1
1956	47.4	42.5	...	4.9	0.0	−0.5	4.6	60.2	9.9
1955	47.4	42.7	...	4.7	−12.0	−13.3	1.3	62.4	10.8
1954	53.9	49.3	...	4.6	−6.0	−6.7	2.1	69.5	13.0
1953	57.3	52.8	...	4.5	11.5	14.6	−15.4	69.4	14.2
1952	51.4	46.1	...	5.3	76.8	95.6	−3.3	68.1	13.2
1951	29.1	23.6	...	5.5	29.0	71.7	−37.4	51.8	7.3

[1]Change from prior year shown; for 1960, change from 1955.
[2]Represents fiscal year GDP.
[3]Fiscal years through 1976 are from July 1 through June 30. Beginning with October 1976 (fiscal year 1977), fiscal years are from October 1 through September 30. The period from July 1 through September 30, 1976 is a separate fiscal period known as the transition quarter (TQ) and not included in any fiscal year.
... = Not available.

Table 31-5. National Defense Outlays and Veterans Benefits, 1900–2007—*Continued*

(For year ending September 30; includes outlays of Department of Defense, Department of Veterans' Affairs, and other agencies for activities primarily related to national defense and veterans programs; minus sign (–) indicates decline.)

Year	National defense and veterans outlays (billion dollars)				Annual percent change[1]			Defense outlays, percent of	
	Total outlays	Defense outlays		Veterans outlays	Total outlays	Defense outlays	Veterans outlays	Federal outlays	Gross domestic product[2]
		Current dollars	Constant (2000) dollars						
1950	22.6	13.7	...	8.8	14.2	4.4	33.9	32.2	5.0
1949	19.7	13.2	...	6.6	26.9	44.4	2.2	33.9	4.8
1948	15.6	9.1	...	6.5	–18.7	–28.9	1.8	30.6	3.5
1947	19.2	12.8	...	6.3	–57.6	–70.0	157.4	37.1	5.5
1946	45.1	42.7	...	2.5	–45.7	–48.6	2 140.9	77.3	19.1
1945	83.1	83.0	...	0.1	5.1	4.8	–187.3	89.5	37.5
1944	79.0	79.1	...	–0.1	18.0	18.7	–145.7	86.7	37.9
1943	67.0	66.7	...	0.3	156.0	160.0	–44.9	84.9	37.1
1942	26.2	25.7	...	0.5	274.0	298.7	–10.5	73.0	17.8
1941	7.0	6.4	...	0.6	213.7	287.7	–1.8	47.1	5.6
1940	2.2	1.7	...	0.6	16.0	21.3	2.7	17.5	1.7
1939	1.9	1.4	...	0.6	5.5	10.3	–4.6	15.5	...
1938	1.8	1.2	...	0.6	3.3	4.7	0.4	18.3	...
1937	1.8	1.2	...	0.6	2.1	3.3	–0.2	15.3	...
1936	1.7	1.1	...	0.6	16.6	24.1	4.2	13.6	...
1935	1.5	0.9	...	0.6	23.2	31.0	12.2	14.2	...
1934	1.2	0.7	...	0.5	–23.2	–10.0	–36.4	10.6	...
1933	1.6	0.8	...	0.8	–3.6	–6.0	–1.1	17.0	...
1932	1.6	0.8	...	0.8	4.4	–0.7	10.5	17.9	...
1931	1.6	0.8	...	0.7	5.1	0.1	11.7	23.5	...
1930	1.5	0.8	...	0.6	4.0	6.1	1.3	25.3	...
1929	1.4	0.8	...	0.6	4.7	7.9	1.0	25.3	...
1928	1.4	0.7	...	0.6	3.9	6.4	1.0	24.7	...
1927	1.3	0.7	...	0.6	0.1	1.7	–1.5	24.1	...
1926	1.3	0.7	...	0.6	–1.5	–5.6	3.5	23.1	...
1925	1.3	0.7	...	0.6	–0.9	4.0	–6.2	24.5	...
1924	1.3	0.7	...	0.6	–8.9	–5.6	–12.2	23.7	...
1923	1.5	0.7	...	0.7	–12.2	–21.9	0.0	23.3	...
1922	1.7	0.9	...	0.7	–31.0	–47.2	13.0	28.4	...
1921	2.4	1.8	...	0.7	–15.1	–25.0	32.0	34.9	...
1920	2.9	2.4	...	0.5	–75.2	–78.6	–1.0	37.1	...
1919	11.5	11.0	...	0.5	79.6	79.1	91.4	59.5	...
1918	6.4	6.1	...	0.3	714.6	895.6	54.1	48.5	...
1917	0.8	0.6	...	0.2	56.0	83.2	1.1	31.6	...
1916	0.5	0.3	...	0.2	–2.6	–2.0	–3.6	47.3	...
1915	0.5	0.3	...	0.2	–2.1	–1.2	–3.9	46.1	...
1914	0.5	0.3	...	0.2	2.0	3.8	–1.2	48.0	...
1913	0.5	0.3	...	0.2	7.6	4.9	13.0	46.9	...
1912	0.5	0.3	...	0.2	–0.4	0.8	–2.6	46.3	...
1911	0.5	0.3	...	0.2	0.2	1.3	–1.8	45.9	...
1910	0.5	0.3	...	0.2	0.6	1.6	–1.1	45.1	...
1909	0.5	0.3	...	0.2	5.1	4.8	5.6	44.4	...
1908	0.5	0.3	...	0.2	15.7	19.0	10.1	44.6	...
1907	0.4	0.2	...	0.1	–0.5	–0.4	–0.6	42.6	...
1906	0.4	0.2	...	0.1	0.4	1.7	–1.6	43.5	...
1905	0.4	0.2	...	0.2	–5.8	–9.1	0.1	42.9	...
1904	0.4	0.3	...	0.2	20.3	33.2	2.5	45.9	...
1903	0.3	0.2	...	0.1	6.6	11.8	0.3	38.9	...
1902	0.3	0.2	...	0.1	–7.3	–12.2	–0.5	37.1	...
1901	0.4	0.2	...	0.1	4.4	7.5	0.3	39.1	...
1900	0.3	0.2	...	0.1	...	...	...	36.6	...

Source: U.S. Census Bureau. U.S. Office of Management and Budget.
[1]Change from prior year shown; for 1960, change from 1955.
[2]Represents fiscal year GDP.
. . . = Not available.

Table 31-6. Department of Homeland Security Total Budget Authority and Personnel by Organization, 2005–2006

(Expenditures in thousands of dollars, for the fiscal year ending September 30. Not all activities carried out by the Department of Homeland Security (DHS) constitute homeland security funding (e.g., Coast Guard search and rescue activities.)

Organization	Expenditures		Full-time employees	
	2005[1]	2006[1]	2005	2006
Adjusted Total Budget Authority[2,3]	38 369 517	40 345 347	179 646	182 131
U.S.–Visitor Immigrant Status Indicator Technology (US - VISIT)	340 000	336 600	102	102
U.S. Customs & Border Protection	6 344 398	7 109 875	40 636	41 986
U.S. Immigration & Customs Enforcement	3 127 078	3 866 443	14 600	15 917
Transportation Security Administration	6 068 275	6 167 014	52 615	50 363
Preparedness Directorate[4]	X	678 395	X	966
Office of Grants and Training	X	3 352 437	X	233
Analysis and Operations[5]	X	252 940	X	406
Federal Law Enforcement Training Center	226 807	279 534	982	1 001
U.S. Coast Guard	7 558 560	8 193 797	46 809	47 121
U.S. Secret Service	1 385 758	1 399 889	6 516	6 564
Federal Emergency Management Agency (FEMA)	5 038 256	4 834 744	4 735	5 708
U.S. Citizenship & Immigration Services	1 775 000	1 887 850	10 052	10 207
Science & Technology Directorate (S&T)	1 115 450	1 487 075	320	387
Office of Screening Coordination and Operation	X	3 960	X	17
Departmental Management and Operations	527 257	559 230	687	846
Counter-Terrorism Fund	8 000	1 980	X	X
Inspector General	82 317	82 187	502	540
Legacy DHS Organizations[6]				
BTS Under Secretary	9 617	X	67	X
Information Analysis and Infrastructure Protection (IAIP) Directorate	887 108	X	803	X
State and Local Government Coordination and Preparedness (SLGCP) (Formerly the Office for Domestic Preparedness (ODP))	3 984 846	X	220	X

Source: U.S. Census Bureau. *Statistical Abstract of the United States: 2007.* U.S. Department of Homeland Security.
[1]Revised enacted total.
[2]Reflects adjustment for recission of prior year carryover funds.
[3]Excludes BioShield funding. The Department of Homeland Security Appropriations Act, 2004, provided $5.6 billion for Project BioShield, to remain available through 2008. Including this uneven funding stream can distort year-over-year comparisons.
[4]The Preparedness Directorate did not exist for FY 2005. Under the Second Stage Review (2SR) changes, elements of IAIP, SLGCP, and Emergency Preparedness and Response (EP&R) were combined to form the Preparedness Directorate.
[5]Analysis and Operations did not exist for FY 2005. Under the Second Stage Review (2SR) changes, the appropriation provides resources for the support of the Office of Intelligence and Analysis and the Directorate of Operations.
[6]For FY 2006, BTS Under Secretary, IAIP Directorate and SLGCP, have become legacy DHS components.
X = Not applicable.

Table 31-7. Homeland Security Funding by Agency, 2004–2006

(Millions of dollars. A total of 32 agencies comprise federal homeland security funding. Department of Homeland Security (DHS) is the designated department to coordinate and centralize the leadership of many homeland security activities under a single department. In addition to DHS, the Departments of Defense (DOD), Energy (DOE), Health and Human Services (HHS), and Justice (DoJ), account for most of the total government-wide homeland security funding.)

Agency	2004	2005[1]	2006[1]
Total budget authority, excluding Bioshield[2,3,4]	**41,307.1**	**52,657.2**	**54,852.9**
Department of Agriculture	326.6	595.9	563.0
Department of Commerce	131.2	166.7	181.1
Department of Defense[5]	7,024.0	16,107.7	16,440.4
Department of Education	8.0	23.9	27.5
Department of Energy	1,362.5	1,562.0	1,705.2
Department of Health and Human Services	4,109.0	4,229.4	4,299.1
Department of Homeland Security[2,3]	23,492.3	23,979.9	25,499.0
Department of Housing and Urban Development	1.8	2.0	1.9
Department of the Interior	67.2	65.0	55.6
Department of Justice	2,165.8	2,690.8	2,975.4
Department of Labor	52.4	56.1	48.3
Department of State	701.3	824.1	1,107.9
Department of Transportation	283.5	219.3	181.0
Department of the Treasury	90.4	101.1	115.8
Department of Veterans Affairs	271.3	249.4	308.8
Corps of Engineers	103.4	89.0	72.0
Environmental Protection Agency	123.3	106.3	129.3
Executive Office of the President	35.0	29.5	20.8
General Services Administration	78.9	65.2	98.6
National Aeronautics and Space Administration	191.0	220.5	212.6
National Science Foundation	327.9	342.2	344.2
Office of Personnel Management	3.0	3.0	2.7
Social Security Administration	143.4	154.7	176.8
District of Columbia	19.0	15.0	13.5
Federal Communications Commission	1.0	1.8	2.3
Intelligence Community Management Account	1.0	72.4	56.0
National Archives and Records Administration	12.0	17.1	18.2
Nuclear Regulatory Commission	66.8	59.2	79.3
Postal Service	X	503.0	X
Securities and Exchange Commission	5.0	5.0	5.0
Smithsonian Institution	78.3	75.0	83.7
United States Holocaust Memorial Museum	8.0	8.0	7.8
Corporation for National and Community Service	22.8	17.0	20.4

Source: U.S. Census Bureau. *Statistical Abstract of the United States: 2007.* U.S. Office of Management and Budget.
[1]Fiscal Year 2005 and 2006 reflect the adjustments made for the Coast Guard and DOD re-estimates.
[2]Enacted Budget.
[3]The federal spending estimates are for the Executive Branch's homeland security efforts. These estimates do not include the efforts of the Legislative or Judicial branches.
[4]The Department of Homeland Security Appropriations Act, 2004, provided $5.6 billion for Project BioShield, to remain available through 2008. Including this uneven funding stream can distort year-over-year comparisons.
[5]In all tables, classified funds for the Intelligence Community are combined with the Department of Defense and titled "Department of Defense".
X = Not applicable.

Table 31-8. Homeland Security Funding by National Strategy Mission Area, 2004–2006

(Millions of dollars. For Homeland Security funding analysis by the Office of Management and Budget (OMB), agencies categorize their funding data based on the critical mission areas defined in the National Strategy.)

Agency	2004	2005[1]	2006[1]
Total Budget Authority excluding Bioshield[2,3]	41 307.1	52 657.2	54 852.9
Intelligence and warning	268.7	349.8	428.2
Border and transportation security	15 322.5	16 652.3	18 348.6
Domestic counterterrorism	2 994.1	3 974.5	4 548.0
Protecting critical infrastructure and key assets	12 571.0	17 835.9	17 851.7
Defending against catastrophic threats	2 827.2	8 146.4	8 639.8
Emergency preparedness and response	7 132.5	5 645.5	4 924.3
Other	191.1	43.8	112.4

Source: U.S. Census Bureau. *Statistical Abstract of the United States: 2007.* U.S. Office of Management and Budget.
[1]Fiscal Years 2005 and 2006 reflect the adjustments made for the Coast Guard and re-estimates for the Department of Defense.
[2]Enacted Budget.
[3]The Department of Homeland Security Appropriations Act, 2004, provided $5.6 billion for Project BioShield, to remain available through 2008. Including this uneven funding stream can distort year-over-year comparisons.

Table 31-9. Homeland Security Grants by State/Territories, 2004–2005

(Thousands of dollars, for the fiscal year ending September 30. Grants consist of the following programs: Citizen Corps Program (CCP), Law Enforcement Terrorism Prevention Program (LETPP), Emergency Management Performance Grant (EMPG), State Homeland Security Program (SHSP), Metropolitan Medical Response System (MMRS), and Urban Areas Security Initiative (UASI). Urban Areas Security Initiative program includes the Urban Areas Program, Transit Security Program, Port Security Grant Program and the Intercity Bus Program. 2005 grants include all the programs as in 2004 except for Port Security Grant Program and the Intercity Bus Program. These programs have not yet been awarded as of May 2005.)

State/Territory	2004	2005
Total	3 115 550	2 518 763
U.S.	3 050 076	2 475 564
Alabama	38 723	28 153
Alaska	21 218	14 879
Arizona	53 371	41 705
Arkansas	28 815	21 561
California	349 894	282 622
Colorado	45 583	36 799
Connecticut	46 523	24 080
Delaware	20 206	14 984
District of Columbia	49 231	96 144
Florida	142 667	101 285
Georgia	70 815	54 918
Hawaii	26 865	23 130
Idaho	22 621	16 805
Illinois	114 925	102 593
Indiana	55 534	38 996
Iowa	29 918	22 291
Kansas	29 064	21 784
Kentucky	45 537	31 419
Louisiana	76 005	42 670
Maine	23 776	16 609
Maryland	64 014	42 250
Massachusetts	69 288	62 436
Michigan	76 981	64 075
Minnesota	60 236	35 311
Mississippi	31 795	22 081
Missouri	66 618	46 952
Montana	20 689	15 318
Nebraska	24 376	23 656
Nevada	37 196	28 386
New Hampshire	24 110	16 776
New Jersey	95 795	60 811
New Mexico	24 946	18 499
New York	178 492	298 351
North Carolina	65 392	46 609
North Dakota	19 421	14 376
Ohio	103 582	77 823
Oklahoma	32 824	29 974
Oregon	41 665	34 820
Pennsylvania	109 866	87 671
Rhode Island	23 485	16 074
South Carolina	40 643	26 284
South Dakota	19 996	14 809
Tennessee	54 157	32 605
Texas	195 671	138 570
Utah	27 033	20 308
Vermont	19 594	14 326
Virginia	61 902	38 185
Washington	73 593	45 330
West Virginia	25 270	18 289
Wisconsin	51 343	37 251
Wyoming	18 809	13 934
Puerto Rico	37 864	25 169
Virgin Islands	6 918	4 612
American Samoa	5 776	4 279
Guam	7 016	4 706
Northern Mariana Islands	7 960	4 333
Republic of the Marshall Islands	0	50
Federated States of Micronesia	0	50

Source: U.S. Census Bureau. *Statistical Abstract of the United States: 2007.* U.S. Department of Homeland Security, State and Local Government Coordination and Preparedness.

Table 31-10. Cost Estimates for Federal Security Classification Activities and Pages Declassified, 1996–2005

(Billions, except as noted. Represents estimates provided by 41 executive branch agencies, including the Department of Defense. Does not include cost estimates of the Central Intelligence Agency (CIA), which that agency has classified.)

Category	2005	2004	2003	2002	2001	2000	1999	1998	1997	1996
Pages declassified (millions)	30	28	43	44	100	75	127	193	204	196
Total cost	7.70	7.20	6.53	5.70	4.70	4.30	3.80	3.60	3.40	2.60
Personnel security[1]	1.15	0.94	0.95	...	...	...	...	...	...	...
Physical security[2]	1.00	0.69	0.54	...	...	...	...	...	...	...
Information security	4.00	4.30	4.00	...	...	...	...	...	...	...
Information technology[3]	3.60	3.90	3.70	...	...	...	...	...	...	...
Classification management[4]	0.31	0.32	0.27	...	...	...	...	...	...	...
Declassification[5]	0.06	0.48	0.05	...	...	...	...	...	...	...
Professional education and training	0.22	0.18	0.16	...	...	...	...	...	...	...
Security management and planning	1.20	1.10	0.86	...	...	...	...	...	...	...
Unique[6]	0.01	0.01	0.03	...	...	...	...	...	...	...

Source: U.S. National Archives and Records Administration, Information Security Oversight Office. *Report on Cost Estimates for Security Classification Activities,* annual. *Report to the President,* annual.

[1]Series of interlocking and mutually supporting program elements that initially establish a government employee's eligibility, and ensure suitability for the continued access to classified information.
[2]Physical measures designed to safeguard and protect classified facilities and information, domestic or foreign.
[3]Protection of information systems against unauthorized access to or modification of information, whether in storage, processing or transit, and against the denial of authorized users, including those measures necessary to detect, document and counter such threats.
[4]Resources used to identify, control, transfer, transmit, retrieve, inventory, archive, or destroy classified information.
[5]Resources used to identify and process information, subject to the automatic, systematic or mandatory review programs authorized by executive order or statute.
[6]Department or agency specific activities that are not reported in any of the primary categories but are nonetheless significant and need to be included.

Table 31-11. Federal Emergency Management Agency (FEMA) Federal Disaster Declarations and Expenditures for Disasters, 1954–2006

(Number, except as noted.)

Year	Major disaster declarations	Emergency declarations	Fire management assistance declarations	National Flood Insurance Program losses paid (thousands of dollars)	Expenditures[1] (thousands of dollars)	Year	Major disaster declarations	Emergency declarations	Fire management assistance declarations	Insurance Program losses paid (thousands of dollars)	Expenditures[1] (thousands of dollars)
2006	52	5	86	...	...	1979	42	6	7	483 281	...
2005	48	68	39	13 101 491	...	1978	25	12	2	147 719	...
2004	68	7	43	2 140 198	5 583 391	1977	22	33	5	...	...
2003	56	19	48	771 794	2 377 908	1976	30	7	7	...	...
2002	49	1	70	433 199	1 883 822	1975	38	4	1	...	...
2001	45	10	45	1 276 846	11 297 969	1974	46	5	2	...	...
2000	45	6	62	251 552	1 747 511	1973	46	0	9	...	...
1999	50	20	40	754 838	...	1972	48	0	0	...	...
1998	65	8	54	886 026	...	1971	17	0	3	...	...
1997	44	0	3	519 512	...	1970	17	0	2	...	...
1996	75	7	75	828 040	...	1969	29	...	...	...	...
1995	32	2	4	1 295 575	...	1968	19	...	...	...	...
1994	36	1	20	411 080	...	1967	11	...	...	...	...
1993	32	19	7	659 092	...	1966	11	...	...	...	...
1992	45	2	6	710 248	...	1965	25	...	...	...	...
1991	43	0	2	353 682	...	1964	25	...	...	...	...
1990	38	0	5	167 920	...	1963	20	...	...	...	...
1989	31	0	1	661 668	...	1962	22	...	...	...	...
1988	11	0	5	51 023	...	1961	12	...	...	...	...
1987	23	1	7	105 423	...	1960	12	...	...	...	...
1986	28	0	1	126 389	...	1959	7	...	...	...	...
1985	27	0	9	368 239	...	1958	7	...	...	...	...
1984	34	4	4	254 643	...	1957	16	...	...	...	...
1983	21	1	2	439 455	...	1956	16	...	...	...	...
1982	24	3	1	198 296	...	1955	18	...	...	...	...
1981	15	0	3	127 118	...	1954	17	...	...	...	...
1980	23	3	2	230 414	...						

Source: U.S. Federal Emergency Management Agency.
[1]Expenditures represent FEMA funding obligated as of 12/31/04. Expenditures for declared disasters within a calendar year represent obligations at the time data was collected. Figures will change as those disasters remaining open receive funding obligated for ongoing recovery and mitigation projects.
... = Not available.

Table 31-12. FEMA Average Total Obligations per Year and per Declaration

(Dollars. Source data is the set of all declarations between October 1, 1998 and January 1, 2007)

Category	Major disaster declaration[1]		Emergency declaration total	
	Average obligations per year	Average obligations per declaration	Average obligations per year	Average obligations per declaration
Total	2 614 167 474	57 157 182	183 877 207	12 159 522
Debris removal	701 022 443	15 320 683	1 806 534	119 440
Protective measures	682 898 462	14 934 736	181 511 649	12 003 121
Roads and bridges	207 272 778	4 533 703	0	0
Water control facilities	74 910 804	1 637 302	. . .	. . .
Public buildings	408 943 220	8 934 627	0	0
Public utilities	249 294 841	5 460 750	26 485	1 751
Recreational or other	106 919 234	2 337 443	6 852	453
State management	182 905 691	3 997 939	525 687	34 756

Source: U.S. Federal Emergency Management Agency.
[1]A World Trade Center insurance Project Worksheet was excluded from the query as its inclusion results in a significantly skewed average.
. . . Not available.

BOX 31 ■ African Americans and Women in the U.S. Military

Women and African Americans are the two minority groups with the longest history of participation in the U.S. military. They have served every war, but historically their participation was often devalued. In the modern military, their roles and visibility have changed dramatically and continue to evolve.

African American slaves fought in the Revolutionary War (an estimated 5,000 on the rebel side) and in the Confederate army in the Civil War with nothing to gain and no reward. The approximately 180,000 who fought with Union troops were paid less than white troops, made to purchase their own uniforms, and were given the worst and most dangerous assignments. Even in World War II, when more than 1 million African Americans enlisted, units were still segregated and even blood products were separated and labeled to assure that white soldiers only got "white" blood. It was not until 1948 and the murder in the U.S. of several African American veterans that President Harry Truman issued an executive order that demanded equal opportunity throughout the military. The last of the all African American units was not disbanded until 1954.

African American enlistment remained high during the Koren War (approximately 600,000 troops) and the Vietnam War. The representation of African Americans in the U.S. military grew to be greater than their representation in the general public and has continued unabated. Despite the fact that in 2004 African Americans composed 21% of the U.S. military, they only accounted for 9% of officers.

During the Iraq War (Operation Iraqi Freedom), the percentage of African Americans in the military began to shrink, as their recruitment declined. African Americans as a percent of new recruits in the U.S. Army dropped from 23% in 2001 to 13% in 2006. One reason may be that the majority of African Americans do not approve of the war (83% surveyed felt the United States should have stayed out of Iraq versus only 46% of whites). Another hypothesis is that as the number of college-educated African Americans rises, there is less need for military service, which was traditionally seen as one of the few careers options and one of the few ways to pay for training and education. The Army countered this decline with modified recruiting techniques and higher enlistment bonuses—up to $20,000 in August 2007.

Because women have traditionally been barred from combat positions, there is a dearth of statistics about their participation in the early wars of the United States. However, since the military was required in 1973 to remove the 2% cap on women, their numbers have more than tripled from 57,518 in 1973 to 212,773 in 2004. Throughout the years, more and more jobs in the military have opened to women. In 2004, 91% of positions in the Army, 96% in the Navy, 93% in the Marines, and 99% in the Air Force were open to women. The Air Force also had the largest proportion of women on active duty (20%) and the highest percentage of active officers (18%) and officer accessions (24%). The Marines had the lowest number of women on active duty (6%), active officers (6%), and officer accessions (10%).

As the Iraq War continues and the number of available troops declines, the role of women in the military is evolving to include duties that are in a technical gray area regarding combat. Because support troops are not separated from combat troops women are taking on tasks traditionally done by men. The Pentagon has stated that it has relaxed its policies because declining numbers of troops require women take on these jobs otherwise the United States cannot sustain its mission. The debate about the roles women should or should not take in combat and the extent of that involvement is ongoing.

Sources:

Abruzzese, Sarah. "Iraq War Begins Drop in Black Enlistees. (National Desk)." *The New York Times* (August 22, 2007): A12(L).

Alvarez, Lizette "Women at War: Officially, American Women Can't Serve in Combat, But in Iraq and Afghanistan They're Fighting—and Dying—as Never Before.(Cover Story)." *New York Times Upfront* 139.11 (March 12, 2007): 18(2).

Manegold, Catherine S. "Unsung Heroes: A Survey of the Role Blacks Have Played in America's Wars." *The New York Times Book Review* 106.20 (May 20, 2001): 8(1).

U.S. Department of Defense, Office of the Undersecretary of Defense, Personnel and Readiness. Population Representation in the Military Services. http://www.defenselink.mil/prhome/poprep2004/

Gilmore, Gerry J. "African-Americans Continue Tradition of Distinguished Service." U.S. Department of Defense, *American Forces Press Service.* http://www.defenselink.mil/news/NewsArticle.aspx?ID=2897

BIBLIOGRAPHY

This bibliography lists in alphabetical order all government sources used to create the tables and boxes in this edition of *Datapedia*. Secondary sources were used for some of the boxes; check the sources at the end of each box for these references.

Administrative Office of the U.S. Courts
2006 Judicial Facts & Figures
  http://www.uscourts.gov/judicialfactsfigures/
Bankruptcy Statistics
  http://www.uscourts.gov/bnkrpctystats/
  bankruptcystats.htm
Federal Judicial Caseload Statistics 2006
  http://www.uscourts.gov/caseload2006/
  contents.html

Executive Office of the President of the United States
News & Policies, January 2006
  http://www.whitehouse.gov/news/releases/2006/
  01/20060131-6.html
Homeownership
  http://www.whitehouse.gov/infocus/
  homeownership/

Council of Economic Advisors
Economic Report of the President
  http://www.whitehouse.gov/cea/pubs.html

Federal Housing Finance Board
Historical Summary Tables
  http://www.fhfb.gov/Default.aspx?Page=53

Federal Communications Commission
Fiscal Year 2008 Budget Estimates Submitted to Congress
  February 2007
    http://www.fcc.gov/Reports/fcc2008budget_
    complete.pdf
Daily Digest News
    http://www.fcc.gov/Daily_Releases/Daily_Digest/
    2007/

National Science Foundation
Division of Science Resources Statistics
Science and Engineering Statistics
  http://www.nsf.gov/statistics/

Smithsonian Institution
Media Library
  http://forces.si.edu/arctic/index.html

U.S. Arctic Research Commission
Report on Goals and Objectives for Arctic Research
  2007, for the U.S. Arctic Research Plan
    http://www.arctic.gov/publications.htm

U.S. Congress

Congressional Budget Office
Causes and Consequences of the Trade Deficit
http://www.cbo.gov/ftpdocs/18xx/doc1897/
tradedef.pdf
Estimated Costs of U.S. Operations in Iraq and
Afghanistan and Other Activities Related to the War
on Terrorism
http://www.cbo.gov/ftpdocs/84xx/doc8497/
07-30-WarCosts_Testimony.pdf
Labor Productivity: Developments Since 1995
http://www.cbo.gov/ftpdocs/79xx/doc7910/
03-26-Labor.pdf

Joint Economic Committee
News
http://www.house.gov/jec/news/2007/
news2007index.html

Library of Congress, Congressional Research Service
The Cost of Iraq, Afghanistan, and Other Global War on
Terror Operations Since 9/11
http://fpc.state.gov/documents/organization/
89927.pdf
CRS Issue Brief for Congress: Campaign Finance
http://fpc.state.gov/documents/organization/
67152.pdf

U.S. House of Representatives
Women in Congress
http://womenincongress.house.gov/

Committee on Education and the Workforce
Testimony of Professor Cheryl Asper Elzy before the
Subcommittee on 21st Century Competitiveness
Committee on Education and the Workforce
http://republicans.edlabor.house.gov/archive/
hearings/109th/21st/piracy092606/elzy.htm

Office of the Clerk
House History
http://clerk.house.gov/art_history/house_history/
index.html

U.S. Senate
Senators, Biographical Characteristics
http://www.senate.gov/pagelayout/reference/
three_column_table/Senators.htm

Office of the Secretary of the Senate
Legislation and Procedure
http://www.senate.gov/pagelayout/reference/
two_column_table/Legislation_and_Procedure.htm

U.S. Department of Agriculture

Center for Nutrition Policy and Promotion
U.S. Food Supply: Nutrients and Other Food Components, per Capita per Day
www.ers.usda.gov/Data/FoodConsumption/
spreadsheets/nutrients.xls

Economic Research Service
Agricultural Outlook: Statistical Indicators
http://www.ers.usda.gov/Publications/Agoutlook/
AOTables/
Amber Waves, Vol. 5, Issue 3, June 2007
http://www.ers.usda.gov/AmberWaves/June07/
PDF/AW_June07.pdf
Farm Income and Costs
http://www.ers.usda.gov/briefing/farmincome/
Food Availability Data Sets
http://www.ers.usda.gov/Data/FoodConsumption/
FoodAvailSpreadsheets.htm
Household Food Security in the United States, 2005
http://www.ers.usda.gov/publications/err29
Organic Production Data Sets
http://www.ers.usda.gov/data/organic/
*Structure and Finances of U.S. Farms: Family Farm Report,
2007 Edition*
http://www.ers.usda.gov/publications/eib24/
U.S. and State Farm Income Data Files: Farm Income
Forecast
http://www.ers.usda.gov/Data/FarmIncome/
finfidmu.htm
U.S. Farm Sector Balance Sheet Data Files
http://www.ers.usda.gov/Data/FarmBalanceSheet/
Fbsdmu.htm

Food and Nutrition Service
Food Stamp Program Participation Rates: 2005
http://www.fns.usda.gov/oane/MENU/
Published/FSP/FILES/Participation/
Trends1999-2005Sum.pdf
National School Lunch Program Fact Sheet.
http://www.fns.usda.gov/cnd/Lunch/
AboutLunch/NSLPFactSheet.pdf
The School Breakfast Program Fact Sheet.
http://www.fns.usda.gov/cnd/breakfast/
AboutBFast/SBPFactSheet.pdf
The Special Supplemental Nutrition Program for Women,
Infants, and Children Program Fact Sheet
http://www.fns.usda.gov/wic/factsheets.htm
Congressional Testimony
http://www.fns.usda.gov/cga/Speeches/
Testimony.htm
The Extent of Trafficking in the Food Stamp Program:
2002-2005, Final Report," December 2006
http://www.fns.usda.gov/oane/menu/Published/
FSP/FILES/ProgramIntegrity/Trafficking2005.pdf

Office of the Inspector General
Management Challenges
http://www.usda.gov/oig/webdocs/
MgmtChallenges2007.pdf

Rural Business-Cooperative Service
USDA Cooperative Information Rpt 1, Section 26 Farm
Marketing, Supply and Service Cooperative Historical
Statistics
http://www.rurdev.usda.gov/rbs/pub/cir1s26.pdf

U.S. Department of Commerce

Bureau of Economic Analysis

International Economic Accounts
http://bea.gov/international/index.htm

National Economic Accounts
http://www.bea.gov/national/Index.htm

National Income and Product Accounts
http://www.bea.gov/national/nipaweb/
SelectTable.asp

Regional Economic Accounts
http://www.bea.gov/regional/index.htm

Survey of Current Business
http://www.bea.gov/scb/about.asp

Census Bureau

65+ in the United States: 2005
http://www.census.gov/prod/2006pubs/
p23-209.pdf

American Community Survey
http://www.census.gov/acs/www/

Annual Survey of Manufactures
http://www.census.gov/prod/2006pubs/
am0531gs1.pdf

E-Stats
http://www.census.gov/eos/www/ebusiness614.htm

The Foreign-Born Population in 2004
http://www.census.gov/population/pop-profile/
dynamic/ForeignBorn.pdf

Historical Income Data
http://www.census.gov/hhes/www/income/
histinc/histinctb.html

Historical Statistics
http://www.census.gov/compendia/statab/
hist_stats.html

Housing Vacancy Survey 2006
http://www.census.gov/hhes/www/housing/hvs/
annual06/ann06ind.html

Income, Earnings, and Poverty: Data from the 2005 American Community Survey
http://www.census.gov/prod/2006pubs/acs-02.pdf

Income, Poverty, and Health Insurance Coverage in the United States: 2005
http://www.census.gov/prod/2006pubs/
p60- 231.pdf

Manufactured Housing Survey
http://www.census.gov/const/www/
mhsindex.html

Married-Couple and Unmarried-Partner Households: 2000
http://www.census.gov/prod/2003pubs/
censr-5.pdf

Number, Timing, and Duration of Marriages and Divorces: 2001
http://www.census.gov/prod/2005pubs/p70-97.pdf

Residential Repairs and Improvement Statistics
http://www.census.gov/const/www/
c50index.html

State and Local Government Finances
http://www.census.gov/govs/www/
estimate.html

Statistical Abstract of the United States: 2007
http://www.census.gov/compendia/statab/
2007edition.html

Statistical Abstract of the United States: 2006
http://www.census.gov/compendia/statab/2006/
2006edition.html

Statistical Abstract of the United States: 2004–2005
http://www.census.gov/prod/www/statistical-
abstract-2001_2005.html

Statistical Abstract of the United States: 2003
http://www.census.gov/prod/www/statistical-
abstract-2001_2005.html

Statistical Abstract of the United States: 2002
http://www.census.gov/prod/www/statistical-
abstract-2001_2005.html

Statistical Abstract of the United States: 2001
http://www.census.gov/prod/www/statistical-
abstract-2001_2005.html

Statistical Abstract of the United States: 2000
http://www.census.gov/prod/www/statistical-
abstract-1995_2000.html

Statistical Abstract of the United States: 1996
http://www.census.gov/prod/www/statistical-
abstract-1995_2000.html

Statistical Abstract of the United States: 1995
http://www.census.gov/prod/www/statistical-
abstract-1995_2000.html

Statistical Abstract of the United States: 1992
http://www2.census.gov/prod2/statcomp/
documents/1992-01.pdf

Statistical Abstract of the United States: 1987
http://www2.census.gov/prod2/statcomp/
documents/1987-01.pdf

Statistical Abstract of the United States: 1980
http://www2.census.gov/prod2/statcomp/
documents/1980-01.pdf

Statistical Abstract of the United States: 1970
http://www2.census.gov/prod2/statcomp/
documents/1970-01.pdf

Technical Note on Same-Sex Unmarried Partner Data from the 1990 and 2000 Censuses.
http://www.census.gov/population/www/cen2000/
samesex.html

U.S. Census Bureau News, Facts for Features
http://www.census.gov/Press-Release/www/
releases/

U.S. Interim Projections by Age, Sex, Race, and Hispanic Origin
http://www.census.gov/ipc/www/usinterimproj/

Working Paper Series No. 56
http://www.census.gov/population/www/
documentation/twps0056.html

Foreign Trade Division

Trade in Goods (Imports, Exports and Trade Balance) with China
http://www.census.gov/foreign-trade/balance/
c5700.html#2006

U.S. Trade in Goods and Services – Balance of Payments (BOP) Basis
http://www.census.gov/foreign-trade/statistics/historical/gands.pdf

National Climatic Data Center
Billion Dollar U.S. Weather Disasters, 1980–2005
http://www.ncdc.noaa.gov/oa/reports/billionz.html

National Hurricane Center
The Deadliest, Costliest, and Most Intense United States Tropical Cyclones from 1851 to 2006.
http://www.nhc.noaa.gov/pdf/NWS-TPC-5.pdf
Tropical Cyclone Report: Hurricane Katrina, 23-30 August, 2005
http://www.nhc.noaa.gov/pdf/TCR-AL122005_Katrina.pdf

National Oceanic and Atmospheric Administration
Hurricane Katrina—Most Destructive Hurricane Ever to Strike the U.S.
http://www.katrina.noaa.gov/
State of the Arctic, Report 2006.
http://www.arctic.noaa.gov/soa2006/

NOAA Fisheries, Office of Science and Technology
Fisheries of the United States: 2005
http://www.st.nmfs.gov/st1/fus/fus05/

U.S. Department of Defense

American Forces Press Service
African-Americans Continue Tradition of Distinguished Service
http://www.defenselink.mil/news/NewsArticle.aspx?ID=2897

Office of the Undersecretary of Defense, Personnel and Readiness
Population Representation in the Military Services
http://www.defenselink.mil/prhome/poprep2004/

Statistical Information Analysis Division
Military Personnel Statistics
http://siadapp.dmdc.osd.mil/personnel/MILITARY/Miltop.htm

U.S. Department of Education

Center for Education Statistics
Digest of Education Statistics: 2005
http://nces.ed.gov/programs/digest/d05/
Forum Guide to Elementary/Secondary Virtual Education
http://nces.ed.gov/pubsearch/pubsinfo.asp?pubid=2006803
Distance Education Courses for Public Elementary and Secondary School Students: 2002-03
http://nces.ed.gov/pubs2005/2005010.pdf
Homeschooling in the United States: 2003
http://nces.ed.gov/pubs2006/2006042.pdf

U.S. Department of Energy

Energy Information Administration
Annual Energy Review 2005
http://tonto.eia.doe.gov/FTPROOT/multifuel/038405.pdf
Emissions of Greenhouse Gases in the United States 2004
http://www.eia.doe.gov/oiaf/1605/gg05rpt/pdf/057304.pdf
Petroleum Navigator, U.S. Crude Oil Field Production
http://tonto.eia.doe.gov/dnav/pet/hist/mcrfpus1M.htm
Retail Gasoline Historical Prices
http://www.eia.doe.gov/oil_gas/petroleum/data_publications/wrgp/mogas_history.html
U.S. Crude Oil, Natural Gas, and Natural Gas Liquids Reserves, 2005 Annual Report
http://www.eia.doe.gov/pub/oil_gas/natural_gas/data_publications/crude_oil_natural_gas_reserves/current/pdf/arr.pdf

U.S. Department of Health and Human Services

Administration on Children, Youth and Families, Children's Bureau
Child Maltreatment 2005
http://www.acf.hhs.gov/programs/cb/pubs/cm05/cm05.pdf

Centers for Disease Control and Prevention, National Center for Health Statistics
Advance Data from Vital and Health Statistics, No. 350, December 10, 2004
http://www.cdc.gov/nchs/data/ad/ad350.pdf
Advance Data from Vital and Health Statistics, No. 260, February 14, 1995
http://www.cdc.gov/nchs/data/ad/ad260.pdf
Advance Data from Vital and Health Statistics, No. 26, April 6, 1978
http://www.cdc.gov/nchs/data/ad/ad026acc.pdf
Health, United States 2006
http://www.cdc.gov/nchs/hus.htm
Health Insurance Coverage: Early Release of Estimates from the National Interview Survey, 2006
http://www.cdc.gov/nchs/data/nhis/earlyrelease/insur200706.pdf
National Vital Statistics Reports, Vol. 55, No. 11, December 28, 2006
http://www.cdc.gov/nchs/data/nvsr/nvsr55/nvsr55_11.pdf
National Vital Statistics Reports, Vol. 55, No. 1, September 29, 2006
http://www.cdc.gov/nchs/data/nvsr/nvsr55/nvsr55_01.pdf
National Vital Statistics Reports, Vol. 54, No. 20, July 21, 2006
http://www.cdc.gov/nchs/data/nvsr/nvsr54/nvsr54_20.pdf

National Vital Statistics Reports, Vol. 54, No. 13, April 19, 2006
http://www.cdc.gov/nchs/data/nvsr/nvsr54/nvsr54_13.pdf
National Vital Statistics Reports, Vol. 53, No. 17, March 7, 2005
http://www.cdc.gov/nchs/data/nvsr/nvsr53/nvsr53_17.pdf
National Vital Statistics Reports, Vol. 54, No. 13, April 19, 2006
http://www.cdc.gov/nchs/data/nvsr/nvsr54/nvsr54_13.pdf
Vital and Health Statistics, Series 23, No. 24, December 2004
http://www.cdc.gov/nchs/data/series/sr_23/sr23_024.pdf

Centers for Medicare and Medicaid Services
National Health Expenditure Data
http://www.cms.hhs.gov/NationalHealthExpendData/
Brief Summaries of Medicare and Medicaid
http://www.cms.hhs.gov/MedicareProgramRatesStats/02_SummaryMedicareMedicaid.asp
Testimonies
http://www.cms.hhs.gov/apps/media/testimonies.asp

Office of Disease Prevention and Health Promotion
Healthy People 2010: Midcourse Review, December 2006
http://www.healthypeople.gov/data/midcourse/default.htm

Office of the Inspector General
OIG News December 5, 2006
http://oig.hhs.gov/publications/docs/semiannual/2006/PRSemiannual%20Final%20FY%202006.pdf
Office of Evaluation and Inspections Reports
http://oig.hhs.gov/oei/oeisearch.html
Hearing Testimony
http://www.oig.hhs.gov/testimony.html

Substance Abuse and Mental Health Services Administration
Mental Health, United States, 2004
http://mentalhealth.samhsa.gov/publications/allpubs/sma06-4195/

U.S. Department of Homeland Security
Homeland Security Budget in Brief, Fiscal Year 2008
http://www.dhs.gov/xlibrary/assets/budget_bib-fy2008.pdf
Hurricane Katrina: What Government is Doing
http://www.dhs.gov/xprepresp/programs/gc_1157649340100.shtm

Federal Emergency Management Administration
Average Total Obligations by Year and by Declaration
http://www.fema.gov/government/grant/pa/stat2.shtm

Declared Disasters by Year or State
http://www.fema.gov/news/disaster_totals_annual.fema
FEMA Public Assistance for Louisiana Recovery, June 1, 2007
http://www.fema.gov/pdf/hazard/hurricane/2005katrina/la_media_report_060107.pdf
FEMA Public Assistance for Mississippi Recovery, June 1, 2007
http://www.fema.gov/pdf/hazard/hurricane/2005katrina/ms_media_report_060107.pdf
Flood Insurance Loss Dollars Paid by Calendar Year
http://www.fema.gov/business/nfip/statistics/cy2005lsdl.shtm
Hurricane Katrina Flood Recovery (Louisiana)
http://www.fema.gov/hazard/flood/recoverydata/katrina/katrina_la_mmds.shtm
Hurricane Katrina Information
http://www.fema.gov/hazard/hurricane/2005katrina/index.shtm

Office of Immigration Statistics
2005 Yearbook of Immigration Statistics
http://www.dhs.gov/xlibrary/assets/statistics/yearbook/2005/OIS_2005_Yearbook.pdf
Estimates of the Unauthorized Immigrant Population Residing in the United States: January 2005
http://www.dhs.gov/xlibrary/assets/statistics/publications/ILL_PE_2005.pdf
Estimates of the Unauthorized Immigrant Population Residing in the United States: 1990 to 2000
http://www.dhs.gov/xlibrary/assets/statistics/publications/Ill_Report_1211.pdf
Illegal Alien Resident Population: Estimates of the Undocumented Immigrant Population Residing in the United States (October, 1996)
http://www.dhs.gov/xlibrary/assets/statistics/illegal.pdf

U.S. Department of the Interior

U.S. Fish and Wildlife Service
Bald Eagle Population Size
http://www.fws.gov/midwest/eagle/population/index.html
Endangered Species Bulletin
http://www.fws.gov/endangered/bulletin.html
News Releases
http://www.fws.gov/news/NewsReleases/

U.S. Department of Justice

Bureau of Justice Statistics
Bureau of Justice Statistics Bulletin
http://www.ojp.usdoj.gov/bjs/
Family Violence Statistics: Including Statistics on Strangers and Acquaintances
http://www.ojp.usdoj.gov/bjs/abstract/fvs.htm

Indicators of School Crime and Safety 2006
    http://www.ojp.usdoj.gov/bjs/pub/pdf/iscs06.pdf

Office of the Attorney General
Combating Identity Theft: A Strategic Plan
    http://www.idtheft.gov/reports/StrategicPlan.pdf

National Drug Intelligence Center
Intelligence Bulletin
    http://www.usdoj.gov/ndic/topics/ibulls.htm

U.S. Department of Labor

Bureau of Labor Statistics
Collective Bargaining
    http://data.bls.gov/cgi-bin/surveymost?ws
Economic News Releases
    http://www.bls.gov/bls/newsrels.htm
Historical Data for the "A" tables of the Employment
    Situation News Release
    http://www.bls.gov/cps/cpsatabs.htm
Historical data for the "B" tables of the Employment
    Situation News Release
    http://www.bls.gov/ces/cesbtabs.htm
Monthly Labor Review
    http://www.bls.gov/opub/mlr/mlrhome.htm
Multiple Jobholders by Selected Demographic and
    Economic Characteristics
    http://www.bls.gov/web/cpseea39.pdf
Unemployment Rates for Previous Years
    http://www.bls.gov/cps/prev_yrs.htm

Mine Safety and Health Administration
    http://www.msha.gov/

U.S. Department of State
*Issues of Democracy "Financing Presidential Election
    Campaigns."*
    http://usinfo.state.gov/journals/itdhr/0996/ijde/
    alex.htm

U.S. Department of Transportation

Bureau of Transportation Statistics
Freedom to Travel
    http://www.bts.gov/publications/freedom_to_travel/
Issue Brief
    http://www.bts.gov/publications/issue_briefs/
    number_03/pdf/entire.pdf
National Transportation Statistics 2007
    http://www.bts.gov/publications/
    national_transportation_statistics/

National Transportation Statistics 2005
    http://www.bts.gov/publications/
    national_transportation_statistics/2005/index.html
National Transportation Statistics 2006
    http://www.bts.gov/publications/
    national_transportation_statistics/2006/index.html
Transportation Statistics Annual Report, December 2006
    http://www.bts.gov/publications/
    transportation_statistics_annual_report/2006/
Travel Patterns of Older Americans with Disabilities.
    http://www.bts.gov/programs/
    bts_working_papers/2004/paper_01/

Maritime Administration
Reports & Statistics: Fleet Statistics
    http://www.marad.dot.gov/MARAD_statistics/
    index.html
World Merchant Fleet 2005
    http://www.marad.dot.gov/MARAD_statistics/
    2005%20STATISTICS/World%20Merchant%20
    Fleet%202005.pdf

U.S. Department of the Treasury
Debt Position and Activity Report
    http://www.treasurydirect.gov/govt/reports/pd/
    pd_debtposactrpt.htm

Bureau of the Public Debt
Public Debt Reports
    http://www.treasurydirect.gov/govt/reports/pd/
    pd.htm

Internal Revenue Service
Tax Statistics
    http://www.irs.gov/taxstats/index.html

U.S. Department of Veterans Affairs
Veteran Data and Information
    http://www1.va.gov/vetdata/

U.S. Environmental Protection Agency
*Municipal Solid Waste Generation, Recycling, and Disposal in
    the United States: Facts and Figures for 2005*
    http://www.epa.gov/epaoswer/osw/conserve/
    resources/msw-2005.pdf

U.S. Government Printing Office
Economic Report of the President, 2007
    http://www.gpoaccess.gov/eop/tables07.html

INDEX

INDEX